Collins

MANDARIN
CHINESE
DICTIONARY
ESSENTIAL EDITION

D0890964

Published by Collins
An imprint of HarperCollins Publishers
Westerhill Road
Bishopbriggs
Glasgow G64 2QT

First Edition 2020

10 9 8 7 6 5 4 3 2 1

© HarperCollins Publishers 2020

ISBN 978-0-00-835985-0

Collins® is a registered trademark of
HarperCollins Publishers Limited

collinsdictionary.com
collins.co.uk/dictionaries

Typeset by Davidson Publishing
Solutions, Glasgow

Printed and bound by CPI Group (UK)
Ltd, Croydon, CR0 4YY

A catalogue record for this book is
available from the British Library.

If you would like to comment on any
aspect of this book, please contact us
at the given address or online.
E-mail: dictionaries@harpercollins.co.uk
 facebook.com/collinsdictionary
 @collinsdict

Acknowledgements

We would like to thank those authors
and publishers who kindly gave
permission for copyright material to be
used in the Collins Corpus. We would
also like to thank Times Newspapers
Ltd for providing valuable data.

目录

CONTENTS

序言	v	Introduction	v
如何使用本词典	xiii	How to Use the Dictionary	viii
略语表	xvii	Reference List	xvii
英语发音指导	xxi	Guide to English Phonetics	xxi
不规则动词	xxii	English Irregular Verbs	xxii
部首检字表	1–42	Radical Index	1–42
汉英词典	1–171	CHINESE–ENGLISH	1–171
汉语活学活用	1–16	Chinese in Action	1–16
英语活学活用	17–32	English in Action	17–32
英汉词典	173–375	ENGLISH–CHINESE	173–375

INTRODUCTION

Learning Chinese is definitely a challenge. However, in some ways Chinese is not particularly complicated. Words do not change with gender, number or even tense, and there are not many complicated grammatical traps for the unwary. However, other things about it make it hard for native English speakers to learn.

CHINESE PRONUNCIATION
THE FOUR TONES
Chinese is a tonal language – the pitch of any syllable affects its meaning.

There are four tones: first tone (high, even pitch); second (rising pitch); third tone (falling and then rising) and fourth tone (falling pitch). There is also a fifth (or neutral) tone, which is pronounced so quietly and quickly that there is no discernible tone at all.

Tones are a very important part of the pronunciation – and wrong tones can cause real confusion.

EXAMPLES OF DIFFERENCES IN TONES:

First tone	Second tone	Third tone	Fourth tone	Neutral tone
mā	má	mǎ	mà	ma
妈	麻	马	骂	吗
mother	hemp	horse	curse; swear	[question particle]

It may seem unnatural to native speakers of English to have pitch so rigidly attached to words, but the tone is as fundamental a part of any syllable as are its vowels and consonants.

PINYIN
Pinyin, the Chinese phonetic alphabet, was first introduced to help children learn to write characters, and foreigners and speakers of non-Mandarin dialects to pronounce Standard Chinese correctly. It is also very useful for dictionaries, as it provides an alphabetical order by which characters can be sorted. However, *Pinyin* is not used much in China. Although signs in China are sometimes written in *Pinyin*, do not expect people to understand *Pinyin* as they would characters – in short, it should not be regarded as a substitute for learning Chinese characters. It is, however, a good, accurate guide to pronunciation.

CHINESE CHARACTERS
The Chinese script has a history that goes back at least three thousand years.

Although there are tens of thousands of known characters, a lot of these are archaic (some so old that even their meanings are unknown). An educated Chinese person will know roughly 4–6000 characters, and 2–3000 is considered sufficient for basic literacy (newspapers and the like).

Each character has to be learned individually – with the shape of the character, the sound of it and the meaning learned together as a unit.

There is no way of predicting the sound and meaning of an unknown Chinese character with any degree of accuracy. This does not mean, however, that there is no system behind the characters at all. All characters contain at least one of the component parts known as "radicals", and almost all radicals have an element of meaning; if you are familiar with these, not only will using a dictionary be much easier, it will also help you identify more of the building blocks of the characters you are trying to learn.

SIMPLIFIED AND COMPLEX CHARACTERS
In the 1950s and 60s the government of the People's Republic of China simplified the Chinese script, in an effort to improve the literacy rate by making characters easier to write. This dictionary uses simplified characters, with traditional or complex character variants given in brackets.

CHINESE GRAMMAR
Compared to many languages, Chinese grammar is not particularly complicated.

Words do not change according to gender, number or case the way they do in many European languages. Sentence structure is generally straightforward, and there are not many exceptions to the grammatical rules (unlike English).

TALKING ABOUT TIME
It is sometimes said that Chinese has no tenses. This is not quite true, but speakers of Chinese talk about time in a way that is quite different from ours.

The English tense system is based on the idea of before and after the point of view of the narrator. Things that happened before the time in which we are talking take the past tense, those that are in the process of going on, the present, and things that have yet to take place, the future. This is shown by a change in the verbs. Chinese verbs, on the other hand, do not change with tense, but an aspect marker is placed before or after the verb. Some of the most common are 了 le (for completed actions – usually *but not always* in the past), 过 guò (for events that have already taken place), 要 yào (for things that are going to happen) and 在 zài (for things that are in the process of happening). These are no more than generalizations, however, and it is important not to use them indiscriminately as substitutes for English tenses, as that is not what they are for.

Adverbs of time are often used to show what time relation events have to each other, such as 已经 yǐjīng (already), 曾经 céngjīng (once), or specific times or dates.

明年我去中国。 Míngnián wǒ qù Zhōngguó.
(literally: Next year I go China). I'm going to China next year.

MEASURE WORDS

These are not unique to Chinese – you occasionally see something similar in English.

> a *gaggle* of geese
> a *piece* of fruit
> six *pints* of milk etc.

They do not occur very often in English. In Chinese, however, measure words are mandatory when giving a number of nouns. It is important to remember to put them in – and also to get them right, as there are a lot of measure words in Chinese.

一只青蛙	yī zhī qīngwā	one frog
三部电影	sān bù diànyǐng	three films
五封信	wǔ fēng xìn	five letters

Different measure words are used for different types of objects.
张 zhāng is used for flat things, such as tickets, sheets and tables.
条 tiáo is used to talk about long, thin things such as ribbons, or fish.
The most common measure word is 个 gè, and it is a useful "default setting" for when you cannot remember the exact term you need.

WORD ORDER

Because of the less specific nature of the Chinese view of time, the tendency to avoid redundancy and the lack of cases to show a word's function in the sentence, word order is important in Chinese. It generally follows a subject-verb-object pattern, although there are certain particles or rhetorical constructions that change the order slightly. If the word order is wrong, it can be very hard to unscramble the sense of a phrase or sentence.

All this may seem a little intimidating to a beginner. However, the challenge of learning Chinese is in direct proportion to the pleasure of being able to use it. Not only is it an absorbing and intriguing language, which can express both brutal frankness and extreme delicacy, it also brings with it great opportunities to learn about a new and very different country and culture. And there could be no better time to begin that exploration than now, when China is taking a greater role in the world.

Esther Tyldesley
University of Edinburgh

HOW TO USE THE DICTIONARY

On the following pages you will find an outline of how information is presented in your Collins Chinese Dictionary. We hope that this will help you to get the most out of your dictionary, not simply from its comprehensive wordlist, but also from the information provided in each entry.

CHINESE-ENGLISH SIDE
HEAD ENTRIES

On the Chinese side, head entries are ordered traditionally, that is by single-character entries with multiple-character entries beginning with the same character nested below them.

标　biāo
　标本　biāoběn
　标点　biāodiǎn
　标记　biāojì
　标题　biāotí
　标志　biāozhì
　标准　biāozhǔn

表　biǎo
　表达　biǎodá

Single character entries are ordered by Pinyin, that is alphabetically and then by tone. In Chinese, there are four tones, each represented by a different mark above the relevant vowel:

‾	first tone	(flat tone)	mā
´	second tone	(rising tone)	má
ˇ	third tone	(falling rising tone)	mǎ
`	fourth tone	(falling tone)	mà
	light or no tone		ma

Where characters have the same Pinyin and tone, they are ordered by the number of strokes in the character, with the smallest number of strokes first.

八	bā
巴	bā
芭	bā
疤	bā

Where characters have the same Pinyin, tone, and number of strokes, they are ordered by the first stroke in the character, as follows:
一 丨 丿 丶 乛

The multiple-character entries nested below single-character entries are similarly ordered by the Pinyin (including tone), and then by the number of strokes.

蒸	**zhēng**
蒸气	**zhēngqì**
蒸汽	**zhēngqì**

Polyphones, that is characters with more than one pronunciation, are cross-referred to the alternative Pinyin.

斗 **dǒu** [名] **1**(指容器) cup **2**(斗状物) ▶ 烟斗 yāndǒu pipe ▶ 漏斗 lòudǒu funnel
→ *see also*/另见 dòu

斗(鬥) **dòu** [动] **1**(打斗) fight ▶ 斗鸡 dòujī cock fighting **2**(战胜) beat
→ *see also*/另见 dǒu

RADICAL AND CHARACTER INDEX

If you do not know the pronunciation for the Chinese character that you are looking for, you can use the index before the start of the Chinese-English side. For further information on how to use the radical index, see the introduction to that section.

THE STRUCTURE OF ENTRIES

On the Chinese side there are two levels of entry (single-character entries and multiple-character entries), both of which have essentially the same entry structure. Pinyin romanization is given for both types of entry.

This dictionary uses simplified characters, with traditional character variants given in round brackets. On the Chinese side, traditional characters are given for single-character entries and multiple-character entries.

Parts of speech are given in square brackets after the Pinyin. Where a word has more than one part of speech, Roman numerals are used. For a full list of all parts of speech used, see page xvii.

Where an entry has more than one meaning, it is divided into categories, which are shown by an Arabic numeral.

When expressing yourself in another language, it is important to be aware of when you can use certain words and expressions and with whom – you would communicate very differently with a business colleague than with a friend. To help you, we have labelled words and expressions appropriately throughout the dictionary.

A full list of field and register labels used in the dictionary is shown on pages xviii–xx.

EXAMPLES

Word examples are preceded by a shaded arrow ▶. Fuller examples are preceded by an empty arrow ▷.

TRANSLATIONS

Translations are shown in normal roman type after the part of speech or indicator. In general, we have only given one translation per meaning, since we believe this is the most accurate and helpful approach.

In a few cases, there is no equivalent at all, and an explanation rather than a translation has to be given. In such cases it is shown in italics:

压(壓)岁(歲)钱(錢) yāsuìqián
[名] *traditional gifts of money given
to children during the Spring Festival*

British and American English variants are shown where appropriate, and alternative parts of translations are preceded by 或 ('or'):

大学(學)生 dàxuéshēng [名]
university (英) 或 college (美) student

ENGLISH-CHINESE SIDE
HEADWORDS

The words you look up in the dictionary – 'headwords' – are listed alphabetically. Homonyms (words which are written in the same way but have different pronunciations) are shown as separate headwords and differentiated by the use of superscript numbers. For example:

bow¹ [bəu] N [c] **1** (*knot*) 蝴蝶结(結)
húdiéjié [个 gè] **2** (*weapon*) 弓
gōng [把 bǎ]
bow² [bau] I vi (*with head, body*) 鞠躬
jūgōng II vt [+ *head*] 低头(頭) dītóu

American spellings of words are always shown, at the headword which is spelled in the British way:

axe, (*US*) **ax** [æks] N [c] 斧 fǔ [把 bǎ]

Irregular past tenses and plural forms are also shown as headwords in their alphabetical position and cross-referred to the base form. For example:

children ['tʃɪldrən] NPL *of* **child**

went [wɛnt] PT *of* **go**

THE STRUCTURE OF ENTRIES

This dictionary uses simplified characters, with traditional character variants given in round brackets. On the English side, traditional characters are given for all translations of headwords and phrases preceded by ▶.

Parts of speech are given in upper case after the phonetic spelling of the headword. We have used the notations C, U and S and PL in square brackets after each noun to show whether nouns are countable, uncountable, singular or plural. C means that the noun is countable, and has a plural form (eg *I'm reading a book; she's bought several books*). U means that the noun is is not normally counted, and is not used in the plural (eg *Lesley refused to give me more information*). S (*for singular noun*) means that the noun is always singular, and is usually preceded by *a*, *an* or *the* (eg *We need to persuade people to repect the environment*). PL means the noun is always plural, and is used with plural verbs or pronouns (eg *These clothes are ready to wear*). For a full list of all parts of speech used, see page xvii.

hairdryer ['hɛədraɪəʳ] N [c] 吹
风(風)机(機) chuīfēngjī [个 gè]

hair gel N [U] 发(髮)胶(膠) fàjiāo

kick-off ['kɪkɔf] N [s] 开(開)场(場)
时(時)间(間) kāichǎng shíjiān

Where an entry has more than one meaning, it is divided into categories, which are shown by an Arabic numeral. You will often find information in round brackets or square brackets and also in *italics* after the meaning category number. This information functions as a 'signpost' to help the user select the right translation when there is more than one to choose from. This 'signpost' or indicator may give a synonym of the headword, typical contexts in which the word might appear or a label indicating the subject field in which the word is used.

A full list of field and register labels used in the dictionary is shown on pages xviii–xx.

link [lɪŋk] I N [c] 1 联(聯)系(繫)
liánxì [种 zhǒng] 2 (*Comput*) (*also:*
hyperlink) 超链(鏈)接 chāoliànjiē
[个 gè] II vт 1 [+ *places, objects*]
连(連)接 liánjiē 2 [+ *people,
situations*] 联(聯)系(繫) liánxì

PHRASES

All phrases are given in bold and preceded by a shaded arrow ▶.

half-time [hɑːf'taɪm] (*Sport*) N [U]
半场(場) bànchǎng ▶ **at half-time**
半场(場)时(時) bànchǎng shí

TRANSLATIONS

Translations are shown in normal roman type after the part of speech or indicator. In general, we have only given one translation per meaning, since we believe this is the most accurate and helpful approach. In a few cases, there is no equivalent at all, and an explanation rather than a translation has to be given.

au pair [ˈəʊˈpɛəʳ] N [c] 为学习语言
而住在当地人家里并提供家政服务
的外国年轻人

PINYIN

Pinyin romanization is given for all translations, except where, as above, there is no real equivalent in Chinese and an explanation rather than a translation has been given.

MEASURE WORDS

Measure words are given after translations of nouns which are countable and take a measure word. They are given in square brackets, with their Pinyin. For more information on measure words, see the introduction on page v–vii.

banknote [ˈbæŋknəʊt] N [c]
纸(紙)币(幣) zhǐbì [张 zhāng]

KEYWORDS

Certain commonly used words, such as *have* and *do*, have been treated in special depth because they constitute basic elements of English and have very many uses and meanings. We have given them a special design to make it easier to find the meaning of construction you are looking for.

 KEYWORD

have [hæv] (*pt, pp* **had**) I ᴠᴛ **1** 有 yǒu ▸ **he
has** *or* **he has got blue eyes/dark hair**
他长(長)着(著)蓝(藍)眼睛/黑头(頭)
发(髮) tā zhǎngzhe lán yǎnjing/hēi
tóufa ▸ **do you have** *or* **have you got a
car/phone?** 你有车(車)/电(電)话(話)

LANGUAGE NOTES

Language notes have been given at certain entries on the Chinese side, for example, 盏 zhǎn and 捌 bā. These are intended to give learners more information about certain important aspects of the Chinese language.

CULTURAL NOTES

A number of entries include cultural notes, giving an insight into Chinese life and culture. These notes cover many subject areas including political institutions and systems, national festivals and Chinese traditions and customs.

如何使用本词典

接下来的几页概要地叙述本词典内容的组织方式。希望此说明能让使用者通过广泛的选词以及每个词条中的信息最有效地使用本词典。

汉英部分
顺序

在汉英部分，词目按传统顺序排列，即单字词条下嵌入以相同汉字开头的多字词条。

标 biāo
  标本 biāoběn
  标点 biāodiǎn
  标记 biāojì
  标题 biāotí
  标志 biāozhì
  标准 biāozhǔn

表 biǎo
  表达 biǎodá

单字词条按拼音字母顺序排序，再按声调顺序排序。注意，轻声排在四声之后。同音字按笔画的多寡排列，笔画少的在前，笔画多的在后。

八	bā
巴	bā
芭	bā
疤	bā

笔画相同的同音字按起笔笔画排列，顺序为：一丨丿丶乛。

单字词条下的多字词条也先按照拼音（包括声调），再按照笔画数进行排序。

蒸	zhēng
蒸气	zhēngqì
蒸汽	zhēngqì

多音字，即有一个以上发音的汉字，会标明"另见"，后接另一个发音。

斗 dǒu [名] **1**(指容器) cup **2**(斗状物) ▶ 烟斗 yāndǒu pipe ▶ 漏斗 lòudǒu funnel
→ see also/另见 dòu

斗(鬥) dòu [动] **1**(打斗) fight ▶ 斗鸡 dòujī cock fighting **2**(战胜) beat
→ see also/另见 dǒu

部首与汉字索引

如果使用者不知道所见汉字的发音，可查阅位于汉英部分之前的部首检字表。详见部首检字表中的检字方法说明。

词条构成

汉语部分的词条有两个层次，单字词条和多字词条，但它们的构成方式基本相同。所有词条都标注汉语拼音。

本词典使用简体字。繁体字附列在圆括号内。在汉英部分，单字词条和多字词条均附有繁体字。

词性在方括号中用中文标注，紧随拼音之后。如果有一个以上的词性，用罗马数字标识。词性列表参见第xxiv页。

如果一个词条有一个以上的词义，则归入不同的义项，用阿拉伯数字标出。当一个词具有多种含义时，读者可以根据阿拉伯数字后圆（方）括号中及斜体字传达的信息找到相关的语境，进而查到正确的翻译。圆括号中的信息起到"路标"的功能，此"路标"标示了主词条的同义词或近义词，以及使用主词条的典型语境。

专业学科领域及修辞色彩缩略语列表见xviii页至xx页。

例子

以词的形式出现的例子，前面用实心灰色箭头 ▶ 标出。更完整的例子，前面用空心箭头 ▷ 标出。

翻译

一般情况下，作为最精确、有效的办法，每个意义只提供一个翻译。在某些情况下，如果根本没有相应的翻译对等语，则提供该词的解释，而不是翻译，用斜体表示。

压(壓)岁(歲)钱(錢) yāsuìqián
   [名] *traditional gifts of money given to children during the Spring Festival*

以-s结尾的名词，若用作复数，则标注为pl，若用作单数，则标注为sg。

奥(奧)林匹克运(運)动(動)
   会(會) Àolínpǐkè Yùndònghuì
   [名] Olympic Games® (*pl*)

算术(術) suànshù [名] maths (英)
   (*sg*) math (美)

必要时，同时给出英式英语和美式英语两种翻译，中间用"或"字隔开。
大学(學)生 dàxuéshēng [名] university (英) 或 college (美) student

英汉部分
同音异义词

书写相同但发音完全不同的单词作为单独的词条出现，并且用数字上标加以区分：

bow[1] [bəʊ] N [c] **1** (*knot*) 蝴蝶结(結)
húdiéjié [个 gè] **2** (*weapon*) 弓
gōng [把 bǎ]
bow[2] [baʊ] I vi (*with head, body*) 鞠躬
jūgōng II vt [+ *head*] 低头(頭) dītóu

如上所示，数字上标明确表明该单词的发音完全不同。

单词的拼写变体也作为单独的词条列出，并参见至首先出现的拼写形式，单词的美式拼写列在英式拼写之后：

pajamas [pəˈdʒɑːməz] (*US*) N PL = **pyjamas**

axe, (*US*) **ax** [æks] N [c] 斧 fǔ [把 bǎ]

不规则动词的时态变化和不规则名词的复数形式作为单独的词条列出，并且指示参照原形：

children [ˈtʃɪldrən] N PL *of* **child**

went [wɛnt] PT *of* **go**

如果一个单词有一个以上的词义，则归入不同的意类，用阿拉伯数字标出。进一步的词义区分在括号中用斜体表示。当一个词条有多种含义时，读者可以根据阿拉伯数字后圆括号中的信息找到相关的语境，进而查到正确的翻译。圆括号中的信息起到"路标"的功能，此"路标"标示了主词条的同义词或近义词，以及使用主词条的典型语境。

专业学科领域及修辞色彩缩略语表见xviii页至xx页。

link [lɪŋk] I N [c] **1** 联(聯)系(繫)
liánxì [种 zhǒng] **2** (*Comput*) (*also*:
hyperlink) 超链(鏈)接 chāoliànjiē
[个 gè] II vt **1** [+ *places, objects*]
连(連)接 liánjiē **2** [+ *people,
situations*] 联(聯)系(繫) liánxì

短语

短语用黑体表示，并跟在实心灰色箭头标志▶后。短语包括不同种类的固定结构、感叹语和其他语法结构：

to have a baby　　　**in the background**　　　**to pack one's bags**

例子

例句用斜体表示，并跟在空心箭头标志▷后。英语中最常用单词，都给出了大量的例子及在相应语境中的翻译，有助于读者在具体的语境中正确使用单词。

翻译

一般情况下，作为最精确、有效的办法，每个意义只提供一个翻译。在某些情况下，如果根本没有相应的翻译对等语，则提供该词的解释，而不是翻译。

au pair [ˈəuˈpɛəʳ] N [c] 为学习语言
而住在当地人家里并提供家政服务
的外国年轻人

拼音

词条及动词词组翻译都标注有拼音。如果该词条没有相应的翻译，则给出相关的解释以帮助读者理解，并省略拼音。

量词

量词在可数名词的翻译之后，和拼音一起括在方括号中。关于量词的详细信息请见序言中的viii页。

banknote [ˈbæŋknəut] N [c]
纸(紙)币(幣) zhǐbì [张 zhāng]

关键词

对于一些极其常用的词，例如have和do, 我们给予了长篇的注释。这类词是构成英语的基本要素，语义众多，用法复杂。本词典对该类词作了特别的外观设计，便于读者查阅。

🔘 **KEYWORD**

have [hæv] (*pt, pp* had) I vt **1** 有 yǒu ▶ he
has *or* he has got blue eyes/dark hair
他长(長)着(著)蓝(藍)眼睛/黑头(頭)
发(髮) tā zhǎngzhe lán yǎnjing/hēi
tóufa ▶ do you have *or* have you got a
car/phone? 你有车(車)/电(電)话(話)

语言注释

为了帮助读者更加准确，熟练地掌握并运用英语，我们对一些易混淆词进行了详细的比较说明。

文化注释

对于英语国家中特有的文化现象，我们都加注了说明和解释。

略语表/REFERENCE LIST

PARTS OF SPEECH		词性
abbreviation	ABBR	简
adjective	ADJ	形
adverb	ADV	副
auxiliary verb	AUX VB	助动
auxiliary word	AUX	助
conjunction	CONJ	连
compound	CPD	复合词
definite article	DEF ART	定冠词
indefinite article	INDEF ART	不定冠词
interjection	INT	叹
noun	N	名
noun abbreviation	N ABBR	名词缩写
singular noun	N SING	单数名词
noun (plural)	N(PL)	名词(复数)
noun plural	NPL	复数名词
numeral	NUM	数
plural	PL	复数
plural adjective	PL ADJ	复数形容词
plural pronoun	PL PRON	复数代词
past participle	PP	过去分词
prefix	PREFIX	前缀
preposition	PREP	介
pres part	PRES PART	现在分词
pronoun	PRON	代
past tense	PT	过去时
suffix	SUFFIX	后缀
verb	VB	动
intransitive verb	VI	不及物动词
transitive verb	VT	及物动词
indicates that particle cannot be separated from the main verb	VT FUS	及物动词

SUBJECT FIELD LABELS   专业学科领域

Administration	*Admin*	行政
Agriculture	*Agr*	农
Anatomy	*Anat*	解剖
Architecture	*Archit*	建筑
Art		艺术
Astrology	*Astrol*	占星术
Astronomy	*Astron*	天文
Motoring	*Aut*	汽车
Aviation	*Aviat*	航空
Badminton		羽毛球
Baseball		棒球
Biology	*Bio*	生物
Bookkeeping		簿记
Botany	*Bot*	植物
Bowls		滚木球
Boxing		拳击
Cards		纸牌
Chemistry	*Chem*	化
Chess		国际象棋
Cinema	*Cine*	电影
Climbing		登山
Clothing		服饰
Commerce	*Comm*	商
Computing	*Comput*	计算机
Cricket		板球
Cooking	*Culin*	烹饪
Drawing		绘画
Drugs		药品
Economics	*Econ*	经济
Electricity	*Elec*	电子
Fencing		击剑
Finance	*Fin*	金融
Fishing		钓鱼
Football		足球

		专业学科领域
Geography	*Geo*	地理
Geology	*Geol*	地质
Geometry	*Geom*	几何
Golf		高尔夫
Grammar	*Gram*	语法
History	*Hist*	历史
Industry	*Ind*	工业
Insurance		保险
Law		法
Linguistics	*Ling*	语言
Literature	*Liter*	文学
Mathematics	*Math*	数
Medicine	*Med*	医
Meteorology	*Met*	气象
Military	*Mil*	军
Mining	*Min*	矿
Music	*Mus*	音
Mythology	*Myth*	神
Nautical	*Naut*	航海
Parliament	*Parl*	议会
Philosophy	*Phil*	哲
Photography	*Phot*	摄影
Physics	*Phys*	物
Physiology	*Physiol*	生理
Politics	*Pol*	政治
Police		警察
Post office	*Post*	邮政
Psychology	*Psych*	心理
Publishing		出版
Radio	*Rad*	广播
Railways	*Rail*	铁路
Religion	*Rel*	宗
Rugby		橄榄球
Science	*Sci*	科学

SUBJECT FIELD LABELS		专业学科领域
School	*Scol*	教育
Sewing		缝纫
Sociology	*Sociol*	社会
Space		宇航
Sport		体育
Technical usage	*Tech*	术语
Telecommunications	*Tel*	电信
Tennis		网球
Texting		手机短信
Theatre	*Theat*	戏剧
Television	*TV*	电视
University	*Univ*	大学
Zoology	*Zool*	动

REGISTER LABELS		修辞色彩缩略语
dialect		方
euphemism		婉
formal	*frm*	正式
formerly		旧
humorous		诙谐
informal	*inf*	非正式
literary	*liter*	文
offensive		侮辱
old-fashioned	*o.f.*	过时
taboo	*inf!*	疑讳/讳
pejorative	*pej*	贬
humble		谦
respectful		敬
slang		俚
spoken language		口
written		书
polite		客套
literal	*lit*	字
figurative	*fig*	喻

英语发音指导/GUIDE TO ENGLISH PHONETICS

辅音/CONSONANTS

[b]   baby
[t]   tent
[d]   daddy
[k]   cork kiss chord
[g]   gag guess
[s]   so rice kiss
[z]   cousin buzz
[ʃ]   sheep sugar
[ʒ]   pleasure beige
[tʃ]   church
[dʒ]   judge general
[f]   farm raffle
[v]   very rev
[θ]   thin maths
[ð]   that other
[l]   little ball
[r]   rat rare
[m]   mummy comb
[n]   no ran
[ŋ]   singing bank
[h]   hat reheat
[x]   loch

半元音/SEMIVOWELS

[j]   yet
[w]   wet

元音/VOWELS

[iː]   heel
[ɪ]   hit pity
[ɛ]   set tent
[æ]   bat apple
[ɑ]   after car calm
[ʌ]   fun cousin
[ə]   over above
[əː]   urn fern work
[ɔ]   wash pot
[ɔː]   born cork
[u]   full soot
[uː]   pool lewd

双元音/DIPHTHONGS

[ɪə]   beer tier
[ɛə]   tear fair there
[eɪ]   date plaice day
[aɪ]   life buy cry
[au]   owl foul now
[əu]   low no
[ɔɪ]   boil boy oily
[uə]   poor tour

不规则动词/ENGLISH IRREGULAR VERBS

PRESENT	PT	PP
arise	arose	arisen
awake	awoke	awoken
be (am, is, are; being)	was, were	been
bear	bore	born(e)
beat	beat	beaten
begin	began	begun
bend	bent	bent
bet	bet, betted	bet, betted
bid (at auction)	bid	bid
bind	bound	bound
bite	bit	bitten
bleed	bled	bled
blow	blew	blown
break	broke	broken
breed	bred	bred
bring	brought	brought
build	built	built
burn	burnt, burned	burnt, burned
burst	burst	burst
buy	bought	bought
can	could	(been able)
cast	cast	cast
catch	caught	caught
choose	chose	chosen
cling	clung	clung
come	came	come
cost	cost	cost
creep	crept	crept
cut	cut	cut
deal	dealt	dealt
dig	dug	dug
do (does)	did	done

PRESENT	PT	PP
draw	drew	drawn
dream	dreamed, dreamt	dreamed, dreamt
drink	drank	drunk
drive	drove	driven
eat	ate	eaten
fall	fell	fallen
feed	fed	fed
feel	felt	felt
fight	fought	fought
find	found	found
fling	flung	flung
fly	flew	flown
forbid	forbad(e)	forbidden
forecast	forecast	forecast
forget	forgot	forgotten
forgive	forgave	forgiven
freeze	froze	frozen
get	got	got, (US) gotten
give	gave	given
go (goes)	went	gone
grind	ground	ground
grow	grew	grown
hang	hung	hung
hang (execute)	hanged	hanged
have	had	had
hear	heard	heard
hide	hid	hidden
hit	hit	hit
hold	held	held
hurt	hurt	hurt
keep	kept	kept
kneel	knelt, kneeled	knelt, kneeled
know	knew	known
lay	laid	laid
lead	led	led

PRESENT	PT	PP
lean	leant, leaned	leant, leaned
leap	leapt, leaped	leapt, leaped
learn	learnt, learned	learnt, learned
leave	left	left
lend	lent	lent
let	let	let
lie (lying)	lay	lain
light	lit, lighted	lit, lighted
lose	lost	lost
make	made	made
may	might	–
mean	meant	meant
meet	met	met
mistake	mistook	mistaken
mow	mowed	mown, mowed
must	(had to)	(had to)
pay	paid	paid
put	put	put
quit	quit, quitted	quit, quited
read	read	read
rid	rid	rid
ride	rode	ridden
ring	rang	rung
rise	rose	risen
run	ran	run
saw	sawed	sawed, sawn
say	said	said
see	saw	seen
sell	sold	sold
send	sent	sent
set	set	set
sew	sewed	sewn
shake	shook	shaken
shear	sheared	shorn, sheared
shed	shed	shed

PRESENT	PT	PP
shine	shone	shone
shoot	shot	shot
show	showed	shown
shrink	shrank	shrunk
shut	shut	shut
sing	sang	sung
sink	sank	sunk
sit	sat	sat
sleep	slept	slept
slide	slid	slid
sling	slung	slung
slit	slit	slit
smell	smelt, smelled	smelt, smelled
sow	sowed	sown, sowed
speak	spoke	spoken
speed	sped, speeded	sped, speeded
spell	spelt, spelled	spelt, spelled
spend	spent	spent
spill	spilt, spilled	spilt, spilled
spin	spun	spun
spit	spat	spat
spoil	spoiled, spoilt	spoiled, spoilt
spread	spread	spread
spring	sprang	sprung
stand	stood	stood
steal	stole	stolen
stick	stuck	stuck
sting	stung	stung
stink	stank	stunk
stride	strode	stridden
strike	struck	struck
swear	swore	sworn
sweep	swept	swept
swell	swelled	swollen, swelled
swim	swam	swum

PRESENT	PT	PP
swing	swung	swung
take	took	taken
teach	taught	taught
tear	tore	torn
tell	told	told
think	thought	thought
throw	threw	thrown
thrust	thrust	thrust
tread	trod	trodden
wake	woke, waked	woken, waked
wear	wore	worn
weave	wove	woven
weep	wept	wept
win	won	won
wind	wound	wound
wring	wrung	wrung
write	wrote	written

Radical Index

部首检字表
Radical Index

检字方法说明:

1 根据字的部首在部首目录中查到该部首所在检字表中的号码;

2 按此号码在检字表中找到该部首,并根据字的笔画
(字的笔画数不含其部首)查到该字的汉语拼音。
繁体字置于括号中。

How to use this index:

1 Use pages 3–4 to identify the radical. Note the number
preceding it.

2 In the index on pages 5–42, use this number to find all the
characters appearing in this dictionary which contain the radical.
Characters are ordered according to the number of strokes.
The Pinyin given will lead you to the correct entry.
Traditional characters are shown in brackets.

部首目录

一画 (1 stroke)

1　一
2　丨
3　丿
4　丶
5　乙
　　(乁乚乛)

二画 (2 strokes)

6　二
7　十
8　十
9　厂
10　匚
11　刂
12　卜 (⺊)
13　冂
14　亻
15　八 (丷)
16　人 (入)
17　勹
18　几
19　儿
20　亠
21　冫
22　冖
23　讠 (言)
24　卩
25　阝
　　(on the left
　　(在左边))
26　阝
　　(on the right
　　(在右边))
27　凵
28　刀
29　力
30　厶
31　又
32　廴

三画 (3 strokes)

33　巛
34　工
35　土
36　士
37　扌
38　艹
39　寸
40　廾
　　(underneath
　　(在下边))
41　大
42　尢
43　小 (⺌)
44　口
45　囗
46　巾
47　山
48　彳
49　彡
50　犭
51　夕
52　夂
53　饣 (食)
54　丬 (爿)
55　广
56　忄
57　门 (門)
58　氵
59　宀
60　辶
61　彐 (彐)
62　尸
63　己 (巳)
64　弓
65　子
66　女
67　纟 (糸)
68　马 (馬)
69　幺

四画 (4 strokes)

70　王
71　毋 (母)
72　殳
73　韦 (韋)
74　木
75　犬
76　歹
77　车 (車)
78　比
79　瓦
80　止
81　支
82　日
83　曰
84　水
85　贝 (貝)
86　见 (見)
87　牛 (牜)
88　手
89　毛
90　气
91　攵
92　片
93　斤
94　爪 (爫)
95　父
96　月
97　欠
98　风 (風)
99　文
100　方
101　火
102　斗
103　灬
104　户 (戶)
105　礻
106　心
107　聿 (肀)
108　戈

五画 **(5 strokes)**
109 用
110 示
111 石
112 龙
113 目
114 田
115 罒
116 皿
117 钅(金)
118 矢
119 禾
120 白
121 瓜
122 鸟(鳥)
123 疒
124 立
125 穴
126 衤
127 疋(疋)
128 皮
129 矛

六画 **(6 strokes)**
130 臣
131 自
132 耒
133 老(耂)
134 耳
135 西(襾)
136 页(頁)
137 虍
138 虫
139 缶
140 舌
141 竹(竹)
142 臼
143 血
144 舟
145 衣
146 羊(羊羊)
147 米
148 艮(食)
149 羽
150 糸
151 (行)

七画 **(7 strokes)**
152 辰
153 赤
154 走
155 豆
156 酉
157 卤(鹵)
158 里
159 足(足)
160 身
161 采
162 豸
163 角
164 言
165 辛

八画 **(8 strokes)**
166 齿(齒)
167 金
168 青
169 雨
170 隹
171 鱼(魚)
172 (長)

九画 **(9 strokes)**
173 音
174 革
175 骨
176 鬼
177 食

十画 **(10 strokes)**
178 髟
179 (鬥)

十一画 **(11 strokes)**
180 鹿
181 麻
182 (麥)

十二画 **(12 strokes)**
183 黑

十三画 **(13 strokes)**
184 鼠

十四画 **(14 strokes)**
185 鼻

十六画 **(16 strokes)**
186 (龍)

十七画 **(17 strokes)**
187 (龜)

1 一

一　yī

一画 (1 stroke)

七　qī

二画 (2 strokes)

三　sān
干　gān; gàn
于　yú
下　xià
丈　zhàng
才　cái
万　wàn
上　shàng
与　yǔ

三画 (3 strokes)

丰　fēng
井　jǐng
开　kāi
夫　fū
天　tiān
无　wú
五　wǔ
专　zhuān
不　bù
互　hù
牙　yá
丑　chǒu

四画 (4 strokes)

业　yè
册　cè
东　dōng
可　kě
平　píng
世　shì
丝　sī
末　mò
未　wèi
正　zhēng; zhèng

五画 (5 strokes)

百　bǎi
而　ér
亚　yà
再　zài
(丢)　diū

六画 (6 strokes)

严　yán
更　gēng; gèng
束　shù
两　liǎng
来　lái
求　qiú

七画 (7 strokes)

表　biǎo
丧　sāng; sàng
事　shì
(並)　bìng

八画 (8 strokes)

甚　shèn
巷　xiàng
歪　wāi
面　miàn

九画 (9 strokes)

哥　gē

十五画 (15 strokes)

整　zhěng

2 丨

三画 (3 strokes)

中　zhōng
内　nèi

四画 (4 strokes)

北　běi
旧　jiù
申　shēn
电　diàn
由　yóu
史　shǐ
出　chū

五画 (5 strokes)

师　shī
曲　qǔ
肉　ròu

六画 (6 strokes)

串　chuàn

3 丿

七画 (7 strokes)

非　fēi

八画 (8 strokes)

临　lín

一画 (1 stroke)

九　jiǔ

二画 (2 strokes)

川　chuān
及　jí
久　jiǔ
千　qiān
丸　wán

三画 (3 strokes)

币　bì
长　cháng; zhǎng
反　fǎn
升　shēng
乌　wū
午　wǔ

四画 (4 strokes)

生　shēng
失　shī
甩　shuǎi
乐　lè; yuè

五画 (5 strokes)

年　nián
丢　diū
乒　pīng
向　xiàng
后　hòu

六画 (6 strokes)

我　wǒ
每　měi
龟　guī
系　xì

七画 (7 strokes)

垂　chuí
乖　guāi
质　zhì
周　zhōu

八画 (8 strokes)

拜	bài
重	chóng; zhòng
复	fù

九画 (9 strokes)

乘	chéng

十一画 (11 strokes)

甥	shēng

十三画 (13 strokes)

舞	wǔ
疑	yí

十四画 (14 strokes)

靠	kào

---

4 丶

二画 (2 strokes)

义	yì
之	zhī

三画 (3 strokes)

为	wéi; wèi

四画 (4 strokes)

半	bàn
主	zhǔ
头	tóu

五画 (5 strokes)

兴	xīng; xìng
农	nóng

六画 (6 strokes)

良	liáng

七画 (7 strokes)

学	xué

八画 (8 strokes)

举	jǔ

---

5 乙 (乁乚乛)

一画 (1 stroke)

了	le; liǎo

二画 (2 strokes)

乞	qǐ
也	yě
飞	fēi
习	xí
乡	xiāng

三画 (3 strokes)

巴	bā
孔	kǒng
书	shū

四画 (4 strokes)

司	sī
民	mín

五画 (5 strokes)

买	mǎi

六画 (6 strokes)

乱	luàn

七画 (7 strokes)

承	chéng

八画 (8 strokes)

(飛)	fēi

十二画 (12 strokes)

(亂)	luàn

---

6 二

二	èr

一画 (1 stroke)

亏	kuī

二画 (2 strokes)

元	yuán
云	yún

六画 (6 strokes)

些	xiē
(亞)	yà

---

7 匕

九画 (9 strokes)

匙	chí

---

8 十

十	shí

二画 (2 strokes)

支	zhī

三画 (3 strokes)

古	gǔ

四画 (4 strokes)

考	kǎo
协	xié
毕	bì
华	huá

五画 (5 strokes)

克	kè

六画 (6 strokes)

直	zhí
卖	mài
(協)	xié

七画 (7 strokes)

南	nán

八画 (8 strokes)

真	zhēn

十画 (10 strokes)

博	bó

十一画 (11 strokes)

(幹)	gàn

---

9 厂

厂	chǎng

二画 (2 strokes)

历	lì
厅	tīng

三画 (3 strokes)

厉	lì

四画 (4 strokes)

压	yā
厌	yàn

六画 (6 strokes)

厕　cè

七画 (7 strokes)

厚　hòu
厘　lí

八画 (8 strokes)

原　yuán

十画 (10 strokes)

厦　shà
厨　chú
雁　yàn

十二画 (12 strokes)

（厴）yàn

十三画 (13 strokes)

（厲）lì

10　匚

二画 (2 strokes)

区　qū
匹　pǐ
巨　jù

五画 (5 strokes)

医　yī

九画 (9 strokes)

（區）qū

十一画 (11 strokes)

（匯）huì

11　刂

三画 (3 strokes)

刊　kān

四画 (4 strokes)

创　chuāng; chuàng
划　huá; huà
刑　xíng
列　liè
刚　gāng

五画 (5 strokes)

别　bié
（別）bié
利　lì
判　pàn
删　shān
（刪）shān

六画 (6 strokes)

刺　cì
到　dào
剁　duò
制　zhì
刮　guā
刻　kè
刹　shā
刷　shuā

七画 (7 strokes)

前　qián
剃　tì
削　xiāo

八画 (8 strokes)

剥　bāo
（剝）bāo
剧　jù
剔　tī
（剛）gāng

九画 (9 strokes)

副　fù

十画 (10 strokes)

割　gē
剩　shèng
（創）chuāng; chuàng

十二画 (12 strokes)

（劃）huà

十三画 (13 strokes)

（劇）jù

12　卜（⼘）

二画 (2 strokes)

卡　kǎ

三画 (3 strokes)

占　zhàn
外　wài

六画 (6 strokes)

卧　wò

八画 (8 strokes)

桌　zhuō

13　冂

三画 (3 strokes)

（冊）cè

四画 (4 strokes)

同　tóng
网　wǎng

14　亻

一画 (1 stroke)

亿　yì

二画 (2 strokes)

仇　chóu
化　huà
什　shén
仍　réng
仅　jǐn

三画 (3 strokes)

代　dài
付　fù
们　men
仨　sā
仪　yí
他　tā
仔　zǐ
仙　xiān

四画 (4 strokes)

传　chuán
份　fèn
仰　yǎng
仿　fǎng
伙　huǒ
价　jià
休　xiū

优　yōu
件　jiàn
伦　lún
任　rèn
伤　shāng
似　sì
伟　wěi
伪　wěi
伍　wǔ

五画 (5 strokes)

估　gū
何　hé
体　tǐ
但　dàn
伸　shēn
作　zuò
伯　bó
佣　yōng; yòng
低　dī
你　nǐ
住　zhù
位　wèi
伴　bàn
佛　fó
(佔)　zhàn

六画 (6 strokes)

侄　zhí
供　gōng
佩　pèi
使　shǐ
佰　bǎi
例　lì
侄　zhí
侧　cè
依　yī

七画 (7 strokes)

修　xiū
保　bǎo
便　biàn; pián
促　cù
俄　é
俩　liǎ
俭　jiǎn
侵　qīn
俗　sú
侮　wǔ
信　xìn

八画 (8 strokes)

倡　chàng
借　jiè
值　zhí
倾　qīng
倒　dǎo; dào
倍　bèi
健　jiàn
俱　jù
(倫)　lún
(們)　men
(個)　gè
(倆)　liǎ

九画 (9 strokes)

偿　cháng
做　zuò
偶　ǒu
偏　piān
偷　tōu
停　tíng
假　jiǎ; jià
(側)　cè
(偽)　wěi
(偉)　wěi

十画 (10 strokes)

傲　ào
傍　bàng
储　chǔ
(備)　bèi

十一画 (11 strokes)

催　cuī
傻　shǎ
(傳)　chuán
(傷)　shāng
(僅)　jǐn
(傾)　qīng
(傭)　yōng

十二画 (12 strokes)

僧　sēng
像　xiàng
(僱)　gù

十三画 (13 strokes)

(價)　jià
(儉)　jiǎn
(憶)　yì

(儀)　yí

十四画 (14 strokes)

儒　rú
(儘)　jǐn

十五画 (15 strokes)

(償)　cháng
(儲)　chǔ
(優)　yōu

15　八（丷）

八　bā

二画 (2 strokes)

分　fēn; fèn
公　gōng

三画 (3 strokes)

只　zhī; zhǐ

四画 (4 strokes)

共　gòng
并　bìng
关　guān

五画 (5 strokes)

兵　bīng
弟　dì
兑　duì

六画 (6 strokes)

其　qí
具　jù
典　diǎn
卷　juǎn
单　dān

七画 (7 strokes)

养　yǎng
首　shǒu

八画 (8 strokes)

益　yì

九画 (9 strokes)

黄　huáng
兽　shòu

十画 (10 strokes)

普	pǔ
曾	céng

---

16 人 (入)

人	rén
入	rù

一画 (1 stroke)

个	gè

二画 (2 strokes)

仓	cāng
介	jiè
从	cóng
今	jīn
以	yǐ
(内)	nèi

三画 (3 strokes)

令	lìng

四画 (4 strokes)

全	quán
会	huì; kuài
合	hé
企	qǐ
伞	sǎn

五画 (5 strokes)

余	yú
含	hán

六画 (6 strokes)

舍	shè
命	mìng
(來)	lái
(兩)	liǎng

八画 (8 strokes)

拿	ná
(倉)	cāng

九画 (9 strokes)

盒	hé

十画 (10 strokes)

舒	shū
(傘)	sǎn

---

17 勹

一画 (1 stroke)

勺	sháo

二画 (2 strokes)

勿	wù
匀	yún
(勻)	yún

三画 (3 strokes)

句	jù
匆	cōng
包	bāo

九画 (9 strokes)

够	gòu

---

18 几

几	jī; jǐ

一画 (1 stroke)

凡	fán

四画 (4 strokes)

朵	duǒ

六画 (6 strokes)

凭	píng

十二画 (12 strokes)

凳	dèng

---

19 儿

儿	ér

二画 (2 strokes)

允	yǔn

三画 (3 strokes)

兄	xiōng

四画 (4 strokes)

光	guāng
先	xiān

五画 (5 strokes)

(兑)	duì

六画 (6 strokes)

(兒)	ér

八画 (8 strokes)

党	dǎng

九画 (9 strokes)

兜	dōu

---

20 亠

一画 (1 stroke)

亡	wáng

二画 (2 strokes)

六	liù

三画 (3 strokes)

市	shì

四画 (4 strokes)

交	jiāo
产	chǎn
充	chōng

六画 (6 strokes)

变	biàn
京	jīng
享	xiǎng
夜	yè

七画 (7 strokes)

哀	āi
亮	liàng
亭	tíng
帝	dì

八画 (8 strokes)

高	gāo
离	lí
旁	páng

九画 (9 strokes)

率	lù; shuài
商	shāng
(產)	chǎn

十画 (10 strokes)

就	jiù

十二画 (12 strokes)

豪	háo
(齊)	qí

十五画 (15 strokes)

赢	yíng

---

21 冫

四画 (4 strokes)

冲	chōng; chòng
次	cì
决	jué
冰	bīng

五画 (5 strokes)

冻	dòng
况	kuàng
冷	lěng

八画 (8 strokes)

凋	diāo
准	zhǔn
凉	liáng; liàng
(凍)	dòng

九画 (9 strokes)

凑	còu
减	jiǎn

十画 (10 strokes)

寒	hán

十三画 (13 strokes)

(凜)	lǐn

---

22 冖

三画 (3 strokes)

写	xiě

四画 (4 strokes)

军	jūn

七画 (7 strokes)

冠	guàn

八画 (8 strokes)

冤	yuān

---

23 讠 (言)

二画 (2 strokes)

讥	jī
计	jì
订	dìng
认	rèn
(計)	jì
(訂)	dìng

三画 (3 strokes)

讨	tǎo
让	ràng
训	xùn
议	yì
记	jì
(記)	jì
(討)	tǎo
(訓)	xùn

四画 (4 strokes)

讽	fěng
讲	jiǎng
许	xǔ
论	lún; lùn
设	shè
访	fǎng
(訪)	fǎng
(設)	shè
(許)	xǔ

五画 (5 strokes)

证	zhèng
评	píng
译	yì
词	cí
识	shí
诉	sù
(詞)	cí
(評)	píng
(訴)	sù

六画 (6 strokes)

诞	dàn
试	shì
诗	shī
诚	chéng
话	huà
询	xún
该	gāi

详	xiáng
(誠)	chéng
(該)	gāi
(話)	huà
(詩)	shī
(試)	shì
(詳)	xiáng
(詢)	xún
(誇)	kuā

七画 (7 strokes)

语	yǔ
误	wù
诱	yòu
说	shuō
(認)	rèn
(說)	shuō
(誘)	yòu
(語)	yǔ
(誤)	wù

八画 (8 strokes)

谁	shéi; shuí
请	qǐng
读	dú
课	kè
调	diào; tiáo
谈	tán
谊	yì
(論)	lùn
(課)	kè
(請)	qǐng
(誰)	shuí
(談)	tán
(調)	tiáo
(誼)	yì
(調)	diào
(誕)	dàn

九画 (9 strokes)

谋	móu
谎	huǎng
谚	yàn
谜	mí
(諷)	fěng
(謀)	móu
(諺)	yàn

十画 (10 strokes)

谢	xiè

谣 yáo
谦 qiān
(謊) huǎng
(謎) mí
(謙) qiān
(謝) xiè
(謠) yáo
(講) jiǎng

十二画 (12 strokes)
(譏) jī
(證) zhèng

十三画 (13 strokes)
(譯) yì
(議) yì

十五画 (15 strokes)
(讀) dú

十七画 (17 strokes)
(讓) ràng

---

24 卩

一画 (1 stroke)
卫 wèi

三画 (3 strokes)
印 yìn

四画 (4 strokes)
危 wēi

五画 (5 strokes)
却 què
即 jí

七画 (7 strokes)
卸 xiè
(卻) què

---

25 阝 *(on the left (在左边))*

二画 (2 strokes)
队 duì

四画 (4 strokes)
阳 yáng
阶 jiē
阴 yīn
防 fáng
阵 zhèn

五画 (5 strokes)
陈 chén
陆 liù; lù
阿 ā
阻 zǔ
附 fù

六画 (6 strokes)
陌 mò
降 jiàng
限 xiàn

七画 (7 strokes)
除 chú
陡 dǒu
险 xiǎn
院 yuàn
(陣) zhèn

八画 (8 strokes)
陪 péi
陶 táo
陷 xiàn
(陳) chén
(陸) liù; lù
(陰) yīn

九画 (9 strokes)
随 suí
隐 yǐn
(階) jiē
(隄) dī
(陽) yáng

十画 (10 strokes)
隔 gé
(隊) duì

十一画 (11 strokes)
障 zhàng

十二画 (12 strokes)
隧 suì

十三画 (13 strokes)
(險) xiǎn
(隨) suí

十四画 (14 strokes)
(隱) yǐn

---

26 阝 *(on the right (在右边))*

四画 (4 strokes)
邪 xié
那 nà

五画 (5 strokes)
邻 lín
邮 yóu

六画 (6 strokes)
耶 yē
郁 yù
郊 jiāo

八画 (8 strokes)
都 dōu; dū
部 bù

九画 (9 strokes)
(郵) yóu
(鄉) xiāng

十二画 (12 strokes)
(鄰) lín

---

27 凵

二画 (2 strokes)
凶 xiōng

六画 (6 strokes)
画 huà

七画 (7 strokes)
幽 yōu

---

28 刀 ( )

十画 (10 strokes)
刀 dāo

二画 (2 strokes)
切   qiē

三画 (3 strokes)
召   zhào

四画 (4 strokes)
争   zhēng
负   fù
色   sè; shǎi

五画 (5 strokes)
免   miǎn
初   chū

六画 (6 strokes)
兔   tù

九画 (9 strokes)
剪   jiǎn
象   xiàng

29 力

力   lì

二画 (2 strokes)
办   bàn

三画 (3 strokes)
功   gōng
务   wù
加   jiā

四画 (4 strokes)
动   dòng
劣   liè

五画 (5 strokes)
劲   jìn
劳   láo
助   zhù
男   nán
努   nǔ
(勁)   jìn

六画 (6 strokes)
势   shì

七画 (7 strokes)
勉   miǎn
勇   yǒng

九画 (9 strokes)
(動)   dòng
(務)   wù

十画 (10 strokes)
募   mù
(勞)   láo

十一画 (11 strokes)
勤   qín
(勸)   quàn
(勢)   shì

30 厶

三画 (3 strokes)
去   qù
台   tái

五画 (5 strokes)
县   xiàn

六画 (6 strokes)
参   cān; shēn
叁   sān

八画 (8 strokes)
能   néng

九画 (9 strokes)
(參)   cān; shēn

31 又

又   yòu chā

二画 (2 strokes)
友   yǒu
劝   quàn
双   shuāng

三画 (3 strokes)
发   fā; fà
圣   shèng
对   duì

四画 (4 strokes)
戏   xì
观   guān
欢   huān

五画 (5 strokes)
鸡   jī

六画 (6 strokes)
艰   jiān
取   qǔ
叔   shū
受   shòu

七画 (7 strokes)
叙   xù

八画 (8 strokes)
难   nán
桑   sāng

十一画 (11 strokes)
叠   dié

32 廴

四画 (4 strokes)
延   yán

六画 (6 strokes)
建   jiàn

33 巛

三画 (3 strokes)
巡   xún

八画 (8 strokes)
巢   cháo

34 工

工   gōng

二画 (2 strokes)
左   zuǒ
巧   qiǎo

三画 (3 strokes)

巩	gǒng
式	shì

四画 (4 strokes)

攻	gōng

六画 (6 strokes)

差	chā; chà; chāi
项	xiàng

九画 (9 strokes)

(項)	xiàng

---

35 土

土	tǔ

三画 (3 strokes)

寺	sì
地	de; dì
场	chǎng
在	zài
至	zhì

四画 (4 strokes)

坏	huài
坟	fén
块	kuài
坚	jiān
坐	zuò
社	shè
坛	tán

五画 (5 strokes)

垃	lā
坡	pō
坦	tǎn
幸	xìng

六画 (6 strokes)

型	xíng
城	chéng
垫	diàn
垮	kuǎ

七画 (7 strokes)

埋	mái; mán

八画 (8 strokes)

域	yù
堵	dǔ
堆	duī
堕	duò
培	péi
基	jī
堂	táng
(堅)	jiān
(執)	zhí

九画 (9 strokes)

堤	dī
塔	tǎ
(報)	bào
(場)	chǎng

十画 (10 strokes)

墓	mù
塑	sù
塌	tā
填	tián
(塊)	kuài
(塗)	tú

十一画 (11 strokes)

墙	qiáng
(塵)	chén
(墊)	diàn

十二画 (12 strokes)

增	zēng
墨	mò

十三画 (13 strokes)

(壇)	tán
(墳)	fén

十四画 (14 strokes)

(獄)	yuè
(壓)	yā

十五画 (15 strokes)

(墮)	duò

十六画 (16 strokes)

(壞)	huài

---

36 士

四画 (4 strokes)

壳	ké
声	shēng

七画 (7 strokes)

壶	hú

九画 (9 strokes)

喜	xǐ
壹	yī
(壺)	hú

十画 (10 strokes)

鼓	gǔ

十一画 (11 strokes)

(壽)	shòu
(臺)	tái

---

37 扌

一画 (1 stroke)

扎	zhā

二画 (2 strokes)

打	dá; dǎ
扑	pū
扔	rēng

三画 (3 strokes)

扛	káng
扣	kòu
执	zhí
扩	kuò
扫	sǎo; sào
托	tuō

四画 (4 strokes)

把	bǎ
扮	bàn
报	bào
抄	chāo
扯	chě
抖	dǒu
扶	fú
护	hù
技	jì
拒	jù

抗　kàng
扭　niǔ
抛　pāo
找　zhǎo
批　pī
扰　rǎo
抢　qiǎng
抑　yì
折　shé; zhē; zhé
抓　zhuā
投　tóu

五画 (5 strokes)
招　zhāo
拔　bá
拌　bàn
抱　bào
拨　bō
拆　chāi
抽　chōu
押　yā
拎　līn
拥　yōng
担　dān; dàn
抵　dǐ
拐　guǎi
拣　jiǎn
拉　lā
拦　lán
抹　mā; mǒ
拧　níng
拍　pāi
拔　pī
抬　tái
拇　mǔ
拖　tuō
拓　tuò
(枴)　guǎi
(抛)　pāo

六画 (6 strokes)
挪　nuó
按　àn
持　chí
挡　dǎng
挂　guà
挥　huī
挤　jǐ
拷　kǎo
括　kuò

拼　pīn
拾　shí
挑　tiāo; tiǎo
指　zhǐ
挣　zhèng
挺　tǐng
挖　wā

七画 (7 strokes)
捣　dǎo
挨　āi; ái
捌　bā
捕　bǔ
振　zhèn
捉　zhuō
挫　cuò
捣　dǎo
换　huàn
捡　jiǎn
捆　kǔn
捞　lāo
损　sǔn
挽　wǎn

八画 (8 strokes)
措　cuò
掺　chān
捶　chuí
掸　dǎn
掉　diào
掂　diān
接　jiē
捷　jié
据　jù
控　kòng
描　miáo
排　pái
捧　pěng
探　tàn
掏　tāo
推　tuī
掀　xiān
(採)　cǎi
(掃)　sǎo; sào
(掙)　zhèng
(掛)　guà
(捲)　juǎn

九画 (9 strokes)
搜　sōu

援　yuán
搓　cuō
搀　chān
提　dī; tí
搁　gē
搭　dā
插　chā
搂　lǒu
搅　jiǎo
揉　róu
握　wò
(揹)　bēi; bèi
(換)　huàn
(揮)　huī
(揀)　jiǎn

十画 (10 strokes)
摇　yáo
摆　bǎi
搬　bān
搞　gǎo
摸　mō
摄　shè
摊　tān
携　xié
(搶)　qiǎng
(損)　sǔn
(搖)　yáo
(搗)　dǎo

十一画 (11 strokes)
摘　zhāi
摔　shuāi
(摻)　chān
(搜)　lǒu

十二画 (12 strokes)
播　bō
撞　zhuàng
撤　chè
撑　chēng
撮　cuō
撒　sā; sǎ
撕　sī
(撥)　bō
(撐)　chēng
(撣)　dǎn
(撈)　lāo
(撲)　pū

十三画 (13 strokes)

操　cāo
擅　shàn
(攩)　dǎng
(撿)　jiǎn
(擔)　dān; dàn
(據)　jù
(擁)　yōng

十四画 (14 strokes)

擦　cā
(擱)　gē
(擰)　níng

十五画 (15 strokes)

(擺)　bǎi
(擠)　jǐ
(擴)　kuò
(擾)　rǎo

十六画 (16 strokes)

攒　zǎn

十七画 (17 strokes)

(攙)　chān
(攝)　shè
(攔)　lán

十八画 (18 strokes)

(攜)　xié

十九画 (19 strokes)

(攤)　tān
(攢)　zǎn

二十画 (20 strokes)

(攪)　jiǎo

38　艹

一画 (1 stroke)

艺　yì

二画 (2 strokes)

艾　ài
节　jié

三画 (3 strokes)

芝　zhī

四画 (4 strokes)

芭　bā
苍　cāng
花　huā
苏　sū
芽　yá

五画 (5 strokes)

茉　mò
苦　kǔ
茂　mào
苹　píng
苗　miáo
英　yīng
范　fàn

六画 (6 strokes)

荤　hūn
草　cǎo
茶　chá
荒　huāng
荣　róng
荫　yìn
荔　lì
药　yào

七画 (7 strokes)

莲　lián
获　huò
(莊)　zhuāng

八画 (8 strokes)

著　zhù
萝　luó
菜　cài
菠　bō
萤　yíng
营　yíng
(華)　huá
(著)　zháo

九画 (9 strokes)

葱　cōng
董　dǒng
葵　kuí
葡　pú
落　là; luò
(葷)　hūn
(葉)　yè
(萬)　wàn

十画 (10 strokes)

蒜　suàn
蓝　lán
蒙　mēng; méng;
　　Měng
蒸　zhēng
(蒼)　cāng
(蓋)　gài

十一画 (11 strokes)

蔫　niān
(蓮)　lián
(蔥)　cōng
(蔭)　yìn

十二画 (12 strokes)

蔬　shū

十三画 (13 strokes)

薯　shǔ
薪　xīn
薄　báo
(薑)　jiāng

十四画 (14 strokes)

藏　cáng
(藍)　lán
(薰)　xūn

十五画 (15 strokes)

藕　ǒu
藤　téng
(藥)　yào
(藝)　yì

十六画 (16 strokes)

蘑　mó
(蘋)　píng
(蘇)　sū

十九画 (19 strokes)

(蘿)　luó

39　寸

寸　cùn

三画 (3 strokes)

寻　xún
导　dǎo

四画 (4 strokes)

寿	shòu

六画 (6 strokes)

封	fēng
耐	nài

七画 (7 strokes)

射	shè

八画 (8 strokes)

(將)	jiāng
(專)	zhuān

九画 (9 strokes)

尊	zūn
(尋)	xún

十一画 (11 strokes)

(對)	duì

十三画 (13 strokes)

(導)	dǎo

---

40 廾 (underneath
(在下边))

三画 (3 strokes)

异	yì

四画 (4 strokes)

弄	nòng

---

41 大

大	dà; dài

一画 (1 stroke)

太	tài

三画 (3 strokes)

夸	kuā
夺	duó
夹	jiā
尖	jiān
(夾)	jiā

五画 (5 strokes)

奉	fèng
奇	qí

奋	fèn
态	tài

六画 (6 strokes)

牵	qiān
美	měi
奖	jiǎng

七画 (7 strokes)

套	tào

八画 (8 strokes)

奢	shē

九画 (9 strokes)

奥	ào

十画 (10 strokes)

(奧)	ào
(態)	tài

十一画 (11 strokes)

(奪)	duó

十三画 (13 strokes)

(奮)	fèn

---

42 尤

一画 (1 stroke)

尤	yóu

二画 (2 strokes)

龙	lóng

---

43 小 (⺌)

小	xiǎo

一画 (1 stroke)

少	shǎo; shào

三画 (3 strokes)

尘	chén
当	dāng; dàng

六画 (6 strokes)

省	shěng
尝	cháng

八画 (8 strokes)

常	cháng

九画 (9 strokes)

掌	zhǎng

---

44 口

口	kǒu

二画 (2 strokes)

叨	dāo
叼	diāo
叮	dīng
号	hào
叫	jiào
另	lìng
右	yòu
叶	yè
叹	tàn

三画 (3 strokes)

吊	diào
吐	tǔ; tù
吓	xià
吃	chī
吸	xī
吗	ma
各	gè
名	míng

四画 (4 strokes)

吧	ba
吵	chǎo
员	yuán
吹	chuī
呆	dāi
吨	dūn
否	fǒu
告	gào
吝	lìn
呕	ǒu
呀	yā
启	qǐ
吩	fēn
听	tīng
吞	tūn
吻	wěn

五画 (5 strokes)

味	wèi
哎	āi
呼	hū
咖	gā; kā
和	hé
呢	ne; ní

六画 (6 strokes)

哆	duō
哈	hā
咳	ké
哪	nǎ
哟	yō
品	pǐn
咽	yān; yàn
咱	zán
虽	suī
咸	xián
哑	yǎ
响	xiǎng
咨	zī
咬	yǎo

七画 (7 strokes)

啊	ā
唇	chún
哼	hēng
唤	huàn
哭	kū
哦	ó; ò
哨	shào
哲	zhé
哮	xiào
(員)	yuán

八画 (8 strokes)

唱	chàng
啦	la
啤	pí
售	shòu
唾	tuò
(唸)	niàn
(喲)	yō
(啞)	yǎ

九画 (9 strokes)

喊	hǎn
喧	xuān
喝	hē

喉	hóu
喇	lǎ
喷	pēn
善	shàn
喂	wèi
(喚)	huàn
(單)	dān
(喪)	sāng; sàng

十画 (10 strokes)

嗝	gé
嗓	sǎng
嗜	shì
(嗎)	ma

十一画 (11 strokes)

嘛	ma
(嘗)	cháng
(嘆)	tàn

十二画 (12 strokes)

嘲	cháo
噎	yē
(嘔)	ǒu

十三画 (13 strokes)

嘴	zuǐ
器	qì
噪	zào
(噸)	dūn

十四画 (14 strokes)

(嚇)	xià

十六画 (16 strokes)

(嚥)	yàn

十七画 (17 strokes)

嚷	rǎng
(嚴)	yán

---

45 口

二画 (2 strokes)

四	sì

三画 (3 strokes)

因	yīn
回	huí
团	tuán

四画 (4 strokes)

园	yuán
围	wéi
困	kùn

五画 (5 strokes)

固	gù
国	guó
图	tú

七画 (7 strokes)

圆	yuán

八画 (8 strokes)

圈	quān
(國)	guó

九画 (9 strokes)

(圍)	wéi

十画 (10 strokes)

(圓)	yuán
(圈)	yuán

十一画 (11 strokes)

(圖)	tú
(團)	tuán

---

46 巾

一画 (1 stroke)

币	bì

二画 (2 strokes)

布	bù
帅	shuài

四画 (4 strokes)

帐	zhàng
希	xī

五画 (5 strokes)

帘	lián

六画 (6 strokes)

帮	bāng
带	dài
(帥)	shuài

七画 (7 strokes)
(師) shī

八画 (8 strokes)
(帶) dài
(帳) zhàng

九画 (9 strokes)
幅 fú
帽 mào
幂 mì

十画 (10 strokes)
幕 mù

十一画 (11 strokes)
(幫) bāng
(幣) bì

十四画 (14 strokes)
(冪) mì

---

47 山

山 shān

三画 (3 strokes)
岁 suì

四画 (4 strokes)
岛 dǎo

五画 (5 strokes)
岸 àn
岳 yuè
岩 yán

六画 (6 strokes)
炭 tàn
峡 xiá

七画 (7 strokes)
(峽) xiá
(島) dǎo

八画 (8 strokes)
崇 chóng
崭 zhǎn
崖 yá

十一画 (11 strokes)
(嶄) zhǎn

十九画 (19 strokes)
(巖) yán

---

48 彳

三画 (3 strokes)
行 háng; xíng

四画 (4 strokes)
彻 chè

五画 (5 strokes)
征 zhēng
往 wǎng
彼 bǐ

六画 (6 strokes)
待 dāi; dài
律 lǜ
很 hěn
(後) hòu

七画 (7 strokes)
徒 tú

八画 (8 strokes)
得 dé; de; děi
(從) cóng

九画 (9 strokes)
循 xún
街 jiē

十画 (10 strokes)
微 wēi

十一画 (11 strokes)
(徹) chè

十二画 (12 strokes)
德 dé

---

49 彡

四画 (4 strokes)
形 xíng

六画 (6 strokes)
须 xū

八画 (8 strokes)
彩 cǎi
(彫) diāo

十二画 (12 strokes)
影 yǐng

---

50 犭

二画 (2 strokes)
犯 fàn

四画 (4 strokes)
狂 kuáng
犹 yóu

五画 (5 strokes)
狐 hú
狗 gǒu

六画 (6 strokes)
狭 xiá
狮 shī
独 dú
狱 yù

七画 (7 strokes)
狼 láng
(狹) xiá

八画 (8 strokes)
猜 cāi
猪 zhū
猎 liè
猫 māo
猛 měng
猕 mí

九画 (9 strokes)
猩 xīng
猴 hóu
(猶) yóu

十画 (10 strokes)
猿 yuán
(獅) shī

十三画 (13 strokes)

獭　tǎ
(獺)　dú

十五画 (15 strokes)

(獵)　liè

十六画 (16 strokes)

(獺)　tǎ

十七画 (17 strokes)

(獼)　mí

---

51 夕

夕　xī

三画 (3 strokes)

多　duō

八画 (8 strokes)

梦　mèng
(夠)　gòu

十一画 (11 strokes)

(夥)　huǒ
(夢)　mèng

---

52 夂

二画 (2 strokes)

处　chǔ; chù
冬　dōng

四画 (4 strokes)

麦　mài
条　tiáo

五画 (5 strokes)

备　bèi

七画 (7 strokes)

夏　xià

---

53 饣 (食)

二画 (2 strokes)

饥　jī
(飢)　jī

四画 (4 strokes)

饮　yǐn
饭　fàn
(飯)　fàn
(飲)　yǐn

五画 (5 strokes)

饱　bǎo
(飽)　bǎo
饰　shì
饲　sì
(飾)　shì

六画 (6 strokes)

饺　jiǎo
饼　bǐng
(餅)　bǐng
(餃)　jiǎo

七画 (7 strokes)

饿　è
(餓)　è
(餘)　yú

八画 (8 strokes)

馄　hún
馅　xiàn
(餛)　hún
(餡)　xiàn

九画 (9 strokes)

馋　chán
(餵)　wèi

十一画 (11 strokes)

馒　mán
(饅)　mán

十七画 (17 strokes)

(饞)　chán

---

54 丬 (爿)

四画 (4 strokes)

状　zhuàng

六画 (6 strokes)

将　jiāng

十三画 (13 strokes)

(牆)　qiáng

---

55 广

广　guǎng

三画 (3 strokes)

庄　zhuāng
庆　qìng

四画 (4 strokes)

床　chuáng
应　yīng; yìng

五画 (5 strokes)

店　diàn
庙　miào
底　dǐ
废　fèi

六画 (6 strokes)

度　dù
庭　tíng

七画 (7 strokes)

席　xí
座　zuò

八画 (8 strokes)

康　kāng
廊　láng
庸　yōng
(廁)　cè

十画 (10 strokes)

(廈)　shà

十一画 (11 strokes)

腐　fǔ

十二画 (12 strokes)

(廠)　chǎng
(廚)　chú
(廢)　fèi
(廣)　guǎng
(廟)　miào

十五画 (15 strokes)

鹰　yīng

二十二画
(22 strokes)

（廳） tīng

---

56 忄 ( )

一画 (1 stroke)

忆　　 yì

三画 (3 strokes)

忙　　 máng

四画 (4 strokes)

怀　　 huái
忧　　 yōu
快　　 kuài

五画 (5 strokes)

性　　 xìng
怕　　 pà
怪　　 guài

六画 (6 strokes)

恭　　 gōng
恢　　 huī
恰　　 qià
恨　　 hèn

七画 (7 strokes)

悄　　 qiāo; qiǎo

八画 (8 strokes)

惭　　 cán
惨　　 cǎn
悼　　 dào
惦　　 diàn
惯　　 guàn
惊　　 jīng
情　　 qíng
惟　　 wéi

九画 (9 strokes)

愤　　 fèn
慌　　 huāng
愉　　 yú

十画 (10 strokes)

慎　　 shèn
（慄） lì

十一画 (11 strokes)

慷　　 kāng
慢　　 màn
（慚） cán
（慘） cǎn
（慣） guàn

十二画 (12 strokes)

懂　　 dǒng
懊　　 ào
（憤） fèn

十三画 (13 strokes)

懒　　 lǎn

十六画 (16 strokes)

（懷） huái
（懶） lǎn

---

57 门 (門)

门　　 mén
（門） mén

二画 (2 strokes)

闪　　 shǎn
（閃） shǎn

三画 (3 strokes)

闯　　 chuǎng
问　　 wèn

四画 (4 strokes)

闲　　 xián
间　　 jiān
闷　　 mēn; mèn
（間） jiān
（問） wèn
（閑） xián
（開） kāi

五画 (5 strokes)

闹　　 nào

六画 (6 strokes)

闻　　 wén
（聞） wén
（閤） hé

七画 (7 strokes)

阅　　 yuè
（閱） yuè

九画 (9 strokes)

阔　　 kuò
（闊） kuò

十画 (10 strokes)

（闖） chuǎng

十一画 (11 strokes)

（關） guān

---

58 氵

二画 (2 strokes)

汉　　 hàn
汇　　 huì

三画 (3 strokes)

池　　 chí
汗　　 hàn
污　　 wū
江　　 jiāng
汤　　 tāng

四画 (4 strokes)

沟　　 gōu
沙　　 shā
汽　　 qì
没　　 méi; mò
沉　　 chén
（決） jué
（沒） méi; mò

五画 (5 strokes)

沫　　 mò
浅　　 qiǎn
法　　 fǎ
泄　　 xiè
河　　 hé
泪　　 lèi
油　　 yóu
沿　　 yán
泡　　 pào
注　　 zhù
泳　　 yǒng
泥　　 ní

波　bō
治　zhì
(況)　kuàng

六画 (6 strokes)

测　cè
洞　dòng
洪　hóng
浑　hún
活　huó
派　pài
洋　yáng
浓　nóng
洒　sǎ
洗　xǐ
(洩)　xiè

七画 (7 strokes)

浮　fú
海　hǎi
浪　làng
浴　yù
流　liú
酒　jiǔ
涩　sè
涉　shè
涂　tú
消　xiāo
涨　zhǎng

八画 (8 strokes)

渔　yú
淡　dàn
混　hùn
渐　jiàn
淋　lín
淹　yān
清　qīng
渠　qú
渔　yú
液　yè
深　shēn
渗　shèn
淘　táo
添　tiān
(淚)　lèi
(淺)　qiǎn
(涼)　liáng; liàng

九画 (9 strokes)

游　yóu
渡　dù
港　gǎng
滑　huá
渴　kě
湖　hú
湿　shī
湾　wān
温　wēn
(測)　cè
(渾)　hún
(湯)　tāng
(湊)　còu
(減)　jiǎn

十画 (10 strokes)

满　mǎn
源　yuán
溪　xī
溜　liū
滚　gǔn
(溝)　gōu
(溫)　wēn
(滅)　miè

十一画 (11 strokes)

滴　dī
演　yǎn
漏　lòu
漫　màn
漂　piāo; piào
漱　shù
(漢)　hàn
(滲)　shèn
(滾)　gǔn
(漸)　jiàn
(滿)　mǎn
(滷)　lǔ
(漲)　zhǎng
(漁)　yú

十二画 (12 strokes)

潮　cháo
澳　ào

十三画 (13 strokes)

激　jī
(濃)　nóng

十四画 (14 strokes)

(濕)　shī
(澀)　sè

十七画 (17 strokes)

灌　guàn

十九画 (19 strokes)

(灑)　sǎ

二十二画
(22 strokes)

(灣)　wān

---

59 宀

二画 (2 strokes)

宁　níng; nìng
它　tā

三画 (3 strokes)

宇　yǔ
字　zì
安　ān
守　shǒu

四画 (4 strokes)

完　wán
灾　zāi

五画 (5 strokes)

审　shěn
宗　zōng
宝　bǎo
定　dìng
宠　chǒng
官　guān
审　shěn
实　shí

六画 (6 strokes)

宣　xuān
室　shì
宫　gōng
宪　xiàn
客　kè

七画 (7 strokes)

宴　yàn
害　hài

宽　kuān
家　jiā
宵　xiāo
宾　bīn
（宫）gōng

八画 (8 strokes)
寄　jì
宿　sù
密　mì

九画 (9 strokes)
寓　yù
富　fù

十画 (10 strokes)
塞　sāi; sài

十一画 (11 strokes)
察　chá
赛　sài
蜜　mì
（寧）níng; nìng
（實）shí

十二画 (12 strokes)
（寬）kuān
（寫）xiě
（審）shěn

十六画 (16 strokes)
（寵）chǒng

十七画 (17 strokes)
（寶）bǎo

---

60 辶

二画 (2 strokes)
边　biān

三画 (3 strokes)
迅　xùn
达　dá
迈　mài
过　guò

四画 (4 strokes)
迎　yíng
远　yuǎn

运　yùn
这　zhè
进　jìn
违　wéi
还　hái; huán
连　lián
近　jìn
返　fǎn
迟　chí

五画 (5 strokes)
迪　dí
迫　pò
述　shù

六画 (6 strokes)
选　xuǎn
追　zhuī
送　sòng
适　shì
逃　táo
迷　mí
退　tuì
（迴）huí

七画 (7 strokes)
造　zào
逐　zhú
逞　chěng
递　dì
逗　dòu
逢　féng
逛　guàng
逝　shì
速　sù
通　tōng
透　tòu
途　tú
（連）lián
（這）zhè

八画 (8 strokes)
逮　dǎi; dài
逻　luó
（進）jìn

九画 (9 strokes)
遗　yí
遇　yù
逼　bī

道　dào
遍　biàn
（過）guò
（運）yùn
（達）dá
（遊）yóu
（違）wéi

十画 (10 strokes)
遥　yáo
遛　liù
（遙）yáo
（遞）dì
（遠）yuǎn

十一画 (11 strokes)
遭　zāo
（適）shì

十二画 (12 strokes)
遵　zūn
（遲）chí
（遺）yí
（選）xuǎn

十三画 (13 strokes)
邀　yāo
避　bì
（邁）mài
（還）huán

十五画 (15 strokes)
（邊）biān

十九画 (19 strokes)
（邏）luó

---

61 彐 (彑)

二画 (2 strokes)
归　guī

四画 (4 strokes)
灵　líng

五画 (5 strokes)
录　lù

62 尸

尸　shī

一画 (1 stroke)
尺　chǐ

三画 (3 strokes)
尽　jǐn; jìn

四画 (4 strokes)
层　céng
尿　niào; suī
屁　pì
尾　wěi
局　jú

五画 (5 strokes)
届　jiè
居　jū
（屆）jiè

六画 (6 strokes)
屋　wū
屎　shǐ
（屍）shī

八画 (8 strokes)
屠　tú

九画 (9 strokes)
犀　xī
属　shǔ

十二画 (12 strokes)
（層）céng

十八画 (18 strokes)
（屬）shǔ

63 己 （巳）

己　jǐ
巳　yǐ

64 弓

一画 (1 stroke)
引　yǐn

四画 (4 strokes)
张　zhāng

五画 (5 strokes)
弥　mí
弦　xián

六画 (6 strokes)
弯　wān

七画 (7 strokes)
弱　ruò

八画 (8 strokes)
弹　dàn; tán
（强）qiáng;
　　　qiǎng
（張）zhāng

九画 (9 strokes)
强　qiáng; qiǎng

十二画 (12 strokes)
（彈）dàn; tán
（彌）mí

十九画 (19 strokes)
（彎）wān

65 子

子　zǐ

二画 (2 strokes)
孕　yùn

三画 (3 strokes)
存　cún
孙　sūn

四画 (4 strokes)
孝　xiào

五画 (5 strokes)
孤　gū

六画 (6 strokes)
孩　hái

七画 (7 strokes)
（孫）sūn

十三画 (13 strokes)
（學）xué

66 女

女　nǚ

二画 (2 strokes)
奶　nǎi

三画 (3 strokes)
如　rú
妇　fù
她　tā
好　hǎo; hào
妈　mā

四画 (4 strokes)
妖　yāo
妨　fáng
妙　miào
妥　tuǒ

五画 (5 strokes)
姓　xìng
妻　qī
妹　mèi
姑　gū
姐　jiě
始　shǐ
委　wěi

六画 (6 strokes)
姨　yí
姿　zī
姜　jiāng
姥　lǎo
耍　shuǎ
威　wēi
娃　wá
（姪）zhí

七画 (7 strokes)
娱　yú
（娛）yú

八画 (8 strokes)

婴	yīng
婚	hūn
娶	qǔ
婶	shěn
(婦)	fù

九画 (9 strokes)

婿	xù
媒	méi
嫂	sǎo

十画 (10 strokes)

媳	xí
嫌	xián

十四画 (14 strokes)

(嬰)	yīng

十五画 (15 strokes)

(嬸)	shěn

---

67 纟 (糹)

二画 (2 strokes)

纠	jiū
(糾)	jiū

三画 (3 strokes)

约	yuē
红	hóng
纤	xiān
级	jí
纪	jì
(級)	jí
(紀)	jì
(約)	yuē
(紅)	hóng

四画 (4 strokes)

纽	niǔ
纱	shā
纸	zhǐ
纯	chún
纺	fǎng
纷	fēn
纱	shā
纬	wěi
(紡)	fǎng

(紛)	fēn
(紐)	niǔ
(紗)	shā
(紙)	zhǐ

五画 (5 strokes)

织	zhī
组	zǔ
线	xiàn
练	liàn
绅	shēn
细	xì
终	zhōng
绊	bàn
(絆)	bàn
经	jīng
(純)	chún
(組)	zǔ
(紳)	shēn
(細)	xì
(終)	zhōng
	huì

六画 (6 strokes)

绝	jué
绑	bǎng
(綁)	bǎng
结	jiē; jié
给	gěi
绕	rào
统	tǒng
(給)	gěi
(結)	jiē; jié
(統)	tǒng
(絕)	jué
(網)	wǎng

七画 (7 strokes)

(經)	jīng
绣	xiù
继	jì
(絧)	kǔn

八画 (8 strokes)

综	zōng
绸	chóu
绳	shéng
维	wéi
绿	lù

(綢)	chóu
(維)	wéi
(綜)	zōng
(綠)	lù

九画 (9 strokes)

缘	yuán
编	biān
(編)	biān
缎	duàn
缓	huǎn
缆	lǎn
缅	miǎn
(緩)	huǎn
(緬)	miǎn
(練)	liàn
(線)	xiàn
(緣)	yuán
(緯)	wěi

十画 (10 strokes)

缠	chán
缝	féng; fèng
(緞)	duàn

十一画 (11 strokes)

缩	suō
(縫)	féng; fèng
(縮)	suō
(總)	zǒng

十二画 (12 strokes)

(繞)	rào
(織)	zhī
(繡)	xiù

十三画 (13 strokes)

(繩)	shéng

十四画 (14 strokes)

(繼)	jì

十五画 (15 strokes)

(纏)	chán

十七画 (17 strokes)

(纖)	xiān

二十二画

(22 strokes)
（纜）lǎn

---

68 马（馬）

马　mǎ
（馬）mǎ

三画 (3 strokes)
驯　xùn
驮　tuó
（馱）tuó
（馴）xùn

四画 (4 strokes)
驴　lú

五画 (5 strokes)
驾　jià
驼　tuó
（駕）jià
（駝）tuó

六画 (6 strokes)
骂　mà
骄　jiāo
骆　luò
（駱）luò

七画 (7 strokes)
验　yàn

八画 (8 strokes)
骑　qí
（騎）qí

九画 (9 strokes)
骗　piàn
骚　sāo
（騙）piàn

十画 (10 strokes)
（騷）sāo

十一画 (11 strokes)
（驕）jiāo

十三画 (13 strokes)
（驚）jīng
（驗）yàn

十四画 (14 strokes)
（驢）lú

---

69 幺

一画 (1 stroke)
幻　huàn

二画 (2 stroke)
幼　yòu

九画 (9 stroke)
（幾）jǐ

---

70 王

王　wáng

一画 (1 stroke)
玉　yù

三画 (3 strokes)
玖　jiǔ

四画 (4 strokes)
玩　wán
环　huán
现　xiàn
玫　méi

五画 (5 strokes)
玻　bō
皇　huáng
珊　shān

六画 (6 strokes)
班　bān

七画 (7 strokes)
球　qiú
理　lǐ
望　wàng
（現）xiàn

八画 (8 strokes)
琴　qín

十三画 (13 strokes)
（環）huán

---

71 毋（母）

母　mǔ

四画 (4 strokes)
毒　dú

---

72 殳

五画 (5 strokes)
段　duàn

七画 (7 strokes)
（殺）shā

八画 (8 strokes)
（殼）ké

九画 (9 strokes)
殿　diàn
毁　huǐ
（毀）huǐ

十一画 (11 strokes)
毅　yì

---

73 韦（韋）

八画 (8 strokes)
韩　hán
（韓）hán

---

74 木

木　mù

一画 (1 stroke)
本　běn
术　shù

二画 (2 strokes)
杂　zá
机　jī
朴　pǔ
权　quán
杀　shā

三画 (3 strokes)
杏　xìng
杈　chà

杆	gān
材	cái
村	cūn
极	jí

四画 (4 strokes)

枕	zhěn
枝	zhī
构	gòu
林	lín
杯	bēi
柜	guì
板	bǎn
松	sōng
枪	qiāng
果	guǒ
采	cǎi
(東)	dōng

五画 (5 strokes)

某	mǒu
柠	níng
标	biāo
查	chá
相	xiāng; xiàng
柳	liǔ
柿	shì
栏	lán
染	rǎn
树	shù
亲	qīn
柒	qī
架	jià
柔	róu

六画 (6 strokes)

栗	lì
样	yàng
案	àn
柴	chái
档	dàng
格	gé
根	gēn
核	hé
框	kuàng
桥	qiáo
桃	táo
校	xiào
栽	zāi

七画 (7 strokes)

检	jiǎn
梳	shū
梯	tī
桶	tǒng
梨	lí
(桿)	gān
(條)	tiáo

八画 (8 strokes)

棍	gùn
棉	mián
椰	yē
椅	yǐ
植	zhí
棒	bàng
集	jí
棵	kē
棋	qí
森	sēn
椭	tuǒ
(極)	jí

九画 (9 strokes)

概	gài
楼	lóu
(業)	yè

十画 (10 strokes)

模	mó; mú
榜	bǎng
(構)	gòu
(槍)	qiāng
(榮)	róng

十一画 (11 strokes)

樱	yīng
横	héng
橡	xiàng
(標)	biāo
(樓)	lóu
(樂)	lè; yuè
(樣)	yàng

十二画 (12 strokes)

橙	chéng
橱	chú
橘	jú
(横)	héng
(樸)	pǔ

(橋)	qiáo
(樹)	shù
(橢)	tuǒ

十三画 (13 strokes)

(檔)	dàng
(檢)	jiǎn

十四画 (14 strokes)

(櫃)	guì
(檸)	níng

十五画 (15 strokes)

(橱)	chú

十七画 (17 strokes)

(櫻)	yīng
(欄)	lán

十八画 (18 strokes)

(機)	jī
(權)	quán

二十五画 (25 strokes)

(鬱)	yù

---

75 犬

四画 (4 strokes)

(狀)	zhuàng

六画 (6 strokes)

臭	chòu; xiù

九画 (9 strokes)

献	xiàn

十画 (10 strokes)

(獃)	dāi

十一画 (11 strokes)

(獎)	jiǎng
(獄)	yù

十五画 (15 strokes)

(獸)	shòu

十六画 (16 strokes)

(獻)	xiàn

76 歹

二画 (2 strokes)
死　sǐ

五画 (5 strokes)
残　cán

十画 (10 strokes)
(殘)　cán

77 车 (車)

车　chē; jū
(車)　chē; jū

一画 (1 stroke)
轧　yà; zhá
(軋)　yà

二画 (2 strokes)
轨　guǐ
(軌)　guǐ

(軍)　jūn

四画 (4 strokes)
转　zhuǎn; zhuàn
轮　lún
软　ruǎn
(軟)　ruǎn

五画 (5 strokes)
轻　qīng

六画 (6 strokes)
较　jiào
(較)　jiào

七画 (7 strokes)
辅　fǔ
辆　liàng
(輔)　fǔ
(輕)　qīng

八画 (8 strokes)
辍　chuò
(輟)　chuò
(輛)　liàng
(輪)　lún

九画 (9 strokes)
输　shū
(輸)　shū

十一画 (11 strokes)
(轉)　zhuǎn; zhuàn

78 比

比　bǐ

二画 (2 strokes)
毕　bì

79 瓦

瓦　wǎ

六画 (6 strokes)
瓷　cí
瓶　píng

80 止

止　zhǐ

二画 (2 strokes)
此　cǐ

三画 (3 strokes)
步　bù

四画 (4 strokes)
武　wǔ
肯　kěn

九画 (9 strokes)
(歲)　suì

十二画 (12 strokes)
(歷)　lì

十四画 (14 strokes)
(歸)　guī

81 支

十画 (10 strokes)
敲　qiāo

82 日

日　rì

二画 (2 strokes)
早　zǎo

三画 (3 strokes)
旱　hàn
旷　kuàng
时　shí

四画 (4 strokes)
易　yì
昏　hūn
昆　kūn
明　míng
旺　wàng

五画 (5 strokes)
昨　zuó
春　chūn
是　shì
显　xiǎn
星　xīng
香　xiāng

六画 (6 strokes)
晃　huǎng; huàng
晕　yūn; yùn
晒　shài
晓　xiǎo
(時)　shí

七画 (7 strokes)
晨　chén
晚　wǎn

八画 (8 strokes)
暂　zàn
智　zhì
量　liáng; liàng
晾　liàng
景　jǐng
晴　qíng
暑　shǔ
替　tì

九画 (9 strokes)
暖　nuǎn
暗　àn

（暈）yūn
（暈）yùn

十画 (10 strokes)
（暢）chàng

十一画 (11 strokes)
暴 bào
（暫）zàn

十二画 (12 strokes)
（曉）xiǎo

十五画 (15 strokes)
（曠）kuàng

十九画 (19 strokes)
（曬）shài

---

83 曰

五画 (5 strokes)
冒 mào

六画 (6 strokes)
（書）shū

七画 (7 strokes)
冕 miǎn

八画 (8 strokes)
最 zuì

九画 (9 strokes)
（會）huì; kuài

---

84 水

水 shuǐ

一画 (1 stroke)
永 yǒng

五画 (5 strokes)
泉 quán

---

85 贝(貝)

贝 bèi

二画 (2 strokes)
（負）fù

三画 (3 strokes)
财 cái
（財）cái
贡 gòng
（貢）gòng

四画 (4 strokes)
责 zé
败 bài
贬 biǎn
（貶）biǎn
购 gòu
贯 guàn
货 huò
贫 pín
贪 tān
（貨）huò
（貧）pín
（貫）guàn
（責）zé
（貪）tān

五画 (5 strokes)
贴 tiē; tiě
贷 dài
贰 èr
费 fèi
贵 guì
贺 hè
贸 mào
（貸）dài
（貿）mào
（費）fèi
（貼）tiē
（貴）guì
（賀）hè
（貳）èr
（買）mǎi

六画 (6 strokes)
贿 huì
资 zī
（資）zī
（賄）huì

七画 (7 strokes)
（賓）bīn

八画 (8 strokes)
赌 dǔ
赔 péi
赏 shǎng
（賭）dǔ
（賠）péi
（賞）shǎng
（賣）mài
（賬）zhàng
（質）zhì

十画 (10 strokes)
赚 zhuàn
（賺）zhuàn
（賽）sài
（贊）zàn
（賸）shèng

十二画 (12 strokes)
赞 zàn
赠 zèng
（購）gòu
（贈）zèng

十三画 (13 strokes)
（贏）yíng

---

86 见(見)

见 jiàn
（見）jiàn

四画 (4 strokes)
规 guī
（規）guī

五画 (5 strokes)
觉 jué

九画 (9 strokes)
（親）qīn

十三画 (13 strokes)
（覺）jué

十八画 (18 strokes)
（觀）guān

87 牛(牛)

牛　niú

四画 (4 strokes)

牧　mù
物　wù

五画 (5 strokes)

牲　shēng

六画 (6 strokes)

特　tè
牺　xī

七画 (7 strokes)

(牵)　qiān

十六画 (16 strokes)

(犧)　xī

88 手

手　shǒu

六画 (6 strokes)

拳　quán

十一画 (11 strokes)

摩　mó

十五画 (15 strokes)

攀　pān

89 毛

毛　máo

七画 (7 strokes)

毫　háo

八画 (8 strokes)

毯　tǎn

90 气

气　qì

六画 (6 strokes)

氧　yǎng

(氣)　qì

91 攵

二画 (2 strokes)

收　shōu

三画 (3 strokes)

改　gǎi

五画 (5 strokes)

政　zhèng
故　gù

六画 (6 strokes)

敌　dí
效　xiào

七画 (7 strokes)

敢　gǎn
教　jiāo; jiào
救　jiù
敏　mǐn
(敗)　bài
(啟)　qǐ
(敘)　xù

八画 (8 strokes)

敞　chǎng
散　sǎn; sàn
敬　jìng

九画 (9 strokes)

数　shǔ; shù

十一画 (11 strokes)

(敵)　dí
(數)　shǔ; shù

92 片

片　piàn

八画 (8 strokes)

牌　pái

93 斤

斤　jīn

四画 (4 strokes)

欣　xīn

七画 (7 strokes)

断　duàn

九画 (9 strokes)

新　xīn

十四画 (14 strokes)

(斷)　duàn

94 爪(爫)

四画 (4 strokes)

爬　pá
(爭)　zhēng

六画 (6 strokes)

爱　ài

95 父

父　fù

二画 (2 strokes)

爷　yé

四画 (4 strokes)

爸　bà

九画 (9 strokes)

(爺)　yé

96 月

月　yuè

二画 (2 strokes)

有　yǒu
肌　jī
肋　lèi

三画 (3 strokes)

肠　cháng
肝　gān
肚　dù

四画 (4 strokes)

育	yù
肮	āng
肥	féi
肺	fèi
服	fú; fù
股	gǔ
肩	jiān
朋	péng
肾	shèn
肿	zhǒng

五画 (5 strokes)

背	bēi; bèi
胆	dǎn
胡	hú
脉	mài
胖	pàng
胜	shèng
胎	tāi
胃	wèi

六画 (6 strokes)

脑	nǎo
胸	xiōng
脏	zāng; zàng
脆	cuì
胳	gē
胶	jiāo
胯	kuà
朗	lǎng
(脉)	mài

七画 (7 strokes)

脚	jiǎo
脖	bó
脸	liǎn
脱	tuō
(脱)	tuō
(唇)	chún

八画 (8 strokes)

朝	cháo
脾	pí
期	qī
腕	wàn
腋	yè
(勝)	shèng

九画 (9 strokes)

腰	yāo
腻	nì
腮	sāi
腥	xīng
腺	xiàn
腿	tuǐ
(腸)	cháng
(腦)	nǎo
(腫)	zhǒng
(腳)	jiǎo

十画 (10 strokes)

膜	mó
(腎)	shèn

十一画 (11 strokes)

膝	xī
(膠)	jiāo

十二画 (12 strokes)

(膩)	nì

十三画 (13 strokes)

臀	tún
(膽)	dǎn
(臉)	liǎn

---

97 欠

欠	qiàn

四画 (4 strokes)

欧	ōu

七画 (7 strokes)

欲	yù

八画 (8 strokes)

款	kuǎn
欺	qī

九画 (9 strokes)

歇	xiē

十画 (10 strokes)

歌	gē

十一画 (11 strokes)

(歐)	ōu

十八画 (18 strokes)

(歡)	huān

---

98 风(風)

风	fēng
(風)	fēng

十一画 (11 strokes)

飘	piāo
(飄)	piāo

---

99 文

文	wén

二画 (2 strokes)

齐	qí

---

100 方

方	fāng

四画 (4 strokes)

放	fàng
房	fáng
(於)	yú

五画 (5 strokes)

施	shī

六画 (6 strokes)

旅	lǚ

七画 (7 strokes)

旋	xuán; xuàn

十画 (10 strokes)

旗	qí

---

101 火

火	huǒ

一画 (1 stroke)

灭	miè

二画 (2 strokes)
灰　huī
灯　dēng

三画 (3 strokes)
灿　càn
(災)　zāi

四画 (4 strokes)
炎　yán
炒　chǎo
炊　chuī
炖　dùn
炉　lú

五画 (5 strokes)
烂　làn
炮　pào

六画 (6 strokes)
烟　yān
烤　kǎo
烦　fán
烧　shāo
烫　tàng
(煩)　fán

八画 (8 strokes)
焰　yàn

九画 (9 strokes)
煤　méi
(煙)　yān

十画 (10 strokes)
熄　xī

十一画 (11 strokes)
熨　yùn
(燦)　càn
(燉)　dùn

十二画 (12 strokes)
燃　rán
(燒)　shāo
(燈)　dēng
(燙)　tàng

十三画 (13 strokes)
(營)　yíng

十五画 (15 strokes)
爆　bào

十六画 (16 strokes)
(爐)　lú

十七画 (17 strokes)
(爛)　làn

---

102 斗

斗　dǒu; dòu

六画 (6 strokes)
料　liào

七画 (7 strokes)
斜　xié

---

103 灬

五画 (5 strokes)
点　diǎn
(為)　wèi; wéi

六画 (6 strokes)
烈　liè
热　rè
(烏)　wū

八画 (8 strokes)
煮　zhǔ
焦　jiāo
然　rán
(無)　wú

九画 (9 strokes)
照　zhào

十画 (10 strokes)
熊　xióng
熬　áo

十一画 (11 strokes)
熟　shú
(熱)　rè

十二画 (12 strokes)
燕　yàn

---

104 户 (戶)

户　hù
(戶)　hù

四画 (4 strokes)
所　suǒ

五画 (5 strokes)
扁　biǎn

六画 (6 strokes)
扇　shān; shàn

---

105 礻

一画 (1 stroke)
礼　lǐ

四画 (4 strokes)
视　shì

五画 (5 strokes)
祝　zhù
祖　zǔ
神　shén
(祕)　mì

七画 (7 strokes)
祸　huò
(視)　shì
(裡)　lǐ

九画 (9 strokes)
福　fú
(禍)　huò

十二画 (12 strokes)
(禮)　lǐ

---

106 心

心　xīn

一画 (1 stroke)
必　bì

三画 (3 strokes)
忘　wàng
忍　rěn

四画 (4 strokes)

念	niàn
忽	hū

五画 (5 strokes)

怒	nù
总	zǒng
急	jí
思	sī

六画 (6 strokes)

恐	kǒng
恶	ě; è
恋	liàn
(恥)	chǐ

七画 (7 strokes)

您	nín
悬	xuán
悠	yōu
患	huàn

八画 (8 strokes)

悲	bēi
惩	chéng
惹	rě
(悶)	mēn; mèn
(惡)	è

九画 (9 strokes)

意	yì
愚	yú
慈	cí
愁	chóu
想	xiǎng
感	gǎn
(愛)	ài

十画 (10 strokes)

愿	yuàn

十一画 (11 strokes)

(慶)	qìng
(憑)	píng
(慾)	yù
(憂)	yōu

十二画 (12 strokes)

(憲)	xiàn

十三画 (13 strokes)

(應)	yīng; yìng

十五画 (15 strokes)

(懲)	chéng
(戀)	liàn

十六画 (16 strokes)

(懸)	xuán

---

107 聿 (聿)

七画 (7 strokes)

肆	sì

---

108 戈

二画 (2 strokes)

成	chéng

四画 (4 strokes)

或	huò

五画 (5 strokes)

战	zhàn

十二画 (12 strokes)

(戰)	zhàn

十三画 (13 strokes)

戴	dài
(戲)	xì

十四画 (14 strokes)

戳	chuō

---

109 用

用	yòng

---

110 示

四画 (4 strokes)

示	shì

六画 (6 strokes)

票	piào

八画 (8 strokes)

禁	jìn

---

111 石

石	shí

三画 (3 strokes)

矿	kuàng
码	mǎ

四画 (4 strokes)

研	yán
砖	zhuān
砍	kǎn
砚	yàn

五画 (5 strokes)

砸	zá
破	pò
(砲)	pào

六画 (6 strokes)

硕	shuò

七画 (7 strokes)

硬	yìng
确	què
(硯)	yàn

八画 (8 strokes)

碑	bēi
碰	pèng
碎	suì
碗	wǎn

九画 (9 strokes)

磁	cí
碟	dié
碳	tàn
(碩)	shuò

十画 (10 strokes)

磅	bàng
磕	kē
(碼)	mǎ
(確)	què

十一画 (11 strokes)

磨　mó; mò
(磚)　zhuān

十五画 (15 strokes)

(礦)　kuàng

---

112 龙

六画 (6 strokes)

聋　lóng
袭　xí

---

113 目

目　mù

二画 (2 strokes)

盯　dīng

三画 (3 strokes)

盲　máng

四画 (4 strokes)

看　kān; kàn
眉　méi
盼　pàn

五画 (5 strokes)

眠　mián

六画 (6 strokes)

眼　yǎn
睁　zhēng
着　zháo
眶　kuàng

八画 (8 strokes)

睦　mù
瞄　miáo
睡　shuì
(睜)　zhēng

九画 (9 strokes)

瞅　chǒu

十画 (10 strokes)

瞒　mán
瞎　xiā

十一画 (11 strokes)

(瞞)　mán

十二画 (12 strokes)

瞪　dèng
瞧　qiáo

十四画 (14 strokes)

(矇)　mēng

十六画 (16 strokes)

(矓)　lóng

---

114 田

二十一画
(21 strokes)

田　tián

三画 (3 strokes)

畅　chàng

四画 (4 strokes)

界　jiè

五画 (5 strokes)

畜　chù; xù
留　liú

六画 (6 strokes)

略　luè
累　lěi; lèi
(畢)　bì
(異)　yì

七画 (7 strokes)

番　fān
(畫)　huà

八画 (8 strokes)

(當)　dāng; dàng

---

115 ㄇㄇ

四画 (4 strokes)

罚　fá

八画 (8 strokes)

罪　zuì

十画 (10 strokes)

(罵)　mà

---

116 皿

三画 (3 strokes)

盂　yú

四画 (4 strokes)

盆　pén

五画 (5 strokes)

盐　yán
盎　àng
监　jiān

六画 (6 strokes)

盛　chéng; shèng
盗　dào
盔　kuī
盘　pán
盖　gài

七画 (7 strokes)

(盜)　dào

八画 (8 strokes)

(盞)　zhǎn

九画 (9 strokes)

(監)　jiān
(盡)　jìn

十画 (10 strokes)

(盤)　pán

---

117 钅 (釒)

二画 (2 strokes)

针　zhēn
钉　dīng
(釘)　dīng
(針)　zhēn

三画 (3 strokes)

钓　diào
(釣)　diào

四画 (4 strokes)

钥	yào
钟	zhōng
钝	dùn
钙	gài
钞	chāo
钢	gāng
钩	gōu
(鈔)	chāo
(鈍)	dùn
(鈣)	gài

五画 (5 strokes)

钻	zuān; zuàn
钱	qián
铁	tiě
铃	líng
铅	qiān
(鉤)	gōu
(鈴)	líng
(鉛)	qiān
(鉅)	jù

六画 (6 strokes)

银	yín
铲	chǎn
铝	lǚ
铜	tóng
(銅)	tóng
(銀)	yín

七画 (7 strokes)

铺	pū; pù
销	xiāo
锁	suǒ
锅	guō
锋	fēng
锈	xiù
(鋒)	fēng
(鋁)	lǚ
(鋪)	pù
(銷)	xiāo

八画 (8 strokes)

锤	chuí
错	cuò
键	jiàn
锯	jù
锚	máo

(錶)	biǎo
(錘)	chuí
(錯)	cuò
(鋼)	gāng
(鋸)	jù
(錢)	qián
(錄)	lù

九画 (9 strokes)

锻	duàn
(鍛)	duàn
(鍋)	guō
(錨)	máo
(鍵)	jiàn

十画 (10 strokes)

镇	zhèn
镑	bàng
(鎊)	bàng
镊	niè
(鎮)	zhèn

十一画 (11 strokes)

镜	jìng
(鏟)	chǎn
(鎖)	suǒ
(鏡)	jìng

十二画 (12 strokes)

(鋪)	pū
(鐘)	zhōng
(鏽)	xiù

十三画 (13 strokes)

(鐵)	tiě

十七画 (17 strokes)

(鑰)	yào

十八画 (18 strokes)

(鑷)	niè

十九画 (19 strokes)

(鑽)	zuān; zuàn

---

118 矢

三画 (3 strokes)

知	zhī

七画 (7 strokes)

短	duǎn

八画 (8 strokes)

矮	ǎi

---

119 禾

二画 (2 strokes)

秀	xiù
私	sī
秃	tū
(禿)	tū

三画 (3 strokes)

季	jì

四画 (4 strokes)

种	zhǒng; zhòng
秒	miǎo
秋	qiū
科	kē

五画 (5 strokes)

秩	zhì
租	zū
称	chèn; chēng
秤	chèng
积	jī
秘	mì

六画 (6 strokes)

移	yí

七画 (7 strokes)

程	chéng
稍	shāo; shào
税	shuì
稀	xī
(稅)	shuì

八画 (8 strokes)

稠	chóu

九画 (9 strokes)

稳	wěn
(稱)	chèn; chēng
(種)	zhǒng; zhòng

十一画 (11 strokes)

穆　mù
(積)　jī

十二画 (12 strokes)

黏　nián

十四画 (14 strokes)

(穩)　wěn
(穫)　huò

---

120 白

白　bái

三画 (3 strokes)

的　de; dí; dì

---

121 瓜

十画 (10 strokes)

瓜　guā

十四画 (14 strokes)

瓣　bàn

---

122 鸟(鳥)

鸟　niǎo
(鳥)　niǎo

四画 (4 strokes)

鸦　yā
(鴉)　yā

五画 (5 stroke)

鸭　yā
鸳　yuān
鸵　tuó
(鴕)　tuó
(鴨)　yā
(鴛)　yuān

六画 (6 strokes)

鸽　gē
(鴿)　gē

七画 (7 strokes)

鹅　é
(鵝)　é

八画 (8 strokes)

鹌　ān
(鵪)　ān

十一画 (11 strokes)

鹦　yīng

十三画 (13 strokes)

(鷹)　yīng

十七画 (17 strokes)

(鸚)　yīng

---

123 疒

四画 (4 strokes)

疤　bā
疮　chuāng
疯　fēng
疫　yì

五画 (5 strokes)

病　bìng
疲　pí
疼　téng

六画 (6 strokes)

痒　yǎng

七画 (7 strokes)

痤　cuó
痛　tòng

八画 (8 strokes)

痴　chī
痰　tán

九画 (9 strokes)

瘦　shòu
(瘋)　fēng

十画 (10 strokes)

瘤　liú
瘫　tān
(瘡)　chuāng

十一画 (11 strokes)

瘾　yǐn
瘸　qué

十二画 (12 strokes)

癌　ái

十四画 (14 strokes)

(癡)　chī

十五画 (15 strokes)

(癢)　yǎng

十七画 (17 strokes)

(癮)　yǐn

十九画 (19 strokes)

(癱)　tān

---

124 立

立　lì

四画 (4 strokes)

竖　shù

五画 (5 strokes)

站　zhàn
竞　jìng

七画 (7 strokes)

童　tóng

九画 (9 strokes)

端　duān

十五画 (15 strokes)

(競)　jìng

---

125 穴

穴　xué

二画 (2 strokes)

究　jiū
穷　qióng

三画 (3 strokes)

空　kōng; kòng

四画 (4 strokes)
突　tū
穿　chuān
窃　qiè

五画 (5 strokes)
容　róng

七画 (7 strokes)
窗　chuāng
窝　wō

九画 (9 strokes)
(窩)　wō

十画 (10 strokes)
(窮)　qióng

十八画 (18 strokes)
(竊)　qiè

---

126 衤

二画 (2 strokes)
补　bǔ

三画 (3 strokes)
衬　chèn

四画 (4 strokes)
袄　ǎo

五画 (5 strokes)
袖　xiù
袜　wà
被　bèi

七画 (7 strokes)
裤　kù
裙　qún
(補)　bǔ

八画 (8 strokes)
褂　guà
裸　luǒ

九画 (9 strokes)
褪　tuì
(複)　fù

十画 (10 strokes)
(褲)　kù

十三画 (13 strokes)
(襖)　ǎo

十五画 (15 strokes)
(襪)　wà

十六画 (16 strokes)
(襯)　chèn

---

127 疋 (⺪)

六画 (6 strokes)
蛋　dàn

---

128 皮

皮　pí

---

129 矛

矛　máo

---

130 臣

二画 (2 strokes)
(臥)　wò

十一画 (11 strokes)
(臨)　lín

---

131 自

自　zì

---

132 耒

四画 (4 strokes)
耕　gēng

---

133 老 (耂)

老　lǎo

---

134 耳

耳　ěr

四画 (4 strokes)
耻　chǐ
耽　dān

五画 (5 strokes)
职　zhí
聊　liáo

六画 (6 strokes)
联　lián

七画 (7 strokes)
(聖)　shèng

九画 (9 strokes)
聪　cōng

十一画 (11 strokes)
(聰)　cōng
(聯)　lián
(聲)　shēng

十二画 (12 strokes)
(職)　zhí

十六画 (16 strokes)
(聽)　tīng

---

135 西 (覀)

西　xī

三画 (3 strokes)
要　yāo; yào

---

136 页 (頁)

页　yè
(頁)　yè

二画 (2 strokes)
顶　dǐng
(頂)　dǐng

三画 (3 strokes)

顺 shùn
(順) shùn
(須) xū

四画 (4 strokes)

预 yù
顿 dùn
顾 gù
顽 wán
(頑) wán
(預) yù
(頓) dùn

五画 (5 strokes)

领 lǐng
(領) lǐng

七画 (7 strokes)

频 pín
(頻) pín
(頭) tóu

八画 (8 strokes)

颗 kē
(顆) kē

九画 (9 strokes)

颜 yán
题 tí
额 é
(額) é
(顏) yán
(題) tí

十画 (10 strokes)

颠 diān
(類) lèi
(願) yuàn

十二画 (12 strokes)

(顧) gù

十三画 (13 strokes)

颤 chàn
(顫) chàn

十四画 (14 strokes)

(顯) xiǎn

---

137 虍

二画 (2 strokes)

虎 hǔ

五画 (5 strokes)

虚 xū
(處) chǔ; chù

六画 (6 strokes)

(虛) xū

七画 (7 strokes)

(號) hào

十一画 (11 strokes)

(虧) kuī

---

138 虫

虫 chóng

二画 (2 stroke)

虱 shī

三画 (3 strokes)

蚁 yǐ
虾 xiā
蚂 mǎ

四画 (4 strokes)

蚕 cán
蚊 wén

五画 (5 strokes)

蛇 shé

六画 (6 strokes)

蛙 wā

七画 (7 strokes)

蛾 é
蜂 fēng
蜗 wō

八画 (8 strokes)

蝇 yíng
蜘 zhī
蝉 chán
蜡 là

九画 (9 strokes)

蝙 biān
蝶 dié
蝴 hú
蝎 xiē
(蝦) xiā
(蝸) wō
(蝨) shī

十画 (10 stroke)

蟒 mǎng
(螞) mǎ
(螢) yíng

十一画 (11 strokes)

螺 luó
(蟬) chán
(蟲) chóng

十三画 (13 strokes)

蟹 xiè
(蠍) xiē
(蠅) yíng
(蟻) yǐ

十五画 (15 strokes)

蠢 chǔn
(蠟) là

十八画 (18 strokes)

(蠶) cán

---

139 缶

三画 (3 strokes)

缸 gāng

四画 (4 strokes)

缺 quē

十七画 (17 strokes)

罐 guàn

---

140 舌

舌 shé

五画 (5 strokes)

甜 tián

七画 (7 strokes)
辞　cí

八画 (8 strokes)
舔　tiǎn

___

141 竹 (⺮)

竹　zhú

三画 (3 strokes)
竿　gān

四画 (4 strokes)
笔　bǐ
笑　xiào
笋　sǔn

五画 (5 strokes)
笨　bèn
笛　dí
笼　lóng
符　fú
第　dì

六画 (6 strokes)
策　cè
等　děng
答　dā; dá
筒　tǒng
(筆) bǐ
(筍) sǔn

七画 (7 strokes)
签　qiān
筷　kuài
简　jiǎn
(節) jié

八画 (8 strokes)
算　suàn
管　guǎn

九画 (9 strokes)
箭　jiàn
箱　xiāng
篇　piān
(範) fàn

十画 (10 strokes)
篮　lán

十二画 (12 strokes)
(簡) jiǎn

十三画 (13 strokes)
(簽) qiān
(簾) lián

十四画 (14 strokes)
(籃) lán

十五画 (15 strokes)
(籐) téng

十六画 (16 strokes)
(籠) lóng

___

142 臼

四画 (4 strokes)
舀　yǎo

七画 (7 strokes)
舅　jiù
舆　yú
(與) yǔ; yù

九画 (9 strokes)
(輿) yú
(興) xīng; xìng

十画 (10 strokes)
(舉) jǔ

十二画 (12 strokes)
(舊) jiù

___

143 血

血　xiě; xuè

___

144 舟

四画 (4 strokes)
舱　cāng
航　háng

五画 (5 strokes)
船　chuán

六画 (6 strokes)
艇　tǐng

十画 (10 strokes)
(艙) cāng

___

145 衣

衣　yī

四画 (4 strokes)
衰　shuāi

五画 (5 strokes)
袋　dài

六画 (6 strokes)
裂　liè
装　zhuāng
裁　cái

七画 (7 strokes)
(裝) zhuāng

八画 (8 strokes)
裹　guǒ
(製) zhì

十六画 (16 strokes)
(襲) xí

___

146 羊 (⺶⺷)

羊　yáng

四画 (4 strokes)
羞　xiū

六画 (6 strokes)
羡　xiàn

七画 (7 strokes)
群　qún
(義) yì
(羨) xiàn

147 米

米　mǐ

三画 (3 strokes)
类　lèi

四画 (4 strokes)
粉　fěn

五画 (5 strokes)
粗　cū
粒　lì

七画 (7 strokes)
粮　liáng

八画 (8 strokes)
粽　zòng
精　jīng

九画 (9 strokes)
糊　hú

十画 (10 strokes)
糙　cāo
糖　táng
糕　gāo

十一画 (11 strokes)
糟　zāo
（糧）liáng

148 艮 (飠)

四画 (4 strokes)
既　jì

十一画 (11 strokes)
（艱）jiān

149 羽

羽　yǔ

四画 (4 strokes)
翅　chì

五画 (5 strokes)
（習）xí

十二画 (12 strokes)
翻　fān

十四画 (14 strokes)
耀　yào

150 糸

四画 (4 strokes)
紧　jǐn
素　sù
索　suǒ

六画 (6 strokes)
紫　zǐ
（紮）zhā
（絲）sī

八画 (8 strokes)
（緊）jǐn

十画 (10 strokes)
（縣）xiàn

十一画 (11 strokes)
繁　fán

151 （行）

五画 (5 strokes)
（術）shù

九画 (9 strokes)
（衝）chōng; chòng
（衛）wèi

152 辰

七画 (7 strokes)
（農）nóng

153 赤

赤　chì

154 走

走　zǒu

三画 (3 strokes)
赶　gǎn
起　qǐ

五画 (5 strokes)
越　yuè
趁　chèn
趋　qū
超　chāo

七画 (7 strokes)
（趕）gǎn

八画 (8 strokes)
趟　tàng
趣　qù

十画 (10 strokes)
（趨）qū

155 豆

豆　dòu

五画 (5 strokes)
登　dēng

八画 (8 strokes)
豌　wān
（豎）shù

十一画 (11 strokes)
（豐）fēng

156 酉

三画 (3 strokes)
配　pèi

四画 (4 strokes)
酗　xù

六画 (6 strokes)
酬　chóu
酱　jiàng

七画 (7 strokes)
酸　suān

八画 (8 strokes)
醉 zuì
醋 cù

九画 (9 strokes)
醒 xǐng

十画 (10 strokes)
(醜) chǒu

十一画 (11 strokes)
(醬) jiàng
(醫) yī

─────────────
157 卤（鹵）

卤 lǔ

九画 (9 stroke)
(鹹) xián

十三画 (13 stroke)
(鹽) yán

─────────────
158 里

里 lǐ

四画 (4 stroke)
野 yě

十一画 (11 stroke)
(釐) lí

─────────────
159 足（⻊）

足 zú

四画 (4 stroke)
跃 yuè
距 jù

五画 (5 strokes)
跌 diē
跑 pǎo

六画 (6 strokes)
跨 kuà
踩 duò
跳 tiào

跪 guì
路 lù
跟 gēn

八画 (8 strokes)
踩 cǎi
踏 tà
踢 tī

九画 (9 strokes)
踹 chuài
蹄 tí

十一画 (11 strokes)
蹦 bèng

十二画 (12 strokes)
蹭 cèng
蹬 dēng
蹲 dūn

十四画 (14 strokes)
(躍) yuè

─────────────
160 身

身 shēn

六画 (6 strokes)
躲 duǒ

八画 (8 strokes)
躺 tǎng

─────────────
161 采

五画 (5 strokes)
释 shì

十三画 (13 strokes)
(釋) shì

─────────────
162 豸

三画 (3 strokes)
豹 bào
豺 chái

七画 (7 strokes)
貌 mào

九画 (9 strokes)
(貓) māo
(豬) zhū

─────────────
163 角

角 jiǎo

六画 (6 strokes)
触 chù
解 jiě

─────────────
164 言（言见 讠）

言 yán

七画 (7 strokes)
誓 shì

十二画 (12 strokes)
警 jǐng

十三画 (13 strokes)
譬 pì
(觸) chù

十四画 (14 strokes)
(護) hù

十六画 (16 strokes)
(變) biàn

─────────────
165 辛

辛 xīn

七画 (7 strokes)
辣 là

九画 (9 strokes)
辩 biàn
辨 biàn
(辦) bàn

十二画 (12 strokes)
(辭) cí

十四画 (14 strokes)
（辯）biàn

---

166 齿(齒)

齿　chǐ
（齒）chǐ

六画 (6 strokes)
龈　yín
（齦）yín

---

167 金

金　jīn

---

168 青

青　qīng

六画 (6 strokes)
静　jìng

八画 (8 strokes)
（靜）jìng

---

169 雨

雨　yǔ

三画 (3 strokes)
雪　xuě

四画 (4 strokes)
（雲）yún

五画 (5 strokes)
雷　léi
零　líng
雾　wù
雹　báo
（電）diàn

六画 (6 strokes)
需　xū

七画 (7 strokes)
霉　méi

九画 (9 strokes)
霜　shuāng

十一画 (11 strokes)
（霧）wù

十三画 (13 strokes)
露　lòu; lù

十六画 (16 strokes)
（靈）líng

---

170 隹

二画 (2 strokes)
（隻）zhī

四画 (4 strokes)
雄　xióng
雇　gù

六画 (6 strokes)
雌　cí

八画 (8 strokes)
雕　diāo

九画 (9 strokes)
（雖）suī

十画 (10 strokes)
（雞）jī
（雜）zá
（雙）shuāng

十一画 (11 strokes)
（離）lí
（難）nán

---

171 鱼(魚)

鱼　yú
（魚）yú

四画 (4 strokes)
鱿　yóu
（魷）yóu

六画 (6 strokes)

鲜　xiān
（鮮）xiān

七画 (7 strokes)
鲨　shā
（鯊）shā

九画 (9 strokes)
鳄　è

十二画 (12 strokes)
鳝　shàn
鳞　lín
（鱔）shàn
（鱗）lín

十六画 (16 strokes)
（鱷）è

---

172 （長）

（長）cháng; zhǎng

---

173 音

音　yīn

十二画 (12 strokes)
（響）xiǎng

---

174 革

革　gé

四画 (4 stroke)
靴　xuē

六画 (6 strokes)
鞋　xié
鞍　ān
（鞏）gǒng

九画 (9 strokes)
鞭　biān

175 骨

骨　gǔ

十三画 (13 strokes)
(髒)　zāng
(體)　tǐ

176 鬼

鬼　guǐ

四画 (4 strokes)
魂　hún
魁　kuí

五画 (5 strokes)
魅　mèi

十一画 (11 strokes)
魔　mó

177 食

食　shí

六画 (6 stroke)
(養)　yǎng

七画 (7 strokes)
餐　cān

178 髟

五画 (5 strokes)
(髮)　fà

八画 (8 strokes)
鬈　quán
(鬆)　sōng

179 (鬥)

(鬥)　dòu

五画 (5 strokes)
(鬧)　nào

180 鹿

鹿　lù

181 麻

麻　má

182 (麥)

(麥)　mài

183 黑

黑　hēi

四画 (4 strokes)
默　mò

五画 (5 srokes)
(點)　diǎn

八画 (8 strokes)
(黨)　dǎng

184 鼠

鼠　shǔ

185 鼻

鼻　bí

186 (龍)

(龍)　lóng

187 (龜)

(龜)　guī

汉英词典

Chinese–English

a

阿 ā [前缀] (方) ▷ 阿爸 ābà dad
  阿拉伯 Ālābó [名] Arabia
  阿拉伯数(數)字 Ālābó shùzì [名]
  Arabic numerals (pl)
  阿姨 āyí [名] (指年长妇女) auntie

啊 ā [叹] oh ▷ 啊! 着火了! Ā! Zháohuǒ
  le! Oh! It's caught fire!

哎 āi [叹] 1 (表示惊讶或不满) oh ▷ 哎!
  这么贵! Āi! Zhème guì! Oh! It's so
  expensive! 2 (表示提醒) hey ▷ 哎! 别踩
  了那朵花。 Āi! Bié cǎile nà duǒ huā.
  Hey! Careful not to tread on that flower.
  哎呀 āiyā [叹] oh ▷ 哎呀，这条路真难
  走! Āiyā, zhè tiáo lù zhēn nán zǒu!
  Oh, this road is hard going!

哀 āi [形] (悲痛) sad
  哀悼 āidào [动] mourn

挨 āi [动] 1 (靠近) be next to ▷ 两个孩子挨
  着门坐。 Liǎng gè háizi āizhe mén zuò.
  The two children sat by the door. 2 (逐个)
  ▷ 挨个儿 āigèr one by one
  → see also/另见 ái

挨 ái [动] 1 (遭受) suffer ▷ 挨饿 ái'è suffer
  from hunger ▷ 挨骂 áimà get told off
  2 (艰难度过) endure
  挨打 áidǎ [动] be beaten up

癌 ái [名] cancer ▷ 癌症 áizhèng cancer

矮 ǎi [形] 1 (指人) short 2 (指物) low

艾 ài [名] (植) mugwort
  艾滋病 àizībìng [名] AIDS

爱(愛) ài [动] 1 (恋) love ▷ 爱人 àiren
  husband or wife, partner ▷ 我爱你。 Wǒ
  ài nǐ. I love you. 2 (喜欢) enjoy ▷ 爱上网
  ài shàngwǎng enjoy surfing the net
  3 (容易) ▷ 她爱晕车。 Tā ài yùnchē. She
  tends to get car sick.
  爱(愛)好 àihào [动] be keen on ▷ 她有
  广泛的爱好。 Tā yǒu guǎngfàn de
  àihào. She has many hobbies.
  爱(愛)护(護) àihù [动] take care of
  爱(愛)情 àiqíng [名] love

安 ān I [形] 1 (安定) quiet ▷ 不安 bù'ān
  anxious 2 (平安) safe ▷ 治安 zhì'ān
  public order II [动] 1 (使安静) calm ▷ 安
  心 ānxīn calm the nerves 2 (安装) fit
  ▷ 门上安把锁 mén shang ān bǎ suǒ fit
  a lock on the door
  安保 ānbǎo [名] security
  安定 āndìng I [形] stable II [动]
  stabilize ▷ 安定局面 āndìng júmiàn
  stabilize the situation
  安家(檢) ānjiā [动] 1 (安置家庭) settle
  2 (结婚) get married
  安检 ānjiǎn [名] security check
  安静(靜) ānjìng [形] 1 (无声) quiet
  2 (平静) peaceful
  安乐(樂)死 ānlèsǐ [名] euthanasia
  安排 ānpái [动] arrange
  安全 ānquán [形] safe ▷ 注意安全。
  Zhùyì ānquán. Be sure to take care.
  ▷ 人身安全 rénshēn ānquán personal
  safety
  安全套 ānquántào [名] condom
  安慰 ānwèi I [动] comfort II [形]
  reassured
  安心 ānxīn [动] (心情安定) stop
  worrying
  安装(裝) ānzhuāng [动] install

鹌(鵪) ān see below/见下文
  鹌(鵪)鹑(鶉) ānchún [名] quail

鞍 ān [名] saddle ▷ 马鞍 mǎ'ān saddle

岸 àn [名] edge ▶ 河岸 hé'àn river bank ▶ 海岸 hǎi'àn seashore

按 àn I [动] 1 (用手压) press ▷ 按电钮 àn diànniǔ press a button ▷ 按门铃 àn ménlíng push a doorbell 2 (人) push ... down 3 (抑制) restrain ▷ 按不住心头怒火 àn bùzhù xīntóu nùhuǒ be unable to restrain one's fury II [介] (依照) according to ▷ 按制度办事 àn zhìdù bànshì do things by the book

按揭 ànjiē [名] mortgage

按摩 ànmó [动] massage

按照 ànzhào [介] according to ▷ 按照课本 ànzhào kèběn according to the textbook

案 àn [名] (案件) case ▶ 案子 ànzi case

案件 ànjiàn [名] case

暗 àn I [形] (昏暗) dim ▷ 今晚月光很暗。 Jīnwǎn yuèguāng hěn àn. Tonight the moon is dim. II [副] secretly

暗号(號) ànhào [名] secret signal

暗杀(殺) ànshā [动] assassinate

暗示 ànshì [动] hint

暗自 ànzì [副] secretly

肮 āng see below/见下文

肮脏(髒) āngzāng [形] 1 (不干净) filthy 2 (喻) (不道德) vile

盎 àng [形] (书) abundant

盎司 àngsī [量] ounce

熬 áo [动] 1 (煮) stew ▶ 熬粥 áozhōu make porridge 2 (忍受) endure

熬夜 áoyè [动] stay up late

袄(襖) ǎo [名] coat ▶ 棉袄 mián'ǎo padded jacket

傲 ào [形] proud

傲慢 àomàn [形] arrogant

傲气(氣) àoqì [名] arrogance

奥(奧) ào [形] profound

奥(奧)林匹克运(運)动(動)会(會) Àolínpǐkè Yùndònghuì [名] Olympic Games® (pl)

澳 ào [名] bay

澳大利亚(亞) Àodàlìyà [名] Australia

澳门 Àomén [名] Macao

懊 ào [形] 1 (后悔) regretful 2 (恼怒) annoyed

懊悔 àohuǐ [动] regret

b

八 bā [数] eight ▸ 八月 bāyuè August

巴 bā [名] ▸ 下巴 xiàba chin ▸ 尾巴 wěiba tail ▸ 嘴巴 zuǐba mouth
巴士 bāshì [名] bus
巴掌 bāzhang [名] (手掌) palm

芭 bā [名] banana
芭蕾舞 bālěiwǔ [名] ballet

疤 bā [名] scar

捌 bā [数] eight

This is the character for eight, which is mainly used in banks, on receipts, cheques etc.

拔 bá [动] 1 (抽出) pull ... up ▸ 拔草 bácǎo weed 2 (取下) pull ... out ▸ 拔牙 báyá pull out a tooth 3 (挑选) choose ▸ 选拔人才 xuǎnbá réncái select talented people 4 (超出) exceed ▸ 海拔 hǎibá height above sea level

把 bǎ I [动] 1 (握住) hold 2 (看守) guard II [名] (把手) handle III [量] 1 ▸ 一把刀 yī bǎ dāo a knife ▸ 一把剪子 yī bǎ jiǎnzi a pair of scissors

measure word, used for objects with a handle

2 handful ▸ 一把米 yī bǎ mǐ a handful of rice

measure word, used for the quantity of something that can be held in a hand

3 ▸ 两把花 liǎng bǎ huā two bunches of flowers

measure word, used for something that can be bundled together

IV [介] ▸ 把门关好 bǎ mén guānhǎo shut the door ▸ 把作业做完 bǎ zuòyè zuòwán finish doing one's homework ▸ 她把书放在桌子上了。Tā bǎ shū fàngzài zhuōzi shang le. She put the book on the table.

把 bǎ is used to alter the word order of a sentence, especially when the verb is a complex one. The normal word order of Subject + Verb + Object, becomes Subject + 把 + Object + Verb. It is very commonly used when the verb implies a change of place, or when the verb is followed by certain complements. For instance, a word-for-word translation of the sentence, 我把书放在那儿。Wǒ bǎ shū fàngzài nàr. (I put the book there) is 'I 把 book put there'.

把手 bǎshou [名] handle
把握 bǎwò I [动] grasp ▸ 把握时机 bǎwò shíjī seize the opportunity II [名] certainty ▸ 没把握 méi bǎwò there is no certainty

爸 bà [名] father
爸爸 bàba [名] dad

吧 ba [助] 1 (在句尾表示建议) ▸ 我们回家吧。Wǒmen huíjiā ba. Let's go home. ▸ 吃吧! Chī ba! Eat! ▸ 再想想吧。Zài xiǎngxiǎng ba. Think about it again. 2 (在句尾表示对推测的肯定) ▸ 你听说了? Nǐ tīngshuōle ba? You may have heard about this. ▸ 他明天走吧? Tā míngtiān zǒu ba? Is he leaving tomorrow?

Adding 吧 ba at the end of a sentence forms a suggestion, e.g. 我们走吧。Wǒmen zǒu ba. (Let's go). But adding 吗 ma at the end of a sentence forms a question, e.g. 我们走吗? Wǒmen zǒu ma? (Shall we go?).

白 bái I [形] 1 (白色) white ▸ 白糖 báitáng white sugar ▸ 白领 báilǐng white-collar 2 (明亮) bright ▸ 白天 báitiān daytime 3 (平淡) plain ▸ 白开水 báikāishuǐ boiled water ▸ 白米饭

báimǐfàn boiled rice II [副] (无结果) in vain ▶ 白费 báifèi waste ▶ 白等 báiděng wait in vain

白菜 báicài [名] Chinese cabbage

白酒 báijiǔ [名] clear spirit

白人 báirén [名] white people (pl)

百 bǎi [数] hundred

百分之百 bǎi fēn zhī bǎi absolutely

百万(萬) bǎiwàn [数] million

佰 bǎi [名] hundred
| This is the character for hundred which is used in banks, on receipts, cheques etc.

摆(擺) bǎi [动] 1 (放置) arrange ▶ 摆放 bǎifàng place 2 (摇动) wave ▶ 摆动 bǎidòng sway ▶ 她向我摆手。Tā xiàng wǒ bǎi shǒu. She waved her hand at me.

摆(擺)设(設) bǎishè [动] furnish and decorate

败(敗) bài [动] (打败) defeat

败(敗)坏(壞) bàihuài I [动] corrupt II [形] corrupt

败(敗)仗 bàizhàng [名] defeat

拜 bài [动] (会见) pay a visit ▶ 拜访 bàifǎng visit

拜年 bàinián [动] pay a New Year call

拜托(託) bàituō [动] ▶ 拜托您给看会儿我女儿。Bàituō nín gěi kān huìr wǒ nǚ'er. Would you be kind enough to look after my daughter for a while?

班 bān I [名] 1 (班级) class ▶ 班长 bānzhǎng class monitor 2 (交通) scheduled trip ▶ 班机 bānjī scheduled flight ▶ 末班车 mòbānchē the last bus 3 (轮班) shift ▶ 上班 shàngbān go to work ▶ 下班 xiàbān finish work ▶ 晚班 wǎnbān night shift 4 (军) squad II [量] ▷ 下一班船 xià yī bān chuán the next boat ▷ 错过一班飞机 cuòguò yī bān fēijī miss a flight
| measure word, used for scheduled transportations

班级(級) bānjí [名] classes (pl)

搬 bān [动] 1 (移动) take ... away ▷ 把这些

东西搬走。Bǎ zhèxiē dōngxi bānzǒu. Take these things away. 2 (迁移) move ▶ 搬家 bānjiā move house

板 bǎn I [名] (片状硬物) board II [动] put on a stern expression

版 bǎn [名] edition ▶ 修订版 xiūdìng bǎn revised edition

办(辦) bàn [动] 1 (处理) handle ▶ 办事 bànshì handle affairs ▷ 我们该怎么办？Wǒmen gāi zěnme bàn? What should we do? 2 (创设) set ... up ▶ 办工厂 bàn gōngchǎng set up a factory 3 (经营) run ▶ 办学 bànxué run a school 4 (展览) stage ▷ 办画展 bàn huàzhǎn stage an art exhibition

办(辦)法 bànfǎ [名] way ▷ 想办法 xiǎng bànfǎ find a way ▷ 联系办法 liánxì bànfǎ means of contact

办(辦)公 bàngōng [动] work

办(辦)理 bànlǐ [动] handle

半 bàn I [数] (二分之一) half ▷ 半价 bànjià half price ▷ 半年 bàn nián half a year II [名] (在中间) middle ▶ 半夜 bànyè midnight III [副] partially ▶ 半新 bànxīn almost new

半导(導)体(體) bàndǎotǐ [名] 1 (指物质) semiconductor 2 (收音机) transistor radio

半岛(島) bàndǎo [名] peninsula

半径(徑) bànjìng [名] radius

半球 bànqiú [名] hemisphere

半天 bàntiān [名] for quite a while ▷ 他等了半天。Tā děngle bàntiān. He waited for quite a while.

伴 bàn [名] company ▶ 做伴 zuòbàn keep company

拌 bàn [动] (搅和) mix

绊(絆) bàn [动] (使跌倒) trip

瓣 bàn I [名] (指花儿) petal II [量] ▷ 几瓣蒜 jǐ bàn suàn a few cloves of garlic ▷ 一瓣橘子 yī bàn júzi a segment of orange
| measure word, used to describe flower petals and segments of fruits

帮(幫)bāng [动] (帮助) help ▷ 我帮他买票。Wǒ bāng tā mǎi piào. I helped him get the tickets.

帮(幫)忙 bāngmáng [动] help ▷ 请您帮我个忙。Qǐng nín bāng wǒ gè máng. Please can you help me out?

帮(幫)助 bāngzhù [动] help ▷ 谢谢您的帮助。Xièxie nín de bāngzhù. Thank you for your help.

绑(綁)bǎng [动] tie up

榜 bǎng [名] list of names
榜样(樣) bǎngyàng [名] model

棒 bàng I [名] (棍子) cudgel ▷ 棒子 bàngzi club II [形] (口) great ▷ 他英语说得很棒。Tā Yīngyǔ shuō de hěn bàng. He speaks great English.

傍 bàng [动] be close to
傍晚 bàngwǎn [名] dusk

磅 bàng [量] pound

镑(鎊)bàng [名] pound

包 bāo I [动] 1 (包裹) wrap 2 (包含) include 3 (担保) guarantee 4 (约定专用) hire ▷ 包车 bāochē hire a car ▷ 包机 bāojī charter a plane II [名] 1 (包裹) parcel 2 (口袋) bag ▷ 背包 bēibāo backpack ▷ 钱包 qiánbāo wallet 3 (疙瘩) lump III [量] packet, bag ▷ 一包烟 yī bāo yān a packet of cigarettes ▷ 一包衣服 yī bāo yīfu a bag of clothes measure word, used to describe things that are wrapped up
包含 bāohán [动] contain
包括 bāokuò [动] include
包子 bāozi [名] *steamed stuffed bun*

包子 bāozi
• 包子 bāozi are bigger than 饺子 jiǎozi. Shaped like buns, they are usually stuffed with meat or vegetable fillings, and are steamed rather than boiled.

剥(剝)bāo [动] peel

雹 báo [名] hail ▷ 雹子 báozi hailstone

薄 báo [形] 1 (不厚) thin 2 (冷淡) cold ▷ 我对她不薄。Wǒ duì tā bù báo. I treat her very well.

宝(寶)bǎo I [名] treasure II [形] precious
宝(寶)贵(貴) bǎoguì [形] valuable

饱(飽)bǎo [形] full ▷ 我吃饱了。Wǒ chībǎo le. I am full.

保 bǎo [动] 1 (保护) protect 2 (保持) keep ▷ 保密 bǎomì keep ... secret ▷ 保鲜膜 bǎoxiānmó Clingfilm® (英), Saran wrap® (美) 3 (保证) ensure
保安 bǎo'ān [名] security guard
保持 bǎochí [动] maintain ▷ 保持警惕 bǎochí jǐngtì stay vigilant
保存 bǎocún [动] preserve
保护(護) bǎohù [动] protect ▷ 保护环境 bǎohù huánjìng protect the environment
保龄(齡)球 bǎolíngqiú [名] (体育运动) bowling
保留 bǎoliú [动] 1 (保存不变) preserve 2 (意见) hold back ▷ 你可以保留自己的意见。Nǐ kěyǐ bǎoliú zìjǐ de yìjiàn. You can keep your opinions to yourself.
保姆 bǎomǔ [名] 1 (做家务的女工) domestic help 2 (保育员) nanny
保守 bǎoshǒu [形] conservative
保卫(衛) bǎowèi [动] defend
保险(險) bǎoxiǎn I [名] insuránce II [形] safe
保证(證) bǎozhèng [动] guarantee
保重 bǎozhòng [动] take care of oneself

报(報)bào I [动] (告诉) report II [名] 1 (报纸) newspaper ▷ 日报 rìbào daily ▷ 报社 bàoshè newspaper office 2 (刊物) periodical ▷ 画报 huàbào glossy magazine
报(報)仇 bàochóu [动] take revenge
报(報)酬 bàochou [名] pay
报(報)到 bàodào [动] register
报(報)道 bàodào I [动] report ▷ 电视台报道了这条新闻。Diànshìtái bàodàole zhè tiáo xīnwén. The television station reported this item of

news. II[名] report ▷ 一篇关于克隆人的报道 yī piān guānyú kèlóngrén de bàodào a report about human cloning

报(報)复(復) bàofù [动] retaliate

报(報)告 bàogào I[动] report ▷ 向主管部门报告 xiàng zhǔguǎn bùmén bàogào report to the department in charge II[名] report ▷ 在大会上作报告 zài dàhuì shang zuò bàogào give a talk at the conference

报(報)关(關) bàoguān [动] declare

报(報)刊 bàokān [名] newspapers and periodicals (pl)

报(報)名 bàomíng [动] sign up

报(報)失 bàoshī [动] report a loss

报(報)销(銷) bàoxiāo [动] (费用) claim for

报(報)纸(紙) bàozhǐ [名] newspaper

抱 bào [动] 1(手臂围住) carry in one's arms 2(领养) adopt 3(心里存有) cherish ▷ 对某事抱幻想 duì mǒushì bào huànxiǎng have illusions about sth

抱歉 bàoqiàn I[形] sorry II[动] apologize

抱怨 bàoyuàn [动] complain

豹 bào [名] leopard

暴 bào [形] (猛烈) violent ▶ 暴雨 bàoyǔ rainstorm

爆 bào [动] 1(猛然破裂) explode ▶ 爆炸 bàozhà explode 2(突然发生) break out ▶ 爆发 bàofā break out

杯 bēi I[名] 1(杯子) cup ▶ 玻璃杯 bōli bēi glass ▶ 酒杯 jiǔbēi wineglass ▶ 杯子 bēizi cup 2(奖杯) cup ▶ 世界杯 Shìjièbēi World Cup II[量] cup, glass ▷ 一杯咖啡 yī bēi kāfēi a cup of coffee ▷ 两杯水 liǎng bēi shuǐ two glasses of water

背(揹) bēi [动] 1(驮) carry ... on one's back 2(担负) take ... on ▷ 背起重任 bēi qǐ zhòngrèn take on great responsibility
→ see also/另见 bèi

悲 bēi [形] (悲伤) sad

悲惨(慘) bēicǎn [形] miserable

悲观(觀) bēiguān [形] pessimistic

悲伤(傷) bēishāng [形] sad

碑 bēi [名] tablet ▶ 纪念碑 jìniànbēi monument

北 běi [名] north ▶ 北方 běifāng the North ▶ 北京 Běijīng Beijing ▶ 北部 běibù the north

北极(極) běijí [名] the North Pole

备(備) bèi [动] 1(具备) have 2(准备) prepare

备(備)份 bèifèn [动] (计算机) keep a backup copy

备(備)用 bèiyòng [动] backup ▷ 备用光盘 bèiyòng guāngpán backup CD

备(備)注(註) bèizhù [名] (注解说明) notes (pl)

背(揹) bèi I[名] 1(指身体) back ▶ 背疼 bèiténg backache 2(指反面) back ▶ 背面 bèimiàn reverse side 3(指后面) behind ▶ 背后 bèihòu behind II[动] (背诵) recite
→ see also/另见 bēi

背景 bèijǐng [名] (指景物、情况) background

背诵(誦) bèisòng [动] recite

被 bèi I[名] quilt ▶ 被子 bèizi quilt II[介] ▷ 他被哥哥打了一顿。 Tā bèi gēge dǎle yī dùn. He was beaten up by his elder brother. III[助] ▷ 他被跟踪了。 Tā bèi gēnzōng le. He was followed.

倍 bèi [名] times (pl) ▷ 这本书比那本书厚三倍。 Zhè běn shū bǐ nà běn shū hòu sān bèi. This book is three times thicker than that one. ▷ 物价涨了一倍。 Wùjià zhǎng le yī bèi. Prices have doubled.

本 běn I[名] 1(本子) book ▶ 笔记本 bǐjìběn notebook 2(版本) edition ▶ 手抄本 shǒuchāoběn hand-written copy II[形] 1(自己的) one's own ▶ 本人 běnrén oneself 2(现今) this ▶ 本月 běnyuè this month III[副] originally ▷ 我本想亲自去一趟。 Wǒ běn xiǎng qīnzì qù yī tàng. I originally wanted to go myself. **IV** [量] ▷ 几本书 jǐ běn shū a few books

■ measure word, used for counting books, magazines, dictionaries, etc.

本地 běndì [名] locality ▷ 她是本地人。Tā shì běndì rén. She is a native of this place.

本科 běnkē [名] undergraduate course ▷ 本科生 běnkēshēng undergraduate

本来 (來) běnlái **I** [形] original ▷ 本来的打算 běnlái de dǎsuàn the original plan **II** [副] (原先) at first ▷ 我本来以为你已经走了。Wǒ běnlái yǐwéi nǐ yǐjīng zǒu le. At first, I thought you had left.

本领 (領) běnlǐng [名] skill

本身 běnshēn [名] itself

本事 běnshi [名] ability

本质 (質) běnzhì [名] essence

笨 bèn [形] **1** (不聪明) stupid **2** (不灵巧) clumsy ▷ 他嘴很笨。Tā zuǐ hěn bèn. He's quite inarticulate.

蹦 bèng [动] leap

逼 bī [动] **1** (强迫) force **2** (强取) press for ▷ 逼债 bīzhài press for repayment of a debt **3** (逼近) close in on
逼近 bījìn [动] close in on
逼迫 bīpò [动] force

鼻 bí [名] (鼻子) nose
鼻涕 bítì [名] mucus
鼻子 bízi [名] nose

比 bǐ **I** [动] **1** (比较) compare ▷ 比比过去，现在的生活好多了。Bǐbǐ guòqù, xiànzài de shēnghuó hǎo duō le. Life now is much better compared to the past. **2** (较量) compete ▷ 他们要比比谁游得快。Tāmen yào bǐbǐ shuí yóu de kuài. They are competing to see who swims the fastest. **II** [介] **1** (指得分) ▷ 零比零 líng bǐ líng nil-nil (英), no score (美) **2** (相对) ▷ 今年冬天比去年冷。Jīnnián dōngtiān bǐ qùnián lěng. It is colder this winter than last winter.

■ 比 bǐ is used to express comparisons: to say that X is taller than Y, simply say X 比 Y 高。e.g. 上海比南京大。

上海比南京大。Shànghǎi bǐ Nánjīng dà. (Shanghai is bigger than Nanjing).

比方 bǐfang [名] analogy ▶ 比方说 bǐfang shuō for example

比分 bǐfēn [名] score

比基尼 bǐjīní [名] bikini

比较 (較) bǐjiào **I** [动] compare **II** [副] relatively ▷ 这里的水果比较新鲜。Zhèlǐ de shuǐguǒ bǐjiào xīnxiān. The fruit here is relatively fresh.

比例 bǐlì [名] proportion

比率 bǐlǜ [名] ratio

比如 bǐrú [连] for instance

比赛 (賽) bǐsài [名] match

彼 bǐ [代] **1** (那个) that **2** (对方) the other side
彼此 bǐcǐ [代] (双方) both sides

笔 (筆) bǐ **I** [名] **1** (工具) pen ▶ 圆珠笔 yuánzhūbǐ ball-point pen **2** (笔画) brush stroke **II** [量] (款项) ▷ 一笔钱 yī bǐ qián a sum of money

■ measure word, used for money

笔 (筆) 记 (記) bǐjì [名] (记录) note ▷ 记笔记 jì bǐjì take notes

笔 (筆) 记 (記) 本电 (電) 脑 (腦) bǐjìběn diànnǎo [名] laptop

币 (幣) bì [名] coin ▶ 货币 huòbì currency ▶ 外币 wàibì foreign currency

必 bì [副] **1** (必然) certainly **2** (必须) ▶ 必修课 bìxiūkè compulsory course
必然 bìrán **I** [形] inevitable **II** [名] necessity
必须 (須) bìxū [副] ▷ 你们必须准时来上班。Nǐmen bìxū zhǔnshí lái shàngbān. You must start work on time.
必要 bìyào [形] essential

毕 (畢) bì [动] finish
毕 (畢) 业 (業) bìyè [动] graduate

避 bì [动] **1** (躲开) avoid ▶ 避风 bìfēng shelter from the wind **2** (防止) prevent
避免 bìmiǎn [动] avoid
避难 (難) bìnàn [动] take refuge
避孕 bìyùn [动] use contraceptives ▷ 避孕药 bìyùnyào the pill

边(邊)biān [名] 1(边线) side ▷ 街两边 jiē liǎngbiān both sides of the street 2(边缘) edge ▷ 路边 lù biān roadside 3(边界) border 4(旁边) side ▷ 在床边 zài chuáng biān by the bed

边(邊)…边(邊)… biān…biān… ▷ 边 吃边谈 biān chī biān tán talk while eating

边(邊)疆 biānjiāng [名] border area
边(邊)界 biānjiè [名] border
边(邊)境 biānjìng [名] border
边(邊)缘(緣) biānyuán [名] edge

编(編)biān [动] 1(编辑) edit ▷ 编程 biānchéng program 2(创作) write ▷ 编 歌词 biān gēcí write lyrics 3(捏造) fabricate ▷ 编谎话 biān huǎnghuà fabricate a lie
编(編)辑(輯) biānjí I [动] edit II [名] editor

蝙 biān see below/见下文
蝙蝠 biānfú [名] bat

鞭 biān [名] 1(鞭子) whip 2(爆竹) firecracker
鞭炮(砲) biānpào [名] firecracker

鞭炮 biānpào
　Firecrackers are believed by the Chinese to scare off evil spirits and attract the god of good fortune to people's doorsteps, especially in the celebration of the Spring Festival and at weddings.

贬(貶)biǎn [动] (降低) reduce ▷ 贬值 biǎnzhí depreciate
贬(貶)义(義)词(詞) biǎnyìcí [名] derogatory expression

扁 biǎn [形] flat ▷ 自行车胎扁了。Zìxíngchē tāi biǎn le. The bicycle tyre is flat.

变(變)biàn [动] 1(改变) change ▷ 小城 的面貌变了。Xiǎochéng de miànmào biàn le. The appearance of the town has changed. 2(变成) become ▷ 他变成熟 了。Tā biàn chéngshú le. He's become quite grown up.

变(變)化 biànhuà I [动] change II [名] change

便 biàn I [形] 1(方便) convenient ▷ 轻便 qīngbiàn portable 2(简单) simple ▷ 便 饭 biànfàn simple meal II [动] excrete ▷ 小便 xiǎobiàn urinate ▷ 大便 dàbiàn defecate III [副] ▷ 稍等片刻演出便开 始。Shāoděng piànkè yǎnchū biàn kāishǐ. The performance is about to start in a moment.
→ see also/另见 pián

便利 biànlì I [形] convenient II [动] facilitate
便士 biànshì [量] pence
便条(條) biàntiáo [名] note
便携(攜)式 biànxiéshì [形] portable
便于(於) biànyú [动] be easy to ▷ 便于联系 biànyú liánxì be easy to contact

遍 biàn I [副] all over ▷ 找了个遍 zhǎole gè biàn searched high and low II [量] ▷ 我说了两遍。Wǒ shuōle liǎng biàn. I said it twice.
　measure word, used for the number of times the same action takes place

辨 biàn [动] distinguish ▷ 辨别 biànbié distinguish
辨认(認) biànrèn [动] identify

辩(辯)biàn [动] debate ▷ 辩论 biànlùn argue

标(標)biāo I [名] 1(记号) mark 2(标准) standard II [动] mark
标(標)本 biāoběn [名] (样品) specimen
标(標)点(點) biāodiǎn [名] punctuation
标(標)记(記) biāojì [名] mark
标(標)题(題) biāotí [名] 1(指文章, 书) title 2(指新闻) headline
标(標)王 biāowáng [名] top bidder
标(標)志(誌) biāozhì [名] sign
标(標)准(準) biāozhǔn I [名] standard ▷ 道德标准 dàodé biāozhǔn moral standard II [形] standard ▷ 标准时间 biāozhǔn shíjiān standard time

表(錶) biǎo [名] **1**(计时器) watch ▸手表 shǒubiǎo wristwatch **2**(计量器) meter ▸电表 diànbiǎo electricity meter **3**(表格) form ▸火车时间表 huǒchē shíjiānbiǎo train timetable ▷填申请表 tián shēnqǐngbiǎo fill in the application form **4**(指亲戚) cousin ▸表哥 biǎogē cousin

表达(達) biǎodá [动] express

表格 biǎogé [名] form

表面 biǎomiàn [名] surface

表明 biǎomíng [动] show

表示 biǎoshì I[动](表达) express II[名] **1**(言行或表情) gesture **2**(意见) attitude

表现(現) biǎoxiàn I[动](显出) show II[名](指行为、作风) performance

表演 biǎoyǎn I[动](演出) perform II[名] performance

表扬(揚) biǎoyáng [动] praise

别(別) bié I[形](其他) other II[副] (不要) ▷别忘了关灯。Bié wàng le guāndēng. Don't forget to turn off the light.

别(別)人 biérén [名] other people

别(別)墅 biéshù [名] villa

别(別)针(針) biézhēn [名] safety pin

宾(賓) bīn [名] guest

宾(賓)馆(館) bīnguǎn [名] hotel

冰 bīng I[名] ice II[动] **1**(使感觉寒冷) be freezing ▷这水冰手。Zhè shuǐ bīng shǒu. This water is freezing. **2**(冰镇) cool ▸冰镇 bīngzhèn iced

冰淇淋 bīngqílín [名] ice cream

冰沙 bīngshā [名] smoothie

冰箱 bīngxiāng [名] fridge

兵 bīng [名] **1**(军队) the army ▷当兵 dāngbīng join the army **2**(士兵) soldier

饼(餅) bǐng [名](面食) cake ▸月饼 yuèbǐng moon cake

饼(餅)干(乾) bǐnggān [名] biscuit (英), cookie(美)

并(並) bìng I[动] **1**(合并) merge **2**(并拢) bring ... together ▷把脚并起来 bǎ jiǎo bìng qǐlái bring your feet together II[副](表示强调) really ▷他今晚并不想出去。Tā jīnwǎn bìng bù xiǎng chūqù. He really doesn't want to go out this evening. III[连] and ▷他会说法语，并在学习西班牙语。Tā huì shuō Fǎyǔ, bìng zài xuéxí Xībānyáyǔ He can speak French, and he is studying Spanish at the moment.

并(並)且 bìngqiě [连] **1**(和) and ▷她聪明并且用功。Tā cōngming bìngqiě yònggōng. She is clever and diligent. **2**(此外) also

病 bìng I[名](疾病) disease ▸心脏病 xīnzàngbìng heart disease ▸生病 shēngbìng become ill ▷他去看病了。Tā qù kànbìng le. He went to see a doctor. II[动] be ill ▷他病得不轻。Tā bìng de bù qīng. He was seriously ill.

病毒 bìngdú [名] virus

病房 bìngfáng [名] ward

病菌 bìngjūn [名] bacteria

病人 bìngrén [名] **1**(指医院里) patient **2**(指家里) invalid

波 bō [名](指水，声音，电) wave

拨(撥) bō [动] **1**(号码) dial ▷拨电话号 bō diànhuà hào dial the phone number **2**(频道) change over to

玻 bō see below/见下文

玻璃 bōli [名] glass

菠 bō see below/见下文

菠菜 bōcài [名] spinach

菠萝(蘿) bōluó [名] pineapple

播 bō [动](电视、收音机) broadcast ▸播放 bōfàng broadcast

伯 bó [名](伯父) uncle

伯伯 bóbo [名] **1**(伯父) uncle **2**(用于称呼) uncle

脖 bó [名] neck ▸脖子 bózi neck

博 bó [形] abundant

博客 bókè [名] blog

博物馆(館) bówùguǎn [名] museum

博主 bózhǔ [名] blogger

补(補) bǔ [动] **1** (衣服、鞋、车胎、袜子) mend **2** (牙) fill **3** (增加) add

补(補)充 bǔchōng I [动] add II [形] supplementary ▷ 补充说明 bǔchōng shuōmíng additional explanation

补(補)考 bǔkǎo [动] resit

补(補)习(習) bǔxí [动] take extra lessons

补(補)助 bǔzhù [名] subsidy

捕 bǔ [动] catch

捕捉 bǔzhuō [动] **1** (抓住) seize **2** (捉拿) hunt down

不 bù [副] **1** (用于否定句) not ▷ 不诚实 bù chéngshí dishonest ▷ 他不抽烟。 Tā bù chōuyān. He doesn't smoke. **2** (用于否定回答) no ▷ "你累了吧？" "不，不累。" "Nǐ lèi le ba?" "Bù, bùlèi." "Are you tired?" – "No, I'm not." **3** (客套) (不用) ▷ 不客气。Bù kèqi. Please don't mention it. ▷ 不谢。Bù xiè. You're welcome.

Negating sentences in Chinese is very straightforward: just use 不 bù before the verb. E.g. 我不喝酒。Wǒ bù hējiǔ (I don't drink alcohol). The only exception is the verb 有 yǒu, to have, for which you must use 没 méi. E.g. 我没有钱。Wǒ méiyǒu qián. (I don't have any money). 不 bù is fourth tone unless it is followed by another fourth tone syllable, in which case it is usually pronounced as a second tone, eg. 不要 búyào. For more information on tones, please see the introduction.

不必 bùbì [副] ▷ 明天你们不必来了。 Míngtiān nǐmen bùbì lái le. You don't have to come tomorrow.

不错 bùcuò [形] correct

不但 bùdàn [连] not only ▷ 这辆车的设计不但美观，而且实用。Zhè liàng chē de shèjì bùdàn měiguān, érqiě shíyòng. The design of this car is not only beautiful, it's also practical.

不得了 bùdéliǎo [形] (表示程度) extreme ▷ 这孩子淘气得不得了。 Zhè háizi táoqì de bùdéliǎo. This child is terribly naughty.

不断(斷) bùduàn [副] continually ▷ 沙漠不断扩大。Shāmò bùduàn kuòdà. The desert is expanding all the time.

不敢 bùgǎn [动] not dare

不管 bùguǎn [连] ▷ 不管出什么事，我们都要保持镇定。Bùguǎn chū shénme shì, wǒmen dōu yào bǎochí zhèndìng. Whatever happens, we must remain calm.

不过(過) bùguò I [副] **1** (仅仅) only ▷ 不过是点小伤。Bùguò shì diǎn xiǎoshāng. It's only a slight injury. **2** (非常) can't be better ▷ 这是最简单不过的方法。Zhè shì zuì jiǎndān bùguò de fāngfǎ. This is by far the easiest method. II [连] but ▷ 他很喜欢新学校，不过离家太远了。Tā hěn xǐhuān xīn xuéxiào, bùguò lí jiā tài yuǎn le. He really likes his new school, but it's a very long way from home.

不仅(僅) bùjǐn [副] **1** (不止) not just ▷ 这不仅是学校的问题。Zhè bùjǐn shì xuéxiào de wèntí. This is not just the school's problem. **2** (不但) not only ▷ 这地毯不仅质量好，而且价格便宜。Zhè dìtǎn bùjǐn zhìliàng hǎo, érqiě jiàgé piányi. Not only is the carpet good quality, it's also cheap.

不久 bùjiǔ [名] ▷ 他们不久就要结婚了。Tāmen bùjiǔ jiùyào jiéhūn le. They are getting married soon.

不论(論) bùlùn [连] no matter ▷ 不论是谁，都必须遵守法规。Bùlùn shì shuí, dōu bìxū zūnshǒu fǎguī. No matter who you are, you have to abide by the regulations.

不满(滿) bùmǎn [形] dissatisfied

不免 bùmiǎn [副] inevitably

不然 bùrán [连] otherwise ▷ 多谢你提醒我，不然我就忘了。Duōxiè nǐ tíxǐng wǒ, bùrán wǒ jiù wàng le. Thanks very much for reminding me, or I would have forgotten about it.

不如 bùrú [动] not be as good as ▷ 城里太吵，不如住在郊区。Chéngli tài chǎo, bùrú zhù zài jiāoqū. The city is too noisy – it's better living in the suburbs.

不少 bùshǎo [形] a lot of ▷ 她有不少好朋友。Tā yǒu bùshǎo hǎo péngyou. She has a lot of good friends.

不舒服 bùshūfu [形] unwell

不同 bùtóng [形] different

不幸(倖) bùxìng I [形] 1(不幸运)
unhappy 2(出人意料) unfortunate
II [名] disaster

不要紧(緊) bùyàojǐn [形] 1(不严重)
not serious ▷ 他的病不要紧。Tā de
bìng bùyàojǐn. His illness is not
serious. 2(没关系) it doesn't matter

不一定 bùyīdìng [副] may not ▷ 她不
一定会回电话。Tā bùyīdìng huì huí
diànhuà. She may not return your call.

不怎么(麼)样(樣) bù zěnmeyàng
[形] not up to much

不止 bùzhǐ [副] 1(不停地) incessantly
▷ 大笑不止 dà xiào bùzhǐ laugh
incessantly 2(多于) more than ▷ 不止
一次 bùzhǐ yī cì on more than one
occasion

布 bù [名] cloth

布(佈)置 bùzhì [动] 1(房间等)
decorate 2(任务, 作业) assign

步 bù [名] 1(脚步) step ▶步伐 bùfá pace
2(阶段) stage ▶步骤 bùzhòu step
3(地步) situation

步行 bùxíng [动] go on foot

部 bù I [名] 1(部分) part ▷ 东部 dōngbù
the eastern part 2(部门) department
▶总部 zǒngbù headquarters (pl) ▶部长
bùzhǎng minister, department head
▷教育部 jiàoyùbù Ministry of Education
II [量] ▷ 一部电话 yī bù diànhuà a
telephone ▷三部电影 sān bù diànyǐng
three films

measure word, used for films,
phones, etc.

部队(隊) bùduì [名] armed forces (pl)

部分 bùfen [名] part

部门(門) bùmén [名] department

部位 bùwèi [名] place

C

擦 cā [动] 1(抹) wipe ... clean 2(指用水)
wash 3(皮鞋) polish 4(摩擦) rub 5(涂)
apply 6(火柴) strike 7(破) scrape ▶擦伤
cāshāng scrape 8(挨着) brush 9(瓜果)
shred

猜 cāi [动] 1(猜测) guess 2(猜疑) suspect

猜测(測) cāicè I [动] speculate II [名]
speculation

猜想 cāixiǎng [动] suppose

猜疑 cāiyí [动] have unfounded
suspicions about

才 cái I [名] 1(才能) ability ▷ 多才多艺
duō cái duō yì multi-talented ▷ (人才)
talent ▶奇才 qícái extraordinary talent
II [副] 1(刚) just ▷ 我才到家, 电话就响
了。Wǒ cái dào jiā, diànhuà jiù xiǎng
le. Just as I arrived home, the phone rang.
2(表示晚) not...until ▷ 我10点才到单
位。Wǒ shídiǎn cái dào dānwèi.
I didn't arrive at work until ten o'clock.
3(表示条件) only...if ▷ 学生只有用功,
才能取得好成绩。Xuéshēng zhǐyǒu
yònggōng, cái néng qǔdé hǎo chéngjì.
Students will only be able to do well if
they study hard. 4(表示情况改变) only
after ▷ 他解释后, 我才明白他为什么那
么难过。Tā jiěshì hòu, wǒ cái míngbai
tā wèi shénme nàme nánguò. It was
only after he explained that I understood
why he was so sad. 5(程度低) only ▷ 他
才学会上网。Tā cái xuéhuì shàngwǎng.

He has only just learned how to use the Internet.

才华(華) cáihuá [名] talent

才能 cáinéng [名] ability

才艺(藝)秀 cáiyì xiù [名] talent contest

才子 cáizǐ [名] talented man

材 cái [名] (指物) material ▶ 教材 jiàocái teaching material

材料 cáiliào [名] 1 (原料) material 2 (资料) material 3 (人才) talent

财(財) cái [名] wealth

财(財)富 cáifù [名] wealth

财(財)政 cáizhèng [名] finance

裁 cái [动] 1 (衣服、纸) cut 2 (减) cut ▶ 裁员 cáiyuán cut staff 3 (判断) decide

裁缝(縫) cáiféng [名] 1 (指男装) tailor 2 (指女装) dressmaker

裁判 cáipàn I [名] 1 (案件) judgment 2 (比赛) referee II [动] make a decision

采(採) cǎi [动] 1 (摘) pick 2 (选) choose 3 (开采) extract 4 (采集) gather

采(採)访(訪) cǎifǎng [动] interview

采(採)购(購) cǎigòu I [动] purchase II [名] buyer

采(採)取 cǎiqǔ [动] adopt

采(採)用 cǎiyòng [动] adopt

彩 cǎi [名] (颜色) colour (英), color (美)

彩电(電) cǎidiàn [名] colour (英) 或 color (美) TV

彩卷 cǎijuǎn [名] colour (英) 或 color (美) film

彩排 cǎipái [动] rehearse

彩票 cǎipiào [名] lottery ticket

彩色 cǎisè [名] colour (英), color (美)

踩 cǎi [动] (脚) step on

菜 cài [名] 1 (植物) vegetable 2 (饭食) dish

菜单(單) càidān [名] menu

菜谱(譜) càipǔ [名] 1 (菜单) menu 2 (指书) cookbook

参(參) cān [动] (加入) join ▶ 参军 cānjūn enlist
→ see also / 另见 shēn

参(參)观(觀) cānguān [动] tour

参(參)加 cānjiā [动] take part in ▶ 参加新年晚会 cānjiā xīnnián wǎnhuì attend a New Year's party ▶ 参加了民主党 cānjiāle Mínzhǔ Dǎng join the Democratic Party

参(參)考 cānkǎo I [动] consult II [名] reference ▶ 参考书 cānkǎoshū reference book

参(參)谋(謀) cānmóu I [名] 1 (顾问) advisor 2 (指军职) staff officer II [动] give advice

参(參)与(與) cānyù [动] participate in

餐 cān I [名] meal II [量] meal

餐车(車) cānchē [名] 1 (指推车) food trolley 2 (指车厢) buffet (英) 或 dining (美) car

餐巾 cānjīn [名] napkin

餐具 cānjù [名] eating utensils (pl)

餐厅(廳) cāntīng [名] canteen

残(殘) cán [形] 1 (指器物) defective 2 (指人或动物) disabled 3 (剩余) remaining

残(殘)次 cáncì [形] damaged ▶ 残次品 cáncì pǐn damaged goods

残(殘)废(廢) cánfèi [动] have a disability

残(殘)疾 cánjí [名] disability ▷ 残疾人 cánjírén people with disabilities

残(殘)酷 cánkù [形] brutal

残(殘)忍 cánrěn [形] cruel

蚕(蠶) cán [名] silkworm

惭(慚) cán see below / 见下文

惭(慚)愧 cánkuì [形] ashamed

惨(慘) cǎn [形] (悲惨) tragic

灿(燦) càn see below / 见下文

灿(燦)烂(爛) cànlàn [形] glorious

仓(倉) cāng [名] store

仓(倉)库 cāngkù [名] storehouse

苍(蒼) cāng [形] (指鬓发) grey (英), gray (美)

苍(蒼)白 cāngbái [形] 1 (脸色) pale

2(文章，表演等) bland

苍(蒼)蝇(蠅) cāngying [名] fly

舱(艙) cāng [名] **1**(用于载人) cabin ▶ 头等舱 tóuděngcāng first-class cabin **2**(用于装物) hold ▶ 货舱 huòcāng cargo hold

藏 cáng [动] **1**(隐藏) hide **2**(储存) store **3**(收集) collect ▶ 藏书 cángshū collect books
→ see also/另见 zàng

操 cāo [名] (体育活动) exercise
操场(場) cāochǎng [名] sports ground
操心 cāoxīn [动] concern
操作 cāozuò [动] operate

糙 cāo [形] poor

草 cǎo [名] **1**(植物) grass ▶ 草地 cǎodì lawn, meadow **2**(用作材料) straw
草稿 cǎogǎo [名] rough draft
草帽 cǎomào [名] straw hat
草莓 cǎoméi [名] strawberry
草率 cǎoshuài [形] rash
草原 cǎoyuán [名] grasslands (pl)

册(冊) cè I [名] book ▶ 手册 shǒucè handbook ▶ 相册 xiàngcè photo album II [量] **1**(指同一本书) copy **2**(指不同本书) volume

厕(廁) cè [名] toilet ▶ 公厕 gōngcè public toilet
厕(廁)所 cèsuǒ [名] toilet

侧(側) cè I [名] side ▶ 两侧 liǎngcè both sides II [动] turn ... away ▷ 我侧过脸去。Wǒ cè guò liǎn qù. I turned my face away.
侧(側)面 cèmiàn I [形] **1**(非官方) unofficial **2**(指方位) side II [名] side

测(測) cè [动] **1**(测量) measure **2**(推测) predict
测(測)量 cèliáng I [动] measure II [名] survey
测(測)试(試) cèshì I [动] test II [名] test

测(測)验(驗) cèyàn I [动] test II [名] test

策 cè [名] suggestion
策划(劃) cèhuà I [动] design II [名] planning
策略 cèlüè I [名] strategy II [形] strategic

层(層) céng I [量] **1**(指建筑物) floor **2**(指覆盖物) layer **3**(步) step **4**(指含义) layer II [名] (指物、状态) layer

曾 céng [副] once
曾经(經) céngjīng [副] once

蹭 cèng [动] **1**(摩擦) rub **2**(沾上) smear **3**(指速度) creep along

叉 chā [名] **1**(器具) fork **2**(餐具) fork **3**(符号) cross
叉子 chāzi [名] **1**(符号) cross **2**(餐具) fork

差 chā [名] difference
→ see also/另见 chà, chāi
差别(別) chābié [名] difference
差错(錯) chācuò [名] **1**(错误) mistake **2**(意外) accident
差距 chājù [名] difference
差异(異) chāyì [名] difference

插 chā [动] insert ▷ 我能不能插一句? Wǒ néng bùnéng chā yī jù? Can I interrupt just a second?
插曲 chāqǔ [名] **1**(音乐) incidental music **2**(事件) interlude
插入 chārù [动] insert
插图(圖) chātú [名] illustration
插销(銷) chāxiāo [名] **1**(门) bolt **2**(插头) electrical plug
插嘴 chāzuǐ [动] interrupt
插座 chāzuò [名] socket (英), outlet (美)

茶 chá [名] tea ▶ 红茶 hóngchá black tea ▶ 茶杯 chábēi teacup ▶ 茶壶 cháhú teapot ▶ 茶馆 cháguǎn teahouse ▷ 泡茶 pào chá make tea
茶具 chájù [名] tea set
茶叶(葉) cháyè [名] tea leaves (pl)

查 chá [动] 1(检查) inspect 2(调查) investigate 3(字典、词典) look ... up
　查号(號)台 cháhàotái [名] directory inquiries (英) 或 assistance (美) (sg)
　查阅(閱) cháyuè [动] look ... up
　查找 cházhǎo [动] look for

察 chá [动] check ▸ 观察 guānchá observe
　察觉(覺) chájué [动] detect

杈 chà [名] branch

差 chà I [动] 1(不相同) be different from ▷ 你和他比差得远了。Nǐ hé tā bǐ chàde yuǎn le. You are not nearly as good as him. 2(缺欠) be short of ▷ 差3个人 chà sān gè rén be three people short II [形] 1(错误) mistaken 2(不好) poor ▷ 质量差 zhìliàng chà poor quality
　→ see also/另见 chā, chāi
　差不多 chàbuduō I [形] very similar II [副] almost

拆 chāi [动] 1(打开) tear ... open 2(拆毁) dismantle

差 chāi [动] send ▸ 出差 chūchāi go on a business trip
　→ see also/另见 chā, chà
　差事 chāishi [名] 1(任务) assignment 2(差使) position

柴 chái [名] firewood
　柴油 cháiyóu [名] diesel

豺 chái [名] jackal

掺(摻) chān [动] mix

搀(攙) chān [动] 1(搀扶) support ... by the arm 2(混合) mix

馋(饞) chán [形] greedy

缠(纏) chán [动] 1(缠绕) twine 2(纠缠) pester

蝉(蟬) chán [名] cicada

产(產) chǎn [动] 1(生育) give birth to 2(出产) produce

产(產)量 chǎnliàng [名] yield
产(產)品 chǎnpǐn [名] product
产(產)权(權) chǎnquán [名] property rights (pl) ▷ 知识产权 zhīshi chǎnquán intellectual property
产(產)生 chǎnshēng [动] produce
产(產)业(業) chǎnyè [名] 1(财产) property 2(工业生产) industry

铲(鏟) chǎn I [名] shovel II [动] shovel

颤(顫) chàn [动] tremble
颤(顫)抖 chàndǒu [动] shiver

长(長) cháng I [形] long II [名] (长度) length
　→ see also/另见 zhǎng
　长(長)城 Chángchéng [名] the Great Wall

长城 Chángchéng

As one of the longest man-made mega structures in the world, the Great Wall of China is nearly 4,000 miles in length, reaching from the border of Xinjiang province in the west to the eastern coast just north of Beijing. It is probably the most famous of China's landmarks, and was made a UNESCO World Heritage site in 1987. There are records of fortifications being built along the route which date from the 3rd century BC, although most of what remains today was built during the Ming dynasty (1368-1644). Built as a defence mechanism, its primary function was to withstand invasions by the northern tribes.

长(長)处(處) chángchu [名] strong point
长(長)度 chángdù [名] length
长(長)江 Cháng Jiāng [名] the Yangtze River
长(長)久 chángjiǔ [形] long-term
长(長)跑 chángpǎo [动] go long-distance running
长(長)寿(壽) chángshòu [形] long-lived ▷ 祝您长寿！ Zhù nín chángshòu! Here's to a long life!

长(長)寿(壽)面(麵) chángshòumiàn [名] long-life noodles (pl)

长寿面 chángshòumiàn
- In the Chinese tradition, long-life noodles are eaten on one's birthday. They are very long, thin noodles symbolizing longevity.

长(長)途 chángtú [形] long-distance ▷ 长途电话 chángtú diànhuà long-distance phone call ▷ 长途旅行 chángtú lǚxíng long journey

肠(腸) cháng [名] intestines (pl)
肠(腸)子 chángzi [名] intestines (pl)

尝(嘗) cháng [动] taste ▶ 品尝 pǐncháng taste
尝(嘗)试(試) chángshì [动] try

常 cháng I [形] 1 (平常) common 2 (经常) frequent ▶ 常客 chángkè regular guest II [副] often
常常 chángcháng [副] often
常识(識) chángshí [名] 1 (非专业知识) general knowledge 2 (生活经验) common sense

偿(償) cháng [动] 1 (归还) repay 2 (满足) fulfil ▷ 如愿以偿 rúyuàn yǐ cháng fulfil one's dreams
偿(償)还(還) chánghuán [动] repay

厂(廠) chǎng [名] (工厂) factory

场(場) chǎng I [名] 1 (地方) ground ▶ 排球场 páiqiú chǎng volleyball court ▶ 市场 shìchǎng market 2 (舞台) stage ▶ 上场 shàngchǎng go on stage 3 (戏剧片段) scene 4 (物) field II [量] 1 (比赛、演出) ▷ 一场足球赛 yī chǎng zúqiú sài a football match ▷ 两场音乐会 liǎng chǎng yīnyuèhuì two concerts
  measure word, used for games and shows
2 (灾害、战争、事故) ▷ 一场火灾 yī chǎng huǒzāi a fire ▷ 一场战争 yī chǎng zhànzhēng a war ▷ 几场事故 jǐ chǎng shìgù several accidents
  measure word, used for afflictions, wars, accidents, etc.

场(場)地 chǎngdì [名] space ▷ 运动场地 yùndòng chǎngdì sports area
场(場)合 chǎnghé [名] occasion
场(場)所 chǎngsuǒ [名] place ▷ 公共场所 gōnggòng chǎngsuǒ public place

敞 chǎng I [形] spacious ▶ 宽敞 kuānchǎng spacious II [动] be open ▷ 大门敞着。Dàmén chǎngzhe. The main door is open.

畅(暢) chàng I [形] 1 (无阻碍) smooth ▶ 畅通 chàngtōng unimpeded 2 (舒适) untroubled ▷ 他心情不畅。Tā xīnqíng bùchàng. He's troubled by something. II [副] uninhibitedly ▶ 畅饮 chàngyǐn drink one's fill
畅(暢)快 chàngkuài [形] carefree
畅(暢)所欲言 chàng suǒ yù yán speak freely
畅(暢)通 chàngtōng [动] be open
畅(暢)销(銷) chàngxiāo [动] have a ready market
畅(暢)销(銷)书(書) chàngxiāo shū [名] best-seller

倡 chàng [动] initiate
倡议(議) chàngyì [动] propose

唱 chàng [动] (发出乐音) sing ▶ 独唱 dúchàng solo ▷ 合唱 héchàng chorus
唱歌 chànggē [动] sing
唱戏(戲) chàngxì [动] perform opera

抄 chāo [动] 1 (誊写) copy 2 (抄袭) plagiarize
抄袭(襲) chāoxí [动] (剽窃) plagiarize

钞(鈔) chāo [名] banknote
钞(鈔)票 chāopiào [名] banknote

超 chāo I [动] 1 (超过) exceed 2 (不受限制) transcend ▶ 超现实 chāoxiànshí surreal II [形] super ▷ 超低温 chāo dīwēn ultra-low temperature
超级(級) chāojí [形] super ▷ 超级大国 chāojí dàguó superpower ▷ 超级市场 chāojí shìchǎng supermarket
超人 chāorén [名] superman

超市 chāoshì [名] supermarket

超重 chāozhòng [动] 1 (超过载重量) overload 2 (超过标准重量) be overweight

巢 cháo [名] nest

朝 cháo I [名] (朝代) dynasty II [动] face III [介] towards ▷ 他朝着我走过来。Tā cháozhe wǒ zǒu guòlái. He was walking towards me.

朝鲜(鮮) Cháoxiǎn [名] North Korea

嘲 cháo [动] ridicule

嘲笑 cháoxiào [动] laugh at

潮 cháo I [名] 1 (潮汐) tide 2 (社会运动) movement ▶ 工潮 gōngcháo labour (英) 或 labor (美) movement ▶ 思潮 sīcháo Zeitgeist II [形] damp

潮流 cháoliú [名] 1 (水流) tide 2 (发展趋势) trend

潮湿(濕) cháoshī [形] damp

潮水 cháoshuǐ [名] tidal waters (pl)

吵 chǎo I [动] 1 (喧闹) make a racket 2 (争吵) squabble II [形] noisy

吵架 chǎojià [动] quarrel

吵闹(鬧) chǎonào [动] 1 (争吵) bicker 2 (打扰) disturb

吵嘴 chǎozuǐ [动] bicker

炒 chǎo [动] 1 (烹调) stir-fry 2 (地皮、外汇等) speculate ▶ 炒股 chǎogǔ speculate in stocks and shares 3 (方) (解雇) sack ▶ 炒鱿鱼 chǎo yóuyú be fired

车(車) chē [名] 1 (运输工具) vehicle ▶ 小汽车 xiǎoqìchē car ▶ 公共汽车 gōnggòng qìchē bus 2 (带轮的装置) wheel ▶ 风车 fēngchē windmill

车(車)本儿(兒) chē běnr [名] driving licence

车(車)费(費) chēfèi [名] fare

车(車)祸(禍) chēhuò [名] traffic accident

车(車)间(間) chējiān [名] workshop

车(車)库 chēkù [名] garage

车(車)辆(輛) chēliàng [名] vehicle

车(車)轮(輪) chēlún [名] wheel

车(車)胎 chētāi [名] tyre (英), tire (美)

车(車)厢(廂) chēxiāng [名] coach

车(車)站 chēzhàn [名] 1 (火车的) railway station 2 (汽车的) bus stop

扯 chě [动] (拉) pull

彻(徹) chè [动] penetrate ▶ 彻夜 chèyè all night

彻(徹)底 chèdǐ [形] thorough

撤 chè [动] 1 (除去) take ... away ▶ 撤职 chèzhí dismiss from one's job 2 (退) move away

撤退 chètuì [动] withdraw

撤销(銷) chèxiāo [动] 1 (职务) dismiss 2 (计划) cancel 3 (法令) rescind

尘(塵) chén [名] 1 (尘土) dirt ▶ 灰尘 huīchén dust 2 (尘世) the material world ▶ 红尘 hóngchén worldly affairs (pl)

尘(塵)土 chéntǔ [名] dust

沉 chén I [动] 1 (向下落) sink 2 (指情绪) become grave II [形] 1 (指程度深) deep ▷ 昨晚我睡得很沉。Zuówǎn wǒ shuì de hěn chén. Last night I slept very deeply. 2 (重) heavy 3 (不舒服) heavy ▷ 我两条腿发沉。Wǒ liǎng tiáo tuǐ fāchén. My legs feel heavy.

沉静(靜) chénjìng [形] 1 (肃静) quiet 2 (指性格) placid

沉闷(悶) chénmèn [形] 1 (天气、气氛) depressing 2 (心情) depressed 3 (指性格) introverted

沉没(沒) chénmò [动] sink

沉默 chénmò I [形] taciturn II [动] be silent

沉痛 chéntòng [形] 1 (心情) grieving 2 (教训) bitter

沉稳(穩) chénwěn [形] 1 (稳重) steady 2 (安稳) peaceful

沉重 chénzhòng [形] heavy

沉着(著) chénzhuó [形] calm

陈(陳) chén [动] 1 (陈列) set ... out 2 (陈述) state

陈(陳)旧(舊) chénjiù [形] out-of-date

陈(陳)列 chénliè [动] display

陈(陳)述 chénshù [动] state

晨 chén [名] morning ▶ 早晨 zǎochén early morning

衬(襯) chèn [名] lining ▶ 衬衫 chènshān shirt

衬(襯)托 chèntuō [动] set ... off

称(稱) chèn [动] match ▶ 相称 xiāngchèn match ▶ 对称 duìchèn be symmetrical
→ see also/另见 chēng

称(稱)心 chènxīn [动] be satisfactory

趁 chèn [介] ▷ 趁这个机会我讲几句话。Chèn zhège jīhuì wǒ jiǎng jǐ jù huà. I would like to take this opportunity to say a few words.

称(稱) chēng I [动] 1(叫) call 2(说) say 3(测量) weigh II [名] name ▶ 简称 jiǎnchēng short form
→ see also/另见 chèn

称(稱)呼 chēnghu I [动] call II [名] form of address

称(稱)赞(讚) chēngzàn [动] praise

撑(撐) chēng [动] 1(抵住) prop ... up 2(船) punt 3(坚持住) keep ... up 4(张开) open 5(容不下) fill to bursting ▷ 少吃点吧，别撑着！Shǎo chī diǎn ba, bié chēngzhe! Don't eat so much, you'll burst!

成 chéng I [动] 1(成功) accomplish ▷ 那件事成了。Nà jiàn shì chéng le. The job is done. 2(成为) become II [形] (可以) OK ▷ 成！就这么定了。Jiù zhème dìng le. OK — that's agreed.

成本 chéngběn [名] cost

成分 chéngfèn [名] 1(组成部分) composition 2(社会阶层) status

成功 chénggōng [动] succeed

成果 chéngguǒ [名] achievement

成绩(績) chéngjì [名] success

成就 chéngjiù I [名] achievement II [动] achieve

成立 chénglì [动] 1(建立) found 2(有根据) be tenable

成年 chéngnián [动] 1(指动植物) mature 2(指人) grow up

成年人 chéngniánrén [名] adult

成人 chéngrén I [名] adult II [动] grow up

成熟 chéngshú [形] 1(指果实) ripe 2(指思想) mature 3(指机会等) ripe

成为(為) chéngwéi [动] become

成问(問)题(題) chéng wèntí be a problem

成语(語) chéngyǔ [名] idiom

成员(員) chéngyuán [名] member

成长(長) chéngzhǎng [动] grow up

诚(誠) chéng [形] honest ▶ 忠诚 zhōngchéng loyal ▶ 诚心 chéngxīn sincere

诚(誠)恳(懇) chéngkěn [形] sincere

诚(誠)实(實) chéngshí [形] honest

承 chéng [动] 1(承受) bear 2(承担) undertake

承担(擔) chéngdān [动] 1(责任) bear 2(工作) undertake 3(费用) bear

承诺(諾) chéngnuò I [动] undertake II [名] commitment

承认(認) chéngrèn [动] 1(认可) acknowledge 2(政权) recognize

承受 chéngshòu [动] 1(禁受) bear 2(经受) experience

城 chéng [名] 1(城墙) city wall ▶ 城外 chéngwài outside the city 2(城市) city ▶ 进城 jìnchéng go to town 3(城镇) town

城堡 chéngbǎo [名] castle

城市 chéngshì [名] city

乘 chéng [动] 1(搭坐) travel by ▷ 乘火车 chéng huǒchē travel by train 2(利用) take advantage of 3(几倍于) multiply ▷ 8乘5等于40。Bā chéng wǔ děngyú sìshí. Eight times five is forty.

乘法 chéngfǎ [名] multiplication

乘方 chéngfāng [名] (数) power

乘客 chéngkè [名] passenger

乘务(務)员(員) chéngwùyuán [名] conductor

盛 chéng [动] 1(装) ladle ... out 2(容纳) contain
→ see also/另见 shèng

程 chéng [名] 1(规矩) rule ▶章程 zhāngchéng constitution 2(程序) procedure ▶议程 yìchéng agenda ▶课程 kèchéng curriculum 3(距离) distance ▶路程 lùchéng journey 4(道路) journey
程度 chéngdù [名] 1(水平) level 2(限度) extent
程式 chéngshì [名] form
程序 chéngxù [名] 1(次序) procedure 2(计算机) program

惩(懲) chéng [动] punish
惩(懲)罚(罰) chéngfá [动] punish

橙 chéng see below/见下文
橙子 chéngzi [名] orange

逞 chěng [动] (夸耀) flaunt
逞能 chěngnéng [动] show off

秤 chèng [名] scales

吃 chī [动] 1(咀嚼吞咽) eat ▶吃药 chīyào take medicine 2(就餐) eat in 3(依靠) live off ▶吃劳保 chī láobǎo live off welfare 4(消灭) wipe ... out 5(耗费) withstand ▶吃力 chīlì strenuous 6(吸收) absorb
吃醋 chīcù [动] be jealous
吃饭(飯) chīfàn [动] have a meal

> To ask **How do you do?**, Chinese people will often ask 你吃饭了吗? Nǐ chī fàn le ma? which literally means **Have you eaten?**

吃惊(驚) chījīng [动] surprise
吃苦 chīkǔ [动] put up with hardship
吃亏(虧) chīkuī [动] 1(受损失) lose out 2(条件不利) be at a disadvantage
吃香 chīxiāng [形] (口) popular

痴(癡) chī I [形] idiotic II [名] obsession
痴(癡)呆(獃) chīdāi [形] idiotic
痴(癡)迷 chīmí [形] infatuated

池 chí [名] (池塘) pond ▶泳池 yǒngchí swimming pool
池塘 chítáng [名] pond

迟(遲) chí [形] 1(慢) slow 2(晚) late
迟(遲)到 chídào [动] be late
迟(遲)钝(鈍) chídùn [形] (贬) slow
迟(遲)早 chízǎo [副] sooner or later

持 chí [动] 1(拿着) hold 2(支持) support ▶坚持 jiānchí maintain
持久 chíjiǔ [形] protracted
持续(續) chíxù [动] go on

匙 chí [名] spoon

尺 chǐ I [量] unit of length, equal to a third of a metre II [名] ruler ▶尺子 chǐzi ruler
尺寸 chǐcun [名] 1(长度) size 2(口) (分寸) sense of propriety
尺码(碼) chǐmǎ [名] (尺寸) size

齿(齒) chǐ [名] (器官) tooth ▶牙齿 yáchǐ tooth

耻(恥) chǐ [名] 1(羞愧) shame 2(耻辱) disgrace
耻(恥)辱 chǐrǔ [名] disgrace

赤 chì [形] (红色) red
赤道 chìdào [名] the equator
赤裸裸 chìluǒluǒ [形] 1(光身子) stark naked 2(喻) (毫无掩饰) undisguised

翅 chì [名] 1(翅膀) wing 2(鳍) fin
翅膀 chìbǎng [名] wing

冲(衝) chōng [动] 1(向前闯) rush forward 2(猛撞) clash ▶冲撞 chōngzhuàng collide 3(浇) pour boiling water on 4(冲洗) rinse 5(指胶片) develop
→ see also/另见 chòng
冲(衝)刺 chōngcì [动] (字) sprint
冲(衝)动(動) chōngdòng [动] be impulsive
冲(衝)浪 chōnglàng [名] surf
冲(衝)突 chōngtū I [动] 1(激烈争斗) conflict 2(相抵触) clash II [名] (矛盾) conflict
冲(沖)洗 chōngxǐ [动] 1(洗涤) wash 2(指胶片) develop

充 chōng [动] 1(满)fill ▶充电 chōngdiàn
charge a battery 2(担任)act as 3(假装)
pass ... off as
充当(當)chōngdāng [动] act as
充分 chōngfèn I [形] ample II [副] fully
充满(滿)chōngmǎn [动] 1(填满)fill
2(有)brim with
充其量 chōngqíliàng [副] at best
充实(實)chōngshí I [形] rich II [动]
enrich
充足 chōngzú [形] sufficient

虫(蟲)chóng [名] insect ▶虫子 chóngzi
insect

重 chóng I [动] 1(重复)repeat 2(重叠)
overlap II [副] again
→ see also/另见 zhòng
重叠 chóngdié [形] overlapping
重逢 chóngféng [动] reunite
重复(複)chóngfù [动] repeat
重新 chóngxīn [副] again

崇 chóng [形] high
崇拜 chóngbài [动] worship
崇高 chónggāo [形] lofty

宠(寵)chǒng [动] spoil
宠(寵)爱(愛)chǒng'ài [动] dote on
宠(寵)物 chǒngwù [名] pet

冲(衝)chòng I [形] 1(指气味刺鼻)
pungent 2(劲儿足)vigorous II [介]
1(对着)at 2(凭)because of III [动] (口)
(正对)face
→ see also/另见 chōng

抽 chōu [动] 1(取出)take ... out 2(取出部
分)take ▶抽时间 chōu shíjiān find time
3(吸)inhale ▶抽烟 chōuyān smoke ▶抽
血 chōuxiě take blood 4(抽缩)shrink
5(打)whip
抽搐 chōuchù [动] twitch
抽风(風)chōufēng [动] 1(指疾病)
have convulsions 2(喻)(不合常理)lose
the plot
抽奖(獎)chōujiǎng [动] draw prizes
抽筋 chōujīn [动] (口)(肌肉痉挛)
have cramp

抽空 chōukòng [动] find time
抽签(籤)chōuqiān [动] draw lots
抽水 chōushuǐ [动] 1(吸水)pump
water 2(缩水)shrink
抽屉(屜)chōuti [名] drawer
抽象 chōuxiàng [形] abstract

仇 chóu [名] 1(仇敌)enemy 2(仇恨)
hatred ▶报仇 bàochóu avenge
仇恨 chóuhèn [动] hate

绸(綢)chóu [名] silk ▶丝绸 sīchóu silk

酬 chóu [动] (报答)reward
酬金 chóujīn [名] remuneration
酬劳(勞)chóuláo I [动] repay II [名]
repayment
酬谢(謝)chóuxiè [动] repay

稠 chóu [形] 1(浓度大)thick 2(稠密)
dense
稠密 chóumì [形] dense

愁 chóu [动] be anxious ▶忧愁 yōuchóu
be worried

丑(醜)chǒu [形] 1(丑陋)ugly 2(令人厌
恶)disgraceful
丑(醜)陋 chǒulòu [形] ugly
丑(醜)闻(聞)chǒuwén [名] scandal

瞅 chǒu [动] (方)look at

臭 chòu [形] 1(指气味)smelly 2(惹人厌
恶)disgusting 3(拙劣)lousy

出 chū [动] 1(与入相对)go out ▶出国
chūguó go abroad ▶出游 chūyóu go
sightseeing 2(来到)appear ▶出庭
chūtíng appear in court 3(超出)exceed
▶出轨 chūguǐ derail 4(给)give out
5(产生)produce 6(发生)occur ▶出事
chūshì have an accident 7(发出)come
out ▶出血 chūxiě bleed ▶出汗 chūhàn
sweat 8(显露)appear ▶出名 chūmíng
become famous
出版 chūbǎn [动] publish
出差 chūchāi [动] go away on business
出发(發)chūfā [动] 1(离开)set out
2(表示着眼点)take ... as a starting
point

出口 chūkǒu I[动] (指贸易) export II[名] exit

出路 chūlù [名] 1(指道路) way out 2(前途) prospects (pl) 3(销路) market

出名 chūmíng [动] become famous

出勤 chūqín [动] (按时到) show up on time ▶ 出勤率 chūqínlǜ ratio of attendance

出去 chūqù [动] go out ▷ 出去吃饭 chūqù chīfàn go out and eat

出色 chūsè [形] outstanding

出身 chūshēn I[动] come from II[名] background

出生 chūshēng [动] be born

出售 chūshòu [动] sell

出席 chūxí [动] attend

出现(現) chūxiàn [动] appear

出院 chūyuàn [动] leave hospital

出租 chūzū [动] let ▷ 有房出租 yǒu fáng chūzū room to let

出租汽车(車) chūzū qìchē [名] taxi

初 chū I[名] original II[形] 1(第一) first ▶ 初恋 chūliàn first love 2(最低) primary 3(开始) early ▶ 初冬 chūdōng early winter

初步 chūbù [形] fundamental

初期 chūqī [名] initial stage

初中 chūzhōng [名] junior middle school ▷ 上初中 shàng chūzhōng go to junior middle school

除 chú I[动] 1(去掉) get rid of ▶ 开除 kāichú dismiss ▶ 去除 qùchú remove 2(指算术) divide ▶ 除法 chúfǎ division ▷ 16除以8等于2。Shíliù chú yǐ bā děngyú èr. Sixteen divided by eight is two. II[介] 1(表示绝对排除关系) except ▷ 除彼得外大家都来了。Chú Bǐdé wài dàjiā dōu lái le. Everyone came except Peter. 2(表示并非唯一) apart from

除非 chúfēi I[连] unless ▷ 除非他要我去，否则我不去。Chúfēi tā yào wǒ qù, fǒuzé wǒ bù qù. I won't go unless he wants me to. II[介] other than

除了 chúle [介] 1(表示不包括) except ▷ 除了你其他人都参加了会议。Chúle nǐ qítā rén dōu cānjiāle huìyì. Everyone else attended the meeting except you. 2(除此以外) apart from ▷ 他除了学习英语，还学习日语。Tā chúle xuéxí Yīngyǔ, hái xuéxí Rìyǔ. Apart from studying English, he also studies Japanese. 3(表示非此即彼) apart from ... the only ... ▷ 他除了工作就是睡觉。Tā chúle gōngzuò jiùshì shuìjiào. The only thing he does apart from work is sleep.

除夕 chúxī [名] New Year's Eve

厨(廚) chú [名] 1(厨房) kitchen ▶ 厨房 chúfáng kitchen 2(厨师) cook

厨(廚)师(師) chúshī [名] cook

橱(櫥) chú [名] cabinet

橱(櫥)窗 chúchuāng [名] 1(指商店的展示窗) shop (英) 或 store (美) window 2(用于展览图片等) display case

橱柜(櫃) chúguì [名] cupboard

处(處) chǔ [动] 1(交往) get on with 2(在) be in 3(办理) deal with 4(处罚) penalize
→ see also/另见 chù

处(處)罚(罰) chǔfá [动] punish

处(處)方 chǔfāng [名] prescription

处(處)分 chǔfèn I[动] punish II[名] punishment

处(處)理 chǔlǐ [动] 1(解决) deal with 2(减价) sell ... at a reduced price ▷ 处理品 chǔlǐpǐn goods sold at a discount 3(加工) treat

处(處)于(於) chǔyú [动] be in a position ▷ 处于困境 chǔyú kùnjìng be in a difficult position

储(儲) chǔ [动] store

储(儲)备(備) chǔbèi I[动] store ... up II[名] reserve

储(儲)藏 chǔcáng [动] 1(保藏) store 2(蕴藏) contain

储(儲)存 chǔcún [动] stockpile

储(儲)蓄 chǔxù I[动] save II[名] savings (pl)

处(處) chù [名] 1(地方) place ▶ 益处 yìchù profit 2(部门) department ▷ 人事处

rénshìchù human resources department
→ see also/另见 chǔ

畜 chù [名] livestock
→ see also/另见 xù
畜生 chùsheng [名] beast

触(觸) chù [动] **1**(接触) touch **2**(触动) move
触(觸)犯 chùfàn [动] violate
触(觸)及 chùjí [动] touch
触(觸)摸 chùmō [动] touch

踹 chuài [动] (踢) kick

川 chuān [名] (河流) river

穿 chuān [动] **1**(破)(纸) pierce **2**(谎言、事实) expose **3**(通过) pass through ▷ 穿过人群 chuān guò rénqún pass through the crowd ▷ 穿针 chuān zhēn thread a needle **4**(串) piece ... together ▷ 穿珍珠 chuān zhēnzhū string pearls together **5**(衣服、鞋帽、首饰等) wear **6**(表示透彻) penetrate
穿着(著) chuānzhuó [名] outfit

传(傳) chuán [动] **1**(交给) hand ... down **2**(传授) pass ... on **3**(传播) spread **4**(传导) conduct **5**(表达) express ▷ 传情 chuánqíng express one's feelings **6**(命令) summon **7**(传染) infect
→ see also/另见 zhuàn
传(傳)播 chuánbō [动] disseminate
传(傳)达(達) chuándá I [动] pass ... on II [名] receptionist ▷ 传达室 chuándáshì reception room
传(傳)单(單) chuándān [名] leaflet
传(傳)媒 chuánméi [名] (传播媒介) media (pl)
传(傳)票 chuánpiào [名] (传唤凭证) summons (sg)
传(傳)奇 chuánqí [形] legendary
传(傳)染 chuánrǎn [动] infect
传(傳)染病 chuánrǎnbìng [名] infectious disease
传(傳)说(說) chuánshuō [名] legend
传(傳)统(統) chuántǒng I [名] tradition II [形] **1**(世代相传) traditional **2**(保守) conservative

传(傳)真 chuánzhēn [动] (指通讯方式) fax ▷ 给我发个传真吧。Gěi wǒ fā gè chuánzhēn ba. Please send me a fax.
传(傳)真机(機) chuánzhēnjī [名] fax machine

船 chuán [名] boat, ship

串 chuàn I [动] **1**(连贯) string ... together **2**(勾结) conspire **3**(指信号) get mixed up **4**(走动) drop by II [量] bunch ▷ 两串钥匙 liǎng chuàn yàoshi two bunches of keys ▷ 一串珍珠 yī chuàn zhēnzhū a string of pearls

创(創) chuāng [名] wound ▶ 创可贴 chuāngkětiē plaster (英), Band-Aid ® (美)
→ see also/另见 chuàng
创(創)伤(傷) chuāngshāng [名] **1**(指肉体) wound **2**(指精神) trauma

疮(瘡) chuāng [名] (指疾病) ulcer ▶ 口疮 kǒuchuāng mouth ulcer ▶ 冻疮 dòngchuāng chilblain

窗 chuāng [名] window ▶ 窗子 chuāngzi window
窗户(戶) chuānghu [名] window
窗口 chuāngkǒu [名] **1**(字) window **2**(喻)(渠道) vehicle **3**(喻)(反映处) window

床 chuáng [名] bed ▶ 单人床 dānrénchuáng single bed ▶ 床单 chuángdān bed sheet ▶ 上床 shàngchuáng go to bed

闯(闖) chuǎng [动] **1**(冲) rush **2**(磨炼) steel oneself **3**(惹) stir ... up ▶ 闯祸 chuǎnghuò cause trouble

创(創) chuàng [动] create ▶ 独创 dúchuàng make an original creation
→ see also/另见 chuāng
创(創)建 chuàngjiàn [动] establish
创(創)立 chuànglì [动] establish
创(創)业(業) chuàngyè [动] carve out a career
创(創)意 chuàngyì [名] creativity
创(創)造 chuàngzào [动] create

创(創)作 chuàngzuò I[动] create II[名] work

吹 chuī [动] 1(出气) blow ▷ 吹蜡烛 chuī làzhú blow out a candle 2(演奏) play ▷ 吹口琴 chuī kǒuqín play the harmonica 3(夸口) boast 4(口)(破裂) fall through ▷ 我和女友吹了。Wǒ hé nǚyǒu chuī le. I've broken up with my girlfriend.
吹风(風) chuīfēng [动](吹干) blow-dry
吹牛 chuīniú [动] brag
吹捧 chuīpěng [动] flatter
吹嘘(噓) chuīxū [动] boast

炊 chuī [动] cook ▷ 炊具 chuījù cooking utensil

垂 chuí [动](一头向下) hang down
垂直 chuízhí [形] vertical

捶 chuí [动] pound

锤(錘) chuí I[名] hammer II[动] hammer

春 chūn [名](春季) spring
春节(節) Chūn Jié [名] Chinese New Year

春节 Chūn Jié
○ Chinese New Year, or Spring Festival, is the most important festival of the year and falls on the first day of the lunar calendar. Traditionally families gather together, children receive money in red envelopes, and in some parts of China everyone helps make and eat a festival feast. On greeting people over this festival it is traditional to wish them wealth and happiness, by saying 恭喜发财 gōngxǐ fācái.

春卷(捲) chūnjuǎn [名] spring roll
春天 chūntiān [名] spring

纯(純) chún [形] 1(纯净) pure 2(纯熟) skilful (英), skillful (美)
纯(純)粹 chúncuì I[形] pure II[副] purely
纯(純)洁(潔) chúnjié I[形] pure II[动] purify

纯(純)净(淨) chúnjìng [形] pure
纯净水 chúnjìngshuǐ [名] pure water

唇(脣) chún [名] lip

蠢 chǔn [形] 1(愚蠢) stupid 2(笨拙) clumsy

戳 chuō I[动](穿过) poke II[名] seal
戳子 chuōzi [名] seal

辍(輟) chuò [动] stop
辍(輟)学(學) chuòxué [动] give up one's studies

词(詞) cí [名] 1(语句) words (pl) ▷ 台词 táicí lines ▷ 闭幕词 bìmùcí closing speech 2(指语言单位) word
词(詞)典 cídiǎn [名] dictionary
词(詞)汇(匯) cíhuì [名] vocabulary
词(詞)语(語) cíyǔ [名] word
词(詞)组(組) cízǔ [名] phrase

瓷 cí [名] porcelain

辞(辭) cí [动] 1(辞职) resign 2(辞退) dismiss
辞(辭)职(職) cízhí [动] resign

慈 cí [形] kind
慈爱(愛) cí'ài [形] affectionate
慈善 císhàn [形] charitable
慈祥 cíxiáng [形] kind

磁 cí [名](物) magnetism
磁场(場) cíchǎng [名] magnetic field
磁盘(盤) cípán [名] disk

雌 cí [形] female ▷ 雌性 cíxìng female

此 cǐ [代](这) this ▷ 此时此刻 cǐshí cǐkè right now
此外 cǐwài [连] apart from this

次 cì I[名] ranking ▷ 档次 dàngcì grade ▷ 名次 míngcì position II[形] 1(第二) second ▷ 次日 cìrì next day 2(差) inferior ▷ 次品 cìpǐn inferior product III[量] time ▷ 初次 chūcì first time ▷ 屡次 lǚcì repeatedly
次序 cìxù [名] order
次要 cìyào [形] secondary

刺 cì [名] sting
　刺耳 cì'ěr [形] **1**(指声音) ear-piercing **2**(喻)(指言语) jarring
　刺激 cìjī [动] **1**(指生物现象) stimulate **2**(推动) stimulate **3**(打击) provoke
　刺猬(蝟) cìwei [名] hedgehog

匆 cōng [副] hastily
　匆忙 cōngmáng [形] hurried

葱(蔥) cōng [名] spring onion

聪(聰) cōng I [名] hearing II [形] **1**(指听力) acute **2**(聪明) clever
　聪(聰)明 cōngmíng [形] clever

从(從) cóng I [动] **1**(跟随) follow **2**(顺从) comply with ▸ 服从 fúcóng obey **3**(从事) participate in II [名] follower III [形] (从属) subordinate ▸ 从犯 cóngfàn accessory IV [介] **1**(起于) from ▷ 从明天起 cóng míngtiān qǐ from tomorrow onwards **2**(经过) ▷ 飞机从我们头顶飞过。Fēijī cóng wǒmen tóudǐng fēiguò. The plane passed over our heads.
　从(從)此 cóngcǐ [副] after that
　从(從)而 cóng'ér [连] thus
　从(從)来(來) cónglái [副] ▷ 她从来未说过。Tā cónglái wèi shuōguo. She never said it.
　从(從)来(來)不 cóngláibù [副] never
　从(從)没 cóngméi [副] never ▷ 他从没见过大海。Tā cóngméi jiànguo dàhǎi. He has never seen the ocean.
　█ When using 从没 cóngméi, 过 guò is placed after the verb.
　从(從)前 cóngqián [名] **1**(过去) past ▷ 希望你比从前快乐。Xīwàng nǐ bǐ cóngqián kuàilè. I hope you are happier than you were before. **2**(很久以前) once upon a time
　从(從)事 cóngshì [动] **1**(投身) undertake **2**(处理) deal with

凑(湊) còu [动] **1**(聚集) gather ... together **2**(碰) encounter **3**(接近) approach
　凑(湊)合 còuhe [动] **1**(聚集) gather ... together **2**(拼凑) improvise **3**(将就) get by
　凑(湊)巧 còuqiǎo [形] lucky

粗 cū [形] **1**(横剖面大) thick **2**(颗粒大) coarse **3**(指声音) gruff **4**(糙) crude
　粗暴 cūbào [形] rough
　粗糙 cūcāo [形] **1**(不光滑) rough **2**(不细致) crude
　粗话(話) cūhuà [名] obscene language
　粗鲁(魯) cūlǔ [形] crude
　粗心 cūxīn [形] careless
　粗野 cūyě [形] rough

促 cù I [形] urgent II [动] **1**(催) press **2**(靠近) be near
　促进(進) cùjìn [动] promote
　促使 cùshǐ [动] press for

醋 cù [名] (指调味品) vinegar

催 cuī [动] **1**(敦促) hurry ▸ 催促 cuīcù hurry **2**(加快) speed ... up ▸ 催眠 cuīmián hypnotize

脆 cuì [形] **1**(易碎) brittle **2**(指食物) crispy
　脆弱 cuìruò [形] fragile

村 cūn [名] village ▸ 村子 cūnzi village

存 cún [动] **1**(存在) exist **2**(储存) store **3**(储蓄) save ▸ 存款 cúnkuǎn savings (pl) **4**(寄存) check ... in ▷ 存行李 cún xínglǐ check in one's bags **5**(保留) retain **6**(心里怀着) harbour (英), harbor (美)
　存档(檔) cúndàng [动] file
　存放 cúnfàng [动] deposit
　存心 cúnxīn [副] deliberately
　存在 cúnzài [动] exist
　存折(摺) cúnzhé [名] passbook

寸 cùn [量] unit of length, approximately 3 cm

搓 cuō [动] rub

撮 cuō [动] (聚集) scoop ... up

痤 cuó see below/见下文
　痤疮(瘡) cuóchuāng [名] acne

挫 cuò [动] (挫折) defeat ▸ 挫折 cuòzhé setback

措 cuò [动] 1(安排) handle 2(筹划) make plans
措施 cuòshī [名] measure

错(錯) cuò I [形] (不正确) incorrect II [动] (避开) miss ▷ 错过机会 cuòguò jīhuì miss an opportunity III [名] fault ▷ 这是我的错。Zhè shì wǒ de cuò. This is my fault.
错(錯)过(過) cuòguò [动] miss ▷ 错过机会 cuòguò jīhuì miss an opportunity
错(錯)误(誤) cuòwù I [形] wrong II [名] mistake

搭 dā [动] 1(建造) put ... up ▷ 搭帐篷 dā zhàngpeng put up a tent 2(挂) hang ▷ 我把大衣搭在胳膊上。Wǒ bǎ dàyī dā zài gēbo shang. I hung my overcoat over my arm. 3(乘) take ▷ 他每个月搭飞机去上海。Tā měigè yuè dā fēijī qù Shànghǎi. He takes the plane to Shanghai every month. ▷ 搭便车 dā biànchē get a lift 4(连接) join ▷ 搭伙 dāhuǒ join forces ▷ 两家公司终于搭上了关系。Liǎng jiā gōngsī zhōngyú dāshàngle guānxì. The two companies finally joined forces. 5(抬) carry
搭档(檔) dādàng I [名] partner II [动] team up
搭配 dāpèi [动] 1(安排) combine 2(配合) pair up 3(指语言) collocate

答 dā [动] answer
→ see also/另见 dá
答理 dāli [动] 1(理睬) bother 2(打招呼) acknowledge
答应(應) dāying [动] 1(回答) answer 2(同意) agree 3(承诺) promise

打 dá [量] dozen
→ see also/另见 dǎ

达(達) dá [动] 1(数量、目标) reach 2(指时间) last 3(通) ▷ 直达 zhídá non-stop journey 4(表示) express ▷ 转达 zhuǎndá convey

达(達)到 dádào [动] 1(要求、水平、目的) achieve ▷ 达到目的 dádào mùdì achieve an aim ▷ 达到要求 dádào yāoqiú satisfy requirements 2(指过程) reach

答 dá [动] 1(回答) answer 2(还报) repay ▷ 报答 bàodá repay
→ see also/另见 dā

答案 dá'àn [名] answer
答复(復) dáfù [动] respond
答卷 dájuàn I [名] answer sheet II [动] answer exam questions

打 dǎ I [动] 1(指暴力) hit ▷ 殴打 ōudǎ beat up ▷ 打人 dǎ rén beat sb up 2(敲) beat ▷ 打鼓 dǎ gǔ beat a drum 3(破) break ▷ 我把暖瓶给打了。Wǒ bǎ nuǎnpíng gěi dǎ le. I broke the Thermos®. 4(发出) send ▷ 打电话 dǎ diànhuà make a phone call ▷ 打手电 dǎ shǒudiàn shine a torch 5(做游戏) play ▷ 打篮球 dǎ lánqiú play basketball 6(表示动作) ▷ 打喷嚏 dǎ pēntì sneeze ▷ 打滚 dǎgǔn roll about ▷ 打针 dǎzhēn have an injection 7(建造) build ▷ 打基础 dǎ jīchǔ build the foundation 8(涂抹) polish ▷ 打蜡 dǎlà wax 9(交涉) deal with ▷ 打交道 dǎ jiāodào socialize ▷ 打官司 dǎ guānsi file a lawsuit 10(制造) make ▷ 打家具 dǎ jiājù make furniture 11(搅拌) beat ▷ 打两个鸡蛋 dǎ liǎng gè jīdàn beat two eggs 12(编织) knit ▷ 打毛衣 dǎ máoyī knit a sweater 13(捕捉) catch ▷ 打猎 dǎliè go hunting 14(画) draw ▷ 打草稿 dǎ cǎogǎo draw up a draft 15(举) hold ▷ 打伞 dǎsǎn hold an umbrella 16(揭) open ▷ 打开 dǎkāi open 17(穿凿) dig ▷ 打耳洞 dǎ ěrdòng pierce one's ears 18(收集) gather ▷ 打柴 dǎchái gather firewood 19(从事) do ▷ 打杂儿 dǎzár do odd jobs 20(用) make ▷ 打比喻 dǎ bǐyù make a comparison 21(捆) pack ▷ 打行李 dǎ xíngli pack one's bags 22(拨动) flick ▷ 打字 dǎzì type ▷ 打字机 dǎzìjī typewriter II [介] from ▷ 打今儿起 dǎ jīnr qǐ from today
→ see also/另见 dá

打败(敗) dǎbài [动] defeat
打扮 dǎban [动] make oneself up
打倒 dǎdǎo [动] 1(击倒在地) knock down 2(指口号) down with 3(推翻) overthrow

打的 dǎ dí [动] take a taxi
打动(動) dǎdòng [动] move
打赌(賭) dǎdǔ [动] bet
打发(發) dǎfa [动] 1(时间) while away 2(哄走) get rid of 3(派) send
打工 dǎgōng [动] temp
打火机(機) dǎhuǒjī [名] lighter
打击(擊) dǎjī I [动] crack down on II [名] (指精神上) blow
打架 dǎjià [动] have a fight
打开(開) dǎkāi [动] 1(开启) open 2(扩展) expand 3(开) turn ... on
打雷 dǎléi [动] thunder
打气(氣) dǎqì [动] (球、轮胎) inflate
打扫(掃) dǎsǎo [动] clean
打算 dǎsuàn I [动] plan II [名] plan
打听(聽) dǎting [动] ask about
打印机(機) dǎyìnjī [名] printer
打仗 dǎzhàng [动] fight a war
打招呼 dǎ zhāohu [动] (问好) greet
打折 dǎzhé [动] discount

大 dà [形] 1(数量、体积、面积) big ▷ 大街 dàjiē street ▷ 一大批 yī dà pī a large amount of 2(指力气) great ▷ 他劲儿真大！Tā jìnr zhēn dà! He's so strong! 3(重要) important 4(强) strong ▷ 大风 dàfēng strong wind 5(指声音) loud ▷ 大声 dàshēng loudly 6(雨、雪) heavy 7(指年龄) old ▷ 你多大了？Nǐ duō dà le? How old are you? ▷ 他比我大。Tā bǐ wǒ dà. He's older than me. 8(指程度) ▷ 大笑 dàxiào roar with laughter 9(老大) eldest ▷ 大姐 dàjiě eldest sister
→ see also/另见 dài

大胆(膽) dàdǎn [形] bold
大地 dàdì [名] the land
大方 dàfang [形] 1(慷慨) generous 2(不拘束) natural 3(不俗气) tasteful
大概 dàgài I [名] general idea II [形] approximate III [副] probably
大伙(夥)儿(兒) dàhuǒr [代] everybody
大家 dàjiā [代] everybody
大款 dàkuǎn [名] (贬) moneybags (sg)

大量 dàliàng [形] (数量多) large amount of ▷ 大量资金 dàliàng zījīn a large investment ▷ 大量裁员 dàliàng cáiyuán lay off a large number of people

大陆(陸) dàlù [名] 1 (指各大洲) continent 2 (指中国) the mainland ▷ 中国大陆 Zhōngguó dàlù mainland China

大米 dàmǐ [名] rice

大人 dàrén [名] adult

大使 dàshǐ [名] ambassador

大使馆(館) dàshǐguǎn [名] embassy

大事 dàshì [名] important event

大提琴 dàtíqín [名] cello

大小 dàxiǎo [名] (尺寸) size

大熊猫 dàxióngmāo [名] panda

大写(寫) dàxiě [名] (指字母) capital letter

大型 dàxíng [形] large-scale

大选(選) dàxuǎn [名] general election

大学(學) dàxué [名] university (英), college (美)

大学(學)生 dàxuéshēng [名] university (英) 或 college (美) student

大雪 dàxuě [名] heavy snow

大衣 dàyī [名] overcoat

大雨 dàyǔ [名] downpour

大约(約) dàyuē [副] 1 (指数量) approximately 2 (可能) probably

大众(眾) dàzhòng [名] the people (pl)

大自然 dàzìrán [名] nature

呆(獃) dāi I [形] 1 (傻) slow-witted 2 (发愣) blank ▷ 发呆 fādāi stare blankly II [动] stay ▷ 我在北京呆了一个星期。 Wǒ zài Běijīng dāile yī gè xīngqī. I stayed in Beijing for a week.

待 dāi [动] stay ▷ 你再多待一会儿。 Nǐ zài duō dāi yīhuǐr. Do stay a little longer.
→ see also/另见 dài

逮 dǎi [动] catch
→ see also/另见 dài

大 dài see below/见下文

大夫 dàifu [名] doctor
→ see also/另见 dà

代 dài I [动] 1 (替) do ... on behalf of 2 (指问候) send regards to ▷ 你见到他时，代我问好。 Nǐ jiàndào tā shí, dài wǒ wènhǎo. When you see him, say hello from me. 3 (代理) act as ▷ 代校长 dài xiàozhǎng acting headmaster II [名] 1 (时代) times (pl) ▷ 古代 gǔdài ancient times 2 (辈分) generation 3 (朝代) dynasty ▷ 清代 Qīng dài Qing Dynasty

代表 dàibiǎo I [名] representative II [动] 1 (代替) stand in for 2 (委托) represent 3 (指意义、概念) be representative of III [形] archetypal

代价(價) dàijià [名] cost

代理 dàilǐ [动] 1 (暂时替代) act on behalf of 2 (委托) represent

代理人 dàilǐrén [名] agent

代码(碼) dàimǎ [名] code

代数(數) dàishù [名] algebra

代替 dàitì [动] substitute for

带(帶) dài I [名] 1 (长条物) strap ▷ 皮带 pídài leather belt ▷ 磁带 cídài cassette ▷ 录像带 lùxiàngdài videotape 2 (轮胎) tyre (英), tire (美) ▷ 车带 chēdài car tyre (英) 或 tire (美) 3 (区域) zone ▷ 热带 rèdài the tropics II [动] 1 (携带) take ▷ 别忘了带钱包！ Bié wàngle dài qiánbāo! Don't forget to take your wallet! 2 (捎带) ▷ 你出去时带点牛奶回来，好吗？ Nǐ chūqù shí dài diǎn niúnǎi huílái, hǎo ma? Can you buy some milk when you're out? 3 (呈现) wear ▷ 面带笑容 miàn dài xiàoróng wear a smile on one's face 4 (含有) have 5 (连带) come with 6 (指导) direct 7 (领) lead 8 (养) bring ... up

带(帶)动(動) dàidòng [动] (指进步) drive

带(帶)领(領) dàilǐng [动] 1 (领着) guide 2 (指挥) lead

带(帶)头(頭) dàitóu [动] take the initiative

待 dài [动] 1 (对待) treat 2 (招待) entertain 3 (等待) wait for
→ see also/另见 dāi

待业(業) dàiyè [动] be unemployed

待遇 dàiyù [名] pay

贷(貸) dài I [动] 1 (指银行) lend 2 (指借钱方) take out a loan II [名] loan

贷(貸)款 dàikuǎn I [动] lend II [名] loan

袋 dài I [名] bag II [量] bag

袋鼠 dàishǔ [名] kangaroo

逮 dài [动] capture
→ see also/另见 dǎi

逮捕 dàibǔ [动] arrest

戴 dài [动] (眼镜、帽子、小装饰品等) wear

单(單) dān I [形] 1 (一个) single ▶ 单身 dānshēn single 2 (奇数) odd 3 (单独) solitary 4 (不复杂) simple 5 (薄弱) weak 6 (衣、裤) thin II [副] only ▷ 成功不能单凭运气。Chénggōng bùnéng dān píng yùnqi. To be successful you can't rely only on luck. III [名] 1 (单子) sheet ▶ 床单 chuángdān bed sheet 2 (列表) list ▶ 菜单 càidān menu

单(單)程 dānchéng [名] single trip

单(單)纯(純) dānchún I [形] simple II [副] merely

单(單)词(詞) dāncí [名] word

单(單)单(單) dāndān [副] only

单(單)调(調) dāndiào [形] monotonous

单(單)独(獨) dāndú [形] 1 (独自) alone 2 (独立) unaided

单(單)位 dānwèi [名] 1 (指标准量) unit 2 (机构) unit

单(單)元 dānyuán [名] unit ▷ 单元房 dānyuánfáng self-contained flat (英) 或 apartment (美)

单(單)子 dānzi [名] 1 (指床上用品) sheet 2 (列表) list

担(擔) dān [动] 1 (挑) carry ... on one's shoulder 2 (负) take ... on
→ see also/另见 dàn

担(擔)保 dānbǎo [动] guarantee

担(擔)当(當) dāndāng [动] take ... on

担(擔)架 dānjià [名] stretcher

担(擔)任 dānrèn [动] hold the post of

担(擔)心 dānxīn [动] worry

耽 dān see below/见下文

耽误(誤) dānwu [动] delay

胆(膽) dǎn [名] (胆量) courage

胆(膽)固醇 dǎngùchún [名] cholesterol

胆(膽)量 dǎnliàng [名] guts (pl)

胆(膽)子 dǎnzi [名] guts (pl)

掸(撣) dǎn [动] brush

掸(撣)子 dǎnzi [名] duster

但 dàn I [连] but II [副] only ▶ 但愿 dànyuàn wish

但是 dànshì [连] but ▷ 虽然下雨, 但是不冷。Suīrán xiàyǔ, dànshì bù lěng. Even though it's raining, it's not cold.

担(擔) dàn [名] load
→ see also/另见 dān

担(擔)子 dànzi [名] (责任) responsibility

诞(誕) dàn [动] be born

诞(誕)生 dànshēng [动] be born

淡 dàn [形] 1 (味道淡) weak 2 (不咸) bland 3 (颜色浅) light 4 (稀薄) light 5 (不热情) indifferent 6 (不红火) slack

淡季 dànjì [名] low season

蛋 dàn [名] (卵) egg ▶ 鸡蛋 jīdàn egg

蛋白质(質) dànbáizhì [名] protein

蛋糕 dàngāo [名] cake

弹(彈) dàn [名] (子弹) bullet ▶ 子弹 zǐdàn bullet ▶ 原子弹 yuánzǐdàn atomic bomb
→ see also/另见 tán

当(當) dāng I [介] 1 (向) in front of ▶ 当众 dāngzhòng in public ▷ 当着全班 dāngzhe quánbān in front of the whole class 2 (正在) ▷ 当我们到时, 电影已开始了。Dāng wǒmen dào shí, diànyǐng yǐ kāishǐ le. When we arrived the film had already started. ▷ 当他在美国时, 他爷爷去世了。Dāng tā zài Měiguó shí, tā yéye qùshì le. His grandfather passed away while he was in America. II [动] 1 (担任) act as ▷ 当经理 dāng jīnglǐ act as manager **2**(掌管) be in charge ▶ 当家 dāngjiā rule the roost → see also/另见 dàng

当(當)场(場) dāngchǎng [副] there and then

当(當)初 dāngchū [名] those days

当(當)代 dāngdài [名] the present ▶ 当代文学 dāngdài wénxué contemporary literature

当(當)地 dāngdì [名] locality ▶ 当地风俗 dāngdì fēngsú local customs

当(當)今 dāngjīn [名] the present

当(當)面 dāngmiàn [动] do ... face to face

当(當)年 dāngnián [名] those days

当(當)前 dāngqián I[动] be faced with II[名] present ▶ 当前的目标 dāngqián de mùbiāo the present aim

当(當)然 dāngrán I[副] of course II[形] natural

当(當)时(時) dāngshí [名] ▶ 我当时高兴极了。 Wǒ dāngshí gāoxìng jí le. I was ecstatic at the time.

当(當)心 dāngxīn [动] be careful

挡(擋) dǎng [动](拦) keep off ▶ 别挡路! Bié dǎnglù! Keep off the road!

党(黨) dǎng [名](政党) party ▶ 党员 dǎngyuán party member

当(當) dàng I[形] appropriate ▶ 不当 bùdàng inappropriate II[动] **1**(作为) treat ... as **2**(认为) assume ▶ 我当你明白了。 Wǒ dàng nǐ míngbai le. I assumed you'd understood. **3**(抵押) pawn **4**(指时间) ▶ 当天 dàngtiān that day → see also/另见 dāng

当(當)年 dàngnián [名] that same year

当(當)铺(舖) dàngpù [名] pawnshop

当(當)做 dàngzuò [动] regard ... as

档(檔) dàng [名] **1**(档案) file **2**(等级) grade

档(檔)案 dàng'àn [名] files (pl)

档(檔)次 dàngcì [名] grade

刀 dāo [名](指工具) knife ▶ 刀子 dāozi knife

叨 dāo see below/见下文

叨唠(嘮) dāolao [动] prattle on

导(導) dǎo [动] **1**(引导) guide **2**(传导) conduct **3**(开导) give guidance **4**(导演) direct

导(導)弹(彈) dǎodàn [名] missile

导(導)火线(線) dǎohuǒxiàn [名] **1**(字) fuse **2**(喻) trigger

导(導)师(師) dǎoshī [名] **1**(字) tutor **2**(喻) mentor

导(導)演 dǎoyǎn I[动] direct II[名] director

导(導)游(遊) dǎoyóu I[动] guide II[名] tour guide

导(導)致 dǎozhì [动] lead to ▶ 粗心导致她没考好。 Cūxīn dǎozhì tā méi kǎohǎo. Because of her carelessness she failed the exam.

岛(島) dǎo [名] island ▶ 岛国 dǎoguó island nation ▶ 半岛 bàndǎo peninsula

倒 dǎo [动] **1**(横躺) fall ▶ 摔倒 shuāidǎo fall down ▶ 卧倒 wòdǎo lie down **2**(失败) fail ▶ 倒闭 dǎobì go bankrupt **3**(食欲) spoil ▶ 倒胃口 dǎo wèikou lose one's appetite **4**(换) change ▶ 倒班 dǎobān change shifts → see also/另见 dào

倒霉 dǎoméi [形] unlucky

倒塌 dǎotā [动] collapse

捣(搗) dǎo [动] **1**(捶打) crush **2**(搅乱) make trouble

捣(搗)乱(亂) dǎoluàn [动] **1**(扰乱) disturb **2**(制造麻烦) make trouble

到 dào [动] **1**(达到) arrive ▶ 火车到了。 Huǒchē dào le. The train has arrived. ▶ 到点了! Dào diǎn le! Time is up! **2**(去) go ▶ 我到厦门旅游。 Wǒ dào Xiàmén lǚyóu. I'm going to Xiamen on a tour. **3**(用作动词的补语) ▶ 听到这个消息我很吃惊。 Tīngdào zhège xiāoxi wǒ hěn chījīng. When I heard the news I was very surprised. ▶ 你的要求我办不到。 Nǐ de yāoqiú wǒ bàn bù dào. I can't handle your demands.

到处(處) dàochù [名] all places (pl)

到达(達) dàodá [动] arrive

到底 dàodǐ I [动] ▷坚持到底 jiānchí dàodǐ keep going until the end II [副] 1(究竟) ▷你到底在干什么？ Nǐ dàodǐ zài gàn shénme? What on earth are you up to? 2(毕竟) after all 3(终于) at last

倒 dào I [动] 1(颠倒) ▷他把地图挂倒了。Tā bǎ dìtú guà dào le. He hung the map up upside down. ▷姓和名写倒了。Xìng hé míng xiě dào le. The first name and surname were written the wrong way round. 2(后退) reverse ▷倒车 dàochē reverse a car 3(倾倒) empty out ▷倒垃圾 dào lājī empty the rubbish out ▷倒杯茶 dào bēi chá pour a cup of tea II [副] 1(表示意料之外) unexpectedly 2(反而) instead 3(表示让步) ▷这房子地段倒好，就是太小。Zhè fángzi dìduàn dào hǎo, jiùshì tài xiǎo. Although the location of the house is good, it's still too small. 4(表示转折) but 5(表示不耐烦) ▷你倒是说呀！Nǐ dàoshì shuō ya! Can you get on with it please! 6(表示责怪) ▷他说得倒漂亮。Tā shuō de dào piàoliang. He's all talk.
→ see also/另见 dǎo

倒立 dàolì [动] 1(物) be upside down 2(人) do a handstand

倒计(計)时(時) dàojìshí [动] count down

倒退 dàotuì [动] go back

倒影 dàoyǐng [名] reflection

悼 dào [动] mourn

悼念(唸) dàoniàn [动] mourn

盗(盜) dào I [动] rob ▷盗窃 dàoqiè steal II [名] robber ▷海盗 hǎidào pirate

盗(盜)版 dàobǎn I [动] pirate ▷盗版软件 dàobǎn ruǎnjiàn pirated software II [名] pirate copy

盗(盜)贼(賊) dàozéi [名] thieves (pl)

道 dào I [名] 1(路) road ▷近道 jìndào shortcut 2(方法) way ▷生财之道 shēngcái zhī dào the road to riches 3(技艺) art ▷茶道 chádào tea ceremony 4(道教) the Tao 5(线) line ▷横道儿

héngdàor horizontal line 6(水流途径) channel ▶下水道 xiàshuǐdào sewer II [量] 1 ▷一道阳光 yī dào yángguāng a beam of sunlight ▷两道泪痕 liǎng dào lèihén two tear streaks
  measure word, used for things in the shape of a long strip
2 ▷第二道门 dì'èr dào mén the second door ▷一道墙 yī dào qiáng a wall
  measure word, used for doors, walls, etc.
3 ▷三道题 sān dào tí three questions ▷两道命令 liǎng dào mìnglìng two orders
  measure word, used for orders, questions, procedures, etc.
4(次) ▷我还要办一道手续 Wǒ háiyào bàn yī dào shǒuxù. I still need to complete one formality. ▷刷了两道漆 shuāle liǎng dào qī paint two coats
5 ▷五道菜 wǔ dào cài five dishes
  measure word, used for dishes or courses of a meal

道德 dàodé [名] morals (pl)

道教 Dàojiào [名] Taoism

道理 dàolǐ [名] 1(规律) principle 2(情理) sense

道路 dàolù [名] path

道歉 dàoqiàn [动] apologize

得 dé I [动] 1(得到) get ▶得奖 déjiǎng win a prize 2(病) catch ▷他得了流感。Tā déle liúgǎn. He caught flu. 3(计算) equal ▷四减二得二。Sì jiǎn èr dé èr. Four minus two equals two. 4(完成) ready ▷晚饭得了。Wǎnfàn dé le. Dinner is ready. 5(适合) be suitable ▶得体 détǐ appropriate II [叹] 1(表示同意、禁止) OK ▷得，就这么决定了。Dé, jiù zhème juédìng le. OK, that's settled then. 2(表示无可奈何) Oh no! ▷得，我又没考及格！Dé, wǒ yòu méi kǎo jígé! Oh no, I failed again! III [助动] ▷版权所有，不得转载。Bǎnquán suǒyǒu, bùdé zhuǎnzǎi. All rights reserved, copying not allowed.
→ see also/另见 de, děi

得到 dédào [动] get ▷得到帮助 dédào bāngzhù get help

得意 déyì [形] pleased with oneself

得罪 dézuì [动] offend

德 dé [名] **1**(品行) morality ▶品德 pǐndé moral character **2**(恩惠) kindness ▶恩德 ēndé kindness **3**(德国) Germany ▶德国 Déguó Germany ▶德语 Déyǔ German
德文 Déwén [名] German language

地 de [助] ▷刻苦地学习 kèkǔ de xuéxí study hard ▷努力地工作 nǔlì de gōngzuò work hard
→ see also/另见 dì

> Use 地 de after adjectives to form adverbs.

的 de [助] **1**(用于定语后) ▷昂贵的价格 ángguì de jiàgé high price ▷他的哥哥 tā de gēge his elder brother ▷经理的秘书 jīnglǐ de mìshū the manager's secretary **2**(名词化) ▷画画的 huàhuà de painter **3**(用于是…的强调结构) ▷我的嗓子是喊哑的。 Wǒ de sǎngzi shì hǎnyǎ de. My voice became hoarse from shouting.
→ see also/另见 dí, dì

> Use 的 de to link descriptive words, phrases and clauses to the noun they describe, e.g. 她是一个很漂亮的女人。 Tā shì yī gè hěn piàoliang de nǚrén. (She is a very beautiful woman.); 这是他昨天给我的书。 Zhè shì tā zuótiān gěi wǒ de shū. (This is the book which he gave me yesterday.)

的话 (話) dehuà [助] ▷见到她的话，替我问好。 Jiàndào tā dehuà, tì wǒ wènhǎo. Please give her my regards if you see her.

得 de [助] **1**(用于动词后面) ▷这种野菜吃得。 Zhè zhǒng yěcài chī de. This wild herb is edible. **2**(动词或补语中间) ▷她抬得动。 Tā tái de dòng. She can carry it. ▷我写得完。 Wǒ xiě de wán. I am able to finish writing it. **3**(动词和形容词后面) ▷他英语学得快。 Tā Yīngyǔ xué de hěn kuài. He's learning English very quickly. ▷风大得很。 Fēng dà de hěn. The wind's very strong.
→ see also/另见 dé, de

> Most adverbial phrases follow the verb and are joined to it by 得 de. Such statements are often evaluations or judgements, and contain the idea of

to the extent of or to the degree that, e.g. 她说得很流利。 Tā shuō de hěn liúlì. (She speaks very fluently.)

得 děi I [动] (口)(需要) need ▷买房得多少钱？ Mǎifáng děi duōshao qián? How much money do you need to buy a house? II [助动] (口) **1**(必要) must ▷我们得6点出发。 Wǒmen děi liùdiǎn chūfā. We have to leave at six. **2**(表示推测) will ▷快走，电影得开始了。 Kuài zǒu, diànyǐng děi kāishǐ le. Get a move on, the film's just about to start.
→ see also/另见 dé, de

灯 (燈) dēng [名] light ▷台灯 táidēng desk lamp ▷红绿灯 hónglùdēng traffic lights (pl)
灯 (燈) 塔 dēngtǎ [名] lighthouse

登 dēng [动] **1**(由低到高) go up **2**(刊登) publish **3**(踩踏板) pedal **4**(踩) get up onto
登记 (記) dēngjì [动] register
登录 (錄) dēnglù [动] log in ▷登录网站 dēnglù wǎngzhàn log in to a website

蹬 dēng [动] pedal

等 děng I [名] **1**(等级) grade ▶中等 zhōngděng medium ▷二等奖 èr děng jiǎng second prize **2**(类) kind II [动] **1**(相同) equal ▶等于 děngyú be equal to **2**(等待) wait ▶等车 děngchē wait for a bus III [连] (等то) ▷等他来了，我们再讨论。 Děng tā lái le, wǒmen zài tǎolùn. We'll talk about it when he comes. IV [助] **1**(列举未尽的) etc. **2**(煞尾的) namely
等待 děngdài [动] wait
等到 děngdào [连] when
等等 děngděng [助] and so on
等号 (號) děnghào [名] (数) equals sign
等候 děnghòu [动] expect
等级 (級) děngjí [名] grade
等于 (於) děngyú [动] **1**(相等于) equal **2**(等同) be equivalent to

凳 dèng [名] stool ▶板凳 bǎndèng wooden stool ▶凳子 dèngzi stool

瞪 dèng [动] 1(表示生气) glare at 2(睁大) open one's eyes wide

低 dī I [形] 1(指高度、程度) low ▷ 他喜欢低声说话。Tā xǐhuan dīshēng shuōhuà. He likes to speak quietly. 2(指等级) junior ▷ 我比她低两届。Wǒ bǐ tā dī liǎngjiè. I am two years below her. II [动] (头) bend

低潮 dīcháo [名] low ebb

低调(調) dīdiào [形] low-key

低级(級) dījí [形] 1(不高级) inferior 2(庸俗) vulgar

堤(隄) dī [名] dyke

提 dī [动] carry
→ see also/另见 tí

提防 dīfang [动] guard against

滴 dī I [动] drip II [名] drop ▷ 水滴 shuǐdī drop of water III [量] drop ▷ 几滴墨水 jǐ dī mòshuǐ a few drops of ink

的 dí see below/见下文
→ see also/另见 de, dì

的确(確) díquè [副] really

迪 dí [动] (书) enlighten

迪斯科 dísīkē [名] disco

敌(敵) dí I [名] enemy II [动] oppose III [形] equal

敌(敵)人 dírén [名] enemy

笛 dí [名] 1(音) flute 2(警笛) siren

笛子 dízi [名] bamboo flute

底 dǐ [名] 1(最下部分) bottom ▷ 鞋底 xiédǐ sole ▷ 底下 dǐxia under 2(末尾) end ▷ 年底 niándǐ the end of the year

底层(層) dǐcéng [名] 1(指建筑) ground floor 2(最下部) bottom

抵 dǐ [动] 1(支撑) support 2(抵抗) resist 3(补偿) compensate for 4(抵押) mortgage 5(抵消) offset 6(代替) be equal to

抵达(達) dǐdá [动] reach

抵抗 dǐkàng [动] resist

抵押 dǐyā [动] mortgage

地 dì [名] 1(地球) the Earth ▷ 地球 dìqiú the Earth 2(陆地) land 3(土地) fields (pl) 4(地点) location ▷ 目的地 mùdìdì destination
→ see also/另见 de

地步 dìbù [名] 1(处境) state, situation 2(程度) extent

地带(帶) dìdài [名] zone

地道 dìdào [名] tunnel

地道 dìdào [形] 1(真正) genuine 2(纯正) pure 3(指质量) well done

地点(點) dìdiǎn [名] location

地方 dìfāng [名] locality ▷ 地方政府 dìfāng zhèngfǔ local government

地方 dìfang [名] 1(区域) place ▷ 你是哪个地方的人？ Nǐ shì nǎge dìfang de rén? Where do you come from? 2(空间) room 3(身体部位) ▷ 我这个地方痛。Wǒ zhège dìfang tòng. I ache here. 4(部分) part ▷ 有不明白的地方吗？ Yǒu bù míngbai de dìfang ma? Are there any parts that are not clear?

地理 dìlǐ [名] geography

地面 dìmiàn [名] 1(地表) the Earth's surface 2(指房屋) floor

地球仪(儀) dìqiúyí [名] globe

地区(區) dìqū [名] area

地摊(攤) dìtān [名] stall

地毯 dìtǎn [名] carpet

地铁(鐵) dìtiě [名] 1(地下铁道) underground (英) 或 subway (美) 2(列车) underground (英) 或 subway (美) train ▷ 坐地铁 zuò dìtiě take the underground (英) 或 subway (美)

地图(圖) dìtú [名] map

地位 dìwèi [名] position ▷ 平等的地位 píngděng de dìwèi equal status ▷ 历史地位 lìshǐ dìwèi place in history

地下 dìxià [名] underground

地下室 dìxiàshì [名] basement

地震 dìzhèn [名] earthquake

地址 dìzhǐ [名] address ▷ 通信地址 tōngxìn dìzhǐ postal address

地址簿 dìzhǐbù [名] address book

地主 dìzhǔ [名] landlord

弟 dì [名] younger brother ▷ 表弟 biǎodì cousin ▷ 弟弟 dìdì younger brother

弟兄 dìxiong [名] brothers (pl)

弟子 dìzǐ [名] disciple

的 dì [名] target ▸ 目的 mùdì goal
→ see also/另见 de, dí

帝 dì [名] (君主) emperor

帝国(國) dìguó [名] empire

递(遞) dì [动] (传送) pass

第 dì [名] ▸ 第三产业 dìsān chǎnyè
tertiary industry ▸ 第三世界 dìsān
shìjiè the Third World ▸ 第一次世界大战
Dìyīcì Shìjiè Dàzhàn the First World War

第六感觉(覺) dìliù gǎnjué [名] sixth
sense

第一手 dìyīshǒu [形] first-hand

掂 diān [动] weigh in one's hand

颠 diān [动] 1 (颠簸) jolt 2 (跌落) fall

颠倒 diāndǎo [动] ▷ 这张照片上下颠倒
了。Zhè zhāng zhàopiàn shàng xià
diāndǎo le. The photo is upside down.

典 diǎn [名] 1 (标准) standard 2 (书籍)
standard work ▸ 词典 cídiǎn dictionary
3 (典故) allusion 4 (典礼) ceremony

典礼(禮) diǎnlǐ [名] ceremony ▷ 毕业
典礼 bìyè diǎnlǐ graduation ceremony

典型 diǎnxíng [形] (代表性)
representative

点(點) diǎn I [名] 1 (时间单位) o'clock
▷ 早上8点 zǎoshang bā diǎn eight
o'clock in the morning 2 (钟点) ▷ 到点
了。Dào diǎn le. It's time. 3 (小滴液体)
drop ▸ 雨点 yǔdiǎn raindrops (pl)
4 (痕迹) stain 5 (指字、画) dot 6 (指几
何) point 7 (小数点) decimal point ▸ 五
点六 wǔ diǎn liù five point six 8 (标志)
point ▸ 终点 zhōngdiǎn end point
9 (方面) point ▸ 优点 yōudiǎn strong
point ▸ 重点 zhòngdiǎn focal point
II [动] 1 (画点) make a dot 2 (头) nod ▸ 点
头 diǎntóu nod one's head 3 (药水等)
apply ▷ 点眼药 diǎn yǎnyào apply eye
drops 4 (查对) check ▸ 点名 diǎnmíng
call the register 5 (指定) select ▸ 点菜
diǎncài order food 6 (灯、火、烟等)
light ▸ 点烟 diǎnyān light a cigarette

7 (点缀) decorate III [量] 1 (少量) a little
▷ 有一点问题。Yǒu yìdiǎn wèntí.
There is a bit of a problem. ▷ 她会说一点
日语。Tā huì shuō yìdiǎn Rìyǔ. She can
speak a little Japanese. 2 (事项) item ▷ 议
事日程上有6点。Yìshì rìchéng shang
yǒu liù diǎn. There are six items on the
agenda. ▷ 我们有4点建议。Wǒmen
yǒu sì diǎn jiànyì. We have four
recommendations.

点(點)击(擊) diǎnjī [动] click

点(點)头(頭) diǎntóu [动] nod

点(點)心 diǎnxin [名] snack

点(點)子 diǎnzi [名] 1 (关键部分) key
point 2 (主意) idea

电(電) diàn I [名] 1 (能源) electricity
▸ 电能 diànnéng electric power ▸ 发电
站 fādiànzhàn electric power station
▷ 停电了。Tíng diàn le. There's been a
power cut. 2 (电报) telegram II [动]
1 (触电) get an electric shock 2 (发电报)
send a telegram ▸ 电贺 diànhè
congratulate by telegram

电(電)报(報) diànbào [名] telegram

电(電)池 diànchí [名] battery

电(電)动(動) diàndòng [形] electric

电(電)话(話) diànhuà [名] 1 (电话机)
telephone ▷ 办公室的电话占线。
Bàngōngshì de diànhuà zhànxiàn.
The office phone is engaged (英) 或
busy (美). ▷ 别挂电话! Bié guà
diànhuà! Don't hang up! 2 (打、接、
回) call ▷ 接电话 jiē diànhuà answer
the phone

电(電)话(話)号(號)码(碼) diànhuà
hàomǎ [名] phone number

电(電)脑(腦) diànnǎo [名] computer
▷ 手提电脑 shǒutí diànnǎo laptop

电(電)器 diànqì [名] electrical
appliance

电(電)视(視) diànshì [名] television,
TV ▷ 彩色电视 cǎisè diànshì colour
(英) 或 color (美) television ▷ 看电视
kàn diànshì watch television

电(電)台(臺) diàntái [名] station

电(電)影 diànyǐng [名] film (英),
movie (美)

电(電)影院 diànyǐngyuàn [名] cinema

电(電)子 diànzǐ [名] electron ▷ 电子表

diànzǐbiǎo digital watch ▷ 电子游戏 diànzǐ yóuxì electronic game ▷ 电子商务 diànzǐ shāngwù e-commerce ▷ 电子图书 diànzǐ túshū e-book ▷ 电子邮件 diànzǐ yóujiàn e-mail

店 diàn [名] 1(商店) shop (英), store (美) 2(旅店) hotel

垫(墊) diàn I [名] cushion ▷ 鞋垫 xiédiàn insole II [动] 1(铺) insert 2(付钱) pay

惦 diàn see below/见下文
惦记(記) diànjì [动] think about

殿 diàn [名] palace ▷ 宫殿 gōngdiàn palace

叼 diāo [动] have ... in one's mouth

凋 diāo [动] wither
凋谢(謝) diāoxiè [动] wither

雕(彫) diāo I [动] carve II [名] 1(指艺术) sculpture ▷ 石雕 shídiāo stone sculpture 2(鸟) vulture
雕(彫)刻 diāokè I [动] carve II [名] carving
雕(彫)塑 diāosù [名] sculpture

吊 diào [动] (悬挂) hang

钓(釣) diào [动] fish ▷ 钓鱼 diàoyú go fishing

调(調) diào I [动] transfer II [名] 1(口音) accent 2(曲调) melody ▷ 走调 zǒudiào be out of tune 3(音) key → see also/另见 tiáo
调(調)查 diàochá [动] investigate

掉 diào [动] 1(落下) fall 2(落后) fall behind 3(遗失) lose 4(减少) reduce 5(转回) turn ... round ▷ 把车头掉过来 bǎ chētóu diào guòlái turn the car round 6(互换) swap ▷ 掉换 diàohuàn swap

跌 diē [动] fall down

叠 dié [动] 1(一层加一层) pile ... up 2(信、纸、衣、被) fold

碟 dié see below/见下文
碟子 diézi [名] saucer

蝶 dié [名] butterfly ▷ 蝴蝶 húdié butterfly

叮 dīng [动] (蚊虫) bite
叮嘱(囑) dīngzhǔ [动] warn

盯 dīng [动] stare at

钉(釘) dīng [名] nail

顶(頂) dǐng I [名] top ▷ 头顶 tóudǐng top of one's head ▷ 山顶 shāndǐng mountain top II [动] 1(指用头) carry ... on one's head 2(拱起) lift ... up 3(支撑) prop ... up 4(撞) butt 5(迎着) face 6(顶撞) be rude to 7(承担) undertake 8(相当) ▷ 他干活一个人能顶两个。Tā gànhuó yī gè rén néng dǐng liǎng gè. He can do as much work as two people. 9(顶替) take the place of III [量] ▷ 一项帽子 yī dǐng màozi a hat ▷ 一顶蚊帐 yī dǐng wénzhàng a mosquito net ▮ measure word, used for things with a pointy tip, such as caps and hats IV [副] extremely ▷ 顶棒 dǐng bàng extremely good
顶(頂)点(點) dǐngdiǎn [名] (最高点) top
顶(頂)峰 dǐngfēng [名] summit
顶(頂)替 dǐngtì [动] 1(替代) take the place of 2(冒名) pose as
顶(頂)嘴 dǐngzuǐ [动] answer back

订(訂) dìng [动] 1(确立) draw ... up 2(预订) order ▷ 订报 dìngbào subscribe to a newspaper 3(校正) revise 4(装订) fasten ... together
订(訂)单(單) dìngdān [名] order form
订(訂)购(購) dìnggòu [动] order
订(訂)婚 dìnghūn [动] get engaged
订(訂)货(貨) dìnghuò [动] order goods
订(訂)金 dìngjīn [名] deposit

定 dìng I [形] 1(平静) calm 2(不变的) settled ▷ 定论 dìnglùn final conclusion 3(规定的) fixed ▷ 定义 dìngyì definition II [动] 1(决定) decide ▷ 定计划 dìng jìhuà decide on a plan **2**(固定) settle **3**(预定) order **III**[副] definitely

定居 dìngjū [动] settle

定期 dìngqī **I**[动] set a date **II**[形] fixed **III**[副] regularly

丢(丢) diū [动] **1**(遗失) lose **2**(扔掉) throw away **3**(投) toss

丢(丢)脸(臉) diūliǎn [动] lose face

丢(丢)人 diūrén [动] lose face

东(東) dōng [名] **1**(方向) east ▷ 东南亚 Dōngnányà Southeast Asia **2**(主人) owner ▶ 股东 gǔdōng shareholder **3**(东道主) host

东(東)北 dōngběi [名] north-east

东(東)边(邊) dōngbiān [名] east side

东(東)方 dōngfāng [名] the East

东(東)道国(國) dōngdàoguó [名] host nation

东(東)西 dōngxi [名] (物品) thing ▷ 今天他买了不少东西。Jīntiān tā mǎile bùshǎo dōngxi. He did quite a bit of shopping today.

冬 dōng [名] winter

冬眠 dōngmián [动] hibernate

冬天 dōngtiān [名] winter

董 dǒng [名] director

董事 dǒngshì [名] director

董事会(會) dǒngshìhuì [名] (指企业) board of directors

懂 dǒng [动] understand ▶ 懂得 dǒngdé understand

懂行 dǒngháng [动] (方) know the ropes

动(動) dòng [动] **1**(指改变位置) move ▷ 不许动! Bùxǔ dòng! Freeze! **2**(行动) act **3**(用作动补) ▷ 她太累了，走不动。 Tā tài lèi le, zǒu bù dòng. She's too tired – she can't go on. **4**(使用) use ▷ 我们得动脑筋。Wǒmen děi dòng nǎojīn. We must use our brains. **5**(触动) affect **6**(感动) move ▶ 动人 dòngrén moving

动(動)机(機) dòngjī [名] motive

动(動)静(靜) dòngjìng [名] **1**(声音) sound **2**(情况) movement

动(動)力 dònglì [名] **1**(指机械) power **2**(力量) strength

动(動)脉(脈) dòngmài [名] artery

动(動)身 dòngshēn [动] set out

动(動)手 dòngshǒu [动] **1**(开始做) get to work **2**(用手摸) touch ▷ 只许看，不许动手。Zhǐxǔ kàn, bùxǔ dòngshǒu. You can look, but don't touch. **3**(打人) strike a blow

动(動)物 dòngwù [名] animal

动(動)物园(園) dòngwùyuán [名] zoo

动(動)员(員) dòngyuán [动] mobilize

动(動)作 dòngzuò **I**[名] movement **II**[动] make a move

冻(凍) dòng [动] freeze ▶ 冻死 dòngsǐ freeze to death

洞 dòng [名] **1**(孔) hole **2**(穴) cave

洞穴 dòngxué [名] cave

都 dōu [副] **1**(全部) all ▷ 全体成员 quántǐ chéngyuán all the members **2**(表示理由) all ▷ 都是他才酿成了车祸。Dōu shì tā de cuò. It's all his fault. **3**(甚至) even ▷ 老师待他比亲生父母都好。Lǎoshī dài tā bǐ qīnshēng fùmǔ dōu hǎo. The teacher treated him even better than his parents. **4**(已经) already ▷ 都到冬天了！Dōu dào dōngtiān le! It's winter already!
→ see also/另见 dū

兜 dōu [名] **1**(衣袋) pocket ▶ 裤兜 kùdōu trouser pocket **2**(拎兜) bag ▶ 网兜 wǎngdōu string bag

兜风(風) dōufēng [动] (游逛) go for a spin

兜圈子 dōuquānzi [动] (喻) (拐弯抹角) beat about the bush

斗 dǒu [名] **1**(指容器) cup **2**(斗状物) ▶ 烟斗 yāndǒu pipe ▶ 漏斗 lòudǒu funnel
→ see also/另见 dòu

抖 dǒu [动] **1**(颤抖) shiver **2**(甩动) shake

陡 dǒu [形] steep

斗(鬥) dòu [动] 1(打斗) fight ▸ 斗鸡 dòujī cock fighting 2(战胜) beat
→ see also/另见 dǒu

斗(鬥)争(爭) dòuzhēng [动] 1(努力战胜) struggle 2(打击) combat 3(奋斗) fight for

豆 dòu [名] bean
豆子 dòuzi [名] (豆类作物) bean

逗 dòu [动] (引逗) tease
逗号(號) dòuhào [名] comma
逗留 dòuliú [动] stay

都 dū [名] (首都) capital
→ see also/另见 dōu
都市 dūshì [名] metropolis

毒 dú I [名] poison II [形] (有毒) poisonous
毒品 dúpǐn [名] drug

独(獨) dú I [形] only ▸ 独生子 dúshēngzǐ only son ▸ 独生女 dúshēngnǚ only daughter II [副] 1(独自) alone 2(唯独) only
独(獨)裁 dúcái [动] dictate
独(獨)立 dúlì [动] 1(指国家) declare independence ▸ 独立宣言 dúlì xuānyán declaration of independence 2(指个人) be independent
独(獨)身 dúshēn [动] be single
独(獨)特 dútè [形] distinctive
独(獨)自 dúzì [副] alone

读(讀) dú [动] 1(朗读) read aloud 2(阅读) read 3(上学) go to school
读(讀)书(書) dúshū [动] 1(阅读) read 2(学习) study 3(上学) go to school
读(讀)者 dúzhě [名] reader

堵 dǔ I [动] 1(堵塞) block ▸ 堵车 dǔchē traffic jam 2(发闷) suffocate II [量] ▸ 一堵墙 yī dǔ qiáng a wall
▐ measure word, used for walls
堵塞 dǔsè [动] block up

赌(賭) dǔ [动] 1(赌博) gamble 2(打赌) bet
赌(賭)博 dǔbó [动] gamble
赌(賭)注 dǔzhù [名] bet

肚 dù [名] belly
肚子 dùzi [名] (腹部) stomach

度 dù I [名] 1(限度) limit 2(气量) tolerance ▸ 大度 dàdù magnanimous 3(考虑) consideration 4(程度) degree ▸ 厚度 hòudù thickness II [量] 1(指经度或纬度) degree ▸ 北纬42度 běiwěi sìshí'èr dù latitude 42 degrees north 2(指电量) kilowatt-hour 3(指温度) degree ▸ 零下十度 língxià shí dù minus ten degrees 4(指弧度或角度) degree 5(次) time III [动] spend

渡 dù [动] 1(越过) cross 2(指用船只) ferry 3(喻)(通过) survive ▸ 渡难关 dù nánguān go through a difficult time

端 duān I [名] 1(头) end 2(开头) beginning ▸ 开端 kāiduān beginning II [动] carry
端午节(節) Duānwǔ Jié [名] Dragon Boat Festival

端午节 Duānwǔ Jié
- Dragon Boat Festival is celebrated on the fifth day of the fifth month of the Chinese lunar calendar. The two main activities which take place at this time are dragon boat racing and eating 粽子 zòngzi.

端正 duānzhèng [形] 1(不歪斜) upright 2(正派) proper

短 duǎn I [形] short ▸ 短期 duǎnqī short-term II [动] owe III [名] weakness
短处(處) duǎnchu [名] weakness
短裤(褲) duǎnkù [名] 1(指女式内裤) pants (pl) 2(指男式内裤) briefs (pl) 3(指夏装) shorts (pl)
短缺 duǎnquē [动] lack
短信 duǎnxìn [名] text message
短暂(暫) duǎnzàn [形] brief

段 duàn [量] 1(用于长条物) ▸ 一段铁轨 yī duàn tiěguǐ a section of railway ▸ 一段木头 yī duàn mùtou a chunk of wood
▐ measure word, used for a part of something that is thin and long
2(指时间) period ▸ 一段时间 yī duàn shíjiān a period of time 3(指路程) stretch 4(部分) piece

断(斷) duàn [动] 1(分成段) break
2(断绝) break ... off 3(判断) decide
断(斷)定 duàndìng [动] determine
断(斷)言 duànyán [动] assert

缎(緞) duàn [名] satin

锻(鍛) duàn [动] forge
锻(鍛)炼(鍊) duànliàn [动] 1(指身体)
work out 2(磨炼) toughen

堆 duī I [动] ▷ 别把垃圾堆在这里。
Bié bǎ lājī duī zài zhèlǐ. Don't pile the
rubbish up here. II [名] pile III [量] pile
▷ 一堆石头 yī duī shítou a pile of stones

队(隊) duì [名] 1(行列) line 2(指集体)
team ▶ 队长 duìzhǎng team leader ▶ 队
员 duìyuán team member
队(隊)伍 duìwu [名] 1(军队) troops (pl)
2(指集体) contingent

对(對) duì I [动] 1(回答) answer
2(对待) treat 3(朝着) face 4(接触) come
into contact with 5(投合) suit ▷ 对脾气
duì píqi suit one's temperament ▷ 今天
的菜很对他的胃口。Jīntiān de cài hěn
duì tā de wèikǒu. Today's meal was
definitely to his liking. 6(调整) adjust
7(核对) check ▷ 对表 duìbiǎo set one's
watch 8(加进) add II [形] 1(对面)
opposite 2(正确) correct III [介] 1(朝) at
2(对于) ▷ 吸烟对健康有害。Xīyān duì
jiànkāng yǒuhài. Smoking is harmful to
your health. IV [量] pair ▷ 一对夫妻 yī
duì fūqī a married couple
对(對)比 duìbǐ [动] contrast ▷ 鲜明的
对比 xiānmíng de duìbǐ marked
contrast
对(對)不起 duìbuqǐ [动] (愧疚) be
sorry ▷ 对不起，借过。Duìbuqǐ,
jièguò. Excuse me – may I just get
through?
对(對)称(稱) duìchèn [形]
symmetrical
对(對)待 duìdài [动] treat
对(對)方 duìfāng [名] other side
对(對)付 duìfu [动] 1(应对) deal with
2(将就) make do
对(對)话(話) duìhuà [名] dialogue

II [动] hold talks
对(對)决(決) duìjué [动] battle for
supremacy
对(對)立 duìlì [动] counter
对(對)面 duìmiàn [名] 1(对过) the
opposite 2(正前方) the front
对(對)手 duìshǒu [名] 1(指比赛)
opponent 2(指能力) match
对(對)象 duìxiàng [名] 1(目标) object
2(指男女朋友) partner
对(對)应(應) duìyìng [动] correspond
对(對)于(於) duìyú [介] ▷ 对于这篇文
章，大家理解不一。Duìyú zhè piān
wénzhāng, dàjiā lǐjiě bù yī. Not
everyone understands this article in
the same way.

兑(兌) duì [动] 1(互换) exchange
2(汇兑) cash
兑(兌)换(換) duìhuàn [动] convert

吨(噸) dūn [量] ton

蹲(蹲) dūn [动] (弯腿) squat

炖(燉) dùn [动] stew

钝(鈍) dùn [形] 1(不锋利) blunt
2(不灵活) dim

顿(頓) dùn I [动] (停顿) pause II [量]
▷ 一顿饭 yī dùn fàn a meal ▷ 挨了一顿
打 áile yī dùn dǎ take a beating
■ measure word, used for meals
顿(頓)时(時) dùnshí [副] immediately

多 duō I [形] 1(数量大) a lot of ▷ 很多书
hěn duō shū a lot of books 2(相差大)
more ▷ 我比你大多了。Wǒ bǐ nǐ dà
duō le. I'm much older than you are.
3(超出) too many ▷ 她喝多了。Tā hē
duō le. She drank too much. 4(过分)
excessive ▶ 多疑 duōyí over-suspicious
II [数] ▷ 两年多前 liǎng nián duō qián
over two years ago III [动] be more than
▷ 多个人就多份力量。Duō gè rén jiù
duō fèn lìliàng. The more people we
have, the stronger we will be. IV [副]
1(用在疑问句中) how ▷ 从北京到上海
有多远？ Cóng Běijīng dào Shànghǎi
yǒu duō yuǎn? How far is it from Beijing

to Shanghai? ▷ 你儿子多大了？ Nǐ érzi duō dà le? How old is your son? **2**(表示感叹) how ▷ 多美的城市！ Duō měi de chéngshì! How beautiful this town is! **3**(表示任何一种程度) however ▷ 给我一把尺，多长都行。 Gěi wǒ yī bǎ chǐ, duō cháng dōu xíng. Give me a ruler – any length will do.

多长(長) duōcháng [副] how long

多媒体(體) duōméitǐ [名] multimedia

多么(麼) duōme [副] **1**(用于询问程度) how ▷ 他到底有多么聪明？ Tā dàodǐ yǒu duōme cōngming? How clever is he really? **2**(用在感叹句) ▷ 多么蓝的天啊！ Duōme lán de tiān a! What a clear day! **3**(表示程度深) no matter how

多少 duōshǎo [副] **1**(或多或少) somewhat ▷ 这笔买卖多少能赚点钱。 Zhè bǐ mǎimài duōshǎo néng zhuàn diǎn qián. We're bound to earn some money from this deal. **2**(稍微) slightly

多少 duōshao I [代] (用于询问数量) ▷ 这台电视机多少钱? Zhè tái diànshìjī duōshao qián? How much is this television? ▷ 今天有多少人到会? Jīntiān yǒu duōshao rén dàohuì? How many people attended the meeting today? II [数] ▷ 你们有多少我们要多少。 Nǐmen yǒu duōshao wǒmen yào duōshao. We want everything you've got.

多数(數) duōshù [名] the majority

多余(餘) duōyú [形] **1**(超过需要量的) surplus **2**(不必要的) redundant

哆 duō see below/见下文

哆嗦 duōsuo [动] tremble

夺(奪) duó [动] **1**(抢) seize **2**(争取) compete for **3**(剥夺) deprive **4**(决定) resolve

夺(奪)取 duóqǔ [动] **1**(武力强取) capture **2**(努力争取) strive for

朵 duǒ [量] ▷ 朵朵白云 duǒduǒ báiyún white clouds ▷ 几朵玫瑰 jǐ duǒ méigui some roses

measure word, used for clouds and flowers

躲 duǒ [动] **1**(隐藏) hide **2**(避让) avoid

躲避 duǒbì [动] **1**(回避) run away from **2**(躲藏) hide

躲藏 duǒcáng [动] hide

剁 duò [动] chop

堕(墮) duò [动] fall

堕(墮)落 duòluò [动] go to the bad

堕(墮)胎 duòtāi [动] have an abortion

跺 duò [动] stamp

e

俄 é[名](俄罗斯)Éluósī Russia ▶ 俄国 Éguó Russia
俄语(語)Éyǔ[名]Russian language

鹅(鵝)é[名]goose

蛾 é[名]moth ▶ 蛾子 ézi moth

额(額)é[名]forehead ▶ 额头 étóu forehead

恶(噁)ě see below/见下文
→ see also/另见 è, wù
恶(噁)心 ěxin I[动]feel nauseous II[形]nauseating

恶(惡)è I[名]evil II[形]1(凶恶) ferocious 2(恶劣)evil
→ see also/另见 ě, wù
恶(惡)搞 è gǎo[名]meme
恶(惡)劣 èliè[形]bad
恶(惡)梦(夢)èmèng[名]nightmare

饿(餓)è I[形]hungry ▷ 我很饿。Wǒ hěn è. I'm very hungry. II[动]starve

鳄(鱷)è[名]crocodile, alligator ▶ 鳄鱼 èyú crocodile, alligator

儿(兒)ér[名]1(小孩子)child 2(儿子) son ▶ 儿子 érzi son
儿(兒)女 érnǚ[名]children (pl)
儿(兒)童 értóng[名]child

而 ér[连]1(并且)and ▷ 美丽而聪明 měilì ér cōngming beautiful and clever 2(但是)but ▷ 浓而不烈 nóng ér bù liè strong but not overpowering ▷ 她不是学生，而是老师。Tā bù shì xuéshēng, ér shì lǎoshī. She isn't a student, but a teacher.
而且 érqiě[连]and what's more ▷ 他会讲英语，而且讲得好。Tā huì jiǎng Yīngyǔ, érqiě jiǎng de hǎo. He can speak English, and what's more he speaks it very well.

耳 ěr[名](耳朵)ear ▶ 耳朵 ěrduo ear

二 èr[数]two ▶ 二月 èryuè February ▷ 第二次 dì èr cì the second time
二十 èrshí[数]twenty

贰(貳)èr[数]two
This is the character for two, which is mainly used in banks, on receipts, cheques etc.

f

tremble **2**(因寒冷等) shiver

发(發)挥(揮) fāhuī [动] **1**(充分利用) bring ... into play **2**(详尽论述) elaborate

发(發)火 fāhuǒ [动] **1**(着火) catch fire **2**(爆炸) detonate **3**(发脾气) lose one's temper

发(發)霉(黴) fāméi [动] go mouldy (英) 或 moldy (美)

发(發)明 fāmíng [动] invent

发(發)票 fāpiào [名] **1**(收据) receipt **2**(发货清单) invoice

发(發)烧(燒) fāshāo [动] have a temperature

发(發)生 fāshēng [动] happen

发(發)现(現) fāxiàn [动] discover

发(發)言 fāyán [动] make a speech

发(發)扬(揚) fāyáng [动] carry on

发(發)音 fāyīn [动] pronounce

发(發)展 fāzhǎn [动] **1**(变化) develop **2**(扩大) expand

发(發) fā [动] **1**(送出) send ▷ 发工资 fā gōngzī pay wages **2**(发射) emit ▶ 发光 fāguāng shine **3**(产生) produce ▶ 发电 fādiàn generate electricity ▶ 发芽 fāyá sprout **4**(表达) express ▶ 发言 fāyán speak **5**(扩大) develop ▶ 发扬 fāyáng carry on **6**(兴旺) prosper ▶ 发家 fājiā make a family fortune **7**(使膨胀) ▶ 发面 fāmiàn leaven dough **8**(散开) spread ▶ 发散 fāsàn diverge **9**(揭开) uncover ▶ 发掘 fājué unearth ▶ 揭发 jiēfā expose **10**(变得) become ▶ 发霉 fāméi go mouldy (英) 或 moldy (美) **11**(流露) ▶ 发愁 fāchóu worry ▶ 发脾气 fā píqì lose one's temper **12**(感到) feel **13**(启程) leave ▶ 出发 chūfā set out → see also/另见 fà

发(發)表 fābiǎo [动] **1**(宣布) announce **2**(刊登) publish

发(發)布 fābù [动] **1**(宣布) issue **2**(指网络) post

发(發)财(財) fācái [动] make a fortune

发(發)出 fāchū [动] **1**(发送) send out **2**(散发) give out

发(發)达(達) fādá I [形] developed II [动] promote

发(發)动(動) fādòng [动] **1**(启动) start **2**(发起) launch **3**(鼓动) mobilize

发(發)动(動)机(機) fādòngjī [名] engine

发(發)抖 fādǒu [动] **1**(因恐惧等)

罚(罰) fá [动] punish ▶ 罚款 fákuǎn fine

罚(罰)款 fákuǎn I [动] fine II [名] fine

法 fǎ [名] **1**(法律) law **2**(方法) method ▶ 用法 yòngfǎ use **3**(标准) model **4**(佛理) Buddhism **5**(法术) magic ▶ 戏法 xìfǎ conjuring tricks

法国(國) Fǎguó [名] France

法律 fǎlǜ [名] law

法庭 fǎtíng [名] court

法语(語) Fǎyǔ [名] French

法院 fǎyuàn [名] court

发(髮) fà [名] hair
→ see also/另见 fā

番 fān [量] ▷ 三番五次 sān fān wǔ cì time and time again ▷ 经过几番挫折他明白了许多道理。 Jīngguò jǐ fān cuòzhé tā míngbaile xǔduō dàolǐ. After a few false starts he picked up quite a lot.

■ measure word, used for actions

番茄 fānqié [名] tomato

翻 fān [动] **1**(换位置) turn over **2**(寻找) rummage **3**(推翻) reverse **4**(越过) get

across **5**(增加) multiply **6**(翻译)
translate **7**(翻脸) fall out
翻译(譯) fānyì I[动] translate II[名]
translator

凡 fán I[名] **1**(人世间) mortal world
2(大概) approximation II[形] ordinary
III[副](总共) in all

烦(煩) fán I[名] trouble II[动](谦)
trouble III[形](厌烦) fed up
烦(煩)恼(惱) fánnǎo [形] worried

繁 fán I[形] numerous II[动] propagate
繁华(華) fánhuá [形] bustling
繁忙 fánmáng [形] busy
繁荣 fánróng [形] flourishing
繁体(體)字 fántǐzì [名] complex
characters (pl)

繁体字 fántǐzì

Complex characters, also known as
traditional Chinese characters, had
been used as the Chinese script for
centuries in all parts of China until
1956 when the government of the
People's Republic of China carried out
a programme of simplifying these
characters in an effort to improve the
literacy rate by making characters
easier to write. Since then, 简体字
jiǎntǐzì 'simplified characters', have
become the dominant form of the
Chinese script. However, for various
cultural and political reasons, some
Chinese-speaking regions and
communities did not accept these
changes, and continue to use the old
system. Hong Kong and Taiwan are
among these regions.

繁殖 fánzhí [动] breed

反 fǎn I[名] **1**(相反) opposite **2**(造反)
rebellion II[动] **1**(转换) turn **2**(回)
return **3**(反对) oppose **4**(背叛) rebel
III[形] opposite IV[副] **1**(相反) on the
contrary **2**(从反面) again ▶ 反思 fǎnsī
review
反动(動) fǎndòng I[形] reactionary
II[名] reaction
反对(對) fǎnduì [动] oppose
反腐 fǎnfǔ [动] tackle corruption
反复(復) fǎnfù [副] **1**(重复) repeatedly
2(多变) capriciously
反抗 fǎnkàng [动] resist
反面 fǎnmiàn I[名] other side II[形]
negative
反应(應) fǎnyìng [名] **1**(反响)
response **2**(指机体) reaction **3**(指物
理、化学) reaction
反映 fǎnyìng [动] **1**(反照) reflect
2(汇报) report
反正 fǎnzhèng [副] anyway

返 fǎn [动] return
返回 fǎnhuí [动] come back

犯 fàn I[动] **1**(违犯) violate **2**(侵犯)
attack **3**(错误、罪行等) commit II[名]
criminal
犯法 fànfǎ [动] break the law
犯规(規) fànguī [动] break the rules
犯人 fànrén [名] prisoner
犯罪 fànzuì [动] commit a crime

饭(飯) fàn [名] **1**(餐) meal ▶ 晚饭
wǎnfàn supper **2**(米饭) rice
饭(飯)店 fàndiàn [名] **1**(住宿) hotel
2(吃饭) restaurant
饭(飯)馆(館) fànguǎn [名] restaurant
饭(飯)厅(廳) fàntīng [名] dining room

范(範) fàn [名] **1**(模范) model ▶ 典范
diǎnfàn model **2**(范围) limit ▶ 规范
guīfàn standard **3**(模子) pattern
范(範)围(圍) fànwéi [名] limit

方 fāng I[名] **1**(方向) direction ▶ 南方
nánfāng the South **2**(方形) square ▶ 长
方形 chángfāngxíng rectangle **3**(方面)
side **4**(方法) method **5**(地方) place
6(方子) prescription **7**(数)(乘方) power
II[形] **1**(方形) square **2**(正直) honest
方案 fāng'àn [名] plan
方便 fāngbiàn [形] **1**(便利) convenient
2(适宜) appropriate
方法 fāngfǎ [名] method
方面 fāngmiàn [名] **1**(指人) side
2(指物) aspect
方式 fāngshì [名] way

方向 fāngxiàng [名] direction
方言 fāngyán [名] dialect
方针(針) fāngzhēn [名] policy

防 fáng I [动] 1 (防备) prevent 2 (防守) defend II [名] dyke
防止 fángzhǐ [动] prevent

妨 fáng [动] obstruct
妨碍(礙) fáng'ài [动] obstruct

房 fáng [名] 1 (房子) house 2 (房间) room ▶ 书房 shūfáng study 3 4 (家族) ▷ 远房亲戚 yuǎnfáng qīnqi a distant relative
房东(東) fángdōng [名] landlord
房屋 fángwū [名] building
房租 fángzū [名] rent

仿 fǎng [动] 1 (仿效) copy 2 (类似) be like
仿佛(彿) fǎngfú I [连] as if II [形] similar

访(訪) fǎng [动] 1 (访问) call on ▶ 访谈 fǎngtán call in for a chat 2 (调查) investigate
访(訪)问(問) fǎngwèn [动] visit

纺(紡) fǎng I [动] spin II [名] silk
纺(紡)织(織) fǎngzhī [动] ▶ 纺织品 fǎngzhīpǐn textiles (pl)

放 fàng [动] 1 (使自由) release ▶ 解放 jiěfàng free 2 (暂时停止) ▷ 放学了。Fàngxué le. School is now over. 3 (放纵) let oneself go 4 (赶牲畜吃草) graze 5 (驱逐) expel ▶ 流放 liúfàng banish 6 (发出) send out ▶ 放炮 fàngpào fire a gun 7 (点燃) set ... off 8 (借出收息) lend 9 (扩展) ▷ 把照片放大 bǎ zhàopiàn fàngdà enlarge a photo 10 (花开) bloom 11 (搁置) put ... to one side 12 (弄倒) cut down 13 (使处于) put 14 (加进) add 15 (控制自己) ▷ 放严肃点 fàng yánsù diǎn become more serious 16 (放映) project 17 (保存) leave
放大 fàngdà [动] enlarge
放假 fàngjià [动] go on holiday (英) 或 vacation (美)
放弃(棄) fàngqì [动] give ... up
放松 fàngsōng [动] relax

放心 fàngxīn [动] set one's mind at rest
放学(學) fàngxué [动] finish school

飞(飛) fēi I [动] 1 (鸟, 虫, 飞机) fly 2 (空中游动) flutter 3 (挥发) evaporate II [副] swiftly
飞(飛)机(機) fēijī [名] aeroplane (英), airplane (美)
飞(飛)行 fēixíng [动] fly

非 fēi I [名] 1 (错误) wrong ▶ 是非 shìfēi right and wrong 2 (非洲) Fēizhōu Africa II [动] 1 (非议) blame 2 (违反) run counter to ▶ 非法 fēifǎ illegal 3 (不是) not be 4 (强硬) insist on III [副] (必须) ▷ 我不让他去, 他非去不可。Wǒ bù ràng tā qù, tā fēi qù bùkě. I've tried to stop him, but he simply has to go.
非常 fēicháng I [形] exceptional II [副] very
非典 fēidiǎn [名] (非典型性肺炎) SARS
非法 fēifǎ [形] illegal
非洲 Fēizhōu [名] Africa

肥 féi I [名] fertilizer II [动] 1 (使肥沃) fertilize 2 (暴富) get rich III [形] 1 (脂肪多) fat 2 (肥沃) fertile 3 (肥大) loose
肥胖 féipàng [形] fat
肥皂 féizào [名] soap

肺 fèi [名] lung

废(廢) fèi I [动] abandon II [形] 1 (不用的) waste 2 (没用的) useless 3 (残废的) disabled

费(費) fèi I [名] fee ▷ 车费 chēfèi bus fare II [形] expensive III [动] spend
费(費)用 fèiyong [名] expense

分 fēn I [动] 1 (分开) divide ▶ 分离 fēnlí separate ▶ 分裂 fēnliè split 2 (分配) assign 3 (辨别) distinguish II [名] 1 (分支) branch 2 (分数) fraction ▶ 分母 fēnmǔ denominator 3 (得分) mark III [量] 1 (分数) fraction ▷ 四分之三 sì fēn zhī sān three quarters 2 (十分之一) one tenth 3 (货币) unit of Chinese currency, equal to a hundredth of a yuan 4 (指时间) minute ▷ 5点过5分 wǔ diǎn guò wǔ fēn 5 minutes past 5 5 (指弧度

或角度) minute ▷ 36度20分角 sānshíliù dù èrshí fēn jiǎo 36 degrees 20 minutes **6**(百分之一) per cent ▷ 月利1分 yuèlì yī fēn monthly interest of 1 per cent
→ see also/另见 fèn

分别(別) fēnbié I [动] **1**(离别) split up **2**(辨别) distinguish II [名] difference

分开(開) fēnkāi [动] separate

分配 fēnpèi [动] assign

分手 fēnshǒu [动] **1**(告别) say goodbye **2**(指男女关系) break up

分数(數) fēnshù [名] mark

分析 fēnxī [动] analyse (英), analyze (美)

分钟(鐘) fēnzhōng [名] minute

吩 fēn see below/见下文
吩咐 fēnfù [动] instruct

纷(紛) fēn [形] **1**(多) numerous ▶ 纷繁 fēnfán numerous **2**(乱) confused ▶ 纷扰 fēnrǎo confusion
纷(紛)纷(紛) fēnfēn I [形] diverse II [副] one after another

坟(墳) fén [名] grave
坟(墳)墓 fénmù [名] grave

粉 fěn I [名] **1**(粉末) powder **2**(粉丝) vermicelli II [动] **1**(成碎末) crumble ▶ 粉碎 fěnsuì crush **2**(变成粉状) pulverize III [形] **1**(白色) white **2**(粉红色) pink
粉笔(筆) fěnbǐ [名] chalk
粉红(紅) fěnhóng [形] pink
粉末 fěnmò [名] powder

分 fèn [名] **1**(成分) component **2**(限度) limit ▶ 过分 guòfèn excessive **3**(情分) feelings (pl)
→ see also/另见 fēn
分量 fènliàng [名] weight

份 fèn I [名] **1**(一部分) part ▶ 股份 gǔfèn share **2**(指划分单位) ▶ 年份 niánfèn year II [量] **1**(指食物) portion **2**(指报刊) copy

奋(奮) fèn [动] **1**(振作) exert oneself ▶ 勤奋 qínfèn diligent **2**(举起) raise
奋(奮)斗(鬥) fèndòu [动] fight

愤(憤) fèn [形] indignant ▶ 气愤 qìfèn indignant
愤(憤)怒 fènnù [形] angry

丰(豐) fēng [形] **1**(丰富) abundant **2**(大) great
丰(豐)富 fēngfù I [形] abundant II [动] enrich
丰(豐)收 fēngshōu [动] have a good harvest

风(風) fēng I [名] **1**(指空气流动) wind **2**(风气) trend **3**(景象) scene ▶ 风光 fēngguāng scenery **4**(态度) manner ▶ 风度 fēngdù bearing **5**(消息) information II [形] rumoured (英), rumored (美) III [动] air ▶ 风干 fēnggān air-dry
风(風)格 fēnggé [名] **1**(气度) manner **2**(特点) style
风(風)景 fēngjǐng [名] scenery
风(風)水 fēngshuǐ [名] feng shui
风(風)俗 fēngsú [名] custom
风(風)险(險) fēngxiǎn [名] risk

封 fēng I [动] (封闭) seal II [名] envelope III [量] ▷ 一封信 yī fēng xìn a letter
封建 fēngjiàn I [名] feudalism II [形] feudal

疯(瘋) fēng I [形] mad II [副] madly
疯(瘋)子 fēngzi [名] lunatic

锋(鋒) fēng [名] **1**(尖端) point **2**(带头的) vanguard **3**(锋面) front
锋(鋒)利 fēnglì [形] **1**(工具) sharp **2**(言论) cutting

蜂 fēng I [名] **1**(黄蜂) wasp **2**(蜜蜂) bee II [副] in swarms
蜂蜜 fēngmì [名] honey

逢 féng [动] come across

缝(縫) féng [动] sew
→ see also/另见 fèng

讽(諷) fěng [动] mock ▶ 讥讽 jīfěng satirize
讽(諷)刺 fěngcì [动] ridicule

奉 fèng [动] 1(献给) present 2(接受) receive 3(尊重) respect 4(信仰) believe in 5(伺候) attend to

奉献(獻) fèngxiàn [动] dedicate

缝(縫) fèng [名] 1(接合处) seam 2(缝隙) crack
→ see also/另见 féng

缝(縫)隙 fèngxì [名] crack

佛 fó [名] 1(佛教) Buddhism 2(佛像) Buddha

佛教 fójiào [名] Buddhism

否 fǒu I [动] deny II [副] 1(书)(不) no 2(是、能、可) or not ▷ 他明天是否来参加聚会？Tā míngtiān shìfǒu lái cānjiā jùhuì? Is he coming to the party tomorrow or not?

否定 fǒudìng I [动] negate II [形] negative

否认(認) fǒurèn [动] deny

否则(則) fǒuzé [连] otherwise

夫 fū [名] 1(丈夫) husband 2(男子) man 3(劳动者) manual worker

夫妇(婦) fūfù [名] husband and wife

夫妻 fūqī [名] husband and wife

夫人 fūrén [名] Mrs

扶 fú [动] 1(稳住) steady 2(搀起) help up 3(扶助) help

服 fú I [名] clothes (pl) II [动] 1(吃) take ▷ 服药 fúyào take medicine 2(担任) serve ▷ 服役 fúyì serve in the army 3(服从) comply with 4(使信服) convince 5(适应) adapt
→ see also/另见 fù

服从(從) fúcóng [动] obey

服务(務) fúwù [动] serve

服务(務)员(員) fúwùyuán [名] 1(指商店里) attendant 2(指饭馆里) waiter, waitress 3(指宾馆里) room attendant

服装(裝) fúzhuāng [名] clothing

浮 fú I [动] float II [形] 1(表面上) superficial 2(可移动) movable 3(暂时) temporary 4(轻浮) slapdash 5(空虚) empty ▷ 浮夸 fúkuā exaggerated 6(多余) surplus

浮肿(腫) fúzhǒng [动] puff up

符 fú I [名] 1(标记) mark 2(图形) Daoist motif II [动] be in keeping with

符号(號) fúhào [名] mark

符合 fúhé [动] match

幅 fú I [名] 1(指布) width 2(泛指大小) size ▷ 幅度 fúdù range II [量] ▷ 一幅画 yī fú huà a painting ▷ 三幅书法 sān fú shūfǎ three calligraphies
measure word, used for paintings, portraits and Chinese calligraphies

福 fú [名] good fortune

辅(輔) fǔ [动] complement

辅(輔)导(導) fǔdǎo [动] coach

腐 fǔ I [形] rotten II [名] bean curd

腐败(敗) fǔbài I [动] rot II [形] corrupt

父 fù [名] 1(父亲) father 2(指男性长辈) senior male relative ▷ 祖父 zǔfù grandfather

父母 fùmǔ [名] parents

父亲(親) fùqīn [名] father

付 fù [动] 1(事物) hand over ▷ 托付 tuōfù entrust 2(钱) pay ▷ 偿付 chángfù pay back

付账(賬) fùzhàng [动] pay the bill

负(負) fù [动] 1(书)(背) carry on one's back ▷ 负重 fùzhòng carry a heavy load 2(担负) bear 3(遭受) suffer 4(享有) enjoy 5(拖欠) be in arrears 6(背弃) turn one's back on 7(失败) lose II [形] negative ▷ 负数 fùshù negative number

负(負)担(擔) fùdān I [动] bear II [名] burden

负(負)责(責) fùzé I [动] be responsible II [形] conscientious

妇(婦) fù [名] 1(妇女) woman ▷ 妇科 fùkē gynaecology (英), gynecology (美) 2(已婚妇女) married woman 3(妻) wife

妇(婦)女 fùnǚ [名] woman

妇(婦)男 fùnán [名] house husband

附 fù [动] 1(附带) attach 2(靠近) get close to 3(依从) depend on
附近 fùjìn I[形] nearby II[名] vicinity

服 fù [量] dose
→ see also/另见 fú

复(複) fù I[形] 1(重复) duplicated ▶复制 fùzhì reproduce 2(繁复) complex II[动] 1(转) turn 2(回答) reply 3(恢复) recover 4(报复) take revenge III[副] again ▶复查 fùchá re-examine
复(復)活节(節) Fùhuó Jié [名](宗) Easter
复(複)习(習) fùxí [动] revise
复(複)印 fùyìn [动] photocopy
复(複)印机(機) fùyìnjī [名] photocopy machine
复(複)杂(雜) fùzá [形] complex

副 fù I[形] 1(辅助) deputy 2(附带) subsidiary ▶副业 fùyè subsidiary business II[名] assistant ▶大副 dàfù first mate III[动] correspond to IV[量] (套) pair ▷一副手套 yī fù shǒutào a pair of gloves ▷一副冷面孔 yī fù lěng miànkǒng a cold expression ▷一副笑脸 yī fù xiàoliǎn a smiling face
▨ measure word, used for expressions
副作用 fùzuòyòng [名] side effect

富 fù I[形] 1(有钱) rich 2(丰富) abundant II[名] wealth III[动] enrich
富有 fùyǒu I[形] wealthy II[动] be full of

g

咖 gā see below/见下文
→ see also/另见 kā
咖喱 gālí [名] curry

该(該) gāi I[动] 1(应当) ought to 2(轮到) be the turn of 3(活该) serve ... right ▶活该 huógāi serve ... right II[助动] 1(应该) should ▷工作明天该完成了。Gōngzuò míngtiān gāi wánchéng le. The work should be finished by tomorrow. 2(表示推测) ▷再不吃的话，菜都该凉了。Zài bù chī dehuà, cài dōu gāi liáng le. If we keep waiting the food is only going to get colder. 3(用于加强语气) ▷要是他能在这儿该多好啊! Yàoshi tā néng zài zhèr gāi duō hǎo a! It would be great if he could be here.

改 gǎi [动] 1(改变) change 2(修改) alter 3(改正) correct
改变(變) gǎibiàn [动] change ▷我改变了主意。Wǒ gǎibiànle zhǔyi. I changed my mind.
改革 gǎigé [动] reform ▷改革开放 gǎigé kāifàng reform and opening up
改善 gǎishàn [动] improve
改正 gǎizhèng [动] correct ▷改正缺点 gǎizhèng quēdiǎn mend one's ways

钙(鈣) gài [名](化) calcium

盖(蓋) gài I [名] (指器皿) cover ▸ 盖子 gàizi lid II [动] 1 (蒙上) cover 2 (遮掩) cover ... up 3 (打上) stamp 4 (压过) block ... out 5 (建造) build

概 gài [名] (大略) outline
概括 gàikuò I [动] summarize II [形] brief
概念 gàiniàn [名] concept

干 gān I [动] have to do with ▸ 这不干我事。Zhè bù gān wǒ shì. This has nothing to do with me. II [形] 1 (无水) dry 2 (不用水) dry ▸ 干洗 gānxǐ dry-clean 3 (干涸) dried-up III [名] ▸ 豆腐干 dòufugān dried tofu ▸ 葡萄干 pútaogān raisin IV [副] (白白) in vain
→ see also / 另见 gàn
干(乾)杯 gānbēi [动] drink a toast ▸ "干杯!" "Gānbēi!" "Cheers!"
干(乾)脆 gāncuì [形] direct
干(乾)旱 gānhàn [形] arid
干(乾)净(淨) gānjìng [形] 1 (无尘) clean 2 (一点不剩) complete ▸ 请把汤喝干净。Qǐng bǎ tāng hē gānjìng. Please finish your soup.
干扰(擾) gānrǎo [动] disturb
干预(預) gānyù [动] interfere
干(乾)燥 gānzào [形] dry

杆(桿) gān [名] post

肝 gān [名] liver

竿 gān [名] pole ▸ 竿子 gānzi pole

赶(趕) gǎn [动] 1 (追) catch ▸ 赶公共汽车 gǎn gōnggòng qìchē catch a bus 2 (加快) rush ▸ 赶着回家 gǎnzhe huíjiā rush home 3 (驱赶) drive 4 (驱逐) drive ... out
赶(趕)紧(緊) gǎnjǐn [副] quickly
赶(趕)快 gǎnkuài [副] at once ▸ 我们得赶快走了! Wǒmen děi gǎnkuài zǒu le! We must go at once!
赶(趕)上 gǎnshàng [动] catch up with
赶(趕)忙 gǎnmáng [副] hurriedly

敢 gǎn [动] 1 (有胆量) dare ▸ 敢于 gǎnyú dare to 2 (有把握) be sure

感 gǎn I [动] 1 (觉得) feel 2 (感动) move ▸ 感人 gǎnrén moving II [名] sense ▸ 成就感 chéngjiùgǎn a sense of achievement ▸ 方向感 fāngxiànggǎn a sense of direction
感到 gǎndào [动] feel ▸ 我感到幸运。Wǒ gǎndào xìngyùn. I feel lucky.
感动(動) gǎndòng [动] move ▸ 他容易被感动。Tā róngyì bèi gǎndòng. He's very easily moved.
感恩节(節) Gǎn'ēn Jié [名] Thanksgiving
感激 gǎnjī [动] appreciate
感觉(覺) gǎnjué I [名] feeling II [动] 1 (感到) feel 2 (认为) sense
感冒 gǎnmào [动] catch a cold
感情 gǎnqíng [名] 1 (心理反应) emotion 2 (喜爱) feelings (pl)
感染 gǎnrǎn [动] (传染) infect
感想 gǎnxiǎng [名] thoughts (pl)
感谢(謝) gǎnxiè [动] thank ▸ 感谢您的指导。Gǎnxiè nín de zhǐdǎo. Thank you for your guidance.
感兴(興)趣 gǎn xìngqù [动] be interested in ▸ 他对绘画感兴趣。Tā duì huìhuà gǎn xìngqù. He's interested in painting.

干(幹) gàn [动] 1 (做) do ▸ 干活 gànhuó work 2 (担任) act as ▸ 他干过队长。Tā gànguo duìzhǎng. He acted as team leader.
→ see also / 另见 gān
干(幹)部 gànbù [名] cadre

刚(剛) gāng I [形] strong II [副] 1 (恰好) just ▸ 水温刚好。Shuǐwēn gāng hǎo. The temperature of the water was just right. 2 (仅仅) just ▸ 这儿刚够放一把椅子。Zhèr gāng gòu fàng yī bǎ yǐzi. There is just enough room for a chair. 3 (不久以前) only just ▸ 小宝宝刚会走路。Xiǎo bǎobao gāng huì zǒulù. The baby has only just started walking.
刚(剛)才 gāngcái [名] just now
刚(剛)刚(剛) gānggāng [副] just
刚(剛)好 gānghǎo I [形] just right II [副] luckily

钢(鋼) gāng [名] steel ▶ 钢铁 gāngtiě steel
钢(鋼)笔(筆) gāngbǐ [名] fountain pen
钢(鋼)琴 gāngqín [名] piano

缸 gāng [名] (器物) vat ▶ 鱼缸 yúgāng fish bowl

港 gǎng [名] 1 (港湾) harbour (英), harbor (美) 2 (香港) Hong Kong ▶ 香港 Xiānggǎng Hong Kong ▶ 港币 gǎngbì Hong Kong dollar
港口 gǎngkǒu [名] port

高 gāo [形] 1 (指高度) tall ▶ 高楼 gāolóu tall building 2 (指标准或程度) high ▶ 高标准 gāo biāozhǔn high standard 3 (指等级) senior ▶ 高中 gāozhōng senior school 4 (指声音) high-pitched 5 (指年龄) old 6 (指价格) high
高大 gāodà [形] (字) huge
高档 gāodàng [形] top quality
高等 gāoděng [形] higher ▷ 高等教育 gāoděng jiàoyù higher education
高级(級) gāojí [形] 1 (指级别) senior ▷ 高级法院 gāojí fǎyuàn high court 2 (超过一般) high-quality ▷ 高级英语 gāojí Yīngyǔ advanced English ▷ 高级宾馆 gāojí bīnguǎn luxury hotel
高考 gāokǎo [名] college entrance examination
高科技 gāokējì [形] hi-tech
高速 gāosù [形] rapid
高速公路 gāosù gōnglù [名] motorway (英), freeway (美)
高兴(興) gāoxìng I [形] happy II [动] enjoy
高原 gāoyuán [名] plateau
高中 gāozhōng [名] (高级中学) senior school (英), high school (美)

糕 gāo [名] cake ▶ 蛋糕 dàngāo cake

搞 gǎo [动] 1 (干) do 2 (弄) get

告 gào [动] 1 (陈述) tell 2 (控诉) sue
告别(別) gàobié [动] say goodbye
告诉(訴) gàosu [动] tell
告状(狀) gàozhuàng [动] (抱怨) complain

哥 gē [名] 1 (哥哥) elder brother 2 (亲热称呼) brother
哥哥 gēge [名] elder brother
哥们(們)儿(兒) gēmenr [名] (朋友) mate (英), buddy (美)

胳 gē see below/见下文
胳膊 gēbo [名] arm

鸽(鴿) gē [名] dove ▶ 鸽子 gēzi dove

搁(擱) gē [动] 1 (放) put 2 (搁置) put aside

割 gē [动] cut

歌 gē I [名] song II [动] sing
歌剧(劇) gējù [名] opera
歌曲 gēqǔ [名] song
歌手 gēshǒu [名] singer

革 gé I [名] leather II [动] (改变) change
革命 gémìng [动] revolutionize ▷ 工业革命 gōngyè gémìng industrial revolution

格 gé [名] (格子) check
格式 géshì [名] format
格外 géwài [副] 1 (特别) especially 2 (额外) additionally

隔 gé [动] 1 (阻隔) separate 2 (间隔) be apart
隔壁 gébì [名] next door ▷ 隔壁邻居 gébì línjū next-door neighbour (英) 或 neighbor (美)

嗝 gé [名] 1 (饱嗝) burp ▶ 打饱嗝 dǎ bǎogé burp 2 (冷嗝) hiccup ▶ 打冷嗝 dǎ lěnggé have a hiccup

个(個) gè I [名] (指身材或大小) size ▶ 个头儿 gètóur build II [量] (表示个数) ▷ 6个桃子 liù gè táozi six peaches ▷ 两个月 liǎng gè yuè two months
This is the most useful and common measure word, and can be used as the default measure word when you are unsure. It can be used for people, objects, fruits, countries, cities, companies, dates, weeks, months, ideas etc.

(表示动量) ▷ 开个会 kāi gè huì have a meeting ▷ 冲个澡 chōng gè zǎo have a shower

▌ the most useful measure word, used for actions

个(個)别(別) gèbié [形] 1(单个) individual 2(少数) a couple

个(個)唱 gè chàng [名] solo concert

个(個)人 gèrén I [名] individual II [代] oneself ▷ 就他个人而言 jiù tā gèrén éryán as far as he's concerned ▷ 在我个人看来, 这是个好主意。Zài wǒ gèrén kànlái, zhè shì gè hǎo zhǔyì. As far as I'm concerned this is a good idea.

个(個)体(體) gètǐ [名] 1(指生物) individual 2(指经济形态) ▷ 个体经营 gètǐ jīngyíng private enterprise

个(個)性 gèxìng [名] personality ▷ 他个性很强。Tā gèxìng hěn qiáng. He has a very strong personality.

个(個)子 gèzi [名] stature ▷ 高个子女人 gāo gèzi nǚrén a tall woman

各 gè I [代] each II [副] individually
各个(個) gègè I [代] each II [副] one by one
各种(種) gèzhǒng [代] all kinds
各自 gèzì [代] each

给(給) gěi I [动] 1(给予) give 2(让) let II [介] 1(为) for ▷ 我给妻子做早餐。Wǒ gěi qīzi zuò zǎocān. I made breakfast for my wife. 2(向) to ▷ 留给他 liú gěi tā leave it to him ▷ 递给我 dì gěi wǒ pass it to me

---

根 gēn I [名] (指植物) root ▷ 祸根 huògēn the root of the problem II [量] ▷ 一根绳子 yī gēn shéngzi a rope ▷ 一根头发 yī gēn tóufa a hair

▌ measure word, used for long thin objects, body parts and plants

根本 gēnběn I [名] root II [形] fundamental III [副] 1(完全) at all 2(彻底) thoroughly ▷ 根本转变态度 gēnběn zhuǎnbiàn tàidu completely change one's attitude

根据(據) gēnjù I [介] according to II [名] basis

根源 gēnyuán [名] cause

跟 gēn I [名] heel II [动] 1(跟随) follow 2(嫁) marry III [介] 1(同) with ▷ 我跟朋友去公园了。Wǒ gēn péngyou qù gōngyuán le. I went to the park with friends. 2(向) ▷ 跟我说说这件事。Gēn wǒ shuōshuo zhè jiàn shì. Tell me what happened. 3(表示比较) as ▷ 他的教育背景跟我相似。Tā de jiàoyù bèijǐng gēn wǒ xiāngsì. His educational background is similar to mine. IV [连] follow

跟随(隨) gēnsuí [动] follow

跟头(頭) gēntou [名] fall ▷ 翻跟头 fān gēntou do a somersault

跟踪(蹤) gēnzōng [动] tail

更 gēng [动] (改变) change ▷ 更正 gēngzhèng correct
→ see also/另见 gèng

更改 gēnggǎi [动] alter

更换(換) gēnghuàn [动] change

更替 gēngtì [动] replace

更新 gēngxīn [动] 1(事物) replace ▷ 更新网站内容 gēngxīn wǎngzhàn nèiróng update web content 2(森林) renew

更衣室 gēngyīshì [名] fitting room

耕 gēng [动] plough
耕地 gēngdì I [动] plough II [名] cultivated land

更 gèng [形] (更加) even more ▷ 天更黑了。Tiān gèng hēi le. It's getting even darker.
→ see also/另见 gēng

更加 gèngjiā [副] even more

工 gōng [名] 1(指人) worker ▷ 童工 tónggōng child labour 2(指阶级) the working class 3(工作或劳动) work 4(工程) project 5(工业) industry

工厂(廠) gōngchǎng [名] factory

工程 gōngchéng [名] engineering project

工程师(師) gōngchéngshī [名] engineer

工夫 gōngfu [名] 1(时间) time 2(空闲) spare time

工具 gōngjù [名] 1(器具) tool 2(喻) instrument

工具栏(欄) gōngjùlán [名] (计算机) toolbar

工人 gōngrén [名] worker

工业(業) gōngyè [名] industry

工艺(藝)品 gōngyìpǐn [名] handicraft item

工资(資) gōngzī [名] pay

工作 gōngzuò [名] 1 (劳动) work 2 (职业) job 3 (业务) work

公 gōng I [形] 1 (非私有) public ▷ 公共 gōnggòng public 2 (共识) general 3 (公正) fair 4 (雄性) male II [名] 1 (公务) official business 2 (敬) (老先生) ▷ 王公 Wáng gōng Mr Wang 3 (丈夫的父亲) father-in-law ▷ 公公 gōnggong father-in-law

公安 gōng'ān [名] public security

公安局 gōng'ānjú [名] 1 (公安机关) Public Security Bureau 2 (派出所) police station

公布(佈) gōngbù [动] announce

公厕(廁) gōngcè [名] public toilet

公尺 gōngchǐ [名] metre (英), meter (美)

公费(費) gōngfèi [名] public expense

公分 gōngfēn [名] centimetre (英), centimeter (美)

公共 gōnggòng [形] public

公共汽车(車) gōnggòng qìchē [名] bus

公共汽车(車)站 gōnggòng qìchēzhàn [名] 1 (指总站) bus station 2 (指路边站) bus stop

公斤 gōngjīn [名] kilogram

公开(開) gōngkāi I [形] public II [动] make public

公里(裡) gōnglǐ [名] kilometre (英), kilometer (美)

公路 gōnglù [名] motorway

公民 gōngmín [名] citizen

公平 gōngpíng [形] fair

公社 gōngshè [名] commune

公司 gōngsī [名] company

公用 gōngyòng [形] public

公寓 gōngyù [名] 1 (旅馆) boarding house 2 (楼房) flat (英), apartment (美)

公元 gōngyuán [名] A.D.

公园(園) gōngyuán [名] park

公正 gōngzhèng [形] impartial

公众(眾) gōngzhòng [名] public

公主 gōngzhǔ [名] princess

功 gōng [名] 1 (功劳) contribution 2 (成效) achievement

功夫 gōngfu [名] martial arts

功课(課) gōngkè [名] homework

功劳(勞) gōngláo [名] contribution

功能 gōngnéng [名] function ▷ 多功能电话 duōgōngnéng diànhuà multi-functional telephone

攻 gōng [动] (攻打) attack

攻击(擊) gōngjī [动] (进攻) attack

供 gōng [动] 1 (供应) supply 2 (提供) provide

供给(給) gōngjǐ [动] supply

供求 gōngqiú [名] supply and demand

供应(應) gōngyìng [动] supply

宫(宮) gōng [名] (皇宫) palace ▷ 宫殿 gōngdiàn palace

恭 gōng [形] respectful

恭维(維) gōngwéi [动] flatter

恭喜 gōngxǐ [动] congratulate

巩(鞏) gǒng see below/见下文

巩(鞏)固 gǒnggù I [形] solid II [动] strengthen

共 gòng I [形] common II [动] share III [副] 1 (一齐) together 2 (总共) altogether IV [名] (共产党) the communist party

共产(產)党(黨) gòngchǎndǎng [名] the communist party

共产(產)主义(義) gòngchǎn zhǔyì [名] communism

共和国(國) gònghéguó [名] republic

共同 gòngtóng I [形] common II [副] together

贡(貢) gòng [名] tribute

贡(貢)献(獻) gòngxiàn I [动] devote II [名] contribution

沟(溝) gōu [名] ditch
沟(溝)通 gōutōng [动] communicate

钩(鉤) gōu [名] 1 (钩子) hook 2 (符号) tick [动] 3 (用钩子挂) hook 4 (编织、缝) crochet

狗 gǒu [名] dog

构(構) gòu I [动] 1 (组成) compose 2 (结成) form 3 (建造) construct II [名] (结构) structure
构(構)成 gòuchéng [动] 1 (造成) constitute 2 (组成) compose
构(構)造 gòuzào [名] structure

购(購) gòu [动] buy
购(購)买(買) gòumǎi [动] buy
购(購)物 gòuwù [动] go shopping ▷ 她爱购物。Tā ài gòuwù. She likes shopping.

够(夠) gòu I [形] enough ▷ 5个就够了。Wǔ gè jiù gòu le. Five is enough. II [动] reach

估 gū [动] guess
估计(計) gūjì [动] reckon

姑 gū [名] 1 (姑母) aunt 2 (丈夫的姐妹) sister-in-law
姑娘 gūniang [名] girl
姑姑 gūgu [名] aunt

孤 gū [形] (孤单) alone
孤单(單) gūdān [形] (寂寞) lonely
孤独(獨) gūdú [形] solitary
孤儿(兒) gū'ér [名] orphan

古 gǔ I [名] ancient times (pl) II [形] ancient
古代 gǔdài [名] antiquity
古典 gǔdiǎn I [名] classics (pl) II [形] classical
古董 gǔdǒng [名] (古代器物) antique
古惑仔 gǔhuòzǎi [名] hooligan
古迹(蹟) gǔjì [名] historic site
古老 gǔlǎo [形] ancient

谷 gǔ [名] 1 (山谷) valley 2 (稻谷) grain
谷歌 Gǔ gē [名] Google®

股 gǔ I [名] 1 (指绳或线) strand 2 (股份) share II [量] (气体) (气味) whiff
股票 gǔpiào [名] share
股市 gǔshì [名] stock market

骨 gǔ [名] bone
骨头(頭) gǔtou [名] (字) bone

鼓 gǔ I [名] drum II [动] 1 ▷ 鼓掌 gǔzhǎng applaud 2 (凸起, 胀大) bulge ▷ 他鼓着嘴。Tā gǔzhe zuǐ. He puffed his cheeks out. III [形] bulging ▷ 她的书包鼓鼓的。Tā de shūbāo gǔgǔ de. Her schoolbag was full to bursting.
鼓励(勵) gǔlì [动] encourage
鼓舞 gǔwǔ I [动] inspire II [形] inspiring

固 gù I [形] strong ▷ 坚固 jiāngù solid ▷ 牢固 láogù firm II [副] (坚定) firmly
固定 gùdìng I [形] fixed II [动] fix
固体(體) gùtǐ [名] solid
固执(執) gùzhí [形] stubborn

故 gù [名] 1 (变故) incident 2 (原因) reason
故宫(宮) Gùgōng [名] the Forbidden City

故宫 Gùgōng
As the largest collection of ancient wooden structures in the world, 故宫 Gùgōng formed the imperial palaces of the Ming (1368-1644) and Qing (1644-1911) dynasties. It is located at what was once the exact centre of the old city of Beijing, just to the north of Tian'anmen Square. It is now a major tourist attraction, both for the architecture of its 800-plus wooden buildings, and for the many artistic and cultural treasures which are housed within them. In 1987 it was declared a World Heritage Site by UNESCO.

故事 gùshi [名] story
故乡(鄉) gùxiāng [名] birthplace
故意 gùyì [副] deliberately
故障 gùzhàng [名] fault ▷ 这台机器出了故障。Zhè tái jīqì chū le gùzhàng. This machine is faulty.

顾(顧)gù [动] 1(看) look ▶回顾 huígù look back ▶环顾 huángù look around 2(注意、照管) attend to ▶照顾 zhàogù attend to

顾(顧)客 gùkè [名] customer

顾(顧)问(問) gùwèn [名] consultant

雇(僱)gù [动] 1(雇佣) employ 2(租赁) hire

雇(僱)员(員) gùyuán [名] employee

雇(僱)主 gùzhǔ [名] employer

瓜 guā [名] (植) melon

刮 guā [动] 1(指用刀) shave 2(涂抹) smear 3(风) blow

挂(掛)guà [动] 1(悬，吊) hang 2(中断电话) hang up

挂(掛)号(號) guàhào I [动] register II [形] registered ▷挂号信 guàhàoxìn registered mail

挂(掛)历(曆) guàlì [名] calendar

褂 guà [名] gown ▶褂子 guàzi gown

乖 guāi [形] (听话) well-behaved

拐(枴)guǎi I [名] 1(拐杖) walking stick 2(拐角处) turning II [动] 1(转变方向) turn ▷向左/右拐 xiàng zuǒ/yòu guǎi turn left/right 2(拐骗) swindle

拐(枴)卖(賣) guǎimài [动] abduct and sell

怪 guài I [形] strange II [动] 1(觉得奇怪) be surprised 2(责怪) blame III [副] (口) really IV [名] monster

怪不得 guàbude [连] no wonder

关(關)guān I [动] 1(合拢) close 2(圈起来) imprison 3(停业) close down 4(断电) turn ... off ▷关灯 guān dēng turn off the light 5(牵连) concern ▷这不关他的事。Zhè bù guān tā de shì. This matter does not concern him. II [名] 1(守卫处所) pass 2(出入境收税处) customs (pl) ▷海关 hǎiguān customs (pl) 4(关联部分) critical point 4(关联部分) ▶关节 guānjié joint ▶关键 guānjiàn key

关(關)闭(閉) guānbì [动] 1(合拢)

close 2(歇业或停办) close down

关(關)怀(懷) guānhuái [动] be concerned about

关(關)税(稅) guānshuì [名] customs duty

关(關)系(係) guānxì I [名] (联系) relation II [动] impact on

关(關)心 guānxīn [动] be concerned about

关(關)于(於) guānyú [介] on

关(關)照 guānzhào [动] (关心照顾) look after

关(關)注 guānzhù [动] 1(关心重视) pay close attention to 2(指社交媒体) follow

观(觀)guān I [动] look ▶围观 wéiguān gather round to watch ▶旁观 pángguān look on II [名] view

观(觀)察 guānchá [动] observe

观(觀)点(點) guāndiǎn [名] point of view

观(觀)看 guānkàn [动] watch

观(觀)念 guānniàn [名] concept

观(觀)众(眾) guānzhòng [名] spectator

官 guān [名] 1(公职人员) official 2(器官) organ

官司 guānsi [名] lawsuit

官员(員) guānyuán [名] official

管 guǎn I [名] 1(管子) pipe ▶水管 shuǐguǎn water pipe ▶管子 guǎnzi tube 2(乐器) wind instrument ▶双簧管 shuānghuángguǎn oboe ▶管状物 guǎnzhuàngwù tube II [动] 1(负责) be in charge of 2(管辖) have jurisdiction over 3(管教) discipline 4(过问) interfere ▷这事不用你管。Zhè shì bù yòng nǐ guǎn. It's no use you interfering in this. 5(保证) guarantee ▶管保 guǎnbǎo guarantee 6(提供) provide

管道 guǎndào [名] pipeline

管理 guǎnlǐ [动] 1(负责) be in charge 2(保管) take care of 3(看管) keep guard over ▷企业管理 qǐyè guǎnlǐ business management

管用 guǎnyòng [形] effective

贯(貫) guàn I [动] 1(贯穿) pass through 2(连贯) keep following II [名] ancestral home ▶ 籍贯 jíguàn place of origin

贯(貫)彻(徹) guànchè [动] implement

贯(貫)穿 guànchuān [动] run through

冠 guàn I [动] crown II [名] crown

冠军(軍) guànjūn [名] champion

惯(慣) guàn [动] 1(习惯) be used to ▷ 我吃西餐已经惯了。Wǒ chī xīcān yǐjīng guàn le. I'm already used to Western food. 2(纵容) spoil ▷ 惯孩子 guàn háizi spoil the children

灌 guàn [动] 1(灌溉) irrigate 2(注入) pour ... into

罐 guàn I [名] 1(盛茶叶、糖等) jar 2(易拉罐) can 3(煤气) cylinder ▶ 煤气罐 méiqìguàn gas cylinder II [量] can ▷ 两罐啤酒 liǎng guàn píjiǔ two cans of beer ▷ 五罐苏打水 wǔ guàn sūdáshuǐ five cans of soda water

罐头(頭) guàntou [名] tin ▷ 金枪鱼罐头 jīnqiāngyú guàntou tinned tuna fish

光 guāng I [名] 1(指物质) light ▶ 月光 yuèguāng moonlight ▶ 阳光 yángguāng sunlight 2(景物) scenery ▶ 风光 fēngguāng scenery 3(荣誉) glory ▶ 增光 zēngguāng bring glory II [动] 1(光大) glorify 2(露出) bare III [形] 1(光滑) smooth ▶ 光滑 guānghuá smooth 2(露着) bare ▶ 光脚 guāngjiǎo barefooted 3(穷尽) used up ▷ 钱都用光了。Qián dōu yòng guāng le. All the money's used up. IV [副] just ▷ 他光说不做。Tā guāng shuō bù zuò. He's all talk.

光临(臨) guānglín [动] be present

光明 guāngmíng I [名] light II [形] bright

光盘(盤) guāngpán [名] CD

光荣 guāngróng [形] glorious

光线(線) guāngxiàn [名] light

广(廣) guǎng [形] 1(宽阔) broad 2(多) numerous

广(廣)播 guǎngbō [动] broadcast

广(廣)场(場) guǎngchǎng [名] square

广(廣)大 guǎngdà [形] 1(宽广) vast 2(众多) numerous

广(廣)泛 guǎngfàn [形] wide-ranging ▷ 广泛开展活动 guǎngfàn kāizhǎn huódòng initiate a wide range of activities

广(廣)告 guǎnggào [名] advertisement

广(廣)阔(闊) guǎngkuò [形] broad

逛 guàng [动] stroll

归(歸) guī [动] 1(返回、还给) return 2(合并) group ... together ▶ 归类 guīlèi categorise 3(属于) be under the charge of ▷ 这本书归他所有。Zhè běn shū guī tā suǒyǒu. This book belongs to him.

归(歸)功 guīgōng [动] give credit to

归(歸)还(還) guīhuán [动] return

龟(龜) guī [名] tortoise ▶ 乌龟 wūguī tortoise

规(規) guī [名] 1(工具) compasses (pl) 2(规则) rule

规(規)定 guīdìng I [动] stipulate II [名] regulation

规(規)范(範) guīfàn [名] standard ▷ 一定要规范市场秩序。Yídìng yào guīfàn shìchǎng zhìxù. We must standardize the market economy.

规(規)矩 guīju I [名] norm II [形] well-behaved ▷ 他办事总是规矩。Tā bànshì zǒngshì guīju. He always plays by the rules.

规(規)律 guīlǜ [名] law

规(規)模 guīmó [名] scale

规(規)则(則) guīzé I [名] regulation II [形] orderly

规(規)章 guīzhāng [名] regulations (pl)

轨(軌) guǐ [名] (轨道) rail ▶ 轨道 guǐdào track

鬼 guǐ [名] 1(灵魂) ghost 2(勾当) dirty trick 3(不良行为者) ▶ 酒鬼 jiǔguǐ drunkard

鬼混 guǐhùn [动] hang around

鬼脸(臉) guǐliǎn [名] grimace ▷ 做鬼脸 zuò guǐliǎn make a funny face

柜(櫃)guì [名] (柜子) cupboard ▸ 衣柜 yīguì wardrobe ▸ 保险柜 bǎoxiǎnguì safe

柜(櫃)台(臺)guìtái [名] counter

贵(貴)guì [形] **1** (指价格) expensive **2** (值得珍视) valuable ▸ 贵宾 guìbīn VIP

贵(貴)重 guìzhòng [形] valuable

贵(貴)族 guìzú [名] aristocrat

跪 guì [动] kneel ▸ 跪下 guìxià kneel down

滚(滾)gǔn I [动] **1** (滚动) roll ▸ 滚动 gǔndòng roll **2** (走开) get lost ▸ 滚烫 gǔntàng boiling hot II [形] **1** (滚动的) rolling **2** (沸腾的) boiling

棍 gùn [名] (棍子) stick ▸ 棍子 gùnzi stick

锅(鍋)guō [名] (指炊具) pot ▸ 炒菜锅 chǎocàiguō wok ▸ 火锅 huǒguō hotpot

国(國)guó I [名] country II [形] (国家) national ▸ 国徽 guóhuī national emblem ▸ 国歌 guógē national anthem ▸ 国旗 guóqí national flag

国(國)产(產)guóchǎn [形] domestic

国(國)画(畫)guóhuà [名] traditional Chinese painting

国(國)会(會)guóhuì [名] parliament

国(國)籍 guójí [名] nationality

国(國)际(際)guójì [形] international

国(國)家 guójiā [名] state

国(國)力 guólì [名] national strength

国(國)民 guómín [名] citizen

国(國)内(內)guónèi [形] domestic

国(國)庆(慶)节(節)Guóqìng jié [名] National Day

国庆节 Guóqìng jié
国庆节 Guóqìng jié (National Day) falls on 1 October, and commemorates the anniversary of the founding of the People's Republic of China in 1949. The PRC was declared by Chairman Mao Zedong, in Tian'anmen Square in Beijing.

国(國)王 guówáng [名] king

国(國)务(務)院 guówùyuàn [名] the State Council

国务院 guówùyuàn
国务院 guówùyuàn, the State Council, is the highest executive and administrative organ of the PRC government, headed by the Premier, and overseeing all the various ministries.

国(國)营(營)guóyíng [形] state-run

果 guǒ [名] **1** (果子) fruit ▸ 果子 guǒzi fruit **2** (结局) outcome ▸ 效果 xiàoguǒ result ▸ 成果 chéngguǒ achievement

果断(斷)guǒduàn [形] resolute

果然 guǒrán [副] really

果实(實)guǒshí [名] **1** (果子) fruit **2** (成果) fruits (pl)

果真 guǒzhēn [副] really

裹 guǒ [动] (缠绕) wrap

过(過)guò I [动] **1** (经过) pass through **2** (度过) spend ▸ 你假期怎么过的？Nǐ jiàqī zěnme guò de? How did you spend your holiday? **3** (过去) pass **4** (超过) be more than ▸ 年过半百 nián guò bàn bǎi over fifty years old **5** (生活) live ▸ 我们过得很好。Wǒmen guò de hěn hǎo. We live well. **6** (庆祝) celebrate ▸ 过生日 guò shēngrì celebrate a birthday II [名] fault III [介] past ▸ 现在是9点过8分。Xiànzài shì jiǔ diǎn guò bā fēn. It is now eight minutes past nine.

> When 过 guò is used as a verb suffix to indicate a past action, it often corresponds to the present perfect tense (e.g. 'I have done') in English, stressing that the subject has experienced something, e.g. 我去过中国三次 Wǒ qùguo Zhōngguó sān cì (I have been to China three times).

过(過)程 guòchéng [名] process

过(過)道 guòdào [名] corridor

过(過)分 guòfèn [形] excessive

过(過)后(後)guòhòu [副] later

过(過)奖(獎)guòjiǎng [动] flatter ▸ 您过奖了。Nín guòjiǎng le. I'm flattered.

过(過)来(來)guòlái [动] come over

过(過)滤(濾)guòlù [动] filter

过(過)敏 guòmǐn [名] (医) allergy

过(過)期 guòqī [动] expire
过(過)年 guònián [动] celebrate the new year
过(過)去 guòqù [名] the past
过(過)去 guòqu [动] pass by
过(過)日子 guò rizi [动] live
过(過)时(時) guòshí [形] outdated
过(過)世 guòshì [动] pass away
过(過)头(頭) guòtóu [形] excessive
过(過)瘾(癮) guòyǐn [动] do to one's heart's content
过(過)于(於) guòyú [副] too

哈 hā I [叹] aha II [拟] ha ha ▷ 哈哈大笑 hā hā dàxiào roar with laughter

还(還) hái [副] 1 (仍旧) still, yet ▷ 那家老饭店还很兴旺。Nà jiā lǎo fàndiàn hái hěn xīngwàng. The old restaurant is still thriving. ▷ 她还没回来。Tā hái méi huílai. She hasn't come back yet. 2 (更加) even more
→ see also/另见 huán
还(還)是 háishì I [副] 1 (仍然) still 2 (最好) had better ▷ 你还是先完成作业吧。Nǐ háishì xiān wánchéng zuòyè ba. You'd better finish your homework first. II [连] or ▷ 你是去巴黎还是去伦敦？Nǐ shì qù Bālí háishì qù Lúndūn? Are you going to Paris or London?

孩 hái [名] child
孩子 háizi [名] child

海 hǎi [名] (海洋) ocean ▷ 地中海 Dìzhōnghǎi the Mediterranean Sea
海边(邊) hǎibiān [名] coast
海拔 hǎibá [名] elevation
海报(報) hǎibào [名] poster
海滨(濱) hǎibīn [名] seaside
海关(關) hǎiguān [名] customs (pl)
海军(軍) hǎijūn [名] the navy
海绵(綿) hǎimián [名] sponge
海滩(灘) hǎitān [名] beach

海峡(峽) hǎixiá [名] strait
海鲜(鮮) hǎixiān [名] seafood
海洋 hǎiyáng [名] ocean

害 hài I [动] 1 (损害) harm 2 (杀害) kill
II [名] harm ▶ 害处 hàichu harm ▶ 灾害
zāihài disaster III [形] harmful ▶ 害虫
hàichóng pest
害怕 hàipà [动] be afraid
害羞 hàixiū [动] be shy

含 hán [动] 1 (用嘴) keep ... in the mouth
2 (包含) contain
含量 hánliàng [名] content
含义(義) hányì [名] meaning

寒 hán [形] (冷) cold ▶ 寒风 hánfēng
chilly wind
寒假 hánjià [名] winter holiday
寒冷 hánlěng [形] cold

韩(韓) hán [名] see below/见下文
韩(韓)国(國) Hánguó [名] South
Korea

喊 hǎn [动] 1 (大声叫) shout ▶ 喊叫
hǎnjiào cry out 2 (叫) call

汉(漢) hàn [名] (汉族) the Han (pl) ▶ 汉
人 Hànrén the Han people (pl)
汉(漢)语(語) Hànyǔ [名] Chinese
汉(漢)字 Hànzì [名] Chinese characters (pl)
汉(漢)族 Hànzú [名] the Han (pl)

汗 hàn [名] sweat ▶ 汗水 hànshuǐ sweat

旱 hàn [形] dry ▶ 旱灾 hànzāi drought

行 háng I [名] 1 (行列) row, first row
2 (行业) profession ▶ 同行 tóngháng
people in the same profession II [量] line
▷ 一行字 yī háng zì a line of words
→ see also/另见 xíng
行业 hángyè [名] industry

航 háng [动] 1 (指船) sail 2 (指飞机) fly
航班 hángbān [名] (指客机) scheduled
flight
航空 hángkōng [动] fly ▷ 航空信
hángkōngxìn airmail ▷ 航空公司
hángkōng gōngsī airline

毫 háo [名] (千分之一) ▶ 毫米 háomǐ
millimetre (英), millimeter (美) ▶ 毫升
háoshēng millilitre (英), milliliter (美)
毫不 háobù [副] not at all
毫无(無) háowú [副] without the
slightest

豪 háo [形] grand ▶ 豪华 háohuá
luxurious

好 hǎo I [形] 1 (令人满意) good ▷ 他脾气
好。Tā píqì hǎo. He's good-natured.
2 (容易) easy ▷ 这事不好办。Zhè shì bù
hǎo bàn. This won't be easy to manage.
3 (健康) well ▷ 你身体好吗? Nǐ shēntǐ
hǎo ma? Are you keeping well? 4 (亲密)
good ▷ 我们是好朋友。Wǒmen shì hǎo
péngyou. We're good friends. 5 (表示问
候) ▷ 你好! Nǐ hǎo! Hello! ▷ 大家好。
Dàjiā hǎo. Hello everyone. 6 (表示完成)
▷ 工作找好了。Gōngzuò zhǎohǎo le.
I've found work. ▷ 衣服洗好了。Yīfu
xǐhǎo le. The clothes have been washed.
7 (表示答应、结束等) ▷ 好，我们现在
就去! Hǎo, wǒmen xiànzài jiù qù!
OK, let's go then! II [副] 1 (强调多或久)
very ▷ 我等了好久她才来。Wǒ děngle
hǎojiǔ tā cái lái. I'd waited for a long
time before she arrived. 2 (表示程度深)
▷ 他话说得好快。Tā huà shuō de hǎo
kuài. He speaks so quickly. III [名] (问候)
regards (pl) ▷ 请代我向你太太问好。
Qǐng dài wǒ xiàng nǐ tàitai wènhǎo.
Please send my regards to your wife.
→ see also/另见 hào
好吃 hǎochī [形] delicious
好处(處) hǎochu [名] 1 (益处) benefit
2 (利益) profit
好久 hǎojiǔ [副] for a long time
好看 hǎokàn [形] 1 (漂亮) nice-looking
2 (精彩) good ▷ 这本书很好看。Zhè
běn shū hěn hǎokàn. This book is very
good.
好受 hǎoshòu [形] comfortable
好容易 hǎoróngyì [副] with great
effort
好听(聽) hǎotīng [形] 1 (指声音、音
乐) lovely 2 (指言语) nice
好玩儿(兒) hǎowánr [形] fun
好像 hǎoxiàng [副] apparently

好笑 hǎoxiào [形] funny
好些 hǎoxiē [形] quite a great deal of

号(號) hào I[名] 1(名称) name ▶外号 wàihào nickname 2(商店) firm ▶商号 shānghào firm 3(标记) sign ▶逗号 dòuhào comma 4(次序) number 5(日期) date ▷6月1号 liùyuè yī hào the first of June 6(大小) size ▷大号 dàhào large-size 7(乐器) brass instrument ▶小号 xiǎohào trumpet II[动](脉) take ▶号脉 hàomài take a pulse
号(號)码(碼) hàomǎ [名] number
号(號)召 hàozhào [动] appeal

好 hào [动] 1(喜爱) like 2(容易) be easy
→ see also/另见 hǎo
好奇 hàoqí [形] curious

喝 hē [动] drink
喝醉 hēzuì [动] get drunk

合(閤) hé [动] 1(闭) close 2(合在一起) join ▶合资 hézī joint venture 3(折合) be equal to 4(符合) tally with
合并(並) hébìng [动] merge
合唱 héchàng [名] chorus
合法 héfǎ [形] legal
合格 hégé [形] qualified
合理 hélǐ [形] rational
合身 héshēn [形] fitted
合适(適) héshì [形] appropriate
合算 hésuàn [动] be worthwhile
合同 hétong [名] contract
合作 hézuò [动] cooperate

何 hé [代](什么) ▶何时 héshí when ▶何人 hérén who ▶何地 hédì where

和 hé I[连] and II[介] with ▷这事和你没关系。Zhè shì hé nǐ méi guānxì. This has nothing to do with you. III[名](总数) total IV[动] draw ▷这场比赛和了。Zhè chǎng bǐsài hé le. The match was a draw.
和蔼(藹) héǎi [形] affable
和好 héhǎo [动] reconcile
和睦 hémù [形] harmonious
和平 hépíng [名](指战争) peace

和气(氣) héqi I[形] polite II[名] peace
和数(數) héshù [名] sum

河 hé [名](河) river

核 hé [名](指水果) stone

盒 hé [名] box
盒子 hézi [名] box

贺(賀) hè [动] congratulate
贺(賀)卡 hèkǎ [名] greetings card

黑 hēi [形] 1(指颜色) black ▶黑板 hēibǎn blackboard 2(暗) dark 3(秘密) secret ▶黑市 hēishì black market 4(反动) ▶黑社会 hēishèhuì gangland ▶黑手党 hēishǒudǎng the Mafia
黑暗 hēi'àn [形] 1(指光线) dark 2(腐败) corrupt
黑人 hēirén [名] black person

很 hěn [副] very

恨 hèn [动] 1(憎恶) hate 2(后悔) regret

哼 hēng [动](轻唱) hum

横(橫) héng I[名] horizontal II[形] 1(梁、线、行) horizontal 2(左右向) sideways ▷▶横躺 héngtǎng lie sideways 3(指横截) across ▷人行横道 rénxíng héngdào zebra crossing III[动] turn ... lengthways

红(紅) hóng I[形] 1(指颜色) red ▶红旗 hóngqí red flag ▶红十字会 Hóngshízìhuì the Red Cross 2(形容受欢迎) popular ▶走红 zǒuhóng be popular ▶红人 hóngrén rising star 3(形容成功) successful ▶红运 hóngyùn lucky II[名] (红利) bonus ▶分红 fēnhóng get a bonus
红(紅)茶 hóngchá [名] black tea
红(紅)绿(綠)灯(燈) hónglùdēng [名] traffic lights (pl)
红(紅)色 hóngsè [形] red

洪 hóng [名](指洪水) flood ▶洪水 hóngshuǐ flood

喉 hóu [名] throat
喉咙(嚨) hóulóng [名] throat

猴 hóu [名] monkey
猴子 hóuzi [名] monkey

后(後) hòu [名] 1(背面) the back ▷ 房后有个车库。Fáng hòu yǒu gè chēkù. At the back of the house is a garage. 2(指时间) ▷ 后天 hòutiān the day after tomorrow 3(指次序) the last ▷ 后排 hòupái the last row
后(後)边(邊) hòubian [名] back
后(後)代 hòudài [名] 1(指时代) later generations (pl) 2(子孙) offspring
后(後)果 hòuguǒ [名] consequence
后(後)悔 hòuhuǐ [动] regret
后(後)来(來) hòulái [副] afterwards ▷ 我后来再也没有见过他。Wǒ hòulái zài yě méiyǒu jiànguo tā. I didn't see him again after that.
后(後)门(門) hòumén [名] back door
后(後)面 hòumiàn I [名] back II [副] later
后(後)年 hòunián [名] the year after next
后(後)退 hòutuì [动] retreat

厚 hòu [形] 1(书、衣服、脸皮) thick 2(雪、土) deep 3(指感情) profound
厚道 hòudao [形] kind

呼 hū [动] 1(排气) exhale 2(喊) shout ▷ 呼喊 hūhǎn shout 3(叫) call ▷ 呼叫 hūjiào call ▷ 呼救 hūjiù call for help
呼机(機) hūjī [名] pager
呼噜 hūlu [名] (口) snore
呼吸 hūxī [动] breathe

忽 hū [副] suddenly
忽然 hūrán [副] suddenly
忽视(視) hūshì [动] ignore

狐 hú see below/见下文
狐狸(貍) húli [名] fox

胡 hú I [名] 1(髭) moustache (英), mustache (美) 2(长在下颚、两腮) beard II [副] recklessly
胡乱(亂) húluàn [副] 1(随便) casually 2(任意) wilfully
胡闹(鬧) húnào [动] play around

胡说(說) húshuō [动] talk nonsense
胡同 hútòng [名] lane
胡(鬍)子 húzi [名] 1(髭) moustache (英), mustache (美) 2(指长在下颚、两腮) beard

壶(壺) hú [名] pot

湖 hú [名] lake

蝴 hú see below/见下文
蝴蝶 húdié [名] butterfly

糊 hú [动] paste
糊里(裡)糊涂(塗) húlihútu confused
糊涂(塗) hútu [形] 1(不明白) confused 2(混乱) chaotic

虎 hǔ [名] tiger

互 hù [副] mutually
互联(聯)网(網) hùliánwǎng [名] the Internet
互相 hùxiāng [副] mutually

户(戶) hù [名] 1(门) door 2(住户) family 3(户头) bank account ▷ 账户 zhànghù account
户(戶)口 hùkǒu [名] (户籍) registered permanent residence

护(護) hù [动] (保护) protect
护(護)理 hùlǐ [动] nurse
护(護)士 hùshi [名] nurse
护(護)照 hùzhào [名] passport

花 huā I [名] 1(指植物) flower 2(烟火) fireworks (pl) II [形] 1(多彩) multi-coloured (英), multi-colored (美) 2(有花的) floral ▷ 花篮 huālán flower basket 3(模糊) blurred ▷ 头昏眼花 tóuhūn yǎnhuā muddle-headed and bleary-eyed 4(虚假) superficial ▷ 花招 huāzhāo trick III [动] spend ▷ 花钱 huā qián spend money ▷ 花工夫 huā gōngfu put in effort
花费(費) huáfèi [动] spend ▷ 留学的花费很大。Liúxué de huāfèi hěn dà. It's very expensive to study abroad.
花生 huāshēng [名] peanut
花纹(紋) huāwén [名] decorative design

花园(園) huāyuán [名] garden

花招 huāzhāo [名] trick

划 huá [动] 1(拨水) row 2(合算) be worthwhile ▷ 划不来 huábulái not worth it 3(擦) scratch
→ see also/另见 huà

华(華) huá [名](中国) China ▷ 华人 huárén Chinese person

华(華)丽(麗) huálì [形] resplendent

华(華)侨(僑) huáqiáo [名] overseas Chinese

华(華)人 huárén [名] Chinese

滑 huá I [形] 1(光滑) slippery 2(油滑) crafty II [动] slip

滑冰 huábīng [动] ice skate

滑动(動) huádòng [动] slide

滑稽 huájī [形] comical

滑坡 huápō [动] 1(字) slide 2(喻) drop

滑雪 huáxuě [动] ski

化 huà I [名] chemistry ▷ 化肥 huàféi chemical fertilizer II [动] 1(变化) change ▷ 化装 huàzhuāng disguise oneself 2(消化) digest

化工 huàgōng [名] chemical industry

化石 huàshí [名] fossil

化学(學) huàxué [名] chemistry

化验(驗) huàyàn [动] test

化妆(妝) huàzhuāng [动] make oneself up

划(劃) huà I [名] 1(划分) demarcate ▷ 划分 huàfēn divide 2(划拨) transfer 3(计划) plan
→ see also/另见 huá

画(畫) huà I [动] 1(用铅笔) draw 2(用刷状，笔画) paint II [名] 1(用铅笔) drawing 2(用刷状，笔画) painting ▷ 油画 yóuhuà oil painting 3(笔画) stroke III [形] painted

画(畫)报(報) huàbào [名] pictorial

画(畫)家 huàjiā [名] painter

画(畫)像 huàxiàng [名] portrait

画(畫)展 huàzhǎn [名] art exhibition

话(話) huà I [名] words (pl) ▷ 说话 shuōhuà talk ▷ 对话 duìhuà conversation ▷ 谎话 huǎnghuà lie II [动] talk about ▷ 话旧 huàjiù reminisce

话(話)剧(劇) huàjù [名] stage play

话(話)题(題) huàtí [名] subject

怀(懷) huái I [名] 1(胸前) bosom 2(胸怀) mind II [动] 1(思念) think of 2(存有) keep ... in mind 3(有孕) become pregnant

怀(懷)念 huáiniàn [动] yearn for

怀(懷)疑 huáiyí [动] 1(认为是真) suspect 2(认为不可能) doubt

怀(懷)孕 huáiyùn [动] be pregnant

坏(壞) huài I [形] 1(不好) bad 2(程度深) extreme II [动] go off ▷ 空调坏了。 Kōngtiáo huài le. The air-conditioning has broken down. III [名] dirty trick

坏(壞)处(處) huàichu [名] harm

坏(壞)蛋 huàidàn [名](讳) bastard

坏(壞)话(話) huàihuà [名](不利的话) bad words (pl)

欢(歡) huān [形] 1(快乐) happy 2(活跃) vigorous

欢(歡)呼 huānhū [动] cheer

欢(歡)快 huānkuài [形] cheerful

欢(歡)乐(樂) huānlè [形] joyful

欢(歡)心 huānxīn [名] favour (英), favor (美)

欢(歡)迎 huānyíng [动] welcome ▷ 欢迎来中国。 Huānyíng lái Zhōngguó. Welcome to China.

还(還) huán [动] 1(回) return 2(归还) return ▷ 还债 huánzhài repay a debt 3(回报) repay ▷ 还价 huánjià haggle ▷ 还击 huánjī fight back
→ see also/另见 hái

环(環) huán I [名] 1(圆圈) ring ▷ 耳环 ěrhuán earring 2(环节) element ▷ 环节 huánjié element II [动] surround

环(環)保 huánbǎo [名](环境保护) huánjìng bǎohù environmental protection

环(環)境 huánjìng [名] environment

▷生活环境 shēnghuó huánjìng living conditions (pl)

环(環)绕(繞) huánrào [动] surround

缓(緩) huǎn I [形] 1 (慢) slow 2 (缓和) relaxed II [动] 1 (推迟) delay 2 (恢复) revive

缓(緩)慢 huǎnmàn [形] slow

幻 huàn [形] unreal

幻想 huànxiǎng I [动] dream II [名] fantasy

换(換) huàn [动] 1 (交换) exchange 2 (更换) replace

唤(喚) huàn [名] summon

唤(喚)醒 huànxǐng [动] (叫醒) wake up

患 huàn I [动] 1 (害) suffer from ▷患者 huànzhě sufferer 2 (忧虑) worry II [名] trouble

荒 huāng [形] 1 (荒芜) waste 2 (荒凉) desolate 3 (短缺) short 4 (荒歉) famine

慌 huāng [形] nervous

慌忙 huāngmáng [形] hurried

慌张(張) huāngzhāng [形] nervous

皇 huáng [名] emperor ▷皇帝 huángdì emperor ▷皇后 huánghòu empress

皇宫(宮) huánggōng [名] palace

黄 huáng I [形] 1 (指颜色) yellow 2 (色情) pornographic II [名] 1 (蛋黄) yolk 2 (黄金) gold

黄瓜 huángguā [名] cucumber

黄河 Huáng Hé [名] Yellow River

黄昏 huánghūn [名] dusk

黄金 huángjīn [名] gold

黄色 huángsè [名] 1 (指颜色) yellow 2 (色情) pornographic

黄油 huángyóu [名] butter

谎(謊) huǎng [名] lie

谎(謊)言 huǎngyán [名] lie

晃 huàng [动] shake

晃动(動) huàngdòng [动] rock

灰 huī I [名] 1 (灰烬) ash 2 (尘土) dust 3 (石灰) lime II [动] (消沉) be disheartened ▷灰暗 huī'àn gloomy

灰尘(塵) huīchén [名] dust

灰色 huīsè [名] (指颜色) grey (英), gray (美)

灰心 huīxīn [动] lose heart

恢 huī [形] vast

恢复(復) huīfù [动] recover

挥(揮) huī [动] 1 (挥舞) wave 2 (抹掉) wipe ... away 3 (指挥) command 4 (散出) scatter ▶挥发 huīfā evaporate

回(迴) huí I [动] 1 (旋转) circle 2 (还) return 3 (掉转) turn around ▷回头 huítóu turn one's head 4 (答复) reply ▷回信 huíxìn reply to a letter II [量] 1 (次数) time ▷我去过两回。 Wǒ qùguo liǎng huí. I have been there twice. 2 (章) chapter

回报(報) huíbào [动] (报答) repay

回(迴)避 huíbì [动] avoid

回答 huídá [动] answer

回(迴)复(復) huífù [动] (答复) reply

回顾(顧) huígù [动] look back

回合 huíhé [名] round

回话(話) huíhuà [动] reply

回扣 huíkòu [名] commission

回教 Huíjiào [名] Islam

回来(來) huílái [动] come back

回去 huíqù [动] go back

回声(聲) huíshēng [名] echo

回收 huíshōu [动] 1 (再利用) recycle 2 (收回) retrieve

回信 huíxìn [动] write in reply

回忆(憶) huíyì [动] recall

毁(毀) huǐ [动] 1 (破坏) destroy 2 (诽谤) defame

毁(毀)坏(壞) huǐhuài [动] destroy

汇(匯) huì I [动] 1 (汇合) converge 2 (聚集) gather 3 (划拨) transfer II [名] 1 (外汇) foreign exchange 2 (聚集物) collection ▶词汇 cíhuì vocabulary

汇(匯)报(報) huìbào [动] report

汇(匯)集 huìjí [动] collect
汇(匯)率 huìlǜ [名] exchange rate

会(會) huì I [动] 1 (聚合) assemble
2 (见面) meet ▸ 会客 huìkè receive a
guest 3 (理解) understand ▸ 领会
lǐnghuì understand 4 (通晓) be able to
▷ 会武术 huì wǔshù be able to do
martial arts II [助动] 1 (能做) can ▷ 我不
会下象棋。Wǒ bùhuì xià xiàngqí.
I can't play chess. 2 (擅长) ▷ 会过日子
huì guò rìzi know how to economize
3 (可能) might ▷ 明天会更热。Míngtiān
huì gèng rè. Tomorrow might be hotter.
III [名] 1 (集会) gathering 2 (团体)
association ▸ 学生会 xuéshēnghuì
student union 3 (城市) city ▸ 大都会
dàdūhuì metropolis 4 (时机)
opportunity ▸ 机会 jīhuì opportunity
→ see also/另见 kuài

Both 会 huì and 要 yào can be used to
express the future tense. 会 huì is
usually used to express a possible or
probable outcome, e.g. 明天会下雨
míngtiān huì xiàyǔ (it might rain
tomorrow); 要 yào refers to
something definite, e.g. 我明天要上
班 wǒ míngtiān yào shàngbān (I am
going to work tomorrow). 会 huì, 能
néng, and 可以 kěyǐ can all be used to
express ability and are sometimes
used interchangeably. Strictly, 会 huì
should express a learned ability, e.g.
我会说法语 wǒ huì shuō Fǎyǔ (I can
speak French), while 能 néng should
be used to express physical ability, e.g.
我能跑得很快 wǒ néng pǎo de hěn
kuài (I can run very fast).

会(會)话(話) huìhuà [动] converse
会(會)见(見) huìjiàn [动] meet
会(會)谈(談) huìtán [动] hold talks
会(會)议(議) huìyì [名] 1 (集会)
meeting 2 (机构) council
会(會)员(員) huìyuán [名] member

贿(賄) huì [名] bribe ▸ 贿赂 huìlù bribe

昏 hūn I [名] dusk II [形] 1 (黑暗) dark
▸ 昏暗 hūn'àn dim 2 (迷糊) muddled
III [动] faint
昏迷 hūnmí [动] be unconscious

荤(葷) hūn [名] meat

婚 hūn I [名] marriage II [动] marry
婚礼(禮) hūnlǐ [名] wedding ceremony
婚姻 hūnyīn [名] marriage

浑(渾) hún [形] 1 (浑浊) muddy 2 (糊涂)
muddled
浑(渾)蛋 húndàn [名] (讳) bastard
浑(渾)身 húnshēn [副] from head to
toe
浑(渾)浊(濁) húnzhuó [形] murky

馄(餛) hún see below/见下文
馄(餛)饨(飩) húntun [名] wonton

馄饨 húntun
In Chinese cooking, 馄饨 húntun is a
kind of dumpling filled with spiced
minced meat and other ingredients
such as chopped mushrooms, shrimps
etc. It is usually served in the soup in
which it is cooked. The English name
for 馄饨 comes from the Cantonese
pronunciation, wantan.

魂 hún [名] (灵魂) soul

混 hùn I [动] 1 (掺杂) mix 2 (蒙混) pass off
... as 3 (苟且生活) drift ▷ 混日子 hùn rìzi
drift through the days II [副] aimlessly
混合 hùnhé [动] mix
混乱(亂) hùnluàn [形] 1 (无秩序)
chaotic 2 (无条理) disordered
混淆 hùnxiáo [动] confuse

活 huó I [动] 1 (生存) live 2 (使生存) keep
... alive II [形] 1 (有生命) alive 2 (不固定)
flexible 3 (不死板) lively 4 (逼真) lifelike
III [副] completely IV [名] 1 (工作) work
2 (产品) product
活动(動) huódòng I [动] 1 (运动) take
exercise 2 (行动) operate 3 (动用关系)
use connections II [名] activity III [形]
movable
活该(該) huógāi [动] (口) serve ... right
活力 huólì [名] vitality
活泼(潑) huópō [形] lively
活期 huóqī [形] current ▷ 活期账号
huóqī zhànghào current account

活跃(躍) huóyuè [动] 1(使有生气) invigorate 2(积极从事) be active

火 huǒ I [名] 1(火焰) fire 2(枪支弹药) ammunition 3(医)(指内火) internal heat 4(喻)(愤怒) rage II [动] be in a rage III [形] 1(红色) flaming red ▶ 火红 huǒhóng flaming red 2(兴旺) prosperous
火柴 huǒchái [名] match
火车(車) huǒchē [名] train
火鸡(雞) huǒjī [名] turkey
火警 huǒjǐng [名] fire alarm
火山 huǒshān [名] volcano
火腿 huǒtuǐ [名] ham
火焰 huǒyàn [名] flame
火药(藥) huǒyào [名] gunpowder

伙(夥) huǒ I [名] 1(同伴) companion 2(指集体) partnership 3(伙食) meals (pl) II [量] group
伙(夥)伴 huǒbàn [名] companion
伙食 huǒshí [名] meals (pl)

或 huò [连] or
或许(許) huòxǔ [副] perhaps
或者 huòzhě I [副] maybe II [连] or

货(貨) huò [名] 1(货币) currency 2(货物) goods (pl) 3(人) person ▶ 蠢货 chǔnhuò idiot
货(貨)币(幣) huòbì [名] currency
货(貨)物 huòwù [名] goods (pl)

获(穫) huò [动] 1(捉住) capture 2(得到) obtain 3(收割) reap ▶ 收获 shōuhuò harvest
获(獲)得 huòdé [动] gain

祸(禍) huò [名] I [名] misfortune II [动] harm

j

几(幾) jī [名] small table ▶ 茶几 chájī tea table
→ see also/另见 jǐ
几(幾)乎 jīhū [副] almost

讥(譏) jī [动] mock
讥(譏)笑 jīxiào [动] jeer

饥(飢) jī I [形] hungry II [名] famine
饥(飢)饿(餓) jī'è [形] starving

机(機) jī I [名] 1(机器) machine ▶ 发动机 fādòngjī engine 2(飞机) aeroplane (英), airplane (美) ▶ 客机 kèjī airliner 3(枢纽) pivot ▶ 转机 zhuǎnjī turning point 4(机会) opportunity 5(机能) ▶ 有机体 yǒujītǐ organism II [形] quick-witted ▶ 机智 jīzhì ingenious
机(機)场(場) jīchǎng [名] airport
机(機)关(關) jīguān [名] 1(部门) department 2(机械) mechanism
机(機)会(會) jīhuì [名] opportunity
机(機)灵(靈) jīling [形] clever
机(機)器 jīqì [名] machine
机(機)械 jīxiè I [名] machinery II [形] rigid
机(機)遇 jīyù [名] opportunity

肌 jī [名] muscle
肌肉 jīròu [名] muscle

鸡(雞) jī [名] chicken ▶ 公鸡 gōngjī

cock (英), rooster (美) ▶ 母鸡 mǔjī hen

鸡(雞)蛋 jīdàn [名] egg

积(積) jī I [动] accumulate II [形] long-standing III [名] (数) product

积(積)极 jījí [形] 1 (肯定的) positive 2 (热心的) active

积(積)极性 jījíxìng [名] positive attitude

积(積)累 jīlěi [动] accumulate

积(積)蓄 jīxù I [动] save II [名] savings (pl)

基 jī I [名] base II [形] primary ▶ 基层 jīcéng grass roots

基本 jīběn I [形] 1 (根本) basic 2 (主要) essential 3 (基础) elementary II [副] basically

基础(礎) jīchǔ I [名] foundation II [形] basic

基督教 Jīdūjiào [名] Christianity

基金 jījīn [名] fund

激 jī I [动] 1 (涌起) surge 2 (刺激) catch a chill 3 (唤起) excite 4 (冰) chill II [形] violent

激动(動) jīdòng [动] excite ▷ 激动的孩子 jīdòng de háizi excited child ▷ 令人激动的电影 lìng rén jīdòng de diànyǐng exciting film

激光 jīguāng [名] laser

激烈 jīliè [形] intense

及 jí I [动] 1 (到达) reach 2 (比得上) be as good as 3 (赶上) be in time for II [连] and

及格 jígé [动] pass

及时(時) jíshí I [形] timely II [副] without delay

级(級) jí I [名] 1 (等级) level 2 (年级) year (英), grade (美) 3 (台阶) step II [量] step ▷ 100多级台阶 yībǎi duō jí táijiē a staircase of more than 100 steps

极(極) jí I [名] 1 (顶点) extreme 2 (指地球或磁体) pole ▶ 南极 nánjí the South Pole II [动] go to an extreme III [形] extreme ▶ 极限 jíxiàn limit IV [副] very

极(極)其 jíqí [副] extremely

即 jí I [动] 1 (书) (就是) mean 2 (靠近) approach 3 (到) ▶ 即位 jíwèi ascend the throne 4 (就着) ▷ 即兴演唱 jíxìng yǎnchàng ad-lib II [形] present ▶ 即日 jírì this very day III [副] immediately

即将(將) jíjiāng [副] soon

即使 jíshǐ [连] even if

急 jí I [形] 1 (着急) anxious 2 (急躁) impatient 3 (猛烈) ▷ 水流很急。shuǐliú hěn jí There's a strong current. 4 (紧急) urgent II [名] priority III [动] worry

急救 jíjiù [动] give first-aid

急忙 jímáng [副] hurriedly

急诊(診) jízhěn [名] emergency treatment

集 jí I [动] gather II [名] 1 (集市) market ▶ 赶集 gǎnjí go to market 2 (集子) anthology ▶ 诗集 shījí an anthology of poems 3 (册) part

集合 jíhé [动] assemble

集体(體) jítǐ [名] collective

集团(團) jítuán [名] group

集中 jízhōng [动] concentrate

几(幾) jǐ [数] 1 (用于疑问句) ▷ 昨天来了几位客人？Zuótiān láile jǐ wèi kèrén? How many customers came yesterday? 2 (用于陈述句) ▷ 几本书 jǐ běn shū several books ▷ 十几本书 shíjǐ běn shū more than ten books ▷ 几十本书 jǐshí běn shū several tens of books
→ see also/另见 jī

己 jǐ [名] self ▶ 自己 zìjǐ oneself

挤(擠) jǐ [动] 1 (拥挤) crowd 2 (时间集中) be close 3 (推人) elbow one's way 4 (贬) (指社交) push one's way 5 (牙膏、颜料) squeeze ... out ▶ 挤奶 jǐ nǎi milk 6 (时间) make 7 (排斥) rob ... of

计(計) jì I [动] 1 (核算) calculate ▶ 共计 gòngjì total 2 (打算) plan 3 (考虑) bother II [名] 1 (计谋) strategy 2 (测量仪器) gauge ▶ 温度计 wēndùjì thermometer

计(計)划(劃) jìhuà I [名] plan II [动] plan

计(計)算 jìsuàn [动] 1(数) calculate 2(筹划) plan 3(暗divide) scheme

计(計)算机(機) jìsuànjī [名] computer

计(計)算器 jìsuànqì [名] calculator

记(記) jì I [动] 1(记住) remember 2(记录) record II [名] 1(指书或文章) record ▶ 游记 yóujì travel journal ▶ 日记 rìjì diary 2(标志) mark 3(指皮肤) birthmark

记(記)得 jìde [动] remember

记(記)号(號) jìhao [名] mark

记(記)录(錄) jìlù I [动] (写下) write ... down II [名] 1(材料) record 2(指人) secretary 3(成绩) record

记(記)忆(憶) jìyì I [动] remember II [名] memory

记(記)者 jìzhě [名] journalist

纪(紀) jì I [名] 1 age ▶ 中世纪 zhōngshìjì the Middle Ages (pl) 2(指地质) period ▶ 侏罗纪 zhūluójì the Jurassic period 3(纪律) discipline II [动] record

纪(紀)律 jìlù [名] discipline

纪(紀)念 jìniàn [动] commemorate [名] memento

技 jì [名] 1(技艺) skill ▶ 技能 jìnéng skill ▶ 技巧 jìqiǎo technique 2(本领) ability ▶ 绝技 juéjì unique ability

技巧 jìqiǎo [名] technique

技术(術) jìshù [名] technology

技术(術)员(員) jìshùyuán [名] technician

季 jì [名] season ▶ 春季 chūnjì spring ▶ 旺季 wàngjì busy season

季节(節) jìjié [名] season

季军(軍)

既 jì I [副] already ▶ 既定 jìdìng fixed II [连] 1(表示兼而有之) ▷ 他既高又壮。 Tā jì gāo yòu zhuàng. He's tall and strong. 2(既然) since

既然 jìrán [连] since

继(繼) jì I [副] 1(接续) continuously ▶ 继任 jìrèn succeed to a post 2(接连) successively ▶ 相继 xiāngjì one after

another II [动] continue

继(繼)承 jìchéng [动] 1(遗产、文化等) inherit 2(遗志、未成事业) take ... on

继(繼)续(續) jìxù I [动] continue II [名] continuation

寄 jì [动] 1(邮递) post (英), mail (美) 2(付托) place 3(依附) depend on

加 jiā [动] 1(相加) ▷ 2加2等于4。 Èr jiā èr děngyú sì. Two plus two is four. 2(增加) increase 3(添加) add

加工 jiāgōng [动] 1(制作) process 2(完善) polish

加拿大 Jiānádà [名] Canada

加强(強) jiāqiáng [动] strengthen

加油 jiāyóu [动] 1(加燃料) refuel 2(加劲儿) make more effort ▷ 快, 加油! Kuài, jiāyóu! Come on, come on!

夹(夾) jiā I [动] 1(固定) get hold of 2(携带) carry ... under one's arm 3(使在中间) ▷ 两边高楼夹着一条狭窄的街道。 Liǎngbiān gāolóu jiāzhe yī tiáo xiázhǎi de jiēdào. A narrow street hemmed in by tall buildings on either side. 4(掺杂) mix ... with II [名] folder

家 jiā I [名] 1(家庭) family 2(住所) home 3(学派) school of thought 4(指人) ▷ 船家 chuánjiā boatman ▶ 农家 nóngjiā peasant ▶ 专家 zhuānjiā expert II [形] 1(饲养的) domestic ▶ 家畜 jiāchù domestic animal 2(嫡亲的) ▷ 家兄 jiāxiōng elder brother III [量] ▷ 一家公司 yī jiā gōngsī a company ▷ 两家人 liǎng jiā rén two families

measure word, used for families, companies, banks, factories, restaurants, hotels etc.

家(傢)伙 jiāhuo [名] 1(工具) tool 2(武器) weapon 3(人) guy

家(傢)具 jiājù [名] furniture

家庭 jiātíng [名] family

家务(務) jiāwù [名] housework

家乡(鄉) jiāxiāng [名] hometown

家长(長) jiāzhǎng [名] 1(一家之长) head of the family 2(父母) parent

假 jiǎ I [形] 1 (虚伪) false 2 (不真) artificial ▶ 假发 jiǎfà wig ▶ 假话 jiǎhuà lie II [连] if ▶ 假如 jiǎrú if
→ see also/另见 jià

假如 jiǎrú [连] if

假设(設) jiǎshè I [动] suppose II [名] hypothesis

假装(裝) jiǎzhuāng [动] pretend

价(價) jià [名] 1 (价格) price ▶ 物价 wùjià price 2 (价值) value

价(價)格 jiàgé [名] price

价(價)钱(錢) jiàqin [名] price

价(價)值 jiàzhí [名] value

驾(駕) jià I [动] 1 (驾驭) harness 2 (驾驶) drive II [代] (敬) ▶ 劳驾 láojià excuse me

驾(駕)驶(駛) jiàshǐ [动] steer

驾(駕)照 jiàzhào [名] driving licence (英), driver's license (美)

架 jià I [名] 1 (架子) frame ▶ 书架 shūjià bookshelf ▶ 脚手架 jiǎoshǒujià scaffolding 2 (指行为) ▶ 吵架 chǎojià quarrel ▶ 打架 dǎjià fight II [动] 1 (撑起) support 2 (招架) ward … off 3 (绑架) kidnap 4 (挽扶) support … under the arm III [量] ▶ 5架飞机 wǔ jià fēijī five planes ▷ 一架钢琴 yī jià gāngqín a piano
measure word, used for pianos, aircraft, machines etc.

假 jià [名] holiday ▶ 暑假 shǔjià summer holiday ▶ 病假 bìngjià sick leave
→ see also/另见 jiǎ

假条(條) jiàtiáo [名] note

尖 jiān I [形] 1 (锐利) pointed 2 (指声音) shrill 3 (敏锐) sensitive 4 (吝啬) stingy 5 (尖刻) biting II [名] 1 (尖端) tip ▶ 笔尖 bǐjiān pen tip 2 (精华) the best

尖锐(銳) jiānruì [形] 1 (锋利) sharp 2 (敏锐) penetrating 3 (刺耳) shrill

坚(堅) jiān I [形] hard II [名] stronghold III [副] firmly ▶ 坚信 jiānxìn firmly believe

坚(堅)持 jiānchí [动] go on

坚(堅)定 jiāndìng [形] steadfast

坚(堅)决(決) jiānjué [副] resolutely

坚(堅)强(強) jiānqiáng [形] strong

坚(堅)硬 jiānyìng [形] hard

间(間) jiān I [介] between ▶ 课间 kèjiān between lessons II [名] 1 (范围) ▶ 晚间 wǎnjiān in the evening ▶ 田间 tiánjiān field 2 (屋子) room ▶ 房间 fángjiān room ▶ 洗手间 xǐshǒujiān toilet III [量] ▷ 两间客厅 liǎng jiān kètīng two living rooms ▷ 一间病房 yī jiān bìngfáng one ward
measure word, used for rooms, lounges, hospital wards etc.

肩 jiān see below/见下文

肩膀 jiānbǎng [名] shoulder

艰(艱) jiān [形] difficult ▶ 艰辛 jiānxīn hardship

艰(艱)巨(鉅) jiānjù [形] formidable

艰(艱)苦 jiānkǔ [形] harsh

艰(艱)难(難) jiānnán [形] hard

监(監) jiān I [动] supervise ▶ 监视 jiānshì keep watch II [名] 1 (监狱) prison ▶ 探监 tànjiān visit a prison 2 (负责人) inspector ▶ 总监 zǒngjiān chief-inspector

监(監)督 jiāndū [动] supervise

监(監)狱(獄) jiānyù [名] prison

拣(揀) jiǎn [动] choose

俭(儉) jiǎn [形] frugal

俭(儉)朴(樸) jiǎnpǔ [形] economical

捡(撿) jiǎn [动] pick … up

检(檢) jiǎn [动] 1 (检查) examine ▶ 体检 tǐjiǎn medical examination 2 (检点) show restraint

检(檢)查 jiǎnchá I [动] examine II [名] self-criticism

减(減) jiǎn [动] 1 (减去) subtract 2 (减少) reduce 3 (降低) decrease ▶ 减退 jiǎntuì fail

减(減)肥 jiǎnféi [动] slim

减(減)轻(輕) jiǎnqīng [动] reduce

减(減)少 jiǎnshǎo [动] reduce

剪 jiǎn I [名] scissors (pl) II [动] 1 (铰) cut 2 (除去) eliminate
剪刀 jiǎndāo [名] scissors (pl)

简(簡) jiǎn I [形] simple II [动] simplify ▸ 简化 jiǎnhuà simplify
简(簡)单(單) jiǎndān [形] 1 (不复杂) simple 2 (草率) casual 3 (平凡) ▷ 这孩子能说两门外语，真不简单。Zhè háizi néng shuō liǎng mén wàiyǔ, zhēn bù jiǎndān. It is quite extraordinary that this child can speak two foreign languages.
简(簡)体(體)字 jiǎntǐzì [名] simplified characters (pl)

简体字 jiǎntǐzì

简体字 jiǎntǐzì (simplified characters) are the type of Chinese characters used today throughout China's Mainland, and mostly derive from the PRC government's efforts during the 1950s and 60s to make the script more accessible and improve literacy. The alternative and older form of the script, known as complex or traditional characters, 繁体字 fántǐzì, is used predominantly in Taiwan, Hong Kong and many overseas Chinese communities. The two systems are closely related and if you have learnt one then, with a little effort, the other form should not pose too many problems!

见(見) jiàn I [动] 1 (看到) see ▸ 罕见 hǎnjiàn rare 2 (接触) come into contact with ▷ 汽油见火就着。Qìyóu jiàn huǒ jiù zháo. Petrol ignites on contact with a flame. 3 (看得出) be visible ▸ 见效 jiànxiào take effect 4 (参照) see ▸ 见上图 jiàn shàngtú see the above diagram 5 (会见) meet ▸ 接见 jiējiàn receive II [名] opinion ▸ 偏见 piānjiàn prejudice III [助动] (书) ▷ 请见谅。Qǐng jiànliàng. Please excuse me.
见(見)面 jiànmiàn [动] meet

件 jiàn I [量] item ▷ 一件衣服 yī jiàn yīfu an item of clothing ▷ 两件事 liǎng jiàn shì two things II [名] correspondence

▷ 急件 jíjiàn urgent letter

建 jiàn [动] 1 (建造) build 2 (建立) found 3 (提出) propose ▸ 建议 jiànyì propose
建立 jiànlì [动] establish
建设(設) jiànshè [动] build
建议(議) jiànyì [动] propose
建筑(築) jiànzhù I [动] build II [名] building
建筑(築)师(師) jiànzhùshī [名] architect

健 jiàn I [形] ▸ 强健 qiángjiàn strong and healthy ▸ 健全 jiànquán sound II [动] 1 (使强健) strengthen ▸ 健身 jiànshēn keep fit 2 (善于) be good at ▸ 健谈 jiàntán be good at small-talk
健康 jiànkāng [形] healthy
健忘 jiànwàng [形] forgetful

渐(漸) jiàn [副] gradually
渐(漸)渐(漸) jiànjiàn [副] gradually

键(鍵) jiàn [名] key
键(鍵)盘(盤) jiànpán [名] keyboard

箭 jiàn [名] arrow

江 jiāng [名] 1 (大河) river 2 (长江) Yangtze

将(將) jiāng I [副] ▷ 他将成为一名医生。Tā jiāng chéngwéi yī míng yīshēng. He is going to become a doctor. II [动] 1 (下棋用语) check 2 (激) egg ... on III [介] with ▷ 请将车停在路边。Qǐng jiāng chē tíng zài lùbiān. Please stop the car by the side of the road.
将(將)军(軍) jiāngjūn [名] general
将(將)来(來) jiānglái [名] future
将(將)要 jiāngyào [副] ▷ 她将要做妈妈了。Tā jiāngyào zuò māma le. She is going to be a mother.

姜(薑) jiāng [名] ginger

讲(講) jiǎng [动] 1 (说) speak 2 (解释) explain 3 (谈) discuss 4 (讲求) emphasize ▷ 讲卫生 jiǎng wèishēng pay attention to hygiene
讲(講)话(話) jiǎnghuà [动] 1 (说话) speak 2 (发言) address

讲(講)台(臺) jiǎngtái [名] dais

讲(講)座 jiǎngzuò [名] course of lectures

奖(獎) jiǎng I [动] encourage ▶ 夸奖 kuājiǎng praise II [动] award

奖(獎)金 jiǎngjīn [名] bonus

奖(獎)励(勵) jiǎnglì [动] encourage and reward

奖(獎)品 jiǎngpǐn [名] trophy

奖(獎)学(學)金 jiǎngxuéjīn [名] scholarship

降 jiàng [动] 1 (落下) drop 2 (降低) reduce ▶ 降价 jiàngjià reduce prices

降低 jiàngdī [动] reduce

降落 jiàngluò [动] land

酱(醬) jiàng I [名] 1 (调味品) soya bean (英) 或 soybean (美) paste 2 (糊状食品) paste ▶ 果酱 guǒjiàng jam II [形] ▶ 酱肘子 jiàngzhǒuzi knuckle of pork in soy sauce

酱(醬)油 jiàngyóu [名] soy sauce

交 jiāo I [动] 1 (交出) hand ... in 2 (付给) pay 3 (托付) entrust 4 (结交) associate with ▶ 交友 jiāoyǒu make friends II [名] (交情) friendship ▶ 深交 shēnjiāo deep friendship

交叉 jiāochā I [动] 1 (相交) intersect 2 (穿插) alternate II [形] overlapping

交换(換) jiāohuàn [动] exchange

交际(際) jiāojì [动] socialize

交警 jiāojǐng [名] traffic police

交流 jiāoliú [动] exchange

交谈(談) jiāotán [动] talk

交通 jiāotōng [名] traffic

交往 jiāowǎng [动] have contact

交易 jiāoyì I [动] trade II [名] transaction

郊 jiāo [名] suburbs (pl) ▶ 郊外 jiāowài outskirts (pl)

郊区(區) jiāoqū [名] suburbs (pl)

骄(驕) jiāo [形] 1 (骄傲) arrogant ▶ 骄气 jiāoqì arrogance 2 (书) (猛烈) fierce

骄(驕)傲 jiāo'ào I [形] 1 (傲慢) arrogant 2 (自豪) proud II [名] pride

胶(膠) jiāo I [名] 1 (黏性物质) glue ▶ 万能胶 wànnéngjiāo all-purpose glue 2 (橡胶) rubber ▶ 胶鞋 jiāoxié rubber boots (pl) II [动] glue

胶(膠)卷 jiāojuǎn [名] film

胶(膠)囊 jiāonáng [名] capsule

教 jiāo [动] teach
→ see also/另见 jiào

焦 jiāo [形] 1 (成黄黑色) burnt 2 (着急) agitated ▶ 心焦 xīnjiāo feel agitated

焦急 jiāojí [形] anxious

角 jiāo [名] 1 (指动物) horn 2 (军号) bugle 3 (数) angle ▶ 直角 zhíjiǎo right angle 4 (角落) corner ▶ 墙角 qiángjiǎo corner of a wall

角度 jiǎodù [名] 1 (数) angle 2 (视角) point of view

角落 jiǎoluò [名] corner

饺(餃) jiǎo [名] Chinese dumpling ▶ 水饺 shuǐjiǎo Chinese dumpling

饺(餃)子 jiǎozi [名] dumpling

饺子 jiǎozi
  Chinese dumplings, wrapped with a
  thin doughy skin, are usually filled
  with minced meat and mixed
  vegetables. They are normally
  steamed or boiled, and served with
  vinegar, soy sauce and other spices.

脚(腳) jiǎo [名] 1 (指人、动物) foot ▶ 脚印 jiǎoyìn footprint 2 (指物体) base ▶ 山脚 shānjiǎo foot of a mountain

搅(攪) jiǎo [动] 1 (搅拌) stir 2 (混杂) mix 3 (搅扰) disturb

搅(攪)拌 jiǎobàn [动] stir

叫 jiào [动] 1 (喊叫) shout 2 (招呼) call 3 (菜、车) order 4 (称为) be called 5 (吩咐) order

叫喊 jiàohǎn [动] yell

叫做 jiàozuò [动] be called

较(較) jiào [动] 1 (比较) compare ▶ 较量 jiàoliàng test one's strength 2 (书) (计较) dispute

教 jiào I[动] teach ▶教导 jiàodǎo
instruct II[名] religion
→ see also/另见 jiāo

教材 jiàocái [名] teaching materials (pl)

教科书(書) jiàokēshū [名] textbook

教练(練) jiàoliàn [名] coach

教师(師) jiàoshī [名] teacher

教室 jiàoshì [名] classroom

教授 jiàoshòu I[名] professor II[动]
lecture in

教学(學) jiàoxué [名] 1(知识传授)
teaching 2(教与学) teaching and
study

教训(訓) jiàoxun I[名] lesson II[动]
teach ... a lesson

教育 jiàoyù I[名] education II[动]
educate

教员(員) jiàoyuán [名] teacher

阶(階) jiē [名] 1(台阶) step 2(官阶) rank

阶(階)段 jiēduàn [名] stage

阶(階)级(級) jiējí [名] class

结(結) jiē [动] bear ▶结果 jiēguǒ bear
fruit
→ see also/另见 jié

结(結)实(實) jiēshi [形] 1(坚固耐用)
sturdy 2(健壮) strong

接 jiē [动] 1(靠近) draw near 2(连接)
connect 3(托住) catch 4(接收) receive
▷接电话 jiē diànhuà answer the phone
5(迎接) meet 6(接替) take over

接触(觸) jiēchù [动] (交往) come into
contact with

接待 jiēdài [动] receive

接到 jiēdào [动] receive

接见(見) jiējiàn [动] have an interview
with

接近 jiējìn I[动] approach II[形]
approachable

接受 jiēshòu [动] accept

接着(著) jiēzhe [动] 1(用手接) catch
2(紧跟着) follow

街 jiē [名] 1(街道) street 2(方)(集市)
market

街道 jiēdào [名] 1(马路) street 2(社区)
neighbourhood (英), neighborhood (美)

节(節) jié I[名] 1(连接处) joint 2(段落)
paragraph 3(节日) festival ▶圣诞节
Shèngdàn Jié Christmas 4(事项) item
▶细节 xìjié details (pl) 5(节操) moral
fibre (英) 或 fiber (美) ▶气节 qìjié
integrity III[动] 1(节约) save 2(删节)
abridge II[量] 1(指部分) section ▷一节
管子 yī jié guǎnzi a length of pipe 2 ▷三
节课 sān jié kè three classes ▷四节车厢
sì jié chēxiāng four carriages ▷两节电
池 liǎng jié diànchí two batteries
measure word, used for school
classes, carriages, batteries etc.

节(節)目 jiémù [名] programme (英),
program (美)

节(節)拍 jiépāi [名] beat

节(節)日 jiérì [名] festival

节(節)省 jiéshěng [动] conserve

节(節)约(約) jiéyuē [动] save

结(結) jié I[动] 1(织编) tie ▶结网
jiéwǎng weave a net 2(结合) unite
3(凝聚) freeze ▶结冰 jiébīng ice up
4(了结) settle up ▶结账 jiézhàng settle
up II[名] 1(绳扣) knot ▶活结 huójié
slip-knot 2(字据) written undertaking
3(生理) node
→ see also/另见 jiē

结(結)构(構) jiégòu [名] composition

结(結)果 jiéguǒ I[名] result II[副] in
the end

结(結)合 jiéhé [动] 1(联系) combine
2(结为夫妇) become husband and wife

结(結)婚 jiéhūn [动] get married

结(結)论(論) jiélùn [名] conclusion

结(結)束 jiéshù [动] end

捷 jié I[形] quick ▶敏捷 mǐnjié nimble
II[名] victory

捷径(徑) jiéjìng [名] short cut

姐 jiě [名] elder sister

姐姐 jiějie [名] elder sister

姐妹 jiěmèi [名] sisters (pl)

解 jiě [动] 1(分开) divide ▶解剖 jiěpōu
dissect 2(解开) untie 3(解除) relieve
4(解答) answer ▶解题 jiětí solve a
problem 5(理解) understand

解答 jiědá [动] answer

解放 jiěfàng [动] liberate
解雇(僱) jiěgù [动] fire
解决(決) jiějué [动] 1(处理) resolve 2(消灭) annihilate
解释(釋) jiěshì [动] explain

介 jiè [动] be situated between
介绍(紹) jièshào [动] 1(使相识) introduce 2(推荐) sponsor 3(使了解) give an introduction to

届(屆) jiè I [动] fall due ▸ 届期 jièqī at the appointed time II [量] 1(指毕业的班级) year ▸ 82届毕业生 bā èr jiè bìyèshēng the class of '82 2(指大会、首脑) ▸ 第10届奥运会 dì shí jiè Àoyùnhuì the tenth Olympic Games® ▸ 第26届总统 dì èrshíliù jiè zǒngtǒng the twenty-sixth president

▌ measure word, used for conferences, sports events, trade fairs, terms of office etc.

界 jiè [名] 1(界限) boundary (pl) 2(阶层) circles (pl) 3(范围) range 4(类别) category

借 jiè [动] 1(借入) borrow 2(借出) lend 3(假托) use ... as a means of 4(凭借) make use of
借口 jièkǒu I [动] use ... as an excuse II [名] excuse
借助 jièzhù [动] enlist the help of

斤 jīn [量] unit of weight, equal to 500 grams

今 jīn I [形] 1(现在的) present 2(当前的) current II [名] today
今后(後) jīnhòu [副] from now on
今年 jīnnián [名] this year
今天 jīntiān [名] today

金 jīn I [名] 1(化) gold 2(金属) metal ▸ 五金 wǔjīn hardware 3(钱) money II [形] 1(金色的) golden ▸ 金发 jīnfà blonde hair
金融 jīnróng [名] finance
金属(屬) jīnshǔ [名] metal
金子 jīnzi [名] gold

仅(僅) jǐn [副] only
仅(僅)仅(僅) jǐnjǐn [副] just

尽(儘) jǐn I [副] 1(尽量) as far as possible ▸ 尽快 jǐnkuài as early as possible 2(最) most 3(表示继续) constantly II [动] 1(不超过) take no more than 2(考虑在先) give priority to
→ see also/另见 jìn
尽(儘)管 jǐnguǎn I [副] without reserve ▸ 有话尽管说。Yǒu huà jǐnguǎn shuō. If there's something you'd like to say please don't hold back. II [连] even though
尽(儘)量 jǐnliàng [副] to the best of one's ability
尽(儘)早 jǐnzǎo [副] as soon as possible

紧(緊) jǐn I [形] 1(不松) tight 2(牢固) secure 3(接近) close 4(急迫) pressing 5(严格) strict 6(拮据) short of money II [动] tighten
紧(緊)急 jǐnjí [形] urgent
紧(緊)张(張) jǐnzhāng [形] 1(激烈) intense 2(不安) nervous 3(不足) in short supply

尽(盡) jìn I [动] 1(完) exhaust 2(达到极限) go to extremes 3(充分发挥) use ... to the full 4(努力完成) strive to accomplish II [形] complete
→ see also/另见 jǐn
尽(盡)力 jìnlì [动] try one's hardest
尽(盡)量 jìnliàng [副] do all one can

进(進) jìn [动] 1(前进) advance 2(进入) enter 3(接收) bring ... in ▸ 进货 jìnhuò stock up 4(吃食) eat 5(呈上) submit 6(攻进) enter ▸ 进球 jìnqiú score a goal
进(進)步 jìnbù I [动] improve II [形] advanced
进(進)攻 jìngōng [动] attack
进(進)化 jìnhuà [动] evolve
进(進)口 jìnkǒu [动] import
进(進)来(來) jìnlái [动] come in
进(進)去 jìnqù [动] enter
进(進)入 jìnrù [动] 1(走进) enter 2(到了) reach 3(到位) get inside
进(進)行 jìnxíng [动] carry ... out
进(進)修 jìnxiū [动] take a refresher course

近 jìn [形] 1(不远) near ▸ 近日 jìnrì recently 2(接近) close 3(亲近) close to
近来(來) jìnlái [副] recently
近视(視) jìnshì [形] short-sighted (英), near-sighted (美)

劲(勁) jìn [名] 1(力气) strength 2(情绪) spirit 3(态度) manner 4(趣味) fun

禁 jìn I [动] 1(禁止) forbid 2(监禁) imprison ▸ 禁闭 jìnbì lock ... up II [名] taboo
→ see also/另见 jīn
禁止 jìnzhǐ [动] forbid

京 jīng [名] 1(首都) capital 2(北京) Beijing
京剧(劇) jīngjù [名] Beijing opera

京剧 jīngjù
京剧 jīngjù is a form of Chinese traditional opera which enjoys a history of over two hundred years, and is regarded as one of the most important Chinese cultural heritages. The performances combine singing, acting, music, dialogue, dancing and acrobatics. Different roles follow different patterns of acting, which are all rather symbolic, suggestive and exaggerated.

经(經) jīng I [名] 1(经线) warp 2(指中医) channels (pl) 3(经度) longitude 4(经典) scripture ▸ 佛经 fójīng Buddhist sutra II [动] 1(经营) run ▸ 经商 jīngshāng be in business 2(经受) endure 3(经过) ▸ 途经西安 tújīng Xī'ān go via Xi'an II [形] regular
经(經)常 jīngcháng I [形] day-to-day II [副] often
经(經)过(過) jīngguò I [动] 1(通过) pass 2(延续) ▸ 经过3年的恋爱，他们终于结婚了。Jīngguò sān nián de liàn'ài, tāmen zhōngyú jiéhūn le. Having been together for three years, they finally got married. 3(经历) ▸ 企业经过裁员缩减了经费开支。Qǐyè jīngguò cáiyuán suōjiǎn le jīngfèi kāizhī. Business expenditure was reduced through staff cutbacks.
II [名] course
经(經)济(濟) jīngjì I [名] 1(社会生产关系) economy 2(个人财政状况) financial situation II [形] 1(有关国民经济) economic 2(实惠) economical ▸ 经济舱 jīngjìcāng economy-class cabin
经(經)理 jīnglǐ [名] manager
经(經)历(歷) jīnglì [动] experience
经(經)验(驗) jīngyàn [名] experience

惊(驚) jīng [动] 1(紧张) start 2(惊动) startle
惊(驚)奇 jīngqí [形] surprised
惊(驚)人 jīngrén [形] amazing
惊(驚)喜 jīngxǐ [动] be pleasantly surprised
惊(驚)讶(訝) jīngyà [形] astonished

精 jīng I [形] 1(经挑选的) refined ▸ 精兵 jīngbīng crack troops 2(完美) excellent 3(细密) precise 4(心细) sharp ▸ 精明 jīngmíng shrewd 5(精通) skilled II [名] 1(精华) essence ▸ 酒精 jiǔjīng alcohol 2(精力) energy III [副] (方) extremely
精彩 jīngcǎi [形] wonderful
精力 jīnglì [名] energy
精确(確) jīngquè [形] precise
精神 jīngshén [名] 1(主观世界) mind 2(宗旨) gist
精神 jīngshen I [名] energy II [形] energetic
精通 jīngtōng [动] be proficient in

井 jǐng I [名] 1(用于取水) well 2(井状物) ▸ 天井 tiānjǐng skylight ▸ 矿井 kuàngjǐng mine shaft II [形] neat

景 jǐng I [名] 1(风景) scenery 2(情形) situation ▸ 背景 bèijǐng background 3(布景) scene ▸ 外景 wàijǐng outdoor scene II [动] admire
景点(點) jǐngdiǎn [名] scenic spot
景色 jǐngsè [名] scenery

警 jǐng I [形] alert ▸ 警惕 jǐngtì on the alert II [动] 1(使警觉) warn 2(戒备) be on the alert III [名] 1(危急) alarm ▸ 报警 bàojǐng raise the alarm 2(警察) police ▸ 巡警 xúnjǐng an officer on the beat

警报(報) jǐngbào [名] alarm
警察 jǐngchá [名] police
警告 jǐnggào [动] warn

竞(競) jìng [动] compete
竞(競)赛(賽) jìngsài [名] competition
竞(競)争(爭) jìngzhēng [动] compete

敬 jìng I [动] 1(尊重) respect 2(恭敬地给) offer II [形] respectful
敬爱(愛) jìng'ài [动] revere
敬礼(禮) jìnglǐ [动] salute

静(靜) jìng [形] 1(不动) still 2(无声) quiet

镜(鏡) jìng [名] 1(镜子) mirror 2(指光学器具) lens ▷ 眼镜 yǎnjìng glasses
镜(鏡)子 jìngzi [名] mirror

纠(糾) jiū [动] 1(缠绕) entangle 2(集合) assemble 3(督察) supervise 4(改正) correct
纠(糾)正 jiūzhèng [动] correct

究 jiū I [动] investigate II [副] actually
究竟 jiūjìng I [名] outcome II [副] actually

九 jiǔ [数] nine
九月 jiǔyuè [名] September

久 jiǔ [形] 1(时间长) long 2(时间长短) long

玖 jiǔ [数] nine
This is the character for "nine", which is mainly used in banks, on receipts etc. to prevent mistakes and forgery.

酒 jiǔ [名] alcohol ▷ 葡萄酒 pútáojiǔ wine ▷ 敬酒 jìngjiǔ propose a toast

旧(舊) jiù I [形] 1(过时) old 2(陈旧) used II [名] old friend

救 jiù [动] save
救护(護)车(車) jiùhùchē [名] ambulance
救命 jiùmìng [动] save a life ▷ 救命啊! Jiùmìng a! Help!

就 jiù I [动] 1(靠近) move close to 2(开始) take ... up 3(完成) accomplish 4(趁) take the opportunity 5(搭配着吃) eat ... with II [副] 1(强调时间短) shortly 2(早已) already 3(表示紧接着) as soon as 4(表示条件关系) then 5(强调数量多) as much as 6(仅仅) only 7(原本) already 8(表示坚决) simply 9(强调事实) exactly 10(表示容忍) even though III [连] even if IV [介] on
就是 jiùshì I [副] 1(表示赞同) exactly 2(表示坚决) still 3(表示强调) really 4(确定范围) only II [助] ▷ 你干就是了，没人说你。Nǐ gàn jiùshì le, méi rén shuō nǐ. Just go ahead and do it — no one will blame you! III [连] even if
就算 jiùsuàn [连] even if

舅 jiù [名] 1(舅父) uncle 2(妻子的弟兄) brother-in-law
舅舅 jiùjiu [名] uncle

居 jū I [动] 1(住) live 2(在) be II [名] house
居住 jūzhù [动] live

局 jú [名] 1(棋盘) chessboard 2(比赛) game ▷ 平局 píngjú a draw 3(形势) situation ▷ 时局 shíjú current political situation 4(聚会) gathering ▷ 饭局 fànjú dinner party 5(圈套) ruse ▷ 骗局 piànjú fraud 6(部分) part 7(机关部门) department 8(业务机构) office II [量] set ▷ 我赢了这局棋。Wǒ yíngle zhè jú qí. I won the chess game.
局长(長) júzhǎng [名] director

橘 jú [名] tangerine
橘子 júzi [名] orange ▷ 橘子汁 júzi zhī orange juice

举(舉) jǔ I [动] 1(往上托) raise ▷ 举重 jǔzhòng weightlifting 2(兴起) mobilize ▷ 举兵 jǔbīng dispatch troops 3(选举) elect 4(提出) cite ▷ 举例 jǔlì cite an example II [名] act III [形] (书) whole
举(舉)办(辦) jǔbàn [动] hold
举(舉)行 jǔxíng [动] hold

巨(鉅) jù [形] huge
巨大 jùdà [形] huge
巨人 jùrén [名] giant

句 jù I [名] sentence II [量] ▷ 说几句话 shuō jǐ jù huà say a few words ▷ 写两句诗 xiě liǎng jù shī write two lines of verse

▌ measure word, used for sentences, and lines in a speech, song or poem

句子 jùzi [名] sentence

拒 jù [动] 1 (抵抗) resist 2 (拒绝) refuse
拒绝(絕) jùjué [动] refuse

具 jù I [动] have II [名] utensil ▶ 玩具 wánjù toy
具备(備) jùbèi [动] have
具体(體) jùtǐ [形] 1 (明确) detailed 2 (特定) particular
具有 jùyǒu [动] have

俱 jù [副] ▷ 面面俱到 miàn miàn jù dào attend to each and every aspect
俱乐(樂)部 jùlèbù [名] club

剧(劇) jù I [名] drama ▶ 喜剧 xǐjù comedy II [形] severe ▶ 剧变 jùbiàn dramatic change
剧(劇)场(場) jùchǎng [名] theatre (英), theater (美)
剧(劇)烈 jùliè [形] severe
剧(劇)院 jùyuàn [名] 1 (剧场) theatre (英), theater (美) 2 (剧团) company

据(據) jù I [动] 1 (占据) occupy ▶ 盘据 pánjù forcibly occupy 2 (凭借) rely on ▶ 据点 jùdiǎn stronghold II [介] according to III [名] evidence ▶ 收据 shōujù receipt
据(據)说(說) jùshuō [动] be said

距 jù [名] distance
距离(離) jùlí [动] be at a distance from

锯(鋸) jù I [名] saw II [动] saw

卷(捲) juǎn I [动] 1 (裹成筒形) roll ... up 2 (撮起) sweep ... up 3 (喻) (牵涉) be swept up in II [名] roll III [量] roll ▷ 一卷卫生纸 yī juǎn wèishēngzhǐ a roll of toilet paper

决(決) jué I [动] 1 (决定) decide 2 (执行死刑) execute 3 (决口) burst 4 (定胜负) decide on a result ▶ 决战 juézhàn decisive battle II [副] under any circumstances III [形] decisive ▶ 果决 guǒjué resolute
决(決)定 juédìng [动] 1 (打定主意) decide 2 (表示条件关系) determine
决(決)心 juéxīn [名] determination

觉(覺) jué I [动] 1 (感觉) feel 2 (觉悟) become aware of II [名] sense ▶ 知觉 zhījué consciousness
觉(覺)得 juéde [动] 1 (感到) feel 2 (认为) think
觉(覺)悟 juéwù [名] awareness

绝(絕) jué I [动] 1 (断绝) cut ... off ▶ 隔绝 géjué isolate 2 (穷尽) exhaust 3 (无后代) have no descendants 4 (死) die II [形] 1 (不通) hopeless ▶ 绝路 juélù blind alley 2 (高超) superb III [副] 1 (最) extremely ▶ 绝密 juémì top secret 2 (绝对) absolutely
绝(絕)对(對) juéduì I [形] absolute II [副] absolutely
绝(絕)望 juéwàng [动] feel desperate

军(軍) jūn I [名] 1 (军队) army ▶ 参军 cānjūn enlist 2 (指军队编制单位) regiment 3 (指集体) forces (pl) II [形] military ▶ 军费 jūnfèi military expenditure
军(軍)队(隊) jūnduì [名] troops (pl)
军(軍)官 jūnguān [名] officer
军(軍)人 jūnrén [名] soldier
军(軍)事 jūnshì [名] military affairs (pl)

k

咖 kā *see below*/见下文
→ *see also*/另见 gā

咖啡 kāfēi [名] coffee ▷ 速溶咖啡 sùróng kāfēi instant coffee

卡 kǎ I [量] (卡路里) calorie II [名] (卡片) card

卡车(車) kǎchē [名] lorry (英), truck (美)

卡拉OK kǎlā'ōukèi [名] karaoke

卡通 kǎtōng [名] cartoon

开(開) kāi [动] 1 (打开) open ▷ 开门 kāimén open the door 2 (银行、商店) be open 3 (绽放) bloom 4 (松开) come undone 5 (驾驶) drive ▷ 开汽车 kāi qìchē drive a car 6 (办) open ... up ▷ 开公司 kāi gōngsī start up a business 7 (开始) start ▷ 开课 kāikè give a course ▷ 开学 kāixué start school ▷ 开演 kāiyǎn start the show 8 (举行) hold ▷ 开会 kāihuì have a meeting 9 (写出) write ... out 10 (灯、电器、煤气) turn on ▷ 开灯 kāidēng turn on the light 11 (沸腾) boil ▷ 水开了。Shuǐ kāi le. The water was just boiled. 12 (饭) serve ▷ 开饭了。Kāifàn le. Dinner is ready.

开(開)刀 kāidāo [动] operate on

开(開)放 kāifàng [动] 1 (解禁) open ▷ 对外开放政策 duìwài kāifàng zhèngcè the opening-up policy 2 (开朗) be open-minded

开(開)关(關) kāiguān [名] switch

开(開)户(戶) kāihù [动] open an account

开(開)会(會) kāihuì [动] have a meeting

开(開)课(課) kāikè [动] 1 (开学) start 2 (授课) teach a course

开(開)朗 kāilǎng [形] (指性格) cheerful

开(開)明 kāimíng [形] enlightened

开(開)幕 kāimù [动] 1 (指演出) start 2 (指会) open

开(開)辟(闢) kāipì [动] 1 (开通) open ... up 2 (开发) develop

开(開)始 kāishǐ I [动] start, begin II [名] beginning

开(開)水 kāishuǐ [名] boiling water

开(開)头(頭) kāitóu I [动] begin II [名] beginning

开(開)玩笑 kāi wánxiào [动] joke ▷ 别拿我开玩笑。Bié ná wǒ kāi wánxiào. Don't make fun of me.

开(開)心 kāixīn [形] happy

开(開)展 kāizhǎn [动] launch

开(開)支 kāizhī [动] spend

刊 kān I [动] (出版) publish II [名] periodical ▷ 报刊 bàokān the press

刊登 kāndēng [动] publish

刊物 kānwù [名] periodical

看 kān [动] 1 (照料) look after ▷ 看家 kānjiā look after the house 2 (看管) watch over
→ *see also*/另见 kàn

砍 kǎn [动] 1 (劈) chop 2 (减) cut

看 kàn [动] 1 (观看) look at ▷ 看到 kàndào see ▷ 看电视 kàn diànshì watch TV 2 (阅读) read 3 (认为) think ▷ 看成 kànchéng consider 4 (拜访) visit ▷ 看望 kànwàng visit 5 (照料) look after 6 (对待) treat 7 (诊治) treat ▷ 看病 kànbìng see a doctor 8 (取决于) depend on
→ *see also*/另见 kān

看不起 kànbuqǐ [动] look down on

看待 kàndài [动] regard ▷ 当朋友看待 dàng péngyou kàndài regard as a friend

看法 kànfǎ [名] opinion
看好 kànhǎo [动] look good
看见(見) kànjiàn [动] see
看来(來) kànlái [动] seem

康 kāng [形] (健康) healthy ▶ 康复 kāngfù recover

慷 kāng see below/见下文
慷慨 kāngkǎi [形] (大方) generous

扛 káng [动] shoulder

抗 kàng [动] 1(抵抗) resist 2(抗拒) refuse
抗议(議) kàngyì [动] protest

考 kǎo [动] 1(测试) have an exam ▶ 考上 kǎoshàng pass the entrance exam
2(检查) check ▶ 考察 kǎochá investigate
考虑(慮) kǎolǜ [动] consider
考试(試) kǎoshì [动] sit an exam
考验(驗) kǎoyàn [动] test

拷 kǎo [动] (拷贝) copy

烤 kǎo [动] 1(指东西) roast ▶ 烤鸭 kǎoyā roast duck 2(指人体) warm oneself ▶ 烤火 kǎohuǒ warm oneself by a fire

靠 kào [动] 1(倚) lean 2(近) keep to 3(依赖) rely on 4(信赖) trust

科 kē [名] 1(指学术) discipline ▶ 文科 wénkē humanities (pl) 2(指部门) department
科技 kējì [名] science and technology
科目 kēmù [名] subject
科学(學) kēxué I [名] science II [形] scientific
科学(學)家 kēxuéjiā [名] scientist
科研 kēyán [名] scientific research

棵 kē [量] ▷ 一棵水仙 yī kē shuǐxiān a narcissus ▷ 三百棵树 sānbǎi kē shù three hundred trees
▌measure word, used for plants, trees and vegetables

颗(顆) kē [量] ▷ 一颗种子 yī kē zhǒngzi a seed ▷ 一颗汗珠 yī kē hànzhū a bead of sweat

▌measure word, used for small, round objects

磕 kē [动] bump

壳(殼) ké [名] shell

咳 ké [动] cough
咳嗽 késou [动] cough

可 kě I [动] (同意) approve II [助动] 1(可以) can 2(值得) III [连] but
可爱(愛) kě'ài [形] adorable
可悲 kěbēi [形] lamentable
可靠 kěkào [形] reliable
可乐(樂) kělè [名] Coke®
可怜(憐) kělián I [形] pitiful II [动] pity
可能 kěnéng I [形] possible II [副] maybe III [名] possibility ▶ 可能性 kěnéngxìng possibility
可怕 kěpà [形] frightening
可是 kěshì [连] but ▷ 这个小镇不大, 可是很热闹。 Zhège xiǎozhèn bù dà, kěshì hěn rènao. This is a small town, but it's very lively.
可惜 kěxī I [形] regrettable II [副] regrettably
可笑 kěxiào [形] 1(令人耻笑) ridiculous 2(引人发笑) funny
可以 kěyǐ I [助动] 1(能够) can 2(有权) may II [形] (不坏) not bad

可以 kěyǐ, 能 néng, and 会 huì can all be used to express ability and are sometimes used interchangeably. Both 可以 kěyǐ and 能 néng can express being able to do something because you have been granted permission, e.g. 你可以/能借我的照相机 nǐ kěyǐ/néng jiè wǒ de zhàoxiàngjī (you may/can borrow my camera). Strictly, 能 néng should be used to express physical ability, e.g. 我能跑得很快 wǒ néng pǎo de hěn kuài (I can run very fast), while 会 huì should express a learned ability, e.g. 我会说法语 wǒ huì shuō Fǎyǔ (I can speak French).

渴 kě I [形] thirsty ▶ 渴望 kěwàng long for II [副] eagerly

克 kè I [动] 1 (克制) restrain 2 (战胜) overcome II [量] gram
克服 kèfú [动] (战胜) overcome
克隆 kèlóng [动] clone

刻 kè I [动] engrave II [名] 1 (雕刻物品) engraving 2 (指十五分钟) quarter
刻苦 kèkǔ [形] hardworking

客 kè [名] 1 (客人) visitor ▶ 客厅 kètīng living room 2 (旅客) traveller (英), traveler (美) ▶ 客车 kèchē passenger train 3 (顾客) customer ▶ 客户 kèhù customer
客观 (觀) kèguān [形] objective
客气 (氣) kèqi I [形] polite II [动] be polite
客人 kèrén [名] guest

课 (課) kè [名] 1 (学科) subject 2 (学时) class 3 (单元) lesson
课 (課) 本 kèběn [名] textbook
课 (課) 程 kèchéng [名] course ▶ 课程表 kèchéngbiǎo school timetable
课 (課) 堂 kètáng [名] classroom
课 (課) 题 (題) kètí [名] (论题) topic
课 (課) 文 kèwén [名] text

肯 kěn [助动] be willing
肯定 kěndìng I [动] confirm II [形] 1 (确定的) affirmative 2 (明确的) clear III [副] certainly

空 kōng I [形] empty ▶ 空虚 kōngxū empty II [名] sky ▶ 空中小姐 kōngzhōng xiǎojiě stewardess
→ see also/另见 kòng
空间 (間) kōngjiān [名] space
空军 (軍) kōngjūn [名] air force
空调 (調) kōngtiáo [名] air conditioner
空气 (氣) kōngqì [名] (大气) air
空前 kōngqián [形] unprecedented

孔 kǒng [名] hole
孔子 Kǒngzǐ [名] Confucius

孔子 Kǒngzǐ
　孔子 Kǒngzǐ, Confucius, (trad. 551-479 BC) was a hugely influential thinker. A posthumous compilation of his sayings, 《论语》 Lúnyǔ, The Analects, is China's most important philosophical work, and was the key text on which much of the traditional Chinese education system was based.

恐 kǒng fear
恐怖 kǒngbù I [形] terrifying II [名] terror ▶ 恐怖主义 kǒngbù zhǔyì terrorism
恐龙 (龍) kǒnglóng [名] dinosaur
恐怕 kǒngpà [副] 1 (担心) fearfully 2 (大概) probably

空 kòng I [动] leave ... empty II [形] vacant ▶ 空白 kòngbái blank ▶ 空缺 kòngquē vacancy III [名] 1 (空间) space 2 (时间) free time ▶ 空儿 kòngr spare time ▶ 有空 yǒu kòng have free time
→ see also/另见 kōng

控 kòng [动] 1 (控制) control 2 (控告) charge
控制 kòngzhì [动] control

口 kǒu I [名] 1 (嘴) mouth ▶ 口才 kǒucái eloquence ▶ 口吃 kǒuchī stammering ▶ 口红 kǒuhóng lipstick 2 (人口) ▶ 家口 jiākǒu family member ▶ 口味 kǒuwèi taste 3 (指容器) rim ▶ 瓶口 píngkǒu the mouth of a bottle 4 (指端口) ▶ 出口 chūkǒu exit ▶ 入口 rùkǒu entrance ▶ 窗口 chuāngkǒu window 5 (缝) split II [量] ▷ 我家有五口人。 Wǒ jiā yǒu wǔ kǒu rén. There are five people in my family.
▌ measure word, used for the number of people in a family
口袋 kǒudài [名] bag
口号 (號) kǒuhào [名] slogan
口渴 kǒukě [形] thirsty ▷ 他口渴了。 Tā kǒukě le. He's thirsty.
口气 (氣) kǒuqì [名] (语气) tone
口试 (試) kǒushì [名] oral exam
口头 (頭) kǒutóu [名] 1 (嘴) word 2 (口语) ▷ 口头作文 kǒutóu zuòwén oral composition
口信 kǒuxìn [名] message
口音 kǒuyīn [名] (方音) accent
口语 (語) kǒuyǔ [名] spoken language

扣 kòu I [动] 1(拉紧) fasten 2(朝下) put ... upside down 3(抓) arrest ▶扣留 kòuliú arrest 4(减) deduct II [名] button ▶扣子 kòuzi button

哭 kū [动] cry

苦 kǔ I [形] 1(苦涩) bitter 2(艰苦) hard II [动] (使受苦) be hard on III [副] painstakingly ▶苦练 kǔ liàn train hard IV [名] suffering ▶吃苦 chīkǔ bear hardships
苦难(難) kǔnàn I [名] hardship II [形] hard
苦恼(惱) kǔnǎo [形] distressed
库(庫)存 kùcún [名] stock

裤(褲) kù [名] trousers (英) (pl) pants (美) (pl) ▶裤子 kùzi trousers (英) (pl) pants (美) (pl)

夸(誇) kuā [动] 1(夸大) exaggerate 2(夸奖) praise
夸(誇)奖(獎) kuājiǎng [动] praise
夸(誇)张(張) kuāzhāng I [形] exaggerated II [名] hyperbole

垮 kuǎ [动] 1(坍塌) collapse ▶垮台 kuǎtái collapse 2(伤身) wear down

胯 kuà [名] hip

跨 kuà [动] 1(迈步) step 2(骑) mount 3(超越) surpass ▶跨国 kuàguó transnational

会(會) kuài [名] accounting ▶财会 cáikuài finance and accounting → see also/另见 huì
会(會)计(計) kuàijì [名] 1(指工作) accounting 2(指人员) accountant

块(塊) kuài I [名] lump II [量] piece ▷一块蛋糕 yī kuài dàngāo a piece of cake ▷一块方糖 yī kuài fāngtáng a lump of sugar

快 kuài I [形] 1(快速) fast 2(赶快) 3(灵敏) quick ▷他脑子快。 Tā nǎozi kuài. He's quick-witted. 4(锋利) sharp 5(直爽) straightforward ▶爽快 shuǎngkuài frank II [副] soon ▶快要

kuàiyào soon
快餐 kuàicān [名] fast food
快活 kuàihuo [形] delighted
快乐(樂) kuàilè [形] happy

筷 kuài [名] chopsticks (pl) ▶筷子 kuàizi chopsticks (pl)

宽(寬) kuān I [形] 1(距离大) wide 2(范围广) broad ▶宽敞 kuānchang spacious 3(宽大) lenient ▶宽容 kuānróng tolerant II [名] width
宽(寬)带(帶) kuāndài [名] broadband

款 kuǎn [名] 1(项目) section 2(钱) sum of money ▶现款 xiànkuǎn cash 3(样式) style ▶款式 kuǎnshì style

狂 kuáng I [形] 1(疯狂) crazy ▶发狂 fākuáng go crazy 2(猛烈) violent ▶狂风 kuángfēng gale 3(狂妄) arrogant 4(狂热) wild II [副] wildly

旷(曠) kuàng I [形] (空阔) spacious ▶旷野 kuàngyě wilderness II [动] neglect ▶旷课 kuàngkè play truant

况(況) kuàng [名] situation ▶状况 zhuàngkuàng condition
况(況)且 kuàngqiě [连] besides

矿(礦) kuàng [名] 1(矿场) mine 2(矿石) ore
矿(礦)泉水 kuàngquánshuǐ [名] mineral water

框 kuàng I [名] 1(框架) frame 2(方框) box II [动] 1(画圈) box 2(口)(限制) limit
框架 kuàngjià [名] 1(指建筑) frame 2(指文书) framework

眶 kuàng [名] socket ▶眼眶 yǎnkuàng eye socket

亏(虧) kuī [动] 1(亏损) lose 2(欠缺) lack 3(亏负) allow ... to suffer losses II [副] luckily ▷亏你把我叫醒，要不我就迟到了。 Kuī nǐ bǎ wǒ jiào xǐng, yàobù wǒ jiù chídào le. It's lucky you woke me up or I would have been late.

盔 kuī [名] helmet

葵 kuí *see below*/见下文
　葵花 kuíhuā [名] sunflower

魁 kuí I [名] head ▸ 夺魁 duókuí win first place II [形] well-built ▸ 魁梧 kuíwú tall and sturdy

昆 kūn *see below*/见下文
　昆虫(蟲) kūnchóng [名] insect

捆(綑) kǔn I [动] tie ... up II [量] bundle ▸ 一捆书 yī kǔn shū a bundle of books

困 kùn I [动] 1(困扰) be stricken 2(限制) trap II [形] 1(瞌睡) sleepy 2(困难) difficult
　困难(難) kùnnan [形] 1(指事情) difficult ▸ 克服困难 kèfú kùnnan overcome difficulties 2(指经济) poor

扩(擴) kuò [动] expand
　扩(擴)大 kuòdà [动] expand

括 kuò [动] 1(包括) include 2(加括号) bracket
　括弧 kuòhú [名] bracket

阔(闊) kuò [形] 1(宽广) wide 2(阔气) wealthy

垃 lā *see below*/见下文
　垃圾 lājī [名] rubbish (英), garbage (美) ▸ 垃圾食品 lājī shípǐn junk food

拉 lā [动] 1(用力移动) pull 2(载运) transport ▸ 出租车司机拉我到了机场。Chūzūchē sījī lā wǒ dàole jīchǎng. The taxi driver took me to the airport. 3(演奏) play ▸ 拉小提琴 lā xiǎotíqín play the violin

喇 lǎ *see below*/见下文
　喇叭 lǎba [名] 1(管乐器) trumpet 2(扩音器) loudspeaker

落 là [动] 1(遗漏) be missing 2(忘记) leave
　→ *see also*/另见 luò

辣 là [形] (指味道) hot ▸ 辣酱 làjiàng chilli sauce ▸ 辣椒 làjiāo chillies

蜡(蠟) là [名] candle ▸ 蜡烛 làzhú candle

啦 la [助] ▸ 你回来啦! Nǐ huílái la! Hey — you're back!

来(來) lái I [动] 1(来到) come ▸ 家里来了几个客人。Jiā li láile jǐ gè kèrén. Some guests came to the house. 2(发生) happen ▸ 刚到家,麻烦来了。Gāng dào jiā, máfan lái le. As soon as I got home, the trouble started. 3(泛指做事)

▷请来碗面条。Qǐng lái wǎn miàntiáo. A bowl of noodles, please. ▷你累了, 让我来。Nǐ lèi le, ràng wǒ lái. You're tired — let me do it. **4**(表示要做) ▷请你来帮个忙。Qǐng nǐ lái bāng gè máng. Can you help me with this? **5**(表示目的) ▷我要想个法子来对付他。Wǒ yào xiǎng gè fǎzi lái duìfu tā. I must think of a way to deal with him. **6**(表示朝向) ▷服务员很快就把饭菜端了上来。Fúwùyuán hěn kuài jiù bǎ fàncài duānle shànglái. Soon the waiter had brought the food to the table. **II**[形] coming ▶ 来年 láinián the coming year **III**[助] **1**(表示持续) ▶近来 jìnlái lately ▷几年来 jǐ nián lái in the last few years **2**(表示概数) about ▷10来公斤重 shí lái gōngjīn zhòng about 10 kilos

来(來)不及 láibùjí [动] lack sufficient time for

来(來)得及 láidejí [动] have enough time for

来(來)回 láihuí **I**[动] **1**(去了再来) make a round trip ▷从住宅小区到市中心来回有多远? Cóng zhùzhái xiǎoqū dào shìzhōngxīn láihuí yǒu duō yuǎn? How far is it from the residential area to town and back? **2**(来来去去) move back and forth **II**[名] round trip ▷我从学校到家一天跑两个来回。Wǒ cóng xuéxiào dào jiā yī tiān pǎo liǎng gè láihuí. I make the round trip from school to home twice a day.

来(來)往 láiwǎng [动] have dealings with

来(來)自 láizì [动] come from

拦(攔) lán [动] stop

栏(欄) lán [名] **1**(栏杆) fence ▶ 栏杆 lángān railing **2**(部分版面) column ▶ 栏目 lánmù column

蓝(藍) lán [形] blue ▶ 蓝色 lánsè blue ▶ 蓝天 lántiān sky

篮(籃) lán [名] (篮子) basket ▶ 篮子 lánzi basket

篮(籃)球 lánqiú [名] basketball

缆(纜) lǎn [名] (似缆之物) cable

缆(纜)车(車) lǎnchē [名] cable car

懒(懶) lǎn [形] **1**(懒惰) lazy **2**(疲倦) lethargic

懒(懶)得 lǎnde [动] not feel like ▷天太热, 我懒得出门。Tiān tài rè, wǒ lǎn de chūmén. I don't feel like going out, it's too hot.

懒(懶)惰 lǎnduò [形] lazy

烂(爛) làn **I**[形] **1**(破烂) worn-out **2**(头绪乱) messy ▶ 烂摊子 làn tānzi a shambles **II**[动] be rotten ▷西瓜烂了。Xīguā làn le. The watermelon has gone off.

狼 láng [名] wolf

廊 láng [名] corridor ▶ 走廊 zǒuláng corridor

朗 lǎng [形] **1**(明亮) bright **2**(响亮) clear

朗读(讀) lǎngdú [动] read ... aloud

朗诵(誦) lǎngsòng [动] recite

浪 làng **I**[名] wave ▶ 浪潮 làngcháo tide **II**[形] wasteful ▶ 浪费 làngfèi squander

浪费(費) làngfèi [动] waste

浪漫 làngmàn [形] romantic

捞(撈) lāo [动] (取) take ▶ 捕捞 bǔlāo fish for

劳(勞) láo [动] **1**(劳动) work **2**(烦劳) trouble ▷劳您帮我看下行李。Láo nín bāng wǒ kān xià xíngli. Would you mind keeping an eye on my luggage?

劳(勞)动(動) láodòng [名] labour (英) 或 labor (美) ▷脑力劳动 nǎolì láodòng brain work

劳(勞)动(動)力 láodònglì [名] **1**(劳动能力) labour (英), labor (美) **2**(人力) workforce

劳(勞)驾(駕) láojià [动] (客套) excuse me

老 lǎo **I**[形] **1**(年岁大的) old **2**(有经验的) experienced ▶ 老手 lǎoshǒu veteran

3(旧的) old ▷ 老同学 lǎo tóngxué old school friend **4**(火候大的) over-done **II**[名](老人) old people **III**[副] **1**(经常) always **2**(长久) for a long time **3**(非常) very ▷ 老远 lǎo yuǎn very far

老百姓 lǎobǎixìng [名] ordinary people

老板(闆) lǎobǎn [名] boss

老虎 lǎohǔ [名] tiger

老家 lǎojiā [名] home ▷ 我老家在上海。Wǒ lǎojiā zài Shànghǎi. Shanghai is my hometown.

老练(練) lǎoliàn [形] experienced

老年 lǎonián [名] old age

老婆 lǎopo [名] wife

老师(師) lǎoshī [名] teacher

老实(實) lǎoshi [形] **1**(诚实规矩) honest **2**(不聪明) naive

老鼠 lǎoshǔ [名] mouse

老外 lǎowài [名] foreigner

姥 lǎo see below/见下文

姥姥 lǎolao [名](口)(母方的) granny

姥爷(爺) lǎoye [名](口)(母方的) grandpa

乐(樂) lè **I**[形] happy **II**[动] **1**(乐于) take pleasure in **2**(笑) laugh
→ see also/另见 yuè

乐(樂)观(觀) lèguān [形] optimistic

乐(樂)趣 lèqù [名] delight

乐(樂)意 lèyì [动] be willing to ▷ 他不乐意帮我们。Tā bù lèyì bāng wǒmen. He's unwilling to help us.
▷ 勒令 lèlìng order

了 le [助] **1**(表示动作或变化已完成) ▷ 他买了这本书。Tā mǎile zhè běn shū. He's bought this book. **2**(表示对未来的假设已完成) ▷ 下个月我考完了试回家。Xià gè yuè wǒ kǎowánle shì huíjiā. I'll go home next month once my exams are over. **3**(在句尾，表示出现变化) ▷ 下雨了。Xiàyǔ le. It's raining. **4**(在句尾，表示提醒、劝说或催促) ▷ 该回家了。Gāi huíjiā le. It's time to go home. ▷ 别喊了！Bié hǎn le! Stop shouting!
→ see also/另见 liǎo

The usage of 了 le is one of the most complex parts of Chinese grammar, partly because it has two completely different functions. It can indicate completion of an action, e.g. 他喝了三杯啤酒 tā hēle sān bēi píjiǔ (he drank three glasses of beer). Sometimes, when placed at the end of a clause or a sentence, it usually indicates a change of some kind, e.g. 天黑了 tiān hēi le (it's gone dark).

雷 léi [名](雷电) thunder ▷ 雷电 léidiàn thunder and lightning

累 léi [动](积累) accumulate ▷ 累积 léijī accumulate

累计(計) léijì [动] add up

肋 lèi [名] rib ▷ 肋骨 lèigǔ rib

泪(淚) lèi [名] tear ▷ 眼泪 yǎnlèi tears (pl) ▷ 流泪 liúlèi shed tears

类(類) lèi **I**[名] kind ▷ 分类 fēnlèi classify ▷ 类型 lèixíng type **II**[动] be similar to ▷ 类似 lèisì similar to

类(類)别(別) lèibié [名] category

类(類)似 lèisì [形] similar

累 lèi **I**[形] tired **II**[动](使劳累) tire ▷ 别累着自己。Bié lèizhe zìjǐ. Don't tire yourself out.
→ see also/另见 léi

冷 lěng [形] **1**(温度低) cold **2**(不热情) frosty ▷ 冷淡 lěngdàn give the cold shoulder to

冷藏 lěngcáng [动] refrigerate

冷冻(凍) lěngdòng [动] freeze ▷ 冷冻食品 lěngdòng shípǐn frozen food

冷静(靜) lěngjìng [形](沉着) cool-headed

冷饮(飲) lěngyǐn [名] cold drink

厘(釐) lí see below/见下文

厘(釐)米 límǐ [量] centimetre (英), centimeter (美)

离(離) lí [动] **1**(分离) leave **2**(距离) be far away from ▷ 我家离办公室不太远。Wǒ jiā lí bàngōngshì bù tài yuǎn.

My home is quite near to the office.

离 lí is used to express separation of two things, or distance of one thing from another: to say that X is far away from Y, say "X 离 Y 远", e.g. 我家离火车站不远 wǒ jiā lí huǒchēzhàn bù yuǎn (my home is not far from the train station).

离(離)婚 líhūn [动] divorce
离(離)开(開) líkāi [动] depart

梨 lí [名] pear

礼(禮) lǐ [名] 1 (仪式) ceremony 2 (礼节) courtesy 3 (礼物) present
礼(禮)拜 lǐbài [名] (星期) week
礼(禮)貌 lǐmào [名] manners (pl)
礼(禮)堂 lǐtáng [名] hall
礼(禮)物 lǐwù [名] present

里(裡) lǐ I [名] 1 (反面) inside 2 (里边) inner ▶ 里屋 lǐwū inner room II [介] in ▷ 屋子里 wūzi lǐ in the room III [副] ▶ 这里 zhèlǐ here ▶ 那里 nàlǐ there IV [量] lǐ, a Chinese unit of length, equal to 1/3 of a mile ▶ 英里 yīnglǐ mile
里(裡)面 lǐmiàn [形] inside

理 lǐ I [名] 1 (道理) reason ▶ 合理 hélǐ reasonable 2 (自然科学) natural science ▶ 理科 lǐkē science II [动] 1 (管理) manage ▶ 理财 lǐcái manage the finances 2 (整理) tidy ▶ 理发 lǐfà get a hair cut 3 (表示态度) acknowledge ▶ 理睬 lǐcái pay attention
理解 lǐjiě [动] understand
理论(論) lǐlùn [名] theory
理想 lǐxiǎng I [名] ideal II [形] ideal
理由 lǐyóu [名] reason

力 lì [名] 1 (物) force 2 (功能) strength 3 (体力) physical strength
力量 lìliàng [名] 1 (力气) strength ▷ 这一拳力量很大。 Zhè yī quán lìliàng hěn dà. That was a very powerful punch. 2 (能力) power 3 (作用) strength ▷ 这种药的力量大。 Zhè zhǒng yào de lìliàng dà. This medicine is very strong.
力气(氣) lìqi [名] strength

历(歷) lì [名] (经历) experience
历(歷)史 lìshǐ [名] history

厉(厲) lì [形] 1 (严格) strict 2 (严肃) stern
厉(厲)害 lìhai [形] 1 (剧烈) terrible ▷ 他口渴得厉害。 Tā kǒukě de lìhai. He was terribly thirsty. 2 (严厉) strict

立 lì I [动] 1 (站) stand 2 (竖立) stand ... up 3 (建立) ▶ 立功 lìgōng make contributions 4 (制定) set ... up ▶ 立法 lìfǎ legislate II [形] upright ▶ 立柜 lìguì wardrobe
立方 lìfāng I [名] cube II [量] cubic ▶ 立方米 lìfāngmǐ cubic metre (英) 或 meter (美)
立即 lìjí [副] immediately
立刻 lìkè [副] immediately

利 lì I [形] (锋利) sharp II [名] 1 (利益) interest ▶ 利弊 lìbì pros and cons (pl) 2 (利润) profit and interest ▶ 暴利 bàolì staggering profits (pl) III [动] benefit
利害 lìhai [形] terrible ▷ 天冷得利害。 Tiān lěng de lìhai. It's terribly cold today.
利率 lìlǜ [名] interest rate
利润(潤) lìrùn [名] profit
利息 lìxī [名] interest
利益 lìyì [名] benefit
利用 lìyòng [动] 1 (物) use 2 (人) exploit

例 lì [名] (例子) example ▶ 举例 jǔlì give an example
例如 lìrú [动] give an example ▷ 大商场货物齐全，例如服装、家电、食品等。 Dà shāngchǎng huòwù qíquán, lìrú fúzhuāng, jiādiàn, shípǐn děng. The big shopping centre sells all kinds of goods, for example, clothes, household appliances and food.
例外 lìwài [动] be an exception
例子 lìzi [名] example

荔 lì see below/见下文
荔枝 lìzhī [名] lychee

栗(慄) lì [名] chestnut ▶ 栗子 lìzi chestnut

粒 lì [量] ▷ 一粒珍珠 yī lì zhēnzhū a pearl ▷ 三粒种子 sān lì zhǒngzi three seeds measure word, used for small round objects, such as sand, grains, pills etc.

俩(倆) liǎ [数] (口) (两个) two ▷ 我俩 wǒ liǎ the two of us

连(連) lián I [动] connect ▶ 连接 liánjiē link II [副] in succession ▷ 连看了几眼 lián kànle jǐ yǎn glance at several times III [介] 1 (包括) including ▷ 连他4人 lián tā sì rén four people, including him 2 (甚至) even

连(連)接 liánjiē [动] connect

连(連)忙 liánmáng [副] at once

连(連)续(續) liánxù [动] go on without stopping ▷ 他连续干了3天，觉得没睡。Tā liánxù gànle sān tiān, jiào dōu méi shuì. He worked for three days in a row without sleeping.

帘(簾) lián [名] curtain (英), drape (美) ▶ 窗帘 chuānglián curtain (英), drape (美)

莲(蓮) lián [名] lotus ▶ 莲花 liánhuā lotus flower

联(聯) lián [动] unite ▶ 联赛 liánsài league match

联(聯)合 liánhé I [动] (人) unite II [形] joint

联(聯)合国(國) Liánhéguó [名] United Nations, UN

联(聯)络(絡) liánluò [动] contact ▷ 联络方式 liánluò fāngshì ways to maintain contact

联(聯)系(繫) liánxì [动] connect ▷ 理论联系实际 lǐlùn liánxì shíjì apply theory to practice ▷ 促进经济贸易联系 cùjìn jīngjì màoyì liánxì encourage economic and trade relations

脸(臉) liǎn [名] 1 (面部) face 2 (前部) front ▶ 门脸 ménliǎn shopfront (英), storefront (美) 3 (情面) face ▶ 脸面 liǎnmiàn face

脸(臉)谱(譜)网(網) Liǎnpǔ wǎng [名] Facebook®

脸(臉)色 liǎnsè [名] (气色) complexion

练(練) liàn I [动] practise (英), practice (美) ▶ 练武 liànwǔ practise martial arts II [形] experienced ▶ 熟练 shúliàn skilful (英), skillful (美)

练(練)习(習) liànxí I [动] practise (英), practice (美) II [名] exercise

恋(戀) liàn 1 (恋爱) love ▶ 相恋 xiāngliàn fall in love with each other 2 (想念) miss ▶ 恋家 liànjiā be homesick

恋(戀)爱(愛) liàn'ài [动] love ▷ 谈恋爱 tán liàn'ài be in love

恋(戀)人 liànrén [名] lover

良 liáng [形] good

良好 liánghǎo [形] good

良心 liángxīn [名] conscience

凉(涼) liáng [形] (冷) cool
→ see also/另见 liàng

凉(涼)快 liángkuai [形] cool

量 liáng [动] (测量) measure
→ see also/另见 liàng

粮(糧) liáng [名] grain

粮(糧)食 liángshi [名] food

两(兩) liǎng I [数] 1 (表示具体数目) two ▷ 两个小时 liǎng gè xiǎoshí two hours 2 (表示不定数目) a few ▷ 说两句 shuō liǎng jù say a few words II [量] liang, a Chinese unit of weight, equal to 50 grams
When citing numbers, including cardinal numbers, ordinal numbers, telephone numbers and serial numbers, 二 èr is used for the number two. However, when you want to talk about two things, you must use 两 liǎng and a measure word, e.g. 两个人 liǎng gè rén (2 people), 两杯茶 liǎng bēi chá (2 cups of tea) etc.

亮 liàng I [形] (光线) bright II [动] (发光) shine ▷ 灯还亮着。Dēng hái liàngzhe. The lights are still lit.

凉(涼) liàng [动] let ... cool
→ see also/另见 liáng

辆(輛) liàng [量] ▷ 一辆汽车 yī liàng qìchē a car ▷ 两辆自行车 liǎng liàng

zìxíngchē two bicycles
measure word, used for vehicles and bicycles

量 liàng [名] 1(限度) capacity 2(数量) quantity
→ see also/另见 liáng

晾 liàng [动] 1(弄干) dry 2(晒干) air

聊 liáo [动] (口) chat ▶ 聊天室 liáotiānshì chat room
聊天儿(兒) liáotiānr [动] (口) chat

了 liǎo [动] 1(完毕) finish 2(放在动词之后表示可能) ▶ 办不了 bànbuliǎo not be able to handle ▶ 受得了 shòu de liǎo be able to bear
→ see also/另见 le
了不起 liǎobuqǐ [形] amazing
了解 liǎojiě [动] 1(知道) understand 2(打听) find ... out

料 liào [名] (材料) material ▶ 木料 mùliào timber

列 liè I [动] 1(排列) set ... out 2(安排) list ▶ 列举 lièjǔ list II [名] 1(行列) rank 2(类别) category
列车(車) lièchē [名] train

劣 liè [形] bad ▶ 恶劣 èliè bad
劣质(質) lièzhì [形] poor-quality

烈 liè [形] (强烈) strong ▶ 激烈 jīliè fierce ▶ 烈性酒 lièxìng jiǔ strong liquor

猎(獵) liè [动] hunt ▶ 打猎 dǎliè go hunting

裂 liè [动] split ▶ 分裂 fēnliè split ▶ 破裂 pòliè break
裂口 lièkǒu [名] split

拎 līn [动] carry

邻(鄰) lín [名] neighbour (英), neighbor (美) ▶ 邻居 línjū neighbour
邻(鄰)近 línjìn [动] be close to
邻(鄰)居 línjū [名] neighbour (英), neighbor (美)

林 lín [名] 1(树林) wood 2(林业) forestry ▶ 林业 línyè forestry

临(臨) lín [动] 1(靠近) face ▶ 临危 línwēi face danger 2(到达) reach ▶ 光临 guānglín presence 3(将要) be about to ▶ 临产 línchǎn be in labour (英) 或 labor (美)
临(臨)近 línjìn [动] be close to ▷ 考试临近了。Kǎoshì línjìn le. The exams are approaching.
临(臨)时(時) línshí [副] temporarily

淋 lín [动] drench
淋浴 línyù [动] take a shower

鳞(鱗) lín [名] scale

凛(凜) lǐn [形] (寒冷) cold ▶ 凛冽 lǐnliè bitterly cold

吝 lìn [形] stingy ▶ 吝啬 lìnsè stingy

灵(靈) líng I [形] 1(灵活) nimble ▶ 灵敏 língmǐn agile 2(灵验) effective II [名] 1(灵魂) soul 2(神灵) deity ▶ 精灵 jīnglíng spirit
灵(靈)活 línghuó [形] 1(敏捷的) agile 2(机动的) flexible

铃(鈴) líng [名] 1(响器) bell ▶ 铃铛 língdang small bell 2(铃状物) ▶ 哑铃 yǎlíng dumb-bell

零 líng I [名] 1(零数) zero 2(零头) odd ▷ 她年纪七十有零。Tā niánjì qīshí yǒu líng. She's seventy-odd years old. II [形] 1(零碎的) odd ▶ 零活 línghuó odd jobs (pl) ▶ 零钱 língqián small change 2(部分的) spare ▶ 零件 língjiàn spare parts (pl) III [连] 1(两年三个月 liǎng nián líng sān gè yuè two years and three months ▷ 五元零二分 wǔ yuán líng èr fēn five yuan two fen
零钱(錢) língqián [名] small change
零食 língshí [名] snack
零售 língshòu [动] retail
零用钱(錢) língyòngqián [名] pocket money (英), allowance (美)

领(領) lǐng I [名] 1(衣领) collar 2(脖颈) neck II [动] 1(带领) lead 2(占有) possess

▶占领 zhànlǐng occupy

领(領)带(帶) lǐngdài [名] tie

领(領)导(導) lǐngdǎo I [动] lead ▷他领导有方。Tā lǐngdǎo yǒu fāng. He's an effective leader. II [名] leader

领(領)土 lǐngtǔ [名] territory

领(領)先 lǐngxiān [动] lead ▷他在比赛中遥遥领先。Tā zài bǐsài zhōng yáoyáo lǐngxiān. He took a runaway lead in the competition.

领(領)袖 lǐngxiù [名] leader

领(領)养(養) lǐngyǎng [动] adopt

另 lìng I [代] another II [副] separately

另外 lìngwài I [代] other ▷我不喜欢这些衣服，我喜欢另外那些。Wǒ bù xǐhuan zhèxiē yīfu, wǒ xǐhuan lìngwài nàxiē. I don't like these clothes — I like the others. II [副] in addition

令 lìng I [名] (命令) order II [动] 1 (命令) order 2 (使) make

溜 liū [动] (走开) sneak off

溜达(達) liūda [动] go for a stroll

留 liú [动] 1 (不走) stay 2 (使留) keep ... back ▶挽留 wǎnliú persuade ... to stay 3 (留意) be careful ▶留神 liúshén be careful 4 (保留) keep 5 (积蓄) grow ▷留胡子 liú húzi grow a beard 6 (接受) accept 7 (遗留) leave ... behind 8 (留学) study abroad ▷留英 liú Yīng study in Britain

留步 liúbù [动] stop here

留念 liúniàn [动] keep as a souvenir

留神 liúshén [动] be on the alert

留心 liúxīn [动] take note

留学(學) liúxué [动] study abroad

留言 liúyán [动] leave a message

留意 liúyì [动] look ... out

流 liú I [动] (流动) flow ▶漂流 piāoliú drift II [名] 1 (水流) current ▶洪流 hóngliú torrent 2 (等级) grade ▶一流 yīliú first-class

流传(傳) liúchuán [动] spread

流动(動) liúdòng [动] (移动) flow

流感 liúgǎn [名] the flu

流利 liúlì [形] fluent

流氓 liúmáng [名] 1 (指行为) perversion 2 (指人) hooligan

流水 liúshuǐ [名] (流动水) running water

流行 liúxíng [动] 1 (广泛传播) be fashionable 2 (热搜) trend

瘤 liú [名] tumour (英), tumor (美) ▶瘤子 liúzi tumour (英), tumor (美)

柳 liǔ [名] willow ▶柳树 liǔshù willow

六 liù [数] six

六月 liùyuè [名] June

陆(陸) liù [数] six
→ see also/另见 lù

This is the character for "six", which is mainly used in banks, on receipts etc. to prevent mistakes and forgery.

遛 liù [动] 1 (指人) take a stroll 2 (指动物) walk ▶遛狗 liùgǒu walk the dog

龙(龍) lóng [名] dragon

龙(龍)卷(捲)风(風) lóngjuǎnfēng [名] tornado

龙(龍)头(頭) lóngtóu [名] tap (英), faucet (美)

聋(聾) lóng [形] deaf

聋(聾)子 lóngzi [名] ▷他是个聋子。Tā shì gè lóngzi. He's deaf.

笼(籠) lóng [名] (笼子) cage ▶笼子 lóngzi cage

隆 lóng [形] (盛大) grand ▶隆重 lóngzhòng solemn

楼(樓) lóu [名] 1 (楼房) tall building ▷教学楼 jiàoxuélóu teaching block 2 (楼层) floor

楼(樓)房 lóufáng [名] multi-storey building

楼(樓)梯 lóutī [名] stairs (pl)

搂(摟) lǒu [动] embrace

漏 lòu [动] 1 (雨、水) leak 2 (消息、风声) divulge 3 (词、句) leave ... out

漏斗 lòudǒu [名] funnel

露 lòu [动] reveal
→ see also/另见 lù
露马(馬)脚(腳) lòu mǎjiǎo [动] give oneself away

炉(爐) lú [名] stove
炉(爐)灶 lúzào [名] kitchen range

卤(滷) lǔ I [名] 1 (盐卤) bittern 2 (卤汁) thick gravy II [动] stew ... in soy sauce

陆(陸) lù [名] land
→ see also/另见 liù
陆(陸)地 lùdì [名] land

录(錄) lù I [名] record II [动] 1 (记载) record ▶ 记录 jìlù take notes 2 (录音) tape-record
录(錄)取 lùqǔ [动] admit ▶ 她被剑桥大学录取了。Tā bèi Jiànqiáo Dàxué lùqǔ le. She was given a place at the University of Cambridge.
录(錄)像 lùxiàng [动] video (英), videotape (美)
录(錄)音 lùyīn [动] record

鹿 lù [名] deer

路 lù [名] 1 (道路) road ▶ 路标 lùbiāo signpost 2 (路程) journey ▶ 一路平安 yī lù píng'ān have a safe journey 3 (门路) means ▶ 财路 cáilù a means of getting rich 4 (条理) sequence ▶ 思路 sīlù train of thought 5 (路线) route ▶ 8路车 bā lù chē No. 8 bus
路程 lùchéng [名] journey
路过(過) lùguò [动] pass through
路口 lùkǒu [名] crossing (英), intersection (美)
路线(線) lùxiàn [名] 1 (指交通) route 2 (指思想) line

露 lù I [名] (水珠) dew II [动] reveal ▶ 暴露 bàolù expose
→ see also/另见 lòu
露天 lùtiān [名] the open air ▶ 露天剧场 lùtiān jùchǎng open-air theatre (英) 或 theater (美)
露营(營) lùyíng [动] camp out

驴(驢) lǘ [名] donkey

旅 lǚ [动] travel ▶ 差旅费 chāilǚfèi travel expenses (pl)
旅馆(館) lǚguǎn [名] hotel
旅客 lǚkè [名] passenger
旅途 lǚtú [名] journey
旅行 lǚxíng [动] travel
旅游(遊) lǚyóu [动] tour ▶ 旅游业 lǚyóuyè tourism ▶ 去国外旅游 qù guówài lǚyóu travel abroad

铝(鋁) lǚ [名] aluminium (英), aluminum (美)

律 lǜ [名] law ▶ 纪律 jìlǜ discipline
律师(師) lǜshī [名] lawyer

绿(綠) lǜ [形] green ▶ 绿灯 lǜdēng green light
绿(綠)化 lǜhuà [动] make ... green ▶ 绿化荒山 lǜhuà huāngshān plant trees on the mountains
绿(綠)卡 lǜkǎ [名] green card
绿(綠)洲 lǜzhōu [名] oasis

乱(亂) luàn I [形] 1 (没有秩序的) disorderly ▶ 杂乱 záluàn messy 2 (心绪不宁的) disturbed II [名] (指冲突) chaos ▶ 战乱 zhànluàn war chaos
乱(亂)哄哄 luànhōnghōng [形] chaotic
乱(亂)七八糟 luànqībāzāo in a mess

略 lüè I [名] 1 (简述) summary 2 (计谋) plan ▶ 策略 cèlüè tactic II [动] 1 (夺取) capture ▶ 侵略 qīnlüè invade 2 (简化) simplify ▶ 省略 shěnglüè omit

伦(倫) lún [名] (人伦) human relationships (pl)
伦(倫)敦 Lúndūn [名] London
伦(倫)理 lúnlǐ [名] ethics (sg)

轮(輪) lún [名] 1 (轮子) wheel 2 (轮船) steamship
轮(輪)船 lúnchuán [名] steamship
轮(輪)换(換) lúnhuàn [动] take turns
轮(輪)廓 lúnkuò [名] outline
轮(輪)流 lúnliú [副] in turns
轮(輪)椅 lúnyǐ [名] wheelchair

论(論)lùn I[名] 1(文章) essay 2(学说) theory ▷ 相对论 xiāngduìlùn theory of relativity II[动](分析) discuss ▷ 评论 pínglùn comment on
论(論)坛(壇)lùntán [名] forum
论(論)文 lùnwén [名] dissertation

萝(蘿)luó [名] trailing plant
萝(蘿)卜(蔔)luóbo [名] turnip ▷ 胡萝卜 húluóbo carrot

逻(邏)luó [动] patrol
逻(邏)辑(輯)luóji [名] logic

螺 luó [名](指动物) snail
螺钉(釘)luódīng [名] screw

裸 luǒ [动] expose
裸体(體)luǒtǐ [形] naked

骆(駱)luò see below/见下文
骆(駱)驼(駝)luòtuo [名] camel

落 luò [动] 1(掉下) fall 2(下降) go down ▷ 降落 jiàngluò descend 3(降下) lower 4(衰败) decline ▷ 衰落 shuāiluò wane 5(落后) fall behind 6(归属) fall to → see also/另见 là
落后(後)luòhòu I[动] fall behind II[形] backward

妈(媽)mā [名](口)(母亲) mum(英), mom(美)
妈(媽)妈(媽)māma [名](口) mum (英), mom(美)

抹 mā [动](擦) wipe → see also/另见 mǒ
抹布 mābù [名] cloth

麻 má I[名](指植物) hemp II[形](麻木) numb
麻烦(煩)máfan I[形] problematic II[名] trouble III[动] trouble ▷ 不好意思，麻烦您了。Bù hǎoyìsi, máfan nín le. Sorry to trouble you.
麻将(將)májiàng [名] mahjong

麻将 májiàng

- The game of mahjong is usually played by four people. 144 tiles appearing like dominoes and bearing various designs are drawn and discarded until one player has an entire hand of winning combinations. The game requires strategy as well as luck. In China, mahjong is also a popular gambling game.

麻醉 mázuì [动](医) anaesthetize(英), anesthetize(美)

马(馬)mǎ [名] horse
马(馬)达(達)mǎdá [名] motor
马(馬)虎 mǎhu [形] careless

马(馬)拉松 mǎlāsōng [名] marathon

马(馬)来(來)西亚(亞) Mǎláixīyà [名] Malaysia

马(馬)路 mǎlù [名] road

马(馬)马(馬)虎虎 mǎmǎhūhū [形] 1 (随随便便) careless 2 (勉强) just passable

马(馬)上 mǎshàng [副] right away ▷ 他马上就到。Tā mǎshàng jiù dào. He'll be here right away.

马(馬)戏(戲) mǎxì [名] circus

码(碼) mǎ [名] numeral ▷ 页码 yèmǎ page number

码(碼)头(頭) mǎtou [名] pier

蚂(螞) mǎ see below/见下文

蚂(螞)蚁(蟻) mǎyǐ [名] ant

骂(罵) mà [动] 1 (侮辱) insult 2 (斥责) tell ... off

吗(嗎) ma [助] (表示疑问) ▷ 你去银行吗？Nǐ qù yínháng ma? Are you going to the bank?

> 吗 ma is added to the end of any statement to turn it into a simple yes/no question, e.g. 你忙吗？Nǐ máng ma? (Are you busy?), whereas 呢 ne is added to the end of a statement to form a tentative question, or to indicate that a response is expected, e.g. 你好吗？我很好，你呢？Nǐ hǎo ma? Wǒ hěn hǎo, nǐ ne? (How are you? Fine, and you?).

嘛 ma [助] 1 (表示显而易见) ▷ 事实就是这样嘛！Shìshí jiùshì zhèyàng ma! That's just the way things are! 2 (表示期望) ▷ 别不高兴嘛！Bié bù gāoxìng ma! Please don't be unhappy.

埋 mái [动] 1 (盖住) bury 2 (隐藏) hide → see also/另见 mán

埋葬 máizàng [动] bury

买(買) mǎi [动] 1 (购买) buy ▷ 不是每个人都买得起房。Bùshì měigè rén dōu mǎi de qǐ fáng. Not everyone can afford to buy a flat. ▷ 我去市场买东西。Wǒ qù shìchǎng mǎi dōngxi. I'm going shopping in the market. 2 (换取) win ... over ▷ 买通 mǎitōng buy ... off

买(買)单(單) mǎidān [动] (方) pay a bill ▷ 买单！Mǎidān! The bill, please!

买(買)卖(賣) mǎimai [名] 1 (生意) business 2 (商店) shop (英), store (美)

迈(邁) mài [动] step ▷ 迈步 màibù stride

麦(麥) mài [名] (麦类粮食) wheat ▷ 燕麦 yànmài oats (pl)

麦(麥)克风(風) màikèfēng [名] microphone, mike (口)

卖(賣) mài [动] (出售) sell ▷ 书都卖完了。Shū dōu màiwán le. The books are all sold out.

卖(賣)弄 màinong [动] show off

脉(脈) mài [名] (脉搏) pulse ▷ 号脉 hàomài feel a pulse

脉(脈)搏 màibó [名] pulse

埋 mán see below/见下文 → see also/另见 mái

埋怨 mányuàn [动] 1 (指责) blame 2 (抱怨) complain

馒(饅) mán see below/见下文

馒(饅)头(頭) mántou [名] steamed bun

瞒(瞞) mán [动] hide the truth from ▷ 别瞒着我们！Bié mánzhe wǒmen! Don't keep us in the dark!

满(滿) mǎn I [形] 1 (充实) full 2 (全) complete II [动] 1 (使充满) fill 2 (到) reach ▷ 孩子刚满六岁。Háizi gāng mǎn liù suì. The child has just turned six years old. III [副] fully

满(滿)意 mǎnyì [动] be satisfied

满(滿)足 mǎnzú [动] 1 (感到满意) be satisfied 2 (使满足) satisfy

漫 màn [动] overflow

漫长(長) màncháng [形] endless

漫画(畫) mànhuà [名] comic strip

漫延 mànyán [动] spread

慢 màn I[形](缓慢) slow II[动] slow 1(指速度) ▷ 慢点儿! Màn diǎnr! Slow down! ▷ 钟慢了十分钟。Zhōng mànle shí fēnzhōng. The clock is ten minutes slow.

忙 máng I[形] busy II[动] be busy with ▷ 你这一段忙什么呢? Nǐ zhè yī duàn máng shénme ne? What's been keeping you busy recently?

盲 máng [形] blind ▶ 文盲 wénmáng illiterate
盲目 mángmù [形] blind
盲文 mángwén [名] braille

蟒 mǎng [名](动物) python

猫(貓) māo [名] cat
猫(貓)儿(兒)眼 māoryǎn [名] spyhole

毛 máo I[名] 1(毛发) hair ▶ 羽毛 yǔmáo feather 2(指食物上) mould (英), mold (美) ▷ 面包上长毛了。Miànbāo shang zhǎng máo le. The bread is mouldy (英) 或 moldy (美). 3(指动物) fur ▶ 毛皮 máopí fur 4(羊毛) wool ▶ 毛衣 máoyī sweater 5(中国货币单位) mao unit of Chinese currency, 1/10 yuan II[形](不纯) gross ▶ 毛重 máozhòng gross weight
毛笔(筆) máobǐ [名] brush pen
毛病 máobìng [名] 1(故障) problem 2(缺点) shortcoming 3(疾病) illness
毛巾 máojīn [名] towel
毛孔 máokǒng [名] pore

矛 máo [名] spear
矛盾 máodùn I[名] 1(相抵之处) conflict 2(哲) contradiction II[形] uncertain

锚(錨) máo [名] anchor

茂 mào [形] 1(茂盛) luxuriant 2(丰富) abundant
茂盛 màoshèng [形] flourishing

冒 mào [动] 1(往外) give ... off ▷ 锅冒烟了。Guō mào yān le. The wok is giving off smoke. 2(不顾) risk ▷ 冒着生命危险 màozhe shēngmìng wēixiǎn putting one's life at risk 3(假充) pretend to be ▶ 冒牌 màopái bogus
冒充 màochōng [动] pass ... off as
冒牌 màopái [动] pirate ▷ 冒牌商品 màopái shāngpǐn pirated goods
冒险(險) màoxiǎn [动] take a risk

贸(貿) mào [动] trade ▷ 外贸 wàimào foreign trade
贸(貿)易 màoyì [名] trade

帽 mào [名](帽子) hat
帽子 màozi [名](字) hat

貌 mào [名](相貌、外表) appearance

没(沒) méi I[动] not have ▷ 没关系 méi guānxi it doesn't matter ▷ 屋子里没人。Wūzi li méi rén. There's no one in the room. II[副] not ▷ 他没看过大海。Tā méi kànguo dàhǎi. He's never seen the sea before.
→ see also/另见 mò

> Constructing negating sentences in Chinese is very straightforward: just use 不 bù before the verb, e.g. 我不喝酒。Wǒ bù hējiǔ. (I don't drink alcohol). The only exception is the verb 有 yǒu, to have, for which you must use 没 méi, e.g. 我没有钱。Wǒ méiyǒu qián. (I don't have any money).

没(沒)错(錯)儿(兒) méicuòr [动] that's right
没(沒)劲(勁) méijìn I[动] have no energy II[形] uninteresting
没(沒)门(門)儿(兒) méiménr [动] (不可能) be impossible
没(沒)事 méishì [动] 1(有空) be free ▷ 我今晚没事。Wǒ jīnwǎn méishì. I'm free tonight. 2(不要紧) be OK ▷ 没事。Méishì. It doesn't matter.
没(沒)有 méiyǒu I[动] 1(不具有) not have 2(不存在) there is not 3(全都不) ▷ 没有一个答案是正确的。Méiyǒu yī gè dá'àn shì zhèngquè de. None of the answers are correct. 4(不如) be not as ... as ... ▷ 他没有你努力。Tā méiyǒu nǐ nǔlì. He's not as hard-working as you. 5(不到) be less than ▷ 他们干了没有两个小时就休息了。Tāmen gànle méiyǒu liǎng gè

xiǎoshí jiù xiūxi le. They had been working for less than two hours when they took a rest. II [副] **1**(尚未) not yet ▷ 她还没有到。Tā hái méiyǒu dào. She hasn't arrived yet. **2**(未曾) never before ▷ 我没有吃过西餐。Wǒ méiyǒu chīguo xīcān. I have never eaten Western food before.

没(沒)辙(轍) méizhé [动] (方) not be able to do anything about

玫 méi see below/见下文

玫瑰 méigui [名] rose

眉 méi [名] (眉毛) eyebrow ▷ 眉毛 méimao eyebrow

媒 méi [名] **1**(媒人) matchmaker ▷ 做媒 zuòméi be a matchmaker **2**(媒介) intermediary

媒体(體) méitǐ [名] media

煤 méi [名] coal

煤气(氣) méiqì [名] **1**(指燃料) gas **2**(有毒气体) carbon monoxide ▷ 煤气中毒 méiqì zhòngdú carbon monoxide poisoning

霉 méi [动] **1**(指食物) mould (英), mold (美) **2**(指衣物) mildew

每 měi I [形] every, each ▷ 每次 měi cì every time ▷ 每个晚上 měigè wǎnshang every evening II [副] every time ▷ 每走一步，他的脚都很疼。Měi zǒu yī bù, tā de jiǎo dōu hěn téng. His feet ache with every step he takes.

美 měi I [形] **1**(美丽) beautiful **2**(好) good ▷ 我们的明天会更美。Wǒmen de míngtiān huì gèng měi. Our future will be even better. II [名] **1**(美丽) beauty **2**(美洲) North and South America ▷ 南美 Nán Měi South America ▷ 北美 Běi Měi North America **3**(美国) the USA

美国(國) Měiguó [名] the US, the USA ▷ 美国人 Měiguórén American

美好 měihǎo [形] wonderful

美甲 měijiǎ [动] get a manicure

美丽(麗) měilì [形] beautiful

美满(滿) měimǎn [形] perfectly satisfactory

美容 měiróng [动] make oneself more beautiful ▷ 美容店 měiróngdiàn beauty salon ▷ 美容手术 měiróng shǒushù cosmetic surgery

美食 měishí [名] delicacy

美术(術) měishù [名] **1**(造型艺术) fine arts (pl) **2**(绘画) painting

美元 měiyuán [名] US dollar

妹 mèi [名] **1**(指直系) younger sister **2**(指亲戚) ▷ 表妹 biǎomèi cousin

妹妹 mèimei (指直系) younger sister

魅 mèi [名] demon

魅力 mèilì [名] charm

闷(悶) mēn I [形] stuffy II [动] **1**(盖) cover ... tightly **2**(不出声) keep silent **3**(呆) shut oneself in
→ see also/另见 mèn

闷(悶)热(熱) mēnrè [形] muggy

门(門) mén I [名] **1**(指出入口) door ▷ 门口 ménkǒu entrance **2**(指开关装置) switch ▷ 电门 diànmén switch II [量] ▷ 5门课 wǔ mén kè five courses ▷ 一门新技术 yī mén xīn jìshù a new technology

measure word, used for academic subjects, courses and technology

门(門)类(類) ménlèi [名] category

门(門)卫(衛) ménwèi [名] guard

门(門)诊(診) ménzhěn [名] outpatient department

闷(悶) mèn [形] **1**(心烦) low **2**(无聊) bored
→ see also/另见 mēn

们(們) men [后缀] ▷ 我们 wǒmen we, us ▷ 你们 nǐmen you ▷ 他们 tāmen they, them

蒙(矇) mēng [动] **1**(欺骗) deceive **2**(乱猜) make a wild guess
→ see also/另见 méng, Měng

蒙(矇)骗(騙) mēngpiàn [动] deceive

蒙 méng I[动] 1(遮盖) cover 2(受到) receive II[形] ignorant ▶ 启蒙 qǐméng enlighten
→ see also/另见 mēng, Měng
蒙(矇)混 ménghùn [动] deceive ▷ 蒙混过关 ménghùn guòguān muddle through

猛 měng [形] 1(凶猛) fierce [副] 2(猛烈) fiercely 3(忽然) suddenly
猛烈 měngliè [形] fierce

蒙 Měng [名] Mongolia ▶ 蒙古 Měnggǔ Mongolia ▶ 蒙古人 Měnggǔrén Mongolian ▶ 内蒙古 Nèiměnggǔ Inner Mongolia
→ see also/另见 mēng, méng

梦(夢) mèng I[名] 1(睡梦) dream ▶ 白日梦 báirìmèng daydream ▶ 做梦 zuòmèng have a dream 2(幻想) illusion II[动] dream
梦(夢)话(話) mènghuà [名] 1(字) ▷ 说梦话 shuō mènghuà talk in one's sleep 2(喻) nonsense
梦(夢)想 mèngxiǎng [动] dream

弥(彌) mí [动] fill
弥(彌)补(補) míbǔ [动] make ... up

迷 mí I[动] 1(迷失) be lost ▶ 迷路 mílù lose one's way 2(迷恋) become obsessed with 3(迷惑) be deluded II[名] fan ▶ 球迷 qiúmí sports fan ▶ 足球迷 zúqiúmí football fan
迷你 mínǐ [形] mini ▷ 迷你裙 mínǐqún mini-skirt
迷信 míxìn [形] 1(鬼神) be superstitious about 2(人或事) have blind faith in

猕(獼) mí see below/见下文
猕(獼)猴桃 míhóutáo [名] kiwi fruit

谜(謎) mí [名] 1(谜语) riddle 2(神秘) mystery
谜(謎)语(語) míyǔ [名] riddle

米 mǐ I[名] (稻米) rice ▶ 米饭 mǐfàn cooked rice II[量] metre(英), meter(美)

秘(祕) mì I[形] secret II[动] keep ... secret III[名] secretary
秘(祕)密 mìmì [名] secret ▷ 一定要保守秘密！ Yídìng yào bǎoshǒu mìmì! You must keep this a secret!
秘(祕)书(書) mìshū [名] secretary

密 mì [形] 1(空隙小) dense 2(关系近) close ▶ 亲密 qīnmì intimate 3(精致) meticulous ▶ 精密 jīngmì precise 4(秘密) secret ▶ 保密 bǎomì keep sth a secret
密度 mìdù [名] density
密封 mìfēng [动] seal ... tightly
密码(碼) mìmǎ [名] 1(口令) password 2(符号系统) code
密切 mìqiè [形] close

幂(冪) mì [名] (数) power

蜜 mì I[名] honey II[形] sweet
蜜蜂 mìfēng [名] bee
蜜月 mìyuè [名] honeymoon

眠 mián [动] 1(睡) sleep ▶ 失眠 shīmián suffer from insomnia 2(冬眠) hibernate

棉 mián [名] cotton
棉花 miánhua [名] (指植物) cotton
棉衣 miányī [名] cotton-padded clothing

免 miǎn [动] 1(除去) exempt ▶ 免试 miǎnshì be exempt from an exam 2(避免) avoid ▶ 免不了 miǎnbuliǎo be unavoidable 3(不要) not be allowed ▷ 闲人免进 xiánrén miǎnjìn staff only
免费(費) miǎnfèi [动] be free of charge ▷ 注册一个免费电子邮箱 zhùcè yī gè miǎnfèi diànzǐ yóuxiāng register for free e-mail
免疫 miǎnyì [名] immunity

勉 miǎn [动] 1(努力) strive 2(勉励) encourage 3(勉强) force ... to carry on
勉强(強) miǎnqiǎng I[动] 1(尽力) push oneself hard ▷ 做事不要太勉强。 Zuòshì bùyào tài miǎnqiǎng. Don't push yourself too hard. 2(强迫) force ▷ 不要勉强孩子学钢琴。 Bùyào

miǎnqiǎng háizi xué gāngqín. Don't force the child to study the piano. **II** [形] **1** (不情愿) reluctant ▷ 我让他帮忙，他勉强答应了。Wǒ ràng tā bāngmáng, tā miǎnqiǎng dāying le. I asked him to help, and he reluctantly agreed. **2** (凑合) barely enough ▷ 他挣的钱勉强够自己花。Tā zhèng de qián miǎnqiǎng gòu zìjǐ huā. The money he earned was barely enough to support himself. **3** (牵强) far-fetched ▷ 这个理论有点勉强。Zhège lǐlùn yǒudiǎn miǎnqiǎng. This theory is a bit far-fetched.

冕 miǎn [名] **1** (皇冠) crown ▷ 加冕 jiāmiǎn be crowned **2** (冠军头衔) title ▷ 卫冕 wèimiǎn defend one's title

缅 (緬) miǎn [形] (书) remote
缅 (緬) 甸 Miǎndiàn [名] Myanmar

面 miàn **I** [名] **1** (脸) face **2** (表面) surface **3** (方位) aspect ▷ 前面 qiánmiàn front **4** (情面) self-respect **5** (粉末) powder ▷ 辣椒面 làjiāomiàn chilli powder **6** (磨成粉的粮食) flour ▷ 面粉 miànfěn flour **7** (面条) noodles (pl) **II** [动] (朝) face **III** [量] **1** (用于扁平物) ▷ 一面墙 yī miàn qiáng a wall ▷ 两面镜子 liǎng miàn jìngzi two mirrors

> measure word, used for objects with a flat surface, such as walls, mirrors, drums etc.

2 (指见面的次数) ▷ 我只见过她一面。Wǒ zhǐ jiànguo tā yī miàn. I've only met her once before. ▷ 我们见过几面。Wǒmen jiànguo jǐ miàn. We've met a few times.

> measure word, used for encounters between two people

面 (麵) 包 miànbāo [名] bread ▷ 面包房 miànbāofáng bakery
面对 (對) miànduì [动] face
面积 (積) miànjī [名] area
面临 (臨) miànlín [动] face
面貌 miànmào [名] **1** (面容) features (pl) **2** (喻) appearance
面前 miànqián [名] ▷ 在困难面前 zài kùnnan miànqián in the face of difficulties

面试 (試) miànshì [动] have an interview
面 (麵) 条 (條) miàntiáo [名] noodles (pl) ▷ 意大利面条 Yìdàlì miàntiáo spaghetti
面子 miànzi [名] **1** (体面) face ▷ 丢面子 diū miànzi lose face **2** (情面) feelings (pl) ▷ 给我点面子，你就答应吧！Gěi wǒ diǎn miànzi, nǐ jiù dāying ba! Show some respect for my feelings and say yes!

苗 miáo [名] (指植物) seedling ▷ 树苗 shùmiáo sapling
苗条 (條) miáotiao [形] slim

描 miáo [动] **1** (画) trace **2** (涂抹) touch … up
描述 miáoshù [动] describe
描写 (寫) miáoxiě [动] describe

瞄 miáo [动] fix one's eyes on
瞄准 (準) miáozhǔn [动] (对准) take aim

秒 miǎo [量] (指时间) second ▷ 5秒 wǔ miǎo five seconds

妙 miào [形] **1** (好) wonderful **2** (巧妙) ingenious

庙 (廟) miào [名] temple

灭 (滅) miè [动] **1** (熄灭) go out **2** (使熄灭) extinguish ▷ 灭火器 mièhuǒqì fire extinguisher **3** (淹没) submerge **4** (消亡) perish **5** (消灭) kill
灭 (滅) 绝 (絕) mièjué [动] (消亡) become extinct

民 mín [名] **1** (人民) the people (pl) **2** (人) person ▷ 网民 wǎngmín Internet user **3** (民间) folk **4** (非军方) civilian
民歌 míngē [名] folk song
民间 (間) mínjiān [名] **1** (百姓中间) folk ▷ 民间传说 mínjiān chuánshuō folklore **2** (非官方) ▷ 民间组织 mínjiān zǔzhī non-governmental organization
民警 mínjǐng [名] civil police
民主 mínzhǔ **I** [名] democracy **II** [形] democratic

民族 mínzú [名] nationality ▷ 少数民族 shǎoshù mínzú ethnic minority

敏 mǐn [形] 1(快) quick ► 敏感 mǐngǎn sensitive 2(聪明) clever ► 机敏 jīmǐn quick-witted

敏捷 mǐnjié [形] quick

名 míng I [名] 1(名字) name ▷ 书名 shūmíng book title 2(名声) reputation II [形] famous ► 名著 míngzhù classics (pl) III [量] 1(指人) ▷ 5名工人 wǔ míng gōngrén five workers ▷ 10名教师 shí míng jiàoshī ten teachers

measure word, used for people of any profession

2(指名次) ▷ 期末考试她得了第一名。 Qīmò kǎoshì tā déle dìyī míng. She came first in the end-of-term exams.

measure word, used for rankings in competitions and exams

名称(稱) míngchēng [名] name
名次 míngcì [名] ranking
名单(單) míngdān [名] list of names
名额(額) míng'é [名] quota
名牌 míngpái [名] famous name ▷ 名牌服装 míngpái fúzhuāng designer clothing
名片 míngpiàn [名] business card
名气(氣) míngqi [名] fame
名人 míngrén [名] famous person
名声(聲) míngshēng [名] reputation
名胜(勝) míngshèng [名] tourist site
名字 míngzi [名] name ▷ 你叫什么名字？ Nǐ jiào shénme míngzi? What's your name?

明 míng I [形] 1(亮) bright 2(清楚) clear 3(公开) open II [名] 1(视力) sight ► 失明 shīmíng lose one's eyesight 2(光明) light III [动] 1(懂) understand ► 明理 mínglǐ be understanding 2(显示) show ► 表明 biǎomíng indicate

明白 míngbai I [形] 1(清楚) clear 2(聪明) sensible 3(公开) explicit II [动] understand
明亮 míngliàng [形] 1(亮堂) bright 2(发亮) shining 3(明白) clear
明确(確) míngquè I [形] clear-cut

II [动] clarify
明天 míngtiān [名] tomorrow
明显(顯) míngxiǎn [形] obvious
明信片 míngxìnpiàn [名] postcard
明星 míngxīng [名] star
明智 míngzhì [形] sensible

命 mìng [名] 1(性命) life 2(命运) fate 3(寿命) lifespan 4(命令) order
命令 mìnglìng [动] order
命名 mìngmíng [动] name
命运(運) mìngyùn [名] fate

摸 mō [动] 1(触摸) stroke 2(摸行动) feel one's way ► 摸索 mōsuǒ grope

模 mó I [名] model ► 模型 móxíng model II [动] imitate
→ see also/另见 mú
模范(範) mófàn [形] model
模仿 mófǎng [动] imitate
模糊 móhu [形] blurred
模拟(擬) mónǐ [动] imitate ► 模拟考试 mónǐ kǎoshì mock exam
模式 móshì [名] pattern
模特儿(兒) mótèr [名] model
模型 móxíng [名] 1(样品) model 2(模具) mould (英), mold (美)

膜 mó [名] (膜状物) film ► 保鲜膜 bǎoxiānmó clingfilm (英), plastic wrap (美)

摩 mó [动] (摩擦) rub ... together
摩擦 mócā I [动] rub II [名] 1(阻力) friction 2(冲突) conflict
摩托车(車) mótuōchē [名] motorbike

磨 mó [动] 1(摩擦) rub 2(指用磨料) grind ► 磨刀 módāo sharpen a knife 3(折磨) wear ... down 4(纠缠) pester 5(拖延) dawdle
→ see also/另见 mò
磨擦 mócā [名] rub
磨蹭 móceng [形] sluggish
磨合 móhé [动] (适应) adapt to each other
磨炼(煉) móliàn [动] steel
磨损(損) mósǔn [动] wear ... out

蘑 mó[名]mushroom
蘑菇 mógu[名]mushroom

魔 mó I[名]1(魔鬼)demon 2(魔法)
magic II[形]magic
魔法 mófǎ[名]magic
魔鬼 móguǐ[名]devil
魔术(術)móshù[名]magic
魔术(術)师(師)móshùshī[名]
magician

抹 mǒ[动]1(涂抹)apply 2(擦)wipe
3(去除)erase
→ see also/另见 mā

末 mò[名](尾)end ▷ 世纪末 shìjì mò
the end of the century
末尾 mòwěi[名]end

没(沒)mò[动]1(沉没)sink 2(漫过)
overflow 3(隐没)disappear ▷ 出没
chūmò appear and disappear
→ see also/另见 méi
没(沒)收 mòshōu[动]confiscate

沫 mò[名]foam ▷ 泡沫 pàomò bubble

茉 mò see below/见下文
茉莉 mòlì[名]jasmine

陌 mò[名](书)footpath
陌生 mòshēng[形]unfamiliar
陌生人 mòshēngrén[名]stranger

墨 mò I[名](墨汁)ink ▷ 墨汁 mòzhī ink
II[形]dark ▷ 墨镜 mòjìng sunglasses

默 mò[动]1(不出声)do ... silently ▷ 默哀
mò'āi pay ... silent tribute 2(默写)write
... from memory

磨 mò I[名](磨)mill ▷ 磨坊 mòfáng mill
II[动]grind
→ see also/另见 mó

谋(謀)móu[名]plan ▷ 阴谋 yīnmóu
plot
谋(謀)杀(殺)móushā[动]murder
谋(謀)生 móushēng[动]make a living

某 mǒu[代](指不确定的人或事)▷ 某人
mǒurén somebody

模 mú[名]mould(英),mold(美)
→ see also/另见 mó
模样(樣)múyàng[名](相貌)looks(pl)

母 mǔ I[名]1(母亲)mother 2(指长辈女
子)▷ 祖母 zǔmǔ grandmother 3(喻)
(基础)origin II[形](雌性)female ▷ 母牛
mǔniú cow
母亲(親)mǔqīn[名]mother

拇 mǔ[名]see below/见下文
拇指 mǔzhǐ[名]1(指手)thumb 2(指脚)
big toe

木 mù I[名]1(树)tree 2(木材)wood
II[形](僵)numb
木材 mùcái[名]timber
木匠 mùjiang[名]carpenter
木偶 mù'ǒu[名]puppet
木头(頭)mùtou[名]wood

目 mù[名]1(眼睛)eye 2(条目)item
目标(標)mùbiāo[名]1(对象)target
2(目的)goal
目的 mùdì[名]1(指地点)destination
2(结果)aim 3(企图)intention
目光 mùguāng[名]1(视线)gaze
2(眼神)look
目录(錄)mùlù[名]1(指事物)
catalogue(英),catalog(美)2(指书刊
中)table of contents
目前 mùqián[名]present ▷ 到目前为
止 dào mùqián wéizhǐ to date ▷ 我们
目前的任务 wǒmen mùqián de
rènwù our current tasks

牧 mù[动]herd
牧民 mùmín[名]herdsman
牧师(師)mùshī[名]priest
牧业(業)mùyè[名]animal husbandry

募 mù[动](募款)raise
募捐 mùjuān[动]collect donations

墓 mù[名]grave
墓碑 mùbēi[名]gravestone
墓地 mùdì[名]graveyard

幕 mù[名](帷幔)curtain ▷ 银幕 yínmù
the silver screen

睦 mù [动] get on ▶ 和睦 hémù harmonious

穆 mù [形] solemn
  穆斯林 mùsīlín [名] Muslim

n

拿 ná [动] 1 (握) hold 2 (得) get

哪 nǎ [代] 1 (什么) which ▷ 你喜欢哪种音乐? Nǐ xǐhuan nǎ zhǒng yīnyuè? What kind of music do you like? ▷ 哪个人是李先生? Nǎge rén shì Lǐ xiānsheng? Which one is Mr Lǐ? 2 (任何一个) any ▷ 你哪天来都行。Nǐ nǎ tiān lái dōu xíng. You can come any day.
  哪个 (個) nǎge [代] which
  哪里 (裡) nǎlǐ [代] 1 (用于问处所) ▷ 你住在哪里? Nǐ zhù zài nǎlǐ? Where do you live? 2 (指某一地方) ▷ 我们应该在哪里见过。Wǒmen yīnggāi zài nǎlǐ jiànguo. I'm sure we've met somewhere before. 3 (谦) ▷ 哪里, 哪里, 你过奖了。Nǎlǐ, nǎlǐ, nǐ guòjiǎng le. No, no, it was nothing.
  哪些 nǎxiē [代] which

那 nà I [代] that ▷ 那些人 nàxiē rén those people II [连] then ▷ 你想买, 那就买吧。Nǐ xiǎng mǎi, nà jiù mǎi ba. If you want to buy it, then buy it.
  那边 (邊) nàbiān [名] that side
  那个 (個) nàge [代] (指代人、事或物) that
  那里 (裡) nàlǐ [代] ▷ 我去过那里。Wǒ qùguo nàlǐ. I've been there. ▷ 我也要去那里吗? Wǒ yě yào qù nàlǐ ma? Shall I go over there as well?
  那么 (麼) nàme [代] 1 (表示程度) ▷ 你不该那么相信他。Nǐ bùgāi nàme

xiāngxìn tā. You shouldn't trust him so much. **2**(表示方式) ▷ 你别那么想。 Nǐ bié nàme xiǎng. Don't think in that way.

那儿(兒) nàr [副] there

那些 nàxiē [代] those

那样(樣) nàyàng [副] ▷ 我没有说过那样的话。Wǒ méiyǒu shuōguo nàyàng de huà. I never said anything like that.

奶 nǎi [名] milk ▶ 酸奶 suānnǎi yoghurt

奶酪 nǎilào [名] cheese

奶奶 nǎinai [名] (父方的) granny

奶农(農) nǎinóng [名] dairy farmer

耐 nài [动] **1**(指人) endure ▶ 耐性 nàixìng patience **2**(指材料) be resistant ▶ 耐用 nàiyòng enduring

耐力 nàilì [名] stamina

耐心 nàixīn [形] patient

男 nán [名] (男性) male

男孩子 nánháizi [名] boy

男朋友 nánpéngyou [名] boyfriend

男人 nánrén [名] man

南 nán [名] south ▶ 东南 dōngnán south-east ▶ 西南 xīnán south-west

南边(邊) nánbiān [名] the south

南部 nánbù [名] southern part

南方 nánfāng [名] the South

南极(極) nánjí [名] South Pole

南面 nánmiàn [名] south

难(難) nán [形] **1**(困难) hard **2**(不好) bad

难(難)道 nándào [副] ▷ 你难道还不明白吗？Nǐ nándào hái bù míngbai ma? How can you not understand? ▷ 难道你就不累？Nándào nǐ jiù bù lèi? Aren't you tired?

难(難)过(過) nánguò I [动] have a hard time II [形] upset

难(難)看 nánkàn [形] **1**(丑) ugly **2**(不体面) ashamed

难(難)免 nánmiǎn [动] be unavoidable

难(難)受 nánshòu [动] **1**(指身体) not feel well **2**(指心情) feel down

脑(腦) nǎo [名] **1**(生理) brain **2**(脑筋) brain **3**(头部) head **4**(头领) leader ▶ 首脑 shǒunǎo head

脑(腦)袋 nǎodai [名] head

脑(腦)子 nǎozi [名] brain

闹(鬧) nào I [形] noisy II [动] **1**(吵闹) have a row ▶ 闹别扭 nào bièniu fall out **2**(病、灾难) suffer from ▶ 闹肚子 nào dùzi have diarrhoea (英) 或 diarrhea (美)

闹(鬧)钟(鐘) nàozhōng [名] alarm clock

呢 ne [助] **1**(表示疑问) ▷ 你们都走，我呢？Nǐmen dōu zǒu, wǒ ne? If you all go, what about me? ▷ 我到底错在哪儿呢？Wǒ dàodǐ cuò zài nǎr ne? What did I actually do wrong? **2**(表示陈述) ▷ 离北京还远着呢。Lí Běijīng hái yuǎnzhe ne. Beijing is still quite far. **3**(表示持续) ▷ 老师还在办公室呢。Lǎoshī hái zài bàngōngshì ne. The teacher is still in the office.

→ see also/另见 ní

呢 ne is added to the end of a statement to form a tentative question, or to indicate that a response is expected, e.g. 你好吗？我很好，你呢？ Nǐ hǎo ma? Wǒ hěn hǎo, nǐ ne? (How are you? Fine, and you?). It may also be used to stress continuity, e.g. 我还在吃饭呢 Wǒ hái zài chīfàn ne (I am still eating dinner), whereas 吗 ma is added to the end of any statement to turn it into a simple yes/no question, e.g. 你忙吗？ Nǐ máng ma? (Are you busy?).

内(內) nèi [名] (里头) inside ▶ 室内 shìnèi indoor ▶ 内地 nèidì inland ▷ 他在一个月内完成了任务。Tā zài yī gè yuè nèi wánchéngle rènwu. He finished the task within a month.

内(內)部 nèibù [形] internal

内(內)服 nèifú [动] take orally

内(內)行 nèiháng [名] expert

内(內)科 nèikē [名] internal medicine

内(內)容 nèiróng [名] content

内(內)向 nèixiàng [形] introverted

能 néng I [名] 1 (能力) ability 2 (物) (能量) energy ▶ 能量 néngliàng energy II [形] capable III [助动] can

能 néng, 会 huì, and 可以 kěyǐ can all be used to express ability and are sometimes used interchangeably. Strictly, 能 néng should be used to express physical ability, e.g. 我能跑得很快 wǒ néng pǎo de hěn kuài (I can run very fast), while 会 huì should express a learned ability, e.g. 我会说法语 wǒ huì shuō Fǎyǔ (I can speak French). Both 能 néng and 可以 kěyǐ can express being able to do something because you have been granted permission, e.g. 你能/可以借我的照相机 nǐ néng/kěyǐ jiè wǒ de zhàoxiàngjī (You can/may borrow my camera).

能干 (幹) nénggàn [形] capable

能够 (夠) nénggòu [动] be able to

能力 nénglì [名] ability

能量饮 (飲) 料 néngliàng yǐnliào [名] energy drink

能源 néngyuán [名] energy

呢 ní [名] woollen cloth
→ see also/另见 ne

呢子 nízi [名] woollen cloth

泥 ní [名] (指土) mud

你 nǐ [代] 1 (称对方) you 2 (你的) your ▷ 你家有几口人? Nǐ jiā yǒu jǐ kǒu rén? How many people are there in your family?

你们 (們) nǐmen [代] you (pl)

你好 nǐhǎo [叹] hello

你好 nǐhǎo is the most common way to say **hello** in Chinese. It is also used to ask **How are you?** 你好吗? Nǐhǎo ma?. The literal translation of **How are you?**, 你怎么样? Nǐ zěnmeyàng?, means **What happened to you?**

腻 (膩) nì [形] (太油) oily

蔫 niān [形] (枯萎) withered

年 nián I [名] 1 (时间单位) year 2 (元旦或春节) New Year 3 (岁数) age II [形] annual

年代 niándài [名] (时代) period

年级 (級) niánjí [名] year (英), grade (美)

年纪 (紀) niánjì [名] age

年龄 (齡) niánlíng [名] age

年轻 (輕) niánqīng [形] young

黏 nián [形] sticky

念 (唸) niàn [动] 1 (读) read 2 (上学) study

念 (唸) 叨 niàndao [动] (唠叨) nag

念 (唸) 书 (書) niànshū [动] study

念 (唸) 头 (頭) niàntou [名] idea

鸟 (鳥) niǎo [名] bird

尿 niào I [名] urine ▶ 撒尿 sāniào urinate II [动] urinate

镊 (鑷) niè [名] tweezers (pl) ▶ 镊子 nièzi tweezers (pl)

您 nín [代] you ▷ 您慢走! nín màn zǒu! Mind how you go!

宁 (寧) níng [形] peaceful
→ see also/另见 nìng

拧 (擰) níng [动] 1 (毛巾、衣服) wring 2 (皮肤) pinch

柠 (檸) níng see below/见下文

柠 (檸) 檬 níngméng [名] lemon

宁 (寧) nìng [副] ▶ 宁愿 nìngyuàn would rather
→ see also/另见 níng

牛 niú [名] 1 (指动物) cow ▶ 公牛 gōngniú bull 2 (指肉) beef ▶ 牛肉 niúròu beef

牛奶 niúnǎi [名] milk

牛仔裤 (褲) niúzǎikù [名] jeans (pl)

扭 niǔ [动] 1 (掉转) turn around 2 (拧) twist 3 (崴) sprain

纽 (紐) niǔ [名] (扣子) button ▶ 纽扣 niǔkòu button

纽 (紐) 约 (約) Niǔyuē [名] New York

农 (農) nóng [名] 1 (农业) agriculture 2 (农民) farmer

农(農)场(場) nóngchǎng [名] farm

农(農)村 nóngcūn [名] the countryside

农(農)历(曆) nónglì [名] lunar calendar

农(農)民 nóngmín [名] farmer

农(農)民工 nóngmíngōng [名] migrant worker

农(農)业(業) nóngyè [名] agriculture

浓(濃) nóng [形] 1 (指气味、味道) strong 2 (指烟雾) thick 3 (指兴趣) great ▷ 他对语言有很浓的兴趣。Tā duì yǔyán yǒu hěn nóng de xìngqù. He has a great interest in languages.

浓(濃)缩(縮) nóngsuō I [动] condense II [形] condensed

弄 nòng [动] 1 (搞) make 2 (设法取得) get

努 nǔ [动] (幼儿) make an effort ▷ 我们再努把力。wǒmen zài nǔ bǎ lì. Let's make one last effort.

努力 nǔlì [动] try hard ▷ 我会尽最大努力。Wǒ huì jìn zuìdà nǔlì. I'll try my very best.

怒 nù I [形] (生气) angry ▷ 恼怒 nǎonù furious II [名] anger ▷ 发怒 fānù lose one's temper

女 nǚ [名] 1 (女子) woman ▷ 女演员 nǚyǎnyuán actress 2 (女儿) daughter ▷ 子女 zǐnǚ children (pl)

女儿(兒) nǚ'ér [名] daughter

女孩儿(兒) nǚháir [名] girl

女孩子 nǚháizi [名] girl

女朋友 nǚpéngyou [名] girlfriend

女人 nǚrén [名] woman

女士 nǚshì [名] 1 (指称呼) Ms. 2 (对妇女的尊称) lady

女婿 nǚxu [名] son-in-law

暖 nuǎn I [形] warm II [动] warm

暖和 nuǎnhuo I [形] warm II [动] warm up

暖气(氣) nuǎnqì [名] heating

暖水瓶 nuǎnshuǐpíng [名] Thermos® flask

挪 nuó [动] move ▷ 挪动 nuódong move

O

哦 ó [叹] oh ▷ 哦, 他也来了。Ó, tā yě lái le. Oh, he's come too.
→ see also/另见 ò

哦 ò [叹] oh ▷ 哦, 我明白了。Ò, wǒ míngbai le. Oh, now I understand.
→ see also/另见 ó

欧(歐) ōu [名] (欧洲) Europe ▷ 欧洲 Ōuzhōu Europe

欧(歐)元 ōuyuán [名] euro

呕(嘔) ǒu [动] vomit

呕(嘔)吐 ǒutù [动] vomit

偶 ǒu [名] 1 (人像) image ▷ 木偶 mù'ǒu puppet 2 (双数) even number ▷ 偶数 ǒushù even number

偶尔(爾) ǒu'ěr [副] occasionally

偶然 ǒurán [形] chance

藕 ǒu [名] lotus root

P

爬 pá [动] 1(前移) crawl 2(上移) climb ▶ 爬山 páshān climb a mountain 3(起床) get up 4(升迁) be promoted

怕 pà [动] 1(惧怕) fear 2(担心) be afraid 3(估计) may be

拍 pāi I [动] 1(击打) beat 2(拍摄) shoot 3(发) send 4(拍马屁) flatter II [名] 1(用具) bat (英), paddle (美) 2(节奏) beat
拍照 pāizhào [动] take a photograph
拍子 pāizi [名] 1(用具) bat (英), paddle (美) ▶ 网球拍子 wǎngqiú pāizi tennis racket 2(节奏) beat

排 pái I [动] 1(摆放) put ... in order 2(排演) rehearse 3(除去) drain II [名] 1(行列) row 2(指军队) platoon 3(指水运) raft III [量] row
排毒 pái dú [动] detox
排队(隊) páiduì [动] queue (英), stand in line (美)
排球 páiqiú [名] volleyball

牌 pái [名] 1(标志板) board ▶ 门牌 ménpái house number ▶ 招牌 zhāopái shop sign 2(商标) brand

派 pài I [名] 1(帮派) group ▶ 学派 xuépài school of thought 2(风度) manner II [动] 1(分配) set 2(委派) send 3(安排) assign
派对(對) pàiduì [名] party

攀 pān [动] 1(向上爬) climb 2(指关系) seek friends in high places ▶ 高攀 gāopān be a social climber 3(拉扯) chat
攀登 pāndēng [动] scale

盘(盤) pán I [名] 1(盘子) tray 2(盘状物) ▶ 棋盘 qípán chessboard 3(行情) quotation II [动] 1(绕) wind ▶ 盘旋 pánxuán wind 2(核查) examine ▶ 盘问 pánwèn interrogate 3(清点) make an inventory ▶ 盘货 pánhuò stocktake 4(转让) transfer III [量] 1(指物量) ▷ 三盘录像带 sān pán lùxiàngdài three videotapes 2(指动量) game
▌ measure word, used for videotapes, cassettes and board games
盘(盤)子 pánzi [名] plate

判 pàn I [动] 1(分辨) distinguish ▶ 判明 pànmíng ascertain 2(评定) judge 3(裁决) sentence ▶ 审判 shěnpàn try II [副] clearly
判断(斷) pànduàn [动] judge

盼 pàn [动] 1(盼望) long 2(看) look ▷ 左顾右盼 zuǒ gù yòu pàn look around
盼望 pànwàng [动] long

旁 páng I [名] side II [形] (口) other
旁边(邊) pángbiān I [名] side II [副] beside

胖 pàng [形] fat

抛(拋) pāo [动] 1(投掷) throw 2(丢下) leave ... behind 3(暴露) bare ▷ 抛头露面 pāo tóu lù miàn appear in public 4(脱手) dispose of
抛(拋)弃(棄) pāoqì [动] desert

跑 pǎo [动] 1(奔) run 2(逃) escape 3(奔波) run around 4(漏) leak
跑步 pǎobù [动] run

泡 pào I [名] 1(指气体) bubble 2(泡状物) ▶ 灯泡 dēngpào light bulb II [动] 1(浸) soak 2(消磨) dawdle 3(沏) infuse ▷ 泡茶 pào chá make tea
泡沫 pàomò [名] foam

炮(砲) pào [名] 1(武器) cannon 2(爆竹) firecracker

陪 péi [动] 1(相伴) go with ▷ 我要陪母亲去医院。wǒ yào péi mǔqīn qù yīyuàn I have to go to the hospital with my mother. 2(协助) assist
陪同 péitóng I [动] accompany II [名] guide

培 péi [动] foster
培训(訓) péixùn [动] train
培养(養) péiyǎng [动] cultivate
培育 péiyù [动] 1(培植养育) cultivate 2(培养教育) nurture

赔(賠) péi [动] 1(赔偿) make good 2(亏本) make a loss
赔(賠)偿(償) péicháng [动] compensate

佩 pèi [动] 1(佩带) wear 2(佩服) admire ▶ 钦佩 qīnpèi esteem
佩服 pèifú [动] admire

配 pèi I [动] 1(指两性) marry 2(指动物) mate 3(调和) mix ▶ 配药 pèiyào make up a prescription 4(分派) allocate ▶ 配售 pèishòu ration 5(衬托) match 6(符合) fit II [名] spouse
配合 pèihé I [动] cooperate II [形] complementary

喷 pēn [动] gush
喷泉 pēnquán [名] fountain
喷嚏 pēntì [名] sneeze

盆 pén [名] 1(盛具) basin ▶ 脸盆 liǎnpén washbasin 2(盆状物) ▶ 骨盆 gǔpén pelvis

朋 péng [名] friend
朋友 péngyou [名] 1(指友谊) friend 2(女友) girlfriend 3(男友) boyfriend
朋友圈 péngyou quān [名] (指社交媒体) moment

捧 pěng I [动] 1(托) hold ... in both hands 2(奉承) flatter II [量] handful

碰 pèng [动] 1(撞击) hit 2(遇见) bump into 3(试探) take a chance
碰见(見) pèngjiàn [动] encounter
碰巧 pèngqiǎo [副] by chance

批 pī I [动] 1(批示) comment ▶ 批示 pīshì comment 2(批评) criticize II [名] wholesale III [量] 1(指人) group 2(指物) batch
批判 pīpàn [动] 1(驳斥) repudiate 2(批评) criticize
批评(評) pīpíng [动] criticize
批准 pīzhǔn [动] approve

披 pī [动] 1(搭) drape ... over one's shoulders 2(开裂) split

皮 pí I [名] 1(表皮) skin 2(皮革) leather ▶ 漆皮 qīpí patent leather 3(外皮) covering 4(表面) surface 5(薄片) sheet ▶ 奶皮 nǎipí skin on the milk 6(指橡胶) rubber II [形] 1(韧) thick-skinned 2(变韧的) rubbery 3(顽皮) naughty
皮包 píbāo [名] leather handbag
皮肤(膚) pífū [名] skin

疲 pí [形] 1(疲劳) tired 2(厌倦) tired of
疲倦 píjuàn [形] tired
疲劳(勞) píláo [形] 1(劳累) weary 2(衰退) weakened

啤 pí see below / 见下文
啤酒 píjiǔ [名] beer

脾 pí [名] spleen
脾气(氣) píqi [名] 1(怒气) temper 2(性情) temperament

匹 pǐ I [动] match II [量] 1(指动物) ▷ 三匹马 sān pǐ mǎ three horses 2(指布料) bolt
measure word, used for horses, mules, donkeys and bolts of silk

屁 pì I [名] wind ▶ 放屁 fàngpì fart II [形] meaningless
屁股 pìgu [名] 1(指人) bottom 2(指后部) rear

譬 pì [名] analogy ▶ 譬如 pìrú for example ▶ 譬喻 pìyù metaphor
譬如 pìrú [动] take ... for example

偏 piān [形] 1(倾斜的) slanting 2(不公的) biased
偏见(見) piānjìn [名] prejudice

偏偏 piānpiān [副] 1(表示主观) persistently 2(表示客观) contrary to expectation 3(表示范围) only

篇 piān I [名] 1(文章) writing ▶ 篇章 piānzhāng sections (pl) 2(单张纸) sheet ▶ 歌篇儿 gēpiān song sheet II [量] ▷ 三篇文章 sān piān wénzhāng three articles measure word, used for articles, essays etc.

便 pián see below/见下文
→ see also/另见 biàn
便便 piánpián [形] fat
便宜 piányi I [形] cheap II [名] small gains (pl) III [动] let ... off lightly

片 piàn I [名] 1(指薄度) piece ▶ 纸片 zhǐpiàn scraps of paper 2(指地区) area II [动] slice III [形] 1(不全) incomplete ▶ 片面 piànmiàn one-sided 2(简短) brief IV [量] 1(指片状物) ▷ 两片药 liǎng piàn yào two tablets ▷ 几片树叶 jǐ piàn shùyè some leaves ▷ 一片面包 yī piàn miànbāo a slice of bread 2(指水陆) stretch measure word, used for thin flat objects
片面 piànmiàn I [名] one side II [形] one-sided
片约(約) piànyuē [名] film contract

骗(騙) piàn [动] 1(欺骗) deceive 2(骗得) swindle ▶ 骗钱 piànqián swindle
骗(騙)子 piànzi [名] swindler

漂 piāo [动] 1(浮) float 2(流动) drift
→ see also/另见 piào

飘(飄) piāo [动] 1(飞扬) flutter 2(发软) wobble
飘(飄)扬(揚) piāoyáng [动] flutter

票 piào [名] 1(作凭证) ticket 2(指钞票) note (英), bill (美) 3(指戏曲) amateur performance

漂 piào see below/见下文
→ see also/另见 piāo
漂亮 piàoliang [形] 1(好看) good-looking 2(精彩) wonderful

拼 pīn [动] 1(合) join together 2(竭尽全力) go all out ▶ 拼命 pīnmìng with all one's might 3(字、词) spell ▷ 你能拼一下这个词吗? nǐ néng pīn yīxià zhège cí ma? Can you spell this word?
拼命 pīnmìng [动] 1(不要命) risk one's life 2(努力) go all out
拼音 pīnyīn [名] Pinyin

贫(貧) pín I [形] 1(穷) poor ▶ 贫民 pínmín the poor 2(少) deficient ▶ 贫血 pínxuè anaemia (英), anemia (美) II [动] (方) be a chatterbox
贫(貧)苦 pínkǔ [形] poverty-stricken
贫(貧)穷(窮) pínqióng [形] poor

频(頻) pín [副] frequently
频(頻)繁 pínfán [形] frequent
频(頻)率 pínlù [名] 1(物) frequency 2(指心脏) rate

品 pǐn I [名] 1(物品) article ▶ 商品 shāngpǐn merchandise 2(等级) grade ▶ 精品 jīngpǐn special product 3(种类) type ▶ 品种 pǐnzhǒng variety 4(品质) character ▶ 品德 pǐndé moral character II [动] taste
品尝(嘗) pǐncháng [动] savour (英), savor (美)
品德 pǐndé [名] moral character
品格 pǐngé [名] character
品质(質) pǐnzhì [名] 1(品德) character 2(质量) quality
品种(種) pǐnzhǒng [名] 1(动) breed 2(植) species 3(指产品) kind

乒 pīng I [拟] bang II [名] (乒乓球) table tennis
乒乓球 pīngpāngqiú [名] table tennis

平 píng I [形] 1(平坦) flat ▶ 平原 píngyuán plain 2(安定) calm 3(普通) ordinary 4(平均) even ▶ 平分 píngfēn fifty-fifty 5(指比分) ▶ 平局 píngjú a draw II [动] 1(夷平) level 2(指成绩) equal 3(镇压) suppress
平安 píng'ān [形] safe and sound
平安夜 píng'ān yè [名] Christmas Eve
平常 píngcháng I [形] common II [副] usually

平等 píngděng [形] equal

平凡 píngfán [形] uneventful

平方 píngfāng [名] 1(数) square 2(平方米) square metre (英) 或 meter (美)

平衡 pínghéng [名] balance ▷ 平衡收支 pínghéng shōuzhī balance revenue and expenditure

平静(靜) píngjìng [形] calm

平均 píngjūn [形] average

平时(時) píngshí [副] usually

平原 píngyuán [名] plain

评(評) píng [动] 1(评论) criticize ▶ 批评 pīpíng criticize ▶ 书评 shūpíng book review 2(评判) judge ▶ 评分 píngfēn mark 3(选) select

评(評)价(價) píngjià [动] evaluate

评(評)论(論) pínglùn [动] review

苹(蘋) píng see below/见下文

苹(蘋)果 píngguǒ [名] apple

凭(憑) píng I [动] rely on II [名] evidence ▶ 凭据 píngjù credentials (pl) III [连] no matter

瓶 píng [名] bottle

瓶子 píngzi [名] bottle

坡 pō [名] slope ▶ 山坡 shānpō slope

迫 pò I [动] 1(逼迫) force 2(接近) approach II [形] urgent

迫切 pòqiè [形] pressing

破 pò I [形] 1(受损) broken 2(烂) lousy II [动] 1(受损) cut 2(破除) break ▶ 破例 pòlì make an exception 3(钱、工夫) spend 4(揭穿) expose ▶ 破案 pò'àn solve a case 5(打败) defeat

破坏(壞) pòhuài [动] 1(建筑、环境、文物、公物) destroy 2(团结、社会秩序) undermine 3(协定、法规、规章) violate 4(计划) bring ... down 5(名誉) damage

破裂 pòliè [动] 1(谈判) break down 2(感情) break up 3(外交关系) break off

扑(撲) pū [动] 1(冲向) rush at 2(专注于) devote 3(扑打) swat 4(翅膀) beat

扑(撲)克 pūkè [名] poker

铺(鋪) pū [动] 1(摊开) spread 2(铺设) lay
→ see also/另见 pù

葡 pú see below/见下文

葡萄 pútáo [名] grape

朴(樸) pǔ see below/见下文

朴(樸)实(實) pǔshí [形] 1(简朴) simple 2(诚实) honest

朴(樸)素 pǔsù [形] 1(衣着) plain 2(生活) simple 3(语言) plain

普 pǔ [形] general

普遍 pǔbiàn I [形] common II [副] commonly

普通 pǔtōng [形] common

普通话(話) pǔtōnghuà [名] Mandarin

铺(鋪) pù [名] 1(商店) shop ▶ 杂货铺 general store 2(床) plank bed ▶ 卧铺 berth
→ see also/另见 pū

q

七 qī [数] seven
七月 qīyuè [名] July

妻 qī [名] wife ▸ 未婚妻 wèihūnqī fiancée
妻子 qīzi [名] wife

柒 qī [数] seven
> This is the character for "seven", which is mainly used in banks, on receipts, etc. to prevent mistakes and forgery.

期 qī I [名] 1(预定时间) time limit ▸ 到期 dàoqī expire 2(一段时间) period of time ▸ 假期 jiàqī holiday II [量] 1(指训练班) class 2(指杂志、报纸) edition III [动] expect
期待 qīdài [动] await
期间(間) qījiān [名] period of time
期望 qīwàng I [名] expectations (pl) II [动] expect

欺 qī [动] 1(欺骗) deceive 2(欺负) bully
欺负(負) qīfu [动] bully
欺骗(騙) qīpiàn [动] deceive

齐(齊) qí I [形] 1(整齐) neat 2(一致) joint 3(完备) ready II [动] 1(达到) reach 2(取齐) level III [副] at the same time

其 qí [代] (书) 1(他的) his 2(她的) her 3(它的) its 4(他们的、她们的、它们的) their 5(他) him 6(她) her 7(它) it 8(他们、她们、它们) them 9(那个) that

其次 qícì [代] 1(下一个) next ▸ 其次要做的事是什么? Qícì yào zuò de shì shì shénme? What are we going to do next? 2(次要的) the second

其实(實) qíshí [副] actually

其他 qítā [代] other ▸ 我不知道, 你问其他人吧。Wǒ bù zhīdào, nǐ wèn qítā rén ba. I don't know, ask someone else. ▸ 还有其他事情没有? Háiyǒu qítā shìqing méiyǒu? Is there anything else?

其余(餘) qíyú [代] the rest

其中 qízhōng [名] among which ▸ 他有六套西服, 其中两套是黑色的。Tā yǒu liù tào xīfú, qízhōng liǎng tào shì hēisè de. He has six suits, of which two are black.

奇 qí I [形] 1(非常少见的) strange ▸ 奇闻 qíwén fantastic story ▸ 奇事 qíshì miracle 2(出人意料的) unexpected ▸ 奇袭 qíxí surprise attack ▸ 奇遇 qíyù lucky encounter II [动] surprise ▸ 惊奇 jīngqí surprise III [副] unusually
奇怪 qíguài [形] strange
奇迹(跡) qíjì [名] miracle

骑(騎) qí I [动] ride II [名] cavalry

棋 qí [名] chess ▸ 围棋 wéiqí go (board game)

旗 qí [名] flag ▸ 锦旗 jǐnqí silk banner
旗袍 qípáo [名] cheongsam
旗子 qízi [名] flag

乞 qǐ [动] beg ▸ 行乞 xíngqǐ go begging
乞丐 qǐgài [名] beggar
乞求 qǐqiú [动] beg

企 qǐ [动] look forward to
企图(圖) qǐtú I [动] plan II [名] (贬) plan
企业(業) qǐyè [名] enterprise

启(啟) qǐ [动] 1(打开) open ▸ 开启 kāiqǐ open 2(开导) enlighten 3(开始) start
启(啟)发(發) qǐfā I [动] inspire II [名] inspiration

起 qǐ I [动] 1 (起来) rise ▸ 起立 qǐlì stand up 2 (取出) remove 3 (长出) form ▸ 脚上起泡 jiǎo shang qǐ pào form a blister on one's foot 4 (产生) become 5 (拟订) sketch out ▸ 起草 qǐcǎo draft 6 (建立) establish II [量] ▷ 一起交通事故 yī qǐ jiāotōng shìgù a traffic accident ▷ 一起火灾 yī qǐ huǒzāi a fire ▊ measure word, used for accidents

起床 qǐchuáng [动] get up

起点 (點) qǐdiǎn [名] starting point

起飞 (飛) qǐfēi [动] take off ▸ 飞机准时起飞。Fēijī zhǔnshí qǐfēi. The plane took off on time.

起来 (來) qǐlái [动] 1 (站起或坐起) get up 2 (起床) get up

气 (氣) qì I [名] 1 (气体) gas ▸ 毒气 dúqì poison gas 2 (空气) air ▷ 这球没气了。Zhè qiú méi qì le. This ball is deflated. 3 (气息) breath 4 (精神) mood 5 (气味) smell ▸ 臭气 chòuqì stink 6 (习气) manner ▸ 孩子气 háiziqì childishness 7 (怒气) anger 8 (中医) qi II [动] 1 (生气) be angry 2 (使生气) provoke

气 (氣) 氛 qìfēn [名] atmosphere

气 (氣) 功 qìgōng [名] qigong

气 (氣) 候 qìhòu [名] climate

气 (氣) 温 (溫) qìwēn [名] temperature

气 (氣) 象 qìxiàng [名] 1 (大气现象) weather 2 (气象学) meteorology 3 (情景) atmosphere

汽 qì [名] 1 (气体) vapour (英), vapor (美) 2 (蒸气) steam

汽车 (車) qìchē [名] car ▸ 公共汽车 gōnggòng qìchē bus

汽水 qìshuǐ [名] fizzy drink

汽油 qìyóu [名] petrol (英), gasoline (美)

器 qì [名] 1 (器具) utensil ▸ 乐器 yuèqì musical instrument ▸ 瓷器 cíqì china 2 (器官) organ

器官 qìguān [名] organ

恰 qià [副] 1 (适当) appropriately 2 (刚好) exactly

恰当 (當) qiàdàng [形] appropriate

恰好 qiàhǎo [副] luckily

千 qiān I [数] thousand II [形] many

千万 (萬) qiānwàn I [数] ten million II [副] ▷ 你千万别做傻事。Nǐ qiānwàn bié zuò shǎshì. You absolutely mustn't do anything stupid.

牵 (牽) qiān [动] 1 (拉住) pull 2 (牵涉) involve

铅 (鉛) qiān [名] (化) lead

铅 (鉛) 笔 (筆) qiānbǐ [名] pencil

谦 (謙) qiān [形] modest

谦 (謙) 虚 (虛) qiānxū I [形] modest II [动] speak modestly

签 (簽) qiān I [动] 1 (名字) sign 2 (意见) endorse II [名] 1 (指占卜、赌博、比赛) lot 2 (标志) label ▸ 书签 shūqiān bookmark 3 (细棍子) stick ▸ 牙签 yáqiān toothpick

签 (簽) 名 qiānmíng [动] sign

签 (簽) 证 (證) qiānzhèng [名] visa

签 (簽) 字 qiānzì [动] sign one's name

前 qián I [形] 1 (正面的) front 2 (指次序) first 3 (从前的) former ▸ 前夫 qiánfū ex-husband 4 (未来的) future II [动] advance

前进 (進) qiánjìn [动] 1 (向前走) advance 2 (发展) make progress

前面 qiánmian [副] in front

前年 qiánnián [名] the year before last

前天 qiántiān [名] the day before yesterday

前头 (頭) qiántou [副] front

前途 qiántú [名] future

前夕 qiánxī [名] eve

钱 (錢) qián [名] money

钱 (錢) 包 qiánbāo [名] 1 (女用) purse 2 (男用) wallet

浅 (淺) qiǎn [形] 1 (指深度) shallow 2 (指难度) easy 3 (指学识) lacking 4 (指颜色) light ▷ 浅蓝色 qiǎnlánsè light blue ▷ 浅绿色 qiǎnlùsè pale green 5 (指时间) short

欠 qiàn [动] 1 (钱、情) owe 2 (缺乏) lack 3 (移动) raise ... slightly

枪(槍) qiāng [名] 1(旧兵器) spear 2(兵器) gun ▶ 手枪 shǒuqiāng pistol

强(強) qiáng I [形] 1(力量大) strong 2(程度高) able 3(好) better 4(略多于) extra ▷ 三分之一强 sān fēn zhī yī qiáng a third extra II [动] force
→ see also/另见 qiǎng
强(強)大 qiángdà [形] powerful
强(強)盗(盗) qiángdào [名] robber
强(強)调(調) qiángdiào [动] stress
强(強)度 qiángdù [名] intensity
强(強)奸(姦) qiángjiān [动] rape
强(強)烈 qiángliè [形] intense

墙(牆) qiáng [名] wall

抢(搶) qiǎng [动] 1(抢劫) rob 2(抢夺) grab 3(抢先) forestall 4(赶紧) rush
抢(搶)劫 qiǎngjié [动] rob

强(強) qiǎng [动] 1(勉强) make an effort 2(迫使) force
→ see also/另见 qiáng
强(強)迫 qiǎngpò [动] force

悄 qiāo see below/见下文
悄悄 qiāoqiāo [副] 1(悄然无声) quietly 2(偷偷) stealthily

敲 qiāo [动] 1(击) knock 2(敲诈) blackmail
敲诈(詐) qiāozhà [动] extort

桥(橋) qiáo [名] bridge
桥(橋)梁(樑) qiáoliáng [名] bridge

瞧 qiáo [动] look

巧 qiǎo [形] 1(手、口) nimble 2(有技能的) skilful (英), skillful (美) 3(恰好) coincidental 4(虚浮的) false
巧克力 qiǎokèlì [名] chocolate
巧妙 qiǎomiào [形] clever

切 qiē [动] cut

茄 qié [名] aubergine (英), eggplant (美)
茄子 qiézi [名] aubergine (英), eggplant (美)

窃(竊) qiè I [动] steal II [副] surreptitiously
窃(竊)听(聽) qiètīng [动] eavesdrop
窃(竊)贼(賊) qièzéi [名] thief

侵 qīn [动] invade
侵略 qīnlüè [动] invade

亲(親) qīn I [名] 1(父母) parent 2(亲戚) relative 3(婚姻) marriage ▶ 定亲 dìngqīn engagement 4(新娘) bride II [形] 1(指血缘近) blood 2(指感情好) intimate III [副] personally IV [动] 1(亲吻) kiss 2(亲近) be close to
亲(親)爱(愛) qīn'ài [形] dear
亲(親)爱(愛)的 qīn'ài de [名] darling (an affectionate term of address)
亲(親)近 qīnjìn [形] close
亲(親)密 qīnmì [形] close ▷ 亲密朋友 qīnmì péngyou close friend ▷ 亲密无间 qīnmì wújiàn be as thick as thieves
亲(親)戚(慼) qīnqi [名] relative
亲(親)切 qīnqiè [形] warm
亲(親)热(熱) qīnrè [形] affectionate
亲(親)自 qīnzì [副] personally

琴 qín [名] ▶ 钢琴 gāngqín piano ▶ 小提琴 xiǎotíqín violin

勤 qín I [形] hard-working II [副] regularly III [名] 1(勤务) duty ▶ 值勤 zhíqín be on duty 2(到场) attendance ▶ 考勤 kǎoqín check attendance
勤奋(奮) qínfèn [形] diligent
勤劳(勞) qínláo [形] hard-working

青 qīng I [形] 1(指绿色) green 2(指黑色) black 3(指年纪) young ▶ 青年 qīngnián youth II [名] 1(指青草) grass 2(指庄稼) unripe crops (pl)
青年 qīngnián [名] youth
青少年 qīngshàonián [名] teenager

轻(輕) qīng I [形] 1(指重量) light 2(指数量或程度) ▷ 他们年纪很轻。Tāmen niánjì hěn qīng. They are quite young. 3(指无足轻重) not important 4(指轻松愉快) relaxed ▶ 轻音乐 qīngyīnyuè light music II [副] 1(指少用力) gently 2(轻率) rashly III [动] disparage

轻(輕)松(鬆) qīngsōng [形] relaxing
轻(輕)易 qīngyì [副] 1(容易) easily 2(随便) rashly

倾(傾) qīng I [动] 1(斜) lean 2(塌) collapse 3(倒出) empty out 4(用尽) exhaust II [名] tendency
倾(傾)向 qīngxiàng I [动] incline to II [名] tendency

清 qīng I [形] 1(纯净) clear 2(寂静) quiet 3(清楚) distinct ▶ 分清 fēnqīng distinguish 4(完全) settled 5(纯洁) pure II [动] 1(清除) get rid of 2(结清) settle 3(清点) check 4(清理) put in order
清楚 qīngchu I [形] clear II [动] understand
清洁(潔) qīngjié [形] clean
清静(靜) qīngjìng [形] quiet
清明节(節) Qīngmíng Jié [名] Tomb Sweeping Festival

清明节 Qīngmíng Jié
  清明节 Qīngmíng Jié, **Tomb Sweeping Festival**, sometimes translated literally as **Clear and Bright Festival**, is celebrated on the 4th, 5th, or 6th of April. It is traditionally the time when Chinese families visit graves to honour their dead ancestors.

情 qíng [名] 1(感情) feeling ▶ 热情 rèqíng warmth 2(情面) kindness 3(爱情) love 4(情况) condition ▶ 实情 shíqíng true state of affairs
情节(節) qíngjié [名] 1(内容) plot 2(事实) circumstances (pl)
情景 qíngjǐng [名] sight
情况(況) qíngkuàng [名] 1(状况) situation 2(变化) military development
情侣(侶) qínglǚ [名] lovers (pl)
情人节(節) Qíngrén Jié [名] Valentine's Day
情形 qíngxíng [名] situation
情绪(緒) qíngxù [名] 1(心理状态) mood 2(不很开心) moodiness

晴 qíng [形] fine
晴朗 qínglǎng [形] sunny

请(請) qīng [动] 1(请求) ask ▷ 请他进来。Qǐng tā jìnlái. Ask him to come in. 2(邀请) invite 3(敬) ▷ 请这边走。Qǐng zhèbiān zǒu. This way, please. ▷ 请大家安静一下。Qǐng dàjiā ānjìng yíxià. Everyone quiet, please.
请(請)假 qǐngjià [动] ask for leave
请(請)教 qǐngjiào [动] consult
请(請)客 qǐngkè [动] treat
请(請)求 qǐngqiú [动] ask
请(請)问(問) qǐngwèn [动] ▷ 请问怎么出去？Qǐngwèn zěnme chūqù? Could you show me the way out, please?
请(請)勿 qǐngwù [动] ▷ 请勿吸烟。Qǐngwù xīyān. No smoking.

庆(慶) qìng I [动] celebrate II [名] festival ▶ 国庆 guóqìng National Day
庆(慶)贺(賀) qìnghè [动] celebrate
庆(慶)祝(祝) qìngzhù [动] celebrate

穷(窮) qióng I [形] poor II [名] limit III [副] 1(彻底) thoroughly 2(极端) extremely

秋 qiū [名] 1(指季节) autumn (英), fall (美) 2(指庄稼) harvest time 3(指一年) year 4(指厄运期) period
秋天 qiūtiān [名] autumn (英), fall (美)

求 qiú I [动] 1(请求) request 2(追求) strive II [名] demand

球 qiú [名] 1(数) (球体) sphere 2(指球状) ball ▶ 雪球 xuěqiú snowball 3(指体育) ball ▶ 篮球 lánqiú basketball ▶ 足球 zúqiú football 4(指比赛) ball game 5(地球) the Earth ▶ 全球 quánqiú the whole world
球场(場) qiúchǎng [名] court
球迷 qiúmí [名] fan

区(區) qū I [动] distinguish II [名] 1(地区) area 2(指行政单位) region ▶ 自治区 zìzhìqū autonomous region
区(區)别(別) qūbié [动] distinguish
区(區)分 qūfēn [动] differentiate
区(區)域 qūyù [名] area

趋(趨) qū [动] 1 (走) hasten 2 (趋向) tend to become
趋(趨)势(勢) qūshì [名] trend
趋(趨)向 qūxiàng I [动] tend to II [名] trend

渠 qú [名] ditch
渠道 qúdào [名] 1 (水道) irrigation ditch 2 (途径) channel

曲 qǔ [名] 1 (指歌曲) song 2 (指乐曲) music
曲子 qǔzi [名] tune

取 qǔ 1 (拿到) take 2 (得到) obtain 3 (采取) adopt 4 (选取) choose
取得 qǔdé [动] get
取消 qǔxiāo [动] cancel

娶 qǔ [动] marry

去 qù I [动] 1 (到) go 2 (除) get rid of 3 (距) be apart 4 (发) send II [形] past
去年 qùnián [名] last year
去世 qùshì [动] pass away

趣 qù I [名] interest ▶志趣 zhìqù interest II [形] interesting
趣味 qùwèi [名] taste

圈 quān I [名] 1 (环形物) circle ▶北极圈 Běijíquān Arctic Circle 2 (范围) circle II [动] circle
圈套 quāntào [名] trap

权(權) quán I [名] 1 (权力) power ▶当权 dāngquán be in power 2 (权利) right 3 (形势) ▶主动权 zhǔdòngquán initiative ▷控制权 kòngzhìquán control 4 (权宜) expediency II [副] for the time being
权(權)力 quánlì [名] power

全 quán I [形] 1 (齐全) complete 2 (整个) whole II [副] entirely III [动] keep ... intact
全部 quánbù [形] whole
全面 quánmiàn [形] comprehensive
全体(體) quántǐ [名] everyone

泉 quán [名] spring ▶温泉 wēnquán hot spring

拳 quán [名] fist
拳头(頭) quántóu [名] fist
拳击(擊) quánjī [名] boxing

鬈 quán [形] curly

劝(勸) quàn [动] 1 (说服) advise 2 (勉励) encourage
劝(勸)告 quàngào [动] advise

缺 quē I [动] 1 (缺乏) lack 2 (残破) be incomplete 3 (缺席) be absent II [名] vacancy ▶补缺 bǔquē fill a vacancy
缺点(點) quēdiǎn [名] shortcoming
缺乏 quēfá [动] lack
缺口 quēkǒu [名] 1 (口子) gap 2 (缺额) shortfall
缺少 quēshǎo [动] lack
缺席 quēxí [动] be absent
缺陷 quēxiàn [名] defect

瘸 qué [动] be lame

却(卻) què I [动] 1 (后退) step back 2 (使退却) drive ... back 3 (拒绝) decline ▶推却 tuīquè decline 4 (表示完成) ▶冷却 lěngquè cool off ▶忘却 wàngquè forget II [副] however

确(確) què I [副] 1 (确实地) really 2 (坚定地) firmly ▶确信 quèxìn firmly believe
确(確)定 quèdìng I [动] determine II [形] definite
确(確)实(實) quèshí I [形] true II [副] really

裙 qún [名] skirt
裙子 qúnzi [名] skirt

群 qún I [名] crowd II [量] 1 (指动物) herd, flock ▷一群绵羊 yī qún miányáng a flock of sheep ▷一群蜜蜂 yī qún mìfēng a swarm of bees ▷一群奶牛 yī qún nǎiniú a herd of cows 2 (指人) group ▷一群学生 yī qún xuésheng a group of students
群众(眾) qúnzhòng [名] the masses (pl)

r

然 rán [代] so
　然而 rán'ér [连] however
　然后(後) ránhòu [连] afterwards

燃 rán [动] 1 (燃烧) burn 2 (点燃) light
　燃料 ránliào [名] fuel
　燃烧(燒) ránshāo [动] burn

染 rǎn [动] 1 (着色) dye 2 (感染) contract 3 (沾染) catch

嚷 rǎng [动] 1 (喊叫) howl 2 (吵闹) make a racket

让(讓) ràng I [动] 1 (退让) make allowances 2 (允许) let 3 (转让) transfer II [介] by

扰(擾) rǎo [动] (搅扰) disturb ▸ 打扰 dǎrǎo disturb

绕(繞) rào [动] 1 (缠绕) wind 2 (围绕) go round 3 (迂回) make a detour

惹 rě [动] 1 (引起) stir up 2 (触动) provoke 3 (招) make

热(熱) rè I [名] 1 (物) heat 2 (高烧) fever ▸ 发热 fārè have a fever II [形] 1 (温度高) hot 2 (走俏) popular III [动] heat
　热(熱)爱(愛) rè'ài [动] love
　热(熱)狗 règǒu [名] hot dog
　热(熱)烈 rèliè [形] heated
　热(熱)闹(鬧) rènao [形] lively
　热(熱)情 rèqíng I [名] passion II [形] enthusiastic
　热(熱)搜 rè sōu [名] trending topic
　热(熱)线(線) rèxiàn [名] 1 (指电话或电报) hotline 2 (指交通) busy route
　热(熱)心 rèxīn [形] warm-hearted

人 rén [名] 1 (人类) human being ▸ 人权 rénquán human rights (pl) 2 (指某种人) person ▸ 军人 jūnrén soldier ▸ 中国人 Zhōngguórén a Chinese person/Chinese people 3 (人手) manpower
　人才 réncái [名] (指能人) talent
　人工 réngōng [形] man-made
　人口 rénkǒu [名] 1 (地区人数) population 2 (家庭人数) people
　人类(類) rénlèi [名] mankind, humankind
　人们(們) rénmen [名] people
　人民 rénmín [名] the people
　人民币(幣) rénmínbì [名] renminbi, RMB
　人生 rénshēng [名] life
　人体(體) réntǐ [名] the human body
　人物 rénwù [名] 1 (能人) figure 2 (艺术形象) character

忍 rěn [动] (忍受) endure
　忍耐 rěnnài [动] show restraint
　忍受 rěnshòu [动] bear

认(認) rèn [动] 1 (识) know 2 (承认) admit
　认(認)得 rènde [动] be acquainted with
　认(認)识(識) rènshi I [动] know II [名] understanding
　认(認)为(為) rènwéi [动] think
　认(認)真 rènzhēn I [形] serious II [动] take ... seriously

任 rèn I [动] 1 (聘) appoint ▸ 任命 wěirèn appoint 2 (听凭) let II [名] (职责) responsibility
　任何 rènhé [形] any ▷ 任何人都不能迟到。Rènhé rén dōu bùnéng chídào. No one can be late.
　任务(務) rènwu [名] task

扔 rēng [动] **1**(掷) throw **2**(丢) throw ... away

仍 réng [副] still

仍然 réngrán [副] (表示继续) still

日 rì [名] **1**(太阳) sun ▶ 日出 rìchū sunrise ▶ 日落 rìluò sunset **2**(白天) daytime **3**(天) day ▶ 明日 míngrì tomorrow **4**(每天) every day ▶ 城市面貌日见改善。Chéngshì miànmào rìjiàn gǎishàn. The city looks better and better every day. **5**(指某一天) day ▶ 生日 shēngrì birthday **6**(日本) Japan

日报(報) rìbào [名] daily paper

日本 Rìběn [名] Japan

日常 rìcháng [形] everyday

日记(記) rìjì [名] diary

日历(曆) rìlì [名] calendar

日期 rìqī [名] date

日用品 rìyòngpǐn [名] daily necessities

日语(語) Rìyǔ [名] Japanese

日元(圓) rìyuán [名] Japanese yen

日子 rìzi [名] **1**(日期) date **2**(时间) day **3**(生活) life

荣(榮) róng [形] (光荣) glorious

荣(榮)幸 róngxìng [形] honoured (英), honored (美) ▷ 认识您，我感到非常荣幸。Rènshi nín, wǒ gǎndào fēicháng róngxìng. I feel honoured to know you.

荣(榮)誉(譽) róngyù [名] (指名声) honour (英), honor (美)

容 róng I [动] **1**(容纳) fit ▶ 容纳 róngnà hold ▶ 容量 róngliàng capacity ▶ 容器 róngqì container **2**(容忍) tolerate ▶ 容忍 róngrěn tolerate **3**(允许) allow II [名] (相貌) appearance ▶ 容貌 róngmào features (pl)

容易 róngyì [形] **1**(简便) easy **2**(较可能) likely

柔 róu [形] **1**(软) soft **2**(柔和) gentle

柔软(軟) róuruǎn [形] soft

揉 róu [动] (搓) rub

肉 ròu [名] **1**(指人) flesh **2**(指动物) meat ▷ 猪肉 zhūròu pork **3**(指瓜果) flesh

如 rú [动] **1**(好似) be like **2**(比得上) be as good as ▶ 不如 bùrú not as good as **3**(例如)

如此 rúcǐ [代] so ▷ 他的态度竟如此恶劣。Tā de tàidu jìng rúcǐ èliè. His attitude was so unpleasant.

如果 rúguǒ [连] if

如何 rúhé [代] ▷ 此事如何解决？Cǐ shì rúhé jiějué? How are we going to sort this out? ▷ 你今后如何打算？Nǐ jīnhòu rúhé dǎsuàn? What are your plans for the future?

儒 rú [名] (儒家) Confucianism ▶ 儒家 Rújiā Confucianism

入 rù [动] **1**(进入) enter ▶ 入场 rùchǎng enter **2**(参加) join ▶ 入学 rùxué enrol

入境 rùjìng [动] enter a country

入口 rùkǒu [名] (门) entrance

软(軟) ruǎn [形] **1**(柔) soft ▶ 软和 ruǎnhuo soft **2**(温和) gentle **3**(柔弱) weak ▶ 软弱 ruǎnruò weak

软(軟)件 ruǎnjiàn [名] (计算机) software

软(軟)卧(臥) ruǎnwò [名] light sleeper

软(軟)饮(飲)料 ruǎnyǐnliào [名] soft drink

弱 ruò [形] **1**(弱小) weak **2**(年幼) young **3**(软弱) weak

弱点(點) ruòdiǎn [名] weakness

S

仨 sā [数] (口) three ▶ 哥仨 gē sā three brothers

撒 sā [动] 1 (手、网) let ... go 2 (贬) (疯、野) lose control of oneself ▶ 撒野 sāyě have a tantrum
→ see also/另见 sǎ

　撒谎(謊) sāhuǎng [动] (口) lie
　撒娇(嬌) sājiāo [动] behave like a spoiled child
　撒气(氣) sāqì [动] 1 (球、车胎) get a puncture 2 (发泄怒气) take one's anger out on ▶ 别拿我撒气! Bié ná wǒ sāqì! Don't take your anger out on me!
　撒手 sāshǒu [动] (松手) let go

洒(灑) sǎ [动] 1 (泼) sprinkle 2 (指不小心) spill
　洒(灑)脱(脫) sǎtuō [形] carefree

撒 sǎ [动] 1 (散布) scatter 2 (散落) spill
→ see also/另见 sā

腮 sāi [名] cheek
　腮帮(幫)子 sāibāngzi [名] (口) cheek

塞 sāi I [动] stuff ... into II [名] cork
　塞车(車) sāichē [名] traffic jam ▶ 长安街上经常塞车。Cháng'ān Jiē shang jīngcháng sāichē. Chang'an Street is often congested.
　塞子 sāizi [名] cork

赛(賽) sài I [名] match ▶ 演讲比赛 yǎnjiǎng bǐsài debating contest II [动] compete
　赛(賽)车(車) sàichē I [动] race II [名] (指汽车) racing car
　赛(賽)季 sàijì [名] season
　赛(賽)跑 sàipǎo [动] race

三 sān [数] 1 (指数目) three ▶ 三月 sānyuè March 2 (表示序数) third 3 (表示多数) several ▶ 三思 sānsī think twice
　三角 sānjiǎo [名] triangle ▶ 三角恋爱 sānjiǎo liàn'ài love triangle
　三明治 sānmíngzhì [名] sandwich
　三围(圍) sānwéi [名] vital statistics (pl)
　三心二意 sān xīn èr yì half-hearted ▶ 他工作三心二意的。Tā gōngzuò sān xīn èr yì de. He's half-hearted about his work.

叁 sān [数] three
　This is the character for "three", which is mainly used in banks, on receipts, etc. to prevent mistakes and forgery.

伞(傘) sǎn [名] umbrella

散 sǎn I [动] loosen II [形] loose
→ see also/另见 sàn
　散漫 sǎnmàn [形] slack
　散文 sǎnwén [名] prose

散 sàn [动] 1 (分离) break up ▶ 乌云散了。Wūyún sàn le. The dark clouds scattered. 2 (散布) give ... out 3 (排除) dispel
→ see also/另见 sǎn
　散布 sànbù [动] 1 (传单) distribute 2 (谣言) spread
　散步 sànbù [动] go for a stroll

丧(喪) sāng [名] funeral
→ see also/另见 sàng
　丧(喪)事 sāngshì [名] funeral arrangements (pl)

桑 sāng [名] mulberry
　桑拿浴 sāngnáyù [名] sauna
　桑那浴 sāngnàyù [名] sauna

嗓 sǎng [名] 1(嗓子) throat 2(嗓音) voice
嗓门(門) sǎngmén [名] voice
嗓子 sǎngzi [名] 1(喉咙) throat 2(嗓音) voice

丧(喪) sàng [动] lose
→ see also/另见 sāng
丧(喪)气(氣) sàngqì [动] lose heart
丧(喪)失 sàngshī [动] lose

骚(騷) sāo [动] disturb
骚(騷)扰(擾) sāorǎo [动] harass ▷ 性骚扰 xìngsāorǎo sexual harassment

扫(掃) sǎo [动] 1(打扫) sweep 2(除去) clear ... away ▷ 扫黄 sǎohuáng crack down on pornography
→ see also/另见 sào
扫(掃)除 sǎochú [动] 1(打扫) sweep ... up 2(除掉) eliminate
扫(掃)盲 sǎománg [动] eliminate illiteracy
扫(掃)描 sǎomiáo [动] scan
扫(掃)描仪(儀) sǎomiáoyí [名] scanner
扫(掃)兴(興) sǎoxìng [形] disappointed

嫂 sǎo [名] (哥哥之妻) sister-in-law
嫂子 sǎozi [名] (口) sister-in-law

扫(掃) sào see below/见下文
→ see also/另见 sǎo
扫(掃)帚 sàozhou [名] broom

色 sè [名] (颜色) colour (英), color (美)
→ see also/另见 shǎi
色彩 sècǎi [名] 1(颜色) colour (英), color (美) 2(指情调) tone
色盲 sèmáng [名] colour (英) 或 color (美) blindness
色情 sèqíng [形] pornographic

涩(澀) sè [形] (味道) astringent

森 sēn [形] (形容树多) wooded
森林 sēnlín [名] forest

僧 sēng [名] Buddhist monk ▷ 僧人 sēngrén Buddhist monk

杀(殺) shā [动] 1(杀死) kill 2(战斗) fight 3(削弱) reduce
杀(殺)毒 shādú [动] get rid of a virus ▷ 杀毒软件 shādú ruǎnjiàn anti-virus software
杀(殺)害 shāhài [动] murder
杀(殺)价(價) shājià [动] bargain ▷ 我很会杀价。 Wǒ hěn huì shājià. I'm a very good bargainer.
杀(殺)手 shāshǒu [名] killer

沙 shā [名] (石粒) sand
沙尘(塵) shāchén [名] dust
沙尘(塵)暴 shāchénbào [名] sandstorm
沙发(發) shāfā [名] sofa
沙锅(鍋) shāguō [名] casserole
沙皇 shāhuáng [名] tsar
沙漠 shāmò [名] desert
沙滩(灘) shātān [名] beach
沙哑(啞) shāyǎ [形] hoarse
沙眼 shāyǎn [名] trachoma
沙子 shāzi [名] sand

纱(紗) shā [名] (指织品) gauze
纱(紗)布 shābù [名] gauze

刹 shā [动] brake
刹车(車) shāchē I [动] 1(停止机器) brake 2(喻) (制止) put a stop to II [名] brake

鲨(鯊) shā [名] shark ▷ 鲨鱼 shāyú shark

傻 shǎ [形] 1(蠢) stupid 2(死心眼) inflexible
傻瓜 shǎguā [名] fool
傻子 shǎzi [名] fool

厦(廈) shà [名] tall building ▷ 摩天大厦 mótiān dàshà skyscraper

色 shǎi [名] colour (英), color (美)
→ see also/另见 sè
色子 shǎizi [名] dice

晒(曬) shài [动] 1(阳光照射) shine upon ▷ 他被晒黑了。 Tā bèi shàihēi le. He's tanned. 2(吸收光热) lie in the sun ▷ 她

在沙滩上晒太阳。Tā zài shātān shang shài tàiyáng. She was sunbathing on the beach.

山 shān [名] (地质) mountain ▸ 小山 xiǎoshān hill

山村 shāncūn [名] mountain village

山洞 shāndòng [名] cave

山峰 shānfēng [名] peak

山谷 shāngǔ [名] valley

山脚(腳) shānjiǎo [名] foothills (pl)

山林 shānlín [名] wooded hill

山脉(脈) shānmài [名] mountain range

山坡 shānpō [名] mountainside

山区(區) shānqū [名] mountainous area

山水 shānshuǐ [名] 1 (风景) scenery 2 (画) landscape painting

山珍海味 shān zhēn hǎi wèi [名] exotic delicacies (pl)

删(刪) shān [动] delete

删(刪)除 shānchú [动] delete

珊 shān see below/见下文

珊瑚 shānhú [名] coral

扇 shān [动] 1 (扇子) fan 2 (耳光) slap
→ see also/另见 shàn

闪(閃) shǎn I [动] 1 (闪避) dodge 2 (受伤) sprain 3 (突然出现) flash 4 (闪耀) shine II [名] lightning ▷ 打闪了。Dǎ shǎn le. Lightning flashed.

闪(閃)电(電) shǎndiàn [名] lightning

闪(閃)动(動) shǎndòng [动] flash

闪(閃)烁(爍) shǎnshuò [动] (忽明忽暗) twinkle

扇 shàn I [名] (扇子) fan II [量] ▷ 一扇窗 yī shàn chuāng a window ▷ 两扇门 liǎng shàn mén two doors

■ measure word, used for doors, windows, screens etc.

→ see also/另见 shān

善 shàn I [形] 1 (善良) kind 2 (良好) good ▸ 善事 shànshì good deeds 3 (友好) friendly II [动] 1 (擅长) be an expert at

2 (容易) be prone to ▸ 善忘 shànwàng forgetful

善良 shànliáng [形] kind-hearted

善于(於) shànyú [动] be good at

擅 shàn [动] be expert at

擅长(長) shàncháng [动] be skilled in

鳝(鱔) shàn [名] eel ▸ 鳝鱼 shànyú eel

伤(傷) shāng I [动] 1 (身体部位) injure ▸ 扭伤 niǔshāng sprain 2 (感情) hurt II [名] injury

伤(傷)残(殘) shāngcán [名] disabled people

伤(傷)风(風) shāngfēng [动] catch a cold

伤(傷)害 shānghài [动] 1 (感情) hurt 2 (身体) damage

伤(傷)痕 shānghén [名] scar

伤(傷)口 shāngkǒu [名] wound

伤(傷)心 shāngxīn [形] sad

商 shāng I [动] discuss ▸ 协商 xiéshāng negotiate II [名] 1 (商业) commerce ▸ 经商 jīngshāng trade 2 (商人) businessman, businesswoman 3 (数) quotient

商标(標) shāngbiāo [名] trademark

商场(場) shāngchǎng [名] shopping centre (英), mall (美)

商店 shāngdiàn [名] shop (英), store (美)

商量 shāngliang [动] discuss

商品 shāngpǐn [名] commodity

商人 shāngrén [名] businessman, businesswoman

商谈(談) shāngtán [动] negotiate

商务(務) shāngwù [名] business ▷ 电子商务 diànzǐ shāngwù e-commerce

商学(學)院 shāngxuéyuàn [名] business school

商业(業) shāngyè [名] commerce

赏(賞) shǎng I [动] 1 (赏赐) award 2 (欣赏) admire 3 (赏识) appreciate II [名] reward

赏(賞)识(識) shǎngshí [动] think highly of

上 shàng I [名] 1 (指方位) upper part
2 (指等级、质量) ▶ 上级 shàngjí higher
authorities (pl) 3 (指时间、次序) ▶ 上星
期 shàng xīngqī last week ▶ 上半年
shàng bànnián the first half of the year
II [动] 1 (向上) go up ▶ 上楼
shànglóu go upstairs 2 (按点前往) go ▶ 上学
shàngxué go to school ▶ 上班
shàngbān go to work 3 (去) go to ▷ 他上
天津开会去了。Tā shàng Tiānjīn
kāihuì qù le. He went to Tianjin to
attend a meeting. 4 (出现) make an
entrance 5 (添补) fill ▶ 上货 shànghuò
stock up 6 (饭、菜) serve ▶ 上菜
shàngcài serve food 7 (安装) fix ▶ 上螺
丝 shàng luósī fix a screw 8 (涂) apply
▷ 上涂料 shàng túliào apply paint
9 (登载) appear ▶ 上杂志 shàng zázhì
appear in a magazine 10 (拧紧) tighten
▷ 我的表已上弦了。Wǒde biǎo yǐ
shàngxián le. I've wound up my watch.
11 (车、船、飞机) board 12 (表示达到目
的) ▷ 当上老师 dāngshàng lǎoshī
become a teacher III [介] 1 (在物体表面)
on ▷ 椅子上 yǐzi shang on the chair
2 (表示范围) in ▷ 报纸上 bàozhǐ shang
in the newspaper

上车 (車) shàngchē [动] get into a
vehicle ▷ 快上车，我们要迟到了。
Kuài shàngchē, wǒmen yào chídào
le. Hurry up and get in the car, we're
going to be late.

上传 (傳) shàngchuán [动] upload
上当 (當) shàngdàng [动] be taken in
上等 shàngděng [形] first-class
上帝 Shàngdì [名] God
上吊 shàngdiào [动] hang oneself
上海 Shànghǎi [名] Shanghai
上级 (級) shàngjí [名] higher
authorities (pl)
上课 (課) shàngkè [动] go to class
上来 (來) shànglái [动] 1 (指动作趋向)
▷ 饭菜端上来了。Fàncài duān
shànglái le. The meal was brought to
the table. 2 (表示成功) ▷ 这个问题我
答不上来。Zhège wèntí wǒ dá bù
shànglái. I can't answer this question.

上面 shàngmiàn [名] 1 (指位置高) ▷ 他
住在我上面。Tā zhù zài wǒ
shàngmiàn. He lives above me.

2 (物体表面) ▷ 墙上面挂着相片。
Qiáng shàngmiàn guàzhe xiàngpiàn.
Photographs were hanging on the
walls. 3 (以上的部分) ▷ 上面我们分析
了各种可能性。Shàngmiàn wǒmen
fēnxīle gè zhǒng kěnéngxìng. As can
be seen above, we have made an
analysis of all possibilities.

上年纪 (紀) shàng niánji [动] get old
上去 shàngqù [动] 1 (指由低到高) go
up 2 (提高) improve
上身 shàngshēn [名] upper body
上升 shàngshēng [动] 1 (往高处移)
ascend 2 (增加) increase
上市 shàngshì [动] appear on the
market
上司 shàngsi [名] superior
上诉 (訴) shàngsù [动] appeal
上网 (網) shàngwǎng [动] go online
上网 (網) 本 shàngwǎngběn [名]
netbook
上午 shàngwǔ [名] morning
上衣 shàngyī [名] top
上瘾 (癮) shàngyǐn [动] be addicted to
上涨 (漲) shàngzhǎng [动] rise

烧 (燒) shāo [动] 1 (着火) burn 2 (加热)
heat ▷ 烧水 shāo shuǐ boil water 3 (烹)
braise 4 (烤) roast ▶ 烧鸡 shāojī roast
chicken 5 (发烧) have a temperature
烧 (燒) 烤 shāokǎo [动] barbecue

稍 shāo [副] slightly
→ see also/另见 shào
稍微 shāowēi [副] a little

勺 sháo [名] ladle

少 shǎo I [形] few ▷ 屋里家具太少。
Wū li jiājù tài shǎo. There is very little
furniture in the room. II [动] 1 (缺) lack
▷ 汤里少了葱。Tāng li shǎole cōng.
There is no onion in the soup. 2 (丢) be
missing ▷ 她发现钱包里的钱少了一百
块。Tā fāxiàn qiánbāo li de qián
shǎole yī bǎi kuài. She discovered that
one hundred kuai were missing from her
purse.
→ see also/另见 shào
少量 shǎoliàng [名] a little

少数(數) shǎoshù [名] minority
少数(數)民族 shǎoshù mínzú [名] ethnic minorities (pl)

少数民族 shǎoshù mínzú
- 少数民族 shǎoshù mínzú refers to China's ethnic minorities. There are 56 distinct ethnic groups in China, of which the Han is by far the largest, accounting for over 90% of the population. The other 55 minorities are mainly located in the southwestern and northwestern provinces. Five regions have been set up as ethnic minorities autonomous regions.

少 shào [形] young ▶ 少女 shàonǚ young girl
→ see also/另见 shǎo
少年 shàonián [名] youth

哨 shào [名] (哨子) whistle
哨子 shàozi [名] whistle

稍 shào see below/见下文
→ see also/另见 shāo
稍息 shàoxī [动] stand at ease

奢 shē [形] extravagant
奢侈 shēchǐ [形] luxurious

舌 shé [名] tongue
舌头(頭) shétou [名] tongue

折 shé [动] (折断) snap ▷ 他的腿折了。Tā de tuǐ shé le. He broke his leg.
→ see also/另见 zhé

蛇 shé [名] snake

设(設) shè [动] 1(设立，布置) set ... up 2(想) plan 3(假定) suppose ▶ 设想 shèxiǎng envisage
设(設)备(備) shèbèi [名] equipment
设(設)计(計) shèjì [动] design ▷ 服装设计 fúzhuāng shèjì fashion design
设(設)施 shèshī [名] facilities (pl)

社 shè [名] organization ▶ 旅行社 lǚxíngshè travel agent

社会(會) shèhuì [名] society ▷ 社会福利 shèhuì fúlì social welfare
社交 shèjiāo [名] social contact
社区(區) shèqū [名] community

舍 shè [名] house ▶ 宿舍 sùshè dormitory

射 shè [动] 1(发) shoot 2(喷) spout 3(放出) emit ▶ 照射 zhàoshè shine
射击(擊) shèjī I [动] fire II [名] shooting
射门(門) shèmén [动] shoot
射线(線) shèxiàn [名] (电磁波) ray

涉 shè [动] (牵涉) involve ▶ 涉嫌 shèxián be a suspect
涉及 shèjí [动] involve

摄(攝) shè [动] 1(吸取) absorb 2(摄影) take a photo
摄(攝)像 shèxiàng [动] make a video
摄(攝)影 shèyǐng [动] 1(照相) take a photo 2(拍电影) shoot a film (英) 或 movie (美)

谁 shéi [代] see below/另见
→ see also/另见 shuí

申 shēn [动] express
申请(請) shēnqǐng [动] apply ▶ 申请工作 shēnqǐng gōngzuò apply for a job

伸 shēn [动] stretch
伸手 shēnshǒu [动] (伸出手) hold out one's hand

身 shēn [名] 1(身体) body 2(生命) life 3(自己) oneself
身材 shēncái [名] figure
身份 shēnfen [名] (地位) position
身份证(證) shēnfènzhèng [名] identity card
身体(體) shēntǐ [名] body

参(參) shēn [名] ginseng ▶ 人参 rénshēn ginseng
→ see also/另见 cān

绅(紳) shēn [名] gentry
绅(紳)士 shēnshì [名] gentleman

深 shēn I[形] 1(指深度) deep 2(指距离) remote 3(深奥) difficult 4(深刻) deep ▷印象深 yìnxiàng shēn a deep impression 5(密切) close 6(浓重) dark ▷深蓝 shēn lán dark blue 7(指时间久) late ▷深夜 shēnyè late at night II[名] depth III[副] very ▷深信 shēnxìn firmly believe

深奥(奧) shēn'ào [形] profound

深度 shēndù I[名] depth II[形] extreme

深化 shēnhuà [动] deepen

深刻 shēnkè [形] deep

深入 shēnrù I[动] penetrate II[形] thorough

深远(遠) shēnyuǎn [形] far-reaching

深造 shēnzào [动] pursue advanced studies

什 shén see below/见下文

什么(麼) shénme [代] 1(表示疑问) what ▷你要什么？ Nǐ yào shénme? What do you want? 2(表示虚指) something ▷他们在商量着什么。 Tāmen zài shāngliangzhe shénme. They are discussing something. 3(表示任指) anything ▷我什么都不怕。 Wǒ shénme dōu bù pà. I'm not afraid of anything. 4(表示惊讶、不满) what ▷什么！他拒绝出席会议！ Shénme! Tā jùjué chūxí huìyì! What! He refused to attend the meeting! 5(表示责难) ▷你在胡说什么! Nǐ zài húshuō shénme! What's that rubbish?

什么(麼)的 shénmede [代] and so on ▷餐桌上摆满了香蕉、李子、苹果什么的。Cānzhuō shang bǎimǎnle xiāngjiāo, lǐzi, píngguǒ shénmede. The dining table was loaded with bananas, plums, apples and so on.

神 shén I[名] 1(宗) god 2(精神) spirit ▶走神 zǒushén be absent-minded II[形] (高超) amazing ▶神奇 shénqí magical

神话(話) shénhuà [名] myth

神经(經) shénjīng [名] nerve

神秘(祕) shénmì [形] mysterious

神气(氣) shénqì I[名] manner II[形] 1(精神) impressive 2(得意) cocky

神圣(聖) shénshèng [形] sacred

神态(態) shéntài [名] look

神仙 shénxiān [名] immortal

神学(學) shénxué [名] theology

审(審) shěn [动] 1(审查) go over 2(审讯) try ▷审案子 shěn ànzi try a case

审(審)查 shěnchá [动] examine

审(審)判 shěnpàn [动] try

审(審)问(問) shěnwèn [动] interrogate

婶(嬸) shěn [名] aunt

肾(腎) shèn [名] kidney

甚 shèn I[形] extreme II[副] very

甚至 shènzhì [副] even

渗(滲) shèn [动] seep

慎 shèn [形] careful

慎重 shènzhòng [形] cautious

升 shēng I[动] 1(由低往高) rise 2(提升) promote ▶升职 shēngzhí be promoted II[量] litre(英), liter(美)

升级(級) shēngjí [动] 1(升高年级) go up 2(规模扩大) escalate 3(指电脑) upgrade

升值 shēngzhí [动] appreciate

生 shēng I[动] 1(生育) give birth to ▷生孩子 shēng háizi have a baby 2(长) grow 3(活) live ▶生死 shēngsǐ life and death 4(患) get ▶生病 shēngbìng get ill 5(点) light ▶生火 shēnghuǒ light a fire II[名] 1(生命) life 2(生平) life ▶今生 jīnshēng this life 3(学生) student ▶新生 xīnshēng new student III[形] 1(活的) living ▶生物 shēngwù 2(未熟的) unripe 3(未煮的) raw 4(生疏) unfamiliar

生产(產) shēngchǎn [动] 1(制造) produce 2(生孩子) give birth to

生存 shēngcún [动] survive

生动(動) shēngdòng [形] lively

生活 shēnghuó I[名] life II[动] 1(居住) live 2(生存) survive

生计(計) shēngjì [名] livelihood

生理 shēnglǐ [名] physiology
生命 shēngmìng [名] life
生命力 shēngmìnglì [名] vitality
生气(氣) shēngqì [动] get angry
生人 shēngrén [名] stranger
生日 shēngrì [名] birthday
生态(態) shēngtài [名] ecology
生物 shēngwù [名] living things (pl)
生物学(學) shēngwùxué [名] biology
生肖 shēngxiào [名] animal of the Chinese zodiac
生效 shēngxiào [动] come into effect
生意 shēngyi [名] business
生育 shēngyù [动] give birth to
生长(長) shēngzhǎng [动] 1(植物) grow 2(生物) grow up

声(聲) shēng [名] 1(声音) sound 2(名声) reputation ▶ 声誉 shēngyù fame 3(声调) tone (of Chinese phonetics)
声(聲)波 shēngbō [名] sound wave
声(聲)调(調) shēngdiào [名] tone
声(聲)明 shēngmíng [动] state
声(聲)望 shēngwàng [名] prestige
声(聲)音 shēngyīn [名] 1(指人) voice 2(指物) sound

牲 shēng [名] (家畜) domestic animal
牲畜 shēngchù [名] livestock

甥 shēng [名] nephew ▶ 外甥 wàishēng nephew ▶ 外甥女 wàishēngnǚ niece

绳(繩) shéng [名] rope
绳(繩)子 shéngzi [名] rope

省 shěng I [动] 1(节约) save ▷ 省钱 shěng qián save money 2(免掉) leave ... out II [名] province
省会(會) shěnghuì [名] provincial capital
省略 shěnglüè [动] leave ... out
省事 shěngshì [动] save trouble
省心 shěngxīn [动] save worry

圣(聖) shèng I [形] holy ▶ 圣诞节 Shèngdàn Jié Christmas II [名] (圣人) sage

圣(聖)诞(誕) Shèngdàn [名] Christmas
圣(聖)经(經) Shèngjīng [名] the Bible

胜(勝) shèng [动] 1(赢) win 2(打败) defeat 3(好于) be better than
胜(勝)利 shènglì [动] 1(打败对方) be victorious 2(获得成功) be successful

盛 shèng [形] 1(兴盛) flourishing 2(强烈) intense 3(盛大) grand ▶ 盛宴 shèngyàn sumptuous dinner 4(深厚) abundant ▶ 盛情 shèngqíng great kindness 5(盛行) popular ▶ 盛行 shèngxíng be in fashion
→ see also/另见 chéng
盛大 shèngdà [形] magnificent

剩(賸) shèng [动] be left ▶ 剩下 shèngxià remain

尸(屍) shī [名] corpse
尸(屍)体(體) shītǐ [名] corpse

失 shī I [动] 1(丢失) lose 2(未得到) fail 3(背弃) break II [名] mistake ▶ 过失 guòshī error
失败(敗) shībài [动] fail
失眠 shīmián [动] be unable to sleep
失眠症 shīmiánzhèng [名] insomnia
失明 shīmíng [动] go blind
失望 shīwàng I [形] disappointed II [动] lose hope
失误(誤) shīwù [动] slip up
失效 shīxiào [动] 1(不起作用) stop working 2(没有效力) be no longer valid
失信 shīxìn [动] go back on one's word
失业(業) shīyè [动] be unemployed, be out of work
失踪(蹤) shīzōng [动] be missing

师(師) shī [名] (老师) teacher
师(師)傅 shīfu [名] (口) master

诗(詩) shī [名] poetry
诗(詩)歌 shīgē [名] poetry
诗(詩)人 shīrén [名] poet

虱(蝨) shī [名] louse

狮(獅) shī see below/见下文
狮(獅)子 shīzi [名] lion

施 shī [动] 1 (实行) carry ... out ▶ 施工 shīgōng construct 2 (给予) exert ▶ 施压 shīyā exert pressure 3 (肥料) apply ▶ 施肥 shīféi spread fertilizer
施行 shīxíng [动] (执行) implement

湿(濕) shī [形] wet
湿(濕)润(潤) shīrùn [形] moist

十 shí [名] ten ▶ 十月 shíyuè October ▶ 十一月 shíyīyuè November ▶ 十二月 shí'èryuè December
十分 shífēn [副] extremely
十字路口 shízì lùkǒu [名] crossroads (pl)

石 shí [名] stone
石油 shíyóu [名] oil

时(時) shí [名] 1 (指时间单位) hour 2 (指规定时间) time ▶ 准时 zhǔnshí on time 3 (时常) ▶ 时不时 shíbùshí from time to time 4 (时尚) fashion ▶ 入时 rùshí fashionable ▶ 过时 guòshí out-of-date 5 (时候) time ▶ 当时 dāngshí at that time 6 (机会) opportunity 7 (语法) tense ▷ 过去时 guòqùshí past tense
时(時)差 shíchā [名] time difference
时(時)常 shícháng [副] often
时(時)代 shídài [名] 1 (指时期) age 2 (指人生) period
时(時)候 shíhou [名] time ▷ 你什么时候上班? Nǐ shénme shíhou shàngbān? What time do you go to work?
时(時)机(機) shíjī [名] opportunity
时(時)间(間) shíjiān [名] time ▷ 时间到了。Shíjiān dào le. Time's up! ▷ 办公时间 bàngōng shíjiān working hours
时(時)刻 shíkè I [名] moment II [副] constantly
时(時)刻表 shíkèbiǎo [名] timetable (英), schedule (美)
时(時)髦 shímáo [形] fashionable
时(時)期 shíqī [名] period

时(時)区(區) shíqū [名] time zone
时(時)事 shíshì [名] current affairs (pl)
时(時)装(裝) shízhuāng [名] fashion

实(實) shí [形] 1 (实心) solid 2 (真实) true ▶ 实话 shíhuà truth
实(實)际(際) shíjì I [名] reality II [形] 1 (实有的) real 2 (合乎事实的) practical
实(實)践(踐) shíjiàn I [动] practise (英), practice (美) II [名] practice
实(實)力 shílì [名] strength
实(實)情 shíqíng [名] actual state of affairs
实(實)施 shíshī [动] implement
实(實)习(習) shíxí [动] practise (英), practice (美)
实(實)习(習)生 shíxíshēng [名] trainee
实(實)现(現) shíxiàn [动] realize
实(實)行 shíxíng [动] put ... into practice
实(實)验(驗) shíyàn I [动] test II [名] experiment
实(實)验(驗)室 shíyànshì [名] laboratory
实(實)用 shíyòng [形] practical
实(實)在 shízài I [形] honest II [副] really

拾 shí I [动] pick ... up II [数] ten
This is the complex character for "ten", which is mainly used in banks, on receipts, etc. to prevent mistakes and forgery.

食 shí I [动] eat II [名] 1 (食物) food ▶ 主食 zhǔshí staple ▶ 狗食 gǒushí dog food 2 (指天体) eclipse ▶ 日食 rìshí solar eclipse
食品 shípǐn [名] food
食谱(譜) shípǔ [名] recipe
食堂 shítáng [名] canteen
食物 shíwù [名] food
食欲(慾) shíyù [名] appetite

史 shǐ [名] history
史诗(詩) shǐshī [名] epic
史实(實) shǐshí [名] historical fact

使 shǐ I [动] 1 (使用) use 2 (让) make II [名] envoy ▶ 大使 dàshǐ ambassador
使馆(館) shǐguǎn [名] embassy
使用 shǐyòng [动] use ▷ 使用说明 shǐyòng shuōmíng operating instructions (pl)

始 shǐ [动] start
始终(終) shǐzhōng [副] all along

屎 shǐ [名] 1 (粪便) excrement 2 (眼、耳) wax ▶ 耳屎 ěrshǐ ear wax

示 shì [动] show
示范(範) shìfàn [动] demonstrate
示威 shìwēi [动] demonstrate

世 shì [名] 1 (生) life ▶ 来世 láishì afterlife 2 (代) generation ▶ 世仇 shìchóu family feud 3 (时期) age 4 (世界) world ▶ 世上 shìshàng in this world
世纪(紀) shìjì [名] century
世界 shìjiè [名] world

市 shì [名] 1 (城市) city 2 (市场) market
市场(場) shìchǎng [名] market
市民 shìmín [名] city residents (pl)

式 shì [名] 1 (样式) style 2 (典礼) ceremony 3 (式子) formula ▶ 公式 gōngshì formula
式样(樣) shìyàng [名] style

事 shì [名] 1 (事情) thing ▶ 私事 sīshì private matter 2 (事故) accident ▶ 出事 chūshì have an accident 3 (事端) trouble ▶ 闹事 nàoshì make trouble 4 (责任) responsibility 5 (工作) job 6 (用于问答) problem ▷ 有事吗? 没事。 Yǒu shì ma? Méishì. Are you OK? — I'm fine.
事故 shìgù [名] accident
事件 shìjiàn [名] event
事情 shìqíng [名] matter
事实(實) shìshí [名] fact ▷ 事实上 shìshíshang in fact
事务(務) shìwù [名] work
事物 shìwù [名] thing
事业(業) shìyè [名] 1 (用于个人) undertaking 2 (用于社会) activity

势(勢) shì [名] 1 (势力) force 2 (姿态) gesture 3 (趋势) tendency
势(勢)力 shìlì [名] power
势(勢)利 shìlì [形] snobbish
势(勢)利眼 shìlìyǎn [名] snob
势(勢)头(頭) shìtóu [名] momentum

饰(飾) shì I [动] 1 (装饰) decorate 2 (扮演) play II [名] ornament ▶ 首饰 shǒushì jewellery (英), jewelry (美)
饰(飾)物 shìwù [名] ornaments (pl)
饰(飾)演 shìyǎn [动] play

试(試) shì I [动] try ▷ 我可以试一下这双鞋吗? Wǒ kěyǐ shì yīxià zhè shuāng xié ma? Can I try on this pair of shoes? II [名] examination
试(試)卷 shìjuàn [名] exam paper
试(試)题(題) shìtí [名] exam question
试(試)验(驗) shìyàn [动] test
试(試)用 shìyòng [动] try ... out
试(試)用期 shìyòngqī [名] probation

视(視) shì [动] 1 (看到) look at 2 (看待) look on
视(視)觉(覺) shìjué [名] vision
视(視)力 shìlì [名] sight

柿 shì see below/见下文
柿子 shìzi [名] persimmon, sharon fruit

是 shì I [动] be ▷ 我是学生。 Wǒ shì xuésheng. I am a student. II [名] right ▶ 是非 shìfēi right and wrong III [副] yes
是 shì is the verb "to be". It is omitted when used with adjectives, e.g. 我很忙 wǒ hěn máng (I am very busy).

适(適) shì [形] 1 (适合) suitable 2 (恰好) right 3 (舒服) well
适(適)当(當) shìdàng [形] appropriate
适(適)合 shìhé [形] suitable
适(適)应(應) shìyìng [动] adapt

室 shì [名] room ▶ 办公室 bàngōngshì office
室外 shìwài [形] outdoor

逝 shì [动] (人) die
逝世 shìshì [动] (书) pass away

释(釋) shì [动] (解释) explain
释(釋)放 shìfàng [动] release

嗜 shì [动] be addicted to
嗜好 shìhào [名] hobby

誓 shì I [动] swear ▶ 发誓 fāshì vow
II [名] vow
誓言 shìyán [名] oath

收 shōu [动] 1 (归拢) put ... away
2 (取回) take ... back 3 (接纳) accept
4 (结束) stop ▶ 收工 shōugōng stop
work 5 (获得) gain ▶ 收入 shōurù
income
收获(穫) shōuhuò [动] 1 (指庄稼)
harvest 2 (指成果) gain
收集 shōují [动] collect
收据(據) shōujù [名] receipt
收拾 shōushi [动] 1 (整顿) tidy 2 (修理)
repair 3 (口) (惩罚) punish
收缩(縮) shōusuō [动] 1 (指物理现象)
contract 2 (紧缩) cut back
收听(聽) shōutīng [动] listen to
收下 shōuxià [动] accept ▷ 我收下了
他的礼物。Wǒ shōuxiàle tā de lǐwù.
I accepted his gift.
收音机(機) shōuyīnjī [名] radio

手 shǒu [名] 1 (指人体) hand 2 (指人)
expert ▶ 选手 xuǎnshǒu player
手表(錶) shǒubiǎo [名] watch
手电(電)筒 shǒudiàntǒng [名] torch
(英), flashlight (美)
手段 shǒuduàn [名] 1 (方法) method
2 (贬) (花招) trick
手风(風)琴 shǒufēngqín [名]
accordion
手工 shǒugōng I [名] craft II [动] make
... by hand
手机(機) shǒujī [名] mobile phone (英),
cell phone (美)
手绢(絹) shǒujuàn [名] handkerchief
手铐(銬) shǒukào [名] handcuffs (pl)
手枪(槍) shǒuqiāng [名] pistol
手势(勢) shǒushì [名] sign

手术(術) shǒushù I [名] operation
II [动] operate
手套 shǒutào [名] glove ▷ 一副手套
yī fù shǒutào a pair of gloves
手提 shǒutí [形] portable
手腕 shǒuwàn [名] (指人体) wrist
手续(續) shǒuxù [名] procedure
手语(語) shǒuyǔ [名] sign language
手掌 shǒuzhǎng [名] palm
手纸(紙) shǒuzhǐ [名] toilet paper
手指 shǒuzhǐ [名] finger
手镯(鐲) shǒuzhuó [名] bracelet

守 shǒu [动] 1 (防卫) guard 2 (遵循)
observe ▶ 守法 shǒufǎ observe the law
守则(則) shǒuzé [名] regulation

首 shǒu I [名] 1 (脑袋) head 2 (头领)
leader II [形] 1 (第一) first ▶ 首富 shǒufù
the richest person 2 (最早) first III [量]
▷ 一首诗 yī shǒu shī one poem ▷ 两首
歌 liǎng shǒu gē two songs
measure word, used for music, songs
and poems
首都 shǒudū [名] capital
首领(領) shǒulǐng [名] chief
首脑(腦) shǒunǎo [名] head of state
首饰(飾) shǒushì [名] jewellery (英),
jewelry (美)
首席 shǒuxí [形] chief
首先 shǒuxiān [副] 1 (最早) first
2 (第一) first
首相 shǒuxiàng [名] prime minister
首要 shǒuyào [形] primary

寿(壽) shòu [名] (寿命) lifespan
寿(壽)命 shòumìng [名] life

受 shòu [动] 1 (接受) receive 2 (遭受)
suffer 3 (忍受) bear
受罪 shòuzuì [动] 1 (指苦难) suffer
2 (指不愉快的事) have a hard time

兽(獸) shòu [名] beast
兽(獸)医(醫) shòuyī [名] vet

售 shòu [动] sell
售货(貨)员(員) shòuhuòyuán [名]
shop assistant

瘦 shòu [形] **1**(指人) thin **2**(指食用肉)
lean **3**(指衣服、鞋袜) tight

书(書) shū I [动] write ▶ 书写 shūxiě
write II [名] **1**(册子) book ▶ 书包
shūbāo school bag ▶ 书架 shūjià
bookcase ▶ 书桌 shūzhuō desk ▶ 精装
书 jīngzhuāngshū hardback **2**(书)(信)
letter ▶ 情书 qíngshū love letter **3**(文件)
document ▶ 申请书 shēnqǐngshū
application documents (pl)
书(書)店 shūdiàn [名] bookshop
书(書)法 shūfǎ [名] calligraphy
书(書)籍 shūjí [名] books (pl)
书(書)记(記) shūjì [名] secretary
书(書)面语(語) shūmiànyǔ [名]
written language
书(書)信 shūxìn [名] letter
书(書)展 shūzhǎn [名] book fair

叔 shū [名] (指父亲的弟弟) uncle
叔叔 shūshu [名] (口) **1**(指亲戚) uncle
2(指父辈男性) uncle

梳 shū I [名] comb ▶ 梳子 shūzi comb,
brush II [动] comb

舒 shū [形] **1**(指身体) stretch out
2(指心情) relax
舒服 shūfu [形] comfortable
舒适(適) shūshì [形] cosy (英),
cozy (美)

输(輸) shū [动] **1**(运送) transport
2(失败) lose
输(輸)出 shūchū [动] (指从内到外)
emit
输(輸)入 shūrù [动] (指从外到内)
enter
输(輸)送 shūsòng [动] **1**(物品) convey
2(人员) transfer

蔬 shū [名] vegetable
蔬菜 shūcài [名] vegetable

熟 shú [形] **1**(指果实) ripe **2**(指食物)
cooked **3**(熟悉) familiar ▶ 他对北京很
熟。Tā duì Běijīng hěn shú. He knows
Beijing well. **4**(熟练) skilled
熟练(練) shúliàn [形] skilled

熟人 shúrén [名] old acquaintance
熟食 shúshí [名] cooked food
熟悉 shúxī [动] know well II [形]
familiar

属(屬) shǔ I [名] **1**(生物) genus **2**(家属)
family member II [动] **1**(隶属) be under
2(指属相) be ▶ 你属什么？Nǐ shǔ
shénme? What sign of the Chinese
zodiac are you?
属(屬)相 shǔxiang [名] (口) sign of the
Chinese zodiac
属(屬)于(於) shǔyú [动] belong to

暑 shǔ [名] **1**(热) heat **2**(盛夏)
midsummer
暑假 shǔjià [名] summer holidays (英)
(pl) vacation (美)

鼠 shǔ [名] **1**(指家鼠) mouse ▶ 老鼠
lǎoshǔ mouse **2**(指田鼠) rat
鼠标(標) shǔbiāo [名] mouse

数(數) shǔ [动] **1**(数目) count **2**(指名
次) rank **3**(列举) list
→ see also/另见 shù

薯 shǔ [名] potato ▶ 红薯 hóngshǔ sweet
potato

术(術) shù [名] **1**(技艺) skill **2**(策略)
tactic
术(術)语(語) shùyǔ [名] terminology

束 shù I [动] **1**(捆) tie **2**(约束) restrain
II [量] **1**(指花) bunch ▶ 一束鲜花 yī shù
xiānhuā a bunch of flowers **2**(指光) ray
▶ 一束阳光 yī shù yángguāng a ray of
sunlight
束缚(縛) shùfù [动] **1**(书)(捆绑) tie
2(局限) restrain

述 shù [动] state
述说(說) shùshuō [动] give an account

树(樹) shù I [名] tree II [动] (建立)
establish
树(樹)立 shùlì [动] establish
树(樹)林 shùlín [名] wood
树(樹)木 shùmù [名] trees (pl)
树(樹)阴(陰) shùyīn [名] shade

竖(豎) shù I [形] vertical II [动] erect III [名] vertical stroke

数(數) shù [名] 1(数目) number 2(语法) ▶ 单数 dānshù singular ▶ 复数 fùshù plural
→ see also/另见 shǔ

数(數)据(據) shùjù [名] data (pl)

数(數)据(據)库(庫) shùjùkù [名] database

数(數)量 shùliàng [名] quantity

数(數)码(碼) shùmǎ I [名] numeral II [形] digital

数(數)码(碼)相机(機) shùmǎ xiàngjī [名] digital camera

数(數)目 shùmù [名] amount

数(數)学(學) shùxué [名] mathematics (sg)

数(數)字 shùzì [名] 1(指系统) numeral 2(数据) figure

漱 shù [动] gargle
漱口 shùkǒu [动] rinse one's mouth out

刷 shuā I [名] brush ▶ 牙刷 yáshuā toothbrush II [动] (清除) scrub
刷卡 shuākǎ [动] swipe a card
刷牙 shuāyá [动] brush one's teeth
刷子 shuāzi [名] brush

耍 shuǎ [动] 1(方)(玩) play 2(戏弄) mess ... around 3(贬)(施展) play ▷ 别再耍小聪明了。Bié zài shuǎ xiǎocōngming le. Don't play those petty tricks again.
耍花招 shuǎ huāzhāo [动] play tricks

衰 shuāi I [形] declining II [动] decline
衰老 shuāilǎo [形] ageing
衰弱 shuāiruò [形] weak

摔 shuāi [动] 1(跌倒) fall 2(下落) fall out ▷ 他从床上摔了下来。Tā cóng chuáng shang shuāile xiàlái. He fell out of bed. 3(砸坏) break
摔跤 shuāijiāo I [动] (摔倒) fall over II [名] wrestling

甩 shuǎi [动] 1(抡) swing 2(扔) fling 3(抛开) throw ... off

甩卖(賣) shuǎimài [动] sell at a reduced price

帅(帥) shuài I [名] commander-in-chief II [形] handsome

率 shuài [动] command
率领(領) shuàilǐng [动] lead

双(雙) shuāng I [形] 1(两个) two 2(偶数) even ▶ 双数 shuāngshù even number 3(加倍) double II [量] pair ▷ 一双鞋 yī shuāng xié a pair of shoes ▷ 一双袜子 yī shuāng wàzi a pair of socks

双(雙)胞胎 shuāngbāotāi [名] twins (pl)

双(雙)方 shuāngfāng [名] both sides (pl)

双(雙)休日 shuāngxiūrì [名] the weekend

霜 shuāng [名] frost

谁(誰) shuí [代] 1(表示问人) who ▷ 谁在门外？Shuí zài mén wài? Who's at the door? 2(指任何一个人) whoever ▷ 谁先到谁买票。Shuí xiān dào shuí mǎi piào. Whoever arrives first buys the tickets.

水 shuǐ [名] 1(物质) water 2(指江河湖海) waters (pl) 3(汁) liquid ▶ 消毒水 xiāodúshuǐ disinfectant ▶ 墨水 mòshuǐ ink

水彩 shuǐcǎi [名] 1(指颜料) watercolour (英), watercolor (美) 2(指画) watercolour (英), watercolor (美)

水果 shuǐguǒ [名] fruit

水晶 shuǐjīng [名] crystal

水库(庫) shuǐkù [名] reservoir

水泥 shuǐní [名] cement

水平 shuǐpíng I [名] standard II [形] horizontal

水手 shuǐshǒu [名] sailor

水银(銀) shuǐyín [名] mercury

水灾(災) shuǐzāi [名] flood

税(稅) shuì [名] tax
税(稅)收 shuìshōu [名] tax revenue

税(稅)务(務)局 shuìwùjú [名]
tax office

睡 shuì [动] sleep
睡觉(覺) shuìjiào [动] sleep
睡眠 shuìmián [名] sleep

顺(順) shùn I [介] 1(指方向) with ▶顺时针 shùnshízhēn clockwise 2(沿) along 3(趁便) ▶顺便 shùnbiàn on the way II [动] 1(朝同一方向) follow 2(使有条理) put ... in order 3(顺从) obey 4(合意) be to one's liking ▶顺心 shùnxīn as one would wish III [形] successful ▷他找工作很顺。Tā zhǎo gōngzuò hěn shùn. His job hunt has been very successful.
顺(順)便 shùnbiàn [副] 1(指乘方便) on the way 2(说、问) by the way ▷顺便问一下，他给你回电话了吗？Shùnbiàn wèn yīxià, tā gěi nǐ huí diànhuà le ma? By the way, did he call you back?
顺(順)风(風) shùnfēng [动] (指祝福) ▷一路顺风! Yīlù shùnfēng! Bon voyage!
顺(順)利 shùnlì [副] smoothly
顺(順)序 shùnxù [名] order

说(說) shuō [动] 1(用语言表达意思) say 2(解释) explain 3(责备) tell ... off
说(說)服 shuōfú [动] persuade
说(說)话(話) shuōhuà I [动] 1(用语言表达意思) talk 2(闲谈) chat II [副] (马上) any minute
说(說)明 shuōmíng I [动] 1(解释明白) explain 2(证明) prove II [名] explanation ▷产品使用说明 chǎnpǐn shǐyòng shuōmíng instruction manual

硕(碩) shuò [形] large
硕(碩)士 shuòshì [名] master's degree

司 sī [动] take charge of
司机(機) sījī [名] driver

丝(絲) sī [名] 1(蚕丝) silk 2(丝状物) thread ▶铁丝 tiěsī wire
丝(絲)绸(綢) sīchóu [名] silk

私 sī [形] 1(个人的) private ▶私事 sīshì private affairs 2(自私的) selfish ▶无私 wúsī unselfish 3(暗地里的) secret 4(非法的) illegal
私人 sīrén [形] 1(属于个人的) private 2(人与人之间的) personal
私生活 sīshēnghuó [名] private life
私下 sīxià [副] privately
私信 sīxìn [名] private message
私营(營) sīyíng [动] run privately
私有 sīyǒu [形] private ▶私有化 sīyǒuhuà privatization
私自 sīzì [副] without permission

思 sī [名] thought ▶思路 sīlù train of thought
思考 sīkǎo [动] think
思念 sīniàn I [动] miss II [名] longing
思维(維) sīwéi [名] thinking
思想 sīxiǎng [名] 1(指体系) thought 2(念头) idea

撕 sī [动] tear

死 sǐ I [动] die II [形] 1(死亡的) dead 2(不可调和的) implacable ▶死敌 sǐdí sworn enemy 3(不能通过的) impassable ▶死胡同 sǐhútòng dead end 4(确切的) fixed 5(脑筋) slow-witted 6(规定) rigid 7(水) still III [副] 1(拼死) to the death ▶死战 sǐzhàn fight to the death 2(表示固执或坚决) stubbornly ▶死等 sǐ děng wait indefinitely 3(表示到达极点) extremely ▶累死我了。Lèisǐ wǒ le. I'm completely exhausted.
死机(機) sǐjī [动] crash
死尸(屍) sǐshī [名] corpse
死亡 sǐwáng [动] die
死刑 sǐxíng [名] death penalty
死者 sǐzhě [名] the deceased

四 sì [数] four
四季 sìjì [名] the four seasons (pl)
四声(聲) sìshēng [名] the four tones of Standard Chinese pronunciation
四月 sìyuè [名] April
四肢 sìzhī [名] limbs (pl)
四周(週) sìzhōu [名] all sides

寺 sì [名] **1**(指佛教) temple, Tibetan Buddhist temple **2**(指伊斯兰教) mosque ▸ 清真寺 qīngzhēnsì mosque

似 sì I [动] (像) be like ▷ 他的脸似纸一样白。Tā de liǎn sì zhǐ yīyàng bái. His face was as white as a sheet of paper. II [副] apparently
似乎 sìhū [副] apparently

饲 sì [动] raise ▸ 饲养 sìyǎng raise
饲料 sìliào [名] fodder

肆 sì [名] four
This is the complex character for "four", which is mainly used in banks, on receipts, etc. to prevent mistakes and forgery.

松(鬆) sōng I [名] (树) pine tree II [动] **1**(放开) relax **2**(鞋带、腰带) loosen III [形] loose
松(鬆) 懈 sōngxiè [形] **1**(放松) relaxed **2**(松散) lax

送 sòng [动] **1**(信、邮包、外卖) deliver **2**(礼物) give ▷ 你准备送他什么结婚物？Nǐ zhǔnbèi sòng tā shénme jiéhūn lǐwù? What are you going to give him as a wedding present? **3**(送行) see ... off ▷ 他把女朋友送到家。Tā bǎ nǚpéngyou sòngdào jiā. He saw his girlfriend home.
送行 sòngxíng [动] see ... off

搜 sōu [动] search
搜查 sōuchá [动] search
搜(蒐) 集 sōují [动] gather
搜索 sōusuǒ [动] search for
搜索引擎 sōusuǒ yǐnqíng [名] search engine

苏(蘇) sū [动] revive
苏(蘇) 打 sūdá [名] soda
苏(蘇) 格兰(蘭) Sūgélán [名] Scotland ▷ 苏格兰短裙 Sūgélán duǎnqún kilt

俗 sú I [名] (风俗) custom ▸ 民俗 mínsú folk custom ▷ 入乡随俗 rù xiāng suí sú when in Rome, do as the Romans do II [形] **1**(大众的) popular **2**(庸俗) vulgar

俗气(氣) súqi [形] vulgar
俗语(語) súyǔ [名] common saying

诉(訴) sù [动] **1**(说给人) tell ▸ 诉说 sùshuō tell **2**(倾吐) pour ... out ▸ 诉苦 sùkǔ complain ▸ 上诉 shàngsù appeal to a higher court

素 sù I [形] plain II [名] **1**(蔬菜、瓜果等食物) vegetable **2**(有根本性质的) element ▸ 维生素 wéishēngsù vitamin
素描 sùmiáo [名] sketch
素食 sùshí [名] vegetarian food
素食者 sùshízhě [名] vegetarian
素质(質) sùzhì [名] character

速 sù I [名] speed II [形] quick ▸ 速算 sùsuàn quick calculation
速成 sùchéng [动] take a crash course
速递(遞) sùdì [动] send by express delivery
速度 sùdù [名] speed
速溶 sùróng [动] dissolve quickly ▷ 速溶咖啡 sùróng kāfēi instant coffee

宿 sù [动] stay
宿舍 sùshè [名] dormitory

塑 sù I [动] model II [名] mould (英), mold (美)
塑料 sùliào [名] plastic
塑料袋 sùliàodài [名] plastic bag
塑像 sùxiàng [名] statue

酸 suān I [形] **1**(指味道) sour **2**(伤心) sad **3**(迂腐) pedantic **4**(疼) sore II [名] acid
酸奶 suānnǎi [名] yoghurt

蒜 suàn [名] garlic

算 suàn [动] **1**(计算) calculate **2**(计算进去) count **3**(谋划) plan ▸ 暗算 ànsuàn plot against **4**(当做) be considered as **5**(由某人负责) blame **6**(算数) count **7**(作罢) ▷ 算了吧! Suànle ba! Forget it! **8**(推测) suppose
算命 suànmìng [动] tell sb's fortune ▷ 算命先生 suànmìng xiānsheng fortune teller
算盘(盤) suànpán [名] (计算用具) abacus

算术(術) suànshù [名] maths (英) (sg) math (美)

算账(賬) suànzhàng [动] 1(计算账目) work out accounts 2(把事情扯平) get even with

虽(雖) suī [连] although ▷ 他个子虽小，力气却很大。Tā gèzi suī xiǎo, lìqi què hěn dà. Although he isn't big, he's very strong.

虽(雖)然 suīrán [连] although ▷ 虽然她很年轻，可是却很成熟。Suīrán tā hěn niánqīng, kěshì què hěn chéngshú. Although she is very young, she is quite mature.

随(隨) suí [动] 1(跟随) follow 2(顺从) go along with 3(任凭) let ... do as they like ▷ 孩子大了，随他去吧。Háizi dà le, suí tā qù ba. The child's grown up — let him do as he wishes.

随(隨)便 suíbiàn I [动] do as one wishes II [形] 1(随意) casual 2(欠考虑的) thoughtless III [副] ▷ 大家随便坐。Dàjiā suíbiàn zuò. Everyone can sit where they like.

随(隨)和 suíhe [形] easygoing

随(隨)身 suíshēn [副] ▷ 随身行李 suíshēn xíngli hand luggage

随(隨)身听(聽) suíshēntīng [名] Walkman®

随(隨)时(時) suíshí [副] at any time

随(隨)手 suíshǒu [副] on one's way ▷ 请随手关门。Qǐng suíshǒu guān mén. Please close the door on your way.

随(隨)着(著) suízhe [动] follow

岁(歲) suì [名] year ▷ 他20岁了。Tā èrshí suì le. He's 20 years old.

岁(歲)数(數) suìshu [名] age

碎 suì I [动] 1(破碎) break 2(使粉碎) smash ▶ 碎纸机 suìzhǐjī shredder II [形] (不完整) broken

隧 suì [名] tunnel

隧道 suìdào [名] tunnel

孙(孫) sūn [名] grandchild

孙(孫)女 sūnnǚ [名] granddaughter

孙(孫)子 sūnzi [名] grandson

损(損) sǔn [动] 1(减少) decrease 2(损害) harm 3(损坏) damage

损(損)害 sǔnhài [动] 1(健康) damage 2(利益) harm 3(名誉) ruin 4(关系) damage

损(損)坏(壞) sǔnhuài [动] damage

损(損)失 sǔnshī I [动] lose II [名] loss

笋(筍) sǔn [名] bamboo shoot

缩(縮) suō [动] 1(收缩) contract 2(收回去) withdraw

缩(縮)减(減) suōjiǎn [动] 1(经费) cut 2(人员) reduce

缩(縮)水 suōshuǐ [动] shrink

缩(縮)写(寫) suōxiě I [名] abbreviation II [动] abridge

所 suǒ I [名] 1(处所) place 2(用于机构名称) office ▶ 派出所 pàichūsuǒ local police station ▶ 诊所 zhěnsuǒ clinic II [量] ▷ 三所医院 sān suǒ yīyuàn three hospitals ▷ 一所大学 yī suǒ dàxué a university

| measure word, used for buildings, houses, hospitals, schools, universities, etc.

III [助] 1(表示被动) ▷ 他被金钱所迷惑。Tā bèi jīnqián suǒ míhuò. He's obsessed with money. 2(表示强调) ▷ 这正是大家所不理解的。Zhè zhèng shì dàjiā suǒ bù lǐjiě de. This is the bit that no-one understands.

所谓(謂) suǒwèi [形] what is known as 1(通常说的) ▷ 中医所谓"上火"不止是指嗓子疼一种症状。Zhōngyī suǒwèi "shànghuǒ" bùzhǐ shì zhǐ sǎngzi téng yī zhǒng zhèngzhuàng. What is known in Chinese medicine as "excess internal heat" covers a lot more than sore throats and the like. 2(形容不认可) so-called

所以 suǒyǐ [连] (表示结果) so ▷ 路上堵车，所以我迟到了。Lùshang dǔchē, suǒyǐ wǒ chídào le. There was a lot of traffic, so I am late.

所有 suǒyǒu I [动] own II [名] possession III [形] all

索 suǒ I [名] **1**(绳子) rope **2**(链子) chain II [动] **1**(找) search ▶ 探索 tànsuǒ explore **2**(要) request
索赔(賠) suǒpéi [动] claim damages
索引 suǒyǐn [名] index

锁(鎖) suǒ I [名] lock II [动] (用锁锁住) lock
锁(鎖)链(鏈) suǒliàn [名] chain

他 tā [代] (另一人) he ▶ 他的包 tā de bāo his bag ▶ 我还记得他。Wǒ hái jìde tā. I still remember him.
他们(們) tāmen [代] they ▶ 他们的老师 tāmen de lǎoshī their teacher ▶ 我给他们写信。Wǒ gěi tāmen xiěxìn. I wrote to them.
他人 tārén [名] others (pl)

它 tā [代] it
它们(們) tāmen [代] they

她 tā [代] she ▶ 她的帽子 tā de màozi her hat ▶ 我给她发了个短信。Wǒ gěi tā fāle gè duǎnxìn. I sent her a text message.
她们(們) tāmen [代] they

塌 tā [动] (倒塌) collapse
塌实(實) tāshi [形] **1**(不浮躁) steady **2**(放心) at peace

塔 tǎ [名] **1**(指佛教建筑物) pagoda **2**(指塔形物) tower
塔楼(樓) tǎlóu [名] tower block

獭(獺) tǎ [名] otter ▶ 水獭 shuǐtǎ otter

踏 tà [动] (踩) step onto

胎 tāi [名] **1**(母体内的幼体) foetus (英), fetus (美) ▶ 怀胎 huáitāi be pregnant **2**(轮胎) tyre (英), tire (美)

胎儿(兒)tāi'ér[名]foetus(英), fetus(美)

台(臺)tái I[名] 1(指建筑) tower ▶ 观测台 guāncètái observation tower 2(指讲话、表演) stage ▶ 舞台 wǔtái stage 3(指作座子用) stand ▶ 蜡台 làtái candlestick 4(台形物) ▶ 窗台 chuāngtái window sill ▶ 站台 zhàntái platform 5(桌子或类似物) table ▶ 梳妆台 shūzhuāngtái dressing table ▶ 写字台 xiězìtái desk 6(指电话服务) telephone service ▷ 查号台 cháhàotái directory inquiries (pl) 7(指广播电视) station ▶ 电视台 diànshìtái television station 8(台湾) Taiwan II[量] 1(指机器) ▷ 一台电脑 yī tái diànnǎo a computer ▷ 一百台电视 yī bǎi tái diànshì one hundred TVs 2(指戏剧、戏曲) ▷ 两台京剧 liǎng tái Jīngjù two Beijing Opera performances ▷ 一台舞剧 yī tái wǔjù a ballet

▌ measure word, used for machines, equipment, stage performances, etc.

台(颱)风(風)táifēng[名]typhoon
台(臺)阶(階)táijiē[名](指建筑)step
台(臺)历(曆)táilì[名]desk calendar
台(臺)球(毬)táiqiú[名] 1(指美式) pool 2(指英式) billiards (sg)
台(臺)湾(灣)Táiwān[名]Taiwan

抬 tái[动] 1(举) raise 2(搬) carry
抬头(頭)táitóu[动](昂头)raise one's head

太 tài I[形] 1(高或大) highest 2(指辈分高) senior ▶ 太爷爷 tài yéye great-grandfather II[副] 1(指程度过分) too ▷ 这部电影太长。Zhè bù diànyǐng tài cháng. This film is too long. 2(指程度极高) so ▷ 我太高兴了。Wǒ tài gāoxìng le. I am so happy.
太极(極)拳 tàijíquán[名]Tai-chi
太空 tàikōng[名]space
太平洋 Tàipíng Yáng[名]the Pacific Ocean
太太 tàitai[名] 1(妻子) wife 2(指老年妇女) lady 3(指已婚妇女) Mrs
太阳(陽)tàiyáng[名]sun

态(態)tài[名] 1(状态) state ▶ 常态 chángtài normality ▶ 体态 tǐtài posture 2(语言) voice
态(態)度 tàidu[名] 1(举止神情) manner 2(看法) attitude

贪(貪)tān I[动] 1(贪污) be corrupt 2(不满足) crave 3(贪图) covet II[形] greedy
贪(貪)吃 tānchī[动] be greedy
贪(貪)婪 tānlán[形] greedy
贪(貪)玩 tānwán be too fond of a good time
贪(貪)污 tānwū[动] embezzle
贪(貪)心 tānxīn I[形] greedy II[名] greed

摊(攤)tān I[动] 1(摆开) spread ... out ▷ 摊开地图 tānkāi dìtú spread out a map 2(指烹调) fry ▷ 他摊了个鸡蛋。Tā tānle gè jīdàn. He fried an egg. 3(分担) share II[名] stall
摊(攤)贩(販)tānfàn[名] street trader

瘫(癱)tān I[名] paralysis II[形] paralysed(英), paralyzed(美)
瘫(癱)痪(瘓)tānhuàn I[名] paralysis II[动] be paralysed(英) or paralyzed(美)

坛(壇)tán[名] 1(土台) raised plot ▶ 花坛 huātán raised flower bed 2(台子) platform ▶ 论坛 lùntán forum

谈(談)tán I[动] talk ▷ 谈生意 tán shēngyì discuss business II[名] talk
谈(談)话(話)tánhuà[动] chat
谈(談)论(論)tánlùn[动] discuss
谈(談)判 tánpàn[动] negotiate
谈(談)心 tánxīn[动] have a heart-to-heart talk

弹(彈)tán[动] 1(指弹性) spring ▷ 球弹不起来了。Qiú tán bù qǐlái le. The ball doesn't bounce. 2(棉花、羊毛) fluff ... up 3(土、灰、球) flick 4(乐器) play ▷ 弹钢琴 tán gāngqín play the piano → see also/另见 dàn
弹(彈)簧 tánhuáng[名] spring
弹(彈)力 tánlì[名] elasticity

弹(彈)性 tánxìng [名] 1(弹力) elasticity 2(喻)flexibility ▷ 弹性工作制 tánxìng gōngzuò zhì flexible working system

痰 tán [名] phlegm

坦 tǎn [形] 1(平整)flat ▶ 平坦 píngtǎn flat 2(直率)candid 3(心里安定)calm ▶ 坦然 tǎnrán composed
坦白 tǎnbái I [形] candid II [动] confess
坦率 tǎnshuài [形] frank

毯 tǎn [名] 1(指地上)carpet ▶ 地毯 dìtǎn carpet 2(指床上)blanket ▶ 毛毯 máotǎn wool blanket 3(指墙上)tapestry ▶ 壁毯 bìtǎn tapestry

叹(嘆)tàn [动] (唉气) sigh
叹(嘆)气(氣)tànqì [动] sigh

炭 tàn [名] charcoal

探 tàn I [动] 1(试图发现)explore ▶ 探险 tànxiǎn explore 2(看望)visit ▶ 探亲 tànqīn visit one's relatives 3(伸出去)stick ... out 4(过问)inquire ▶ 打探 dǎtàn scout II [名] scout ▶ 侦探 zhēntàn detective
探测(測)tàncè [动] survey
探索 tànsuǒ [动] probe
探讨(討)tàntǎo [动] investigate
探望 tànwàng [动] (看望) visit

碳 tàn [名] carbon

汤(湯)tāng [名] (指食物) soup
汤(湯)药(藥)tāngyào [名] decoction of herbal medicine

堂 táng I [名] 1(房屋)hall ▶ 礼堂 lǐtáng auditorium ▶ 课堂 kètáng classroom ▶ 教堂 jiàotáng church 2(厅)hall II [量] ▷ 两堂课 liǎng táng kè two lessons
■ measure word, used for school lessons

糖 táng [名] 1(指做饭)sugar 2(糖果)sweet

躺 tǎng [动] lie

烫(燙)tàng I [形] very hot ▷ 这汤真烫。Zhè tāng zhēn tàng. This soup is boiling hot. II [动] 1(人)scald 2(加热)heat ... up 3(熨)iron 4(头发)perm
烫(燙)手 tàngshǒu [形] scalding

趟 tàng [量] 1(指旅程) ▷ 我已经去了好几趟。Wǒ yǐjīng qùle hǎo jǐ tàng. I've made several trips. 2(指公交车、地铁等) ▷ 他错过了一趟车。Tā cuòguòle yī tàng chē. He missed the bus.
■ measure word, used for journeys, visits, scheduled public transport, etc.

掏 tāo [动] 1(拿出)take ... out 2(挖)dig 3(偷)steal

逃 táo [动] 1(逃跑)run away 2(逃避)flee
逃避 táobì [动] escape ▷ 逃避责任 táobì zérèn shirk responsibility ▷ 逃避关税 táobì guānshuì evade customs duties
逃跑 táopǎo [动] escape

桃 táo [名] peach ▶ 桃子 táozi peach

陶 táo [名] pottery
陶瓷 táocí [名] ceramics (pl)
陶器 táoqì [名] pottery
陶醉 táozuì [动] be intoxicated

淘 táo I [动] 1(米)wash 2(金子)pan for ▶ 淘金 táojīn pan for gold II [形] naughty
淘气(氣)táoqì [形] naughty
淘汰 táotài [动] eliminate

讨(討)tǎo [动] 1(债)demand 2(饭、钱)beg 3(讨论)discuss
讨(討)论(論)tǎolùn [动] discuss
讨(討)厌(厭)tǎoyàn I [形] 1(可恶)disgusting 2(指难办)nasty II [动] dislike

套 tào I [名] (套子)cover ▶ 手套 shǒutào glove ▶ 避孕套 bìyùntào condom II [动] (罩在外面)slip ... on III [量] set ▷ 一套西装 yī tào xīzhuāng a suit ▷ 两套邮票 liǎng tào yóupiào two sets of stamps
■ measure word, used for suits, collections of books, tools, etc.
套餐 tàocān [名] set meal

特 tè I[形] special II[副] **1**(特地) especially **2**(非常) extremely

特别(別) tèbié I[形] peculiar II[副] **1**(格外) exceptionally **2**(特地) specially

特此 tècǐ [副] hereby

特地 tèdì [副] especially

特点(點) tèdiǎn [名] characteristic

特价(價) tèjià [名] bargain price ▷ 特价商品 tèjià shāngpǐn bargain

特例 tèlì [名] special case

特区(區) tèqū [名] special zone

特权(權) tèquán [名] privilege

特色 tèsè [名] characteristic

特殊 tèshū [形] special

特务(務) tèwu [名] special agent

特征(徵) tèzhēng [名] characteristic

疼 téng I[形] sore ▷ 我牙疼。Wǒ yá téng. I have toothache. II[动] love

藤(籐) téng [名] vine ▷ 藤椅 téngyǐ cane chair

剔 tī [动] (牙、指甲) pick

梯 tī [名] ladder ▷ 电梯 diàntī lift (英), elevator (美) ▷ 楼梯 lóutī stairs (pl)

踢 tī [动] kick ▷ 踢足球 tī zúqiú play football

提 tí [动] **1**(拿) carry **2**(升) raise ▷ 提拔 tíbá promote **3**(提前) bring forward **4**(提出) put ... forward ▷ 他提了个建议。Tā tíle gè jiànyì. He put forward a proposal. **5**(提取) collect **6**(谈起) mention ▷ 别再提那件事了。Bié zài tí nà jiàn shì le. Don't mention that subject again.

提倡 tíchàng [动] promote

提出 tíchū [动] put ... forward

提纲(綱) tígāng [名] synopsis

提高 tígāo [动] raise ▷ 提高效率 tígāo xiàolù increase efficiency

提供 tígōng [动] provide

提前 tíqián I[动] bring ... forward II[副] early

提问(問) tíwèn [动] ask a question

提醒 tíxǐng [动] remind

提议(議) tíyì I[动] propose II[名] proposal

题(題) tí I[名] subject ▷ 标题 biāotí title II[动] inscribe

题(題)材 tícái [名] theme

题(題)目 tímù [名] **1**(标题) title **2**(考题) question

蹄 tí [名] hoof

体(體) tǐ [名] **1**(身体) body ▷ 人体 réntǐ human body **2**(物体) substance ▷ 液体 yètǐ liquid

体(體)操 tǐcāo [名] gymnastics (sg)

体(體)会(會) tǐhuì I[动] come to understand II[名] understanding

体(體)积(積) tǐjī [名] volume

体(體)检(檢) tǐjiǎn [名] physical examination

体(體)力 tǐlì [名] physical strength

体(體)贴(貼) tǐtiē [动] show consideration for

体(體)温(溫) tǐwēn [名] temperature

体(體)系 tǐxì [名] system

体(體)现(現) tǐxiàn [动] embody

体(體)型 tǐxíng [名] physique

体(體)验(驗) tǐyàn [动] learn from experience

体(體)育 tǐyù [名] **1**(课程) P.E. **2**(运动) sport ▷ 体育比赛 tǐyù bǐsài sports event

体(體)育场(場) tǐyùchǎng [名] stadium

体(體)育馆(館) tǐyùguǎn [名] gym

体(體)重 tǐzhòng [名] weight

剃 tì [动] shave

替 tì I[动] (代) replace II[介] for ▷ 别替他操心了。Bié tì tā cāoxīn le. Don't worry about him.

替代 tìdài [动] replace

天 tiān I[名] **1**(天空) sky **2**(一昼夜) day ▷ 昨天 zuótiān yesterday **3**(一段时间) ▷ 天还早呢。Tiān hái zǎo ne. It's still so early. **4**(季节) season ▷ 秋天 qiūtiān autumn (英), fall (美) **5**(天气) weather

▶阴天 yīntiān overcast weather ▷天很
热。Tiān hěn rè. It's a very hot day.
6(自然) nature **7**(造物主) God ▷天知
道！Tiān zhīdào! God knows! **8**(神的住
所) Heaven **II**[形](指位于顶部的)
overhead ▶天桥 tiānqiáo overhead
walkway

天才 tiāncái [名] **1**(才能) talent **2**(人)
genius

天鹅(鵝) tiān'é [名] swan

天空 tiānkōng [名] sky

天气(氣) tiānqì [名] weather ▷天气预
报 tiānqì yùbào weather forecast

天然 tiānrán [形] natural

天生 tiānshēng [形] inherent ▷这孩子
天生聋哑。Zhè háizi tiānshēng
lóngyǎ. This child was born with
hearing and speech difficulties.

天使 tiānshǐ [名] angel

天堂 tiāntáng [名] Heaven

天天 tiāntiān [副] every day

天下 tiānxià [名] the world

天线(線) tiānxiàn [名] aerial

天性 tiānxìng [名] nature

天真 tiānzhēn [形] innocent

添 tiān [动](增加) add

田 tián [名] **1**(耕地) field **2**(开采地) field
▶油田 yóutián oilfield

田径(徑) tiánjìng [名] track and field
sports (pl)

田野 tiányě [名] open country

甜 tián [形] **1**(指味道) sweet **2**(指睡觉)
sound

甜点(點) tiándiǎn [名] dessert

甜食 tiánshí [名] sweet

填 tián [动] **1**(塞满) fill **2**(填写) complete
▷填表格 tián biǎogé fill in a form

填充 tiánchōng [动] **1**(填上) stuff
2(补足) fill ... in

填空 tiánkòng [动](指考试) fill in the
blanks

填写(寫) tiánxiě [动] fill ... in

舔 tiǎn [动] lick

挑 tiāo [动] **1**(肩扛) carry ... on a carrying
pole **2**(挑选) choose **3**(挑剔) nitpick
→ see also/另见 tiǎo

挑食 tiāoshí [动] be a fussy eater

挑剔 tiāoti [动] nitpick

挑选(選) tiāoxuǎn [动] select

条(條) tiáo **I**[名] **1**(细树枝) twig
2(长条) strip **3**(层次) order **4**(分项) item
5(律令) article **6**(短书信) note **II**[量]
1(用于细长东西) ▷两条腿 liǎng tiáo tuǐ
two legs ▷一条烟 yī tiáo yān a
multipack of cigarettes **2**(指分事项)
▷一条新闻 yī tiáo xīnwén an item of
news **3**(指与人有关) ▷一条人命 yī tiáo
rénmìng a life

▋ measure word, used for long thin
things, news, human lives, etc.

条(條)件 tiáojiàn [名] **1**(客观因素)
condition **2**(要求) requirement
3(状况) circumstances (pl)

条(條)理 tiáolǐ [名] order

条(條)约(約) tiáoyuē [名] treaty

调(調) tiáo [动] **1**(使和谐) harmonize
▶失调 shītiáo imbalance **2**(使均匀)
blend ▷给钢琴调音 gěi gāngqín tiáo
yīn tune a piano **3**(调解) mediate
→ see also/另见 diào

调(調)节(節) tiáojié [动] adjust

调(調)料 tiáoliào [名] seasoning

调(調)皮 tiáopí [形](顽皮) naughty

调(調)整 tiáozhěng [动] adjust

挑 tiǎo [动] **1**(扯起一头) raise **2**(向上拨)
prick
→ see also/另见 tiāo

挑战(戰) tiǎozhàn [动] challenge ▷面
临新挑战 miànlín xīn tiǎozhàn face a
new challenge

跳 tiào [动] **1**(跃) jump ▶跳高 tiàogāo
high jump ▶跳水 tiàoshuǐ diving ▶跳远
tiàoyuǎn long jump ▶跳远(弹起) bounce
3(起伏地动) beat ▶心跳 xīntiào
heartbeat **4**(越过) jump over ▷跳过几
页 tiàoguò jǐ yè skip a few pages

跳槽 tiàocáo [动] change jobs

跳舞 tiàowǔ [动] dance

跳跃(躍) tiàoyuè [动] jump

贴(貼) tiē I [动] 1 (粘) stick 2 (紧挨) be close to 3 (贴补) subsidize II [名] allowance

帖 tiě [名] 1 (请帖) invitation ▸ 请帖 qǐngtiě invitation 2 (小卡片) card

铁(鐵) tiě [名] (金属) iron
铁(鐵)道 tiědào [名] railway (英), railroad (美)
铁(鐵)路 tiělù [名] railway (英), railroad (美)

厅(廳) tīng [名] 1 (大堂) hall ▸ 客厅 kètīng sitting room ▸ 餐厅 cāntīng canteen 2 (机关) office

听(聽) tīng I [动] 1 (收听) listen to 2 (听从) obey ▷ 听老师的话 tīng lǎoshī de huà do as the teacher says II [名] tin III [量] can ▷ 一听啤酒 yī tīng píjiǔ a can of beer
听(聽)话(話) tīnghuà I [动] obey II [形] obedient
听(聽)见(見) tīngjiàn [动] hear
听(聽)讲(講) tīngjiǎng [动] attend a lecture
听(聽)说(說) tīngshuō [动] hear
听(聽)众(眾) tīngzhòng [名] audience

亭 tíng [名] 1 (亭子) pavilion 2 (小房子) kiosk ▸ 电话亭 diànhuàtíng phone box (英), phone booth (美)

庭 tíng [名] 1 (书) (厅堂) hall 2 (院子) courtyard 3 (法庭) law court
庭院 tíngyuàn [名] courtyard

停 tíng [动] 1 (止) stop 2 (停留) stop off 3 (停放) park
停车(車)场(場) tíngchēchǎng [名] car park (英), car lot (美)
停顿(頓) tíngdùn [动] 1 (中止) halt 2 (指说话) pause II [名] pause
停止 tíngzhǐ [动] stop ▷ 停止营业 tíngzhǐ yíngyè cease trading

挺 tǐng [副] very

艇 tǐng [名] boat ▸ 游艇 yóutǐng yacht ▸ 救生艇 jiùshēngtǐng lifeboat

通 tōng I [动] 1 (连接) connect with ▸ 通商 tōngshāng have trade relations with ▸ 通风 tōngfēng ventilate 2 (使不堵) clear ... out ▷ 通下水道 tōng xiàshuǐdào clear out a drain 3 (传达) inform ▸ 通信 tōngxìn correspond by letter ▷ 通电话 tōng diànhuà communicate by telephone 4 (通晓) understand ▸ 精通 jīngtōng be expert in II [名] expert ▷ 外语通 wàiyǔ tōng an expert in foreign languages III [形] 1 (没有障碍) open ▷ 电话打通了。Diànhuà dǎ tōng le. The call has been put through. 2 (顺畅) workable 3 (顺通) coherent 4 (普通) common 5 (整个) overall IV [副] 1 (全部) completely 2 (一般) normally
通常 tōngcháng I [形] normal II [名] normal circumstances (pl) ▷ 我通常7点起床。Wǒ tōngcháng qī diǎn qǐchuáng. Under normal circumstances, I get up at seven o'clock.
通道 tōngdào [名] (指出入) passageway ▷ 地下通道 dìxià tōngdào tunnel
通过(過) tōngguò I [动] 1 (经过) pass ▷ 通过边境线 tōngguò biānjìngxiàn cross the border 2 (同意) pass II [介] by means of
通俗 tōngsú [形] popular
通宵 tōngxiāo [名] all night
通信 tōngxìn [动] correspond
通讯(訊) tōngxùn I [名] dispatch II [动] communicate
通用 tōngyòng [动] be in common use
通知 tōngzhī [名] notification

同 tóng I [动] 1 (一样) be the same ▸ 不同 bù tóng be different 2 (共同) do ... together ▸ 同居 tóngjū cohabit II [介] 1 (跟) with 2 (指比较) as
同伴 tóngbàn [名] companion
同等 tóngděng [形] of the same level
同类(類) tónglèi I [形] of the same kind II [名] the same kind
同盟 tóngméng [名] alliance
同情 tóngqíng [动] sympathize ▷ 表示同情 biǎoshì tóngqíng express sympathy

同时(時)tóngshí I[名] at the same time ▷ 同时发生 tóngshí fāshēng occur simultaneously II[连] besides

同事 tóngshì [名] colleague

同性恋(戀)tóngxìngliàn [名] homosexuality

同学(學)tóngxué [名] 1(指同校) fellow student 2(指同班) classmate

同样(樣)tóngyàng [形] 1(一样) same 2(情况类似) similar

同意 tóngyì [动] agree

同志 tóngzhì [名] comrade

铜(銅)tóng [名] copper

铜(銅)牌 tóngpái [名] bronze medal

童 tóng [名] (小孩) child ▷ 神童 shéntóng child prodigy

童话(話)tónghuà [名] fairy tale

童年 tóngnián [名] childhood

统(統)tǒng I[名] ▷ 系统 xìtǒng system ▷ 血统 xuètǒng bloodline II[动] command III[副] all

统(統)计(計)tǒngjì [名] statistics (pl) ▷ 人口统计 rénkǒu tǒngjì census II[动] count

统(統)统(統)tǒngtǒng [副] entirely

统(統)一 tǒngyī I[动] 1(使成一体) unite 2(使一致) unify ▷ 统一思想 tǒngyī sīxiǎng reach a common understanding II[形] unified

统(統)治 tǒngzhì [动] rule

桶 tǒng I[名] bucket ▷ 汽油桶 qìyóu tǒng petrol (英) 或 gasoline (美) drum ▷ 啤酒桶 píjiǔ tǒng beer barrel II[量] barrel ▷ 一桶柴油 yī tǒng cháiyóu a barrel of diesel oil ▷ 两桶牛奶 liǎng tǒng niúnǎi two churns of milk

筒 tǒng [名] 1(竹管) bamboo tube 2(粗管状物) ▷ 笔筒 bǐtǒng pen holder ▷ 邮筒 yóutǒng post box (英), mailbox (美) 3(指衣服) ▷ 长筒袜 chángtǒngwà stockings (pl)

痛 tòng I[动] 1(疼) ache ▷ 头痛 tóutòng have a headache ▷ 胃痛 wèitòng have a stomach ache 2(悲伤) grieve ▷ 哀痛 āitòng sorrow II[副] deeply ▷ 痛打 tòngdǎ give a sound beating to

痛苦 tòngkǔ [形] painful

痛快 tòngkuài [形] 1(高兴) joyful 2(尽兴) to one's heart's content ▷ 玩个痛快 wán gè tòngkuài play to one's heart's content 3(爽快) straightforward

偷 tōu I[动] (窃) steal II[副] stealthily

偷空 tōukòng [动] take time off

偷懒(懶)tōulǎn [动] be lazy

偷窃(竊)tōuqiè [动] steal

偷偷 tōutōu [副] secretly

头(頭)tóu I[名] 1(脑袋) head ▷ 点头 diǎntóu nod one's head 2(头发) hair ▷ 分头 fēntóu parted hair ▷ 平头 píngtóu crew cut ▷ 梳头 shūtóu comb one's hair 4(开始) beginning 5(头目) head ▷ 谁是你们的头儿? Shuí shì nǐmen de tóur? Who's your boss? II[形] 1(第一) first ▷ 头奖 tóujiǎng first prize ▷ 头等 tóuděng first class 2(领头) leading 3(时间在前) first ▷ 头几年 tóu jǐ nián first few years III[量] 1(指动物) ▷ 三头母牛 sān tóu mǔniú three cows 2(指蒜) bulb ▷ 一头蒜 yī tóu suàn a bulb of garlic

▍measure word, used for cows, bulls and vegetable bulbs

头(頭)发(髮)tóufa [名] hair

头(頭)领(領)tóulǐng [名] leader

头(頭)脑(腦)tóunǎo [名] brains (pl)

头(頭)衔(銜)tóuxián [名] title

头(頭)像 tóuxiàng [名] 1(头部的像) bust 2(指社交媒体) profile picture

投 tóu [动] 1(扔) throw 2(放进去) put ... in 3(跳下去) throw oneself 4(投射) cast 5(寄) post

投入 tóurù I[形] (指专注) engrossed II[动] 1(放入) put ... in 2(参加) throw oneself into

投诉(訴)tóusù I[动] lodge a complaint II[名] appeal

投降 tóuxiáng [动] surrender

投资(資)tóuzī I[动] invest II[名] investment

透 tòu I [动] 1(渗透) penetrate 2(泄露) leak out 3(显露) appear II [形] 1(透彻) thorough 2(程度深) complete ▷ 我浑身都湿透了。Wǒ húnshēn dōu shītòu le. I'm soaked to the skin.

透彻(徹) tòuchè [形] incisive
透露 tòulù [动] disclose
透明 tòumíng [形] transparent

秃(禿) tū [形] 1(指毛发) bald 2(指山) barren 3(指树) bare

秃(禿)顶(頂) tūdǐng [动] be bald
秃(禿)子 tūzi [名] (口) baldy

突 tū [副] suddenly

突出 tūchū I [动] give prominence to ▷ 他从不突出自己。Tā cóng bù tūchū zìjǐ. He never pushes himself forward. II [形] (明显) noticeable ▷ 突出的特点 tūchū de tèdiǎn prominent feature

突击(擊) tūjī I [动] 1(突然袭击) assault 2(加快完成) do a rush job II [副] from nowhere

突破 tūpò [动] 1(防线、界线) break through 2(僵局、难关) make a breakthrough 3(限额) surpass 4(记录) break

突然 tūrán I [形] sudden II [副] suddenly

图(圖) tú I [名] 1(图画) picture 2(地图) map 3(计划) plan II [动] 1(贪图) seek ▷ 图一时痛快 tú yīshí tòngkuài seek momentary gratification 2(谋划) scheme

图(圖)案 tú'àn [名] design
图(圖)画(畫) túhuà [名] picture
图(圖)书(書) túshū [名] books (pl)
图(圖)书(書)馆(館) túshūguǎn [名] library
图(圖)像 túxiàng [名] image
图(圖)章 túzhāng [名] seal

徒 tú [名] (徒弟) apprentice ▷ 徒弟 túdì apprentice

途 tú [名] way ▷ 旅途 lǚtú journey ▷ 前途 qiántú prospect

途径(徑) tújìng [名] channel

涂(塗) tú [动] 1(抹) spread ... on ▷ 涂油漆 tú yóuqī apply paint 2(乱写乱画) scribble 3(改动) cross ... out

涂(塗)改 túgǎi [动] alter
涂(塗)料 túliào [名] paint

屠 tú I [动] 1(动物) slaughter 2(人) massacre II [名] butcher

屠夫 túfū [名] (字) butcher
屠杀(殺) túshā [动] massacre

土 tǔ I [名] 1(泥) soil 2(土地) land ▷ 领土 lǐngtǔ territory II [形] 1(地方) local 2(民间) folk 3(不时髦) unfashionable

土地 tǔdì [名] 1(田地) land 2(疆域) territory
土豆 tǔdòu [名] potato
土话(話) tǔhuà [名] local dialect
土壤 tǔrǎng [名] soil
土著 tǔzhù [名] indigenous peoples (pl)

吐 tǔ [动] (排出口外) spit
→ see also/另见 tù

吐 tù [动] vomit
→ see also/另见 tǔ

吐沫 tùmo [名] saliva

兔 tù [名] 1(野兔) hare 2(家兔) rabbit

团(團) tuán I [名] 1(球形物) ball 2(组织) group ▷ 剧团 jùtuán drama company 3(军) regiment II [动] 1(聚合) unite ▷ 团聚 tuánjù reunite 2(揉成球状) roll into a ball III [形] round IV [量] ▷ 一团面 yī tuán miàn a lump of dough ▷ 一团毛线 yī tuán máoxiàn a ball of wool

■ measure word, used for rolled up round things

团(團)伙(夥) tuánhuǒ [名] gang
团(團)结(結) tuánjié [动] unite
团(團)体(體) tuántǐ [名] organization
团(團)圆(圓) tuányuán [动] reunite

推 tuī [动] 1(门、窗、车) push 2(指用工具) scrape ▷ 他推了个光头。Tā tuīle gè guāngtóu. He's shaved his head. 3(开展) push forward 4(推断) deduce 5(辞让) decline 6(推诿) shift 7(推迟) postpone

8 (举荐) elect
推测(測) tuīcè [动] infer
推辞(辭) tuīcí [动] decline
推迟(遲) tuīchí [动] put ... off
推出 tuīchū [动] bring ... out
推动(動) tuīdòng [动] promote
推广(廣) tuīguǎng [动] popularize
推荐(薦) tuījiàn [动] recommend
推特 Tuītè [名] Twitter®
推销(銷) tuīxiāo [动] promote

腿 tuǐ [名] **1** (下肢) leg ▸ 大腿 dàtuǐ thigh ▸ 小腿 xiǎotuǐ calf **2** (支撑物) leg

退 tuì [动] **1** (后移) retreat **2** (使后移) cause ... to withdraw **3** (退出) quit **4** (减退) recede **5** (减弱) fade **6** (退还) return **7** (撤销) cancel
退步 tuìbù I [动] **1** (落后) lag behind **2** (让步) give way II [名] leeway
退让(讓) tuìràng [动] make a concession
退缩(縮) tuìsuō [动] hold back
退休 tuìxiū [动] retire

褪 tuì [动] **1** (衣服) take ... off **2** (毛) shed **3** (颜色) fade

吞 tūn [动] **1** (整个咽下) swallow **2** (吞并) take over
吞并(併) tūnbìng [动] annex
吞没(沒) tūnmò [动] **1** (据为己有) misappropriate **2** (淹没) engulf

臀 tún [名] buttock

托 tuō I [动] **1** (撑) support **2** (委托) entrust **3** (依赖) rely on II [名] tray
托儿(兒)所 tuō'érsuǒ [名] nursery
托福 tuōfú [名] TOEFL, Test of English as a Foreign Language
托(託)付 tuōfù [动] entrust
托(託)运(運) tuōyùn [动] ship

拖 tuō [动] **1** (拉) pull **2** (地板) mop **3** (下垂) trail **4** (拖延) delay
拖鞋 tuōxié [名] slipper
In many Chinese homes, slippers are worn to keep both the floor and your socks clean.

拖延 tuōyán [动] delay

脱(脫) tuō [动] **1** (皮肤、毛发) shed **2** (衣服、鞋帽) take ... off **3** (摆脱) escape **4** (颜色) fade **5** (油脂) skim
脱(脫)臼 tuōjiù [动] dislocate
脱(脫)离(離) tuōlí [动] **1** (关系) break off **2** (危险) get away from
脱(脫)落 tuōluò [动] **1** (毛发、牙齿) lose **2** (油漆、墙皮) come off
脱(脫)水 tuōshuǐ [动] dehydrate

驮(馱) tuó [动] carry on one's back

驼(駝) tuó I [名] camel ▸ 骆驼 luòtuo camel II [形] hunchbacked ▸ 驼背 tuóbèi be hunchbacked

鸵(鴕) tuó see below/见下文
鸵(鴕)鸟(鳥) tuóniǎo [名] ostrich

妥 tuǒ [形] **1** (适当) appropriate **2** (停当) ready
妥当(當) tuǒdang [形] appropriate
妥善 tuǒshàn [形] appropriate
妥协(協) tuǒxié [动] compromise

椭(橢) tuǒ see below/见下文
椭(橢)圆(圓) tuǒyuán [名] oval

拓 tuò [动] open ... up
拓展 tuòzhǎn [动] expand

唾 tuò I [名] saliva II [动] spit
唾沫 tuòmo [名] (口) saliva

W

挖 wā [动] 1 (掘) dig ▶ 挖掘 wājué excavate 2 (耳朵、鼻子) pick

蛙 wā [名] frog
蛙泳 wāyǒng [名] breaststroke

娃 wá [名] (方) baby
娃娃 wáwa [名] 1 (小孩) baby 2 (玩具) doll

瓦 wǎ [名] tile
瓦斯 wǎsī [名] gas

袜 (襪) wà [名] socks (pl) ▶ 长筒袜 chángtǒngwà stockings (pl)
袜 (襪) 子 wàzi [名] socks (pl)

歪 wāi [形] (倾斜) slanting
歪斜 wāixié [形] crooked

外 wài I [名] 1 (范围以外) outside ▶ 外边 wàibian outside 2 (外国) foreign country II [形] 1 (外国的) foreign 2 (疏远) other ▶ 外人 wàirén outsider III [副] besides
外表 wàibiǎo [名] exterior
外地 wàidì [名] other parts of the country ▶ 外地人 wàidìrén person from another part of the country
外公 wàigōng [名] maternal grandfather
外国 (國) wàiguó [名] foreign country
外国 (國) 人 wàiguórén [名] foreigner
外号 (號) wàihào [名] nickname
外汇 (匯) wàihuì [名] (外币) foreign currency
外交 wàijiāo [名] foreign affairs ▶ 外交部 wàijiāobù Ministry of Foreign Affairs
外交官 wàijiāoguān [名] diplomat
外科 wàikē [名] surgery ▶ 外科医生 wàikē yīshēng surgeon
外卖 (賣) wàimài [名] takeaway (英), takeout (美)
外贸 (貿) wàimào [名] foreign trade
外婆 wàipó [名] maternal grandmother
外企 wàiqǐ [名] foreign enterprise
外伤 (傷) wàishāng [名] injury
外商 wàishāng [名] foreign businessman
外甥 wàisheng [名] nephew
外孙 (孫) wàisūn [名] grandson
外套 wàitào [名] overcoat
外文 wàiwén [名] foreign language
外向 wàixiàng [形] (指性格) extrovert
外语 (語) wàiyǔ [名] foreign language

弯 (彎) wān I [形] curved II [动] bend III [名] bend

湾 (灣) wān [名] bay

豌 wān see below / 见下文
豌豆 wāndòu [名] pea

丸 wán I [名] (指药) pill ▶ 丸药 wányào pill II [量] pill ▶ 他服了一丸药。 Tā fúle yī wán yào. He took a pill.

完 wán I [形] whole II [动] 1 (完成) complete 2 (耗尽) run out 3 (了结) finish
完成 wánchéng [动] complete
完美 wánměi [形] perfect
完全 wánquán I [形] complete II [副] completely
完整 wánzhěng [形] complete

玩 wán [动] 1 (玩耍) play 2 (游玩) have a good time ▶ 我去泰国玩了一个星期。 Wǒ qù Tàiguó wánle yī gè xīngqī. I went to Thailand for a week's holiday. 3 (做客) visit 4 (表示祝愿) enjoy ▶ 玩得好! Wán de hǎo! Enjoy yourself!

玩具 wánjù [名] toy

玩笑 wánxiào [名] joke ▷ 他喜欢跟人开玩笑。Tā xǐhuan gēn rén kāi wánxiào. He likes to play jokes on people.

玩意儿(兒) wányìr [名] (口) 1(东西) thing 2(玩具) toy 3(器械) gadget

顽(頑) wán [形] 1(难以摆脱的) stubborn ▷ 顽固 wángù stubborn 2(淘气) naughty

挽 wǎn [动] 1(拉) hold 2(卷起) roll ... up

晚 wǎn I [形] late ▷ 晚秋 wǎnqiū autumn ▷ 我起晚了。Wǒ qǐ wǎn le. I got up late. II [名] evening

晚安 wǎn'ān [形] good night

晚饭(飯) wǎnfàn [名] dinner

晚会(會) wǎnhuì [名] party

晚年 wǎnnián [名] old age

晚上 wǎnshang [名] evening

碗 wǎn [名] bowl

万(萬) wàn [数] ten thousand

万(萬)岁(歲) wànsuì [叹] long live

万(萬)一 wànyī [连] if by any chance

腕 wàn [名] 1(指手) wrist 2(指脚) ankle

腕子 wànzi [名] 1(指手) wrist 2(指脚) ankle

亡 wáng [动] die ▷ 死亡 sǐwáng die

王 wáng [名] king

王国(國) wángguó [名] kingdom

王子 wángzǐ [名] prince

网(網) wǎng [名] 1(工具) net 2(网状物) web 3(系统) network ▷ 互联网 hùliánwǎng the Internet

网(網)吧 wǎngbā [名] Internet café

网(網)络(絡) wǎngluò [名] network

网(網)民 wǎngmín [名] Internet user

网(網)球 wǎngqiú [名] tennis ▷ 网球场 wǎngqiúchǎng tennis court

网(網)页(頁) wǎngyè [名] web page

网(網)站 wǎngzhàn [名] website

网(網)址 wǎngzhǐ [名] web address

往 wǎng I [介] to II [形] past ▷ 往事 wǎngshì past events (pl)

往往 wǎngwǎng [副] often

忘 wàng [动] forget

忘记(記) wàngjì [动] forget

旺 wàng [形] 1(火) roaring 2(人、生意) flourishing 3(花) blooming

旺季 wàngjì [名] 1(指生意) peak season 2(指水果、蔬菜) season

旺盛 wàngshèng [形] 1(精力、生命力) full of energy 2(植物) thriving

望 wàng [动] 1(向远处看) look into the distance 2(察看) watch 3(希望) hope

危 wēi I [形] dangerous II [动] endanger

危害 wēihài [动] harm

危机(機) wēijī [名] crisis

危险(險) wēixiǎn I [形] dangerous II [名] danger

威 wēi [名] power

威力 wēilì [名] power

威士忌 wēishìjì [名] whisky

威胁(脅) wēixié [动] threaten

威信 wēixìn [名] prestige

威严(嚴) wēiyán I [形] dignified II [名] dignity

微 wēi I [形] tiny ▷ 微米 wēimǐ micron ▷ 微秒 wēimiǎo microsecond II [副] slightly

微波炉(爐) wēibōlú [名] microwave oven

微博 wēi bó [名] micro-blog

微风(風) wēifēng [名] gentle breeze

微件 wēijiàn [名] (计算机) widget

微量元素 wēiliàng yuánsù [名] trace element

微妙 wēimiào [形] delicate

微弱 wēiruò [形] faint

微生物 wēishēngwù [名] micro-organism

微小 wēixiǎo [形] tiny

微笑 wēixiào [动] smile

微型 wēixíng [形] mini

为(為) wéi I [动] 1(是) be 2(充当) act as II [介] by
→ see also/另见 wèi

为(為)难(難) wéinán I [形] embarrassed II [动] make things difficult for

为(為)期 wéiqī be scheduled for

为(為)生 wéishēng [动] make a living

为(為)止 wéizhǐ ▷ 到上周末为止 dào shàngzhōu mò wéizhǐ by the end of last week

违(違) wéi [动] break ▷ 违者必究。 Wéizhě bì jiū. Violations will not be tolerated.

违(違)背 wéibèi [动] go against

违(違)法 wéifǎ I [动] break the law II [形] illegal

违(違)反 wéifǎn [动] go against

违(違)犯 wéifàn [动] violate

围(圍) wéi I [动] surround II [名] 1(四周) all sides 2(周长) measurement ▷ 三围 sānwéi vital statistics ▷ 胸围 xiōngwéi chest measurement

围(圍)棋 wéiqí [名] go (board game)

围棋 wéiqí
- 围棋 wéiqí is a popular strategic board game in China, Japan and other East-Asian countries. It originated in ancient China. It is known as go in Japan. It is played by two players alternately placing black and white round stone pieces on the intersections of a square grid on a square game board. To win, the player must control a larger area on the game board than his/her opponent.

围(圍)绕(繞) wéirào [动] 1(物体) revolve around 2(话题) centre (英) 或 center (美) on

唯 wéi [副] 1(单单) only 2(书) (只是) but only

唯一 wéiyī [形] only

维(維) wéi I [动] 1(连接) hold ... together 2(保持) maintain II [名] dimension

维(維)持 wéichí [动] 1(保持) maintain 2(资助) support

维(維)护(護) wéihù [动] safeguard

维(維)生素 wéishēngsù [名] vitamin

维(維)修 wéixiū [动] maintain

伟(偉) wěi [形] great

伟(偉)大 wěidà [形] great

伟(偉)哥 wěigē [名] (医) Viagra®

伟(偉)人 wěirén [名] great man

伪(偽) wěi [形] false

伪(偽)钞(鈔) wěichāo [名] counterfeit note (英) 或 bill (美)

伪(偽)君子 wěijūnzǐ [名] hypocrite

伪(偽)造 wěizào [动] forge

伪(偽)装(裝) wěizhuāng I [动] disguise II [名] disguise

尾 wěi [名] 1(尾巴) tail ▷ 尾巴 wěiba tail 2(末端) end 3(残余) remainder ▷ 扫尾 sǎowěi finish off

尾气(氣) wěiqì [名] exhaust (英), tailpipe (美)

纬(緯) wěi [名] (地理) latitude ▷ 纬线 wěixiàn latitude

纬(緯)度 wěidù [名] latitude

委 wěi I [动] entrust II [名] 1(委员) committee member ▷ 委员 wěiyuán committee member 2(委员会) committee ▷ 委员会 wěiyuánhuì committee

委屈 wěiqū [名] unjust treatment

委托(託) wěituō [动] entrust

委婉 wěiwǎn [形] (指言词) tactful

卫(衛) wèi [动] protect

卫(衛)生 wèishēng I [名] 1(干净) hygiene 2(扫除) clean-up II [形] hygienic

卫(衛)生间(間) wèishēngjiān [名] toilet (英), rest room (美)

卫(衛)生纸(紙) wèishēngzhǐ [名] toilet paper (英) 或 tissue (美)

卫(衛)星 wèixīng [名] satellite

为(為) wèi [介] for ▷ 我真为你高兴！
Wǒ zhēn wèi nǐ gāoxìng! I am really
happy for you!
→ see also/另见 wéi

为(為)了 wèile [介] in order to

为(為)什么(麼) wèi shénme [副] why

未 wèi [副] not

未必 wèibì [副] not necessarily

未成年人 wèichéngniánrén [名]
minor

未婚夫 wèihūnfū [名] fiancé

未婚妻 wèihūnqī [名] fiancée

未来(來) wèilái [名] future

位 wèi I [名] 1 (位置) location 2 (地位)
position 3 (数学) digit ▷ 两位 liǎng
wèi shù two-digit number II [量] ▷ 两位
教授 liǎng wèi jiàoshòu two professors
▷ 一位父亲 yī wèi fùqīn a father
measure word, used for people

位于(於) wèiyú [动] be located

位置 wèizhì [名] 1 (地点) location
2 (地位) place 3 (职位) position

位子 wèizi [名] 1 (座位) seat 2 (职位)
position

味 wèi [名] 1 (滋味) taste 2 (气味) smell

味道 wèidào [名] (滋味) taste

味精 wèijīng [名] monosodium
glutamate

胃 wèi [名] stomach

胃口 wèikǒu [名] 1 (食欲) appetite
2 (喜好) liking

喂(餵) wèi I [动] feed ▷ 喂养 wèiyǎng
raise II [叹] 1 (指打电话) hello 2 (指招呼)
hey

温(溫) wēn I [形] 1 (不冷不热) warm
2 (平和) mild II [动] (加热) warm ... up
III [名] temperature

温(溫)度 wēndù [名] temperature

温(溫)和 wēnhé [形] 1 (指性情、态度)
mild 2 (指气候) temperate

温(溫)暖 wēnnuǎn [形] warm

温(溫)泉 wēnquán [名] hot spring

温(溫)柔 wēnróu [形] gentle

温(溫)室 wēnshì [名] greenhouse
▷ 温室效应 wēnshì xiàoyìng the
greenhouse effect

文 wén [名] 1 (字) writing 2 (书面语)
written language ▷ 中文 Zhōngwén the
Chinese language 3 (文章) essay 4 (指社
会产物) culture 5 (文科) humanities (pl)

文化 wénhuà [名] 1 (精神财富) culture
2 (知识) education

文件 wénjiàn [名] 1 (公文) document
2 (计算机) file

文具 wénjù [名] stationery

文科 wénkē [名] humanities (pl)

文盲 wénmáng [形] illiterate

文明 wénmíng I [名] civilization II [形]
civilized

文凭(憑) wénpíng [名] diploma

文物 wénwù [名] cultural relic

文学(學) wénxué [名] literature

文艺(藝) wényì [名] 1 (文学艺术) art
and literature 2 (文学) literature
3 (演艺) performing arts (pl)

文章 wénzhāng [名] (著作) essay

文字 wénzì [名] 1 (指符号) script
2 (指文章) writing

闻(聞) wén I [动] (嗅) smell II [名]
(消息) news (sg) ▷ 新闻 xīnwén news

蚊 wén [名] mosquito ▷ 蚊子 wénzi
mosquito

吻 wěn I [名] (嘴唇) lip ▷ 接吻 jiēwěn kiss
II [动] kiss

稳(穩) wěn I [形] 1 (平稳) steady
2 (坚定) firm 3 (稳重) composed 4 (可靠)
reliable 5 (肯定) sure II [动] keep calm

稳(穩)定 wěndìng I [形] steady II [动]
settle

问(問) wèn I [动] 1 (提问) ask 2 (问候)
send regards to 3 (干预) ask about II [名]
question ▷ 疑问 yíwèn doubt

问(問)候 wènhòu [动] send regards to

问(問)题(題) wèntí [名] 1 (疑问)
question 2 (困难) problem 3 (故障)
fault 4 (分项) issue

窝(窩) wō [名](栖息地) nest

蜗(蝸) wō see below/见下文
蜗(蝸)牛 wōniú [名] snail

我 wǒ [代] 1(自己, 作主语) I 2(自己, 作宾语) me
我们(們) wǒmen [代] 1(作主语) we 2(作宾语) us

卧(臥) wò I [动] 1(躺) lie 2(趴伏) sit II [名] berth
卧(臥)铺(鋪) wòpù [名] berth
卧(臥)室 wòshì [名] bedroom

握 wò [动] 1(抓) grasp 2(掌握) master
握手 wòshǒu [动] shake hands

乌(烏) wū I [名] crow ▶乌鸦 wūyā crow II [形] black ▶乌云 wūyún black cloud
乌(烏)龟(龜) wūguī [名] tortoise
乌(烏)黑 wūhēi [形] jet-black

污 wū [形] 1(肮脏) dirty 2(腐败) corrupt ▶贪污 tānwū be corrupt
污染 wūrǎn [动] pollute
污辱 wūrǔ [动](侮辱) insult

屋 wū [名] 1(房子) house 2(房间) room
屋顶(頂) wūdǐng [名] roof
屋子 wūzi [名] room

无(無) wú I [动](没有) not have ▶无效 wúxiào invalid ▶无形 wúxíng invisible II [副] not ▶无论如何 wúlùn rúhé in any case
无(無)耻(恥) wúchǐ [形] shameless
无(無)辜 wúgū I [动] be innocent II [名] the innocent
无(無)关(關) wúguān [动] have nothing to do with
无(無)赖(賴) wúlài [名] rascal
无(無)论(論) wúlùn [连] no matter what
无(無)情 wúqíng [形] 1(指感情) heartless 2(不留情) ruthless
无(無)数(數) wúshù I [形] countless II [动] be uncertain
无(無)所谓(謂) wúsuǒwèi [动] 1(谈不上) never mind 2(不在乎) be indifferent
无(無)限 wúxiàn [形] boundless
无(無)线(線)电(電) wúxiàndiàn [名] radio
无(無)线(線)网(網)络(絡) wúxiàn wǎngluò [名] Wi-Fi
无(無)须(須) wúxū [副] needlessly
无(無)知 wúzhī [形] ignorant

五 wǔ [名] five ▶五月 wǔyuè May ▶五分之一 wǔ fēn zhī yī one fifth
五官 wǔguān [名] the five sense organs

午 wǔ [名] noon
午饭(飯) wǔfàn [名] lunch
午夜 wǔyè [名] midnight

伍 wǔ [名](五) five
This is the character for "five", which is mainly used in banks, on receipts, cheques, etc. to prevent mistakes and forgery.

武 wǔ [形] 1(军事的) military 2(勇猛) valiant ▶威武 wēiwǔ powerful
武力 wǔlì [名] 1(军事力量) military strength 2(暴力) force
武器 wǔqì [名] weapon
武士 wǔshì [名] warrior
武术(術) wǔshù [名] martial arts circles (pl)

侮 wǔ [动](侮辱) insult ▶侮辱 wǔrǔ insult

舞 wǔ I [名] dance II [动](跳舞) dance
舞蹈 wǔdǎo [名] dance
舞台(臺) wǔtái [名] stage

勿 wù [副] not ▷请勿吸烟 qǐng wù xī yān no smoking

务(務) wù I [名] business ▶任务 rènwù task II [副] without fail
务(務)必 wùbì [副] without fail

物 wù [名] 1(东西) thing ▶物体 wùtǐ body 2(物产) produce ▶物产 wùchǎn produce 3(动物) creature 4(指哲学) matter

物价(價) wùjià [名] price
物理 wùlǐ [名] (指学科) physics (sg)
物业(業) wùyè [名] property
物质(質) wùzhì [名] 1 (哲) matter
2 (非精神) material things (pl)
物种(種) wùzhǒng [名] species (sg)

误(誤) wù I [名] mistake II [形]
erroneous III [副] accidentally ▶ 误伤
wùshāng accidentally injure IV [动]
(耽误) miss ▶ 快点儿，别误了火车！
Kuài diǎnr, bié wùle huǒchē! Hurry up
— we don't want to miss the train!

雾(霧) wù [名] fog

夕 xī [名] 1 (傍晚) sunset ▶ 夕照 xīzhào
evening glow 2 (晚上) evening ▶ 除夕
chúxī New Year's Eve

西 xī [名] 1 (方向) west ▶ 西北 xīběi
northwest ▶ 西南 xīnán southwest
2 (疆域) the West ▶ 西藏 Xīzàng Tibet
西班牙 Xībānyá [名] Spain ▷ 西班牙人
Xībānyárén Spaniard ▷ 西班牙语
Xībānyáyǔ the Spanish language
西餐 xīcān [名] Western food
西方 xīfāng [名] the West
西服 xīfú [名] suit
西瓜 xīguā [名] watermelon
西红(紅)柿 xīhóngshì [名] tomato
西药(藥) xīyào [名] Western medicine
西医(醫) xīyī [名] (药品) Western
medicine

吸 xī [动] 1 (气、水等) draw ... in ▶ 吸烟
xīyān smoke cigarettes 2 (吸收) absorb
3 (吸引) attract
吸尘(塵)器 xīchénqì [名] vacuum
cleaner
吸收 xīshōu [动] 1 (摄取) absorb
2 (接纳) recruit
吸引 xīyǐn [动] attract

希 xī [动] hope
希望 xīwàng I [动] hope II [名] hope

牺(犧) xī see below/见下文

牺(犧)牲 xīshēng [动] 1(献身) sacrifice oneself 2(放弃) sacrifice

稀 xī [形] 1(稀有) rare 2(稀疏) sparse 3(水多的) watery ▶稀饭 xīfàn rice porridge
稀少 xīshǎo [形] sparse
稀有 xīyǒu [形] rare

犀 xī [名] rhinoceros ▶犀牛 xīniú rhinoceros

溪 xī [名] brook

熄 xī [动] put ... out ▶熄灯 xīdēng put out the light
熄灭(滅) xīmiè [动] put ... out

膝 xī [名] knee ▶膝盖 xīgài knee

习(習) xí I [动] 1(学习) practise (英), practice (美) ▶习武 xí wǔ study martial arts 2(熟悉) be used to ▶习以为常 xí yǐ wéi cháng become used to II [名] (习惯) custom ▶陋习 lòuxí bad habit
习(習)惯(慣) xíguàn I [动] be used to II [名] habit
习(習)性 xíxìng [名] habits (pl)

席 xí [名] 1(编织物) mat ▶竹席 zhúxí bamboo mat 2(座位) seat ▶席位 xíwèi seat ▶出席 chūxí be present 3(宴席) feast ▶酒席 jiǔxí banquet

袭(襲) xí [动] 1(攻击) make a surprise attack ▶空袭 kōngxí air raid 2(仿做) follow the pattern of ▶抄袭 chāoxí plagiarize
袭(襲)击(擊) xíjī [动] attack

媳 xí [名] daughter-in-law
媳妇(婦) xífù [名] 1(儿子的妻子) daughter-in-law 2(晚辈的妻子) wife

洗 xǐ [动] 1(衣、碗等) wash ▶洗衣店 xǐyīdiàn Launderette ® (英), Laundromat ® (美) 2(胶卷) develop 3(录音、录像) wipe 4(麻将、扑克) shuffle
洗衣机(機) xǐyījī [名] washing machine
洗澡 xǐzǎo [动] have a bath

喜 xǐ I [形] 1(高兴) happy 2(可贺的) celebratory II [动] 1(爱好) like ▶喜好 xǐhào like 2(适宜) suit
喜爱(愛) xǐ'ài [动] like
喜欢(歡) xǐhuan [动] like
喜剧(劇) xǐjù [名] comedy

戏(戲) xì I [动] (嘲弄) joke ▶戏弄 xìnòng tease II [名] show ▶京戏 jīngxì Beijing Opera ▶马戏 mǎxì circus
戏(戲)法 xìfǎ [名] magic
戏(戲)剧(劇) xìjù [名] theatre (英), theater (美)
戏(戲)曲 xìqǔ [名] Chinese opera
戏(戲)院 xìyuàn [名] theatre (英), theater (美)

系(繫) xì I [名] 1(系统) system 2(部门) department II [动] (拴) tie
→ see also/另见 jì
系列 xìliè [名] series (sg)
系统(統) xìtǒng [名] system

细(細) xì I [形] 1(绳、线等) thin 2(颗粒小) fine 3(音量小语等) gentle 4(细微) detailed ▶细节 xìjié details (pl) II [副] minutely ▶细想 xìxiǎng consider carefully
细(細)胞 xìbāo [名] cell
细(細)菌 xìjūn [名] germ
细(細)心 xìxīn [形] careful
细(細)致(緻) xìzhì [副] meticulously

虾(蝦) xiā [名] shrimp ▶龙虾 lóngxiā lobster ▶对虾 duìxiā prawn

瞎 xiā [形] (失明) blind
瞎话(話) xiāhuà [名] lie

峡(峽) xiá [名] gorge ▶海峡 hǎixiá strait
峡(峽)谷 xiágǔ [名] canyon

狭(狹) xiá [形] narrow ▶狭窄 xiázhǎi narrow

下 xià I [动] 1(走下) go down ▷ 下山 xià shān go down the mountain ▷ 下楼 xià lóu go downstairs ▷ 下船 xià chuán disembark from a boat ▷ 下床 xià chuáng get out of bed **2**(落下) fall ▶下雨 xiàyǔ rain ▶下雪 xiàxuě snow **3**(传发) issue **4**(下锅煮) put … in **5**(给出) give **6**(开始) begin ▶下笔 xiàbǐ start to write **7**(结束) finish ▶下班 xiàbān finish work ▶下课 xiàkè finish class **8**(生下) ▶下蛋 xià dàn lay an egg **9**(用于动词后, 表示脱离物体) ▶拧下灯泡 nǐng xià dēngpào unscrew a light bulb **10**(用于动词后, 表示动作完成) ▶记录下会议内容 jìlù xià huìyì nèiróng take the minutes at a meeting **II**[名] **1**(低) ▶下层 xiàcéng lower level **2**(另) ▶下次 xiàcì next time ▶下个星期 xià gè xīngqī next week **3**(指方位或时间) ▶楼下 lóuxià downstairs ▶树下 shù xià under the tree **4**(指范围、情况、条件) ▶在朋友的帮助下 zài péngyou de bāngzhù xià with help from friends ▶在压力下 zài yālì xià under pressure **III**[量] time ▶拍了几下 pāile jǐ xià tapped a few times ▶拧了两下 nǐngle liǎng xià turned a couple of times

下岗(崗) xiàgǎng [动] **1**(完工) leave one's post **2**(失业) be laid off

下海 xiàhǎi [动] (指经商) go into business

下级(級) xiàjí [名] subordinate

下来(來) xiàlái [动] **1**(指由高到低) come down ▷我不上去了, 你下来吧。 Wǒ bù shàngqù le, nǐ xiàlái ba. I won't come up – you come down. **2**(指作物成熟) be harvested **3**(用于动词后, 指脱离物体) ▷他把眼镜摘了下来。 Tā bǎ yǎnjìng zhāile xiàlái. He took off his glasses. **4**(用于动词后, 表示动作完成) ▷暴乱平息下来了。 Bàoluàn píngxī xiàlái le. The riot has calmed down. **5**(表示出现某种状态) ▷灯光暗了下来。 Dēngguāng ànle xiàlái. The light started to fade.

下流 xiàliú [形] dirty

下面 xiàmiàn **I**[副] **1**(指位置) underneath **2**(指次序) next **II**[名] lower levels (pl)

下去 xiàqù [动] **1**(指由高到低) go down **2**(指时间的延续) continue **3**(用于动词后, 指空间上) ▷从楼上跳下去 cóng lóu shang tiào xiàqù jump from a building **4**(时间上的持续) ▷唱下去

chàng xiàqù keep singing **5**(指数量下降) ▷高烧已经退下去了。 Gāoshāo yǐjīng tuì xiàqù le. His temperature has already gone down. **6**(指程度深化) ▷天气有可能热下去。 Tiānqì yǒu kěnéng rè xiàqù. The weather will probably go on getting hotter.

下网(網) xiàwǎng (计算机) go offline

下午 xiàwǔ [名] afternoon

下载(載) xiàzǎi [动] download

吓(嚇) xià [动] frighten ▶吓人 xiàrén scary

吓(嚇)唬 xiàhu [动] frighten

夏 xià [名] summer

夏令营(營) xiàlìngyíng [名] summer camp

夏天 xiàtiān [名] summer

仙 xiān [名] immortal ▶仙人 xiānrén immortal

先 xiān [名] (指时间) earlier ▶事先 shìxiān beforehand

先后(後) xiānhòu [副] successively

先进(進) xiānjìn [形] advanced

先生 xiānsheng [名] **1**(指男士) Mr **2**(老师) teacher **3**(丈夫) husband

纤(纖) xiān [形] fine

纤(纖)维(維) xiānwéi [名] fibre

掀 xiān [动] lift

掀起 xiānqǐ [动] **1**(揭起) lift **2**(涌起) surge

鲜(鮮) xiān **I**[形] **1**(新鲜) fresh **2**(鲜美) delicious **II**[名] delicacy ▶海鲜 hǎixiān seafood

鲜(鮮)艳(豔) xiānyàn [形] brightly-coloured (英), brightly-colored (美)

闲(閒) xián **I**[形] **1**(不忙) idle **2**(安静) quiet **3**(闲置) unused ▶闲房 xiánfáng empty house **II**[名] leisure

闲(閒)话(話) xiánhuà [名] **1**(流言) gossip **2**(废话) digression

闲(閒)事 xiánshì [名] other people's business

弦 xián [名] 1 (指乐器) string 2 (指钟表) spring

咸 (鹹) xián [形] salted ▷ 咸菜 xiáncài pickled vegetables (pl)

嫌 xián [动] dislike ▷ 他嫌这儿吵，搬走了。Tā xián zhèr chǎo, bānzǒu le. He found it too noisy here and moved away.
嫌弃 (棄) xiánqì [动] cold-shoulder
嫌疑 xiányí [名] suspicion

显 (顯) xiǎn [动] 1 (表现) display 2 (呈现) be apparent
显 (顯) 然 xiǎnrán [形] obvious
显 (顯) 示 xiǎnshì [动] demonstrate
显 (顯) 眼 xiǎnyǎn [形] conspicuous
显 (顯) 著 xiǎnzhù [形] striking

险 (險) xiǎn [形] 1 (险要) strategic 2 (危险) dangerous

县 (縣) xiàn [名] county

现 (現) xiàn [形] 1 (现在) present ▷ 现状 xiànzhuàng present situation 2 (现有) ready ▷ 现金 xiànjīn cash
现 (現) 场 (場) xiànchǎng [名] scene ▷ 现场报道 xiànchǎng bàodào live report
现 (現) 成 xiànchéng [形] ready-made
现 (現) 代 xiàndài [名] modern times (pl)
现 (現) 代化 xiàndàihuà [名] modernization
现 (現) 实 (實) xiànshí [名] reality
现 (現) 象 xiànxiàng [名] phenomenon
现 (現) 在 xiànzài [名] now
现 (現) 状 (狀) xiànzhuàng [名] the current situation

限 xiàn I [动] limit II [名] limit
限期 xiànqī I [动] set a deadline II [名] deadline
限制 xiànzhì [动] restrict

线 (線) xiàn [名] 1 (指细长状物) thread ▷ 电线 diànxiàn electric wire 2 (交通干线) line
线 (線) 索 xiànsuǒ [名] clue

宪 (憲) xiàn [名] constitution
宪 (憲) 法 xiànfǎ [名] constitution

陷 xiàn I [名] 1 (书) (陷阱) trap 2 (过失) fault ▶ 缺陷 quēxiàn defect II [动] 1 (沉入) get bogged down 2 (凹进) sink 3 (卷入) get involved
陷害 xiànhài [动] frame
陷阱 xiànjǐng [名] trap

馅 (餡) xiàn [名] stuffing ▷ 饺子馅 jiǎozi xiàn jiaozi filling

羡 (羨) xiàn [动] admire
羡 (羨) 慕 xiànmù [动] envy

献 (獻) xiàn [动] 1 (给) give ▶ 献血 xiànxiě donate blood 2 (表演) show

腺 xiàn [名] gland

乡 (鄉) xiāng [名] 1 (乡村) countryside 2 (家乡) home town
乡 (鄉) 村 xiāngcūn [名] village
乡 (鄉) 下 xiāngxia [名] countryside

相 xiāng [副] (互相) mutually ▶ 相差 xiāngchà differ
→ see also / 另见 xiàng
相处 (處) xiāngchǔ [动] get along
相当 (當) xiāngdāng I [动] match II [形] appropriate III [副] quite
相对 (對) xiāngduì I [动] be opposite II [形] 1 (非绝对的) relative 2 (比较的) comparative
相反 xiāngfǎn I [形] opposite II [连] on the contrary
相关 (關) xiāngguān [动] be related
相互 xiānghù I [形] mutual II [副] ▷ 相互理解 xiānghù lǐjiě understand each other
相识 (識) xiāngshí [动] be acquainted
相似 xiāngsì [形] similar
相同 xiāngtóng [形] identical
相像 xiāngxiàng [动] be alike
相信 xiāngxìn [动] believe

香 xiāng I [形] 1 (芬芳) fragrant 2 (美味) delicious 3 (睡得熟的) sound II [名] 1 (香料) spice 2 (烧的香) incense

香波 xiāngbō [名] shampoo

香肠(腸) xiāngcháng [名] sausage

香港 Xiānggǎng [名] Hong Kong

香蕉 xiāngjiāo [名] banana

香料 xiāngliào [名] spice

香水 xiāngshuǐ [名] perfume

香烟(煙) xiāngyān [名](卷烟) cigarette

香皂 xiāngzào [名] soap

箱 xiāng [名] 1(箱子) box 2(箱状物) ▷ 信箱 xìnxiāng postbox(英), mailbox(美)

箱子 xiāngzi [名] box

详(詳) xiáng [形] detailed

详(詳)情 xiángqíng [名] details (pl)

详(詳)细(細) xiángxì [形] detailed

享 xiǎng [动] enjoy

享受 xiǎngshòu [动] enjoy

响(響) xiǎng I [名] 1(回声) echo 2(声音) sound II [动] sound ▷ 手机响了。Shǒujī xiǎng le. The mobile (英) 或 cell (美) phone was ringing. III [形] loud

响(響)亮 xiǎngliàng [形] loud and clear

响(響)应(應) xiǎngyìng [动] respond

想 xiǎng [动] 1(思考) think ▷ 想办法 xiǎng bànfǎ think of a way 2(推测) reckon 3(打算) want to 4(想念) miss

In a positive sentence, both 想 xiǎng and 要 yào can be used to express "want to". To express "I don't want to", it is more common to use 不想 bù xiǎng, as the expression 不要 bù yào is stronger and indicates a definite decision, meaning "I shall not (under any circumstances)".

想法 xiǎngfǎ [名] opinion

想念 xiǎngniàn [动] miss

想象(像) xiǎngxiàng I [动] imagine II [名] imagination

向 xiàng I [名] direction II [动] 1(对着) face 2(偏袒) side with III [介] to ▷ 我向他表示了感谢。Wǒ xiàng tā biǎoshìle gǎnxiè. I expressed my thanks to him.

向(嚮)导(導) xiàngdǎo [名] guide

向来(來) xiànglái [副] always

项(項) xiàng I [名](项目) item ▷ 事项 shìxiàng item II [量] item ▷ 3项要求 sān xiàng yāoqiú three requirements ▷ 2项任务 liǎng xiàng rènwu two tasks

项(項)链(鏈) xiàngliàn [名] necklace

项(項)目 xiàngmù [名] 1(事项) item 2(指工程计划) project

巷 xiàng [名] lane

相 xiàng [名] 1(相貌) appearance 2(姿势) posture 3(官位) minister ▷ 外相 wàixiàng foreign minister 4(相片) photograph ▷ 照相 zhàoxiàng take a photograph

→ see also/另见 xiāng

相貌 xiàngmào [名] appearance

相片 xiàngpiàn [名] photograph

象 xiàng [名] 1(大象) elephant 2(样子) appearance

象棋 xiàngqí [名] Chinese chess

象棋 xiàngqí is a very popular board game in China. It is a game of skill, played by two players on a board which imitates a battle field with a river in between two opposing sides. There are some similarities between the Chinese chess and international chess.

象牙 xiàngyá [名] ivory

象征(徵) xiàngzhēng [动] symbolize

像 xiàng I [名] portrait ▷ 画像 huàxiàng paint portraits ▷ 雕像 diāoxiàng statue II [动] 1(相似) look like 2(比如) ▷ 像他这样的好孩子，谁不喜欢呢！Xiàng tā zhèyàng de hǎo háizi, shuí bù xǐhuan ne! Who doesn't like good children like this one! III [副] as if ▷ 像要下雪了。Xiàng yào xià xuě le. It looks as if it might snow.

橡 xiàng [名] 1(橡树) oak 2(橡胶树) rubber tree

橡胶(膠) xiàngjiāo [名] rubber

橡皮 xiàngpí [名] rubber (英), eraser (美)

削 xiāo [动] peel

消 xiāo [动] **1**(消失) disappear **2**(使消失) remove
消除 xiāochú [动] eliminate
消防 xiāofáng [名] fire fighting
消费(費) xiāofèi [动] consume
消耗 xiāohào [动] consume
消化 xiāohuà [动] digest
消极(極) xiāojí [形] **1**(反面) negative **2**(消沉) demoralized
消灭(滅) xiāomiè [动] **1**(消失) die out **2**(除掉) eradicate
消失 xiāoshī [动] vanish
消息 xiāoxi [名] news (sg)

宵 xiāo [名] night ▶ 通宵 tōngxiāo all night

销(銷) xiāo [动] **1**(熔化) melt **2**(除去) cancel **3**(销售) market **4**(消费) spend
销(銷)路 xiāolù [名] market
销(銷)售 xiāoshòu [动] sell

小 xiǎo [形] (不大) small ▶ 年龄小 niánlíng xiǎo young
小便 xiǎobiàn I [动] urinate II [名] urine
小吃 xiǎochī [名] **1**(非正餐) snack **2**(冷盘) cold dish
小丑 xiǎochǒu [名] (滑稽演员) clown
小儿(兒)科 xiǎo'érkē [名] (医) paediatrics (英) 或 pediatrics (美) department
小费(費) xiǎofèi [名] tip
小伙(夥)子 xiǎohuǒzi [名] lad
小姐 xiǎojiě [名] **1**(称呼) Miss **2**(女子) young lady
小看 xiǎokàn [动] underestimate
小麦(麥) xiǎomài [名] wheat
小名 xiǎomíng [名] pet name
小气(氣) xiǎoqi [形] **1**(气量小) petty **2**(吝啬) stingy
小区(區) xiǎoqū [名] housing estate
小时(時) xiǎoshí [名] hour
小说(說) xiǎoshuō [名] novel
小提琴 xiǎotíqín [名] violin
小偷 xiǎotōu [名] thief

小心 xiǎoxīn I [动] be careful II [形] careful
小学(學) xiǎoxué [名] primary school (英), elementary school (美)
小学(學)生 xiǎoxuéshēng [名] primary school pupil (英), elementary school student (美)
小组(組) xiǎozǔ [名] group

晓(曉) xiǎo I [名] dawn II [动] **1**(知道) know **2**(使人知道) tell
晓(曉)得 xiǎode [动] know

孝 xiào I [动] be dutiful ▶ 孝子 xiàozǐ a filial son II [名] filial piety
孝顺(順) xiàoshùn I [动] show filial obedience II [形] filial

校 xiào [名] (学校) school
校长(長) xiàozhǎng [名] principal

哮 xiào I [名] wheezing II [动] wheeze
哮喘 xiàochuǎn [名] asthma

笑 xiào [动] **1**(欢笑) laugh **2**(嘲笑) laugh at
笑话(話) xiàohua I [名] joke II [动] laugh at

效 xiào I [名] effect II [动] **1**(仿效) imitate **2**(献出) devote ... to
效果 xiàoguǒ [名] **1**(结果) effect **2**(戏剧) effects (pl)
效率 xiàolǜ [名] efficiency
效益 xiàoyì [名] returns (pl)

些 xiē [量] **1**(不定量) some **2**(略微) a little

歇 xiē [动] (休息) rest
歇息 xiēxi [动] **1**(休息) have a rest **2**(睡觉) go to sleep

蝎(蠍) xiē [名] scorpion ▶ 蝎子 xiēzi scorpion

协(協) xié I [动] assist II [副] jointly ▶ 协议 xiéyì agree on
协(協)会(會) xiéhuì [名] association
协(協)调(調) xiétiáo I [动] coordinate II [形] coordinated
协(協)议(議) xiéyì [名] agreement

协(協)助 xiézhù [动] help

协(協)作 xiézuò [动] collaborate

邪 xié [形] (不正当) evil

邪恶(惡) xié'è [形] evil

斜 xié I [形] slanting II [动] slant

斜坡 xiépō [名] slope

携(攜) xié [动] 1 (携带) carry 2 (拉着) hold

携(攜)带(帶) xiédài [动] carry

鞋 xié [名] shoe

鞋匠 xiéjiàng [名] cobbler

写(寫) xiě [动] 1 (书写) write 2 (写作) write 3 (描写) describe 4 (绘画) draw

写(寫)作 xiězuò [动] write

血 xiě [名] (口) blood
→ see also/另见 xuè

泄(洩) xiè [动] (泄露) let ... out

泄(洩)露 xièlòu [动] let ... out

卸 xiè [动] 1 (搬下) unload ▷ 卸车 xièchē unload a vehicle 2 (除去) remove ▷ 卸妆 xièzhuāng remove one's makeup 3 (拆卸) strip 4 (解除) be relieved of ▷ 卸任 xièrèn step down

谢(謝) xiè [动] 1 (感谢) thank ▷ 多谢！ Duō xiè! Thanks a lot! 2 (认错) apologize 3 (拒绝) decline ▷ 谢绝 xièjué decline 4 (脱落) wither

谢(謝)谢(謝) xièxie [动] thank you, thanks (口)

蟹 xiè [名] crab ▷ 螃蟹 pángxiè crab

心 xīn [名] 1 (心脏) heart 2 (思想) mind ▷ 用心 yòngxīn attentively ▷ 谈心 tánxīn heart-to-heart talk 3 (中心) centre (英), center (美)

心得 xīndé [名] what one has learned

心理 xīnlǐ [名] psychology

心灵(靈) xīnlíng [名] mind

心情 xīnqíng [名] frame of mind

心愿(願) xīnyuàn [名] one's heart's desire

心脏(臟) xīnzàng [名] heart

心脏(臟)病 xīnzàngbìng [名] heart disease

辛 xīn [形] 1 (辣) hot 2 (辛苦) laborious 3 (痛苦) bitter

辛苦 xīnkǔ I [形] laborious II [动] trouble ▷ 辛苦你了！ Xīnkǔ nǐ le! Thanks for taking the trouble!

辛勤 xīnqín [形] hardworking

欣 xīn [形] glad

欣赏(賞) xīnshǎng [动] 1 (赏识) admire 2 (享受) enjoy

新 xīn I [形] (跟旧相对) new II [副] newly

新潮 xīncháo I [形] fashionable II [名] new trend

新陈(陳)代谢(謝) xīn chén dàixiè [名] metabolism

新加坡 Xīnjiāpō [名] Singapore

新郎 xīnláng [名] bridegroom

新年 xīnnián [名] 1 (指一段时间) New Year 2 (指元旦当天) New Year's Day

新娘 xīnniáng [名] bride

新闻(聞) xīnwén [名] news (sg)

新鲜(鮮) xīnxiān [形] 1 (指食物) fresh 2 (指植物) tender 3 (清新) fresh 4 (新奇) novel

新颖(穎) xīnyǐng [形] original

薪 xīn [名] (薪水) salary

薪水 xīnshui [名] salary

信 xìn I [动] 1 (相信) believe ▷ 轻信 qīngxìn readily believe 2 (信奉) believe in ▷ 信教 xìnjiào be religious II [名] 1 (书信) letter ▷ 信箱 xìnxiāng letterbox (英), mailbox (美) 2 (信息) information ▷ 口信 kǒuxìn verbal message 3 (信用) trust ▷ 失信 shīxìn lose trust

信贷(貸) xìndài [名] credit

信封 xìnfēng [名] envelope

信号(號) xìnhào [名] signal

信件 xìnjiàn [名] letter

信赖(賴) xìnlài [动] trust

信任 xìnrèn [动] trust

信息 xìnxī [名] information

信心 xìnxīn [名] faith

信仰 xìnyǎng [动] believe in ▷ 他没有宗教信仰。Tā méiyǒu zōngjiào xìnyǎng. He has no religious faith.

信用 xìnyòng [名] 1(指信任) word 2(指借贷) credit

信用卡 xìnyòngkǎ [名] credit card

信誉(譽) xìnyù [名] reputation

兴(興) xīng [动] 1(旺盛) prosper 2(流行) be popular 3(使盛行) promote
→ see also/另见 xìng

兴(興)奋(奮) xīngfèn [动] be excited

兴(興)盛 xīngshèng [形] prosperous

兴(興)旺 xīngwàng [形] prosperous

星 xīng [名] 1(指天体) star ▶ 星星 xīngxing star 2(指名人) star ▶ 球星 qiúxīng football star

星期 xīngqī [名] 1(周) week 2(指某天) ▶ 星期天 xīngqītiān Sunday ▶ 星期三 xīngqīsān Wednesday ▷ 明天星期几? Míngtiān xīngqī jǐ? What day is it tomorrow?

猩 xīng [名] orang-utan ▶ 黑猩猩 hēixīngxing chimpanzee

腥 xīng [形] fishy

刑 xíng [名] (刑罚) punishment ▶ 死刑 sǐxíng the death penalty

行 xíng I [动] 1(走) walk ▶ 步行 bùxíng go on foot 2(流通) be current ▶ 发行 fāxíng issue 3(做) do ▶ 行医 xíngyī practise (英) 或 practice (美) medicine II [形] 1(可以) OK 2(能干) capable III [名] 1(旅行) travel 2(行为) conduct ▶ 暴行 bàoxíng act of cruelty
→ see also/另见 háng

行动(動) xíngdòng [动] 1(行走) move about 2(活动) take action

行李 xíngli [名] luggage

行人 xíngrén [名] pedestrian

行驶(駛) xíngshǐ [动] travel

行为(為) xíngwéi [名] behaviour (英), behavior (美)

行走 xíngzǒu [动] walk

形 xíng [名] 1(形状) shape 2(形体) body

形成 xíngchéng [动] form

形容 xíngróng [动] describe

形式 xíngshì [名] form

形象 xíngxiàng [名] image

形状(狀) xíngzhuàng [名] shape

型 xíng [名] type ▶ 体型 tǐxíng build ▶ 血型 xuèxíng blood group

型号(號) xínghào [名] model

醒 xǐng [动] 1(神志恢复) come to 2(睡醒) wake up 3(醒悟) become aware ▶ 提醒 tíxǐng remind

兴(興) xìng [名] excitement
→ see also/另见 xīng

兴(興)趣 xìngqù [名] interest ▷ 他对集邮有浓厚的兴趣。Tā duì jíyóu yǒu nónghòu de xìngqù. He has a deep interest in stamp-collecting.

杏 xìng [名] apricot

幸 xìng I [形] lucky II [副] fortunately

幸福 xìngfú I [名] happiness II [形] happy

幸亏(虧) xìngkuī [副] fortunately

幸运(運) xìngyùn I [名] good luck II [形] lucky

性 xìng [名] 1(性格) character ▶ 任性 rènxìng stubborn 2(性能) function ▶ 酸性 suānxìng acidity 3(性别) gender ▶ 男性 nánxìng male 4(情欲) sex 5(性质) ▶ 可靠性 kěkàoxìng reliability ▶ 实用性 shíyòngxìng utility 6(语法) gender ▶ 阳性 yángxìng masculine

性别(別) xìngbié [名] sex

性感 xìnggǎn [形] sexy

性格 xìnggé [名] personality

性质(質) xìngzhì [名] character

姓 xìng I [动] ▷ 我姓李。Wǒ xìng Lǐ. My surname is Li. II [名] surname

姓名 xìngmíng [名] full name

凶 xiōng [形] 1(不幸的) unlucky 2(凶恶) ferocious ▶ 凶相 xiōngxiàng fierce look 3(厉害) terrible

凶狠 xiōnghěn [形] vicious

凶手 xiōngshǒu [名] murderer

兄 xiōng [名] brother
兄弟 xiōngdì [名] brother

胸 xiōng [名] 1 (胸部) chest 2 (心胸) heart
胸脯 xiōngpú [名] chest

雄 xióng [形] 1 (公的) male ▶ 雄性 xióngxìng male 2 (有气魄的) imposing 3 (强有力的) strong

熊 xióng [名] bear
熊猫(貓) xióngmāo [名] panda

休 xiū [动] 1 (停止) stop 2 (休息) rest
休息 xiūxi [动] rest
休闲(閒) xiūxián [动] (悠闲) be at leisure ▷ 休闲服装 xiūxián fúzhuāng casual clothes

修 xiū [动] 1 (修理) mend 2 (兴建) build 3 (剪) trim
修改 xiūgǎi [动] alter
修建 xiūjiàn [动] build
修理 xiūlǐ [动] repair
修饰(飾) xiūshì [动] 1 (修整装饰) decorate 2 (修改润饰) polish
修养(養) xiūyǎng [名] 1 (水平) accomplishments (pl) 2 (指态度) gentility

羞 xiū [形] shy ▶ 害羞 hàixiū be shy

秀 xiù I [形] 1 (清秀) elegant 2 (优异) outstanding II [名] talent ▶ 新秀 xīnxiù new talent
秀气(氣) xiùqi [形] 1 (清秀) delicate 2 (文雅) refined

袖 xiù [名] sleeve ▶ 袖子 xiùzi sleeve
袖珍 xiùzhēn [形] pocket-sized ▷ 袖珍收音机 xiùzhēn shōuyīnjī pocket radio

绣(繡) xiù I [动] embroider II [名] embroidery

锈(鏽) xiù [名] rust ▶ 生锈 shēngxiù go rusty

须(須) xū I [副] ▶ 必须 bìxū must II [名] beard

须(須)要 xūyào [动] need
须(須)知 xūzhī [名] essentials (pl)

虚(虛) xū [形] 1 (空着) empty 2 (胆怯) timid 3 (虚假) false 4 (虚心) modest 5 (弱) weak
虚(虛)构(構) xūgòu [动] fabricate
虚(虛)假 xūjiǎ [形] false
虚(虛)荣(榮) xūróng [名] vanity
虚(虛)弱 xūruò [形] frail
虚(虛)伪(偽) xūwěi [形] hypocritical
虚(虛)心 xūxīn [形] open-minded

需 xū I [动] need II [名] needs (pl) ▶ 军需 jūnxū military requirements (pl)
需求 xūqiú [名] demand
需要 xūyào I [动] need II [名] needs (pl) ▷ 日常生活需要 rìcháng shēnghuó xūyào necessities of life

许(許) xǔ [动] 1 (称赞) praise 2 (答应) promise 3 (允许) allow
许(許)多 xǔduō [形] many ▷ 他养了许多金鱼。Tā yǎngle xǔduō jīnyú. He keeps a lot of goldfish.

叙(敘) xù [动] 1 (谈) chat 2 (记述) recount
叙(敘)事 xùshì [动] narrate
叙(敘)述 xùshù [动] recount

畜 xù [动] raise
→ see also/另见 chù
畜牧 xùmù [动] rear ▷ 畜牧业 xùmùyè animal husbandry

酗 xù see below/见下文
酗酒 xùjiǔ [动] get drunk

婿 xù [名] (女婿) son-in-law ▶ 女婿 nǚxù son-in-law

宣 xuān [动] 1 (宣布) announce 2 (疏导) lead ... off ▶ 宣泄 xuānxiè get ... off one's chest
宣布 xuānbù [动] announce
宣称(稱) xuānchēng [动] announce
宣传(傳) xuānchuán [动] disseminate ▷ 宣传工具 xuānchuán gōngjù means of dissemination

宣告 xuāngào [动] proclaim
宣誓 xuānshì [动] take an oath
宣言 xuānyán [名] declaration
宣扬(揚) xuānyáng [动] advocate
宣战(戰) xuānzhàn [动] declare war

喧 xuān [动] make a noise
喧哗(譁) xuānhuá I [形] riotous
II [动] create a disturbance
喧闹(鬧) xuānnào [形] rowdy

悬(懸) xuán [动] 1 (挂) hang 2 (设想)
imagine 3 (挂念) be concerned about
4 (未定) be unresolved
悬(懸)挂(掛) xuánguà [动] hang
悬(懸)念 xuánniàn [名] suspense
悬(懸)崖 xuányá [名] precipice

旋 xuán I [动] 1 (旋转) revolve 2 (返回)
return II [名] spiral
→ see also/另见 xuàn
旋律 xuánlǜ [名] melody
旋钮(鈕) xuánniǔ [名] knob
旋涡(渦) xuánwō [名] whirlpool
旋转(轉) xuánzhuǎn [动] revolve

选(選) xuǎn I [动] 1 (挑选) choose
2 (选举) vote II [名] 1 (指人) selection
▶ 人选 rénxuǎn selection of people
2 (作品集) collection ▶ 文选 wénxuǎn
collected works (pl)
选(選)拔 xuǎnbá [动] select
选(選)举(舉) xuǎnjǔ [动] elect
选(選)民 xuǎnmín [名] electorate
选(選)手 xuǎnshǒu [名] contestant
选(選)修 xuǎnxiū [动] choose to study
▷ 选修课程 xuǎnxiū kèchéng
optional course
选(選)择(擇) xuǎnzé [动] choose
▷ 别无选择 bié wú xuǎnzé have no
choice

旋 xuàn [动] spin
→ see also/另见 xuán
旋风(風) xuànfēng [名] whirlwind

靴 xuē [名] boot
靴子 xuēzi [名] boot

穴 xué [名] 1 (洞) den 2 (穴位)
acupuncture point
穴位 xuéwèi [名] acupuncture point

学(學) xué I [动] 1 (学习) study ▷ 学英
语 xué Yīngyǔ learn English 2 (模仿)
imitate II [名] 1 (学问) learning ▶ 博学
bóxué erudition 2 (学科) science ▶ 生物
学 shēngwùxué biology ▶ 化学 huàxué
chemistry 3 (学校) school ▶ 大学 dàxué
university ▶ 中学 zhōngxué senior
school (英), high school (美) ▶ 小学
xiǎoxué primary school (英), elementary
school (美)
学(學)费(費) xuéfèi [名] tuition fee
学(學)科 xuékē [名] subject
学(學)历(歷) xuélì [名] educational
background
学(學)生 xuésheng [名] student
学(學)士 xuéshì [名] (指学位)
bachelor's degree
学(學)术(術) xuéshù [名] learning
学(學)说(說) xuéshuō [名] theory
学(學)位 xuéwèi [名] degree
学(學)问(問) xuéwen [名] learning
学(學)院 xuéyuàn [名] college
学(學)习(習) xuéxí [动] study
学(學)校 xuéxiào [名] school
学(學)业(業) xuéyè [名] studies (pl)
学(學)者 xuézhě [名] scholar

雪 xuě [名] snow ▶ 下雪 xiàxuě to snow
雪花 xuěhuā [名] snowflake

血 xuè [名] (血液) blood
→ see also/另见 xiě
血统(統) xuètǒng [名] blood relation
血型 xuèxíng [名] blood type
血压(壓) xuèyā [名] blood pressure
血液 xuèyè [名] 1 (血) blood 2 (主要力
量) lifeblood
血缘(緣) xuèyuán [名] blood relation

熏(薰) xūn [动] 1 (烟气接触物体)
blacken 2 (熏制) smoke ▶ 熏肉 xūnròu
smoked meat

寻(尋) xún [动] search
寻(尋)常 xúncháng [形] usual

寻(尋)求 xúnqiú [动] seek
寻(尋)找 xúnzhǎo [动] look for

巡 xún [动] patrol
巡逻(邏) xúnluó [动] patrol

询(詢) xún [动] inquire
询(詢)问(問) xúnwèn [动] ask

循 xún [动] abide by
循环(環) xúnhuán [动] circulate

训(訓) xùn I [动] 1 (教导) teach 2 (训练) train II [名] rule
训(訓)练(練) xùnliàn [动] train

迅 xùn [形] swift
迅速 xùnsù [形] swift

驯(馴) xùn I [形] tame II [动] tame
驯(馴)服 xùnfú I [形] tame II [动] tame

压(壓) yā I [动] 1 (施力) press 2 (超越) outdo 3 (使稳定) control 4 (压制) suppress 5 (积压) put ... off II [名] pressure
压(壓)力 yālì [名] 1 (物) pressure 2 (指对人) pressure 3 (负担) burden
压(壓)迫 yāpò [动] 1 (压制) oppress 2 (挤压) put pressure on
压(壓)岁(歲)钱(錢) yāsuìqián [名] traditional gifts of money given to children during the Spring Festival
压(壓)抑 yāyì [动] suppress

呀 yā [叹] (表示惊异) oh ▷ 呀！已经12点了！ Yā! Yǐjīng shí'èr diǎn le! Oh! It's 12 o'clock already!

押 yā [动] (抵押) leave ... as a security
押金 yājīn [名] deposit

鸦(鴉) yā [名] crow
鸦(鴉)片 yāpiàn [名] opium

鸭(鴨) yā [名] duck

牙 yá [名] (牙齿) tooth
牙齿(齒) yáchǐ [名] tooth
牙床 yáchuáng [名] gum
牙膏 yágāo [名] toothpaste
牙签(籤) yáqiān [名] toothpick
牙刷 yáshuā [名] toothbrush
牙痛 yátòng [名] toothache

牙医(醫) yáyī [名] dentist

芽 yá [名] (指植物) sprout

崖 yá [名] cliff

哑(啞) yǎ [形] 1(不能说话) mute 2(不说话) speechless 3(嘶哑) hoarse
哑(啞)巴 yǎba [名] person with speech difficulties
哑(啞)铃(鈴) yǎlíng [名] dumbbell
哑(啞)语(語) yǎyǔ [名] sign language

轧(軋) yà [动] (碾) roll

亚(亞) yà I [形] inferior ▶ 亚军 yàjūn runner-up II [名] Asia
亚(亞)洲 Yàzhōu [名] Asia ▷ 她是亚洲人。Tā shì Yàzhōurén. She's Asian.

咽 yān [名] pharynx
→ see also/另见 yàn
咽喉 yānhóu [名] (字) throat

烟(煙) yān [名] 1(指气体) smoke 2(烟草) tobacco ▶ 香烟 xiāngyān cigarette
烟(煙)草 yāncǎo [名] 1(指植物) tobacco plant 2(烟草制品) tobacco
烟(煙)花 yānhuā [名] firework
烟(煙)灰缸 yānhuīgāng [名] ashtray
烟(煙)民 yānmín [名] smokers (pl)

淹 yān [动] (淹没) flood
淹没(沒) yānmò [动] 1(漫过) submerge 2(喻) drown ... out

延 yán [动] 1(延长) extend 2(推迟) delay
延长(長) yáncháng [动] extend
延迟(遲) yánchí [动] delay

严(嚴) yán [形] 1(严密) tight 2(严格) strict
严(嚴)格 yángé [形] strict
严(嚴)谨(謹) yánjǐn [形] (严密谨慎) meticulous
严(嚴)厉(厲) yánlì [形] severe
严(嚴)肃(肅) yánsù [形] 1(庄重) solemn 2(严格认真) severe
严(嚴)重 yánzhòng [形] serious

言 yán I [动] speak II [名] 1(话) speech 2(字) words (pl)
言论(論) yánlùn [名] speech ▷ 言论自由 yánlùn zìyóu freedom of speech
言情片 yánqíngpiàn [名] romantic film (英) 或 movie (美)
言语(語) yányǔ [名] language

岩(巖) yán [名] rock

炎 yán I [形] scorching II [名] (炎症) inflammation
炎黄子孙(孫) Yán-Huáng zǐsūn [名] Chinese people
炎热(熱) yánrè [形] scorching hot
炎症 yánzhèng [名] inflammation

沿 yán I [介] along II [动] (依照) follow III [名] edge
沿岸 yán'àn [名] bank
沿海 yánhǎi [名] coast

研 yán [动] (研究) research ▶ 研究院 yánjiūyuàn research institute ▶ 研究生 yánjiūshēng postgraduate student
研究 yánjiū [动] 1(探求) research 2(商讨) discuss

盐(鹽) yán [名] salt

颜(顔) yán [名] 1(脸) face 2(颜色) colour (英), color (美)
颜(顔)料 yánliào [名] colouring (英), coloring (美)
颜(顔)色 yánsè [名] (色彩) colour (英), color (美)

眼 yǎn [名] 1(眼睛) eye 2(小洞) small hole
眼光 yǎnguāng [名] 1(视线) gaze 2(观察能力) vision 3(观点) perspective
眼红(紅) yǎnhóng [动] be jealous
眼界 yǎnjiè [名] horizons (pl)
眼睛 yǎnjing [名] eye
眼镜(鏡) yǎnjìng [名] glasses (pl)
眼泪(淚) yǎnlèi [名] tear
眼力 yǎnlì [名] 1(视力) eyesight 2(鉴别能力) judgement
眼神 yǎnshén [名] 1(指神态) expression 2(方)(视力) eyesight

演 yǎn [动] (表演) perform
演出 yǎnchū [动] perform
演讲(講) yǎnjiǎng [动] make a speech
演示 yǎnshì [动] demonstrate
演说(說) yǎnshuō [动] make a speech
演员(員) yǎnyuán [名] performer
演奏 yǎnzòu [动] perform

厌(厭) yàn [动] (厌恶) detest
厌(厭)烦(煩) yànfán [动] be sick of
厌(厭)恶(惡) yànwù [动] loathe

砚(硯) yàn [名] ink stone

咽(嚥) yàn [动] swallow
→ see also/另见 yān

宴 yàn [动] host a dinner ▶ 宴请 yànqǐng invite ... to dinner
宴会(會) yànhuì [名] banquet

验(驗) yàn [动] (检查) test
验(驗)光 yànguāng [动] have an eye test
验(驗)血 yànxiě [动] have a blood test

谚(諺) yàn [名] saying ▶ 谚语 yànyǔ proverb

雁 yàn [名] wild goose

焰 yàn [名] flame

燕 yàn [名] swallow
燕麦(麥) yànmài [名] oats (pl)
燕尾服 yànwěifú [名] tailcoat

羊 yáng [名] sheep ▶ 山羊 shānyáng goat
羊毛 yángmáo [名] wool
羊绒(絨)衫 yángróngshān [名] cashmere
羊肉 yángròu [名] mutton

阳(陽) yáng [名] 1 (阴的对立面) Yang (from Yin and Yang) 2 (太阳) sun ▶ 阳光 yángguāng sunlight
阳(陽)台(臺) yángtái [名] balcony
阳(陽)性 yángxìng [名] 1 (医) positive 2 (语言) masculine

洋 yáng I [名] (海洋) ocean II [形] (外国的) foreign
洋白菜 yángbáicài [名] cabbage
洋葱(蔥) yángcōng [名] onion

仰 yǎng [动] (脸向上) look up
仰望 yǎngwàng [动] look up

养(養) yǎng I [动] 1 (供给) provide for 2 (饲养) keep ▷ 我爱养花。Wǒ ài yǎng huā. I like growing flowers. 3 (生育) give birth to 4 (培养) form ▷ 养成习惯 yǎngchéng xíguàn form a habit II [形] foster ▶ 养母 yǎngmǔ foster mother ▶ 养子 yǎngzǐ adopted son
养(養)活 yǎnghuo [动] (口) 1 (提供生活费用) support 2 (饲养) raise 3 (生育) give birth to
养(養)料 yǎngliào [名] nourishment
养(養)育 yǎngyù [动] bring up
养(養)殖 yǎngzhí [动] breed

氧 yǎng [名] oxygen ▶ 氧气 yǎngqì oxygen

痒(癢) yǎng [动] itch

样(樣) yàng I [名] 1 (模样) style 2 (标准物) sample II [量] type ▷ 3样水果 sān yàng shuǐguǒ three types of fruit
样(樣)品 yàngpǐn [名] sample
样(樣)式 yàngshì [名] style
样(樣)子 yàngzi [名] 1 (模样) appearance 2 (神情) expression

妖 yāo [名] evil spirit
妖精 yāojing [名] (妖怪) demon

要 yāo [动] 1 (求) ask 2 (邀请) invite
→ see also/另见 yào

Both 要 yào and 会 huì can be used to express the future tense. 要 yào refers to something definite, e.g. 我明天要上班 wǒ míngtiān yào shàngbān (I am going to work tomorrow); 会 huì is usually used to express a possible, or probable outcome, e.g. 明天会下雨 míngtiān huì xiàyǔ (It might rain tomorrow).

要求 yāoqiú I [动] demand II [名] request

腰 yāo [名] **1**(身体中部) waist **2**(裤腰) waist

腰包 yāobāo [名] wallet

腰带(帶) yāodài [名] belt

腰果 yāoguǒ [名] cashew nut

腰围(圍) yāowéi [名] waistline

腰子 yāozi [名] (口) kidney

邀 yāo [动] (邀请) invite

邀请(請) yāoqǐng [动] invite

谣(謠) yáo [名] **1**(歌谣) folk song ▷ 歌谣 gēyáo folk song **2**(谣言) rumour (英), rumor (美) ▷ 谣言 yáoyán hearsay

谣(謠)传(傳) yáochuán I [动] be rumoured (英) 或 rumored (美) II [名] rumour (英), rumor (美)

摇(搖) yáo [动] shake

摇(搖)动(動) yáodòng [动] **1**(摇东西) wave **2**(晃) shake

摇(搖)滚(滾)乐(樂) yáogǔnyuè [名] rock and roll

摇(搖)晃 yáohuàng [动] shake

摇(搖)篮(籃) yáolán [名] cradle

遥(遙) yáo [形] distant ▷ 遥控器 yáokòngqì remote control

遥(遙)控 yáokòng [动] operate by remote control

遥(遙)远(遠) yáoyuǎn [形] **1**(指距离) distant **2**(指时间) far-off

咬 yǎo [动] **1**(指用嘴) bite **2**(夹住) grip

舀 yǎo [动] ladle

药(藥) yào [名] **1**(指治病) medicine **2**(指化学物品) chemical

药(藥)材 yàocái [名] herbal medicine

药(藥)店 yàodiàn [名] chemist's

药(藥)方 yàofāng [名] prescription

药(藥)物 yàowù [名] medicine

要 yào I [形] important II [动] **1**(想得到) want ▷ 我女儿要一个新书包。Wǒ nǚ'ér yào yī gè xīn shūbāo. My daughter wants a new schoolbag. **2**(要求) ask ▷ 老师要我们安静。Lǎoshī yào wǒmen ānjìng. The teacher asked us to be quiet. III [助动] **1**(应该) should ▷ 饭前要洗手。Fàn qián yào xǐ shǒu. You should wash your hands before you eat. **2**(需要) need ▷ 我要上厕所。Wǒ yào shàng cèsuǒ. I need the toilet. **3**(表示意志) want ▷ 我要学开车。Wǒ yào xué kāichē. I want to learn to drive. **4**(将要) be about to ▷ 我们要放暑假了。Wǒmen yào fàng shǔjià le. We're about to break for summer vacation. IV [连] (如果) if ▷ 你要碰见他，替我问声好。Nǐ yào pèngjiàn tā, tì wǒ wèn shēng hǎo. If you meet him, say hello from me.
→ see also/另见 yāo

> In a positive sentence, both 要 yào and 想 xiǎng can be used to express "want to". To express "I don't want to", it is more common to use 不想 bù xiǎng, as the expression 不要 bù yào is stronger and indicates a definite decision, meaning "I shall not (under any circumstances)".

要不 yàobù [连] **1**(否则) otherwise ▷ 快点走，要不你要迟到了。Kuài diǎn zǒu, yàobù nǐ yào chídào le. Go quickly, otherwise you'll be late. **2**(要么) either ... or ▷ 我们要不去看电影，要不去咖啡厅，你说呢? Wǒmen yàobù qù kàn diànyǐng, yàobù qù kāfēitīng, nǐ shuō ne? We can either go to see a film or go to a coffee shop — which would you prefer?

要紧(緊) yàojǐn [形] **1**(重要) important **2**(严重) serious

要领(領) yàolǐng [名] **1**(要点) gist **2**(基本要求) main points (pl)

要么(麼) yàome [连] either ... or ▷ 你要么学文，要么学理。Nǐ yàome xué wén, yàome xué lǐ. You either study arts or science.

要是 yàoshi [连] if ▷ 要是你不满意，可以随时退货。Yàoshi nǐ bù mǎnyì, kěyǐ suíshí tuì huò. If you're not satisfied, you can return the goods at any time.

钥(鑰) yào see below/见下文

钥(鑰)匙 yàoshi [名] key

耀 yào [动] (照射) shine

耶 yē *see below*/见下文
　耶稣(穌) Yēsū [名] Jesus

椰 yē [名] coconut
　椰子 yēzi [名] **1**(树) coconut tree
　2(果实) coconut

噎 yē [动](堵塞) choke

爷(爺) yé [名](祖父)(paternal)
　grandfather
　爷(爺)爷(爺) yéye [名](口)(祖父)
　(paternal) granddad

也 yě [副] **1**(同样) also ▷ 他也去过中国。
　Tā yě qùguo Zhōngguó. He's been to
　China too. **2**(表示转折) still ▷ 即使他来
　了，也帮不上忙。Jíshǐ tā lái le, yě
　bāng bù shàng máng. Even if he comes,
　it still won't be of any use.
　也许(許) yěxǔ [副] perhaps

野 yě I [名](野外) open country ▶ 野餐
　yěcān picnic II [形] **1**(野生) wild ▶ 野菜
　yěcài wild herbs (pl) **2**(蛮横) rude ▶ 粗
　野 cūyě rough **3**(无约束) unruly
　野餐 yěcān [动] have a picnic
　野蛮(蠻) yěmán [形] **1**(蒙昧)
　uncivilized **2**(残暴) brutal
　野生 yěshēng [形] wild
　野兽(獸) yěshòu [名] wild animal
　野外 yěwài [名] open country
　野心 yěxīn [名] ambition
　野营(營) yěyíng [名] camp

业(業) yè [名] **1**(行业) industry ▷ 饮食
　业 yǐnshíyè the food and drink industry
　2(职业) job ▷ 就业 jiùyè obtain
　employment ▶ 失业 shīyè be
　unemployed **3**(学业) studies (pl) ▷ 毕业
　bìyè graduate **4**(产业) property ▷ 家业
　jiāyè family property
　业(業)务(務) yèwù [名] profession
　业(業)余(餘) yèyú I [名] spare time
　II [形] amateurish
　业(業)主 yèzhǔ [名] owner

叶(葉) yè [名](叶子) leaf

页(頁) yè I [名] page II [量] page
　页(頁)码(碼) yèmǎ [名] page number

夜 yè [名] night
　夜班 yèbān [名] night shift
　夜猫(貓)子 yèmāozi [名](方) **1**(猫头
　鹰) owl **2**(喻)(晚睡者) night owl
　夜生活 yèshēnghuó [名] nightlife
　夜市 yèshì [名] night market
　夜宵 yèxiāo [名] late-night snack
　夜总(總)会(會) yèzǒnghuì [名]
　nightclub

液 yè [名] liquid
　液体(體) yètǐ [名] liquid

腋 yè [名](夹肢窝) armpit ▶ 腋毛 yèmáo
　underarm hair

一 yī [数] **1**(指数目) one ▶ 一辈子 yībèizi
　a lifetime **2**(相同) ▷ 一类人 yī lèi rén
　the same sort of people **3**(全) ▷ 一屋子
　烟 yī wūzi yān full of smoke

> 一 yī is pronounced as 1st tone when it
> is used by itself to mean the number
> one for example in telephone numbers
> etc. When it is followed by another
> syllable it changes its tone depending
> on the tone of the subsequent syllable.
> If the subsequent syllable is 1st, 2nd or
> 3rd tone then it is pronounced as 4th
> tone yì. If the subsequent syllable is a
> 4th tone, then it is pronounced as a
> 2nd tone yí. For consistency, changes
> of tone in pinyin are not shown in this
> book.

　一般 yībān [形] **1**(一样) same ▷ 他们俩
　一般大。Tāmen liǎ yībān dà. The
　two of them are the same age. **2**(普通)
　ordinary
　一半 yībàn [名] half
　一边(邊) yībiān I [名](一面) side
　II [副] at the same time
　一道 yīdào [副] together
　一点(點)儿(兒) yīdiǎnr [量] **1**(一些)
　some ▷ 你行李太多，我帮你提一点
　儿吧。Nǐ xíngli tài duō, wǒ bāng nǐ
　tí yīdiǎnr ba. You've got so much
　luggage – let me help you with some of
　it. **2**(很少) a little ▷ 这件事我一点儿都
　不知道。Zhè jiàn shì wǒ yīdiǎnr dōu
　bù zhīdào. I know nothing about this.
　一定 yīdìng I [形] **1**(规定的) definite

2(固定的) fixed **3**(相当) certain **4**(特定) given II[副] definitely ▷ 放心，我一定去机场接你。Fàngxīn, wǒ yīdìng qù jīchǎng jiē nǐ. Don't worry, I'll definitely pick you up at the airport.

一共 yīgòng [副] altogether ▷ 这套书一共多少本？Zhè tào shū yīgòng duōshao běn? How many books are there in this set?

一…就… yī…jiù… [副] as soon as ▷ 我一到家就给你打电话。Wǒ yī dào jiā jiù gěi nǐ dǎ diànhuà. I'll call you as soon as I get home.

一连(連) yīlián [副] on end ▷ 一连下了几个月的雨。Yīlián xiàle jǐ gè yuè de yǔ. It's been raining for months on end.

一路 yīlù [名] **1**(行程) journey ▷ 一路顺利吗？Yīlù shùnlì ma? Did you have a good journey? **2**(一起) the same way ▷ 咱俩是一路。Zán liǎ shì yīlù. We're going the same way.

一面 yīmiàn I[名] aspect ▷ 积极的一面 jíjí de yīmiàn a positive aspect II[副] at the same time ▷ 她一面听音乐，一面看小说。Tā yīmiàn tīng yīnyuè, yīmiàn kàn xiǎoshuō. She was listening to music and reading a novel at the same time.

一齐(齊) yīqí [副] simultaneously

一起 yīqǐ I[名] the same place II[副] together

一切 yīqiè [代] **1**(全部) all **2**(全部事物) everything

一时(時) yīshí I[名] **1**(一个时期) time **2**(短暂时间) moment II[副] **1**(临时) for the moment **2**(时而) sometimes

一同 yītóng [副] together

一下 yīxià I[量] ▷ 我去问一下。Wǒ qù wèn yīxià. I'll just go and ask.

| measure word, used after verbs to indicate one's attempts to do something

II[副] at once ▷ 天一下就冷了。Tiān yīxià jiù lěng le. All at once the weather turned cold.

一向 yīxiàng [副] always

一些 yīxiē [量] **1**(部分) some **2**(几个) a few **3**(稍微) a little ▷ 她感觉好一些了。Tā gǎnjué hǎo yīxiē le. She feels a little better.

一样(樣) yīyàng [形] same ▷ 他俩爱好一样。Tā liǎ àihào yīyàng. They have the same hobbies.

一月 yīyuè [名] January

一再 yīzài [副] repeatedly

一直 yīzhí [副] **1**(不变向) straight **2**(不间断) always ▷ 大风一直刮了两天两夜。Dàfēng yīzhí guāle liǎng tiān liǎng yè. The gale blew for two days and two nights. **3**(指一定范围) all the way ▷ 从南一直到北 cóng nán yīzhí dào běi from the north all way to the south

一致 yīzhì I[形] unanimous II[副] unanimously

衣 yī [名] (衣服) clothing ▷ 衣裳 yīshang clothes (pl)

衣服 yīfu [名] clothes (pl)

衣柜(櫃) yīguì [名] wardrobe

医(醫) yī I[名] **1**(医生) doctor **2**(医学) medicine ▷ 中医 zhōngyī Chinese traditional medicine II[动] treat

医(醫)疗(療) yīliáo [动] treat ▷ 免费医疗制度 miǎnfèi yīliáo zhìdù system of free medical care

医(醫)生 yīshēng [名] doctor

医(醫)术(術) yīshù [名] medical skill

医(醫)务(務)室 yīwùshì [名] clinic

医(醫)学(學) yīxué [名] medicine

医(醫)药(藥) yīyào [名] medicine

医(醫)院 yīyuàn [名] hospital

医(醫)治 yīzhì [动] cure

依 yī [动] **1**(依靠) depend on **2**(依从) comply with

依旧(舊) yījiù [副] still

依据(據) yījù I[动] go by II[名] basis

依靠 yīkào I[动] rely on II[名] support

依赖(賴) yīlài [动] depend on

依然 yīrán [副] still

依照 yīzhào [介] according to

壹 yī [数] one

| This is the character for "one", which is mainly used in banks, on receipts, etc. to prevent mistakes and forgery.

仪(儀)yí[名] **1**(外表)appearance **2**(礼节)ceremony **3**(仪器)meter

仪(儀)器 yíqì[名]meter

仪(儀)式 yíshì[名]ceremony

姨 yí[名] **1**(母亲的姐妹)aunt **2**(妻子的姐妹)sister-in-law

移 yí[动] **1**(移动)move **2**(改变)change

移动(動)yídòng[动]move

移民 yímín I[动]emigrate II[名] immigrant

遗(遺)yí[动] **1**(遗失)lose **2**(留下)leave ... behind

遗(遺)产(產)yíchǎn[名]legacy

遗(遺)传(傳)yíchuán[动]inherit

遗(遺)憾 yíhàn I[名]regret II[动]be a pity

遗(遺)弃(棄)yíqì[动] **1**(车、船等) abandon **2**(妻、子女等)desert

遗(遺)书(書)yíshū[名] **1**(书面遗言) last letter (of dying man)

遗(遺)体(體)yítǐ[名]remains (pl)

遗(遺)忘 yíwàng[动]forget

遗(遺)址(阯)yízhǐ[名]ruins (pl)

遗(遺)嘱(囑)yízhǔ[名]will

疑 yí[动]doubt

疑难(難)yínán[形]knotty

疑问(問)yíwèn[名]question

疑心 yíxīn I[名]suspicion II[动] suspect

已 yǐ[副]already

已经(經)yǐjīng[副]already

以 yǐ(书)I[动]use ▷ 以强凌弱 yǐ qiáng líng ruò use one's strength to humiliate the weak II[介] **1**(依照)by **2**(因为)for **3**(表示界限) ▶ 以内 yǐnèi within ▷ 以南 yǐnán to the south III[连] ▷ 我们要改进技术，以提高生产效率。Wǒmen yào gǎijìn jìshù, yǐ tígāo shēngchǎn xiàolù. We should improve the technology so as to increase production.

以便 yǐbiàn[连]in order that

以后(後)yǐhòu[名] ▷ 两年以后 liǎng nián yǐhòu two years later ▷ 以后我们去看电影。Yǐhòu wǒmen qù kàn diànyǐng. Afterwards we're going to see a film.

以及 yǐjí[连]as well as

以来(來)yǐlái[名] ▷ 入冬以来 rù dōng yǐlái since the beginning of the winter

以免 yǐmiǎn[连]in case

以前 yǐqián[名] ▷ 10年以前 shí nián yǐqián ten years ago ▷ 她以前是老师。Tā yǐqián shì lǎoshī. She was a teacher before.

以为(為)yǐwéi[动]think

以下 yǐxià[名](低于某点) ▷ 30岁以下 sānshí suì yǐxià under thirty

以致 yǐzhì[连]so that

蚁(蟻)yǐ[名]ant ▶ 蚂蚁 mǎyǐ ant

椅 yǐ[名]chair

椅子 yǐzi[名]chair

亿(億)yì[数]hundred million

义(義)yì[名] **1**(正义)righteousness **2**(情谊)human relationship **3**(意义) meaning II[形] **1**(正义的)just **2**(拜认的)adopted ▶ 义父 yìfù adoptive father

义(義)卖(賣)yìmài[动]sell ... for charity

义(義)气(氣)yìqi I[名]loyalty II[形]loyal

义(義)务(務)yìwù I[名]duty II[形]compulsory

艺(藝)yì[名] **1**(技能)skill ▶ 手艺 shǒuyì craftsmanship **2**(艺术)art

艺(藝)人 yìrén[名](表演者)performer

艺(藝)术(術)yìshù I[名] **1**(文艺)art **2**(方法)skill ▷ 管理艺术 guǎnlǐ yìshù management skills II[形]artistic

艺(藝)术(術)家 yìshùjiā[名]artist

忆(憶)yì[动]remember ▶ 记忆 jìyì memory

议(議)yì I[名]opinion ▶ 建议 jiànyì propose II[动]discuss ▶ 商议 shāngyì discuss

议(議)程 yìchéng[名]agenda

议(議)会(會)yìhuì[名]parliament

议(議)论(論) yìlùn I[动] discuss II[名] talk

议(議)题(題) yìtí [名] topic

议(議)员(員) yìyuán [名] MP(英), congressman, congresswoman(美)

异(異) yì I[形] 1(不同) different ▶ 差异 chāyì difference 2(奇异) strange 3(另外) other ▶ 异国 yìguó foreign country II[动] separate ▶ 离异 líyì separate

异(異)常 yìcháng [形] unusual

异(異)性 yìxìng [名] (指性别) the opposite sex

译(譯) yì [动] translate

译(譯)文 yìwén [名] translation

译(譯)者 yìzhě [名] translator

译(譯)制(製) yìzhì [动] dub

抑 yì [动] repress

抑郁(鬱) yìyù [形] depressed

抑制 yìzhì [动] 1(生理) inhibit 2(控制) control

易 yì [形] (容易) easy ▷ 易传染 yì chuánrǎn easily transmissible

易拉罐 yìlāguàn [名] can

疫 yì [名] epidemic

疫苗 yìmiáo [名] inoculation

益 yì I[名] benefit II[形] beneficial III[动] increase IV[副] increasingly

益处(處) yìchu [名] benefit

谊(誼) yì [名] friendship ▶ 友谊 yǒuyì friendship

意 yì [名] 1(意思) meaning 2(心愿) wish ▶ 好意 hǎoyì good intention

意见(見) yìjiàn [名] 1(看法) opinion 2(不满) objection

意识(識) yìshí I[名] consciousness II[动] realize

意思 yìsi [名] 1(意义) meaning 2(意见) idea 3(愿望) wish 4(趣味) interest ▶ 有意思 yǒu yìsi interesting ▶ 没意思 méi yìsi boring 5(心意) token

意图(圖) yìtú [名] intention

意外 yìwài I[名] accident II[形] unexpected

意义(義) yìyì 1(含义) meaning 2(作用) significance

毅 yì [形] resolute

毅力 yìlì [名] perseverance

因 yīn I[连] because II[介] because of ▷ 昨天他因病缺课。Zuótiān tā yīn bìng quē kè. He missed a class yesterday because of illness. III[名] cause ▶ 病因 bìngyīn cause of the illness

因此 yīncǐ [连] so

因而 yīn'ér [连] therefore

因素 yīnsù [名] 1(成分) element 2(原因) factor

因特网(網) Yīntèwǎng [名] the Internet

因为(為) yīnwèi [连] because

阴(陰) yīn I[形] 1(指天气) overcast 2(阴险的) insidious ▶ 阴谋 yīnmóu plot 3(物) negative ▶ 阴性 yīnxìng negative II[名] 1(阳的对立面) Yin (from Yin and Yang) 2(指月亮) the moon ▶ 阴历 yīnlì lunar calendar 3(阴凉处) shade ▶ 树阴 shùyīn the shade

阴(陰)暗 yīn'àn [形] gloomy

阴(陰)部 yīnbù [名] private parts (pl)

阴(陰)凉(涼) yīnliáng [形] shady and cool

音 yīn [名] 1(声音) sound 2(消息) news (sg)

音量 yīnliàng [名] volume

音响(響) yīnxiǎng [名] (指设备) acoustics (pl)

音像 yīnxiàng [名] audio and video

音乐(樂) yīnyuè [名] music

音乐(樂)会(會) yīnyuèhuì [名] concert

银(銀) yín I[名] 1(指金属) silver 2(指货币) money ▶ 收银台 shōuyíntái cashier's desk II[形] silver

银(銀)行 yínháng [名] bank

银(銀)河 yínhé [名] the Milky Way

银(銀)幕 yínmù [名] screen

银(銀)牌 yínpái [名] silver medal

龈(齦) yín [名] gum ▸ 牙龈 yáyín gum

引 yǐn [动] 1(牵引) draw 2(引导) lead
▸ 引路 yǐnlù lead the way 3(引起) cause
4(引用) cite

引导(導) yǐndǎo [动] 1(带领) lead
2(启发诱导) guide

引进(進) yǐnjìn [动] 1(人) recommend
2(物) import

引力 yǐnlì [名] gravitation

引起 yǐnqǐ [动] cause

引擎 yǐnqíng [名] engine

引用 yǐnyòng [动] (引述) quote

引诱(誘) yǐnyòu [动] 1(诱导) induce
2(诱惑) tempt

饮(飲) yǐn I [动] drink II [名] drink

饮(飲)料 yǐnliào [名] drink

饮(飲)食 yǐnshí [名] food and drink

饮(飲)用水 yǐnyòngshuǐ [名] drinking
water

隐(隱) yǐn [动] conceal

隐(隱)藏 yǐncáng [动] conceal

隐(隱)瞒(瞞) yǐnmán [动] cover
... up

隐(隱)私 yǐnsī [名] private matters (pl)

瘾(癮) yǐn [名] (嗜好) addiction ▸ 上瘾
shàng yǐn be addicted to

印 yìn I [名] 1(图章) stamp 2(痕迹) print
II [动] (留下痕迹) print

印度 Yìndù [名] India

印刷 yìnshuā [动] print

印象 yìnxiàng [名] impression

印章 yìnzhāng [名] seal

荫(蔭) yìn [形] shady

荫(蔭)凉(涼) yìnliáng [形] shady and
cool

应(應) yīng I [动] 1(答应) answer
2(应允) agree II [助动] should
→ see also/另见 yìng

应(應)当(當) yīngdāng [助动] should

应(應)该(該) yīnggāi [助动] should

应(應)允 yīngyǔn [动] consent

英 yīng [名] 1(才能出众者) hero ▸ 精英
jīngyīng elite 2(英国) Britain

英镑(鎊) yīngbàng [名] pound sterling

英格兰(蘭) Yīnggélán [名] England

英国(國) Yīngguó [名] Great Britain
▸ 英国的 Yīngguó de British

英国(國)人 Yīngguórén [名] the
British

英俊 yīngjùn [形] (漂亮的) handsome

英文 Yīngwén [名] English

> 英文 Yīngwén generally refers to the
written English language, whereas 英
语 Yīngyǔ refers to the spoken English
language, although they are to some
extent interchangeable. This is the
same for all languages.

英雄 yīngxióng I [名] hero II [形] heroic

英勇 yīngyǒng [形] brave

英语(語) Yīngyǔ [名] English

婴(嬰) yīng [名] baby

婴(嬰)儿(兒) yīng'ér [名] baby

樱(櫻) yīng [名] 1(樱桃) cherry ▸ 樱桃
yīngtáo cherry 2(樱花) cherry blossom
▸ 樱花 yīnghuā cherry blossom

鹦(鸚) yīng see below/见下文

鹦(鸚)鹉(鵡) yīngwǔ [名] parrot

鹰(鷹) yīng [名] eagle

迎 yíng [动] 1(迎接) welcome 2(对着)
meet

迎合 yínghé [动] cater to

迎接 yíngjiē [动] welcome

萤(螢) yíng [名] firefly ▸ 萤火虫
yínghuǒchóng firefly

营(營) yíng I [动] (经营) operate II [名]
1(军队驻地) barracks (pl) 2(军队编制)
battalion 3(营地) camp ▸ 营地 yíngdì
camp

营(營)救 yíngjiù [动] rescue

营(營)销(銷) yíngxiāo [动] sell

营(營)养(養) yíngyǎng [名]
nourishment

营(營)业(業) yíngyè [动] do business

蝇(蠅) yíng [名] fly ▶ 苍蝇 cāngying fly

赢(贏) yíng [动] 1(胜) win 2(获利) gain
赢(贏) 利 yínglì [名] gain

影 yǐng [名] 1(影子) shadow 2(照片)
photograph 3(电影) film(英), movie(美)
影片 yǐngpiàn [名] 1(胶片) film(英), movie(美) 2(电影)
film(英), movie(美)
影响(響) yǐngxiǎng I [动] affect II [名]
influence
影印 yǐngyìn [动] photocopy

应(應) yìng [动] 1(回答) answer ▶回应
huíyìng answer 2(满足) respond to
3(顺应) comply with 4(应付) handle
▶应急 yìngjí handle an emergency
→ see also/另见 yīng
应(應) 酬 yìngchou I [动] socialize with
II [名] social engagement
应(應) 付 yìngfu [动] 1(采取办法)
handle 2(敷衍) do half-heartedly
3(将就) make do with
应(應) 聘 yìngpìn [动] accept an offer
应(應) 用 yìngyòng I [动] apply II [形]
applied
应(應) 用软(軟) 件 yìngyòng
ruǎnjiàn [名] app

硬 yìng I [形] 1(坚固) hard 2(刚强) firm
3(能干的) strong II [副] obstinately
硬币(幣) yìngbì [名] coin
硬件 yìngjiàn [名] 1(计算机) hardware
2(设备) equipment
硬盘(盤) yìngpán [名] hard disk

哟(喲) yō [叹] (表示轻微的惊异或赞叹)
oh

佣(傭) yōng I [动] hire II [名] servant
▶ 女佣 nǚyōng maid
→ see also/另见 yòng

拥(擁) yōng [动] 1(抱) embrace 2(围着)
gather round 3(拥挤) swarm 4(拥护)
support
拥(擁) 抱 yōngbào [动] embrace
拥(擁) 护(護) yōnghù [动] support
拥(擁) 挤(擠) yōngjǐ I [形] crowded
II [动] crowd
拥(擁) 有 yōngyǒu [动] have

庸 yōng [形] (不高明) mediocre
庸俗 yōngsú [形] vulgar

永 yǒng I [形] (书) everlasting II [副]
forever
永恒(恆) yǒnghéng [形] everlasting
永久 yǒngjiǔ [形] eternal
永远(遠) yǒngyuǎn [副] eternally

泳 yǒng [名] swim ▶ 蛙泳 wāyǒng
breaststroke
泳道 yǒngdào [名] lane

勇 yǒng [形] brave
勇敢 yǒnggǎn [形] brave
勇气(氣) yǒngqì [名] courage

用 yòng I [动] 1(使用) use 2(需要) need
3(消费) consume ▶用餐 yòng cān have
a meal II [名] 1(费用) expense ▶家用
jiāyòng household expenses (pl) 2(用处)
use ▶没用 méiyòng useless
用处(處) yòngchu [名] use
用功 yònggōng I [形] hardworking
II [动] work hard
用户(戶) yònghù [名] user ▷网络用户
wǎngluò yònghù internet user
用户名 yònghùmíng [名] (计算机)
username
用具 yòngjù [名] tool
用力 yònglì [动] exert oneself
用品 yòngpǐn [名] goods (pl)
用途 yòngtú [名] use

佣 yòng see below/见下文
→ see also/另见 yōng
佣金 yòngjīn [名] commission

优(優) yōu [形] (优良) excellent
优(優) 点(點) yōudiǎn [名] strong
point
优(優) 良 yōuliáng [形] fine
优(優) 美 yōuměi [形] elegant
优(優) 势(勢) yōushì [名]
advantage
优(優) 先 yōuxiān [动] have priority
优(優) 秀 yōuxiù [形] outstanding
优(優) 越 yōuyuè [形] superior

忧(憂) yōu I [形] anxious II [动] worry
III [名] anxiety
忧(憂)伤(傷) yōushāng [形] sad
忧(憂)郁(鬱) yōuyù [形] depressed

幽 yōu [形] (暗) dim ▶ 幽暗 yōu'àn
gloomy
幽默 yōumò [形] humorous

悠 yōu [形] 1 (久远) remote 2 (闲适)
leisurely
悠久 yōujiǔ [形] long-standing
悠闲(閒) yōuxián [形] leisurely

尤 yóu [副] especially
尤其 yóuqí [副] especially

由 yóu I [动] 1 (听凭) give in to 2 (经过) go
through II [介] 1 (归) by 2 (根据) ▷ 由此
可见… yóu cǐ kě jiàn… from this we
can see… 3 (从) from 4 (由于) due to
III [名] cause ▶ 理由 lǐyóu reason
由于(於) yóuyú [介] as a result of

邮(郵) yóu I [动] post (英), mail (美)
II [名] 1 (邮务) post (英), mail (美)
2 (邮票) stamp
邮(郵)递(遞) yóudì [动] send ... by
post (英) 或 mail (美)
邮(郵)电(電) yóudiàn [名] post and
telecommunications
邮(郵)寄 yóujì [动] post (英), mail (美)
邮(郵)件 yóujiàn [名] post (英), mail (美)
邮(郵)局 yóujú [名] post office
邮(郵)票 yóupiào [名] stamp
邮(郵)政 yóuzhèng [名] postal service
邮(郵)资(資) yóuzī [名] postage

犹(猶) yóu [副] still
犹(猶)豫 yóuyù [形] hesitant

油 yóu I [名] oil II [形] oily
油滑 yóuhuá [形] slippery
油腻(膩) yóunì I [形] greasy II [名]
greasy food
油漆 yóuqī I [名] varnish II [动] varnish

鱿(魷) yóu [名] squid
鱿(魷)鱼(魚) yóuyú [名] squid

游(遊) yóu [动] 1 (游泳) swim 2 (游览)
tour
游(遊)客 yóukè [名] tourist
游(遊)览(覽) yóulǎn [动] tour
游牧 yóumù [动] live a nomadic life
游(遊)说(說) yóushuì [动] lobby
游(遊)戏(戲) yóuxì I [名] game
II [动] play
游(遊)行 yóuxíng [动] march
游泳 yóuyǒng I [动] swim II [名]
swimming
游泳池 yóuyǒngchí [名] swimming
pool

友 yǒu I [名] friend ▶ 男友 nányǒu
boyfriend II [形] friendly ▶ 友好 yǒuhǎo
friendly
友爱(愛) yǒu'ài [形] affectionate
友情 yǒuqíng [名] friendship
友人 yǒurén [名] friend
友谊(誼) yǒuyì [名] friendship

有 yǒu [动] 1 (具有) have 2 (存在) ▷ 院子
里有一棵大树。 Yuànzi lǐ yǒu yī kē dà
shù. There's a big tree in the courtyard.
3 (发生) occur ▷ 我的生活有了一些变
化。 Wǒ de shēnghuó yǒule yīxiē
biànhuà. A few changes have occurred in
my life. (表示程度) have ▷ 他特别有学
问。 Tā tèbié yǒu xuéwèn. He's
extremely knowledgeable. 4 (某) ▶ 有时
候 yǒushíhou sometimes ▷ 有一次,
他得了冠军。 Yǒu yī cì, tā déle
guànjūn. He won a prize once.
有的 yǒude [名] some ▷ 展出的作品,
有的来自本土,有的来自海外。
Zhǎnchū de zuòpǐn, yǒude láizì
běntǔ, yǒude láizì hǎiwài. Of the
articles on display, some are local,
others are from overseas.
有点(點)儿(兒) yǒudiǎnr [副]
somewhat
有关(關) yǒuguān [动] 1 (有关系) be
relevant 2 (涉及到) be about
有利 yǒulì [形] favourable (英),
favorable (美)
有名 yǒumíng [形] famous
有趣 yǒuqù [形] interesting
有限 yǒuxiàn [形] limited

有限公司 yǒuxiàn gōngsī [名] limited company

有线(線)电(電)视(視) yǒuxiàn diànshì [名] cable TV

有幸 yǒuxìng [形] fortunate

有意思 yǒu yìsi I [形] 1 (有意义) significant 2 (有趣味) interesting II [动] be interested in

又 yòu [副] 1 (重复) again 2 (同时) ▷ 她是一个好教师，又是一个好妈妈。Tā shì yī gè hǎo jiàoshī, yòu shì yī gè hǎo māma. She's both a good teacher and a great mother. 3 (也) too 4 (另外) another 5 (再加上) and ▷ 一又三分之二 yī yòu sān fēn zhī èr one and two thirds 6 (可是) but

右 yòu [名] 1 (右边) right ▷ 右边 yòubian right side ▷ 请向右转。Qǐng xiàng yòu zhuǎn. Please turn right. 2 (右翼) the Right

幼 yòu I [形] young II [名] child ▷ 幼儿园 yòu'éryuán nursery school (英), kindergarten (美)

幼儿(兒) yòu'ér [名] small child

幼年 yòunián [名] infancy

幼小 yòuxiǎo [形] young

幼稚 yòuzhì [形] 1 (书) (年龄很小) young 2 (头脑简单) naive

诱(誘) yòu [动] 1 (诱导) guide 2 (引诱) entice

诱(誘)饵(餌) yòu'ěr [名] bait

诱(誘)惑 yòuhuò [动] 1 (引诱) entice 2 (吸引) attract

于(於) yú [介] 1 (在) in 2 (向) from 3 (对) to 4 (从) from 5 (比) than ▷ 大于 dàyú bigger than

于(於)是 yúshì [连] so

余(餘) yú [名] 1 (零头) ▷ 500余人 wǔ bǎi yú rén more than five hundred people 2 (指时间) ▷ 课余 kèyú extra-curricular

余(餘)地 yúdì [名] room

盂 yú [名] jar ▷ 痰盂 tányú spittoon (英), cuspidor (美)

鱼(魚) yú [名] fish ▷ 鱼肉 yúròu fish

娱(娛) yú I [动] amuse II [名] amusement

娱(娛)乐(樂) yúlè I [动] have fun II [名] entertainment

渔(漁) yú [动] (捕鱼) fish ▷ 渔业 yúyè fisheries

愉 yú [形] happy

愉快 yúkuài [形] happy ▷ 祝你旅行愉快! Zhù nǐ lǚxíng yúkuài! Have a pleasant journey!

愚 yú I [形] foolish ▷ 愚蠢 yúchǔn foolish II [名] fool

愚昧 yúmèi [形] ignorant

舆(輿) yú [形] popular

舆(輿)论(論) yúlùn [名] public opinion

与(與) yǔ I [介] with II [连] and → see also/另见 yù

宇 yǔ [名] 1 (房屋) house 2 (四方) the universe

宇航 yǔháng I [动] travel through space II [名] space travel

宇航员(員) yǔhángyuán [名] astronaut

宇宙 yǔzhòu [名] universe

羽 yǔ [名] 1 (羽毛) feather 2 (翅膀) wing

羽毛 yǔmáo [名] feather

羽毛球 yǔmáoqiú [名] 1 (指运动) badminton 2 (指球体) shuttlecock

雨 yǔ [名] rain ▷ 下雨 xiàyǔ to rain

雨具 yǔjù [名] waterproofs (pl)

雨水 yǔshuǐ [名] (降水) rain

语(語) yǔ I [名] (语言) language ▷ 手语 shǒuyǔ sign language II [动] talk

语(語)调(調) yǔdiào [名] tone

语(語)法 yǔfǎ [名] grammar

语(語)句 yǔjù [名] sentence

语(語)气(氣) yǔqì [名] 1 (口气) tone of voice 2 (语法) mood

语(語)文 yǔwén [名] 1 (语言文字) language 2 (中文) Chinese 3 (语言与文学) language and literature

语(語)言 yǔyán [名] language
语(語)音 yǔyīn [名] pronunciation
语(語)音信箱 yǔyīn xìnxiāng [名] voice mail
语(語)种(種) yǔzhǒng [名] language

与(與) yù [动] take part in ▶ 与会 yùhuì participate in a conference ▶ 与会者 yùhuìzhě conferee
→ see also/另见 yǔ

玉 yù [名] (玉石) jade
玉米 yùmǐ [名] (指植物) maize (英), corn (美)

郁(鬱) yù [形] (烦闷) gloomy
郁(鬱)闷(悶) yùmèn [形] melancholy

育 yù I [动] 1 (生育) give birth to 2 (养活) raise ▶ 养育 yǎngyù bring up II [名] education ▶ 教育 jiàoyù education

狱(獄) yù [名] (监狱) prison ▶ 监狱 jiānyù prison

浴 yù [动] wash
浴盆 yùpén [名] bath
浴室 yùshì [名] bathroom

预(預) yù [副] in advance
预(預)报(報) yùbào [动] predict ▷ 天气预报 tiānqì yùbào weather forecast
预(預)备(備) yùbèi [动] prepare
预(預)测(測) yùcè [动] predict
预(預)防 yùfáng [动] prevent
预(預)感 yùgǎn [动] have a premonition
预(預)计(計) yùjì [动] estimate
预(預)见(見) yùjiàn [动] foresee
预(預)科 yùkē [名] foundation course
预(預)料 yùliào [动] predict
预(預)算 yùsuàn [名] budget
预(預)习(習) yùxí [动] prepare for lessons
预(預)言 yùyán [动] predict

域 yù [名] region ▶ 领域 lǐngyù realm

欲(慾) yù [名] desire
欲(慾)望 yùwàng [名] desire

遇 yù I [动] meet ▶ 遇到 yùdào meet II [名] 1 (待遇) treatment 2 (机会) opportunity

寓 yù I [动] 1 (居住) live 2 (寄托) imply II [名] residence ▶ 公寓 gōngyù flat (英), apartment (美)
寓言 yùyán [名] fable

鸳(鴛) yuān [名] mandarin duck
鸳(鴛)鸯(鴦) yuānyāng [名] (指鸟) mandarin duck

冤 yuān [名] 1 (冤枉) injustice ▶ 冤枉 yuānwang treat unfairly 2 (冤仇) enmity

元 yuán I [名] 1 (始) first 2 (首) chief ▶ 元首 yuánshǒu head of state 3 (主) fundamental ▶ 元素 yuánsù element 4 (整体) component ▶ 单元 dānyuán unit 5 (圆形货币) coin ▶ 金元 jīnyuán gold coin II [量] yuan ▷ 5元钱 wǔ yuán qián five yuan
元旦 Yuándàn [名] New Year's Day
元件 yuánjiàn [名] part
元帅(帥) yuánshuài [名] commander-in-chief
元宵 yuánxiāo [名] sweet round dumplings made of glutinous rice, usually eaten with the broth in which they are cooked
元宵节(節) Yuánxiāo Jié [名] the Lantern Festival

元宵节 Yuánxiāo Jié
 The Lantern Festival is celebrated on the 15th day of the Lunar Chinese New Year. The traditional food which is eaten at this festival is called 元宵 yuánxiāo or 汤圆 tāngyuán, a traditional sweet dumpling made of glutinous rice, with various sweet fillings.

园(園) yuán [名] 1 (指菜地或果林) garden 2 (指游乐场所) park
园(園)丁 yuándīng [名] (园艺工人) gardener
园(園)林 yuánlín [名] garden
园(園)艺(藝) yuányì [名] gardening

员(員) yuán [名] 1(指工作或学习的人) ▶炊事员 chuīshìyuán cook 2(成员) member

员(員)工 yuángōng [名] staff (pl)

原 yuán [形] 1(本来的) original 2(未加工的) raw ▶原油 yuányóu crude oil

原来(來) yuánlái I [形] original II [副] 1(起初) originally 2(其实) all along

原理 yuánlǐ [名] principle

原谅(諒) yuánliàng [动] forgive

原料 yuánliào [名] (指烹饪) ingredient

原始 yuánshǐ [形] 1(古老) primitive 2(最初) original

原先 yuánxiān I [形] original II [副] originally

原因 yuányīn [名] reason

原则(則) yuánzé [名] principle

原著 yuánzhù [名] the original

原子 yuánzǐ [名] atom

圆(圆) yuán I [形] 1(圆形的) round ▶圆圈 yuánquān circle 2(球形的) spherical 3(圆满的) satisfactory II [名] (数) (圆周) circle

圆(圆)规(規) yuánguī [名] compasses (pl)

圆(圆)满(滿) yuánmǎn [形] satisfactory

圆(圆)舞曲 yuánwǔqǔ [名] waltz

援 yuán [动] (援助) help ▶支援 zhīyuán support

援救 yuánjiù [动] rescue

援助 yuánzhù [动] help

缘(緣) yuán [名] 1(缘故) cause 2(缘分) fate 3(边缘) edge

缘(緣)分 yuánfèn [名] fate

缘(緣)故 yuángù [名] cause

猿 yuán [名] ape

猿猴 yuánhóu [名] apes and monkeys (pl)

猿人 yuánrén [名] ape-man

源 yuán [名] source ▶水源 shuǐyuán source

远(遠) yuǎn [形] 1(指距离) far ▶远程 yuǎnchéng long-distance 2(指血统) distant 3(指程度) far

远(遠)大 yuǎndà [形] far-reaching

远(遠)方 yuǎnfāng [名] afar

远(遠)见(見) yuǎnjiàn [名] foresight

远(遠)亲(親) yuǎnqīn [名] distant relative

远(遠)视(視) yuǎnshì [名] (医) long sightedness

远(遠)足 yuǎnzú [动] hike

院 yuàn [名] 1(院落) courtyard ▶院子 yuànzi yard 2(指机关和处所) ▶电影院 diànyǐngyuàn cinema (英), movie theater (美) 3(学院) college 4(医院) hospital

愿(願) yuàn I [名] (愿望) wish II [助动] ▷我不愿说。Wǒ bù yuàn shuō. I don't want to say anything.

愿(願)望 yuànwàng [名] wish

愿(願)意 yuànyì [动] 1(同意) be willing to 2(希望) wish

约(約) yuē I [动] 1(束缚) restrict 2(商定) arrange 3(邀请) invite II [形] brief ▶简约 jiǎnyuē brief III [副] about

约(約)会(會) yuēhuì [名] 1(指工作) appointment 2(指恋人) date

约(約)束 yuēshù [动] bind

月 yuè [名] 1(月球) the moon ▶满月 mǎnyuè full moon 2(月份) month ▶3月 sānyuè March 3(每月) monthly ▶月薪 yuèxīn monthly salary

月饼(餅) yuèbing [名] mooncake

月饼 yuèbing

● Mooncakes, the traditional festival food for 中秋节 Zhōngqiū Jié (the Mid-Autumn Festival), are round cakes made of a variety of sweet fillings including beanpaste, egg and peanut.

月份 yuèfèn [名] month

月光 yuèguāng [名] moonlight

月经(經) yuèjīng [名] (例假) period

月亮 yuèliang [名] the moon

月票 yuèpiào [名] monthly ticket

乐(樂) yuè [名] music ▶ 器乐 qìyuè
instrumental music ▶ 民乐 mínyuè folk
music
→ see also/另见 lè
乐(樂)队(隊) yuèduì [名] band
乐(樂)器 yuèqì [名] musical
instrument
乐(樂)曲 yuèqǔ [名] music
乐(樂)团(團) yuètuán [名]
philharmonic orchestra

岳(嶽) yuè [名] 1 (高山) mountain
2 (妻子的父母) parents-in-law (pl)
岳父 yuèfù [名] father-in-law
岳母 yuèmǔ [名] mother-in-law

阅(閱) yuè [动] 1 (看) read 2 (检阅)
inspect 3 (经历) experience
阅(閱)读(讀) yuèdú [动] read
阅(閱)览(覽) yuèlǎn [动] read
阅(閱)历(歷) yuèlì [动] experience

跃(躍) yuè [动] leap ▶ 跳跃 tiàoyuè
jump

越 yuè I [动] 1 (跨过) jump over 2 (超过)
exceed II [副] ▶ 越发 yuèfā increasingly
越来(來)越 yuèláiyuè [副] more and
more ▷ 天气越来越暖和了。Tiānqì
yuèláiyuè nuǎnhuo le. The weather is
getting warmer and warmer.
越野 yuèyě [动] go cross-country
越…越… yuè…yuè… [副] the more …
the more … ▷ 越早越好 yuè zǎo yuè
hǎo the earlier the better

晕(暈) yūn [动] 1 (晕眩) feel dizzy
2 (昏迷) faint ▷ 她晕过去了。Tā yūn
guòqù le. She passed out.
→ see also/另见 yùn

云(雲) yún [名] cloud
云(雲)彩 yúncai [名] (口) cloud

匀(勻) yún I [形] even II [动] 1 (使均匀)
even … out 2 (分) apportion
匀(勻)称(稱) yúnchèn [形]
well-proportioned

允 yǔn [动] allow
允许(許) yǔnxǔ [动] allow

孕 yùn I [动] be pregnant ▶ 怀孕 huáiyùn
be pregnant II [名] pregnancy

运(運) yùn I [动] 1 (运动) move 2 (搬运)
transport 3 (运用) use II [名] luck ▶ 好运
hǎoyùn good luck
运(運)动(動) yùndòng I [动] (物)
move II [名] 1 (体育活动) sport 2 (群众
性活动) movement
运(運)动(動)鞋 yùndòngxié [名]
trainer
运(運)动(動)员(員) yùndòngyuán
[名] athlete
运(運)河 yùnhé [名] canal
运(運)气(氣) yùnqi [名] luck
运(運)输(輸) yùnshū [动] transport
运(運)算 yùnsuàn [动] calculate
运(運)行 yùnxíng [动] move
运(運)用 yùnyòng [动] make use of
运(運)转(轉) yùnzhuǎn [动] (指机器)
run
运(運)作 yùnzuò [动] operate

晕(暈) yùn [动] feel giddy ▶ 晕机 yùnjī
be airsick ▶ 晕车 yùnchē be carsick
▶ 晕船 yùnchuán be seasick
→ see also/另见 yūn

熨 yùn [动] iron
熨斗 yùndǒu [名] iron

Z

杂(雜) zá I [形] miscellaneous ▷ 复杂 fùzá complicated II [动] mix
杂(雜)货(貨) záhuò [名] groceries (pl)
杂(雜)技 zájì [名] acrobatics (pl)
杂(雜)志(誌) zázhì [名] magazine

砸 zá [动] 1 (撞击) pound 2 (打破) break ▷ 杯子砸坏了。Bēizi záhuài le. The cup was broken.

灾(災) zāi [名] 1 (灾害) disaster ▷ 水灾 shuǐzāi flood 2 (不幸) misfortune
灾(災)害 zāihài [名] disaster
灾(災)难(難) zāinàn [名] disaster

栽 zāi [动] 1 (种) plant ▷ 栽花 zāi huā grow flowers 2 (摔倒) tumble

再 zài [副] 1 (又) again ▷ 你再说一遍。Nǐ zài shuō yī biàn. Say that again. 2 (更) more ▷ 请把音量放得再大些。Qǐng bǎ yīnliàng fàng de zài dà xiē. Please turn the volume up a bit. 3 (继续) ▷ 我不能再等了。Wǒ bùnéng zài děng le. I can't wait any longer. 4 (接着) then ▷ 你做完功课再看小说。Nǐ zuòwán gōngkè zài kàn xiǎoshuō. You can read your book when you've finished your homework. 5 (另外) ▷ 再说 zàishuō besides
再见(見) zàijiàn [动] say goodbye ▷ 再见！Zàijiàn! Goodbye!
再三 zàisān [副] again and again

在 zài I [动] 1 (存在) live 2 (处于) be ▷ 你的书在桌子上。Nǐ de shū zài zhuōzi shang. Your book is on the table. ▷ 我父母在纽约。Wǒ fùmǔ zài Niǔyuē. My parents are in New York. 3 (在于) rest with II [副] ▷ 情况在改变。Qíngkuàng zài gǎibiàn. Things are changing. ▷ 他们在看电视。Tāmen zài kàn diànshì. They're watching TV. III [介] at ▷ 在机场等候 zài jīchǎng děnghòu wait at the airport ▷ 在历史上 zài lìshǐ shang in history
在乎 zàihu [动] care
在于(於) zàiyú [动] 1 (存在) lie in 2 (取决于) depend on

咱 zán [代] 1 (咱们) we 2 (方) (我) I
咱们(們) zánmen [代] 1 (我们) we 2 (方) (我) I

攒(攢) zǎn [动] save

暂(暫) zàn I [形] brief II [副] temporarily
暂(暫)时(時) zànshí [名] ▷ 暂时的需要 zànshí de xūyào temporary need

赞(贊) zàn [动] 1 (帮助) assist ▷ 赞助 zànzhù assistance 2 (称颂) commend ▷ 赞赏 zànshǎng admire
赞(贊)成 zànchéng [动] approve
赞(讚)美 zànměi [动] praise
赞(贊)同 zàntóng [动] approve of
赞(讚)扬(揚) zànyáng [动] pay tribute to

脏(髒) zāng [形] dirty ▷ 脏话 zānghuà dirty word

遭 zāo [动] meet with ▷ 遭殃 zāoyāng suffer
遭到 zāodào [动] encounter
遭受 zāoshòu [动] suffer

糟 zāo I [名] dregs (pl) II [动] 1 (浪费) waste ▷ 糟蹋 zāota spoil 2 (腌制) flavour (英) 或 flavor (美) with alcohol III [形] 1 (腐烂) rotten 2 (弄坏) messy
糟糕 zāogāo [形] terrible ▷ 真糟糕，我的钥匙丢了。Zhēn zāogāo, wǒ de yàoshi diū le. Oh no, I've lost my key!

早 zǎo I[名] morning II[副] a long time ago III[形] early
　早安 zǎo'ān[名] ▷ 早安! Zǎo'ān! Good morning!
　早餐 zǎocān[名] breakfast
　早晨 zǎochen[名] morning
　早饭(飯) zǎofàn[名] breakfast
　早晚 zǎowǎn I[名] morning and evening II[副] 1(迟早) sooner or later 2(方)(将来) some day
　早上 zǎoshang[名] morning

造 zào[动] 1(制造) make 2(瞎编) concoct ▶造谣 zàoyáo start a rumour(英) 或 rumor(美)
　造成 zàochéng[动] cause
　造反 zàofǎn[动] rebel
　造型 zàoxíng[名] model

噪 zào[动](嚷) clamour(英), clamor(美) ▶噪音 zàoyīn noise

责(責) zé I[名] responsibility ▶负责 fùzé be responsible for II[动](责备) blame ▶指责 zhǐzé censure
　责(責)备(備) zébèi[动] blame
　责(責)任 zérèn[名] responsibility

怎 zěn[代](口) ▷你怎能相信他的话? Nǐ zěn néng xiāngxìn tā de huà? How can you believe him?
　怎么(麼) zěnme I[代] ▷你看这事我该怎么办? Nǐ kàn zhè shì wǒ gāi zěnme bàn? What do you think I should do about this? ▷你昨天怎么没来上课? Nǐ zuótiān zěnme méi lái shàngkè? Why weren't you in class yesterday? II[副](泛指方式) ▷我是怎么想就怎么说。 Wǒ shì zěnme xiǎng jiù zěnme shuō. I say whatever I think. ▷他最近怎么样? Tā zuìjìn zěnme yàng? How has he been doing?
　怎样(樣) zěnyàng[副] how

增 zēng[动] increase
　增加 zēngjiā[动] increase
　增长(長) zēngzhǎng[动] increase

赠(贈) zèng[动] present ▶捐赠 juānzèng donate

赠(贈)品 zèngpǐn[名] gift

扎(紮) zhā[动] 1(刺) prick 2(住下) set up camp 3(钻进) plunge into
　扎(紮)实(實) zhāshi[形] 1(结实) sturdy 2(实在) solid

炸 zhá[动] fry
　→ see also/另见 zhà

炸 zhà[动] 1(爆破) blow ... up 2(破裂) explode 3(逃离) run scared
　→ see also/另见 zhá
　炸弹(彈) zhàdàn[名] bomb
　炸药(藥) zhàyào[名] explosive

摘 zhāi[动] 1(取) pick 2(选) select 3(借) borrow

窄 zhǎi[形] 1(不宽敞) narrow 2(气量小) narrow-minded 3(不宽裕) hard up

粘 zhān[动] stick

盏(盞) zhǎn I[名] small cup II[量] ▷一盏灯 yī zhǎn dēng a lamp
▌ measure word, used for lamps and lights

展 zhǎn I[动] 1(进行) develop 2(施展) give free rein to 3(暂缓) postpone II[名] exhibition
　展出 zhǎnchū[动] exhibit
　展开(開) zhǎnkāi[动] 1(张开) spread 2(进行) develop
　展览(覽) zhǎnlǎn[名] exhibition
　展品 zhǎnpǐn[名] exhibit

崭(嶄) zhǎn see below/见下文
　崭(嶄)新 zhǎnxīn[形] brand-new

占(佔) zhàn[动](占用) occupy

战(戰) zhàn I[名] war II[动] 1(战斗) fight 2(发抖) shiver
　战(戰)斗(鬥) zhàndòu[动] fight
　战(戰)胜(勝) zhànshèng[动] overcome
　战(戰)士 zhànshì[名] soldier
　战(戰)争(爭) zhànzhēng[名] war

站 zhàn I[动] 1(站立) stand 2(停下) stop II[名] 1(停车地点) stop ▷ 公共汽车站 gōnggòng qìchēzhàn bus stop 2(服务机构) centre(英), center(美)

张(張) zhāng I[动] 1(打开) open 2(展开) extend ▷ 扩张 kuòzhāng stretch 3(夸大) exaggerate ▷ 夸张 kuāzhāng exaggerate 4(看) look 5(开业) open for business 6(陈设) lay ... on II[量] 1(指平的物体) ▷ 一张海报 yī zhāng hǎibào a poster ▷ 一张书桌 yī zhāng shūzhuō a desk 2(指嘴或脸) ▷ 一张大嘴 yī zhāng dà zuǐ a big mouth ▷ 一张脸 yī zhāng liǎn a face

| measure word, used for flat objects such as newspaper, maps, paintings, cards, tickets, pancakes; furniture such as beds, desks, sofas; mouths and faces

章 zhāng [名] 1(作品) article ▷ 文章 wénzhāng article 2(章节) chapter 3(条理) order 4(章程) regulation ▷ 宪章 xiànzhāng charter 5(图章) seal 6(标志) badge(英), button(美)

长(長) zhǎng I[形] 1(大) older ▷ 他年长我3岁。 Tā nián zhǎng wǒ sān suì. He's three years older than me. 2(排行第一) oldest ▷ 长兄 zhǎngxiōng oldest brother II[名] 1(年长者) 兄长 xiōngzhǎng elder brother 2(头领) head ▷ 校长 xiàozhǎng head teacher III[动] 1(生) form 2(发育) grow 3(增加) acquire → see also/另见 cháng

涨(漲) zhǎng [动] increase

掌 zhǎng I[名] 1(手掌) palm 2(人的脚掌) sole 3(动物的脚掌) foot 4(掌形物) ▷ 仙人掌 xiānrénzhǎng cactus 5(U型铁) horseshoe 6(鞋掌) sole II[动] 1(打) slap 2(钉) sole 3(主持) be in charge of 掌握 zhǎngwò [动] control

丈 zhàng [名] (长度单位) Chinese unit of length, equal to 3.3 metres 丈夫 zhàngfu [名] husband

帐(帳) zhàng [名] (布幔) curtain ▷ 蚊帐 wénzhàng mosquito net

帐(帳)篷 zhàngpeng [名] tent

账(賬) zhàng [名] 1(账目) accounts (pl) 2(账簿) ledger 3(债务) credit ▷ 赊账 shēzhàng buy on credit 账(賬)单(單) zhàngdān [名] bill 账(賬)号(號) zhànghào [名] account number

障 zhàng I[名] barrier II[动] hinder 障碍(礙) zhàng'ài I[动] hinder II[名] obstacle

招 zhāo I[动] 1(挥动) beckon 2(招收) recruit 3(引来) attract 4(惹怒) provoke 5(坦白) confess II[名] 1(计谋) trick 2(指下棋) move 招待 zhāodài [动] entertain ▷ 招待会 zhāodàihuì reception 招呼 zhāohu [动] 1(呼唤) call 2(问候) greet 3(吩咐) tell

着(著) zháo [动] 1(挨) touch 2(受到) be affected by 3(燃烧) be lit 4(入睡) fall asleep 着(著)急 zháojí [形] worried

找 zhǎo [动] 1(寻找) look for 2(退余额) give change ▷ 找钱 zhǎoqián give change 3(求见) call on

召 zhào [动] summon 召开(開) zhàokāi [动] hold

照 zhào I[动] 1(照射) light up 2(映照) reflect 3(拍摄) take a photograph 4(照料) look after 5(对照) contrast 6(遵照) refer to ▷ 参照 cānzhào consult 7(明白) understand II[名] 1(照片) photograph 2(执照) licence(英), license(美) III[介] 1(按照) according to 2(向着) in the direction of 照常 zhàocháng [副] as usual 照顾(顧) zhàogù [动] 1(照料) look after 2(考虑) consider 照看 zhàokàn [动] look after 照料 zhàoliào [动] take care of 照片 zhàopiàn [名] photograph 照相 zhàoxiàng [动] take a picture 照相机(機) zhàoxiàngjī [名] camera

折 zhé I [动] 1 (折断) break 2 (损失) lose 3 (弯曲) wind 4 (回转) turn back 5 (使信服) convince 6 (折合) convert ... into 7 (折叠) fold II [名] 1 (折子) notebook ▶ 存折 cúnzhé bank book 2 (折扣) discount
→ see also/另见 shé

折叠 zhédié [动] fold

折扣 zhékòu [名] discount

折磨 zhémó [动] torment

哲 zhé I [形] wise II [名] sage

哲学(學) zhéxué [名] philosophy

这(這) zhè [代] (指人或事物) this

这(這)边(邊) zhèbian [副] here

这(這)个(個) zhège [代] this ▷ 这个可比那个好多了。Zhège kě bǐ nàge hǎo duō le. This one is much better than that one.

这(這)么(麼) zhème [代] 1 (程度) so ▷ 今天这么热。Jīntiān zhème rè. It's so hot today. 2 (指方式) such ▷ 我看就应该这么做。Wǒ kàn jiù yīnggāi zhème zuò. I think it should be done this way.

这(這)儿(兒) zhèr [副] here

这(這)些 zhèxiē [代] these (pl)

这(這)样(樣) zhèyàng [代] 1 (指程度) so ▷ 乡村的风景这样美。Xiāngcūn de fēngjǐng zhèyàng měi. The scenery in the countryside is so beautiful. 2 (指状态) such ▷ 再这样下去可不行。Zài zhèyàng xiàqù kě bùxíng. It really won't do to carry on like this.

针(針) zhēn [名] 1 (工具) needle 2 (针状物) ▶ 表针 biǎozhēn hand (on watch) ▶ 别针 biézhēn safety pin 3 (针剂) injection 4 (缝合) stitch

针(針)对(對) zhēnduì [动] 1 (对准) be aimed at 2 (按照) have ... in mind

真 zhēn I [形] true ▶ 真话 zhēnhuà truth ▶ 真品 zhēnpǐn genuine product II [副] really ▷ 他真勇敢。Tā zhēn yǒnggǎn. He is really brave.

真的 zhēnde [副] really

真理 zhēnlǐ [名] truth

真实(實) zhēnshí [形] true

真正 zhēnzhèng [形] true

枕 zhěn I [名] pillow II [动] rest one's head on

枕头(頭) zhěntou [名] pillow

阵(陣) zhèn [名] 1 (军) (阵形) battle formation 2 (军) (阵地) position 3 (时间) a while

振 zhèn [动] 1 (振动) vibrate 2 (振作) boost

振动(動) zhèndòng [动] vibrate

镇(鎮) zhèn I [名] 1 (城镇) town 2 (重地) garrison II [动] 1 (抑制) suppress 2 (守卫) guard 3 (安定) calm 4 (冷却) cool III [形] calm ▶ 镇静 zhènjìng calm

镇(鎮)定 zhèndìng [形] calm

正 zhēng see below/见下文
→ see also/另见 zhèng

正月 zhēngyuè [名] first month of the lunar year

争(爭) zhēng [动] 1 (争夺) contend 2 (争论) argue

争(爭)论(論) zhēnglùn [动] argue

争(爭)取 zhēngqǔ [动] strive for

征 zhēng I [动] 1 (征讨) mount a military expedition 2 (召集) draft ▶ 征兵 zhēngbīng conscript 3 (征收) levy ▶ 征税 zhēngshuì levy taxes 4 (征求) solicit ▶ 征订 zhēngdìng solicit subscriptions II [名] 1 (征程) journey ▶ 长征 chángzhēng the Long March 2 (迹象) sign ▶ 特征 tèzhēng feature

征服 zhēngfú [动] conquer

征(徵)求 zhēngqiú [动] solicit

征(徵)兆 zhēngzhào [名] sign

睁(睜) zhēng [动] open

蒸 zhēng [动] 1 (指烹饪方法) steam 2 (蒸发) evaporate

蒸气(氣) zhēngqì [名] vapour (英), vapor (美)

蒸汽 zhēngqì [名] steam

整 zhěng I[形] 1(完整) whole 2(规整) tidy II[动] 1(整理) sort ... out 2(修理) repair 3(刁难) punish

整个(個) zhěnggè [形] whole

整理 zhěnglǐ [动] sort ... out

整齐(齊) zhěngqí [形] 1(有序的) orderly 2(均匀的) even

正 zhèng I[形] 1(不偏不斜) straight ▷ 正前方 zhèng qiánfāng directly ahead ▷ 这照片挂得不正。Zhè zhàopiàn guà de bù zhèng. This photograph is not hung straight. 2(居中的) main 3(正面) right 4(正直) upright ▷ 公正 gōngzhèng just 5(正当) right ▷ 正轨 zhèngguǐ the right track 6(纯正) pure ▷ 这道菜的味儿不正。Zhè dào cài de wèir bù zhèng. This dish does not taste authentic. 7(规范的) regular 8(主要的) principal ▷ 正餐 zhèngcān main meal 9(指图形) regular 10(物) positive 11(数)(大于零的) positive ▷ 正数 zhèngshù positive number II[动] 1(使不歪) straighten 2(改正) put ... right III[副] 1(恰好) just 2(正在) right now ▷ 天正刮着风。Tiān zhèng guāzhe fēng. It's windy right now.
→ see also/另见 zhēng

正常 zhèngcháng [形] normal

正当(當) zhèngdàng [形] legitimate

正念 zhèngniàn [名] mindfulness

正确(確) zhèngquè [形] correct

正式 zhèngshì [形] official

正在 zhèngzài [副] right now

证(證) zhèng I[动] prove II[名] 1(证据) evidence ▷ 物证 wùzhèng material evidence 2(证件) ▷ 身份证 shēnfènzhèng identity card

证(證)明 zhèngmíng I[动] prove II[名] certificate

政 zhèng [名] 1(政治) politics (sg) 2(事务) affairs (pl)

政策 zhèngcè [名] policy

政党(黨) zhèngdǎng [名] political party

政府 zhèngfǔ [名] government

政权(權) zhèngquán [名] political power

政治 zhèngzhì [名] politics (sg)

挣(掙) zhèng [动] 1(赚得) earn ▷ 挣钱 zhèngqián earn money 2(摆脱) break free

之 zhī [助] (的) ▷ 父母之爱 fùmǔ zhī ài parental love

之后(後) zhīhòu [介] after

之间(間) zhījiān [介] 1(指两者) between 2(指三者或三者以上) among

之前 zhīqián [介] before

之上 zhīshàng [介] above

之下 zhīxià [介] below

之一 zhī yī [代] one of

之中 zhīzhōng [介] amid

支 zhī I[动] 1(支撑) prop ... up 2(伸出) raise 3(支持) bear 4(调度) send 5(付出) pay ... out 6(领取) get II[量] 1(指乐曲) ▷ 一支钢琴曲 yī zhī gāngqínqǔ a piano tune 2(指细长物) ▷ 一支钢笔 yī zhī gāngbǐ a pen 3(指队伍) ▷ 一支部队 yī zhī bùduì an army unit

▍measure word, used for songs, tunes, troops and stick-like objects

支持 zhīchí [动] 1(鼓励) support 2(支撑) hold out

支出 zhīchū I[动] spend II[名] expenditure

支付 zhīfù [动] pay

支票 zhīpiào [名] cheque (英), check (美) ▷ 把支票兑付成现金 bǎ zhīpiào duìhuànchéng xiànjīn cash a cheque

支援 zhīyuán [动] help

只(隻) zhī [量] ▷ 一只拖鞋 yī zhī tuōxié a slipper ▷ 两只小船 liǎng zhī xiǎochuán two boats ▷ 小鸟 sān zhī xiǎo niǎo three birds
→ see also/另见 zhǐ

▍measure word, used for one of a pair such as gloves, eyes, feet; also used for animals, insects, birds and boats

芝 zhī see below/见下文

芝麻 zhīma [名] sesame

枝 zhī [名] branch

知 zhī I [动] 1 (知道) know 2 (使知道) inform II [名] knowledge
知道 zhīdào [动] know ▷ 这事我可不知道。Zhè shì wǒ kě bù zhīdào. I really know nothing about this.
知识(識) zhīshi [名] knowledge

织(織) zhī [动] knit

蜘 zhī see below/见下文
蜘蛛 zhīzhū [名] spider

执(執) zhí I [动] 1 (拿着) hold 2 (执掌) take charge of 3 (坚持) stick to 4 (执行) carry out II [名] written acknowledgment ▷ 回执 huízhí receipt
执(執)行 zhíxíng [动] carry out
执(執)照 zhízhào [名] licence (英), license (美)

直 zhí I [形] 1 (不弯曲) straight 2 (竖的) vertical 3 (公正) upstanding 4 (直爽) candid II [动] straighten III [副] 1 (直接) straight 2 (不断地) continuously 3 (简直) simply
直到 zhídào [介] until
直接 zhíjiē [形] direct
直升机(機) zhíshēngjī [名] helicopter

侄(姪) zhí [名] nephew
侄(姪)女 zhínǚ [名] niece
侄(姪)子 zhízi [名] nephew

值 zhí I [名] 1 (价值) value 2 (数) value II [动] 1 (值得) be worth 2 (碰上) just happen to be 3 (轮到) be on duty
值班 zhíbān [动] be on duty
值得 zhídé [动] be worth ▷ 这书值得买。Zhè shū zhídé mǎi. This book is worth buying.

职(職) zhí [名] 1 (职位) post 2 (职责) duty
职(職)工 zhígōng [名] 1 (员工) staff 2 (工人) blue-collar worker
职(職)业(業) zhíyè [名] occupation
职(職)员(員) zhíyuán [名] member of staff

植 zhí [动] 1 (栽种) plant 2 (树立) establish

植物 zhíwù [名] plant ▷ 草本植物 cǎoběn zhíwù herbs

止 zhǐ I [动] 1 (停止) stop 2 (截止) end II [副] only

只 zhǐ [副] only ▷ 我只在周末有时间。Wǒ zhǐ zài zhōumò yǒu shíjiān. I only have time at the weekend.
→ see also/另见 zhī
只好 zhǐhǎo [副] have to
只是 zhǐshì I [副] merely II [连] but
只要 zhǐyào [连] so long as
只有 zhǐyǒu [副] only

纸(紙) zhǐ [名] paper
纸(紙)币(幣) zhǐbì [名] note (英), bill (美)

指 zhǐ I [名] finger ▷ 中指 zhōngzhǐ middle finger ▷ 无名指 wúmíngzhǐ ring finger II [动] 1 (对着) point to 2 (点明) point ... out 3 (针对) refer to 4 (依靠) rely on
指出 zhǐchū [动] point ... out
指导(導) zhǐdǎo [动] instruct
指挥(揮) zhǐhuī I [动] command II [名] 1 (指挥官) commander 2 (乐队指挥) conductor
指南针(針) zhǐnánzhēn [名] compass
指示 zhǐshì [动] instruct
指责(責) zhǐzé [动] criticize

至 zhì I [动] arrive II [介] to ▷ 从东至西 cóng dōng zhì xī from east to west III [副] 1 (至于) ▷ 至于 zhìyú as to 2 (最) extremely ▷ 至少 zhìshǎo at least
至今 zhìjīn [副] so far
至少 zhìshǎo [副] at least
至于(於) zhìyú [介] as to

制(製) zhì I [动] 1 (制造) make 2 (拟订) work ... out 3 (约束) restrict II [名] system
制订(訂) zhìdìng [动] work ... out
制定 zhìdìng [动] draw ... up
制度 zhìdù [名] system
制(製)造 zhìzào [动] 1 (物品) manufacture 2 (气氛、局势) create

制(製)作 zhìzuò [动] make ▷ 制作网页 zhìzuò wǎngyè create a web page ▷ 制作商 zhìzuòshāng manufacturer

质(質) zhì I [名] 1 (性质) nature ▶ 本质 běnzhì nature 2 (质量) quality 3 (物质) matter 4 (抵押品) pledge ▶ 人质 rénzhì hostage II [形] simple III [动] question ▶ 质疑 zhìyí cast doubt on

质(質)量 zhìliàng [名] 1 (物) mass 2 (优劣) quality

治 zhì [动] 1 (治理) control 2 (医治) cure 3 (消灭) exterminate 4 (惩办) punish 5 (研究) research

治安 zhì'ān [名] security ▶ 社会治安 shèhuì zhì'ān public order

治疗(療) zhìliáo [动] cure

秩 zhì [名] order

秩序 zhìxù [名] sequence

智 zhì I [形] wise II [名] wisdom

智慧 zhìhuì [名] intelligence

智力 zhìlì [名] intelligence

智商 zhìshāng [名] IQ

中 zhōng I [名] 1 (中心) centre (英), center (美) ▶ 中央 zhōngyāng central 2 (中国) China ▶ 中餐 zhōngcān Chinese food 3 (两端之间的) the middle ▶ 中层 zhōngcéng mid-level 4 (不偏不倚) impartial ▶ 适中 shìzhōng moderate 5 (在过程里的) course II [动] be suitable for

中国(國) Zhōngguó [名] China

中国(國)人 Zhōngguórén [名] Chinese person

中华(華) Zhōnghuá [名] China

中华(華)人民共和国(國) Zhōnghuá Rénmín Gònghéguó [名] People's Republic of China

中华人民共和国 Zhōnghuá Rénmín Gònghéguó

The People's Republic of China was declared in Tian'anmen Square on October 1st 1949 by Chairman Mao Zedong.

中间(間) zhōngjiān [名] 1 (中心) middle 2 (之间) ▷ 我站在他俩中间。 Wǒ zhàn zài tā liǎ zhōngjiān. I was standing in between the both of them.

中介 zhōngjiè [名] agency ▷ 房产中介 fángchǎn zhōngjiè estate agent

中年 zhōngnián [名] middle age

中秋节(節) Zhōngqiū Jié [名] Mid-Autumn Festival

中秋节 Zhōngqiū Jié

The Mid-Autumn Festival is celebrated on the 15th day of the 8th month of the Chinese lunar calendar. Traditionally families gather to observe the moon and eat 月饼 yuèbǐng, mooncakes. The roundness of both the full moon and the cakes symbolize the unity of the family.

中文 Zhōngwén [名] Chinese

中午 zhōngwǔ [名] noon

中心 zhōngxīn [名] centre (英), center (美)

中学(學) zhōngxué [名] high school (英), senior school (美)

中旬 zhōngxún [名] the middle ten days of a month

中央 zhōngyāng [名] 1 (中心地) centre (英), center (美) 2 (最高机构) central government

中药(藥) zhōngyào [名] Chinese medicine

中医(醫) zhōngyī [名] 1 (医学) traditional Chinese medicine 2 (医生) doctor of traditional Chinese medicine

终(終) zhōng I [动] die II [副] in the end III [形] all ▶ 终身 zhōngshēn all one's life

终(終)点(點) zhōngdiǎn [名] 1 (尽头) terminus 2 (体育) finish

终(終)于(於) zhōngyú [副] finally

终(終)止 zhōngzhǐ [动] stop

钟(鐘) zhōng [名] 1 (响器) bell 2 (记时器) clock 3 (指时间) ▷ 5点钟 wǔ diǎn zhōng five o'clock

钟(鐘)表(錶) zhōngbiǎo [名] clocks and watches

钟(鐘)头(頭) zhōngtóu [名] hour

肿(腫) zhǒng [动] swell

种(種) zhǒng I[名] 1(物种) species (sg) 2(人种) race 3(种子) seed 4(胆量) courage II[量] kind, type ▷各种商品 gè zhǒng shāngpǐn all kinds of commodities ▷3种选择 sān zhǒng xuǎnzé three choices
→ see also/另见 zhòng

种(種)子 zhǒngzi [名] seed

种(種)族 zhǒngzú [名] race

种(種) zhòng [动] sow ▶种田 zhòngtián farm ▶种痘 zhòngdòu vaccinate
→ see also/另见 zhǒng

众(眾) zhòng I[形] numerous II[名] multitude

众(眾)筹(籌) zhòngchóu [名] crowdfunding

重 zhòng I[名] weight II[形] 1(重量大) heavy 2(程度深) strong 3(重要) important ▶重任 zhòngrèn important task 4(不轻率) serious ▶稳重 wěnzhòng staid III[动] stress ▶注重 zhùzhòng pay attention to
→ see also/另见 chóng

重大 zhòngdà [形] major

重点(點) zhòngdiǎn [名] key point

重量 zhòngliàng [名] weight

重视(視) zhòngshì [动] attach importance to

重要 zhòngyào [形] important

周 zhōu I[名] 1(圈子) circle 2(星期) week II[动] 1(环绕) circle 2(接济) give ... financial help III[形] 1(普遍) widespread 2(完备) thorough

周到 zhōudào [形] thorough

周(週)末 zhōumò [名] weekend

周(週)围(圍) zhōuwéi [名] the vicinity

猪(豬) zhū [名] pig

猪(豬)肉 zhūròu [名] pork

竹 zhú [名] bamboo

竹子 zhúzi [名] bamboo

逐 zhú I[动] 1(追赶) chase 2(驱逐) drive ... away II[副] one after another

逐步 zhúbù [副] step by step

逐渐(漸) zhújiàn [副] gradually

主 zhǔ I[名] 1(接待者) host ▶东道主 dōngdàozhǔ host 2(所有者) owner ▶房主 fángzhǔ home-owner 3(当事人) person concerned 4(主宰) idea 5(上帝) God II[形] main III[动] 1(主持) take charge ▶主办 zhǔbàn take charge of 2(主张) be in favour (英) 或 favor (美) of 3(从自身出发) look at ... subjectively ▶主观 zhǔguān subjective

主动(動) zhǔdòng [形] voluntary

主观(觀) zhǔguān [形] subjective

主人 zhǔrén [名] 1(接待者) host 2(雇佣者) master ▶女主人 nǚzhǔrén mistress 3(所有者) owner

主任 zhǔrèn [名] director

主题(題) zhǔtí [名] 1(主旨) theme 2(指社交媒体) thread

主席 zhǔxí [名] chairperson

主要 zhǔyào [形] major

主义(義) zhǔyì [名] doctrine ▶社会主义 shèhuì zhǔyì socialism ▶浪漫主义 làngmàn zhǔyì romanticism

主意 zhǔyi [名] 1(办法) idea 2(主见) opinion

主张(張) zhǔzhāng I[动] advocate II[名] standpoint

煮 zhǔ [动] boil

煮饭(飯) zhǔ fàn [动] cook

助 zhù [动] help

助手 zhùshǒu [名] assistant

住 zhù [动] 1(居住) live 2(停住) stop 3(用作动词补语)

住宿 zhùsù [动] stay

住院 zhùyuàn [动] be hospitalized

住宅 zhùzhái [名] house

住址 zhùzhǐ [名] address

注 zhù I[动] 1(灌入) pour ▶注射 zhùshè inject 2(集中) concentrate 3(解释) explain II[名] 1(记载) record ▶注册 zhùcè enrol (英), enroll (美) 2(赌注) bet

注意 zhùyì [动] be careful

祝 zhù [动] wish
祝贺(賀) zhùhè [动] congratulate

著 zhù I [形] marked II [动] 1 (显出) show 2 (写作) write III [名] work
著名 zhùmíng [形] famous
著作 zhùzuò [名] writings (pl)

抓 zhuā [动] 1 (拿住) grab 2 (划过) scratch 3 (捉拿) catch 4 (着重) take control of 5 (吸引) attract 6 (把握住) seize
抓紧(緊) zhuājǐn [动] make the most of

专(專) zhuān [动] 1 (集中) concentrate 2 (独占) dominate ▶ 专卖 zhuānmài monopoly
专(專)家 zhuānjiā [名] expert
专(專)门(門) zhuānmén I [形] specialized II [副] especially
专(專)心 zhuānxīn [形] single-minded
专(專)业(業) zhuānyè [名] special field of study

砖(磚) zhuān [名] brick

转(轉) zhuǎn [动] 1 (改换) turn ▶ 转弯 zhuǎnwān turn a corner ▶ 转学 zhuǎnxué change schools 2 (传送) pass ... on ▶ 转送 zhuǎnsòng deliver
→ see also/另见 zhuàn
转(轉)变(變) zhuǎnbiàn [动] transform
转(轉)告 zhuǎngào [动] pass on

转(轉) zhuàn [动] turn
→ see also/另见 zhuǎn

赚(賺) zhuàn [动] 1 (获得利润) make a profit 2 (挣钱) earn

庄(莊) zhuāng [名] 1 (指村庄) village 2 (指土地) manor ▶ 庄园 zhuāngyuán manor 3 (指商店) store ▶ 茶庄 cházhuāng teahouse ▶ 饭庄 fànzhuāng restaurant
庄(莊)稼 zhuāngjia [名] crops (pl)
庄(莊)严(嚴) zhuāngyán [形] solemn

装(裝) zhuāng I [动] 1 (修饰) dress up ▶ 装饰 zhuāngshì decorate 2 (假装) pretend 3 (装载) load 4 (装配) install II [名] (服装) clothing ▶ 套装 tàozhuāng matching outfit

状(狀) zhuàng [名] 1 (形状) shape 2 (情况) state ▶ 症状 zhèngzhuàng symptom 3 (诉状) complaint ▶ 告状 gàozhuàng bring a case 4 (证书) certificate ▶ 奖状 jiǎngzhuàng certificate
状(狀)况(況) zhuàngkuàng [名] condition
状(狀)态(態) zhuàngtài [名] condition

撞 zhuàng [动] 1 (碰撞) collide 2 (碰见) bump into 3 (试探) try 4 (闯) dash
撞车(車) zhuàngchē [动] 1 (车辆相撞) collide 2 (发生分歧) clash

追 zhuī [动] 1 (追赶) chase 2 (追究) investigate 3 (追求) seek 4 (回溯) reminisce
追捕 zhuībǔ [动] pursue and capture
追求 zhuīqiú [动] 1 (争取) seek 2 (求爱) chase after

准 zhǔn I [动] 1 (准许) allow ▶ 批准 pīzhǔn ratify 2 (依据) be in accord with II [名] standard III [形] 1 (准确) accurate ▶ 准时 zhǔnshí punctual 2 (类似) quasi
准(準)备(備) zhǔnbèi [动] 1 (筹划) prepare 2 (打算) plan
准(準)确(確) zhǔnquè [形] accurate
准(準)时(時) zhǔnshí [形] punctual

捉 zhuō [动] 1 (握住) clutch 2 (捕捉) catch

桌 zhuō I [名] table ▶ 书桌 shūzhuō desk II [量] table ▶ 一桌菜 yī zhuō cài a table covered in dishes
桌子 zhuōzi [名] table

咨 zī [动] consult
咨询(詢) zīxún [动] seek advice from

姿 zī [名] 1 (容貌) looks (pl) 2 (姿势) posture
姿势(勢) zīshì [名] posture

资(資) zī I [名] 1 (钱财) money ▶ 外资 wàizī foreign capital ▶ 邮资 yóuzī postage 2 (资质) ability ▶ 天资 tiānzī natural ability 3 (资格) qualifications (pl) ▶ 资历 zīlì record of service II [动] 1 (资助) aid ... financially 2 (提供) provide

资(資)本 zīběn [名] (优势)

资(資)格 zīgé [名] 1 (条件) qualifications (pl) 2 (身份) seniority

资(資)金 zījīn [名] funds (pl)

资(資)料 zīliào [名] 1 (必需品) means (pl) 2 (材料) material

资(資)源 zīyuán [名] resources (pl)

子 zǐ I [名] 1 (儿子) son ▶ 母子 mǔzǐ mother and son 2 (人) person ▶ 男子 nánzǐ man 3 (种子) seed ▶ 瓜子 guāzǐ melon seed 4 (卵) egg ▶ 鱼子 yúzǐ fish roe 5 (粒状物) ▶ 棋子 qízǐ chess piece 6 (铜子) coin II [形] 1 (幼小) young 2 (附属) affiliated

子女 zǐnǚ [名] children

仔 zǐ [形] young

仔细(細) zǐxì [形] 1 (细心) thorough 2 (小心) careful

紫 zǐ [形] purple

自 zì I [代] oneself II [副] certainly III [介] from

自从(從) zìcóng [介] since

自动(動) zìdòng [形] 1 (主动的) voluntary 2 (机械的) automatic

自动(動)取款机(機) zìdòng qǔkuǎnjī [名] cashpoint (英), ATM (美)

自费(費) zìfèi [形] self-funded

自己 zìjǐ I [代] oneself II [形] our

自觉(覺) zìjué I [动] be aware of II [形] conscientious

自来(來)水 zìláishuǐ [名] tap water

自拍 zìpāi [动] take a selfie

自然 zìrán I [名] nature II [形] natural III [副] naturally

自杀(殺) zìshā [动] commit suicide

自私 zìsī [形] selfish

自我 zìwǒ [代] self

自信 zìxìn [形] self-confident

自行车(車) zìxíngchē [名] bicycle

自学(學) zìxué [动] teach oneself

自由 zìyóu I [名] freedom II [形] free

自愿(願) zìyuàn [动] volunteer

自助餐 zìzhùcān [名] self-service buffet

字 zì [名] 1 (文字) character 2 (字音) pronunciation 3 (书法作品) calligraphy ▶ 字画 zìhuà painting and calligraphy 4 (字体) script 5 (字据) written pledge

字典 zìdiǎn [名] dictionary

字母 zìmǔ [名] letter

宗 zōng [名] 1 (祖宗) ancestor 2 (家族) clan 3 (宗派) school ▶ 正宗 zhèngzōng orthodox school 4 (宗旨) purpose

宗教 zōngjiào [名] religion

综(綜) zōng [动] summarize ▶ 综述 zōngshù sum … up

综(綜)合 zōnghé I [动] synthesize II [形] comprehensive

总(總) zǒng I [动] gather ▶ 总括 zǒngkuò sum … up II [形] 1 (全部的) total 2 (为首的) chief ▶ 总部 zǒngbù headquarters (pl) III [副] 1 (一直) always 2 (毕竟) after all

总(總)理 zǒnglǐ [名] premier

总(總)是 zǒngshì [副] always

总(總)算 zǒngsuàn [副] 1 (最终) finally 2 (大体上) all things considered

总(總)统(統) zǒngtǒng [名] president

粽 zòng [名] see below/见下文

粽子 zòngzi [名] glutinous rice dumplings

粽子 zòngzi

 * The traditional festival food for the
 * Dragon Boat Festival is large
 * pyramid-shaped glutinous rice
 * dumplings wrapped in reed or
 * bamboo leaves, often with sweet or
 * meat fillings.

走 zǒu [动] 1 (行走) walk ▶ 走路 zǒulù walk ▷ 出去走走 chūqù zǒuzou go out for a walk 2 (跑动) run 3 (运行) move 4 (离开) leave ▷ 我先走。 Wǒ xiān zǒu. I'll be off. 5 (来往) visit 6 (通过) go through 7 (漏出) leak 8 (改变) depart from 9 (去世) die

走道 zǒudào [名] path

走动(動) zǒudòng [动] 1 (行走) walk about 2 (来往) visit each other

走后(後)门(門) zǒu hòumén use one's connections

走廊 zǒuláng [名] corridor

租 zū I [动] 1(租用)(房屋) rent 2(租用)(汽车、自行车、录像带) hire(英), rent(美) 3(出租) rent out II [名] rent ▸ 房租 fángzū rent

足 zú I [名] foot ▸ 足迹 zújì footprint II [形] ample ▸ 充足 chōngzú adequate III [副] 1(达到某种程度) as much as 2(足以) enough

足够(夠) zúgòu [动] be enough

足球 zúqiú [名] football

阻 zǔ [动] block

阻止 zǔzhǐ [动] stop

组(組) zǔ I [动] form II [名] group

组(組)成 zǔchéng [动] form

组(組)织(織) zǔzhī I [动] organize II [名] 1(集体) organization 2(指器官) tissue 3(指纱线) weave

祖 zǔ [名] 1(祖辈) grandparent 2(祖宗) ancestor 3(首创者) founder

祖父 zǔfù [名] grandfather

祖国(國) zǔguó [名] motherland

祖母 zǔmǔ [名] grandmother

祖先 zǔxiān [名] ancestors (pl)

钻(鑽) zuān [动] 1(打洞) drill 2(穿过) go through 3(钻研) bury one's head in → see also/另见 zuàn

钻(鑽)研 zuānyán [动] study ... intensively

钻(鑽) zuàn [名] 1(工具) drill 2(钻石) diamond → see also/另见 zuān

钻(鑽)石 zuànshí [名] 1(金刚石) diamond 2(宝石) jewel

嘴 zuǐ [名] 1(口) mouth 2(嘴状物) ▸ 茶壶嘴 cháhú zuǐ spout of a teapot 3(话) words (pl) ▸ 插嘴 chāzuǐ interrupt

最 zuì [副] most ▸ 最难忘的海外之旅 zuì nánwàng de hǎiwài zhī lǚ the most unforgettable trip abroad ▸ 这家饭店服务最好。Zhè jiā fàndiàn fúwù zuì hǎo. The service at this restaurant is the best.

最初 zuìchū I [形] initial II [副] at first

最好 zuìhǎo I [形] best II [副] had better

最后(後) zuìhòu I [形] final II [副] at last

最近 zuìjìn [形] recent

罪 zuì I [名] 1(恶行) crime ▸ 犯罪 fànzuì commit a crime 2(过失) blame 3(苦难) hardship 4(刑罚) punishment ▸ 死罪 sǐzuì death sentence II [动] blame

罪犯 zuìfàn [名] criminal

醉 zuì I [形] 1(饮酒过量的) drunk ▸ 醉鬼 zuìguǐ drunk 2(用酒泡制) steeped in wine II [动] drink too much

尊 zūn I [形] senior II [动] respect

尊敬 zūnjìng [动] respect

尊重 zūnzhòng I [动] respect II [形] serious ▸ 放尊重些！Fàng zūnzhòng xiē! Behave yourself!

遵 zūn [动] follow

遵守 zūnshǒu [动] observe

昨 zuó [名] 1(昨天) yesterday ▸ 昨日 zuórì yesterday 2(过去) the past

昨天 zuótiān [名] yesterday

左 zuǒ I [名] left ▸ 左边 zuǒbian the left II [形] 1(相反的) conflicting 2(进步的) leftist ▸ 左派 zuǒpài left-wing

左边(邊) zuǒbian [名] the left side

左右 zuǒyòu I [名] 1(左和右) left and right 2(跟随者) attendants (pl) 3(上下) ▸ 他身高1点75米左右。Tā shēngāo yī diǎn qī wǔ mǐ zuǒyòu. He is about 1.75 metres (英) 或 meters (美) tall. II [动] control

作 zuò I [动] 1(起) rise 2(写) write ▸ 作家 zuòjiā writer ▸ 作曲 zuòqǔ compose music 3(装) pretend 4(犯) do 5(当) take ... as ▸ 作废 zuòfèi become invalid 6(发作) feel II [名] work ▸ 杰作 jiézuò masterpiece

作罢(罷) zuòbà [动] drop

作家 zuòjiā [名] writer

作品 zuòpǐn [名] work

作为(為) zuòwéi I [名] 1 (行为) action 2 (成绩) accomplishment 3 (干头儿) scope II [动] (当作) regard ... as

作文 zuòwén [动] write an essay

作业(業) zuòyè I [名] work II [动] do work

作用 zuòyòng I [动] affect II [名] 1 (影响) effect 2 (活动) action

作者 zuòzhě [名] author

坐 zuò [动] 1 (坐下) sit ▷ 坐在窗口 zuò zài chuāngkǒu sit by the window 2 (乘坐) travel by ▷ 坐飞机 zuò fēijī travel by plane

座 zuò I [名] 1 (坐位) seat ▷ 座号 zuòhào seat number 2 (垫子) stand 3 (星座) constellation ▷ 双子座 Shuāngzǐ Zuò Gemini II [量] ▷ 一座山 yī zuò shān a mountain ▷ 三座桥 sān zuò qiáo three bridges ▷ 五座办公楼 wǔ zuò bàngōnglóu five office buildings
measure word, used for mountains, buildings, bridges, etc.

座谈(談) zuòtán [动] discuss

座位 zuòwèi [名] seat

做 zuò [动] 1 (制造) make 2 (写作) write 3 (从事) do ▷ 做生意 zuò shēngyi do business 4 (举行) hold ▷ 做寿 zuòshòu hold a birthday party 5 (充当) be ▷ 做大会主席 zuò dàhuì zhǔxí chair a meeting 6 (用作) be used as 7 (结成) become ▷ 做朋友 zuò péngyou be friends

做法 zuòfǎ [名] method

做饭(飯) zuòfàn [动] cook

做客 zuòkè [动] be a guest

做梦(夢) zuòmèng [动] dream

Chinese
in Action

1	Greetings	2
2	Telephone	6
3	Correspondence	8
4	Numbers	12
5	Date	14
6	Time	16

1 Greetings

1.1 Meeting people

It is very important to use the appropriate form of greeting in China. As with other cultures, the way that you greet somebody will depend on whether you know them or whether they are a stranger. The most common greeting is:

你好	(nǐ hǎo), *or*
您好	(nín hǎo)

The form 您好 (nín hǎo) is more formal and should be used when you want to show particular respect.

Chinese people show great respect for the wisdom and experience of their elders. The senior people present will usually initiate the greetings, and you should greet the oldest, most senior person before any others.

1.2 Some typical greetings

你好！(nǐ hǎo)	*Hello!*
嗨！(hēi)	*Hi!*
喂！(wèi)	*Hello! (usually on the phone)*
早上好！(zǎoshang hǎo)	*Good morning!*
早！(zǎo)	*Morning!*
最近身体怎么样？(zuìjìn shēntǐ zěnmeyàng)	
	How have you been?
还不错，谢谢。(hái bùcuò, xièxie)	*Fine, thanks.*
好久不见！最近还好吗？(hǎojiǔ bù jiàn! zuìjìn hái hǎo ma?)	
	Long time no see! How are you doing?
很好，谢谢，你怎么样？(hěn hǎo, xièxie, nǐ zěnmeyàng)	
	Very well, thank you, and you?
挺好的，多谢。(tǐng hǎo de, duōxiè)	*Fine, thanks.*
棒极了！(bàng jí le)	*Great!*
一般。(yībān)	*So-so.*

1.3 Chinese names

Chinese family names are placed first, followed by the given name. For instance, in the name "Zhao Li," "Zhao" is the family name, "Li" the given name. Family names usually consist of one syllable, whereas given names can have either one or two syllables.

Chinese people call their close friends and family members by their given names. For example, "Ma Wenli" may be addressed by close friends as "Wenli."

In formal situations you should address Chinese people by their family name or full name and the appropriate courtesy title. Unlike English, professional, social, and family titles always follow the name:

Mr. Liu would be 刘先生 (Liú xiānsheng)

Mr. Li Nan 李楠先生 (Lǐ Nán xiānsheng)

Mrs. Liu 刘夫人 (Liú fūrén)

Miss Liu 刘小姐 (Liú xiǎojiě)

Ms. Liu 刘女士 (Liú nǚshì)

Dr. Ma would be 马医生 (Mǎ yīshēng)

Professor Xu would be 徐教授 (Xú jiàoshòu)

Chinese people will often address people by their surname followed by their job title, for example:

叶主任 (Yè zhǔrèn)　　Director Ye

林老师 (Lín lǎoshī)　　Teacher Lin

Most Chinese women continue using their maiden names even after marriage, but they may indicate their marital status by using 太太 (tàitai) or 夫人 (fūrén) with their maiden name. 小姐 (xiǎojiě) is a polite and common form of address for a woman. An older woman can be addressed as 大姐 (dàjiě).

If you want to address a group of people formally – for example, at a meeting – you say 女士们先生们 (nǚshìmen xiānshengmen) meaning 'Ladies and Gentlemen' (or just 女士们 ('Ladies') or 先生们 ('Gentlemen') if the group is not mixed).

When you are not sure about someone's name or title, you should address him or her as 先生 (xiānsheng) (Sir) or 女士 (nǚshì) (Madam or Miss).

1.4 Introductions

让我把你介绍给我的朋友们。
(ràng wǒ bǎ nǐ jièshào gěi wǒ de péngyoumen)
Let me introduce you to my friends.

我想让你认识一下我的丈夫。
(wǒ xiǎng ràng nǐ rènshi yīxià wǒ de zhàngfu)
I'd like you to meet my husband.

请允许我介绍一下到场的嘉宾。
(qǐng yǔnxǔ wǒ jièshào yīxià dàochǎng de jiābīn)
Please allow me to introduce these distinguished guests.

这是珍妮特。(zhè shì ɛhēnnítè) *This is Janet.*

In response:

很高兴见到您。(hěn gāoxìng jiàndào nín) *Pleased to meet you.*
嗨，你好。(hēi, nǐ hǎo) *Hi, how are you doing?*
您好。(nín hǎo) *How do you do?*

If you want to attract the attention of someone you do not know – for example, in the street or in a shop – you say 劳驾 (láojià).

1.5 Parting

The most common way to say goodbye to someone is 再见 (zàijiàn). Other alternatives are 回见 (huíjiàn) and 再会 (zàihuì).

再见！(zàijiàn) *Goodbye!*

再会！(zàihuì) *Bye!*

7点见。(qī diǎn jiàn) *See you at seven.*

晚安！(wǎn'ān) *Good night!*

明天见！(míngtiān jiàn) *See you tomorrow!*

星期一见！(xīngqīyī jiàn) *See you on Monday!*

"回见!" "好，再会" (huíjiàn – hǎo, zàihuì) *'See you later.'* – *'Okay, bye.'*

1.6 Business cards

Business/name cards are frequently used in business circles in China and will almost always be exchanged when meeting someone for the first time on business.

Cards should be held in both hands when they are being offered or received. When receiving another person's card, you should take the time to look at it attentively before putting it away.

Business cards are often printed in English on one side and Chinese on the other.

Huan Yu Import & Export Co. Ltd.

Wang Changhai   General Manager

Address: No. 15 Heping Road, Beijing, China
Zip Code: 100082
Tel.: +8610 64446666
Fax: +8610 64446688
E-mail: wangchanghai@huanyu.com

寰宇进出口有限责任公司

王长海   总经理

地址：北京市和平路15号
邮编：100082
电话：+8610 64446666
传真：+8610 64446688
E-mail: wangchanghai@huanyu.com

2   Telephone

2.1   Making a phone call

When Chinese people make a phone call, they ask for the person they wish to speak to by name. It is not the Chinese caller's habit to give their own name first when making or receiving a call.

When answering the telephone the standard response upon picking up the receiver is 喂 (wèi).

When giving telephone numbers, Chinese speakers normally read out the numbers one by one so that 020 7900 0283 would be read:

零二零 七九零零 零二八三
líng'èrlíng qījiǔlínglíng líng'èrbāsān

When making a phone call, you might want to say:

喂？(wèi) *Hello?*

请问…在吗？(qǐngwèn...zài ma) *Could I speak to ... please?*

是…吗？(shì...ma) *Is that ...?*

我怎么拨外线电话？(wǒ zěnme bō wàixiàn diànhuà) *How do I make an outside call?*

…的区号是多少？(...de qūhào shì duōshao) *What is the code for ... ?*

我5分钟后打回来。(wǒ wǔ fēnzhōng hòu dǎ huílái) *I'll call back in 5 minutes.*

他回来时，可否让他给我回电话？(tā huílái shí, kěfǒu ràng tā gěi wǒ huí diànhuà) *Could you ask him to call me when he gets back?*

对不起，我拨错号了。(duìbuqǐ, wǒ bōcuò hào le) *Sorry, I must have dialled the wrong number.*

电话掉线了。(diànhuà diàoxiàn le) *We were cut off.*

线路很不清楚。(xiànlù hěn bù qīngchu) *This is a very bad line.*

You might hear:

请讲。(qǐng jiǎng) *Speaking.*

请问您是哪位？(qǐngwèn nín shì nǎ wèi) *Who's speaking?*

请问您找哪位？(qǐngwèn nín zhǎo nǎ wèi) *Who would you like to speak to?*

请别挂断。(qǐng bié guàduàn) *Please hold (the line).*

没人接听。(méi rén jiētīng) *There's no reply.*

电话占线。(diànhuà zhànxiàn) *The line is engaged (Brit) or busy (US).*

请问您是哪位?(qǐngwèn nín shì nǎ wèi) *Who shall I say is calling?*

您要留言吗?(nín yào liúyán ma) *Would you like to leave a message?*

2.2 An example conversation

您好,这里是北京饭店。
Hello, Beijing Hotel.

请转二零一六房间分机,我找张先生。
Please could you put me through to room number 2016? I'd like to speak to Mr. Zhang.

好的,请稍等。
Hold on one moment, please.

他不在,您能帮我给他捎个话吗?
He doesn't seem to be in at the moment. Can I leave a message?

当然可以。
Of course.

请让他给约翰·史密斯回电话,电话号码是零零四四二零七三零六三八九二。
Could you ask him to call John Smith back? The phone number is 00442073063892.

好的。
Okay.

2.3 Useful telephone vocabulary

打电话 (dǎ diànhuà) *make a phone call*

电话号码 (diànhuà hàomǎ) *phone number*

分机号码 (fēnjī hàomǎ) *extension number*

市话 (shìhuà) *local call*

长途电话 (chángtú diànhuà) *national call*

国际长途电话 (guójì chángtú diànhuà) *international call*

3 Correspondence

3.1 Personal letters

Starting and ending a personal letter

Opening lines:
亲爱的妈妈: *Dear Mum*
小强: *Dear Xiao Qiang*

Closing lines:
祝身体健康! *Take care!*
祝万事如意! *All the best*

Sample letter

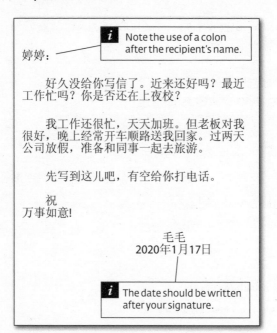

婷婷:

> *i* Note the use of a colon after the recipient's name.

　　好久没给你写信了。近来还好吗？最近工作忙吗？你是否还在上夜校？

　　我工作还很忙，天天加班。但老板对我很好，晚上经常开车顺路送我回家。过两天公司放假，准备和同事一起去旅游。

　　先写到这儿吧，有空给你打电话。

　　祝
万事如意!

毛毛
2020年1月17日

> *i* The date should be written after your signature.

Useful expressions

真高兴收到你的来信。*It was lovely to hear from you.*
对不起，没能及时给你回信，只因… *Sorry I didn't reply sooner but …*
代我向…问好。*Give my regards to …*
东东谨祝一切安好。*Dong Dong sends his best wishes.*
盼早日回信。*Looking forward to hearing from you.*

3.2 Formal letters

Starting and ending a formal letter

Opening lines:

致启者: *Dear Sir or Madam*

致有关人: *To whom it may concern*

Closing lines:

敬上 *Regards*

此致 敬礼! *Yours sincerely*

Sample letter

长江商贸公司
山东省青岛市市南区香港中路16号 （250920）

王先生：

 　　不胜感激您在10月14日的来信中确认收到旅游费的定金。

 　　可否告知余款的到期日？根据贵方提供信息，全部款项应于本月底付讫，我将尽早支付其余款项。

 　　此致
敬礼!

　　　　　　　　　　　　　　苏眉莉
　　　　　　　　　　　　　2019年10月25日

i Note that the closing line is split over two lines.

Useful expressions

现答复您…的来信。 *In reply to your letter of ...*

有关… *With reference to ...*

收到您…来信不胜感激。 *Thank you for your letter of ...*

我们荣幸地通知您… *We are pleased to inform you that ...*

我们很遗憾地通知您… *We regret to inform you that ...*

为…致信给您。 *I am writing to you to ...*

如需详情，尽请与我联系。 *If you require any further information, please do not hesitate to contact me.*

切盼回复。 *I look forward to hearing from you.*

3.3 Addressing an envelope in Chinese

You should start in the upper left-hand corner with the addressee's post code. The address is written in the middle of the envelope, followed by the name of the addressee.

Note that the address is written in the order:

> province, city
> street, house number
> addressee's name

The sender's address and name, followed by their postcode, should be written in the lower right-hand corner of the envelope.

Sample envelope

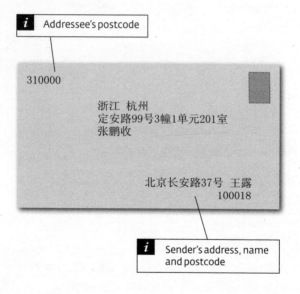

i Addressee's postcode

310000

浙江　杭州
定安路99号3幢1单元201室
张鹏收

北京长安路37号　王露
100018

i Sender's address, name and postcode

3.4 Email

Email is very popular in China for formal business purposes.

Sample email

收件人：		To:
抄送：		Cc:
密送：		Bcc:
主题：		Subject:

For more informal communication, the instant messenger tools, QQ and WeChat (微信) are the most popular platforms in China. QQ was originally designed for desktop (桌面) use, and contains a wide range of features including language-learning groups and apps. WeChat was designed specially for smartphones (智能手机) and mobile devices (移动设备). Both tools allow users to exchange messages, photos, and so on.

4 Numbers

4.1 Cardinal numbers

0	零 (líng)		40	四十 (sìshí)
1	一 (yī)		50	五十 (wǔshí)
2	二 (èr)		60	六十 (liùshí)
3	三 (sān)		70	七十 (qīshí)
4	四 (sì)		80	八十 (bāshí)
5	五 (wǔ)		90	九十 (jiǔshí)
6	六 (liù)		100	一百 (yībǎi)
7	七 (qī)			
8	八 (bā)		101	一百零一 (yībǎi líng yī)
9	九 (jiǔ)		212	二百一十二 (èrbǎi yīshí'èr)
10	十 (shí)			
11	十一 (shíyī)		1,000	一千 (yīqiān)
12	十二 (shí'èr)		1,001	一千零一 (yīqiān líng yī)
13	十三 (shísān)		2,500	二千五百 (èrqiān wǔbǎi)
14	十四 (shísì)			
15	十五 (shíwǔ)		100,000	十万 (shíwàn)
16	十六 (shíliù)		1,000,000	一百万 (yībǎi wàn)
17	十七 (shíqī)		1,000,000,000	十亿 (shíyì)
18	十八 (shíbā)			
19	十九 (shíjiǔ)			
20	二十 (èrshí)			
21	二十一 (èrshíyī)			
22	二十二 (èrshí'èr)			
23	二十三 (èrshísān)			
24	二十四 (èrshísì)			
25	二十五 (èrshíwǔ)			
30	三十 (sānshí)			
31	三十一 (sānshíyī)			

4.2 Ordinal numbers

1st	第一 (dì-yī)
2nd	第二 (dì-èr)
3rd	第三 (dì-sān)
4th	第四 (dì-sì)
5th	第五 (dì-wǔ)
6th	第六 (dì-liù)
7th	第七 (dì-qī)
8th	第八 (dì-bā)
9th	第九 (dì-jiǔ)
10th	第十 (dì-shí)
15th	第十五 (dì-shíwǔ)
20th	第二十 (dì-èrshí)
50th	第五十 (dì-wǔshí)
100th	第一百 (dì-yībǎi)
101st	第一百零一 (dì-yībǎi líng yī)
110th	第一百一十 (dì yībǎi yīshí)
1,000th	第一千 (dì-yīqiān)

4.3 Fractions, decimals and percentages

½	二分之一 (èr fēn zhī yī)
⅓	三分之一 (sān fēn zhī yī)
¼	四分之一 (sì fēn zhī yī)
⅔	三分之二 (sān fēn zhī èr)
0.5	零点五 (líng diǎn wǔ)
3.5	三点五 (sān diǎn wǔ)
6.89	六点八九 (liù diǎn bājiǔ)
10%	百分之十 (bǎi fēn zhī shí)
100%	百分之百 (bǎi fēn zhī bǎi)

5 Date

5.1 Days of the week

星期一 (xīngqīyī)	Monday
星期二 (xīngqī'èr)	Tuesday
星期三 (xīngqīsān)	Wednesday
星期四 (xīngqīsì)	Thursday
星期五 (xīngqīwǔ)	Friday
星期六 (xīngqīliù)	Saturday
星期日 (xīngqīrì)	Sunday

5.2 Months of the year

一月 (yīyuè)	January
二月 (èryuè)	February
三月 (sānyuè)	March
四月 (sìyuè)	April
五月 (wǔyuè)	May
六月 (liùyuè)	June
七月 (qīyuè)	July
八月 (bāyuè)	August
九月 (jiǔyuè)	September
十月 (shíyuè)	October
十一月 (shíyīyuè)	November
十二月 (shí'èryuè)	December

5.3 Talking about the date

今天几号?	What's the date today?
今天星期几?	What day is it today?
今天是2020年1月20日。	It's the 20th of January 2020.
在20日	on the 20th
1月1日	the first of January
在2月	in February
在2025年	in 2025
在十九世纪	in the nineteenth century
在九十年代	in the nineties

5.4 When?

今天	today
昨天	yesterday
明天	tomorrow
前天	the day before yesterday
后天	the day after tomorrow
昨天上午/下午/晚上	yesterday morning/afternoon/evening
明天上午/下午/晚上	tomorrow morning/afternoon/evening
第二天	the next day
每个星期六	every Saturday
下周日	next Sunday
上周二	last Tuesday

6 Time

6.1 What time is it?

几点了? (jǐ diǎn le?)

1点
(yī diǎn)

1点15分 / 1点一刻
(yī diǎn shíwǔ fēn / yī diǎn yīkè)

1点25分
(yī diǎn èrshíwǔ fēn)

1点30分 / 1点半
(yī diǎn sānshí fēn / yī diǎn
bàn)

1点45分 / 2点差一刻
(yī diǎn sìshíwǔ fēn /
liǎng diǎn chà yī kè)

1点50分 / 2点差10分
(yī diǎn wǔshí fēn /
liǎng diǎn chà shí fēn)

上午9点 / 晚上9点
(shàngwǔ jiǔ diǎn /
wǎnshang jiǔ diǎn)

中午12点 / 凌晨零点
(zhōngwǔ shí'èr diǎn /
língchén líng diǎn)

6.2 Useful expressions

几点开始? What time does it start?
20分钟后 in twenty minutes
大约在8点钟 at around eight o'clock
上午 in the morning
下午 in the afternoon
傍晚 in the evening

英语活学活用

1　日常交流　　　　　　　　18

2　信件和电话　　　　　　　22

3　数字　　　　　　　　　　27

4　星期和日期　　　　　　　30

5　时间　　　　　　　　　　32

1 日常交流

1.1 姓名和称谓

姓名

在说英语的国家中，姓名是由父母取的 *first name*（名字）和父母双方或一方的 *surname*（姓氏）组成。*forename* 即 *first name*。

> ***i*** 许多人还有 *middle name*（中名）。*middle name* 也是由父母取的，通常用缩略形式，而不用全称：*John F Kennedy*。

先生、夫人等

如果某人不是你的朋友，你可以用头衔加姓氏礼貌地称呼他。*Mr*（先生）用于男士的姓氏前。已婚女士被称为 *Mrs*（夫人），未婚女士使用 *Miss*（小姐）或 *Ms*（女士）。

Mr Nichols can see you now.（用于办公室会话）

> ***i*** 过去，已婚的女性总是改用夫姓。如今，一些女性婚后仍延用自己的姓氏。如果不清楚一位女士是否已婚，可使用称呼 *Ms*。一些较年轻的女性更倾向于使用 *Ms*，而不是 *Mrs* 或 *Miss*，但是较年长的女性则不喜欢使用 *Ms* 这一称呼。

知名人士

一般只用姓氏来称呼作家、作曲家、艺术家和其他知名人士。

the works of Shakespeare

昵称

人们常用 *nickname*，名字的非正式形式，来称呼他人，在会话中更是如此。许多名字都有约定俗成的简短形式。例如，如果某人的名字是 *James*，人们可以称他为 *Jamie*，*Jim* 或 *Jimmy*。

1.2 称呼他人

称呼不认识的人

- 如果你想引起某个不认识的人的注意 —— 比如，在大街上或在商店里 —— 通常说 *Excuse me*。

  Excuse me. You've dropped your scarf.

称呼认识的人

- 如果你知道对方的姓氏，你可用头衔（通常是 *Mr*，*Mrs* 或 *Miss*）加姓氏称呼他们。这用法相当正式。

  Thank you, Mr Jones.   *Goodbye, Dr Kirk.*

- 在英国、美国、澳大利亚等国的工作场所中，人们通常直呼名字，甚至对老板也是如此。

  What do you think, John?
  Are you going to the meeting with the new Finance Director?

> ⚠ 在 *Mr*，*Mrs* 和 *Miss* 后，只能加姓氏，而绝对不能加名。

1.3 问候

与人打招呼

- 与人打招呼通常用 hello。这个词既非太正式，又不会太随便，适用于大多数场合。在 hello 的后面，通常加上对方的名字或寒暄的话。

  'Hello, Tina.' — 'Hello. How are you today?'

- hi 或 hiya 是更为随便的问候方式，在年轻人中以及美式英语中尤为常用。

  Hiya, Tommy. How are you doing?

- 若要以正式方式问候他人，所用的词要视一天里的具体时间而定。中午12点钟之前说 good morning。

  Good morning, Mr Wright. How are you today?

  中午12点钟和6点钟之间说 good afternoon，6点之后人们说 good evening。

  Good afternoon. Could I speak to Ms Duff, please?
  Good evening. I'd like a table for four, please.

⚠️ 只有晚间与人告别，或当自己或他人上床睡觉之前，才能说 good night。它不能用来问候别人。

- 如果某人说 How are you?，你可以简单地回答 Very well, thank you. 或 Fine, thanks.。你也可以礼貌地反问一声 How are you?，或更随便些 And you?。

  'Hello, John. How are you?' — 'Fine, thanks, Mark. And you?'

- 在见面问候或告别时显得热情而有礼貌，人们有时说 Nice to see you.。

  'Hello, it's nice to see you again. How are you?' — 'Nice to see you too, Mr Bates.'

特别的日子

- 在某人的生日见到其人时，可以说 Happy Birthday! 或 Many happy returns!。

- 在圣诞节见到别人时，可以说 Merry Christmas! 或 Happy Christmas!。

- 在新年，你可以祝愿人们 Happy New Year!。

分别

- 与人分别时，说 goodbye。这种表达方式有点正式。

  'Goodbye, John,' Miss Saunders said.

- bye 是更常用的告别方式，而且比较随便。

  See you about seven. Bye.

- 如果你认为很快再次见到对方，可以说 See you later.。

  'See you later.' — 'Okay, bye.'   See you on Monday.

- 许多讲美式英语的人会用 have a nice day 向他们不太熟识的人道别。例如，在商店或酒店中工作的人员会对顾客这样说。

ℹ️ 在正式场合，比如商务会议，人们通常用握手以示问候或道别。在不太正式的场合下表示问候或道别，男士们也会握手，或者，互相轻拍后背或肩膀，而女士们则常常亲吻女性或男性亲友。

1.4 自我介绍和介绍他人

自我介绍

- 与陌生人初次见面，在自我介绍时，可以告诉对方你的姓名或介绍你是谁。你需要先说 *hello* 或其他客套的话。

  'Hello. I'm Harry,' said the boy.

  'I don't think we've met, have we? Are you visiting?' — 'Yes, I'm Peter Taylor.'

- 如果想显得正式些，则说 *May I introduce myself?*。

介绍他人

- 在介绍从未谋面的人相互认识时，说 *This is …*。介绍时，使用何种姓名形式可以视场合的正式程度而定（见第18页）。

  This is Shirley , Mr McKay. Shirley, this is Mr McKay.

- 如果需要正式些，则说 *I'd like to introduce …*。

  Mr Anderson, I'd like to introduce my wife.

> ⚠ 用手指指着别人介绍是很无礼的行为。但是，可以用手指指着物品或指示方向。

1.5 邀请

邀请某人做某事

- 通常，礼貌地邀请某人做某事，应说 *Would you like to …?*。

  Would you like to come to my party on Saturday?

  Well, would you like to comment on that, Tessa? (在会议或讨论中)

- 另一种礼貌的邀请形式是，祈使句与 *please* 连用。

  Please help yourself to a drink.

- 也可用 *How would you like to …?* 或 *Why don't you …?* 间接地邀请某人，或用以 *how about* 开头的问句邀请。

  How would you like to come and work for me?

  Why don't you come to the States with us in November?

  How about coming to stay for a few days?

> ℹ 如果应邀到某人家中做客，通常要带小礼物，比如鲜花或蛋糕。如被邀请就餐，大多数人会顺便带一瓶酒。主人通常会当面打开礼物。

回应邀请

- 如果接受邀请，就说 *thank you*。如果更加随便的话，就说声 *thanks*。也可加一句 *Yes, I'd love to.* 或 *I'd like that very much.*。

  'Won't you join me for lunch?' — 'Thanks, I'd like that very much.'

- 如果拒绝邀请，不愿拜访某人或随人去某地，则说 *I'm sorry, I can't.*。如果想解释原因，则用 *I'm afraid …* 或 *I'd like to but …*，再加上原因。

  'Can you come and spend the day with me on Sunday?' — 'Oh, I'm sorry. I can't.'

  'We're having a party on Saturday. Can you come?' — 'I'm afraid I'm busy.'

1.6　感谢他人

表示感谢

- 如果别人刚刚为你做了某事，或送给你某物，表示感谢的常用方式是说 thank you，或更随意地说声 thanks。

  'Don't worry. I've given you a good reference.' — 'Thank you, Mr Dillon.'

- 人们常常加上 very much 以加强语气。

  'Here you are.' — 'Thank you very much.'

  你也可以说 Thanks a lot. (但不能说 Thank you a lot. 或 Thanks lots.)。

- 如果需要解释为何感谢对方，则说 Thank you for ... 或 Thanks for ... 。

  Thanks for helping out.

> *i*　你会听到一些讲英式英语的人说 cheers 或 ta 表示感谢，这是非正式的表达方式。

如果某人请你吃东西，表示拒绝时，可以说 No, thank you. 或 No, thanks. (不能只说 Thank you.)。

'Would you like a coffee?' — 'No, thank you.'

如何回答感谢

- 如果某人因你帮忙而表示感谢，则应回答 That's all right. 或 That's OK.。

  'Thank you, Charles.' — 'That's all right, David.'

  如果想显得既礼貌又友好，可以说 It's a pleasure. 或 Pleasure.。

  'Thank you very much for talking to us about your research.' — 'It's a pleasure.'

1.7　道歉

致歉

- 如果打扰了某人或麻烦了某人，有多种道歉方式。最常用的是 sorry 或 I'm sorry。

  Sorry I'm late.

  可以在 I'm sorry 中加上副词 very，so，terribly 或 extremely，加强语势。

  I'm very sorry if I worried you.
  I'm terribly sorry but I have to leave.

> *i*　当不小心做了某事，例如踩了某人的脚，可以说 sorry 或 I'm sorry。讲美式英语的人则说 excuse me。

- 当打搅了某人或打断了某人的工作时，用 Excuse me, I'm sorry to disturb you.。这是礼貌的道歉方式。

  I'm sorry to disturb you but I need your signature.

- 如果想请某人让一下路，或想同陌生人讲话时，可以用 excuse me。一些说美式英语的人则会说 pardon me。

  Excuse me, do you mind if I squeeze past you?
  Pardon me, Sergeant. I wonder if you'd do me a favor? (美)

- 如果因需要做某事而不得不离开片刻，例如在商务环境中，或与不太熟识的人在一起时，也可以说 *Excuse me*。

    Excuse me for a moment. I have to make a telephone call.

> **i** 如果做了令人尴尬或失礼的事，譬如打饱嗝、打嗝、打喷嚏或吃东西时发出声音，应该道歉。人们通常会说 *excuse me* 或 *I beg your pardon*。

接受道歉

- 接受道歉通常有固定的表达形式，例如 *That's okay.*，*Don't worry about it.*，或 *It doesn't matter.*。

    'I'm sorry.' — 'That's okay.'
    'I apologize for what I said.' — 'Don't worry about it.'

2 信件和电话

2.1 写信该如何开头和结尾

给公司或组织机构的信件

称谓	结束语
Dear Sir	
Dear Madam	*Yours faithfully* (英)
Dear Sir or Madam	*Yours truly* (美)

写给已知姓名的个人正式信件

称谓	结束语
Dear Ms Roberts	*Yours sincerely* (英)
Dear Dr Jones	*Sincerely yours / Yours truly* (美)

结尾可用下列表达方式，显得不那么正式：

Yours
Kind regards
(With) best wishes

给朋友或熟人的信件

称谓	结束语
Dear Jeremy	*All the best*
Dear Aunt Jane	*Love (from)*
Dear Granny	*Lots of love (from)*
Hi Josh	*All my love*

电子邮件

尽管有时也需要用电子邮件发送正式信函，但是，当人们写电子邮件时，普遍比写信要随意。信件的开头和结尾方式同样适用于电子邮件。

> **i** 人们在给关系亲密的朋友或男/女朋友写信或电子邮件时，往往在落款后加几个X。X代表吻。

2.2 英国地址

Ms S Wilkins
10 Osprey Close
Guildford
Surrey
GL4 2PX

Nicola Thornbury
64 Newbridge Gardens
Bristol
BS7 4BT

i 邮政编码写在城市名称或地区名称的下面。

2.3 美国地址

Mark Smith
968 Michigan St
Seattle WA 98060-1024
USA

i 邮政编码写在城市名称和州名之后，州名用缩略形式。

- 寄往海外的信件通常要写发件人的地址。发件人的地址写在信封的背面，并在地址前加注 sender 或 from。
- 称呼通常由收信人的头衔、名字的首字母及姓氏组成：

  Ms S Wilkins
  Dr P Smith

- 如果是非正式书信，可以只写收信人的名和姓：

  Sarah Wilkins

2.4 给朋友的电子邮件

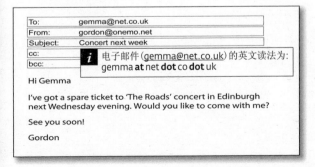

To:	gemma@net.co.uk
From:	gordon@onemo.net
Subject:	Concert next week
cc:	
bcc:	

i 电子邮件 (gemma@net.co.uk) 的英文读法为：
gemma **at** net **dot** co **dot** uk

Hi Gemma

I've got a spare ticket to 'The Roads' concert in Edinburgh next Wednesday evening. Would you like to come with me?

See you soon!

Gordon

2.5 商业电子信函

To:kevin.morrison@unt.com
From:charles.stimpson@unt.com
Subject:Budget meeting
cc:
bcc:

Following on from our phone conversation this morning, the Budget meeting will now be held on Wednesday at 10 a.m. in the South Meeting Room. I hope that you can attend.

Charles

重点词组

To	收件人	Send	发送
From	发件人	Forward	转发
Subject	主题	Reply	答复发件人
Cc	抄送	Compose	撰写
Bcc	密送	Delete	删除
Attachment	附件		

短信 text message
发短信 to send a text message
微博 Weibo (China's Twitter)
发微博 to tweet (on Weibo)
微信 WeChat

发微信 to send a WeChat message
移动设备 mobile device
智能手机 smartphone
应用程序/软件 app

2.6 感谢信（英式）

 在非正式信件中，地址和日期写在右上角，或只写日期。参见第31页日期的写法。

41 Mallard Crescent
Leeds
LS6 9BR
2 January 2020

Dear Tom and Lucy

Thank you for the lovely Christmas presents you sent me. The scarf is beautiful and the book is just what I wanted. As you know, J K Rowling is my favourite author.

I hear you're off to Spain soon. I'm so envious! I haven't got any holidays planned, but I'm going to London next weekend to see my aunt and uncle.

Thanks again for the presents, and have a great time in Spain. Don't forget to send me a postcard!

Lots of love

Carolyn

重点词组

可以用下列方式开头：
It was lovely to hear from you.
Thanks for your letter.
Sorry I haven't written sooner.
It was great to see you last weekend.

可以用下列方式结尾：
Write soon.
Look forward to seeing you soon.
Give my regards to Sally.
Julia sends you a big hug.

2.7 酒店预订函（英式）

26 Guanghua Road
Chaoyang District
Beijing 100027
China

Mrs Elaine Hudson
Manager
Poppywell Cottage
Devon
DV3 9SP

23rd June 2020

Dear Mrs Hudson

i 在商务信函的右上角，写上发信人自己的地址，但不要写发信人的姓名。日期紧跟在收信人地址的下一行。在信纸的左上角，通常在日期的下一行，写上收信人的姓名和／或职务头衔。如果使用带信头的信纸，日期写在收信人地址的上一行或下一行，或写在信纸的右上角。参见第31页有关日期的写法。

My sister stayed with you last year and has recommended your guest house very highly.

I would like to reserve a room for one week from 18th–24th August. I would be very grateful if you would let me know how much this would be for two adults and two children and whether you have a room free between these dates.

Yours sincerely

Ming Li

2.8 打电话

开始通话

接听电话

● 接听电话时，通常先说 *hello*，或使用比较正式的问候方式（参见第19页）。如果当时你在工作，可以给出自己的姓名，所在部门或公司的名称，或给出电话号码或分机号码。

> *Hello?*
> *Hello, Li Xin speaking.*
> *Good morning, Lotus Blossom Hotel. Can I help you?*
> *Eight six nine two three five seven. Hello?*

如何问候接听电话的人

● 当对方接听电话并致以问候后，打电话的人通常也要问候对方，然后说 *It's ...* 或 *This is ...* 以表明自己的身份。

> *Oh, hello. It's Mei Rong here.*

结束通话

● 可以用第19页中任何一种告别方式结束通话。也可以说 *Speak to you soon.* 或 *Thanks for ringing.*。

25

在办公室

要求接通某人

- 如果你知道对方联系人的姓名或分机号码，或想转接到某个特定部门，可以使用下列的短语。

  Hello. Could I speak to Susan, please?
  Can I have extension 5443, please?

- 如果你认为自己知道接听电话的人是谁，则可以问 *Is that ...?*。
  如果正是其人，对方则会回答 *Speaking.*。

  'Hello. Is that Emma?' — 'Speaking.'

接线员或秘书可能会说…

- 如果是与接线员或秘书通话，他们可能会使用以下表达方式：

  Who shall I say is calling?　　　　　*Dr Jackson is on another line.*
  Hold the line, please.　　　　　　　*Do you want to hold?*
  One moment, please.　　　　　　　　*I'm sorry. Mr Green isn't here at*
  I'm putting you through now.　　　　　*the moment.*
  　　　　　　　　　　　　　　　　　　Would you like to leave a message?

留言

- 如果想找的人不在，你可以留言，告知晚些时候会再打，或者让别人转告，请他回电话。

  Could I leave a message, please?
  I'll call back in half an hour.
  Would you ask him to call me when he gets back?

通话故障

- 如果无法接通想拨打的号码，可以用下列惯用语解释问题所在：

  I can't get through.　　　　　　　　*I must have dialled the wrong number.*
  I can't get a signal here.　　　　　　*We were cut off.*

- 也有可能无法听清对方的话：

  We've got a crossed line.
  The line is breaking up.

录音留言

- 录音留言在英国和美国非常普遍，在大型公司或组织里就更加常见。
  无人接听电话时就会听到：

  Your call is in a queue and will be answered shortly.
  All our operators (英)/operatives (美) are busy at the moment. Please hold.
  The number you are calling is engaged (英)/busy (美). Please try again later.
  The number you have dialled has not been recognized.

- 人们通常也会在家中的电话答录机上录下个人留言，以下是告知拨打电话的人何时开始录音的标准方式：

  Please speak after the tone (英)/beep (美).

2.9　手机短信

随着手机的出现，一种新的短信"语言"诞生了，并且因其迅捷、有趣，尤其受到年轻人的青睐。它的特点是根据类似的发音，采用简短的拼写方式：例如，*U* 代表 *you*，*R* 代表 *are*，*d8* 代表 *date* 以及 *2nite* 代表 *tonight*。新的表达方式总是不断地出现。

3 数字

3.1 基数

下列的数字称作基数。根据此表，你可以知道如何构成其他数字。数字可用作形容词（用于名词前，有时也称作限定词）或代词（用于代替名词）。

1	one	18	eighteen	80	eighty
2	two	19	nineteen	90	ninety
3	three	20	twenty	100	one hundred/
4	four	21	twenty-one		a hundred
5	five	22	twenty-two	101	one hundred and one/
6	six	23	twenty-three		a hundred and one
7	seven	24	twenty-four	102	one hundred and two/
8	eight	25	twenty-five		a hundred and two
9	nine	26	twenty-six	110	one hundred and ten/
10	ten	27	twenty-seven		a hundred and ten
11	eleven	28	twenty-eight	120	one hundred and
12	twelve	29	twenty-nine		twenty/a hundred
13	thirteen	30	thirty		and twenty
14	fourteen	40	forty	200	two hundred
15	fifteen	50	fifty	300	three hundred
16	sixteen	60	sixty	400	four hundred
17	seventeen	70	seventy	500	five hundred

1000	one thousand/a thousand
1001	one thousand and one/a thousand and one
1010	one thousand and ten/a thousand and ten
1100	one thousand one hundred
1200	one thousand two hundred
1500	one thousand five hundred
2000	two thousand
5000	five thousand
10,000	ten thousand
20,000	twenty thousand
100,000	one hundred thousand/a hundred thousand
150,000	one hundred and fifty thousand/ a hundred and fifty thousand
1,000,000	one million/a million
2,000,000	two million
1,000,000,000	one billion/a billion

3.2 重点短语

She's fifteen (years old).
on page two hundred and fifty-six
two plus seven are nine
eight minus two are six
hundreds of years

the two women
all five candidates
two small children
in fives
They sold the house for £150,000.

- **one** 作为数字用在名词前，强调只有一个事物，或用于表示表达的精确性。当谈论一个团体中的特定一员时也用 one。否则，就用 a。

  There was only one gate into the palace.
  One member said that he would never vote for such a proposal.
  A car came slowly up the road.

- 数字0有如下几种表达方式：

  在温度、税率、利率中，用 *zero*

  It was fourteen below zero when they woke up.

  在小数点前，用 *nought* (英式)/*naught* (美式)

  nought point eight nine (0.89)

  表示计算，在口语中用 *nothing*

  five minus five is nothing

  当一个一个地报数字，或在小数点后时，用 *oh* 或字母 *o*

  point oh eight nine (.089)

  在体育比分中，用 *nil*

  England beat Germany one-nil.

- 介于100和999之间的数字通常用阿拉伯数字表示。当朗读或写成单词时，在英式英语中，百位数和十位数之间用 and 连接，而在美式英语中，省略 *and*。

  261 → *two hundred and sixty-one* (英)/*two hundred sixty-one* (美)

- 当大于 9999 的数字写成阿拉伯数字时，通常在右起第3位数字前加逗号，在右起第6位数字前加逗号，依次类推，从而把数字分成3个数字一组的几组：15,000　　　　　1,986,000

3.3　序数词

序数词用于表明某物在一个系列或序列中所处的位置, 可以用作形容词(用于名词前, the 或 her 一类的限定词之后)、代词(代替名词)或副词(在谈论赛跑或其他比赛时, 与某些动词连用, 比如 come 或 finish)。大多数分数的分母用序数词表示。

1st	first	27th	twenty-seventh
2nd	second	28th	twenty-eighth
3rd	third	29th	twenty-ninth
4th	fourth	30th	thirtieth
5th	fifth	31st	thirty-first
6th	sixth	32nd	thirty-second
7th	seventh	40th	fortieth
8th	eighth	41st	forty-first
9th	ninth	42nd	forty-second
10th	tenth	50th	fiftieth
11th	eleventh	60th	sixtieth
12th	twelfth	70th	seventieth
13th	thirteenth	80th	eightieth
14th	fourteenth	90th	ninetieth
15th	fifteenth	100th	hundredth
16th	sixteenth	101st	hundred and first
17th	seventeenth	102nd	hundred and second
18th	eighteenth	103rd	hundred and third
19th	nineteenth	110th	hundred and tenth
20th	twentieth	200th	two hundredth
21st	twenty-first	1000th	thousandth
22nd	twenty-second	2000th	two thousandth
23rd	twenty-third	10,000th	ten thousandth
24th	twenty-fourth	1,000,000th	millionth
25th	twenty-fifth	1,000,000,000th	billionth
26th	twenty-sixth		

> *We live on the fourth floor.*
> *in the twelfth century*
> *on her twenty-first birthday*

> *An Italian came second.*
> *I was the first to arrive.*
> *the third of a series of documentaries*

- 如上表所示, 序数词常用缩略形式表示, 1加 st 为 first, 2加 nd 为 second, 3加 rd 为 third, fourth 到 ninth 分别用相应的基数词加 th 表示 —— 例如, 6th。这些缩写形式在日期中尤为常用。

- 10 以上不是 10 的倍数的序数词, 由基数词加序数词构成, 之间用连字符分开。
  > *my thirty-third birthday*
  > *our forty-fifth wedding anniversary*

> *i*   楼房的第一层, 在英式英语中被称为 ground floor, 在美式英语中则被称为 first floor。在英式英语中, 再往上的一层为 first floor, 在美式英语中则为 second floor。

3.4 分数、小数和百分数

$\frac{1}{2}$	a half	0.5	(nought) point five (英)/
$\frac{1}{3}$	a third		(naught) point five (美)
$\frac{1}{4}$	a quarter	3.5	three point five
$\frac{1}{5}$	a fifth	6.89	six point eight nine
$\frac{1}{6}$	a sixth	10%	ten per cent (英)/
$\frac{1}{10}$	a tenth		ten percent (美)
$\frac{2}{3}$	two-thirds	100%	one hundred per cent (英)/
$\frac{5}{8}$	five-eigths		one hundred percent (美)

- 除了 half (一半)和 quarter (四分之一)以外, 分数的分母用序数词表示。
  > *four and a half centuries*
  > *The state produces a third of the nation's oil.*
  > *More than two-thirds of the Earth is water.*

- 分数的分子通常可以用不定冠词 a。
  > *The country spends over a fifth of its budget on education.*

  正式用语和书面语中, 或需要强调数量时, 用 one。
  > *one quarter of the total population*

- 分子大于1时, 通常要加连字符。
  > *He's due at the office in three-quarters of an hour.*

4 星期和日期

4.1 星期

Monday	星期一	Friday	星期五
Tuesday	星期二	Saturday	星期六
Wednesday	星期三	Sunday	星期日
Thursday	星期四		

What day is it today? It's Thursday.
I'm usually here on Mondays and Fridays.
Deliveries usually arrive on a Thursday.
The attack took place last Thursday.
Talks are likely to start next Tuesday.
We meet here every Saturday morning.
I'll be away from Monday to Friday.
I'll need an answer by Monday.
We're having a party on the last Sunday in May.

4.2 月份

January	一月	July	七月
February	二月	August	八月
March	三月	September	九月
April	四月	October	十月
May	五月	November	十一月
June	六月	December	十二月

● 月份前用介词 in。

It always snows in January.
I flew to London in early March.
It happened in late May, and the apple trees were in bloom.
He spent two weeks with us in July 2015.

⚠ next（下一个）或 last（上一个）加月份，前面不用介词 in。
　Staff were on strike last June.　*I don't know where I'll be next November.*

● 某月中的具体日子前用介词 on。

His exhibition opens on 5 February（英）/February 5（美）.
The trial will begin on August the twenty-second.

ℹ 在英国，一学年分为三个 terms（学期），夏季有长假期，圣诞节和复活节
各有一个较短的假期。在美国，一学年分为两个 semesters（学期），十
月、四月以及圣诞节和复活节都会放假。

4.3 季节

spring	春季	autumn（英）/fall（美）	秋季
summer	夏季	winter	冬季

- 季节前的介词用 in。
  In winter the nights are extremely cold.
  It's nice to get away in the spring.

⚠️ next（下一个）或 last（上一个）加上季节, 前面不用介词 in。
The final report is due out next autumn（英）/fall（美）.

4.4 日期的写法

- 书写日期有几种不同的方式:

  13 September   September 13
  13th September   September 13th

- 若想给出年份, 则将年份放在最后。如果将日放在月后, 则用逗号将年份与日期分开。

  13th September 2019 (in a letter)
  My date of birth is 13 September 1997.
  I was born on September 13th, 1997.

4.5 日期的读法

- 即使日期是用基数词表示, 也要读作序数词。

  September 13 读作 *September the thirteenth*（英）

- 若月放在表示日的数字之后, 月份前要加介词 of。

  13 September 读作 *the thirteenth of September*

4.6 年的读法

- 读年份时一般分成两部分。例如:

  1957 读作 *nineteen fifty-seven*   1860 读作 *eighteen sixty*

  以"20-"开头的年份 —— 例如, 2003 和 2010 —— 可以读作 *two thousand and ...*。例如:

  2003 读作 *two thousand and three*   2010 读作 *two thousand and ten*

  以"20-"开头的年份也可以分成两部分读, 例如:

  2020 可读作 *twenty twenty*   2004 可读作 *twenty oh four*

- 以"-oo"结尾的年份, 可将第二部分读作 *hundred*。例如:

  1900 读作 *nineteen hundred*

- 以"01-09"结尾的年份有两种读法。例如:

  1807 可以读作 *eighteen oh seven* 或 *eighteen hundred and seven*。

4.7 年代和世纪

- 1970 –1979 可以读作 *the nineteen seventies*, 或非正式的读法为 *the seventies*。

- 说到 20 世纪的年代时, 不必指出世纪。例如, 1920s 可以读作 *the twenties*。它可以写作 *the '20s, the 20s* 或 *the Twenties*。

- 世纪还可以写作序数词, 例如, *the 20th century*。

5　时间

5.1　几点了?

It's one o'clock

It's a quarter past one (英)
It's a quarter after one (美)
It's one fifteen

It's twenty-five past one (英)
It's twenty-five after one (美)
It's one twenty-five

It's half past one (英)
It's half after one (美)
It's one thirty

It's a quarter to two (英)
It's a quarter of two (美)
It's one forty-five

It's ten to two (英)
It's ten of two (美)
It's one fifty

> ⚠ o'clock 只用在表示整点的时间后。例如,可以说 five o'clock,但不能说
> "ten past five o'clock"或"a quarter past five o'clock"。
> • 可以用 minutes 表示5分钟以内的时间,或精确地表示时间。
>   *It was twenty-four minutes past ten..*

• 如果过整点的分钟数小于10,许多人在分钟数前用 o,读作 oh。例如:
   10.07 可以读作 *ten oh seven* 或 *ten seven*。
   注意,在写时间时,英国人在小时后加圆点,譬如:10.07。而美国人多用冒号,7:35。
• 若所指的钟点很明确,在介词 past 或 to 之后不必加钟点。
   'What time does the train leave?' —'I think it's at quarter to.'

问时间	回答
What time is it?	*It's nearly ten past twelve.* (英)
	It's nearly ten after twelve. (美)
What's the time now?	*It's three o'clock exactly.*
What time do you make it?	*I make it four twenty-seven.*
Do you have the time (on you)?	*Yes, it's half past nine.*
Can you tell me the time?	*Yes, it's nearly quarter to eight.*

`04:00`	four in the morning 4 a.m.	`16:00`	four in the afternoon 4 p.m.
`12:00`	twelve in the morning/ midday 12 a.m./noon	`21:00`	nine in the evening 9 p.m.

• 可以加 a.m. 表示午夜到中午之间的时间。同样,p.m. 表示中午到午夜之间的
   时间。这些缩写通常不用于对话中,而且从不与 o'clock 连用。

   He finally got home at 11.30 p.m., having set out at 6 a.m.

English–Chinese

英汉词典

a

KEYWORD

a [eɪ, ə] *(before vowel or silent h:* **an)** INDEF ART **1** *(article)* 一个(個) yī gè ▸ **a man** 一个(個)男人 yī gè nánrén ▸ **a girl** 一个(個)女孩 yī gè nǚhái ▸ **an elephant** 一只(隻)大象 yī zhǐ dàxiàng ▸ **she's a doctor** 她是一名医(醫)生 tā shì yī míng yīshēng ▸ **they haven't got a television** 他们(們)没(沒)有电(電)视(視) tāmen méiyǒu diànshì **2** *(one)* 一 yī ▸ **a year ago** 一年前 yī nián qián **3** *(expressing ratios, prices etc)* ▸ **five hours a day/week** 一天/一周(週)5个(個)小时(時) yī tiān/yī zhōu wǔ gè xiǎoshí ▸ **100 km an hour** 每小时(時)100公里 měi xiǎoshí yībǎi gōnglǐ

A & E *(Brit)* N ABBR *(= accident and emergency)* 急诊(診)室 jízhěnshì

abbey ['æbɪ] N [c] 大修道院 dà xiūdàoyuàn [座 zuò]

abbreviation [əbriːvɪ'eɪʃən] N [c] 缩(縮) 写(寫) suōxiě [个 gè]

ability [ə'bɪlɪtɪ] N [s] ▸ **ability (to do sth)** (做某事的)能力 (zuò mǒushì de) nénglì

able ['eɪbl] ADJ ▸ **to be able to do sth** *(have skill, ability)* 能够(夠)做某事 nénggòu zuò mǒushì; *(have opportunity)* 可以做某事 kěyǐ zuò mǒushì

abolish [ə'bɒlɪʃ] VT *[+ system, practice]* 废(廢)止 fèizhǐ

abortion [ə'bɔːʃən] *(Med)* N [c/u] 流产(產) liúchǎn [次 cì] ▸ **to have an abortion** 流产(產) liúchǎn

KEYWORD

about [ə'baut] I PREP *(relating to)* 关(關) 于(於) guānyú ▸ **a book about London** 关(關)于(於)伦(倫)敦的一本书(書) guānyú Lúndūn de yī běn shū ▸ **what's it about?** (这)是关(關)于(於)什 么(麼)的? zhè shì guānyú shénme de? ▸ **we talked about it** 我们(們)谈(談)到 了这(這)事 wǒmen tándàole zhè shì ▸ **to be sorry/pleased/angry about sth** 对(對)某事感到抱歉/开(開)心/生 气(氣) duì mǒushì gǎndào bàoqiàn/ kāixīn/shēngqì ▸ **what** *or* **how about eating out?** 出去吃怎么(麼)样(樣)? chūqù chī zěnmeyàng? II ADV **1** *(approximately)* 大约(約) dàyuē ▸ **about a hundred/thousand people** 大约(約)100/1000人 dàyuē yībǎi/yīqiān rén **2** *(place)* 在 zài ▸ **to leave things lying about** 把东(東)西到处(處)乱(亂)放 bǎ dōngxi dàochù luànfàng ▸ **to be about to do sth** 正要做某事 zhèng yào zuò mǒushì

above [ə'bʌv] I PREP *(higher than)* 在…上 面 zài…shàngmian II ADV *(in position)* 在 上面 zài shàngmian III ADJ ▸ **the above address** 上述地址 shàngshù dìzhǐ ▸ **above all** 首先 shǒuxiān

abroad [ə'brɔːd] ADV **1** *[be +]* 在国(國)外 zài guówài **2** *[go +]* 到国(國)外 dào guówài

absence ['æbsəns] N **1** [c/u] *[of person]* 缺 席 quēxí [次 cì] **2** [s] *[of thing]* 缺乏 quēfá

absent ['æbsənt] ADJ 缺席的 quēxí de ▸ **to be absent** 不在 bùzài

absolutely [æbsə'luːtlɪ] ADV *(utterly)* 绝(絕)对(對)地 juéduì de

absorbent cotton [əb'zɔːbənt-] *(US)* [u] 脱(脫)脂棉 tuōzhīmián

abuse [n ə'bjuːs, vb ə'bjuːz] I N **1** [u] *(insults)* 辱骂(罵) rǔmà **2** [u] *(ill-treatment: physical)* 虐待 nüèdài; *(sexual)* 猥亵(褻) wěixiè **3** [c/u] *(misuse)* [of power, alcohol, drug] 滥(濫)用 lànyòng [种 zhǒng] II VT 1 (ill-treat: physically) 虐待 nüèdài 2 (sexually) [+ child] 摧残(殘) cuīcán

academic [ækə'dɛmɪk] I ADJ 学(學)术(術)的 xuéshù de II N 大学(學)教师(師) dàxué jiàoshī

academy [ə'kædəmɪ] N [c] 1 学(學)会(會) xuéhuì [个 gè] 2 (school, college) 学(學)院 xuéyuàn [个 gè]

accelerate [æk'sɛləreɪt] VI (Aut) 加速 jiāsù

accelerator [æk'sɛləreɪtər] (Aut) N [c] 加速器 jiāsùqì [个 gè]

accent ['æksənt] N [c] 口音 kǒuyīn [种 zhǒng] ▷ to speak with an (Irish/French) accent 讲(講)话(話)带(帶)(爱(愛)尔(爾)兰(蘭)/法国(國))口音 jiǎnghuà dài (Ài'ěrlán/Fǎguó) kǒuyīn

accept [ək'sɛpt] VT 接受 jiēshòu

access ['æksɛs] I N [u] ▷ access (to sth) (to building, room) 进(進)入(某物) jìnrù (mǒuwù); (to information, papers) (某物的) 使用权(權) (mǒuwù de) shǐyòngquán II VT (Comput) 存取 cúnqǔ

accident ['æksɪdənt] N [c] 1 (involving vehicle) 事故 shìgù [个 gè] 2 (mishap) 意外 yìwài [个 gè] ▷ to have an accident 出事故 chū shìgù ▷ by accident (unintentionally) 无(無)意中 wúyì zhōng; (by chance) 偶然 ǒurán

accidental [æksɪ'dɛntl] ADJ 意外的 yìwài de

accident and emergency (Brit) N [c] 急诊(診)室 jízhěnshì [个 gè]

accommodation [əkɒmə'deɪʃən] I N [u] 住处(處) zhùchù II **accommodations** (US) NPL = **accommodation**

accompany [ə'kʌmpənɪ] VT 1 (frm: escort) 陪伴 péibàn 2 (Mus) 为(為)…伴奏 wèi…bànzòu

according [ə'kɔːdɪŋ] ▷ **according to** PREP [+ person] 据(據)…所说(說) jù…suǒshuō; [+ account, information] 根据(據) gēnjù

account [ə'kaunt] N [c] 1 (with bank, at shop) 账(賬)户(戶) zhànghù [个 gè] 2 (report) 描述 miáoshù [番 fān] ▷ to take sth into account, take account of sth 考虑(慮)到某事 kǎolǜ dào mǒushì

accountancy [ə'kauntənsɪ] N [u]

会(會)计(計)学(學) kuàijìxué

accountant [ə'kauntənt] N [c] 会(會)计(計)师(師) kuàijìshī [位 wèi]

accuracy ['ækjurəsɪ] N [u] 1 [of information, measurements] 准(準)确(確) zhǔnquè 2 [of person, device] 精确(確) jīngquè

accurate ['ækjurɪt] ADJ [+ information, measurement, instrument] 精确(確)的 jīngquè de; [+ description, account, person, aim] 准(準)确(確)的 zhǔnquè de

accuse [ə'kjuːz] VT 1 ▷ to accuse sb of (doing) sth 指责(責)某人(做)某事 zhǐzé mǒurén (zuò) mǒushì 2 ▷ to be accused of sth (of crime) 被指控某事 bèi zhǐkòng mǒushì

ache [eɪk] I VI 痛 tòng II N [c] 疼痛 téngtòng [种 zhǒng] ▷ I've got (a) stomach/toothache 我胃/牙痛 wǒ wèi/yá tòng

achieve [ə'tʃiːv] VT [+ victory, success, result] 取得 qǔdé

achievement [ə'tʃiːvmənt] N [c] 成就 chéngjiù [个 gè]

acid ['æsɪd] N [c/u] (Chem) 酸 suān [种 zhǒng]

acrobat ['ækrəbæt] N [c] 杂(雜)技演员(員) zájì yǎnyuán [位 wèi] ▷ He's an acrobat. 他是一位杂技演员。 Tā shì yī wèi zájì yǎnyuán.

across [ə'krɒs] I PREP 1 (moving from one side to the other of) 穿过(過) chuānguò 2 (situated on the other side of) 在…对(對)面 zài…duìmiàn 3 (extending from one side to the other of) 跨越 kuàyuè II ADV 1 (from one side to the other) 从(從)一边(邊)到另一边(邊) cóng yībiān dào lìngyībiān 2 ▷ **across from** (opposite) 在…对(對)面 zài…duìmiàn 3 ▷ **across at/to** (towards) 朝向 cháoxiàng 4 (in width) 宽(寬) kuān

act [ækt] VI 1 (take action) 行动(動) xíngdòng 2 (behave) 举(舉)止 jǔzhǐ ▷ They were acting suspiciously. 他们举止可疑。 Tāmen jǔzhǐ kěyí. 3 (in play, film) 演戏(戲) yǎnxì ▷ **acts of sabotage** 破坏(壞)行动(動) pòhuài xíngdòng

action ['ækʃən] N [u] 1 (steps, measures) 行动(動) xíngdòng [次 cì] 2 [c] (deed) 行为(為) xíngwéi [种 zhǒng] ▷ to take action 采(採)取行动(動) cǎiqǔ xíngdòng

active ['æktɪv] ADJ **1** 活跃(躍)的 huóyuè de **2** [+ volcano] 活的 huó de

activity [æk'tɪvɪtɪ] I N [c] 活动(動) huódòng [项 xiàng] II **activities** NPL 活动(動) huódòng

actor ['æktə^r] N [c] 演员(員) yǎnyuán [个 gè]

actress ['æktrɪs] N [c] 女演员(員) nǚ yǎnyuán [个 gè]

actual ['æktjuəl] ADJ 真实(實)的 zhēnshí de

actually ['æktjuəlɪ] ADV **1** 实(實)际(際)地 shíjì de **2** (in fact) 事实(實)上 shìshíshang ▸ actually, we have the same opinion 实(實)际(際)上我们(們)有同样(樣)的观(觀)点(點) shíjìshang wǒmen yǒu tóngyàng de guāndiǎn

AD ADV ABBR (= Anno Domini) 公元 gōngyuán

ad [æd] (inf) N (advertisement) 广(廣)告 guǎnggào

adapt [ə'dæpt] I VT 使适(適)合 shǐ shìhé II VI ▸ to adapt (to) 适(適)应(應) shìyìng

adaptor [ə'dæptə^r] (Elec) N [c] 转(轉)接器 zhuǎnjiēqì [个 gè]

add [æd] VT **1** (put in, put on) 加入 jiārù **2** ▸ to add (together) (calculate total of) 加(起来(來)) jiā (qǐlai)

addict ['ædɪkt] N [c] ▸ drug/heroin addict 吸毒/海洛因成瘾(癮)的人 xīdú/hǎiluòyīn chéngyǐn de rén [个 gè]

addicted [ə'dɪktɪd] ADJ ▸ to be addicted to sth 对(對)某事上瘾(癮) duì mǒushì shàngyǐn

addition [ə'dɪʃən] N [u] (Math) 加法 jiāfǎ ▸ in addition to 除…之外 chú…zhīwài

address [ə'drɛs] N [c] 地址 dìzhǐ [个 gè]

adjective ['ædʒɛktɪv] N [c] 形容词(詞) xíngróngcí [个 gè]

adjust [ə'dʒʌst] VT [+ device, position, setting] 校准(準) jiàozhǔn

adjustable [ə'dʒʌstəbl] ADJ 可调(調)节(節)的 kě tiáojié de

admire [əd'maɪə^r] VT 钦(欽)佩 qīnpèi

admit [əd'mɪt] VT **1** (confess) 承认(認) chéngrèn **2** (accept) [+ defeat, responsibility] 接受 jiēshòu ▸ he admits that... 他承认(認)… tā chéngrèn… ▸ to be admitted to hospital 住进(進)医(醫)院 zhùjìn yīyuàn

adolescent [ædəu'lɛsnt] N [c] 青少年 qīngshàonián [个 gè]

adopt [ə'dɔpt] VT **1** [+ plan, approach, attitude] 采(採)用 cǎiyòng **2** [+ child] 收养(養) shōuyǎng

adopted [ə'dɔptɪd] ADJ 被收养(養)的 bèi shōuyǎng de

adoption [ə'dɔpʃən] N [c/u] [of child] 收养(養) shōuyǎng

adult ['ædʌlt] I N [c] 成年人 chéngniánrén [个 gè] II ADJ (grown-up) 成年的 chéngnián de

advance [əd'vɑ:ns] ADJ [+ notice, warning] 预(預)先的 yùxiān de ▸ in advance [book, prepare, plan +] 提前 tíqián

advanced [əd'vɑ:nst] ADJ **1** (highly developed) 先进(進)的 xiānjìn de **2** (Scol) [+ student, pupil] 高年级(級)的 gāoniánjí de; [+ course, work] 高等的 gāoděng de

advantage [əd'vɑ:ntɪdʒ] N **1** (benefit) 好处(處) hǎochù [种 zhǒng] **2** (favourable factor) 有利因素 yǒulì yīnsù [个 gè] ▸ to take advantage of [+ person] 利用 lìyòng; [+ opportunity] 利用 lìyòng

adventure [əd'vɛntʃə^r] N [c] 冒险(險)活动(動) màoxiǎn huódòng [次 cì]

adverb ['ædvə:b] N [c] 副词(詞) fùcí [个 gè]

advert ['ædvə:t] (Brit) N 广(廣)告 guǎnggào

advertise ['ædvətaɪz] I VI 做广(廣)告 zuò guǎnggào II VT **1** [+ product, event] 为(為)…做广(廣)告 wèi…zuò guǎnggào **2** [+ job] 刊登 kāndēng

advertisement [əd'və:tɪsmənt] (Comm) N [c] 广(廣)告 guǎnggào [则 zé]

advice [əd'vaɪs] N [u] 忠告 zhōnggào ▸ a piece of advice 一条(條)建议(議) yītiáo jiànyì

advise [əd'vaɪz] VT ▸ to advise sb to do sth 劝(勸)某人做某事 quàn mǒurén zuò mǒushì

aerial ['ɛərɪəl] (Brit) N [c] 天线(線) tiānxiàn [根 gēn]

aerobics [ɛə'rəubɪks] N [u] 有氧健身操 yǒuyǎng jiànshēncāo

aeroplane ['ɛərəpleɪn] (Brit) N [c] 飞(飛)机(機) fēijī [架 jià]

affair [ə'fɛə^r] I N **1** [s] (matter, business) 事情 shìqing **2** [c] (romance) 风(風)流韵(韻)事 fēngliú yùnshì [桩 zhuāng] II **affairs** NPL **1** (matters) 事务(務) shìwù

2 (*personal concerns*) 私事 sīshì ▸ **to have an affair (with sb)** (和某人) 发(發)生暧昧关(關)系(係) (hé mǒurén) fāshēng àimèi guānxi

affect [əˈfɛkt] VT ▸ 影响(響) yǐngxiǎng

afford [əˈfɔːd] VT ▸ **to be able to afford (to buy/pay) sth** 买(買)/支付得起某物 mǎi/zhīfùdeqǐ mǒuwù

afraid [əˈfreɪd] ADJ (*frightened*) 害怕的 hàipà de ▸ **to be afraid of sb/sth** 害怕某人/某物 hàipà mǒurén/mǒuwù ▸ **to be afraid to do sth/of doing sth** 怕做某事 pà zuò mǒushì ▸ **to be afraid that...** (*worry, fear*) 担(擔)心… dānxīn…; (*expressing apology, disagreement*) 恐怕… kǒngpà… ▸ **I'm afraid so/not** 恐怕是/不是的 kǒngpà shì/bùshì de

Africa [ˈæfrɪkə] N ▸ 非洲 Fēizhōu

African [ˈæfrɪkən] **I** ADJ ▸ 非洲的 Fēizhōu de **II** N [c] (*person*) 非洲人 Fēizhōurén [个 gè]

after [ˈɑːftəʳ] **I** PREP **1** (*in time*) 在…以后(後) zài…yǐhòu **2** (*in place, order*) 在…后(後)面 zài…hòumiàn **II** ADV (*afterwards*) 以后(後) yǐhòu **III** CONJ (*once*) 在…以后(後) zài…yǐhòu ▸ **the day after tomorrow** 后(後)天 hòutiān ▸ **it's ten after eight** (US) (現)在是8点(點)过(過)10分 xiànzài shì bādiǎn guò shífēn ▸ **after all** 毕(畢)竟 bìjìng ▸ **after doing sth** 做完某事后(後) zuòwán mǒushì hòu

> **after, afterwards** 和 **later** 用于表示某事发生在说话的时间, 或者某个特定事情之后。**after** 可以和 **not long**、**shortly** 等连用。*After dinner she spoke to him...Shortly after, she called me.* 在无须指明某个特定时间或事件时, 可以用 **afterwards**。*Afterwards we went to a night club...You'd better come and see me later.* **afterwards** 可以和 **soon**、**shortly** 等连用。*Soon afterwards, he came to the clinic.* **later** 表示某事发生在说话之后, 可以和 **a little**、**much** 或 **not much** 等连用。*A little later, the lights went out... I learned all this much later.* 可以用 **after**、**afterwards** 和 **later** 后跟表示时间段的词语, 表示某事发生的时间。*...five years after his death...She wrote about it six years later/afterwards.*

afternoon [ˈɑːftəˈnuːn] N [c/u] ▸ 下午 xiàwǔ [个 gè] ▸ **this afternoon** 今天下午 jīntiān xiàwǔ ▸ **tomorrow/yesterday afternoon** 明天/昨天下午 míngtiān/zuótiān xiàwǔ ▸ (*good*) **afternoon!** (*hello*) 下午好! xiàwǔ hǎo!

after-shave (lotion) [ˈɑːftəʃeɪv-] N [u] ▸ 须(鬚)后(後) (润(潤)肤(膚)) 水 xūhòu (rùnfū) shuǐ

afterwards [ˈɑːftəwədz], (US) **afterward** [ˈɑːftəwəd] ADV ▸ 以后(後) yǐhòu

again [əˈɡɛn] ADV ▸ 又一次地 yòu yī cì de ▸ **again and again/time and again** 一再 yīzài

against [əˈɡɛnst] PREP **1** (*leaning on, touching*) 紧(緊)靠在 jǐnkào zài **2** (*opposed to*) 反对(對) fǎnduì **3** (*in game or competition*) 同…对(對)抗 tóng…duìkàng **4** ▸ **to protect against sth** 保护(護)免受某种(種)伤(傷)害 bǎohù miǎnshòu mǒu zhǒng shānghài ▸ **they'll be playing against Australia** 他们(們)将(將)在比赛(賽)中同澳大利亚(亞)队(隊)对(對)抗 tāmen jiāng zài bǐsài zhōng tóng Àodàlìyà duì duìkàng ▸ **against the law/rules** 违(違)法律(律)/规(規)则(則) wéifǎn fǎlǜ/guīzé ▸ **against one's will** 违(違)背自己的意愿(願) wéibèi zìjǐ de yìyuàn

age [eɪdʒ] N **1** [c/u] 年龄(齡) niánlíng **2** [c] (*period in history*) 时(時)代 shídài [个 gè] ▸ **what age is he?** 他多大了? tā duōdà le? ▸ **at the age of 20** 20岁(歲) èrshí suì shí ▸ **an age, ages** (*inf*) 很长(長)时(時)间(間) hěn cháng shíjiān ▸ **the Stone/Bronze/Iron Age** 石器/铜(銅)器/铁(鐵)器时(時)代 shíqì/tóngqì/tiěqì shídài

aged[1] [ˈeɪdʒd] ADJ ▸ **aged 10** 10岁(歲) shí suì

aged[2] [ˈeɪdʒɪd] NPL ▸ **the aged** 老人 lǎorén

agent [ˈeɪdʒənt] N [c] ▸ 代理人 dàilǐrén [个 gè]

aggressive [əˈɡrɛsɪv] ADJ ▸ 好斗(鬥)的 hàodòu de

ago [əˈɡəu] ADV ▸ **2 days ago** 两(兩)天前 liǎngtiān qián ▸ **long ago/a long time ago** 很久以前 hěnjiǔ yǐqián ▸ **how long ago?** 多久以前? duōjiǔ yǐqián?

agony ['ægənɪ] N [c/u] 痛苦 tòngkǔ [种 zhǒng]

agree [ə'griː] VI 1 (*have same opinion*) 同意 tóngyì 2 ▶ **to agree to sth/to do sth** 同意某事/做某事 tóngyì mǒushì/ zuò mǒushì ▶ **to agree with sb about sth** 关(關)于(於)某事(贊)成某人的 看法 guānyú mǒushì zànchéng mǒurén de kànfǎ ▶ **to agree on sth** [+ *price, arrangement*] 商定某事 shāngdìng mǒushì

agreement [ə'griːmənt] N 1 [c] ▶ **an agreement (on sth)** (*decision, arrangement*) (关(關)于(於)某事的) 协(協)议(議) (guānyú mǒushì de) xiéyì [个 gè] 2 [u] (*consent*) 同意 tóngyì

agricultural [ægrɪ'kʌltʃərəl] ADJ 农(農) 业(業)的 nóngyè de

agriculture ['ægrɪkʌltʃəʳ] N [u] 农(農) 业(業) nóngyè

ahead [ə'hɛd] ADV 1 (*in front*) 在前地 zàiqián de 2 (*in work, achievements*) 提前 地 tíqián de 3 (*in competition*) 领(領)先 地 lǐngxiān de 4 (*in the future*) 在未 来(來) zài wèilái ▶ **the days/months ahead** 今后(後)几(幾)天/几(幾)个(個) 月 jīnhòu jǐ tiān/jǐ gè yuè ▶ **ahead of time/schedule** 提前 tíqián ▶ **right** or **straight ahead** 笔(筆)直向前 bǐzhí xiàngqián ▶ **go ahead!** (*giving permission*) 干(幹)吧! gànba!

aid [eɪd] N [u] 援助 yuánzhù

AIDS [eɪdz] N ABBR (= *acquired immune deficiency syndrome*) 艾滋病 àizībìng

aim [eɪm] I VT ▶ **to aim sth (at sb/sth)** [+ *gun, camera*] 将(將)某物瞄准(準) (某人/某物) jiāng mǒuwù miáozhǔn (mǒurén/mǒuwù) II VI (*with weapon*) 瞄 准(準) miáozhǔn III N [c] (*objective*) 目 标(標) mùbiāo [个 gè] ▶ **to aim at sth** (*with weapon*) 瞄准(準)某物 miáozhǔn mǒuwù ▶ **to aim to do sth** 打算做某事 dǎsuàn zuò mǒushì

air [εəʳ] I N [u] 空气(氣) kōngqì II CPD [+ *travel*] 乘飞(飛)机(機)的 chéng fēijī de; [+ *fare*] 飞(飛)机(機)的 fēijī de ▶ **in/into/ through the air** 在/进(進)入/穿过(過) 天空 zài/jìnrù/chuānguò tiānkōng ▶ **by air** (*flying*) 乘飞(飛)机(機) chéng fēijī

air-conditioned ['εəkən'dɪʃənd] ADJ 装(裝)有空调(調)的 zhuāngyǒu kōngtiáo de

air conditioning [-kən'dɪʃənɪŋ] N [u] 空 气(氣)调(調)节(節) kōngqì tiáojié

air force N [c] 空军(軍) kōngjūn [支 zhī]

air hostess (*Brit*) N [c] 空中小姐 kōngzhōng xiǎojiě [位 wèi]

airline ['εəlaɪn] N [c] 航空公司 hángkōng gōngsī [家 jiā]

airmail ['εəmeɪl] N [u] ▶ **by airmail** 航空 邮(郵)寄 hángkōng yóujì

airplane ['εəpleɪn] (*US*) N [c] 飞(飛) 机(機) fēijī [架 jià]

airport ['εəpɔːt] N [c] 飞(飛)机(機) 场(場) fēijīchǎng [个 gè]

aisle [aɪl] N [c] 过(過)道 guòdào [条 tiáo] ▶ **aisle seat** (*on plane*) 靠过(過)道的座位 kào guòdào de zuòwèi

alarm [ə'lɑːm] N 1 (*warning device*) 警 报(報) jǐngbào [个 gè] 2 (*on clock*) 闹(鬧)钟(鐘) nàozhōng [个 gè]

alarm clock N [c] 闹(鬧)钟(鐘) nàozhōng [个 gè]

Albania [æl'beɪnɪə] N 阿尔(爾)巴尼 亚(亞) Ā'ěrbāníyà

album ['ælbəm] N [c] 1 册(冊)子 cèzi [本 běn] 2 (*LP*) 唱片 chàngpiàn [张 zhāng]

alcohol ['ælkəhɒl] N [u] 酒 jiǔ

alcoholic [ælkə'hɒlɪk] I N [c] 酒鬼 jiǔguǐ [个 gè] II ADJ [+ *drink*] 含酒精的 hán jiǔjīng de

alert [ə'lɜːt] N [c] (*situation*) ▶ **a security alert** 安全警戒 ānquán jǐngjiè [个 gè]

A level (*Brit*) N [c/u] 中学中级考试

Algeria [æl'dʒɪərɪə] N 阿尔(爾)及利 亚(亞) Ā'ěrjílìyà

alike [ə'laɪk] ADJ ▶ **to be/look alike** 是/看 起来(來)相似的 shì/kànqǐlái xiāngsì de

alive [ə'laɪv] ADJ (*living*) ▶ **to be alive** 活 着(著)的 huózhe de ▶ **alive and well** 安 然无(無)恙的 ānrán wúyàng de

⊙ **KEYWORD**

all [ɔːl] I ADJ 所有的 suǒyǒu de ▶ **all day/ night** 整日/夜 zhěngrì/yè ▶ **all big cities** 所有的大城市 suǒyǒu de dàchéngshì

II PRON 1 全部 quánbù ▶ **all I could do was apologize** 我所能做的全部就是道 歉 wǒ suǒ néng zuò de quánbù jiùshì dàoqiàn ▸ **I ate it all, I ate all of it** 我把它全都吃了 wǒ bǎ tā quán dōu chī le ▸ **all of us** 我们(們)中的所有人 wǒmen zhōng de suǒyǒu rén ▸ **we all sat down** 我们(們)都坐下了 wǒmen dōu zuòxià le ▸ **is that all?** 那就是全部吗(嗎)? nà jiùshì quánbù ma?

2 (in expressions) ▸ **after all** (considering) 毕(畢)竟 bìjìng ▸ **in all** 总(總)共 zǒnggòng ▸ **best of all** 最好不过(過)的是 zuì hǎo bùguò de shì

III ADV **1** (emphatic) 完全 wánquán ▸ **he was doing it all by himself** 他完全是自己做的 tā wánquán shì zìjǐ zuò de ▸ **all alone** 孤零零的 gūlínglíng de **2** (in scores) ▸ **the score is 2 all** 比分2比2平 bǐfēn èr bǐ èr píng

allergic [əˈləːdʒɪk] ADJ [+ reaction, response] 过(過)敏的 guòmǐn de ▸ **to be allergic to sth** 对(對)某物过(過)敏 duì mǒuwù guòmǐn

allergy [ˈælədʒɪ] (Med) N [c/U] 过(過)敏症 guòmǐnzhèng [种 zhǒng] ▸ **to have an allergy to sth** 对(對)某物有过(過)敏症 duì mǒuwù yǒu guòmǐnzhèng

allow [əˈlau] VT **1** (permit) 允许(許) yǔnxǔ **2** [+ sum, time, amount] 留出 liúchū ▸ **to allow sb to do sth** 允许(許)某人做某事 yǔnxǔ mǒurén zuò mǒushì

all right I ADJ **1** ▸ **to be all right** (satisfactory) 还(還)不错(錯)的 hái bùcuò de; (well, safe) 安然无(無)恙的 ānrán wúyàng de **II** ADV **1** [go, work out +] 顺(順)利地 shùnlì de **2** [see, hear, work +] 没(沒)问(問)题(題)地 méi wèntí de **3** (as answer) 可以 kěyǐ

almond [ˈɑːmənd] N [c/U] (nut) 杏仁 xìngrén [颗 kē]

almost [ˈɔːlməust] ADV 差不多 chàbùduō

alone [əˈləun] I ADJ 独(獨)自的 dúzì de **II** ADV (unaided) 独(獨)自地 dúzì de ▸ **to leave sb/sth alone** (undisturbed) 不要打扰(擾)某人/某物 bùyào dǎrǎo mǒurén/mǒuwù

along [əˈlɔŋ] I PREP **1** 沿着(著) yánzhe **2** [+ road, corridor, river] 沿着(著) yánzhe **II** ADV 沿着(著) yánzhe ▸ **along with** (together with) 与(與)…一起 yǔ…yìqǐ

alphabet [ˈælfəbɛt] N ▸ **the alphabet** 字母表 zìmǔbiǎo

already [ɔːlˈrɛdɪ] ADV 已经(經) yǐjīng ▸ **I have already started making dinner** 我已经(經)开(開)始做晚餐了 wǒ yǐjīng kāishǐ zuò wǎncān le ▸ **is it five o'clock already?** (expressing surprise) 已经(經)到5点(點)了吗(嗎)? yǐjīng dào wǔ diǎn le ma?

also [ˈɔːlsəu] ADV **1** (too) 也 yě **2** (moreover) 同样(樣) tóngyàng

alternate [ɔlˈtəːnɪt] ADJ **1** 交替的 jiāotì de **2** (US: alternative) 供替换(換)的 gōng tìhuàn de

alternative [ɔlˈtəːnətɪv] I ADJ **1** (Brit) 另外的 lìngwài de **2** (non-conventional) 非常规(規)的 fēi chángguī de **II** N [c] ▸ **(an) alternative (to)** …的替代 …de tìdài [个 gè] ▸ **to have no alternative (but to)** (除…外)别(別)无(無)选(選)择(擇) (chú…wài) bié wú xuǎnzé

alternatively [ɔlˈtəːnətɪvlɪ] ADV 或者 huòzhě

although [ɔːlˈðəu] CONJ **1** 尽(儘)管 jǐnguǎn **2** (but) 但是 dànshì

altogether [ɔːltəˈgɛðəʳ] ADV **1** (completely) 完全 wánquán **2** (in total) 总(總)共 zǒnggòng ▸ **how much is that altogether?** 总(總)共多少钱(錢)? zǒnggòng duōshǎo qián?

aluminium [æljuˈmɪnɪəm], (US) **aluminum** [əˈluːmɪnəm] N [U] 铝(鋁) lǚ

always [ˈɔːlweɪz] ADV 总(總)是 zǒngshì ▸ **He's always late** 他总(總)是迟(遲)到 tā zǒngshì chídào

am [æm] VB see **be**

a.m. ADV ABBR (= ante meridiem) 上午 shàngwǔ

amateur [ˈæmətəʳ] N [c] 业(業)余(餘)爱(愛)好者 yèyú àihàozhě [个 gè]

amaze [əˈmeɪz] VT 使惊(驚)讶(訝) shǐ jīngyà ▸ **to be amazed (at/by/that…)** (对(對)/被…)惊(驚)讶(訝) (duì/bèi…) jīngyà

amazing [əˈmeɪzɪŋ] ADJ 令人惊(驚)讶(訝)的 lìng rén jīngyà de

ambassador [æmˈbæsədəʳ] N [c] 大使 dàshǐ [位 wèi]

ambition [æmˈbɪʃən] N [c] ▸ **an ambition (to do sth)** (做某事的)志向 (zuò mǒushì de) zhìxiàng [个 gè] ▸ **to achieve one's ambition** 实(實)现(現)自

己的抱负(負) shíxiàn zìjǐ de bàofù

ambitious [æmˈbɪʃəs] ADJ 雄心勃勃的 xióngxīn bóbó de

ambulance [ˈæmbjuləns] N [c] 救护(護)车(車) jiùhùchē [辆 liàng]

America [əˈmɛrɪkə] N 美洲 Měizhōu

American [əˈmɛrɪkən] I ADJ 美国(國)的 Měiguó de II N [c] (person) 美国(國)人 Měiguórén [个 gè]

among(st) [əˈmʌŋ(st)] PREP 在…当(當)中 zài…dāngzhōng

> 如果指两个以上的人或物，用 **among** 或 **amongst**。如果只指两个人或物，用 **between**。…an area between Mars and Jupiter…an opportunity to discuss these issues amongst themselves. **amongst** 是有些过时的表达方式。注意，如果你 **between** 某些东西或某些人，他们在你的两侧。如果你 **among** 或 **amongst** 某些东西或某些人，他们在你的周围。…the bag standing on the floor between us…the sound of a pigeon among the trees…

amount [əˈmaunt] N [c/u] (quantity) 数(數)量 shùliàng; [of money] 数(數)额(額) shù'é [个 gè]; [of work] 总(總)量 zǒngliàng [个 gè]

amp [æmp] N [c] 安培 ānpéi

amplifier [ˈæmplɪfaɪər] N [c] 扬(揚)声(聲)器 yángshēngqì [个 gè]

amuse [əˈmjuːz] VT (distract, entertain) 给(給)…消遣 gěi…xiāoqiǎn ▸ to be amused at/by sth 被某事逗乐(樂) bèi mǒushì dòulè

amusement arcade N [c] 游(遊)乐(樂)场(場) yóulèchǎng [个 gè]

an [æn, ən] DEF ART see **a**

anaesthetic, (US) **anesthetic** [ænɪsˈθɛtɪk] N [c/u] 麻醉剂(劑) mázuìjì [种 zhǒng] ▸ local anaesthetic 局部麻醉 júbù mázuì ▸ general anaesthetic 全身麻醉 quánshēn mázuì

analyse, (US) **analyze** [ˈænəlaɪz] VT 分析 fēnxī

analysis [əˈnæləsɪs] (pl **analyses** [əˈnæləsiːz]) N [c/u] 分析 fēnxī [种 zhǒng]

analyze [ˈænəlaɪz] (US) VT = **analyse**

ancestor [ˈænsɪstər] N [c] 祖先 zǔxiān [位 wèi]

ancient [ˈeɪnʃənt] ADJ 1 [+ Greece, Rome, monument] 古代的 gǔdài de 2 (very old) 古老的 gǔlǎo de

and [ænd] CONJ 和 hé ▸ men and women 男人和女人 nánrén hé nǔrén ▸ better and better 越来(來)越好 yuèláiyuè hǎo ▸ to try and do sth 试(試)着(著)做某事 shìzhe zuò mǒushì

Android® [ˈændrɔɪd] N 安卓 ān zhuó

anesthetic [ænɪsˈθɛtɪk] (US) = **anaesthetic**

anger [ˈæŋgər] N [u] 生气(氣) shēngqì

angry [ˈæŋgrɪ] ADJ 生气(氣)的 shēngqì de ▸ to be angry with sb/about sth 对(對)某人/某事生气(氣) duì mǒurén/mǒushì shēngqì ▸ to make sb angry 使某人生气(氣) shǐ mǒurén shēngqì

animal [ˈænɪməl] N [c] 动(動)物 dòngwù [只 zhī]

ankle [ˈæŋkl] (Anat) N [c] 踝 huái [个 gè]

anniversary [ænɪˈvɜːsərɪ] N [c] 1 ▸ anniversary (of sth) (某事的)周(週)年纪(紀)念 (mǒushì de) zhōunián jìniàn [个 gè] 2 (also: wedding anniversary) 结(結)婚周(週)年纪(紀)念 jiéhūn zhōunián jìniàn [个 gè]

announce [əˈnauns] VT 宣布(佈) xuānbù ▸ the government has announced that… 政府宣称(稱)… zhèngfǔ xuānchēng…

announcement [əˈnaunsmənt] N [c] 1 宣布(佈) xuānbù 2 (at airport or station) 通告 tōnggào [个 gè] ▸ to make an announcement 发(發)表声(聲)明 fābiǎo shēngmíng

annoy [əˈnɔɪ] VT 使烦(煩)恼(惱) shǐ fánnǎo

annoyed [əˈnɔɪd] ADJ 厌(厭)烦(煩)的 yànfán de ▸ to be annoyed at sth/with sb 对(對)某事/某人感到厌(厭)烦(煩) duì mǒushì/mǒurén gǎndào yànfán

annoying [əˈnɔɪɪŋ] ADJ [+ noise, habit, person] 讨(討)厌(厭)的 tǎoyàn de

annual [ˈænjuəl] ADJ 1 [+ meeting, report] 每年的 měinián de 2 [+ sales, income, rate] 年度的 niándù de

anorak [ˈænəræk] N [c] 连(連)帽防风(風)夹(夾)克 liánmào fángfēng jiákè [件 jiàn]

another [əˈnʌðər] I ADJ 1 ▸ another book (one more) 另一本书(書) lìng yī běn shū 2 (a different one) 另外的 lìngwài de

3 ▶ another 5 years/miles/kilos 再有5年/英里/公斤 zài yǒu wǔ nián/yīnglǐ/gōngjīn **II** PRON **1** (one more) 再一个(個) zài yī gè **2** (a different one) 不同的一个(個) bùtóng de yī gè ▶ one another 相互 xiānghù

answer ['ɑːnsər] **I** N [c] **1** (reply) 回答 huídá [个 gè]; (to letter) 回信 huíxìn [封 fēng] **2** (solution) 答案 dá'àn [个 gè] **II** VI (reply) 回答 huídá; (to telephone ringing, knock at door) 应(應)答 yìngdá **III** VT [+ person] 答复(復) dáfù; [+ question] 回答 huídá; [+ letter] 回复(復) huífù ▶ to answer the phone 接听(聽)电(電)话(話) jiētīng diànhuà

answering machine ['ɑːnsərɪŋ-] N [c] 电(電)话(話)答录(錄)机(機) diànhuà dálùjī [台 tái]

Antarctic [ænt'ɑːktɪk] N ▶ the Antarctic 南极(極) Nánjí

anthem ['ænθəm] N [c] 赞(讚)美诗(詩) zànměishī 国(國)歌 guógē [首 shǒu]

antibiotic ['æntɪbaɪ'ɔtɪk] N [c] 抗生素 kàngshēngsù [种 zhǒng]

antique [æn'tiːk] N [c] 古董 gǔdǒng [件 jiàn]

antiseptic [æntɪ'sɛptɪk] N [c/u] 杀(殺)菌剂(劑) shājūnjì [种 zhǒng]

antivirus [] N [c] (program) 抗病毒素 kàngbìng dúsù [个 gè]

anxious ['æŋkʃəs] ADJ 忧(憂)虑(慮)的 yōulǜ de

 KEYWORD

any ['ɛnɪ] **I** ADJ **1** (in negatives, in questions) 一些的 yìxiē de ▶ I haven't any chocolate/sweets 我没(沒)有巧克力/糖了 wǒ méiyǒu qiǎokèlì/táng le ▶ there was hardly any food 几(幾)乎没(沒)有食物了 jīhū méiyǒu shíwù le ▶ have you got any chocolate/sweets? 你有巧克力/糖吗(嗎)? nǐ yǒu qiǎokèlì/táng ma?
2 (in "if" clauses) 任何的 rènhé de ▶ if there are any tickets left 如果有票剩下的话(話) rúguǒ yǒu piào shèngxia de huà
3 (no matter which) 任意的 rènyì de ▶ take any card you like 拿你喜欢(歡)的任意一张(張)卡 ná nǐ xǐhuan de

rènyì yī zhāng kǎ
4 (in expressions) ▶ any day now 从(從)现(現)在起的任何一天 cóng xiànzài qǐ de rènhé yītiān ▶ (at) any moment (在)任何时(時)刻 (zài) rènhé shíkè ▶ any time (whenever) 不论(論)何时(時) bùlùn héshí; (also: at any time) 在任何时(時)候 zài rènhé shíhou

II PRON **1** (in negatives) 一些 yìxiē ▶ I didn't eat any (of it) 我(这(這))一点(點)也没(沒)吃 wǒ (zhè) yīdiǎn yě méi chī ▶ I haven't any (of them) 我一个(個)也没(沒)有 wǒ yī gè yě méiyǒu
2 (in questions) 一些 yìxiē ▶ have you got any? 你有吗(嗎)? nǐ yǒu ma?
3 (in "if" clauses) 任何 rènhé ▶ if any of you would like to take part, ... 如果你们(們)中任何人想参(參)加的话(話), ... rúguǒ nǐmen zhōng rènhé rén xiǎng cānjiā de huà, ...
4 (no matter which ones) 无(無)论(論)哪一个(個) wúlùn nǎ yī gè ▶ help yourself to any of the books 无(無)论(論)哪本书(書)你随(隨)便拿 wúlùn nǎ běn shū nǐ suíbiàn ná

III ADV **1** (with negative) 丝(絲)毫 sīháo ▶ I don't play tennis any more 我不再打网(網)球了 wǒ bùzài dǎ wǎngqiú le ▶ don't wait any longer 不再等了 bùzài děng le
2 (in questions) …一点(點) …yīdiǎn ▶ do you want any more soup/sandwiches? 你还(還)想再要点(點)汤(湯)/三明治吗(嗎)? nǐ hái xiǎng zài yào diǎn tāng/sānmíngzhì ma?

anybody ['ɛnɪbɔdɪ] PRON = anyone
anyhow ['ɛnɪhau] ADV = anyway
anyone ['ɛnɪwʌn] PRON **1** (in negatives, "if" clauses) 任何人 rènhé rén **2** (in questions) 任何一个(個) rènhé yī gè rén ▶ I can't see anyone 我见(見)不到任何人 wǒ jiàn bù dào rènhé rén ▶ did anyone see you? 有人看到你吗(嗎)? yǒurén kàndào nǐ ma? ▶ anyone could do it 任何人都能做到 rènhé rén dōunéng zuòdào
anything ['ɛnɪθɪŋ] PRON (in negatives, questions, "if" clauses) 任何事 rènhé shì ▶ I can't see anything 我什么(麼)也看不见(見) wǒ shénme yě kàn bù jiàn

▶ **hardly anything** 几(幾)乎没(沒)有任何东(東)西 jīhū méiyǒu rènhé dōngxi
▶ **did you find anything?** 你找到些什么(麼)吗(嗎)？ nǐ zhǎodào xiē shénme ma? ▶ **if anything happens to me...** 如果任何事情发(發)生在我身上… rúguǒ rènhé shìqing fāshēng zài wǒ shēnshang... ▶ **you can say anything you like** 你可以畅(暢)所欲言 nǐ kěyǐ chàng suǒ yù yán

anyway ['ɛnɪweɪ] ADV **1** (besides) 无(無)论(論)如何 wúlùn rúhé **2** (all the same) 还(還)是 háishi **3** (in short) 总(總)之 zǒngzhī ▶ **I shall go anyway** 无论(論)如何我要走了 wúlùn rúhé wǒ yào zǒu le

anywhere ['ɛnɪwɛə'] ADV (in negatives, questions, "if" clauses) 任何地方 rènhé dìfang ▶ **I can't see him anywhere** 我哪里(裡)都见(見)不到他 wǒ nǎlǐ dōu jiàn bù dào tā

apart [ə'pɑːt] ADV [couple, family +] 分开(開) fēnkāi ▶ **to take sth apart** 拆卸某物 chāixiè mǒuwù ▶ **apart from** 除去 chúqù

apartment [ə'pɑːtmənt] N [c] (US) 公寓 gōngyù [处(處) chù]

apologize [ə'pɔlədʒaɪz] VI 道歉 dàoqiàn ▶ **to apologize to sb (for sth)** 向某人(为(為)某事)道歉 xiàng mǒurén (wèi mǒushì) dàoqiàn

apology [ə'pɔlədʒɪ] N [c/u] 道歉 dàoqiàn [个 gè]

apostrophe [ə'pɔstrəfɪ] N [c] 撇号(號) piěhào [个 gè]

app [æp] N [c] 应(應)用软(軟)件 yìngyòng ruǎnjiàn [个 gè]

apparently [ə'pærəntlɪ] ADV 表面看来(來) biǎomiàn kànlái

appear [ə'pɪə'] VI **1** (seem) 看起来(來) kànqǐlái **2** (come into view, begin to develop) 出现(現) chūxiàn ▶ **to appear to be/have** 看起来(來)是/有 kànqǐlái shì/yǒu

appendicitis [əpɛndɪ'saɪtɪs] N [u] 阑(闌)尾炎 lánwěiyán

appetite ['æpɪtaɪt] N [c/u] 食欲(慾) shíyù

applause [ə'plɔːz] N [u] 掌声(聲) zhǎngshēng

apple ['æpl] N [c] 苹(蘋)果 píngguǒ [个 gè]

appliance [ə'plaɪəns] (frm) N [c] 器具 qìjù [件 jiàn]

applicant ['æplɪkənt] N [c] 申请(請)人 shēnqǐngrén [个 gè]

application [æplɪ'keɪʃən] N **1** [c] 申请(請) shēnqǐng [份 fèn] **2** [c] (Comput: program) 应(應)用程序 yìngyòng chéngxù [个 gè]

application form N [c] 申请(請)表格 shēnqǐng biǎogé [份 fèn]

apply [ə'plaɪ] VI (make application) 提出申请(請) tíchū shēnqǐng ▶ **to apply for sth** [+job, grant, membership] 申请(請)某事 shēnqǐng mǒushì

appointment [ə'pɔɪntmənt] N [c] (arranged meeting) 约(約)会(會) yuēhuì [个 gè]; (with hairdresser, dentist, doctor) 预(預)约(約) yùyuē [个 gè] ▶ **to make an appointment (with sb)** (to see hairdresser, dentist, doctor) (和某人)预(預)约(約) (hé mǒurén) yùyuē

appreciate [ə'priːʃɪeɪt] VT (be grateful for) 感谢(謝) gǎnxiè ▶ **I (really) appreciate your help** 我(十分)感谢(謝)你的帮(幫)助 wǒ (shífēn) gǎnxiè nǐde bāngzhù

approach [ə'prəutʃ] I VI [person, car +] 走近 zǒu jìn; [event, time +] 临(臨)近 línjìn II VT **1** (draw near to) 向…靠近 xiàng...kàojìn **2** [+ situation, problem] 处(處)理 chǔlǐ III N [c] (to a problem, situation) 方式 fāngshì [种 zhǒng]

approval [ə'pruːvəl] N [u] 批准 pīzhǔn

approve [ə'pruːv] VI 赞(贊)成 zànchéng

approximate [ə'prɔksɪmɪt] ADJ 近似的 jìnsì de

apricot ['eɪprɪkɔt] N [c/u] 杏子 xìngzi [个 gè]

April ['eɪprəl] N [c/u] 四月 sìyuè; see also/ 另见 **July**

apron ['eɪprən] N [c] 围(圍)裙 wéiqún [条 tiáo]

Aquarius [ə'kwɛərɪəs] N [u] (sign) 宝(寶)瓶座 Bǎopíng Zuò gè

Arab ['ærəb] I ADJ 阿拉伯的 Ālābó de II N [c] 阿拉伯人 Ālābórén [个 gè]

Arabic ['ærəbɪk] N [u] (language) 阿拉伯语(語) Ālābóyǔ

arch [ɑːtʃ] N [c] 拱 gǒng [个 gè]

archaeology [ɑːkɪ'ɔlədʒɪ] N [u] 考古学(學) kǎogǔxué

archeology [ɑːkɪ'ɔlədʒɪ] (US) = **archaeology**

architect ['ɑ:kɪtekt] N [c] 建筑(築)师(師) jiànzhùshī [位 wèi]

architecture ['ɑ:kɪtektʃəʳ] N [u] 建筑(築)学(學) jiànzhùxué

Arctic ['ɑ:ktɪk] N ▸ the Arctic 北极(極) Běijí

are [ɑ:ʳ] VB see be

area ['ɛərɪə] N 1 [c] (region, zone) 地区(區) dìqū [个 gè] 2 [c] (of room, building etc) 区(區)域 qūyù [个 gè] 3 [c/u] (Math, Geom) 面积(積) miànjī [个 gè] 4 [c] (part) 部分 bùfen [个 gè] ▸ in the London area 在伦(倫)敦周边(邊)地区(區) zài Lúndūn zhōubiān dìqū

area code (esp US) N [c] 区(區)号(號) qūhào [个 gè]

Argentina [ɑ:dʒən'ti:nə] N 阿根廷 Āgēntíng

argue ['ɑ:gju:] VI (quarrel) ▸ to argue (with sb) (about sth) (为(為)某事) (和某人) 争(爭)吵 (wèi mǒushì) (hé mǒurén) zhēngchǎo

argument ['ɑ:gjumənt] N [c/u] (quarrel) 争(爭)吵 zhēngchǎo [阵 zhèn] ▸ an argument for/against sth 赞(贊)成/反对(對)某事的论(論)据(據) zànchéng/fǎnduì mǒushì de lùnjù

Aries ['ɛəriz] N [u] (sign) 白羊座 Báiyáng Zuò

arithmetic [ə'rɪθmətɪk] N [u] (Math) 算术(術) suànshù

arm [ɑ:m] I N [c] 1 胳膊 gēbo [条 tiáo] 2 (of jacket, shirt etc) 袖子 xiùzi [只 zhī] II arms NPL (weapons) 武器 wǔqì

armchair ['ɑ:mtʃɛəʳ] N [c] 扶手椅 fúshǒuyǐ [把 bǎ]

armed [ɑ:md] ADJ 武装(裝)的 wǔzhuāng de

army ['ɑ:mɪ] N ▸ the army 军(軍)队(隊) jūnduì

around [ə'raund] I ADV (about) 到处(處) dàochù II PREP 1 (encircling) 围(圍)绕(繞) wéirào 2 (near) 在附近 zài fùjìn 3 大约(約) dàyuē

arrange [ə'reɪndʒ] I VT 1 (organize) 安排 ānpái 2 (put in order) 整理 zhěnglǐ II VI ▸ to arrange to do sth 安排做某事 ānpái zuò mǒushì

arrangement [ə'reɪndʒmənt] I N [c] 1 (agreement) 约(約)定 yuēdìng [个 gè] 2 (grouping, layout) 布(佈)置 bùzhì [种 zhǒng] II arrangements NPL (plans, preparations) 安排 ānpái

arrest [ə'rɛst] VT 逮捕 dàibǔ ▸ to be under arrest 被逮捕 bèi dàibǔ

arrival [ə'raɪvl] N [c/u] 到达(達) dàodá

arrive [ə'raɪv] VI 1 到 dào 2 (letter, meal +) 来(來) lái

arrow ['ærəu] N [c] 1 (weapon) 箭 jiàn [支 zhī] 2 (sign) 箭头(頭)标(標)志(誌) jiàntóu biāozhì [个 gè]

art [ɑ:t] I N 1 (activity of drawing, painting etc) 美术(術) měishù 2 [u] 艺(藝)术(術) yìshù 3 [c] (skill) 技艺(藝) jìyì [项 xiàng] II arts NPL ▸ the arts 艺(藝)术(術)活动(動) yìshù huódòng III CPD ▸ arts [+ graduate, student, course] 文科 wénkē ▸ work of art 艺(藝)术(術)品 yìshùpǐn

art gallery N [c] 美术(術)馆(館) měishùguǎn [个 gè]

article ['ɑ:tɪkl] N [c] 1 物品 wùpǐn [件 jiàn] 2 (in newspaper) 文章 wénzhāng [篇 piān] 3 (Ling) 冠词(詞) guàncí [个 gè]

artificial [ɑ:tɪ'fɪʃəl] ADJ 人造的 rénzào de

artist ['ɑ:tɪst] N [c] 画(畫)家 huàjiā [位 wèi]

○ **KEYWORD**

as [æz, əz] I CONJ 1 (referring to time) 当(當)…时(時) dāng…shí ▸ he came in as I was leaving 我离(離)开(開)时(時)他进(進)来(來)了 wǒ líkāi shí tā jìnlai le 2 (since, because) 因为(為) yīnwèi ▸ as you can't come, I'll go on my own 既然你不能来(來), 我就自己去 jìrán nǐ bùnéng lái, wǒ jiù zìjǐ qù 3 (referring to manner, way) 像…一样(樣) xiàng…yīyàng ▸ as you can see 如你所见(見)到的 rú nǐ suǒ jiàndào de ▸ it's on the left as you go in 在你进(進)入时(時)的左侧(側) zài nǐ jìnrù shí de zuǒcè II PREP 1 (in the capacity of) 作为(為) zuòwéi ▸ he works as a salesman 他做推销(銷)员(員)的工作 tā zuò tuīxiāoyuán de gōngzuò 2 (when) 在…时(時) zài…shí ▸ he was very energetic as a child 他小时(時)候精力很旺盛 tā xiǎoshíhou jīnglì hěn wàngshèng

III ADV **1** (in comparisons) ▸ as big/good/easy etc as... 像…一样(樣)大/好/容易〔等〕 xiàng...yīyàng dà/hǎo/róngyì děng ▸ you're as tall as he is or as him 你和他一样(樣)高 nǐ hé tā yīyàng gāo ▸ as soon as ……就… yī...jiù... **2** (in expressions) ▸ as if or though 好像 hǎoxiàng

ash [æʃ] N [U] 灰末 huīmò

ashamed [ə'feɪmd] ADJ ▸ to be/feel ashamed 感到羞愧 gǎndào xiūkuì ▸ to be ashamed of sb/sth 对(對)某人/某事感到羞愧 duì mǒurén/mǒushì gǎndào xiūkuì

ashtray ['æʃtreɪ] N [C] 烟(煙)灰缸 yānhuīgāng [个 gè]

Asia ['eɪʃə] N 亚(亞)洲 Yàzhōu

Asian ['eɪʃən] I ADJ 亚(亞)洲的 Yàzhōu de II N [C] (person) 亚(亞)洲人 Yàzhōurén [个 gè]

ask [ɑːsk] I VT **1** ▸ to ask (sb) a question 问(問)(某人)一个(個)问(問)题(題) wèn (mǒurén) yī gè wèntí **2** (invite) 邀请(請) yāoqǐng II VI 问(問) wèn ▸ to ask (sb) whether/why... 问(問)(某人)是否/为(為)什么(麼)… wèn (mǒurén) shìfǒu/wèishénme... ▸ to ask sb to do sth 请(請)求某人做某事 qǐngqiú mǒurén zuò mǒushì ▸ to ask to do sth 要求做某事 yāoqiú zuò mǒushì ▸ to ask sb the time 向某人询(詢)问(問)时(時)间(間) xiàng mǒurén xúnwèn shíjiān ▸ to ask sb about sth 向某人打听(聽)某事 xiàng mǒurén dǎtīng mǒushì ▸ I asked him his name 我问(問)他叫什么(麼) wǒ wèn tā jiào shénme
▸ **ask for** VT FUS **1** (+ thing) 要 yào **2** (+ person) 找 zhǎo

asleep [ə'sliːp] ADJ 睡着(著)的 shuìzháo de ▸ to be asleep 睡着(著) shuìzháo le ▸ to fall asleep 入睡 rùshuì

aspirin ['æsprɪn] N [C] (tablet) 阿司匹林药(藥)片 āsīpǐlín yàopiàn [片 piàn]

assemble [ə'sɛmbl] I VT (+ machinery, object) 装(裝)配 zhuāngpèi II VI (gather) 聚集 jùjí

assembly [ə'sɛmblɪ] N **1** [C] (meeting) 集会(會) jíhuì [个 gè] **2** [U] (of vehicles) 装(裝)配 zhuāngpèi

assignment [ə'saɪnmənt] N [C] 任务(務) rènwù [项 xiàng]; (for student) 作业 zuòyè [个 gè]

assistance [ə'sɪstəns] N [U] 帮助 bāngzhù

assistant [ə'sɪstənt] N [C] **1** (helper) 助手 zhùshǒu [个 gè] **2** (Brit: in shop) 营(營)业(業)员(員) yíngyèyuán [个 gè]

assortment [ə'sɔːtmənt] N [C] ▸ an assortment of sth 各种(種)各样(樣)的某物 gèzhǒng gèyàng de mǒuwù [件 jiàn]

assume [ə'sjuːm] VT 假设(設) jiǎshè

assure [ə'ʃuəʳ] VT 使确(確)信 shǐ quèxìn

asterisk ['æstərɪsk] N [C] 星号(號) xīnghào [个 gè]

asthma ['æsmə] N [U] 哮喘 xiàochuǎn

astonishing [ə'stɔnɪʃɪŋ] ADJ 惊(驚)人的 jīngrén de

astronaut ['æstrənɔːt] N [C] 宇航员(員) yǔhángyuán [位 wèi]

astronomy [ə'strɔnəmɪ] N [U] 天文学(學) tiānwénxué

◯ **KEYWORD**

at [æt] PREP **1** (position, time, age) 在 zài ▸ we had dinner at a restaurant 我们(們)在一家饭(飯)店吃了饭(飯) wǒmen zài yì jiā fàndiàn chīle fàn ▸ at home 在家 zàijiā ▸ at work 在工作 zài gōngzuò ▸ to be sitting at a table/desk 坐在桌边(邊)/书(書)桌边(邊) zuòzài zhuōbiān/shūzhuōbiān ▸ there's someone at the door 门(門)口有人 ménkǒu yǒurén; (towards) ▸ to throw sth at sb 向某人扔某物 xiàng mǒurén rēng mǒuwù ▸ at four o'clock 在4点(點)钟(鐘) zài sì diǎn zhōng ▸ at Christmas 在圣(聖)诞(誕)节(節) zài Shèngdànjié **2** (referring to price, speed) 以 yǐ ▸ apples at £2 a kilo 苹(蘋)果每公斤两(兩)镑(鎊) píngguǒ měi gōngjīn liǎng bàng ▸ at 50 km/h 以每小时(時)50公里的速度 yǐ měi xiǎoshí wǔshí gōnglǐ de sùdù **3** (in expressions) ▸ not at all (in answer to question) 一点(點)也不 yìdiǎn yě bù; (in answer to thanks) 别(別)客气(氣) bié kèqì

ate [eɪt] PT of eat

athlete ['æθliːt] N [C] 运(運)动(動)员(員) yùndòngyuán [名 míng]

athletics [æθˈlɛtɪks] N [U] 田径(徑)
运(運)动(動) tiánjìng yùndòng

Atlantic [ətˈlæntɪk] I ADJ ▶ 大西洋的
Dàxīyáng de II N ▶ the Atlantic (Ocean)
大西洋 Dàxīyáng

atlas [ˈætləs] N [c] 地图(圖)册(冊) dìtúcè
[本 běn]

atmosphere [ˈætməsfɪəʳ] N 1 [c] [of
planet] 大气(氣)层(層) dàqìcéng [个 gè]
2 [of place] 气(氣)氛 qìfēn

attach [əˈtætʃ] VT ▶ 附上 fùshàng

attachment [əˈtætʃmənt] N [c] [of tool,
computer file] 附件 fùjiàn [个 gè]

attack [əˈtæk] I VT 1 [+ person] 袭(襲)
击(擊) xíjī 2 [+ place, troops] 攻击(擊)
gōngjī 3 (criticise) 抨击(擊) pēngjī II VI
(Mil, Sport) 进(進)攻 jìngōng III N 1 [c/U]
(on person) 袭(襲)击(擊) xíjī [次 cì]
2 [c/U] (military assault) 攻击(擊) gōngjī
[次 cì] 3 [c/U] [of illness] 发(發)作 fāzuò
[阵 zhèn] ▶ an attack on sb (assault)
袭(襲)击(擊)某人 xíjī mǒurén; (criticism)
抨击(擊)某人 pēngjī mǒurén

attempt [əˈtɛmpt] I N [c] (try) 尝(嘗)
试(試) chángshì [个 gè] II VI ▶ to
attempt to do sth 试(試)图(圖)做某事
shìtú zuò mǒushì ▶ an attempt to do
sth 做某事的企图(圖) zuò mǒushì de
qǐtú

attend [əˈtɛnd] VT 1 [+ school, church,
course] 上 shàng 2 [+ lecture, conference]
参(參)加 cānjiā

attention [əˈtɛnʃən] N [U]
1 (concentration) 注意 zhùyì 2 (care) 照料
zhàoliào ▶ to pay attention (to sth/sb)
关(關)注(某事/某人) guānzhù
(mǒushì/mǒurén)

attitude [ˈætɪtjuːd] N [c/U] 看法 kànfǎ
[个 gè]

attorney [əˈtəːnɪ] (US) N [c] (lawyer) 律
师(師) lǜshī [位 wèi]

attract [əˈtrækt] VT ▶ 吸引 xīyǐn

attraction [əˈtrækʃən] I N [U] (charm,
appeal) 吸引力 xīyǐnlì II **attractions**
N PL (also: **tourist attractions**)
(amusements) 游(遊)览(覽)胜(勝)地
yóulǎn shèngdì

attractive [əˈtræktɪv] ADJ [+ man, woman]
有魅力的 yǒu mèilì de; [+ thing, place]
吸引人的 xīyǐn rén de ▶ he was very
attractive to women 他对(對)女人很

auburn [ˈɔːbən] ADJ 赤褐色的 chìhèsè
de

auction [ˈɔːkʃən] I N [c] 拍卖(賣) pāimài
[次 cì] II VT 拍卖(賣) pāimài

audience [ˈɔːdɪəns] N [c] 1 (in theatre)
观(觀)众(眾) guānzhòng [位 wèi] 2 (Rad,
TV) 听(聽)众(眾) tīngzhòng [位 wèi]

August [ˈɔːgəst] N [c/U] 八月 bāyuè; see
also/另见 **July**

aunt [ɑːnt] N [c] (father's sister) 姑母
gūmǔ [位 wèi]; (father's older brother's
wife) 伯母 bómǔ [位 wèi]; (father's
younger brother's wife) 婶(嬸)母 shěnmǔ
[位 wèi]; (mother's sister) 姨母 yímǔ [位
wèi]; (mother's brother's wife) 舅母 jiùmǔ
[位 wèi]

auntie, aunty [ˈɑːntɪ] (inf) N = **aunt**

au pair [ˈəuˈpɛəʳ] N [c] 为学习语言而住
在当地人家里并提供家政服务的外国年
轻人

Australia [ɔsˈtreɪlɪə] N 澳大利亚(亞)
Àodàlìyà

Australian [ɔsˈtreɪlɪən] I ADJ 澳大利
亚(亞)的 Àodàlìyà de II N [c] (person) 澳
大利亚(亞)人 Àodàlìyàrén [个 gè]

Austria [ˈɔstrɪə] N 奥(奧)地利 Àodìlì

author [ˈɔːθəʳ] N [c] (writer) [of novel] 作家
zuòjiā [位 wèi]; [of text] 作者 zuòzhě [个
gè]

autobiography [ɔːtəbaɪˈɔgrəfɪ] N [c] 自
传(傳) zìzhuàn [部 bù]

automatic [ɔːtəˈmætɪk] I ADJ 自动(動)
的 zìdòng de II N [c] (car) 自动(動)
挡(擋) zìdòngdǎng [个 gè]

automatically [ɔːtəˈmætɪklɪ] ADV 1 (by
itself) 自动(動)地 zìdòng de 2 (without
thinking) 无(無)意识(識)地 wú yìshí de
3 (as a matter of course) 自然而然地 zìrán
ér rán de

automobile [ˈɔːtəməbiːl] (US) N [c] 汽
车(車) qìchē [辆 liàng]

autumn [ˈɔːtəm] (Brit) N [c/U] 秋季 qiūjì
[个 gè] ▶ in (the) autumn 在秋季 zài
qiūjì

available [əˈveɪləbl] ADJ 1 可用的 kě
yòng de 2 [+ person] 有空的 yǒukòng de

avalanche [ˈævəlɑːnʃ] N [c] 雪崩
xuěbēng [次 cì]

avatar [ˈævətɑːʳ] N [c] 虚(虛)拟(擬)化身
xūnǐ huàshēn [个 gè]

average ['ævərɪdʒ] **I** N [c] **1** (Math: mean) 平均数(數) píngjūnshù [个 gè] **2** ▸ the **average (for sth/sb)** (某物/某人的) 平均水平 (mǒuwù/mǒurén de) píngjūn shuǐpíng [个 gè] **II** ADJ (ordinary) 普通的 pǔtōng de ▸ on **average** 平均 píngjūn ▸ above/below (the) **average** 高于(於)/低于(於)平均水平 gāoyú/dīyú píngjūn shuǐpíng

avoid [ə'vɔɪd] VT **1** [+ person, obstacle] 避免 bìmiǎn **2** [+ trouble, danger] 防止 fángzhǐ ▸ to **avoid doing sth** 避免做某事 bìmiǎn zuò mǒushì

awake [ə'weɪk] (pt **awoke**, pp **awoken** or **awakened**) ADJ ▸ to be **awake** 醒着(著)的 xǐngzhe de

award [ə'wɔːd] **I** N [c] (prize) 奖(獎) jiǎng [个 gè] **II** VT [+ prize] 授予 shòuyǔ

aware [ə'wɛər] ADJ ▸ to be **aware of sth** (know about) 意识(識)到某事 yìshi dào mǒushì; (be conscious of) 觉(覺)察到某事 juéchá dào mǒushì ▸ to be **aware that...** 知道… zhīdào…

away [ə'weɪ] **I** ADV **1** (move, walk +) …开(開) …kāi **2** (not present) 不在 bùzài **II** ADJ (match, game) 客场(場)的 kèchǎng de ▸ a **week/month away** 还(還)有一个(個)星期/月 háiyǒu yī gè xīngqī/yuè ▸ **two kilometres away** 离(離)这(這)里(裡)两(兩)公里远(遠) lí zhèlǐ liǎng gōnglǐ yuǎn

awful ['ɔːfəl] **I** ADJ **1** 糟糕的 zāogāo de **2** [+ shock, crime] 可怕的 kěpà de **3** ▸ to **look/feel awful** (ill) 看起来(來)/感觉(覺)很糟糕的 kàn qǐlái/gǎnjué hěn zāogāo de **II** ADV (US: inf: very) 十分地 shífēn de ▸ an **awful lot (of)** (amount) 大量的 dàliàng de; (number) 非常多的 fēicháng duō de

awkward ['ɔːkwəd] ADJ **1** [+ movement] 笨拙的 bènzhuō de **2** [+ time, question] 令人尴(尷)尬的 lìng rén gāngà de

axe, (US) **ax** [æks] N [c] 斧 fǔ [把 bǎ]

baby ['beɪbɪ] N [c] 婴(嬰)儿(兒) yīng'ér [个 gè] ▸ to **have a baby** 生孩子 shēng háizi

baby carriage (US) N [c] 婴(嬰)儿(兒)车(車) yīng'ér chē [辆 liàng]

babysit ['beɪbɪsɪt] (pt, pp **babysat**) VI 代人照看孩子 dài rén zhàokàn háizi

babysitter ['beɪbɪsɪtər] N [c] 代人照看孩子的人 dài rén zhàokàn háizi de rén [个 gè]

bachelor ['bætʃələr] N [c] **1** (unmarried man) 单(單)身汉(漢) dānshēnhàn [个 gè] **2** ▸ **Bachelor of Arts/Science** 文/科学(學)士学(學)位 wén/lǐkē xuéshì xuéwèi [个 gè]

back [bæk] **I** N [c] **1** 背部 bèibù [个 gè] **2** [of hand, neck, legs] 背面 bèimiàn [个 gè]; [of house, door, book] 后(後)面 hòumiàn [个 gè]; [of car] 后(後)部 hòubù [个 gè] **II** VT **1** (support) 支持 zhīchí; (financially) 资(資)助 zīzhù **2** (reverse) 倒 dào **III** ADJ [+ garden, door, room, wheels] 后(後)面的 hòumiàn de **IV** ADV **1** (not forward) 向后(後) xiàng hòu **2** (returned) 回 huí ▸ to be **back** 回来(來) huílái ▸ **can I have it back?** 我能要回它吗(嗎)? wǒ néng yàohuí tā ma?

▸ **back down** VI 做出让(讓)步 zuòchū ràngbù

▸ **back out** VI (withdraw) 退出 tuìchū

▸ **back up** VT **1** [+ statement, theory] 证(證)实(實) zhèngshí **2** (Comput) [+ disk] 备(備)份 bèifèn

backache ['bækeɪk] N [C/U] 背痛 bèitòng [阵 zhèn]

background ['bækgraʊnd] N **1** [C] (of picture, scene, events) 背景 bèijǐng [个 gè] **2** [C/U] (of person) (origins) 出身 chūshēn [种 zhǒng]; (experience) 经(經)验(驗) jīngyàn [种 zhǒng] ▸ **in the background** 在背后(後) zài bèihòu

backing ['bækɪŋ] N [U] (support) 支持 zhīchí; (financial) 资(資)助 zīzhù

backpack ['bækpæk] N [C] 双(雙)肩背包 shuāngjiān bēibāo [个 gè]

backpacker ['bækpækə'] N [C] 背包旅行者 bēibāo lǚxíngzhě [名 míng]

BACKPACKER

backpacker 一词指预算紧张的青年旅行者。他们把全部的随身物品放在一个背包里,尽可能地节省开支,为的是能延长旅行时间多了解一个地区,多看一些地方。

backstroke ['bækstrəʊk] N [U] (also: **the backstroke**) 仰泳 yǎngyǒng

backup ['bækʌp] **I** ADJ (Comput) (+ copy, file, disk) 备(備)份的 bèifèn de **II** N [U] (support) 支持 zhīchí

backward ['bækwəd] ADV (esp US) = **backwards**

backwards ['bækwədz] ADV 向后(後)地 xiàng hòu de

backyard [bæk'jɑːd] N [C] 后(後)院 hòuyuàn [个 gè]

bacon ['beɪkən] N [U] 腌(醃)猪(豬)肉 yān zhūròu

bad [bæd] ADJ **1** [+ weather, health, conditions, temper] 坏(壞)的 huài de; [+ actor, driver] 不胜(勝)任的 bù shèngrèn de; [+ behaviour, habit] 不良的 bùliáng de **2** (wicked) 恶(惡)的 è de **3** (naughty) 不听(聽)话(話)的 bù tīnghuà de **4** [+ mistake, accident, headache] 严(嚴)重的 yánzhòng de **5** [+ back, arm] 有病的 yǒubìng de **6** (rotten) 腐烂(爛)的 fǔlàn de ▸ **to be bad for sth/sb** 对(對)某事/某物有害 duì mǒushì/mǒuwù yǒuhài ▸ **not bad** 不错(錯) bùcuò

badge [bædʒ] N [C] (Brit) 徽章 huīzhāng [个 gè]

badly ['bædlɪ] ADV **1** (poorly) 不令人满(滿)意地 bù lìng rén mǎnyì de **2** [+ damaged, injured] 严(嚴)重地 yánzhòng de

badminton ['bædmɪntən] N [U] 羽毛球 yǔmáoqiú

bad-tempered ['bæd'tempəd] ADJ 脾气(氣)坏(壞)的 píqì huài de

bag [bæg] N [C] **1** 袋 dài [个 gè] **2** (suitcase) 行李箱 xínglixiāng [个 gè] **3** (handbag) 手袋 shǒudài [个 gè] ▸ **to pack one's bags** 准(準)备(備)离(離)开(開) zhǔnbèi líkāi

baggage ['bægɪdʒ] N [U] 行李 xíngli

baggage (re)claim N [U] 行李领(領)取 xíngli lǐngqǔ

bake [beɪk] VT 烤 kǎo

baker ['beɪkə'] N [C] (also: **baker's**) 面(麵)包店 miànbāodiàn [家 jiā]

bakery ['beɪkərɪ] N [C] 面(麵)包房 miànbāofáng [个 gè]

balance ['bæləns] N **1** [U] (of person, object) 平衡 pínghéng **2** [C] (in bank account) 余(餘)额(額) yú'é [笔 bǐ] **3** [S] (remainder to be paid) 余(餘)欠之数(數) yúqiàn zhī shù ▸ **to keep/lose one's balance** 保持/失去平衡 bǎochí/shīqù pínghéng

balcony ['bælkənɪ] N [C] (open) 露台(臺) lùtái [个 gè]; (covered) 阳(陽)台(臺) yángtái [个 gè]

bald [bɔːld] ADJ 秃(秃)的 tū de ▸ **to go bald** 变(變)秃(秃) biàntū

ball [bɔːl] N [C] 球 qiú [个 gè]

ballet ['bæleɪ, US bæ'leɪ] N [U] 芭蕾舞 bāléiwǔ

ballet dancer N [C] 芭蕾舞演员(員) bāléiwǔ yǎnyuán [位 wèi]

balloon [bə'luːn] N [C] 气(氣)球 qìqiú [只 zhī]

ballpoint (pen) ['bɔːlpɔɪnt(-)] N [C] 圆(圓)珠笔(筆) yuánzhūbǐ [支 zhī]

ban [bæn] **I** N [C] 禁止 jìnzhǐ [种 zhǒng] **II** VT 禁止 jìnzhǐ

banana [bə'nɑːnə] N [C] 香蕉 xiāngjiāo [只 zhī]

band [bænd] N [C] **1** (group) 群 qún **2** (Mus) 乐(樂)队(隊) yuèduì [个 gè]

bandage ['bændɪdʒ] N [C] 绷(繃)带(帶) bēngdài [条 tiáo]

Band-Aid® ['bændeɪd] (US) N [C] 邦迪

创(創)可贴(貼) Bāngdí chuāngkětiē [贴 tiē]

bang [bæŋ] I N [c] 1 (noise) 砰的一声(聲) pēng de yī shēng; [of gun, exhaust] 爆炸声(聲) bàozhà shēng [阵 zhèn] 2 (blow) 撞击(擊) zhuàngjī [下 xià] II VT [+ one's head, elbow] 撞 zhuàng III bangs NPL (US: fringe) 刘(劉)海 liúhǎi ▶ to bang into sth/sb 猛撞某物/某人 měngzhuàng mǒuwù/mǒurén

Bangladesh [bæŋɡlə'deʃ] N 孟加拉国(國) Mèngjiālāguó

bank [bæŋk] N [c] 1 (Fin) 银(銀)行 yínháng [家 jiā] 2 [of river, lake] 岸 àn [个 gè]

bank account N [c] 银(銀)行账(賬)户(戶) yínháng zhànghù [个 gè]

bank card N [c] 1 (Brit: for cash machine) 银(銀)行卡 yínhángkǎ [张 zhāng] 2 (US: credit card) 银(銀)行信用卡 yínháng xìnyòngkǎ [张 zhāng]

bank holiday (Brit) N [c] 法定假期 fǎdìng jiàqī [个 gè]

banknote ['bæŋknəʊt] N [c] 纸(紙)币(幣) zhǐbì [张 zhāng]

bar [bɑːʳ] N [c] 1 (pub) 酒吧 jiǔbā [个 gè] 2 (counter) 吧台(臺) bātái [个 gè] 3 [of metal] 条(條) tiáo 4 (tablet) [of soap, chocolate] 块(塊) kuài

barbecue ['bɑːbɪkjuː] N [c] 烧(燒)烤聚会(會) shāokǎo jùhuì [次 cì]

barefoot(ed) ['bɛəfʊt(ɪd)] ADV 赤脚(腳)地 chìjiǎo de

barely ['bɛəlɪ] ADV 几(幾)乎不 jīhū bù

bargain ['bɑːɡɪn] N [c] 1 (good buy) 廉价(價)品 liánjiàpǐn [件 jiàn] 2 (deal, agreement) 协(協)议(議) xiéyì [个 gè]

barge [bɑːdʒ] N [c] 驳(駁)船 bóchuán [艘 sōu]

bark [bɑːk] VI [dog +] 叫 jiào

barmaid ['bɑːmeɪd] (esp Brit) N [c] 酒吧女侍 jiǔbā nǚshì [个 gè]

barman ['bɑːmən] (pl barmen) (esp Brit) N [c] 酒吧男侍 jiǔbā nánshì [个 gè]

barrel ['bærəl] N [c] 桶 tǒng [个 gè]

barrier ['bærɪəʳ] N [c] 关(關)口 guānkǒu [个 gè]

bartender ['bɑːtɛndəʳ] (US) N [c] 酒吧侍者 jiǔbā shìzhě [个 gè]

base [beɪs] N [c] 1 (bottom) 底部 dǐbù [个 gè] 2 (basis) 根基 gēnjī [个 gè] 3 基地 jīdì [个 gè]; (for individual, organization) 总(總)部 zǒngbù [个 gè] ▶ to be based on sth 以某物为(為)根据(據) yǐ mǒuwù wéi gēnjù ▶ I'm based in London 我长(長)驻(駐)伦(倫)敦 wǒ chángzhù Lúndūn

baseball ['beɪsbɔːl] N [U] 棒球 bàngqiú

basement ['beɪsmənt] N [c] 地下室 dìxiàshì [间 jiān]

basic ['beɪsɪk] ADJ 基本的 jīběn de; see also/另见 **basics**

basically ['beɪsɪklɪ] ADV 1 (fundamentally) 基本上 jīběnshang 2 (in fact, put simply) 简(簡)而言之 jiǎnéryánzhī

basics ['beɪsɪks] NPL ▶ the basics 基本点(點) jīběndiǎn

basin ['beɪsn] N [c] 1 (bowl) 盆 pén [个 gè] 2 (also: wash basin) 洗脸(臉)盆 xǐliǎnpén [个 gè] 3 [of river, lake] 流域 liúyù [个 gè]

basket ['bɑːskɪt] N [c] 筐 kuāng [个 gè]

basketball ['bɑːskɪtbɔːl] N [U] 篮(籃)球 lánqiú

bat [bæt] N [c] 1 (animal) 蝙蝠 biānfú [只 zhī] 2 (for cricket, baseball) 球板/棒 qiúbǎn/bàng [只 zhī] 3 (Brit: for table tennis) 球拍 qiúpāi [只 zhī]

bath [bɑːθ] N [c] 1 (Brit: bathtub) 浴缸 yùgāng [个 gè] 2 (act of bathing) 洗澡 xǐzǎo [次 cì] ▶ to have or take a bath 洗澡 xǐzǎo

bathe [beɪð] VI 1 (esp Brit) 戏(戲)水 xìshuǐ 2 (esp US: have a bath) 洗澡 xǐzǎo

bathroom ['bɑːθrʊm] N [c] 1 卫(衛)生间(間) wèishēngjiān [个 gè] 2 (US: toilet) 厕(廁)所 cèsuǒ [处 chù] ▶ to go to the bathroom (US) 去卫(衛)生间(間) qù wèishēngjiān

bathtub ['bɑːθtʌb] (US) N [c] 浴缸 yùgāng [个 gè]

battery ['bætərɪ] N 1 电(電)池 diànchí [块 kuài] 2 (in car) 电(電)瓶 diànpíng [个 gè]

battle ['bætl] N [c] 1 (Mil) 战(戰)役 zhànyì [场 cháng] 2 (fig: struggle) 斗(鬥)争(爭) dòuzhēng [场 cháng]

bay [beɪ] N [c] 湾(灣) wān [个 gè]

BC ADV ABBR (= before Christ) 公元前 gōngyuán qián

⭕ **KEYWORD**

be [bi:] (*pt* **was, were,** *pp* **been**) **I** vi **1** (*with complement*) 是 shì ▶ **I'm English/ Chinese** 我是英国(國)人/中国(國)人 wǒ shì Yīngguórén/Zhōngguórén ▶ **she's tall/pretty** 她长(長)得高/漂亮 tā zhǎngde gāo/piàoliang ▶ **this is my mother** 这(這)是我妈(媽)妈(媽) zhèshì wǒ māma ▶ **who is it?** 是谁(誰)啊? shì shuí a? ▶ **be careful/ quiet!** 当(當)心/安静(靜)! dāngxīn/ānjìng!
2 (*referring to time, date*) 是 shì ▶ **it's 5 o'clock** 现(現)在是5点(點)钟(鐘) xiànzài shì wǔ diǎn zhōng
3 (*describing weather*) ▶ **it's hot/cold** 天热(熱)/冷 tiān rè/lěng
4 (*talking about health*) ▶ **how are you?** 你身体(體)怎么(麼)样(樣)? nǐ shēntǐ zěnmeyàng?
5 (*talking about age*) 有 yǒu ▶ **how old are you?** 你多大了? nǐ duō dà le?
6 (*talking about place*) 在 zài ▶ **Madrid is in Spain** 马(馬)德里在西班牙 Mǎdélǐ zài Xībānyá ▶ **the supermarket isn't far from here** 超市离(離)这(這)儿(兒)不远(遠) chāoshì lí zhèr bù yuǎn ▶ **I won't be here tomorrow** 我明天不在这(這)儿(兒) wǒ míngtiān bùzài zhèr ▶ **have you been to Beijing** 你去过(過)北京吗(嗎)? nǐ qùguo Běijīng ma? ▶ **we've been here for ages** 我们(們)已经(經)在这(這)里(裡)好久了 wǒmen yǐjīng zài zhèlǐ hǎojiǔ le ▶ **the meeting will be in the canteen** 会(會)议(議)将(將)在食堂举(舉)行 huìyì jiāng zài shítáng jǔxíng
7 (*referring to distance*) 有 yǒu ▶ **it's 10 km to the village** 这(這)儿(兒)离(離)村庄(莊)有10公里 zhèr lí cūnzhuāng yǒu shí gōnglǐ
8 (*cost*) 花 huā ▶ **how much was the meal?** 这(這)顿(頓)饭(飯)花了多少钱(錢)? zhè dùn fàn huāle duōshao qián? ▶ **that'll be £5 please** 请(請)付5英镑(鎊) qǐngfù wǔ yīngbàng
9 (*linking clauses*) 是 shì ▶ **the problem is that ...** 问(問)题(題)是… wèntí shì…
II AUX VB **1** (*forming continuous tenses*) ▶ **what are you doing?** 你在干(幹)什么(麼)? nǐ zài gàn shénme? ▶ **they're coming tomorrow** 他们(們)明天来(來) tāmen míngtiān lái
2 (*forming passives*) ▶ **to be murdered** 被谋(謀)杀(殺) bèi móushā ▶ **he was killed in a car crash** 他在一场(場)车(車)祸(禍)中丧(喪)生 tā zài yī chǎng chēhuò zhōng sàngshēng
3 (*in tag questions*) ▶ **it was fun, wasn't it?** 有意思，是不是? yǒu yìsi, shì bù shì? ▶ **he's good-looking, isn't he?** 他长(長)得不错(錯)，是不是? tā zhǎng de bùcuò, shì bù shì?

beach [bi:tʃ] N [c] 海滩(灘) hǎitān [片 piàn]

beads [bi:dz] NPL (*necklace*) 项(項)链(鏈) xiàngliàn

beam [bi:m] N [c] [*of wood, metal*] 梁 liáng [根 gēn]

bean [bi:n] N [c] 豆 dòu [粒 lì] ▶ **coffee/ cocoa beans** 咖啡/可可豆 kāfēi/kěkě dòu

bear [bɛəʳ] (*pt* **bore,** *pp* **borne**) **I** N [c] 熊 xióng [头 tóu] **II** VT **1** (*tolerate*) 容忍 róngrěn **2** (*endure*) 忍受 rěnshòu

beard [bɪəd] N [c] 胡(鬍)须(鬚) húxū [根 gēn]

beat [bi:t] (*pt* **beat,** *pp* **beaten**) VT [+ *opponent, record*] 击(擊)败(敗) jībài

beaten ['bi:tn] PP *of* **beat**

beautiful ['bju:tɪful] ADJ **1** 美丽(麗)的 měilì de **2** [+ *shot, performance*] 精彩的 jīngcǎi de

beautifully ['bju:tɪflɪ] ADV 极(極)好地 jíhǎo de

beauty ['bju:tɪ] N [U] 美 měi

became [bɪ'keɪm] PT *of* **become**

because [bɪ'kɔz] CONJ 因为(為) yīnwéi ▶ **because of** 因为(為) yīnwèi

> 我们在解释一件事发生的原因时，可以使用 **because**、**as** 或 **since**。**because** 最为常用，并且是唯一可以回答以 **why** 提出的问题。*"Why can't you come?" — "Because I'm too busy."* 在引出含有原因的从句时，尤其是在书面语中，我们可以用 **as** 或 **since** 代替 **because**。*I was rather nervous, as I hadn't seen her for a long time...Since the juice is quite strong, you should always dilute it.*

become [bɪ'kʌm] (*pt* **became,** *pp* **become**)

VI **1**(+ *noun*) 成为(為) chéngwéi **2**(+ *adj*) 变(變) biàn

bed [bed] N [c] 床 chuáng [张 zhāng] ▸ **to go to bed** 去睡觉(覺) qù shuìjiào

bed and breakfast N [U] 住宿加早餐 zhùsù jiā zǎocān

bedding ['bedɪŋ] N [U] 床上用品 chuángshàng yòngpǐn

bedroom ['bedrum] N [c] 卧(臥)室 wòshì [间 jiān]

bee [bi:] N [c] 蜜蜂 mìfēng [只 zhī]

beef [bi:f] N [U] 牛肉 niúròu ▸ **roast beef** 烤牛肉 kǎo niúròu

beefburger ['bi:fbə:gəʳ] (*Brit*) N [c] 牛肉汉(漢)堡包 niúròu hànbǎobāo [个 gè]

been [bi:n] PP *of* **be**

beer [bɪəʳ] N [U] 啤酒 píjiǔ ▸ **would you like a beer?** 你想喝一瓶啤酒吗(嗎)? nǐ xiǎng hē yī píng píjiǔ ma?

beet [bi:t] N (*US: red vegetable*) 甜菜根 tiáncàigēn [根 gēn]

beetle ['bi:tl] N [c] 甲虫(蟲) jiǎchóng [只 zhī]

beetroot ['bi:tru:t] (*Brit*) N [c/U] 甜菜根 tiáncàigēn [根 gēn]

before [bɪ'fɔ:ʳ] I PREP 之前 zhīqián II CONJ 在…之前 zài…zhīqián III ADV 以前 yǐqián ▸ **before doing sth** 在做某事之前 zài zuò mǒushì zhīqián ▸ **I've never seen it before** 我以前从(從)没(沒)见(見)过(過) wǒ yǐqián cóng méi jiànguo

beg [beg] VI (*beggar+*) 乞讨(討) qǐtǎo ▸ **I beg your pardon** (*apologizing*) 对(對)不起 duìbuqǐ; (*not hearing*) 请(請)再说(說)一遍 qǐng zài shuō yī biàn

began [bɪ'gæn] PT *of* **begin**

beggar ['begəʳ] N [c] 乞丐 qǐgài [个 gè]

begin [bɪ'gɪn] (*pt* began, *pp* begun) I VT 开(開)始 kāishǐ II VI 开(開)始 kāishǐ ▸ **to begin doing** *or* **to do sth** 开(開)始做某事 kāishǐ zuò mǒushì

beginner [bɪ'gɪnəʳ] N [c] 初学(學)者 chūxuézhě [位 wèi]

beginning [bɪ'gɪnɪŋ] N [c] 开(開)始 kāishǐ [个 gè] ▸ **at the beginning** 开(開)始时(時) kāishǐ shí

begun [bɪ'gʌn] PP *of* **begin**

behave [bɪ'heɪv] VI 表现(現) biǎoxiàn

behaviour, (*US*) **behavior** [bɪ'heɪvjəʳ] N [U] 举(舉)止 jǔzhǐ

behind [bɪ'haɪnd] I PREP 在…后(後)面 zài…hòumiàn II ADV (*at/towards the back*) 在/向后(後)面 zài/xiàng hòumiàn ▸ **to be behind** (*schedule*) 落后(後)于(於)(计(計)划(劃)) luòhòu yú (jìhuà) ▸ **to leave sth behind** (*forget*) 落下某物 làxià mǒuwù

beige [beɪʒ] ADJ 灰棕色的 huīzōngsè de

Beijing ['beɪ'dʒɪŋ] N 北京 Běijīng

Belgian ['beldʒən] I ADJ 比利时(時)的 Bǐlìshí de II N [c](*person*) 比利时(時)人 Bǐlìshírén [个 gè]

Belgium ['beldʒəm] N 比利时(時) Bǐlìshí

believe [bɪ'li:v] VT 相信 xiāngxìn ▸ **to believe that …** 认(認)为(為)… rènwéi…

bell [bel] N [c] (*on door*) 门(門)铃(鈴) ménlíng [个 gè]

belong [bɪ'lɔŋ] VI ▸ **to belong to** [+ *person*] 属(屬)于(於) shǔyú; [+ *club, society*] 是…的成员(員) shì…de chéngyuán

belongings [bɪ'lɔŋɪŋz] NPL 所有物 suǒyǒuwù

below [bɪ'ləu] I PREP **1**(*beneath*) 在…之下 zài…zhīxià **2**(*less than*) 低于(於) dīyú II ADV **1**(*beneath*) 下面 xiàmian **2**(*less*) 以下 yǐxià ▸ **below zero** 零度以下 língdù yǐxià ▸ **temperatures below normal** *or* **average** 低于(於)正常(或)平均温(溫)度 dīyú zhèngcháng (huò) píngjūn wēndù

belt [belt] N [c] 腰带(帶) yāodài [条 tiáo]

bench [bentʃ] N [c] 长(長)椅 chángyǐ [条 tiáo]

bend [bend] (*pt, pp* bent) I VT 使弯(彎)曲 shǐ wānqū II VI **1** 屈身 qūshēn **2** [*road, river* +] 转(轉)弯(彎) zhuǎnwān III N [c] (*in road, river*) 弯(彎) wān [个 gè]
▸ **bend down** VI 弯(彎)腰 wānyāo

beneath [bɪ'ni:θ] I PREP 在…之下 zài…zhīxià II ADV 在下面 zài xiàmian

benefit ['benɪfɪt] I N [c/U] 好处(處) hǎochù [个 gè] II VI ▸ **to benefit from sth** 从(從)某事中获(獲)益 cóng mǒushì zhōng huòyì

bent [bent] I PT, PP *of* **bend** II ADJ 弯(彎)曲的 wānqū de

berth [bə:θ] N [c] 卧(臥)铺(鋪) wòpù [张 zhāng]

beside [bɪ'saɪd] PREP 在…旁边(邊) zài…pángbiān; *see also*/另见 **besides**

besides [bɪˈsaɪdz] I ADV (*also*: **beside**) (*in addition*) 另外 lìngwài II PREP (*also*: **beside**) (*in addition to, as well as*) 除…之外 chú…zhīwài

> **besides** 引ას的事物包括在我们所谈及的事情之内。*She is very intelligent besides being very beautiful.* 不过，当我们说 **the only person besides** 另外某人时，或 **the only thing besides** 另外某物时，我们指在某一特定场合或上下文中的唯一其他人或物。*There was only one person besides me who knew where the money was hidden.* 介词 **except** 后面通常跟我们的陈述中不包括的那些物、人、事的名词或代词形式。*She spoke to everyone except me.* **except** 也可作连词，引导从句或副词短语。*There was nothing more to do now except wait.* **except** 还可以引出由连词 **that**、**when** 或 **if** 引导的从句。*The house stayed empty, except when we came for the holidays.* **except for** 是用在名词前的介词短语，用来引出某人或某物，说明要不是有某人或某物，所陈述的便为全部事实。*Everyone was late except for Richard.*

best [bɛst] I ADJ 最好的 zuì hǎo de II ADV 最 zuì III N ▶ **the best** 最好的事物 zuì hǎo de shìwù ▶ **the best thing to do is …** 最好是… zuì hǎo shì… ▶ **to do** or **try one's best** 尽(盡)某人最大的努力 jìn mǒurén zuì dà de nǔlì

bet [bɛt] (*pt, pp* **bet** or **betted**) I N [c] 赌(賭)注 dǔzhù [个 gè] II VT 1 ▶ **to bet sb 100 pounds that…** 就…和某人赌(賭)100英镑(鎊) jiù…hé mǒurén dǔ yībǎi yīngbàng 2 (*expect, guess*) ▶ **to bet (that)** 断(斷)定 duàndìng III VI ▶ **to bet on** [+ *horse, result*] 下赌(賭)注于(於) xià dǔzhù yú

better [ˈbɛtəʳ] I ADJ 1 (*comparative of good*) 更好的 gèng hǎo de 2 (*after an illness or injury*) 好转(轉)的 hǎozhuǎn de II ADV (*comparative of well*) 更好地 gèng hǎo de ▶ **to get better** (*improve*) 变(變)得更好 biàn de gèng hǎo; (*sick person* +) 渐(漸)愈(癒) jiànyù ▶ **to feel better** 感觉(覺)好一些 gǎnjué hǎo yīxiē ▶ **I'd better go** or **I had better go** 我得走了 wǒ děi zǒu le

between [bɪˈtwiːn] I PREP 1 (*in space*) 在…中间(間) zài…zhōngjiān 2 (*in time*) 介于(於)…之间(間) jièyú…zhījiān 3 (*in amount, age*) 介于(於)…之间(間) jièyú…zhījiān II ADV ▶ **in between** (*in space*) 在…中间(間) zài…zhōngjiān; (*in time*) 期间(間) qījiān ▶ **to choose between** 从(從)中选(選)一个(個) cóngzhōng xuǎn yī gè ▶ **to be shared/ divided between people** 由大家一起分享/分用 yóu dàjiā yīqǐ fēnxiǎng/fēnyòng

beyond [bɪˈjɒnd] I PREP 1 在…的另一边(邊) zài…de lìng yībiān 2 [+ *time, date, age*] 迟(遲)于(於) chíyú II ADV 1 (*in space*) 在另一边(邊) zài lìng yībiān 2 (*in time*) 在…之后(後) zài…zhīhòu

Bible [ˈbaɪbl] (*Rel*) N [c] ▶ **the Bible** 圣(聖)经(經) Shèngjīng [部 bù]

bicycle [ˈbaɪsɪkl] N [c] 自行车(車) zìxíngchē [辆 liàng] ▶ **to ride a bicycle** 骑(騎)自行车(車) qí zìxíngchē

big [bɪg] ADJ 1 大的 dà de 2 [+ *change, increase, problem*] 大的 dà de

bike [baɪk] N [c] 1 (*bicycle*) 自行车(車) zìxíngchē [辆 liàng] 2 (*motorcycle*) 摩托车(車) mótuōchē [部 bù]

bikini [bɪˈkiːnɪ] N [c] 比基尼 bǐjīní [套 tào]

bill [bɪl] N [c] 1 (*requesting payment*) 账(賬)单(單) zhàngdān [个 gè] 2 (*Brit: in restaurant*) 账(賬)单(單) zhàngdān [个 gè] 3 (*US: banknote*) 钞(鈔)票 chāopiào [张 zhāng]

billfold [ˈbɪlfəʊld] (*US*) N [c] 钱(錢)夹(夾) qiánjiā [个 gè]

billion [ˈbɪljən] N [c] 十亿(億) shíyì

bin [bɪn] N [c] (*Brit*) 垃圾箱 lājīxiāng [个 gè]

binoculars [bɪˈnɒkjʊləz] NPL 双(雙)筒望远(遠)镜(鏡) shuāngtǒng wàngyuǎnjìng

biochemistry [baɪəˈkɛmɪstrɪ] N [U] 生物化学(學) shēngwù huàxué

biography [baɪˈɒgrəfɪ] N [c] 传(傳)记(記) zhuànjì [部 bù]

biology [baɪˈɒlədʒɪ] N [U] 生物学(學) shēngwùxué

bird [bɜːd] N [c] 鸟(鳥) niǎo [只 zhī]

Biro® [ˈbaɪərəʊ] (*Brit*) N [c] 圆(圓)珠笔(筆) yuánzhūbǐ [支 zhī]

birth [bɜːθ] N [c/U] 出生 chūshēng

birth certificate N [C] 出生证(證)明 chūshēng zhèngmíng [个 gè]

birth control II [U] 节(節)育 jiéyù

birthday ['bɜːθdeɪ] I N [C] 生日 shēngrì [个 gè] II CPD [+ cake, card, present] 生日 shēngrì

biscuit ['bɪskɪt] N [C] 1 (Brit) 饼(餅)干(乾) bǐnggān [片 piàn] 2 (US) 小圆(圓) 饼(餅) xiǎo yuánbǐng [张 zhāng]

bishop ['bɪʃəp] N [C] 主教 zhǔjiào [位 wèi]

bit [bɪt] I PT of **bite** II N [C] 1 (esp Brit: piece) 少许(許) shǎoxǔ 2 (esp Brit: part) 部分 bùfen [个 gè] 3 (Comput) 比特 bǐtè [个 gè] ▸ **a bit mad/dangerous** 有点(點) 疯(瘋)狂/危险(險) yǒu diǎn fēngkuáng/ wēixiǎn ▸ **for a bit** (inf) 一会(會)儿(兒) yīhuìr ▸ **quite a bit** 不少 bù shǎo

bite [baɪt] (pt **bit**, pp **bitten** ['bɪtn]) I VT 咬 yǎo II N [C] 1 (mouthful) 一口 kǒu 2 (from dog) 咬伤(傷) yǎoshāng [处 chù] 3 (from snake, mosquito) 咬痕 yǎohén [个 gè] ▸ **to bite one's nails** 咬指甲 yǎo zhǐjia

bitter ['bɪtəʳ] ADJ [+ taste] 苦的 kǔ de

black [blæk] I ADJ 1 黑色的 hēisè de 2 [+ person] 黑人的 hēirén de 3 [+ tea, coffee] 不加牛奶的 bù jiā niúnǎi de II N [U] 黑色 hēisè ▸ **black out** VI (faint) 暂(暫)时(時)失去 知觉(覺) zànshí shīqù zhījué

blackboard ['blækbɔːd] N [C] 黑板 hēibǎn [个 gè]

blackmail ['blækmeɪl] I N [U] 敲诈(詐) qiāozhà II VT 敲诈(詐) qiāozhà

blade [bleɪd] N [C] 刃 rèn

blame [bleɪm] I N [U] (for mistake, crime) 责(責)备(備) zébèi II VT ▸ **to blame sb for sth** 为(為)某事责(責)备(備)某人 wèi mǒushì zébèi mǒurén ▸ **to be to blame (for sth)** 该(該)(为(為)某事) 负(負)责(責)任 gāi (wèi mǒushì) fù zérèn ▸ **to blame sth on sb** 把某事 归(歸)咎于(於)某人 bǎ mǒushì guījiù yú mǒurén

blank [blæŋk] ADJ 空白的 kòngbái de

blanket ['blæŋkɪt] N [C] 毛毯 máotǎn [床 chuáng]

blast [blɑːst] N [C] (explosion) 爆炸 bàozhà [次 cì]

blaze [bleɪz] I N [C] 大火 dàhuǒ [场 cháng] II VI [fire +] 熊熊燃烧(燒) xióngxióng ránshāo

blazer ['bleɪzəʳ] N [C] 上装(裝) shàngzhuāng [件 jiàn]

bleed [bliːd] (pt, pp **bled** [blɛd]) VI 流血 liúxuè ▸ **my nose is bleeding** 我流鼻血 了 wǒ liú bíxuè le

blender ['blɛndəʳ] N [C] 搅(攪)拌器 jiǎobànqì [个 gè]

bless [blɛs] VT (Rel) 赐(賜)福 cìfú ▸ **bless you!** (after sneeze) 上帝保佑(祐)! shàngdì bǎoyòu!

blew [bluː] PT of **blow**

blind [blaɪnd] I ADJ 失明的 shīmíng de II N (for window) 向上卷(捲)的帘(簾)子 xiàng shàng juǎn de liánzi ▸ **blind people** 盲人 mángrén ▸ **to go blind** 失 明 shīmíng

blink [blɪŋk] VI 眨眼睛 zhǎ yǎnjīng

blister ['blɪstəʳ] N [C] 水泡 shuǐpào [个 gè]

blizzard ['blɪzəd] N [C] 暴风(風)雪 bàofēngxuě [场 cháng]

block [blɔk] I N [C] 1 街区(區) jiēqū [个 gè] 2 [of stone, wood, ice] 块(塊) kuài II VT [+ entrance, road] 堵塞 dǔsè ▸ **block of flats** or (US) **apartment block** 公寓 楼(樓) gōngyùlóu ▸ **3 blocks from here** 离(離)这(這)里(裡)有3个(個)街区(區)那 么(麼)远(遠) lí zhèlǐ yǒu sān gè jiēqū nàme yuǎn

blog ['blɔg] I N [C] 博客 bókè II VI 写(寫) 博客 xiě bókè

blogger ['blɔgə] N [C] 博主 bó zhǔ [名 míng]

blogging ['blɔgɪŋ] I N [U] (写(寫))博客 (xiě) bókè II ADJ (写(寫))博客的 (xiě)bókè de

blogosphere ['blɔgəsfɪəʳ] N [C] 博客圈 bókè quān

blogpost ['blɔgpəust] N [C] 博文 bó wén [篇 piān]

blond(e) [blɔnd] ADJ 1 [+ hair] 金色的 jīnsè de 2 [+ person] 金发(髮)的人 jīnfà de rén

blood [blʌd] N [U] 血液 xuèyè

blood pressure N [U] 血压(壓) xuèyā ▸ **to have high/low blood pressure** 有 高/低血压(壓) yǒu gāo/dī xuèyā ▸ **to take sb's blood pressure** 量某人的血 压(壓) liáng mǒurén de xuèyā

blood test N [C] 验(驗)血 yànxiě [次 cì] ▸ **to have a blood test** 验(驗)血 yànxiě

blouse [blauz, US blaus] N [C] 女士 衬(襯)衫 nǚshì chènshān [件 jiàn]

blow [bləʊ] (*pt* blew, *pp* blown) I N [c]
1 (*punch*) 拳打 quándǎ [顿 dùn] **2** 打
击(擊) dǎjī [个 gè] II vi **1** [*wind, sand, dust
etc* +] 吹 chuī **2** [*person* +] 吹气(氣)
chuīqì III vt [*wind* +] 吹 chuī ▸ **to blow
one's nose** 擤鼻子 xǐng bízi
▸ **blow away** I vt 吹走 chuīzǒu II vi
刮(颳)跑 guāpǎo
▸ **blow down** vt 刮(颳)倒 guādǎo
▸ **blow out** vt 吹灭(滅) chuīmiè
▸ **blow up** I vi (*explode*) 爆炸 bàozhà
II vt **1** (*destroy*) 使爆炸 shǐ bàozhà
2 (*inflate*) 充气(氣) chōngqì

blow-dry ['bləʊdraɪ] N [c] 吹风(風)定型
chuīfēng dìngxíng

blown [bləʊn] pp *of* blow

blue [bluː] I ADJ 蓝(藍)色的 lánsè de II N
[u] 蓝(藍)色 lánsè III blues NPL (*Mus*)
▸ **the blues** 蓝(藍)调(調) lándiào

blunt [blʌnt] ADJ **1** (*not sharp*) 钝(鈍)的
dùn de **2** [+ *person, remark*] 直率的
zhíshuài de

blush [blʌʃ] vi 脸(臉)红(紅) liǎnhóng

board [bɔːd] I N [c] **1** (*piece of wood*) 木板
mùbǎn [块 kuài] **2** [c] (*also*: noticeboard)
公告板 gōnggàobǎn [块 kuài] **3** [c] (*also*:
blackboard) 黑板 hēibǎn [个 gè] **4** [c]
(*for chess*) 盘(盤) pán **5** [u] (*at hotel*) 膳
食 shànshí II vt [+ *ship, train, plane*] 上
shàng III vi (*frm: on ship, train, plane*) 登
上 dēngshàng ▸ **board and lodging** 食
宿 shísù ▸ **on board**
在船/车(車)/飞(飛)机(機)上 zài chuán/
chē/fēijī shang

boarding card ['bɔːdɪŋ-] N [c] 登机(機)
卡 dēngjīkǎ [张 zhāng]

boarding school N [c/u] 寄宿学(學)校
jìsù xuéxiào [个 gè]

boast [bəʊst] I vi ▸ **to boast (about or of)**
说(說)(关(關)于(於)某事的)大话(話)
shuō (guānyú mǒushì de) dàhuà II N [c]
自夸 zìkuā [种 zhǒng]

boat [bəʊt] N [c] **1** (*small vessel*) 船 chuán
[艘 sōu] **2** (*ship*) 轮(輪)船 lúnchuán [艘
sōu] ▸ **to go by boat** 乘船去
chéngchuán qù

body ['bɔdɪ] N **1** [c] (*of person*) 身体(體) shēntǐ
[个 gè] **2** [c] (*corpse*) 尸(屍)体(體) shītǐ
[具 jù]

bodybuilding ['bɔdɪ'bɪldɪŋ] N [u]
健身 jiànshēn

bodyguard ['bɔdɪgɑːd] N [c] 保镖(鏢)
bǎobiāo [个 gè]

boil [bɔɪl] I vt **1** [+ *water*] 烧(燒)开(開)
shāokāi **2** [+ *eggs, potatoes*] 煮 zhǔ II vi
[*liquid* +] 沸腾(騰) fèiténg III N (*Med*)
疖(癤)子 jiēzi ▸ **to boil a kettle** 烧(燒)
开(開)水 shāokāi shuǐ

boiler ['bɔɪləʳ] N [c] (*device*) 锅(鍋)炉(爐)
guōlú [个 gè]

boiling (hot) ['bɔɪlɪŋ-] (*inf*) ADJ ▸ **I'm
boiling (hot)** 我太热(熱)了 wǒ tài rè le

bolt [bəʊlt] N [c] **1** (*to lock door*) 插销(銷)
chāxiāo [个 gè] **2** (*used with nut*) 螺
钉(釘) luódīng [颗 kē]

bomb [bɔm] I N [c] 炸弹(彈) zhàdàn [颗
kē] II vt 轰(轟)炸 hōngzhà

bomber ['bɔməʳ] N [c] **1** (*Aviat*) 轰(轟)炸
机(機) hōngzhàjī [架 jià] **2** (*terrorist*) 投
放炸弹(彈)的人 tóufàng zhàdàn de rén
[个 gè]

bombing ['bɔmɪŋ] N [c/u] 轰(轟)炸
hōngzhà [阵 zhèn]

bone [bəʊn] N **1** [c/u] 骨头(頭) gǔtou [根
gēn] **2** [c] (*in fish*) 刺 cì [根 gēn]

bonfire ['bɔnfaɪəʳ] N [c] **1** (*as part of a
celebration*) 篝火 gōuhuǒ [堆 duī] **2** (*to
burn rubbish*) 火堆 huǒduī [个 gè]

bonnet ['bɔnɪt] N [c] (*Brit*) [*of car*] 引擎罩
yǐnqíngzhào [个 gè]

bonus ['bəʊnəs] N [c] **1** (*extra payment*)
红(紅)利 hónglì [份 fèn] **2** (*additional
benefit*) 额(額)外收获(穫) éwài
shōuhuò [份 fèn]

book [buk] I N [c] **1** (*novel etc*) 书(書) shū
[本 běn] **2** [*of stamps, tickets*] 册(冊) cè
II vt [+ *table, seat, room*] 预(預)
订(訂) yùdìng ▸ **fully booked** 预(預)
订(訂)一空 yùdìng yīkōng
▸ **book into** (*Brit*) vt FUS [+ *hotel*] 登
记(記)入住 dēngjì rùzhù

bookcase ['bukkeɪs] N [c] 书(書)橱
shūchú [个 gè]

booklet ['buklɪt] N [c] 小册(冊)子
xiǎocèzi [本 běn]

bookshelf ['bukʃelf] N [c] 书(書)架
shūjià [个 gè]

bookshop ['bukʃɔp] (*Brit*) N [c] 书(書)店
shūdiàn [家 jiā]

bookstore ['bukstɔːʳ] (*esp US*) N
= bookshop

boot [buːt] I N [c] **1** 靴子 xuēzi [双

shuāng]; (for football, walking) 鞋 xié [双
shuāng] **2** (Brit) (of car) 车(車)后(後)行
李箱 chē hòu xínglǐxiāng [个 gè]
▶ **boot up** (Comput) I VT 使运(運)行 shǐ
yùnxíng II VI 开(開)始运(運)行 kāishǐ
yùnxíng

border ['bɔːdəʳ] N [c] 边(邊)界 biānjiè [条
tiáo]

bore [bɔːʳ] I PT of **bear** II VT **1** [+ hole]
钻(鑽) zuàn **2** [+ oil well, tunnel] 开(開)
凿(鑿) kāizáo **3** [+ person] 使厌(厭)
烦(煩) shǐ yànfán ▶ **to be bored (with
sth)** (对(對)某事) 不感兴(興)趣 (duì
mǒushì) bù gǎn xìngqù

boring ['bɔːrɪŋ] ADJ 乏味的 fáwèi de

born [bɔːn] ADJ ▶ **to be born** [baby +] 出生
chūshēng

borrow ['bɒrəu] VT 借 jiè

Bosnia ['bɒznɪə] N 波斯尼亚(亞)
Bōsīníyà

Bosnian ['bɒznɪən] ADJ 波斯尼亚(亞)的
Bōsīníyà de

boss [bɒs] N [c] **1** (employer) 老板 lǎobǎn
[个 gè] **2** (inf: leader) 领(領)导(導)
lǐngdǎo [位 wèi]

both [bəuθ] I ADJ 两(兩)都 liǎngzhě
dōu II PRON **1** (things) 两(兩)者 liǎngzhě
2 (people) 两(兩)个(個) liǎng gè III CONJ
▶ **both A and B** A和B两(兩)都 A hé B
liǎngzhě dōu ▶ **both of us went** or **we
both went** 我们(們)两(兩)个(個)都去
了 wǒmen liǎng gè dōuqù le

bother ['bɒðəʳ] I VT **1** (worry) 烦(煩)
扰(擾) fánrǎo **2** (disturb) 打扰(擾) dǎrǎo
II VI 在乎 zàihu III N [U] (trouble) 麻
烦(煩) máfan ▶ **don't bother** 不用于
bùyòng le

bottle ['bɒtl] N **1** [c] 瓶子 píngzi [个 gè]
2 [c] (amount contained) 瓶 píng **3** [c]
[baby's] 奶瓶 nǎipíng [个 gè] ▶ **a bottle
of wine/milk** 一瓶葡萄酒/牛奶 yī píng
pútáojiǔ/niúnǎi

bottle opener N [c] 开(開)瓶器
kāipíngqì [个 gè]

bottom ['bɒtəm] I N **1** [c] [of container, sea]
底部 dǐbù [个 gè] **2** [c] [of page, list] 下端
xiàduān [个 gè] **3** [U/s] [of class, league]
最后(後)一名 zuìhòu yī míng **4** [c] [of
hill, tree, stairs] 最底部 zuìdǐbù [个 gè]
5 [c] (buttocks) 臀部 túnbù [个 gè] II ADJ
(lowest) 最下面的 zuì xiàmiàn de ▶ **at**

the bottom of 在···的底部 zài...de
dǐbù

bought [bɔːt] PT, PP of **buy**

bound [baund] ADJ ▶ **to be bound to do
sth** (certain) 一定做某事 yīdìng zuò
mǒushì

boundary ['baundrɪ] N [c] 边(邊)界
biānjiè [个 gè]

bow¹ [bəu] N [c] **1** (knot) 蝴蝶结(結)
húdiéjié [个 gè] **2** (weapon) 弓 gōng
[把 bǎ]

bow² [bau] I VI (with head, body) 鞠躬
jūgōng II VT [+ head] 低头(頭) dītóu

bowl [bəul] N [c] **1** 碗 wǎn [个 gè]
2 (contents) 一碗的量 yī wǎn de liàng
3 (for washing clothes/dishes) 盆 pén [个 gè]

bowling ['bəulɪŋ] N [U] 保龄(齡)球
bǎolíngqiú ▶ **to go bowling** 打保龄(齡)
球 dǎ bǎolíngqiú

bow tie [bəu-] N [c] 蝶形领(領)结(結)
diéxíng lǐngjié [个 gè]

box [bɒks] I N [c] **1** (container) 盒子 hézi
[个 gè] **2** (contents) 盒 hé **3** (also:
cardboard box) 纸(紙)箱 zhǐxiāng [个
gè] **4** (crate) 箱 xiāng II VI (Sport) 拳
击(擊) quánjī

boxer ['bɒksəʳ] N [c] 拳击(擊)运(運)
动(動)员(員) quánjī yùndòngyuán
[位 wèi]

boxer shorts, boxers N PL 平角裤(褲)
píngjiǎokù

boxing ['bɒksɪŋ] (Sport) N [U] 拳击(擊)
quánjī

Boxing Day (Brit) N [c/u] 圣诞节后的第
一天，是公共假日

boy [bɔɪ] N [c] **1** (male child) 男孩 nánhái
[个 gè] **2** (young man) 男青年 nán
qīngnián [个 gè]

boyfriend ['bɔɪfrɛnd] N [c] 男朋友
nánpéngyou [个 gè]

bra [brɑː] N [c] 胸罩 xiōngzhào [件 jiàn]

bracelet ['breɪslɪt] N [c] 手镯(鐲)
shǒuzhuó [只 zhī]

braid [breɪd] N [c] (US: plait) 辫(辮)子
biànzi [条 tiáo]

brain [breɪn] N [c] 脑(腦)脑 nǎo [个 gè]

brainy ['breɪnɪ] ADJ (inf) 聪(聰)明的
cōngming de

brake [breɪk] I N [c] (Aut) 刹车(車)
shāchē [个 gè] II VI (driver, vehicle +)
刹车(車) shāchē

branch [brɑːntʃ] N [c] **1** [of tree] 树(樹)枝 shùzhī [条 tiáo] **2** [of shop] 分店 fēndiàn [家 jiā]; [of bank, company] 分支机(機)构(構) fēnzhī jīgòu [个 gè]

brand [brænd] N [c] 牌子 páizi [块 kuài]

brand-new ['brænd'njuː] ADJ 全新的 quánxīn de

brandy ['brændɪ] N [c/u] 白兰(蘭)地酒 báilándìjiǔ [瓶 píng]

brass [brɑːs] N [u] 铜(銅) tóng

brave [breɪv] ADJ **1** 勇敢的 yǒnggǎn de **2** [+ attempt, smile, action] 英勇的 yīngyǒng de

Brazil [brə'zɪl] N 巴西 Bāxī

bread [brɛd] N [u] 面(麵)包 miànbāo

break [breɪk] (pt **broke**, pp **broken**) I VT **1** 打碎 dǎsuì **2** [+ leg, arm] 弄断(斷) nòngduàn **3** [+ promise, contract] 违(違)背 wéibèi **4** [+ law, rule] 违(違)反 wéifàn **5** [+ record] 打破 dǎpò II VI 破碎 pòsuì III N **1** [c] (rest) 休息 xiūxi [次 cì] **2** [c] (pause, interval) 间(間)歇 jiànxiē [个 gè] **3** [c] (fracture) 骨折 gǔzhé [次 cì] **4** [c] (holiday) 休假 xiūjià [次 cì] ▸ **to break the news to sb** 委婉地向某人透露消息 wěiwǎn de xiàng mǒurén tòulù xiāoxi ▸ **to take a break** (for a few minutes) 休息一下 xiūxi yīxià ▸ **without a break** 连(連)续(續)不断(斷) liánxù bùduàn
▸ **break down** VI **1** 坏(壞)掉 huàidiào
▸ **break in** VI [burglar +] 破门(門)而入 pòmén ér rù
▸ **break into** VT FUS [+ house] 强(強)行进(進)入 qiángxíng jìnrù
▸ **break off** VT **1** [+ branch, piece of chocolate] 折断(斷) zhéduàn **2** [+ engagement, relationship] 断(斷)绝(絕) duànjué
▸ **break out** VI **1** (begin) 爆发(發) bàofā **2** (escape) 逃脱(脫) táotuō
▸ **break up** I VI **1** [couple, marriage +] 破裂 pòliè **2** [meeting, party +] 纷(紛)纷(紛)离(離)去 fēnfēn líqù II VT **1** [+ fight] 调(調)停 tiáotíng **2** [+ meeting, demonstration] 驱(驅)散 qūsàn ▸ **to break up with sb** 同某人分手 tóng mǒurén fēnshǒu

breakdown ['breɪkdaʊn] N [c] **1** (Aut) 故障 gùzhàng [个 gè] **2** [of system, talks] 中断(斷) zhōngduàn [次 cì] **3** [of marriage] 破裂 pòliè [个 gè] **4** (Med) (also: **nervous breakdown**) 精神崩溃(潰) jīngshén bēngkuì [阵 zhèn] ▸ **to have a breakdown** 精神崩溃(潰) jīngshén bēngkuì

breakfast ['brɛkfəst] N [c/u] 早餐 zǎocān [顿 dùn]

break-in ['breɪkɪn] N [c] 闯(闖)入 chuǎngrù

breast [brɛst] N **1** [c] [of woman] 乳房 rǔfáng [个 gè] **2** [c/u] 胸脯肉 xiōngpúròu [块 kuài]

breath [brɛθ] N **1** [c/u] (intake of air) 呼吸 hūxī [下 xià] **2** [u] (air from mouth) 口气(氣) kǒuqì ▸ **out of breath** 上气(氣)不接下气(氣) shàngqì bùjiē xiàqì ▸ **bad breath** 口臭 kǒuchòu ▸ **to get one's breath back** (Brit) 恢复(復)正常呼吸 huīfù zhèngcháng hūxī ▸ **to hold one's breath** 屏住呼吸 bǐngzhù hūxī

breathe [briːð] I VT [+ air] 呼吸 hūxī II VI 呼吸 hūxī
▸ **breathe in** VI 吸入 xīrù
▸ **breathe out** VI 呼出 hūchū

breed [briːd] (pt, pp **bred** [brɛd]) I VT [+ animals] 繁殖 fánzhí II N [c] 品种(種) pǐnzhǒng [个 gè]

breeze [briːz] N [c] 微风(風) wēifēng [阵 zhèn]

brewery ['bruːərɪ] N [c] 啤酒厂(廠) píjiǔchǎng [家 jiā]

bribe [braɪb] I N [c] 贿(賄)赂(賂) huìlù [种 zhǒng] II VT 行贿(賄) xínghuì ▸ **to bribe sb to do sth** 贿(賄)赂(賂)某人去做某事 huìlù mǒurén qù zuò mǒushì

brick [brɪk] N [c/u] 砖(磚) zhuān [块 kuài]

bride [braɪd] N [c] 新娘 xīnniáng [个 gè]

bridegroom ['braɪdgruːm] N [c] 新郎 xīnláng [个 gè]

bridesmaid ['braɪdzmeɪd] N [c] 伴娘 bànniáng [个 gè]

bridge [brɪdʒ] N **1** [c] 桥(橋) qiáo [座 zuò] **2** [u] (Cards) 桥(橋)牌 qiáopái

brief [briːf] I ADJ **1** 短暂(暫)的 duǎnzàn de **2** [+ description, speech] 简(簡)短的 jiǎnduǎn de II **briefs** NPL **1** (for men) 男式三角内(內)裤(褲) nánshì sānjiǎo nèikù **2** (for women) 女式三角内(內)裤(褲) nǚshì sānjiǎo nèikù

briefcase ['briːfkeɪs] N [c] 公事包 gōngshìbāo [个 gè]

briefly ['briːflɪ] ADV 简(簡)短地 jiǎnduǎn de

bright [braɪt] ADJ **1** [+ light] 亮的 liàng de **2** [+ person] 聪(聰)明的 cōngmíng de; [+ idea] 巧妙的 qiǎomiào de **3** [+ colour] 鲜(鮮)亮的 xiānliàng de

brilliant ['brɪljənt] ADJ **1** [+ person, mind] 才华(華)横(横)溢的 cáihuá héngyì de **2** [+ idea, performance] 出色的 chūsè de **3** (esp Brit: inf: wonderful) 棒极(極)了的 bàngjíle de

bring [brɪŋ] (pt, pp **brought**) VT (with you) 带(帶)来(來) dàilái; (to sb) 拿来(來) nálái

▶ **bring along** VT 随(隨)身携(攜)带(帶) suíshēn xiédài

▶ **bring back** VT (return) 带(帶)回来(來) dài huílái

▶ **bring forward** VT [+ meeting] 提前 tíqián

▶ **bring round** VT [+ unconscious person] 使苏(甦)醒 shǐ sūxǐng

▶ **bring up** VT **1** [+ child] 抚(撫)养(養) fǔyǎng **2** [+ question, subject] 提出 tíchū

Britain ['brɪtən] N (also: **Great Britain**) 英国(國) Yīngguó ▶ **in Britain** 在英国(國) zài Yīngguó

British ['brɪtɪʃ] I ADJ 英国(國)的 Yīngguó de II NPL ▶ **the British** 英国(國)人 Yīngguórén

broad [brɔːd] ADJ 宽(寬)的 kuān de ▶ **in broad daylight** 光天化日之下 guāng tiān huà rì zhī xià

broadcast ['brɔːdkɑːst] (pt, pp **broadcast**) I N [c] 广(廣)播 guǎngbō [段 duàn] II VT 播送 bōsòng

broccoli ['brɒkəlɪ] N [U] 花椰菜 huāyēcài

brochure ['brəuʃuəʳ, US brəu'ʃʌr] N [c] 小册(冊)子 xiǎocèzi [本 běn]

broil [brɔɪl] (US) VT 烤 kǎo

broke [brəuk] I PT of **break** II ADJ (inf: penniless) 身无(無)分文的 shēn wú fēnwén de

broken ['brəukn] I PP of **break** II ADJ **1** 破碎的 pòsuì de **2** [+ machine] 坏(壞)损(損)的 huàisǔn de ▶ **a broken leg** 折断(斷)的腿 zhéduàn de tuǐ

bronchitis [brɒŋ'kaɪtɪs] N [U] 支气(氣)管炎 zhīqìguǎnyán

bronze [brɒnz] N **1** [U] (metal) 青铜(銅) qīngtóng **2** [c] (Sport) (also: **bronze medal**) 铜(銅)牌 tóngpái [块 kuài]

brooch [brəutʃ] N [c] 胸针(針) xiōngzhēn [枚 méi]

brother ['brʌðəʳ] N [c] 兄弟 xiōngdì [个 gè]; (elder) 哥哥 gēge [个 gè]; (younger) 弟弟 dìdi [个 gè]

brother-in-law ['brʌðərɪnlɔː] N [c] (older sister's husband) 姐夫 jiěfu [个 gè]; (younger sister's husband) 妹夫 mèifu [个 gè]; (husband's older brother) 大伯子 dàbǎizi [个 gè]; (husband's younger brother) 小叔子 xiǎoshūzi [个 gè]; (wife's older brother) 内(內)兄 nèixiōng [个 gè]; (wife's younger brother) 内(內)弟 nèidì [个 gè]

brought [brɔːt] PT, PP of **bring**

brown [braun] I ADJ **1** 褐色的 hèsè de; [+ hair, eyes] 棕色的 zōngsè de **2** (tanned) 晒黑的 shàihēi de II N [U] (colour) 褐色 hèsè

browse [brauz] VI (on the internet) 浏(瀏)览(覽) liúlǎn

bruise [bruːz] N [c] 青瘀 qīngyū [块 kuài]

brush [brʌʃ] I N [c] 刷子 shuāzi [把 bǎ]; (for hair) 发(髮)刷 fàshuā [把 bǎ]; [artist's] 画(畫)笔(筆) huàbǐ [支 zhī] II VT **1** [+ carpet etc] 刷 shuā **2** [+ hair] 梳 shū ▶ **to brush one's teeth** 刷牙 shuāyá

Brussels sprout ['brʌslz-] N [c] 芽甘蓝(藍) yágānlán [个 gè]

bubble ['bʌbl] N [c] 泡泡 pào pào [个 gè]

bubble gum N [U] 泡泡糖 pàopàotáng

bucket ['bʌkɪt] N [c] **1** (pail) 桶 tǒng [个 gè] **2** (contents) 一桶 yī tǒng

buckle ['bʌkl] I N [c] (on shoe, belt) 扣(釦)环(環) kòuhuán [个 gè] II VT [+ shoe, belt] 扣住 kòuzhù

Buddhism ['budɪzəm] N [U] 佛教 Fójiào

Buddhist ['budɪst] I ADJ 佛教的 Fójiào de II N [c] 佛教徒 Fójiàotú [个 gè]

buffet ['bufeɪ, US bu'feɪ] N [c] **1** (in station) 餐厅(廳) cāntīng [个 gè] **2** (food) 自助餐 zìzhùcān [顿 dùn]

bug [bʌg] N [c] **1** (esp US: insect) 虫(蟲)子 chóngzi [只 zhī] **2** (Comput: in program) 病毒 bìngdú [种 zhǒng] **3** (inf: virus) 病菌 bìngjūn [种 zhǒng]

build [bɪld] (pt, pp **built**) I N [c/U] [of person] 体(體)格 tǐgé [种 zhǒng] II VT [+ house, machine] 建造 jiànzào
▶ **build up** VI (accumulate) 积(積)聚 jījù

builder ['bɪldəʳ] N [c] (worker) 建筑(築)工人 jiànzhù gōngrén [位 wèi]

building ['bɪldɪŋ] N [c] 建筑(築)物 jiànzhùwù [座 zuò]

built [bɪlt] I PT, PP of **build** II ADJ ▶ **well-/heavily-built** [+ person] 体(體)态(態)优(優)美/粗笨的 tǐtài yōuměi/cūbèn de

bulb [bʌlb] N [c] **1** (Elec) 电(電)灯(燈)泡 diàndēngpào [个 gè] **2** (Bot) 球茎(莖) qiújīng [个 gè]

Bulgaria [bʌl'gɛərɪə] N 保加利亚(亞) Bǎojiālìyà

bull [bul] N [c] 公牛 gōngniú [头 tóu]

bullet ['bulɪt] N [c] 子弹(彈) zǐdàn [发 fā]

bulletin ['bulɪtɪn] N [c] 公告 gōnggào [个 gè]

bulletin board c **1** (Comput) 公共留言板 gōnggòng liúyánbǎn **2** (US: noticeboard) 布(佈)告栏(欄) bùgàolán

bully ['bulɪ] I N [c] 恃强(強)凌(淩)弱者 shìqiáng língruò zhě [个 gè] II VT 欺侮 qīwǔ

bum [bʌm] (inf) N [c] **1** (Brit: backside) 屁股 pìgu [个 gè] **2** (esp US: tramp) 流浪汉(漢) liúlànghàn [个 gè]

bump [bʌmp] I N [c] **1** 肿(腫)包 zhǒngbāo [个 gè] **2** (on road) 隆起物 lóngqǐwù [个 gè] II VT (strike) 碰 pèng
▶ **bump into** VT FUS **1** [+ obstacle, person] 撞到 zhuàngdào **2** (inf: meet) 碰见(見) pèngjiàn

bumpy ['bʌmpɪ] ADJ 崎岖(嶇)不平的 qíqū bùpíng de

bunch [bʌntʃ] N [c] **1** [of flowers] 束 shù **2** [of keys, bananas, grapes] 串 chuàn

bungalow ['bʌŋgələu] N [c] 平房 píngfáng [间 jiān]

bunk [bʌŋk] N [c] 铺(鋪)位 pùwèi [个 gè]

burger ['bə:gəʳ] N [c] 汉(漢)堡包 hànbǎobāo [个 gè]

burglar ['bə:gləʳ] N [c] 窃(竊)贼(賊) qièzéi [个 gè]

burglary ['bə:glərɪ] N **1** [c] (act) 盗(盜)窃(竊) dàoqiè [次 cì] **2** [U] (crime) 盗(盜)窃(竊)罪 dàoqièzuì

burn [bə:n] I VT **1** 焚烧(燒) fénshāo **2** [+ fuel] 燃烧(燒) ránshāo II VI **1** [fire, flame +] 燃烧(燒) ránshāo **2** [house, car +] 烧(燒)着(著) shāozháo III N [c] 烧(燒)伤(傷) shāoshāng [次 cì] ▶ **I've burnt myself!** 我把自己烫(燙)伤(傷)了！ wǒ bǎ zìjǐ tàngshāng le!
▶ **burn down** VI [house +] 烧(燒)毁(毀) shāohuǐ

burnt [bə:nt] PT, PP of **burn**

burqa ['bə:kə] N [c] 布卡（伊斯兰(蘭)国(國)家妇(婦)女穿的蒙面长(長)袍 bù kǎ (Yīsīlán guójiā fùnǚ chuān de méngmiàn chángpáo)

burst [bə:st] (pt, pp **burst**) VI [pipe, tyre +] 爆裂 bàoliè ▶ **to burst into flames** 突然着(著)火 tūrán zháohuǒ ▶ **to burst into tears** 突然大哭起来(來) tūrán dàkū qǐlái ▶ **to burst out laughing** 突然大笑起来(來) tūrán dàxiào qǐlái

bury ['bɛrɪ] VT **1** 掩埋 yǎnmái **2** [+ dead person] 埋葬 máizàng

bus [bʌs] N [c] 公共汽车(車) gōnggòng qìchē [辆 liàng]

bus driver N [c] 公共汽车(車)司机(機) gōnggòng qìchē sījī [位 wèi]

bush [buʃ] N [c] 灌木 guànmù [棵 kē]

business ['bɪznɪs] N **1** [c] (firm) 公司 gōngsī [家 jiā] **2** [U] (occupation) 商业(業) shāngyè **3** [U] (trade) 生意 shēngyì ▶ **to be away on business** 出差 chūchāi ▶ **to do business with sb** 和某人做生意 hé mǒurén zuò shēngyì

businessman ['bɪznɪsmən] (pl **businessmen**) N [c] 商人 shāngrén [个 gè]

businesswoman ['bɪznɪswumən] (pl **businesswomen**) N [c] 女商人 nǚ shāngrén [个 gè]

bus station N [c] 公共汽车(車)车(車)站 gōnggòngqìchē chēzhàn [个 gè]

bus stop N [c] 公共汽车(車)站 gōnggòngqìchē zhàn [个 gè]

bust [bʌst] N [c] 胸部 xiōngbù

busy ['bɪzi] ADJ **1** 忙的 máng de **2** [+ shop, street] 繁忙的 fánmáng de **3** [+ schedule, time, day] 忙碌(碌)的 mánglù de **4** (esp US: Tel) 占(佔)线(線)的 zhànxiàn de ▸ **I'm busy** 我正忙着(著)呢 wǒ zhèng mángzhe ne

KEYWORD

but [bʌt] CONJ (yet, however) 但是 dànshì ▸ **I'd love to come, but I'm busy** 我想来(來)，但是有事 wǒ xiǎng lái, dànshì yǒushì ▸ **not only ... but also** 不但…而且 bùdàn…érqiě

butcher ['butʃər] N [c] **1** 肉商 ròushāng [个 gè] **2** (shop) (also: **butcher's**) 肉铺(鋪) ròupù [个 gè]

butter ['bʌtər] N [u] 黄油 huángyóu

butterfly ['bʌtəflaɪ] N [c] 蝴蝶 húdié [只 zhī]

button ['bʌtn] N [c] **1** (on clothes) 纽扣 niǔkòu [颗 kē] **2** (on machine) 按钮(鈕) ànniǔ [个 gè] **3** (US: badge) 徽章 huīzhāng [个 gè]

buy [baɪ] (pt, pp **bought**) I VT 买(買) mǎi II N [c] (purchase) 所买(買)之物 suǒ mǎi zhī wù [件 jiàn] ▸ **to buy sb sth** 给(給)某人买(買)某物 gěi mǒurén mǎi mǒuwù ▸ **to buy sth off or from sb** 从(從)某人处(處)购(購)买(買)某物 cóng mǒurén chù gòumǎi mǒuwù

buzz [bʌz] VI (insect, machine +) 发(發)出嗡嗡声(聲) fāchū wēngwēng shēng

KEYWORD

by [baɪ] I PREP **1** (referring to cause, agent) 被 bèi ▸ **a painting by Picasso** 毕(畢)加索的画(畫) Bìjiāsuǒ de huà ▸ **surrounded by a fence** 由篱(籬)笆围(圍)着(著) yóu líba wéizhe

2 (referring to method, manner, means) ▸ **by bus/car/train** 乘公共汽车(車)/汽车(車)/火车(車) chéng gōnggòngqìchē/qìchē/huǒchē ▸ **to pay by cheque** 以支票支付 yǐ zhīpiào zhīfù ▸ **by moonlight/candlelight** 借助月光/烛(燭)光 jièzhù yuèguāng/zhúguāng

3 (via, through) 经(經)由 jīngyóu ▸ **he**

came in by the back door 他从(從)后(後)门(門)进(進)来(來) tā cóng hòumén jìnlai

4 (close to, beside) 靠近 kàojìn ▸ **he was standing by the door** 他正站在门(門)边(邊) tā zhèng zhànzài ménbiān ▸ **the house by the river** 河边(邊)的房子 hébiān de fángzi

5 (with times, dates, years) 以前 yǐqián ▸ **by 4 o'clock** 4点(點)以前 sì diǎn yǐqián ▸ **by April 7** 4月7号(號)以前 sì yuè qī hào yǐqián ▸ **by now/then** 到如今/那时(時) dào rújīn/nàshí

6 (during) ▸ **by day/night** 在白天/晚上 zài báitiān/wǎnshang

7 (specifying degree of change) 相差 xiāngchà ▸ **crime has increased by 10 per cent** 犯罪率上升了10% fànzuìlǜ shàngshēngle bǎi fēn zhī shí

8 (in measurements) ▸ **a room 3 metres by 4** 一间(間)长(長)3米宽(寬)4米的房间(間) yī jiān cháng sān mǐ kuān sì mǐ de fángjiān

9 (Math) ▸ **to divide/multiply by 3** 被3除/乘 bèi sān chú/chéng

10 ▸ **by myself/himself** etc (unaided) 我/他 {等} 自己 wǒ/tā děng zìjǐ; (alone) 我/他 {等} 单(單)独(獨) wǒ/tā děng dāndú

II ADV see **go by, pass by** etc

> 如果你说 I'll be home by ten o'clock，你的意思是你要在10点或10点以前到家，但绝不会晚于10点。如果你说 I'll be home before ten o'clock，你的意思是10点是你到家的最晚时间，你可能9点以前就到家了。如果你说 I'll be at home until ten o'clock，你的意思是10点以前你会在家里，但10点以后就不在了。当我们谈论某人写了一本书或剧本、导演了一部电影、作了一部乐曲或画了一幅画时，我们说一部作品是 **by** 那个人或是 **written by** 那个人。a collection of piano pieces by Mozart 当我们谈到某人给你写信或留言时，我们说信或留言是 **from** 那个人。He received a letter from his brother.

bye(-bye) ['baɪ('baɪ)] (inf) INT 再见(見) zàijiàn

C

cab [kæb] N [c] 出租车(車) chūzūchē [辆 liàng]

cabbage ['kæbɪdʒ] N [c/u] 卷(捲)心菜 juǎnxīncài [头 tóu]

cabin ['kæbɪn] N [c] **1** (on ship) 船舱(艙) chuáncāng [个 gè] **2** (on plane) 机(機)舱(艙) jīcāng [个 gè]

cable ['keɪbl] N **1** [c/u] (rope) 缆(纜)绳(繩) lǎnshéng [根 gēn] **2** [c/u] (Elec) 电(電)缆(纜) diànlǎn [根 gēn]

cable television N [u] 有线(線)电(電)视(視) yǒuxiàn diànshì

cactus ['kæktəs] (pl cactuses or cacti ['kæktaɪ]) N [c] 仙人掌 xiānrénzhǎng [棵 kē]

cafeteria [kæfɪ'tɪərɪə] N [c] 自助餐厅(廳) zìzhù cāntīng [个 gè]

cage [keɪdʒ] N [c] 笼(籠)子 lóngzi [个 gè]

cagoule [kə'guːl] N [c] 连(連)帽防雨长(長)夹(夾)克衫 liánmào fángyǔ cháng jiākèshān [件 jiàn]

cake [keɪk] N [c/u] 蛋糕 dàngāo [块 kuài]; (small) 糕点(點) gāodiǎn [块 kuài]

calculate ['kælkjuleɪt] VT 计(計)算 jìsuàn

calculation [kælkju'leɪʃən] N [c/u] (Math) 计(計)算 jìsuàn

calculator ['kælkjuleɪtə'] N [c] 计(計)算器 jìsuànqì [个 gè]

calendar ['kæləndə'] N [c] 日历(曆) rìlì [本 běn]

calf [kɑːf] (pl calves) N [c] **1** 小牛 xiǎoniú [头 tóu] **2** (Anat) 腿肚 tuǐdù [个 gè]

call [kɔːl] I VT **1** (name) 为(為)…取名 wèi…qǔmíng **2** (address as) 称(稱)呼 chēnghū **3** (describe as) 说(說)成是 shuōchéng shì **4** (shout) 喊 hǎn **5** (Tel) 打电(電)话(話) dǎ diànhuà **6** (summon) 召唤(喚) zhàohuàn II VI (telephone) 打电(電)话(話) dǎ diànhuà III N **1** [c] (shout) 大喊 dà hǎn **2** [c] (Tel) 电(電)话(話) diànhuà [次 cì] **3** [c] (visit) 探访(訪) tànfǎng [次 cì] ▶ to be called sth [person +] 被叫某名 bèijiào mǒu míng; [object +] 被称(稱)为(為)某物 bèi chēngwéi mǒuwù ▶ who's calling? (Tel) 请(請)问(問)是谁(誰)? qǐngwèn shìshuí? ▶ to make a phone call 打电(電)话(話) dǎ diànhuà ▶ to give sb a call 打电(電)话(話)给(給)某人 dǎ diànhuà gěi mǒurén
▶ **call back** I VI (Tel) 再打电(電)话(話) zài dǎ diànhuà II VT (Tel) 给(給)…回电(電)话(話) gěi…huí diànhuà
▶ **call off** VT 取消 qǔxiāo

call centre, (US) **call center** N [c] (Tel) 电(電)话(話)中心 diànhuà zhōngxīn [个 gè]

calm [kɑːm] ADJ **1** 冷静(靜)的 lěngjìng de **2** [+ sea] 平静(靜)的 píngjìng de
▶ **calm down** I VT [+ person, animal] 使平静(靜) shǐ píngjìng II VI [person +] 平静(靜)下来(來) píngjìng xiàlái

calorie ['kælərɪ] N [c] 卡路里 kǎlùlǐ

calves [kɑːvz] N PL of calf

Cambodia [kæm'bəudɪə] N 柬埔寨 Jiǎnpǔzhài

camcorder ['kæmkɔːdə'] N [c] 摄(攝)像放像机(機) shèxiàng fàngxiàng jī [部 bù]

came [keɪm] PT of come

camel ['kæməl] N [c] 骆(駱)驼(駝) luòtuo [头 tóu]

camera ['kæmərə] N [c] **1** (Phot) 照相机(機) zhàoxiàngjī [架 jià] **2** (Cine, TV) 摄(攝)影机(機) shèyǐngjī [部 bù]

cameraman ['kæmərəmæn] (pl cameramen) N [c] 摄(攝)影师(師) shèyǐngshī [位 wèi]

camp [kæmp] I N [c] (for refugees, prisoners, soldiers) 营(營) yíng II VI 扎(紮)营(營) zhāyíng ▶ to go camping 外出露营(營) wàichū lùyíng

campaign [kæm'peɪn] N [c] 运(運)动(動) yùndòng [场 cháng]

camper ['kæmpə^r] N [c] **1** (person) 野营(營)者 yěyíngzhě [个 gè] **2** (also: **camper van**) 野营(營)车(車) yěyíngchē [辆 liàng]

camping ['kæmpɪŋ] N [U] 野营(營) yěyíng

campsite ['kæmpsaɪt] N [c] 营(營)地 yíngdì [个 gè]

campus ['kæmpəs] N [c] 校园(園) xiàoyuán [个 gè]

can¹ [kæn] N [c] **1** (for food, drinks) 罐头(頭) guàntou [个 gè]; (for petrol, oil) 罐 guàn [个 gè] **2** (contents) 一听(聽)所装(裝)的量 yī tīng suǒ zhuāng de liàng [听 tīng] **3** (contents and container) 一罐 yīguàn

KEYWORD

can² [kæn] (negative **cannot, can't**, conditional, pt **could**) AUX VB **1** (be able to) 能 néng ▸ **can I help you?** (in shop) 您要买(買)点(點)儿(兒)什么(麼)? nín yào mǎi diǎnr shénme?; (in general) 我能帮(幫)你吗(嗎)? wǒ néng bāng nǐ ma? ▸ **you can do it if you try** 如果试(試)试(試)的话(話)你是能做的 rúguǒ shìshì de huà nǐ shì néng zuò de ▸ **I can't hear/see anything** 我什么(麼)也听(聽)不见/看不见(見) wǒ shénme yě tīng bù jiàn/kàn bù jiàn **2** (know how to) 会(會) huì ▸ **I can swim/drive** 我会(會)游泳/开(開)车(車) wǒ huì yóuyǒng/kāichē **3** (permission, requests) 可以 kěyǐ ▸ **can I use your phone?** 我可以用你的电(電)话(話)吗(嗎)? wǒ kěyǐ yòng nǐ de diànhuà ma? ▸ **can you help me?** 你可以帮(幫)我一下吗(嗎)? nǐ kěyǐ bāng wǒ yīxià ma? **4** (possibility) 可能 kěnéng ▸ **he can be very unpleasant** 他有时(時)会(會)非常不高兴(興) tā yǒushí huì fēicháng bù gāoxìng

> can、could 和 be able to 都是用来表示某人有能力做某事，后接原形动词。can 或 be able to 的现在式都可以指现在，但 can 更为常用。They can all read and write...The snake is able to catch small mammals. could 或 be

> able to 的过去式可用来指过去。will 或 shall 加 be able to 则用于表示将来。指在某一特定时间能够做某事，用 be able to。After treatment he was able to return to work. can 和 could 用于表示可能性。could 指的是某个特定情况下的可能性，而 can 则表示一般情况下的可能性。Many jobs could be lost...Too much salt can be harmful. 在谈论过去的时候，用 could have 加过去分词形式。It could have been much worse. 在谈论规则或表示许可的时候，用 can 表示现在，用 could 表示过去。They can leave at any time. 注意，当表示请求时，can 和 could 两者都可。Can I have a drink?...Can we put the fire on? 但表示建议时只能使用 could。You could phone her and ask.

Canada ['kænədə] N 加拿大 Jiānádà

Canadian [kə'neɪdɪən] I ADJ 加拿大的 Jiānádà de II N [c] (person) 加拿大人 Jiānádàrén [个 gè]

canal [kə'næl] N [c] 运(運)河 yùnhé [条 tiáo]

cancel ['kænsəl] VT 取消 qǔxiāo

cancer ['kænsə^r] N **1** [c/U] (Med) 癌症 áizhèng [种 zhǒng] **2** (Astrol) ▸ **Cancer** [U] (sign) 巨蟹座 Jùxiè Zuò

candidate ['kændɪdeɪt] N [c] **1** (for job) 候选(選)人 hòuxuǎnrén [位 wèi] **2** (in exam) 报(報)考者 bàokǎozhě [个 gè]

candle ['kændl] N [c] 蜡(蠟)烛(燭) làzhú [根 gēn]

candy ['kændɪ] (US) N [c/U] 糖果 tángguǒ [块 kuài]

canned [kænd] ADJ 罐装(裝)的 guànzhuāng de

cannot ['kænɔt] = **can not**

canoe [kə'nuː] N [c] 独(獨)木船 dúmùchuán [艘 sōu]

canoeing [kə'nuːɪŋ] N [U] 划独(獨)木船 huá dúmùchuán

can opener [-'əupnə^r] N [c] 开(開)罐器 kāiguànqì [个 gè]

can't [kɑːnt] = **can not**

canteen [kæn'tiːn] N [c] 食堂 shítáng [个 gè]

canvas ['kænvəs] N [U] 帆布 fānbù

cap [kæp] N [c] 帽 mào [顶 dǐng]

capable ['keɪpəbl] ADJ 有能力的 yǒu nénglì de ▸ **to be capable of doing sth**

有做某事的能力 yǒu zuò mǒushì de nénglì

capacity ['kə'pæsɪtɪ] N [s] (of container, ship) 容量 róngliàng; (of stadium, theatre) 可容纳(納)人数(數) kě róngnà rénshù

capital ['kæpɪtl] N 1 [c] (city) 首都 shǒudū [个 gè] 2 [U] (money) 资(資)本 zīběn 3 [c] (also: **capital letter**) 大写(寫)字母 dàxiě zìmǔ [个 gè] ▸ **capital R/L** etc 大写(寫)字母 R/L {等} dàxiě zìmǔ R/L děng

capitalism ['kæpɪtəlɪzəm] N [U] 资(資)本主义(義) zīběn zhǔyì

Capricorn ['kæprɪkɔ:n] N [U] (sign) 摩羯座 Mójié Zuò

captain ['kæptɪn] N [c] 1 (of ship) 船长(長) chuánzhǎng [位 wèi] 2 (of plane) 机(機)长(長) jīzhǎng [位 wèi] 3 (of team) 队(隊)长(長) duìzhǎng [个 gè]

capture ['kæptʃəʳ] VT 1 (+ animal) 捕获(獲)bǔhuò; (+ person) 俘虏(虜)fúlǔ

car [kɑːʳ] N [c] 1 (Aut) 汽车(車) qìchē [辆 liàng; 2 (US: Rail) 车(車)厢(廂) chēxiāng [节 jié] ▸ **by car** 乘汽车(車) chéng qìchē

caravan ['kærəvæn] N [c] (Brit) 活动(動)住房 huódòng zhùfáng [处 chù]

carbon-neutral [kɑ:bn'nju:trəl] ADJ 碳中和 tàn zhōnghé

card [kɑ:d] N 1 [c] 卡片 kǎpiàn [张 zhāng] 2 [c] (also: **playing card**) 扑(撲)克牌 pūkèpái [张 zhāng] 3 [c] (greetings card) 贺(賀)卡 hèkǎ [张 zhāng] 4 [c] (also: **business card**) 名片 míngpiàn [张 zhāng] 5 [c] (bank card, credit card) 信用卡 xìnyòngkǎ [张 zhāng] ▸ **to play cards** 打牌 dǎpái

cardigan ['kɑ:dɪgən] N [c] 开(開)襟毛衣 kāijīn máoyī [件 jiàn]

care [kɛəʳ] I N [U] 照顾(顧) zhàogù II VI 关(關)心 guānxīn ▸ **with care** 小心 xiǎoxīn ▸ **take care!** (saying goodbye) 慢走! mànzǒu! ▸ **to take care of sb** 照顾(顧)某人 zhàogù mǒurén ▸ **to take care of sth** (+ possession, clothes) 保管某物 bǎoguǎn mǒuwù; (+ problem, situation) 处(處)理某物 chǔlǐ mǒuwù ▸ **I don't care** 我不在乎 wǒ bù zàihu

▸ **care about** VT FUS (+ person, thing, idea) 关(關)心 guānxīn

▸ **care for** VT FUS 照顾(顧) zhàogù

career [kə'rɪəʳ] N [c] 1 (job, profession) 事业(業) shìyè [项 xiàng] 2 (working life) 生涯 shēngyá [个 gè]

careful ['kɛəful] ADJ 1 小心的 xiǎoxīn de 2 [+ work, thought, analysis] 仔细(細)的 zǐxì de ▸ **(be) careful!** 小心! xiǎoxīn! ▸ **to be careful with sth** [+ money] 谨(謹)慎地使用某物 jǐnshèn de shǐyòng mǒuwù; [+ fragile object] 小心对(對)待某物 xiǎoxīn duìdài mǒuwù

carefully ['kɛəfəlɪ] ADV 1 (cautiously) 小心地 xiǎoxīn de 2 (methodically) 用心地 yòngxīn de

careless ['kɛəlɪs] ADJ [+ person, worker] 粗心的 cūxīn de; [+ driving] 疏忽的 shūhu de; [+ mistake] 疏忽造成的 shūhu zàochéng de ▸ **it was careless of him to let the dog out** 他真不当(當)心，把狗放了出去 tā zhēn bù dāngxīn, bǎ gǒu fàngle chūqù

caretaker ['kɛəteɪkəʳ] N [c] (Brit) 看门(門)人 kānménrén [个 gè]

car ferry N [c] 汽车(車)渡轮(輪) qìchē dùlún [艘 sōu]

cargo ['kɑ:gəu] (pl **cargoes**) N [c/U] 货(貨)物 huòwù [批 pī]

car hire (Brit) N [U] 汽车(車)出租 qìchē chūzū

Caribbean [kærɪ'bi:ən] N ▸ **the Caribbean (Sea)** 加勒比海 Jiālèbǐ Hǎi

carnival ['kɑ:nɪvl] N 1 [c/U] (festival) 狂欢(歡)节(節) kuánghuānjié [个 gè] 2 [c] (US) 游(遊)艺(藝)团(團) yóuyìtuán [个 gè]

car park (Brit) N [c] 停车(車)场(場) tíngchēchǎng [处 chù]

carpenter ['kɑ:pɪntəʳ] N [c] 木匠 mùjiàng [个 gè]

carpet ['kɑ:pɪt] N [c] (fitted) 地毯 dìtǎn [条 tiáo]; (rug) 小地毯 xiǎo dìtǎn [块 kuài]

car rental N [U] 汽车(車)出租 qìchē chūzū

carriage ['kærɪdʒ] N [c] (Brit: Rail) 车(車)厢(廂) chēxiāng [节 jié]

carrier bag (Brit) N [c] 购(購)物袋 gòuwùdài [个 gè]

carrot ['kærət] N [c/U] 胡萝(蘿)卜(蔔) húluóbo [根 gēn]

carry ['kærɪ] VT 1 (+ person) 抱 bào; (by hand with the arm down) 提 tí; (on one's

back) 背(揹) bēi; (by hand) 拿 ná **2** (transport) [ship, plane +] 运(運)载(載) yùnzài
▶ **carry on** I VI (continue) 继(繼)续(續) jìxù II VT (continue) [+ work, tradition] ▶ **to carry on with sth** 继(繼)续(續)做某事 jìxù zuò mǒushì ▶ **to carry on doing sth** 继(繼)续(續)做某事 jìxù zuò mǒushì
▶ **carry out** VT [+ order, instruction] 执(執)行 zhíxíng

cart [kɑːt] N [c] **1** 大车(車) dàchē [辆(輛) liàng] **2** (US) (also: **shopping cart**) 手推车(車) shǒutuīchē [辆(輛) liàng]

carton ['kɑːtən] N [c] **1** (esp US: cardboard box) 纸(紙)箱 zhǐxiāng [个(個) gè] **2** (of milk, juice, yoghurt) 容器 róngqì [个(個) gè]

cartoon [kɑːˈtuːn] N [c] **1** (drawing) 漫画(畫) mànhuà [幅 fú] **2** (Brit: comic strip) 系列幽默画(畫) xìliè yōumò huà [套 tào] **3** (animated) 卡通片 kǎtōngpiàn [部 bù]

cartridge ['kɑːtrɪdʒ] N [c] **1** (for gun) 弹(彈)壳(殼) dànké [个(個) gè] **2** (for printer) 墨盒 mòhé [个(個) gè]

case [keɪs] N **1** [c] (instance) 情况(況) qíngkuàng [种(種) zhǒng] **2** [c] (container) 盒子 hézi [个(個) gè] **3** (Brit) (also: **suitcase**) 行李箱 xínglixiāng [个(個) gè]
▶ **lower/upper case** 小/大写(寫) xiǎo/dàxiě ▶ **in case he comes** 以防万(萬)一他会(會)来(來) yǐfáng wànyī tā huì lái ▶ **in any case** 无(無)论(論)如何 wúlùn rúhé ▶ **just in case** 以防万(萬)一 yǐfáng wànyī ▶ **in that case** 既然是那样(樣) jìrán shì nàyàng

cash [kæʃ] I N [u] **1** (notes and coins) 现(現)金 xiànjīn **2** (money) 现(現)款 xiànkuǎn II VT 兑(兌)现(現) duìxiàn
▶ **to pay (in) cash** 付现(現)金 fù xiànjīn

cashew [kæˈʃuː] N [c] (also: **cashew nut**) 腰果 yāoguǒ [颗 kē]

cashier [kæˈʃɪəʳ] N [c] 出纳(納)员(員) chūnàyuán [个(個) gè]

casino [kəˈsiːnəu] N [c] 赌(賭)场(場) dǔchǎng [个(個) gè]

cassette [kæˈsɛt] N [c] 磁带(帶) cídài [盘 pán]

cast [kɑːst] (pt, pp **cast**) N [c] (Theat) 演员(員)表 yǎnyuánbiǎo [份 fèn]

castle ['kɑːsl] N [c] 城堡 chéngbǎo [座 zuò]

casual ['kæʒjul] ADJ **1** (chance) 漫不经(經)心的 màn bù jīngxīn de **2** (unconcerned) 随(隨)便的 suíbiàn de **3** (informal) 非正式的 fēizhèngshì de

casualty ['kæʒjultɪ] N **1** [c] (of war, accident) (injured) 伤(傷)病员(員) shāngbìngyuán [个(個) gè]; (dead) 伤(傷)亡人员(員) shāngwáng rényuán [批 pī] **2** [u] (Brit: in hospital) 急诊(診)室 jízhěnshì

cat [kæt] N [c] 猫(貓) māo [只 zhī]

catalogue, (US) **catalog** ['kætəlɔg] N [c] **1** (for mail order) 目录(錄) mùlù [个(個) gè] **2** (of exhibition) 目录 mùlù [个(個) gè] **3** (of library) 书(書)目 shūmù [个(個) gè]

catastrophe [kəˈtæstrəfɪ] N [c] 大灾(災)难(難) dàzāinàn [场 cháng]

catch [kætʃ] (pt, pp **caught**) VT **1** [+ animal, fish] 捕获(獲) bǔhuò; [+ thief, criminal] 抓获(獲) zhuāhuò **2** [+ ball] 接 jiē **3** [+ bus, train, plane] 赶(趕)上 gǎnshàng **4** (discover) [+ person] 发(發)现(現) fāxiàn **5** [+ flu, illness] 染上 rǎnshàng
▶ **to catch sb doing sth** 撞见(見)某人做某事 zhuàngjiàn mǒurén zuò mǒushì
▶ **catch up** VI 追上 zhuīshàng

category ['kætɪgərɪ] N [c] 种(種)类(類) zhǒnglèi [个(個) gè]

catering ['keɪtərɪŋ] N [u] 饮(飲)食业(業) yǐnshíyè

cathedral [kəˈθiːdrəl] N [c] 大教堂 dàjiàotáng [个(個) gè]

Catholic ['kæθəlɪk] I ADJ 天主教的 Tiānzhǔjiào de II N [c] 天主教徒 Tiānzhǔjiàotú [个(個) gè]

cattle ['kætl] NPL 牛 niú

caught [kɔːt] PT, PP of **catch**

cauliflower ['kɔlɪflauəʳ] N [c/u] 菜花 càihuā [头 tóu]

cause [kɔːz] I N [c] 起因 qǐyīn [个(個) gè] II VT 导(導)致 dǎozhì ▶ **to cause sb to do sth** 促使某人做某事 cùshǐ mǒurén zuò mǒushì ▶ **to cause sth to happen** 导(導)致某事发(發)生 dǎozhì mǒushì fāshēng

cautious ['kɔːʃəs] ADJ 谨(謹)慎的 jǐnshèn de

cave [keɪv] N [c] 山洞 shāndòng [个(個) gè]

CCTV ['si:si:ti:'vi:] N ABBR (= **closed-circuit television**) 闭(閉)路电(電)视(視) bìlù diànshì [个(個) gè]

CD N ABBR (= compact disc) 激光唱片 jīguāng chàngpiàn

CD player N [c] 激光唱机(機) jīguāng chàngjī [部 bù]

CD-ROM [ˌsiːdiːˈrɔm] N ABBR (= compact disc read-only memory) 光盘(盤)只读(讀)存储(儲)器 guāngpán zhǐdú cúnchǔ qì ▸ **on CD-ROM** 光盘(盤)版 guāngpán bǎn

ceiling [ˈsiːlɪŋ] N [c] 天花板 tiānhuābǎn [块 kuài]

celebrate [ˈsɛlɪbreɪt] VT 庆(慶)祝 qìngzhù

celebrity [sɪˈlɛbrɪtɪ] N [c] 名人 míngrén [位 wèi]

cell [sɛl] N [c] 1 (Bio) 细(細)胞 xìbāo [个 gè] 2 (in prison) 牢房 láofáng [间 jiān]

cellar [ˈsɛləʳ] N [c] 地下室 dìxiàshì [间 jiān]; (for wine) 酒窖 jiǔjiào [个 gè]

cello [ˈtʃɛləʊ] N [c] 大提琴 dàtíqín [把 bǎ]

cement [səˈmɛnt] N [U] (concrete) 水泥 shuǐní

cemetery [ˈsɛmɪtrɪ] N [c] 墓地 mùdì [处 chù]

cent [sɛnt] N [c] 分 fēn

center [ˈsɛntəʳ] (US) N = centre

centigrade [ˈsɛntɪɡreɪd] ADJ 摄(攝)氏的 Shèshì de

centimetre, (US) **centimeter** [ˈsɛntɪmiːtəʳ] N [c] 厘(釐)米 límǐ

central [ˈsɛntrəl] ADJ 中心的 zhōngxīn de

central heating N [U] 中央供暖系统(統) zhōngyāng gōngnuǎn xìtǒng

centre, (US) **center** [ˈsɛntəʳ] N [c] 1 (of) 中心 zhōngxīn [个 gè] 2 [c] (building) 中心 zhōngxīn [个 gè] ▸ **to be at the centre of sth** 是某事的关(關)键(鍵) shì mǒushì de guānjiàn ▸ **to centre** or **be centred on** (focus on) 集中于(於) jízhōng yú

century [ˈsɛntjʊrɪ] N [c] 世纪(紀) shìjì [个 gè] ▸ **the 21st century** 21世纪(紀) èrshíyī shìjì ▸ **in the twenty-first century** 在21世纪(紀) zài èrshíyī shìjì

cereal [ˈsiːrɪəl] N 1 [c/U] (plant, crop) 谷(穀)类(類)植物 gǔlèi zhíwù [种 zhǒng] 2 [c/U] (also: breakfast cereal) 谷(穀)类(類)食品 gǔlèi shípǐn [种 zhǒng]

ceremony [ˈsɛrɪmənɪ] N [c] 典礼(禮) diǎnlǐ [个 gè]

certain [ˈsəːtən] ADJ 1 (sure) 肯定的 kěndìng de 2 (some) 某些 mǒuxiē ▸ **to be certain that...** 肯定… kěndìng… ▸ **to make certain that...** 证(證)实(實)… zhèngshí… ▸ **to be certain of sth** 肯定 kěndìng ▸ **a certain amount of sth** 一定量的某物 yídìng liàng de mǒuwù ▸ **to know sth for certain** 确(確)定某事 quèdìng mǒushì

certainly [ˈsəːtənlɪ] ADV 1 (undoubtedly) 无(無)疑地 wúyí de 2 (of course) 当(當)然 dāngrán ▸ **certainly not** 绝(絕)对(對)不行 juéduì bùxíng

certificate [səˈtɪfɪkɪt] N [c] 1 (of birth, marriage) 证(證)书 zhèng [张 zhāng] 2 (diploma) 结(結)业(業)证(證)书(書) jiéyè zhèngshū [个 gè]

chain [tʃeɪn] N 1 [c/U] 链(鏈)条(條) liàntiáo [根 gēn] 2 [c] (jewellery) 链(鏈)子 liànzi [条 tiáo]

chair [tʃɛəʳ] N [c] 椅子 yǐzi [把 bǎ]; (armchair) 扶手椅 fúshǒuyǐ [把 bǎ]

chairperson [ˈtʃɛəpəːsn] (pl **chairpersons**) N [c] 主席 zhǔxí [位 wèi]

chalk [tʃɔːk] N [c/U] (for writing) 粉笔(筆) fěnbǐ [支 zhī]

challenge [ˈtʃælɪndʒ] I N [c/U] 1 (hard task) 挑战(戰) tiǎozhàn [个 gè] 2 (to rival, competitor) 挑战(戰) tiǎozhàn [个 gè] II VT [+ rival, competitor] 向…挑战(戰) xiàng…tiǎozhàn ▸ **to challenge sb to a fight/game** 挑战(戰)某人打架/比赛(賽) tiǎnzhàn mǒurén dǎjià/bǐsài

champagne [ʃæmˈpeɪn] N [c/U] 香槟(檳)酒 xiāngbīnjiǔ [瓶 píng]

champion [ˈtʃæmpɪən] N [c] 冠军(軍) guànjūn [位 wèi]

championship [ˈtʃæmpɪənʃɪp] N [c] 锦(錦)标(標)赛(賽) jǐnbiāosài [届 jiè]

chance [tʃɑːns] I N 1 [c/U] (likelihood, possibility) 可能性 kěnéngxìng [种 zhǒng] 2 [s] (opportunity) 机(機)会(會) jīhuì 3 [U] (luck) 运(運)气(氣) yùnqì II ADJ [+ meeting, discovery] 偶然的 ǒurán de ▸ **he hasn't much chance of winning** 他赢(贏)的机(機)会(會)不大 tā yíng de jīhuì bù dà ▸ **the chance to do sth** 做某事的机(機)会(會) zuò mǒushì de jīhuì ▸ **by chance** 偶然 ǒurán

change [tʃeɪndʒ] I VT 1 改变(變) gǎibiàn 2 [+ wheel, battery] 换(換) huàn 3 [+ trains, buses] 换(換) huàn

4 [+ *clothes*] 换(換) huàn **5** [+ *job, address*] 更改 gēnggǎi **6** [+ *nappy*] 换(換) huàn **7** [+ *money*] 兑(兑)换(換) duìhuàn **II** vi **1** 变(變)化 biànhuà **2** (*change clothes*) 换(換)衣服 huànyī **3** (*on bus, train*) 换(換)车(車) huànchē **III** N **1** [c/u] (*alteration*) 转(轉)变(變) zhuǎnbiàn [种 zhǒng] **2** [s] (*novelty*) 变(變)化 biànhuà **3** [u] 零钱(錢) língqián; (*money returned*) 找头(頭) zhǎotou ▸ **to change one's mind** 改变(變)主意 gǎibiàn zhǔyì ▸ **for a change** 为(為)了改变(變)一下 wèile gǎibiàn yīxià ▸ **a change of clothes/ underwear** 一套换(換)洗的衣服/内(內)衣 yī tào huànxǐ de yīfu/nèiyī ▸ **small change** 零钱(錢) língqián ▸ **to give sb change for** *or* **of 10 pounds** 给(給)某人10英镑(鎊)的零钱(錢) gěi mǒurén shí yīngbàng de língqián ▸ **keep the change!** 不用找了！ bùyòng zhǎo le!

changing room (*Brit*) N [c] **1** (*in shop*) 试(試)衣室 shìyīshì [间 jiān] **2** (*Sport*) 更衣室 gēngyīshì [间 jiān]

channel ['tʃænl] N [c] **1** (*TV*) 频(頻)道 píndào [个 gè] **2** (*for water*) 沟(溝)渠 gōuqú [条 tiáo] ▸ **the (English) Channel** 英吉利海峡(峽) Yīngjílì hǎixiá

chaos ['keɪɔs] N [u] 混乱(亂) hùnluàn

chapel ['tʃæpl] N [c] (*in hospital, prison, school*) 附属(屬)教堂 fùshǔ jiàotáng [个 gè]

chapter ['tʃæptəʳ] N [c] 章 zhāng

character ['kærɪktəʳ] N **1** [c] 特性 tèxìng [种 zhǒng] **2** [c] (*in novel, film*) 角色 juésè [个 gè] **3** [c] (*letter, symbol*) 字母 zìmǔ [个 gè]

characteristic [kærɪktə'rɪstɪk] N [c] 特征(徵) tèzhēng [个 gè] ▸ **to be characteristic of sb/sth** 反映某人/某物的特性 fǎnyìng mǒurén/mǒuwù de tèxìng

charge [tʃɑːdʒ] I N [c] **1** 费(費)用 fèiyòng [笔 bǐ] II vt **1** [+ *sum of money*] 要价(價) yàojià; [+ *customer, client*] 收费(費) shōufèi **2** (*also*: **charge up**) [+ *battery*] 使充电(電) shǐ chōngdiàn III **charges** N PL 费(費) fèi ▸ **free of charge** 免费(費) miǎnfèi ▸ **to be in charge (of sth/sb)** (*of person, machine*) 主管(某事/某人) zhǔguǎn (mǒushì/mǒurén) ▸ **how much**

do you charge? 你收费(費)多少？ nǐ shōufèi duōshao? ▸ **to charge sb £20 for sth** 因某物收某人20英镑(鎊) yīn mǒuwù shōu mǒurén èrshí yīngbàng

charity ['tʃærɪtɪ] N [c] (*organization*) 慈善机(機)构(構) císhàn jīgòu [个 gè] ▸ **to give money to charity** 把钱(錢)捐给(給)慈善团(團)体(體) bǎ qián juāngěi císhàn tuántǐ

charm [tʃɑːm] N [c/u] [*of place, thing*] 魅力 mèilì [种 zhǒng]; [*of person*] 迷人的特性 mírén de tèxìng [个 gè]

charming ['tʃɑːmɪŋ] ADJ [+ *person*] 迷人的 mírén de; [+ *place, custom*] 吸引人的 xīyǐn rén de

chart [tʃɑːt] N [c] 图(圖)表 túbiǎo [个 gè]

charter flight N [c] 包机(機) bāojī [架 jià]

chase [tʃeɪs] vt 追赶(趕) zhuīgǎn

chat [tʃæt] I vi (*also*: **have a chat**) 聊天 liáotiān II N [c] (*conversation*) 聊天 liáotiān [次 cì]

chatroom (*Comput*) N [c] 聊天室 liáotiānshì [个 gè]

chat show (*Brit*) N [c] 访(訪)谈(談)节(節)目 fǎngtán jiémù [个 gè]

chauvinist ['ʃəuvɪnɪst] N [c] (*also*: **male chauvinist**) 大男子主义(義)者 dànánzǐzhǔyìzhě [个 gè]

cheap [tʃiːp] ADJ **1** 便宜的 piányi de **2** [+ *ticket*] 降价(價)的 jiàngjià de; [+ *fare, rate*] 廉价(價)的 liánjià de

cheat [tʃiːt] I vi 作弊 zuòbì II vt 欺骗(騙) qīpiàn III N [c] (*in games, exams*) 作弊者 zuòbìzhě [个 gè] ▸ **cheat on** (*inf*) vt FUS 不忠实(實)于(於) bù zhōngshí yú

check [tʃɛk] I vt **1** 核(覈)对(對) héduì; [+ *passport, ticket*] 检(檢)查 jiǎnchá **2** (*also*: **check in**) [+ *luggage*] 托运(運) tuōyùn II vi (*investigate*) 检(檢)查 jiǎnchá III N [c] **1** (*inspection*) 检(檢)查 jiǎnchá [次 cì] **2** (*US: in restaurant*) 账(賬)单(單) zhàngdān [张 zhāng] **3** (*US*) = **cheque 4** (*pattern: gen pl*) 方格图(圖)案 fānggé tú'àn [个 gè] = **cheque 5** (*US: mark*) 勾号(號) gōuhào [个 gè] IV ADJ (*also*: **checked**) [+ *pattern, cloth*] 方格图(圖)案的 fānggé tú'àn de ▸ **to check sth against sth** 将(將)某物与(與)某物相比较(較) jiāng mǒuwù yǔ mǒuwù xiāng bǐjiào ▸ **to check with sb** 向某人证(證)实(實) xiàng mǒurén zhèngshí ▸ **to keep a check on sb/sth** (watch) 监(監)视(視)某人/某物 jiānshì mǒurén/mǒuwù

▸ **check in** VI (at hotel, clinic) 登记(記)dēngjì; (at airport) 办(辦)理登机(機)手续(續) bànlǐ dēngjī shǒuxù

▸ **check into** VT 登记(記)入住 dēngjì rùzhù

▸ **check out** VI (of hotel) 结(結)账(賬)离(離)开(開) jiézhàng líkāi

checkbook ['tʃɛkbʊk] (US) N = **cheque book**

checked [tʃɛkt] ADJ see **check**

checkers ['tʃɛkəz] (US) NPL 西洋跳棋 xīyáng tiàoqí

check-in ['tʃɛkɪn] (also: **check-in desk**) N [c] 旅客验(驗)票台(臺) lǚkè yànpiàotái [个 gè]

checkout ['tʃɛkaʊt] N [c] 付款台(臺) fùkuǎntái [个 gè]

check-up ['tʃɛkʌp] N [c] (by doctor) 体(體)检(檢) tǐjiǎn [次 cì]; (by dentist) 牙科检(檢)查 yákē jiǎnchá [次 cì]

cheek [tʃiːk] N 1 [c] 面颊(頰) miànjiá [个 gè] 2 [U] 厚颜(顏)无(無)耻(恥) hòuyán wúchǐ ▸ **to have the cheek to do sth** 居然有脸(臉)做某事 jūrán yǒu liǎn zuò mǒushì

cheeky ['tʃiːkɪ] (esp Brit) ADJ 恬不知耻(恥)的 tián bù zhī chǐ de

cheer [tʃɪəʳ] I VI 欢(歡)呼 huānhū II N [c] 喝彩 hècǎi [阵 zhèn] ▸ **cheers!** (esp Brit: toast) 干(乾)杯! gānbēi!

▸ **cheer up** VI 振作起来(來) zhènzuò qǐlái

cheerful ['tʃɪəfʊl] ADJ 兴(興)高采烈的 xìng gāo cǎi liè de

cheese [tʃiːz] N [c/U] 干(乾)酪 gānlào [块 kuài]

chef [ʃɛf] N [c] 厨(廚)师(師) chúshī [位 wèi]

chemical ['kɛmɪkl] N [c] 化学(學)剂(劑) huàxuéjì [种 zhǒng]

chemist ['kɛmɪst] N [c] 1 (Brit) (also: **chemist's**) 药(藥)商 yàoshāng [个 gè] 2 (scientist) 化学(學)家 huàxuéjiā [位 wèi]

chemistry ['kɛmɪstrɪ] N [U] 化学(學) huàxué

cheque, (US) **check** [tʃɛk] N [c] 支票 zhīpiào [张 zhāng] ▸ **to pay by cheque** 用支票付款 yòng zhīpiào fùkuǎn

cheque book, (US) **checkbook** ['tʃɛkbʊk] N [c] 支票簿 zhīpiàobù [本 běn]

cherry ['tʃɛrɪ] N [c] 1 (fruit) 樱(櫻)桃 yīngtáo [颗 kē] 2 (also: **cherry tree**) 樱(櫻)桃树(樹) yīngtáo shù [棵 kē]

chess [tʃɛs] N [U] 象棋 xiàngqí

chest [tʃɛst] N [c] 1 胸部 xiōngbù 2 (box) 箱子 xiāngzi [个 gè]

chestnut ['tʃɛsnʌt] N [c] 栗子 lìzi [颗 kē]

chew [tʃuː] VT 嚼 jiáo

chewing gum ['tʃuːɪŋ-] N [U] 口香糖 kǒuxiāngtáng

chick [tʃɪk] N [c] 小鸟(鳥) xiǎoniǎo [只 zhī]

chicken ['tʃɪkɪn] N 1 [c] 鸡(雞) jī [只 zhī] 2 [c/U] (meat) 鸡(雞)肉 jīròu [块 kuài]

chickenpox ['tʃɪkɪnpɒks] N [U] 水痘 shuǐdòu

chief [tʃiːf] I N [c] 首领(領) shǒulǐng [个 gè] II ADJ 首要的 shǒuyào de

child [tʃaɪld] (pl **children**) N [c] 1 儿(兒)童 értóng [个 gè] 2 (son, daughter) 孩子 háizi [个 gè] ▸ **she's just had her second child** 她刚(剛)生了第二个(個)孩子 tā gāng shēngle dì'èr gè háizi

child minder (Brit) N [c] 保姆 bǎomǔ [个 gè]

children ['tʃɪldrən] NPL of **child**

Chile ['tʃɪlɪ] N 智利 Zhìlì

chill [tʃɪl] VT [+ food, drinks] 使冷冻(凍) shǐ lěngdòng ▸ **to catch a chill** 着(著)凉(涼) zháoliáng

chilli, (US) **chili** ['tʃɪlɪ] N [c/U] 辣椒 làjiāo [个 gè]

chilly ['tʃɪlɪ] ADJ 相当(當)冷的 xiāngdāng lěng de

chimney ['tʃɪmnɪ] N [c] 烟(煙)囱(囪) yāncōng [节 jié]

chin [tʃɪn] N [c] 下巴 xiàbā [个 gè]

China ['tʃaɪnə] N 中国(國) Zhōngguó

china ['tʃaɪnə] N [U] (crockery) 瓷器 cíqì

Chinese [tʃaɪ'niːz] (pl **Chinese**) I ADJ 中国(國)的 Zhōngguó de II N 1 [c] (person) 中国(國)人 Zhōngguórén [个 gè] 2 [U] (language) 汉(漢)语(語) Hànyǔ

chip [tʃɪp] N [c] 1 (Brit) 薯条(條) shǔtiáo [根 gēn] 2 (US: snack) 薯片 shǔpiàn [片

piàn 3 (Comput)(also: **microchip**) 集成电(電)路片 jíchéngdiànlù piàn [块 kuài]

chiropodist [kɪˈrɒpədɪst] (Brit) N [c] 足医(醫) zúyī [位 wèi]

chocolate [ˈtʃɒklɪt] I N **1** [u] 巧克力 qiǎokèlì **2** [c/u] (drinking chocolate) 巧克力饮(飲)料 qiǎokèlì yǐnliào [瓶 píng] **3** [c] (piece of confectionery) 巧克力糖 qiǎokèlì táng [块 kuài] II CPD [+ cake, pudding, mousse] 巧克力 qiǎokèlì ▶ **bar of chocolate** 巧克力条(條) qiǎokèlì tiáo ▶ **piece of chocolate** 一块(塊)巧克力 yī kuài qiǎokèlì

choice [tʃɔɪs] N **1** [c/u] (between items) 选(選)择(擇) xuǎnzé [个 gè] **2** [c] (option) 选(選)择(擇) xuǎnzé ▶ **a wide choice** 多种(種)多样(樣) duōzhǒng duōyàng ▶ **to have no/little choice** 没(沒)有/没(沒)有太多选(選)择(擇) méiyǒu/méiyǒu tàiduō xuǎnzé

choir [ˈkwaɪəʳ] N [c] 合唱团(團) héchàngtuán [个 gè]

choke [tʃəuk] VI (on food, drink) 噎住 yēzhù; (with smoke, dust) 呛(嗆) qiàng ▶ **to choke on sth** 被某物噎了 bèi mǒuwù yē le

choose [tʃuːz] (pt chose, pp chosen) I VT 挑选(選) tiāoxuǎn II VI ▶ **to choose between** 在…之间(間)作出选(選)择(擇) zài…zhījiān zuòchū xuǎnzé ▶ **to choose to do sth** 选(選)择(擇)做某事 xuǎnzé zuò mǒushì

chop [tʃɒp] I VT [+ vegetables, fruit, meat] 切 qiē II N [c] (Culin) 排骨 páigǔ [根 gēn]
▶ **chop down** VT [+ tree] 砍倒 kǎndǎo
▶ **chop up** VT 切 qiē

chopsticks [ˈtʃɒpstɪks] NPL 筷子 kuàizi

chose [tʃəuz] PT of **choose**

chosen [ˈtʃəuzn] PP of **choose**

Christ [kraɪst] N 耶稣(穌) Yēsū

christening [ˈkrɪsnɪŋ] N [c] 洗礼(禮) xǐlǐ [次 cì]

Christian [ˈkrɪstɪən] I ADJ 基督教的 Jīdūjiào de II N [c] 基督徒 Jīdūtú [个 gè]

Christian name N [c] 教名 jiàomíng [个 gè]

Christmas [ˈkrɪsməs] N [c/u] **1** 圣(聖)诞(誕)节(節) Shèngdàn Jié [个 gè] **2** (period) 圣(聖)诞(誕)节(節)期间(間) Shèngdàn Jié qījiān ▶ **Happy** or **Merry Christmas!** 圣(聖)诞(誕)快乐(樂)! Shèngdàn Kuàilè! ▶ **at Christmas** 在圣(聖)诞(誕)节(節) zài Shèngdàn Jié ▶ **for Christmas** 为(為)了圣(聖)诞(誕)节(節) wèile Shèngdàn Jié

Christmas Eve N [c/u] 圣(聖)诞(誕)夜 Shèngdàn Yè [个 gè]

Christmas tree N [c] 圣(聖)诞(誕)树(樹) Shèngdàn shù [棵 kē]

church [tʃəːtʃ] N [c/u] 教堂 jiàotáng [座 zuò]

cider [ˈsaɪdəʳ] N [c/u] **1** (Brit: alcoholic) 苹(蘋)果酒 píngguǒjiǔ [瓶 píng] **2** (US: non-alcoholic) 苹(蘋)果汁 píngguǒzhī [瓶 píng]

cigar [sɪˈgɑːʳ] N [c] 雪茄烟(煙) xuějiā yān [支 zhī]

cigarette [sɪgəˈrɛt] N [c] 香烟(煙) xiāngyān [支 zhī]

cinema [ˈsɪnəmə] N [c] (Brit) 电(電)影院 diànyǐngyuàn [个 gè]

circle [ˈsəːkl] N [c] 圆(圓)圈 yuánquān [个 gè]

circular [ˈsəːkjuləʳ] N [c] (letter) 供传(傳)阅(閱)的函件 gōng chuányuè de hánjiàn [封 fēng]

circumstances [ˈsəːkəmstənsɪz] NPL 情况(況) qíngkuàng ▶ **in** or **under the circumstances** 在这(這)种(種)情况(況)下 zài zhè zhǒng qíngkuàng xià

circus [ˈsəːkəs] N [c] 马(馬)戏(戲)团(團) mǎxìtuán [个 gè]

citizen [ˈsɪtɪzn] N [c] 公民 gōngmín [个 gè]

citizenship [ˈsɪtɪznʃɪp] N [u] 公民身份 gōngmín shēnfèn

city [ˈsɪtɪ] N [c] 城市 chéngshì [座 zuò] ▶ **the City** (Brit: Fin) 英国(國)伦(倫)敦商业(業)区(區) Yīngguó Lúndūn shāngyèqū

THE CITY

the City (伦敦商业区)是伦敦的一部分, 位于市中心的东部。很多重要的金融机构都将总部设在这里, 譬如英格兰银行、伦敦证券交易所和其他几个主要银行。这些金融机构的所在地通常统称为 **the City**。在历史上, 这个地区是伦敦的心脏, 有自己的市长和警力。

city centre (esp Brit) N [c] 市中心 shì zhōngxīn [个 gè]

civilization [sɪvɪlaɪˈzeɪʃən] N [c/u] 文明 wénmíng [种 zhǒng]

civilized [ˈsɪvɪlaɪzd] ADJ [+ society, people] 文明的 wénmíng de

civil partnership N [c/u] 民事伴侣(侶) 关(關)系 mínshì bànlǚ guānxi

civil war N [c/u] 内(内)战(戰) nèizhàn [场 cháng]

claim [kleɪm] I VT 1 [+ expenses, rights, inheritance] 要求 yāoqiú 2 [+ compensation, damages, benefit] 索取 suǒqǔ II VI (for insurance) 提出索赔(賠) tíchū suǒpéi III N [c] 索赔(賠) suǒpéi [项 xiàng] ▸ to claim or make a claim on one's insurance 提出保险(險)索赔(賠) 的要求 tíchū bǎoxiǎn suǒpéi de yāoqiú ▸ insurance claim 保险(險)索赔(賠)要求 bǎoxiǎn suǒpéi de yāoqiú

clap [klæp] VI 鼓掌 gǔzhǎng

clarinet [klærɪˈnɛt] (Mus) N [c] 单(單)簧管 dānhuángguǎn [根 gēn]

class [klɑːs] I N 1 [c] (Scol: group of pupils) 班级(級) bānjí [个 gè]; (lesson) 课(課) kè [堂 táng] 2 [c/u] (social) 阶(階)级(級) jiējí [个 gè] II VT (categorize) ▸ to class sb/sth as 将(將)某人/某物分类(類) 为(為) jiāng mǒurén/mǒuwù fēnlèi wéi

classic [ˈklæsɪk] N [c] 经(經)典 jīngdiǎn [种 zhǒng]

classical [ˈklæsɪkl] ADJ 1 (traditional) 传(傳)统(統)的 chuántǒng de 2 (Mus) 古典的 gǔdiǎn de

classmate [ˈklɑːsmeɪt] N [c] 同学(學) tóngxué [位 wèi]

classroom [ˈklɑːsrʊm] N [c] 教室 jiàoshì [间 jiān]

claw [klɔː] N [c] 爪子 zhuǎzi [只 zhī]

clay [kleɪ] N [u] 黏土 niántǔ

clean [kliːn] I ADJ 1 干(乾)净(淨)的 gānjìng de; [+ water] 清洁(潔)的 qīngjié de II VT [+ car, cooker] 弄干(乾)净(淨) nòng gānjìng; [+ room] 打扫(掃) dǎsǎo ▸ a clean driving licence or (US) record 未有违(違)章记(記)录(錄)的驾(駕)照 wèiyǒu wéizhāng jìlù de jiàzhào ▸ to clean one's teeth (Brit) 刷牙 shuāyá ▸ clean up VT [+ room, place] 打扫(掃) 干(乾)净(淨) dǎsǎo gānjìng; [+ mess] 整理 zhěnglǐ

cleaner [ˈkliːnər] N [c] (person) 清洁(潔)工 qīngjié gōng [位 wèi]

clear [klɪər] I ADJ 1 [+ explanation, account] 明确(確)的 míngquè de 2 (visible) 清晰的 qīngxī de 3 (audible) 清晰的 qīngxī de 4 (obvious) 无(無)疑的 wúyí de 5 (transparent) 透明的 tòumíng de 6 (unobstructed) 畅(暢)通的 chàngtōng de II VT [+ place, room] 清空 qīngkōng III VI [weather, sky +] 变(變)晴 biànqíng; [fog, smoke +] 消散 xiāosàn ▸ to be clear about sth 很明确(確)某事 hěn míngquè mǒushì ▸ to make o.s. clear 表达(達)清楚 biǎodá qīngchǔ ▸ to clear the table 收拾饭(飯)桌 shōushi fànzhuō ▸ clear away 清除 qīngchú ▸ clear off (inf) VI (leave) 走开(開) zǒukāi ▸ clear up I VT 1 [+ room, mess] 清理 qīnglǐ 2 [+ mystery, problem] 澄清 chéngqīng II VI (tidy up) 清理 qīnglǐ

clearly [ˈklɪəlɪ] ADV 1 [explain +] 明确(確)地 míngquè de; [think +] 清醒地 qīngxǐng de; [see +] 清楚地 qīngchu de; [speak, hear +] 清晰地 qīngxī de 2 [+ visible, audible] 清楚地 qīngchu de 3 (obviously) 显(顯)然 xiǎnrán

clever [ˈklɛvər] ADJ 1 聪(聰)明的 cōngmíng de 2 (sly, crafty) 耍小聪(聰)明的 shuǎ xiǎocōngmíng de 3 [+ device, arrangement] 巧妙的 qiǎomiào de

click [klɪk] N [c] (Comput) ▸ with a click of one's mouse 按一下鼠标(標) àn yīxià shǔbiāo [下 xià] ▸ to click on sth (Comput) 点(點)击(擊)某处(處) diǎnjī mǒuchù

client [ˈklaɪənt] N [c] [of lawyer] 委托(託)人 wěituōrén [个 gè]; [of company, restaurant, shop] 顾(顧)客 gùkè [位 wèi]

cliff [klɪf] N [c] 悬(懸)崖 xuányá [个 gè]

climate [ˈklaɪmɪt] N [c/u] 气(氣)候 qìhòu [种 zhǒng]

climate change N [u] 气(氣)候变(變)化 qìhòu biànhuà

climb [klaɪm] I VT (also: climb up) [+ tree] 爬 pá; [+ mountain, hill] 攀登 pāndēng; [+ ladder] 登 dēng; [+ stairs, steps] 上 shàng II VI [person +] 攀爬 pānpá III N [c] 攀登 pāndēng [次 cì] ▸ to go climbing 去爬山 qù páshān

climber ['klaɪmə'] N [c] 登山者 dēngshānzhě [个 gè]

climbing ['klaɪmɪŋ] N [u] 攀登 pāndēng

clingfilm ['klɪŋfɪlm] (Brit) N [u] 保鲜(鲜)纸(纸) bǎoxiān zhǐ

clinic ['klɪnɪk] (Med) N [c] 诊(诊)所 zhěnsuǒ [家 jiā]

cloakroom ['kləʊkrum] N [c] **1** (for coats) 衣帽间(间) yīmàojiān [个 gè] **2** (Brit: bathroom) 厕(厕)所 cèsuǒ [处 chù]

clock [klɒk] N [c] 钟(钟) zhōng [个 gè]
▸ **around the clock** [work, guard +] 日夜不停 rìyè bùtíng
▸ **clock in, clock on** VI (for work) 打卡上班 dǎkǎ shàngbān
▸ **clock off, clock out** VI (from work) 打卡下班 dǎkǎ xiàbān

close¹ [kləʊs] I ADJ **1** 近的 jìn de **2** [+relative] 直系的 zhíxì de **3** [+contest] 势(势)均力敌(敌)的 shì jūn lì dí de II ADV (near) 紧(紧)紧(紧)地 jǐnjǐn de
▸ **close to** (near) 近 jìn ▸ **a close friend** 一位密友 yī wèi mìyǒu ▸ **close by, close at hand** 在近旁 zài jìnpáng

close² [kləʊz] I VT **1** 关(关) guān **2** [+shop, factory] 关(关)闭(闭) guānbì II VI **1** 关(关) guān **2** [+shop, library +] 关(关)门(门) guānmén
▸ **close down** VI [factory, business +] 关(关)闭(闭) guānbì

closed [kləʊzd] ADJ [+door, window] 关(关)着(着)的 guānzhe de; [+shop, library] 关(关)着(着)门(门)的 guānzhe mén de; [+road] 封锁(锁)着(着)的 fēngsuǒzhe de

closely ['kləʊslɪ] ADV **1** [examine, watch +] 仔细(细)地 zǐxì de **2** [+connected] 密切地 mìqiè de

closet ['klɒzɪt] N [c] (US) 壁橱(橱) bìchú [个 gè]

cloth [klɒθ] N [c/u] **1** (fabric) 布料 bùliào [块 kuài] **2** [c] (for cleaning, dusting) 布布 bù bù [块 kuài] **3** [c] (tablecloth) 桌布 zhuōbù [块 kuài]

clothes [kləʊðz] N PL 衣服 yīfu ▸ **to take one's clothes off** 脱(脱)衣服 tuō yīfu

cloud [klaʊd] N **1** 云(云) yún [片 piàn] **2** [c] [of smoke, dust] 雾(雾) wù [团 tuán]
▸ **cloud over** VI 阴(阴)云(云)密布(布) yīnyún mìbù

cloudy ['klaʊdɪ] ADJ 多云(云)的 duōyún de ▸ **it's cloudy** 天阴(阴) tiānyīn

clown [klaʊn] N [c] 小丑(丑) xiǎochǒu [个 gè]

club [klʌb] N [c] **1** 俱乐(乐)部 jùlèbù [个 gè] **2** (Sport) 俱乐(乐)部 jùlèbù [个 gè] **3** (nightclub) 夜总(总)会(会) yèzǒnghuì [家 jiā]

clue [klu:] N [c] **1** (in investigation) 线(线)索 xiànsuǒ [条 tiáo] **2** (in crossword, game) 提示 tíshì [个 gè] ▸ **I haven't a clue** (inf) 我一无(无)所知 wǒ yī wú suǒ zhī

clumsy ['klʌmzɪ] ADJ 笨手笨脚(脚)的 bèn shǒu bèn jiǎo de

clutch [klʌtʃ] N [c] (Aut) 离(离)合器 líhéqì [个 gè]

coach [kəʊtʃ] I N [c] **1** (Brit) 长(长)途汽车(车) chángtú qìchē [辆 liàng] **2** (Sport) 教练(练) jiàoliàn [位 wèi] II VT (Sport) 训(训)练(练) xùnliàn

coal [kəʊl] N [u] 煤 méi

coast [kəʊst] N [c] 海岸 hǎi'àn [个 gè]

coat [kəʊt] N [c] **1** (overcoat) 外套 wàitào [件 jiàn] **2** [of animal] 皮毛 pímáo [层 céng]

coat hanger N [c] 衣架 yījià [个 gè]

cocaine [kəˈkeɪn] N [u] 可卡因 kěkǎyīn

cock [kɒk] N [c] (Brit) 公鸡(鸡) gōngjī [只 zhī]

cocoa ['kəʊkəʊ] N [u] 可可 kěkě

coconut ['kəʊkənʌt] N [c] (nut) 椰子 yēzi [个 gè]

cod [kɒd] (pl cod or cods) N [c] (fish) 鳕(鳕)鱼(鱼) xuěyú [条 tiáo]

code [kəʊd] N **1** [c] (cipher) 密码(码) mìmǎ [个 gè] **2** [c] (Tel) 区(区)号(号) qūhào [个 gè] **3** [c/u] (Comput, Sci) 编(编)码(码) biānmǎ [个 gè]

coffee ['kɒfɪ] N **1** [u] 咖啡 kāfēi **2** [c] (cup of coffee) 一杯咖啡 yī bēi kāfēi [杯 bēi] ▸ **black coffee** 黑咖啡 hēi kāfēi ▸ **white coffee** 牛奶咖啡 niúnǎi kāfēi

coffin ['kɒfɪn] N [c] 棺材 guāncai [口 kǒu]

coin [kɔɪn] N [c] 硬币(币) yìngbì [枚 méi]

coincidence [kəʊˈɪnsɪdəns] N [c/u] 巧合 qiǎohé [种 zhǒng]

Coke® [kəʊk] N [u] (drink) 可口可乐(乐) Kěkǒu Kělè

cold [kəʊld] I ADJ [+water, object] 凉(凉)

的 liáng de; [+ weather, room, meat] 冷的 lěng de II N 1 [U] (weather) ▶ the cold 寒冷天气(氣) hánlěng tiānqì 2 (c) (illness) 感冒 gǎnmào [次 cì] ▶ it's cold 天气(氣)寒冷 tiānqì hánlěng ▶ to be or feel cold [person +] 感到冷 gǎndào lěng ▶ to catch (a) cold 患感冒 huàn gǎnmào

collapse [kə'læps] VI 倒塌 dǎotān; [person +] 倒下 dǎoxià

collar ['kɒlə'] N [c] 领(領)子 lǐngzi [个 gè]

collarbone ['kɒləbəun] N [c] 锁(鎖)骨 suǒgǔ [根 gēn]

colleague ['kɒli:g] N [c] 同事 tóngshì [个 gè]

collect [kə'lɛkt] VT 1 采(採)集 cǎijí 2 (as hobby) 收集 shōují 3 (Brit: fetch) [+ person] 接 jiē; [+ object] 取 qǔ 4 [+ money, donations] 募捐 mùjuān ▶ to call collect, make a collect call (US: Tel) 打对(對)方付款的电(電)话(話) dǎ duìfāng fùkuǎn de diànhuà

collection [kə'lɛkʃən] N 1 [c] (of art, stamps) 收藏品 shōucángpǐn [件 jiàn] 2 [c] (for charity, gift) 募捐 mùjuān [次 cì]

collector [kə'lɛktə'] N [c] 收藏家 shōucángjiā [位 wèi]

college ['kɒlɪdʒ] N 1 [c/u] (for further education) 学(學)院 xuéyuàn [个 gè] 2 [c] (of university) 学(學)院 xuéyuàn [个 gè] ▶ to go to college 上大学(學) shàng dàxué

collide [kə'laɪd] VI 碰撞 pèngzhuàng ▶ to collide with sth/sb 与(與)某物/某人碰撞 yǔ mǒuwù/mǒurén pèngzhuàng

collision [kə'lɪʒən] N [c/u] (of vehicles) 碰撞 pèngzhuàng [下 xià]

colonel ['kə:nl] N [c] 上校 shàngxiào [位 wèi]

color etc ['kʌlə'] (US) = **colour** etc

colour, (US) **color** ['kʌlə'] I N 1 [c] 颜(顏)色 yánsè [种 zhǒng] 2 [c] (skin colour) 肤(膚)色 fūsè [种 zhǒng] II VT 给(給)…着(著)色 gěi...zhuósè III CPD [+ film, photograph, television] 彩色 cǎisè ▶ in colour [+ film, illustrations] 彩色 cǎisè

colourful, (US) **colorful** ['kʌləful] ADJ 色泽(澤)鲜(鮮)艳(豔)的 sèzé xiānyàn de

colour television, (US) **color television** N [c/u] 彩色电(電)视(視) cǎisè diànshì [台 tái]

column ['kɒləm] N [c] (Archit) 支柱 zhīzhù [个 gè]

comb [kəum] I N [c] 梳子 shūzi [把 bǎ] II VT 梳理 shūlǐ

combination [kɒmbɪ'neɪʃən] N [c] 混合 hùnhé [种 zhǒng]

combine [kəm'baɪn] I VT ▶ to combine sth with sth 将(將)某物与(與)某物结(結)合起来(來) jiāng mǒuwù yǔ mǒuwù jiéhé qǐlái II VI [qualities, situations +] 结(結)合 jiéhé; [people, groups +] 组(組)合 zǔhé ▶ a combined effort 协(協)力 xiélì

○ **KEYWORD**

come [kʌm] (pt came, pp come) VI
1 来(來) lái ▶ come here! 到这(這)儿(兒)来(來)! dào zhèr lái! ▶ can I come too? 我也能来(來)吗(嗎)? wǒ yě néng lái ma? ▶ come with me 跟我来(來) gēn wǒ lái ▶ a girl came into the room 一个(個)女孩进(進)了房间(間) yī gè nǚhái jìnle fángjiān ▶ why don't you come to lunch on Saturday? 何不星期六过(過)来(來)吃午饭(飯)呢? hé bù xīngqīliù guòlái chī wǔfàn ne? ▶ he's come here to work 他已经(經)到了这(這)儿(兒)工作 tā yǐjīng dàole zhèr gōngzuò
2 ▶ to come to (reach) 到达(達) dàodá; (amount to) 达(達)到 dádào ▶ to come to a decision 做出决(決)定 zuòchū juédìng ▶ the bill came to £40 账(賬)单(單)共计(計)40英镑(鎊) zhàngdān gòngjì sìshí yīngbàng
3 (be, become) ▶ to come first/second/last etc (in series) 排在第一/第二/最后(後){等} páizài dìyī/dì'èr/zuìhòu děng; (in competition, race) 位居第一/第二/最后(後){等} wèijū dìyī/dì'èr/zuìhòu děng
▶ **come across** VT FUS 偶然发(發)现(現) ǒurán fāxiàn
▶ **come apart** VI 裂成碎片 lièchéng suìpiàn
▶ **come back** VI (return) 回来(來) huílái
▶ **come down** VI 1 [price +] 降低 jiàngdī 2 [plane +] 坠(墜)落 zhuìluò 3 (descend) 降下 jiàngxià
▶ **come forward** VI (volunteer) 自告奋(奮)勇 zì gào fènyǒng

▶**come from** VT FUS 来(來)自 láizì ▶I come from London 我来(來)自伦(倫)敦 wǒ láizì Lúndūn ▶ where do you come from? 你是哪里(裡)人？nǐ shì nǎlǐ rén?

▶**come in** VI 进(進)入 jìnrù ▶ come in! 进(進)来(來)！jìnlai!

▶**come off** VI [button, handle +] 脱(脫)落 tuōluò

▶**come on** VI (progress) 进(進)展 jìnzhǎn ▶ come on! (giving encouragement) 来(來)！lái!; (hurry up) 快一点(點)！kuài yīdiǎn!

▶**come out** VI 1 [person +] 出去 chūqù 2 [sun +] 出现(現) chūxiàn 3 [book +] 出版 chūbǎn; [film +] 上映 shàngyìng

▶**come through** VT FUS (survive) 经(經)历(歷)…而幸存 jīnglì…ér xìngcún

▶**come to** VI (regain consciousness) 苏(甦)醒 sūxǐng

▶**come up** VI 1 (approach) 走近 zǒujìn 2 [problem, opportunity +] 突然出现(現) tūrán chūxiàn

▶**come up to** VT FUS 1 (approach) 走近 zǒujìn 2 (meet) ▶ the film didn't come up to our expectations 电(電)影没(沒)有我们(們)预(預)期的那么(麼)好 diànyǐng méiyǒu wǒmen yùqī de nàme hǎo

comedian [kə'miːdiən] (Theat, TV) N [c] 喜剧(劇)演员(員) xǐjù yǎnyuán [个 gè]

comedy ['kɒmɪdɪ] N 1 [U] (humour) 幽默 yōumò 2 [c] (play, film) 喜剧(劇) xǐjù [部 bù]

comfortable ['kʌmfətəbl] ADJ 1 [person +] ▶ to be comfortable 舒服的 shūfu de 2 [+ furniture, room, clothes] 使人舒服的 shǐ rén shūfu de ▶ to make o.s. comfortable 自在点(點) zìzài diǎn

comma ['kɒmə] N [c] 逗号(號) dòuhào [个 gè]

command [kə'mɑːnd] N 1 [c] (order) 命令 mìnglìng [项 xiàng] 2 [c] (Comput) 指令 zhǐlìng [个 gè]

comment ['kɒment] I N [c/U] (evaluation) 评(評)论(論) pínglùn [种 zhǒng] II VI ▶ to comment (on sth) (对(對)某事) 发(發)表意见(見) (duì mǒushì) fābiǎo yìjiàn

▶"no comment" "无(無)可奉告"wú kě fèng gào"

commentary ['kɒməntərɪ] N [c/U] 实(實)况(況)报(報)道 shíkuàng bàodào [段 duàn]

commentator ['kɒmenteɪtəʳ] N [c] 解说(說)员(員) jiěshuōyuán [位 wèi]

commercial [kə'məːʃəl] I ADJ [+ success, failure] 从(從)盈利角度出发(發) cóng yínglì jiǎodù chūfā; [+ television, radio] 商业(業)性的 shāngyèxìng de II N [c] (advertisement) 广(廣)告 guǎnggào [则 zé]

commit [kə'mɪt] VT 犯 fàn ▶ to commit suicide 自杀(殺) zìshā

committee [kə'mɪtɪ] N [c] 委员(員)会(會) wěiyuánhuì [个 gè]

common ['kɒmən] ADJ 常见(見)的 chángjiàn de ▶ to have sth in common [+ people] 有某些共同点(點) yǒu mǒuxiē gòngtóngdiǎn; [things +] 有共同的某特征(徵) yǒu gòngtóng de mǒu tèzhēng ▶ to have sth in common with sb/sth 与(與)某人/某物有某共同点(點) yǔ mǒurén/mǒuwù yǒu mǒu gòngtóngdiǎn

common sense N [U] 常识(識) chángshí

communicate [kə'mjuːnɪkeɪt] VI 联(聯)络(絡) liánluò

communication [kəmjuːnɪ'keɪʃən] I N [U] 交流 jiāoliú II communications N PL 通讯(訊) tōngxùn

communism ['kɒmjunɪzəm] N [U] 共产(產)主义(義) gòngchǎn zhǔyì

community [kə'mjuːnɪtɪ] N [c] 社区(區) shèqū [个 gè]

commute [kə'mjuːt] VI 乘车(車)上下班 chéngchē shàngxià bān ▶ to commute to/from London/Brighton 去/从(從)伦(倫)敦/布赖(賴)顿(頓)乘车(車)上下班 qù/cóng Lúndūn/Bùlàidùn chéngchē shang xià bān

compact disc N [c] 激光唱片 jīguāng chàngpiàn [张 zhāng]

company ['kʌmpənɪ] N [c] (firm) 公司 gōngsī [个 gè] 2 [U] (companionship) 交往 jiāowǎng ▶ to keep sb company 陪伴某人 péibàn mǒurén

comparatively [kəm'pærətɪvlɪ] ADV [+ easy, safe, peaceful] 相对(對)地 xiāngduì de

compare [kəm'peə^r] I VT 比较(較) bǐjiào II VI ▶ to compare favourably/unfavourably (with sth/sb) 比得上/比不上(某物/某人) bǐdeshang/bǐbùshang (mǒuwù/mǒurén) ▶ to compare sb/sth to 把某人/某物比作 bǎ mǒurén/mǒuwù bǐzuò ▶ compared with or to 与(與)…相比 yǔ…xiāngbǐ ▶ how does he compare with his predecessor? 和他前任比起来(來)他怎么(麼)样(樣)? hé tā qiánrèn bǐ qǐlái tā zěnmeyàng?

comparison [kəm'pærɪsn] N [c/u] 比较(較) bǐjiào [种 zhǒng] ▶ in or by comparison (with) (与(與)…) 比较(較)起来(來) (yǔ…) bǐjiào qǐlái

compartment [kəm'pɑ:tmənt] N [c] (Rail) 隔间(間) géjiān [个 gè]

compass ['kʌmpəs] N [c] 指南针(針) zhǐnánzhēn [个 gè]

compatible [kəm'pætɪbl] ADJ [+ people] 意气(氣)相投的 yìqì xiāngtóu de; (Comput) 兼容的 jiānróng de ▶ to be compatible with sth (Comput) 与(與)某物兼容 yǔ mǒuwù jiānróng

compensation [kɔmpən'seɪʃən] N [u] 赔(賠)偿(償)金 péichángjīn ▶ compensation for sth 因某事而获(獲)得的赔(賠)偿(償)金 yīn mǒushì ér huòdé de péichángjīn

compete [kəm'pi:t] VI [companies, rivals +] 竞(競)争(爭) jìngzhēng; (in contest, game) 比赛(賽) bǐsài ▶ to compete for sth [companies, rivals +] 争(爭)夺(奪)某物 zhēngduó mǒuwù; (in contest, game) 争(爭)夺(奪)某物 zhēngduó mǒuwù ▶ to compete with sb/sth (for sth) [companies, rivals +] 与(與)某人/某物竞(競)争(爭)(以得到某物) yǔ mǒurén/mǒuwù jìngzhēng (yǐ dédào mǒuwù); (in contest, game) 与(與)某人/某物竞(競)争(爭)(以获(獲)得某奖(獎)项(項)) yǔ mǒurén/mǒuwù jìngzhēng (yǐ huòdé mǒu jiǎngxiàng)

competent ['kɔmpɪtənt] ADJ 称(稱)职(職)的 chènzhí de; [+ piece of work] 合格的 hégé de

competition [kɔmpɪ'tɪʃən] N 1 [u] (rivalry) 竞(競)争(爭) jìngzhēng 2 [c] (contest) 竞(競)赛(賽) jìngsài [项 xiàng]

▶ in competition with 与(與)…竞(競)争(爭) yǔ…jìngzhēng

competitive [kəm'pɛtɪtɪv] ADJ 1 [+ industry, society] 竞(競)争(爭)性的 jìngzhēngxìng de 2 [+ person] 求胜(勝)心切的 qiúshèngxīnqiè de

competitor [kəm'pɛtɪtə^r] N [c] 1 (in business) 竞(競)争(爭)对(對)手 jìngzhēng duìshǒu [个 gè] 2 (participant) 参(參)赛(賽)者 cānsàizhě [个 gè]

complain [kəm'pleɪn] VI ▶ to complain (about sth) (就某事) 投诉(訴) (jiù mǒushì) tóusù; (grumble) (就某事) 诉(訴)苦 (jiù mǒushì) sùkǔ ▶ to complain to sb (about sth) (就某事) 向某人投诉(訴) (jiù mǒushì) xiàng mǒurén tóusù

complaint [kəm'pleɪnt] N [c] 抱怨 bàoyuàn [个 gè] ▶ to make a complaint (to sb) (向某人) 投诉(訴) (xiàng mǒurén) tóusù

complete [kəm'pli:t] I ADJ 1 完全的 wánquán de 2 (whole) 完整的 wánzhěng de 3 (finished) 完成的 wánchéng de II VT 1 完成 wánchéng 2 [+ form, coupon] 填写(寫) tiánxiě ▶ complete with 附带(帶) fùdài

completely [kəm'pli:tlɪ] ADV [+ different, satisfied, untrue] 完全 wánquán; [forget, destroy +] 彻(徹)底 chèdǐ

complexion [kəm'plɛkʃən] N [c] 面色 miànsè [种 zhǒng]

complicated ['kɔmplɪkeɪtɪd] ADJ 复(複)杂(雜)的 fùzá de

compliment [n 'kɔmplɪmənt, vb 'kɔmplɪment] I N [c] 赞(讚)美 zànměi [种 zhǒng] II VT 赞(讚)美 zànměi ▶ to pay sb a compliment 赞(讚)美某人 zànměi mǒurén ▶ to compliment sb on sth 为(為)某事赞(讚)美某人 wèi mǒushì zànměi mǒurén

composer [kəm'pəuzə^r] N [c] 作曲家 zuòqǔjiā [位 wèi]

comprehension [kɔmprɪ'hɛnʃən] N 1 [u] (understanding) 理解 lǐjiě 2 [c/u] (Scol) 理解力练(練)习(習) lǐjiělì liànxí [项 xiàng]

comprehensive [kɔmprɪ'hɛnsɪv] I ADJ 1 [+ review, list] 全面的 quánmiàn de 2 [+ insurance] 综(綜)合的 zōnghé de II N [c] (Brit) (also: **comprehensive**

school) 综(綜)合性中学(學)
zōnghéxìng zhōngxué [所 suǒ]

compulsory [kəm'pʌlsərɪ] ADJ 必须(須)
的 bìxū de; [+ course] 必修的 bìxiū de

computer [kəm'pju:tə^r] I N [c] 计(計)算
机(機) jìsuànjī [台 tái] II CPD [+ language,
program, system, technology etc] 电(電)
脑(腦) diànnǎo

computer game N [c] 电(電)脑(腦)
游(遊)戏(戲) diànnǎo yóuxì [局 jú]

computer programmer N [c] 电(電)
脑(腦)编(編)程员(員) diànnǎo
biānchéngyuán [位 wèi]

computer science N [U] 计(計)算
机(機)科学(學) jìsuànjī kēxué

computing [kəm'pju:tɪŋ] I N [U] 计(計)
算机(機)运(運)用 jìsuànjī yùnyòng;
(also: **computing studies**) 计(計)算
机(機)学(學) jìsuànjīxué II CPD [+ course,
skills] 电(電)脑(腦) diànnǎo

concentrate ['kɔnsəntreɪt] VI 集中精力
jízhōng jīnglì ▸ **to concentrate on sth**
(keep attention on) 全神贯(貫)注于(於)
某事 quán shén guàn zhù yú mǒushì;
(focus on) 集中注意力于(於)某事
jízhōng zhùyìlì yú mǒushì

concentration [kɔnsən'treɪʃən] N [U]
专(專)心 zhuānxīn

concern [kən'sə:n] I N [U] (anxiety)
担(擔)忧(憂) dānyōu II VT (worry) 使
担(擔)忧(憂) shǐ dānyōu ▸ **concern for
sb** 为(為)某人担(擔)心 wèi mǒurén
dānxīn ▸ **as far as I'm concerned**
据(據)我看来(來) jù wǒ kànlái ▸ **the
people concerned** (in question) 有关(關)
人士 yǒuguān rénshì

concerned [kən'sə:nd] ADJ (worried)
担(擔)心的 dānxīn de ▸ **to be
concerned about sb/sth** 担(擔)心某
人/某事 dānxīn mǒurén/mǒushì

concerning [kən'sə:nɪŋ] PREP 关(關)
于(於) guānyú

concert ['kɔnsət] N [c] 音乐(樂)会(會)
yīnyuèhuì [个 gè]

concert hall N [c] 音乐(樂)厅(廳)
yīnyuètīng [个 gè]

conclusion [kən'klu:ʒən] N 1 [s] (end)
结(結)尾 jiéwěi 2 [c] (deduction) 结(結)
论(論) jiélùn [个 gè] ▸ **to come to the
conclusion that...** 得出的结(結)论(論)
是… déchū de jiélùn shì...

concrete ['kɔnkri:t] I N [U] 混凝土
hùnníngtǔ II ADJ 1 [+ block, floor] 混凝土
的 hùnníngtǔ de 2 [+ proposal, evidence]
确(確)实(實)的 quèshí de

condemn [kən'dɛm] VT (denounce)
谴(譴)责(責) qiǎnzé

condition [kən'dɪʃən] I N 1 [s] (state)
状(狀)态(態) zhuàngtài 2 [c] (stipulation)
条(條)件 tiáojiàn [个 gè] II **conditions**
NPL 环(環)境 huánjìng ▸ **in good/poor
condition** 状(狀)况(況)良好/不好
zhuàngkuàng liánghǎo/bùhǎo
▸ **weather conditions** 天气(氣)形
势(勢) tiānqì xíngshì ▸ **on condition
that...** 在…条(條)件下 zài...tiáojiàn
xià

conditional [kən'dɪʃənl] I ADJ 有条(條)
件的 yǒu tiáojiàn de II N (Ling) ▸ **the
conditional** 条(條)件从(從)句 tiáojiàn
cóngjù

conditioner [kən'dɪʃənə^r] N [c/U] 护(護)
发(髮)素 hùfàsù [种 zhǒng]

condom ['kɔndəm] N [c] 安全套
ānquántào [只 zhī]

conduct [kən'dʌkt] VT [+ orchestra, choir]
指挥(揮) zhǐhuī

conductor [kən'dʌktə^r] N [c] 1 [of
orchestra] 指挥(揮)家 zhǐhuījiā [位 wèi]
2 (US: on train) 列车(車)员(員)
lièchēyuán [位 wèi] 3 (on bus) 售票
员(員) shòupiàoyuán [位 wèi]

cone [kəun] N [c] 1 (shape) 圆(圓)锥(錐)
体(體) yuánzhuītǐ [个 gè] 2 (also: **ice
cream cone**) 锥(錐)形蛋卷(捲)冰淇淋
zhuīxíng dànjuǎn bīngqílín [个 gè]

conference ['kɔnfərəns] N [c] 会(會)
议(議) huìyì [次 cì]

confess [kən'fɛs] VI 坦白 tǎnbái ▸ **to
confess to sth/to doing sth** 承认(認)某
事/做了某事 chéngrèn mǒushì/zuòle
mǒushì

confession [kən'fɛʃən] N [c/U] (admission)
坦白 tǎnbái [种 zhǒng] ▸ **to make a
confession** 坦白 tǎnbái

confidence ['kɔnfɪdns] N 1 [U] (faith) 信
赖(賴) xìnlài 2 [U] (self-assurance) 自信
zìxìn ▸ **in confidence** 秘(祕)密地 mìmì
de

confident ['kɔnfɪdənt] ADJ (self-assured)
自信的 zìxìn de ▸ **to be confident that...**
有信心… yǒu xìnxīn...

confidential [kɔnfɪˈdɛnʃəl] ADJ 机(機)密的 jīmì de

confirm [kənˈfəːm] VT 肯定 kěndìng; [+ appointment, date] 确(確)认(認) quèrèn

confiscate [ˈkɔnfɪskeɪt] VT 没(沒)收 mòshōu ▸ to confiscate sth from sb 没(沒)收某人的某物 mòshōu mǒurén de mǒuwù

confuse [kənˈfjuːz] VT 1 (perplex) 把…弄糊涂(塗) bǎ...nòng hútu 2 (mix up) 混淆 hùnxiáo

confused [kənˈfjuːzd] ADJ 困惑的 kùnhuò de

confusing [kənˈfjuːzɪŋ] ADJ 含混不清的 hánhùn bù qīng de

confusion [kənˈfjuːʒən] N 1 [c/u] (uncertainty) 惶惑 huánghuò [种 zhǒng] 2 [u] (mix-up) 混淆 hùnxiáo

congratulate [kənˈgrætjuleɪt] VT 祝贺(賀) zhùhè ▸ to congratulate sb on sth/on doing sth 祝贺(賀)某人某事/做某事 zhùhè mǒurén mǒushì/zuò mǒushì

congratulations [kəngrætjuˈleɪʃənz] NPL 祝贺(賀) zhùhè ▸ congratulations on your engagement! 祝贺(賀)你订(訂)婚了！zhùhè nǐ dìnghūn le!

Congress [ˈkɔŋgrɛs] N (US) ▸ Congress 国(國)会(會) guóhuì

congressman [ˈkɔŋgrɛsmən] (pl congressmen) (US) N [c] 国(國)会(會)议(議)员(員) guóhuì yìyuán [位 wèi]

congresswoman [ˈkɔŋgrɛswumən] (pl congresswomen) (US) N [c] 女国(國)会(會)议(議)员(員) nǚ guóhuì yìyuán [位 wèi]

connection [kəˈnɛkʃən] N 1 [c/u] (link) 联(聯)系(繫) liánxì [种 zhǒng] 2 [c] (Elec) 接头(頭) jiētóu [个 gè] 3 [c] (train, plane) 联(聯)运(運) liányùn [种 zhǒng] ▸ what is the connection between them? 他们(們)之间(間)有什么(麼)关(關)系(係)？tāmen zhījiān yǒu shénme guānxì?

conscience [ˈkɔnʃəns] N [c] 是非感 shìfēi gǎn [种 zhǒng] ▸ to have a guilty/clear conscience 感到内(內)疚/问(問)心无(無)愧 gǎndào nèijiù/wèn xīn wú kuì

conscientious [kɔnʃɪˈɛnʃəs] ADJ 认(認)真的 rènzhēn de

conscious [ˈkɔnʃəs] ADJ 1 (awake) 清醒的 qīngxǐng de 2 [+ decision, effort] 蓄意的 xùyì de ▸ to be conscious of sth 意识(識)到某事 yìshí dào mǒushì

consciousness [ˈkɔnʃəsnɪs] N [u] (Med) 知觉(覺) zhījué ▸ to lose consciousness 失去知觉(覺) shīqù zhījué

consequence [ˈkɔnsɪkwəns] N [c] 后(後)果 hòuguǒ [种 zhǒng]

consequently [ˈkɔnsɪkwəntlɪ] ADV 所以 suǒyǐ

conservation [kɔnsəˈveɪʃən] N [u] [of environment] 环(環)保 huánbǎo; [of energy] 节(節)约(約) jiéyuē

conservative [kənˈsəːvətɪv] I ADJ 1 (traditional) 保守的 bǎoshǒu de 2 (Brit: Pol) ▸ Conservative 保守党(黨) bǎoshǒudǎng II N [c] (Brit: Pol) ▸ Conservative 保守党(黨)人士 bǎoshǒudǎng rénshì [名 míng]

conservatory [kənˈsəːvətrɪ] N [c] 暖房 nuǎnfáng [间 jiān]

consider [kənˈsɪdəʳ] VT 1 (think about) 考虑(慮) kǎolù 2 (take into account) 考虑(慮)到 kǎolù dào

considerate [kənˈsɪdərɪt] ADJ 体(體)贴(貼)的 tǐtiē de

considering [kənˈsɪdərɪŋ] I PREP 考虑(慮)到 kǎolù dào II CONJ ▸ considering (that)... 考虑(慮)到… kǎolù dào...

consist [kənˈsɪst] VI ▸ to consist of 由…组(組)成 yóu...zǔchéng

consonant [ˈkɔnsənənt] N [c] 辅(輔)音 fǔyīn [个 gè]

constant [ˈkɔnstənt] ADJ 1 [+ threat, pressure, pain, reminder] 不断(斷)的 búduàn de 2 [+ interruptions, demands] 重复(復)的 chóngfù de 3 [+ temperature, speed] 恒(恆)定的 héngdìng de

constantly [ˈkɔnstəntlɪ] ADV 1 (repeatedly) 不断(斷)地 búduàn de 2 (uninterruptedly) 持续(續)地 chíxù de

constipated [ˈkɔnstɪpeɪtɪd] ADJ 便秘(祕)的 biànmì de

construct [kənˈstrʌkt] VT 建造 jiànzào

construction [kənˈstrʌkʃən] N 1 [u] [of building, road, machine] 建造 jiànzào 2 [c] (structure) 建筑(築) jiànzhù [座 zuò]

consult [kənˈsʌlt] VT [+ doctor, lawyer, friend] 咨询(詢) zīxún; [+ book, map] 查阅(閱) cháyuè

consumer [kən'sju:məʳ] N [c] [of goods, services] 消费(費)者 xiāofèizhě [个 gè]; [of resources] 使用者 shǐyòngzhě [个 gè]

contact ['kɒntækt] I N **1** [c/u] (communication) 联(聯)络(絡) liánluò [种 zhǒng] **2** [c] (person) 熟人 shúrén [个 gè] II VT 联(聯)系(繫) liánxì ▸ **to be in contact with sb** 与(與)某人有联(聯)络(絡) yǔ mǒurén yǒu liánluò

contactless ['kɒntæktlɪs] ADJ [+ payment] 非接触(觸)式支付 fēi jiēchù shì zhīfù

contact lenses NPL 隐(隱)形眼镜(鏡) yǐnxíng yǎnjìng

contain [kən'teɪn] VT [+ objects] 装(裝)有 zhuāngyǒu; [+ component, ingredient] 含有 hányǒu

container [kən'teɪnəʳ] N [c] **1** (box, jar etc) 容器 róngqì [个 gè] **2** (for transport) 集装(裝)箱 jízhuāngxiāng [个 gè]

content¹ ['kɒntɛnt] I N [u] 内(內)容 nèiróng II **contents** NPL [of bottle, packet] 所含之物 suǒhán zhī wù

content² [kən'tɛnt] ADJ 满(滿)足的 mǎnzú de

contest ['kɒntɛst] N [c] 比赛(賽) bǐsài [项 xiàng]

contestant [kən'tɛstənt] N [c] 参(參)赛(賽)者 cānsàizhě [位 wèi]

context ['kɒntɛkst] N [c/u] [of word, phrase] 上下文 shàngxiàwén [个 gè]

continent ['kɒntɪnənt] N [c] 大陆(陸) dàlù [个 gè] ▸ **on the Continent** (Brit) 在欧(歐)洲大陆(陸) zài Ōuzhōu dàlù

continental breakfast N [c] 欧(歐)洲大陆(陸)式早餐 Ōuzhōu dàlù shì zǎocān [顿 dùn]

continue [kən'tɪnju:] VI **1** 继(繼)续(續) jìxù **2** [speaker +] 继(繼)续(續)说(說) jìxù shuō ▸ **to continue to do sth** or **doing sth** 持续(續)做某事 chíxù zuò mǒushì ▸ **to continue with sth** 继(繼)续(續)某事 jìxù mǒushì

continuous [kən'tɪnjuəs] ADJ 连(連)续(續)不停的 liánxù bù tíng de

contraception [kɒntrə'sɛpʃən] N [u] 避孕 bìyùn

contraceptive [kɒntrə'sɛptɪv] N [c] (drug) 避孕药(藥) bìyùnyào [片 piàn]; (device) 避孕工具 bìyùn gōngjù [种 zhǒng]

contract ['kɒntrækt] N [c] 合同 hétong [份 fèn]

contradict [kɒntrə'dɪkt] VT 驳(駁)斥 bóchì

contradiction [kɒntrə'dɪkʃən] N [c/u] 矛盾 máodùn [种 zhǒng]

contrary ['kɒntrərɪ] N [c/u] ▸ **the contrary** 相反 xiāngfǎn ▸ **on the contrary** 正相反 zhèng xiāngfǎn

contrast [n 'kɒntrɑ:st, vb kən'trɑ:st] I N [c/u] **1** 明显(顯)的差异(異) míngxiǎn de chāyì [种 zhǒng] **2** ▸ **to be a contrast to sth** 与(與)某物截然不同 yǔ mǒuwù jiérán bùtóng II VI ▸ **to contrast with sth** 与(與)某物形成对(對)照 yǔ mǒuwù xíngchéng duìzhào ▸ **to contrast sth with sth** 将(將)某物与(與)某物进(進)行对(對)比 jiāng mǒuwù yǔ mǒuwù jìnxíng duìbǐ

contribute [kən'trɪbju:t] I VI ▸ **to contribute (to sth)** (with money) (给(給)某事)捐助 (gěi mǒushì) juānzhù II VT ▸ **to contribute 10 pounds (to sth)** (给(給)某事)捐献(獻)10英镑(鎊) (gěi mǒushì) juānxiàn shí yīngbàng

contribution [kɒntrɪ'bju:ʃən] N [c] 捐献(獻) juānxiàn [次 cì]

control [kən'trəul] I VT [+ country, organization] 统(統)治 tǒngzhì; [+ person, emotion, disease, fire] 控制 kòngzhì II N [u] [of country, organization] 控制权(權) kòngzhì quán III **controls** NPL [of vehicle, machine, TV] 操纵(縱)装(裝)置 cāozòng zhuāngzhì ▸ **to control o.s.** 克制自己 kèzhì zìjǐ ▸ **to be in control of sth** (of situation, car) 控制着(著)(某事) kòngzhì zhe (mǒushì) ▸ **to be under control** [fire, situation +] 处(處)于(於)控制之下 chǔ yú kòngzhì zhī xià ▸ **circumstances beyond our control** 不在我们(們)控制之中的情况(況) bù zài wǒmen kòngzhì zhī zhōng de qíngkuàng

controversial [kɒntrə'və:ʃl] ADJ 有争(爭)议(議)的 yǒu zhēngyì de; [+ book, film] 引起争(爭)论(論)的 yǐnqǐ zhēnglùn de

convenient [kən'vi:nɪənt] ADJ [+ method, system, time] 方便的 fāngbiàn de; [+ place] 近便的 jìnbiàn de

conventional [kən'vɛnʃənl] ADJ 符合

习(習)俗的 fúhé xísú de; [+ *method, product*] 传(傳)统(統)的 chuántǒng de

conversation [kɒnvəˈseɪʃən] N [c/u] 交谈(談) jiāotán [次 cì] ▸ **to have a conversation** (about sth/with sb) (和某人) 谈(談) (某事) (hé mǒurén) tán (mǒushì)

convert [kənˈvəːt] VT **1** (*transform*) [+ *substance*] 使转(轉)化 shǐ zhuǎnhuà; [+ *building*] 改建 gǎijiàn ▸ **to convert sth into sth** [+ *substance*] 将(將)某物转(轉)化成某物 jiāng mǒuwù zhuǎnhuà chéng mǒuwù; [+ *building*] 将(將)某建筑(築)改建成某建筑(築) jiāng mǒu jiànzhù gǎijiàn chéng mǒu jiànzhù

convince [kənˈvɪns] VT **1** (*cause to believe*) 使信服 shǐ xìnfú **2** 说(說)服 shuōfú ▸ **to convince sb to do sth** 说(說)服某人去做某事 shuōfú mǒurén qù zuò mǒushì

cook [kuk] I VT [+ *food, meat, vegetables*] 烹调(調) pēngtiáo; [+ *meal*] 做饭(飯) zuòfàn II VI **1** [*person* +] 做饭(飯) zuòfàn **2** [*food* +] 烧(燒) shāo III N [c] 厨(廚)师(師) chúshī [位 wèi] ▸ **a good cook** 会(會)做饭(飯)的人 huì zuòfàn de rén

cooker [ˈkukəʳ] (*Brit*) N [c] 厨(廚)灶 chúzào [个 gè]

cookie [ˈkukɪ] N [c] **1** (*US: for eating*) 小甜饼(餅) xiǎotiánbǐng [块 kuài] **2** (*Comput*) 记(記)忆(憶)块(塊) jìyì kuài [个 gè]

cooking [ˈkukɪŋ] N [u] 烹调(調) pēngtiáo

cool [kuːl] I ADJ **1** 凉(涼)的 liáng de **2** (*calm, unemotional*) 冷静(靜)的 lěngjìng de **3** (*inf: good*) 顶(頂)呱呱的 dǐngguāguā de; (*fashionable*) 酷的 kù de II VT 使变(變)凉(涼) shǐ biànliáng III VI 冷下来(來) lěngxiàlái IV N ▸ **to keep/lose one's cool** (*inf*) 保持冷静(靜)/失去自制而激动(動)起来(來) bǎochí lěngjìng/shīqù zìzhì ér jīdòng qǐlái ▸ **to keep sth cool** 保持某物的凉(涼)度 bǎochí mǒuwù de liángdù
▸ **cool down** VI 变(變)凉(涼) biànliáng

co-operate [kəuˈɒpəreɪt] VI **1** (*collaborate*) 合作 hézuò **2** (*be helpful*) 配合 pèihé

cope [kəup] VI 对(對)付 duìfù

copper [ˈkɒpəʳ] N [u] 铜(銅) tóng

copy [ˈkɒpɪ] I N **1** [c] 复(複)制(製)品 fùzhìpǐn [件 jiàn] **2** [c] (*of book, record, newspaper*) 本/张(張)/份 běn/zhāng/fèn II VT 模仿 mófǎng ▸ **to make a copy of sth** 复(複)印某物 fùyìn mǒuwù

cork [kɔːk] N [c] 瓶塞 péngsāi [个 gè]

corkscrew [ˈkɔːkskruː] N [c] 瓶塞钻(鑽) píngsāizuàn [个 gè]

corn [kɔːn] N **1** (*Brit: cereal crop*) 谷(穀)物 gǔwù **2** [u] (*US: maize*) 玉米 yùmǐ ▸ **corn on the cob** 玉米(棒子) yùmǐ (bàngzi)

corner [ˈkɔːnəʳ] N [c] **1** 角落 jiǎoluò [个 gè] **2** [*of road*] 街角 jiējiǎo [个 gè]

corpse [kɔːps] N [c] 死尸(屍) sǐshī [具 jù]

correct [kəˈrɛkt] I ADJ **1** 正确(確)的 zhèngquè de; [+ *decision, means, procedure*] 适(適)当(當)的 shìdàng de II VT [+ *mistake, fault, person*] 纠(糾)正 jiūzhèng

correction [kəˈrɛkʃən] N [c] 修改 xiūgǎi [次 cì]

corridor [ˈkɔrɪdɔːʳ] N [c] (*in house, building*) 走廊 zǒuláng [条 tiáo]; (*on train*) 车(車)厢(廂)过(過)道 chēxiāng guòdào [个 gè]

corruption [kəˈrʌpʃən] N [u] 贪(貪)赃(贓)舞弊 tānzāng wǔbì

cosmetics [kɒzˈmɛtɪks] N PL (*beauty products*) 化妆(妝)品 huàzhuāngpǐn

cost [kɒst] I N [c] 价(價)格 jiàgé [种 zhǒng] II VT 价(價)格为(為) jiàgé wéi ▸ **how much does it cost?** 这(這)多少钱(錢)? zhè duōshao qián? ▸ **it costs 5 pounds/too much** 价(價)格为(為)5英镑(鎊)/太高 jiàgé wéi wǔ yīngbàng/tàigāo ▸ **the cost of living** 生活费(費)用 shēnghuó fèiyòng

costume [ˈkɒstjuːm] N [c/u] 戏(戲)装(裝) xìzhuāng [套 tào]

cot [kɒt] N [c] **1** (*Brit: child's*) 幼儿(兒)床 yòu'ér chuáng [张 zhāng] **2** (*US: bed*) 帆布床 fānbù chuáng [张 zhāng]

cottage [ˈkɒtɪdʒ] N [c] 村舍 cūnshè [个 gè]

cotton [ˈkɒtn] I N [u] **1** (*fabric*) 棉布 miánbù **2** (*thread*) 棉线(線) miánxiàn II CPD [+ *dress, sheets*] 棉布 miánbù

cotton wool (*Brit*) N [u] 脱(脫)脂棉 tuōzhī mián

couch [kautʃ] N [c] 长(長)沙发(發) cháng shāfā [个 gè]

cough [kɒf] I VI 咳嗽 késou II N [c] 咳嗽 késou [阵 zhèn] ▸ **to have a cough** 咳嗽 késou

KEYWORD

could [kʊd] AUX VB **1** (referring to past) ▸ **we couldn't go to the party** 我们(們) 没(沒)能去参(參)加聚会(會) wǒmen méi néng qù cānjiā jùhuì ▸ **he couldn't read or write** 他不会(會)读(讀)也不会(會)写(寫) tā bù huì dú yě bù huì xiě **2** (possibility) ▸ **he could be in the library** 他可能在图(圖)书(書)馆(館)里 tā kěnéng zài túshūguǎn ▸ **you could have been killed!** 可能你连(連)命都没(沒)了! kěnéng nǐ lián mìng dōu méile! **3** (in conditionals with "if") ▸ **if we had more time, I could finish this** 如果有更多时(時)间(間),我能够(夠)完成的 rúguǒ yǒu gèng duō shíjiān, wǒ nénggòu wánchéng de ▸ **we'd have a holiday, if we could afford it** 如果能支付得起的话(話),我们(們)就去度假了 rúguǒ néng zhīfù de qǐ de huà, wǒmen jiù qù dùjià le **4** (in offers, suggestions, requests) 可以 kěyǐ ▸ **I could call a doctor** 我可以叫个(個)医(醫)生 wǒ kěyǐ jiào gè yīshēng ▸ **could I borrow the car?** 我可以借一下车(車)吗(嗎)? wǒ kěyǐ jiè yīxià chē ma? ▸ **he asked if he could make a phone call** 他问(問)是否可以打个(個)电(電)话(話) tā wèn shìfǒu kěyǐ dǎ gè diànhuà

council ['kaʊnsl] N [c] 议(議)会(會) yìhuì [个 gè]

count [kaʊnt] I VT **1** (also: count up) 数(數) shǔ **2** (include) 把…算在内(內) bǎ…jìsuàn zài nèi II VI **1** (数(數)) shǔ **2** (matter) 有价(價)值 yǒu jiàzhí ▸ **to count (up) to 10** 数(數)到10 shǔdào shí

▸ **count on** VT FUS [+ support, help] 指望 zhǐwàng; [+ person] 依靠 yīkào

counter ['kaʊntər] N [c] 柜(櫃)台(臺) guìtái [个 gè]

country ['kʌntrɪ] N **1** [c] (nation) 国(國)家 guójiā [个 gè] **2** (countryside) ▸ **the country** 乡(鄉) xiāng **3** (native land) 家乡(鄉) jiāxiāng [个 gè]

countryside ['kʌntrɪsaɪd] N [u] 农(農)村 nóngcūn

couple ['kʌpl] N [c] **1** (married) 夫妻 fūqī [对 duì]; (living together) 情侣(侶) qínglǚ [对 duì] **2** ▸ **a couple of** (two) 两(兩)个(個) liǎng gè

courage ['kʌrɪdʒ] N [u] 勇气(氣) yǒngqì

courier ['kʊrɪər] N [c] **1** (messenger) 信使 xìnshǐ [个 gè] **2** (rep) 旅游(遊)团(團)的服务(務)员(員) lǚyóutuán de fúwùyuán [个 gè]

course [kɔːs] N **1** [c] 课(課)程 kèchéng [个 gè] **2** (of meal) ▸ **first/next/last course** 第一/下一/最后(後)一道菜 dìyī/xià yī/zuìhòu yī dào cài [道 dào] **3** [c] (for golf, horse-racing) 场(場) chǎng ▸ **of course** (naturally) 自然 zìrán; (certainly) 当(當)然 dāngrán ▸ **of course!** 没(沒)问(問)题(題)! méi wèntí! ▸ **of course not!** 当(當)然不行! dāngrán bù xíng!

court [kɔːt] N [c] **1** (Law) 法庭 fǎtíng [个 gè] **2** (for tennis, badminton) 球场(場) qiúchǎng [个 gè]

courthouse ['kɔːthaʊs] (US) N [c] 法院 fǎyuàn [个 gè]

courtyard ['kɔːtjɑːd] N [c] 庭院 tíngyuàn [个 gè]

cousin ['kʌzn] N [c] (older male on father's side) 堂兄 tángxiōng [个 gè]; (younger male on father's side) 堂弟 tángdì [个 gè]; (older female on father's side) 堂姐 tángjiě [个 gè]; (younger female on father's side) 堂妹 tángmèi [个 gè]; (older male on mother's side) 表兄 biǎoxiōng [个 gè]; (younger male on mother's side) 表弟 biǎodi [个 gè]; (older female on mother's side) 表姐 biǎojiě [个 gè]; (younger female on mother's side) 表妹 biǎomèi [个 gè]

cover ['kʌvər] I VT **1** ▸ **to cover sth (with sth)** (用某物) 盖(蓋)着(著)某物 (yòng mǒuwù) gàizhe mǒuwù **2** (in insurance) ▸ **to cover sb (against sth)** 给(給)某人保(某事)的险(險) gěi mǒurén bǎo (mǒushì de) xiǎn II N **1** [c] 套子 tàozi [个 gè] **2** [c] (of book, magazine) 封面 fēngmiàn [个 gè] **3** [u] (insurance) 保险(險) bǎoxiǎn III **covers** NPL (on bed) 铺(鋪)盖(蓋) pūgai ▸ **to be covered in or with sth** 被某物覆盖(蓋) bèi mǒuwù fùgài

▸ **cover up** VT [+ facts, feelings, mistakes] (用某事)掩饰(飾)某事 (yòng mǒushì) yǎnshì mǒushì

cow [kau] N [c] 奶牛 nǎiniú [头 tóu]

coward ['kauəd] N [c] 胆(膽)小鬼 dǎnxiǎoguǐ [个 gè]

cowboy ['kaubɔɪ] N [c] 牛仔 niúzǎi [个 gè]

crab [kræb] N 1 [c] (creature) 螃蟹 pángxiè [只 zhī] 2 [u] (meat) 蟹肉 xièròu

crack [kræk] N [c] 裂缝(縫) lièfèng [条 tiáo]
▶ **crack down on** VT FUS 对(對)…严(嚴)惩(懲)不贷(貸) duì…yánchéng bùdài

cracked [krækt] ADJ 破裂的 pòliè de

cracker ['krækər] N [c] (biscuit) 薄脆饼(餅)干(乾) báocuì bǐnggān [块 kuài]

cradle ['kreɪdl] N [c] 摇(搖)篮(籃) yáolán [个 gè]

craft [krɑːft] N [c] (weaving, pottery etc) 工艺(藝) gōngyì [道 dào]

cramp [kræmp] N [c/u] 抽筋 chōujīn [阵 zhèn]

crane [kreɪn] N [c] 起重机(機) qǐzhòngjī [部 bù]

crash [kræʃ] I N [c] 1 (of car) 撞击(擊) zhuàngjī [下 xià]; (of plane) 坠(墜)机(機) zhuìjī [次 cì] 2 (noise) 哗(嘩)啦声(聲) huālā shēng [声 shēng] II VT (+ car, plane) 使撞毁(毀) shǐ zhuànghuǐ III VI 1 (car, driver +) 撞击(擊) zhuàngjī; (plane +) 坠(墜)毁(毀) zhuìhuǐ 2 (Comput) 死机(機) sǐjī ▶ **a car/plane crash** 撞车(車)/飞(飛)机(機)失事 zhuàngchē/fēijī shīshì ▶ **to crash into sth** 猛地撞上某物 měngde zhuàngshàng mǒuwù

crawl [krɔːl] VI 爬 pá

crazy ['kreɪzɪ] (inf) ADJ 发(發)疯(瘋)的 fāfēng de ▶ **to go crazy** 发(發)疯(瘋) fāfēng

cream [kriːm] I N 1 [u] (dairy cream) 奶油 nǎiyóu 2 [c/u] (for skin) 乳霜 rǔshuāng [瓶 píng] II ADJ (in colour) 乳白色的 rǔbáisè de

crease [kriːs] N [c] (in cloth, paper: fold) 折痕 zhéhén [道 dào]; (wrinkle) 皱(皺)纹(紋) zhòuwén [条 tiáo]

create [kriːˈeɪt] VT 创(創)造 chuàngzào

creative [kriːˈeɪtɪv] ADJ 有创(創)造力的 yǒu chuàngzàolì de

creature ['kriːtʃər] N [c] 动(動)物 dòngwù [种 zhǒng]

crèche [krɛʃ] (Brit) N [c] 托儿(兒)所 tuō'érsuǒ [个 gè]

credit ['krɛdɪt] N 1 [u] (financial) 贷(貸)款 dàikuǎn 2 [u] (recognition) 赞(讚)扬(揚) zànyáng 3 [c] (Scol, Univ) 学(學)分 xuéfēn [个 gè] ▶ **on credit** 赊(賒)账(賬) shēzhàng

credit card N [c] 信用卡 xìnyòngkǎ [张 zhāng]

crew [kruː] N 1 [c] 全体(體)工作人员(員) quántǐ gōngzuò rényuán 2 [c] (TV) 组(組) zǔ [个 gè]

crib [krɪb] N [c] (US) 有围(圍)栏(欄)的童床 yǒu wéilán de tóngchuáng [张 zhāng]

cricket ['krɪkɪt] N [u] (sport) 板球 bǎnqiú

> **CRICKET**
>
> 在大英帝国时代，cricket（板球）作为一种夏季运动引入印度、巴基斯坦和澳大利亚等国。如今，板球在这些国家依然十分盛行。比赛两队各11名队员，通常为男性。队员通常穿着传统的白色运动服。板球的规则以复杂著称。两队轮流击球。击球的队尽力争取最多次数的 **run**（跑垒），其击球手在两组称为 **stump**（三门柱）的柱子间跑。另一队争取在击球手跑到门柱前用球击中门柱，还可以在球触地前接住球将该击球手淘汰出局。

crime [kraɪm] N 1 [c] (illegal act) 罪行 zuìxíng [种 zhǒng] 2 [u] (illegal activities) 犯罪活动(動) fànzuì huódòng

criminal ['krɪmɪnl] N [c] 罪犯 zuìfàn [个 gè]

crisis ['kraɪsɪs] (pl crises ['kraɪsiːz]) N [c/u] 危机(機) wēijī [种 zhǒng]

crisp [krɪsp] N [c] (Brit: potato crisp) 薯片 shǔpiàn [片 piàn]

critical ['krɪtɪkl] ADJ 1 (crucial) 关(關)键(鍵)的 guānjiàn de 2 (serious) 危急的 wēijí de

criticism ['krɪtɪsɪzəm] N 1 [u] (censure) 批评(評) pīpíng 2 [c] (complaint) 指责(責) zhǐzé [种 zhǒng]

criticize ['krɪtɪsaɪz] VT 批评(評) pīpíng

Croatia [krəuˈeɪʃə] N 克罗(羅)地亚(亞) Kèluódìyà

crocodile ['krɔkədaɪl] N [c] 鳄(鱷)鱼(魚) èyú [只 zhī]

crooked ['krukɪd] ADJ (off-centre) 歪的 wāi de

crop [krɒp] N 1 [c] (plants) 庄(莊)稼 zhuāngjia [种 zhǒng] 2 [c] (amount produced) 收成 shōuchéng [个 gè]

cross [krɒs] I N [c] 1 (x shape) 交叉符号(號) jiāochā fúhào [个 gè]; (showing disagreement) 叉号(號) chāhào [个 gè] 2 (crucifix shape) 十字 shízì [个 gè] 3 (Rel) 十字架 shízìjià [个 gè] II VT [+ street, room] 横(橫)穿 héngchuān III VI (roads, lines +) 相交 xiāngjiāo IV ADJ (angry) 生气(氣)的 shēngqì de
▶ **cross out** VT (delete) 取消 qǔxiāo
▶ **cross over** VI (cross the street) 过(過)马(馬)路 guò mǎlù

crossing ['krɒsɪŋ] N [c] 1 (voyage) 横(橫)渡 héngdù [次 cì] 2 (Brit) (also: pedestrian crossing) 人行横(橫)道 rénxíng héngdào [个 gè]

crossroads ['krɒsrəudz] (pl crossroads) N [c] 十字路口 shízì lùkǒu [个 gè]

crosswalk ['krɒswɔːk] (US) N [c] 人行横(橫)道 rénxíng héngdào [个 gè]

crossword ['krɒswəːd] N [c] (also: crossword puzzle) 填字游(遊)戏(戲) tiánzì yóuxì [个 gè]

crowd [kraud] N [c] 人群 rénqún [个 gè]
▶ **crowds of people** 大批人群 dàpī rénqún

crowded ['kraudɪd] ADJ 拥(擁)挤(擠)的 yōngjǐ de

crowdfunding ['kraudfʌndɪŋ] N [U] 众(眾)筹(籌) zhòng chóu

crown [kraun] N [c] 皇冠 huángguān [个 gè]

cruel ['kruəl] ADJ 残(殘)忍的 cánrěn de; [+ treatment, behaviour] 恶(惡)毒的 èdú de ▶ **to be cruel to sb** 残(殘)酷地对(對)待某人 cánkù de duìdài mǒurén

cruelty ['kruəltɪ] N [U] 残(殘)忍 cánrěn

cruise [kruːz] N [c] 游(遊)船 yóuchuán [艘 sōu] ▶ **to be/go on a cruise** 乘游(遊)船旅行 chéng yóuchuán lǚxíng

crush [krʌʃ] VT 1 [+ garlic] 压(壓)碎 yāsuì 2 [+ person] 使挤(擠)在一起 shǐ jǐ zài yīqǐ

cry [kraɪ] VI (weep) 哭 kū ▶ **what are you crying about?** 你哭什么(麼)? nǐ kū shénme?

cub [kʌb] N [c] 1 幼兽(獸) yòushòu [只 zhī] 2 (also: cub scout) 幼童军(軍) yòutóngjūn [名 míng]

cube [kjuːb] N [c] 立方体(體) lìfāngtǐ [个 gè]

cucumber ['kjuːkʌmbər] N [c/U] 黄瓜 huángguā [根 gēn]

cuddle ['kʌdl] I VT, VI 搂(摟)抱 lǒubào II N [c] 拥(擁)抱 yōngbào [个 gè]

cultural ['kʌltʃərəl] ADJ 文化的 wénhuà de

culture ['kʌltʃər] N [c/U] 文化 wénhuà [种 zhǒng]

cunning ['kʌnɪŋ] ADJ 狡猾的 jiǎohuá de

cup [kʌp] N [c] 1 (for drinking) 杯子 bēizi [个 gè] 2 (trophy) 奖(獎)杯(盃) jiǎngbēi [个 gè] ▶ **a cup of tea** 一杯茶 yī bēi chá

cupboard ['kʌbəd] N [c] 柜(櫃)子 guìzi [个 gè]

curb [kəːb] N [c] (US) = **kerb**

cure [kjuər] I VT (Med) 治好 zhìhǎo; [+ patient] 治愈(癒) zhìyù II N [c] (Med) 疗(療)法 liáofǎ [种 zhǒng]

curious ['kjuərɪəs] ADJ 好奇的 hàoqí de
▶ **to be curious about sb/sth** 对(對)某人/某物感到好奇 duì mǒurén/mǒuwù gǎndào hàoqí

curl [kəːl] N [c] 卷(捲)发(髮) juǎnfà [头 tóu] 蜷作一团(團) quán zuò yī tuán

curly ['kəːlɪ] ADJ 卷(捲)曲的 juǎnqū de

currant ['kʌrnt] N [c] 无(無)子葡萄干(乾) wúzǐ pútáogān [粒 lì]

currency ['kʌrnsɪ] N [c/U] 货(貨)币(幣) huòbì [种 zhǒng]

current ['kʌrnt] I N [c] 1 [of air, water] 流 liú [股 gǔ] 2 (Elec) 电(電)流 diànliú [股 gǔ] II ADJ [+ situation, tendency, policy] 目前的 mùqián de

current affairs NPL 时(時)事 shíshì ▶ **a current affairs programme** 时(時)事讨(討)论(論)节(節)目 shíshì tǎolùn jiémù

curriculum [kə'rɪkjuləm] (pl curriculums or curricula [kə'rɪkjulə]) N [c] 1 全部课(課)程 quánbù kèchéng 2 (for particular subject) 课(課)程 kèchéng [门 mén]

curriculum vitae [-'viːtaɪ] (esp Brit) N [c] 简(簡)历(歷) jiǎnlì [份 fèn]

curry ['kʌrɪ] N [c/U] (dish) 咖哩 gālí [种 zhǒng]

cursor ['kəːsər] (Comput) N [c] 光标(標) guāngbiāo [个 gè]

curtain ['kəːtn] N [c] (esp Brit) 窗帘(簾)

chuānglián [幅 fú] ▶ **to draw the curtains** (together) 拉上窗帘(簾) lāshàng chuānglián; (apart) 拉开(開)窗帘(簾) lākāi chuānglián

cushion ['kʊʃən] N [c] 靠垫(墊) kàodiàn [个 gè]

custom ['kʌstəm] I N 1 [c/u] (tradition) 传(傳)统(統) chuántǒng [个 gè] 2 [c/u] (convention) 惯(慣)例 guànlì [个 gè] II **customs** NPL 海关(關) hǎiguān ▶ **to go through customs** 过(過)海关(關) guò hǎiguān

customer ['kʌstəmə^r] N [c] 顾(顧)客 gùkè [位 wèi]

customs officer N [c] 海关(關)官员(員) hǎiguān guānyuán [位 wèi]

cut [kʌt] (pt, pp **cut**) I VT 1 切 qiē 2 (injure) ▶ **to cut one's hand/knee** 割破手/膝盖(蓋) gēpò shǒu/xīgài 3 [+ grass, hair, nails] 修剪 xiūjiǎn 4 [+ scene, episode, paragraph] 删(刪)剪 shānjiǎn 5 [+ prices, spending] 削减(減) xuējiǎn II N 1 [c] (injury) 伤(傷)口 shāngkǒu [个 gè] 2 [c] (reduction) 削减(減) xuējiǎn [次 cì] ▶ **to cut sth in half** 将(將)某物切成两(兩)半 jiāng mǒuwù qiēchéng liǎng bàn ▶ **to cut o.s.** 割破自己 gēpò zìjǐ ▶ **to get or have one's hair cut** 剪发(髮) jiǎnfà ▶ **a cut and blow-dry** 剪发(髮)吹干(乾) jiǎnfà chuīgān

▶ **cut down** VT 1 [+ tree] 砍倒 kǎndǎo 2 (reduce) 减(減)少 jiǎnshǎo
▶ **cut down on** VT FUS [+ alcohol, coffee, cigarettes] 减(減)少 jiǎnshǎo
▶ **cut off** 1 VT [+ part of sth] 切掉 qiēdiào 2 [+ supply] 停止供应(應) tíngzhǐ gōngyìng
▶ **cut up** VT 切碎 qiēsuì

cute [kjuːt] ADJ 1 (inf) [+ child, dog, house] 可爱(愛)的 kě'ài de 2 (esp US: inf: attractive) 迷人的 mírén de

cutlery ['kʌtləri] (Brit) N [u] 餐具 cānjù

CV N ABBR (= **curriculum vitae**) 简(簡)历(歷) jiǎnlì

cyberbullying ['saɪbəbuliɪŋ] N [u] 网(網)络(絡)霸凌(淩) wǎngluò bàlíng

cybercafé ['saɪbəkæfeɪ] N [c] 网(網)吧 wǎngbā [家 jiā]

cycle ['saɪkl] I N [c] 自行车(車) zìxíngchē [辆 liàng] II VI 骑(騎)自行车(車) qí zìxíngchē III CPD [+ shop, helmet, ride] 自行车(車) zìxíngchē ▶ **to go cycling** 骑(騎)自行车(車) qí zìxíngchē

cycle lane N [c] 自行车(車)道 zìxíngchēdào [条 tiáo]

cycling ['saɪklɪŋ] N [u] 骑(騎)自行车(車) qí zìxíngchē

cyclist ['saɪklɪst] N [c] 骑(騎)自行车(車)的人 qí zìxíngchē de rén [个 gè]

cylinder ['sɪlɪndə^r] N [c] [of gas] 罐 guàn [个 gè]

cynical ['sɪnɪkl] ADJ 愤(憤)世嫉俗的 fèn shì jí sú de

Cyprus ['saɪprəs] N 塞浦路斯 Sàipǔlùsī

Czech Republic N ▶ **the Czech Republic** 捷克共和国(國) Jiékè Gònghéguó

d

dad [dæd] (*inf*) N [c] 爸爸 bàba [个 gè]

daffodil ['dæfədɪl] N [c] 黄水仙 huángshuǐxiān [支 zhī]

daily ['deɪlɪ] I ADJ 每日的 měi rì de II ADV 每日 měi rì

daisy ['deɪzɪ] N [c] 雏(雛)菊 chújú [朵 duǒ]

dam [dæm] N [c] 水坝(壩) shuǐbà [个 gè]

damage ['dæmɪdʒ] I N [u] **1** 损(損) 坏(壞) sǔnhuài **2** (*dents, scratches*) 损(損)伤(傷) sǔnshāng II VT 毁(毁) 坏(壞) huǐhuài

damp [dæmp] ADJ 潮湿(濕)的 cháoshī de

dance [dɑːns] I N **1** [c] (*waltz, tango*) 舞蹈 wǔdǎo [曲 qǔ] **2** [c] (*social event*) 舞 会(會) wǔhuì [个 gè] II VI 跳舞 tiàowǔ

dancer ['dɑːnsər] N [c] 舞蹈演员(員) wǔdǎo yǎnyuán [位 wèi]

dancing ['dɑːnsɪŋ] N [u] 跳舞 tiàowǔ

dandruff ['dændrəf] N [u] 头(頭)皮屑 tóupíxiè

danger ['deɪndʒər] N **1** [u] (*unsafe situation*) 危险(險) wēixiǎn **2** [c] (*hazard, risk*) 威胁(脅) wēixié [个 gè] ▶ there is a danger of/that... 有…的危险(險) yǒu...de wēixiǎn ▶ to be in danger of doing sth 有…的危险(險) yǒu...de wēixiǎn

dangerous ['deɪndʒrəs] ADJ 危险(險)的 wēixiǎn de ▶ it's dangerous to... …是 危险(險)的 ...shì wēixiǎn de

Danish ['deɪnɪʃ] I ADJ 丹麦(麥)的

Dānmài de II N [u] (*language*) 丹麦(麥) 语(語) Dānmàiyǔ

dare [dɛər] I VT ▶ to dare sb to do sth 激 某人做某事 jī mǒurén zuò mǒushì II VI ▶ to dare (to) do sth 敢做某事 gǎn zuò mǒushì ▶ I daren't tell him (*Brit*) 我不敢 告诉(訴)他 wǒ bù gǎn gàosù tā ▶ I dare say (*I suppose*) 我相信 wǒ xiāngxìn ▶ how dare you! 你怎敢! nǐ zěn gǎn!

daring ['dɛərɪŋ] ADJ 勇敢的 yǒnggǎn de

dark [dɑːk] I ADJ **1** (*+ room, night*) 黑暗的 hēi'àn de **2** (*+ eyes, hair, skin*) 黑色的 hēisè de; (*+ person*) 头(頭)发(髮)和皮 肤(膚)深色的 tóufa hé pífū shēnsè de **3** (*+ suit, fabric*) 深色的 shēnsè de II N ▶ the dark 黑暗 hēi'àn ▶ dark blue/ green 深蓝(藍)色/绿(綠)色 shēnlán sè/ lǜsè ▶ it is/is getting dark 天黑了 tiān hēile

darling ['dɑːlɪŋ] N 亲(親)爱(愛)的 qīn'ài de

dart [dɑːt] ▶ darts N PL 投镖(鏢)游(遊) 戏(戲) tóubiāo yóuxì

dashcam ['dæʃkæm] N [c] 行车(車) 记(記)录(錄)仪(儀) xíngchē jìlù yí [台 tái]

data ['deɪtə] N PL 数(數)据(據) shùjù

database ['deɪtəbeɪs] N [c] 数(數)据(據) 库(庫) shùjùkù [个 gè]

date [deɪt] I N [c] **1** 日期 rìqī [个 gè] **2** (*meeting with friend*) 约(約)会(會) yuēhuì [个 gè] **3** (*fruit*) 红(紅)枣(棗) hóngzǎo [颗 kē] II VT (*+ letter, cheque*) 给(給)…注明日期 gěi...zhùmíng rìqī ▶ what's the date today?, what's today's date? 今天几(幾)号(號)？ jīntiān jǐ hào? ▶ date of birth 出生日期 chūshēng rìqī ▶ to be out of date (*old-fashioned*) 落伍 luòwǔ; (*expired*) 过(過)期 guòqī ▶ to be up to date (*modern*) 时(時)新 shíxīn

daughter ['dɔːtər] N [c] 女儿(兒) nǚ'ér [个 gè]

daughter-in-law ['dɔːtərɪnlɔː] (*pl* daughters-in-law) N [c] 媳妇(婦) xífu [个 gè]

dawn [dɔːn] N [c/u] 黎明 límíng [个 gè]

day [deɪ] N **1** [c] 天 tiān **2** [c/u] (*daylight hours*) 白天 báitiān [个 gè] ▶ during the day 在白天 zài báitiān ▶ the day before/after 前/后(後)一天 qián/hòu yī tiān ▸ **the day after tomorrow** 后(後)天 hòutiān ▸ **these days** (nowadays) 现(現)在 xiànzài ▸ **the following day** 第二天 dì'èr tiān ▸ **one day/some day/one of these days** 有一天 yǒu yī tiān ▸ **by day** 在白天 zài báitiān ▸ **all day (long)** 一天到晚 yītiān dàowǎn ▸ **to work an 8 hour day** 每天工作8小时(時) měi tiān gōngzuò bā xiǎoshí

daylight ['deɪlaɪt] N [U] 白昼(晝) báizhòu

dead [dɛd] ADJ **1** 死的 sǐ de **2** [+ battery] 不能再用的 bùnéng zài yòng de

deadline ['dɛdlaɪn] N [c] 截止日期 jiézhǐ rìqī [个 gè] ▸ **to meet a deadline** 如期 rúqī

deaf [dɛf] ADJ 聋(聾)的 lóng de; (partially) 耳背的 ěrbèi de

deafening ['dɛfnɪŋ] ADJ [+ noise] 震耳欲(慾)聋(聾)的 zhèn ěr yù lóng de

deal [di:l] (pt, pp dealt) N [c] 协(協)议(議) xiéyì [个 gè] ▸ **to do/make/strike a deal with sb** 和某人做买(買)卖(賣) hé mǒurén zuò mǎimài ▸ **it's a deal!** (inf) 成交! chéngjiāo! ▸ **a good or great deal (of)** 大量(的…) dàliàng(de…)
▸ **deal with** VT FUS [+ problem] 处(處)理 chǔlǐ

dealer ['di:lə'] N [c] **1** 商人 shāngrén [个 gè] **2** (in drugs) 毒品贩(販)子 dúpǐn fànzi [个 gè]

dealt [dɛlt] PT, PP of **deal**

dear [dɪə'] **I** ADJ **1** 亲(親)爱(愛)的 qīn'ài de **2** (esp Brit: expensive) 昂贵(貴)的 ángguì de **II** N 亲(親)爱(愛)的 qīn'ài de **III** INT ▸ **oh dear/dear dear/dear me!** 呵/哎呀! hè/āiyā!
▸ **Dear Sir/Madam** (in letter) 亲(親)爱(愛)的先生/女士 qīn'ài de xiānsheng/nǚshì ▸ **Dear Peter/Jane** 亲(親)爱(愛)的彼得/简(簡) qīn'ài de Bǐdé/Jiǎn

death [dɛθ] N [c/U] 死亡 sǐwáng [个 gè] ▸ **(a matter of) life and death** 生死攸关(關)(的事情) shēngsǐ yōuguān (de shìqíng) ▸ **to scare/bore sb to death** 吓(嚇)死某人/使某人感到无(無)聊之极(極) xiàsǐ mǒurén/shǐ mǒurén gǎndào wúliáo zhī jí

death penalty N ▸ **the death penalty** 死刑 sǐxíng

debate [dɪ'beɪt] N [c/U] 讨(討)论(論) tǎolùn [次 cì]

debt [dɛt] N [c] **1** (sum of money owed) 债(債)务(務) zhàiwù [笔 bǐ] **2** [U] (state of owing money) 欠债(債) qiànzhài ▸ **to be in/get into debt** 负(負)债(債) fùzhài

decade ['dɛkeɪd] N [c] 十年 shínián [个 gè]

decaffeinated [dɪ'kæfɪneɪtɪd] ADJ 不含咖啡因的 bù hán kāfēiyīn de

deceive [dɪ'si:v] VT 欺骗(騙) qīpiàn

December [dɪ'sɛmbə'] N [c/U] 十二月 shí'èryuè; see also/另见 **July**

decent ['di:sənt] ADJ [+ person] 受尊重的 shòu zūnzhòng de

decide [dɪ'saɪd] **I** VT [+ question, argument] 解决(決) jiějué **II** VI 决(決)定 juédìng ▸ **to decide to do sth** 决(決)定做某事 juédìng zuò mǒushì ▸ **I can't decide whether...** 我无(無)法决(決)定是否… wǒ wúfǎ juédìng shìfǒu…

decimal ['dɛsɪməl] **I** ADJ [+ system, currency] 十进(進)位的 shíjìnwèi de **II** N [c] 小数(數) xiǎoshù [个 gè]

decision [dɪ'sɪʒən] N [c] 决(決)定 juédìng [个 gè] ▸ **to make a decision** 作出决(決)定 zuòchū juédìng

deck [dɛk] N [c] 甲板 jiǎbǎn [个 gè]

deckchair ['dɛktʃɛə'] N [c] 折叠(疊)式躺椅 zhédiéshì tǎngyǐ [把 bǎ]

declare [dɪ'klɛə'] VT **1** [+ intention, attitude] 宣布(佈) xuānbù; [+ support] 表明 biǎomíng **2** (at customs) 报(報)关(關) bàoguān ▸ **to declare war (on sb)** (向某人)宣战(戰) (xiàng mǒurén) xuānzhàn

decorate ['dɛkəreɪt] VT **1** ▸ **to decorate (with)** (用…)装(裝)饰(飾) (yòng…) zhuāngshì **2** (paint etc) 装(裝)潢 zhuānghuáng

decoration [dɛkə'reɪʃən] N [c/U] 装(裝)饰(飾) zhuāngshì [种 zhǒng]

decrease [n 'di:kri:s, vb di:'kri:s] **I** N ▸ **decrease (in sth)** (某物的)减(減)少 (mǒuwù de) jiǎnshǎo **II** VT, VI 减(減)少 jiǎnshǎo

deduct [dɪ'dʌkt] VT ▸ **to deduct sth (from sth)** (从(從)某物中)减(減)去某物 (cóng mǒuwù zhōng) jiǎnqù mǒuwù

deep [di:p] **I** ADJ **1** 深的 shēn de **2** [+ voice, sound] 低沉的 dīchén de **3** [+ sleep] 酣

睡的 hānshuì de **II** ADV 深 shēn ▶ it is
1 m deep 它有1米深 tā yǒu yī mǐ shēn
▶ to take a deep breath 深呼吸 shēn
hūxī

deeply ['di:plɪ] ADV **1** [breathe, sigh +] 深深
地 shēnshēn de **2** [sleep +] 沉沉地
chénchén de

deer [dɪəʳ] (pl deer) N [c] 鹿 lù [头 tóu]

defeat [dɪ'fi:t] I N [c/u] **1** [of army] 战(戰)
败(敗) zhànbài [次 cì] **2** [of team] 击(擊)
败(敗) jībài [次 cì] II VT **1** [+ enemy,
opposition] 战(戰)胜(勝) zhànshèng
2 [+ team] 击(擊)败(敗) jībài

defect ['di:fɛkt] N [c] 缺点(點) quēdiǎn
[个 gè]

defence, (US) **defense** [dɪ'fɛns] N **1** [u]
(protection) 防御 fángyù **2** [u] (Mil)
国(國)防措施 guófáng cuòshī ▶ the
Ministry of Defence, (US) the
Department of Defense 国(國)防部
Guófángbù

defend [dɪ'fɛnd] VT 防御 fángyù ▶ to
defend o.s. 自卫(衛) zìwèi

defender [dɪ'fɛndəʳ] N [c] (in team) 防守
队(隊)员(員) fángshǒu duìyuán [个 gè]

defense [dɪ'fɛns] (US) N = **defence**

definite ['dɛfɪnɪt] ADJ **1** [+ plan, answer,
views] 明确(確)的 míngquè de
2 [+ improvement, possibility, advantage]
肯定的 kěndìng de ▶ is that definite?
肯定吗(嗎)? kěndìng ma

definitely ['dɛfɪnɪtlɪ] ADV 确(確)定地
quèdìng de

defy [dɪ'faɪ] VT [+ law, ban] 蔑视(視)
mièshì

degree [dɪ'gri:] N [c] **1** ▶ degree (of sth)
(level) (某事的)程度 (mǒushì de)
chéngdù [种 zhǒng] **2** (measure of
temperature, angle, latitude) 度 dù **3** (at
university) 学(學)位 xuéwèi [个 gè] ▶ to
some degree/a certain degree 从(從)
某种(種)/一定程度上来(來)说(說) cóng
mǒu zhǒng/yīdìng chéngdù shàng lái
shuō ▶ 10 degrees below (zero) 零下10
度 língxià shí dù ▶ a degree in maths
数(數)学(學)学(學)位 shùxué xuéwèi

delay [dɪ'leɪ] I VT **1** [+ decision, ceremony]
推迟(遲) tuīchí **2** [+ person] 耽搁(擱)
dānge; [+ plane, train] 延误(誤) yánwù
II VI 耽搁(擱) dānge III N [c/u] 延
误(誤) yánwù [件 jiàn] ▶ to be delayed

[person, flight, departure +] 被耽搁(擱)了
bèi dānge le ▶ without delay 立即 lìjí

delete [dɪ'li:t] VT 删(刪)除 shānchú

deliberate [dɪ'lɪbərɪt] ADJ 故意的 gùyì
de ▶ it wasn't deliberate 那不是故意的
nà bù shì gùyì de

deliberately [dɪ'lɪbərɪtlɪ] ADV 故意地
gùyì de

delicate ['dɛlɪkɪt] ADJ **1** (fragile) 易碎的
yìsuì de **2** [+ problem, situation, issue] 微
妙的 wēimiào de **3** [+ colour, flavour,
smell] 清淡可口的 qīngdàn kěkǒu de

delicious [dɪ'lɪʃəs] ADJ 美味的 měiwèi de

delight [dɪ'laɪt] N [u] 快乐(樂) kuàilè

delighted [dɪ'laɪtɪd] ADJ ▶ delighted (at
or with sth) (对(對)某事)感到高兴(興)
(duì mǒushì) gǎndào gāoxìng ▶ to be
delighted to do sth 乐(樂)意做某事
lèyì zuò mǒushì

deliver [dɪ'lɪvəʳ] VT **1** [+ letter, parcel]
传(傳)送 chuánsòng **2** [+ baby] 接生
jiēshēng

delivery [dɪ'lɪvərɪ] N **1** [u] 传(傳)送
chuánsòng **2** [c] (consignment) 递(遞)送
的货(貨)物 dìsòng de huòwù [件 jiàn]

demand [dɪ'mɑ:nd] I VT [+ apology,
explanation, pay rise] 要求 yāoqiú II N
1 [c] (request) 要求 yāoqiú [个 gè] **2** [u]
(for product) 需求量 xūqiúliàng ▶ to
make demands on sb/sth 对(對)某人/
某事提出要求 duì mǒurén/mǒushì tíchū
yāoqiú ▶ to be in demand 受欢(歡)迎
shòu huānyíng

democracy [dɪ'mɔkrəsɪ] N **1** [u] (system)
民主 mínzhǔ **2** [c] (country) 民主国(國)
mínzhǔ guó [个 gè]

democratic [dɛmə'krætɪk] ADJ 民主的
mínzhǔ de

demolish [dɪ'mɔlɪʃ] VT 拆毁(毀) chāihuǐ

demonstrate ['dɛmənstreɪt] I VT [+ skill,
appliance] 演示 yǎnshì II VI ▶ to
demonstrate (for/against sth) 示威
(支持/反对(對)某事) shìwēi (zhīchí/
fǎnduì mǒushì) ▶ to demonstrate how
to do sth 演示如何做某事 yǎnshì rúhé
zuò mǒushì

demonstration [dɛmən'streɪʃən] N [c]
1 示威 shìwēi [次 cì] **2** [of appliance,
cooking] 演示 yǎnshì [个 gè]

demonstrator ['dɛmənstreɪtəʳ] N [c] 示
威者 shìwēizhě [个 gè]

denim ['dɛnɪm] N [U] 斜纹(紋)粗棉布 xiéwén cū miánbù

Denmark ['dɛnmɑːk] N 丹麦(麥) Dānmài

dent [dɛnt] N [c] 凹部 āobù [个 gè]

dental ['dɛntl] ADJ 牙齿(齒)的 yáchǐ de

dentist ['dɛntɪst] N [c] 1 (person) 牙医(醫) yáyī [位 wèi] 2 ▸ the dentist('s) 牙医(醫)诊(診)所 yáyī zhěnsuǒ [家 jiā]

deny [dɪ'naɪ] VT 否定 fǒudìng

deodorant [diː'əudərənt] N [c/U] 除臭剂(劑) chúchòujì [种 zhǒng]

depart [dɪ'pɑːt] VI ▸ to depart (from/for somewhere) (从(從)某地)出发(發)/出发(發)(赶(趕)往某地) (cóng mǒudì) chūfā/chūfā (gǎnwǎng mǒudì)

department [dɪ'pɑːtmənt] N [c] 1 (in shop) 部 bù [个 gè] 2 (in school or college) 系 xì [个 gè]

department store N [c] 百货(貨)商店 bǎihuò shāngdiàn [家 jiā]

departure [dɪ'pɑːtʃər] N [c/U] 出发(發) chūfā

departure lounge N [c] 候机(機)厅(廳) hòujītīng [个 gè]

depend [dɪ'pɛnd] VI 1 ▸ to depend on sth 依某物而定 yī mǒuwù ér dìng 2 ▸ you can depend on me/him (rely on, trust) 你可以信赖(賴)我/他 nǐ kěyǐ xìnlài wǒ/tā 3 ▸ to depend on sb/sth (for survival) 依靠某人/某物为(為)生 yīkào mǒurén/mǒuwù wéishēng ▸ it (all) depends 要看情况(況)而定 yào kàn qíngkuàng ér dìng

deposit [dɪ'pɒzɪt] N [c] 储(儲)蓄 chǔxù [笔 bǐ]; (on house, bottle, when hiring) 押金 yājīn [份 fèn] ▸ to put down a deposit of 50 pounds 支付50英镑(鎊)的保证(證)金 zhīfù wǔshí yīngbàng de bǎozhèngjīn

depressed [dɪ'prɛst] ADJ 沮丧(喪)的 jǔsàng de

depressing [dɪ'prɛsɪŋ] ADJ 令人沮丧(喪)的 lìng rén jǔsàng de

deprive [dɪ'praɪv] VT ▸ to deprive sb of sth 剥(剝)夺(奪)某人某物 bōduó mǒurén mǒuwù

depth [dɛpθ] N [c/U] 深 shēn ▸ at/to/from a depth of 3 metres 在/到/从(從)3米深处(處) zài/dào/cóng sān mǐ shēn chù ▸ to study/analyse sth

in depth 深入研究/分析某事 shēnrù yánjiū/fēnxī mǒushì

descend [dɪ'sɛnd] VI (frm) 下来(來) xiàlái ▸ to be descended from 是…的后(後)裔 shì…de hòuyì

describe [dɪs'kraɪb] VT 描述 miáoshù

description [dɪs'krɪpʃən] N [c/U] 描述 miáoshù [种 zhǒng]

desert [N 'dɛzət] N [c/U] (Geo) 沙漠 shāmò [片 piàn] 2 [c] (fig: wasteland) 荒地 huāngdì [片 piàn]

deserve [dɪ'zəːv] VT 应(應)受 yīng shòu ▸ to deserve to do sth 应(應)该(該)获(獲)得某事 yīnggāi huòdé mǒuwù

design [dɪ'zaɪn] I N 1 [c] (art, process, layout, shape) 设(設)计(計) shèjì 2 [c] (pattern) 图(圖)案 tú'àn [种 zhǒng] II VT 设(設)计(計) shèjì ▸ to be designed for sb/to do sth 专(專)门(門)为(為)某人/做某事设(設)计(計) zhuānmén wèi mǒurén/zuò mǒushì shèjì

designer [dɪ'zaɪnər] I N [c] 设(設)计(計)者 shèjìzhě [位 wèi] II CPD [+ clothes, label, jeans] 名师(師)设(設)计(計)的 míngshī shèjì de

desk [dɛsk] N [c] 1 (in office) 办(辦)公桌 bàngōngzhuō [张 zhāng] 2 (for pupil) 书(書)桌 shūzhuō [张 zhāng] 3 (in hotel, at airport, hospital) 服务(務)台(臺) fúwùtái [个 gè]

desk clerk (US) N [c] 接待员(員) jiēdàiyuán [位 wèi]

desktop ['dɛsktɒp] N [c] (computer) 桌面 zhuōmiàn [张(張) zhāng]

despair [dɪs'pɛər] N [U] 绝(絕)望 juéwàng ▸ in despair 绝(絕)望地 juéwàngde

desperate ['dɛspərɪt] ADJ 1 [+ person] 绝(絕)望的 juéwàng de 2 [+ attempt, effort] 铤(鋌)而走险(險)的 tǐng ér zǒu xiǎn de 3 [+ situation] 危急的 wēijí de

desperately ['dɛspərɪtlɪ] ADV [struggle, shout +] 拼命地 pīnmìng de

despise [dɪs'paɪz] VT 鄙视(視) bǐshì

despite [dɪs'paɪt] PREP 尽(儘)管 jǐnguǎn

dessert [dɪ'zəːt] N [c/U] 饭(飯)后(後)甜点(點) fànhòu tiándiǎn [份 fèn]

destination [dɛstɪ'neɪʃən] N [c] 目的地 mùdìdì [个 gè]

destroy [dɪs'trɔɪ] VT 破坏(壞) pòhuài

destruction [dɪsˈtrʌkʃən] N [U] 破坏(壞) pòhuài

detail [ˈdiːteɪl] I N [c] 细(細)节(節) xìjié [个 gè] II **details** N PL 详(詳)情 xiángqíng ▸ **in detail** 详(詳)细(細)地 xiángxì de

detailed [ˈdiːteɪld] ADJ 详(詳)细(細)的 xiángxì de

detective [dɪˈtɛktɪv] N [c] 侦(偵)探 zhēntàn [个 gè]

detective story, detective novel N [c] 侦(偵)探小说(說) zhēntàn xiǎoshuō [部 bù]

detergent [dɪˈtəːdʒənt] N [c/u] 清洁(潔)剂(劑) qīngjiéjì [种 zhǒng]

determined [dɪˈtəːmɪnd] ADJ 坚(堅)定的 jiāndìng de ▸ **to be determined to do sth** 决(決)心做某事 juéxīn zuò mǒushì

detour [ˈdiːtuə˞] N [c] 1 ▸ **to make a detour** 绕(繞)道 ràodào [次 cì] 2 (US: on road) 绕(繞)行道路 ràoxíng dàolù [条 tiáo]

detox [ˈdiːtɔks] I N [U] 脱(脫)瘾治疗(療) tuō yǐn zhìliáo II VB 脱(脫)瘾 tuō yǐn

develop [dɪˈvɛləp] I VT 1 [+ business, idea, relationship] 发(發)展 fāzhǎn; [+ land, resource] 开(開)发(發) kāifā 2 [+ product, weapon] 开(開)发(發) kāifā 3 (Phot) 冲(沖)洗 chōngxǐ II VI [person +] 成长(長) chéngzhǎng; [country, situation, friendship, skill +] 发(發)展 fāzhǎn

development [dɪˈvɛləpmənt] N 1 [U] (growth) 成长(長) chéngzhǎng; (political, economic) 发(發)展 fāzhǎn 2 [c] (event) 新形势(勢) xīn xíngshì [种 zhǒng]

devil [ˈdɛvl] N ▸ **the Devil** 撒旦 Sādàn [个 gè]

devoted [dɪˈvəutɪd] ADJ 1 [+ husband, daughter] 忠诚(誠)的 zhōngchéng de 2 ▸ **devoted to sth** (specialising in) 致力于(於)某事的 zhìlì yú mǒushì de

diabetes [daɪəˈbiːtiːz] N [U] 糖尿病 tángniàobìng

diabetic [daɪəˈbɛtɪk] N [c] 糖尿病患者 tángniàobìng huànzhě [个 gè]

diagonal [daɪˈægənl] ADJ 斜的 xié de

diagram [ˈdaɪəgræm] N [c] 图(圖)解 tújiě [个 gè]

dial [ˈdaɪəl] I N [c] (on clock or meter) 标(標)度盘(盤) biāodùpán [个 gè] II VT [+ number] 拨(撥) bō III VI 拨(撥)号(號) bōhào

dialling code [ˈdaɪəlɪŋ-] (Brit) N [c] 电(電)话(話)区(區)号(號) diànhuà qūhào [个 gè]

dialogue, (US) **dialog** [ˈdaɪəlɔg] N [c/u] (conversation) 对(對)话(話) duìhuà [次 cì]

diamond [ˈdaɪəmənd] N [c] 钻(鑽)石 zuànshí [颗 kē]

diaper [ˈdaɪəpə˞] (US) N [c] 尿布 niàobù [块 kuài]

diarrhoea, (US) **diarrhea** [daɪəˈriːə] N [U] 腹泻(瀉) fùxiè ▸ **to have diarrhoea** 腹泻(瀉) fùxiè

diary [ˈdaɪərɪ] N [c] 1 日记(記)簿 rìjìbù [个 gè] 2 (daily account) 日记(記) rìjì [篇 piān]

dice [daɪs] (pl dice) N [c] 骰子 tóuzi [个 gè]

dictation [dɪkˈteɪʃən] N [c/u] (at school, college) 听(聽)写(寫) tīngxiě [次 cì]

dictionary [ˈdɪkʃənrɪ] N [c] 词(詞)典 cídiǎn [本 běn]

did [dɪd] PT of **do**

die [daɪ] VI 死亡 ▸ **to die of or from sth** 死于(於)某事 sǐ yú mǒushì ▸ **to be dying** 奄奄一息 yǎnyǎn yī xī ▸ **to be dying for sth/to do sth** 渴望某事/做某事 kěwàng mǒushì/zuò mǒushì ▸ **die out** VI 1 [custom, way of life +] 灭(滅)亡 mièwáng 2 [species +] 灭(滅)绝(絕) mièjué

diesel [ˈdiːzl] N 1 [U] (also: diesel oil) 柴油 cháiyóu 2 [c] (vehicle) 柴油机(機)驱(驅)动(動)的车(車)辆(輛) cháiyóujī qūdòng de chēliàng [辆 liàng]

diet [ˈdaɪət] N 1 [c/u] (food) 饮(飲)食 yǐnshí [种 zhǒng] 2 [c] (slimming) 减(減)肥饮(飲)食 jiǎnféi yǐnshí [份 fèn] II VI ▸ **to be on a diet** 实(實)行减(減)肥节(節)食 shíxíng jiǎnféi jiéshí

difference [ˈdɪfrəns] N [c] 差异(異) chāyì [种 zhǒng] ▸ **the difference in size/colour** 尺寸/颜(顏)色上的差异(異) chǐcùn/yánsè shang de chāyì ▸ **to make a/no difference (to sb/sth)** (对(對)某人/某事) 有/无(無)影响(響) (duì mǒurén/mǒushì) yǒu/wú yǐngxiǎng

different ['dɪfrənt] ADJ 不同的 bù
tóng de

difficult ['dɪfɪkəlt] ADJ **1** 困难(難)的
kùnnan de **2** [+ person, child] 执(執)拗的
zhíniù de ▸ **it is difficult for us to
understand her** 我们(們)很难(難)理解
她 wǒmen hěn nán lǐjiě tā

difficulty ['dɪfɪkəltɪ] N [c] 困难(難)
kùnnan [个 gè] ▸ **to have difficulty/
difficulties** 有困难(難) yǒu kùnnan

dig [dɪg] (pt, pp **dug**) I VT **1** [+ hole] 挖 wā
2 [+ garden] 掘土 juétǔ II VI (with spade)
挖掘 wājué
▸ **dig up** VT [+ plant, body] 挖出 wāchū

digital ['dɪdʒɪtl] ADJ **1** [+ clock, watch]
数(數)字的 shùzì de **2** [+ recording,
technology] 数(數)码(碼)的 shùmǎ de

digital camera N [c] 数(數)码(碼)相
机(機) shùmǎ xiàngjī [台 tái]

digital radio N [U] 数(數)码(碼)收音
机(機) shùmǎ shōuyīnjī [台 tái]

digital television N [U] 数(數)字电(電)
视(視) shùzì diànshì

dim [dɪm] ADJ **1** 暗淡的 àndàn de **2** (inf:
stupid) 迟(遲)钝(鈍)的 chídùn de

dime [daɪm] (US) N [c] 一角银(銀)币(幣)
yī jiǎo yínbì [枚 méi]

dimension [daɪ'mɛnʃən] I N [c] (aspect)
方面(麵) fāngmiàn [个 gè]
II **dimensions** NPL (measurements) 面
积(積) miànjī

diner ['daɪnəʳ] N [c] (US: restaurant) 廉
价(價)餐馆(館) liánjià cānguǎn [家 jiā]

dinghy ['dɪŋgɪ] N [c] (also: rubber dinghy)
橡皮筏 xiàngpífá [个 gè]

dining room N [c] **1** (in house) 饭(飯)
厅(廳) fàntīng [个 gè] **2** (in hotel) 餐
厅(廳) cāntīng [个 gè]

dinner ['dɪnəʳ] N [c/U] **1** 晚餐 wǎncān [顿
dùn] **2** (formal meal) 正餐 zhèngcān
[顿 dùn]

dinner party N [c] 宴会(會) yànhuì
[个 gè]

dinner time N [c/U] 晚饭(飯)时(時)
间(間) wǎnfàn shíjiān [段 duàn]

dinosaur ['daɪnəsɔːʳ] N [c] 恐龙(龍)
kǒnglóng [只 zhī]

dip [dɪp] VT 蘸 zhàn

diploma [dɪ'pləumə] N [c] 毕(畢)业(業)
文凭(憑) bìyè wénpíng [张 zhāng]

direct [daɪ'rɛkt] I ADJ 直达(達)的 zhídá

de II VT **1** (show) 给(給)…指路
gěi…zhǐlù **2** (manage) 管理 guǎnlǐ
3 [+ play, film, programme] 导(導)演
dǎoyǎn III ADV [go, write, fly +] 直接地
zhíjiē de

direction [dɪ'rɛkʃən] I N [c] 方向
fāngxiàng [个 gè] II **directions** NPL **1** (to
get somewhere) 指路说(說)明 zhǐlù
shuōmíng **2** (for doing something) 用法
说(說)明 yòngfǎ shuōmíng ▸ **in the
direction of** 朝 cháo

director [dɪ'rɛktəʳ] N [c] **1** [of company]
经(經)理 jīnglǐ [位 wèi] **2** [of organization,
public authority] 主任 zhǔrèn [位 wèi]
3 [of play, film] 导(導)演 dǎoyǎn
[位 wèi]

directory [dɪ'rɛktərɪ] N [c] **1** 电(電)
话(話)号(號)码(碼)簿 diànhuà
hàomǎbù [个 gè] **2** (on computer) 文件名
录(錄) wénjiàn mínglù [个 gè]

dirt [dəːt] N [U] 污物 wūwù

dirty ['dəːtɪ] ADJ 脏(髒)的 zāng de

disabled [dɪs'eɪbld] ADJ **1** 伤(傷)残(殘)的
shāngcán de **2** (mentally) 残(殘)疾的
cánjí de

disadvantage [dɪsəd'vɑːntɪdʒ] N [c/U]
(drawback) 不利 bùlì [种 zhǒng]

disagree [dɪsə'griː] VI ▸ **to disagree
(with sb)** 不同意(某人的观(觀)点(點))
bù tóngyì (mǒurén de guāndiǎn) ▸ **to
disagree (with sth)** (对(對)某事表示)
不同意 (duì mǒushì biǎoshì) bù tóngyì

disagreement [dɪsə'griːmənt] N [c]
(argument) 争(爭)执(執) zhēngzhí
[个 gè]

disappear [dɪsə'pɪəʳ] VI **1** (from view) 消
失 xiāoshī **2** (go missing) 失踪(蹤)
shīzōng **3** (cease to exist) 消失 xiāoshī

disappearance [dɪsə'pɪərəns] N [c/U]
[of person] 失踪(蹤) shīzōng [次 cì]

disappoint [dɪsə'pɔɪnt] VT [+ person]
使失望 shǐ shīwàng

disappointed [dɪsə'pɔɪntɪd] ADJ 失望的
shīwàng de

disappointment [dɪsə'pɔɪnt-
mənt] N **1** [U] (emotion) 失望 shīwàng
2 [c] (cause) 令人失望的人/事 lìng rén
shīwàng de rén/shì [个/件 gè/jiàn]

disapprove [dɪsə'pruːv] VI ▸ **to
disapprove (of sb/sth)** 不同意(某人/
某事) bù tóngyì (mǒurén/mǒushì)

disaster [dɪ'zɑːstə^r] N [c/u] **1** (*earthquake, flood*) 灾(災)难(難) zāinàn [次 cì] **2** (*accident, crash etc*) 灾(災)祸(禍) zāihuò [场 cháng] **3** (*fiasco*) 惨(慘)败(敗) cǎnbài [次 cì] **4** (*serious situation*) 灾(災)难(難) zāinàn [个 gè]

disastrous [dɪ'zɑːstrəs] ADJ **1** (*catastrophic*) 灾(災)难(難)性的 zāinànxìng de **2** (*unsuccessful*) 惨(慘)败(敗)的 cǎnbài de

disc [dɪsk] N [c] **1** 圆(圓)盘(盤) yuánpán [个 gè] **2** (*Comput*) = **disk**

discipline ['dɪsɪplɪn] N [u] 纪(紀)律 jìlù

disc jockey N [c] 简称为DJ, 意为广播电台或迪斯科舞厅流行音乐唱片播放及介绍人

disco ['dɪskəu] N (*event*) 迪斯科 dísìkē

disconnect [dɪskə'nɛkt] VT **1** [+ *pipe, tap, hose*] 拆开(開) chāikāi **2** [+ *computer, cooker, TV*] 断(斷)开(開) duànkāi

discount ['dɪskaunt] N [c/u] 折扣 zhékòu [个 gè]

discourage [dɪs'kʌrɪdʒ] VT 使泄(洩)气(氣) shǐ xièqì

discover [dɪs'kʌvə^r] VT 发(發)现(現) fāxiàn

discovery [dɪs'kʌvərɪ] N **1** [c/u] [*of treasure, cure*] 发(發)现(現) **2** [c] (*thing found*) 被发(發)现(現)的事物 bèi fāxiàn de shìwù [个 gè]

discrimination [dɪskrɪmɪ'neɪʃən] N [u] 歧视(視) qíshì ▸ **racial/sexual discrimination** 种(種)族/性别(別)歧视(視) zhǒngzú/xìngbié qíshì

discuss [dɪs'kʌs] VT 讨(討)论(論) tǎolùn

discussion [dɪs'kʌʃən] N [c/u] 讨(討)论(論) tǎolùn [次 cì]

disease [dɪ'ziːz] N [c/u] (*illness*) 病 bìng [场 cháng]

disgraceful [dɪs'greɪsful] ADJ 可耻(恥)的 kěchǐ de

disguise [dɪs'gaɪz] I N [c] (*costume*) 伪(偽)装(裝)品 wěizhuāngpǐn [件 jiàn] II VT ▸ **(to be) disguised (as sth/sb)** [+ *person*] 假扮成(某物/某人) jiǎbàn chéng (mǒuwù/mǒurén) ▸ **in disguise** 乔(喬)装(裝)着(著) qiáozhuāng zhe

disgusted [dɪs'gʌstɪd] ADJ 感到厌(厭)恶(惡)的 gǎndào yànwù de

disgusting [dɪs'gʌstɪŋ] ADJ **1** [+ *food, habit*] 令人作呕(嘔)的 lìng rén zuò'ǒu

de **2** [+ *behaviour, situation*] 讨(討)厌(厭)的 tǎoyàn de

dish [dɪʃ] I N [c] **1** 盘(盤) pán [个 gè]; (*for eating*) 碟 dié [个 gè] **2** (*recipe, food*) 一道菜 yī dào cài [道 dào] **3** (*also*: **satellite dish**) 盘(盤)形物 pánxíngwù [个 gè] II **dishes** NPL 碗碟 wǎndié ▸ **to do** or **wash the dishes** 刷洗碗碟 shuāxǐ wǎndié

dishonest [dɪs'ɔnɪst] ADJ **1** 不诚(誠)实(實)的 bù chéngshí de **2** [+ *behaviour*] 不正直的 bù zhèngzhí de

dishwasher ['dɪʃwɔʃə^r] N [c] 洗碗机(機) xǐwǎnjī [台 tái]

dishwashing liquid ['dɪʃwɔʃɪŋ-] (US) N [u] 洗洁(潔)剂(劑) xǐjiéjì

disinfectant [dɪsɪn'fɛktənt] N [c/u] 消毒剂(劑) xiāodújì [种 zhǒng]

disk [dɪsk] N [c] (*Comput: hard*) 硬盘(盤) yìngpán [个 gè]; (*floppy*) 软(軟)盘(盤) ruǎnpán [张 zhāng]

dislike [dɪs'laɪk] VT 不喜欢(歡) bù xǐhuan ▸ **one's likes and dislikes** 某人的爱(愛)好和厌(厭)恶(惡) mǒurén de àihào hé yànwù

dismiss [dɪs'mɪs] VT 解雇(僱) jiěgù

disobedient [dɪsə'biːdɪənt] ADJ 不服从(從)的 bù fúcóng de

disobey [dɪsə'beɪ] VT **1** 不顺(順)从(從) bù shùncóng **2** [+ *order*] 不服从(從) bù fúcóng

display [dɪs'pleɪ] I N **1** [c/u] (*in shop, at exhibition*) 陈(陳)列 chénliè [种 zhǒng] **2** [c] (*information on screen*) 显(顯)示 xiǎnshì [个 gè] **3** [c] (*screen*) 显(顯)示屏 xiǎnshìpíng [个 gè] II VT **1** [+ *exhibits*] 陈(陳)列 chénliè **2** [+ *results, information*] 显(顯)示 xiǎnshì

disposable [dɪs'pəuzəbl] ADJ 一次性的 yīcìxìng de

dispute [dɪs'pjuːt] N (*industrial*) 争(爭)执(執) zhēngzhí

disqualify [dɪs'kwɔlɪfaɪ] VT 取消…的资(資)格 qǔxiāo…de zīgé

disrupt [dɪs'rʌpt] VT **1** [+ *conversation, meeting*] 扰(擾)乱(亂) rǎoluàn **2** [+ *plan, process*] 妨碍(礙) fáng'ài

dissolve [dɪ'zɔlv] VT (*in liquid*) 溶解 róngjiě

distance ['dɪstns] N [c/u] 距离(離) jùlí [个 gè] ▸ **within walking distance** 步行可到 bùxíng kě dào

distinct [dɪ'stɪŋkt] ADJ [+ *advantage, change*] 明确(確)的 míngquè de

distinguish [dɪ'stɪŋgwɪʃ] VT ▶ to distinguish one thing from another 将(將)一事物与(與)另一事物区(區)别(別)开(開)来(來) jiāng yī shìwù yǔ lìng yī shìwù qūbié kāilái

distract [dɪs'trækt] VT [+ *person*] 使分心 shǐ fēnxīn ▶ to distract sb's attention 分散某人的注意力 fēnsàn mǒurén de zhùyìlì

distribute [dɪs'trɪbjuːt] VT **1** (*hand out*) 分发(發) fēnfā **2** (*share out*) 分配 fēnpèi

district [dɪstrɪkt] N [c] 地区(區) dìqū [个 gè]

disturb [dɪs'təːb] VT (*interrupt*) 打扰(擾) dǎrǎo

disturbing [dɪs'təːbɪŋ] ADJ 令人不安的 lìng rén bù'ān de

ditch [dɪtʃ] N [c] 沟(溝) gōu [条 tiáo]

dive [daɪv] VI (*into water*) 跳水 tiàoshuǐ; (*under water*) 潜(潛)水 qiánshuǐ

diver ['daɪvə'] N [c] 潜(潛)水员(員) qiánshuǐyuán [位 wèi]

diversion [daɪ'vəːʃən] N [c] (*Brit*) 临(臨)时(時)改道 línshí gǎidào [次 cì]

divide [dɪ'vaɪd] I VT **1** ▶ to divide (up) 划(劃)分 huàfēn **2** (*in maths*) 除 chú **3** ▶ to divide sth between/among sb/sth (*share*) 在两(兩)个(個)/3个(個)以上的人/物之间(間)分配某物 zài liǎng gè/sān gè yǐshàng de rén/wù zhījiān fēnpèi mǒuwù II VI (*into groups*) 分开(開) fēnkāi ▶ to divide sth in half 将(將)某物一分为(為)二 jiāng mǒuwù yī fēn wéi èr ▶ 40 divided by 5 40除以5 sìshí chú yǐ wǔ

diving ['daɪvɪŋ] N [U] **1** (*underwater*) 潜(潛)水 qiánshuǐ **2** (*from board*) 跳水 tiàoshuǐ

division [dɪ'vɪʒən] N [U] **1** (*Math*) 除法 chúfǎ **2** [U] (*sharing out*) [*of labour, resources*] 分配 fēnpèi

divorce [dɪ'vɔːs] I N [c/U] 离(離)婚 líhūn [次 cì] II VT [+ *spouse*] 与(與)…离(離)婚 yǔ…líhūn III VI 离(離)婚 líhūn

divorced [dɪ'vɔːst] ADJ 离(離)异(異)的 líyì de ▶ to get divorced 离(離)婚 líhūn

DIY (*Brit*) N ABBR (= do-it-yourself) 自己动(動)手的活计(計) zìjǐ dòngshǒu de huójì ▶ to do DIY 自己动(動)手做 zìjǐ dòngshǒu zuò

DIY

英国人对 **DIY** 很上瘾，有时幽默地称其为一种全民性消遣。**DIY** 是 **do-it-yourself**，是指自己动手制作和修理东西，尤其是在家里。房主不雇佣专业的建筑工人，木匠或油漆匠，这样不仅省钱，还能从自己动手改进家里的设备、环境中得到莫大的满足感。专门的 **DIY** 商店销售工具、油漆和其他能满足 **DIY** 爱好者嗜好的用品。

dizzy ['dɪzɪ] ADJ ▶ to feel dizzy 感到头(頭)晕(暈) gǎndào tóuyūn

DJ N ABBR (= disc jockey) 简称为DJ，意为广播电台或迪斯科舞厅流行音乐唱片播放及介绍人

○ **KEYWORD**

do [duː] (*pt* did, *pp* done) I VT **1** 做 zuò ▶ what are you doing? 你在做什么(麼)呢？nǐ zài zuò shénme ne? ▶ are you doing anything tomorrow evening? 你明晚有什么(麼)打算？nǐ míngwǎn yǒu shénme dǎsuàn? ▶ what did you do with the money? (*how did you spend it?*) 你怎么(麼)用这(這)笔(筆)钱(錢)的？nǐ zěnme yòng zhè bǐ qián de? ▶ what are you going to do about this? 你打算对(對)此怎么(麼)办(辦)？nǐ dǎsuàn duì cǐ zěnmebàn?

2 (*for a living*) ▶ what do you do? 你做什么(麼)工作？nǐ zuò shénme gōngzuò?

3 (*with noun*) ▶ to do the cooking 做饭(飯) zuòfàn

4 (*referring to speed, distance*) ▶ the car was doing 100 汽车(車)以100英里(裡)的时(時)速行进(進) qìchē yǐ yībǎi yīnglǐ de shísù xíngjìn ▶ we've done 200 km already 我们(們)的时(時)速已达(達)到了200公里(裡) wǒmen de shísù yǐ dádàole èrbǎi gōnglǐ

5 (*cause*) ▶ the explosion did a lot of damage 爆炸造成了很大损(損)失 bàozhà zàochéngle hěn dà sǔnshī ▶ a holiday will do you good 休次假会(會)对(對)你有好处(處) xiū cì jià huì duì nǐ yǒu hǎochù

II VI **1** (*act, behave*) 做 zuò ▶ do as I tell

you 按我告诉(訴)你的做 àn wǒ gàosù nǐ de zuò

2 (get on) ▶ 进(進)展 jìnzhǎn ▶ **he's doing well/badly at school** 他的学(學)习(習)成绩(績)很好/很差 tā de xuéxí chéngjī hěn hǎo/hěn chà ▶ **"how do you do?" —"how do you do?"** "你好" "你好" "nǐ hǎo" "nǐ hǎo"

3 (suit) 行 xíng ▶ **will it do?** 行吗(嗎)? xíng ma?

4 (be sufficient) 足够(夠) zúgòu ▶ **will £5 do?** 15镑(鎊)够(夠)吗(嗎)? shíwǔ bàng gòu ma?

III AUX VB **1** (in negative constructions) ▶ **I don't understand** 我不懂 wǒ bù dǒng ▶ **she doesn't want it** 她不想要这(這)个(個) tā bù xiǎng yào zhège ▶ **don't be silly!** 别(別)傻了! bié shǎ le!

2 (to form questions) ▶ **do you like jazz?** 你喜欢(歡)爵士乐(樂)吗(嗎)? nǐ xǐhuan juéshìyuè ma? ▶ **what do you think?** 你怎么(麼)想? nǐ zěnme xiǎng? ▶ **why didn't you come?** 你为(為)什么(麼)没(沒)来(來)? nǐ wèi shénme méi lái?

3 (for emphasis, in polite expressions) ▶ **do sit down/help yourself** 赶(趕)快坐啊/千万(萬)别(別)客气(氣) gǎnkuài zuò a/qiānwàn bié kèqi

4 (used to avoid repeating vb) 用于避免动词的重复 ▶ **they say they don't care, but they do** 他们(們)说(說)不在乎, 但实(實)际(際)是在乎的 tāmen shuō bù zàihu, dàn shíjì shì zàihu de ▶ **(and) so do I** 我也是 wǒ yě shì ▶ **and neither did we** 我们(們)也不 wǒmen yě bù ▶ **"who made this mess?" —"I did"** "是谁(誰)弄得乱(亂)七八糟的?" "是我" "shuí nòng de luànqībāzāo de" "shì wǒ"

5 (in question tags) ▶ **I don't know him, do I?** 我不认(認)识(識)他, 是吗(嗎)? wǒ bù rènshi tā, shì ma? ▶ **she lives in London, doesn't she?** 她住在伦(倫)敦, 不是吗(嗎)? tā zhù zài Lúndūn, bù shì ma?

▶ **do up** VT FUS **1** [+ laces] 系(繫)紧(緊) jìjǐn; [+ dress, coat, buttons] 扣上 kòushàng

2 (esp Brit) [+ room, house] 装(裝)修 zhuāngxiū

▶ **do with** VT FUS **1** (need) ▶ **I could do**

with a drink/some help 我想喝一杯/需要帮(幫)助 wǒ xiǎng hē yī bēi/xūyào bāngzhù

2 (be connected) ▶ **to have to do with** 与(與)…有关(關) yǔ…yǒuguān ▶ **what has it got to do with you?** 这(這)跟你有什么(麼)关(關)系(係)? zhè gēn nǐ yǒu shénme guānxi?

▶ **do without** VT FUS 没(沒)有…也行 méiyǒu…yě xíng

dock [dɔk] N [c] (Naut) 船坞(塢) chuánwù [个 gè]

doctor ['dɔktə'] N [c] **1** 医(醫)生 yīshēng [位 wèi] **2** ▶ **the doctor's** 诊(診)所 zhěnsuǒ [家 jiā]

document ['dɔkjumənt N [c] **1** 文件 wénjiàn [份 fèn] **2** (Comput) 文档(檔) wéndàng [个 gè]

documentary [dɔkju'mentəri] N [c] 纪(紀)录(錄)片 jìlùpiàn [部 bù]

does [dʌz] VB see **do**

doesn't ['dʌznt] = **does not**

dog [dɔg] N [c] **1** 狗 gǒu [只 zhī] **2** (male) 雄兽(獸) xióngshòu [头 tóu]

do-it-yourself ['du:ɪtjɔ:'self] I N [U] 自己动(動)手的活计(計) zìjǐ dòngshǒu de huójì II ADJ [+ store] 出售供购(購)买(買)者自行装(裝)配物品的 chūshòu gōng gòumǎizhě zìxíng zhuāngpèi wùpǐn de

dole [dəul] (inf) N [U] (Brit) ▶ **(the) dole** (payment) 失业(業)救济(濟) shīyè jiùjìjīn ▶ **(to be) on the dole** (Brit) 靠失业(業)救济(濟)金生活 kào shīyè jiùjìjīn shēnghuó

doll [dɔl] N [c] 娃娃 wáwa [个 gè]

dollar ['dɔlə'] N [c] 元 yuán

dolphin ['dɔlfɪn] N [c] 海豚 hǎitún [只 zhī]

dominoes ['dɔmɪnəuz] N [U] 多米诺(諾)骨牌游(遊)戏(戲) duōmǐnuò gǔpái yóuxì

donate [də'neɪt] VT **1** ▶ **to donate (to sb)** [+ money, clothes] 捐赠(贈)(给(給)某人) juānzèng (gěi mǒurén) **2** [+ blood, organs] 捐献(獻) juānxiàn

done [dʌn] PP of **do**

donkey ['dɔŋkɪ] N [c] 驴(驢) lú [头 tóu]

don't [dəunt] = **do not**

donut ['dəunʌt] (US) N = **doughnut**

door [dɔ:'] N [c] 门(門) mén [扇 shàn]

▶**to answer the door** 应(應)门(門) yìngmén

doorbell ['dɔːbel] N [c] 门(門)铃(鈴) ménlíng [个 gè]

dormitory ['dɔːmɪtrɪ] N [c] **1**(room) 宿舍 sùshè [间 jiān] **2**(US: building) 宿舍 楼(樓) sùshèlóu [座 zuò]

dose [dəus] N [c] 一剂(劑) yī jì

dot [dɒt] N [c] 圆(圓)点(點) yuándiǎn [个 gè] ▶**on the dot** (punctually) 准(準) 时(時)地 zhǔnshí de

dot-com [dɒt'kɒm] N [c] 网(網)络(絡)公 司 wǎngluò gōngsī [家 jiā]

double ['dʌbl] I ADJ **1**(amount) 双(雙)份的 shuāngfèn de II V [population, size +] 变(變)成两(兩)倍 biànchéng liǎng bèi ▶**it's spelt with a double "M"** 它的拼写(寫)中有两(兩)个(個) "M" tā de pīnxiě zhōng yǒu liǎng gè "M" ▶**double the size/number (of sth)** (是某物)大小/数(數)量的两(兩)倍 (shì mǒuwù) dàxiǎo/shùliàng de liǎng bèi

double bass N [c/u] 低音提琴 dīyīn tíqín [把 bǎ]

double-click ['dʌbl'klɪk] V 双(雙) 击(擊) shuāngjī

double-decker ['dʌbl'dɛkə'] (esp Brit) N [c] (bus) 双(雙)层(層)公共汽车(車) shuāngcéng gōnggòng qìchē [辆 liàng]

double glazing [-'gleɪzɪŋ] (Brit) N [u] 双(雙)层(層)玻璃 shuāngcéng bōli

double room N [c] 双(雙)人房 shuāngrénfáng

doubt [daut] I N [c/u] (uncertainty) 怀(懷)疑 huáiyí [种 zhǒng] II V [+ person's word] 不信 bù xìn ▶**to doubt if** or **whether...** 拿不准(準)是否... ná bù zhǔn shìfǒu... ▶**I doubt it (very much)** 我(很)怀(懷)疑 wǒ (hěn) huáiyí

doubtful ['dautful] ADJ **1**(questionable) ▶**it is doubtful that/whether...** 不能 确(確)定...是否... bùnéng quèdìng.../ shìfǒu... **2**(unconvinced) ▶**to be doubtful that/whether...** 怀(懷)疑...是否... huáiyí.../shìfǒu... ▶**to be doubtful about sth** 对(對)某事有怀(懷)疑 duì mǒushì yǒu huáiyí

doughnut, (US) **donut** ['dəunʌt] N [c] 炸面(麵)饼(餅)圈 zhá miànbǐngquān [个 gè]

down [daun] I ADV **1**(downwards) 向下

xiàngxià **2** (in a lower place) 在下面 zài xiàmiàn II PREP **1**(towards lower level) 沿着(著)...往下 yánzhe...wǎng xià **2**(at lower part of) 在下面 zài xiàmiàn **3**(along) 沿着(著) yánzhe ▶**she looked down** 她向下看 tā xiàng xià kàn ▶**he walked down the road** 他沿街走去 tā yán jiē zǒuqù ▶**down there** 在那 儿(兒) zài nàr ▶**down** (behind) 英格兰(蘭)落后(後) 两(兩)球 Yīnggélán luòhòu liǎng qiú

download ['daunləud] V 下载(載) xiàzài

downstairs ['daun'stɛəz] ADV **1**(on or to floor below) 楼(樓)下 lóuxià **2**(on or to ground level) 在一层(層) zài yī céng

downtown ['daun'taun] (US) I ADV **1**[be, work +] 在市中心 zài shì zhōngxīn **2**[go +] 去市中心 qù shì zhōngxīn II ADJ ▶**downtown Chicago** 芝加哥的市中心 Zhījiāgē de shì zhōngxīn

dozen ['dʌzn] N [c] 一打 yī dá ▶**two dozen eggs** 两(兩)打鸡(雞)蛋 liǎng dá jīdàn ▶**dozens of** 许(許)多 xǔduō

draft [drɑːft] N **1** [c] (first version) 草稿 cǎogǎo **2** [c] (bank draft) 汇(匯)票 huìpiào [张 zhāng]; see also/另见 **draught**

drag [dræg] V [pull] [+ large object, body] 拖 tuō

dragon ['drægn] N [c] 龙(龍) lóng [条 tiáo]

drain [dreɪn] I N [c] (in street) 排水沟(溝) páishuǐgōu [条 tiáo] II V [+ vegetables] 使...流干(乾) shǐ...liúgān III V [liquid +] 流入 liúrù

drama ['drɑːmə] N **1** [u] (theatre) 戏(戲) 剧(劇) xìjù **2** [c] (play) 一出(齣)戏(戲) 剧(劇) yī chū xìjù [幕 mù] **3** [c/u] (excitement) 戏(戲)剧(劇)性 xìjùxìng [种 zhǒng]

dramatic [drə'mætɪk] ADJ **1**(marked, sudden) 戏(戲)剧(劇)性的 xìjùxìng de **2**(exciting, impressive) 激动(動)人心的 jīdòng rénxīn de **3**(theatrical) 戏(戲) 剧(劇)的 xìjù de

drank [dræŋk] PT of **drink**

drapes [dreɪps] (US) N PL 窗帘(簾) chuānglián

draught, (US) **draft** [drɑːft] N [c] 气(氣) 流 qìliú [股 gǔ]

draughts [drɑːfts] (Brit) N [U] 西洋跳棋 xīyáng tiàoqí

draw [drɔː] (pt **drew**, pp **drawn**) I VT 1 画(畫) huà 2 [+ curtains, blinds] (close) 拉上 lāshàng; (open) 拉开(開) lākāi II VI 1 (with pen, pencil etc) 画(畫)画(畫) huàhuà 2 ▶ **to draw (with/against sb)** (esp Brit: Sport) (与(與)某人)打成平局 (yǔ mǒurén) dǎchéng píngjú III N [c] 1 (esp Brit: Sport) 平局 píngjú [个(個) gè] 2 (lottery) 抽奖(獎) chōujiǎng [次 cì] ▶ **draw up** VT [+ document, plan] 草拟(擬) cǎonǐ

drawback ['drɔːbæk] N [c] 欠缺 qiànquē [个(個) gè]

drawer [drɔːʳ] N [c] 抽屉(屜) chōuti [个(個) gè]

drawing ['drɔːɪŋ] N 1 [c] (picture) 素描 sùmiáo [幅 fú] 2 [U] (skill, discipline) 绘(繪)画(畫) huìhuà

drawing pin (Brit) N [c] 图(圖)钉(釘) túdīng [枚 méi]

drawn [drɔːn] PP of **draw**

dread [drɛd] VT (fear) 惧(懼)怕 jùpà

dreadful ['drɛdful] ADJ 糟透的 zāotòu de

dream [driːm] (pt, pp **dreamed** or **dreamt**) I N [c] 1 梦(夢) mèng [场 cháng] 2 (ambition) 梦(夢)想 mèngxiǎng [个(個) gè] II VI ▶ **to dream about** (when asleep) 梦(夢)到 mèngdào

dreamt [drɛmt] PT, PP of **dream**

drench [drɛntʃ] VT (soak) 使湿(濕)透 shī shītòu

dress [drɛs] I N [c] 连(連)衣裙 liányīqún [条 tiáo] II VT 1 [+ child] 给(給)…穿衣 gěi...chuānyī 2 [+ salad] 拌 bàn III VI 穿衣 chuānyī ▶ **to dress o.s., get dressed** 穿好衣服 chuānhǎo yīfu ▶ **dress up** VI 1 (wear best clothes) 穿上盛装(裝) chuānshàng shèngzhuāng 2 ▶ **to dress up as** 化装(裝)成 huàzhuāng chéng

dresser ['drɛsəʳ] N [c] 1 (Brit: cupboard) 碗橱(櫥) wǎnchú [个(個) gè] 2 (US: chest of drawers) 梳妆(妝)台(臺) shūzhuāngtái [个(個) gè]

dressing gown N [c] 晨衣 chényī [套 tào]

dressing table N [c] 梳妆(妝)台(臺) shūzhuāngtái [个(個) gè]

drew [druː] PT of **draw**

dried [draɪd] ADJ [+ fruit, herbs] 干(乾)的 gān de; [+ eggs, milk] 粉状(狀)的 fěnzhuàng de

drier ['draɪəʳ] N = **dryer**

drill [drɪl] I N [c] 钻(鑽) zuàn [个 gè]; [of dentist] 钻(鑽)头(頭) zuàntóu [个 gè] II VT 在…上钻(鑽)孔 zài...shang zuānkǒng

drink [drɪŋk] (pt **drank**, pp **drunk**) I N 1 [c] (tea, water etc) 饮(飲)料 yǐnliào [种 zhǒng] 2 [c] (alcoholic) 酒 jiǔ [瓶 píng] II VT 喝 hē III VI (drink alcohol) 喝酒 hējiǔ ▶ **to have a drink** 喝一杯 hē yībēi; (alcoholic) 喝酒 hējiǔ

drive [draɪv] (pt **drove**, pp **driven**) I N 1 [c] (journey) 车(車)程 chēchéng [段 duàn] 2 [c] (also: **driveway**) 私家车(車)道 sījiā chēdào [条 tiáo] 3 [c] (also: **CD ROM/ disk drive**) 驱(驅)动(動)器 qūdòngqì [个(個) gè] II VT 1 [+ vehicle] 驾(駕)驶(駛) jiàshǐ 2 ▶ **to drive sb to the station/ airport** 驱(驅)车(車)送某人去车(車)站/飞(飛)机(機)场(場) qūchē sòng mǒurén qù chēzhàn/fēijīchǎng III VI 开(開)车(車) kāichē ▶ **to go for a drive** 开(開)车(車)兜风(風) kāichē dōufēng ▶ **it's a 3-hour drive from London** 到伦(倫)敦要3个(個)小时(時)的车(車)程 dào Lúndūn yào sān gè xiǎoshí de chēchéng ▶ **to drive sb mad/to desperation** 逼得某人发(發)疯(瘋)/绝(絕)望 bī de mǒurén fāfēng/juéwàng ▶ **to drive at 50 km an hour** 以每小时(時)50公里(裡)的速度驾(駕)车(車) yǐ měi xiǎoshí wǔshí gōnglǐ de sùdù jiàchē

driver ['draɪvəʳ] N [c] 1 [of own car] 驾(駕)驶(駛)员(員) jiàshǐyuán [位 wèi] 2 [of taxi, bus, lorry, train] 司机(機) sījī [位 wèi]

driver's license ['draɪvəz-] (US) N [c] 驾(駕)驶(駛)执(執)照(炤) jiàshǐ zhízhào [本 běn]

driveway ['draɪvweɪ] N [c] 车(車)道 chēdào [条 tiáo]

driving instructor N [c] 驾(駕)驶(駛)教练(練) jiàshǐ jiàoliàn [位 wèi]

driving licence (Brit) N [c] 驾(駕)驶(駛)执(執)照(炤) jiàshǐ zhízhào [本 běn]

driving test N [c] 驾(駕)驶(駛)执(執)

照(炤)考试(試) jiàshǐ zhízhào kǎoshì [次 cì]

drizzle ['drɪzl] vɪ ▸ **it is drizzling** 下着(著)毛毛雨 xiàzhe máomaoyǔ

drop [drɔp] I N **1** [c] (of liquid) 滴 dī **2** (reduction) ▸ **a drop in sth** 某物的下降 mǒuwù de xiàjiàng II vт **1** 失手落下 shīshǒu luòxià; (deliberately) 放 fàng **2** 将(將)…送到 jiāng…sòngdào III vɪ (amount, level +) 下降 xiàjiàng; [object +] 落下 luòxià
▸ **drop in** (inf) vɪ ▸ **to drop in (on sb)** 顺(順)便拜访(訪)(某人) shùnbiàn bàifǎng (mǒurén)
▸ **drop off** I vɪ (fall asleep) 睡着(著) shuìzháo II vт [+ passenger] 将(將)…送到 jiāng…sòngdào
▸ **drop out** vɪ (of college, university) 辍(輟)学(學) chuòxué

drought [draut] N [c/u] 旱灾(災) hànzāi [场 cháng]

drove [drəuv] PT of **drive**

drown [draun] I vт ▸ **to be drowned** 被淹死 bèi yānsǐ II vɪ [person, animal +] 溺死 nìsǐ

drug [drʌg] N [c] **1** (prescribed) 药(藥) yào [片 piàn] **2** (recreational) 毒品 dúpǐn [种 zhǒng] ▸ **to take drugs** 吸毒 xīdú
▸ **hard/soft drugs** 硬/软(軟)毒品 yìng/ruǎn dúpǐn

drug addict N [c] 吸毒成瘾(癮)者 xīdú chéngyǐnzhě [个 gè]

drug dealer N [c] 毒品贩(販)子 dúpǐn fànzi

drug-driving N [u] 吸毒驾(駕)车(車) xīdú jiàchē

druggist ['drʌgɪst] (US) N [c] **1** 药(藥)剂(劑)师(師) yàojìshī [位 wèi] **2** ▸ **druggist('s) (shop)** 药(藥)店 yàodiàn [家 jiā]

drugstore ['drʌgstɔːʳ] (US) N [c] 杂(雜)货(貨)店 záhuòdiàn [家 jiā]

drum [drʌm] I N [c] 鼓 gǔ [面 miàn] II **drums** NPL (kit) 鼓 gǔ

drummer ['drʌməʳ] N [c] 鼓手 gǔshǒu [位 wèi]

drunk [drʌŋk] I PP of **drink** II ADJ 醉的 zuì de ▸ **to get drunk** 喝醉了 hēzuì le

dry [draɪ] I ADJ **1** 干(乾)的 gān de **2** [+ climate, weather, day] 干(乾)燥的 gānzào de II vт 把…弄干(乾)

bǎ…nònggān III vɪ [paint, washing +] 变(變)干(乾) biàngān ▸ **to dry one's hands/hair** 擦干(乾)手/头(頭)发(髮) cāgān shǒu/tóufa

dry-cleaner ['draɪ'kliːnəʳ] N [c] (also: **dry cleaner's**) 干(乾)洗店 gānxǐdiàn [家 jiā]

dryer ['draɪəʳ] N [c] **1** (tumble dryer, spin-dryer) 干(乾)衣机(機) gānyījī [台 tái] **2** (hair dryer) 吹风(風)机(機) chuīfēngjī [个 gè]

duck [dʌk] N **1** [c] (bird) 鸭(鴨) yā [只 zhī] **2** [u] (as food) 鸭(鴨)肉 yāròu

due [djuː] I ADJ ▸ **to be due** [person, train, bus +] 应(應)到 yīng dào; [baby +] 预(預)期 yùqī; [rent, payment +] 应(應)支付 yīng zhīfù II ADV ▸ **due north/south** 正北方/南方 zhèng běifāng/nánfāng
▸ **due to…** (because of) 由于(於)… yóuyú…

dug [dʌg] PT, PP of **dig**

dull [dʌl] ADJ **1** [+ weather, day] 阴(陰)沉的 yīnchén de **2** (boring) 单(單)调(調)乏味的 dāndiào fáwèi de

dumb [dʌm] ADJ **1** 哑(啞)的 yǎ de **2** (pej: stupid, foolish) 愚蠢的 yúchǔn de

dump [dʌmp] I N [c] 垃圾场(場) lājīchǎng [个 gè] II vт **1** (get rid of) 倾(傾)倒 qīngdào **2** [+ computer data] 转(轉)储(儲) zhuǎnchǔ

Dumpster® ['dʌmpstəʳ] (US) N [c] (用以装(裝)运(運)工地废(廢)料的无(無)盖(蓋))废(廢)料筒 (yòngyǐ zhuāngyùn gōngdì fèiliào de wú gài) fèiliàotǒng [个 gè]

during ['djuərɪŋ] PREP **1** 在…期间(間) zài…qījiān **2** (at some point in) 在…时(時)候 zài…shíhou

dusk [dʌsk] N [u] 黄昏 huánghūn ▸ **at dusk** 黄昏时刻 huánghūn shíkè

dust [dʌst] N [u] (dirt: outdoors) 尘(塵)土 chéntǔ; (indoors) 灰尘(塵) huīchén

dustbin ['dʌstbɪn] (Brit) N [c] 垃圾箱 lājīxiāng [个 gè]

dustman ['dʌstmən] (Brit) (pl dustmen) N [c] 清洁(潔)工 qīngjiégōng [位 wèi]

dusty ['dʌstɪ] ADJ 满(滿)是尘(塵)土的 mǎn shì chéntǔ de

Dutch [dʌtʃ] I ADJ 荷兰(蘭)的 Hélán de II N [u] (language) 荷兰(蘭)语(語) Hélányǔ III **the Dutch** NPL (people) 荷兰(蘭)人 Hélánrén

duty ['djuːtɪ] I N [c/u] **1** (responsibility) 责(責)任 zérèn [个 gè] **2** (tax) 税(稅) shuì [种 zhǒng] II **duties** NPL (tasks) 任务(務) rènwù

duty-free ['djuːtɪ'friː] ADJ [+ drink, cigarettes] 免税(稅)的 miǎnshuì de
▶ **duty-free shop** 免税(稅)商店 miǎnshuì shāngdiàn

duvet ['duːveɪ] (Brit) N [c] 羽绒(絨)被 yǔróngbèi [床 chuáng]

DVD ['diːviː'diː] N [c] 光碟 guāngdié [张(張) zhāng] ▷ I've got that film on DVD. 我有那部电影的光碟。Wǒ yǒu nà bù diànyǐng de guāngdié.

DVD player N [c] DVD播放器 DVD bōfàngqì [台 tái]

dye [daɪ] I N [c/u] 染料 rǎnliào [种 zhǒng] II VT 染色 rǎnsè

dynamic [daɪ'næmɪk] ADJ 生气(氣)勃勃 的 shēngqì bóbó de

dyslexia [dɪs'lɛksɪə] N [u] 诵(誦)读(讀) 困难(難) sòngdú kùnnan

dyslexic [dɪs'lɛksɪk] ADJ 诵(誦)读(讀)有 困难(難)的 sòngdú yǒu kùnnan de

each [iːtʃ] I ADJ 每 měi II PRON (each one) 每个(個) měigè ▶ **each one of them** 他 们(們)中的每一个(個) tāmen zhōng de měi yī gè ▶ **each other** 互相 hùxiāng ▶ **they have 2 books each** 他们(們)每人 有两(兩)本书(書) tāmen měi rén yǒu liǎng běn shū ▶ **they cost 5 pounds each** 每个(個)售价(價)5镑(鎊) měigè shòujià wǔ bàng

> **each** 表示一个群体中的每一个人或物，强调的是每一个个体。**every** 指由两个以上的个体组成的群体中的所有的人或物，强调的是整体。He listened to every news bulletin...an equal chance for every child... 注意 **each** 指两个当中的任何一个。Each apartment has two bedrooms...We each carried a suitcase. **each** 和 **every** 后面都只能跟名词单数形式。

ear [ɪəʳ] N [c] 耳朵 ěrduo [只 zhī]

earache ['ɪəreɪk] N [c/u] 耳朵痛 ěrduo tòng

earlier ['əːlɪəʳ] I ADJ [+ date, time] 较(較) 早的 jiàozǎo de II ADV [leave, go +] 提早 tízǎo ▶ **earlier this year** 本年初 běn nián chū

early ['əːlɪ] I ADV **1** (in day, month) 在初期 zài chūqī **2** (before usual time) [get up, go to bed, arrive, leave +] 早 zǎo II ADJ [+ stage, career] 早期的 zǎoqī de ▶ **I usually get up early** 我通常早起床。wǒ tōngcháng zǎo qǐchuáng ▶ **early this morning** 今天一大早 jīntiān yīdàzǎo

▶**early in the morning** 清早 qīngzǎo
▶**you're early!** 你怎么(麼)这(這)么(麼)早！nǐ zěnme zhème zǎo!

earn [əːn] VT 挣(掙)得 zhèngdé ▶**to earn one's** or **a living** 谋(謀)生 móushēng

earnings ['əːnɪŋz] NPL 收入 shōurù

earphones ['ɪəfəunz] NPL 耳机(機) ěrjī

earring ['ɪərɪŋ] N [c] 耳环(環) ěrhuán [只 zhī]

earth [əːθ] N 1 [U/S] (also: **the Earth**) 地球 dìqiú 2 [U] (land surface) 陆(陸)地 lùdì 3 [U] (soil) 泥土 nítǔ

earthquake ['əːθkweɪk] N [c] 地震 dìzhèn [次 cì]

easily ['iːzɪlɪ] ADV 不费(費)力地 bù fèilì de

east [iːst] I N 1 [s/U] 东(東)方 dōngfāng 2 ▶**the East** (the Orient) 东(東)方国(國)家 dōngfāng guójiā II ADJ 东(東)部的 dōngbù de III ADV 向东(東)方 xiàng dōngfāng ▶**the east of Spain** 西班牙东(東)部 Xībānyá dōngbù ▶**to the east** 以东(東) yǐdōng ▶**east of ...** …以东(東) …yǐdōng

Easter ['iːstəʳ] N [U] 复(復)活节(節) Fùhuó Jié ▶**the Easter holidays** 复(復)活节(節)假期 Fùhuó Jié jiàqī

eastern ['iːstən] ADJ 1 (Geo) 东(東)部的 dōngbù de 2 ▶**Eastern** (oriental) 东(東)方的 Dōngfāng de

easy ['iːzɪ] ADJ 1 容易的 róngyì de 2 [+ life, time] 安逸的 ānyì de ▶**dogs are easy to train** 狗很容易训(訓)练(練) gǒu hěn róngyì xùnliàn ▶**it's easy to train dogs** 驯狗是容易的 xùngǒu shì róngyì de

eat [iːt] (pt ate, pp eaten ['iːtn]) I VT 吃 chī II VI 1 吃 chī 2 (have a meal) 吃饭(飯) chīfàn

eaten ['iːtn] PP of **eat**

e-book ['iːbuk] N [c] (also: **electronic book**) 电子书 diànzǐshū [本 běn]

echo ['ɛkəu] (pl echoes) N [c] 回音 huíyīn [个 gè]

e-cigarette ['iːsɪgəˌrɛt] N [c] 电(電)子香烟(煙) diànzǐ xiāngyān [支 zhǐ]

ecology [ɪ'kɔlədʒɪ] N [U] 1 (environment) 生态(態) shēngtài 2 (subject) 生态(態)学(學) shēngtàixué

economic [iːkə'nɔmɪk] ADJ 1 经(經)济(濟)的 jīngjì de 2 (profitable) 有利可图(圖)的 yǒulì-kětú de

economical [iːkə'nɔmɪkl] ADJ 节(節)约(約)的 jiéyuē de

economics [iːkə'nɔmɪks] N [U] 经(經)济(濟)学(學) jīngjìxué

economy [ɪ'kɔnəmɪ] N 1 [c] 经(經)济(濟) jīngjì [种 zhǒng] 2 [U] (thrift) 节(節)约(約) jiéyuē

eczema ['ɛksɪmə] N [U] 湿(濕)疹 shīzhěn

edge [ɛdʒ] N [c] 1 [of road, town] 边(邊)缘(緣) biānyuán [个 gè] 2 [of table, chair] 棱(稜) léng

Edinburgh ['ɛdɪnbərə] N 爱(愛)丁堡 Àidīngbǎo

editor ['ɛdɪtəʳ] N [c] 编(編)辑(輯) biānjí [个 gè]

educate ['ɛdjukeɪt] VT 教育 jiàoyù

education [ɛdju'keɪʃən] N [U/S] 教育 jiàoyù

effect [ɪ'fɛkt] I N [c/U] 影响(響) yǐngxiǎng [个 gè] II **effects** NPL (Cine) 特别(別)效果 tèbié xiàoguǒ ▶**to take effect** [drug +] 见(見)效 jiànxiào ▶**to have an effect on sb/sth** 对(對)某人/某事产(產)生影响(響) duì mǒurén/mǒushì chǎnshēng yǐngxiǎng

effective [ɪ'fɛktɪv] ADJ 有效的 yǒuxiào de

efficiency [ɪ'fɪʃənsɪ] N [U] 效率 xiàolù

efficient [ɪ'fɪʃənt] ADJ 效率高的 xiàolùgāo de

effort ['ɛfət] N 1 [U] 努力 nǔlì 2 [c] (attempt) 尝(嘗)试(試) chángshì [个 gè] ▶**to make an effort to do sth** 努力做某事 nǔlì zuò mǒushì

e.g. ADV ABBR (= exempli gratia) (for example) 举(舉)例来(來)说(說) jǔlì lái shuō

egg [ɛg] N [c] 蛋 dàn [个 gè]

eggplant ['ɛgplɑːnt] (US) N [c/U] 茄子 qiézi [个 gè]

Egypt ['iːdʒɪpt] N 埃及 Āijí

eight [eɪt] NUM 八 bā; see also/另见 **five**

eighteen [eɪ'tiːn] NUM 十八 shíbā; see also/另见 **fifteen**

eighteenth [eɪ'tiːnθ] NUM 第十八 dìshíbā; see also/另见 **fifth**

eighth [eɪtθ] NUM 1 第八 dìbā 2 (fraction) 八分之一 bā fēn zhī yī; see also/另见 **fifth**

eighty ['eɪtɪ] NUM 八十 bāshí; see also/另见 **fifty**

Eire ['εərə] N 爱(愛)尔(爾)兰(蘭)共和国(國) Ài'ěrlán Gònghéguó

either ['aɪðə'] I ADJ **1** (one or other) 两(兩)者任何一个(個) liǎngzhě rèn yī de **2** (both, each) 两(兩)者中每一方的 liǎngzhě zhōng měi yī fāng de ▸ **on either side** 在两(兩)边(邊) zài liǎng biān II PRON **1** (after negative) 两(兩)者之中任何一个(個) liǎngzhě zhī zhōng rènhé yī gè ▸ **I don't like either of them** 两(兩)个(個)我都不喜欢(歡) liǎng gè wǒ dōu bù xǐhuan **2** (after interrogative) 两(兩)者之中任何一个(個) liǎngzhě zhī zhōng rènhé yī gè III ADV (in negative statements) 也也 yě IV CONJ ▸ **either... or...** 要么(麼)…要么(麼)… yàome... yàome... ▸ **no, I don't either** 不，我也不 bù, wǒ yě bù

elastic [ɪ'læstɪk] N [U] 橡皮 xiàngpí

elastic band (Brit) N [c] 橡皮筋 xiàngpíjīn [根 gēn]

elbow ['εlbəu] N [c] (Anat) 肘 zhǒu [个 gè]

elder ['εldə'] ADJ [+ brother, sister] 年龄(齡)较(較)大的 niánlíng jiào dà de

elderly ['εldəlɪ] ADJ 年长(長)的 niánzhǎng de ▸ **elderly people** 老人家 lǎorenjia

eldest ['εldɪst] I ADJ 年龄(齡)最大的 niánlíng zuì dà de II N [s/pL] 年龄(齡)最大的孩子 niánlíng zuì dà de háizi

elect [ɪ'lεkt] VT 选(選)举(舉) xuǎnjǔ

election [ɪ'lεkʃən] N [c] 选(選)举(舉) xuǎnjǔ [次 cì] ▸ **to hold an election** 举(舉)行选(選)举(舉) jǔxíng xuǎnjǔ

electric [ɪ'lεktrɪk] ADJ **1** 电(電)动(動)的 diàndòng de **2** [+ current, charge, socket] 电(電)的 diàn de

electrical [ɪ'lεktrɪkl] ADJ 电(電)动(動)的 diàndòng de

electric guitar N [c/u] 电(電)吉他 diànjítā [把 bǎ]

electrician [ɪlεk'trɪʃən] N [c] 电(電)工 diàngōng [个 gè]

electricity [ɪlεk'trɪsɪtɪ] N [U] **1** (energy) 电(電) diàn **2** (supply) 供电(電) gōngdiàn

electric shock N [c] 触(觸)电(電) chùdiàn [次 cì]

electronic [ɪlεk'trɔnɪk] ADJ 电(電)子的 diànzǐ de

electronics [ɪlεk'trɔnɪks] N [U] 电(電)子学(學) diànzǐxué

elegant ['εlɪgənt] ADJ 优(優)雅的 yōuyǎ de

elementary school (US) N [c/u] 小学(學) xiǎoxué

elephant ['εlɪfənt] N [c] 大象 dàxiàng [头 tóu]

elevator ['εlɪveɪtə'] (US) N [c] 电(電)梯 diàntī [部 bù]

eleven [ɪ'lεvn] NUM 十一 shíyī; see also/另见 **five**

eleventh [ɪ'lεvnθ] NUM 第十一 dìshíyī; see also/另见 **fifth**

eliminate [ɪ'lɪmɪneɪt] VT **1** [+ poverty] 消除 xiāochú **2** [+ team, contestant, candidate] 淘汰 táotài

else [εls] ADV ▸ **or else** (otherwise) 否则(則) fǒuzé; (threatening) 要不然 yàobùrán ▸ Don't talk to me like that again, or else! 别这么跟我说话，要不够你受的！ Bié zhème gēn wǒ shuōhuà, yàobù gòu nǐ shòu de! ▸ **something else** 其他东(東)西 qítā dōngxi ▸ **anything else** 任何其他东(東)西 qítā dōngxi ▸ **what else?** 其他什么(麼)？ qítā shénme? ▸ **everywhere else** 其他任何地方 qítā rènhé dìngfang ▸ **everyone else** 其他人 qítā rén ▸ **nobody else** 没(沒)有其他人 méiyǒu qítā rén

elsewhere [εls'wεə'] ADV [be +] 在别(別)处(處) zài biéchù **2** [go +] 到别(別)处(處) dào biéchù

email ['i:meɪl] I N [c/u] 电(電)子邮(郵)件 diànzǐ yóujiàn [封 fēng] II VT **1** [+ person] 给(給)…发(發)电(電)子邮(郵)件 gěi...fā diànzǐ yóujiàn **2** [+ file, document] 用电(電)子邮(郵)件寄 yòng diànzǐ yóujiàn jì

email account N [c] 电(電)子邮(郵)件账(賬)号(號) diànzǐ yóujiàn zhànghào [个 gè]

email address N [c] 电(電)子邮(郵)件地址(阯) diànzǐ yóujiǎn dìzhǐ [个 gè]

embarrassed [ɪm'bærəst] ADJ ▸ **to be embarrassed** 不好意思的 bù hǎoyìsi de

embarrassing [ɪm'bærəsɪŋ] ADJ 令人尴(尷)尬的 lìng rén gāngà de

embassy ['εmbəsɪ] N [c] 大使馆(館) dàshǐguǎn [个 gè]

emergency [ɪˈməːdʒənsɪ] N [c] (*crisis*) 紧(緊)急情况(況) jǐnjí qíngkuàng [个 gè] ▸ **in an emergency** 在紧(緊)急情况(況)下 zài jǐnjí qíngkuàng xià

emergency room (US) N [c] 急诊(診)室 jízhěnshì [个 gè]

emigrate [ˈɛmɪgreɪt] VI 移居外国(國) yíjū wàiguó

emoji [ɪˈməʊdʒɪ] N [c] 表情符号(號) biǎoqíng fúhào [个 gè]

emotion [ɪˈməʊʃən] N [c/u] 感情 gǎnqíng [种 zhǒng]

emotional [ɪˈməʊʃənl] ADJ 易动(動)感情的 yì dòng gǎnqíng de

emperor [ˈɛmpərər] N [c] 皇帝 huángdì [个 gè]

emphasize [ˈɛmfəsaɪz] VT 强(強)调(調) qiángdiào

empire [ˈɛmpaɪər] N [c] 帝国(國) dìguó [个 gè]

employ [ɪmˈplɔɪ] VT 雇(僱)用 gùyòng ▸ **he was employed as a technician** 他受雇(僱)做技师(師) tā shòugù zuò jìshī

employee [ɪmplɔɪˈiː] N [c] 雇(僱)员(員) gùyuán [个 gè]

employer [ɪmˈplɔɪər] N [c] 雇(僱)主 gùzhǔ [个 gè]

employment [ɪmˈplɔɪmənt] N [u] 工作 gōngzuò

empty [ˈɛmptɪ] I ADJ 空的 kōng de II VT 倒空 dàokōng

encourage [ɪnˈkʌrɪdʒ] VT 1 [+ *person*] 鼓励(勵) gǔlì 2 [+ *activity, attitude*] 支持 zhīchí 3 [+ *growth, industry*] 助长(長) zhùzhǎng ▸ **to encourage sb to do sth** 鼓励(勵)某人去做某事 gǔlì mǒurén qù zuò mǒushì

encouragement [ɪnˈkʌrɪdʒmənt] N [u] 鼓励(勵) gǔlì

encyclop(a)edia [ɛnsaɪkləʊˈpiːdɪə] N [c] 百科全书(書) bǎikē quánshū

end [ɛnd] I N 1 [s] (*of period, event*) 末期 mòqī 2 [s] (*of film, book*) 末尾 mòwěi 3 [c] (*of street, queue, rope, table*) 尽(盡)头(頭) jìntóu [个 gè] 4 [c] (*of town*) 端 duān II VT (*finish, stop*) 终(終)止 zhōngzhǐ III VI [*meeting, film, book* +] 结(結)束 jiéshù ▸ **at the end of August** 在8月末 zài bāyuè mò ▸ **to come to an end** 完结(結) wánjié ▸ **in the end** 最终(終) zuìzhōng

▸ **end up** VI ▸ **to end up in/at** [+ *place*] 最终(終)到了 zuìzhōng dàole

ending [ˈɛndɪŋ] N [c] 结(結)局 jiéjú [个 gè] ▸ **a happy ending** 美满(滿)结(結)局 měimǎn jiéjú

enemy [ˈɛnəmɪ] N [c] 敌(敵)人 dírén [个 gè]

energetic [ɛnəˈdʒɛtɪk] ADJ 1 精力充沛的 jīnglì chōngpèi de 2 [+ *activity*] 生机(機)勃勃的 shēngjī bóbó de

energy [ˈɛnədʒɪ] N [u] 能源 néngyuán

engaged [ɪnˈgeɪdʒd] ADJ 1 (*to be married*) 已订(訂)婚的 yǐ dìnghūn de 2 (*Brit: Tel*) 被占(佔)用的 bèi zhànyòng de 3 (*Brit*) [+ *toilet*] 被占(佔)用的 bèi zhànyòng de ▸ **to get engaged (to)** 订(訂)婚 (与(與)…) dìnghūn (yǔ…)

engagement [ɪnˈgeɪdʒmənt] N [c] (*to marry*) 婚约(約) hūnyuē [个 gè]

engagement ring N [c] 订(訂)婚戒指 dìnghūn jièzhǐ [枚 méi]

engine [ˈɛndʒɪn] N [c] 1 (*Aut*) 发(發)动(動)机(機) fādòngjī [台 tái] 2 (*Rail*) 机(機)车(車) jīchē [部 bù]

engineer [ɛndʒɪˈnɪər] N [c] 1 (*who designs machines, bridges*) 工程师(師) gōngchéngshī [位 wèi] 2 (*who repairs machines, phones etc*) 机(機)械师(師) jīxièshī [位 wèi]

engineering [ɛndʒɪˈnɪərɪŋ] N [u] 1 工程 gōngchéng 2 (*science*) 工程学(學) gōngchéngxué

England [ˈɪŋglənd] N 英格兰(蘭) Yīnggélán

English [ˈɪŋglɪʃ] I ADJ 英国(國)的 Yīngguó de II N (*language*) 英语(語) Yīngyǔ III **the English** NPL (*people*) 英国(國)人 Yīngguórén ▸ **an English speaker** 一个(個)讲(講)英语(語)的人 yī gè jiǎng yīngyǔ de rén

Englishman [ˈɪŋglɪʃmən] N [c] (*pl* Englishmen) 英格兰(蘭)男人 Yīnggélán nánrén [个 gè]

Englishwoman [ˈɪŋglɪʃwumən] N [c] (*pl* Englishwomen) 英格兰(蘭)女人 Yīnggélán nǚrén [个 gè]

enjoy [ɪnˈdʒɔɪ] VT (*take pleasure in*) 享受…的乐(樂)趣 xiǎngshòu…de lèqù ▸ **to enjoy doing sth** 喜欢(歡)做某事 xǐhuān zuò mǒushì ▸ **to enjoy o.s.** 过(過)得快活 guò de kuàihuó

▶**enjoy your meal!** 吃好！chīhǎo!

enjoyable [ɪn'dʒɔɪəbl] ADJ 有乐(樂)趣的 yǒu lèqù de

enormous [ɪ'nɔːməs] ADJ **1** 庞(龐)大的 pángdà de **2** [+ pleasure, success, disappointment] 巨大的 jùdà de

enough [ɪ'nʌf] I ADJ [+ time, books, people] 足够(夠)的 zúgòu de II PRON (sufficient, more than desired) 足够(夠)的东(東)西 zúgòu de dōngxi III ADV ▶**big/old/tall enough** 足够(夠)大/到年龄(齡)了/足够(夠)高 zúgòu dà/dào niánlíng le/zúgòu gāo ▶**enough time/money to do sth** 有足够(夠)的时(時)间(間)/金钱(錢)去做某事 yǒu zúgòu de shíjiān/jīnqián qù zuò mǒushì ▶**have you got enough?** 你够(夠)吗(嗎)？nǐ gòu ma ▶**enough to eat** 够(夠)吃 gòuchī ▶**will 5 be enough?** 5个(個)够(夠)吗(嗎)？wǔ gè gòu ma? ▶**I've had enough!** 我受够(夠)了！wǒ shòugòu le! ▶**that's enough, thanks** 足矣，谢(謝)谢(謝) zúyǐ, xièxie

enquiry [ɪn'kwaɪərɪ] N = **inquiry**

enrol, (US) **enroll** [ɪn'rəul] I VT **1** 招…入学(學) zhāo…rùxué **2** (on course, in club) 注(註)册(冊) zhùcè II VI (at school, university, on course, in club) 注(註)册(冊) zhùcè

en suite ['ɔnswiːt] (Brit) ADJ [+ bathroom] 接连(連)的 jiēlián de

ensure [ɪn'ʃuər] (frm) VT 保证(證) bǎozhèng

enter ['ɛntər] I VT **1** [+ room, building] 进(進)入 jìnrù **2** [+ race, competition] 参(參)加 cānjiā **3** (Comput) [+ data] 输(輸)入 shūrù II VI 进(進)来(來) jìnlái

entertain [ɛntə'teɪn] VT **1** (amuse) 给(給)…娱(娛)乐(樂) gěi…yúlè **2** (invite) [+ guest] 招待 zhāodài

entertainment [ɛntə'teɪnmənt] N [U] 娱(娛)乐(樂)活动(動) yúlè huódòng

enthusiasm [ɪn'θuːzɪæzəm] N [U] 热(熱)情 rèqíng ▶**enthusiasm for sth** 对(對)某事的热(熱)情 duì mǒushì de rèqíng

enthusiastic [ɪnθuːzɪ'æstɪk] ADJ 极(極)感兴(興)趣的 jí gǎn xìngqù de; [+ response, reception] 热(熱)情的 rèqíng de ▶**to be enthusiastic about sth** 对(對)某事满(滿)怀(懷)热(熱)情

duì mǒushì mǎnhuái rèqíng

entire [ɪn'taɪər] ADJ 整个(個)的 zhěnggè de

entirely [ɪn'taɪəlɪ] ADV 完全地 wánquán de

entrance ['ɛntrns] N [C] 入口 rùkǒu [个 gè] ▶**the entrance to sth** 某处(處)的入口 mǒuchù de rùkǒu

entry ['ɛntrɪ] N **1** [C] (way in) 入口 rùkǒu [个 gè] **2** [C] (in competition) 登记(記) dēngjì [个 gè] **3** [C] (item) (in diary) 项(項)目 xiàngmù [个 gè] (Comput) 输(輸)入 shūrù [项 xiàng] ▶**"no entry"** (to land, room) "禁止入内(內)" "jìnzhǐ rùnèi"; (Aut) "禁止通行" "jìnzhǐ tōngxíng"

envelope ['ɛnvələup] N [C] 信封 xìnfēng [个 gè]

environment [ɪn'vaɪərnmənt] N [C/U] 环(環)境 huánjìng [个 gè] ▶**the environment** (natural world) 自然环(環)境 zìrán huánjìng

environmental [ɪnvaɪərn'mɛntl] ADJ 环(環)境保护(護)的 huánjìng bǎohù de

environmentally friendly [ɪnvaɪərn'mɛntl-] ADJ 不污染环(環)境的 bù wūrǎn huánjìng de

envy ['ɛnvɪ] I N [U] 羡(羨)慕 xiànmù II VT (be jealous of) 羡(羨)慕 xiànmù ▶**to envy sb sth** 羡(羨)慕某人的某物 xiànmù mǒurén de mǒuwù

epilepsy ['ɛpɪlɛpsɪ] N [U] 癫(癲)痫(癇) diānxián

epileptic [ɛpɪ'lɛptɪk] N [C] 癫(癲)痫(癇)病人 diānxián bìngrén [个 gè]

episode ['ɛpɪsəud] N [C] (TV, Rad) 集 jí

equal ['iːkwl] I ADJ **1** 相等的 xiāngděng de **2** [+ intensity, importance] 同样(樣)的 tóngyàng de II VT **1** [+ number, amount] 等于(於) děngyú **2** (match, rival) 比得上 bǐ de shàng ▶**they are roughly equal in size** 它们(們)大小差不多 tāmen dàxiǎo chàbuduō ▶**to be equal to** (the same as) 与(與)…相同 yǔ…xiāngtóng ▶**79 minus 14 equals 65** 79减(減)14等于(於)65 qīshíjiǔ jiǎn shísì děngyú liùshíwǔ

equality [iː'kwɔlɪtɪ] N [U] 平等 píngděng

equally ['iːkwəlɪ] ADV **1** (share, divide +) 平等地 píngděng de **2** [+ good, important] 同样(樣)地 tóngyàng de

equator [ɪˈkweɪtə^r] N ▸ **the equator** 赤道 chìdào

equipment [ɪˈkwɪpmənt] N [U] 设(設)备(備) shèbèi

equivalent [ɪˈkwɪvələnt] I ADJ 相同的 xiāngtóng de II N [c] 相当(當)的人/物 xiāngdāng de rén/wù [个 gè]

ER N ABBR (US: Med: = **emergency room**) 急诊(診)室 jízhěnshì [个 gè]

eraser [ɪˈreɪzə^r] (esp US) N [c] 橡皮 xiàngpí [块 kuài]

e-reader, eReader [ˈiːriːdə^r] N [c] 电(電)子阅(閱)读(讀)器 diànzǐ yuèdú qì [台 tái]

error [ˈɛrə^r] N [c/U] 差错(錯) chācuò [个 gè] ▸ **to make an error** 犯错(錯)误(誤) fàn cuòwù

escalator [ˈeskəleɪtə^r] N [c] 自动(動)扶梯 zìdòng fútī [部 bù]

escape [ɪsˈkeɪp] I VI 1 (get away) 逃走 táozǒu 2 (from jail) 逃跑 táopǎo 3 (from accident) ▸ **to escape unhurt** 安然逃脱(脫) ānrán táotuō II VT [+ injury] 避免 bìmiǎn ▸ **to escape from** [+ place] 从(從)…逃跑 cóng…táopǎo; [+ person] 避开(開) bìkāi

especially [ɪsˈpɛʃlɪ] ADV 尤其 yóuqí

essay [ˈeseɪ] N (Scol) 论(論)文 lùnwén

essential [ɪˈsɛnʃl] I ADJ 1 (necessary, vital) 必要的 bìyào de 2 (basic) 基本的 jīběn de II **essentials** N PL (necessities) 必需品 bìxūpǐn ▸ **it is essential to…** 必须(須)… bìxū…

estate [ɪsˈteɪt] N [c] 1 (land) 庄(莊)园(園) zhuāngyuán [个 gè] 2 (Brit) (also: **housing estate**) 住宅区(區) zhùzháiqū

estate agent (Brit) N [c] 房地产(產)经(經)纪(紀)人 fángdìchǎn jīngjìrén [个 gè]

estimate [n ˈɛstɪmət, vb ˈɛstɪmeɪt] I N [c] 估计(計) gūjì [种 zhǒng] II VT (reckon, calculate) 估计(計) gūjì ▸ **the damage was estimated at 300 million pounds** 估计(計)损(損)失为(為)3亿(億)英镑(鎊) gūjì sǔnshī wéi sānyì yīngbàng

etc. (esp US) **etc.** ABBR (= **et cetera**) 等等 děngděng

Ethiopia [iːθɪˈəʊpɪə] N 埃塞俄比亚(亞) Āisài'ébǐyà

ethnic [ˈeθnɪk] ADJ 种(種)族的 zhǒngzú de

e-ticket [ˈiːtɪkɪt] N [c] 电(電)子客票 diànzǐ kèpiào [张 zhāng]

EU N ABBR (= **European Union**) ▸ **the EU** 欧(歐)洲联(聯)盟 Ōuzhōu Liánméng

euro [ˈjuərəu] (pl **euros**) N [c] 欧(歐)元 Ōuyuán [个 gè]

Europe [ˈjuərəp] N 欧(歐)洲 Ōuzhōu

European [juərəˈpiːən] I ADJ 欧(歐)洲的 Ōuzhōu de II N [c] (person) 欧(歐)洲人 Ōuzhōurén [个 gè]

European Union N ▸ **the European Union** 欧(歐)洲联(聯)盟 Ōuzhōu Liánméng

evacuate [ɪˈvækjueɪt] VT 1 [+ people] 疏散 shūsàn 2 [+ place] 撤离(離) chèlí

evaluate [ɪˈvæljueɪt] VT 评(評)估 pínggū

even [ˈiːvn] I ADV 甚至 shènzhì II ADJ 1 (flat) 平坦的 píngtǎn de 2 [+ number] 偶数(數)的 ǒushù de ▸ **he didn't even hear what I said** 他甚至根本没(沒)听(聽)见(見)我的话(話) tā shènzhì gēnběn méi tīngjiàn wǒ de huà ▸ **even more** 甚至更多 shènzhì gèng duō ▸ **even if** 即使 jíshǐ ▸ **even though** 尽(儘)管 jǐnguǎn ▸ **not even** 连(連)…也不 lián…yě bù ▸ **even on Sundays** 甚至星期天 shènzhì xīngqītiān

evening [ˈiːvnɪŋ] N [c/U] 1 (early) 傍晚 bàngwǎn [个 gè] 2 (late) 晚上 wǎnshang [个 gè] 3 (whole period, event) 晚上 wǎnshang [个 gè] ▸ **in the evening** 在晚上 zài wǎnshang ▸ **this evening** 今晚 jīnwǎn ▸ **tomorrow/yesterday evening** 明/昨晚 míng/zuówǎn

evening class N [c] 夜校 yèxiào [个 gè]

event [ɪˈvent] N [c] 事件 shìjiàn [个 gè]

eventually [ɪˈventʃuəlɪ] ADV 1 (finally) 终(終)于(於) zhōngyú 2 (ultimately) 最终(終) zuìzhōng

> 请勿将 eventually 和 finally 混淆。如果某事拖延了很久，或者经历了相当复杂的过程后终于发生了，可以说 eventually 发生了，Eventually, they got to the hospital… I found Victoria Avenue eventually. eventually 还可以表示某一系列事情中的最后一件事，通常这最后的一件事是前面一系列事情的结果。Eventually, they were forced to return to England. 在经历了长期等待或期盼后，某事终于发生了，可

以说它 **finally** 发生了。*Finally, I went to bed... The heat of the sun finally became too much for me.* **finally** 还可以表示发生的一系列事情当中最后的一件事。*The sky turned red, then purple, and finally black.*

ever ['evə^r] ADV 从(從)来(來) cónglái ▸ **have you ever seen it/been there** *etc*? 你曾经(經)见(見)过(過)它/去过(過)那儿(兒)吗(嗎)? nǐ céngjīng jiànguo tā/qùguo nàr děng ma? ▸ **ever since** *(adv)* 从(從)…以来(來) cóng… yǐlái ▸ *We have been friends ever since.* 我们从那时以来一直是朋友。Wǒmen cóng nàshí yǐlái yīzhí shì péngyou.; *(conj)* 自从(從) zìcóng ▸ *Jack has loved trains ever since he was a boy.* 杰克自小就喜爱火车。Jiékè zìxiǎo jiù xǐ'ài huǒchē. ▸ **the best ever** 迄今最佳 qìjīn zuìjiā ▸ **hardly ever** 几(幾)乎从(從)不 jīhū cóngbù

KEYWORD

every ['evrɪ] ADJ **1** *(each)* 每个(個) měigè ▸ **every village should have a post office** 每个(個)村庄(莊)都应(應)该(該)有一个(個)邮(郵)局 měigè cūnzhuāng dōu yīnggāi yǒu yī gè yóujú **2** *(all possible)* 一切可能的 yīqiè kěnéng de ▸ **recipes for every occasion** 各个(個)场(場)合均适(適)用的菜谱(譜) gègè chǎnghé jūn shìyòng de càipǔ **3** *(with time words)* 每 měi ▸ **every day/week** 每天/周(週) měi tiān/zhōu ▸ **every Sunday** 每个(個)星期天 měigè xīngqītiān ▸ **every now and then** *or* **again** 不时(時)地 bùshí de

everybody ['evrɪbɒdɪ] PRON 每人 měirén ▸ **everybody knows about it** 谁(誰)都知道 shuí dōu zhīdào ▸ **everybody else** 其他所有人 qítā suǒyǒurén

everyone ['evrɪwʌn] PRON = **everybody** 请勿将 **everyone** 和 **every one** 混淆。**everyone** 总是指人，并且用作单数名词。*Everyone likes him...On behalf of everyone in the school, I'd like to thank you.* 在短语 **every one** 中，**one** 是代词，在不同的上下文当中，它能够指

代任何人或事物。其后经常紧随单词 *of*，*We've saved seeds from every one of our plants...Every one of them phoned me.* 在这些例子当中，**every one** 是表达 **all** 的含义，而且语气更强烈。

everything ['evrɪθɪŋ] PRON 所有事物 suǒyǒu shìwù ▸ **is everything OK?** 都还(還)好吧? dōu hái hǎo ba? ▸ **everything is ready** 所有都准(準)备(備)就绪(緒) suǒyǒu dōu zhǔnbèi jiùxù ▸ **he did everything possible** 他尽(盡)了最大努力 tā jìnle zuìdà nǔlì

everywhere ['evrɪweə^r] **I** ADV 处(處)处(處) chùchù **II** PRON 所有地方 suǒyǒu dìfang ▸ **there's rubbish everywhere** 到处(處)都是垃圾 dàochù dōu shì lājī ▸ **everywhere you go** 无(無)论(論)你去哪里(裡) wúlùn nǐ qù nǎlǐ

evidence ['evɪdns] N [U] **1** *(proof)* 根据(據) gēnjù **2** *(signs, indications)* 迹(跡)象 jìxiàng

evil ['iːvl] ADJ 邪恶(惡)的 xié'è de

ex- [eks] PREFIX [+ *husband, president etc*] 前 qián ▸ **my ex-wife** 我的前妻 wǒ de qiánqī

exact [ɪg'zækt] ADJ 确(確)切的 quèqiè de

exactly [ɪg'zæktlɪ] ADV **1** *(precisely)* 确(確)切地 quèqiè de **2** *(indicating agreement)* 一点(點)不错(錯) yìdiǎn bùcuò ▸ **at 5 o'clock exactly** 在5点(點)整时(時) zài wǔ diǎn zhěng shí ▸ **not exactly** 不完全是 bù wánquán shì

exaggerate [ɪg'zædʒəreɪt] **I** VI 夸(誇)张(張) kuāzhāng **II** VT *(overemphasize)* 夸(誇)大 kuādà

exam [ɪg'zæm] N 测(測)验(驗) cèyàn ▸ **pass an exam** 表示考试通过，若没通过，则说 **fail an exam**。参加考试，用动词 **take**，在英式英语中则用 **sit an exam**。

examination [ɪgzæmɪ'neɪʃən] N **1** [C] *(frm: Scol, Univ)* 考试(試) kǎoshì [次 cì] **2** [C/U] *(Med)* 体(體)检(檢) tǐjiǎn [次 cì]

examine [ɪg'zæmɪn] VT **1** *(inspect)* 检(檢)查 jiǎnchá **2** *(Scol, Univ)* 对(對)…进(進)行测(測)验(驗) duì…jìnxíng cèyàn **3** *(Med)* 检(檢)查 jiǎnchá

example [ɪg'zɑːmpl] N [C] 例子 lìzi [个 gè] ▸ **for example** 例如 lìrú ▸ **an**

example of sth 某物的例子 mǒuwù de lìzi

excellence [ˈɛksələns] N [U] 卓越 zhuóyuè

excellent [ˈɛksələnt] I ADJ 极(極)好的 jí hǎo de II INT ▶ excellent! 太好了! tài hǎo le!

except [ɪkˈsɛpt] PREP 除了 chúle
▶ except for 除了…外 chúle…wài
▶ except if/when …时(時)例外 …shí lìwài

exception [ɪkˈsɛpʃən] N [C] 例外 lìwài [个 gè]

exchange [ɪksˈtʃeɪndʒ] I VT 1 [+ gifts, addresses] 交换(換) jiāohuàn 2 ▶ to exchange sth (for sth) [+ goods] 用某物 交换(換) (某物) yòng mǒuwù jiāohuàn (mǒuwù) II N [C/U] [of students, sportspeople] 交流 jiāoliú [次 cì] ▶ in exchange (for) 作为(為)(对(對)…的) 交换(換) zuòwéi (duì…de) jiāohuàn

exchange rate N [C] 汇(匯)率 huìlǜ [个 gè]

excited [ɪkˈsaɪtɪd] ADJ 兴(興)奋(奮)的 xīngfèn de ▶ to be excited about sth/ about doing sth 对(對)某事/做某事感 到激动(動) duì mǒushì/zuò mǒushì gǎndào jīdòng ▶ to get excited 激 动(動)兴(興)奋(奮) jīdòng xīngfèn

excitement [ɪkˈsaɪtmənt] N [U] 兴(興) 奋(奮) xīngfèn

exciting [ɪkˈsaɪtɪŋ] ADJ 令人兴(興) 奋(奮)的 lìng rén xīngfèn de

exclamation mark, (Brit)
exclamation point (US)
[ɛkskləˈmeɪʃən (-)] N [C] 感叹(嘆)号(號) gǎntànhào [个 gè]

excluding [ɪksˈkluːdɪŋ] PREP 不包括 bù bāokuò

excuse [n ɪksˈkjuːs, vb ɪksˈkjuːz] I N [C/U] 借口 jièkǒu [个 gè] II VT 1 (justify) 是… 的正当(當)理由 shì…de zhèngdàng lǐyóu 2 (forgive) 原谅(諒) yuánliàng ▶ to make an excuse 找借口 zhǎo jièkǒu
▶ excuse me! (attracting attention) 劳(勞)驾(駕)! láojià; (as apology) 对(對)不起! duìbuqǐ ▶ excuse me, please 请(請)原谅(諒) qǐng yuánliàng
▶ excuse me? (US) 对(對)不起, 你说(說)什么(麼)? duìbuqǐ, nǐ shuō shénme?

exercise [ˈɛksəsaɪz] I N 1 [U] (physical exertion) 运(運)动(動) yùndòng 2 [C] (series of movements) 练(練)习(習) liànxí [个 gè] 3 [C] (Scol, Mus) 练(練)习(習) liànxí [个 gè] II VT [+ muscles] 锻(鍛) 炼(鍊) duànliàn; [+ mind] 运(運)用 yùnyòng III VI [person +] 锻(鍛)炼(鍊) duànliàn ▶ to take or get exercise 做健 身活动(動) zuò jiànshēn huódòng ▶ to do exercises (Sport) 锻(鍛)炼(鍊)身 体(體) duànliàn shēntǐ

exhaust [ɪgˈzɔːst] N (esp Brit) 1 [C] (also: exhaust pipe) 排气(氣)管 páiqìguǎn [根 gēn] 2 [U] (fumes) 废(廢)气(氣) fèiqì

exhausted [ɪgˈzɔːstɪd] ADJ 精疲力竭的 jīng pí lì jié de

exhibition [ɛksɪˈbɪʃən] N [C] 展览(覽) 会(會) zhǎnlǎnhuì [个 gè]

exist [ɪgˈzɪst] VI 1 (be present) 存在 cúnzài 2 (live, subsist) 生存 shēngcún

exit [ˈɛksɪt] I N [C] 出口 chūkǒu [个 gè] II VT (Comput) 退出 tuìchū ▶ to exit from sth [+ room, motorway] 离(離) 开(開)某处(處) líkāi mǒuchù

expect [ɪksˈpɛkt] I VT 1 (anticipate) 预(預)料 yùliào 2 (await) 期待 qīdài 3 [+ baby] 怀(懷)有 huáiyǒu 4 (suppose) 料想 liàoxiǎng II VI ▶ to be expecting (be pregnant) 怀(懷)孕 huáiyùn ▶ to expect sth to happen 预(預)期某事 将(將)发(發)生 yùqī mǒushì jiāng fāshēng ▶ I expect so 我想会(會)的 wǒ xiǎng huì de

expense [ɪksˈpɛns] I N [C/U] 费(費) 用 fèiyòng [笔 bǐ] II expenses NPL 经(經) 费(費) jīngfèi

expensive [ɪksˈpɛnsɪv] ADJ 1 昂贵(貴)的 ángguì de 2 [+ mistake] 代价(價)高的 dàijià gāo de

experience [ɪksˈpɪərɪəns] I N 1 [U] (in job) 经(經)验(驗) jīngyàn 2 [U] (of life) 阅(閱)历(歷) yuèlì 3 [C] (individual event) 经(經)历(歷) jīnglì [个 gè] II VT [+ feeling, problem] 体(體)验(驗) tǐyàn

experienced [ɪksˈpɪərɪənst] ADJ 有 经(經)验(驗)的 yǒu jīngyàn de

experiment [n ɪksˈpɛrɪmənt, vb ɪksˈpɛrɪment] I N [C] 1 (Sci) 实(實) 验(驗) shíyàn [个 gè] 2 (trial) 试(試)用 shìyòng [次 cì] II VI (试(試)验(驗) shìyàn ▶ to perform or conduct or carry out an

experiment 做实(實)验(驗) zuò shíyàn

expert ['ɛkspəːt] I N [c] 专(專)家 zhuānjiā [位 wèi] II ADJ [+ opinion, help, advice] 专(專)家的 zhuānjiā de ▸ an expert on sth 某事的专(專)家 mǒushì de zhuānjiā

expertise [ɛkspəː'tiːz] N [U] 专(專)门(門)知识(識) zhuānmén zhīshi

expire [ɪks'paɪəʳ] VI [passport, licence +] 过(過)期 guòqī

explain [ɪks'pleɪn] VT 1 [+ situation, contract] 解释(釋) jiěshì 2 [+ decision, actions] 阐(闡)明 chǎnmíng ▸ to explain why/how etc 解释(釋)为(為)什么(麼)/如何[等] jiěshì wèi shénme/rúhé děng ▸ to explain sth to sb 向某人解释(釋)某事 xiàng mǒurén jiěshì mǒushì

explanation [ɛksplə'neɪʃən] N 1 [c/u] (reason) ▸ explanation (for) (对(對)···的)解释(釋) (duì...de) jiěshì 2 [c] (description) ▸ explanation (of) (···的)说(說)明 (...de) shuōmíng [个 gè]

explode [ɪks'pləud] I VI 爆炸 bàozhà II VT [+ bomb, tank] 使爆炸 shǐ bàozhà

exploit [ɪks'plɔɪt] VT [+ resources] 开(開)发(發) kāifā; [+ person, idea] 剥(剝)削 bōxuē

explore [ɪks'plɔːʳ] I VT 探索 tànsuǒ II VI 探险(險) tànxiǎn

explosion [ɪks'pləuʒən] N [c] 1 爆炸 bàozhà [个 gè] 2 (of population) 激增 jīzēng [个 gè]

export [vb ɛks'pɔːt, n 'ɛkspɔːt] VT 输(輸)出 shūchū II N 1 [U] (process) 出口 chūkǒu 2 [c] (product) 出口物 chūkǒuwù [宗 zōng]

express [ɪks'prɛs] VT 表达(達) biǎodá; [+ service, mail] 特快的 tèkuài de ▸ to express o.s. 表达(達)自己的意思 biǎodá zìjǐ de yìsi

expression [ɪks'prɛʃən] N 1 [c] (word, phrase) 言辞(辭) yáncí [种 zhǒng] 2 [c/u] (on face) 表情 biǎoqíng [种 zhǒng]

extension [ɪks'tɛnʃən] N [c] 1 (of building) 扩(擴)建部分 kuòjiàn bùfen [个 gè] 2 (of contract, visa) 延期 yánqī [次 cì] 3 (Tel) 分机(機) fēnjī [部 bù] ▸ extension 3718 (Tel) 3718分机(機) sān qī yī bā fēnjī

extent [ɪks'tɛnt] N [U/s] (of problem, damage) 程度 chéngdù ▸ to a certain extent 在一定程度上 zài yīdìng chéngdù shang

extinct [ɪks'tɪŋkt] ADJ [+ animal, plant] 灭(滅)绝(絕)的 mièjué de

extra ['ɛkstrə] I ADJ 额(額)外的 éwài de II ADV (in addition) 额(額)外地 éwài de III N [c] 1 (luxury) 额(額)外的事物 éwài de shìwù [件 jiàn] 2 (surcharge) 另外的收费(費) lìngwài de shōufèi [项 xiàng] ▸ wine will cost extra 酒另外收钱(錢) jiǔ lìngwài shōuqián

extraordinary [ɪks'trɔːdnrɪ] ADJ 非凡的 fēifán de

extreme [ɪks'triːm] ADJ 1 极(極)度的 jídù de 2 [+ opinions, methods] 极端的 jíduān de

extremely [ɪks'triːmlɪ] ADV 非常 fēicháng

extremist [ɪks'triːmɪst] N [c] 过(過)激分子 guòjī fènzǐ [个 gè]

eye [aɪ] N [c] (Anat) 眼睛 yǎnjing [只 zhī] ▸ to keep an eye on sb/sth 密切注意某人/某事 mìqiè zhùyì mǒurén/mǒushì

eyebrow ['aɪbrau] N [c] 眉毛 méimao [个 gè]

eyelash ['aɪlæʃ] N [c] 眼睫毛 yǎnjiémáo [根 gēn]

eyelid ['aɪlɪd] N [c] 眼皮 yǎnpí [个 gè]

eyeliner ['aɪlaɪnəʳ] N [c/u] 眼线(線)笔(筆) yǎnxiànbǐ

eyeshadow ['aɪʃædəu] N [c/u] 眼影 yǎnyǐng

eyesight ['aɪsaɪt] N [U] 视(視)力 shìlì

f

fabric ['fæbrɪk] N [c/u] 织(織)物 zhīwù [件 jiàn]

fabulous ['fæbjuləs] ADJ (inf) 极(極)好的 jíhǎo de

face [feɪs] I N 1 [c] (Anat) 脸(臉) liǎn [张 zhāng] 2 [c] (expression) 表情 biǎoqíng [个 gè] II VT 1 [+ direction] 面向 miànxiàng 2 [+ unpleasant situation] 面对(對) miànduì ▶ I can't or couldn't face it 我应(應)付不了 wǒ yìngfù bùliǎo ▶ to come face to face with [+ person] 与(與)⋯⋯面对(對)面 yǔ⋯miàn duì miàn ▶ face up to VT FUS 1 [+ truth, facts] 接受 jiēshòu 2 [+ responsibilities, duties] 承担(擔) chéngdān

Facebook® ['feɪsbʊk] N [u] 脸(臉)谱(譜)网(網) Liǎnpǔ wǎng

face cloth (Brit) N [c] 洗脸(臉)毛巾 xǐliǎn máojīn [条 tiáo]

FaceTime® ['feɪs,taɪm] N [u] 视(視)频(頻)通话(話) shìpín tōnghuà

facility [fə'sɪlɪtɪ] N [c] (service) 设(設)施 shèshī [种 zhǒng]

fact [fækt] N [c] 真相 zhēnxiàng [个 gè] ▶ in (actual) fact, as a matter of fact (for emphasis) 实(實)际(際)上 shíjìshang ▶ facts and figures 精确(確)的资(資)料 jīngquè de zīliào

factory ['fæktərɪ] N [c] 工厂(廠) gōngchǎng [家 jiā]

fail [feɪl] I VT [+ exam, test] 没(沒)有通过(過) méiyǒu tōngguò II VI 1 [candidate +] 没(沒)通过(過) méi

tōngguò 2 [attempt, plan, remedy +] 失败(敗) shībài ▶ to fail to do sth 未能做某事 wèi néng zuò mǒushì

failure ['feɪljəʳ] N 1 [c/u] (lack of success) 失败(敗) shībài 2 [c] ▶ failure to do sth 没(沒)有做某事 méiyǒu zuò mǒushì

faint [feɪnt] I ADJ 1 [+ sound, light, smell, hope] 微弱的 wēiruò de 2 [+ mark, trace] 隐(隱)约(約)的 yǐnyuē de II VI 晕(暈)倒 yūndǎo ▶ to feel faint 感到眩晕(暈) gǎndào xuànyūn

fair [fɛəʳ] I ADJ 1 (just, right) 公平的 gōngpíng de 2 (quite large) 相当(當)的 xiāngdāng de 3 (quite good) 大体(體)的 dàtǐ de 4 [+ skin, complexion] 白皙的 báixī de; [+ hair] 金色的 jīnsè de II N [c] 1 (trade fair) 交易会(會) jiāoyìhuì [届 jiè] 2 (Brit) (also: funfair) 游(遊)乐(樂)场(場) yóulèchǎng [座 zuò] ▶ it's not fair! 太不公平了! tài bù gōngpíng le!

fairground ['fɛəgraʊnd] N [c] 游(遊)乐(樂)场(場) yóulèchǎng [座 zuò]

fairly ['fɛəlɪ] ADV 1 (justly) 公平地 gōngpíng de 2 (quite) 相当(當) xiāngdāng

faith [feɪθ] N 1 [u] (trust) 信任 xìnrèn 2 [u] (religious belief) 信仰 xìnyǎng ▶ to have faith in sb/sth 相信某人/某事 xiāngxìn mǒurén/mǒushì

faithful ['feɪθful] ADJ 忠实(實)的 zhōngshí de

faithfully ['feɪθfəlɪ] ADV ▶ Yours faithfully (Brit) 您忠实(實)的 nín zhōngshí de

fake [feɪk] I N [c] 赝(贗)品 yànpǐn [件 jiàn] II ADJ 假的 jiǎ de

fall [fɔːl] (pt fell, pp fallen) I VI 1 掉 diào 2 [snow, rain +] 下 xià 3 [price, temperature, currency +] 下降 xiàjiàng II N 1 [c] [of person] 摔倒 shuāidǎo [次 cì] 2 [c] (in price, temperature) 下降 xiàjiàng [次 cì] 3 [c/u] (US: autumn) 秋天 qiūtiān [个 gè] ▶ to fall in love (with sb/sth) 爱(愛)上(某人/某事) àishàng (mǒurén/mǒushì) ▶ fall down VI 1 [person +] 摔倒 shuāidǎo 2 [building +] 倒塌 dǎotā ▶ fall off VI [person, object +] 掉下 diàoxià ▶ fall over VI [person, object +] 跌倒 diēdǎo

▶**fall through** VI [*plan* +] 落空 luòkōng

fallen ['fɔːlən] PP of **fall**

false [fɔːls] ADJ 假的 jiǎ de

fame [feɪm] N [U] 声(聲)誉(譽) shēngyù

familiar [fə'mɪlɪəʳ] ADJ 熟悉的 shúxī de
▶**to be familiar with** 对(對)…熟悉 duì…shúxī

family ['fæmɪlɪ] N [c] **1** (*relations*) 家庭 jiātíng [个 gè] **2** (*children*) 孩子 háizi [个 gè]

famine ['fæmɪn] N [c/u] 饥(飢)荒 jīhuang [阵 zhèn]

famous ['feɪməs] ADJ 著名的 zhùmíng de

fan [fæn] N [c] **1** [*of pop star*] 迷 mí [个 gè]; (*Sport*) 球迷 qiúmí [个 gè] **2** (*Elec*) 风(風)扇 fēngshàn [台 tái] **3** (*handheld*) 扇子 shànzi [把 bǎ] shān

fanatic [fə'nætɪk] N [c] 狂热(熱)者 kuángrèzhě [名 míng]

fancy-dress party ['fænsɪdrɛs-] N [c] 化装(裝)舞会(會) huàzhuāng wǔhuì [个 gè]

fantastic [fæn'tæstɪk] ADJ **1** 极(極)好的 jí hǎo de **2** [+ *sum, amount, profit*] 巨大的 jùdà de

FAQ N ABBR (= **frequently asked question**) 常见(見)问(問)题(題) chángjiàn wèntí

far [fɑːʳ] I ADJ **1** 远(遠)的 yuǎn de **2** ▶**the far end/side** 尽(盡)头(頭)的 jìntóu de II ADV **1** 远(遠) yuǎn; (*in time*) 久远(遠)地 jiǔyuǎn de **2** (*much, greatly*) …得多 …de duō ▶**as far as I know** 据(據)我所知 jù wǒ suǒ zhī ▶**by far** …得多 …de duō ▶**so far** 迄今为(為)止 qìjīn wéizhǐ ▶**it's not far from here** 离(離)这(這)里(裡)不远(遠) lí zhèlǐ bù yuǎn ▶**how far?** 多远(遠)? duō yuǎn? ▶**far away** 遥(遙)远(遠) yáoyuǎn ▶**far better** 好得多 hǎo de duō

fare [fɛəʳ] N [c] 票价(價) piàojià [种 zhǒng]; (*in taxi*) 乘客 chéngkè [位 wèi] ▶**half/full fare** 半/全价(價) bàn/quánjià

Far East N ▶**the Far East** 远(遠)东(東) Yuǎndōng

farm [fɑːm] N [c] 农(農)场(場) nóngchǎng [个 gè]

farmer ['fɑːməʳ] N [c] 农(農)民 nóngmín [个 gè]

farming ['fɑːmɪŋ] N [U] 农(農)业(業) nóngyè

fascinating ['fæsɪneɪtɪŋ] ADJ 迷人的 mírén de

fashion ['fæʃən] N [U/s] 流行的式样(樣) liúxíng de shìyàng ▶**in fashion** 流行 liúxíng

fashionable ['fæʃnəbl] ADJ 流行的 liúxíng de

fast [fɑːst] I ADJ 快的 kuài de II ADV 快 kuài ▶**my watch is 5 minutes fast** 我的表(錶)快5分钟(鐘) wǒ de biǎo kuài wǔ fēnzhōng ▶**fast asleep** 酣睡 hānshuì

fasten ['fɑːsn] VT [+ *coat, jacket, belt*] 系(繫) jì

fast food N [U] 快餐 kuàicān

fat [fæt] I ADJ 肥胖的 féipàng de; [+ *animal*] 肥的 féi de II N **1** [U] (*on person, animal, meat*) 脂肪 zhīfáng **2** [c/u] (*for cooking*) 食用油 shíyòngyóu [桶 tǒng]

> 用 **fat** 形容某人胖，显得过于直接，甚至有些粗鲁。比较礼貌而又含蓄的说法是 **plump** 或 **chubby**，后者更为正式。**overweight** 和 **obese** 暗示某人因为肥胖而有健康问题。**obese** 是医学术语，表示某人极度肥胖或超重。一般而言，应尽量避免当面使用任何表示肥胖的词语。

fatal ['feɪtl] ADJ **1** 致命的 zhìmìng de **2** [+ *mistake*] 严(嚴)重的 yánzhòng de

father ['fɑːðəʳ] N [c] 父亲(親) fùqīn [位 wèi]

Father Christmas (*Brit*) N 圣(聖)诞(誕)老人 Shèngdàn lǎorén

father-in-law ['fɑːðərənlɔː] (*pl* **fathers-in-law**) N [c] [*of woman*] 公公 gōnggong; [*of man*] 岳父 yuèfù

faucet ['fɔːsɪt] (*US*) N [c] 水龙(龍)头(頭) shuǐlóngtóu [个 gè]

fault [fɔːlt] N **1** [s] 错(錯)误(誤) cuòwù **2** [c] (*defect: in person*) 缺点(點) quēdiǎn [个 gè]; (*in machine*) 故障 gùzhàng [个 gè] ▶**it's my fault** 是我的错(錯) shì wǒ de cuò

fava bean ['fɑːvə-] (*US*) N [c] 蚕(蠶)豆 cándòu [颗 kē]

favour, (*US*) **favor** ['feɪvəʳ] N [c] 恩惠 ēnhuì [种 zhǒng] ▶**to do sb a favour** 帮(幫)某人的忙 bāng mǒurén de máng ▶**to be in favour of sth/doing sth** 赞(贊)成某事/做某事 zànchéng mǒushì/zuò mǒushì

favourite, (US) **favorite** ['feɪvrɪt] I ADJ 最喜欢(歡)的 zuì xǐhuan de II N [c] 偏爱(愛) piān'ài [种 zhǒng]

fax [fæks] I N [c] 1 (传(傳)真 chuánzhēn [份 fèn] 2 (also: **fax machine**) 传(傳)真机(機) chuánzhēnjī [台 tái] II VT [+ document] 用传(傳)真发(發)送 yòng chuánzhēn fāsòng

fear [fɪər] N 1 [c/u] (terror) 害怕 hàipà [种 zhǒng] 2 [c/u] (anxiety) 焦虑(慮) jiāolù [种 zhǒng]

feather ['fɛðər] N [c] 羽毛 yǔmáo [根 gēn]

feature ['fi:tʃər] N [c] 特点(點) tèdiǎn [个 gè]

February ['fɛbruərɪ] N [c/u] 二月 èryuè; see also/另见 **July**

fed [fɛd] PT, PP of **feed**

fed up (inf) ADJ ▸ to be fed up 厌(厭)倦 yànjuàn

fee [fi:] N [c] 费(費)费 fèi [种 zhǒng]; [+ of doctor, lawyer] 费(費)用 fèiyòng [项 xiàng]

feeble ['fi:bl] ADJ 1 虚(虛)弱的 xūruò de 2 [+ attempt, excuse, argument] 无(無)力的 wúlì de

feed [fi:d] (pt, pp fed) I VT 喂(餵) wèi II N [c] (Comput) 实(實)时(時)动(動)态(態) shíshí dòngtài [条 tiáo]

feel [fi:l] (pt, pp felt) VT 1 (touch) [+ object, face] 摸 mō 2 [+ pain] 感到 gǎndào 3 (think, believe) 认(認)为(為) rènwéi ▸ to feel that... 感到… gǎndào... ▸ to feel hungry 觉(覺)得饿(餓) juéde è ▸ to feel cold 觉(覺)得冷 juéde lěng ▸ to feel lonely/better 感到孤独(獨)/感觉(覺)好多了 gǎndào gūdú/gǎnjué hǎo duō le ▸ I don't feel well 我觉(覺)得身体(體)不适(適) wǒ juéde shēntǐ bùshì ▸ to feel sorry for sb 同情某人 tóngqíng mǒurén ▸ to feel like (want) 想要 xiǎng yào

feeling ['fi:lɪŋ] I N 1 [c] (emotion) 感受 gǎnshòu [种 zhǒng] 2 [c] (physical sensation) 感觉(覺) gǎnjué [种 zhǒng] 3 [s] (impression) 感觉(覺) gǎnjué II **feelings** NPL 1 (attitude) 看法 kànfǎ 2 (emotions) 情感 qínggǎn ▸ I have a feeling that... 我有种(種)感觉(覺)… wǒ yǒu zhǒng gǎnjué... ▸ to hurt sb's feelings 伤(傷)害某人的感情 shānghài mǒurén de gǎnqíng

feet [fi:t] NPL of **foot**

fell [fɛl] PT of **fall**

felt [fɛlt] PT, PP of **feel**

felt-tip pen, felt-tip ['fɛlttɪp-] N [c] 毡(氈)头(頭)墨水笔(筆) zhāntóu mòshuǐbǐ [支 zhī]

female ['fi:meɪl] I N [c] 1 (Zool) 雌兽(獸) císhòu [头 tóu] 2 (woman) 女性 nǚxìng [位 wèi] II ADJ 1 (Zool) 雌性的 cíxìng de 2 (relating to women) 妇(婦)女的 fùnǚ de ▸ male and female students 男女学(學)生 nánnǚ xuéshēng

feminine ['fɛmɪnɪn] ADJ 1 女性的 nǚxìng de 2 (Ling) 阴(陰)性的 yīnxìng de

feminist ['fɛmɪnɪst] N [c] 女权(權)主义(義)者 nǚquán zhǔyìzhě [位 wèi]

fence [fɛns] N [c] 篱(籬)笆 líba [道 dào]

fencing ['fɛnsɪŋ] N [u] (Sport) 击(擊)剑(劍) jījiàn

ferry ['fɛrɪ] N [c] (small) 摆(擺)渡 bǎidù [个 gè]; (large) (also: **ferryboat**) 渡船 dùchuán [艘 sōu]

festival ['fɛstɪvəl] N [c] 1 (Rel) 节(節)日 jiérì [个 gè] 2 (Theat, Mus) 艺(藝)术(術)节(節) yìshùjié [届 jiè]

fetch [fɛtʃ] VT 去拿来(來) qù nálái ▸ to fetch sth for sb, fetch sb sth 去给(給)某人拿来(來)某物 qù gěi mǒurén nálái mǒuwù

fever ['fi:vər] N [c/u] (Med) 发(發)烧(燒) fāshāo [次 cì]

few [fju:] I ADJ 1 (not many) 少数(數)的 shǎoshù de 2 ▸ a few (some) 几(幾)个(個) jǐ gè II PRON 1 ▸ a few (some) 几(幾)个(個) jǐ gè 2 ▸ in the next few days 在接下来(來)的几(幾)天里(裡) zài jiēxiàlái de jǐ tiān li ▸ in the past few days 在过(過)去的几(幾)天里(裡) zài guòqù de jǐ tiān li ▸ a few of us/them 我们(們)/他们(們)中的几(幾)个(個) wǒmen/tāmen zhōng de jǐ gè ▸ a few more 再多几(幾)个(個) zài duō jǐ gè ▸ very few survive 极(極)少幸(倖)存 jí shǎo xìngcún

fewer ['fju:ər] ADJ 较(較)少的 jiào shǎo de ▸ no fewer than 不少于(於) bù shǎo yú

fiancé [fɪ'ɒnseɪ] N [c] 未婚夫 wèihūnfū [个 gè]

fiancée [fɪ'ɒnseɪ] N [c] 未婚妻 wèihūnqī [个 gè]

fiction ['fɪkʃən] N [U] 小说(說) xiǎoshuō

field [fiːld] N [c] **1** (grassland) 草地 cǎodì [块 kuài] **2** (cultivated) 田地 tiándì [片 piàn] **3** (Sport) 场(場)地 chǎngdì [块 kuài] **4** (subject, area of interest) 领(領)域 lǐngyù [个 gè]

fierce [fɪəs] ADJ **1** 凶猛的 xiōngměng de **2** [+ loyalty, resistance, competition] 强(強)烈的 qiángliè de

fifteen [fɪf'tiːn] NUM 十五 shíwǔ ▸ **she's fifteen (years old)** 她15岁(歲)了 tā shíwǔ suì le

fifteenth [fɪf'tiːnθ] NUM 第十五 dìshíwǔ; see also/另见 **fifth**

fifth [fɪfθ] NUM **1** (in series) 第五 dìwǔ **2** (fraction) 五分之一 wǔ fēn zhī yī ▸ **on July fifth, on the fifth of July** 在7月5日 zài qīyuè wǔrì

fifty ['fɪftɪ] NUM 五十 wǔshí ▸ **he's in his fifties** 他50多岁(歲) tā wǔshí duō suì

fight [faɪt] (pt, pp **fought**) I N [c] **1** (punch-up) 斗(鬥)殴(毆) dòu'ōu [场 cháng] **2** 斗(鬥)争(爭) dòuzhēng [场 cháng] II VT **1** 与(與)…对(對)打 yǔ…duìdǎ III VI **1** 战(戰)斗(鬥) zhàndòu **2** (struggle) 奋(奮)斗(鬥) fèndòu ▸ **to fight for/against sth** 为(為)支持/反对(對)某事而斗(鬥)争(爭) wèi zhīchí/fǎnduì mǒushì ér dòuzhēng

figure ['fɪɡəʳ] I N [c] **1** (number, statistic) 统(統)计(計)数(數)字 tǒngjì shùzì [个 gè] **2** (digit) 数(數)字 shùzì [个 gè] **3** (body, shape) 身材 shēncái [种 zhǒng] II VT (esp US: inf: reckon) 估计(計) gūjì ▸ **that figures** (inf) 那不足为(為)怪 nà bùzú wéi guài

file [faɪl] I N [c] **1** (dossier) 档(檔)案 dàng'àn [份 fèn] **2** (folder) 文件夹(夾) wénjiànjiā [个 gè] **3** (Comput) 文件 wénjiàn [份 fèn] II VT **1** (also: file away) [+ papers, document] 把…归(歸)档(檔) bǎ…guīdàng **2** [+ wood, metal, fingernails] 把…锉(銼)平 bǎ…cuòpíng

fill [fɪl] I VT **1** [+ container] 装(裝)满(滿) zhuāngmǎn **2** [+ space, area] 占(佔)满(滿) zhànmǎn **3** [+ tooth] 补(補)bǔ ▸ **to fill sth with sth** 用某物填满(滿)某物 yòng mǒuwù tiánmǎn mǒuwù ▸ **fill in** VT (esp Brit) [+ form, name] 填写(寫) tiánxiě ▸ **fill out** VT [+ form] 填写(寫) tiánxiě

filling ['fɪlɪŋ] N [c] (in tooth) 填补(補)物 tiánbǔwù [种 zhǒng]

film [fɪlm] I N [c] **1** (esp Brit) 影片 yǐngpiàn [部 bù] **2** [c/U] (Phot) 胶(膠)卷 jiāojuǎn [卷 juǎn] II VT 把…拍成影片 bǎ…pāichéng yǐngpiàn

film star N [c] (esp Brit) 影星 yǐngxīng [位 wèi]

filthy ['fɪlθɪ] ADJ 污秽(穢)的 wūhuì de

final ['faɪnl] I ADJ **1** 最后(後)的 zuìhòu de **2** [+ decision, offer] 不可变(變)更的 bùkě biàngēng de II N [c] (Sport) 决(決)赛(賽) juésài [场 cháng]

finally ['faɪnəlɪ] ADV **1** (eventually) 终(終)于(於) zhōngyú **2** (lastly) 最后(後) zuìhòu **3** (in conclusion) 总(總)之 zǒngzhī

find [faɪnd] (pt, pp **found**) I VT **1** [+ person, object, exit] 找到 zhǎodào; [+ lost object] 找回 zhǎohuí **2** (discover) [+ answer, solution] 找出 zhǎochū; [+ object, person] 发(發)现(現) fāxiàn **3** [+ work, job] 得到 dédào; [+ time] 有 yǒu ▸ **to find sb guilty/not guilty** 判决(決)某人有罪/无(無)罪 pànjué mǒurén yǒuzuì/wúzuì ▸ **to find one's way** 认(認)得路 rènde lù ▸ **find out** I VT [+ fact, truth] 查明 chámíng II VT ▸ **to find out about sth** (deliberately) 获(獲)知某事 huòzhī mǒushì; (by chance) 偶然发(發)现(現)某物 ǒurán fāxiàn mǒuwù

fine [faɪn] I ADJ **1** (satisfactory) 还(還)不错(錯)的 hái bùcuò de **2** (excellent) 好的 hǎo de **3** (in texture) 细(細)的 xì de **4** [+ weather, day] 晴朗的 qínglǎng de II ADV (well) 不错(錯)地 bùcuò de III N [c] (Law) 罚(罰)款 fákuǎn [笔 bǐ] IV VT (Law) 处(處)以…罚(罰)金 chǔ…yǐ fájīn ▸ **(I'm) fine** (我)很好 (wǒ) hěn hǎo ▸ **(that's) fine** (那)好吧 (nà) hǎoba ▸ **you're doing fine** 你做得很好 nǐ zuò de hěn hǎo

finger ['fɪŋɡəʳ] N [c] 手指 shǒuzhǐ [根 gēn]

finish ['fɪnɪʃ] I N **1** [s] (end) 结(結)束 jiéshù **2** [c] (Sport) 终(終)点(點) zhōngdiǎn [个 gè] II VT [+ work] 结(結)束 jiéshù; [+ task, report, book] 完成 wánchéng III VI **1** [course, event +] 结(結)束 jiéshù **2** [person +] 说(說)完 shuōwán ▸ **to finish doing sth** 做完某事 zuòwán mǒushì

Finland ['fɪnlənd] N 芬兰(蘭) Fēnlán

fir [fɜːʳ] N [c] (also: **fir tree**) 冷杉 lěngshān [棵 kē]

fire ['faɪəʳ] I N 1 [u] (flames) 火 huǒ 2 [c] (in fireplace, hearth) 炉(爐)火 lúhuǒ [团 tuán] 3 [c/u] (accidental) 火灾(災) huǒzāi [场 cháng] II VT 1 (shoot) 射出 shèchū 2 (inf: dismiss) 解雇(僱) jiěgù III VI (shoot) 开(開)火 kāihuǒ ▸ **on fire** 起火 qǐhuǒ ▸ **to catch fire** 着(著)火 zháohuǒ

fire alarm N [c] 火警警报(報) huǒjǐng jǐngbào [个 gè]

fire brigade N [c] 消防队(隊) xiāofángduì [支 zhī]

fire engine (Brit) N [c] 救火车(車) jiùhuǒchē [辆 liàng]

firefighter ['faɪəfaɪtəʳ] N [c] 消防队(隊) 员(員) xiāofáng duìyuán [位 wèi]

fireman ['faɪəmən] (pl **firemen**) N [c] 消防队(隊)员(員) xiāofáng duìyuán [位 wèi]

fire station N [c] 消防站 xiāofángzhàn [个 gè]

fire truck (US) N [c] 救火车(車) jiùhuǒchē [辆 liàng]

firework ['faɪəwɜːk] I N [c] 烟(煙)火 yānhuǒ [团 tuán] II **fireworks** NPL (display) 烟(煙)火表演 yānhuǒ biǎoyǎn

firm [fɜːm] I ADJ 1 [+ mattress, ground] 硬 实(實)的 yìngshí de 2 [+ person] 坚(堅) 定的 jiāndìng de II N [c] 公司 gōngsī [家 jiā]

first [fɜːst] I ADJ 1 (in series) 第一的 dìyī de 2 [+ reaction, impression] 最初的 zuìchū de 3 [+ prize, division] 头(頭)等的 tóuděng de II ADV 1 (before anyone else) 首先 shǒuxiān 2 (before other things) 首 先 shǒuxiān 3 (when listing reasons) 第一 dìyī 4 (for the first time) 第一次 dìyī cì 5 (in race, competition) [come, finish +] 第 一名 dìyī míng ▸ **at first** 起先 qǐxiān ▸ **the first of January** 1月1号(號) yī yuè yī hào

first aid N [u] 急救 jíjiù

first-class [fɜːst'klɑːs] I ADJ 1 (excellent) 第一流的 dìyīliú de 2 [+ carriage, ticket, stamp] 一类(類)的 yīlèi de II ADV [travel, send +] 作为(為)一类(類) zuòwéi yīlèi

firstly ['fɜːstlɪ] ADV 首先 shǒuxiān

first name N [c] 名 míng [个 gè]

fish [fɪʃ] I N 1 [c] 鱼(魚) yú [条 tiáo] 2 [u] (food) 鱼(魚)肉 yúròu II VI (commercially) 捕鱼(魚) bǔyú; (as sport, hobby) 钓(釣) 鱼(魚) diàoyú ▸ **to go fishing** 去钓(釣) 鱼(魚) qù diàoyú

fisherman ['fɪʃəmən] (pl **fishermen**) N [c] 渔(漁)民 yúmín [位 wèi]

fishing ['fɪʃɪŋ] N [u] 钓(釣)鱼(魚) diàoyú

fishing boat N [c] 渔(漁)船 yúchuán [条 tiáo]

fist [fɪst] N [c] 拳 quán [个 gè]

fit [fɪt] I ADJ 1 (healthy) 健康的 jiànkāng de II VI 1 [clothes, shoes +] 合身 héshēn 2 (in space, gap) 适(適)合 shìhé ▸ **to keep fit** 保持健康 bǎochí jiànkāng ▸ **to have a fit** (Med) 癫(癲)痫(癇)病发(發)作 diānxiánbìng fāzuò ▸ **to be a good fit** 很合身 hěn héshēn
▸ **fit in** I VI (lit) 容纳(納) róngnà II VT [+ appointment, visitor] 定时(時)间(間) dìng shíjiān yú

fitness ['fɪtnɪs] N [u] 健康 jiànkāng

five [faɪv] NUM 五 wǔ ▸ **that will be five pounds, please** 请(請)付5镑(鎊) qǐng fù wǔ bàng ▸ **she's five (years old)** 她5 岁(歲) tā wǔ suì le ▸ **it's five o'clock** 5点(點)了 wǔ diǎn le

fix [fɪks] VT 1 [+ date, price, meeting] 确(確) 定 quèdìng 2 (mend) 修理 xiūlǐ 3 [+ problem] 解决(決) jiějué

fizzy ['fɪzɪ] (Brit) ADJ 带(帶)气(氣)的 dàiqì de

flag [flæg] N [c] 旗 qí [面 miàn]

flame [fleɪm] N [c/u] 火焰 huǒyàn [团 tuán] ▸ **in flames** 燃烧(燒)着(著) ránshāozhe

flash [flæʃ] I VI 闪(閃)光 shǎnguāng II N [c] 1 闪(閃)光 shǎnguāng [阵 zhèn] 2 (Phot) 闪(閃)光灯(燈) shǎnguāngdēng [个 gè] ▸ **to flash one's headlights** 亮起车(車)头(頭)灯(燈) liàngqǐ chētóudēng

flashlight ['flæʃlaɪt] (esp US) N [c] 手 电(電)筒 shǒudiàntǒng [个 gè]

flask [flɑːsk] N [c] (also: **vacuum flask**) 保温(溫)瓶 bǎowēnpíng [个 gè]

flat [flæt] I ADJ 1 (level) 平的 píng de 2 [+ tyre, ball] 气(氣)不足的 qì bùzú de 3 (Brit) [+ battery] 没(沒)电(電)的 méi diàn de II N [c] (Brit) 公寓 gōngyù [套 tào]

flatter ['flætəʳ] VT 奉承 fèngchéng

flavour, (US) **flavor** ['fleɪvəʳ] I N [c/u] 味
道[种 zhǒng] II VT 给(給)…调(調)味
gěi…tiáowèi

flea [fliː] N [c] 跳蚤 tiàozao [只 zhī]

flew [fluː] PT of **fly**

flexible ['flɛksəbl] ADJ **1** 柔韧(韌)的
róurèn de **2** [+ person, schedule] 机(機)
动(動)的 jīdòng de

flight [flaɪt] N **1** 班机 hángbān [个 gè]
2 [c] (also: **flight of stairs, flight of steps**)
一段楼(樓)梯 yī duàn lóutī [段 duàn]

flight attendant N [c] (male) 男空服人
员(員) nán kōngfú rényuán [位 wèi];
(female) 空姐 kōngjiě [位 wèi]

float [fləʊt] VI **1** 漂浮 piāofú **2** (stay
afloat) 浮着(著) fúzhe

flock [flɔk] N [c] 群 qún

flood [flʌd] I N [c/u] 洪水 hóngshuǐ [次
cì] II VT 淹没(沒) yānmò III

floor [flɔːʳ] N **1** [c] (storey) 楼(樓)层(層) lóucéng [个
gè] ▶ **on the floor** 在地板上 zài dìbǎn
shang ▶ **ground floor** (Brit) 一楼(樓) yī
lóu ▶ **first floor** (Brit) 二楼(樓) èr lóu;
(US) 一楼(樓) yī lóu

> 在英式英语中，建筑的 **ground floor**
> 是指紧贴地面的那个楼层。它上面的一
> 层叫 **first floor**。在美式英语中，**first
> floor** 是指紧贴地面的楼层，它上面的
> 一层是 **second floor**。

floppy ['flɔpɪ] N [c] (also: **floppy disk**)
软(軟)盘(盤) ruǎnpán [张 zhāng]

florist ['flɔrɪst] N [c] **1** 花商 huāshāng
[个 gè] **2** (also: **florist's**) 花店 huādiàn
[家 jiā]

flour ['flaʊəʳ] N [u] 面(麵)粉 miànfěn

flow [fləʊ] I VI 流动(動) liúdòng II N
[c/u] **1** 流动(動) liúdòng **2** (of traffic) 川
流不息 chuān liú bù xī

flower ['flaʊəʳ] I N [c] 花 huā [朵 duǒ]
II VI 开(開)花 kāihuā ▶ **in flower** 正
开(開)着(著)花 zhèng kāizhe huā

flown [fləʊn] PP of **fly**

flu [fluː] N [u] 流感 liúgǎn

fluent ['fluːənt] ADJ **1** [+ speech, reading,
writing] 流畅(暢)的 liúchàng de **2** ▶ **to
speak fluent French, be fluent in
French** 讲(講)流利的法语(語) jiǎng
liúlì de Fǎyǔ

flush [flʌʃ] VT ▶ **to flush the toilet** 冲(沖)
厕(廁)所 chōng cèsuǒ

flute [fluːt] N [c] 长(長)笛 chángdí [支 zhī]

fly [flaɪ] (pt **flew**, pp **flown**) I VT [+ plane]
驾(駕)驶(駛) jiàshǐ II VI [bird, insect,
plane +] 飞(飛) fēi **2** [passengers +] 乘
飞(飛)机(機) chéng fēijī III N [c] (insect)
苍(蒼)蝇(蠅) cāngying [只 zhī]
▶ **fly away** VI 飞(飛)走 fēizǒu

focus ['fəʊkəs] (pl **focuses**) I N **1** [u] (Phot)
聚焦 jùjiāo **2** [c] 重点(點) zhòngdiǎn
[个 gè] II VI ▶ **to focus (on)** (with camera)
聚焦(于(於)) jùjiāo (yú) 集中
(于(於)) jízhōng (yú) ▶ **in focus/out of
focus** 焦点(點)对(對)准(準)/没(沒)
对(對)准(準) jiāodiǎn duìzhǔn/méi
duìzhǔn ▶ **to be the focus of attention**
为(為)关(關)注的焦点(點) wéi guānzhù
de jiāodiǎn

fog [fɔg] N [c/u] 雾(霧) wù [场 chǎng]

foggy ['fɔgɪ] ADJ [+ day, climate] 有雾(霧)
的 yǒu wù de ▶ **it's foggy** 今天有雾(霧)
jīntiān yǒu wù

fold [fəʊld] VT (also: **fold up**) 折叠(疊)
zhédié

folder ['fəʊldəʳ] N [c] 文件夹(夾)
wénjiànjiā [个 gè]

follow ['fɔləʊ] VT **1** [+ person] 跟随(隨) gēnsuí
2 [+ example, advice, instructions] 遵循
zūnxún **3** [+ route, path] 沿着(著)…行
进(進) yánzhe…xíngjìn **4** (Comput)
关(關)注 guānzhù ▶ **I don't quite follow
you** 我不太理解你的意思 wǒ bù tài
lǐjiě nǐ de yìsi ▶ **as follows** (when listing)
如下 rúxià; (in this way) 按如下方式 àn
rúxià fāngshì ▶ **followed by** 接着(著)是
jiēzhe shì

following ['fɔləʊɪŋ] I PREP (after) 在…之
后(後) zài…zhīhòu II ADJ **1** [+ day, week]
接着(著)的 jiēzhe de **2** (next-mentioned)
下述的 xiàshù de

fond [fɔnd] ADJ ▶ **to be fond of** [+ person]
喜爱(愛) xǐ'ài; [+ food, walking] 喜欢(歡)
xǐhuan

food [fuːd] N [c/u] 食物 shíwù [种 zhǒng]

fool [fuːl] I N [c] 白痴(癡) báichī [个 gè]
II VT (deceive) 欺骗(騙) qīpiàn

foot [fut] (pl **feet**) N **1** [c] (measure) 英尺
yīngchǐ **2** [c] (of person) 脚(腳) jiǎo [只
zhī] ▶ **on foot** 步行 bùxíng

football ['futbɔːl] N **1** [c] (ball) 足球 zúqiú
[只 zhī] **2** [u] (sport: Brit) 足球 zúqiú; (US)
美式足球 měishì zúqiú

footballer ['futbɔːlə'] (Brit) N [c] 足球运(運)动(動)员(員) zúqiú yùndòngyuán [位 wèi]

footpath ['futpɑːθ] N [c] 人行小径(徑) rénxíng xiǎojìng [条 tiáo]

footprint ['futprɪnt] N [c] 足迹(跡) zújì [个 gè]

O **KEYWORD**

for [fɔː'] PREP **1** 为(為) wèi ▸ is this for me? 这(這)是为(為)我准(準)备(備)的吗(嗎)? zhè shì wèi wǒ zhǔnbèi de ma? ▸ a table for two 供两(兩)人用的桌子 gōng liǎng rén yòng de zhuōzi **2** (purpose) 为(為)了 wèile ▸ what's it for? 它有什么(麼)用途? tā yǒu shénme yòngtú? ▸ it's time for lunch 该(該)吃午饭(飯)了 gāi chī wǔfàn le ▸ what for? 为(為)什么(麼)呢? wèi shénme ne? ▸ a knife for chopping vegetables 用于(於)切菜的刀 yòngyú qiēcài de dāo **3** (time) ▸ he was away for two years 他离(離)开(開)两(兩)年了 tā líkāi liǎng nián le ▸ it hasn't rained for three weeks 已经(經)有3周(週)没(沒)下雨了 yǐjīng yǒu sān zhōu méi xiàyǔ le ▸ the trip is scheduled for June 5 旅行安排在6月5日 lǚxíng ānpái zài liù yuè wǔ rì **4** (in exchange for) ▸ I sold it for £50 我以五十镑(鎊)卖(賣)掉了它 wǒ yǐ wǔshí bàng màidiàole tā ▸ to pay 50 pence for a ticket 花50便士买(買)张(張)票 huā wǔshí biànshì mǎi zhāng piào **5** (reason) 因为(為) yīnwèi **6** (on behalf of, representing) 为(為) wèi ▸ he works for a local firm 他为(為)一家当(當)地公司工作 tā wèi yī jiā dāngdì gōngsī gōngzuò ▸ G for George George中的G George zhōng de G **7** (destination) 前往 qiánwǎng ▸ he left for Rome 他前往罗(羅)马(馬) tā qiánwǎng Luómǎ **8** (with infinitive clause) ▸ it is not for me to decide 这(這)不是由我来(來)决(決)定的 zhè bùshì yóu wǒ lái juédìng de ▸ there is still time for you to do it 你还(還)有时(時)间(間)去做 nǐ hái yǒu shíjiān qù zuò **9** (in favour of) 赞(贊)成 zànchéng **10** (referring to distance) 达(達) dá ▸ there are roadworks for 50 km 长(長)跑练(練)习(習)长(長)达(達)50公里 chángpǎo liànxí chángdá wǔshí gōnglǐ

> for 和 to 都可用于表示某人的目的,但后接不同的语言结构。for 用于表示目的时,后面必须跟名词。 *Occasionally I go to the pub for a drink.* for 通常不用在动词前面。不能说 *I go to the pub for to have a drink.* for 用在 -ing 形式前表示某物的用途。 *...a small machine for weighing the letters...* 与动词连用时,不定式前不加 for。 *She went off to fetch help.*

forbid [fə'bɪd] (pt forbade, pp forbidden) VT 禁止 jìnzhǐ ▸ to forbid sb to do sth 禁止某人做某事 jìnzhǐ mǒurén zuò mǒushì

forbidden [fə'bɪdn] PP of forbid

force [fɔːs] I N **1** [U] (violence) 武力 wǔlì **2** [U] (strength) 力量 lìliàng II VT 强(強)迫 qiǎngpò III forces NPL (Mil) 部队(隊) bùduì ▸ to force sb to do sth 强(強)迫某人做某事 qiǎngpò mǒurén zuò mǒushì

forecast ['fɔːkɑːst] (pt, pp forecast or forecasted) I N [c] 预(預)报(報) yùbào [个 gè] II VT (predict) 预(預)测(測) yùcè

forehead ['fɔrɪd] N [c] 额(額) é [个 gè]

foreign ['fɔrɪn] ADJ 外国(國)的 wàiguó de

foreigner ['fɔrɪnə'] N [c] 外国(國)人 wàiguórén [个 gè]

forest ['fɔrɪst] N [c/U] 森林 sēnlín [片 piàn]

forever [fə'rɛvə'] ADV 永远(遠) yǒngyuǎn

forgave [fə'geɪv] PT of forgive

forge [fɔːdʒ] VT [+ signature, banknote] 伪(偽)造 wěizào

forget [fə'gɛt] (pt forgot, pp forgotten) I VT **1** 忘记(記) wàngjì **2** (leave behind) [+ object] 忘带(帶) wàng dài II VI (fail to remember) 忘记(記) wàngjì ▸ to forget to do sth 忘记(記)做某事 wàngjì zuò mǒushì ▸ to forget that... 忘记(記)… wàngjì...

forgive [fə'gɪv] (pt forgave, pp forgiven [fə'gɪvn]) VT 原谅(諒) yuánliàng ▸ to forgive sb for sth 原谅(諒)某人某事 yuánliàng mǒurén mǒushì

forgot [fə'gɒt] PT of **forget**

forgotten [fə'gɒtn] PP of **forget**

fork [fɔːk] N [c] **1** 餐叉 cānchā [把 bǎ] **2** (in road, river, railway) 岔路 chàlù [条 tiáo]

form [fɔːm] I N **1** [c] (type) 类(類)型 lèixíng [种 zhǒng] **2** [c] (Brit: Scol: class) 年级(級) niánjí [个 gè] **3** [c] (document) 表格 biǎogé [张 zhāng] II VT **1** (make) 组(組)成 zǔchéng **2** (create) [+ group, organization, company] 成立 chénglì ▸ **in the form of** 通过(過)⋯方式 tōngguò…fāngshì

formal ['fɔːməl] ADJ 正式的 zhèngshì de

former ['fɔːmə'] ADJ 前任的 qiánrèn de ▸ **in former times/years** 以前 yǐqián

fortnight ['fɔːtnaɪt] (Brit) N [c] 两(兩)星期 liǎng xīngqī

fortunate ['fɔːtʃənɪt] ADJ 幸运(運)的 xìngyùn de

fortunately ['fɔːtʃənɪtlɪ] ADV 幸运(運)的是 xìngyùn de shì

fortune ['fɔːtʃən] N [c] 大笔(筆)钱(錢) dà bǐ qián ▸ **to make a fortune** 发(發)大财(財) fā dà cái

forty ['fɔːtɪ] NUM 四十 sìshí

forum ['fɔːrəm] N [c] (Comput) 论(論)坛(壇) lùntán [个 gè]

forward ['fɔːwəd] ADV = **forwards**

forwards ['fɔːwədz] ADV 向前 xiàngqián

fought [fɔːt] PT, PP of **fight**

found [faund] I PT, PP of **find** II VT [+ organization, company] 创(創)办(辦) chuàngbàn

fountain ['fauntɪn] N [c] 喷(噴)泉 pēnquán [个 gè]

four [fɔː'] NUM 四 sì; see also/另见 **five**

fourteen ['fɔː'tiːn] NUM 十四 shísì; see also/另见 **fifteen**

fourteenth ['fɔː'tiːnθ] NUM 第十四 dìshísì; see also/另见 **fifth**

fourth ['fɔːθ] NUM **1** 第四 dìsì **2** (US: quarter) 四分之一 sì fēn zhī yī; see also/另见 **fifth**

fox [fɔks] N [c] 狐狸 húlí [只 zhī]

fracking ['frækɪŋ] N [u] 水力压(壓)裂 shuǐlì yā liè

fragile ['frædʒaɪl] ADJ 易损(損)的 yìsǔn de

frame [freɪm] N [c] **1** 框 kuàng [个 gè] **2** (also: **frames**) [of spectacles] 眼镜(鏡)架 yǎnjìngjià [副 fù] 逆(逕)陷

France [frɑːns] N 法国(國) Fǎguó

fraud [frɔːd] N [c/u] 诈(詐)骗(騙) zhàpiàn [种 zhǒng]

freckle ['frekl] N [c] 雀斑 quèbān [个 gè]

free [friː] ADJ **1** (costing nothing) 免费(費)的 miǎnfèi de **2** [+ person] 自由的 zìyóu de **3** [+ time] 空闲(閒)的 kòngxián de **4** [+ seat, table] 空余(餘)的 kòngyú de ▸ **free (of charge), for free** 免费(費) miǎnfèi ▸ **to be free of** or **from sth** 没(沒)有某物 méiyǒu mǒuwù ▸ **to be free to do sth** 随(隨)意做某事 suíyì zuò mǒushì

freedom ['friːdəm] N [u] 自由 zìyóu

freeway ['friːweɪ] (US) N [c] 高速公路 gāosù gōnglù [条 tiáo]

freeze [friːz] (pt froze, pp frozen) I VI **1** [liquid, weather +] 结(結)冰 jiébīng **2** [pipe +] 冻(凍)住 dòngzhù II VT **1** [+ food] 冷冻(凍) lěngdòng

freezer ['friːzə'] N [c] 冰柜(櫃) bīngguì [个 gè]

freezing ['friːzɪŋ] ADJ (also: **freezing cold**) [+ day, weather] 极(極)冷的 jílěng de; [+ person, hands] 冰冻(凍)的 bīngdòng de ▸ **I'm freezing** 冻(凍)死我了 dòngsǐ wǒ le

French [frentʃ] I ADJ 法国(國)的 Fǎguó de II N [u] (language) 法语(語) Fǎyǔ III **the French** NPL (people) 法国(國)人 Fǎguórén

French fries [-fraɪz] (esp US) NPL 炸薯条(條) zháshǔtiáo

Frenchman ['frentʃmən] (pl **Frenchmen**) N [c] 法国(國)男人 Fǎguó nánrén [个 gè]

Frenchwoman ['frentʃwumən] (pl **Frenchwomen**) N [c] 法国(國)女人 Fǎguó nǚrén [个 gè]

frequent ['friːkwənt] ADJ 频(頻)繁的 pínfán de

fresh [freʃ] ADJ **1** 新鲜(鮮)的 xīnxiān de **2** [+ approach, way] 新颖(穎)的 xīnyǐng de ▸ **fresh air** 新鲜(鮮)空气(氣) xīnxiān kōngqì

Friday ['fraɪdɪ] N [c/u] 星期五 xīngqīwǔ [个 gè]; see also/另见 **Tuesday**

fridge [fridʒ] (Brit) N [c] 冰箱 bīngxiāng [台 tái]

fried [fraɪd] I PT, PP of **fry** II ADJ [+ food] 炒的 chǎo de

friend [frɛnd] I N [c] 朋友 péngyou [个 gè] II VT 加为(爲)好友 jiā wéi hǎoyǒu ▸ **to make friends with sb** 与(與)某人 交朋友 yǔ mǒurén jiāo péngyou

friendly ['frɛndlɪ] ADJ 友善的 yǒushàn de ▸ **to be friendly with** 跟…友好 gēn…yǒuhǎo

friendship ['frɛndʃɪp] N [c] 友情 yǒuqíng [种 zhǒng]

fright [fraɪt] N [c] 惊(驚)吓(嚇) jīngxià [个 gè] ▸ **to give sb a fright** 吓(嚇)唬某 人一下 xiàhu mǒurén yíxià

frighten ['fraɪtn] VT 使惊(驚)恐 shǐ jīngkǒng

frightened ['fraɪtnd] ADJ ▸ **to be frightened** 被吓(嚇)倒 bèi xiàdǎo ▸ **to be frightened of sth/of doing sth** or **to do sth** 害怕某事/做某事 hàipà mǒushì/ zuò mǒushì

frightening ['fraɪtnɪŋ] ADJ 令人恐 惧(懼)的 lìngrén kǒngjù de

frog [frɔg] (Zool) N [c] 青蛙 qīngwā [只 zhī]

KEYWORD

from [frɔm] PREP **1** (indicating starting place) 来(來)自 láizì ▸ **where are you from?** 你来(來)自哪里(裡)？ nǐ láizì nǎlǐ? ▸ **from London to Glasgow** 从(從) 伦(倫)敦到格拉斯哥 cóng Lúndūn dào Gélāsīgē

2 (indicating origin) 来(來)自 láizì ▸ **a present/telephone call/letter from sb** 来(來)自某人的礼(禮)物/电(電) 话(話)/信 láizì mǒurén de lǐwù/diànhuà/ xìn

3 (with time, distance, price, numbers) 从(從) cóng ▸ **from one o'clock to** or **until two** 从(從)1点(點)直到2点(點) cóng yīdiǎn zhídào liǎngdiǎn ▸ **it's 1 km from the beach** 这(這)儿(兒)有1公里 cóng hǎitān dào zhèr yǒu yī gōnglǐ

front [frʌnt] I N [c] (of house, dress) 前面 qiánmiàn; (of coach, train, car) 前部 qiánbù II ADJ 前面的 qiánmiàn de ▸ **in front** 在前面 zài qiánmiàn ▸ **in front of** (facing) 在…前面 zài…qiánmiàn; (in the presence of) 在…面前 zài…miànqián

front door N [c] 前门(門) qiánmén [个 gè]

frontier ['frʌntɪər] N [c] (Brit) 国(國)界 guójiè

front page N [c] (Publishing) 头(頭)版 tóubǎn

frost [frɔst] N [c] 霜 shuāng [场 cháng]

frosty ['frɔstɪ] ADJ 有霜冻(凍)的 yǒu shuāngdòng de

froze [frəuz] PT of **freeze**

frozen ['frəuzn] I PP of **freeze** II ADJ **1** [+ food] 冷冻(凍)的 lěngdòng de; [+ ground, lake] 结(結)冰的 jiébīng de **2** [+ person, fingers] 冰冷的 bīnglěng de

fruit [fruːt] (pl **fruit** or **fruits**) N [c/u] 水果 shuǐguǒ [种 zhǒng]

frustrated [frʌsˈtreɪtɪd] ADJ 泄(洩) 气(氣)的 xièqì de

fry [fraɪ] (pt, pp **fried**) I VT 油煎 yóujiān II **fries** NPL = **French fries**

frying pan ['fraɪɪŋ-] N [c] 平底煎锅(鍋) píngdǐ jiānguō [个 gè]

fuel ['fjuəl] N [c/u] 燃料 ránliào [种 zhǒng]

full [ful] ADJ **1** 满(滿)的 mǎn de; [+ cinema, car, restaurant] 满(滿)的 mǎn de **2** [+ details] 全部的 quánbù de; [+ information, name] 完全的 wánquán de ▸ **I'm full (up)** 我吃饱(飽)了 wǒ chībǎo le ▸ **full of** 充满(滿) chōngmǎn

full stop (Brit) N [c] 句号(號) jùhào [个 gè]

full-time ['ful'taɪm] I ADJ [+ work, study] 全职(職)的 quánzhí de; [+ student, staff] 全日制的 quánrìzhì de II ADV [work, study +] 全日地 quánrì de

fully ['fulɪ] ADV 完全地 wánquán de

fumes [fjuːmz] NPL 浓(濃)烈的烟(煙) 气(氣) nóngliè de yānqì

fun [fʌn] N [u] 乐(樂)趣 lèqù ▸ **to have fun** 玩得开(開)心 wán de kāixīn ▸ **to do sth for fun** 为(為)找乐(樂)而做某事 wèi zhǎolè ěr zuò mǒushì ▸ **to make fun of sb/sth** 取笑某人/某物 qǔxiào mǒurén/mǒuwù

fund [fʌnd] I N [c] 基金 jījīn [项 xiàng] II **funds** NPL (money) 资(資)金 zījīn

funeral ['fjuːnərəl] N [c] 葬礼(禮) zànglǐ [个 gè]

funfair ['fʌnfɛər] (Brit) N [c] 露天游(遊) 乐(樂)场(場) lùtiān yóulèchǎng [个 gè]

funny ['fʌnɪ] ADJ **1**(*amusing*) 可笑的 kěxiào de **2**(*strange*) 奇怪的 qíguài de

fur [fɜːʳ] N [c/u] 毛 máo [根 gēn]

furious ['fjʊərɪəs] ADJ 大发(發)雷霆的 dà fā léitíng de

furniture ['fɜːnɪtʃəʳ] N [u] 家具 jiājù ▸ a piece of furniture 一件家具 yī jiàn jiājù

further ['fɜːðəʳ] ADV 更远(遠)地 gèngyuǎn de ▸ how much further is it? 还(還)有多远(遠)? háiyǒu duōyuǎn?

further education N [u] 继(繼)续(續) 教育 jìxù jiàoyù

fuse, (*US*) **fuze** [fjuːz] N [c] 保险(險) 丝(絲) bǎoxiǎnsī [根 gēn] ▸ a fuse has blown 保险(險)丝(絲)烧(燒)断(斷)了 bǎoxiǎnsī shāoduàn le

fuss [fʌs] N [s/u] 大惊(驚)小怪 dà jīng xiǎo guài ▸ to make *or* kick up a fuss (about sth) (对(對)某事)小题(題)大做 (duì mǒushì) xiǎo tí dà zuò

future ['fjuːtʃəʳ] I ADJ 将(將)来(來)的 jiānglái de II N **1** ▸ the future 未来(來) wèilái **2** (*Ling*) (*also:* future tense) ▸ the future 将(將)来(來)时(時) jiāngláishí ▸ in (the) future (*from now on*) 从(從)今以后(後) cóngjīn yǐhòu ▸ in the near/foreseeable future 在不久/可预(預)见(見)的未来(來) zài bùjiǔ/kě yùjiàn de wèilái

fuze [fjuːz] (*US*) N [c] VT, VI = fuse

gallery ['gælərɪ] N [c] (*also:* art gallery) 美术(術)馆(館) měishùguǎn [个 gè]

gamble ['gæmbl] I VI **1**(*bet*) 赌(賭)博 dǔbó **2**(*take a risk*) 投机(機) tóujī II N [c] (*risk*) 冒险(險) màoxiǎn [次 cì] ▸ to gamble on sth 对(對)某事打赌(賭) duì mǒushì dǎdǔ; [+ success, outcome] 对(對)某事冒险(險) duì mǒushì màoxiǎn

gambling ['gæmblɪŋ] N [u] 赌(賭)博 dǔbó

game [geɪm] N **1** [c] (*sport*) 运(運)动(動) yùndòng [项 xiàng] **2** [c] (*activity*) (*children's*) 游(遊)戏(戲) yóuxì [个 gè] **3** [c] (*also:* board game) 棋盘(盤)游(遊) 戏(戲) qípán yóuxì [项 xiàng]; (*also:* computer game) 电(電)脑(腦)游(遊) 戏(戲) diànnǎo yóuxì [个 gè] **4** [c] (*match*) 比赛(賽) bǐsài [场 chǎng] ▸ a game of football/tennis 一场(場)足球/网(網)球赛(賽) yī chǎng zúqiú/wǎngqiú sài

gamer ['geɪməʳ] N [c] (*on computer*) 游(遊)戏(戲)玩家 yóuxì wánjiā [个 gè]

gaming ['geɪmɪŋ] N [c] (*on computer*) 游(遊)戏(戲) yóuxì

gang [gæŋ] N [c] 一帮 yī bāng

gangster ['gæŋstəʳ] N [c] 歹徒 dǎitú [个 gè]

gap [gæp] N [c] 缝(縫)隙 fèngxì [个 gè]

gap year (*Brit*) N [c] 高中和大学之间的 空隙年

GAP YEAR

在高中毕业以后、进入大学继续接受高等教育之前，学生可以休息一年，这一年被称为 **gap year**。在 **gap year** 期间，很多人选择去旅游或去国外生活，也有人更愿意工作。无论如何选择，他们都能从学校学习生活之外获得宝贵的生活经验。

garage ['gærɑːʒ] N [c] 1 (of private house) 车(車)库 chēkù [个 gè] 2 (for car repairs) 汽车(車)修理厂(廠) qìchē xiūlǐchǎng [个 gè] 3 (Brit: petrol station) 加油站 jiāyóuzhàn [个 gè]

garbage ['gɑːbɪdʒ] N [U] 1 (esp US: rubbish) 垃圾 lājī 2 (nonsense) 废(廢)话(話) fèihuà

garbage can (US) N [c] 垃圾箱 lājīxiāng [个 gè]

garbage man (pl garbage men) (US) N [c] 清洁(潔)工 qīngjiégōng [位 wèi]

garden ['gɑːdn] N [c] 花园(園) huāyuán [个 gè]

gardener ['gɑːdnə'] N [c] (professional) 园(園)丁 yuándīng [位 wèi]; (amateur) 园(園)艺(藝)爱(愛)好者 yuányì àihàozhě [个 gè]

gardening ['gɑːdnɪŋ] N [U] 园(園)艺(藝) yuányì

garlic ['gɑːlɪk] N [U] 大蒜 dàsuàn

gas [gæs] N 1 [U] (for cooking, heating) 煤气(氣) méiqì 2 [U] (US) (also: **gasoline**) 汽油 qìyóu

gasoline ['gæsəliːn] (US) N [U] 汽油 qìyóu

gas station (US) N [c] 加油站 jiāyóuzhàn [个 gè]

gate [geɪt] N [c] 1 门(門) mén [个 gè]; (of building) 大门(門) dàmén [个 gè] 2 (at airport) 登机(機)口 dēngjīkǒu [个 gè]

gather ['gæðə'] I vt (understand) ▶ to gather (that)... 获(獲)悉… huòxī… II vi 聚集 jùjí

gave [geɪv] pt of **give**

gay [geɪ] I adj 同性恋(戀)的 tóngxìngliàn de II N [c] 同性恋(戀) tóngxìngliàn [个 gè]

gay marriage N [c/U] 同性婚姻 tóngxìng hūnyīn [次 cì]

GCSE (Brit) N ABBR (= General Certificate

of Secondary Education) 普通中等教育证(證)书(書) Pǔtōng Zhōngděng Jiàoyù Zhèngshū

gear [ɡɪə'] N 1 [c] (of car, bicycle) 排挡(檔) páidǎng [个 gè] 2 [U] (equipment) 装(裝)备(備) zhuāngbèi 3 [U] (clothing) 服装(裝) fúzhuāng ▶ to change or (US) shift gear 换(換)挡(檔) huàndǎng

geese [giːs] N PL of **goose**

gel [dʒɛl] N [c/U] 啫喱 zélí [瓶 píng] ▶ bath/shower gel 浴液 yùyè

Gemini ['dʒɛmɪnaɪ] N [U] (sign) 双(雙)子座 Shuāngzǐ Zuò

general ['dʒɛnərl] adj 1 (overall) [+ situation] 总(總)的 zǒng de; [+ decline, standard] 一般的 yībān de 2 [+ terms, outline, idea] 笼(籠)统(統)的 lǒngtǒng de

general election N [c] (in Britain, United States) 大选（選）dàxuǎn [届 jiè]

generally ['dʒɛnrəlɪ] adv 1 (on the whole) 大体(體)上 dàtǐshang 2 (usually) 通常 tōngcháng

generation [dʒɛnə'reɪʃən] N [c] 一代人 yīdàirén [代 dài]

generous ['dʒɛnərəs] adj 大方的 dàfang de

Geneva [dʒɪ'niːvə] N 日内(內)瓦 Rìnèiwǎ

genius ['dʒiːnɪəs] N [c] 天才 tiāncái [位 wèi]

gentle ['dʒɛntl] adj 温(溫)和的 wēnhé de

gentleman ['dʒɛntlmən] (pl gentlemen) N [c] 先生 xiānsheng [位 wèi]

gents [dʒɛnts] N ▶ the gents (Brit: inf) 男厕(廁) náncè

genuine ['dʒɛnjuɪn] adj (real) 真正的 zhēnzhèng de; [+ emotion, interest] 实(實)实(實)在在的 shíshí-zàizài de

geography [dʒɪ'ɔɡrəfɪ] N [U] 1 地理 dìlǐ 2 (school/university subject) 地理学(學) dìlǐxué

gerbil ['dʒəːbɪl] N [c] 沙鼠 shāshǔ [只 zhī]

germ [dʒəːm] (Bio) N [c] 细(細)菌 xìjūn [种 zhǒng]

German ['dʒəːmən] I adj 德国(國)的 Déguó de II N 1 [c] (person) 德国(國)人 Déguórén [个 gè] 2 [U] (language) 德语(語) Déyǔ

Germany ['dʒəːmənɪ] N 德国(國) Déguó

KEYWORD

get [gɛt] (*pt, pp* got, (*US*) *pp* gotten) I VT

1 ▸ **to have got;** *see also*/另见 **have, got**

2 [+ *money, permission, results, information*] 获(獲)得 huòdé; [+ *job, flat, room*] 得到 dédào ▸ **he got a job in London** 他在伦(倫)敦得到一份工作 tā zài Lúndūn dédào yī fèn gōngzuò

3 (*fetch*) 去拿 qùná ▸ **to get sth for sb** 为(為)某人去拿某物 wèi mǒurén qù ná mǒuwù ▸ **can I get you a coffee?** 要我给(給)你拿杯咖啡吗(嗎)？ yào wǒ gěi nǐ ná bēi kāfēi ma? ▸ **I'll come and get you** 我会(會)来(來)接你的 wǒ huì lái jiē nǐ de

4 [+ *present, letter, prize, TV channel*] 收到 shōudào ▸ **what did you get for your birthday?** 你生日时(時)得到了什么(麼)礼(禮)物？ nǐ shēngrì shí dédàole shénme lǐwù?

5 [+ *plane, bus*] 乘坐 chéngzuò ▸ **I'll get the bus** 我会(會)乘坐公共汽车(車)wǒ huì chéngzuò gōnggòng qìchē

6 (*cause to be/become*) ▸ **to get sth/sb ready** 使某事/某人准(準)备(備)就绪(緒) shǐ mǒurén/mǒushì zhǔnbèi jiùxù

7 (*take, move*) 把…送到 bǎ…sòngdào ▸ **we must get him to hospital** 我们(們)必须(須)把他送到医(醫)院 wǒmen bìxū bǎ tā sòngdào yīyuàn

8 (*buy*) 买(買) mǎi; (*regularly*) 买(買)到 mǎidào ▸ **I'll get some milk from the supermarket** 我要去超市买(買)牛奶 wǒ yào qù chāoshì mǎi niúnǎi

9 (*be infected by*) [+ *cold, measles*] 染上 rǎnshàng ▸ **you'll get a cold** 你会(會)得感冒的 nǐ huì dé gǎnmào de

10 [+ *time, opportunity*] 有 yǒu

11 ▸ **to get sth done** (*do oneself*) 做某事 zuò mǒushì; (*have done*) 完成某事 wánchéng mǒushì ▸ **to get one's hair cut** 理发(髮) lǐfà ▸ **to get sb to do sth** 让(讓)某人做某事 ràng mǒurén zuò mǒushì

II VI 1 (*become, be*: + *adj*) 变(變)得 biàn de ▸ **to get old/tired/cold/dirty** 变(變)老/变(變)得疲倦/变(變)冷/变(變)脏(髒) biànlǎo/biànde píjuàn/biànlěng/biànzāng ▸ **to get**

drunk 喝醉了 hēzuì le

2 (*go*) ▸ **to get to work/the airport/Beijing** *etc* 到办(辦)公室/到达(達)机(機)场(場)/到达(達)北京｛等｝dào bàngōngshì/dàodá jīchǎng/dàodá Běijīng děng ▸ **how did you get here?** 你是怎么(麼)到这(這)儿(兒)的？ nǐ shì zěnme dào zhèr de? ▸ **he didn't get home till 10pm** 他直到晚上10点(點)才到家 tā zhídào wǎnshang shí diǎn cái dàojiā ▸ **how long does it take to get from London to Paris?** 从(從)伦(倫)敦到巴黎需要多久？ cóng Lúndūn dào Bālí xūyào duō jiǔ?

3 (*begin*) ▸ **to get to know sb** 开(開)始了解某人 kāishǐ liǎojiě mǒurén ▸ **let's get going** *or* **started!** 开(開)始吧！ kāishǐ ba!

III AUX VB 1 ▸ **to have got to;** *see also*/另见 **have, got**

2 (*passive use*) 作为(為)构成被动语态的助动词 ▸ **to get killed** 被杀(殺) bèishā

▸ **get away** VI 逃跑 táopǎo

▸ **get back** I VI (*return*) 回来(來) huílái

II VT (*reclaim*) 重新得到 chóngxīn dédào

▸ **get back to** VT FUS (*return to*) [+ *activity, work*] 回到 huídào; [+ *subject*] 重新回到 chóngxīn huídào ▸ **to get back to sleep** 重又睡着(著) chóng yòu shuìzháo

▸ **get in** VI 1 [*train, bus, plane* +] 抵达(達) dǐdá

2 (*arrive home*) 到家 dàojiā

▸ **get into** VT FUS [+ *vehicle*] 乘坐 chéngzuò

▸ **get off** I VI (*from train, bus*) 下车(車) xiàchē

II VT (*as holiday*) 放假 fàngjià ▸ **we get three days off at Christmas** 圣(聖)诞(誕)节(節)时(時)我们(們)放了3天假 Shèngdàn Jié shí wǒmen fàngle sān tiān jià

III VT FUS [+ *train, bus*] 从(從)…下来(來) cóng…xiàlái

▸ **get on** I VI 1 (*be friends*) 和睦相处(處) hémù xiāngchǔ ▸ **to get on well with sb** 与(與)某人相处(處)融洽 yǔ mǒurén xiāngchǔ róngqià

2 (*progress*) 进(進)展 jìnzhǎn ▸ **how are you getting on?** 你过(過)得怎么(麼)样(樣)？ nǐ guò de zěnmeyàng?

II VT FUS [+ *bus, train*] 上 shàng

▶ **get on with** VT FUS (continue, start) 开(開)始继续(繼續)做 kāishǐ jìxù zuò
▶ **get out** I VI (of vehicle) 下车(車) xiàchē
II VT (take out) 拿出 náchū
▶ **get out of** VT FUS [+ vehicle] 从(從)…下来(來) cóng…xiàlái
▶ **get over** VT FUS [+ illness, shock] 从(從)…中恢复(復)过(過)来(來) cóng…zhōng huīfù guòlái
▶ **get through** I VI (Tel) 接通 jiētōng
II VT FUS [+ work, book] 完成 wánchéng
▶ **get together** VI [people +] 聚在一起 jù zài yīqǐ
▶ **get up** VI 站起来(來) zhànqǐlái; (out of bed) 起床 qǐchuáng

ghost [ɡəʊst] N [c] 鬼神 guǐshén [种(種)zhǒng]

giant [ˈdʒaɪənt] I N [c] 巨人 jùrén [个(個)gè]
II ADJ (huge) 巨大的 jùdà de

gift [ɡɪft] N [c] 1 礼(禮)物 lǐwù [件 jiàn]
2 (talent) 天赋(賦) tiānfù [种(種)zhǒng]

gin [dʒɪn] N [U] 杜松子酒 dùsōngzǐjiǔ

ginger [ˈdʒɪndʒəʳ] I N [U] (spice) 姜(薑) jiāng II ADJ (colour) 姜(薑)色的 jiāngsè de

girl [ɡəːl] N [c] 1 (child) 女孩 nǚhái [个(個)gè]; (young woman, woman) 姑娘 gūniang [个(個)gè] 2 (daughter) 女儿(兒) nǚ'ér [个(個)gè]

girlfriend [ˈɡəːlfrɛnd] N [c] 1 [of girl] 女性朋友 nǚxìng péngyou [个(個)gè] 2 [of boy] 女朋友 nǚpéngyou [个(個)gè]

⊙ **KEYWORD**

give [ɡɪv] (pt **gave**, pp **given**) VT 1 ▶ to give sb sth, give sth to sb 给(給)某人某物 gěi mǒurén mǒuwù; (as gift) 送给(給)某人某物 sònggěi mǒurén mǒuwù ▶ I gave David the book, I gave the book to David 我把这(這)本书(書)送给(給)了戴维(維) wǒ bǎ zhè běn shū sònggěile Dàiwéi ▶ give it to him 把它送给(給)他 bǎ tā sònggěi tā
2 [+ advice, details] 提供 tígōng ▶ to give sb sth [+ opportunity, surprise, shock, job] 给(給)某人某物 gěi mǒurén mǒuwù
3 (deliver) ▶ to give a speech/a lecture 作演讲(講)/讲(講)座 zuò yǎnjiǎng/jiǎngzuò

4 (organize) ▶ to give a party/dinner party etc 做东(東)办(辦)一个(個)聚会(會)/宴会(會){等} zuòdōng bàn yī gè jùhuì/yànhuì děng
▶ **give back** VT 交还(還) jiāohuán ▶ to give sth back to sb 把某物交还(還)给(給)某人 bǎ mǒuwù jiāohuán gěi mǒurén
▶ **give in** VI (yield) 屈服 qūfú
▶ **give up** I VI 放弃(棄) fàngqì
II VT [+ job] 辞(辭)掉 cídiào ▶ to give up smoking 戒烟(煙) jièyān

glad [ɡlæd] ADJ 高兴(興)的 gāoxìng de ▶ I'd be glad to help you 我很愿(願)意帮(幫)助你 wǒ hěn yuànyì bāngzhù nǐ

glamorous [ˈɡlæmərəs] ADJ 富有魅力的 fùyǒu mèilì de

glass [ɡlɑːs] I N 1 [U] (substance) 玻璃 bōli
2 [c] (container) 玻璃杯 bōlibēi [个(個)gè]
3 [c] (glassful) 一杯 yī bēi II **glasses** NPL (spectacles) 眼镜(鏡) yǎnjìng ▶ a pair of glasses 一副眼镜(鏡) yī fù yǎnjìng

global [ˈɡləʊbl] ADJ 全球的 quánqiú de

global warming [-ˈwɔːmɪŋ] N [U] 全球变(變)暖 quánqiú biànnuǎn

glove [ɡlʌv] N [c] 手套 shǒutào [副 fù] ▶ a pair of gloves 一副手套 yī fù shǒutào

glue [ɡluː] N [c/U] 胶(膠) jiāo [种(種)zhǒng]

⊙ **KEYWORD**

go [ɡəʊ] (pt **went**, pp **gone**, pl **goes**) I VI
1 去 qù ▶ he's going to New York 他要去纽(紐)约(約) tā yào qù Niǔyuē ▶ where's he gone? 他去哪儿(兒)了? tā qù nǎr le? ▶ shall we go by car or train? 我们(們)开(開)车(車)去还(還)是坐火车(車)去? wǒmen kāichē qù háishi zuò huǒchē qù?
2 (depart) 离(離)开(開) líkāi ▶ let's go 我们(們)走吧 wǒmen zǒu ba ▶ I must be going 我必须(須)得走了 wǒ bìxū děi zǒu le ▶ our plane goes at 11pm 我们(們)的飞(飛)机(機)晚上11点(點)起飞(飛) wǒmen de fēijī wǎnshang shíyī diǎn qǐfēi
3 (disappear) 消失 xiāoshī ▶ all her jewellery had gone 她所有的珠宝(寶)首饰(飾)都不见(見)了 tā suǒyǒu de

zhūbǎo shǒushì dōu bùjiàn le

4 (attend) ▸ **to go to school/university** 上学(學)/上大学(學) shàngxué/shàng dàxué

5 (with activity) ▸ **to go for a walk** 去散步 qù sànbù ▸ **to go on a trip** 去旅行 qù lǚxíng

6 (work) 运(運)转(轉) yùnzhuǎn

7 (become) ▸ **to go pale/mouldy/bald** 变(變)得苍(蒼)白/发(發)霉(黴)/秃(禿)顶(頂) biàn de cāngbái/fāméi/tūdǐng

8 (be about to, intend to) ▸ **are you going to come?** 你要来(來)吗(嗎)? nǐ yào lái ma? ▸ **I think it's going to rain** 我想天要下雨了 wǒ xiǎng tiān yào xiàyǔ le

9 (progress) 进(進)行 jìnxíng ▸ **how did it go?** 这(這)事进(進)展如何? zhè shì jìnzhǎn rúhé?

10 (lead) [road, path +] 通向 tōngxiàng

11 (in other expressions) ▸ **there's still a week to go before the exams** 考试(試)前还(還)有一个(個)星期的时(時)间(間) kǎoshì qián hái yǒu yī gè xīngqī de shíjiān ▸ **to keep going** 继(繼)续(續)下去 jìxù xiàqù

II N **1** [c] (try) 尝(嘗)试(試) chángshì [次 cì] ▸ **to have a go (at sth/at doing sth)** 试(試)一下 (某事/做某事) shì yīxià (mǒushì/zuò mǒushì)

2 [c] (turn) 轮(輪)流 lúnliú [次 cì] ▸ **whose go is it?** 轮(輪)到谁(誰)了? lúndào shuí le?

▸ **go ahead** VI **1** [event +] 发(發)生 fāshēng

2 (press on) ▸ **to go ahead with sth** 着(著)手做某事 zhuóshǒu zuò mǒushì

▸ **go ahead!** (encouraging) 干(幹)吧! gànba!

▸ **go around** VI **1** [news, rumour +] 传(傳)播 chuánbō

2 (revolve) 转(轉)动(動) zhuàndòng

▸ **go away** VI **1** (leave) 离(離)开(開) líkāi

2 (on holiday) 外出 wàichū

▸ **go back** VI 返回 fǎnhuí

▸ **go back to** VT FUS [+ activity, work, school] 回到 huídào

▸ **go down** I VI [price, level, amount +] 下降 xiàjiàng

2 [sun +] 落下 luòxià

3 [computer +] 死机(機) sǐjī

II VT FUS [+ stairs, ladder] 从(從)…下来(來) cóng…xiàlái

▸ **go for** VT FUS (fetch) 去取 qù qǔ

▸ **go in** VI 进(進)去 jìnqù

▸ **go in for** VT FUS [+ competition] 参(參)加 cānjiā

▸ **go into** VT FUS (enter) 进(進)入 jìnrù

▸ **go off** VI **1** (leave) 离(離)去 líqù ▸ **he's gone off to work** 他已经(經)去上班了 tā yǐjīng qù shàngbān le

2 (explode) 爆炸 bàozhà

3 [alarm +] 响(響)起 xiǎngqǐ

4 [lights +] 熄灭(滅) xīmiè

▸ **go on** VI **1** (continue) 继(繼)续(續) jìxù ▸ **to go on with one's work** 继(繼)续(續)自己的工作 jìxù zìjǐ de gōngzuò ▸ **to go on doing sth** 继(繼)续(續)做某事 jìxù zuò mǒushì

2 (happen) 发(發)生 fāshēng ▸ **what's going on here?** 这(這)里(裡)发(發)生什么(麼)事了? zhèlǐ fāshēng shénme shì le?

▸ **go out** VI **1** [person +] 离(離)开(開) líkāi; (to party, club) 出去消遣 chūqù xiāoqiǎn ▸ **are you going out tonight?** 你今晚出去吗(嗎)? nǐ jīnwǎn chūqù ma?

2 [couple +] 和…交往 hé…jiāowǎng ▸ **to go out with sb** 和某人交往 hé mǒurén jiāowǎng

3 [light, fire +] 熄灭(滅) xīmiè

▸ **go over** VI 过(過)去 guòqù

▸ **go round** VI = **go around**

▸ **go through** VT FUS [+ place, town] 路过(過) lùguò

▸ **go up** VI [price, level, value +] 上涨(漲) shàngzhǎng

2 (go upstairs) 上楼(樓) shànglóu

▸ **go up to** VT FUS 向…走过(過)去 xiàng…zǒuguòqù

▸ **go with** VT FUS (accompany) 与(與)…相伴共存 yǔ…xiāngbàn gòngcún

▸ **go without** VT FUS [+ food, treats] 没(沒)有 méiyǒu…

goal [gəʊl] N [c] **1** (Sport) 进(進)球得分 jìnqiú défēn [次 cì] **2** (aim) 目标(標) mùbiāo [个 gè] ▸ **to score a goal** 进(進)一球 jìn yī qiú

goalkeeper ['gəʊlkiːpəʳ] N [c] 守门(門)员(員) shǒuményuán [个 gè]

goat [gəʊt] N [c] 山羊 shānyáng [只 zhī]

God [gɒd] N 上帝 Shàngdì

goggles ['gɒglz] NPL 护(護)目镜(鏡) hùmùjìng

gold [gəʊld] I N [u] (metal) 黄金 huángjīn II ADJ [+ ring, watch, tooth] 金的 jīn de

golf [gɒlf] N [u] 高尔(爾)夫球 gāo'ěrfúqiú ▸ **to play golf** 打高尔(爾)夫球 dǎ gāo'ěrfúqiú

golf course N [c] 高尔(爾)夫球场(場) gāo'ěrfúqiúchǎng [个 gè]

gone [gɒn] I PP of **go** II ADJ 离(離)去的 líqù de III PREP (Brit: inf: after) 过(過) guò ▸ **the food's all gone** 食物都没(沒) 了 shíwù dōu méi le

good [gʊd] I ADJ 1 (pleasant) 令人愉快的 lìng rén yúkuài de 2 [+ food, school, job] 好的 hǎo de 3 (well-behaved) 乖的 guāi de 4 [+ idea, reason, advice] 好的 hǎo de 5 (skilful) 好的 hǎo de 6 [+ news, luck, example] 好的 hǎo de 7 (morally correct) 公正的 gōngzhèng de II N [u] (right) 善 shàn ▸ **good!** 好! hǎo! ▸ **to be good at (doing) sth** 精于(於)(做)某事 jīng yú (zuò) mǒushì ▸ **to be no good at (doing) sth** 不擅长(長)(做)某事 bù shàncháng (zuò) mǒushì ▸ **it's no good doing...** 做…没(沒)有用 zuò...méiyǒu yòng ▸ **it's good for you** 对(對)你有益 duì nǐ yǒuyì ▸ **it's good to see you** 很高兴(興)见(見)到你 hěn gāoxìng jiàndào nǐ ▸ **good morning/afternoon!** 早上/下午好! zǎoshang/xiàwǔ hǎo! ▸ **good night!** (before going home) 再见(見)! zàijiàn!; (before going to bed) 晚安! wǎn'ān! ▸ **for good** (forever) 永久地 yǒngjiǔ de; see also/另见 **goods**

goodbye [gʊd'baɪ] INT 再见(見) zàijiàn ▸ **to say goodbye** 告别(別) gàobié

good-looking ['gʊd'lʊkɪŋ] ADJ 好看的 hǎokàn de

goods [gʊdz] NPL 商品 shāngpǐn

goose [guːs] (pl **geese**) N [c] 鹅(鵝) é [只 zhī]

gorgeous ['gɔːdʒəs] ADJ [+ weather, day] 宜人的 yírén de

gossip ['gɒsɪp] I N [u] (rumours) 流言蜚语(語) liúyán fēiyǔ II VI (chat) 闲(閒) 谈(談) xiántán

got [gɒt] PT, PP of **get** ▸ **have you got your umbrella?** 你有伞(傘)吗(嗎)? nǐ yǒu

sǎn ma? ▸ **he has got to accept the situation** 他只得接受现(現)状(狀) tā zhǐdé jiēshòu xiànzhuàng

gotten ['gɒtn] (US) PP of **get**

government ['gʌvnmənt] N [c] (institution) 政府 zhèngfǔ [届 jiè]

GP N ABBR [c] (= general practitioner) 家庭医(醫)生 jiātíng yīshēng [位 wèi]

graceful ['greɪsful] ADJ 优(優)美的 yōuměi de

grade [greɪd] N [c] 1 (school mark) 分数(數) fēnshù [个 gè] 2 (US: school class) 年级(級) niánjí [个 gè]

grade crossing (US) N [c] 铁路线与公路交叉处 jiāochā chù

grade school (US) N [c/u] 小学(學) xiǎoxué [座 zuò]

gradual ['grædjuəl] ADJ 逐渐(漸)的 zhújiàn de

gradually ['grædjuəlɪ] ADV 逐渐(漸)地 zhújiàn de

gram [græm] N [c] 克 kè

grammar ['græmə] N [u] 语(語)法 yǔfǎ

gramme [græm] (Brit) N = **gram**

grand [grænd] ADJ 壮(壯)丽(麗)的 zhuànglì de

grandchild ['græntʃaɪld] (pl **grandchildren**) N [c] (male on father's side) 孙(孫)子 sūnzi [个 gè]; (female on father's side) 孙(孫)女 sūnnǚ [个 gè]; (male on mother's side) 外孙(孫) wàisūn [个 gè]; (female on mother's side) 外孙(孫)女 wàisūnnǚ [个 gè]

grandfather ['grændfɑːðə'] N [c] (on mother's side) 外公 wàigōng [位 wèi]; (on father's side) 爷(爺)爷(爺) yéye [位 wèi]

grandmother ['grænmʌðə'] N [c] (on father's side) 外婆 wàipó [位 wèi]; (on father's side) 奶奶 nǎinai [位 wèi]

grandson ['grænsʌn] N [c] (on father's side) 孙(孫)子 sūnzi [个 gè]; (on mother's side) 外孙(孫) wàisūn [个 gè]

grape [greɪp] N [c] 葡萄 pútáo [串 chuàn] ▸ **a bunch of grapes** 一串葡萄 yī chuàn pútáo

grapefruit ['greɪpfruːt] (pl **grapefruit** or **grapefruits**) N [c/u] 葡萄柚 pútáoyòu [个 gè]

graph [grɑːf] N [c] 图(圖)表 túbiǎo [幅 fú]

graphics ['græfɪks] I N [u] (design)

制(製)图(圖)学(學) zhìtúxué II N PL
(images) 图(圖)形 túxíng

grass [grɑːs] N [c/u] (Bot) 草 cǎo [株 zhū]
▸ **the grass** (the lawn) 草坪 cǎopíng

grate [greɪt] VT [+ food] 磨碎 mósuì

grateful ['greɪtful] ADJ 感激的 gǎnjī de
▸ **to be grateful to sb for sth** 为(為)某
事感激某人 wèi mǒushì gǎnjī mǒurén

grave [greɪv] N [c] 坟(墳)墓 fénmù [座
zuò]

graveyard ['greɪvjɑːd] N [c] 墓地 mùdì
[块 kuài]

gray [greɪ] (US) ADJ = **grey**

greasy ['griːsɪ] ADJ **1** [+ food] 油腻(膩)的
yóunì de **2** [+ skin, hair] 多油脂的 duō
yóuzhī de

great [greɪt] I ADJ **1** (large) 巨大的 jùdà
de **2** [+ success, achievement] 重大的
zhòngdà de; [+ pleasure, difficulty, value]
极(極)大的 jídà de; [+ risk] 超乎寻(尋)
常的 chāohū xúncháng de [+ city,
person, work of art] 伟(偉)大的 wěidà de
4 (terrific) [+ person, place] 好极了的
hǎojíle de; [+ idea] 棒极了的 bàngjíle de
II INT ▸ **great!** 太好了! tài hǎo le! ▸ **we
had a great time** 我们(們)玩得很快活
wǒmen wán de hěn kuàihuo

Great Britain N 大不列颠(顛)
Dàbùlièdiān

Greece [griːs] N 希腊(臘) Xīlà

greedy ['griːdɪ] ADJ 贪(貪)心的 tānxīn de

Greek [griːk] I ADJ 希腊(臘)的 Xīlà de
II N **1** [c] (person) 希腊(臘)人 Xīlàrén [个
gè] **2** [u] (modern language) 希腊(臘)
语(語) Xīlàyǔ

green [griːn] I ADJ **1** 绿(綠)色的 lǜsè de
2 (environmental) 环(環)保的 huánbǎo
de II N **1** [c/u] 绿(綠)色 lǜsè [抹 mǒ]

greengrocer ['griːnɡrəusə'] (esp Brit) N
[c] (shop) (also: **greengrocer's**) 果蔬店
guǒshūdiàn [家 jiā]

greenhouse ['griːnhaus] I N [c] 暖房
nuǎnfáng [间 jiān] II CPD [+ gas,
emissions] 温(溫)室 wēnshì

green tax N [c/u] 环(環)保税(稅)
huánbǎo shuì

grew [gruː] PT of **grow**

grey, (US) **gray** [greɪ] I ADJ **1** 灰色的
huīsè de; [+ hair] 灰白的 huībái de
2 [+ weather, day] 阴(陰)沉的 yīnchén de
II N [c/u] 灰色 huīsè [种 zhǒng]

grey-haired [greɪ'hɛəd] ADJ 灰白头(頭)
发(髮)的 huībái tóufa de

grief [griːf] N [u] 悲痛 bēitòng

grill [grɪl] VT (Brit) [+ food] 烤 kǎo

grit [grɪt] N [u] 沙粒 shālì

groan [ɡrəun] VI 呻吟 shēnyín

grocer ['grəusə'] N [c] **1** (person) 食品
杂(雜)货(貨)商 shípǐn záhuòshāng [个
gè] **2** (shop) (also: **grocer's**) 食品杂(雜)
货(貨)店 shípǐn záhuòdiàn [家 jiā]

grocery ['grəusərɪ] I N [c] (also: **grocery
shop** (Brit), **grocery store** (esp US)) 食品
杂(雜)货(貨)店 shípǐn záhuòdiàn [家
jiā] II **groceries** N PL (provisions) 食品
杂(雜)货(貨) shípǐn záhuò

groom [gruːm] N [c] (also: **bridegroom**)
新郎 xīnláng [位 wèi]

ground [graund] I PT, PP of **grind** II N
1 (floor) ▸ **the ground** 地面 dìmiàn
2 (earth, soil, land) ▸ **the ground** 土地
tǔdì **3** [c] (Sport) 场(場) chǎng ▸ **on the
ground** 在地面上 zài dìmiàn shang

ground floor N [c] 一楼(樓) yīlóu [层
céng]

group [gruːp] N [c] **1** 组(組) zǔ [个 gè]
2 (also: **pop group, rock group**) 组(組)合
zǔhé [个 gè] ▸ **in groups** 成组(組)地
chéngzǔ de

grow [grəu] (pt **grew**, pp **grown**) I VI
1 [plant, tree +] 生长(長) shēngzhǎng;
[person, animal +] 长(長)大 zhǎngdà
2 [amount, feeling, problem +] 扩(擴)大
kuòdà II VT [+ flowers, vegetables] 栽
种(種) zāizhòng ▸ **to grow by 10%** 增
长(長)10% zēngzhǎng bǎi fēn zhī shí
▸ **grow up** VI (be brought up) 长(長)大
zhǎngdà; (be mature) 成熟 chéngshú

grown [ɡrəun] PP of **grow**

grown-up [grəun'ʌp] N [c] 成年人
chéngniánrén [个 gè]

growth [grəuθ] N **1** [u/s] [of economy,
industry] 发(發)展 fāzhǎn **2** [u] [of child,
animal, plant] 生长(長) shēngzhǎng ▸ **a
growth in sth** 某方面的发(發)展 mǒu
fāngmiàn de fāzhǎn

grumble ['grʌmbl] VI (complain) 抱怨
bàoyuàn

guarantee [gærən'tiː] N [c] (Comm:
warranty) 质(質)保承诺(諾) zhìbǎo
chéngnuò [个 gè]

guard [gɑːd] I N [c] (sentry) 警卫(衛)

jīngwèi [个 gè] II vt [+ building, entrance, door] 守卫(衛) shǒuwèi; [+ person] 保护(護) bǎohù ▸ to be on one's guard (against) 提防 dīfáng

guess [ges] I vt, vi (conjecture) 猜测(測) cāicè II N [c] 猜测(測) cāicè [种 zhǒng] ▸ I guess so 我想是吧 wǒxiǎng shì ba

guest [gest] N [c] (at home) 客人 kèrén [位 wèi]; (at special event) 宾(賓)客 bīnkè [位 wèi]; (in hotel) 房客 fángkè [位 wèi]

guide [gaɪd] I N [c] 1 (tour guide) 导(導)游(遊) dǎoyóu [位 wèi] 2 (local guide) 向导(導) xiàngdǎo [位 wèi] 3 (also: guide book) 指南 zhǐnán [本 běn] II vt 1 (round city, museum) 给(給)…导(導)游(遊) gěi…dǎoyóu 2 (lead) 给(給)…领(領)路 gěi…lǐnglù

guidebook ['gaɪdbʊk] N [c] 旅游(遊)指南 lǚyóu zhǐnán [本 běn]

guided tour ['gaɪdɪd-] N [c] 有导(導)游(遊)的游(遊)览(覽) yǒu dǎoyóu de yóulǎn [次 cì]

guilty ['gɪltɪ] ADJ 1 [+ person, feelings] 内(內)疚的 nèijiù de 2 [+ secret, conscience] 自知有过(過)错(錯)的 zìzhī yǒu guòcuò de 3 (responsible) 有过(過)失的 yǒu guòshī de 4 (Law) 有罪的 yǒuzuì de ▸ guilty of murder/manslaughter 谋(謀)杀(殺)/误(誤)杀(殺)罪 móushā/wùshā zuì

guitar [gɪ'tɑːʳ] N [c] 吉他 jítā [把 bǎ]

gum [gʌm] N 1 [c] (Anat) 牙床 yáchuáng 2 [u] (also: chewing gum/bubblegum) 口香糖 kǒuxiāngtáng

gun [gʌn] N [c] (small, medium-sized) 枪(槍) qiāng [支 zhī]; (large) 炮(砲) pào [架 jià]

guy [gaɪ] N [c] (man) 家(傢)伙 jiāhuo [个 gè] ▸ (you) guys 伙(夥)计(計)们(們) huǒjìmen

gym [dʒɪm] N 1 [c] (also: gymnasium) 健身房 jiànshēnfáng [个 gè] 2 [u] (also: gymnastics) 体(體)操 tǐcāo

gymnast ['dʒɪmnæst] N [c] 体(體)操运(運)动(動)员(員) tǐcāo yùndòngyuán [位 wèi]

gymnastics [dʒɪm'næstɪks] N [u] 体(體)操 tǐcāo

gypsy ['dʒɪpsɪ] N [c] 吉卜赛(賽)人 Jípǔsàirén [个 gè]

h

habit ['hæbɪt] N [c/u] 习(習)惯(慣) xíguàn [个 gè] ▸ to be in the habit of doing sth 有做某事的习(習)惯(慣) yǒu zuò mǒushì de xíguàn ▸ a bad habit 坏(壞)习(習)惯(慣) huài xíguàn

hacker ['hækəʳ] (Comput) N [c] 黑客 hēikè

had [hæd] pt, pp of **have**

hadn't ['hædnt] = had not

hail [heɪl] I N [u] 冰雹 bīngbáo II vi 下雹 xiàbáo

hair [hɛəʳ] N [u] 头(頭)发(髮) tóufa [c] (single strand) 毛发(髮) máofà [根 gēn] ▸ to do one's hair 梳头(頭) shūtóu ▸ to have or get one's hair cut 剪头(頭)发(髮) jiǎn tóufa

hairbrush ['hɛəbrʌʃ] N [c] 发(髮)刷 fàshuā [把 bǎ]

haircut ['hɛəkʌt] N [c] 1 理发(髮) lǐfà [次 cì] 2 (hairstyle) 发(髮)型 fàxíng [种 zhǒng] ▸ to have or get a haircut 剪头(頭)发(髮) jiǎn tóufa

hairdresser ['hɛədresəʳ] N [c] 1 美发(髮)师(師) měifàshī [位 wèi] 2 (also: hairdresser's) 发(髮)廊 fàláng [个 gè]

hairdryer ['hɛədraɪəʳ] N [c] 吹风(風)机(機) chuīfēngjī [个 gè]

hair gel N [u] 发(髮)胶(膠) fàjiāo

hairspray ['hɛəspreɪ] N [u] 喷发(髮)定型剂(劑) pēnfà dìngxíngjì

hairstyle ['hɛəstaɪl] N [c] 发(髮)型 fàxíng [种 zhǒng]

half [hɑːf] (pl **halves**) I N, PRON [c] 1 一半

yībàn **2** (Brit: child's ticket) 半票 bànpiào [张 zhāng] **II** ADJ [+ bottle] 一半的 yībàn de **III** ADV [+ empty, closed, open, asleep] 半 bàn ▶ to cut sth in half 把某物切成 两(兩)半 bǎ mǒuwù qiēchéng liǎng bàn ▶ two/three etc and a half 二/三 {等} 点(點)五 èr/sān děng diǎn wǔ ▶ half a pound/kilo/mile 半磅/公斤/英里 bàn bàng/gōngjīn/yīnglǐ ▶ a day/week/ pound etc and a half 一天/星期/磅 {等} 半 yī tiān/xīngqī/bàng děng bàn ▶ half an hour 半小时(時) bàn xiǎoshí ▶ half past three/four etc 三/四 {等} 点(點)半 sān/sì děng diǎn bàn

half-hour [hɑːˈfaʊəʳ] N [c] 半小时(時) bàn xiǎoshí [个 gè]

half price [ˈhɑːfˈpraɪs] **I** ADJ 半价(價) 的 bànjià de **II** ADV 半价(價)地 bànjià de

half-term [hɑːˈftɜːm] (Brit: Scol) N [c/u] 期中假 qīzhōngjià [段 duàn] ▶ at half-term 期中假时(時) qīzhōngjià shí

half-time [hɑːˈftaɪm] (Sport) N [u] 半场(場) bànchǎng ▶ at half-time 半场(場)时(時) bànchǎng shí

halfway [ˈhɑːˈfweɪ] ADV (between two points) 到一半 dào yībàn ▶ halfway through sth 在某事过(過)了一半 时(時) zài mǒushì guòle yībàn shí

hall [hɔːl] N **1** [c] (esp Brit: entrance) 门(門) 厅(廳) méntīng [个 gè] **2** [c] (room) 礼(禮)堂 lǐtáng [个 gè]

ham [hæm] **I** N [c] 火腿 huǒtuǐ **II** CPD [+ sandwich, roll, salad] 火腿 huǒtuǐ

hamburger [ˈhæmbɜːɡəʳ] N [c] 汉(漢)堡 包 hànbǎobāo [个 gè]

hammer [ˈhæməʳ] N [c] 锤(錘)子 chuízi [把 bǎ]

hand [hænd] **I** N **1** [c] 手 shǒu [双 shuāng] **2** [c] [of clock] 指针(針) zhǐzhēn [个 gè] **II** VT 递(遞) dì ▶ to do sth by hand 手工制(製)作 shǒugōng zhìzuò ▶ to give or lend sb a hand (with sth) 帮(幫)某人(做某事) bāng mǒurén (zuò mǒushì) ▶ on the one hand..., on the other hand... 一方面…, 另一方面… yī fāngmiàn…, lìng yī fāngmiàn…
▶ hand in VT 上交 shàngjiāo
▶ hand out VT 分配 fēnpèi
▶ hand over VT 交给(給) jiāogěi

handbag [ˈhændbæg] (Brit) N [c] 手包 shǒubāo [个 gè]

handcuffs [ˈhændkʌfs] NPL 手铐(銬) shǒukào ▶ in handcuffs 带(帶)手 铐(銬) dài shǒukào

handkerchief [ˈhæŋkətʃɪf] N [c] 手帕 shǒupà [条 tiáo]

handle [ˈhændl] **I** N [c] [of bag] 把手 bǎshǒu [个 gè]; [of cup, knife, paintbrush, broom, spade] 柄 bǐng [个 gè]; [of door, window] 拉手 lāshǒu [个 gè] **II** VT [+ problem, job, responsibility] 处(處)理 chǔlǐ

handlebars [ˈhændlbɑːz] NPL 把手 bǎshǒu

handmade [ˈhændˈmeɪd] ADJ 手工 制(製)作的 shǒugōng zhìzuò de

handsome [ˈhænsəm] ADJ 英俊的 yīngjùn de

handwriting [ˈhændraɪtɪŋ] N [u] 笔(筆)迹(跡) bǐjì

handy [ˈhændɪ] ADJ **1** (useful) 方便的 fāngbiàn de **2** (close at hand) 手边(邊)的 shǒubiān de

hang [hæŋ] (pt, pp hung) **I** VT 挂(掛) guà **II** VI (be suspended) 悬(懸)挂(掛) xuánguà
▶ hang about VI = hang around
▶ hang around (inf) **I** VI 闲(閒)荡(蕩) xiándàng
▶ hang on VI (wait) 稍等 shāoděng
▶ hang round VI = hang around
▶ hang up **I** VI (Tel) 挂(掛)断(斷)电(電) 话(話) guàduàn diànhuà **II** VT [+ coat, hat, clothes] 挂(掛)起 guàqǐ

hanger [ˈhæŋəʳ] N [c] (also: coat hanger) 衣架 yījià [个 gè]

hangover [ˈhæŋəʊvəʳ] N [c] 宿醉 sùzuì [次 cì]

happen [ˈhæpən] VI 发(發)生 fāshēng ▶ what will happen if...? 如果…会(會) 怎么(麼)样(樣)? rúguǒ…huì zěnmeyàng? ▶ tell me what happened 告诉(訴)我发(發)生了什么(麼)事 gàosù wǒ fāshēngle shénme shì

happiness [ˈhæpɪnɪs] N [u] 幸福 xìngfú

happy [ˈhæpɪ] ADJ **1** 高兴(興)的 gāoxìng de [+ life, childhood, marriage, place] 美 满(滿)的 měimǎn de **2** ▶ to be happy with sth (satisfied) 对(對)某事满(滿)意 duì mǒushì mǎnyì ▶ to be happy to do sth (willing) 乐(樂)意做某事 lèyì zuò mǒushì ▶ happy birthday! 生日快

乐(樂)! shēngrì kuàilè! ▶ **happy Christmas!** 圣(聖)诞(誕)快乐(樂)! Shèngdàn kuàilè!

harassment ['hærəsmənt] N [U] 骚(騷)扰(擾) sāorǎo

harbour, (US) **harbor** ['hɑːbəʳ] N [c] 港口 gǎngkǒu [个 gè]

hard [hɑːd] I ADJ **1** [+ surface, object] 硬的 yìng de **2** [+ question, problem] 困难(難)的 kùnnan de; [+ work] 费(費)力的 fèilì de **3** [+ push, punch, kick] 用力的 yònglì de II ADV **1** [work, try, think +] 努力地 nǔlì de **2** [hit, punch, kick +] 用力地 yònglì de ▶ **it's hard to tell/say/know** 很难(難)讲(講)/说(說)/知道 hěn nán jiǎng/shuō/zhīdào ▶ **such events are hard to understand** 这(這)种(種)事很难(難)理解 zhè zhǒng shì hěn nán lǐjiě ▶ **it's hard work serving in a shop** 商店工作很难(難)做 shāngdiàn gōngzuò hěn nán zuò

hard disk (Comput) N [c] 硬盘(盤) yìngpán [个 gè]

hardly ['hɑːdlɪ] ADV **1** (scarcely) 几(幾)乎不 jīhū bù **2** (no sooner) ▶ **he had hardly sat down when the door burst open** 他一坐下门(門)就被猛地打开(開)了 tā yī zuòxià mén jiù bèi měng de dǎkāi le ▶ **hardly ever/any/anyone** 几(幾)乎从(從)不/没(沒)有/没(沒)有任何人 jīhū cóngbù/méiyǒu/méiyǒu rènhé rén ▶ **I can hardly believe it** 我简(簡)直不能相信 wǒ jiǎnzhí bùnéng xiāngxìn

hardware ['hɑːdwɛəʳ] N [U] (Comput) 硬件 yìngjiàn

hardworking [hɑːdˈwəːkɪŋ] ADJ 勤奋(奮)的 qínfèn de

harm [hɑːm] VT **1** (damage) 损(損)坏(壞) sǔnhuài **2** (injure) 伤(傷)害 shānghài

harmful ['hɑːmful] ADJ 有害的 yǒuhài de

harp [hɑːp] N [c] (Mus) 竖(豎)琴 shùqín [架 jià]

harvest ['hɑːvɪst] N **1** [c/U] (harvest time) 收获(穫) shōuhuò [种 zhǒng] **2** [c] (crop) 收成 shōucheng [个 gè]

has [hæz] VB see **have**

hashtag ['hæʃtˌhæg] N [c] (Comput only) 主题(題)标(標)签(簽) zhǔtí biāoqiān [个 gè]

hasn't ['hæznt] = **has not**

hat [hæt] N [c] 帽子 màozi [顶 dǐng]

hate [heɪt] VT [+ person] 恨 hèn; [+ food, activity, sensation] 讨(討)厌(厭) tǎoyàn ▶ **to hate doing/to do sth** 不喜欢(歡)做某事 bù xǐhuan zuò mǒushì

hatred ['heɪtrɪd] N [U] 仇恨 chóuhèn

 KEYWORD

have [hæv] (pt, pp had) I VT **1** 有 yǒu ▶ **he has** or **he has got blue eyes/dark hair** 他长(長)着(著)蓝(藍)眼睛/黑头(頭)发(髮) tā zhǎngzhe lán yǎnjing/hēi tóufa ▶ **do you have** or **have you got a car/phone?** 你有车(車)/电(電)话(話)吗(嗎)? nǐ yǒu chē/diànhuà ma? ▶ **to have** or **have got sth to do** 有必须(須)得做的事 yǒu bìxū děi zuò de shì ▶ **she had her eyes closed** 她闭(閉)上了眼睛 tā bìshàng le yǎnjing

2 ▶ **to have breakfast** 吃早饭(飯) chī zǎofàn ▶ **to have a drink/a cigarette** 喝一杯/抽支烟(煙) hē yì bēi/chōu zhī yān

3 ▶ **to have a swim/bath** 游泳/洗澡 yóuyǒng/xǐzǎo ▶ **to have a meeting/party** 开(開)会(會)/开(開)派对(對) kāihuì/kāi pàiduì

4 (receive, obtain) 得到 dédào ▶ **can I have your address?** 能告诉(訴)我你的地址吗(嗎)? néng gàosù wǒ nǐ de dìzhǐ ma? ▶ **you can have it for £5** 付5英镑(鎊)它就是你的了 fù wǔ yīngbàng tā jiùshì nǐ de le

5 ▶ **to have a baby** 生孩子 shēng háizi

6 ▶ **to have sth done** 指使/安排做某事 zhǐshǐ/ānpái zuò mǒushì ▶ **to have one's hair cut** 理发(髮) lǐfà

7 ▶ **to have a headache** 头(頭)痛 tóutòng ▶ **to have an operation** 动(動)手术(術) dòng shǒushù

II AUX VB **1** ▶ **to have arrived/gone** 已到了/走了 yǐ dàole/zǒule ▶ **has he told you?** 他已经(經)告诉(訴)你了吗(嗎)? tā yǐjīng gàosù nǐ le ma? ▶ **when she had dressed, she went downstairs** 穿好衣服后(後),她下了楼(樓) chuānhǎo yīfu hòu, tā xiàle lóu ▶ **I haven't seen him for ages/since July** 我已经(經)很久/自7月以来(來)就没(沒)见(見)过(過)他了 wǒ yǐjīng hěn jiǔ/zì qīyuè yǐlái jiù méi jiànguo tā le

2 (in tag questions) ▸ **you've done it, haven't you?** 你已经(經)做了，是不是？ nǐ yǐjīng zuò le, shì bù shì?
3 (in short answers and questions) ▸ **yes, I have**, 是的，我有/已做了 shì de, wǒ yǒu/yǐzuò le ▸ **no I haven't!** 不，我还(還)没(沒)有/没(沒)做呢! bù, wǒ hái méiyǒu/méi zuò ne! ▸ **so have I!** 我也一样(樣)! wǒ yě yīyàng! ▸ **neither have I** 我也没(沒)有过(過) wǒ yě méiyǒuguo ▸ **I've finished, have you?** 我已经(經)完成了，你呢? wǒ yǐjīng wánchéng le, nǐ ne?
4 (be obliged) ▸ **to have (got) to do sth** 不得不做某事 bù dé bù zuò mǒushì ▸ **she has (got) to do it** 她必须(須)得这(這)么(麼)做 tā bìxū děi zhème zuò ▸ **have on** VT [+ clothes] 穿着(著) chuānzhe ▸ **he didn't have anything on** 他什么(麼)都没(沒)穿 tā shénme dōu méi chuān

haven't ['hævnt] = have not
hay fever N [U] 花粉病 huāfěnbìng
hazel ['heɪzl] ADJ [+ eyes] 淡褐色的 dàn hèsè de
he [hiː] PRON 他 tā
head [hed] I N [c] **1** 头(頭) tóu [个 gè] **2** [of company, organization, department] 领(領)导(導) lǐngdǎo [个 gè] **3** (Brit: head teacher) 校长(長) xiàozhǎng [位 wèi] II VT **1** [+ list, group] 以…打头(頭) yǐ…dǎtóu **2** (Football) [+ ball] 用头(頭)顶(頂) yòng tóu dǐng ▸ **10 pounds a** or **per head** 每人10英镑(鎊) měi rén shí yīngbàng ▸ **from head to foot** or **toe** 从(從)头(頭)到脚(腳) cóng tóu dào jiǎo ▸ **heads or tails?** 正面还(還)是反面? zhèngmiàn háishi fǎnmiàn?
▸ **head for** VT FUS 前往 qiánwǎng ▸ **to be heading** or **headed for Glasgow** 正前往格拉斯哥 zhèng qiánwǎng Gélāsīgē
headache ['hedeɪk] N [c] 头(頭)痛 tóutòng [阵 zhèn] ▸ **to have a headache** 头(頭)痛 tóutòng
headlight ['hedlaɪt] N [c] 前灯(燈) qiándēng [个 gè]
headline ['hedlaɪn] N [c] 标(標)题(題) biāotí [个 gè] ▸ **the headlines** (Publishing) 头(頭)条(條)新闻(聞)

tóutiáo xīnwén; (TV, Rad) 内(內)容提要 nèiróng tíyào
headmaster [hed'mɑːstəʳ] (Brit) N [c] 校长(長) xiàozhǎng [位 wèi]
headmistress [hed'mɪstrɪs] (Brit) N [c] 女校长(長) nǚxiàozhǎng [位 wèi]
head office N [c/U] [of company] 总(總)部 zǒngbù
headphones ['hedfəʊnz] NPL 耳机(機) ěrjī
headquarters ['hedkwɔːtəz] NPL 总(總)部 zǒngbù
heal [hiːl] VI 痊愈(癒) quányù
health [helθ] N [U] 健康 jiànkāng ▸ **to be good/bad for one's health** 对(對)人的健康有益/不利 duì mǒurén de jiànkāng yǒuyì/bùlì ▸ **to drink (to) sb's health** 举(舉)杯祝某人健康 jǔbēi zhù mǒurén jiànkāng
healthy ['helθɪ] ADJ **1** 健康的 jiànkāng de **2** [+ diet, lifestyle] 对(對)健康有益的 duì jiànkāng yǒuyì de
heap [hiːp] N [c] 堆 duī [个 gè]
hear [hɪəʳ] (pt, pp heard [həːd]) VT **1** 听(聽)见(見) tīngjiàn **2** [+ news, lecture, concert] 听(聽)听 tīng ▸ **to hear sb doing sth** 听(聽)见(見)某人做某事 tīngjiàn mǒurén zuò mǒushì ▸ **to hear that…** 听(聽)说(說)… tīngshuō… ▸ **to hear about sth/sb** 听(聽)说(說)某事/某人 tīngshuō mǒushì/mǒurén ▸ **to hear from sb** 得到某人的消息 dédào mǒurén de xiāoxi ▸ **I've never heard of him** 我从(從)来(來)没(沒)听(聽)说(說)过(過)他 wǒ cónglái méi tīngshuō guo tā
heart [hɑːt] N **1** [c] 心脏(臟) xīnzàng [颗 kē] **2** [c] (emotions) 感情 gǎnqíng [种 zhǒng] **3** [c] (shape) 心形物 xīnxíngwù [个 gè] ▸ **to learn/know sth (off) by heart** 背诵(誦)某事 bèisòng mǒushì ▸ **to break sb's heart** 使某人伤(傷)心 shǐ mǒurén shāngxīn
heart attack N [c] 心脏(臟)病发(發)作 xīnzàngbìng fāzuò [阵 zhèn] ▸ **to have a heart attack** 心脏(臟)病发(發)作 xīnzàngbìng fāzuò
heat [hiːt] I N **1** [U] 热(熱) rè **2** [U] (temperature) 热(熱)度 rèdù **3** [c] (Sport) (also: **qualifying heat**) 预(預)赛(賽) yùsài [场 chǎng] II VT [+ water, food] 加

热(熱) jiārè; [+ room, house] 取暖 qǔnuǎn ▶ I find the heat unbearable 热(熱)得我实(實)在受不了 rè de wǒ shízài shòu bù liǎo
▶ heat up VT [+ food] 加热(熱) jiārè

heater ['hi:tər] N [c] (electric heater, gas heater) 供暖装(裝)置 gōngnuǎn zhuāngzhì [个 gè]; (in car) 暖气(氣) 设(設)备(備) nuǎnqì shèbèi [套 tào]

heating ['hi:tɪŋ] N [U] (system) 暖气(氣) nuǎnqì

heatwave ['hi:tweɪv] N [c] 酷暑时(時) 期 kùshǔ shíqí [段 duàn]

heaven ['hɛvn] N [U] 天堂 tiāntáng

heavy ['hɛvɪ] ADJ 1 重的 zhòng de 2 [+ traffic] 拥(擁)挤(擠)的 yōngjǐ de; [+ fine, penalty, sentence] 重的 zhòng de; [+ drinking, smoking, gambling] 过(過)度 的 guòdù de; [+ rain, snow] 大的 dà de ▶ how heavy are you/is it? 你/它有多 重? nǐ/tā yǒu duō zhòng?

he'd [hi:d] = he would, he had

hedge [hɛdʒ] N [c] 树(樹)篱(籬) shùlí [道 dào]

heel [hi:l] N [c] 1 [of foot] 脚(腳)后(後)跟 jiǎohòugēn [个 gè] 2 [of shoe] 鞋跟 xiégēn [个 gè]

height [haɪt] N 1 [c/u] 高度 gāodù [个 gè] 2 [c] (altitude) 高处(處) gāochù ▶ of average/medium height 平均/中等高 度 píngjūn/zhōngděng gāodù

held [hɛld] PT, PP OF hold

helicopter ['hɛlɪkɒptər] N [c] 直升 机(機) zhíshēngjī [架 jià]

hell [hɛl] I N [U] 地狱(獄) dìyù II INT (inf!) 天啊 tiān a ▶ it was hell (inf) 糟糕 极(極)了 zāogāo jí le

he'll [hi:l] = he will, he shall

hello [hə'ləu] INT (as greeting) 你好 nǐ hǎo; (Tel) 喂 wèi; (to attract attention) 劳(勞)驾(駕) láojià

helmet ['hɛlmɪt] N [c] 1 头(頭)盔 tóukuī [个 gè]; [of soldier, police officer, firefighter] 钢(鋼)盔 gāngkuī [个 gè]

help [hɛlp] I N [U] 帮(幫)助 bāngzhù II VT [+ person] 帮(幫)助 bāngzhù III VI 1 (assist) 帮忙 bāngmáng 2 (be useful) 有用 yǒuyòng ▶ thanks, you've been a great help 谢(謝)谢(謝), 你帮(幫)了 很大忙 xièxie, nǐ bāngle hěn dà máng ▶ I helped him (to) fix his car 我帮(幫)

助他修了他的车(車) wǒ bāngzhù tā xiūle tā de chē ▶ help! 救命! jiùmìng! ▶ can I help you? (in shop) 我能为(為)您 效劳(勞)吗(嗎)? wǒ néng wèi nín xiàoláo ma? ▶ I can't help feeling sorry for him 我情不自禁地同情他 wǒ qíng bù zì jīn de tóngqíng tā ▶ it can't be helped 没(沒)办(辦)法 méi bànfǎ

helpful ['hɛlpful] ADJ 有用的 yǒuyòng de; [+ advice, suggestion] 有建设(設)性的 yǒu jiànshèxìng de

helping ['hɛlpɪŋ] N [c] (of food) 一份 yī fèn

helpless ['hɛlplɪs] ADJ 无(無)依无(無)靠 的 wúyīwúkào de

hen [hɛn] N [c] 母鸡(雞) mǔjī [只 zhī]

her [hə:r] I PRON 她 tā II ADJ 她的 tā de ▶ I haven't seen her 我还(還)没(沒) 见(見)到她。wǒ hái méi jiàndào tā ▶ they gave her the job 他们(們)给(給) 了她那份工作 tāmen gěile tā nà fèn gōngzuò ▶ her face was very red 她的 脸(臉)很红(紅) tā de liǎn hěn hóng

herb [hə:b, US ə:rb] N [c] 草本植物 cǎoběn zhíwù [株 zhū]

herd [hə:d] N [c] 牧群 mùqún [群 qún]

here [hɪər] ADV 1 (in/to this place) 在 这(這)里(裡) zài zhèlǐ 2 (near me) 到 这(這)里(裡) dào zhèlǐ ▶ here's my phone number 这(這)是我的电(電) 话(話)号(號)码(碼) zhè shì wǒ de diànhuà hàomǎ ▶ here he is 他到了 tā dào le ▶ here you are (take this) 给(給) 你 gěi nǐ ▶ here and there 各处(處) gèchù

hero ['hɪərəu] (pl heroes) N [c] 1 男主人 公 nán zhǔréngōng [个 gè] 2 [of battle, struggle] 英雄 yīngxióng [位 wèi]

heroin ['hɛrəuɪn] N [U] 海洛因 hǎiluòyīn

heroine ['hɛrəuɪn] N [c] 1 女主人公 nǚzhǔréngōng [个 gè] 2 (of battle, struggle) 女英雄 nǚyīngxióng [位 wèi]

hers [hə:z] PRON 她的 tā de ▶ this is hers 这(這)是她的。zhè shì tā de ▶ a friend of hers 她的一个(個)朋友 tā de yī gè péngyou

herself [hə:'sɛlf] PRON 1 她自己 tā zìjǐ 2 (emphatic) 她本人 tā běnrén ▶ she hurt herself 她伤(傷)了自己。tā shāngle zìjǐ ▶ she made the dress herself 她自己做的这(這)件连(連)衣 裙。tā zìjǐ zuò de zhè jiàn liányīqún

▶ she lives by herself 她独(獨)自一人住 tā dúzì yī rén zhù

he's [hiːz] = he is, he has

hesitate ['hezɪteɪt] VI 犹(猶)豫 yóuyù ▶ he did not hesitate to take action 毫不迟(遲)疑地采(採)取了行动(動) tā háo bù chíyí de cáiqǔ le xíngdòng ▶ don't hesitate to contact me 请(請)务(務)必和我联(聯)系(繫) qǐng wùbì hé wǒ liánxì

heterosexual ['hetərəu'seksjuəl] N [c] 异(異)性恋(戀)者 yìxìngliànzhě [个 gè]

hi [haɪ] INT (as greeting) 嘿 hēi; (in email) 你好 nǐhǎo

hiccup ['hɪkʌp]: **hiccups** NPL ▶ to have/ get (the) hiccups 打嗝 dǎgé

hidden ['hɪdn] PP of **hide**

hide [haɪd] (pt hid, pp hidden) I VT 隐(隱) 藏 yǐncáng; [+ feeling, information] 隐(隱)瞒(瞞) yǐnmán II VI 藏起来(來) cáng qǐlái ▶ to hide from sb 躲着(著) 人 duǒzhe mǒurén

hi-fi ['haɪfaɪ] N [c] 高保真音响(響)设(設) 备(備) gāobǎozhēn yīnxiǎng shèbèi [套 tào]

high [haɪ] I ADJ 高的 gāo de II ADV [reach, throw +] 高高地 gāogāo de; [fly, climb +] 高 gāo ▶ it is 20 m high 有20米高 yǒu èrshí mǐ gāo ▶ foods that are high in fat 脂肪含量高的食品 zhīfáng hánliàng gāo de shípǐn ▶ safety has always been our highest priority 安全 一直是我们(們)最重视(視)的问(問) 题(題) ānquán yīzhí shì wǒmen zuì zhòngshì de wèntí ▶ high up 离(離)地 面高的 lí dìmiàn gāo de

> high 不能用于描写人，动物和植物，
> 而应用 tall。She was rather tall for a
> woman。tall 还可以用来描写建筑物
> （如摩天大楼等）以及其他高度大于宽度
> 的东西。...tall pine trees...a tall glass
> vase...

higher education ['haɪə'-] N [U] 高等教 育 gāoděng jiàoyù

high-rise ['haɪraɪz] ADJ 高层(層)的 gāocéng de

high school N [c/U] 中学(學) zhōngxué [所 suǒ]

hijack ['haɪdʒæk] VT 劫持 jiéchí

hijacker ['haɪdʒækə'] N [c] 劫持者 jiéchízhě [个 gè]

hike [haɪk] I VI 步行 bùxíng II N [c] (walk) 徒步旅行 túbù lǚxíng ▶ to go hiking 做徒步旅行 zuò túbù lǚxíng

hiking ['haɪkɪŋ] N 步行 bùxíng

hill [hɪl] N [c] 小山 xiǎoshān [座 zuò]; (slope) 坡 pō [个 gè]

him [hɪm] PRON 他 tā ▶ I haven't seen him 我还(還)没(沒)看见(見)他 wǒ hái méi kànjiàn tā ▶ they gave him the job 他们(們)给(給)了他那份工作 tāmen gěile tā nà fèn gōngzuò

himself [hɪm'self] PRON 1 他自己 tā zìjǐ 2 (emphatic) 他本人 tā běnrén ▶ he hurt himself 他伤(傷)了自己 tā shāngle zìjǐ ▶ he prepared the supper himself 他自 己准(準)备(備)了晚餐 tā zìjǐ zhǔnbèile wǎncān ▶ he lives by himself 他独(獨) 自一人住 tā dúzì yīrén zhù

Hindu ['hɪnduː] N [c] 印度教信徒 Yìndùjiào xìntú [位 wèi] II ADJ 与(與)印 度教有关(關)的 yǔ Yìndùjiào yǒuguān de

hip [hɪp] N [c] 髋(髖)部 kuānbù [个 gè]

hippie ['hɪpɪ] N [c] 嬉皮士 xīpíshì [个 gè]

hire ['haɪə'] I VT (esp Brit) 租用 zūyòng; [+ worker] 雇(僱)用 gùyòng II N [U] (Brit) [of car, hall] 租用 zūyòng

hire car (Brit) N [c] 租的车(車) zū de chē

his [hɪz] I ADJ 他的 tā de II PRON 他的 tā de ▶ his face was very red 他的脸(臉) 很红(紅) tā de liǎn hěn hóng ▶ these are his 这(這)些是他的 zhèxiē shì tā de ▶ a friend of his 他的一个(個)朋友 tā de yī gè péngyou

history ['hɪstərɪ] N [U] 历(歷)史 lìshǐ

hit [hɪt] I VT 1 (strike) 打 dǎ 2 (collide with) 碰撞 pèngzhuàng 3 [+ target] 击(擊)中 jīzhòng II N [c] 1 (on website) 点(點)击(擊) diǎnjī [次 cì] 2 (hit song) 成功而风(風)行一时(時)的事物 chénggōng ér fēngxíng yīshí de shìwù [个 gè]

hitchhike ['hɪtʃhaɪk] VI 搭便车(車)旅行 dā biànchē lǚxíng

hitchhiker ['hɪtʃhaɪkə'] N [c] 搭便 车(車)旅行者 dā biànchē lǚxíngzhě [个 gè]

HIV N ABBR (= human immunodeficiency virus) 艾滋病病毒 àizībìng bìngdú

hoarse [hɔːs] ADJ 嘶哑(啞)的 sīyǎ de

hobby ['hɔbɪ] N [c] 爱(愛)好 àihào [种 zhǒng]

hockey ['hɒkɪ] N [U] **1** (*Brit*) 曲棍球 qūgùnqiú **2** (*US: on ice*) 冰球 bīngqiú

hold [həʊld] (*pt, pp* held) I VT **1** 拿 ná **2** (*contain*) 容纳(納) róngnà II VI (*Tel*) 等着(著) děngzhe III N [C] (*of ship, plane*) 货(貨)舱(艙) huòcāng [个 gè] ▶ **hold the line!** (*Tel*) 别(別)挂(掛)线(線)! bié guàxiàn! ▶ **to hold sb prisoner/hostage** 扣(釦)留某人作为(為)囚犯/人质(質) kòuliú mǒurén zuòwéi qiúfàn/rénzhì ▶ **to get/grab/take hold of sb/sth** 紧(緊)紧(緊)拿着(著)/抓着(著)/握着(著)某人/某物 jǐnjǐn názhe/zhuāzhe/wòzhe mǒurén/mǒuwù ▶ **I need to get hold of Bob** 我需要找到鲍(鮑)勃 wǒ xūyào zhǎodào Bàobó

▶ **hold on** VI **1** (*keep hold*) 抓牢 zhuāláo **2** 等一会(會)儿(兒) děng yīhuìr

▶ **hold up** VT **1** (*lift up*) 举(舉)起 jǔqǐ **2** (*delay*) 阻碍(礙) zǔ'ài

hold-up ['həʊldʌp] N [C] **1** (*robbery*) 持械抢(搶)劫 chíxiè qiǎngjié [次 cì] **2** (*delay*) 延搁(擱) yángē [次 cì]; (*in traffic*) 交通阻塞 jiāotōng zǔsè [阵 zhèn]

hole [həʊl] N [C] **1** (*space, gap*) 洞 dòng [个 gè] **2** (*tear*) 破洞 pòdòng [个 gè]

holiday ['hɒlɪdeɪ] (*Brit*) N [C/U] 假期 jiàqī [个 gè] ▶ **public holiday** 公共假期 gōnggòng jiàqī ▶ **the school/summer/Christmas holidays** (*Brit: Scol*) 学(學)校/暑(暑)/圣(聖)诞(誕)假期 xuéxiào/shǔ/Shèngdàn jiàqī ▶ **to be on holiday** 在度假 zài dùjià

Holland ['hɒlənd] N 荷兰(蘭) Hélán

hollow ['hɒləʊ] ADJ (*not solid*) 空的 kōng de

holy ['həʊlɪ] ADJ 神圣(聖)的 shénshèng de

home [həʊm] I N **1** [C/U] (*house*) 家 jiā [个 gè] **2** [C/U] (*country, area*) 家乡(鄉) jiāxiāng [个 gè] **3** [C] (*institution*) 收容院 shōuróngyuàn [个 gè] II ADV [*be, go, get etc* +] 在家 zàijiā ▶ **at home** (*in house*) 在家 zàijiā

homeless ['həʊmlɪs] I ADJ 无(無)家可归(歸)的 wú jiā kě guī de II NPL ▶ **the homeless** 无(無)家可归(歸)的人 wú jiā kě guī de rén

homepage ['həʊmpeɪdʒ] N [C] 主页(頁) zhǔyè [个 gè]

homesick ['həʊmsɪk] ADJ 想家的 xiǎngjiā de

homework ['həʊmwəːk] N [U] 家庭作业(業) jiātíng zuòyè

homosexual [hɒməʊ'sɛksjʊəl] I ADJ 同性恋(戀)的 tóngxìngliàn de II N [C] 同性恋(戀)者 tóngxìngliànzhě [个 gè]

honest ['ɒnɪst] ADJ 诚(誠)实(實)的 chéngshí de ▶ **to be honest,...** 说(說)实(實)话(話), … shuō shíhuà, …

honesty ['ɒnɪstɪ] N [U] 诚(誠)实(實) chéngshí

honey ['hʌnɪ] N [U] 蜂蜜 fēngmì

honeymoon ['hʌnɪmuːn] N [C] 蜜月 mìyuè [个 gè]

Hong Kong ['hɒŋ'kɒŋ] N 香港 Xiānggǎng

hood [hʊd] N [C] **1** 兜帽 dōumào [个 gè] **2** (*US: Aut*) 发(發)动(動)机(機)罩 fādòngjī zhào [个 gè]

hoof [huːf] (*pl* hooves) N 蹄 tí

hook [hʊk] N [C] 钩(鉤) gōu [个 gè] ▶ **to take the phone off the hook** 不把电(電)话(話)听(聽)筒挂(掛)上 bù bǎ diànhuà tīngtǒng guàshàng

hooray [huː'reɪ] INT 好哇 hǎo wa

Hoover® ['huːvə'] (*Brit*) I N [C] 吸尘(塵)器 xīchénqì [台 tái] II VT [+ *carpet*] 用吸尘(塵)器吸 yòng xīchénqì xī

hooves [huːvz] NPL *of* hoof

hop [hɒp] VI 单(單)脚(腳)跳 dānjiǎo tiào

hope [həʊp] I VT 希望 xīwàng II VI 盼望 pànwàng III N [U] 希望 xīwàng ▶ **I hope so/not** 希望是(這)样(樣)/希望不会(會) xīwàng shì zhèyàng/xīwàng bùhuì ▶ **to hope that...** 希望… xīwàng… ▶ **to hope to do sth** 希望能做某事 xīwàng néng zuò mǒushì

hopefully ['həʊpfʊlɪ] ADV ▶ **hopefully,...** 如果运(運)气(氣)好… rúguǒ yùnqì hǎo…

hopeless ['həʊplɪs] ADJ **1** [+ *situation, position*] 糟糕的 zāogāo de **2** (*inf: useless*) 无(無)能的 wúnéng de

horizon [hə'raɪzn] N ▶ **the horizon** 地平线(線) dìpíngxiàn

horizontal [hɒrɪ'zɒntl] ADJ 水平的 shuǐpíng de

horn [hɔːn] N **1** [C] (*of animal*) 角 jiǎo [个 gè] **2** [C] (*Aut*) 喇叭 lǎba [个 gè]

horoscope ['hɒrəskəʊp] N [C] 占星术(術) zhānxīngshù [种 zhǒng]

horrible ['hɒrɪbl] ADJ [+ *colour, food, mess*]

糟透的 zāotòu de; [+ accident, crime] 可怕的 kěpà de; [+ experience, moment, situation, dream] 令人恐惧(懼)的 lìng rén kǒngjù de

horror film N [c] 恐怖片 kǒngbùpiàn [部 bù]

horse [hɔːs] N [c] 马(馬) mǎ [匹 pǐ]

horse racing N [c] 赛(賽)马(馬) sàimǎ

hose [həuz] N [c] (also: hosepipe) 输(輸)水软(軟)管 shūshuǐ ruǎnguǎn [根 gēn]

hospital ['hɔspɪtl] N [c/u] 医(醫)院 yīyuàn [家 jiā] ▸ to be in hospital or (US) in the hospital 住院 zhùyuàn

hospitality [hɔspɪ'tælɪtɪ] N [U] 好客 hàokè

host [həust] N [c] 主人 zhǔrén [位 wèi]

hostage ['hɔstɪdʒ] N [c] 人质(質) rénzhì [个 gè] ▸ to be taken/held hostage 被绑(綁)架/扣押做人质(質) bèi bǎngjià/kòuyā zuò rénzhì

hostel ['hɔstl] N [c] (esp Brit) 招待所 zhāodàisuǒ [个 gè]

hostess ['həustɪs] N [c] 女主人 nǚzhǔrén [位 wèi]

hot [hɔt] ADJ 1 [+ object] 烫(燙)的 tàng de; [+ weather, person] 热(熱)的 rè de 2 (spicy) 辣的 là de

hotel [həu'tɛl] N [c] 旅馆(館) lǚguǎn [个 gè] ▸ to stay at a hotel 住旅馆(館) zhù lǚguǎn

hour ['auər] I N [c] 小时(時) xiǎoshí [个 gè] II hours NPL (ages) 很长(長)时(時)间(間) hěn cháng shíjiān ▸ the buses leave on the hour 每小时(時)正点(點)有一班公共汽车(車) měi xiǎoshí zhèngdiǎn yǒu yī bān gōnggòng qìchē ▸ for three/four hours 三/四个(個)小时(時) sān/sì gè xiǎoshí ▸ (at) 60 kilometres/miles an or per hour 每小时(時)60公里/英里 měi xiǎoshí liùshí gōnglǐ/yīnglǐ ▸ to pay sb by the hour 按小时(時)付费(費)给(給)某人 àn xiǎoshí fùfèi gěi mǒurén ▸ lunch hour 午餐时(時)间(間) wǔcān shíjiān

house [haus] N [c] 家 jiā [个 gè] ▸ at/to my house 在/到我家 zài/dào wǒjiā

housewife ['hauswaɪf] (pl housewives) N [c] 家庭主妇(婦) jiātíng zhǔfù [个 gè]

housework ['hauswəːk] N [U] 家务(務)劳(勞)动(動) jiāwù láodòng

housing estate (Brit) N [c] 住宅区(區) zhùzháiqū [个 gè]

hovercraft ['hɔvəkrɑːft] (pl hovercraft) N [c] 气(氣)垫(墊)船 qìdiànchuán [艘 sōu]

🅚 **KEYWORD**

how [hau] I ADV 1 (in questions) 怎样(樣) zěnyàng ▸ how did you do it? 你是怎么(麼)做的? nǐ shì zěnme zuò de? ▸ how are you? 你好吗(嗎)? nǐ hǎo ma? ▸ how long have you lived here? 你在这(這)儿(兒)住了多久了? nǐ zài zhèr zhùle duō jiǔ le? ▸ how much milk/many people? 有多少奶/人? yǒu duōshǎo nǎi/rén? ▸ how old are you? 你多大了? nǐ duō dà le? ▸ how tall is he? 他有多高? tā yǒu duō gāo? 2 (in suggestions) ▸ how about a cup of tea/a walk etc? 来(來)杯茶/去散步{等}好吗(嗎)? lái bēi chá/qù sànbù děng hǎo ma?
II CONJ 怎么(麼) zěnme ▸ I know how you did it 我知道你怎么(麼)做的 wǒ zhīdào nǐ zěnme zuò de ▸ to know how to do sth 知道如何做某事 zhīdào rúhé zuò mǒushì

however [hau'ɛvər] ADV 1 (but) 但是 dànshì 2 (with adj, adv) 不管怎样(樣) bùguǎn zěnyàng 3 (in questions) 究竟怎样(樣) jiūjìng zěnyàng

hug [hʌg] I VT [+ person] 拥(擁)抱 yōngbào II N [c] 拥(擁)抱 yōngbào [个 gè] ▸ to give sb a hug 拥(擁)抱某人 yōngbào mǒurén

huge [hjuːdʒ] ADJ 巨大的 jùdà de; [+ amount, profit, debt] 巨额(額)的 jù'é de; [+ task] 庞(龐)大的 pángdà de

human ['hjuːmən] I ADJ 人的 rén de II N [c] (also: human being) 人 rén [个 gè] ▸ the human race 人类(類) rénlèi ▸ human nature 人性 rénxìng

humor ['hjuːmər] (US) N = humour

humour, (US) **humor** ['hjuːmər] N [U] 幽默 yōumò ▸ sense of humour 幽默感 yōumògǎn

hundred ['hʌndrəd] I NUM 百 bǎi II hundreds NPL 几(幾)百 jǐbǎi ▸ a or one hundred books/people/

dollars 一百本书(書)/个(個)人/美元 yībǎi běn shū/gè rén/měiyuán

hung [hʌŋ] PT, PP of **hang**

Hungary ['hʌŋgərɪ] N 匈牙利 Xiōngyálì

hungry ['hʌŋgrɪ] ADJ 饥(飢)饿(餓)的 jī'è de ▸ **to be hungry** 饿(餓)了 èle

hunt [hʌnt] I VT (for food, sport) 打猎(獵) dǎliè II VI (for food, sport) 打猎(獵) dǎliè III N [c] **1** (for food, sport) 狩猎(獵) shòuliè [次 cì] **2** (for missing person) 搜(蒐)寻(尋) sōuxún [次 cì] **3** (for criminal) 追捕 zhuībǔ [次 cì]

hunting ['hʌntɪŋ] N [U] (for food, sport) 打猎(獵) dǎliè ▸ **job/house/bargain hunting** 到处(處)找工作/住房/便宜货(貨) dàochù zhǎo gōngzuò/zhùfáng/piányihuò

hurricane ['hʌrɪkən] N [c] 飓风(風) jùfēng [场 chǎng] ▸ **hurricane Charley/Tessa** 查理/特萨(薩)号(號)台(颱)风(風) Chálǐ/Tèsà hào táifēng

hurry ['hʌrɪ] I VI 赶(趕)紧(緊) gǎnjǐn II N ▸ **to be in a hurry (to do sth)** 急于(於)(做某事) jíyú (zuò mǒushì) ▸ **to do sth in a hurry** 匆忙地做某事 cōngmáng de zuò mǒushì ▸ **hurry up** I VI 赶(趕)快 gǎnkuài

hurt [həːt] (pt, pp **hurt**) I VT **1** (cause pain to) 弄痛 nòngtòng **2** (injure) 使受伤(傷) shǐ shòushāng **3** (emotionally) 使伤(傷)心 shǐ shāngxīn II VI (be painful) 痛 tòng III ADJ **1** (injured) 受伤(傷)的 shòushāng de **2** (emotionally) 受委屈的 shòu wěiqū de ▸ **to hurt o.s.** 伤(傷)了自己 shāngle zìjǐ ▸ **I didn't want to hurt your feelings** 我并(並)不想伤(傷)害你的感情 wǒ bìng bù xiǎng shānghài nǐ de gǎnqíng ▸ **where does it hurt?** 哪儿(兒)疼? nǎr téng?

husband ['hʌzbənd] N [c] 丈夫 zhàngfu [个 gè]

hut [hʌt] N [c] (shed) 木棚 mùpéng [个 gè]

hyphen ['haɪfn] N [c] 连(連)字符 liánzìfú [个 gè]

I [aɪ] PRON 我 wǒ

ice [aɪs] N [U] 冰 bīng; (for drink) 冰块(塊) bīngkuài

iceberg ['aɪsbəːg] N [c] 冰山 bīngshān [座 zuò] ▸ **the tip of the iceberg** (fig) 冰山一角 bīngshān yījiǎo

ice cream N [c/U] 冰激凌 bīngjīlíng [个 gè]

ice cube N [c] 冰块(塊) bīngkuài [块 kuài]

ice hockey (esp Brit) N [U] 冰球 bīngqiú

Iceland ['aɪslənd] N 冰岛(島) Bīngdǎo

ice rink N [c] 溜冰场(場) liūbīngchǎng [个 gè]

ice-skating ['aɪsskeɪtɪŋ] N [U] 溜冰 liūbīng

icing (Culin) N [U] 糖霜 tángshuāng

icon ['aɪkɔn] N [c] (Comput) 图(圖)符 túfú [个 gè]

ICT (Brit) N ABBR (= information and communication technology) 通信技术(術) tōngxìn jìshù

ID N ABBR (= identification) 身份证(證)明 shēnfèn zhèngmíng ▸ **do you have any ID?** 你有证(證)件吗(嗎)? nǐ yǒu zhèngjiàn ma?

I'd [aɪd] = **I would, I had**

idea [aɪˈdɪə] N **1** [c] (scheme) 主意 zhǔyi [个 gè] **2** [c] (opinion, theory) 看法 kànfǎ [种 zhǒng] **3** [c/U] (notion) 概念 gàiniàn [个 gè] ▸ **(what a) good idea!** (真是

个(個)）好主意! (zhēn shì gè)hǎo zhǔyi! ► **I haven't the slightest** or **faintest idea** 我根本就不知道 wǒ gēnběn jiù bù zhīdào

ideal [aɪˈdɪəl] ADJ 理想的 lǐxiǎng de

identical [aɪˈdɛntɪkl] ADJ 完全相同的 wánquán xiāngtóng de ► **identical to** 和…完全相同 hé…wánquán xiāngtóng

identification [aɪdɛntɪfɪˈkeɪʃən] N [U] (proof of identity) 身份证(證)明 shēnfèn zhèngmíng

identify [aɪˈdɛntɪfaɪ] VT (recognize) 识(識)别(別) shíbié

identity card N [c] 身份证(證) shēnfènzhèng [个 gè]

idiot [ˈɪdɪət] N [c] 傻子 shǎzi [个 gè]

i.e. ABBR (= id est) 也就是 yě jiù shì

◯ **KEYWORD**

if [ɪf] CONJ **1** (conditional use) 如果 rúguǒ ► **I'll go if you come with me** 如果你和我一起的话(話)我就去 rúguǒ nǐ hé wǒ yīqǐ de huà wǒ jiù qù ► **if I were you** 如果我是你的话(話) rúguǒ wǒ shì nǐ de huà ► **if necessary** 如有必要 rú yǒu bìyào ► **if so** 如果是这(這)样(樣)的话(話) rúguǒ shì zhèyàng de huà ► **if not** 如果不行的话(話) rúguǒ bùxíng de huà **2** (whenever) 无(無)论(論)何时(時) wúlùn héshí ► **if we are in Hong Kong, we always go to see her** 我们(們)无(無)论(論)何时(時)去港, 都会(會)去看她 wǒmen wúlùn héshí qù Xiānggǎng, dōu huì qù kàn tā **3** (whether) 是否 shìfǒu ► **ask him if he can come** 问(問)他是否能来(來) wèn tā shìfǒu néng lái **4** (in expressions) ► **if only we had more time!** 要是我们(們)再多点(點)时(時)间(間)就好了! yàoshi wǒmen zài duō diǎn shíjiān jiù hǎo le!

ignore [ɪgˈnɔːʳ] VT [+ person] 不理 bù lǐ; [+ advice, event] 不顾(顧) bù gù

I'll [aɪl] = I will, I shall

ill [ɪl] I ADJ 有病的 yǒubìng de II **the ill** NPL ► **the mentally/terminally ill** 精神/晚期病人 jīngshén/wǎnqī bìngrén ► **to fall** or **be taken ill** 生病 shēngbìng

单词 ill 和 sick 在语意上很相近, 但使用方法略有不同。ill 通常不用在名词前, 但可用在动词词组中, 比如 fall ill 和 be taken ill。He fell ill shortly before Christmas...One of the jury members was taken ill. sick 经常用在名词前。...sick children... 在英式英语中, ill 比 sick 更为文雅和委婉。sick 常常指实际的身体病痛, 例如晕船或呕吐。I spent the next 24 hours in bed, groaning and being sick. 美式英语中, sick 经常用在英国人说 ill 的地方。Some people get hurt in accidents or get sick.

illegal [ɪˈliːgl] ADJ 非法的 fēifǎ de

illness [ˈɪlnɪs] N [c/u] 病 bìng [场 chǎng]

illusion [ɪˈluːʒən] N [c] 幻想 huànxiǎng [个 gè]

illustration [ɪləˈstreɪʃən] N [c] 插图(圖) chātú [幅 fú]

imagination [ɪmædʒɪˈneɪʃən] N [c/u] 想象力 xiǎngxiànglì [种 zhǒng] **2** [c] (mind's eye) 想象 xiǎngxiàng [个 gè]

imagine [ɪˈmædʒɪn] VT **1** (envisage) 想象 xiǎngxiàng **2** (suppose) 设(設)想 shèxiǎng

imitate [ˈɪmɪteɪt] VT **1** (copy) 效仿 xiàofǎng **2** [+ person, sound, gesture] 模仿 mófǎng

imitation [ɪmɪˈteɪʃən] I N [c] 仿制(製)品 fǎngzhìpǐn [件 jiàn] II ADJ 仿制(製)的 fǎngzhì de

immediate [ɪˈmiːdɪət] ADJ 立即的 lìjí de

immediately [ɪˈmiːdɪətlɪ] I ADV (at once) 立即地 lìjí de II CONJ ► **immediately he had said it, he regretted it** 他刚(剛)一说(說)完马(馬)上就后(後)悔了 tā gāng yī shuōwán mǎshàng jiù hòuhuǐ le ► **immediately before/after** 紧(緊)接着(著)…之前/后(後) jǐnjiēzhe…zhīqián/hòu

immigrant [ˈɪmɪgrənt] N [c] 移民 yímín [个 gè]

immigration [ɪmɪˈgreɪʃən] I N [U] **1** (process) 移民 yímín **2** (also: immigration control) 移民局检(檢)查 yímínjú jiǎnchá II CPD [+ authorities, policy, controls, officer] 移民 yímín

impatient [ɪmˈpeɪʃənt] ADJ 急躁的 jízào de ► **to get impatient (at** or **with sth)** (对(對)某事) 不耐烦(煩) (duì mǒushì) bù nàifán

import [ɪmˈpɔːt] VT 进(進)口 jìnkǒu

importance [ɪmˈpɔːtns] N [U]
1 (*significance*) 重要性 zhòngyàoxìng
2 (*influence*) 影响(響) yǐngxiǎng

important [ɪmˈpɔːtənt] ADJ **1** 重要的 zhòngyào de **2** (*influential*) 有影响(響) 的 yǒu yǐngxiǎng de ▸ **it is important to eat sensibly** 合理进(進)食是很重要的 hélǐ jìnshí shì hěn zhòngyào de ▸ **it's not important** 不重要的 bù zhòngyào de

impossible [ɪmˈpɔsɪbl] ADJ 不可能的 bù kěnéng de ▸ **it is impossible to understand what's going on** 不可能了解事情的进(進)展情况(況) bù kěnéng liǎojiě shìqing de jìnzhǎn qíngkuàng

impress [ɪmˈprɛs] VT [+ *person*] 给(給)…极(極)深的印象 gěi…jíshēn de yìnxiàng ▸ **to be impressed by** or **with sb/sth** 对(對)某人/某物印象深刻 duì mǒurén/mǒuwù yìnxiàng shēnkè

impression [ɪmˈprɛʃən] N [c] 印象 yìnxiàng [个 gè] ▸ **to make** or **create a good/bad impression** 留下好/不良印象 liúxià hǎo/bùliáng yìnxiàng

impressive [ɪmˈprɛsɪv] ADJ 给(給)人深刻印象的 gěi rén shēnkè yìnxiàng de

improve [ɪmˈpruːv] I VT 改进(進) gǎijìn II VI [*weather, situation* +] 改善 gǎishàn; [*pupil, performance* +] 进(進)步 jìnbù

improvement [ɪmˈpruːvmənt] N [c/U] 改进(進) gǎijìn [个 gè] ▸ **improvement in** [+ *person, thing*] 进(進)步 jìnbù

🔵 **KEYWORD**

in [ɪn] I PREP **1** 在…里(裡) zài…li ▸ **it's in the house/garden/box** 它在房子/花园(園)/盒子里(裡) tā zài fángzi/huāyuán/hézi li ▸ **put it in the house/garden/box** 把它放在房子/花园(園)/盒子里(裡) bǎ tā fàng zài fángzi/huāyuán/hézi li ▸ **in here/there** 在这(這)儿(兒)/那儿(兒) zài zhèr/nàr
2 (*with place names*) 在 zài ▸ **in London/England** 在伦(倫)敦/英格兰(蘭) zài Lúndūn/Yīnggélán
3 (*time: during*) 在 zài; (*within*) (*referring to future*) 在…之后(後) zài…zhīhòu; (*referring to past*) 在…之内(內) zài…zhīnèi ▸ **in 1988/May** 在1988年/5

月 zài yī jiǔ bā bā nián/wǔ yuè ▸ **in the morning/afternoon** 在上午/下午 zài shàngwǔ/xiàwǔ ▸ **I'll see you in two weeks' time** or **in two weeks** 我两(兩)周(週)后(後)见(見)你 wǒ liǎng zhōu hòu jiàn nǐ ▸ **I did it in 3 hours/days** 我花了3小时(時)/天完成 wǒ huāle sān xiǎoshí/tiān wánchéng
4 (*indicating manner, material etc*) 以 yǐ ▸ **in pencil/ink** 用铅(鉛)笔(筆)/墨水笔(筆) yòng qiānbǐ/mòshuǐbǐ ▸ **the boy in the blue shirt** 穿蓝(藍)衬(襯)衫的男孩儿(兒) chuān lán chènshān de nánhái'r ▸ **in the sun/rain** 在阳(陽)光下/雨中 zài yángguāng xià/yǔ zhōng
5 (*with languages*) 用 yòng ▸ **in English/French** 用英语(語)/法语(語) yòng yīngyǔ/fǎyǔ
6 (*with ratios, numbers*) 每 měi ▸ **one in ten people** 十分之一的人 shí fēn zhī yī de rén
7 (*amongst*) [+ *group, collection*] 在…中 zài…zhōng ▸ **the best athlete in the team** 该(該)队(隊)中最好的运(運)动(動)员(員) gāiduì zhōng zuìhǎo de yùndòngyuán
II ADV ▸ **to be in** (*at home, work*) 在 zài ▸ **to ask sb in** 把某人请(請)到家中 bǎ mǒurén qǐngdào jiāzhōng

inbox [ˈɪnbɒks] N [c] (*of email*) 收件箱 shōujiànxiāng [个 gè]

inch [ɪntʃ] N [c] 英寸 yīngcùn

include [ɪnˈkluːd] VT 包括 bāokuò

including [ɪnˈkluːdɪŋ] PREP 包括 bāokuò ▸ **nine people were injured, including two Britons** 九个(個)人受了伤(傷)，包括两(兩)个(個)英国(國)人 jiǔ gè rén shòule shāng, bāokuò liǎng gè Yīngguórén

income [ˈɪnkʌm] N [c/U] 收入 shōurù [笔 bǐ]

income tax N [U] 所得税(稅) suǒdéshuì

inconvenient [ɪnkənˈviːnjənt] ADJ [+ *time, moment*] 不合时(時)宜的 bùhé shíyí de

incorrect [ɪnkəˈrɛkt] ADJ 错(錯)误(誤)的 cuòwù de

increase [n ˈɪnkriːs, vb ɪnˈkriːs] I N [c] 增长(長) zēngzhǎng [成 chéng] II VI 增长(長) zēngzhǎng III VT [+ *price, number*, level] 提高 tígāo ▸ **a 5% increase, an increase of 5%** 百分之五的增长(長) bǎi fēn zhī wǔ de zēngzhǎng

incredible [ɪnˈkrɛdɪbl] ADJ (amazing, wonderful) 不可思议(議)的 bù kě sīyì de

indeed [ɪnˈdiːd] ADV (as a reply) 是的 shì de ▸ **yes indeed!** 的确(確)如此！díquè rúcǐ!

independence [ɪndɪˈpɛndns] N [U] 独(獨)立 dúlì

independent [ɪndɪˈpɛndnt] ADJ 独(獨)立的 dúlì de

index [ˈɪndɛks] (pl indexes) N [C] 索引 suǒyǐn [条 tiáo]

India [ˈɪndɪə] N 印度 Yìndù

Indian [ˈɪndɪən] I ADJ 印度的 Yìndù de II N [C] (person from India) 印度人 Yìndùrén [个 gè]

indicate [ˈɪndɪkeɪt] VT 1 表明 biǎomíng 2 (point to) 指向 zhǐxiàng

indifferent [ɪnˈdɪfrənt] ADJ 1 没(沒)兴(興)趣的 méi xìngqù de 2 (mediocre) 平庸的 píngyōng de

indigestion [ɪndɪˈdʒɛstʃən] N [U] 消化不良 xiāohuà bùliáng

individual [ɪndɪˈvɪdjuəl] I N 个(個)人 gèrén II ADJ (personal) 个(個)人的 gèrén de

indoor [ˈɪndɔːʳ] ADJ 室内(內)的 shìnèi de

indoors [ɪnˈdɔːz] ADV 在室内(內) zài shìnèi

industrial [ɪnˈdʌstrɪəl] ADJ 工业(業)的 gōngyè de; [+ accident] 因工的 yīngōng de

industrial estate (Brit) N [C] 工业(業)区(區) gōngyèqū [个 gè]

industrial park (US) N [C] 工业(業)区(區) gōngyèqū [个 gè]

industry [ˈɪndəstrɪ] N 1 [U] (manufacturing) 工业(業) gōngyè 2 [C] (business) 行业(業) hángyè [种 zhǒng]

inevitable [ɪnˈɛvɪtəbl] ADJ 不可避免的 bù kě bìmiǎn de

infection [ɪnˈfɛkʃən] N [C] 感染 gǎnrǎn [处 chù] ▸ **to have an ear/a throat infection** 耳朵/咽喉感染 ěrduo/yānhóu gǎnrǎn

infectious [ɪnˈfɛkʃəs] ADJ 传(傳)染的 chuánrǎn de

inflation [ɪnˈfleɪʃən] N [U] 通货(貨)膨胀(脹) tōnghuò péngzhàng

influence [ˈɪnfluəns] I N 1 [C/U] (power) 权(權)势(勢) quánshì [种 zhǒng] 2 [C] (effect) 影响(響) yǐngxiǎng [个 gè] II VT 影响(響) yǐngxiǎng

inform [ɪnˈfɔːm] VT 告诉(訴) gàosù ▸ **to inform sb that...** 告诉(訴)某人··· gàosù mǒurén...

informal [ɪnˈfɔːml] ADJ 1 (relaxed) 不拘礼(禮)节(節)的 bùjū lǐjié de 2 [+ clothes, party] 日常的 rìcháng de 3 [+ meeting, discussions, agreement] 非正式的 fēi zhèngshì de

information [ɪnfəˈmeɪʃən] N [U] 信息 xìnxī ▸ **a piece of information** 一条(條)信息 yī tiáo xìnxī

information technology N [U] 信息技术(術) xìnxī jìshù

ingredient [ɪnˈgriːdɪənt] N [C] 配料 pèiliào [种 zhǒng]

inhabitant [ɪnˈhæbɪtnt] N [C] 居民 jūmín [个 gè]

inherit [ɪnˈhɛrɪt] VT 继(繼)承 jìchéng

initial [ɪˈnɪʃl] I N [C] (letter) 首字母 shǒuzìmǔ [个 gè] II **initials** NPL [of name] 首字母 shǒuzìmǔ

injection [ɪnˈdʒɛkʃən] N [C] 注射 zhùshè ▸ **to give sb an injection** 给(給)某人注射 gěi mǒurén zhùshè

injure [ˈɪndʒəʳ] VT [+ person] 伤(傷)害 shānghài ▸ **he was badly injured in the attack** 他在进(進)攻中受了重伤(傷) tā zài jìngōng zhōng shòule zhòngshāng

injury [ˈɪndʒərɪ] N [C/U] (wound) 伤(傷)害 shānghài [个 gè] ▸ **to escape without injury** 安然脱(脫)险(險) ānrán tuōxiǎn

ink [ɪŋk] N [C/U] 墨水 mòshuǐ [瓶 píng]

in-laws [ˈɪnlɔːz] NPL 姻亲(親) yīnqīn

innocent [ˈɪnəsnt] ADJ 清白的 qīngbái de

insect [ˈɪnsɛkt] N [C] 昆虫(蟲) kūnchóng [只 zhī]

insect repellent N [C/U] 杀(殺)虫(蟲)剂(劑) shāchóngjì [瓶 píng]

inside [ˈɪnˈsaɪd] I N 内(內)部 nèibù II ADJ [+ wall, surface] 内(內)部的 nèibù de III ADV [go+] 里(裡)面 lǐmiàn; [be +] 在里(裡)面 zài lǐmiàn 2 (indoors) 在屋内(內) zài wū nèi IV PREP [+ place, container] 在···的里(裡)面 zài...de lǐmiàn

insist [ɪn'sɪst] VI, VT 坚(堅)持 jiānchí ▸ **to insist on sth/doing sth** 坚(堅)持要求某事/做某事 jiānchí yāoqiú mǒushì/zuò mǒushì

inspector [ɪn'spɛktər] N [c] **1** (official) 检(檢)查员(員) jiǎncháyuán [位 wèi] **2** (Brit) (also: **ticket inspector**) 查票员(員) chápiàoyuán [位 wèi]

install, instal [ɪn'stɔːl] VT 安装(裝) ānzhuāng

instalment, (US) **installment** [ɪn'stɔːlmənt] N [c] 分期付款 fēnqī fùkuǎn [期 qī]

instance ['ɪnstəns] N [c] (example) 例子 lìzi [个 gè] ▸ **for instance** 例如 lìrú

instant ['ɪnstənt] I N [c] (moment) 瞬息 shùnxī [个 gè] II ADJ **1** [+ reaction, success] 立即的 lìjí de **2** [+ coffee, soup, noodles] 速食的 sùshí de ▸ **for an instant** 一瞬间(間) yī shùnjiān

instantly ['ɪnstəntlɪ] ADV 立即 lìjí

instead [ɪn'stɛd] ADV 代替 dàitì ▸ **instead of** 而不是 ér bù shì

instinct ['ɪnstɪŋkt] N [c/u] 本能 běnnéng [种 zhǒng]

instruct [ɪn'strʌkt] VT ▸ **to instruct sb to do sth** 命令某人做某事 mìnglìng mǒurén zuò mǒushì

instruction [ɪn'strʌkʃən] I CPD [+ manual, leaflet] 说(說)明 shuōmíng II **instructions** NPL 说(說)明 shuōmíng

instructor [ɪn'strʌktər] N [c] 教员(員) jiàoyuán [位 wèi]

instrument ['ɪnstrumənt] N [c] **1** 器械 qìxiè [件 jiàn] **2** (Mus) 乐(樂)器 yuèqì [件 jiàn]

insulin ['ɪnsjulɪn] N [u] 胰岛(島)素 yídǎosù

insult [n 'ɪnsʌlt, vb ɪn'sʌlt] I N [c] 侮辱 wǔrǔ [个 gè] II VT 侮辱 wǔrǔ

insurance [ɪn'ʃuərəns] N [u] 保险(險) bǎoxiǎn ▸ **fire/life/health insurance** 火/人寿(壽)/健康险(險) huǒ/rénshòu/jiànkāngxiǎn

insure [ɪn'ʃuər] VT [+ house, car] 给(給)…保险(險) gěi…bǎoxiǎn

intelligent [ɪn'tɛlɪdʒənt] ADJ 聪(聰)明的 cōngmíng de

intend [ɪn'tɛnd] VT ▸ **to intend to do sth** 打算做某事 dǎsuàn zuò mǒushì

intense [ɪn'tɛns] ADJ [+ heat, pain] 剧(劇) 烈的 jùliè de; [+ competition] 激烈的 jīliè de

intensive care N ▸ **to be in intensive care** 接受重病特别(別)护(護)理 jiēshòu zhòngbìng tèbié hùlǐ

intention [ɪn'tɛnʃən] N [c/u] 打算 dǎsuàn [个 gè]

interest ['ɪntrɪst] N **1** [u/s] (in subject, idea, person) 兴(興)趣 xìngqù **2** [c] (pastime, hobby) 爱(愛)好 àihào [个 gè] **3** [u] (on loan, savings) 利息 lìxī ▸ **to take an interest in sth/sb** 对(對)某事/某人感兴(興)趣 duì mǒushì/mǒurén gǎn xìngqù

interested ['ɪntrɪstɪd] ADJ ▸ **to be interested (in sth/doing sth)** 对(對)(某事/做某事)有兴(興)趣 duì (mǒushì/zuò mǒushì) yǒu xìngqù

> 请勿将 **interested** 和 **interesting** 混淆。如果你 **interested in** 某事，说明你对它很感兴趣，很想了解或知道更多关于它的事情，或者想花更多的时间来做这件事。Not all of the children were interested in animals...She asked him how he became interested in politics. 如果你发现某事 **interesting**，表示它令人感兴趣，引人注意，使你乐于更多地了解这件事或者去做这件事。It must be an awfully interesting job...The interesting thing is that this is exactly the answer we got before.

interesting ['ɪntrɪstɪŋ] ADJ 有趣的 yǒuqù de

interfere [ɪntə'fɪər] VI (meddle) 干涉 gānshè ▸ **to interfere with sth** [+ plans, career, duty] 妨碍(礙)某事 fáng'ài mǒushì

interior [ɪn'tɪərɪər] N [c] 内(內)部 nèibù

intermission [ɪntə'mɪʃən] N [c] (Cine) 休息时(時)间(間) xiūxi shíjiān [段 duàn]

international [ɪntə'næʃənl] ADJ 国(國)际(際)的 guójì de

internet ['ɪntənɛt] N ▸ **the internet** 因特网(網) yīntèwǎng

internet café N [c] 网(網)吧 wǎngbā [个 gè]

interpret [ɪn'tə:prɪt] VI 口译(譯) kǒuyì

interpreter [ɪn'tə:prɪtər] N [c] 口译(譯)者 kǒuyìzhě [位 wèi]

interrupt [ɪntə'rʌpt] I VT **1** 打断(斷) dǎduàn **2** [+ activity] 中断(斷)

zhōngduàn II VI (in conversation) 打岔 dǎchà

interruption [ɪntəˈrʌpʃən] N [C/U] 打 扰(擾) dǎrǎo [种 zhǒng]

interval [ˈɪntəvl] N [C] **1** (break, pause) 间(間)隔 jiàngé [个 gè] **2** (Brit: Theat, Mus, Sport) 幕间(間)休息 mùjiān xiūxi [个 gè]

interview [ˈɪntəvjuː] I N [C/U] **1** (for job) 面试(試) miànshì [次 cì] **2** (Publishing, Rad, TV) 采(採)访(訪) cǎifǎng [次 cì] II VT **1** (for job) 面试(試) miànshì **2** (Publishing, Rad, TV) 采(採)访(訪) cǎifǎng ▸ **to go for/have an interview** 参(參)加面试(試) cānjiā miànshì

interviewer [ˈɪntəvjuə] N [C] 采(採) 访(訪)者 cǎifǎngzhě [位 wèi]

intimidate [ɪnˈtɪmɪdeɪt] VT 恐吓(嚇) kǒnghè

into [ˈɪntu] PREP 到…里(裡)面 dào…lǐmiàn ▸ **come into the house/ garden** 走进(進)房子/花园(園)里(裡) zǒujìn fángzi/huāyuán li ▸ **get into the car** 进(進)入车(車)子 jìnrù chēzi ▸ **let's go into town** 我们(們)进(進)城吧 wǒmen jìnchéng ba ▸ **to translate Chinese into French** 把汉(漢)语(語)翻 译(譯)成法语(語) bǎ Hànyǔ fānyì chéng Fǎyǔ ▸ **research into cancer** 对(對)癌 症的深入研究 duì áizhèng de shēnrù yánjiū ▸ **I'd like to change some dollars into euros** 我想把一些美元换(換)成 欧(歐)元 wǒ xiǎng bǎ yīxiē měiyuán huànchéng ōuyuán

introduce [ɪntrəˈdjuːs] VT **1** [+ new idea, measure, technology] 引进(進) yǐnjìn **2** ▸ **to introduce sb (to sb)** 给(給)某人 介绍(紹)（某人）gěi mǒurén jièshào (mǒurén) ▸ **may I introduce you (to...)?** 让(讓)我介绍(紹)你（认(認)识(識)…) 好吗(嗎)? ràng wǒ jièshào nǐ (rènshi…) hǎo ma?

introduction [ɪntrəˈdʌkʃən] N **1** [U] [of new idea, measure, technology] 引进(進) yǐnjìn **2** [C] [of person] 介绍(紹) jièshào [个 gè] **3** [C] [of book, talk] 引言 yǐnyán [个 gè]

invade [ɪnˈveɪd] VT 侵略 qīnlüè

invalid [ˈɪnvəlɪd] N [C] 病弱者 bìngruòzhě [个 gè]

invent [ɪnˈvɛnt] VT 发(發)明 fāmíng

invention [ɪnˈvɛnʃən] N [C] 发(發)明 fāmíng [项 xiàng]

investigate [ɪnˈvɛstɪgeɪt] VT 调(調)查 diàochá

investigation [ɪnvɛstɪˈgeɪʃən] N [C/U] 调(調)查 diàochá [项 xiàng]

invisible [ɪnˈvɪzɪbl] ADJ 看不见(見)的 kàn bù jiàn de

invitation [ɪnvɪˈteɪʃən] N [C] **1** 邀请(請) yāoqǐng [个 gè] **2** [C] (card) 请(請)柬 qǐngjiǎn [封 fēng]

invite [ɪnˈvaɪt] VT 邀请(請) yāoqǐng ▸ **to invite sb to do sth** 邀请(請)某人做某事 yāoqǐng mǒurén zuò mǒushì ▸ **to invite sb to dinner** 请(請)某人赴宴 qǐng mǒurén fùyàn

involve [ɪnˈvɒlv] VT **1** (entail) 包含 bāohán **2** (concern, affect) 使卷(捲)入 shǐ juǎnrù ▸ **to involve sb (in sth)** 使某人 参(參)与(與)（某事）shǐ mǒurén cānyù (mǒushì)

iPad® [ˈaɪpæd] N [C] 苹(蘋)果平板电(電) 脑(腦) Píngguǒ píngbǎn diànnǎo [部 bù]

iPhone® [ˈaɪfəʊn] N [C] 苹(蘋)果手机(機) Píngguǒ shǒujī [部 bù]

iPod® [ˈaɪpɒd] N . 数(數)码(碼)随(隨)身 听(聽) shùmǎ suíshēntīng [个 gè]

Iran [ɪˈrɑːn] N 伊朗 Yīlǎng

Iraq [ɪˈrɑːk] N 伊拉克 Yīlākè

Iraqi [ɪˈrɑːkɪ] I ADJ 伊拉克的 Yīlākè de II N [C] (person) 伊拉克人 Yīlākèrén [名 míng]

Ireland [ˈaɪələnd] N 爱(愛)尔(爾)兰(蘭) Ài'ěrlán ▸ **the Republic of Ireland** 爱(愛)尔(爾)兰(蘭)共和国(國) Ài'ěrlán Gònghéguó

Irish [ˈaɪrɪʃ] I ADJ 爱(愛)尔(爾)兰(蘭)的 Ài'ěrlán de II N [U] (language) 爱(愛) 尔(爾)兰(蘭)语(語) Ài'ěrlányǔ III **the Irish** NPL 爱(愛)尔(爾)兰(蘭)人 Ài'ěrlánrén

Irishman [ˈaɪrɪʃmən] (pl **Irishmen**) N [C] 爱(愛)尔(爾)兰(蘭)男人 Ài'ěrlán nánrén [个 gè]

Irishwoman [ˈaɪrɪʃwumən] (pl **Irishwomen**) N [C] 爱(愛)尔(爾)兰(蘭) 女人 Ài'ěrlán nǚrén [个 gè]

iron [ˈaɪən] I N **1** [U] (metal) 铁(鐵) tiě **2** [C] (for clothes) 熨斗 yùndǒu [个 gè] II ADJ [+ bar, railings] 铁(鐵)的 tiě de

III VT [+ clothes] 熨 yùn

irresponsible [ɪrɪ'spɒnsɪbl] ADJ [+ person, driver] 无(無)责(責)任感的 wú zérèngǎn de; [+ attitude, behaviour] 不负(負)责(責)任的 bù fù zérèn de

irritating ['ɪrɪteɪtɪŋ] ADJ 烦(煩)人的 fánrén de

is [ɪz] VB of be

Islam ['ɪzlɑːm] N [U] 伊斯兰(蘭)教 Yīsīlánjiào

Islamic [ɪz'læmɪk] ADJ [+ law, faith] 伊斯兰(蘭)教的 Yīsīlánjiào de; [+ country] 伊斯兰(蘭)的 Yīsīlán de

island ['aɪlənd] N [C] 岛(島) dǎo [个 gè]

isolated ['aɪsəleɪtɪd] ADJ 1 [+ place] 孤零零的 gūlínglíng de 2 [+ person] 孤立的 gūlì de 3 [+ incident, case, example] 个(個)别(別)的 gèbié de

Israel ['ɪzreɪl] N 以色列 Yīsèliè

Israeli [ɪz'reɪlɪ] I ADJ 以色列的 Yīsèliè de II N [C] (person) 以色列人 Yīsèlièrén [名 míng]

issue ['ɪʃjuː] N [C] (problem, subject) 问(問)题(題) wèntí [个 gè]

IT N ABBR (= Information Technology) 信息技术(術) xìnxī jìshù

it [ɪt] PRON 1 (object or animal) 它 tā; (referring to baby) 他/她 tā/tā 2 (weather, date, time) ▶ **it's raining** 正在下雨 zhèngzài xiàyǔ 3 (impersonal) ▶ **it doesn't matter** 没(沒)关(關)系(係) méi guānxi ▶ **I can't find it** 我找不到 wǒ zhǎo bù dào ▶ **what is it?** (thing) 是什么(麼)东(東)西? shì shénme dōngxi?; (what's the matter?) 怎么(麼)了? zěnme le? ▶ **"who is it?" — "it's me"** "是谁(誰)?" "是我。" "shì shuí?" "shì wǒ."

Italian [ɪ'tæljən] I ADJ 意大利的 Yìdàlì de II N 1 [C] (person) 意大利人 Yìdàlìrén [名 míng] 2 [U] (language) 意大利语(語) Yìdàlìyǔ

Italy ['ɪtəlɪ] N 意大利 Yìdàlì

itch [ɪtʃ] VI 发(發)痒(癢) fāyǎng

itchy ['ɪtʃɪ] ADJ 发(發)痒(癢)的 fāyǎng de

it'd ['ɪtd] = **it would, it had**

item ['aɪtəm] N [C] 项(項)目 xiàngmù [个 gè]; (on bill) 项(項)项(項) xiàng ▶ **items of clothing** 几(幾)件衣服 jǐ jiàn yīfu

it'll ['ɪtl] = **it will**

its [ɪts] ADJ 1 (of animal) 它的 tā de 2 (of baby) 他/她的 tā/tā de

it's [ɪts] = **it is, it has**

itself [ɪt'self] PRON 1 (reflexive) 它自己 tā zìjǐ 2 (emphatic) 本身 běnshēn ▶ **it switches itself on automatically** 它自动(動)接通 tā zìdòng jiētōng ▶ **I think life itself is a learning process** 我认(認)为(為)生活本身是个(個)学(學)习(習)的过(過)程。 wǒ rènwéi shēnghuó běnshēn shì gè xuéxí de guòchéng. ▶ **by itself** (alone) 单(單)独(獨)地 dāndú de

I've [aɪv] = **I have**

j

jack [dʒæk] N [c] (Aut) 千斤顶(頂) qiānjīndǐng [个 gè]

jacket ['dʒækɪt] N [c] 夹(夾)克 jiākè [件 jiàn]

jail [dʒeɪl] I N [c/u] 监(監)狱(獄) jiānyù [个 gè] II VT 监(監)禁 jiānjìn

jam [dʒæm] N [c/u] (Brit: preserve) 果酱(醬) guǒjiàng [瓶 píng]

janitor ['dʒænɪtəʳ] N [c] 看门(門)人 kānménrén [个 gè]

January ['dʒænjuərɪ] N [c/u] 一月 yīyuè; see also/另见 **July**

Japan [dʒə'pæn] N 日本 Rìběn

Japanese [dʒæpə'niːz] (pl **Japanese**) I ADJ 日本的 Rìběn de II N 1 [c] (person) 日本人 Rìběnrén [个 gè] 2 [u] (language) 日语(語) Rìyǔ

jar [dʒɑːʳ] N [c] 广(廣)口瓶 guǎngkǒupíng [个 gè]

jaw [dʒɔː] (Anat) I N [c] 颌 hé [个 gè] II **jaws** NPL 嘴巴 zuǐba

jazz [dʒæz] N [u] (Mus) 爵士乐(樂) juéshìyuè

jealous ['dʒɛləs] ADJ 1 [+ husband, wife] 爱(愛)妒忌的 ài dùjì de 2 (envious) 妒忌的 dùjì de

jeans [dʒiːnz] NPL 牛仔裤(褲) niúzǎikù ▸ **a pair of jeans** 一条(條)牛仔裤(褲) yī tiáo niúzǎikù

jelly ['dʒɛlɪ] N [c/u] (US) 果酱(醬) guǒjiàng [瓶 píng]

jersey ['dʒəːzɪ] N [c] 针(針)织(織)毛衫 zhēnzhī máoshān [件 jiàn]

Jesus ['dʒiːzəs] N (Rel) 耶稣(穌) Yēsū ▸ **Jesus Christ** 耶稣(穌)基督 Yēsū Jīdū

jet [dʒɛt] N [c] (aeroplane) 喷(噴)气(氣)式飞(飛)机(機) pēnqìshì fēijī [架 jià]

jet lag N [u] 时(時)差反应(應) shíchā fǎnyìng

Jew [dʒuː] N [c] 犹(猶)太人 Yóutàirén [个 gè]

jewel ['dʒuːəl] N [c] 宝(寶)石 bǎoshí [块 kuài]

jewellery, (US) **jewelry** ['dʒuːəlrɪ] N [u] 首饰(飾) shǒushì

Jewish ['dʒuːɪʃ] ADJ 犹(猶)太的 Yóutài de

jigsaw ['dʒɪgsɔː] N [c] (also: **jigsaw puzzle**) 拼图(圖)玩具 pīntú wánjù [套 tào]

job [dʒɔb] N [c] 1 (position) 工作 gōngzuò [份 fèn] 2 (task) 任务(務) rènwù [项 xiàng] ▸ **Gladys got a job as a secretary** 格拉迪斯找到了一份秘书(書)工作 Gélādísī zhǎodào le yī fèn mìshū gōngzuò ▸ **a part-time/full-time job** 半职(職)/全职(職)工作 bànzhí/quánzhí gōngzuò

jockey ['dʒɔkɪ] N [c] (Sport) 赛(賽)马(馬)骑(騎)师(師) sàimǎ qíshī [位 wèi]

jog [dʒɔg] VI 慢跑 mànpǎo

jogging ['dʒɔgɪŋ] N [u] 慢跑 mànpǎo

join [dʒɔɪn] I VT 1 [+ club, party, army, navy, queue] 加入 jiārù 2 [+ person] 会(會)面 huìmiàn ▸ **will you join us for dinner?** 你想不想和我们(們)一起吃晚饭(飯)? nǐ xiǎng bù xiǎng hé wǒmen yīqǐ chī wǎnfàn? ▸ **join in** VI 参(參)与(與) cānyù

joint [dʒɔɪnt] N [c] 1 (Anat) 关(關)节(節) guānjié [个 gè]; (Brit: Culin) [of beef, lamb] 大块(塊)肉 dàkuàiròu [块 kuài]

joke [dʒəuk] I N [c] 笑话(話) xiàohua [个 gè] II VI 开(開)玩笑 kāi wánxiào ▸ **you're joking** or **you must be joking!** (inf) 你在开(開)玩笑{或}你一定在开(開)玩笑吧! nǐ zài kāi wánxiào huò nǐ yīdìng zài kāi wánxiào ba!

Jordan ['dʒɔːdən] N 约(約)旦 Yuēdàn

journalist ['dʒəːnəlɪst] N [c] 新闻(聞)工作者 xīnwén gōngzuòzhě [位 wèi]

journey ['dʒəːnɪ] N [c] 旅程 lǚchéng [段 duàn] ▸ **a 5-hour journey** 5个(個)小时(時)的路程 wǔ gè xiǎoshí de lùchéng ▸ **to go on a journey** 去旅行 qù lǚxíng

请勿将 **journey**, **voyage** 和 **trip** 混淆。**journey** 是指从一地搭乘车船或飞机到另一地的过程。...*a journey of over 2000 miles*... 如果你 **journey** 到某地，你就是去那里。这是书面的用法。*The nights became colder as they journeyed north.* **voyage** 是指从一地到另一地的长途行程，通常指乘船旅行或者太空旅行。...*the voyage to the moon in 1972*... **trip** 是指从一地到另一地的旅行过程，在目的地作短暂的停留后返回。...*a business trip to Milan*...

joy [dʒɔɪ] N [U] 快乐(樂) kuàilè

judge [dʒʌdʒ] I N [c] 1 (*Law*) 法官 fǎguān [位 wèi] 2 (*in competition*) 裁判 cáipàn [个 gè] II VT 1 [+ *exhibits, competition*] 评(評)定 píngdìng

judo ['dʒuːdəu] N [U] 柔道 róudào

jug [dʒʌg] N [c] 壶(壺) hú [把 bǎ]

juice [dʒuːs] N [c/U] 汁 zhī [杯 bēi]

July [dʒuːˈlaɪ] N [c/U] 七月 qīyuè ▶ **the first of July** 七月一日 qīyuè yī rì ▶ **at the beginning/end of July** 在七月初/末 zài qīyuè chū/mò ▶ **each** *or* **every July** 每年七月 měi nián qīyuè

jump [dʒʌmp] I VI 跳 tiào II N [c] 跳 tiào ▶ **to jump over sth** 跳过(過)某物 tiàoguò mǒuwù ▶ **to jump out of a window** 从(從)窗户(戶)跳下 cóng chuānghu tiàoxià ▶ **to jump on/off sth** 跳上/下某物 tiàoshàng/xià mǒuwù ▶ **to jump the queue** (*Brit*) 加塞儿(兒) jiāsāir

jumper ['dʒʌmpə'] N [c] (*Brit*) 毛衣 máoyī [件 jiàn]

junction ['dʒʌŋkʃən] (*Brit*) N [c] 交叉点(點) jiāochādiǎn [个 gè]

June [dʒuːn] N [c/U] 六月 liùyuè; *see also/* 另见 **July**

jungle ['dʒʌŋgl] N [c/U] 丛(叢)林 cónglín [片 piàn]

junior ['dʒuːnɪə'] ADJ 级(級)别(別)低的 jíbié dī de ▶ **George Bush Junior** (*US*) 小乔(喬)治・布什 xiǎo Qiáozhì Bùshí

junior high, (*US*) **junior high school** N [c/U] 初中 chūzhōng [所 suǒ]

junior school (*Brit*) N [c/U] 小学(學) xiǎoxué [所 suǒ]

junk [dʒʌŋk] N [U] (*inf: rubbish*) 废(廢)旧(舊)杂(雜)物 fèijiù záwù

jury ['dʒuərɪ] N [c] 1 (*Law*) 陪审(審)团(團) péishěntuán [个 gè] 2 (*in competition*) 评(評)审(審)团(團) píngshěntuán [个 gè]

just [dʒʌst] I ADJ (*frm*) [+ *decision, punishment, reward*] 公平的 gōngpíng de; [+ *society, cause*] 公正的 gōngzhèng de II ADV 1 (*exactly*) 正好 zhènghǎo 2 (*merely*) 仅(僅)仅(僅) jǐnjǐn 3 (*for emphasis*) 简(簡)直 jiǎnzhí 4 (*in instructions, requests*) 只是 zhǐshì ▶ **it's just right** 正合适(適) zhèng héshì ▶ **I'm just finishing this** 我马(馬)上就做完了 wǒ mǎshàng jiù zuòwán le ▶ **we were just going** 我们(們)正要走 wǒmen zhèng yào zǒu ▶ **to have just done sth** 刚(剛)刚(剛)做完某事 gānggāng zuòwán mǒushì ▶ **just now** (*a moment ago*) 刚(剛)才 gāngcái; (*at the present time*) 现(現)在 xiànzài ▶ **just about everything/everyone** 差不多所有东(東)西/所有人 chàbuduō suǒyǒu dōngxi/suǒyǒu rén ▶ **just before/after...** 就在…以前/以后(後) jiùzài...yǐqián/yǐhòu ▶ **just enough time/money** 时(時)间(間)/钱(錢)正好够(夠) shíjiān/qián zhènghǎo gòu ▶ **just a minute, just one moment** (*asking someone to wait*) 等一下 děng yīxià; (*interrupting*) 慢着(著) mànzhe

justice ['dʒʌstɪs] N 1 [U] (*Law: system*) 司法 sīfǎ 2 [U] (*fairness*) 正义(義) zhèngyì

K

K ABBR **1** (inf) (= **thousands**) 千 qiān **2** (Comput) (= **kilobytes**) 千字节(節) qiānzìjié

kangaroo [kæŋɡə'ruː] N [c] 袋鼠 dàishǔ [只 zhī]

karaoke [kɑːrə'əʊkɪ] N [U] 卡拉OK kǎlāOukèi

karate [kə'rɑːtɪ] N [U] 空手道 kōngshǒudào

keen [kiːn] ADJ 热(熱)衷的 rèzhōng de
▶ **to be keen to do sth** 渴望做某事 kěwàng zuò mǒushì ▶ **to be keen on sth** 热(熱)衷于(於)某事 rèzhōng yú mǒushì

keep [kiːp] (pt, pp **kept**) I VT **1** [+ receipt, money, job] 保留 bǎoliú **2** (store) 保存 bǎocún **3** (detain) 留 liú ▶ **to keep doing sth** (repeatedly) 总(總)是做某事 zǒng shì zuò mǒushì; (continuously) 不停做某事 bùtíng zuò mǒushì ▶ **to keep sb waiting** 让(讓)某人等着(著) ràng mǒurén děngzhe ▶ **to keep the room tidy** 保持房间(間)整洁(潔) bǎochí fángjiān zhěngjié ▶ **to keep a promise** 履行诺(諾)言 lǚxíng nuòyán ▶ **can you keep a secret?** 你能保守秘(祕)密吗(嗎)? nǐ néng bǎoshǒu mìmì ma? ▶ **to keep a record (of sth)** 记(記)录(錄)(某事) jìlù (mǒushì) ▶ **how are you keeping?** (inf) 你还(還)好吗(嗎)? nǐ hái hǎo ma?
▶ **keep away** VI ▶ **to keep away (from sth)** 不接近(某处(處)) bù jiējìn (mǒuchù)
▶ **keep off** VT FUS ▶ **keep off the grass!** 请(請)勿进(進)入草坪! qǐng wù jìnrù cǎopíng!
▶ **keep on** VI ▶ **to keep on doing sth** 继(繼)续(續)做某事 jìxù zuò mǒushì
▶ **keep up** VI ▶ **to keep up** 跟上 gēnshàng ▶ **to keep up with sb** (walking, moving) 跟上某人 gēnshàng mǒurén; (in work) 跟上某人 gēnshàng mǒurén

keep-fit [kiːp'fɪt] CPD [+ class, session, course] 健身 jiànshēn

kept [kept] PT, PP of **keep**

kerb, (US) **curb** [kəːb] N [c] 路缘(緣) lùyuán [个 gè]

ketchup ['ketʃəp] N [U] 番茄酱(醬) fānqiéjiàng

kettle ['ketl] N [c] 水壶(壺) shuǐhú [把 bǎ]

key [kiː] N [c] **1** (for lock, mechanism) 钥(鑰)匙 yàoshi [把 bǎ] **2** [of computer, typewriter, piano] 键(鍵) jiàn [个 gè]

keyboard ['kiːbɔːd] N [c] 键(鍵)盘(盤) jiànpán [个 gè]

keyhole ['kiːhəul] N [c] 钥(鑰)匙孔 yàoshikǒng [个 gè]

kick [kɪk] I VT [+ person, ball] 踢 tī II N [c] 踢 tī [顿 dùn]
▶ **kick off** VI 开(開)赛(賽) kāisài

kick-off ['kɪkɔf] N [s] 开(開)场(場)时(時)间(間) kāichǎng shíjiān

kid [kɪd] I N [c] (inf: child) 小孩 xiǎohái [个 gè]; (teenager) 年轻(輕)人 niánqīngrén [个 gè] II VI ▶ **you're kidding!** 你一定是在开(開)玩笑吧! nǐ yīdìng shì zài kāi wánxiào ba!

kidnap ['kɪdnæp] VT 绑(綁)架 bǎngjià

kidney ['kɪdnɪ] N **1** [c] (Anat) 肾(腎)脏(臟) shènzàng [个 gè] **2** [c/U] (Culin) 腰子 yāozi [个 gè]

kill [kɪl] VT **1** [+ person, animal, plant] 致死 zhìsǐ **2** (murder) 谋(謀)杀(殺) móushā
▶ **my back's killing me** (inf) 我的背疼死了 wǒ de bèi téng sǐ le

killer ['kɪlə'] N [c] 凶手 xiōngshǒu [个 gè]

kilo ['kiːləu] N [c] 公斤 gōngjīn

kilometre, (US) **kilometer** ['kɪləmiːtə'] N [c] 公里 gōnglǐ

kind [kaɪnd] I ADJ 友好的 yǒuhǎo de II N [c] (type, sort) 种(種)类(類) zhǒnglèi [个 gè] ▶ **an opportunity to meet all kinds of people** 与(與)各种(種)各样(樣)的人见(見)面的机(機)会(會) yǔ gè zhǒng gè yàng de rén jiànmiàn de jīhuì ► it was kind of them to help 他们(們)来(來)帮(幫)忙真是太好了 tāmen lái bāngmáng zhēn shì tài hǎo le

kindness ['kaɪndnɪs] N [U] 仁慈 réncí

king [kɪŋ] N [c] 国(國)王 guówáng [位 wèi]

kingdom ['kɪŋdəm] N [c] 王国(國) wángguó [个 gè]

kiss [kɪs] I N [c] 吻 wěn [个 gè] II VT 吻 wěn ► to give sb a kiss 吻某人一下 wěn mǒurén yíxià ► to kiss sb goodbye/goodnight 与(與)某人吻别(別)/吻某人一下，道晚安 yǔ mǒurén wěnbié/wěn mǒurén yíxià, dào wǎn'ān

kit [kɪt] N [U] (esp Brit: equipment) 成套用品 chéngtào yòngpǐn; (clothing) 服装(裝) fúzhuāng

kitchen ['kɪtʃɪn] N [c] 厨(廚)房 chúfáng [个 gè]

kite [kaɪt] N [c] 风(風)筝(箏) fēngzheng [个 gè]

kitten ['kɪtn] N [c] 小猫(貓) xiǎomāo [只 zhī]

knee [ni:] N [c] 膝盖(蓋) xīgài [个 gè]

kneel [ni:l] (pt, pp knelt) VI (also: kneel down) 跪下 guìxià

knew [nju:] PT of know

knickers ['nɪkəz] (Brit) NPL 女式内(內)裤(褲) nǚshì nèikù ► a pair of knickers 一条(條)女式内(內)裤(褲) yī tiáo nǚshì nèikù

knife [naɪf] (pl knives) N [c] 刀 dāo [把 bǎ] ► knife and fork 刀叉 dāochā

knit [nɪt] VI 织(織) zhī

knives [naɪvz] NPL of knife

knob [nɔb] N [c] 球形把手 qiúxíng bǎshǒu [个 gè]

knock [nɔk] I VT (strike) 碰撞 pèngzhuàng II VI (on door, window) 敲 qiāo III N [c] 1 (blow, bump) 碰撞 pèngzhuàng [下 xià] 2 (on door) 敲门(門)声(聲) qiāoménshēng [声 shēng] ► to knock sb unconscious [blow, blast +] 把某人打昏 bǎ mǒurén dǎhūn

► knock down VT 1 (run over) 撞倒 zhuàngdǎo 2 (demolish) 拆除 chāichú

► knock out VT 1 (make unconscious) 打昏 dǎhūn 2 (Boxing) 击(擊)昏 jīhūn 3 (eliminate) (in game, competition) 淘汰 táotài

► knock over VT 撞倒 zhuàngdǎo

knot [nɔt] N [c] 结(結) jié [个 gè] ► to tie a knot 打个(個)结(結) dǎ gè jié

know [nəu] (pt knew, pp known) VT 1 [+ facts, dates] 知道 zhīdào 2 [+ language] 懂 dǒng 3 [+ person, place, subject] 认(認)识(識) rènshi ► to know that... 知道… zhīdào… ► to know where/when 知道何处(處)/何时(時)… zhīdào héchù/héshí… ► to get to know sb 逐渐(漸)开(開)始了解某人 zhújiàn kāishǐ liǎojiě mǒurén ► to know about sth 听(聽)说(說)过(過)某事 tīngshuō guo mǒushì ► yes, I know 对(對)，的确(確)如此 duì, díquè rúcǐ ► you never know (难(難)讲(講)) 很难(難)讲(講) hěn nán jiǎng ► you know (used for emphasis) 你得知道 nǐ děi zhīdào

knowledge ['nɔlɪdʒ] N [U] 知识(識) zhīshi ► to (the best of) my knowledge 据(據)我所知 jù wǒ suǒ zhī

known [nəun] PP of know

Koran [kɔ'rɑːn] N ► the Koran 《古兰(蘭)经(經)》 Gǔlánjīng

Korea [kə'rɪə] N see North Korea, South Korea

Korean [kə'rɪən] I ADJ 朝鲜(鮮)的 Cháoxiān de II N 1 (person) 朝鲜(鮮)人 Cháoxiǎnrén 2 (language) 朝鲜(鮮)语(語) Cháoxiǎnyǔ

label ['leɪbl] I N [c] 标(標)签(籤) biāoqiān [个 gè] II VT 用标(標)签(籤)标(標)明 yòng biāoqiān biāomíng

labor ['leɪbə'] (US) N = **labour**

laboratory [ləˈbɔrətərɪ] N [c] 研究室 yánjiūshì [个 gè]

labor union (US) N [c] 工会(會) gōnghuì [个 gè]

labour, (US) **labor** ['leɪbə'] N [U] 1 (manpower) 劳(勞)动(動)力 láodònglì 2 ▶ Labour (Labour Party) 工党(黨) Gōngdǎng ▶ to be in labour (Med) 处(處)于(於)阵(陣)痛期 chǔyú zhèntòng qī

lace [leɪs] N 1 [U] (fabric) 花边(邊) huābiān 2 [c] (of shoe) 系(繫)带(帶) jìdài [根 gēn]

lack [læk] I N [s/U] 缺乏 quēfá II VT [+ means, skills, experience, confidence] 缺乏 quēfá

ladder ['lædə'] N [c] 梯子 tīzi [个 gè]

lady ['leɪdɪ] N [c] 女士 nǚshì [位 wèi] ▶ ladies and gentlemen... 女士们(們), 先生们(們)... nǚshìmen, xiānshēngmen... ▶ the ladies' (Brit), the ladies' room (US) 女厕(廁)所 nǚcèsuǒ

lager ['lɑːɡə'] (Brit) N [c/U] 淡啤酒 dànpíjiǔ [瓶 píng]

laid [leɪd] PT, PP of **lay**

lain [leɪn] PP of **lie**

lake [leɪk] N [c] 湖 hú [个 gè]

lamb [læm] N 1 [c] (animal) 羔羊

gāoyáng [只 zhī] 2 [U] (meat) 羔羊肉 gāoyángròu

lamp [læmp] N [c] 灯(燈) dēng [盏 zhǎn]

lamp-post ['læmppəust] (Brit) N [c] 灯(燈)柱 lùdēngzhù [个 gè]

lampshade ['læmpʃeɪd] N [c] 灯(燈)罩 dēngzhào [个 gè]

land [lænd] I N 1 [U] (area of open ground) 土地 tǔdì 2 [U] (not sea) 陆(陸)地 lùdì II VI 1 (Aviat, Space) 降落 jiàngluò 2 (from ship) 登陆(陸) dēnglù

landing ['lændɪŋ] N [c/U] (Aviat) 降落 jiàngluò [次 cì]

landlady ['lændleɪdɪ] N [c] 女房东(東) nǚfángdōng [位 wèi]

landlord ['lændlɔːd] N [c] 男房东(東) nánfángdōng [位 wèi]

landscape ['lændskeɪp] N [c/U] 风(風)景 fēngjǐng [道 dào]

lane [leɪn] N [c] 1 (in country) 小路 xiǎolù [条 tiáo] 2 (Aut) (of road) 车(車)道 chēdào [条 tiáo]

language ['læŋɡwɪdʒ] N 1 [c] (English, Russian etc) 语(語)言 yǔyán [种 zhǒng] 2 [U] (speech) 语(語)言表达(達)能力 yǔyán biǎodá nénglì

language laboratory N [c] 语(語)言实(實)验(驗)室 yǔyán shíyànshì [个 gè]

lap [læp] N [c] 1 (of person) 大腿的上方 dàtuǐ de shàngfāng 2 (in race) 圈 quān

laptop ['læptɒp] N [c] (also: laptop computer) 笔(筆)记(記)本电(電)脑(腦) bǐjìběn diànnǎo [个 gè]

large [lɑːdʒ] ADJ [+ house, person] 大的 dà de; [+ number, amount] 大量的 dàliàng de

laser ['leɪzə'] N 1 [c/U] (beam) 激光 jīguāng [束 shù] 2 [c] (machine) 激光器 jīguāngqì [台 tái]

last [lɑːst] I ADJ 1 (most recent) 最近的 zuìjìn de; [+ Monday, July, weekend etc] 上 shàng 2 (final) 最后(後)的 zuìhòu de; (of series, row) 最后(後)的 zuìhòu de II PRON (final one) 最后(後)一个(個) zuìhòu yī gè III ADV 1 (most recently) 最近 zuìjìn 2 (at the end) 最后(後) zuìhòu 3 (in final position) 最后(後) zuìhòu IV VI (continue) 持续(續) chíxù ▶ last week 上个(個)星期 shàng gè xīngqī ▶ last night (yesterday evening) 昨晚 zuówǎn; (during the night) 昨天夜里(裡) zuótiān yèlǐ ▶ the last time (the previous time) 上

一次 shàng yī cì ▸ **at (long) last** (finally) 终(終)于(於) zhōngyú ▸ **our house is the last but one** 我们(們)的房子是倒数(數)第二个(個) wǒmen de fángzi shì dàoshǔ dì'èr gè ▸ **it lasts (for) 2 hours** 持续(續)了两(兩)个(個)小时(時) chíxùle liǎng gè xiǎoshí

lastly ['lɑːstlɪ] ADV 最后(後) zuìhòu

late [leɪt] I ADJ **1** (not on time) 迟(遲)的 chí de **2** (after the usual time) 稍晚的 shāowǎn de II ADV **1** (not on time) 迟(遲) chí **2** (after the usual time) 晚 wǎn ▸ **we're late** 我们(們)迟(遲)到了 wǒmen chídào le ▸ **sorry I'm late** 对(對)不起，我迟(遲)到了 duìbuqǐ, wǒ chídào le ▸ **to be 10 minutes late** 迟(遲)到10分钟(鐘) chídào shí fēnzhōng ▸ **in late May** 5月下旬 wǔyuè xiàxún

lately ['leɪtlɪ] ADV 最近 zuìjìn

later ['leɪtəʳ] ADV 以后(後) yǐhòu ▸ **some time/weeks/years later** 一些时(時)候/几(幾)个(個)星期/几(幾)年以后(後) yīxiē shíhou/jǐ gè xīngqī/jǐ nián yǐhòu ▸ **later on** 以后(後) yǐhòu

latest ['leɪtɪst] ADJ **1** [+ book, film, news] 最新的 zuìxīn de **2** (most up-to-date) 最新式的 zuì xīnshì de ▸ **at the latest** 最迟(遲) zuì chí

Latin ['lætɪn] N [U] 拉丁语(語) Lādīngyǔ

Latin America N 拉丁美洲 Lādīngměizhōu

Latin American I ADJ 拉丁美洲的 Lādīngměizhōu de II N [c] (person) 拉丁美洲人 Lādīngměizhōurén [个 gè]

latter ['lætəʳ] N ▸ **the latter** 后(後)者 hòuzhě

laugh [lɑːf] I N [c] 笑 xiào [阵 zhèn] II VI 笑 xiào ▸ **laugh at** VT FUS 对(對)…发(發)笑 duì…fāxiào

launch [lɔːntʃ] VT **1** [+ rocket, missile, satellite] 发(發)射 fāshè **2** [+ product, publication] 推出 tuīchū

laundry ['lɔːndrɪ] N [U] (dirty washing) 待洗的衣物 dàixǐ de yīwù; (clean washing) 洗好的衣物 xǐhǎo de yīwù

laundry detergent (US) N [U/c] 洗衣粉 xǐyīfěn

lavatory ['lævətərɪ] (Brit) N [c] 卫(衛)生间(間) wèishēngjiān [个 gè]

law [lɔː] N **1** [s/U] (legal system) 法律 fǎlǜ **2** [c] (regulation) 法规(規) fǎguī [条 tiáo] ▸ **against the law** 违(違)法 wéifǎ ▸ **to break the law** 违(違)法 wéifǎ ▸ **by law** 依照法律 yīzhào fǎlǜ ▸ **to study law** 学(學)习(習)法律 xuéxí fǎlǜ

lawn [lɔːn] N [c] 草坪 cǎopíng [片 piàn]

lawnmower ['lɔːnməʊəʳ] N [c] 割草机(機) gēcǎojī [部 bù]

lawyer ['lɔːjəʳ] N [c] 律师(師) lǜshī [位 wèi]

lay [leɪ] I PT of **lie** II VT III (put) 放 fàng ▸ **to lay the table** 摆(擺)放餐具 bǎifàng cānjù ▸ **lay down** VT (put down) 放下 fàngxià ▸ **lay off** VT 解雇(僱) jiěgù

layer ['leɪəʳ] N [c] 层(層) céng

layout ['leɪaʊt] N [c] 布(佈)局 bùjú [个 gè]

lazy ['leɪzɪ] ADJ 懒(懶)惰的 lǎnduò de

lead¹ [liːd] (pt, pp led) I N **1** [c] [for dog] 皮带(帶) pídài [条 tiáo] **2** [c] (Elec) 导(導)线(線) dǎoxiàn [根 gēn] II VT **1** (guide) 带(帶)领(領) dàilǐng **2** [+ group, party, organization] 领(領)导(導) lǐngdǎo; [+ march, demonstration, parade] 带(帶)领(領) dàilǐng III VT (in race, competition) 领(領)先 lǐngxiān ▸ **to be in the lead** 领(領)先 lǐngxiān ▸ **to lead the way** (lit) 引路 yǐnlù; (fig) 率先 shuàixiān ▸ **lead away** VT [+ prisoner] 带(帶)走 dàizǒu ▸ **lead to** VT FUS (result in) 导(導)致 dǎozhì

lead² [lɛd] N [U] (metal) 铅(鉛) qiān

leader ['liːdəʳ] N [c] 领(領)导(導)人 lǐngdǎorén [位 wèi]

leaf [liːf] (pl **leaves**) N [c] 叶(葉) yè [片 piàn]

leaflet ['liːflɪt] N [c] (booklet) 小册(冊)子 xiǎocèzi [本 běn]; (single sheet) 传(傳)单(單) chuándān [份 fèn]

league [liːg] N [c] (Sport) 联(聯)赛(賽) liánsài [季 jì]

leak [liːk] I N [c] [of liquid, gas] 裂隙 lièxì [条 tiáo] II VI [shoes, pipe, liquid, gas +] 漏 lòu

lean [liːn] (pt, pp **leaned** or **leant**) I VT ▸ **to lean sth on/against sth** 把某物靠在某物上 bǎ mǒuwù kào zài mǒuwù shang

II ADJ [+ *meat*] 瘦的 shòu de **III** VI ▸ **to lean against sth** [*person* +] 靠在某物上 kào zài mǒuwù shang ▸ **to lean forward/back** 向前/后(後)倾(傾) xiàng qián/hòu qīng
▸ **lean on** VT FUS 倚 yǐ

leap year N [c] 闰(閏)年 rùnnián [个 gè]

learn [lə:n] (*pt, pp* **learned** *or* **learnt**) **I** VT (*study*) [+ *skill*] 学(學) xué; [+ *poem, song*] 背 bèi **II** VI (*study*) 学(學) xué ▸ **to learn about sth** (*study*) 学(學)到某物 xuédào mǒuwù ▸ **to learn to do sth/how to do sth** 学(學)做某事/怎样(樣)做某事 xuézuò mǒushì/zěnyàng zuò mǒushì

learnt [lə:nt] PT, PP *of* **learn**

least [li:st] **I** ADJ (*noun*) 最少的 zuì shǎo de **II** ADV **1** (*with adjective*) ▸ **the least expensive/attractive/interesting** 最便宜/没(沒)有魅力/没(沒)趣的 zuì piányi/méiyǒu mèilì/méiqù de **2** (*with verb*) 最不 zuì bù **III** PRON ▸ **the least** 最少 zuìshǎo ▸ **at least** (*in expressions of quantity, comparisons*) 至少 zhìshǎo

leather [ˈlɛðəʳ] **I** N [U] 皮革 pígé **II** CPD [+ *jacket, shoes, chair*] 皮 pí

leave [li:v] (*pt, pp* **left**) **I** VT **1** [+ *place*] 离(離)开(開) líkāi **2** [+ *school, job, group*] 放弃(棄) fàngqì **3** (*leave behind: deliberately*) 留下 liúxià; (*accidentally*) 落 luò **4** [+ *message*] 留 liú **II** VI **1** (*depart*) [*person* +] 离(離)开(開) líkāi; [*bus, train* +] 出发(發) chūfā **2** (*give up school*) 辍(輟)学(學) chuòxué; (*give up job*) 辞(辭)职(職) cízhí **III** N [U] 休假 xiūjià; (*Mil*) 假期 jiàqī ▸ **to leave sth to sb** 把某物留给(給)某人 bǎ mǒuwù liú gěi mǒurén ▸ **to leave sb/sth alone** 不理会(會)某人/某物 bù lǐhuì mǒurén/mǒuwù ▸ **to leave for** [+ *destination*] 前往 qiánwǎng
▸ **leave behind** VT (*forget*) 忘带(帶) wàngdài
▸ **leave on** VT [+ *light, heating*] 开(開)着(著) kāizhe
▸ **leave out** VT 删(刪)掉 shāndiào

leaves [li:vz] NPL *of* **leaf**

Lebanon, the Lebanon [ˈlɛbənən] N 黎巴嫩 Líbānèn

lecture [ˈlɛktʃəʳ] N [c] (*talk*) 讲(講)座 jiǎngzuò [个 gè] ▸ **to give a lecture (on sth)** 作(某方面的)讲(講)座 zuò (mǒu fāngmiàn de) jiǎngzuò

lecturer [ˈlɛktʃərəʳ] N [c] 讲(講)师(師) jiǎngshī [位 wèi]

led [lɛd] PT, PP *of* **lead'**

left' [lɛft] **I** ADJ (*not right*) 左的 zuǒ de **II** N ▸ **the left** 左侧(側) zuǒcè **III** ADV [*turn, go, look* +] 向左 xiàngzuǒ ▸ **on the left** 在左边(邊) zài zuǒbiān ▸ **to the left** 靠左边(邊) kào zuǒbiān

left² [lɛft] **I** PT, PP *of* **leave II** ADJ ▸ **to be left over** 剩下 shèngxià

left-hand [ˈlɛfthænd] ADJ [+ *side, corner*] 左侧(側)的 zuǒcè de

left-handed [lɛftˈhændɪd] ADJ 左撇子的 zuǒpiězi de

left-luggage [lɛftˈlʌgɪdʒ] (*Brit*) N [U] ▸ **left-luggage locker** 行李寄存柜(櫃) xíngli jìcúnguì

leg [lɛg] N [c] **1** 腿 tuǐ [条 tiáo] **2** [c/U] [*of lamb, chicken*] 腿 tuǐ [根 gēn]

legal [ˈliːgl] ADJ **1** [+ *system, requirement*] 法律的 fǎlǜ de **2** [+ *action, situation*] 合法的 héfǎ de

legal holiday (*US*) N [c] 法定假期 fǎdìng jiàqī [个 gè]

leisure [ˈlɛʒəʳ, *US* ˈliːʒəʳ] N [U] 闲(閒)暇 xiánxiá

leisure centre (*Brit*) N [c] 娱(娛)乐(樂)中心 yúlè zhōngxīn [个 gè]

lemon [ˈlɛmən] N [c] 柠(檸)檬 níngméng [个 gè]

lemonade [lɛməˈneɪd] N [U] 柠(檸)檬汽水 níngméng qìshuǐ

lend [lɛnd] (*pt, pp* **lent**) VT **1** ▸ **to lend sth to sb** 把某物借给(給)某人 bǎ jiègěi mǒurén **2** [*bank* +] 贷(貸) dài

length [lɛŋθ] N **1** [c/U] [*of object, animal*] 长(長)度 chángdù [个 gè]; [*of sentence, article*] 篇幅 piānfu [个 gè] **2** [c/U] (*duration*) 期间(間) qíjiān [个 gè]

lens [lɛnz] N [c] [*of spectacles*] 镜(鏡)片 jìngpiàn [片 piàn]; [*of telescope, camera*] 镜(鏡)头(頭) jìngtóu [个 gè]

Lent [lɛnt] N [U] 大斋(齋)节(節) Dàzhāijié

lent [lɛnt] PT, PP *of* **lend**

lentil [ˈlɛntɪl] N [c] 小扁豆 xiǎobiǎndòu [颗 kē]

Leo [ˈliːəu] N [U] (*sign*) 狮(獅)子座 Shīzi Zuò

leopard ['lɛpəd] N [c] 豹 bào [只 zhī]

lesbian ['lɛzbɪən] I ADJ 女同性恋(戀)的 nǚtóngxìngliàn de II N [c] 女同性恋(戀)者 nǚtóngxìngliànzhě [个 gè]

less [lɛs] I ADJ (noun) 更少的 gèng shǎo de II ADV **1** (with adjective/adverb) 较(較)少地 jiàoshǎo de **2** (with verb) 较(較)少 jiàoshǎo III PRON 较(較)少的东(東)西 jiàoshǎo de dōngxi IV PREP ▸ less tax/10% discount 去掉税(稅)/10%的折扣 qùdiào shuì/bǎi fēn zhī shí de zhékòu ▸ less than half 不到一半 bù dào yībàn

lesson ['lɛsn] N [c] 课(課)kè [堂 táng]

let [lɛt] (pt, pp let) VT **1** ▸ to let sb do sth (give permission) 允许(許)某人做某事 yǔnxǔ mǒurén zuò mǒushì **2** ▸ to let sth happen 让(讓)某事发(發)生 ràng mǒushì fāshēng ▸ to let sb know that... 告诉(訴)某人... gàosù mǒurén... **3** ▸ to let sb in/out 让(讓)某人进(進)去/出去 ràng mǒurén jìnqù/chūqù ▸ let's go/eat 我们(們)走/吃吧 wǒmen zǒu/chī ba ▸ "to let" "现(現)房待租" "xiànfáng dàizū" ▸ to let go (release one's grip) 松(鬆)开(開) sōngkāi ▸ to let sb/sth go (release) 放走某人/某物 fàngzǒu mǒurén/mǒuwù
  ▸ **let down** VT [+ person] 令…失望 lìng…shīwàng
  ▸ **let in** VT **1** [+ water, air] 允许(許)进(進)来(來) yǔnxǔ jìnlái **2** [+ person] 给(給)…开(開)门(門) gěi…kāimén

letter ['lɛtə^r] N [c] **1** (note) 信 xìn [封 fēng] **2** (of alphabet) 字母 zìmǔ [个 gè]

letterbox ['lɛtəbɔks] (Brit) N [c] 信箱 xìnxiāng [个 gè]

lettuce ['lɛtɪs] N [c/u] 生菜 shēngcài [棵 kē]

level ['lɛvl] I ADJ **1** 平的 píng de II N [c] **1** (standard) 水平 shuǐpíng [种 zhǒng] **2** (height) 水位 shuǐwèi [个 gè]

level crossing (Brit) N [c] 平交道口 píngjiāodàokǒu [个 gè]

lever ['li:və^r, US 'lɛvə^r] N [c] 杆(桿)gǎn [根 gēn]

liar ['laɪə^r] N [c] 说(說)谎(謊)者 shuōhuǎngzhě [个 gè]

liberal ['lɪbərl] I ADJ [+ person, attitude] 开(開)明的 kāimíng de II N [c] (Pol)
  ▸ **Liberal** 自由党(黨)党(黨)员(員)

Zìyóudǎng dǎngyuán [名 míng]

Libra ['li:brə] N [u] (sign) 天秤座 Tiānchèng Zuò

librarian [laɪ'brɛərɪən] N [c] 图(圖)书(書)管理员(員) túshū guǎnlǐyuán [位 wèi]

library ['laɪbrərɪ] N [c] 图(圖)书(書)馆(館) túshūguǎn [个 gè]

licence, (US) **license** ['laɪsns] N **1** [c] (permit) 许(許)可证(證) xǔkězhèng [张 zhāng] **2** [c] (also: driving licence) 驾(駕)驶(駛)执(執)照 jiàshǐ zhízhào [本 běn]

license plate (US) N [c] 车(車)牌照 chēpáizhào [个 gè]

lick [lɪk] VT 舔 tiǎn

lid [lɪd] N [c] **1** (of box, case, pan) 盖(蓋)gài [个 gè] **2** (eyelid) 眼睑(瞼)yǎnjiǎn [个 gè]

lie¹ [laɪ] (pt lay, pp lain) VI **1** (person +) 躺 tǎng
  ▸ **lie about** (Brit) VI = lie around
  ▸ **lie around** VI 乱(亂)放 luànfàng
  ▸ **lie down** VI (person +) 躺下 tǎngxià

lie² [laɪ] I (say) 说(說)谎(謊) shuōhuǎng II N [c] 谎(謊)言 huǎngyán [个 gè] ▸ to tell lies 说(說)谎(謊) shuōhuǎng

life [laɪf] (pl lives) N **1** [c/u] (living, existence) 生命 shēngmìng [个 gè] **2** [c] (lifespan) 一生 yīshēng [个 gè] ▸ his personal/working life 他的个(個)人/工作生活 tāde gèrén/gōngzuò shēnghuó

lifeboat ['laɪfbəut] N [c] 救生船 jiùshēngchuán [艘 sōu]

life preserver [-prɪ'zə:və^r] (US) N [c] (lifebelt) 救生用具 jiùshēng yòngjù [件 jiàn]; (life jacket) 救生衣 jiùshēngyī [件 jiàn]

lifestyle ['laɪfstaɪl] N [c/u] 生活方式 shēnghuó fāngshì [种 zhǒng]

lift [lɪft] I VT 举(舉)起 jǔqǐ II N [c] (Brit) 电(電)梯 diàntī [部 bù] ▸ to give sb a lift (esp Brit) 让(讓)某人搭便车(車) ràng mǒurén dā biànchē
  ▸ **lift up** VT [+ person, thing] 举(舉)起 jǔqǐ

light [laɪt] (pt, pp lit) I N **1** [u] (from sun, moon, lamp, fire) 光 guāng **2** [c] (Elec, Aut) 灯(燈)dēng [盏 zhǎn] **3** [s] (for cigarette) 打火机(機)dǎhuǒjī II VT [+ candle, fire, cigarette] 点(點)燃 diǎnrán III ADJ

1 [+ *colour*] 淡的 dàn de **2** (*not heavy*) 轻(輕)的 qīng de **IV lights** NPL (*also:* **traffic lights**) 交通指示灯(燈) jiāotōng zhǐshìdēng ▶ **to turn** or **switch the light on/off** 开(開)/关(關)灯(燈) kāi/guān dēng

light bulb N [c] 灯(燈)泡 dēngpào [个 gè]

lighter ['laɪtə^r] N [c] (*also:* **cigarette lighter**) 打火机(機) dǎhuǒjī [个 gè]

lighthouse ['laɪthaus] N [c] 灯(燈)塔 dēngtǎ [座 zuò]

lightning ['laɪtnɪŋ] N [U] 闪(閃)电(電) shǎndiàn

like¹ [laɪk] PREP **1** (*similar to*) 像 xiàng **2** (*in similes*) 像⋯一样(樣) xiàng…yīyàng **3** (*such as*) 如 rú ▶ **a house like ours** 像我们(們)这(這)样(樣)的房子 xiàng wǒmen zhèyàng de fángzi ▶ **to be like sth/sb** 像某物/某人 xiàng mǒuwù/mǒurén ▶ **what's he/the weather like?** 他/天气(氣)怎么(麼)样(樣)? tā/tiānqì zěnmeyàng? ▶ **to look like** [+ *person*] 长(長)得像 zhǎngde xiàng; [+ *thing*] 类(類)似 lèisì ▶ **what does it look/sound/taste like?** 看/听(聽)/尝(嘗)起来(來)怎么(麼)样(樣)? kàn/tīng/cháng qǐlái zěnmeyàng? ▶ **like this** 像这(這)样(樣) xiàng zhèyàng

like² [laɪk] I VT [+ *person, thing*] 喜欢(歡) xǐhuan II N ▶ **his likes and dislikes** 他的好恶(惡) tā de hàowù ▶ **to like doing sth** 喜欢(歡)做某事 xǐhuan zuò mǒushì ▶ **I would** or **I'd like an ice-cream/to go for a walk** 我想吃个(個)冰激凌(淩)/去散步。wǒxiǎng chī gè bīngjīlíng/qù sànbù. ▶ **would you like a coffee?** 你想不想(來)喝咖啡? nǐ xiǎng bù xiǎng lái bēi kāfēi? ▶ **if you like** (*in offers, suggestions*) 如果你愿(願)意的话(話) rúguǒ nǐ yuànyì de huà

likely ['laɪklɪ] ADJ 很可能的 hěn kěnéng de ▶ **it is likely that...** 有可能⋯ yǒu kěnéng… ▶ **to be likely to do sth** 很可能做某事 hěn yǒu kěnéng zuò mǒushì

lime [laɪm] N [c] (*fruit*) 酸橙 suānchéng [个 gè]

limit ['lɪmɪt] N [c] **1** (*maximum point*) 限度 xiàndù [个 gè] **2** 限定 xiàndìng [种 zhǒng]

limp [lɪmp] VI 跛行 bǒxíng

line [laɪn] N [c] **1** (*long thin mark*) 线(線) xiàn [条 tiáo] **2** 排 pái **3** (*of words*) 行 háng **4** (*Tel*) 线(線)路 xiànlù [条 tiáo] **5** (*railway track*) 铁(鐵)路线(線) tiělù xiànlù [条 tiáo] ▶ **hold the line please!** (*Tel*) 请(請)稍等! qǐng shāoděng! ▶ **to stand** or **wait in line** 排队(隊)等候 páiduì děnghòu ▶ **on the right lines** 大体(體)正确(確) dàtǐ zhèngquè

linen ['lɪnɪn] I N [U] **1** (*cloth*) 亚(亞)麻布 yàmábù **2** (*tablecloths, sheets*) 亚(亞)麻制(製)品 yàmá zhìpǐn II CPD [+ *jacket, sheets*] 亚(亞)麻料 yàmáliào

lining ['laɪnɪŋ] N [c/U] 衬(襯)里(裡) chènlǐ [个 gè]

link [lɪŋk] I N [c] **1** 联(聯)系(繫) liánxì [种 zhǒng] **2** (*Comput*) (*also:* **hyperlink**) 超链(鏈)接 chāoliànjiē [个 gè] II VT **1** [+ *places, objects*] 连(連)接 liánjiē **2** [+ *people, situations*] 联(聯)系(繫) liánxì

lion ['laɪən] N [c] 狮(獅)子 shīzi [头 tóu]

lip [lɪp] N [c] 唇(脣) chún [个 gè]

lip-read ['lɪpri:d] VI 唇(脣)读(讀) chúndú

lipstick ['lɪpstɪk] N [c/U] 口红(紅) kǒuhóng [支 zhī]

liquid ['lɪkwɪd] N [c/U] 液体(體) yètǐ [种 zhǒng]

liquidizer ['lɪkwɪdaɪzə^r] N [c] 榨(搾)汁机(機) zhàzhījī [个 gè]

liquor ['lɪkə^r] (US) N [U] 酒 jiǔ

list [lɪst] I N [c] (*list*) 单(單)子 dānzi [个 gè] II VT **1** (*record*) [*person* +] 列出 lièchū **2** (*Comput*) 列出 lièchū

listen ['lɪsn] VI **1** 听(聽) tīng; (*to speaker*) 听(聽)⋯说(說) tīng…shuō **2** (*follow advice*) 听(聽)从(從) tīngcóng ▶ **to listen to sb** (*pay attention to*) 留神听(聽)某人说(說)话(話) liúshén tīng mǒurén shuōhuà; (*follow advice of*) 听(聽)从(從)某人 tīngcóng mǒurén ▶ **to listen to sth** 听(聽)某事 tīng mǒushì

lit [lɪt] PT, PP of **light**

liter ['li:tə^r] (US) N = **litre**

literature ['lɪtrɪtʃə^r] N [U] 文学(學) wénxué

litre, (US) **liter** ['li:tə^r] N [c] 升 shēng

litter ['lɪtə^r] N [U] 垃圾 lājī

litter bin (*Brit*) N [c] 垃圾箱 lājīxiāng [个 gè]

little ['lɪtl] I ADJ 1 (*small*) 小的 xiǎo de 2 (*young*) [+ *child*] 小的 xiǎo de 3 (*younger*) ▸ **little brother/sister** 弟弟/妹妹 dìdi/mèimei 4 (*quantifier*) ▸ **to have little time/money** 没(沒)有多少时(時)间(間)/金钱(錢) méiyǒu duōshao shíjiān/jīnqián II ADV 少 shǎo ▸ **a little** (*small amount*) 一点(點) yīdiǎn; (*noun*) 一点(點) yīdiǎn; [*sleep, eat* +] 一点(點) yīdiǎn ▸ **a little boy of 8** 一个(個)8岁(歲)的小男孩 yī gè bāsuì de xiǎo nánhái ▸ **a little bit** (*adj*) 有点(點) yǒudiǎn ▸ **little by little** 逐渐(漸)地 zhújiàn de

live¹ [lɪv] I VI 1 (*reside*) 住 zhù 2 (*lead one's life*) 生活 shēnghuó II VT [+ *life*] 过(過)guò ▸ **live on** VT FUS 靠…维(維)持生活 kào…wéichí shēnghuó ▸ **live together** VI 同居 tóngjū ▸ **live with** VT FUS [+ *partner*] 与(與)…同居 yǔ…tóngjū

live² [laɪv] I ADJ [+ *animal, plant*] 活的 huó de II ADV [*broadcast* +] 实(實)况(況)地 shíkuàng de

lively ['laɪvli] ADJ [+ *person*] 活泼(潑)的 huópo de; [+ *place, event, discussion*] 活跃(躍)的 huóyuè de

liver ['lɪvəʳ] N 1 [c] (*liver*) 肝脏(臟)gānzàng [个(個) gè] 2 [c/u] (*Culin*) 肝 gān [个(個) gè]

lives [laɪvz] NPL of **life**

livestream [laɪvstri:m] N [c] 网(網)络(絡)直播 wǎngluò zhíbō

living ['lɪvɪŋ] N [u] (*life*) 生活 shēnghuó ▸ **for a living** 作为(為)谋(謀)生之道 zuòwéi móushēng zhī dào ▸ **to earn** or **make a/one's living** 谋(謀)生 móushēng

living room N [c] 起居室 qǐjūshì [间(間) jiān]

load [ləʊd] I N [c] (*thing carried*) [*of vehicle*] 装(裝)载(載)量 zhuāngzàiliàng [车(車) chē] II VT 1 (*also*: **load up**) [+ *vehicle, ship*] 装(裝) zhuāng 2 [+ *program, data*] 下载(載) xiàzài ▸ **loads of** or **a load of money/people** (*inf*) 很多钱(錢)/人 hěnduō qián/rén

loaf [ləʊf] (*pl* **loaves**) N [c] ▸ **a loaf (of bread)** 一条(條)(面(麵)包) yī tiáo (miànbāo)

loan [ləʊn] I N [c] 贷(貸)款 dàikuǎn

[笔(筆) bǐ] II VT ▸ **to loan sth (out) to sb** [+ *money, thing*] 把某人物借给(給)某人 bǎ mǒuwù jiègěi mǒurén

loaves [ləʊvz] NPL of **loaf**

local ['ləʊkl] ADJ [+ *council, newspaper, library*] 当(當)地的 dāngdì de; [+ *residents*] 本地的 běndì de

lock [lɔk] I N [c] 锁(鎖) suǒ [把 bǎ] II VT 1 锁(鎖) suǒ 2 [+ *screen*] 锁(鎖) suǒ ▸ **lock out** VT [+ *person*] (*deliberately*) 把…锁(鎖)在外面 bǎ…suǒ zài wàimiàn ▸ **to lock o.s. out** 把自己锁(鎖)在外面 bǎ zìjǐ suǒ zài wàimiàn ▸ **lock up** VT 锁(鎖)好 suǒhǎo

locker ['lɔkəʳ] N [c] 小柜(櫃) xiǎoguì [个(個) gè]

lodger ['lɔdʒəʳ] N [c] 房客 fángkè [个(個) gè]

loft [lɔft] N [c] (*attic*) 阁(閣)楼(樓) gélóu [座 zuò]

log [lɔg] N [c] (*for fuel*) 木柴 mùchái [根 gēn] ▸ **log in, log on** (*Comput*) VI 登录(錄) dēnglù ▸ **log into** (*Comput*) VT FUS 登入 dēngrù ▸ **log out, log off** (*Comput*) VI 退出系统(統) tuìchū xìtǒng

logical ['lɔdʒɪkl] ADJ [+ *argument, analysis*] 逻(邏)辑(輯)的 luóji de; [+ *conclusion, result*] 合逻(邏)辑(輯)的 hé luóji de; [+ *course of action*] 合乎情理的 héhū qínglǐ de

London ['lʌndən] N 伦(倫)敦 Lúndūn

Londoner ['lʌndənəʳ] N [c] 伦(倫)敦人 Lúndūnrén [个(個) gè]

lonely ['ləʊnlɪ] ADJ 1 [+ *person*] 孤独(獨)的 gūdú de 2 [+ *place*] 人迹(跡)罕至的 rénjì hǎn zhì de

long [lɔŋ] I ADJ 1 [+ *rope, hair, table, tunnel*] 长(長)的 cháng de 2 [+ *meeting, discussion, film, time*] 长(長)的 cháng de 3 [+ *book, poem*] 长(長)的 cháng de II ADV (*time*) 长(長)久 chángjiǔ ▸ **how long is the lesson?** 这(這)节(節)课(課)多长(長)时(時)间(間)? zhè jié kè duō cháng shíjiān? ▸ **6 metres long** 6米长(長) liù mǐ cháng ▸ **so** or **as long as** (*provided*) 只要 zhǐyào ▸ **long ago** 很久以前 hěn jiǔ yǐqián ▸ **it won't take long** 这(這)不需花很多时(時)间(間) zhè bù xūyào huā hěn duō shíjiān ▸ **a long way** 很远(遠) hěn yuǎn

loo [luː] (Brit: inf) N [C] 厕(廁)所 cèsuǒ [个(個) gè]

look [luk] I VI **1** (glance, gaze) 看 kàn **2** (search) 找 zhǎo **3** (seem, appear) 看起来(來) kàn qǐlái II N (expression) 表情 biǎoqíng [副 fù] ▸ **to look out of the window** 望向窗外 wàng xiàng chuāngwài ▸ **look out!** 当(當)心! dāngxīn! ▸ **to look like sb** 长(長)得像某人 zhǎng de xiàng mǒurén ▸ **to look like sth** 看起来(來)像某物 kàn qǐlái xiàng mǒuwù ▸ **it looks as if...** 看来(來)… kànlái… ▸ **to have** or **take a look at** 看一看 kàn yī kàn ▸ **look after** VT FUS 照顾(顧) zhàogù ▸ **look at** VT FUS 看一看 kàn yī kàn ▸ **look for** VT FUS [+ person, thing] 寻(尋)找 xúnzhǎo ▸ **look forward to** VT FUS 盼望 pànwàng ▸ **to look forward to doing sth** 盼望做某事 pànwàng zuò mǒushì ▸ **we look forward to hearing from you** 我们(們)盼望收到你的回音 wǒmen pànwàng shōudào nǐ de huíyīn ▸ **look into** VT FUS (investigate) 调(調)查 diàochá ▸ **look round, look around** I VI **1** (turn head) 环(環)顾(顧) huángù **2** (in building) 看看 kànkan II VT FUS [+ place, building] 游(遊)览(覽) yóulǎn ▸ **look through** VT FUS [+ book, magazine, papers] 翻阅(閱) fānyuè ▸ **look up** VT [+ information, meaning] 查 chá

loose [luːs] ADJ **1** [+ screw, connection, tooth] 松(鬆)动(動)的 sōngdòng de **2** [+ hair] 散开(開)的 sǎnkāi de **3** [+ clothes, trousers] 宽(寬)松(鬆)的 kuānsōng de

lord [lɔːd] (Brit) N [C] (peer) 贵(貴)族 guìzú [位 wèi]

lorry ['lɔrɪ] (Brit) N [C] 卡车(車) kǎchē [辆 liàng]

lorry driver (Brit) N [C] 卡车(車)司机(機) kǎchē sījī [位 wèi]

lose [luːz] (pt, pp lost) I VT **1** (mislay) 丢(丟)失 diūshī **2** (not win) [+ contest, fight, argument] 输(輸) shū **3** (through death) [+ relative, wife etc] 失去 shīqù II VI 输(輸) shū ▸ **to lose weight** 减(減)重 jiǎnzhòng

loss [lɒs] N [C/U] 丧(喪)失 sàngshī [种 zhǒng]

lost [lɒst] I PT, PP of **lose** II ADJ [+ object] 丢(丟)失的 diūshī de; [+ person, animal] 走失的 zǒushī de ▸ **to get lost** 迷路 mílù

lost and found (US) N = **lost property**

lost property N [U] **1** (things) 招领(領)的失物 zhāolǐng de shīwù **2** (Brit: office) 失物招领(領)处(處) shīwù zhāolǐngchù

lot [lɒt] N [C] ▸ **a lot** (many) 许(許)多 xǔduō; (much) 很多 hěn duō ▸ **a lot of** 许(許)多 xǔduō ▸ **lots of** 许(許)多 xǔduō ▸ **he reads/smokes a lot** 他读(讀)得/烟(煙)抽得很多 tā shū dú de/yān chōu de hěn duō

lottery ['lɒtərɪ] N [C] 彩票 cǎipiào [张 zhāng]

loud [laud] I ADJ 响(響)亮的 xiǎngliàng de II ADV [speak +] 大声(聲)地 dàshēng de

loudly ['laudlɪ] ADV 大声(聲)地 dàshēng de

loudspeaker [laud'spiːkəʳ] N [C] 扬(揚)声(聲)器 yángshēngqì [个 gè]

lounge [laundʒ] N [C] **1** (in hotel) 休息室 xiūxishì [间 jiān] **2** (at airport, station) 等候室 děnghòushì [间 jiān] **3** 起居室 qǐjūshì [间 jiān]

love [lʌv] I N [U] (for partner, sweetheart) 爱(愛)情 àiqíng; (for child, pet) 爱(愛) ài II VT [+ partner, child, pet] 爱(愛) ài; [+ thing, food, activity] 热(熱)爱(愛) rè'ài ▸ **to be in love (with sb)** (与(與)某人)恋(戀)爱(愛) (yǔ mǒurén) liàn'ài ▸ **to fall in love (with sb)** 爱(愛)上(某人) àishàng (mǒurén) ▸ **to make love** 做爱(愛) zuò'ài ▸ **love (from) Anne** (on letter) 爱(愛)你的，安妮 ài nǐ de, Ānní ▸ **to love doing/to do sth** 喜爱(愛)做某事 xǐ'ài zuò mǒushì ▸ **I'd love to come** 我非常想来(來) wǒ fēicháng xiǎng lái

lovely ['lʌvlɪ] (esp Brit) ADJ **1** [+ place, person, music] 漂亮的 piàoliang de **2** [+ holiday, meal, present] 令人愉快的 lìng rén yúkuài de; [+ person] 可爱(愛)的 kě'ài de

lover ['lʌvəʳ] N [C] 情人 qíngrén [个 gè] ▸ **a lover of art** or **an art lover** 钟(鐘)爱(愛)艺(藝)术(術)的人 zhōng'ài yìshù de rén

low [ləʊ] ADJ **1** [+ *wall, hill, heel*] 矮的 ǎi de **2** [+ *temperature, price, level, speed*] 低的 dī de **3** [+ *standard, quality*] 低劣的 dīliè de ▸ **low in calories/salt/fat** 低卡路里/盐(鹽)/脂肪 dī kǎlùlǐ/yán/zhīfáng

low-carb ['ləʊ'ka:b] ADJ (*food*) 低碳水化合物的 dī tànshuǐhuàhéwù de

lower ['ləʊəʳ] VT (*reduce*) 降低 jiàngdī

loyal ['lɔɪəl] ADJ 忠实(實)的 zhōngshí de

loyalty ['lɔɪəltɪ] N [U] 忠诚(誠) zhōngchéng

luck [lʌk] N [U] **1** (*chance*) 运(運)气(氣) yùnqì **2** (*good fortune*) 幸运(運) xìngyùn ▸ **good luck** 好运(運) hǎoyùn ▸ **good luck!** or **best of luck!** 祝你好运(運)! zhùnǐ hǎoyùn! ▸ **bad luck** 不走运(運) bù zǒuyùn

luckily ['lʌkɪlɪ] ADV 幸运(運)的是 xìngyùn de shì

lucky ['lʌkɪ] ADJ [+ *person*] 幸运(運)的 xìngyùn de ▸ **to be lucky** 走运(運) zǒuyùn ▸ **it is lucky that...** 侥(僥)幸(倖)的是··· jiǎoxìng de shì... ▸ **to have a lucky escape** 侥(僥)幸(倖)逃脱(脫) jiǎoxìng táotuō

luggage ['lʌgɪdʒ] N [U] 行李 xíngli ▸ **piece of luggage** 一件行李 yī jiàn xíngli

lunch [lʌntʃ] N **1** [c/U] (*meal*) 午餐 wǔcān [顿(頓) dùn] **2** [U] (*lunchtime*) 午餐时(時)间(間) wǔcān shíjiān ▸ **to have lunch (with sb)** (与(與)某人)共进(進)午餐 (yǔ mǒurén) gòng jìn wǔcān

lung [lʌŋ] N [c] 肺 fèi [片 piàn]

Luxembourg ['lʌksəmbəːg] N 卢(盧)森堡 Lúsēnbǎo

luxurious [lʌg'zjʊərɪəs] ADJ 豪华(華)的 háohuá de

luxury ['lʌkʃərɪ] I N [U] (*comfort*) 奢华(華) shēhuá II CPD [+ *hotel, car, goods*] 豪华(華) háohuá

lying ['laɪɪŋ] VB *see* lie¹, lie²

lyrics ['lɪrɪks] NPL 词(詞)句 cíjù

mac [mæk] (*Brit: inf*) N [c] 雨衣 yǔyī [件 jiàn]

machine [məˈʃiːn] N [c] 机(機)器 jīqì [台 tái]

machine gun N [c] 机(機)关(關)枪(槍) jīguānqiāng [架 jià]

machinery [məˈʃiːnərɪ] N [U] 机(機)器 jīqì

mad [mæd] ADJ **1** (*insane*) 精神失常的 jīngshén shīcháng de **2** (*inf: angry*) 恼(惱)怒的 nǎonù de ▸ **to go mad** 发(發)疯(瘋) fāfēng; (*get angry*) 发(發)火 fāhuǒ ▸ **to be mad about** or **on sth** (*inf*) 狂热(熱)地爱(愛)好某物 kuángrè de àihào mǒuwù

madam ['mædəm] N 女士 nǚshì ▸ **Dear Madam** 尊敬的女士 zūnjìng de nǚshì

made [meɪd] PT, PP *of* make

madness ['mædnɪs] N [U] **1** (*insanity*) 疯(瘋)狂 fēngkuáng **2** (*foolishness*) 愚蠢 yúchǔn

magazine [mægə'zi:n] N [c] 杂(雜)志(誌) zázhì [份 fèn]

magic ['mædʒɪk] I N [U] 魔法 mófǎ II ADJ **1** [+ *formula, solution, cure*] 神奇的 shénqí de **2** (*supernatural*) 魔法的 mófǎ de

magnet ['mægnɪt] N [c] 磁铁(鐵) cítiě [块 kuài]

maid [meɪd] N [c] (*servant*) 女仆(僕) nǚpú [个 gè]

maiden name ['meɪdn-] N [c] 娘家姓 niángjiā xìng [个 gè]

mail [meɪl] I N [U] **1** ▸ **the mail** 邮(郵)政 yóuzhèng **2** (letters) 邮(郵)件 yóujiàn **3** (email) 电(電)子邮(郵)件 diànzǐ yóujiàn II VT **1** (esp US: post) 寄出 jìchū **2** (email) 发(發)电(電)邮(郵)给(給) fā diànyóu gěi ▸ **by mail** 以邮(郵)寄方式 yǐ yóujì fāngshì

mailbox ['meɪlbɒks] N [c] **1** (US: for letters) 信箱 xìnxiāng [个 gè] **2** (US) 邮(郵)筒 yóutǒng [个 gè] **3** (Comput) 电(電)子信箱 diànzǐ xìnxiāng [个 gè]

mailman ['meɪlmæn] (pl **mailmen**) (US) N [c] 邮(郵)差 yóuchāi [个 gè]

mailwoman ['meɪlwʊmən] (US) N [c] (pl **mailwomen**) 女邮(郵)递(遞)员(員) nǚyóudìyuán [位 wèi]

main [meɪn] ADJ 主要的 zhǔyào de

main course N [c] 主菜 zhǔcài [道 dào]

mainly ['meɪnlɪ] ADV 主要地 zhǔyào de

main road N [c] 主干(幹)道 zhǔgàndào [条 tiáo]

majesty ['mædʒɪstɪ] N (title) ▸ **Your/His/Her Majesty** 陛下 bìxià

major ['meɪdʒər] I ADJ 重要的 zhòngyào de II N [c] **1** (Mil) 少校 shàoxiào [位 wèi] **2** (US) 专(專)业 zhuānyè [个 gè]

Majorca [mə'jɔːkə] N 马(馬)略卡岛(島) Mǎluèkǎ dǎo

majority [mə'dʒɔrɪtɪ] N [s + PL VB] 大多数(數) dàduōshù

make [meɪk] (pt, pp **made**) I VT **1** [+ object, clothes, cake] 做 zuò; [+ noise] 制(製)造 zhìzào; [+ mistake] 犯 fàn **2** (manufacture) 生产(產) shēngchǎn **3** (cause to be) ▸ **to make sb sad** 使某人难(難)过(過) shǐ mǒurén nánguò ▸ **to make sb do sth** 促使某人做事 cùshǐ mǒurén zuò mǒushì **5** [+ money] 挣(掙) zhèng **6** (equal) ▸ **2 and 2 make 4** 2加2等于(於)4 èr jiā èr děngyú sì II N [c] (brand) 牌子 páizi [个 gè] ▸ **to make a profit/loss** 赢(贏)利/赔(賠)钱(錢) yínglì/péiqián ▸ **what time do you make it?** 你表(錶)几(幾)点(點)了? nǐ biǎo jǐdiǎn le? ▸ **it's made (out) of glass** 是玻璃做的 shì bōli zuò de

▸ **make out** VT [+ cheque] 开(開)出 kāichū

▸ **make up** VT **1** [+ story, excuse] 捏造 niēzào **2** (with cosmetics) 化妆(妝) huàzhuāng ▸ **to make up one's mind** 下

定决(決)心 xià dìng juéxīn ▸ **to make o.s. up** 化妆(妝) huàzhuāng

make-up ['meɪkʌp] N [U] (cosmetics) 化妆(妝)品 huàzhuāngpǐn

Malaysia [mə'leɪzɪə] N 马(馬)来(來)西亚(亞) Mǎláixīyà

male [meɪl] ADJ [+ employee, child, model, friend, population] 男的 nán de; [+ animal, insect, plant, tree] 雄性的 xióngxìng de

mall [mɔːl] N (also: **shopping mall**) 大型购(購)物中心 dàxíng gòuwù zhōngxīn [个 gè]

Malta ['mɔːltə] N 马(馬)耳他岛 Mǎ'ěrtā

mammal ['mæml] N [c] 哺乳动(動)物 bǔrǔ dòngwù [个 gè]

man [mæn] (pl **men**) N **1** [c] (person) 男人 nánrén [个 gè] **2** [U] (mankind) 人类(類) rénlèi

manage ['mænɪdʒ] I VT [+ business, shop, time, money] 管理 guǎnlǐ II VI (cope) 应(應)付 yìngfù ▸ **to manage to do sth** 设(設)法做到某事 shèfǎ zuòdào mǒushì

management ['mænɪdʒmənt] N **1** [U] (managing) 管理 guǎnlǐ **2** [U/s] (managers) 管理人员(員) guǎnlǐ rényuán

manager ['mænɪdʒər] N [c] **1** 经(經)理 jīnglǐ [位 wèi] **2** (Sport) 球队(隊)经(經)理 qiúduì jīnglǐ [位 wèi]

mandarin ['mændərɪn] N **1** [U] ▸ **Mandarin (Chinese)** 普通话(話) Pǔtōnghuà **2** [c] (also: **mandarin orange**) 柑橘 gānjú [个 gè]

maniac ['meɪnɪæk] N [c] (lunatic) 疯(瘋)子 fēngzi [个 gè]

manner ['mænər] I N [s] (way) 方式 fāngshì II **manners** NPL 礼(禮)貌 lǐmào ▸ **it's good/bad manners to arrive on time** 准(準)时(時)是有礼(禮)貌/无(無)礼(禮)的表现(現) zhǔnshí shì yǒu lǐmào/wúlǐ de biǎoxiàn

manual ['mænjuəl] N [c] (handbook) 手册(冊) shǒucè [本 běn]

manufacture [mænjuˈfæktʃər] VT 生产(產) shēngchǎn

manufacturer [mænjuˈfæktʃərər] N [c] 制(製)造商 zhìzàoshāng [个 gè]

many ['mɛnɪ] I ADJ (a lot of) 许(許)多的 xǔduō de II PRON 许(許)多的 xǔduō de ▸ **how many** (direct question) 多少

map | 284

duōshao ▸ **twice as many (as)** (是…的)两(兩)倍 (shì…de) liǎng bèi

map [mæp] N [c] 地图(圖) dìtú [张 zhāng]

marathon ['mærəθən] N [c] (race) 马(馬)拉松长(長)跑 mǎlāsōng chángpǎo [次 cì]

marble ['mɑːbl] I N [U] 大理石 dàlǐshí II **marbles** N PL (game) 弹(彈)子游(遊) 戏(戲) dànzǐ yóuxì

March [mɑːtʃ] N [c/U] 三月 sānyuè; see also/另见 **July**

march [mɑːtʃ] VI 行军(軍) xíngjūn

margarine [mɑːdʒəˈriːn] N [U] 人造黄油 rénzào huángyóu

marijuana [mærɪˈwɑːnə] N [U] 大麻 dàmá

mark [mɑːk] I N [c] **1** (cross, tick) 记(記) 号(號) jìhao [个 gè] **2** [c] (stain) 污 点(點) wūdiǎn [个 gè] **3** [c] (Brit: grade, score) 分数(數) fēnshù [个 gè] II VT **1** (indicate) [+ place] 标(標)示 biāoshì **2** (Brit: Scol) 评(評)分 píngfēn

market ['mɑːkɪt] N [c] 集市 jíshì [个 gè]

marketing ['mɑːkɪtɪŋ] N [U] 市场(場) 营(營)销(銷) shìchǎng yíngxiāo

marriage ['mærɪdʒ] N **1** [c/U] (relationship, institution) 婚姻 hūnyīn [个 gè] **2** [c] (wedding) 婚礼(禮) hūnlǐ [场 chǎng]

married ['mærɪd] ADJ 已婚的 yǐhūn de ▸ **to be married to sb** 和某人结(結)婚 hé mǒurén jiéhūn ▸ **to get married** 结(結)婚 jiéhūn

marry ['mærɪ] VT 和…结(結)婚 hé…jiéhūn

marvellous, (US) **marvelous** ['mɑːvləs] ADJ 极好的 jí hǎo de

masculine ['mæskjulɪn] ADJ **1** [+ characteristic, value] 男性的 nánxìng de **2** (Ling) [+ pronoun] 阳(陽)性的 yángxìng de

mashed potato [mæʃt-] N [c/U] 土豆泥 tǔdòuní [份 fèn]

mask [mɑːsk] N [c] **1** (disguise) 面罩 miànzhào [个 gè] **2** (protection) 口罩 kǒuzhào [个 gè]

mass [mæs] N [c] (large amount, number) 大量 dàliàng ▸ **masses of** (inf) 大量 dàliàng

massage ['mæsɑːʒ] N [c/U] 按摩 ànmó [次 cì]

massive ['mæsɪv] ADJ [+ amount, increase] 巨大的 jùdà de; [+ explosion] 大规(規)模 的 dàguīmó de

master ['mɑːstə[r]] VT (learn) [+ skill, language] 掌握 zhǎngwò

masterpiece ['mɑːstəpiːs] N [c] 杰(傑) 作 jiézuò [部 bù]

mat [mæt] N [c] 席(蓆) xí [张 zhāng]

match [mætʃ] I N **1** [c] (game) 比赛(賽) bǐsài [场 chǎng] **2** [c] (for lighting fire) 火 柴 huǒchái [根 gēn] II VI (go together) [colours, materials +] 相配 xiāngpèi

mate [meɪt] N [c] (animal) 配偶 pèi'ǒu [个 gè]

material [məˈtɪərɪəl] I N **1** [c/U] (cloth) 衣 料 yīliào [块 kuài] **2** [U] (information, data) 资(資)料 zīliào II **materials** N PL (equipment) 用具 yòngjù

math [mæθ] (US) N = **maths**

mathematics [mæθəˈmætɪks] (frm) N [U] 数(數)学(學) shùxué

maths [mæθs] (Brit) N [U] 数(數)学(學) shùxué

matter ['mætə[r]] I N [c] 事件 shìjiàn [个 gè] II VI (be important) 要紧(緊) yàojǐn ▸ **what's the matter (with...)?** (…)怎 么(麼)了? (…)zěnme le? ▸ **it doesn't matter** 没(沒)关(關)系(係) méi guānxi

mattress ['mætrɪs] N [c] 床(牀)垫(墊) chuángdiàn [个 gè]

maximum ['mæksɪməm] I ADJ [+ speed, height] 最高的 zuì gāo de; [+ weight] 最 重的 zuì zhòng de II N [c] 最大量 zuì dà liàng

May [meɪ] N [c/U] 五月 wǔyuè; see also/ 另见 **July**

⬤ **KEYWORD**

may [meɪ] AUX VB **1** (possibility) ▸ **it may rain later** 等会(會)儿(兒)可能要下雨 děnghuìr kěnéng yào xiàyǔ ▸ **we may not be able to come** 我们(們)可能来(來)不了 wǒmen kěnéng lái bù liǎo ▸ **he may have hurt himself** 他可能 伤(傷)了自己 tā kěnéng shāngle zìjǐ **2** (permission) ▸ **may I come in?** 我可以 进(進)来(來)吗(嗎)? wǒ kěyǐ jìnlái ma?

maybe ['meɪbiː] ADV **1** 可能 kěnéng **2** (making suggestions) 也许(許) yěxǔ

3 (estimating) 大概 dàgài ▸ **maybe so/ not** 也许(許)如此/不是 yěxǔ rúcǐ/bù shì

mayor [mɛəʳ] N [c] 市长(長) shìzhǎng [位 wèi]

me [miː] PRON 我 wǒ ▸ **it's me** 是我 shì wǒ

meal [miːl] N **1** [c] (occasion) 一餐 yī cān [顿 dùn] **2** [c] (food) 膳食 shànshí [顿 dùn] ▸ **to go out for a meal** 出去吃 饭(飯) chūqù chīfàn

mean [miːn] (pt, pp meant) I VT **1** (signify) 表示…意思 biǎoshì…yìsi **2** (refer to) 意 指 yìzhǐ **3** (intend) ▸ **to mean to do sth** 意欲做某事 yìyù zuò mǒushì II ADJ **1** (not generous) 吝啬(嗇)的 lìnsè de **2** (unkind) 刻薄的 kèbó de ▸ **what do you mean?** 你什么(麼)意思？nǐ shénme yìsi?; see also/ 另见 **means**

meaning [ˈmiːnɪŋ] N [c/u] (of word, expression) 意思 yìsi [层 céng]; (of symbol, dream, gesture) 含义(義) hányì [个 gè]

means [miːnz] (pl means) N [c] (method) 方法 fāngfǎ [个 gè]

meant [mɛnt] PT, PP of mean

meanwhile [ˈmiːnwaɪl] ADV 同时(時) tóngshí

measles [ˈmiːzlz] N [u] 麻疹 mázhěn

measure [ˈmɛʒəʳ] VT 测(測)量 cèliáng

measurement [ˈmɛʒəmənt] I N [c] (length, width etc) 尺寸 chǐcùn II **measurements** NPL (of person) 三 围(圍) sānwéi

meat [miːt] N [u] 肉 ròu

Mecca [ˈmɛkə] N 麦(麥)加 Màijiā

mechanic [mɪˈkænɪk] N [c] 机(機)械工 jīxiègōng [位 wèi]

medal [ˈmɛdl] N [c] 奖(奬)章 jiǎngzhāng [枚 méi]

media [ˈmiːdɪə] I PL of medium II NPL ▸ **the media** 媒体(體) méitǐ

medical [ˈmɛdɪkl] I ADJ 医(醫)疗(療)的 yīliáo de II N [c] (examination) 体(體)格 检查 tǐgé jiǎnchá [次 cì]

medicine [ˈmɛdsɪn] N **1** [u] (science) 医(醫)学(學) yīxué **2** [c/u] (medication) 药(藥) yào [种 zhǒng]

Mediterranean [mɛdɪtəˈreɪnɪən] N ▸ **the Mediterranean** (sea) 地中海 Dìzhōnghǎi; (region) 地中海沿岸地

区(區) Dìzhōnghǎi yán'àn dìqū

medium [ˈmiːdɪəm] ADJ **1** (average) 中等 的 zhōngděng de **2** (clothing size) 中 码(碼)的 zhōngmǎ de

medium-sized [ˈmiːdɪəmˈsaɪzd] ADJ 中 等大小的 zhōngděng dàxiǎo de

meet [miːt] (pt, pp met) I VT **1** (accidentally) 遇见(見) yùjiàn; (by arrangement) 和…见(見)面 hé…jiànmiàn **2** (for the first time) 结(結) 识(識) jiéshí; (be introduced to) 认(認) 识(識) rènshi **3** 接 jiē II VI **1** (accidentally) 相遇 xiāngyù; (by arrangement) 见(見)面 jiànmiàn **2** (for the first time) 认(認) 识(識) rènshi ▸ **pleased to meet you** 见(見)到你很高兴(興) jiàndào nǐ hěn gāoxìng ▸ **meet up** VI 会(會)面 huìmiàn

meeting [ˈmiːtɪŋ] N [c] **1** (of club, committee) 会(會)议(議) huìyì [次 cì] **2** [c] (encounter) 会(會)面 huìmiàn [次 cì]

megabyte [ˈmɛgəbaɪt] N [c] 兆字节(節) zhàozìjié [个 gè]

melon [ˈmɛlən] N [c/u] 瓜 guā [个 gè]

melt [mɛlt] I VI 融化 rónghuà II VT 使融化 shǐ rónghuà

member [ˈmɛmbəʳ] N [c] **1** (of family, staff, public) 一员(員) yīyuán **2** (of club, party) 成员(員) chéngyuán [个 gè]

meme [miːm] N [c] 恶(惡)搞 è gǎo

memorial [mɪˈmɔːrɪəl] N [c] 纪(紀)念碑 jìniànbēi [座 zuò]

memorize [ˈmɛməraɪz] VT 记(記)住 jìzhù

memory [ˈmɛmərɪ] N **1** [c/u] (ability to remember) 记(記)忆(憶)力 jìyìlì [种 zhǒng] **2** [c] (thing remembered) 记(記) 忆(憶) jìyì [个 gè] **3** [c/u] (Comput) 存 储(儲)器 cúnchǔqì [个 gè] ▸ **to have a good/bad memory (for sth)** (对(對)某 事) 记(記)忆(憶)力好/差 (duì mǒushì) jìyìlì hǎo/chà

men [mɛn] NPL of man

mend [mɛnd] VT 修理 xiūlǐ

mental [ˈmɛntl] ADJ [+ illness, health] 精 神的 jīngshén de

mental hospital N [c] 精神病院 jīngshénbìngyuàn [个 gè]

mention [ˈmɛnʃən] VT 提到 tídào ▸ **don't mention it!** 不客气(氣)! bù kèqi!

menu ['mɛnjuː] N [c] **1** 菜单(單) càidān [个 gè] **2** (Comput) 选(選)择(擇)菜单(單) xuǎnzé càidān [个 gè]

merry ['mɛrɪ] ADJ ▸ Merry Christmas! 圣(聖)诞(誕)快乐(樂)！Shèngdàn Kuàilè!

mess [mɛs] N **1** [s/u] (untidiness) 凌(淩)乱(亂) língluàn **2** [s/u] (chaotic situation) 混乱(亂)的局面 hùnluàn de júmiàn ▸ **mess about, mess around** (inf) VI 混日子 hùn rìzi

message ['mɛsɪdʒ] N [c] 消息 xiāoxi [条 tiáo] ▸ **to leave (sb) a message** (给(給)某人)留个(個)信 (gěi mǒurén)liú gè xìn

met [mɛt] PT, PP of **meet**

metal ['mɛtl] N [c/u] 金属(屬) jīnshǔ [种 zhǒng]

meter ['miːtər] N [c] **1** 仪(儀)表 yíbiǎo [个 gè]; (also: **parking meter**) 停车(車)计(計)时(時)器 tíngchē jìshíqì [个 gè] **2** (US: unit) = **metre**

method ['mɛθəd] N [c/u] 方法 fāngfǎ [种 zhǒng]

metre, (US) **meter** ['miːtər] N [c] (unit) 米 mǐ

metric ['mɛtrɪk] ADJ 公制的 gōngzhì de

Mexico ['mɛksɪkəu] N 墨西哥 Mòxīgē

mice [maɪs] NPL of **mouse**

microchip ['maɪkrəutʃɪp] N [c] 集成电(電)路块(塊) jíchéngdiànlù kuài [个 gè]

microphone ['maɪkrəfəun] N [c] 话(話)筒 huàtǒng [个 gè]

microscope ['maɪkrəskəup] N [c] 显(顯)微镜(鏡) xiǎnwēijìng [个 gè]

microwave ['maɪkrəuweɪv] N [c] (also: **microwave oven**) 微波炉(爐) wēibōlú [个 gè]

midday [mɪd'deɪ] N [u] 正午 zhèngwǔ ▸ **at midday** 在正午 zài zhèngwǔ

middle ['mɪdl] I N **1** [c] (centre) 中央 zhōngyāng [个 gè] **2** [s] (of month, event) 中 zhōng II ADJ [+ position, event, period] 中间(間)的 zhōngjiān de ▸ **in the middle of the night** 在半夜 zài bànyè

middle-aged [mɪdl'eɪdʒd] ADJ 中年的 zhōngnián de

middle class ADJ (also: **middle-class**) 中层(層)社会(會)的 zhōngcéng shèhuì de

Middle East N ▸ **the Middle East** 中东(東) Zhōngdōng

middle name N [c] 中间(間)名字 zhōngjiān míngzi [个 gè]

MIDDLE NAME

first name 是由父母取的名字。**last name** 或 **surname** 是家族的姓氏。在说英语的国家中,名在姓之前。在 **first name** 和 **last name** 之间,还可能有 **middle name** (中名),这是你父母给你取的第二个 "名"。**middle name** 通常只用于正式场合,例如在选课或签署文件时。

midnight ['mɪdnaɪt] N [u] 半夜 bànyè ▸ **at midnight** 在午夜 zài wǔyè

midwife ['mɪdwaɪf] (pl **midwives**) N [c] 助产(產)士 zhùchǎnshì [位 wèi]

might [maɪt] AUX VB (possibility) ▸ I might get home late 我可能会(會)晚回家 wǒ kěnéng huì wǎn huíjiā ▸ **it might have been an accident** 可能是个(個)事故 kěnéng shì gè shìgù

migraine ['miːgreɪn] N [c/u] 偏头(頭)痛 piāntóutòng [阵 zhèn]

mild [maɪld] ADJ **1** [+ infection, illness] 轻(輕)微的 qīngwēi de **2** [+ climate, weather] 温(溫)暖的 wēnnuǎn de

mile [maɪl] I N [c] 英里 yīnglǐ II **miles** NPL (inf: a long way) 很远(遠)的距离(離) hěn yuǎn de jùlí ▸ **70 miles per** or **an hour** 每小时(時)70英里 měi xiǎoshí qīshí yīnglǐ

military ['mɪlɪtərɪ] ADJ 军(軍)事的 jūnshì de

milk [mɪlk] N [u] 奶 nǎi

milkshake ['mɪlkʃeɪk] N [c/u] 奶昔 nǎixī [份 fèn]

millimetre, (US) **millimeter** ['mɪlɪmiːtər] N [c] 毫米 háomǐ

million ['mɪljən] I NUM 百万(萬) bǎiwàn II **millions** NPL (lit) 数(數)百万(萬) shùbǎi wàn; (inf: fig) 无(無)数(數) wúshù ▸ **a** or **one million books/people/dollars** 100万(萬)本书(書)/个(個)人/元 yìbǎi wàn běn shū/gè rén/yuán

millionaire [mɪljə'nɛər] N [c] 百万(萬)富翁 bǎiwàn fùwēng [个 gè]

mind [maɪnd] I N [c] 智力 zhìlì [种 zhǒng] II VT **1** (Brit: look after) [+ child, shop] 照看 zhàokàn **2** (be careful of) 当(當)心

dāngxīn **3** (object to) 介意 jièyì **4** (have a preference) ▸ I don't mind (what/who...) 我不在乎 (什么(麼)/谁(誰)…) wǒ bù zàihu (shénme/shéi...) **5** ▸ do/would you mind (if...)? (如果…) 你介意吗 (嗎)？ (rúguǒ...) nǐ jièyì ma? ▸ to make up one's mind or make one's mind up 下定决(決)心 xiàdìng juéxīn ▸ to change one's/sb's mind 改变(變)主意 gǎibiàn zhǔyi ▸ I wouldn't mind a coffee 我挺想喝杯咖啡 wǒ tǐng xiǎng hē bēi kāfēi ▸ mind the step 小心脚(腳)下 xiǎoxīn jiǎoxia

mindfulness ['maɪndfʊlnɪs] N [U] 正念 zhèngniàn

KEYWORD

mine¹ [maɪn] PRON 我的 wǒ de ▸ this is mine 这(這)是我的 zhè shì wǒ de ▸ these are mine 这(這)些是我的 zhèxiē shì wǒ de

mine² [maɪn] N [c] 矿(礦) kuàng [座 zuò]

mineral water ['mɪnərəl-] N [U/c] 矿(礦)泉水 kuàngquánshuǐ

miniature ['mɪnətʃəʳ] ADJ 微型的 wēixíng de

minibus ['mɪnɪbʌs] N [c] 小公共汽车(車) xiǎo gōnggòng qìchē [辆 liàng]

minimum ['mɪnɪməm] I ADJ 最低的 zuì dī de II N [c] 最少量 zuì shǎo liàng

miniskirt ['mɪnɪskəːt] N [c] 超短裙 chāoduǎnqún [条 tiáo]

minister ['mɪnɪstəʳ] N [c] **1** (Brit: Pol) 部长(長) bùzhǎng [位 wèi] **2** (Rel) 牧师(師) mùshī [位 wèi]

minor ['maɪnəʳ] ADJ [+ repairs, changes] 不重要的 bù zhòngyào de; [+ injuries] 不严(嚴)重的 bù yánzhòng de

minority [maɪˈnɔrɪtɪ] N **1** [S + PL VB] [of group, society] 少数(數) shǎoshù **2** [c] (ethnic, cultural, religious) 少数(數)民族 shǎoshù mínzú [个 gè]

mint [mɪnt] N **1** [U] (plant) 薄荷 bòhe **2** [U] (sweet) 薄荷糖 bòhe táng

minus ['maɪnəs] PREP (inf: without) 没(沒)有 méiyǒu ▸ 12 minus 3 (is or equals 9) 12减(減)3 (等于(於)9) shí'èr jiǎn sān (děngyú jiǔ) ▸ minus 24 (degrees C/F) (temperature) 零下

24 (摄(攝)氏/华(華)氏度) língxià èrshísì (shèshì/huáshì dù) ▸ B minus (Scol) B减(減)bì jiǎn

minute ['mɪnɪt] N [c] **1** (unit) 分钟(鐘) fēnzhōng **2** 一会(會)儿(兒) yīhuìr ▸ wait or just a minute! 等一会(會)儿(兒)！ děng yīhuìr!

miracle ['mɪrəkl] N [c] **1** (Rel) 圣(聖)迹(蹟) shèngjì [处 chù] **2** (marvel) 奇迹(蹟) qíjì [个 gè]

mirror ['mɪrəʳ] N [c] **1** 镜(鏡)子 jìngzi [面 miàn]; [in car] 后(後)视(視)镜(鏡) hòushìjìng [个 gè]

misbehave [mɪsbɪˈheɪv] VI 行为(為)无(無)礼(禮) xíngwéi wúlǐ

miscellaneous [mɪsɪˈleɪnɪəs] ADJ 形形色色的 xíngxíng-sèsè de

miserable ['mɪzərəbl] ADJ **1** [+ person] 痛苦的 tòngkǔ de **2** [+ weather, day] 恶(惡)劣的 èliè de

Miss [mɪs] N **1** 小姐 xiǎojiě **2** (esp Brit: as form of address) 小姐 xiǎojiě ▸ Dear Miss Smith 亲(親)爱(愛)的史密斯小姐 qīn'ài de Shǐmìsī xiǎojiě

○ **MISS, MRS, MS**
○
○ 在说英语的国家中，Mrs (夫人)用于
○ 已婚女士的姓名前。Miss (小姐)用于
○ 未婚女士。有些女士认为，让
○ 人们知道她是否结婚并不重要，所以往
○ 往用 Ms (女士)称呼自己。与 Mr
○ (先生)类似，Ms 不表明任何婚姻状
○ 况。

miss [mɪs] VT **1** (fail to hit) 未击(擊)中 wèi jīzhòng **2** [+ train, bus, plane] 错(錯)过(過) cuòguò **3** [+ chance, opportunity] 错(錯)过(過) cuòguò ▸ you can't miss it 你不会(會)找不到 nǐ bù huì zhǎo bù dào

missing ['mɪsɪŋ] ADJ [+ person] 失踪(蹤)的 shīzōng de; [+ object] 丢(丟)失的 diūshī de

mist [mɪst] N [c/U] 薄雾(霧) bówù [场 chǎng]

mistake [mɪsˈteɪk] N [c] **1** (error) 错(錯)误(誤) cuòwù [个 gè] **2** (blunder) 过(過)失 guòshī [个 gè] ▸ to make a mistake 犯错(錯) fàncuò ▸ to do sth by mistake 误(誤)做某事 wùzuò mǒushì

mistaken [mɪsˈteɪkən] I PP of **mistake**
II ADJ ▸ **to be mistaken (about sth)**
[*person +*] (把某事) 搞错(錯) (bǎ
mǒushì) gǎocuò

mistook [mɪsˈtuk] PT of **mistake**

misty [ˈmɪstɪ] ADJ 有雾(霧)的 yǒuwù de

misunderstand [mɪsʌndəˈstænd]
(*pt, pp* **misunderstood**) VT, VI 误(誤)解
wùjiě

misunderstanding [ˈmɪsʌndəˈstændɪŋ]
N [c/u] 误(誤)会(會) wùhuì [个 gè]

misunderstood [mɪsʌndəˈstud] PT, PP of
misunderstand

mix [mɪks] I VT 混合 hùnhé II VI (*socially*)
▸ **to mix (with sb)** (和某人) 相处(處)
(hé mǒurén) xiāngchǔ III N [c] 混合
hùnhé [种 zhǒng] ▸ **to mix sth with sth**
[*+ activities*] 将(將)某物同某物混淆
jiāng mǒuwù tóng mǒuwù hùnxiáo
▸ **mix up** VT [*+ people*] 分辨不出 fēnbiàn
bù chū; [*+ things*] 混淆 hùnxiáo

mixed [mɪkst] ADJ 1 [*+ salad, herbs*] 什
锦(錦)的 shíjǐn de 2 [*+ group, community*]
形形色色的 xíngxíng sèsè de 3 [*+ school,
education*] 男女混合的 nánnǚ hùnhé de

mixture [ˈmɪkstʃəʳ] N [c/u] 混合物
hùnhéwù [种 zhǒng]

mix-up [ˈmɪksʌp] (*inf*) N [c] 混乱(亂)
hùnluàn [种 zhǒng]

mobile phone (*Brit*) N [c] 手机(機)
shǒujī [部 bù]

model [ˈmɒdl] I N [c] 1 (*of boat, building*)
模型 móxíng [个 gè] 2 (*fashion model*)
时(時)装(裝)模特 shízhuāng mótè [位
wèi] II ADJ (*miniature*) ▸ **model aircraft/
train** 模型飞(飛)机(機)/火车(車)
móxíng fēijī/huǒchē III VT [*+ clothes*] 展
示 zhǎnshì

modem [ˈməudɛm] N [c] 调(調)制(製)解
调(調)器 tiáozhì jiětiáo qì [个 gè]

moderate [ˈmɒdərət] ADJ 中庸的
zhōngyōng de

modern [ˈmɒdən] ADJ 1 [*+ world, times,
society*] 现(現)代的 xiàndài de
2 [*+ technology, design*] 新式的 xīnshì de

modernize [ˈmɒdənaɪz] VT 使现(現)代
化 shǐ xiàndàihuà

modern languages NPL 现(現)代
语(語)言 xiàndài yǔyán

modest [ˈmɒdɪst] ADJ 谦(謙)虚(虛)的
qiānxū de

moisturizer [ˈmɔɪstʃəraɪzəʳ] N [c/u] 保
湿(濕)霜 bǎoshīshuāng [瓶 píng]

moment [ˈməumənt] N 1 [c] (*period of
time*) 片刻 piànkè 2 [c] (*point in time*) 瞬
间(間) shùnjiān ▸ **at the/this (present)
moment** 此刻/当(當)前 cǐkè/dāngqián
▸ **at the last moment** 在最后(後)一刻
zài zuìhòu yīkè

Monday [ˈmʌndɪ] N [c/u] 星期一
xīngqīyī [个 gè]; see also/另见 **Tuesday**

money [ˈmʌnɪ] N [u] 1 (*cash*) 钱(錢) qián
2 (*in the bank*) 存款 cúnkuǎn 3 (*currency*)
货(貨)币(幣) huòbì ▸ **to make money**
[*person, business +*] 赚(賺)钱(錢)
zhuànqián

monitor [ˈmɒnɪtəʳ] N [c] 显(顯)示屏
xiǎnshìpíng [个 gè]

monkey [ˈmʌŋkɪ] N [c] (*Zool*) 猴 hóu [只
zhī]

monotonous [məˈnɒtənəs] ADJ [*+ life, job
etc, voice, tune*] 单(單)调(調)的 dāndiào de

month [mʌnθ] N [c] 月 yuè [个 gè]
▸ **every month** 每个(個)月 měigè yuè

monthly [ˈmʌnθlɪ] I ADJ 每月的 měi yuè
de II ADV (*every month*) 按月 àn yuè

monument [ˈmɒnjumənt] N [c] 纪(紀)
念碑 jìniànbēi [座 zuò]

mood [muːd] N [c] 心情 xīnqíng [种
zhǒng] ▸ **to be in a good/bad/awkward
mood** 心情好/坏(壞)/不痛快 xīnqíng
hǎo/huài/bù tòngkuài

moon [muːn] N ▸ **the moon** 月球 yuèqiú

moonlight [ˈmuːnlaɪt] N [u] 月光
yuèguāng

moped [ˈməupɛd] N [c] 机(機)动(動)自
行车(車) jīdòng zìxíngchē [辆 liàng]

moral [ˈmɒrl] ADJ [*+ issues, values*] 道德的
dàodé de; [*+ behaviour, person*] 品行端正
的 pǐnxíng duānzhèng de

⊙ KEYWORD

more [mɔːʳ] I ADJ 1 更多的 gèng duō de
▸ **I get more money/holidays than you
do** 我比你有更多的钱(錢)/假期 wǒ bǐ
nǐ yǒu gèng duō de qián/jiàqī
2 (*additional*) 再一些的 zài yīxiē de
▸ **would you like some more tea/
peanuts?** 你要再来(來)点(點)茶/花生
吗(嗎)? nǐ yào zài lái diǎn chá/
huāshēng ma? ▸ **is there any more**

wine? 还(還)有酒吗(嗎)? háiyǒu jiǔ ma? ▸ **a few more weeks** 再几(幾)个(個)星期 zài jǐ gè xīngqī
II PRON 1 (in comparisons) 更多的量 gèng duō de liàng ▸ **there's/there are more than I thought** 比我想得更多 bǐ wǒ xiǎng de gèng duō ▸ **more than 20** 大于(於)20 dà yú èrshí ▸ **she's got more than me** 她比我得到的多 tā bǐ wǒ dédào de duō
2 (further, additional) 额(額)外的量 éwài de liàng ▸ **is there/are there any more?** 还(還)有多的吗(嗎)? háiyǒu duō de ma? ▸ **have you got any more of it/them?** 你(還)有吗(嗎)? nǐ hái yǒu ma? ▸ **much/many more** 多得多 duō de duō
III ADV 1 (to form comparative) 更 gèng ▸ **more dangerous/difficult (than)** (比…)更危险(險)/难(難) (bǐ…) gèng wēixiǎn/nán
2 (in expressions) ▸ **more and more** 越来(來)越 yuèláiyuè ▸ **more or less** (adj, adv) 差不多 chàbuduō ▸ **more than ever** 空前的多 kōngqián de duō ▸ **once more** 再一次 zài yīcì

morning ['mɔ:nɪŋ] N [c/u] (early in the morning) 早晨 zǎochén [个 gè]; (later in the morning) 上午 shàngwǔ [个 gè] ▸ **good morning!** 早上好! zǎoshang hǎo! ▸ **at 3 o'clock/7 o'clock in the morning** 凌(淩)晨3点(點)/早上7点(點) língchén sān diǎn/zǎoshang qī diǎn ▸ **this morning** 今天上午 jīntiān shàngwǔ ▸ **on Monday morning** 星期一上午 Xīngqīyī shàngwǔ

Morocco [mə'rɔkəu] N 摩洛哥 Móluògē

mortgage ['mɔ:gɪdʒ] N [c] 抵押贷(貸)款 dǐyā dàikuǎn [笔 bǐ]

Moscow ['mɔskəu] N 莫斯科 Mòsīkē

Moslem ['mɔzləm] ADJ, N = Muslim

mosque [mɔsk] N [c] 清真寺 qīngzhēnsì [座 zuò]

mosquito [mɔs'ki:təu] (pl mosquitoes) N [c] 蚊 wén [只 zhī]

⊙ KEYWORD

most [məust] I ADJ 1 (almost all) 大部分的 dàbùfen de ▸ **most people** 大多数(數)人 dàduōshù rén

2 (in comparisons) ▸ **the) most** 最 zuì ▸ **who won the most money/prizes?** 谁(誰)赢(贏)了最多的钱(錢)/奖(獎)品? shuí yíngle zuì duō de qián/jiǎngpǐn?
II PRON 大部分 dàbùfen; (plural) 大多数(數) dàduōshù ▸ **most of it/them** 它/他们(們)的大部分 tā/tāmen de dàbùfen ▸ **I paid the most** 我付了大部分 wǒ fùle dàbùfen ▸ **to make the most of sth** 充分利用某物 chōngfèn lìyòng mǒuwù ▸ **at the (very) most** 顶(頂)多 dǐngduō
III ADV (superlative) 1 (with verb) ▸ **the) most** 最 zuì ▸ **what I miss (the) most is...** 我最想念的是… wǒ zuì xiǎngniàn de shì…
2 (with adj) ▸ **the most comfortable/expensive sofa in the shop** 店里(裡)最舒服/贵(貴)的沙发(發) diànli zuì shūfu/guì de shāfā
3 (with adv) ▸ **most efficiently/effectively** 最有效率/有效地 zuì yǒu xiàolǜ/yǒuxiào de ▸ **most of all** 最起码(碼)的 zuì qǐmǎ de

mother ['mʌðər] N [c] 母亲(親) mǔqīn [位 wèi]

mother-in-law ['mʌðərɪnlɔ:] (pl mothers-in-law) N [c] (of woman) 婆婆 pópo [位 wèi]; (of man) 岳母 yuèmǔ [位 wèi]

Mother's Day (Brit) N [c/u] 母亲(親)节(節) Mǔqīn Jié [个 gè]

motivated ['məutɪveɪtɪd] ADJ 士气(氣)高涨(漲)的 shìqì gāozhǎng de

motor ['məutər] N [c] 发(發)动(動)机(機) fādòngjī [个 gè]

motorbike ['məutəbaɪk] N [c] 摩托车(車) mótuōchē [辆 liàng]

motorboat ['məutəbəut] N [c] 摩托艇 mótuōtǐng [艘 sōu]

motorcycle ['məutəsaɪkl] (frm) N [c] 摩托车(車) mótuōchē [辆 liàng]

motorcyclist ['məutəsaɪklɪst] N [c] 摩托车(車)手 mótuōchēshǒu [位 wèi]

motorist ['məutərɪst] (esp Brit) N [c] 开(開)汽车(車)的人 kāi qìchē de rén [个 gè]

motor racing (Brit) N [u] 赛(賽)车(車) sàichē

motorway ['məutəweɪ] (Brit) N [c] 高速公路 gāosù gōnglù [条 tiáo]

mountain ['mauntɪn] N [c] 山 shān [座 zuò]

mountain bike N [c] 山地自行车(車) shāndì zìxíngchē [辆 liàng]

mountainous ['mauntɪnəs] ADJ 多山的 duōshān de

mouse [maus] (pl **mice**) N [c] **1** 鼠 shǔ [只 zhī] **2** (Comput) 鼠标(標) shǔbiāo [个 gè]

mouse mat ['mausmæt] N [c] 鼠标(標)垫(墊) shǔbiāo diàn [个 gè]

moustache, (US) **mustache** [məs'tɑːʃ] N [c] 髭 zī [根 gēn]

mouth [n mauθ] N [c] **1** 嘴 zuǐ [张 zhāng] **2** (of river) 河口 hékǒu [个 gè]

mouthful ['mauθful] N [c] 一口 yī kǒu

move [muːv] I VI **1** [vehicle +] 行进(進) xíngjìn; [person, object +] 动(動) dòng **2** (relocate) 搬家 bānjiā; (from activity) 改换(換) gǎihuàn II VT **1** [+ furniture, car] 移动(動) nuódòng **2** (affect emotionally) 感动(動) gǎndòng III N [c] **1** [of house] 搬家 bānjiā [次 cì] **2** (in game) 一步 yī bù ▸ **to move house/jobs/offices** 搬家/换(換)工作/更换(換)办(辦)公地点(點) bānjiā/huàn gōngzuò/gēnghuàn bàngōng dìdiǎn ▸ **to get a move on** (inf) 快点(點) kuàidiǎn
▸ **move away** VI (from town, area) 离(離)开(開) líkāi; (from window, door) 走开(開) zǒukāi
▸ **move back** VI **1** (return) 回来(來) huílái **2** (backwards) 后(後)退 hòutuì
▸ **move forward** VI [person, troops, vehicle +] 向前移动(動) xiàng qián yídòng
▸ **move in** VI (into house) 搬入 bānrù
▸ **move into** VT FUS (house, area) 搬进(進) bānjìn
▸ **move out** VI (of house) 搬出去 bānchūqù
▸ **move over** VI (to make room) 让(讓)开(開)些 ràngkāi xiē

movement ['muːvmənt] N **1** [c] 团(團)体(體) tuántǐ [个 gè] **2** [c] (gesture) 动(動)作 dòngzuò [个 gè]

movie ['muːvɪ] (US) N [c] 电(電)影 diànyǐng [部 bù] ▸ **the movies** 电(電)影 diànyǐng

movie theater (US) N [c] 电(電)影院 diànyǐngyuàn [个 gè]

moving ['muːvɪŋ] ADJ **1** (emotionally) 动(動)人的 dòngrén de **2** (not static) 活动(動)的 huódòng de

MP N ABBR (= **Member of Parliament**) 下院议(議)员(員) Xiàyuàn Yìyuán

MP3 [ɛmpiː'θriː] N **1** (format) 一种音频压缩格式 yī zhǒng yīnpín yāsuō géshì **2** (file) 以这种音频压缩格式储存的声音文件 yǐ zhè zhǒng yīnpín yāsuō géshì chǔcún de shēngyīn wénjiàn

MP3 player ['ɛmpiːθriː-] N [c] MP3 播放器 M P sān bōfàngqì [个 gè] ▸ I need a new MP3 player. 我需要一个新MP3播放器。Wǒ xūyào yī gè xīn M P sān bōfàngqì.

mph ABBR (= **miles per hour**) 每小时(時)…英里 měi xiǎoshí…yīnglǐ

Mr ['mɪstəʳ], (US) **Mr.** N ▸ **Mr Smith** 史密斯先生 Shǐmìsī xiānsheng

Mrs ['mɪsɪz], (US) **Mrs.** N ▸ **Mrs Smith** 史密斯太太 Shǐmìsī tàitai

Ms [mɪz], (US) **Ms.** N (Miss or Mrs) ▸ **Ms Smith** 史密斯女士 Shǐmìsī nǚshì

KEYWORD

much [mʌtʃ] I ADJ 大量的 dàliàng de ▸ **we haven't got much time/money** 我们(們)没(沒)有多少时(時)间(間)/钱(錢) wǒmen méiyǒu duōshao shíjiān/qián
II PRON 大量 dàliàng ▸ **there isn't much left** 剩下的不多了 shèngxià de bù duō le ▸ **he doesn't do much at the weekends** 周(週)末他不做太多事 zhōumò tā bù zuò tài duō shì
III ADV **1** (a great deal) 许(許)多 xǔduō ▸ **he hasn't changed much** 他没(沒)变(變)很多 tā méi biàn hěn duō ▸ **"did you like her?" — "not much"** "你喜欢(歡)她吗(嗎)？" "不太喜欢(歡)" "nǐ xǐhuan tā ma?" "bù tài xǐhuan" **2** (far) …得多 …de duō ▸ **I'm much better now** 我感觉(覺)好多了 wǒ gǎnjué hǎo duō le **3** (often) 经(經)常 jīngcháng ▸ **do you go out much?** 你经(經)常出去吗(嗎)？nǐ jīngcháng chūqù ma?

mud [mʌd] N [U] 泥 ní

muddle ['mʌdl] N [c/u] **1** [of papers, figures, things] 混乱(亂)状(狀)态(態) hùnluàn zhuàngtài [个 gè] **2** (situation) 糟糕局面 zāogāo júmiàn [个 gè] ▶ **to be in a muddle** 一片混乱(亂) yī piàn hùnluàn

muddy ['mʌdɪ] ADJ 沾满(滿)烂(爛)泥的 zhānmǎn lànní de

muesli ['mju:zlɪ] N [u] 穆兹利，和干水果混在一起的燕麦早餐

mug [mʌg] I N [c] 大杯子 dà bēizi [个 gè] II VT (rob) 行凶抢(搶)劫 xíngxiōng qiǎngjié

mugging ['mʌgɪŋ] N [c/u] 行凶抢(搶)劫 xíngxiōng qiǎngjié [次 cì]

multiply ['mʌltɪplaɪ] I VT (Math) ▶ **to multiply sth (by sth)** (某数(數))乘以某数(數) (mǒushù) chéng yǐ mǒushù II VI (increase) 增加 zēngjiā

mum [mʌm] N (Brit: inf) 妈(媽)妈(媽) māma

mummy ['mʌmɪ] N [c] (Brit: inf) 妈(媽)妈(媽) māma [位 wèi]

murder ['mə:dər] I N [c/u] 谋(謀)杀(殺) móushā [个 gè] II VT 谋(謀)杀(殺) móushā

murderer ['mə:dərər] N [c] 凶手 xiōngshǒu [个 gè]

muscle ['mʌsl] N [c/u] 肌肉 jīròu [块 kuài]

museum [mju:'zɪəm] N [c] 博物馆(館) bówùguǎn [个 gè]

mushroom ['mʌʃrum] N [c] 蘑菇 mógu [个 gè]

music ['mju:zɪk] N [u] **1** 音乐(樂) yīnyuè **2** (Scol, Univ) 音乐(樂)课(課) yīnyuèkè

musical ['mju:zɪkl] ADJ **1** (related to music) 音乐(樂)的 yīnyuè de **2** (musically gifted) 有音乐(樂)天赋(賦)的 yǒu yīnyuè tiānfù de

musical instrument N [c] 乐(樂)器 yuèqì [件 jiàn]

musician [mju:'zɪʃən] N [c] 音乐(樂)家 yīnyuèjiā [位 wèi]

Muslim, Moslem ['muzlɪm] I N [c] 穆斯林 Mùsīlín [个 gè] II ADJ 穆斯林的 Mùsīlín de

must [mʌst] AUX VB **1** (expressing importance or necessity) 必须(須) bìxū **2** (expressing intention) 得 děi **3** (expressing presumption) 一定 yīdìng **4** ▶ **you must be joking** 你准(準)是在开(開)玩笑 nǐ zhǔn shì zài kāi wánxiào ▶ **the doctor must allow the patient to decide** 医(醫)生必须(須)让(讓)病人来(來)决(決)定 yīshēng bìxū ràng bìngrén lái juédìng ▶ **I really must be getting back** 我真得回去了 wǒ zhēn děi huíqù le

mustache ['mʌstæʃ] (US) N = **moustache**

mustard ['mʌstəd] N [u] 芥末 jièmo

mustn't ['mʌsnt] = **must not**

my [maɪ] ADJ 我的 wǒ de

myself [maɪ'self] PRON **1** 我自己 wǒ zìjǐ **2** (me) 我 wǒ ▶ **I hurt myself** 我伤(傷)了自己。 wǒ shāngle zìjǐ ▶ **by myself** (unaided) 我独(獨)力地 wǒ dúlì de; (alone) 我独(獨)自 wǒ dúzì

mysterious [mɪs'tɪərɪəs] ADJ 神秘(祕)的 shénmì de

mystery ['mɪstərɪ] N **1** [c] (puzzle) 谜(謎) mí [个 gè] **2** [c] (story) 推理作品 tuīlǐ zuòpǐn [部 bù]

myth [mɪθ] N [c] **1** (legend, story) 神话(話) shénhuà [个 gè] **2** (fallacy) 谬(謬)论(論) miùlùn [个 gè]

n

nail [neɪl] N [c] **1** [of finger, toe] 指甲 zhǐjia [个 gè] **2** (for hammering) 钉(釘)子 dīngzi [个 gè]

nailfile ['neɪlfaɪl] N [c] 指甲锉(銼) zhǐjiacuò [个 gè]

nail polish N [U] 指甲油 zhǐjiayóu

nail varnish (Brit) N = **nail polish**

naked ['neɪkɪd] ADJ 裸体(體)的 luǒtǐ de

name [neɪm] N [c] 名字 míngzi [个 gè]
▸ **what's your name?** 你叫什么(麼)名字? nǐ jiào shénme míngzi? ▸ **my name is Peter** 我叫彼得 wǒ jiào Bǐdé ▸ **to give one's name and address** 留下姓名和地址 liúxià xìngmíng hé dìzhǐ

nanny ['nænɪ] N [c] 保姆 bǎomǔ [个 gè]

napkin ['næpkɪn] N [c] 餐巾 cānjīn [张 zhāng]

nappy ['næpɪ] (Brit) N [c] 尿布 niàobù [块 kuài]

narrow ['nærəʊ] ADJ 窄的 zhǎi de

nasty ['nɑːstɪ] ADJ **1** [+ taste, smell] 恶(噁)心的 ěxīn de **2** [+ injury, accident, disease] 严(嚴)重的 yánzhòng de

nation ['neɪʃən] N [c] 国(國)家 guójiā [个 gè]

national ['næʃənl] I ADJ 国(國)家的 guójiā de II N [c] 公民 gōngmín [个 gè]

national anthem N [c] 国(國)歌 guógē [首 shǒu]

national holiday (US) N [c] 法定假期 fǎdìng jiàqī [个 gè]

nationality [næʃə'nælɪtɪ] N [c/U] 国(國)籍 guójí [个 gè]

national park N [c] 国(國)家公园(園) guójiā gōngyuán [个 gè]

native ['neɪtɪv] ADJ [+ country] 本国(國)的 běnguó de; [+ language, tongue] 母语(語)的 mǔyǔ de

natural ['nætʃrəl] ADJ **1** (normal) 正常的 zhèngcháng de **2** [+ material, product, food] 天然的 tiānrán de

naturally ['nætʃrəlɪ] ADV **1** (unsurprisingly) 自然地 zìrán de **2** (occur, happen +) 自然而然地 zìrán ér rán de

nature ['neɪtʃəʳ] N [U] (also: Nature) 自然界 zìránjiè

naughty ['nɔːtɪ] ADJ 淘气(氣)的 táoqì de

navy ['neɪvɪ] I N **1** ▸ **the navy** (service) 海军(軍) hǎijūn **2** [U] (also: navy-blue) 藏青色 zàngqīngsè II ADJ (also: navy-blue) 藏青色的 zàngqīngsè de

near [nɪəʳ] I ADJ 近的 jìn de II ADV (close) 近 jìn III PREP (also: near to) **1** (physically) 近 jìn **2** (just before/after) 临(臨)近 línjìn ▸ **the nearest shops are 5 km away** 最近的商店离(離)这(這)里(裡)有5公里远(遠) zuìjìn de shāngdiàn lí zhèlǐ yǒu wǔ gōnglǐ yuǎn ▸ **in the near future** 在不远(遠)的将(將)来(來) zài bù yuǎn de jiānglái

nearby [nɪə'baɪ] I ADJ 附近的 fùjìn de II ADV 在附近 zài fùjìn

nearly ['nɪəlɪ] ADV 差不多 chàbuduō ▸ **you're nearly as tall as I am** 你跟我差不多高了 nǐ gēn wǒ chàbuduō gāo le ▸ **nearly always** 几(幾)乎总(總)是 jīhū zǒngshì

near-sighted [nɪə'saɪtɪd] (US) ADJ (short-sighted) 近视(視)的 jìnshì de

neat [niːt] ADJ **1** 整洁(潔)的 zhěngjié de; [+ handwriting] 工整的 gōngzhěng de **2** (US: inf: great) 绝(絕)妙的 juémiào de

neatly ['niːtlɪ] ADV 整齐(齊)地 zhěngqí de

necessarily ['nɛsɪsrɪlɪ] ADV 必然 bìrán

necessary ['nɛsɪsrɪ] ADJ 必要的 bìyào de ▸ **if/when/where necessary** 如有必要/必要时(時)/在必要处(處) rú yǒu bìyào/bìyào shí/zài bìyào chù

neck [nɛk] N [c] **1** (Anat) 颈(頸) jǐng **2** [of shirt, dress, jumper] 领(領)子 lǐngzi [个 gè]

necklace ['nɛklɪs] N [c] 项(項)链(鏈) xiàngliàn [条 tiáo]

necktie ['nɛktaɪ] (US) N [c] 领(領)带(帶)
lǐngdài [条 tiáo]

need [ni:d] VT 1 (require) 需要 xūyào
2 (want) [+ drink, holiday, cigarette] 想要
xiǎng yào 3 [+ a haircut, a bath, a wash]
得 děi ▸ **to need to do sth** 必须(須)做
某事 bìxū zuò mǒushì ▸ **the car needs
servicing** 这(這)辆(輛)车(車)需要
维(維)修(脩)了 zhè liàng chē xūyào
wéixiū le

needle ['ni:dl] N [c] 1 (for sewing) 针(針)
zhēn [根 gēn] 2 (for injections) 注射
针(針) zhùshèzhēn [只 zhī]

negative ['nɛgətɪv] I ADJ 1 [+ test, result]
阴(陰)性的 yīnxìng de 2 [+ person,
attitude, view] 消极的 xiāojí de
3 [+ answer, response] 否定的 fǒudìng de
II N [c] (Ling) 否定词(詞) fǒudìngcí
[个 gè]

negotiate [nɪ'gəuʃɪeɪt] VI 商讨(討)
shāngtǎo

neighbour, (US) **neighbor** ['neɪbər] N [c]
邻(鄰)居 línjū [个 gè]

neighbourhood, (US) **neighborhood**
['neɪbəhud] N [c] 地区(區) dìqū [个 gè]

neither ['naɪðər] I PRON (person) 两(兩)
人都不 liǎng rén dōu bù; (thing) 两(兩)
者都不 liǎng zhě dōu bù II CONJ ▸ **I
didn't move and neither did John** 我和
约(約)翰都没(沒)动(動) wǒ hé Yuēhàn
dōu méi dòng ▸ **neither do/have I** 我也
不/没(沒) wǒ yě bù/méi ▸ **neither...
nor...** 既不…也不… jì bù…yě bù…

neither 和 none 作代词的时候用法
不同。用 neither 指两个人或事物，
表示否定含义。*Neither had close friends
at university.* neither 的用法与之相
同，后接代词或名词词组。*Neither of
them spoke…Neither of these options is
desirable.* 注意，也可以把 neither 用
在单数可数名词之前。*Neither side can
win.* none 可以指代三个或者三个以
上的人或事物，表示否定含义。*None
could afford the food.* none of 的用法与
之相同，后接代词或名词词组。*None
of them had learned anything.*

nephew ['nɛvju:] N [c] (brother's son)
侄(姪)子 zhízi [个 gè]; (sister's son) 外甥
wàisheng [个 gè]

nerve [nə:v] N 1 [c] (Anat) 神经(經)
shénjīng [根 gēn] 2 [U] (courage) 勇
气(氣) yǒngqì ▸ **to get on sb's nerves**
使某人心烦(煩) shǐ mǒurén xīnfán

nervous ['nə:vəs] ADJ 1 紧(緊)张(張)的
jǐnzhāng de ▸ **to be nervous about sth/
about doing sth** 对(對)某事/做某事感
到紧(緊)张(張)不安 duì mǒushì/zuò
mǒushì gǎndào jǐnzhāng bù'ān

nest [nɛst] N [c] 巢 cháo [个 gè]

net [nɛt] N 1 [c] 网(網) wǎng [张 zhāng]
2 (Comput) ▸ **the Net** 网(網)络(絡)
wǎngluò [个 gè]

Netherlands ['nɛðələndz] NPL ▸ **the
Netherlands** 荷兰(蘭) Hélán

network ['nɛtwə:k] N [c] 1 网(網)状(狀)
系统(統) wǎngzhuàng xìtǒng [个 gè]
2 (system) 网(網)络(絡) wǎngluò [个 gè]

never ['nɛvər] ADV 从(從)未 cóngwèi
▸ **we never saw him again** 我们(們)再
没(沒)有见(見)过(過)他 wǒmen zài
méiyǒu jiànguo tā

new [nju:] ADJ 1 崭(嶄)新的 zhǎnxīn de
2 [+ product, system, method] 新式的
xīnshì de 3 [+ job, address, boss, president]
新的 xīn de ▸ **this concept is new to me**
我对(對)这(這)个(個)概念不熟悉 wǒ
duì zhège gàiniàn bù shúxī

news [nju:z] N [U] 消息 xiāoxi ▸ **a piece
of news** 一条(條)消息 yī tiáo xiāoxi
▸ **good/bad news** 好/坏(壞)消息 hǎo/
huài xiāoxi ▸ **the news** (TV, Rad) 新
闻(聞) xīnwén

newsagent ['nju:zeɪdʒənt] (Brit) N [c]
(also: **newsagent's**) 报(報)刊店
bàokāndiàn [家 jiā]

newspaper ['nju:zpeɪpər] N [c] 报(報)
纸(紙) bàozhǐ [份 fèn]

New Year N [U] ▸ **(the) New Year** 新年
Xīnnián ▸ **in the New Year** 在新的一年
中 zài xīn de yī nián zhōng ▸ **Happy
New Year!** 新年快乐(樂)! Xīnnián
Kuàilè!

New Year's Day, (US) **New Year's** N [U]
元旦 Yuándàn

New Year's Eve, (US) **New Year's** N [U]
元旦前夜 Yuándàn qiányè

New Zealand [-'zi:lənd] I N 新西兰(蘭)
Xīnxīlán II ADJ 新西兰(蘭)的 Xīnxīlán de

next [nɛkst] I ADJ 1 下一个(個)的 xià yī
gè de 2 [+ house, street, room] 旁边(邊)的
pángbiān de II ADV 接下来(來)地
jiēxiàlái de ▸ **the next day/morning** 第

二天/天早晨 dì'er tiān/tiān zǎochén ▶ **the next five years/weeks will be very important** 接下来(來)的5年/周(週)将(將)是至关(關)重要的 jiēxiàlái de wǔ nián/zhōu jiāng shì zhì guān zhòngyào de ▶ **the next flight/prime minister** 下一次航班/下一任首相 xià yī cì hángbān/xià yī rèn shǒuxiàng ▶ **next time, be a bit more careful** 下一次，要更谨(謹)慎些 xià yī cì, yào gèng jǐnshèn xiē ▶ **who's next?** 下一位是谁(誰)？ xià yī wèi shì shuí? ▶ **the week after next** 下下个(個)星期 xiàxià gè xīngqī ▶ **next to** (beside) 旁边(邊) pángbiān

next door ADV 隔壁 gébì

NHS (Brit) N ABBR (= National Health Service) ▶ **the NHS** 英国国民医疗服务制度

nice [naɪs] ADJ **1** 好的 hǎo de **2** [+ person] (likeable) 和蔼(藹)的 hé'ǎi de; (friendly) 友好的 yǒuhǎo de ▶ **to look nice** 看上去不错(錯) kànshàngqù bùcuò ▶ **it's nice to see you** 很高兴(興)见(見)到你 hěn gāoxìng jiàndào nǐ

nickname ['nɪkneɪm] N [c] 绰(綽)号(號) chuòhào [个 gè]

niece [niːs] N [c] (brother's daughter) 侄(姪)女 zhínǔ [个 gè]; (sister's daughter) 甥女 shēngnǔ [个 gè]

Nigeria [naɪ'dʒɪərɪə] N 尼日利亚(亞) Nírìlìyà

night [naɪt] N **1** [c/u] 黑夜 hēiyè [个 gè] **2** [c] (evening) 晚上 wǎnshang [个 gè] ▶ **at night** 夜间(間) yèjiān ▶ **in/during the night** 夜里(裡) yèlǐ

nightclub ['naɪtklʌb] N [c] 夜总(總)会(會) yèzǒnghuì [个 gè]

nightie ['naɪtɪ] N [c] 睡衣 shuìyī [件 jiàn]

nightmare ['naɪtmɛər] N [c] 恶(惡)梦(夢) èmèng [场 chǎng]

nil [nɪl] N **1** [u] (Brit: Sport) 零 líng ▶ **they lost two nil to Italy** 他们(們)以0比2输(輸)给(給)意大利队(隊) tāmen yǐ líng bǐ èr shūgěi Yìdàlì duì **2** ▶ **their chances of survival are nil** 他们(們)没(沒)有幸(倖)存的可能 tāmen méiyǒu xìngcún de kěnéng

nine [naɪn] NUM 九 jiǔ; see also/另见 **five**

nineteen ['naɪn'tiːn] NUM 十九 shíjiǔ; see also/另见 **fifteen**

ninety ['naɪntɪ] NUM 九十 jiǔshí; see also/另见 **fifty**

KEYWORD

no [nəʊ] (pl noes) **I** ADV (opposite of "yes") 不 bù ▶ **"did you see it?" — "no (I didn't)"** "你看见(見)了吗(嗎)?" "不(我没(沒)见(見)到)" "nǐ kànjiàn le mǎ?" "bù (wǒ méi jiàndào)" ▶ **no thank you, no thanks** 不用，谢(謝)谢(謝)你 bùyòng, xièxie nǐ
II ADJ (not any) 没(沒)有 méiyǒu ▶ **I have no milk/books** 我没(沒)有牛奶/书(書) wǒ méiyǒu niúnǎi/shū ▶ **"no smoking"** "严(嚴)禁吸烟(煙)" "yánjìn xīyān" ▶ **no way!** 没(沒)门(門)儿(兒)! méiménr!

nobody ['nəʊbədɪ] PRON 没(沒)有人 méiyǒu rén

noise [nɔɪz] N **1** [c] (sound) 响(響)声(聲) xiǎngshēng [阵 zhèn] **2** [u] (din) 噪音 zàoyīn

noisy ['nɔɪzɪ] ADJ 嘈杂(雜)的 cáozá de; [+ place] 喧闹(鬧)的 xuānnào de

none [nʌn] PRON **1** (not one) 没(沒)有一个(個) méiyǒu yī gè **2** (not any) 没(沒)一点(點)儿(兒) méiyǒu yīdiǎnr ▶ **none of us/them** 我们(們)/他们(們)谁(誰)也没(沒) wǒmen/tāmen shuí yě méi ▶ **I've/there's none left** 我一点(點)也没(沒)有了/一点(點)也没(沒)剩 wǒ yīdiǎn yě méiyǒu le/yīdiǎn yě méi shèng

nonsense ['nɒnsəns] N [u] 胡说(說)八道 húshuō bādào

non-smoking ['nɒn'sməʊkɪŋ] ADJ 禁烟(煙)的 jìnyān de

non-stop ['nɒn'stɒp] ADV **1** (ceaselessly) 不断(斷)地 bùduàn de **2** [fly, drive +] 不停地 bùtíng de

noodles ['nuːdlz] NPL 面(麵)条(條) miàntiáo

noon [nuːn] N [u] 中午 zhōngwǔ ▶ **at noon** 中午 zhōngwǔ

no-one ['nəʊwʌn] PRON = **nobody**

nor [nɔːr] CONJ 也不 yě bù; see also/另见 **neither**

normal ['nɔːməl] ADJ 正常的 zhèngcháng de ▶ **more/higher/worse**

than normal 比正常的多/高/糟糕 bǐ zhèngcháng de duō/gāo/zāogāo

normally ['nɔ:məlɪ] ADV (usually) 通常地 tōngcháng de

north [nɔ:θ] I N [u/s] 北方 běifāng II ADJ 北部的 běibù de III ADV 向北方 xiàng běifāng ▶ to the north 以北 yǐběi ▶ north of …以北 …yǐběi

North America N 北美 Běiměi

north-east [nɔ:θ'i:st] I N 东(東)北 dōngběi II ADJ 东(東)北的 dōngběi de III ADV 向东(東)北 xiàng dōngběi

northern ['nɔ:ðən] ADJ 北方的 běifāng de ▶ the northern hemisphere 北半球 běibànqiú

Northern Ireland N 北爱(愛)尔(爾)兰(蘭) Běi'ài'ěrlán

North Korea N 朝鲜(鮮) Cháoxiǎn

North Pole N ▶ the North Pole 北极(極) Běijí

north-west [nɔ:θ'wɛst] I N 西北 xīběi II ADJ 西北的 xīběi de III ADV 向西北 xiàng xīběi

Norway ['nɔ:weɪ] N 挪威 Nuówēi

nose [nəuz] N [c] 鼻子 bízi [个 gè]

not [nɔt] ADV 不 bù ▶ he is not here 他不在这(這)儿(兒) tā bù zài zhèr ▶ it's too late, isn't it? 现(現)在太晚了,不是吗(嗎)? xiànzài tài wǎn le, bùshì ma? ▶ he asked me not to do it 他叫我不要这(這)么(麼)做 tā jiào wǒ bù yào zhème zuò ▶ are you coming or not? 你来(來)不来(來)? nǐ lái bù lái? ▶ not at all (in answer to thanks) 不客气(氣) bù kèqi ▶ not yet/now 还(還)没(沒)/现(現)在不 hái méi/xiànzài bù ▶ not really 并(並)不是的 bìng bù shì de

note [nəut] I N [c] 1 (message) 便条(條) biàntiáo [张 zhāng] 2 (Brit: banknote) 纸(紙)币(幣) zhǐbì [张 zhāng] II VT (observe) 留意 liúyì III **notes** NPL (from or for lecture) 笔(筆)记(記) bǐjì ▶ to make a note of sth 记(記)下某事 jìxià mǒushì ▶ to take notes 记(記)笔(筆)记(記) jì bǐjì

notebook ['nəutbuk] N [c] 笔(筆)记(記)本 bǐjìběn [个 gè]

notepad ['nəutpæd] N [c] 1 (pad of paper) 记(記)事本 jìshìběn [个 gè] 2 (Comput) 记(記)事簿 jìshìbù [个 gè]

nothing ['nʌθɪŋ] PRON 什么(麼)也没(沒)有 shénme yě méiyǒu ▶ nothing new/serious/to worry about 没(沒)有什么(麼)新的/要紧(緊)的/值得担(擔)忧(憂)的 méiyǒu shénme xīn de/yàojǐn de/zhídé dānyōu de ▶ nothing else 没(沒)有别(別)的 méiyǒu bié de ▶ for nothing 免费(費) miǎnfèi ▶ nothing at all 什么(麼)也没(沒)有 shénme yě méiyǒu

notice ['nəutɪs] I VT 注意到 zhùyì dào II N [c] 公告 gōnggào [个 gè] ▶ to notice that... 注意到… zhùyì dào… ▶ to take no notice of sb/sth 不理某人/某事 bù lǐ mǒurén/mǒushì ▶ without notice 不事先通知 bù shìxiān tōngzhī

noticeboard ['nəutɪsbɔ:d] (Brit) N [c] 布(佈)告栏(欄) bùgàolán [个 gè]

notification [nəutɪfɪ'keɪʃən] N [c] 通知 tōngzhī [个 gè]

nought [nɔ:t] (esp Brit) NUM 零 líng

noun [naun] N [c] 名词(詞) míngcí [个 gè]

novel ['nɔvl] N [c] 小说(說) xiǎoshuō [部 bù]

novelist ['nɔvəlɪst] N [c] 小说(說)家 xiǎoshuōjiā [位 wèi]

November [nəu'vɛmbər] N [c/u] 十一月 shíyīyuè [个 gè]; see also/另见 July

now [nau] I ADV 1 现(現)在 xiànzài 2 (these days) 如今 rújīn II CONJ ▶ now (that) 既然 jìrán ▶ right now 这(這)时(時) zhèshí ▶ by now 到现(現)在 dào xiànzài ▶ just now 眼下 yǎnxià ▶ from now on 从(從)现(現)在起 cóng xiànzài qǐ ▶ that's all for now 到此这(這)里(裡) jiù dào zhèlǐ

nowhere ['nəuwɛər] ADV 无(無)处(處) wúchù ▶ nowhere else 没(沒)有其他地方 méiyǒu qítā dìfang

nuclear ['nju:klɪər] ADJ 核能的 hénéng de

nuisance ['nju:sns] N ▶ to be a nuisance [thing +] 讨(討)厌(厭)的东(東)西 tǎoyàn de dōngxi

numb [nʌm] ADJ 麻木的 mámù de

number ['nʌmbər] I N 1 [c] (Math) 数(數) shù [个 gè] 2 [c] (telephone number) 电(電)话(話)号(號)码(碼) diànhuà hàomǎ [个 gè] 3 [c] [of house, bank

account, bus] 号(號) hào [个 gè] **4** [c/u]
(*quantity*) 数(數)量 shùliàng **II** VT
[+ *pages*] 给(給)…标(標)号(號)码(碼)
gěi…biāo hàomǎ ▸ **a number of** (*several*)
几(幾)个(個) jǐ gè ▸ **a large/small**
number of 大量/少数(數) dàliàng/
shǎoshù

number plate (*Brit*) N [c] 车(車)号(號)
牌 chēhàopái [个 gè]

nun [nʌn] N [c] 修女 xiūnǚ [名 míng]

nurse [nə:s] N [c] 护(護)士 hùshi [位 wèi]

nursery ['nə:sərɪ] N [c] 幼儿(兒)园(園)
yòu'éryuán [个 gè]

nursery school N [c/u] 幼儿(兒)园(園)
yòu'éryuán [个 gè]

nut [nʌt] N [c] **1** (*Bot, Culin*) 坚(堅)果
jiānguǒ [枚 méi] **2** (*Tech*) 螺母 luómǔ
[个 gè]

nylon ['naɪlɔn] N [u] 尼龙(龍) nílóng

oak [əuk] N **1** [c] (*also:* **oak tree**) 橡树(樹)
xiàngshù [棵 kē] **2** [u] (*wood*) 橡木
xiàngmù

oar [ɔːʳ] N [c] 桨(槳) jiǎng [只 zhī]

oats [əuts] NPL 燕麦(麥) yànmài

obedient [ə'biːdɪənt] ADJ 顺(順)从(從)的
shùncóng de

obey [ə'beɪ] **I** VT [+ *person, orders*] 听(聽)
从(從) tīngcóng; [+ *law, regulations*] 服
从(從) fúcóng **II** VI 服从(從) fúcóng

object [n 'ɔbdʒɛkt, vb əb'dʒɛkt] **I** N [c]
1 (*thing*) 物体(體) wùtǐ [个 gè] **2** (*Ling*)
宾(賓)语(語) bīnyǔ [个 gè] **II** VI 反
对(對) fǎnduì

objection [əb'dʒɛkʃən] N [c] 异(異)
议(議) yìyì [个 gè]

obsess [əb'sɛs] VT 使着(著)迷 shǐ
zháomí

obsession [əb'sɛʃən] N [c] 着(著)迷
zháomí [种 zhǒng]

obtain [əb'teɪn] VT 获(獲)得 huòdé

obvious ['ɔbvɪəs] ADJ 明显(顯)的
míngxiǎn de

obviously ['ɔbvɪəslɪ] ADV (*of course*)
显(顯)然地 xiǎnrán de

occasion [ə'keɪʒən] N [c] **1** (*moment*)
时(時)刻 shíkè [个 gè] **2** (*event,
celebration*) 场(場)合 chǎnghé [种
zhǒng]

occasionally [ə'keɪʒənəlɪ] ADV 偶尔(爾)
地 ǒu'ěr de

occupation [ɔkju'peɪʃən] N [c] 职(職)
业(業) zhíyè [种 zhǒng]

occupy ['ɔkjupaɪ] VT **1** (inhabit) [+ house, office] 占(佔)用 zhànyòng **2** ▸ **to be occupied** [seat, place etc +] 被占(佔)用 bèi zhànyòng **3** (fill) [+ time] 占(佔)用 zhànyòng

occur [ə'kə:ʳ] VI 发(發)生 fāshēng ▸ **to occur to sb** 某人想到 mǒurén xiǎngdào

ocean ['əʊʃən] N [c] 海洋 hǎiyáng [片 piàn]

o'clock [ə'klɔk] ADV ▸ **six o'clock** 6点(點) 钟(鐘) liùdiǎnzhōng

October [ɔk'təʊbəʳ] N [c/u] 十月 shíyuè; see also/另见 **July**

octopus ['ɔktəpəs] N [c] 章鱼(魚) zhāngyú [只 zhī]

odd [ɔd] ADJ **1** (strange) 奇怪的 qíguài de **2** [+ number] 奇数(數)的 jīshù de

odour, (US) **odor** ['əʊdəʳ] N [c/u] 气(氣) 味 qìwèi [种 zhǒng]

○ **KEYWORD**

of [ɔv, əv] PREP **1** (gen) 的 de ▸ **the history of China** 中国(國)历(歷)史 Zhōngguó lìshǐ ▸ **at the end of the street** 在街的尽(盡)头(頭) zài jiē de jìntóu ▸ **the city of New York** 纽(紐) 约(約)城 Niǔyuēchéng

2 (expressing quantity, amount) ▸ **a kilo of flour** 一公斤面(麵)粉 yī gōngjīn miànfěn ▸ **a cup of tea/vase of flowers** 一杯茶/一瓶花 yī bēi chá/yī píng huā ▸ **there were three of them** 他们(們)有 3个(個) tāmen yǒu sān gè ▸ **an annual income of $30,000** 每年3万(萬)美元的 收入 měinián sānwàn měiyuán de shōurù

3 (in dates) ▸ **the 5th of July** 7月5日 qīyuè wǔ rì

4 (US: in times) ▸ **at five of three** 3点(點) 差5分 sān diǎn chà wǔ fēn

---

○ **KEYWORD**

off [ɔf] I ADJ **1** (not turned on) 关(關)着(著) 的 guānzhe de

2 (cancelled) 取消的 qǔxiāo de

II ADV **1** (away) ▸ **I must be off** 我必 须(須)得走了 wǒ bìxū děi zǒu le ▸ **where are you off to?** 你上哪儿(兒)

去? nǐ shàng nǎr qù?

2 (not at work) ▸ **to have a day off** (as holiday) 休假一天 xiūjià yī tiān; (because ill) 休病假一天 xiū bìngjià yī tiān

3 (Comm) ▸ **10% off** 10%的折扣 bǎi fēn zhī shí de zhékòu

III PREP (indicating motion, removal etc) ▸ **to take a picture off the wall** 把 画(畫)像从(從)墙(墻)上取下来(來) bǎ huàxiàng cóng qiángshang qǔ xiàlái

offence, (US) **offense** [ə'fɛns] N [c] (crime) 罪行 zuìxíng [种 zhǒng]

offend [ə'fɛnd] VT (upset) 得罪 dézuì

offense [ə'fɛns] N [US] = **offence**

offer ['ɔfəʳ] I VT **1** 给(給) gěi **2** (bid) 出 价(價) chūjià II N [c] **1** 提议(議) tíyì [项 xiàng] **2** (special deal) 特价(價) tèjià [个 gè]

office ['ɔfɪs] N **1** [c] (room) 办(辦)公室 bàngōngshì [间 jiān] **2** [c] (department) 部门(門) bùmén [个 gè] **3** [c] (US) [of doctor, dentist] 诊(診)所 zhěnsuǒ [家 jiā]

office block N [c] 办(辦)公大楼(樓) bàngōng dàlóu [座 zuò]

officer ['ɔfɪsəʳ] N [c] **1** (Mil) 军(軍)官 jūnguān [位 wèi] **2** (also: police officer) 警官 jǐngguān [位 wèi]

office worker N [c] 职(職)员(員) zhíyuán [个 gè]

official [ə'fɪʃl] ADJ 官方的 guānfāng de

often ['ɔfn] ADV (frequently) 经(經)常 jīngcháng ▸ **how often do you wash the car?** 你多久洗一次车(車)? nǐ duō jiǔ xǐ yī cì chē?

oil [ɔɪl] I N [c/u] 油 yóu [桶 tǒng] II VT [+ engine, machine] 给(給)…加油 gěi…jiāyóu

oil rig N [c] (on land) 石油钻(鑽)塔 shíyóu zuàntǎ [个 gè]; (at sea) 钻(鑽)井平 台(臺) zuànjǐng píngtái [个 gè]

okay [əʊ'keɪ] I ADJ **1** (acceptable) 可以的 kěyǐ de **2** (safe and well) 好的 hǎo de

II ADV (acceptably) 不错(錯) bùcuò

III INT **1** (expressing agreement) 行 xíng **2** (in questions) 好吗(嗎) hǎo ma ▸ **are you okay?** 你还(還)好吗(嗎)? nǐ hái hǎo ma? ▸ **it's okay with or by me** 这(這)对(對)我没(沒)问(問)题(題) zhè duì wǒ méi wèntí

old [əʊld] ADJ **1** [+ person] 年老的 niánlǎo de **2** (not new, not recent) 古老的 gǔlǎo

de 3 (*worn out*) 破旧(舊)的 pòjiù de
4 (*former*) 以前的 yǐqián de 5 [+ *friend, enemy, rival*] 老的 lǎo de ▸ **how old are you?** 你多大了? nǐ duō dà le? ▸ **he's 10 years old** 他10岁(歲)了 tā shísuì le ▸ **older brother/sister** 哥哥/姐姐 gēge/jiějie

old age pensioner (*Brit*) N [c] 拿退休金的人 ná tuìxiūjīn de rén [位 wèi]

old-fashioned [ˈəʊldˈfæʃnd] ADJ [+ *object, custom, idea*] 老式的 lǎoshì de; [+ *person*] 守旧(舊)的 shǒujiù de

olive [ˈɒlɪv] N [c] 橄榄(欖) gǎnlǎn [棵 kē]

olive oil N [U] 橄榄(欖)油 gǎnlǎnyóu

Olympic® [əʊˈlɪmpɪk] ADJ 奥(奧)林匹克的 Àolínpǐkè de II **the Olympics®** NPL 奥(奧)林匹克运(運)动(動)会(會) Àolínpǐkè Yùndònghuì

omelette, (*US*) **omelet** [ˈɒmlɪt] N [c] 煎蛋饼(餅) jiāndànbǐng [个 gè]

KEYWORD

on [ɒn] I PREP 1 (*indicating position*) 在…上 zài...shang ▸ **it's on the table/wall** 它在桌上/墙(牆)上 tā zài zhuōshang/qiángshang ▸ **the house is on the main road** 房子在主路旁 fángzi zài zhǔlù páng ▸ **on the left/right** 在左边(邊)/右边(邊) zài zuǒbiān/yòubiān ▸ **on the top floor** 在顶(頂)楼(樓)zài dǐnglóu 2 (*indicating means, method, condition etc*) ▸ **on foot** 步行 bùxíng ▸ **on the train/bus** [*be, sit* +] 在火车(車)/公共汽车(車)上 zài huǒchē/gōnggòng qìchē shang; [*travel, go* +] 乘坐 chéngzuò ▸ **on the television/radio** 在电(電)视(視)上/广(廣)播中 zài diànshì shang/guǎngbō zhōng ▸ **on the internet** 在因特网(網)上 zài Yīntèwǎng shang ▸ **to be on antibiotics** 定期服用抗生素 dìngqī fúyòng kàngshēngsù 3 (*referring to time*) 在 zài ▸ **on Friday** 在星期五 zài xīngqīwǔ ▸ **on Friday, June 20th** 在6月20日, 星期五 zài liùyuè èrshí rì, xīngqīwǔ II ADV 1 (*clothes*) ▸ **to have one's coat on** 穿着(著)外套 chuānzhe wàitào ▸ **what's she got on?** 她穿着(著)什么(麼)? tā chuānzhe shénme?

2 (*covering, lid etc*) ▸ **screw the lid on tightly** 把盖(蓋)子旋紧(緊) bǎ gàizi xuánjǐn III ADJ 1 (*turned on*) 打开(開)的 dǎkāi de 2 (*happening*) ▸ **is the meeting still on?** 会(會)议(議)还(還)在进(進)行吗(嗎)? huìyì hái zài jìnxíng ma? ▸ **there's a good film on at the cinema** 电(電)影院正在上映一部好电(電)影 diànyǐngyuàn zhèngzài shàngyìng yī bù hǎo diànyǐng

once [wʌns] I ADV 1 (*one time only*) 一次 yīcì 2 (*at one time*) 曾经(經) céngjīng 3 (*on one occasion*) 有一次 yǒu yī cì II CONJ (*as soon as*) 立刻 lìkè ▸ **once a** or **every month** 每月一次 měi yuè yī cì ▸ **once upon a time** (*in stories*) 很久以前 hěnjiǔ yǐqián ▸ **once in a while** 偶尔(爾) ǒu'ěr ▸ **once or twice** (*a few times*) 一两(兩)次 yī liǎng cì

KEYWORD

one [wʌn] I ADJ 1 (*number*) 一 yī ▸ **it's one o'clock** 现(現)在1点(點) xiànzài yī diǎn ▸ **one hundred/thousand children** 100/1000个(個)孩子 yībǎi/yīqiān gè háizi 2 (*same*) 同一的 tóngyī de ▸ **shall I put it all on the one plate?** 要我把它都放在同一个(個)盘(盤)子里(裡)吗(嗎)? yào wǒ bǎ tā dōu fàng zài tóng yī gè pánzi li ma? II PRON 1 (*number*) 一 yī ▸ **I've already got one** 我已经(經)有一个(個)了 wǒ yǐjīng yǒu yī gè le ▸ **one of them/of the boys** 他们(們)中的一个(個)/男孩中的一个(個) tāmen zhōng de yī gè/nánhái zhōng de yī gè ▸ **one by one** 一个(個)一个(個)地 yī gè yī gè de 2 (*with adj*) 一个(個) yī gè ▸ **I've already got a red one** 我已经(經)有一个(個)红(紅)的了 wǒ yǐjīng yǒu yī gè hóng de le 3 (*in generalizations*) 人人 rénrén ▸ **what can one do?** 一个(個)人能做什么(麼)呢? yī gè rén néng zuò shénme ne? ▸ **this one** 这(這)个(個) zhège ▸ **that one** 那个(個) nàge III N (*numeral*) 一 yī

KEYWORD

oneself PRON 自己 zìjǐ ▶ **to hurt oneself** 伤(傷)了自己 shāngle zìjǐ ▶ **by oneself** (unaided) 独(獨)力地 dúlì de; (alone) 独(獨)自 dúzì

one-way ['wʌnwei] ADJ **1** [+ street, traffic] 单(單)行的 dānxíng de **2** [+ ticket, trip] 单(單)程的 dānchéng de

onion ['ʌnjən] N [c] 洋葱(蔥) yángcōng [个 gè]

online, on-line ['ɒnlain] (Comput) ADV (on the internet) 网(網)上 wǎngshang

only ['əunlɪ] I ADV **1** 仅(僅)仅(僅) jǐnjǐn **2** (emphasizing insignificance) 只 zhǐ II ADJ (sole) 唯一的 wéiyī de III CONJ (but) 可是 kěshì ▶ **I was only joking** 我只是在开(開)玩笑。wǒ zhǐshì zài kāi wánxiào ▶ **not only... but (also)...** 不但...而且... búdàn...érqiě... ▶ **an only child** 独(獨)生子女 dúshēng zǐnǔ

onto, on to ['ɒntu] PREP 到…上 dào…shàng

open ['əupn] I ADJ **1** [+ door, window] 开(開)着(著)的 kāizhe de; [+ mouth, eyes] 张(張)着(著)的 zhāngzhe de **2** [+ shop] 营(營)业(業)的 yíngyè de II VT [+ container] 打开(開) dǎkāi; [+ door, lid] 开(開) kāi; [+ letter] 拆开(開) chāikāi; [+ book, hand, mouth, eyes] 开(開) kāi III VI **1** [door, lid +] 开(開) kāi **2** [public building +] 开(開)门(門) kāimén ▶ **in the open (air)** 在户(戶)外 zài hùwài

opening hours NPL 营(營)业(業)时(時)间(間) yíngyè shíjiān

open-minded [əupn'maindid] ADJ 开(開)明的 kāimíng de

opera ['ɒpərə] N [c] 歌剧(劇) gējù [部 bù]

operate ['ɒpəreit] I VT [+ machine, vehicle, system] 操作 cāozuò II VI **1** [machine, vehicle, system +] 工作 gōngzuò; [company, organization +] 运(運)作 yùnzuò **2** (Med) 动(動)手术(術) dòng shǒushù ▶ **to operate on sb** (Med) 给(給)某人动(動)手术(術) gěi mǒurén dòng shǒushù

operation [ɒpə'reiʃən] N **1** [c] (procedure) 实(實)施步骤(驟) shíshī bùzhòu [个 gè] **2** [c] (Med) 手术(術) shǒushù [次 cì] ▶ **to have an operation** (Med) 接受手术(術) jiēshòu shǒushù

operator ['ɒpəreitər] N [c] (Tel) 接线(線)员(員) jiēxiànyuán [位 wèi]

opinion [ə'pinjən] N [c] (individual view) 观(觀)点(點) guāndiǎn [个 gè] ▶ **in my/her opinion** 按我的/她的意见(見) àn wǒ de/tā de yìjiàn

opinion poll N [c] 民意测(測)验(驗) mínyì cèyàn [次 cì]

opponent [ə'pəunənt] N [c] 对(對)手 duìshǒu [个 gè]

opportunity [ɒpə'tju:niti] N [c/U] 机(機)会(會) jīhuì [个 gè] ▶ **to take the opportunity of doing sth or to do sth** 趁机(機)会(會)做某事 chèn jīhuì zuò mǒushì

oppose [ə'pəuz] VT [+ person, idea] 反对(對) fǎnduì ▶ **to be opposed to sth** 反对(對)某事 fǎnduì mǒushì

opposite ['ɒpəzit] I ADJ **1** [+ side, house] 对(對)面的 duìmiàn de **2** [+ end, corner] 最远(遠)的 zuì yuǎn de **3** [+ meaning, direction] 相反的 xiāngfǎn de II ADV [live, work, sit +] 在对(對)面 zài duìmiàn III PREP 在…的对(對)面 zài…de duìmiàn IV N ▶ **the opposite** 对(對)立面 duìlìmiàn ▶ **the opposite sex** 异(異)性 yìxìng

opposition [ɒpə'ziʃən] N [U] 反对(對) fǎnduì

optician [ɒp'tiʃən] N [c] **1** 眼镜(鏡)商 yǎnjìngshāng [个 gè] **2** (also: **optician's**) 眼镜(鏡)店 yǎnjìngdiàn [家 jiā]

optimistic [ɒpti'mistik] ADJ 乐(樂)观(觀)的 lèguān de

option ['ɒpʃən] N [c] **1** (choice) 选(選)择(擇) xuǎnzé [种 zhǒng] **2** (Scol, Univ) 选(選)修课(課) xuǎnxiūkè [门 mén]

or [ɔ:r] CONJ **1** 还(還)是 háishì **2** (also: **or else**) 否则(則) fǒuzé

oral ['ɔ:rəl] I ADJ [+ test, report] 口头(頭)的 kǒutóu de II N [c] 口试(試) kǒushì [次 cì]

orange ['ɒrindʒ] I N [c] (fruit) 柑橘 gānjú [只 zhǐ] II ADJ (in colour) 橙色的 chéngsè de

orange juice ['ɒrindʒdʒu:s] N [U] 橘子汁 júzizhī

orchard ['ɔ:tʃəd] N [c] 果园(園) guǒyuán [个 gè]

orchestra [ˈɔːkɪstrə] N [c] 管弦乐(樂)
队(隊) guǎnxián yuèduì [支 zhī]

order [ˈɔːdəʳ] I N 1 [c] (command) 命令
mìnglìng [个 gè] 2 [c] (Comm: in
restaurant) 点(點)菜 diǎncài [份 fèn]
3 [U] (sequence) 次序 cìxù II VT
1 (command) 命令 mìnglìng 2 (Comm:
from shop, company) 定购(購) dìnggòu;
(in restaurant) 点(點)菜 diǎncài III VI (in
restaurant) 点(點)菜 diǎncài ▶ in
alphabetical/numerical order 按字
母/数(數)字顺(順)序 àn zìmǔ/shùzì
shùnxù ▶ out of order (not working) 已
坏(壞)停用 yǐhuài tíngyòng ▶ in order
to do sth (为(為)了做某事 wèile zuò
mǒushì ▶ to order sb to do sth 命令某
人做某事 mìnglìng mǒurén zuò mǒushì

ordinary [ˈɔːdɪnrɪ] ADJ 普通的 pǔtōng de

organ [ˈɔːɡən] N [c] 1 (Anat) 器官 qìguān
[个 gè] 2 (Mus) 管风(風)琴 guǎnfēngqín
[架 jià]

organic [ɔːˈɡænɪk] ADJ 1 [+ food, farming]
有机(機)的 yǒujī de 2 [+ substance] 有
机(機)物的 yǒujīwù de

organization [ˌɔːɡənaɪˈzeɪʃən] N [c]
组(組)织(織) zǔzhī [个 gè]

organize [ˈɔːɡənaɪz] VT 组(組)织(織)
zǔzhī

original [əˈrɪdʒɪnl] ADJ 1 (first, earliest) 最
初的 zuìchū de 2 (imaginative) 独(獨)
创(創)的 dúchuàng de

originally [əˈrɪdʒɪnəlɪ] ADV 起初 qǐchū

ornament [ˈɔːnəmənt] N [c] 装(裝)
饰(飾)物 zhuāngshìwù [件 jiàn]

orphan [ˈɔːfn] N [c] 孤儿(兒) gū'ér
[个 gè]

other [ˈʌðəʳ] I ADJ 1 (additional) 另外的
lìngwài de 2 (not this one) 其他的 qítā
de 3 ▶ the other... (of two things or people)
另一... lìng yī... 4 (apart from oneself) 其
他的 qítā de II PRON 1 (additional one,
different one) 其他 qítā 2 (of two things or
people) ▶ the other 另一个(個) lìng yī
gè ▶ the other day/week (inf: recently)
几(幾)天/星期前 jǐtiān/xīngqī qián

otherwise [ˈʌðəwaɪz] ADV 1 (if not) 否
则(則) fǒuzé 2 (apart from that) 除此以
外 chú cǐ yǐwài

ought [ɔːt] (pt ought) AUX VB 1 (indicating
advisability) ▶ you ought to see a doctor
你应(應)该(該)去看医(醫)生 nǐ yīnggāi

qù kàn yīshēng 2 (indicating likelihood)
▶ he ought to be there now 他现(現)在
应(應)该(該)到那儿(兒)了 tā xiànzài
yīnggāi dào nàr le

our [ˈauəʳ] ADJ 我们(們)的 wǒmen de

ours [auəz] PRON 我们(們)的 wǒmen de

ourselves [auəˈselvz] PRON PL 我们(們)
自己 wǒmen zìjǐ ▶ we didn't hurt
ourselves 我们(們)没(沒)伤(傷)到自己
wǒmen méi shāngdào zìjǐ ▶ by
ourselves (unaided) 我们(們)独(獨)力来
wǒmen dúlì de; (alone) 我们(們)单(單)
独(獨)地 wǒmen dāndú de

KEYWORD

out [aut] I ADV 1 (outside) 在外面 zài
wàimiàn ▶ out here/there 这(這)
儿(兒)/那儿(兒) zhèr/nàr
2 (absent, not in) 不在 bù zài ▶ Mr Green
is out at the moment 格林先生这(這)
会(會)儿(兒)不在 Gélín xiānsheng
zhèhuìr bù zài ▶ to have a day/night
out 外出玩一天/一晚 wàichū wán yī
tiān/yī wǎn
3 (Sport) ▶ the ball was out 球出界了
qiú chūjiè le
II ADJ ▶ to be out (out of game) 出局的
chūjú de; (extinguished) [fire, light, gas +]
熄灭(滅)的 xīmiè de
III ▶ out of PREP 1 (outside: with
movement) 出 chū; (beyond) 朝…外
cháo...wài ▶ to go/come out of the
house 从(從)房子里(裡)走出去/来(來)
cóng fángzi lǐ zǒu chūqù/lái
2 (from among) …中的 …zhōng de ▶ one
out of every three smokers 每3个(個)
烟(煙)民中的1个(個) měi sān gè
yānmín zhōng de yīgè
3 (without) ▶ to be out of milk/petrol 牛
奶喝完了/汽油用完了 niúnǎi hēwán le/
qìyóu yòngwán le

outdoor [autˈdɔːʳ] ADJ 1 [+ activity]
户(戶)外的 hùwài de 2 [+ swimming pool,
toilet] 露天的 lùtiān de

outdoors [autˈdɔːz] ADV 在户(戶)外 zài
hùwài

outing [ˈautɪŋ] N [c] 出游(遊) chūyóu
[次 cì]

outlet [ˈautlɛt] N [c] 1 (hole, pipe) 排放口

páifàngkǒu [个 (個) gè] **2** (US: Elec) 电 (電) 源 插座 diànyuán chāzuò [个 (個) gè]

outline ['autlaɪn] N [c] **1** (shape) 轮 (輪) 廓 lúnkuò [个 (個) gè] **2** (brief explanation) 概要 gàiyào [篇 piān]

outside [aut'saɪd] I N [c] [of container] 外 面 wàimiàn [个 (個) gè]; [of building] 外表 wàibiǎo [个 (個) gè] II ADJ (exterior) 外部的 wàibù de III ADV **1** [be, wait +] 在外面 zài wàimiàn **2** [go +] 向外面 xiàng wàimiàn IV PREP **1** [+ place] 在…外 zài…wài; [+ organization] 在…以外 zài…yǐwài **2** [+ larger place] 在…附近 zài…fùjìn

outskirts ['autskɜːts] NPL ▶ the outskirts 郊区 (區) jiāoqū ▶ on the outskirts of... 在…的郊区 (區) zài…de jiāoqū

outstanding [aut'stændɪŋ] ADJ 杰 (傑) 出的 jiéchū de

oval ['əuvl] ADJ 椭 (橢) 圆 (圓) 形的 tuǒyuánxíng de

oven ['ʌvn] N [c] 烤箱 kǎoxiāng [个 (個) gè]

 KEYWORD

over ['əuvəʳ] I ADJ (finished) 结 (結) 束的 jiéshù de
II PREP **1** (more than) 超过 (過) chāoguò
▶ **over 200 people came** 超过 (過) 二百 人来 (來) 了 zhāoguò èrbǎi rén lái le
2 在…上 zài…shang; (spanning) 横 (橫) 横 (橫) 跨 héngkuà; (across) 穿过 (過) chuānguò; (on the other side of) 在…对 (對) 面 zài…duìmiàn ▶ **a bridge over the river** 横 (橫) 跨河流的一座桥 (橋) héngkuà héliú de yī zuò qiáo
3 (during) 在…期间 (間) zài…qījiān
▶ **we talked about it over dinner** 我 们 (們) 边 (邊) 吃晚饭 (飯) 边 (邊) 讨 (討) 论 (論) wǒmen biān chī wǎnfàn biān tǎolùn
4 [+ illness, shock, trauma] 康复 (復) kāngfù
5 ▶ **all over the town/house/floor** 全 镇 (鎮) /满 (滿) 屋子/满 (滿) 地 quánzhèn/ mǎn wūzi/mǎn dì
III ADV **1** [walk, jump, fly etc +] 过 (過) guò
▶ **over here/there** 在这 (這) 里 (裡) /那 里 (裡) zài zhèlǐ/nàlǐ
2 (more, above) 超过 (過) chāoguò
▶ **people aged 65 and over** 65岁 (歲) 及

以上年龄 (齡) 的人 liùshíwǔ suì jí yǐshàng niánlíng de rén
3 (US: again) 再 zài
4 ▶ **all over** (everywhere) 到处 (處) dàochù

overcast ['əuvəkɑːst] ADJ 多云 (雲) 的 duōyún de

overdose ['əuvədəus] N [c] 过 (過) 量用 药 (藥) guòliàng yòngyào [剂 jì]

overseas [əuvə'siːz] ADV 向海外 xiàng hǎiwài

overtake [əuvə'teɪk] (pt overtook, pp overtaken) I VT (esp Brit: Aut) 超过 (過) chāoguò II VI (esp Brit: Aut) 超车 (車) chāochē

overtime ['əuvətaɪm] N [U] 加班时 (時) 间 (間) jiābān shíjiān

overtook [əuvə'tuk] PT of **overtake**

overweight [əuvə'weɪt] ADJ 超重的 chāozhòng de

owe [əu] VT [+ money] 欠 qiàn ▶ **to owe sb sth** 欠某人某物 qiàn mǒurén mǒuwù

owing to ['əuɪŋ-] PREP (because of) 因 为 (為) yīnwèi

owl [aul] N [c] 猫 (貓) 头 (頭) 鹰 (鷹) māotóuyīng [只 zhī]

own [əun] I ADJ 自己的 zìjǐ de II VT [+ house, land, car etc] 拥 (擁) 有 yōngyǒu
▶ **a room of my own** 我自己的房间 (間) wǒ zìjǐ de fángjiān ▶ **on one's own** (alone) 独 (獨) 自地 dúzì de; (without help) 独 (獨) 立地 dúlì de
▶ **own up** VI (confess) 坦白 tǎnbái

owner ['əunəʳ] N [c] 物主 wùzhǔ [位 wèi]

oxygen ['ɔksɪdʒən] N [U] 氧气 (氣) yǎngqì

oyster ['ɔɪstəʳ] N [c] 牡蛎 (蠣) mǔlì 蚝 (蠔) háo [个 (個) gè]

ozone layer N [c] 臭氧层 (層) chòuyǎngcéng [层 céng]

Pacific [pə'sɪfɪk] N ▸ **the Pacific (Ocean)** 太平洋 Tàipíngyáng

pack [pæk] I VT 1 [+ clothes] 把…打包 bǎ…dǎbāo 2 [+ suitcase, bag] 把…装(裝)箱 bǎ…zhuāngxiāng II VI 打点(點)行装(裝) dǎdiǎn xíngzhuāng III N [of cards] 副 fù
▸ **pack up** VI (Brit) 打点(點)行装(裝) dǎdiǎn xíngzhuāng

package ['pækɪdʒ] N [c] 1 包裹 bāoguǒ [个 gè] 2 (Comput) 程序包 chéngxùbāo [个 gè]

packed [pækt] ADJ 拥(擁)挤(擠)的 yōngjǐ de

packet ['pækɪt] N [c] [of cigarettes, biscuits] 盒 hé [个 gè]; [of crisps, sweets, seeds] 袋 dài [个 gè]

pad [pæd] N [c] 便笺(牋)簿 biànjiānbù

paddle ['pædl] N [c] 1 (for canoe) 短桨(槳) duǎnjiǎng [个 gè] 2 (US: for table tennis) 球拍 qiúpāi [只 zhī]

padlock ['pædlɔk] N [c] 挂(掛)锁(鎖) guàsuǒ [个 gè]

paedophile, (US) **pedophile** ['piːdəufaɪl] N [c] 恋(戀)童癖者 liàntóngpǐzhě [个 gè]

page [peɪdʒ] N [c] 页(頁) yè

pain [peɪn] N [c/u] 疼痛 téngtòng [阵 zhèn] ▸ **to have a pain in one's chest/arm** 胸痛/胳膊疼 xiōng tòng/gēbo téng ▸ **to be in pain** 在苦恼(惱)中 zài kǔnǎo zhōng

painful ['peɪnful] ADJ [+ back, joint, swelling] 疼痛的 téngtòng de

painkiller ['peɪnkɪləʳ] N [c] 止痛药(藥) zhǐtòngyào [片 piàn]

paint [peɪnt] I N [c/u] 1 (decorator's) 油漆 yóuqī [桶 tǒng] 2 (artist's) 颜(顔)料 yánliào [罐 guàn] II VT 1 [+ wall, door, house] 油漆 yóuqī 2 [+ person, object] 描绘(繪) miáohuì 3 [+ picture, portrait] 用颜(顔)料画(畫) yòng yánliào huà III VI (creatively) 绘(繪)画(畫) huìhuà ▸ **a tin of paint** 一罐颜(顔)料 yī guàn yánliào ▸ **to paint sth blue/white** etc 把某物涂(塗)成蓝(藍)色/白色﹛等﹜ bǎ mǒuwù túchéng lánsè/báisè děng

paintbrush ['peɪntbrʌʃ] N [c] 1 (decorator's) 漆刷 qīshuā [个 gè] 2 (artist's) 画(畫)笔(筆) huàbǐ [支 zhī]

painter ['peɪntəʳ] N [c] 1 (artist) 画(畫)家 huàjiā [位 wèi] 2 (decorator) 油漆工 yóuqīgōng [个 gè]

painting ['peɪntɪŋ] N 1 [u] 绘(繪)画(畫) huìhuà; (decorating walls, doors etc) 上油漆 shàng yóuqī 2 [c] (picture) 画(畫) huà [幅 fú]

pair [pɛəʳ] N [c] 1 [of shoes, gloves, socks] 双(雙) shuāng 2 (two people) 对(對) duì ▸ **a pair of scissors** 一把剪刀 yī bǎ jiǎndāo ▸ **a pair of trousers** 一条(條)裤(褲)子 yī tiáo kùzi

pajamas [pə'dʒɑːməz] (US) N PL = **pyjamas**

Pakistan [pɑːkɪ'stɑːn] N 巴基斯坦 Bājīsītǎn

Pakistani [pɑːkɪ'stɑːnɪ] I ADJ 巴基斯坦的 Bājīsītǎn de II N [c] 巴基斯坦人 Bājīsītǎnrén [个 gè]

palace ['pæləs] N [c] 宫(宮)殿 gōngdiàn [座 zuò]

pale [peɪl] ADJ 1 [+ colour] 淡的 dàn de 2 [+ skin, complexion] 白皙的 báixī de 3 (from sickness, fear) 苍(蒼)白的 cāngbái de ▸ **pale blue/pink/green** 淡蓝(藍)色/粉红(紅)色/绿(綠)色 dàn lánsè/fěnhóngsè/lǜsè

Palestine ['pæləstaɪn] N 巴勒斯坦 Bālèsītǎn

Palestinian [pælɪs'tɪnɪən] I ADJ 巴勒斯坦的 Bālèsītǎn de II N [c] 巴勒斯坦人 Bālèsītǎnrén [个 gè]

pan [pæn] N [c] (*also:* **saucepan**) 炖(燉)
锅(鍋) dùnguō [口 kǒu]

pancake ['pænkeɪk] N [c] 薄煎饼(餅)
báo jiānbing [张 zhāng]

> **PANCAKE**
>
> 如果你要求英国厨师和美国厨师为你做
> 一张 **pancake**，饼的样子决不会是一
> 模一样。在这两个国家，**pancake** 都
> 呈扁平圆形，用牛奶、面粉和鸡蛋打成
> 面糊，油炸后，趁热吃。英国的饼很
> 薄，经常卷起来，或者夹有甜味或其他
> 口味的馅儿。很多人在 **Shrove**
> **Tuesday** (忏悔星期二) 即 **Lent** (大
> 斋节) 开始前的一天吃饼，这一天就是
> 人们熟知的 **Pancake Day** (煎饼节)。
> (**Lent** 是指复活节前的40天，从前基
> 督教徒在这段时间里斋戒 的传统。)
> 在美国，**pancake** 相对较小、较厚，
> 通常在早餐时就着黄油和枫糖浆吃。

panda ['pændə] N [c] 熊猫(貓)
xióngmāo [只 zhī]

panic ['pænɪk] I N [U] 惊(驚)恐 jīngkǒng
II v 惊(驚)慌 jīnghuāng

pants [pænts] NPL **1** (*Brit: underwear*)
内(內)裤(褲) nèikù **2** (*US: trousers*)
裤(褲)子 kùzi

pantyhose ['pæntɪhəuz] (*US*) NPL
连(連)裤(褲)袜(襪) liánkùwà ► **a pair
of pantyhose** 一条(條)连(連)裤(褲)
袜(襪) yī tiáo liánkùwà

paper ['peɪpəʳ] I N [U] **1** 纸(紙) zhǐ
2 [c] (*also:* **newspaper**) 报(報)纸(紙)
bàozhǐ [份 fèn] ► **a piece of paper**
(*odd bit, sheet*) 一张(張)纸(紙)
yī zhāng zhǐ

paperback ['peɪpəbæk] N [c] 平装(裝)
书(書) píngzhuāngshū [本 běn]

paper clip N [c] 回(迴)形针(針)
huíxíngzhēn [枚 méi]

parachute ['pærəʃu:t] N [c] 降落伞(傘)
jiàngluòsǎn [个 gè]

parade [pə'reɪd] N [c] 游(遊)行 yóuxíng
[次 cì]

paradise ['pærədaɪs] N **1** [U] (*Rel*) 天堂
tiāntáng **2** [c/U] (*fig*) 乐(樂)园(園)
lèyuán [个 gè]

paragraph ['pærəgrɑ:f] N [c] 段落
duànluò [个 gè]

parallel ['pærəlɛl] ADJ **1** 平行的 píngxíng
de **2** (*Comput*) 并(並)行的 bìngxíng de

paralysed, (*US*) **paralyzed** ['pærəlaɪzd]
(*Med*) ADJ 瘫(癱)痪(瘓)的 tānhuàn de

paramedic [pærə'mɛdɪk] N [c] 护(護)理
人员(員) hùlǐ rényuán [位 wèi]

parcel ['pɑ:sl] N [c] 包裹 bāoguǒ [个 gè]

pardon ['pɑ:dn] N [c] ► **(I beg your)
pardon?**, (*US*) **pardon me?** 请(請)问(問)
您刚(剛)才说(說)什么(麼)？ qǐngwèn
nín gāngcái shuō shénme?

parent ['pɛərənt] I N [c] **1** (*father*) 父
亲(親) fùqīn [位 wèi] **2** (*mother*) 母
亲(親) mǔqīn [位 wèi] II **parents** NPL
父母 fùmǔ

Paris ['pærɪs] N 巴黎 Bālí

park [pɑ:k] I N [c] 公园(園) gōngyuán
[个 gè] II vt 停放 tíngfàng III vi 停
车(車) tíngchē

parking ['pɑ:kɪŋ] N [U] 停车(車) tíngchē
► **"no parking"** "严(嚴)禁停车(車)"
"yánjìn tíngchē"

parking lot (*US*) N [c] 停车(車)场(場)
tíngchēchǎng [个 gè]

parking meter N [c] 停车(車)计(計)
时(時)器 tíngchē jìshíqì [个 gè]

parking ticket N [c] 违(違)章停车(車)
罚(罰)款单(單) wéizhāng tíngchē
fákuǎndān [张 zhāng]

parliament ['pɑ:ləmənt] (*Brit*) N [c/U]
议(議)会(會) yìhuì [个 gè]

parrot ['pærət] N [c] 鹦(鸚)鹉(鵡)
yīngwǔ [只 zhī]

part [pɑ:t] N **1** [c/U] (*section, division*) 部分
bùfen [个 gè] **2** [c] (*of machine, vehicle*) 部
件 bùjiàn [个 gè] ► **to take part in**
(*participate in*) 参(參)加 cānjiā
► **part with** VT FUS [+ *possessions*]
放弃(棄) fàngqì; [+ *money, cash*]
花 huā

participate [pɑ:'tɪsɪpeɪt] vi 参(參)
与(與) cānyù ► **to participate in sth**
[+ *activity, discussion*] 参(參)加某事
cānjiā mǒushì

particular [pə'tɪkjuləʳ] ADJ 特定的
tèdìng de

partly ['pɑ:tlɪ] ADV 部分地 bùfen de

partner ['pɑ:tnəʳ] N [c] **1** (*wife, husband,
girlfriend, boyfriend*) 伴侣(侶) bànlǚ [个
gè] **2** (*in firm*) 合伙(夥)人 héhuǒrén [个
gè] **3** (*Sport*) 搭档(檔) dādàng [个 gè]

4 (for cards, games) 对(對)家 duìjiā [个 gè] **5** (at dance) 舞伴 wǔbàn [个 gè]

part-time ['pɑːtaɪm] I ADJ 兼职(職)的 jiānzhí de [work, study +] 部分时(時)间(間)地 bùfen shíjiān de

party ['pɑːtɪ] N [c] **1** (Pol) 党(黨) dǎng [个 gè] **2** (social event) 聚会(會) jùhuì [次 cì]
▶ **birthday party** 生日聚会(會) shēngrì jùhuì

pass [pɑːs] I VT **1** (hand) ▶ **to pass sb sth** [+ salt, glass, newspaper, tool] 把某物递(遞)给(給)某人 bǎ mǒuwù dìgěi mǒurén **2** (go past) 经(經)过(過) jīngguò **3** [+ exam, test] 通过(過) tōngguò II VI **1** (go past) 经(經)过(過) jīngguò **2** (in exam) 及格 jígé ▶ **to get a pass (in sth)** (Scol, Univ) (某考试(試)) 达(達)到及格标(標)准(準) (mǒu kǎoshì) dádào jígé biāozhǔn
▶ **pass away** VI (die) 去世 qùshì

passage ['pæsɪdʒ] N [c] 走廊 zǒuláng [条 tiáo]

passenger ['pæsɪndʒəʳ] N [c] 乘客 chéngkè [位 wèi]

passive ['pæsɪv] N [U] ▶ **the passive** (Ling) 被动(動)语(語)态(態) bèidòng yǔtài

Passover ['pɑːsəʊvəʳ] N [U] 逾越节(節) Yúyuèjié

passport ['pɑːspɔːt] N [c] 护(護)照 hùzhào [本 běn]

password ['pɑːswɜːd] N [c] 密码(碼) mìmǎ [个 gè]

past [pɑːst] I PREP (in front of, beyond, later than) 过(過) guò II ADV (by) ▶ **to go/walk/drive past** 经(經)/走/开(開)过(過) jīng/zǒu/kāiguò III ADJ [+ week, month, year] 刚(剛)过(過)去的 gāng guòqù de IV N [c] ▶ **the past** 过(過)去 guòqù [个 gè]; (tense) 过(過)去时(時) guòqùshí ▶ **it's past midnight** 过(過)了午夜 guòle wǔyè ▶ **ten/(a) quarter past eight** 8点(點)10/15分 bā diǎn shí/shíwǔ fēn ▶ **for the past few/3 days** 过(過)去几(幾)/3天以来(來) guòqù jǐ/sān tiān yǐlái ▶ **the past tense** 过(過)去时(時) guòqùshí ▶ **in the past** (before now) 在过(過)去 zài guòqù

pasta ['pæstə] N [U] 意大利面食 Yìdàlì miànshí

pastry ['peɪstrɪ] N **1** [U] (dough) 油酥面(麵)团(團) yóusū miàntuán **2** [c] (cake)

酥皮糕点(點) sūpí gāodiǎn [块 kuài]

patch [pætʃ] N [c] **1** (piece of material) 补(補)丁 bǔdīng [个 gè] **2** (area) 斑片 bānpiàn [块 kuài]

path [pɑːθ] N [c] **1** (track) 小路 xiǎolù [条 tiáo]; (in garden) 小径(徑) xiǎojìng [条 tiáo]

pathetic [pə'θɛtɪk] ADJ [+ excuse, effort, attempt] 不足道的 bùzúdào de

patience ['peɪʃns] N [U] 耐心 nàixīn

patient ['peɪʃnt] I N [c] (Med) 病人 bìngrén [个 gè] II ADJ [+ person] 耐心的 nàixīn de

patrol [pə'trəʊl] VT 在…巡逻(邏) zài…xúnluó ▶ **to be on patrol** 在巡逻(邏)中 zài xúnluó zhōng

pattern ['pætən] N [c] **1** 花样(樣) huāyàng [种 zhǒng] **2** (for sewing, knitting) 样(樣)式 yàngshì [个 gè]

pause [pɔːz] VI (when speaking) 停顿(頓) tíngdùn; (when doing sth) 暂(暫)停 zàntíng

pavement ['peɪvmənt] N [c] (Brit) 人行道 rénxíngdào [条 tiáo]

pay [peɪ] (pt, pp paid) I N [U] 工资(資) gōngzī II VT **1** [+ debt, bill, tax] 付 fù **2** [+ person] ▶ **to get paid** 发(發)工资(資) fā gōngzī **3** ▶ **to pay sb sth** (as wage, salary, for goods, services) 付给(給)某人某物 fùgěi mǒurén mǒuwù ▶ **how much did you pay for it?** 你买(買)那个(個)花了多少钱(錢)? nǐ mǎi nàge huāle duōshǎo qián?
▶ **pay back** VT **1** [+ money, loan] 偿(償)还(還) chánghuán **2** [+ person] (with money) 还(還)给(給)某人 huángěi
▶ **pay for** VT FUS 买(買) mǎi

payment ['peɪmənt] N [c] 付款额(額) fùkuǎn é [笔 bǐ]

payphone ['peɪfəʊn] N [c] 公用电(電)话(話) gōngyòng diànhuà [部 bù]

PC N ABBR (= personal computer) 个(個)人电(電)脑(腦) gèrén diànnǎo

PDA N ABBR (= personal digital assistant) 掌上电(電)脑(腦) zhǎngshàng diànnǎo

PE (Scol) N ABBR (= physical education) 体(體)育 tǐyù

pea [piː] N [c] 豌豆 wāndòu [粒 lì]

peace [piːs] N [U] **1** (not war) 和平 hépíng **2** [of place, surroundings] 宁(寧)静(靜) níngjìng

peaceful ['piːsful] ADJ 安静(靜)的 ānjìng de

peach [piːtʃ] N [c] 桃 táo [个 gè]

peak [piːk] I N [c] 山顶(頂) shāndǐng [个 gè] II ADJ [+ level, times] 高峰的 gāofēng de

peanut ['piːnʌt] N [c] 花生 huāshēng [粒 lì]

pear [pɛəʳ] N [c] 梨 lí [个 gè]

pearl [pəːl] N [c] 珍珠 zhēnzhū [颗 kē]

pebble ['pɛbl] N [c] 卵石 luǎnshí [块 kuài]

peculiar [pɪ'kjuːliəʳ] ADJ 奇怪的 qíguài de

pedal ['pɛdl] N [c] 1 (on bicycle) 脚(腳)蹬子 jiǎodēngzi [个 gè] 2 (in car, on piano) 踏板 tàbǎn [个 gè]

pedestrian [pɪ'dɛstrɪən] N [c] 行人 xíngrén [个 gè]

pedestrian crossing (Brit) N [c] 人行横(橫)道 rénxíng héngdào [条 tiáo]

pedophile ['piːdəufaɪl] (US) N = **paedophile**

pee [piː] (inf) VI 撒尿 sāniào

peel [piːl] I N [U] 皮 pí II VT [+ vegetables, fruit] 削 xiāo

peg [pɛg] N [c] 1 (for coat, hat, bag) 挂(掛)钉(釘) guàdīng [枚 méi] 2 (Brit) (also: **clothes peg**) 衣夹(夾) yījiā [个 gè]

pen [pɛn] N [c] 笔(筆) bǐ [支 zhī]; (also: **fountain pen**) 自来(來)水笔(筆) zìláishuǐbǐ [支 zhī]; (also: **ballpoint pen**) 圆(圓)珠笔(筆) yuánzhūbǐ [支 zhī]

penalty ['pɛnltɪ] N [c] 1 处(處)罚(罰) chǔfá [次 cì] 2 (Football, Rugby) 罚(罰)球 fáqiú [个 gè]

pence [pɛns] (Brit) NPL of **penny**

pencil ['pɛnsl] N [c] 铅(鉛)笔(筆) qiānbǐ [支 zhī]

pencil sharpener N [c] 铅(鉛)笔(筆)刀 qiānbǐdāo [把 bǎ]

penguin ['pɛŋgwɪn] N [c] 企鹅(鵝) qǐé [只 zhī]

penicillin [pɛnɪ'sɪlɪn] N [U] 青霉(黴)素 qīngméisù

penknife ['pɛnnaɪf] (pl **penknives**) N [c] 小刀 xiǎodāo [把 bǎ]

penny ['pɛnɪ] (pl **pennies** or (Brit) **pence**) N [c] 便士 biànshì [枚 méi]

pension ['pɛnʃən] N [c] (from state) 养(養)老金 yǎnglǎojīn [份 fèn]; (from employer) 退休金 tuìxiūjīn [份 fèn]

pensioner ['pɛnʃənəʳ] (Brit) N [c] 领(領)养(養)老金的人 lǐng yǎnglǎojīn de rén [个 gè]

people ['piːpl] NPL 1 人 rén 2 (generalizing) 人们(們) rénmen ▸ **old people** 老人 lǎorén ▸ **many people** 许(許)多人 xǔduō rén ▸ **people say that...** 有人说(說)… yǒurén shuō…

pepper ['pɛpəʳ] N 1 [U] (spice) 胡椒粉 hújiāofěn 2 [c] (vegetable) 胡椒 hújiāo [个 gè]

peppermint ['pɛpəmɪnt] N [c] 薄荷糖 bòhetáng [块 kuài]

per [pəːʳ] PREP 每 měi ▸ **per day** 每天 měi tiān ▸ **per person** 每人 měi rén ▸ **per annum** 每年 měi nián

per cent, percent [pə'sɛnt] (pl **per cent**) N [c] 百分之… bǎi fēn zhī… ▸ **by 15 per cent** 以百分之十五 yǐ bǎi fēn zhī shíwǔ

perfect ['pəːfɪkt] I ADJ 1 [+ weather, behaviour] 完美的 wánměi de; [+ sauce, skin, teeth] 无(無)瑕的 wúxiá de 2 [+ crime, solution, example] 理想的 lǐxiǎng de II N ▸ **the perfect (tense)** 完成(时)(時) wánchéng(shí)

perfectly ['pəːfɪktlɪ] ADV 1 非常好地 fēicháng hǎo de 2 [+ honest, reasonable, clear] 绝(絕)对(對)地 juéduì de

perform [pə'fɔːm] I VT 表演 biǎoyǎn II VI (function) 1 [actor, musician, singer, dancer +] 演出 yǎnchū

performance [pə'fɔːməns] N 1 [c] (Theat: by actor, musician, singer, dancer) 表演 biǎoyǎn [次 cì]; [of play, show] 演出 yǎnchū [场 chǎng] 2 [U] [of employee, surgeon, athlete, team] 表现(現) biǎoxiàn

perfume ['pəːfjuːm] N 1 [c/U] 香水 xiāngshuǐ [瓶 píng] 2 [c] 芳香 fāngxiāng [种 zhǒng]

perhaps [pə'hæps] ADV 可能 kěnéng ▸ **perhaps not** 未必 wèibì

period ['pɪərɪəd] N [c] 1 (interval, stretch) 周(週)期 zhōuqī [个 gè] 2 (time) 时(時)期 shíqī [段 duàn] 3 (era) 时(時)代 shídài [个 gè] 4 (esp US: punctuation mark) 句号(號) jùhào [个 gè] 5 (also: **menstrual period**) 月经(經)期 yuèjīngqī [个 gè] ▸ **to have one's period** 来(來)例假 lái lìjià

permanent ['pəːmənənt] ADJ 持久的 chíjiǔ de; [+ damage] 永久的 yǒngjiǔ de;

[+ *state, job, position*] 长(長)期的 chángqī de

permission [pəˈmɪʃən] N [U] **1** (*consent*) 准许(許) zhǔnxǔ **2** (*official authorization*) 批准 pīzhǔn

permit [ˈpəːmɪt N [C] (*authorization*) 许(許)可证(證) xǔkězhèng [个 gè]

persecute [ˈpəːsɪkjuːt] VT 迫害 pòhài

person [ˈpəːsn] (*pl gen* **people**) N [C] 人 rén [个 gè] ▸ **in person** 亲(親)自 qīnzì ▸ **first/second/third person** 第一/二/三人称(稱) dìyī/èr/sān rénchēng

personal [ˈpəːsnl] ADJ **1** [+ *telephone number, bodyguard*] 私人的 sīrén de; [+ *opinion, habits*] 个(個)人的 gèrén de; [+ *care, contact, appearance, appeal*] 亲(親)自的 qīnzì de **2** [+ *life, matter, relationship*] 私人的 sīrén de

personality [pəːsəˈnælɪtɪ] N [C/U] 个(個)性 gèxìng [种 zhǒng]

personally [ˈpəːsnəlɪ] ADV 就我个(個)人来(來)说(說) jiù wǒ gèrén lái shuō

personal stereo N [C] 随(隨)身听(聽) suíshēntīng [个 gè]

perspiration [pəːspɪˈreɪʃən] N [U] 汗 hàn

persuade [pəˈsweɪd] VT ▸ **to persuade sb to do sth** 劝(勸)说(說)某人做某事 quànshuō mǒurén zuò mǒushì

pessimistic [pɛsɪˈmɪstɪk] ADJ 悲观(觀)的 bēiguān de

pest [pɛst] N [C] (*insect*) 害虫(蟲) hàichóng [只 zhī]

pester [ˈpɛstəʳ] VT 烦(煩)扰(擾) fánrǎo

pet [pɛt] N [C] 宠(寵)物 chǒngwù [只 zhī]

petrol [ˈpɛtrəl] (*Brit*) N [U] 汽油 qìyóu

petrol station (*Brit*) N [C] 加油站 jiāyóuzhàn [个 gè]

pharmacy [ˈfɑːməsɪ] N **1** (*shop*) 药(藥)店 yàodiàn [家 jiā] **2** [U] (*science*) 药(藥)学(學) yàoxué

philosophy [fɪˈlɒsəfɪ] N [U] (*subject*) 哲学(學) zhéxué

phone [fəun] I N [C] 电(電)话(話) diànhuà [部 bù] II VT 打电(電)话(話) 给(給)…dǎ diànhuà gěi VI 打电(電)话(話) dǎ diànhuà ▸ **to be on the phone** (*be calling*) 在通话(話) zài tōnghuà ▸ **by phone** 通过(過)电(電)话(話) tōngguò diànhuà

▸ **phone back** I VT 给(給)…回电(電)话(話) gěi…huí diànhuà VI 回电(電)话(話) huídiàn

phone bill N [C] 话(話)费(費)单(單) huàfèidān [张 zhāng]

phone book N [C] 电(電)话(話)簿 diànhuàbù [本 běn]

phone booth (*US*) N [C] 电(電)话(話)亭 diànhuàtíng [个 gè]

phone box (*Brit*) N [C] 电(電)话(話)亭 diànhuàtíng [个 gè]

phone call N [C] 电(電)话(話) diànhuà [部 bù] ▸ **to make a phone call** 打电(電)话(話) dǎ diànhuà

phonecard [ˈfəunkɑːd] N [C] 电(電)话(話)卡 diànhuàkǎ [张 zhāng]

phone number N [C] 电(電)话(話)号(號)码(碼) diànhuà hàomǎ [个 gè]

photo [ˈfəutəu] N [C] 照片 zhàopiàn [张 zhāng] ▸ **to take a photo (of sb/sth)** 给(給)(某人/某物)拍照片 gěi(mǒurén/mǒuwù)pāi zhàopiàn

photobomb [ˈfəutəubɒm] I N [C] 照片炸弹(彈) zhàopiàn zhàdàn II VB 意外被拍进(進)照片 yìwài bèi pāi jìn zhàopiàn

photocopier [ˈfəutəukɒpɪəʳ] N [C] 影印机(機) yǐngyìnjī [台 tái]

photocopy [ˈfəutəukɒpɪ] I N [C] 影印本 yǐngyìnběn [个 gè] II VT [+ *document, picture*] 影印 yǐngyìn

photograph [ˈfəutəgræf] N [C] 照片 zhàopiàn [张 zhāng]

photographer [fəˈtɒgrəfəʳ] N [C] 摄(攝)影师(師) shèyǐngshī [位 wèi]

photography [fəˈtɒgrəfɪ] N [U] 摄(攝)影 shèyǐng

phrase [freɪz] N [C] **1** (*expression*) 习(習)语(語) xíyǔ [个 gè] **2** (*in phrase book, dictionary*) 短语(語) duǎnyǔ [个 gè]

phrase book N [C] 常用词(詞)手册(冊) chángyòngcí shǒucè [本 běn]

physical [ˈfɪzɪkl] ADJ 生理的 shēnglǐ de

physician [fɪˈzɪʃən] (*US*) N [C] 医(醫)生 yīshēng [位 wèi]

physicist [ˈfɪzɪsɪst] N [C] 物理学(學)家 wùlǐxuéjiā [位 wèi]

physics [ˈfɪzɪks] N [U] 物理学(學) wùlǐxué

physiotherapist [fɪzɪəuˈθɛrəpɪst] N [C] 理疗(療)师(師) lǐliáoshī [位 wèi]

physiotherapy [fɪzɪəuˈθɛrəpɪ] N [U] 物理疗(療)法 wùlǐ liáofǎ

pianist ['pi:ənɪst] N [c] (*professional*) 钢(鋼)琴家 gāngqínjiā [位 wèi]; (*amateur*) 钢(鋼)琴演奏者 gāngqín yǎnzòuzhě [位 wèi]

piano [pɪˈænəu] N [c] 钢(鋼)琴 gāngqín [架 jià]

pick [pɪk] VT **1** (*choose*) 选(選)择(擇) xuǎnzé **2** [+ *fruit, flowers*] 采(採)摘 cǎizhāi ▸ **take your pick** 随(隨)意挑选(選) suíyì tiāoxuǎn
  ▸ **pick out** VT (*select*) [+ *person, thing*] 挑中 tiāozhòng
  ▸ **pick up** VT **1** [+ *object*] (*take hold of*) 拿起 náqǐ; (*from floor, ground*) 捡(撿)起 jiǎnqǐ **2** (*collect*) [+ *person, parcel*] 接 jiē

pickpocket ['pɪkpɔkɪt] N [c] 扒手 páshǒu [个 gè]

picnic ['pɪknɪk] N [c] (*meal*) 野餐 yěcān [顿 dùn]

picture ['pɪktʃə'] I N [c] **1** (*painting, drawing, print*) 画(畫)huà [幅 fú] **2** (*photograph*) 照片 zhàopiàn [张 zhāng] **3** (*film, movie*) 电(電)影 diànyǐng [部 bù] II **the pictures** NPL (*Brit: inf: the cinema*) 电(電)影院 diànyǐngyuàn

picture messaging [-ˈmɛsɪdʒɪŋ] N [U] 彩信 cǎixìn

piece [pi:s] N [c] **1** (*fragment*) 块(塊) kuài **2** [*of string, ribbon, sticky tape*] 段 duàn **3** [*of cake, bread, chocolate*] 块(塊) kuài ▸ **a piece of paper** 一张(張)纸(紙) yī zhāng zhǐ ▸ **a 10p piece** (*Brit*) 一枚10便士硬币(幣) yī méi shí biànshì yìngbì

pierced [pɪəst] ADJ [+ *ears, nose, lip*] 穿孔的 chuānkǒng de

piercing ['pɪəsɪŋ] N [c] 人体(體)穿孔 réntǐ chuānkǒng [个 gè]

pig [pɪg] N [c] 猪(豬) zhū [头 tóu]

pigeon ['pɪdʒən] N [c] 鸽(鴿)子 gēzi [只 zhī]

pile [paɪl] I N [c] 堆 duī [个 gè] II VT 堆起 duīqǐ ▸ **piles of** or **a pile of sth** (*inf*) 一大堆某物 yī dàduī mǒuwù

pill [pɪl] N [c] 药(藥)丸 yàowán [粒 lì] ▸ **the pill** (*contraceptive pill*) 避孕药(藥) bìyùnyào ▸ **to be on the pill** 服避孕药(藥) fú bìyùnyào

pillow ['pɪləu] N [c] 枕头(頭) zhěntou [个 gè]

pilot ['paɪlət] N [c] 飞(飛)行员(員) fēixíngyuán [个 gè]

PIN [pɪn] N ABBR (= **personal identification number**) 密码(碼) mìmǎ

pin [pɪn] I N [c] **1** (*used in sewing*) 大头(頭)针(針) dàtóuzhēn [枚 méi] **2** (*badge*) 饰(飾)针(針) shìzhēn [枚 méi] II VT (*on wall, door, board*) 钉(釘)住 dìngzhù
  ▸ **pins and needles** 发(發)麻 fāmá

pinch [pɪntʃ] VT [+ *person*] 捏 niē

pine [paɪn] N [c] **1** (*also: pine tree*) 松树(樹) sōngshù [棵 kē] **2** [U] (*wood*) 松木 sōngmù

pineapple ['paɪnæpl] N [c] 菠萝(蘿) bōluó 凤(鳳)梨 fènglí [个 gè]

pink [pɪŋk] I ADJ 粉红(紅)色的 fěnhóngsè de II [c/U] 粉红(紅)色 fěnhóngsè [种 zhǒng]

pint [paɪnt] N [c] (*measure: Brit: 568 cc*) 品脱(脫) pǐntuō; (*US: 473 cc*) 品脱(脫) pǐntuō

pipe [paɪp] N [c] **1** (*for water, gas*) 管子 guǎnzi [根 gēn] **2** (*for smoking*) 烟(煙)斗 yāndǒu [个 gè]

pirate ['paɪərət] N [c] 海盗(盜) hǎidào [个 gè]

pirated ['paɪərətɪd] (*Comm*) ADJ 盗(盜)版的 dàobǎn de

Pisces ['paɪsi:z] N [U] (*sign*) 双(雙)鱼(魚)座 Shuāngyú Zuò

pitch [pɪtʃ] N [c] (*Brit*) 球场(場) qiúchǎng [个 gè]

pity ['pɪtɪ] I N **1** [U] (*compassion*) 同情 tóngqíng **2** (*misfortune*) ▸ **it is a pity that...** 真遗(遺)憾··· zhēn yíhàn... II VT [+ *person*] 同情 tóngqíng ▸ **what a pity!** 真可惜! zhēn kěxī!

pizza ['pi:tsə] N [c] 比萨(薩)饼(餅) bǐsàbǐng [个 gè]

place [pleɪs] I N **1** [c] (*location*) 地方 dìfang [个 gè] **2** [c] 空位 kòngwèi [个 gè]; (*seat*) 座位 zuòwèi [个 gè]; (*at university, on course, on committee, in team*) 名额(額) míng'é [个 gè] **3** [c] (*in competition*) 名次 míngcì [个 gè] **4** (*US: inf*) ▸ **some/every/no/any place** 某些/每个(個)/没(沒)有/任何地方 mǒuxiē/měigè/méiyǒu/rènhé dìfang II VT (*put*) 放 fàng; (*classify*) ▸ **in places** 有几(幾)处(處) yǒu jǐ chù ▸ **at sb's place** (*home*) 在某人的家里(裡) zài mǒurén de jiāli
  ▸ **to take sb's/sth's place** 代替某人/某

物 dàitì mǒurén/mǒuwù ▸ to take place (happen) 发(發)生 fāshēng

plain [pleɪn] I ADJ **1** (not patterned) 无(無)图(圖)案花纹(紋)的 wú tú'àn huāwén de II N [C] **1** (area of land) 平原 píngyuán [个 gè]

plait [plæt] I N [C] 辫(辮)子 biànzi [条 tiáo] II VT 编(編).biān

plan [plæn] I N [C] (scheme, project) 计(計)划(劃)jìhuà [个 gè] **2** (drawing) 详(詳)图(圖) xiángtú [张 zhāng] II VT 计(計)划(劃)jìhuà III VI (think ahead) 打算 dǎsuàn IV **plans** NPL (intentions) 计(計)划(劃)jìhuà ▸ to plan to do sth 计(計)划(劃)做某事 jìhuà zuò mǒushì

plane [pleɪn] N [C] 飞(飛)机(機)fēijī [架 jià]

planet ['plænɪt] N [C] 行星 xíngxīng [个 gè]

plant [plɑːnt] I N **1** [C] 植物 zhíwù [株 zhū] **2** [C] (factory, power station) 工厂(廠) gōngchǎng [个 gè] II VT 栽种(種) zāizhòng

plaster ['plɑːstəʳ] N **1** [U] 灰泥 huīní **2** [C/U] (Brit) (also: sticking plaster) 橡皮膏 xiàngpígāo [块 kuài] ▸ in plaster (Brit) 打了石膏的 dǎle shígāo de

plastic ['plæstɪk] I N [C/U] 塑料 sùliào [种 zhǒng] II ADJ [+ bucket, chair, cup] 塑料的 sùliào de

plastic wrap (US) N [U] 保鲜(鮮)膜 bǎoxiānmó

plate [pleɪt] N [C] 碟 dié [个 gè]

platform ['plætfɔːm] N [C] **1** (stage) 平台(臺) píngtái [个 gè] **2** (Rail) 站台(臺) zhàntái [个 gè] ▸ the train leaves from platform 7 火车(車)从(從)7号(號)站台(臺)出发(發) huǒchē cóng qī hào zhàntái chūfā

play [pleɪ] I N [C] 戏(戲)剧(劇) xìjù [出chū] II VT **1** [+ game, chess] 玩 wán; [+ football] 踢 tī; [+ cricket, tennis] 打 dǎ **2** [+ team, opponent] 同…比赛(賽) tóng…bǐsài **3** [+ part, role, character] 扮演 bànyǎn **4** [+ instrument, piece of music] 演奏 yǎnzòu **5** [+ CD, record, tape] 播放 bōfàng III VI **1** [children +] 玩耍 wánshuǎ **2** [orchestra, band +] 演奏 yǎnzòu ▸ to play cards 玩纸(紙)牌 wán zhǐpái ▸ **play back** VT 回放 huífàng

player ['pleɪəʳ] N [C] **1** (Sport) 选(選)手 xuǎnshǒu [名 míng] **2** (Mus) ▸ a trumpet/flute/piano player 小号(號)/长(長)笛/钢(鋼)琴演奏者 xiǎohào/chángdí/gāngqín yǎnzòuzhě [位 wèi]

playground ['pleɪgraʊnd] N [C] (at school) 运(運)动(動)场(場) yùndòngchǎng [个 gè]; (in park) 游(遊)戏(戲)场(場) yóuxìchǎng [个 gè]

playing card ['pleɪɪŋ-] N [C] 纸(紙)牌 zhǐpái [张 zhāng]

pleasant ['plɛznt] ADJ **1** (agreeable) 令人愉快的 lìng rén yúkuài de **2** (friendly) 友善的 yǒushàn de

please [pliːz] I INT 请(請) qǐng II VT (satisfy) 使高兴(興) shǐ gāoxìng ▸ yes, please 好的 hǎode

pleased [pliːzd] ADJ 开(開)心的 kāixīn de ▸ pleased to meet you 见(見)到你很高兴(興) jiàndào nǐ hěn gāoxìng ▸ pleased with sth 对(對)某事满(滿)意 duì mǒushì mǎnyì

pleasure ['plɛʒəʳ] N **1** [U] (happiness, satisfaction) 高兴(興) gāoxìng **2** [U] (fun) 享乐(樂) xiǎnglè ▸ "it's a pleasure", "my pleasure" "乐(樂)意效劳(勞)" "lèyì xiàoláo"

plenty ['plɛntɪ] PRON **1** (lots) 大量 dàliàng **2** (sufficient) 充足 chōngzú ▸ plenty of [+ food, money, time] 很多 hěn duō; [+ jobs, people, houses] 许(許)多 xǔduō

plot [plɔt] I N **1** [C] (secret plan) ▸ a plot (to do sth) (做某事的)阴(陰)谋(謀)(zuò mǒushì de) yīnmóu [个 gè] **2** [C/U] (of story, play, film) 情节(節) qíngjié [个 gè] II VI (conspire) 密谋(謀) mìmóu ▸ to plot to do sth 密谋(謀)做某事 mìmóu zuò mǒushì

plug [plʌg] N [C] **1** (Elec: on appliance) 插头(頭) chātóu [个 gè] 插座 chāzuò [个 gè] **2** (in sink, bath) 塞子 sāizi [个 gè] ▸ **plug in** (Elec) VT 插上…的插头(頭) chāshàng…de chātóu

plum [plʌm] N [C] (fruit) 梅子 méizi [颗 kē]

plumber ['plʌməʳ] N [C] 管子工 guǎnzigōng [位 wèi]

plural ['plʊərl] I ADJ 复(複)数(數)的 fùshù de II N [C] 复(複)数(數) fùshù [个 gè]

plus [plʌs] I CONJ **1** (added to) 加 jiā **2** (as well as) 和 hé II ADV (additionally) 此外 cǐwài III N [c] (inf) ▸ **it's a plus** 这(這)是个(個)附加的好处(處) zhè shì gè fùjiā de hǎochù [个 gè] ▸ **B plus** (Scol) B加 bǐjiā

p.m. ADV ABBR (= post meridiem) 下午 xiàwǔ

pneumonia [nju:'məunɪə] N [U] 肺炎 fèiyán

pocket ['pɒkɪt] N [c] 口袋 kǒudài [个 gè]

pocketbook ['pɒkɪtbuk] (US) N [c] **1** (wallet) 皮夹(夾) píjiā [个 gè] **2** (handbag) 手提包 shǒutíbāo [个 gè]

poem ['pəʊɪm] N [c] 诗(詩) shī [首 shǒu]

poet ['pəʊɪt] N [c] 诗(詩)人 shīrén [位 wèi]

poetry ['pəʊɪtrɪ] N [U] **1** (poems) 诗(詩) shī **2** (form of literature) 诗(詩)歌 shīgē

point [pɔɪnt] I N [c/u] **1** (in report, lecture, interview) 论(論)点(點) lùndiǎn [个 gè] **2** [s] (significant part) [of argument, discussion] 要害 yàohài **3** [s] (purpose) [of action] 目的 mùdì **4** [c] (place) 位置 wèizhì [个 gè] **5** [s] (moment) 时(時)刻 shíkè **6** [c] (sharp end) 尖端 jiānduān [个 gè] **7** [c] (in score, competition, game, sport) 分 fēn **8** [c] (also: **decimal point**) 小数(數)点(點) xiǎoshùdiǎn [个 gè] II VI (with finger, stick) 指出 zhǐchū III VT **1** ▸ **to point sth at sb** 把某物瞄准(準)某人 bǎ mǒuwù miáozhǔn mǒurén ▸ **there's no point (in doing that)** (那样(樣)做)毫无(無)意义(義) (nàyàng zuò) háo wú yìyì ▸ **two point five** (2.5) 二点(點)五 èr diǎn wǔ ▸ **to point at sth/sb** (with finger, stick) 指着(著)某物/某人 zhǐzhe mǒuwù/mǒurén
▸ **point out** VT 指出 zhǐchū ▸ **to point out that...** 指出… zhǐchū…

pointless ['pɔɪntlɪs] ADJ 无(無)意义(義)的 wú yìyì de

poison ['pɔɪzn] I N [c/u] 毒药(藥) dúyào [种 zhǒng] II VT 下毒 xiàdú

poisonous ['pɔɪznəs] ADJ (lit) 有毒的 yǒudú de

poker ['pəʊkəʳ] N [U] 扑(撲)克牌 pūkèpái

Poland ['pəʊlənd] N 波兰(蘭) Bōlán

polar bear ['pəʊlə-] N [c] 北极(極)熊 běijíxióng [头 tóu]

Pole [pəʊl] N [c] 波兰(蘭)人 Bōlánrén [个 gè]

pole [pəʊl] N [c] **1** (stick) 杆(桿) gān [根 gēn] **2** (Geo) 地极 dìjí [个 gè]

police [pə'li:s] NPL **1** (organization) 警方 jǐngfāng **2** (members) 警察 jǐngchá

policeman [pə'li:smən] (pl policemen) N [c] 男警察 nán jǐngchá [名 míng]

police officer N [c] 警察 jǐngchá [名 míng]

police station N [c] 警察局 jǐngchájú [个 gè]

policewoman [pə'li:swumən] (pl policewomen) N [c] 女警察 nǚjǐngchá [名 míng]

Polish ['pəʊlɪʃ] I ADJ 波兰(蘭)的 Bōlán de II N [U] (language) 波兰(蘭)语(語) Bōlányǔ

polish ['pɒlɪʃ] I N [c/u] 上光剂(劑) shàngguāngjì [盒 hé] II VT [+ shoes] 擦亮 cāliàng; [+ furniture, floor] 上光 shàngguāng

polite [pə'laɪt] ADJ 有礼(禮)貌的 yǒu lǐmào de

political [pə'lɪtɪkl] ADJ 政治的 zhèngzhì de

politician [pɒlɪ'tɪʃən] N [c] 政治家 zhèngzhìjiā [位 wèi]

politics ['pɒlɪtɪks] N [U] **1** (activity) 政治 zhèngzhì **2** (subject) 政治学(學) zhèngzhìxué

pollute [pə'lu:t] VT 污染 wūrǎn

polluted [pə'lu:tɪd] ADJ 被污染的 bèi wūrǎn de

pollution [pə'lu:ʃən] N [U] **1** (process) 污染 wūrǎn **2** (substances) 污染物 wūrǎnwù

polythene bag ['pɒlɪθi:n-] N [c] 聚乙烯塑料袋 jùyǐxī sùliàodài [个 gè]

pond [pɒnd] N [c] 池塘 chítáng [个 gè]

pony [pəʊnɪ] N [c] 小马(馬) xiǎomǎ [匹 pǐ]

ponytail ['pəʊnɪteɪl] N [c] 马(馬)尾辫(辮) mǎwěibiàn [条 tiáo]

pool [pu:l] N **1** [c] (pond) 水塘 shuǐtáng [个 gè] **2** [c] (also: **swimming pool**) 游(遊)泳池 yóuyǒngchí [个 gè] **3** [U] (game) 美式台(臺)球 měishì táiqiú

poor [puəʳ] I ADJ **1** [+ person] 贫(貧)穷(窮)的 pínqióng de; [+ country, area] 贫(貧)困的 pínkùn de **2** (bad) [+ quality, performance] 低水平的 dī shuǐpíng de; [+ wages, conditions, results, attendance]

差的 chà de II NPL ▶ **the poor** 穷(窮)人 qióngrén ▶ **poor (old) Bill** 可怜(憐)的(老)比尔(爾) kělián de (lǎo) Bǐ'ěr

pop [pɒp] N 1 [u] (Mus) 流行音乐(樂) liúxíng yīnyuè 2 [c] (US: inf: father) 爸爸 bàba [个 gè]

popcorn ['pɒpkɔːn] N [u] 爆米花 bàomǐhuā

pope [pəup] N [c] 教皇 jiàohuáng [位 wèi]

popular ['pɒpjulə'] ADJ 1 [+ person, place, thing] 流行的 liúxíng de 2 [+ name, activity] 时(時)髦的 shímáo de

population [pɒpju'leɪʃən] N [c] 人口 rénkǒu [个 gè]

pork [pɔːk] N [u] 猪(豬)肉 zhūròu

port [pɔːt] N 1 [c] (harbour) 港口 gǎngkǒu [个 gè] 2 [c] (town) 港市 gǎngshì [座 zuò]

portable ['pɔːtəbl] ADJ 便携(攜)式的 biànxiéshì de

porter ['pɔːtə'] N [c] 1 (Brit: doorkeeper) 门(門)房 ménfáng [个 gè] 2 (US: on train) 列车(車)员(員) lièchēyuán [位 wèi]

portion ['pɔːʃən] N [c] 份 fèn

portrait ['pɔːtreɪt] N [c] (picture) 画(畫)像 huàxiàng [幅 fú]

Portugal ['pɔːtjugəl] N 葡萄牙 Pútáoyá

Portuguese [pɔːtju'giːz] (pl Portuguese) I ADJ 葡萄牙的 Pútáoyá de II N 1 [c] (person) 葡萄牙人 Pútáoyárén [个 gè] 2 [u] (language) 葡萄牙语(語) Pútáoyáyǔ

posh [pɒʃ] (inf) ADJ [+ hotel, car, restaurant] 豪华(華)的 háohuá de

position [pə'zɪʃən] N [c] 1 [of house, person, thing] 位置 wèizhì [个 gè] 2 (posture) [of person's body] 姿势(勢) zīshì [种 zhǒng]

positive ['pɒzɪtɪv] ADJ 1 (good) 有益的 yǒuyì de 2 (affirmative) [+ test, result] 阳(陽)性的 yángxìng de 3 (sure) ▶ **to be positive (about sth)** 确(確)信(某事) quèxìn (mǒushì)

possession [pə'zɛʃən] I N [u] (ownership) 拥(擁)有 yōngyǒu II **possessions** NPL (belongings) 财(財)产(產) cáichǎn

possibility [pɒsɪ'bɪlɪtɪ] N [c] 1 可能性 kěnéngxìng [种 zhǒng]; (of sth happening) 可能的事 kěnéng de shì [件 jiàn] 2 (option) 可选(選)性 kěxuǎnxìng [种 zhǒng]

possible ['pɒsɪbl] ADJ [+ event, reaction, effect, consequence] 可能的 kěnéng de; [+ risk, danger] 潜(潛)在的 qiánzài de; [+ answer, cause, solution] 可接受的 kě jiēshòu de ▶ **it's possible (that...)** 可能(…) kěnéng… ▶ **if possible** 如有可能 rú yǒu kěnéng ▶ **as soon as possible** 尽(盡)快 jìnkuài

possibly ['pɒsɪblɪ] ADV (perhaps) 大概 dàgài

post [pəust] I N 1 (Brit) ▶ **the post** (service, system) 邮(郵)政 yóuzhèng; (letters, delivery) 邮(郵)件 yóujiàn 2 [c] (pole) 柱子 zhùzi [根 gēn] 3 [c] (job) 职(職)位 zhíwèi [个 gè] II VT 1 (Brit) [+ letter] 邮(郵)寄 yóujì 2 [on social media] 发(發)布 fābù ▶ **by post** (Brit) 以邮(郵)件的方式 yǐ yóujiàn de fāngshì

postbox ['pəustbɒks] (Brit) N [c] (in street) 邮(郵)筒 yóutǒng [个 gè]

postcard ['pəustkɑːd] N [c] 明信片 míngxìnpiàn [张 zhāng]

postcode ['pəustkəud] (Brit) N [c] 邮(郵)政编(編)码(碼) yóuzhèng biānmǎ [个 gè]

poster ['pəustə'] N [c] 海报(報) hǎibào [张 zhāng]

postman ['pəustmən] (pl postmen) (Brit) N [c] 邮(郵)递(遞)员(員) yóudìyuán [位 wèi]

post office N [c] 邮(郵)局 yóujú [个 gè]

postpone [pəus'pəun] VT 推迟(遲) tuīchí

postwoman ['pəustwumən] (pl postwomen) (Brit) N [c] 女邮(郵)递(遞)员(員) nǚyóudìyuán [位 wèi]

pot [pɒt] N 1 [c] (for cooking) 锅(鍋) guō [口 kǒu] 2 [c] (also: teapot) 茶壶(壺) cháhú [个 gè] 3 [c] (also: coffeepot) 咖啡壶(壺) kāfēihú [个 gè] 4 [c] (for paint, jam, marmalade, honey) 罐 guàn [个 gè] 5 [c] (also: flowerpot) 花盆 huāpén [个 gè]

potato [pə'teɪtəu] (pl potatoes) N [c/u] 马(馬)铃(鈴)薯 mǎlíngshǔ [个 gè] 土豆 tǔdòu [个 gè]

potato chips (US) NPL 薯片 shǔpiàn

pottery ['pɒtərɪ] N 1 [u] (work, hobby) 陶艺(藝) táoyì 2 [c] (factory, workshop) 制(製)陶厂(廠) zhìtáochǎng [家 jiā]

pound [paund] N [c] 1 (unit of money)

镑(鎊) bàng **2** (unit of weight) 磅 bàng ▸ **a pound coin** 1镑(鎊)硬币(幣) yī bàng yìngbì ▸ **a five-pound note** 5 镑(鎊)纸(紙)币(幣) wǔ bàng zhǐbì ▸ **half a pound (of sth)** 半磅(某物) bànbàng (mǒuwù)

pour [pɔːʳ] VT ▸ **to pour sth (into/onto sth)** 灌某物（到某物里(裡)/上）guàn mǒuwù (dào mǒuwù li/shang) ▸ **it is pouring (with rain), it is pouring down** 大雨如注 dàyǔ rúzhù

poverty ['pɒvətɪ] N [U] 贫(貧)穷(窮) pínqióng

powder ['paʊdəʳ] N [C/U] 粉 fěn [袋 dài]

power ['paʊəʳ] N [U] **1** (control) 权(權)力 quánlì **2** (electricity) 电(電)力 diànlì

powerful ['paʊəful] ADJ **1** (influential) 有影响(響)力的 yǒu yǐngxiǎnglì de **2** (physically strong) 强(強)健的 qiángjiàn de **3** [+ engine, machine] 大功率的 dà gōnglǜ de

practical ['præktɪkl] ADJ **1** [+ difficulties, experience] 实(實)践(踐)的 shíjiàn de **2** [+ ideas, methods, advice, suggestions] 切合实(實)际(際)的 qièhé shíjì de **3** [+ person, mind] 有实(實)际(際)经(經)验(驗)的 yǒu shíjì jīngyàn de

practically ['præktɪklɪ] ADV 几(幾)乎 jīhū

practice ['præktɪs] I N [U] (exercise, training) 练(練)习(習) liànxí **2** [c] (training session) 实(實)习(習) shíxí [次 cì] II VT, VI (US) = **practise** ▸ **in practice** (in reality) 实(實)际(際)上 shíjìshang ▸ **2 hours' piano practice** 2小时(時)的练(練)琴时(時)间(間) èr xiǎoshí de liànqín shíjiān

practise, (US) **practice** ['præktɪs] I VT 练(練)习(習) liànxí II VI 练(練)习(習) liànxí

praise [preɪz] VT 称(稱)赞(讚) chēngzàn

pram [præm] (Brit) N [C] 婴(嬰)儿(兒)车(車) yīng'érchē [辆 liàng]

prawn [prɔːn] (Brit) N [C] 虾(蝦)xiā [只 zhī]

pray [preɪ] VI 祷(禱)告 dǎogào

prayer [prɛəʳ] (Rel) N [C] (words) 祈祷(禱)文 qídǎowén [篇 piān]

precaution [prɪ'kɔːʃən] N [C] 预(預)防措施 yùfáng cuòshī [项 xiàng]

precious ['prɛʃəs] ADJ [+ time, resource,

memories] 宝(寶)贵(貴)的 bǎoguì de; (financially) 贵(貴)重的 guìzhòng de

precise [prɪ'saɪs] ADJ **1** [+ time, nature, position, circumstances] 精确(確)的 jīngquè de; [+ figure, definition] 准(準)确(確)的 zhǔnquè de; [+ explanation] 清晰的 qīngxī de **2** [+ instructions, plans] 详(詳)尽(盡)的 xiángjìn de

precisely [prɪ'saɪslɪ] ADV (exactly) 确(確)地 quèdì de; (referring to time) 正好 zhènghǎo

predict [prɪ'dɪkt] VT 预(預)言 yùyán

prediction [prɪ'dɪkʃən] N [C] 预(預)言 yùyán [种 zhǒng]

prefer [prɪ'fəːʳ] VT 偏爱(愛) piān'ài ▸ **to prefer coffee to tea** 喜欢(歡)咖啡胜(勝)于(於)茶 xǐhuan kāfēi shèngyú chá ▸ **I'd prefer to go by train** 我宁(寧)愿(願)坐火车(車)去 wǒ nìngyuàn zuò huǒchē qù

pregnant ['prɛgnənt] ADJ 怀(懷)孕的 huáiyùn de ▸ **3 months pregnant** 怀(懷)孕3个(個)月 huáiyùn sān gè yuè

prejudice ['prɛdʒudɪs] N [C/U] 偏见(見) piānjiàn [个 gè]

Premier League (Brit: Football) N ▸ **the Premier League** 超级(級)联(聯)赛(賽) Chāojí Liánsài

preparation [prɛpə'reɪʃən] I N [U] 准(準)备(備) zhǔnbèi II **preparations** N PL (arrangements) ▸ **preparations (for sth)** （为(為)某事的）准(準)备(備)工作 (wèi mǒushì de) zhǔnbèi gōngzuò ▸ **in preparation for sth** 为(為)某事而准(準)备(備)的 wèi mǒushì ér zhǔnbèi de

prepare [prɪ'pɛəʳ] I VT 准(準)备(備) zhǔnbèi; [+ food, meal] 预(預)备(備) yùbèi II VI ▸ **to prepare (for sth)** （为(為)某事）做准(準)备(備) (wèi mǒushì) zuò zhǔnbèi ▸ **to prepare to do sth** (get ready) 准(準)备(備)好做某事 zhǔnbèihǎo zuò mǒushì

prepared [prɪ'pɛəd] ADJ ▸ **to be prepared to do sth** (willing) 有意做某事 yǒuyì zuò mǒushì ▸ **prepared (for sth)** (ready) （对(對)某事）有所准(準)备(備)的 (duì mǒushì) yǒu suǒ zhǔnbèi de

prescribe [prɪ'skraɪb] VT (Med) 开(開) kāi

prescription [prɪ'skrɪpʃən] N [C] (Med: slip of paper) 处(處)方 chǔfāng [个 gè];

(*medicine*) 药(藥)方 yàofāng [个 gè]

present ['preznt I ADJ 1 (*current*) 现(現)有的 xiànyǒu de **2** (*in attendance*) 在场(場)的 zàichǎng de II N **1** (*not past*) ▸ **the present** 目前 mùqián **2** [c] (*gift*) 礼(禮)物 lǐwù [件 jiàn] **3** ▸ **the present** (*also: present tense*) 现(現)在时(時)态(態) xiànzài shítài [个 gè] ▸ **to be present at sth** 出席某事 chūxí mǒushì ▸ **to give sb a present** 给(給)某人礼(禮)物 gěi mǒurén lǐwù

president ['prezɪdənt] N [c] (*Pol*) 总(總)统(統) zǒngtǒng [位 wèi]

press [pres] I N ▸ **the press** 新闻(聞)界 xīnwénjiè II VT **1** [+ *button, switch, bell*] 按 àn **2** (*iron*) 熨平 yùnpíng ▸ **to be pressed for time/money** 时(時)间(間)紧(緊)迫/手头(頭)紧(緊) shíjiān jǐnpò/shǒutóu jǐn

pressure ['preʃəʳ] N **1** [U] (*physical force*) 压(壓)力 yālì **2** [U] ▸ **pressure (to do sth)** (做某事的)压(壓)力 (zuò mǒushì de) yālì **3** [c/U] (*stress*) 压(壓)力 yālì [种 zhǒng] ▸ **to put pressure on sb (to do sth)** 对(對)某人施加压(壓)力(去做某事) duì mǒurén shījiā yālì (qù zuò mǒushì)

pretend [prɪ'tend] VT ▸ **to pretend to do sth/pretend that...** 假装(裝)做某事/假装(裝)… jiǎzhuāng zuò mǒushì/jiǎzhuāng...

pretty ['prɪtɪ] I ADJ 漂亮的 piàoliang de II ADV [+ *good, happy, soon etc*] 相当(當) xiāngdāng

prevent [prɪ'vent] VT [+ *war, disease, situation*] 防止 zǔzhǐ; [+ *accident, fire*] 防止 fángzhǐ ▸ **to prevent sb (from) doing sth** 阻止某人做某事 zǔzhǐ mǒurén zuò mǒushì ▸ **to prevent sth (from) happening** 防止某事发(發)生 fángzhǐ mǒushì fāshēng

previous ['pri:vɪəs] ADJ **1** [+ *marriage, relationship, experience, owner*] 前的 qián de **2** [+ *chapter, week, day*] 以前的 yǐqián de

previously ['pri:vɪəslɪ] ADV **1** 以前 yǐqián **2** ▸ **10 days previously** 10天前 shí tiān qián

price [praɪs] N [c/U] 价(價)格 jiàgé [种 zhǒng]

pride [praɪd] N [U] 自豪 zìháo ▸ **to take (a) pride in sb/sth** 因某人/某事而自豪 yīn mǒurén/mǒushì ér zìháo

priest [pri:st] N [c] 神职(職)人员(員) shénzhí rényuán [位 wèi]

primarily ['praɪmərɪlɪ] ADV 主要地 zhǔyào de

primary school ['praɪmərɪ-] (*Brit*) N [c/U] 小学(學) xiǎoxué [所 suǒ]

Prime Minister [praɪm-] N [c] 总(總)理 zǒnglǐ [位 wèi]

prince [prɪns] N [c] 王子 wángzǐ [位 wèi]

princess [prɪn'ses] N [c] 公主 gōngzhǔ [位 wèi]

principal ['prɪnsɪpl] I ADJ 主要的 zhǔyào de II N [c] (*of school, college*) 校长(長) xiàozhǎng [位 wèi]

principle ['prɪnsɪpl] N [c/U] 准(準)则(則) zhǔnzé [个 gè] ▸ **in principle** (*in theory*) 原则(則)上 yuánzé shang

print [prɪnt] I N [c] (*photograph*) 照片 zhàopiàn [张 zhāng] II VT **1** [+ *story, article*] 出版 chūbǎn **2** (*stamp*) 印 yìn **3** (*write*) 用印刷体(體)写(寫) yòng yìnshuātǐ xiě **4** (*Comput*) 打印 dǎyìn ▸ **print out** VT 打印出 dǎyìnchū

printer ['prɪntəʳ] N [c] 打印机(機) dǎyìnjī [台 tái]

printout ['prɪntaut] N [c] 打印输(輸)出 dǎyìn shūchū [次 cì]

priority [praɪ'ɔrɪtɪ] I N [c] (*concern*) 重点(點) zhòngdiǎn [个 gè] II **priorities** NPL 优(優)先考虑(慮)的事 yōuxiān kǎolǜ de shì ▸ **to give priority to sth/sb** 给(給)某事/某人以优(優)先权(權) gěi mǒushì/mǒurén yǐ yōuxiānquán

prison ['prɪzn] N **1** [c/U] (*institution*) 监(監)狱(獄) jiānyù [所 suǒ] **2** [U] (*imprisonment*) 坐牢 zuòláo ▸ **in prison** 坐牢 zuòláo

prisoner ['prɪznəʳ] N [c] 囚犯 qiúfàn [个 gè]

private ['praɪvɪt] ADJ **1** [+ *property, land, plane*] 私人的 sīrén de **2** [+ *education, housing, health care, industries*] 私有的 sīyǒu de **3** (*confidential*) 秘(祕)密的 mìmì de **4** [+ *life, thoughts, plans, affairs, belongings*] 私人的 sīrén de ▸ **in private** 私下 sīxià

prize [praɪz] N [c] 奖(獎)金 jiǎng [个 gè]

prizewinner ['praɪzwɪnəʳ] N [c] 获(獲)
奖(獎)者 huòjiǎngzhě [位 wèi]
pro [prəʊ] PREP (in favour of) 赞(贊)成
zànchéng
probability [prɒbə'bɪlɪtɪ] N [c/u]
▸ probability (of sth/that...)
(某事/…的) 可能性 (mǒushì/…de)
kěnéngxìng [种 zhǒng]
probable ['prɒbəbl] ADJ 可能的
kěnéng de
probably ['prɒbəblɪ] ADV 可能 kěnéng
problem ['prɒbləm] N [c] 难(難)题(題)
nántí [个 gè] ▸ what's the problem?
有什么(麼)问(問)题(題)吗(嗎)? yǒu
shénme wèntí ma ▸ I had no problem
finding her 我要找她不难(難) wǒ yào
zhǎo tā bù nán ▸ no problem! (inf)
没(沒)问(問)题(題)! méi wèntí!
process ['prəʊsɛs] I N [c] (procedure)
过(過)程 guòchéng [个 gè] II VT
(Comput) [+ data] 处(處)理 chǔlǐ ▸ to be
in the process of doing sth 在从(從)事
某事的过(過)程中 zài cóngshì mǒushì
de guòchéng zhōng
produce prə'djuːs] VT 1 [+ effect, result]
促成 cùchéng 2 [+ goods, commodity]
生产(產) shēngchǎn 3 [+ play, film,
programme] 上演 shàngyǎn
producer [prə'djuːsəʳ] N [c] 1 [of film, play,
programme] 制(製)片人 zhìpiànrén [位
wèi] 2 [of food, material] (country) 产(產)
地 chǎndì [个 gè]; (company) 制(製)造
zhìzàoshāng [个 gè]
product ['prɒdʌkt] N [c] 产(產)品
chǎnpǐn [个 gè]
production [prə'dʌkʃən] N 1 [u] 生
产(產) shēngchǎn 2 (amount produced,
amount grown) 产(產)量 chǎnliàng
2 [c] (play, show) 作品 zuòpǐn [部 bù]
profession [prə'fɛʃən] N [c] 职(職)
业(業) zhíyè [种 zhǒng]
professional [prə'fɛʃənl] ADJ
1 [+ photographer, musician, footballer]
职(職)业(業)的 zhíyè de; [+ advice, help]
专(專)业(業)的 zhuānyè de 2 (skilful)
专(專)业(業)水平的 zhuānyè shuǐpíng de
professor [prə'fɛsəʳ] N [c] 1 (Brit) 教授
jiàoshòu [位 wèi] 2 (US) 教员(員)
jiàoyuán [位 wèi]
profile ['prəʊfaɪl] N [c] (Comput) 个(個)人
资(資)料 gèrén zīliào

profile picture N [c] (Comput) 头(頭)像
tóuxiàng
profit ['prɒfɪt] N [c/u] 利润(潤) lìrùn ▸ to
make a profit 赚(賺)钱(錢) zhuànqián
profitable ['prɒfɪtəbl] ADJ 有利润(潤)的
yǒu lìrùn de
program ['prəʊgræm] I N [c] 1 (also:
computer program) 程序 chéngxù [个
gè] 2 (US) = **programme** II VT 1 (Comput)
▸ to program sth (to do sth) 为(為)某
物编(編)程 (做某事) wèi mǒuwù
biānchéng (zuò mǒushì) 2 (US)
= **programme**
programme, (US) **program** ['prə
ʊgræm] I N [c] 1 (Rad, TV) 节(節)目
jiémù [个 gè] 2 (for theatre, concert)
节(節)目宣传(傳)(册(冊)) jiémù
xuānchuáncè [本 běn] 3 [of talks, events,
performances] 节(節)目单(單) jiémùdān
[个 gè] II VT ▸ to programme sth (to do
sth) [+ machine, system] 设(設)定某事
(做某事) shèdìng mǒushì (zuò
mǒushì); see also/另见 **program**
programmer ['prəʊgræməʳ] (Comput)
N [c] 程序员(員) chéngxùyuán
[位 wèi]
progress ['prəʊgrɛs N [u] 1 (headway)
进(進)展 jìnzhǎn 2 (advances) 进(進)步
jìnbù ▸ to make progress (with sth)
(对(對)某事)取得进(進)步 (duì
mǒushì) qǔdé jìnbù
project ['prɒdʒɛkt] N [c] 工程
gōngchéng [个 gè]
promise ['prɒmɪs] I N [c] 许(許)诺(諾)
xǔnuò [个 gè] II VI 保证(證) bǎozhèng
III VT ▸ to promise sb sth, promise sth
to sb 保证(證)给(給)某人某物
bǎozhèng gěi mǒurén mǒuwù ▸ to
break/keep a promise (to do sth)
违(違)背/遵守(做某事的)诺(諾)言
wéibèi/zūnshǒu (zuò mǒushì de)
nuòyán ▸ to promise to do sth 保
证(證)做某事 bǎozhèng zuò mǒushì
promotion [prə'məʊʃən] N [c/u] 晋(晉)
级(級) jìnjí [次 cì]
prompt [prɒmpt] I ADJ 1 (on time) 干(乾)
脆的 gāncuì de 2 (for rapid) [+ action,
response] 迅速的 xùnsù de II N [c]
(Comput) 提示符 tíshìfú [个 gè]
▸ at 8 o'clock prompt 8点(點)整
bā diǎn zhěng

pronoun ['prəunaun] N [c] 代词(詞)
dàicí [个 gè]

pronounce [prə'nauns] VT 发(發)音
fāyīn

pronunciation [prənʌnsɪ'eɪʃən] N [c/u]
发(發)音 fāyīn [个 gè]

proof [pru:f] N [u] 证(證)据(據) zhèngjù

proper ['prɒpəʳ] ADJ [+ procedure, place,
word] 恰当(當)的 qiàdàng de

properly ['prɒpəlɪ] ADV 1 [eat, work,
concentrate +] 充分地 chōngfèn de
2 [behave +] 体(體)面地 tǐmiàn de

property ['prɒpətɪ] N 1 [u] (possessions)
财(財)产(產) cáichǎn 2 [c/u] (buildings
and land) 地产(產) dìchǎn [处 chù]

prostitute ['prɒstɪtjuːt] N [c] (female) 妓
女 jìnǚ [个 gè] ▶ a male prostitute 男妓
nánjì

protect [prə'tɛkt] VT 保护(護) bǎohù
▶ to protect sb/sth from or against sth
保护(護)某人/某物不受某物的伤(傷)害
bǎohù mǒurén/mǒuwù bù shòu mǒuwù
de shānghài

protection [prə'tɛkʃən] N [c/u]
▶ protection (from or against sth)
（免受某物侵害的）保护(護)（miǎnshòu
mǒuwù qīnhài de）bǎohù [种 zhǒng]

protest [n 'prəutɛst, vb prə'tɛst] I N [c/u]
抗议(議) kàngyì [个 gè] II VI ▶ to
protest about/against/at sth (Brit) 抗
议(議)某事 kàngyì mǒushì III VT (US:
voice opposition to) 示威 shìwēi

Protestant ['prɒtɪstənt] I N [c] 新教徒
Xīnjiàotú [个 gè] II ADJ 新教的 Xīnjiào de

protester [prə'tɛstəʳ] N [c] 抗议(議)者
kàngyìzhě [名 míng]

proud [praud] ADJ 1 [+ parents, owner] 自
豪的 zìháo de 2 (arrogant) 骄(驕)傲的
jiāo'ào de ▶ to be proud of sb/sth
为(為)某人/某事感到自豪 wèi mǒurén/
mǒushì gǎndào zìháo

prove [pruːv] I VT [+ idea, theory] 证(證)明
zhèngmíng II VI ▶ to prove that...
[person +] 证(證)明… zhèngmíng…;
[situation, experiment, calculations +]
显(顯)示… xiǎnshì… ▶ to prove sb
right/wrong 证(證)明某人是对(對)
的/错(錯)的 zhèngmíng mǒurén shì duì
de/cuò de

provide [prə'vaɪd] VT [+ food, money,
shelter] 供应(應) gōngyìng; [+ answer,

opportunity, details] 提供 tígōng ▶ to
provide sb with sth 提供某人某物
tígōng mǒurén mǒuwù

provided (that) [prə'vaɪd-] CONJ 假
如 jiǎrú

PS ABBR (= postscript) 附言 fùyán

psychiatrist [saɪ'kaɪətrɪst] N [c] 精神病
医(醫)生 jīngshénbìng yīshēng [位 wèi]

psychological [saɪkə'lɒdʒɪkl] ADJ 心理
的 xīnlǐ de

psychologist [saɪ'kɒlədʒɪst] N [c] 心理
学(學)家 xīnlǐxuéjiā [位 wèi]

psychology [saɪ'kɒlədʒɪ] N [u] 心理
学(學) xīnlǐxué

PTO ABBR (= please turn over) 请(請)翻
过(過)来(來) qǐng fān guòlái

pub [pʌb] (Brit) N [c] 酒吧 jiǔbā [个 gè]

public ['pʌblɪk] I ADJ 1 [+ support, opinion,
interest] 公众(眾)的 gōngzhòng de
2 [+ building, service, library] 公共的
gōnggòng de 3 [+ announcement, meeting]
公开(開)的 gōngkāi de II N [s + PL VB]
▶ the (general) public 民众(眾)
mínzhòng

public holiday N [c] 法定假期 fǎdìng
jiàqī [个 gè]

publicity [pʌb'lɪsɪtɪ] N [u] 1 (information,
advertising) 宣传(傳) xuānchuán
2 (attention) 关(關)注 guānzhù

public school N [c/u] 1 (Brit: private
school) 私立中学(學) sīlì zhōngxué [所
suǒ] 2 (US: state school) 公立学(學)校
gōnglì xuéxiào [所 suǒ]

public transport N [u] 公共交通
gōnggòng jiāotōng

publish ['pʌblɪʃ] VT [+ book, magazine] 出
版 chūbǎn

publisher ['pʌblɪʃəʳ] N [c] (company) 出版
社 chūbǎnshè [家 jiā]

pudding ['pudɪŋ] N [c/u] (Brit: dessert in
general) 甜点(點) tiándiǎn [份 fèn]

puddle ['pʌdl] N [c] 水坑 shuǐkēng [个 gè]

pull [pul] I VT 1 [+ rope, hair] 拖 tuō;
[+ handle, door, cart, carriage] 拉 lā
2 [+ trigger] 扣(釦) kòu II VI 猛拉
měnglā ▶ to pull a muscle 扭伤(傷)肌
肉 niǔshāng jīròu ▶ to pull sb's leg (fig)
开(開)某人的玩笑 kāi mǒurén de
wánxiào
▶ **pull down** VT [+ building] 拆毁(毀)
chāihuǐ

▶ **pull in** vɪ (*at the kerb*) 停了下来(來) tíngle xiàlái

▶ **pull out** vɪ **1** (*Aut: from kerb*) 开(開)出 kāichū; (*when overtaking*) 超车(車) chāochē **2** 退出 tuìchū

▶ **pull through** vɪ (*from illness*) 恢复(復) 健康 huīfù jiànkāng; (*from difficulties*) 渡 过(過)难(難)关(關) dùguò nánguān

▶ **pull up** I vɪ (*stop*) 停下 tíngxià II vᴛ **1** (*raise*) (*socks, trousers*) 拉起 lāqǐ **2** (*+ plant, weed*) 拔除 báchú

pull-off ['pʊlɔf] (*US*) N [c] 路侧(側)停 车(車)处(處) lùcè tíngchēchù [个 gè]

pullover ['pʊləʊvəʳ] N [c] 套头(頭)衫 tàotóushān [件 jiàn]

pulse [pʌls] N [c] (*Anat*) 脉(脈)搏 màibó [下 xià] ▶ **to take** *or* **feel sb's pulse** 给(給)某人诊(診)脉(脈) gěi mǒurén zhěnmài

pump [pʌmp] N [c] **1** (*for liquid, gas*) 泵 bèng [个 gè] **2** (*for getting water*) 抽水 机(機) chōushuǐjī [台 tái] **3** (*for inflating sth*) 打气(氣)筒 dǎqìtǒng [个 gè]

▶ **water/petrol pump** 水/油泵 shuǐ/ yóubèng

▶ **pump up** vᴛ 打气(氣) dǎqì

punch [pʌntʃ] I N [c] **1** (*for liquid, gas*) 拳打 quándǎ [顿 dùn] II vᴛ **1** (*hit*) 用拳打击(擊) yòng quán dǎjī **2** (*+ button, keyboard*) 敲 击(擊) qiāojī **3** (*+ ticket, paper*) 在…上打 孔 zài…shang dǎkǒng

▶ **punch in** vᴛ 敲入 qiāorù

punctual ['pʌŋktjʊəl] ADJ 准(準)时(時) 的 zhǔnshí de

punctuation [pʌŋktjuˈeɪʃən] N [u] 标(標)点(點) biāodiǎn

puncture ['pʌŋktʃəʳ] I N [c] 刺孔 cìkǒng [个 gè] II vᴛ (*+ tyre, lung*) 戳破 chuōpò ▶ **to have a puncture** 轮(輪)胎被扎破 了 lúntāi bèi zhāpò le

punish ['pʌnɪʃ] vᴛ 惩(懲)罚(罰) chéngfá ▶ **to punish sb for sth/for doing sth** 因某事/做某事而惩(懲)罚(罰)某人 yīn mǒushì/zuò mǒushì ér chéngfá mǒurén

punishment ['pʌnɪʃmənt] N **1** [u] 惩(懲)罚(罰) chéngfá **2** [c/u] (*penalty*) 处(處)罚(罰) chǔfá [次 cì]

pupil ['pju:pl] N [c] 学(學)生 xuésheng [名 míng]

puppy ['pʌpɪ] N [c] 小狗 xiǎogǒu [只 zhī]

purchase ['pə:tʃɪs] (*frm*) vᴛ 购(購)买(買) gòumǎi

pure [pjʊəʳ] ADJ **1** (*+ silk, gold, wool*) 纯(純) 的 chún de **2** (*clean*) 纯(純)净(淨)的 chúnjìng de

purple ['pə:pl] I ADJ 紫色的 zǐsè de II N [c/u] 紫色 zǐsè [种 zhǒng]

purpose ['pə:pəs] N [c] **1** (*of person*) 目的 mùdì [个 gè] **2** (*of act, meeting, visit*) 意 义(義) yìyì [个 gè] ▶ **on purpose** 故意地 gùyì de

purse [pə:s] N [c] **1** (*Brit: for money*) 钱(錢) 包 qiánbāo [个 gè] **2** (*US: handbag*) 手袋 shǒudài [个 gè]

push [pʊʃ] I N [c] 推 tuī II vᴛ **1** (*+ button*) 按 àn **2** (*+ car, door, person*) 推 tuī III vɪ **1** (*press*) 按 àn **2** (*shove*) 推 tuī ▶ **at the push of a button** 只要按一下按钮(鈕) zhǐyào àn yīxià ànniǔ ▶ **to push one's way through the crowd** 挤(擠)过(過) 人群 jǐguò rénqún ▶ **to push sth/sb out of the way** 把某物/某人推开(開) bǎ mǒuwù/mǒurén tuīkāi ▶ **to push a door open/shut** 把门(門)推开(開)/上 bǎ mén tuīkāi/shàng ▶ **to be pushed for time/money** (*inf*) 赶(趕)时(時)间(間)/ 缺钱(錢) gǎn shíjiān/quēqián ▶ **to push forward/push through the crowd** 挤(擠)向/过(過)人群 jǐxiàng/guò rénqún

▶ **push in** vɪ (*in queue*) 插队(隊) chāduì

▶ **push over** vᴛ (*+ person, wall, furniture*) 推倒 tuīdǎo

▶ **push up** vᴛ (*+ total, prices*) 提高 tígāo

pushchair ['pʊʃtʃeəʳ] (*Brit*) N [c] 幼儿(兒) 车(車) yòu'érchē [辆 liàng]

put [pʊt] (*pt, pp* **put**) vᴛ **1** (*+ thing*) 放 fàng; (*+ person*) (*in institution*) 安置 ānzhì **2** (*write, type*) 写(寫) xiě ▶ **to put a lot of time/energy/effort into sth/into doing sth** 投入大量的时(時)间(間)/精力/努 力于(於)某事/做某事 tóurù dàliàng de shíjiān/jīnglì/nǔlì yú mǒushì/zuò mǒushì ▶ **how shall I put it?** 我该(該)怎么(麼) 说(說)呢? wǒ gāi zěnme shuō ne?

▶ **put across, put over** vᴛ (*+ ideas, argument*) 讲(講)清 jiǎngqīng

▶ **put away** vᴛ 把…收起 bǎ…shōuqǐ

▶ **put back** vᴛ **1** (*replace*) 放回 fànghuí **2** (*+ watch, clock*) 倒拨(撥) dàobō

▶ **put down** vᴛ **1** (*on floor, table*) 放下

fàngxià **2** (*in writing*) 写(寫)下 xiěxià

▶ **put forward** VT [+ *ideas, proposal, name*] 提出 tíchū

▶ **put in** VT **1** [+ *request, complaint, application*] 提出 tíchū **2** (*install*) 安装(裝) ānzhuāng

▶ **put off** VT (*delay*) 推迟(遲) tuīchí; (*Brit: distract*) 使分心 shǐ fēnxīn; (*discourage*) 使失去兴(興)趣 shǐ shīqù xìngqù ▶ **to put off doing sth** (*postpone*) 推迟(遲)做某事 tuīchí zuò mǒushì

▶ **put on** VT **1** [+ *clothes, make-up, glasses*] 穿戴 chuāndài **2** [+ *light, TV, radio, oven*] 开(開) kāi; [+ *CD, video*] 放 fàng ▶ **to put on weight/three kilos** *etc* 增重/增加了3公斤{等} zēngzhòng/zēngjiāle sān gōngjīn {děng}

▶ **put out** VT **1** [+ *candle, cigarette*] 熄灭(滅) xīmiè; [+ *fire, blaze*] 扑(撲)灭(滅) pūmiè **2** (*switch off*) 关(關) guān **3** 麻烦(煩) máfan

▶ **put over** VT = **put across**

▶ **put through** VT (*Tel*) 接通 jiētōng ▶ **put me through to Miss Blair** 请(請)帮(幫)我接布莱(萊)尔(爾)小姐 qǐng bāng wǒ jiē Bùláiěr xiǎojiě

▶ **put up** VT **1** [+ *fence, building, tent*] 建造 jiànzào; [+ *poster, sign*] 张(張)贴(貼) zhāngtiē **2** [+ *umbrella, hood*] 撑(撐)起 chēngqǐ **3** [+ *price, cost*] 增加 zēngjiā **4** (*accommodate*) 为(為)…提供住宿 wèi…tígōng zhùsù ▶ **to put up one's hand** 举(舉)手 jǔshǒu

▶ **put up with** VT FUS 容忍 róngrěn

puzzle ['pʌzl] N [c] 谜(謎) mí [个 gè]; (*toy*) 测(測)智玩具 cèzhì wánjù [套 tào] **2** [s] (*mystery*) 谜(謎)团(團) mítuán

puzzled ['pʌzld] ADJ 茫然的 mángrán de

pyjamas, (US) **pajamas** [pə'dʒɑ:məz] NPL 睡衣裤(褲) shuìyīkù ▶ **a pair of pyjamas** 一套睡衣裤(褲) yī tào shuìyīkù

pylon ['paɪlən] N [c] 电(電)缆(纜)塔 diànlǎntǎ [座 zuò]

pyramid ['pɪrəmɪd] N [c] 金字塔 jīnzìtǎ [座 zuò]

q

qualification [kwɔlɪfɪ'keɪʃən] N [c] 资(資)格证(證)明 zīgé zhèngmíng [个 gè]

qualified ['kwɔlɪfaɪd] ADJ 合格的 hégé de ▶ **fully qualified** 完全合格的 wánquán hégé de

qualify ['kwɔlɪfaɪ] VI **1** (*pass examinations*) 取得资(資)格 qǔdé zīgé **2** (*in competition*) 具备(備)资(資)格 jùbèi zīgé ▶ **to qualify as an engineer/a nurse** *etc* 取得工程师(師)/护(護)士{等}的资(資)格 qǔdé gōngchéngshī/hùshì děng de zīgé

quality ['kwɔlɪtɪ] N **1** [U] (*standard*) 质(質)量 zhìliàng **2** [c] (*characteristic*) [*of person*] 素质(質) sùzhì [种 zhǒng] ▶ **quality of life** 生活质(質)量 shēnghuó zhìliàng

quantity ['kwɔntɪtɪ] N **1** [c/U] (*amount*) 数(數)量 shùliàng **2** [U] (*volume*) 容量 róngliàng ▶ **in large/small quantities** 大/少量 dà/shǎoliàng

quarantine ['kwɔrənti:n] N [U] 检(檢)疫隔离(離) jiǎnyì ▶ **in quarantine** 被隔离(離) bèi gélí

quarrel ['kwɔrəl] I N [c] 吵架 chǎojià [场 chǎng] II VI 争(爭)吵 zhēngchǎo

quarry ['kwɔrɪ] N [c] 采(採)石场(場) cǎishíchǎng [座 zuò]

quarter ['kwɔ:təʳ] N [c] 四分之一 sìfēnzhīyī ▶ **to cut/divide sth into quarters** 把某物切/分为(為)4份 bǎ mǒuwù qiē/fēnwéi sì fèn ▶ **a quarter of**

an hour 一刻钟(鐘) yīkèzhōng ▸ **it's a quarter to three** or (US) **of three** 现(現)在是三点(點)差一刻 xiànzài shì sān diǎn chà yīkè ▸ **it's a quarter past three** or (US) **after three** 现(現)在是三点(點)一刻 xiànzài shì sān diǎn yīkè

quarter-final [ˈkwɔːtəˈfaɪnl] N [c] 四分之一决(決)赛(賽) sìfēnzhīyī juésài [场(場) chǎng]

quay [kiː] N [c] 码(碼)头(頭) mǎtóu [个 gè]

queen [kwiːn] N [c] **1** (monarch) 女王 nǚwáng [位 wèi] **2** (king's wife) 王后 wánghòu [位 wèi]

query [ˈkwɪərɪ] I N [c] 疑问(問) yíwèn [个 gè] II VT [+ figures, bill, expenses] 询(詢)问(問) xúnwèn

question [ˈkwɛstʃən] I N **1** [c] (query) 问(問)题(題) wèntí [个 gè] **2** [c] (issue) 议(議)题(題) yìtí [项 xiàng] **3** [c] (in written exam) 试(試)题(題) shìtí [道 dào] II VT (interrogate) 盘(盤)问(問) pánwèn ▸ **to ask sb a question, to put a question to sb** 问(問)某人一个(個)问(問)题(題), 向某人提出问(問)题(題) wèn mǒurén yī gè wèntí, xiàng mǒurén tíchū wèntí ▸ **to be out of the question** 不可能的 bù kěnéng de

question mark N [c] 问(問)号(號) wènhào [个 gè]

questionnaire [kwɛstʃəˈnɛəʳ] N [c] 问(問)卷 wènjuàn [份 fèn]

queue [kjuː] (esp Brit) I N [c] 队(隊)伍 duì [支 zhī] II VI (also: queue up) 排队(隊) páiduì ▸ **to queue for sth** 为(為)某事排队(隊) wèi mǒushì páiduì

quick [kwɪk] I ADJ **1** (fast) 快的 kuài de **2** [+ look] 快速的 kuàisù de; [+ visit] 短时(時)间(間)的 duǎn shíjiān de **3** [+ reply, response, decision] 迅速的 xùnsù de II ADV (inf: quickly) 快地 kuài de ▸ **be quick!** 快点(點)! kuài diǎn!

quickly [ˈkwɪklɪ] ADV **1** [walk, grow, speak, work +] 快地 kuài de **2** [realize, change, react, finish +] 迅速地 xùnsù de

quiet [ˈkwaɪət] ADJ **1** [+ voice, music] 悄声(聲)的 qiāoshēng de **2** [+ place] 安静(靜)的 ānjìng de **2** [+ person] 平静(靜)的 píngjìng de **3** (silent) ▸ **to be quiet** 沉默的 chénmò de ▸ **be quiet!** 请(請)安静(靜)! qǐng ānjìng!

quietly [ˈkwaɪətlɪ] ADV **1** [speak, play +] 安静(靜)地 ānjìng de **2** (silently) 默默地 mòmò de

quilt [kwɪlt] N [c] **1** 被子 bèizi [床 chuáng] **2** (Brit: duvet) 羽绒(絨)被 yǔróngbèi [床 chuáng]

quit [kwɪt] (pt, pp quit or quitted) I VT **1** (esp US: give up) [+ habit, activity] 摆(擺)脱(脫) bǎituō **2** (inf: leave) [+ job] 辞(辭)去 cíqù II VI (give up) 放弃(棄) fàngqì **2** (resign) 辞(辭)职(職) cízhí

quite [kwaɪt] ADV **1** (rather) 相当(當) xiāngdāng **2** (completely) 十分 shífēn ▸ **I see them quite a lot** 我常常见(見)到他们(們) wǒ chángcháng jiàndào tāmen ▸ **quite a lot of money** 很多钱(錢) hěn duō qián ▸ **quite a few** 相当(當)多 xiāngdāng duō ▸ **it's not quite finished** 像是还(還)没(沒)结(結)束 xiàng shì hái méi jiéshù ▸ **quite (so)!** 的确(確)(是这(這)样(樣))! díquè (shì zhèyàng)! ▸ **it was quite a sight** 景色十分壮观(觀) jǐngsè shífēn zhuàngguān

quite 可用在 a 或 an 之前，后接形容词加名词结构。例如，可以说 It's quite an old car 或者 The car is quite old，以及 It was quite a warm day 或者 The day was quite warm。如前例所示，quite 应放在不定冠词之前。例如，不能说 It's a quite old car。quite 可以用来修饰形容词和副词，而且程度比 fairly 更强烈，但是比 very 弱。quite 暗示某事物的某种特性超出预料。Nobody here's ever heard of it but it is actually quite common。注意，不要混淆 quite 和 quiet。

quiz [kwɪz] N [c] (game) 知识竞赛 zhīshi jìngsài [次 cì]

quotation [kwəuˈteɪʃən] N [c] **1** 引语(語) yǐnyǔ [句 jù] **2** (estimate) 报(報)价(價) bàojià [个 gè]

quote [kwəut] I VT [+ politician, author] 引用 yǐnyòng; [+ line] 引述 yǐnshù II N [c] 引语(語) yǐnyǔ [句 jù] III **quotes** NPL (inf: quotation marks) 引号(號) yǐnhào ▸ **in quotes** 在引号(號)里(裡) zài yǐnhào li

r

rabbi ['ræbaɪ] N [c] 拉比(犹太教教师或法学导师)

rabbit ['ræbɪt] N [c] 兔子 tùzi [只 zhī]

rabies ['reɪbiːz] N [u] 狂犬病 kuángquǎnbìng

race [reɪs] I N **1** [c] (*speed contest*) 速度竞(競)赛(賽) sùdù jìngsài [场 chǎng] **2** [c/u] (*ethnic group*) 种(種)族 zhǒngzú [个 gè] II vɪ 参(參)赛(賽) cānsài III vт 与(與)…进(進)行速度竞(競)赛(賽) yǔ…jìnxíng sùdù jìngsài ▸ **a race against time** 抢(搶)时(時)间(間) qiǎng shíjiān

race car (*US*) N = **racing car**

racecourse ['reɪskɔːs] (*Brit*) N [c] 赛(賽)马(馬)场(場) sàimǎchǎng [个 gè]

racehorse ['reɪshɔːs] N [c] 赛(賽)马(馬) sàimǎ [匹 pǐ]

racetrack ['reɪstræk] N [c] (*for cars*) 赛(賽)道 sàidào [条 tiáo]; (*US: for horses*) 赛(賽)马(馬)场(場) sàimǎchǎng [个 gè]

racial ['reɪʃl] ADJ 种(種)族的 zhǒngzú de

racing driver ['reɪsɪŋ-] (*Brit*) N [c] 赛(賽)车(車)手 sàichēshǒu [位 wèi]

racism ['reɪsɪzəm] N [u] 种(種)族歧视(視) zhǒngzú qíshì

racist ['reɪsɪst] I ADJ [+ *policy, attack, behaviour, idea*] 种(種)族主义(義)的 zhǒngzú zhǔyì de; [+ *person, organization*] 有种(種)族偏见(見)的 yǒu zhǒngzú piānjiàn de II N [c] 种(種)族主义(義)者 zhǒngzú zhǔyìzhě [个 gè]

rack [ræk] N [c] **1** (*also*: **luggage rack**) 行李架 xínglijià [个 gè] **2** (*for hanging clothes, dishes*) 架 jià [个 gè]

racket ['rækɪt] N [c] 球拍 qiúpāi [副 fù]

racquet ['rækɪt] N [c] 球拍 qiúpāi [副 fù]

radar ['reɪdɑːʳ] N [c/u] 雷达(達) léidá [个 gè]

radiation [reɪdɪ'eɪʃən] N [u] 辐(輻)射 fúshè

radiator ['reɪdɪeɪtəʳ] N [c] 暖气(氣)片 nuǎnqìpiàn [个 gè]

radio ['reɪdɪəu] N **1** [c] (*receiver*) 收音机(機) shōuyīnjī [台 tái] **2** [u] (*broadcasting*) 广(廣)播 guǎngbō ▸ **on the radio** 广(廣)播中 guǎngbō zhōng

radioactive ['reɪdɪəu'æktɪv] ADJ 放射性的 fàngshèxìng de

radio station N [c] 广(廣)播电(電)台(臺) guǎngbō diàntái [个 gè]

RAF (*Brit*) N ABBR (= **Royal Air Force**) ▸ **the RAF** 皇家空军(軍) Huángjiā Kōngjūn

rag [ræg] N [c/u] 破布 pòbù [块 kuài]

rage [reɪdʒ] N [c/u] 盛怒 shèngnù [阵 zhèn]

raid [reɪd] vт [*soldiers, police* +] 突袭(襲) tūxí; [*criminal* +] 袭(襲)击(擊) xíjí

rail [reɪl] N [c] **1** (*for safety on stairs*) 扶手 fúshǒu [个 gè]; (*on bridge, balcony*) 横(横)栏(欄) hénglán [个 gè] **2** (*for hanging clothes*) 横(横)杆 hénggān [根 gēn] **3** (*for trains*) 铁(鐵)轨(軌) tiěguǐ [条 tiáo] ▸ **by rail** 乘火车(車) chéng huǒchē

railroad ['reɪlrəud] (*US*) N [c] = **railway**

railway ['reɪlweɪ] (*Brit*) N [c] **1** (*system*) 铁(鐵)路 tiělù **2** (*line*) 铁(鐵)道 tiědào [条 tiáo]

railway line (*Brit*) N [c] 铁(鐵)路线(線) tiělùxiàn [条 tiáo]

railway station (*Brit*) N [c] 火车(車)站 huǒchēzhàn [个 gè]

rain [reɪn] I N [u] 雨 yǔ II vɪ 下雨 xiàyǔ ▸ **in the rain** 在雨中 zài yǔ zhōng ▸ **it's raining** 正在下雨 zhèng zài xiàyǔ

rainbow ['reɪnbəu] N [c] 彩虹 cǎihóng [道 dào]

raincoat ['reɪnkəut] N [c] 雨衣 yǔyī [件 jiàn]

rainforest ['reɪnfɔrɪst] N [c/u] 雨林 yǔlín [片 piàn]

rainy ['reɪnɪ] ADJ 多雨的 duōyǔ de

raise [reɪz] I vт **1** (*lift*) [+ *hand, glass*]

举(舉)起 jǔqǐ **2** (increase) [+ salary, rate, speed limit] 增加 zēngjiā; [+ morale, standards] 提高 tígāo **3** (rear) [+ child, family] 抚(撫)养(養) fǔyǎng **II** N [C] (US: payrise) 加薪 jiāxīn [次 cì]

rally ['rælɪ] N [C] **1** (public meeting) 集会(會) jíhuì [次 cì] **2** (Aut) 拉力赛(賽) lālìsài [场 chǎng]

Ramadan [ræmə'dɑːn] N [U] 斋(齋)月 zhāiyuè

rambler ['ræmblə'] N [C] (Brit) 漫步者 mànbùzhě [个 gè]

ramp [ræmp] N [C] 坡道 pōdào [条 tiáo]

ran [ræn] PT of **run**

rang [ræŋ] PT of **ring**

range [reɪndʒ] **I** N [C] **1** [of ages, prices] 范(範)围(圍) fànwéi [个 gè]; [of subjects, possibilities] 系列 xìliè [个 gè] **2** (also: **mountain range**) 山脉(脈) shānmài [个 gè] **II** vi ▶ to range from... to... 在…到…之间(間) zài…dào…zhījiān

rape [reɪp] **I** N [C/U] 强(強)奸(姦) qiángjiān [次 cì] **II** vt 强(強)奸(姦) qiángjiān

rapids ['ræpɪdz] NPL 湍流 tuānliú

rare [rɛə'] ADJ **1** 稀有的 xīyǒu de **2** [+ steak] 半熟的 bànshóu de

rarely ['rɛəlɪ] ADV 很少 hěn shǎo

raspberry ['rɑːzbərɪ] N [C] 山莓 shānméi [颗 kē]

rat [ræt] N [C] 田鼠 tiánshǔ [只 zhī]

rather ['rɑːðə'] ADV 相当(當) xiāngdāng ▶ **rather a lot** 相当(當)多 xiāngdāng duō ▶ **I would rather go than stay** 我宁(寧)愿(願)走开而不愿(願)留下来(來) wǒ nìngyuàn zǒu ér bù yuàn liú xiàlái ▶ **I'd rather not say** 我宁(寧)可不说(說) wǒ nìngkě bù shuō

raw [rɔː] ADJ 生的 shēng de

raw materials NPL 原材料 yuáncáiliào

razor ['reɪzə'] N [C] **1** (also: **safety razor**) 剃须(鬚)刀 tìxūdāo [个 gè] **2** (also: **electric razor**) 电(電)动(動)剃(鬚)刀 diàndòng tìxūdāo [个 gè]

razor blade N [C] 剃须(鬚)刀刀片 tìxūdāo dāopiàn [个 gè]

reach [riːtʃ] vt [+ place, destination] 到达(達) dàodá; [+ conclusion, agreement, decision] 达(達)成 dáchéng; [+ stage, level, age] 达(達)到 dádào

react [riː'ækt] vi 反应(應) fǎnyìng

reaction [riː'ækʃn] N [C/U] 反应(應) fǎnyìng [种 zhǒng]

reactor [riː'æktə'] N [C] 反应(應)器 fǎnyìngqì [个 gè]

read [riːd] (pt, pp read [rɛd]) **I** vi 阅(閱)读(讀) yuèdú **II** vt **1** 读(讀) dú **2** (study at university: Brit) 攻读(讀) gōngdú ▶ **read through** vt **1** (quickly) 浏(瀏)览(覽) liúlǎn **2** (thoroughly) 仔细(細)阅(閱)读(讀) zǐxì yuèdú

reading ['riːdɪŋ] N [U] 阅(閱)读(讀) yuèdú

ready ['rɛdɪ] ADJ 做好准(準)备(備)的 zuòhǎo zhǔnbèi de ▶ **to get ready** 准(準)备(備)好 zhǔnbèihǎo ▶ **to get sb/sth ready** 使某人/某物准(準)备(備)就绪(緒) shǐ mǒurén/mǒuwù zhǔnbèi jiùxù ▶ **to be ready to do sth** (prepared) 准(準)备(備)做某事 zhǔnbèi zuò mǒushì; (willing) 愿(願)意做某事 yuànyì zuò mǒushì

real [rɪəl] ADJ **1** [+ leather, gold] 真正的 zhēnzhèng de **2** [+ reason, interest, name] 真实(實)的 zhēnshí de **3** [+ life, feeling] 真实(實)的 zhēnshí de

realistic [rɪə'lɪstɪk] ADJ **1** 现(現)实(實)的 xiànshí de **2** (convincing) [+ book, film, portrayal] 逼真的 bīzhēn de

reality [riː'ælɪtɪ] N [U] (real things) 现(現)实(實) xiànshí ▶ **in reality** 事实(實)上 shìshí shang

realize ['rɪəlaɪz] vt 意识(識)到 yìshídào ▶ **to realize that...** 意识(識)到… yìshídào…

really ['rɪəlɪ] ADV **1** (very) ▶ **really good/delighted** 真好/真高兴(興) zhēn hǎo/zhēn gāoxìng **2** (genuinely) 确(確)实(實) quèshí **3** (after negative) 真正地 zhēnzhèng de ▶ **really?** (indicating surprise, interest) 真的吗(嗎)? zhēnde ma?

realtor ['rɪəltɔː'] (US) N [C] 房地产(產)商 fángdìchǎnshāng [个 gè]

rear [rɪə'] **I** N [s] (back) 后(後)面 hòumian **II** vt [+ cattle, chickens] (esp Brit) 饲养(養) sìyǎng

reason ['riːzn] N [C] 原因 yuányīn [个 gè] ▶ **the reason for sth** 某事的(動)机(機) mǒushì de dòngjī ▶ **the reason why** …的原因 …de yuányīn

reasonable ['riːznəbl] ADJ **1** [+ person,

decision] 合情合理的 héqíng hélǐ de; [+ *number, amount*] 相当(當)的 xiāngdāng de; [+ *price*] 合理的 hélǐ de **2** (*not bad*) 凑(湊)合的 còuhe de ▶ **be reasonable!** 理智些! lǐzhì xie!

reasonably [ˈriːznəblɪ] ADV (*moderately*) 相当(當)地 xiāngdāng de

reassure [riːəˈʃuəʳ] VT 使安心 shǐ ānxīn

receipt [rɪˈsiːt] N [c] 收据(據) shōujù [张 zhāng]

receive [rɪˈsiːv] VT 收到 shōudào

recent [ˈriːsnt] ADJ 最近的 zuìjìn de

recently [ˈriːsntlɪ] ADV 最近 zuìjìn ▶ **until recently** 直到最近 zhídào zuìjìn

reception [rɪˈsɛpʃən] N [s] (*in public building*) 接待处(處) jiēdàichù **2** [c] (*party*) 欢(歡)迎会(會) huānyínghuì [个 gè] **3** [c] (*welcome*) 反响(響) fǎnxiǎng [种 zhǒng]

receptionist [rɪˈsɛpʃənɪst] (*esp Brit*) N [c] 接待员(員) jiēdàiyuán [位 wèi]

recipe [ˈrɛsɪpɪ] (*Culin*) N [c] 食谱(譜) shípǔ [个 gè]

recognize [ˈrɛkəgnaɪz] VT 认(認)出 rènchū

recommend [rɛkəˈmɛnd] VT 推荐(薦) tuījiàn

record [*n, adj* ˈrɛkɔːd, *vb* rɪˈkɔːd] I N [c] **1** (*sound-recording*) 唱片 chàngpiàn [张 zhāng] **2** (*unbeaten statistic*) 记(記) 录(錄) jìlù [个 gè] II **records** NPL 记(記) 录(錄) jìlù III VT (*make recording of*) 录(錄)制(製) lùzhì IV ADJ [+ *sales, profits, levels*] 创(創)记(記)录(錄)的 chuàng jìlù de ▶ **in record time** 破记(記)录(錄)地 pò jìlù de ▶ **to keep a record of sth** 记(記)录(錄)某事 jìlù mǒushì

recover [rɪˈkʌvəʳ] VI 恢复(復) huīfù

recovery [rɪˈkʌvərɪ] N [c/u] 康复(復) kāngfù

recycle [riːˈsaɪkl] VT 再生利用 zàishēng lìyòng

recycling [riːˈsaɪklɪŋ] N [u] 循环(環)利 用 xúnhuán lìyòng

red [rɛd] I ADJ **1** (紅)色的 hóngsè de **2** [+ *face, person*] 涨(漲)红(紅)的 zhànghóng de **3** [+ *hair*] 红(紅)褐色的 hónghèsè de **4** [+ *wine*] 红(紅)的 hóng de II N [c/u] 红(紅)色 hóngsè [种 zhǒng]

Red Cross N ▶ **the Red Cross** 红(紅)十 字会(會) Hóngshízìhuì

red-haired [rɛdˈhɛəd] ADJ 红(紅)棕色 头(頭)发(髮)的 hóngzōngsè tóufa de

reduce [rɪˈdjuːs] VT 减(減)少 jiǎnshǎo ▶ **to reduce sth by/to** 将(將)某物 减(減)少⋯/将(將)某物减(減)少到⋯ jiāng mǒuwù jiǎnshǎo.../jiāng mǒuwù jiǎnshǎodào...

reduction [rɪˈdʌkʃən] N **1** [c/u] (*decrease*) 减(減)少 jiǎnshǎo **2** [c] (*discount*) 减(減)价(價) jiǎnjià [次 cì]

redundant [rɪˈdʌndnt] ADJ (*Brit*) 被裁 员(員)的 bèi cáiyuán de ▶ **to be made redundant** 被裁员(員) bèi cáiyuán

refer [rɪˈfəːʳ] VT ▶ **to refer sb to** [+ *book*] 叫 某人参(參)看 jiào mǒurén cānkàn ▶ **refer to** VT FUS 提到 tídào

referee [rɛfəˈriː] N [c] (*Sport*) 裁判员(員) cáipànyuán [位 wèi]

reference [ˈrɛfrəns] N [c] **1** (*mention*) 提 到 tídào [次 cì] **2** (*for job application: letter*) 证(證)明人 zhèngmíngrén [位 wèi]

refill [riːˈfɪl] VT 再装(裝)满(滿) zài zhuāngmǎn

reflect [rɪˈflɛkt] VT [+ *image*] 映出 yìngchū; [+ *light, heat*] 反射 fǎnshè

reflection [rɪˈflɛkʃən] N **1** [c] (*image*) 影 像 yǐngxiàng [个 gè] **2** [u] (*thought*) 沉 思 chénsī

refreshing [rɪˈfrɛʃɪŋ] ADJ 提神的 tíshén de

refreshments [rɪˈfrɛʃmənts] NPL 饮(飲)料及小吃 yǐnliào jí xiǎochī

refrigerator [rɪˈfrɪdʒəreɪtəʳ] N [c] 冰箱 bīngxiāng [个 gè]

refugee [rɛfjuˈdʒiː] N [c] 难(難)民 nànmín [批 pī] ▶ **a political refugee** 政 治难(難)民 yī gè zhèngzhì nànmín

refund [*n* ˈriːfʌnd, *vb* rɪˈfʌnd] I N [c] 退款 tuìkuǎn [笔 bǐ] II VT 偿(償)还(還) chánghuán

refuse¹ [rɪˈfjuːz] VT, VI 拒绝(絕) jùjué ▶ **to refuse to do sth** 拒绝(絕)做某事 jùjué zuò mǒushì ▶ **to refuse sb permission** 不批准某人 bù pīzhǔn mǒurén

refuse² [ˈrɛfjuːs] N [u] 垃圾 lājī

regard [rɪˈgɑːd] I VT (*consider, view*) 认(認)为(為) rènwéi II N ▶ **to give one's regards to** 向⋯表示问(問)候 xiàng...biǎoshì wènhòu

region ['ri:dʒən] N [c] 区(區)域 qūyù [个 gè]

regional ['ri:dʒənl] ADJ 地区(區)的 dìqū de

register ['rɛdʒɪstər] N [c] **1** (at hotel) 登记(記) dēngjì [个 gè] **2** (in school) 注(註)册(冊) zhùcè [个 gè]

registered ['rɛdʒɪstəd] ADJ (Post) 挂(掛)号(號)的 guàhào de [个 gè] [位 wèi]

registration [rɛdʒɪs'treɪʃən] N [c/u] [of birth, death, students] 登记(記) dēngjì [个 gè]

regret [rɪ'grɛt] VT 后(後)悔 hòuhuǐ ▸ to have no regrets 没(沒)有遗(遺)憾 méiyǒu yíhàn ▸ to regret that... 对(對)…感到后(後)悔 duì...gǎndào hòuhuǐ

regular ['rɛgjulər] ADJ **1** [+ breathing, intervals] 有规(規)律的 yǒu guīlǜ de **2** [+ event] 有规(規)律的 yǒu guīlǜ de; [+ visitor] 经(經)常的 jīngcháng de **3** (normal) 正常的 zhèngcháng de

regularly ['rɛgjuləlɪ] ADV 经(經)常 jīngcháng

regulation [rɛgju'leɪʃən] N [c] 规(規)章 guīzhāng [套 tào]

rehearsal [rɪ'hə:səl] N [c/u] 排练(練) páiliàn [次 cì]

rehearse [rɪ'hə:s] VT, VI 排练(練) páiliàn

reject [rɪ'dʒɛkt VT **1** 拒绝(絕)接受 jùjué jiēshòu **2** [+ applicant, admirer] 拒绝(絕) jùjué

related [rɪ'leɪtɪd] ADJ [+ people] 有亲(親)缘(緣)关(關)系(係)的 yǒu qīnyuán guānxì de ▸ to be related to sb 和某人有关(關)连(連) hé mǒurén yǒu guānlián

relation [rɪ'leɪʃən] N [c] **1** (relative) 亲(親)戚(慼) qīnqi [个 gè] **2** (connection) 关(關)系(係) guānxì [种 zhǒng] ▸ in relation to 与(與)…相比 yǔ...xiāngbǐ

relationship [rɪ'leɪʃənʃɪp] N [c] **1** (connection) 关(關)系(係) guānxì [个 gè] **2** (rapport) (between two people, countries) 关(關)系(係) guānxì [种 zhǒng] **3** (affair) 亲(親)密的关(關)系(係) qīnmì de guānxì [种 zhǒng] ▸ to have a good relationship 关(關)系(係)亲(親)密 guānxì qīnmì

relative ['rɛlətɪv] N [c] 亲(親)戚(慼) qīnqi [个 gè]

relatively ['rɛlətɪvlɪ] ADV 相对(對) xiāngduì

relax [rɪ'læks] VI 放松 fàngsōng

relaxation [ri:læk'seɪʃən] N [u] 消遣 xiāoqiǎn

relaxed [rɪ'lækst] ADJ 放松(鬆)的 fàngsōng de; [+ discussion, atmosphere] 轻(輕)松(鬆)的 qīngsōng de

relaxing [rɪ'læksɪŋ] ADJ 令人放松(鬆)的 lìng rén fàngsōng de

release [rɪ'li:s] I N [c] 释(釋)放 shìfàng [次 cì] II VT **1** 释(釋)放 shìfàng **2** [+ record, film] 发(發)行 fāxíng

relevant ['rɛləvənt] ADJ 切题(題)的 qiètí de ▸ relevant to 和…有关(關)的 hé...yǒuguān de

reliable [rɪ'laɪəbl] ADJ 可靠的 kěkào de; [+ method, machine] 可信赖(賴)的 kě xìnlài de

relief [rɪ'li:f] N [u] 如释(釋)重负(負) rú shì zhòng fù

relieved [rɪ'li:vd] ADJ 宽(寬)慰的 kuānwèi de ▸ to be relieved that... 对(對)…感到放心 duì...gǎndào fàngxīn

religion [rɪ'lɪdʒən] N **1** (belief) 宗教信仰 zōngjiào xìnyǎng **2** [c] (set of beliefs) 宗教 zōngjiào [种 zhǒng]

religious [rɪ'lɪdʒəs] ADJ **1** [+ activities, faith] 宗教的 zōngjiào de **2** [+ person] 笃(篤)信宗教的 dǔxìn zōngjiào de

reluctant [rɪ'lʌktənt] ADJ 不情愿(願)的 bù qíngyuàn de ▸ to be reluctant to do sth 不愿(願)做某事 bùyuàn zuò mǒushì

reluctantly [rɪ'lʌktəntlɪ] ADV 不情愿(願)地 bù qíngyuàn de

rely on [rɪ'laɪ-] VT FUS **1** (be dependent on) 依赖(賴) yīlài **2** (trust) 信赖(賴) xìnlài

remain [rɪ'meɪn] VI **1** (continue to be) 仍然是 réngrán shì **2** (stay) 逗留 dòuliú ▸ to remain silent/in control 保持沉默/仍然控制局面 bǎochí chénmò/réngrán kòngzhì júmiàn

remaining [rɪ'meɪnɪŋ] ADJ 剩下的 shèngxià de

remark [rɪ'mɑ:k] N [c] (comment) 评(評)论(論) pínglùn [个 gè]

remarkable [rɪ'mɑ:kəbl] ADJ 不寻(尋)常的 bù xúncháng de

remarkably [rɪ'mɑ:kəblɪ] ADV 极(極)其地 jíqí de

remember [rɪ'mɛmbər] VT **1** [+ person, name, event] 记(記)住 jìzhù **2** (bring back to mind) 回想起 huíxiǎngqǐ **3** (bear in mind) 牢记(記) láojì ▸ she remembered to do it 她记(記)得要做某事 tā jìde yào zuò mǒushì

remind [rɪ'maɪnd] VT 提醒 tíxǐng ▸ to remind sb to do sth 提醒某人做某事 tíxǐng mǒurén zuò mǒushì ▸ to remind sb of sb/sth 使某人想起某人/某事 shǐ mǒurén xiǎngqǐ mǒurén/mǒushì

remote [rɪ'məʊt] ADJ 遥(遙)远(遠)的 yáoyuǎn de

remote control N [c] 遥(遙)控器 yáokòngqì [个 gè]

remove [rɪ'muːv] VT **1** [+ object, organ] 移走 yízǒu **2** [+ clothing, bandage] 脱(脫)下 tuōxià **3** [+ stain] 清除 qīngchú

renew [rɪ'njuː] VT [+ loan, contract] 延长(長) yáncháng

renewable [rɪ'njuːəbl] ADJ (energy, resource) 可更新的 kě gēngxīn de

rent [rɛnt] I N [c/u] 租金 zūjīn [笔 bǐ] II VT **1** 租用 zūyòng **2** (also: rent out) [+ house, room] 出租 chūzū

reorganize [riː'ɔːgənaɪz] VT 重组(組) chóngzǔ

rep [rɛp] N (also: sales rep) 商品经(經)销(銷)代理 shāngpǐn jīngxiāo dàilǐ [位 wèi]

repair [rɪ'pɛər] I N [c/u] 修理 xiūlǐ [次 cì] II VT **1** 修补(補) xiūbǔ **2** [+ damage] 维(維)修 wéixiū

repay [riː'peɪ] (pt, pp repaid) VT 偿(償)还(還) chánghuán

repeat [rɪ'piːt] VT **1** 重复(複) chóngfù **2** [+ action, mistake] 重做 chóngzuò

repeatedly [rɪ'piːtɪdlɪ] ADV 反复(復)地 fǎnfù de

replace [rɪ'pleɪs] VT **1** (put back) 将(將)⋯放回 jiāng…fànghuí **2** (take the place of) 代替 dàitì

replay [n 'riːpleɪ, vb riː'pleɪ] I N [c] [of match] 重新比赛(賽) chóngxīn bǐsài [场 chǎng] II VT [+ track, song] (on tape) 重新播放 chóngxīn bōfàng ▸ to replay a match 重新比赛(賽) chóngxīn bǐsài

reply [rɪ'plaɪ] I N [c] 回答 huídá [个 gè] II VI 答复(復) dáfù ▸ there's no reply (Tel) 无(無)人接听(聽) wúrén jiētīng

report [rɪ'pɔːt] I N [c] **1** (account) 报(報)告 bàogào [个 gè] **2** (Brit) (also: school report) 成绩(績)单(單) chéngjìdān [份 fèn] II VT [+ theft, accident, death] 报(報)案 bào'àn; [+ person] 告发(發) gàofā

report card (US) N [c] 学(學)生成绩(績)报(報)告单(單) xuéshēng chéngjì bàogàodān [份 fèn]

reporter [rɪ'pɔːtər] N [c] 记(記)者 jìzhě [名 míng]

represent [rɛprɪ'zɛnt] VT [+ person, nation] 代表 dàibiǎo

representative [rɛprɪ'zɛntətɪv] N [c] 代表 dàibiǎo [个 gè]

republic [rɪ'pʌblɪk] N [c] 共和国(國) gònghéguó [个 gè]

reputation [rɛpju'teɪʃən] N [c] 名声(聲) míngshēng [种 zhǒng]

request [rɪ'kwɛst] I N [c] 要求 yāoqiú [个 gè] II VT 要求 yāoqiú

require [rɪ'kwaɪər] VT (need) 需要 xūyào ▸ to be required [approval, permission +] 必须(須)有 bìxū yǒu

rescue ['rɛskjuː] I N [c/u] 营(營)救 yíngjiù [次 cì] II VT 解救 jiějiù

research [rɪ'səːtʃ] N [u] 研究 yánjiū ▸ to do research 从(從)事研究 cóngshì yánjiū

resemblance [rɪ'zɛmbləns] N [c/u] 相似 xiāngsì [种 zhǒng]

reservation [rɛzə'veɪʃən] N [c] 预(預)定 yùdìng [个 gè] ▸ to make a reservation (in hotel, restaurant, on train) 预(預)定 yùdìng

reservation desk (US) N [c] 预(預)定台(臺) yùdìngtái [个 gè]

reserve [rɪ'zəːv] VT 预(預)定 yùdìng

reserved [rɪ'zəːvd] ADJ **1** [+ seat] 已预(預)定的 yǐ yùdìng de **2** (restrained) 矜持的 jīnchí de

resident ['rɛzɪdənt] N [c] 居民 jūmín [位 wèi]

resign [rɪ'zaɪn] VI 辞(辭)职(職) cízhí

resist [rɪ'zɪst] VT [+ temptation, urge] 克制 kèzhì

resit [riː'sɪt] (Brit) VT [+ exam] 补(補)考 bǔkǎo

resolution [rɛzə'luːʃən] N [c/u] 决(決)心 juéxīn [个 gè] ▸ New Year's resolution 新年决(決)心 xīnnián juéxīn

resort [rɪ'zɔːt] N [c] (also: holiday resort) 度假胜(勝)地 dùjià shèngdì [个 gè]

▶ a seaside/winter sports resort 海边(邊)/冬季运(運)动(動)胜(勝)地 yī ge hǎibiān/dōngjì yùndòng shèngdì ▶ as a last resort 作为(為)最后(後)手段 zuòwéi zuìhòu shǒuduàn

resource [rɪ'zɔ:s]: **resources** NPL **1** (coal, iron, oil) 资(資)源 zīyuán **2** (money) 财(財)力 cáilì ▶ **natural resources** 自然资(資)源 zìrán zīyuán

respect [rɪs'pɛkt] I N [U] 尊敬 zūnjìng II VT 尊敬 zūnjìng ▶ **to have respect for sb/sth** 对(對)某人/某事怀(懷)有敬意 duì mǒurén/mǒushì huáiyǒu jìngyì

respectable [rɪs'pɛktəbl] ADJ **1** [+ area, background] 体(體)面的 tǐmiàn de **2** [+ person] 受人尊敬的 shòurén zūnjìng de

responsibility [rɪspɒnsɪ'bɪlɪtɪ] I N **1** [s] (duty) 职(職)责(責) zhízé **2** [s] (obligation) 义(義)务(務) yìwù II **responsibilities** NPL 责(責)任 zérèn

responsible [rɪs'pɒnsɪbl] ADJ **1** (at fault) 负(負)有责(責)任的 fùyǒu zérèn de **2** (in charge) 负(負)责(責)的 fùzé de **3** (sensible, trustworthy) 可靠的 kěkào de

rest [rɛst] I N **1** [U] (relaxation) 休息 xiūxi **2** [c] (break) 休息 xiūxi [次 cì] **3** [s] (remainder) 剩余(餘) shèngyú II VI (relax) 休息 xiūxi III VT [+ eyes, legs, muscles] 休息 xiūxi ▶ **to rest sth on/ against sth** (lean) 把某物靠在某物上 bǎ mǒuwù kào zài mǒuwù shang ▶ **the rest (of them)** (他们(們)当(當)中)其余(餘)的 (tāmen dāngzhōng)qíyú de

rest area (US) N [c] 路边(邊)服务(務)站 lùbiān fúwùzhàn [个 gè]

restaurant ['rɛstərɒn] N [c] 餐馆(館) cānguǎn [家 jiā]

restless ['rɛstlɪs] ADJ (fidgety) 坐立不安的 zuòlì bù'ān de

restore [rɪ'stɔ:ʳ] VT 修复(復) xiūfù

restrict [rɪs'trɪkt] VT **1** [+ growth, membership, privilege] 限制 xiànzhì **2** [+ activities] 约(約)束 yuēshù

rest room (US) N [c] 洗手间(間) xǐshǒujiān [个 gè]

result [rɪ'zʌlt] I N [c] [of event, action] 后(後)果 hòuguǒ [种 zhǒng]; [of match, election, exam, competition] 结(結)果 jiéguǒ [个 gè]; [of calculation] 答案 dá'àn [个 gè] II VI 产(產)生 chǎnshēng ▶ **to**

result in 导(導)致 dǎozhì ▶ **as a result of** 由于(於) yóuyú ▶ **to result from** 因…而产(產)生 yīn…ér chǎnshēng

résumé ['reɪzju:meɪ] N [c] (US: CV) 简(簡)历(歷) jiǎnlì [份 fèn]

retire [rɪ'taɪəʳ] VI 退休 tuìxiū

retired [rɪ'taɪəd] ADJ 退休的 tuìxiū de

retiree [rɪtaɪə'ri:] (US) N [c] 领(領)养(養)老金的人 lǐng yǎnglǎojīn de rén [位 wèi]

retirement [rɪ'taɪəmənt] N [c/U] 退休 tuìxiū

return [rɪ'tə:n] I VI 返回 fǎnhuí II VT 归(歸)还(還) guīhuán III N **1** [s] [of person] 返回 fǎnhuí **2** [s] [of something borrowed or stolen] 归(歸)还(還) guīhuán **3** [U] (Comput: key) 回车(車)键(鍵) huíchējiàn ▶ **in return (for)** 作为(為)(对(對)…)的回报(報) zuòwéi(duì…)de huíbào ▶ **many happy returns (of the day)!** 生日快乐(樂)! shēngrì kuàilè! IV CPD (Brit) [+ journey, ticket] 往返 wǎngfǎn

retweet [ri:'twi:t] VB (on Twitter®) 转(轉)发(發) zhuǎn fā

reunion [ri:'ju:nɪən] N [c] 团(團)聚 tuánjù [次 cì]

reveal [rɪ'vi:l] VT (make known) 透露 tòulù

revenge [rɪ'vɛndʒ] N [U] 复(復)仇 fùchóu ▶ **to take (one's) revenge (on sb)** (对(對)某人)进(進)行报(報)复(復) (duì mǒurén)jìnxíng bàofù

review [rɪ'vju:] N [c] [of book, film] 评(評)论(論) pínglùn [个 gè]

revise [rɪ'vaɪz] I VT (study) 复(復)习(習) fùxí II VI (study: Brit) 复(復)习(習) fùxí

revision [rɪ'vɪʒən] N [U] (Brit: studying) 复(復)习(習) fùxí

revolution [rɛvə'lu:ʃən] N **1** [c/U] (Pol) 革命 gémìng [场 chǎng] **2** [c] 变(變)革 biàngé [场 chǎng]

reward [rɪ'wɔ:d] I N [c] 奖(獎)励(勵) jiǎnglì [种 zhǒng] II VT 奖(獎)赏(賞) jiǎngshǎng

rewarding [rɪ'wɔ:dɪŋ] ADJ 值得做的 zhídé zuò de

rewind [ri:'waɪnd] (pt, pp rewound) VT 倒带(帶) dàodài

rhythm ['rɪðm] N [c/U] 节(節)奏 jiézòu [个 gè]

rib [rɪb] N [c] 肋骨 lèigǔ [根 gēn]

ribbon ['rɪbən] N [c/u] 饰(飾)带(帶) shìdài [条 tiáo]

rice [raɪs] N [c/u] **1** (grain) 大米 dàmǐ [粒 lì] **2** (when cooked) 米饭(飯) mǐfàn [碗 wǎn]

rich [rɪtʃ] ADJ [+ person, country] 富有的 fùyǒu de

rid [rɪd] (pt, pp rid) VT ▸ to get rid of sth/ sb [+ smell, dirt, car etc] 摆(擺)脱(脫)某物/某人 bǎituō mǒuwù/mǒurén

ride [raɪd] (pt rode, pp ridden ['rɪdn]) I N [c] **1** (in car, on bicycle) 兜风(風) dōufēng [次 cì] **2** (on horse, bus, train) 出行 chūxíng [次 cì] II VI **1** (on horse) 骑(騎)马(馬) qímǎ; (on bicycle) 骑(騎)车(車) qíchē; (in car) 乘坐 chéngzuò III VT **1** [+ horse, bicycle, motorcycle] 骑(騎) qí **2** [+ distance] 行进(進) xíngjìn ▸ to give sb a ride (US) 让(讓)某人搭车(車) ràng mǒurén dāchē [个 gè]

ridiculous [rɪ'dɪkjuləs] ADJ 荒谬(謬)的 huāngmiù de

rifle ['raɪfl] N [c] 步枪(槍) bùqiāng [支 zhī]

right [raɪt] I ADJ **1** (not left) 右边(邊)的 yòubiān de **2** (correct) 正确(確)的 zhèngquè de; [+ person, place, clothes] 合适(適)的 héshì de; [+ decision, direction, time] 最适(適)宜的 zuì shìyí de II N **1** [s] (not left) 右边(邊) yòubiān **2** [c] (entitlement) 权(權)利 quánlì [项 xiàng] III ADV **1** (correctly) 正确(確)地 zhèngquè de **2** (properly, fairly) 恰当(當) qiàdàng **3** (not to/on the left) 右边(邊)地 yòubiān de IV INT 好 hǎo ▸ do you have the right time? 你的表(錶)几(幾)点(點)了？ nǐ de biǎo jǐdiǎn le? ▸ to be right [person +] 正确(確) zhèngquè; [answer, fact +] 对(對) duì; [clock +] 准(準)确(確) zhǔnquè ▸ you did the right thing 你做对(對)了 nǐ zuò de duì ▸ to or on the right (position) 靠〔或〕在右侧(側) kào huò zài yòucè ▸ to the right (movement) 向右 xiàngyòu

right-handed [raɪt'hændɪd] ADJ 惯(慣)用右手的 guànyòng yòushǒu de

ring [rɪŋ] (pt rang, pp rung) I N [c] (on finger) 戒指 jièzhǐ [枚 méi] II VI **1** [bell +] 鸣(鳴)响(響) míngxiǎng **2** [telephone +] 响(響) xiǎng **3** (Brit) 打电(電)话(話) dǎ diànhuà III VT **1** [+ bell, doorbell] 使…响(響) shǐ…xiǎng **2** (Brit: Tel) 给(給)…打电(電)话(話) gěi…dǎ diànhuà ▸ there was a ring at the door, the doorbell rang 有人按门(門)铃(鈴) yǒurén àn ménlíng ▸ to give sb a ring (Brit: Tel) 给(給)某人打电(電)话(話) gěi mǒurén dǎ diànhuà

▸ **ring back** (Brit: Tel) I VT 回电(電)话(話) huí diànhuà II VI 再打电(電)话(話) zài dǎ diànhuà

▸ **ring up** (Brit: Tel) VT 给(給)…打电(電)话(話) gěi…dǎ diànhuà

ring-fence ['rɪŋfɛns] VT 使…专(專)门(門)用于 shǐ … zhuānmén yòngyú

rinse [rɪns] VT [+ dishes, clothes] 漂洗 piǎoxǐ

riot ['raɪət] I N [c] (disturbance) 暴乱(亂) bàoluàn [次 cì] II VI 闹(鬧)事 nàoshì

ripe [raɪp] ADJ 成熟的 chéngshú de

rise [raɪz] (pt rose, pp risen ['rɪzn]) I N **1** [c] (Brit: salary increase) 加薪 jiāxīn [次 cì] **2** [c] (in prices, temperature, crime rate) 上升 shàngshēng [次 cì] II VI **1** (move upwards) 上升 shàngshēng **2** [prices, numbers +] 上升 shàngshēng **3** [sun, moon +] 升起 shēngqǐ **4** (from chair) 起身 qǐshēn

risk [rɪsk] I N [c/u] (danger) 危险(險) wēixiǎn [个 gè] **2** [c] (possibility, chance) 风(風)险(險) fēngxiǎn [种 zhǒng] II VT **1** (take the chance of) 冒险(險)做 màoxiǎn zuò ▸ to take a risk 担(擔)风(風)险(險) dān fēngxiǎn ▸ to risk it (inf) 冒险(險)一试(試) màoxiǎn yī shì

rival ['raɪvl] I N [c] 竞(競)争(爭)对(對)手 jìngzhēng duìshǒu [个 gè] II ADJ [+ teams, groups, supporters] 对(對)立的 duìlì de

river ['rɪvəʳ] N [c] 河 hé [条 tiáo]

river bank N [c] 河岸 hé'àn

road [rəʊd] N [c] **1** (in country) 公路 gōnglù [条 tiáo] **2** (in town) 路 lù [条 tiáo] ▸ it takes four hours by road 要花4小时(時)的车(車)程 yào huā sì xiǎoshí de chēchéng

road map N [c] 道路图(圖) dàolùtú [张 zhāng]

road sign N [c] 交通标(標)志(誌) jiāotōng biāozhì [个 gè]

roast [rəʊst] VT 烤 kǎo

rob [rɒb] VT 抢(搶)劫 qiǎngjié ▸ **to rob sb of sth** 剥(剝)夺(奪)某人的某物 bōduó mǒurén de mǒuwù

robber ['rɒbəʳ] N [c] 强(強)盗(盜) qiángdào [个 gè]

robbery ['rɒbərɪ] N [c/u] 抢(搶)劫 qiǎngjié [次 cì]

robot ['rəubɒt] N [c] 机(機)器人 jīqìrén [个 gè]

rock [rɒk] N 1 [c] (boulder) 巨石 jùshí [块 kuài] 2 [c] (esp US: small stone) 小石子 xiǎoshízǐ [块 kuài] 3 [u] (Mus) (also: **rock music**) 摇(搖)滚(滾)乐(樂) yáogǔnyuè

rocket ['rɒkɪt] N [c] 1 (Space) 火箭 huǒjiàn [枚 méi] 2 (firework) 火箭式礼(禮)花 huǒjiànshì lǐhuā [个 gè]

rod [rɒd] N 1 (pole) 杆 gān [根 gēn] 2 (also: **fishing rod**) 钓(釣)鱼(魚)竿 diàoyúgān [根 gēn]

rode [rəud] PT of **ride**

role [rəul] N [c] 1 (function) 作用 zuòyòng [个 gè] 2 (Theat: part) 角色 juésè [个 gè]

roll [rəul] I N [c] 1 一卷 yī juǎn 2 (also: **bread roll**) 小圆(圓)面(麵)包 xiǎo yuánmiànbāo [个 gè] II VT 使滚(滾)动(動) shǐ gǔndòng III VI [ball, stone +] 滚(滾)动(動) gǔndòng ▸ **cheese/ham roll** 奶酪/火腿面(麵)包卷(捲) nǎilào/huǒtuǐ miànbāojuǎn

rollerblades ['rəuləbleɪdz] N PL 直排轮(輪)溜冰鞋 zhípáilún liūbīngxié

roller coaster [-'kəustəʳ] N [c] (at funfair) 过(過)山车(車) guòshānchē [辆 liàng]

roller skates N PL 旱冰鞋 hànbīngxié

roller skating N [u] 滑旱冰 huá hànbīng

Roman ['rəumən] I ADJ 1 (of ancient Rome) 古罗(羅)马(馬)的 gǔ Luómǎ de 2 (of modern Rome) 罗(羅)马(馬)的 Luómǎ de II N [c] (in ancient Rome) 古罗(羅)马(馬)人 gǔ Luómǎrén [个 gè]

Roman Catholic I ADJ 天主教的 Tiānzhǔjiào de II N [c] 天主教教徒 Tiānzhǔjiào jiàotú [个 gè]

romance [rə'mæns] N 1 [c] (affair) 恋(戀)情 liànqíng [种 zhǒng] 2 [u] (charm, excitement) 迷人之处(處) mírén zhī chù

Romania [rə'meɪnɪə] N 罗(羅)马(馬)尼亚(亞) Luómǎníyà

Romanian [rə'meɪnɪən] I ADJ 罗(羅)马(馬)尼亚(亞)的 Luómǎníyà de II N 1 [c] (person) 罗(羅)马(馬)尼亚(亞)人 Luómǎníyàrén [个 gè] 2 [u] (language) 罗(羅)马(馬)尼亚(亞)语(語) Luómǎníyàyǔ

romantic [rə'mæntɪk] ADJ 1 [+ person] 浪漫的 làngmàn de 2 (connected with love) [+ play, story etc] 爱(愛)情的 àiqíng de 3 (charming, exciting) [+ setting, holiday, dinner etc] 浪漫的 làngmàn de

roof [ru:f] N [c] 1 [of building] 屋顶(頂) wūdǐng [个 gè] 2 [of cave, mine, vehicle] 顶(頂) dǐng [个 gè]

room [ru:m] N 1 [c] (in house) 房间 fángjiān [个 gè] 2 [c] (also: **bedroom**) 卧(臥)室 wòshì [个 gè] 3 [u] (space) 空间(間) kōngjiān ▸ **single/double room** 单(單)人/双(雙)人间(間) dānrén/shuāngrén jiān

root [ru:t] N [c] 根 gēn [个 gè]

rope [rəup] N [c/u] 绳(繩)子 shéngzi [根 gēn]

rose [rəuz] I PT of **rise** II N [c] (flower) 玫瑰 méigui [朵 duǒ]

rot [rɒt] I VT (cause to decay) 使腐坏(壞) shǐ fǔhuài II VI (decay) [teeth, wood, fruit +] 腐烂(爛) fǔlàn

rotten ['rɒtn] ADJ 1 (decayed) 腐烂(爛)的 fǔlàn de 2 (inf: awful) 糟透的 zāotòu de

rough [rʌf] ADJ 1 [+ skin, surface, cloth] 粗糙的 cūcāo de 2 [+ terrain] 崎岖(嶇)的 qíqū de 3 [+ sea, crossing] 波涛(濤)汹(洶)涌(湧)的 bōtāo xiōngyǒng de 4 (violent) [+ person] 粗鲁(魯)的 cūlǔ de; [+ town, area] 治安混乱(亂)的 zhì'ān hùnluàn de 5 [+ outline, plan, idea] 粗略的 cūlüè de

roughly ['rʌflɪ] ADV 1 (violently) 粗暴地 cūbào de 2 (approximately) 大约(約) dàyuē ▸ **roughly speaking** 粗略地说(說) cūlüè de shuō

round [raund] I ADJ 1 (circular) 圆(圓)的 yuán de 2 (spherical) 球形的 qiúxíng de 3 [+ figure, sum] 不计(計)尾数(數)的 bù jì wěishù de II N [c] 1 (stage) (in competition) 一轮(輪) yī lún 2 (Golf) 一场(場) yī chǎng III PREP 1 (surrounding) 围(圍)绕(繞) wéirào 2 (near) 在…附近 zài…fùjìn 3 (on or from the other side of) 绕(繞)过(過) ràoguò ▸ **to move round the room/sail round the world** 绕(繞)

房间(間)一周(週)/环(環)球航行 rào fángjiān yī zhōu/huánqiú hángxíng ▸ **all round** 在…周围(圍) zài…zhōuwéi ▸ **to go round (sth)** 绕(繞)过(過)(某物) ràoguò (mǒuwù) ▸ **to go round to sb's (house)** 造访(訪)某人(的家) zàofǎng mǒurén (de jiā) ▸ **all (the) year round** 一年到头(頭) yī nián dàotóu ▸ **I'll be round at 6 o'clock** 我会(會)在6点(點)钟(鐘)到你家 wǒ huì zài liù diǎnzhōng dào nǐ jiā ▸ **round about** (esp Brit: approximately) 大约(約) dàyuē ▸ **round the clock** 连(連)续(續)24小时(時) liánxù èrshísì xiǎoshí ▸ **a round of applause** 掌声(聲)雷动(動) zhǎngshēng léidòng

▸ **round off** VT [+ meal, evening] 圆(圓)满(滿)结(結)束 yuánmǎn jiéshù

▸ **round up** I N [c] (Brit: Aut) 环(環)形交叉路 huánxíng jiāochàlù [个 gè]

round trip I N [c] 往返旅行 wǎngfǎn lǚxíng [次 cì] II ADJ (US) 往返的 wǎngfǎn de

route [ruːt] N [c] **1** (path, journey) 路 lù [条 tiáo] **2** (of bus, train) 路线(線) lùxiàn [条 tiáo]

router [ˈruːtəʳ] N (Comput) 路由器 lùyóuqì

routine [ruːˈtiːn] I N [c/u] 例行公事 lìxíng gōngshì [次 cì]

row[1] [rəu] I N [c] **1** (of people, houses) 一排 yī pái **2** (of seats in theatre, cinema) 一排 yī pái II VI (in boat) 划船 huáchuán III VT [+ boat] 划 huá ▸ **in a row** 连(連)续(續) liánxù

row[2] [rau] N **1** [s] (noise: Brit: inf) 吵闹(鬧)声(聲) chǎonàoshēng **2** [c] (noisy quarrel) 吵架 chǎojià [场 chǎng]

rowboat [ˈrəubəut] (US) N [c] 划艇 huátǐng [艘 sōu]

rowing [ˈrəuɪŋ] (Sport) N [u] 赛(賽)艇运(運)动(動) sàitǐng yùndòng

rowing boat (Brit) N [c] 划艇 huátǐng [艘 sōu]

royal [ˈrɔɪəl] ADJ 皇家的 huángjiā de ▸ **the royal family** 王室 wángshì

ROYAL FAMILY

royal family （英国王室）以伊丽莎白女王二世为首。女王于1953年登基。她的丈夫是菲利普亲王，即爱丁堡公爵。他们育有四名成年子女：查尔斯王子、安妮公主、安德鲁王子和爱德华王子。查尔斯王子，即威尔士亲王是王位的继承人。他有两个孩子，威廉王子和哈利王子。他们的母亲是已故的威尔士王妃戴安娜。

rub [rʌb] VT (with hand, fingers) 揉 róu; (with cloth, substance) 擦 cā ▸ **rub out** VT (erase) 擦掉 cādiào

rubber [ˈrʌbəʳ] N **1** [u] (substance) 橡胶(膠) xiàngjiāo **2** [c] (Brit) 橡皮擦 xiàngpícā [个 gè]

rubber boot (US) N [c] 橡胶(膠)长(長)统(統)靴 xiàngjiāo chángtǒngxuē [双 shuāng]

rubbish [ˈrʌbɪʃ] (Brit) I N [u] **1** (refuse) 垃圾 lājī **2** (inferior material) 垃圾 lājī **3** (nonsense) 废(廢)话(話) fèihuà II ADJ (Brit; inf) ▸ **I'm rubbish at golf** 我高尔(爾)夫球打得很糟糕 wǒ gāo'ěrfūqiú dǎ de hěn zāogāo ▸ **rubbish!** 胡说(說)! húshuō!

rubbish bin (Brit) N [c] 垃圾箱 lājīxiāng [个 gè]

rucksack [ˈrʌksæk] N [c] 背包 bēibāo [个 gè]

rude [ruːd] ADJ **1** 无(無)礼(禮)的 wúlǐ de **2** [+ word, joke, noise] 粗鄙的 cūbǐ de ▸ **to be rude to sb** 对(對)某人无(無)礼(禮) duì mǒurén wúlǐ

rug [rʌg] N [c] 小地毯 xiǎodìtǎn [块 kuài]

rugby [ˈrʌgbɪ] N [u] (also: rugby football) 英式橄榄(欖)球 yīngshì gǎnlǎnqiú

ruin [ˈruːɪn] I N [u] (of person, institution) 毁(毀)坏(壞) huǐhuài II VT [+ clothes, carpet] 毁(毀)坏(壞) huǐhuài; [+ plans, prospects] 葬送 zàngsòng III ruins N PL [of building, castle] 废(廢)墟 fèixū ▸ **to be in ruins** [building, town +] 破败(敗)不堪 pòbài bùkān

rule [ruːl] N **1** [c] (regulation) 规(規)则(則) guīzé [条 tiáo] **2** [c] (of language, science) 规(規)则(則) guīzé [条 tiáo] ▸ **it's against the rules** 这(這)是不合规(規)定的 zhè shì bù hé guīdìng de ▸ **as a rule** 通常 tōngcháng

ruler ['ru:lə'] N [c] (for measuring) 直尺 zhíchǐ [把 bǎ]

rum [rʌm] N [U] 朗姆酒 lǎngmǔjiǔ

rumour, (US) **rumor** ['ru:mə'] N [c/U] 谣(謠)言 yáoyán [个 gè]

run [rʌn] (pt ran, pp run) I N [c] **1** (as exercise, sport) 跑步 pǎobù [次 cì] **2** (Cricket, Baseball) 跑动(動)得分 pǎodòng défēn [次 cì] II VT **1** [+ race, distance] 跑 pǎo **2** (operate) [+ business, shop, country] 经(經)营(營) jīngyíng **3** [+ water, bath] 流 liú **4** [+ program, test] 进(進)行 jìnxíng III VI **1** 跑 pǎo **2** (flee) 逃跑 táopǎo **3** [bus, train +] 行驶(駛) xíngshǐ **4** (in combination) 变(變)得 biàn de ▸ **to go for a run** (as exercise) 跑步 锻(鍛)炼(鍊) pǎobù duànliàn ▸ **in the long run** 终(終)究 zhōngjiū ▸ **I'll run you to the station** 我开(開)车(車)送你 去车(車)站 wǒ kāichē sòng nǐ qù chēzhàn ▸ **to run on** or **off petrol/ batteries** 以汽油/电(電)池为(為)能源 yǐ qìyóu/diànchí wéi néngyuán

▸ **run after** VT FUS (chase) 追赶(趕) zhuīgǎn

▸ **run away** VI (from home, situation) 出 走 chūzǒu

▸ **run into** VT FUS (meet) [+ person] 偶然 碰见(見) ǒurán pèngjiàn; [+ trouble, problems] 遭遇 zāoyù

▸ **run off** VI 跑掉 pǎodiào

▸ **run out** VI **1** [time, money, luck +] 用完 yòngwán **2** [lease, passport +] 到期 dàoqī

▸ **run out of** VT FUS 耗尽(盡) hàojìn

▸ **run over** VT (Aut) [+ person] 撞倒 zhuàngdǎo

rung [rʌŋ] PP of **ring**

runner ['rʌnə'] N [c] (in race) 赛(賽)跑者 sàipǎozhě [个 gè]

runner-up [rʌnər'ʌp] N [c] 亚(亞)军(軍) yàjūn [个 gè]

running ['rʌnɪŋ] N [U] (sport) 赛(賽)跑 sàipǎo ▸ **6 days running** 连(連)续(續)6 天 liánxù liù tiān

run-up ['rʌnʌp] N ▸ **the run-up to...** [+ election etc] …的前期 …de qiánqī

runway ['rʌnweɪ] N [c] 跑道 pǎodào [条 tiáo]

rush [rʌʃ] I N [s] (hurry) 匆忙 cōngmáng II VI [person +] 急速前往 jísù qiánwǎng

rush hour N [c] 高峰时(時)间(間) gāofēng shíjiān [段 duàn]

Russia ['rʌʃə] N 俄罗(羅)斯 Éluósī

Russian ['rʌʃən] I ADJ 俄罗(羅)斯的 Éluósī de II N **1** [c] (person) 俄罗(羅)斯人 Éluósīrén [个 gè] **2** [U] (language) 俄 语(語) Éyǔ

rust [rʌst] N [U] 铁(鐵)锈(鏽) tiěxiù

rusty ['rʌstɪ] ADJ **1** [+ surface, object] 生 锈(鏽)的 shēngxiù de **2** [+ skill] 荒疏的 huāngshū de

RV (US) N ABBR (= recreational vehicle) 娱(娛)乐(樂)车(車) yúlèchē

rye [raɪ] N [U] (cereal) 黑麦(麥) hēimài

S

sack [sæk] I N [c] 麻袋 mádài [个 gè] II VT 解雇(僱) jiěgù

sad [sæd] ADJ 1 伤(傷)心的 shāngxīn de 2 (distressing) 令人悲伤(傷)的 lìng rén bēishāng de

saddle ['sædl] N [c] (for horse) 马(馬)鞍 mǎ'ān [副 fù]; (on bike, motorbike) 车(車)座 chēzuò [个 gè]

safe [seɪf] I ADJ 1 (not dangerous) 安全的 ānquán de 2 (out of danger) 脱(脫)险(險)的 tuōxiǎn de 3 [+ place] 保险(險)的 bǎoxiǎn de II N [c] 保险(險)箱 bǎoxiǎnxiāng [个 gè]

safety ['seɪftɪ] N [u] 1 安全 ānquán 2 [of person, crew] 平安 píng'ān

Sagittarius [sædʒɪ'tɛərɪəs] N [u] (sign) 人马(馬)座 Rénmǎ Zuò

said [sɛd] PT, PP of say

sail [seɪl] I N [c] 帆 fān [张 zhāng] II VI [ship +] 航行 hángxíng; [passenger +] 乘船航行 chéngchuán hángxíng ▸ to go sailing 去航行 qù hángxíng

sailing ['seɪlɪŋ] N [u] 帆船运(運)动(動) fānchuán yùndòng

sailor ['seɪləʳ] N [c] 水手 shuǐshǒu [名 míng]

saint [seɪnt] N [c] 圣(聖)徒 shèngtú [位 wèi]

salad ['sæləd] N [c/u] 色拉 sèlā [份 fèn]

salary ['sælərɪ] N [c/u] 薪水 xīnshuǐ [份 fèn]

sale [seɪl] I N 1 [s] (selling) 出售 chūshòu 2 [c] (with reductions) 贱(賤)卖(賣) jiànmài [次 cì] II **sales** N PL (quantity sold) 销(銷)售量 xiāoshòuliàng ▸ to be (up) for sale 待售 dàishòu ▸ to be on sale (Brit) 上市 shàngshì; (US: reduced) 廉价(價)出售 liánjià chūshòu

salesman ['seɪlzmən] (pl **salesmen**) N [c] 推销(銷)员(員) tuīxiāoyuán [位 wèi]

salmon ['sæmən] (pl **salmon**) N [c/u] 大马(馬)哈鱼(魚) dàmǎhāyú [条 tiáo]

salon ['sælɔn] N [c] 发(髮)廊 fàláng [家 jiā]

salt [sɔːlt] N [u] 盐(鹽) yán

salty ['sɔːltɪ] ADJ [+ food] 咸(鹹)的 xián de

same [seɪm] I ADJ 1 [+ size, colour, age] 相同的 xiāngtóng de 2 [+ place, person, time] 同一个(個)的 tóng yī gè de II PRON ▸ the same 1 (similar) 一样(樣) yīyàng 2 (also: the same thing) 同样(樣) tóngyàng ▸ the same as 与(與)…一样(樣) yǔ…yīyàng ▸ the same book/place as 与(與)…一样(樣)的书(書)/地方 yǔ…yīyàng de shū/dìfang ▸ at the same time 同时(時) tóngshí

same-sex ['seɪm,sɛks] ADJ 同性的 tóngxìng de ▸ same-sex marriage/relationship 同性婚姻/关(關)系 tóngxìng hūnyīn/guānxi

sample ['sɑːmpl] N [c] 样(樣)品 yàngpǐn [件 jiàn]; [of blood, urine] 采(採)样(樣) cǎiyàng [个 gè]

sand [sænd] N [u] 沙子 shāzi

sandal ['sændl] N [c] 凉(涼)鞋 liángxié [双 shuāng]

sandwich ['sændwɪtʃ] N [c] 三明治 sānmíngzhì [份 fèn] ▸ a cheese/ham/jam sandwich 奶酪/火腿/果酱(醬)三明治 nǎilào/huǒtuǐ/guǒjiàng sānmíngzhì

sang [sæŋ] PT of sing

sanitary napkin ['sænɪtərɪ-] (US) N [c] 卫(衛)生巾 wèishēngjīn [块 kuài]

sanitary towel (Brit) N [c] 卫(衛)生巾 wèishēngjīn [块 kuài]

sank [sæŋk] PT of sink

Santa (Claus) ['sæntə('klɔːz)] N 圣(聖)诞(誕)老人 Shèngdàn Lǎorén

sardine [sɑː'diːn] N [c] 沙丁鱼(魚) shādīngyú [条 tiáo]

SARS [sɑːz] N ABBR (= severe acute respiratory syndrome) 非典型性肺炎 fēidiǎnxíngxìng fèiyán

SAT N ABBR (US) (= Scholastic Aptitude Test) 学(學)业能力倾(傾)向测(測)试(試) Xuéyè Nénglì Qīngxiàng Cèshì

sat [sæt] PT, PP of **sit**

satellite ['sætəlaɪt] N 1 [c] 人造卫(衛)星 rénzào wèixīng [颗 kē] 2 [c] (also: **satellite television**) 卫(衛)星电(電)视(視) wèixīng diànshì

satisfactory [sætɪsˈfæktərɪ] ADJ 令人满(滿)意的 lìng rén mǎnyì de

satisfied ['sætɪsfaɪd] ADJ 满(滿)足的 mǎnzú de ▶ **to be satisfied with sth** 对(對)某事满(滿)意 duì mǒushì mǎnyì

sat nav ['sætnæv] N [c] 卫(衛)星导(導)航 wèixīng dǎoháng

Saturday ['sætədɪ] N [c/u] 星期六 xīngqīliù [个 gè]; see also/另见 **Tuesday**

sauce [sɔːs] N [c/u] 酱(醬) jiàng [种 zhǒng]

saucepan ['sɔːspən] N [c] 深平底锅(鍋) shēnpíngdǐguō [个 gè]

saucer ['sɔːsər] N [c] 茶杯碟 chábēidié [个 gè]

Saudi Arabia [saʊdɪˈreɪbɪə] N 沙特阿拉伯 Shātè Ālābó

sausage ['sɔsɪdʒ] N [c/u] 香肠(腸) xiāngcháng [根 gēn]

save [seɪv] I VT 1 [+ person] 救 jiù 2 (also: **save up**) 积(積)攒(攢) jīzǎn 3 (economize on) [+ money, time] 节(節)省 jiéshěng 4 (Comput) 存储(儲) cúnchǔ II VI (also: **save up**) 积(積)攒(攢) jīzǎn ▶ **to save sb's life** 挽救某人的生命 wǎnjiù mǒurén de shēngmìng

savings ['seɪvɪŋz] NPL (money) 存款 cúnkuǎn

savoury, (US) **savory** ['seɪvərɪ] ADJ 咸(鹹)辣的 xiánlà de

saw [sɔː] (pt sawed, pp sawed or sawn) I PT of **see** II VT 锯(鋸) jù III N [c] 锯(鋸)子 jùzi [把 bǎ]

sawn [sɔːn] PP of **saw**

saxophone ['sæksəfəʊn] N [c] 萨(薩)克斯管 sàkèsīguǎn [根 gēn]

say [seɪ] (pt, pp said) VT 1 说(說) shuō 2 (clock, watch +) 表明 biǎomíng; [sign +] 写(寫)着(著) xiězhe ▶ **to say sth to sb** 告诉(訴)某人某事 gàosù mǒurén mǒushì ▶ **to say yes/no** 同意/不同意 tóngyì/bù tóngyì

scale [skeɪl] N [s] (size, extent) 规(規)模

guīmó scales NPL 秤 chèng ▶ **on a large/small scale** 以大/小规(規)模 yǐ dà/xiǎo guīmó

scandal ['skændl] N [c] 丑(醜)闻(聞) chǒuwén [条 tiáo]

Scandinavia [skændɪˈneɪvɪə] N 斯堪的纳(納)维(維)亚(亞) Sīkāndìnàwéiyà

scanner ['skænər] N [c] (Comput) 扫(掃)描仪(儀) sǎomiáoyí [台 tái]

scar [skɑː] N [c] 伤(傷)疤 shāngbā [个 gè]

scarce [skɛəs] ADJ 短缺的 duǎnquē de

scarcely ['skɛəslɪ] ADV 几(幾)乎不 jīhū bù

scare [skɛər] VT 使害怕 shǐ hàipà

scared ['skɛəd] ADJ ▶ **to be scared (of sb/ sth)** 害怕 (某人/某物) hàipà (mǒurén/mǒuwù)

scarf [skɑːf] (pl **scarfs** or **scarves**) N [c] (long) 围(圍)巾 wéijīn [条 tiáo]; (square) 头(頭)巾 tóujīn [块 kuài]

scarves [skɑːvz] NPL of **scarf**

scenery ['siːnərɪ] N [u] 风(風)景 fēngjǐng

schedule ['ʃedjuːl, US'skedjuːl] N [c] 1 (agenda) 日程安排 rìchéng ānpái [个 gè] 2 (US) [of trains, buses] 时(時)间(間)表 shíjiānbiǎo [个 gè] ▶ **on schedule** 准(準)时(時) zhǔnshí ▶ **to be ahead of/ behind schedule** 提前/落后(後)于(於)计(計)划(劃) tíqián/luòhòu yú jìhuà

scheme [skiːm] N [c] (plan) 方案 fāng'àn [个 gè]

scholarship ['skɒləʃɪp] N [c] 奖(獎)学(學)金 jiǎngxuéjīn [项 xiàng]

school [skuːl] N 1 [c/u] (place) 学(學)校 xuéxiào [所 suǒ]; (pupils and staff) 全体(體)师(師)生 quántǐ shīshēng 2 [c/u] (US) 大学(學) dàxué [所 suǒ] ▶ **to go to school** [child +] 上学(學) shàngxué ▶ **to leave school** [child +] 结(結)束义(義)务(務)教育 jiéshù yìwù jiàoyù

schoolboy ['skuːlbɔɪ] N [c] 男生 nánshēng [个 gè]

schoolchildren ['skuːltʃɪldrən] NPL 学(學)童 xuétóng

schoolgirl ['skuːlgəːl] N [c] 女生 nǚshēng [个 gè]

science ['saɪəns] N 1 [u] (scientific study) 科学(學) kēxué 2 [c/u] (branch of science, school subject) 学(學)科 xuékē [个 gè]

science fiction N [U] 科幻小说(說) kēhuàn xiǎoshuō

scientific [saɪən'tɪfɪk] ADJ 科学(學)的 kēxué de

scientist ['saɪəntɪst] N [c] 科学(學)家 kēxuéjiā [位 wèi]

scissors ['sɪzəz] NPL 剪刀 jiǎndāo ▸ **a pair of scissors** 一把剪刀 yī bǎ jiǎndāo

scooter ['sku:tə'] N [c] (also: **motor scooter**) 小型摩托车(車) xiǎoxíng mótuōchē [辆 liàng]

score [skɔː'] I N [c] 比分 bǐfēn [个 gè] II VT [+ goal, point] 得 dé III VI (in game, sport) 得分 défēn

Scorpio ['skɔːpɪəu] N [U] (sign) 天蝎(蠍) 座 Tiānxiē Zuò

Scotch tape® (US) N [U] 透明胶(膠) 带(帶) tòumíng jiāodài

Scotland ['skɔtlənd] N 苏(蘇)格兰(蘭) Sūgélán

Scottish ['skɔtɪʃ] ADJ 苏(蘇)格兰(蘭)的 Súgélán de

scrambled egg ['skræmbld-] N [c/U] 炒 鸡(雞)蛋 chǎo jīdàn [盘 pán]

scrap [skræp] VT **1** [+ car, ship] 报(報) 废(廢) bàofèi **2** [+ project, idea, system, tax] 废(廢)弃(棄) fèiqì

scratch [skrætʃ] I N [c] **1** (on car, furniture) 刮痕 guāhén [条 tiáo] **2** (on body) 擦 伤(傷) cāshāng [处 chù] II VT **1** (damage) 划(劃)破 huápò **2** (because of itch) 搔 sāo

scream [skri:m] VI 尖声(聲)喊叫 jiānshēng hǎnjiào

screen [skri:n] N [c] **1** (at cinema) 银(銀) 幕 yínmù [块 kuài] **2** (of television, computer) 屏幕 píngmù [个 gè]

screw [skru:] N [c] 螺丝(絲) luósī [个 gè]

screwdriver ['skru:draɪvə'] N [c] 螺 丝(絲)起子 luósī qǐzi [把 bǎ]

scroll [skrəul] (Comput) VT 滚(滾)屏 gǔn píng

▸ **scroll down** VI 向下滚(滾)屏 xiàng xià gǔn píng

▸ **scroll up** VI 向上滚(滾)屏 xiàng shàng gǔn píng

sculpture ['skʌlptʃə'] N [U] 雕塑 diāosù

sea [si:] N ▸ **the sea** 海洋 hǎiyáng ▸ **by sea** 由海路 yóu hǎilù

seafood ['si:fu:d] N [U] 海味 hǎiwèi

seagull ['si:gʌl] N [c] 海鸥(鷗) hǎi'ōu [只 zhī]

seal [si:l] N [c] 海豹 hǎibào [只 zhī]

search [sə:tʃ] I N [c] **1** (for missing person) 搜(蒐)寻(尋) sōuxún [次 cì] **2** (Comput) 检(檢)索 jiǎnsuǒ [次 cì] II VT 搜查 sōuchá

seashore ['si:ʃɔː'] N [c] 海岸 hǎi'àn

seasick ['si:sɪk] ADJ 晕(暈)船的 yùnchuán de ▸ **to be or feel seasick** 感 到晕(暈)船恶(噁)心 gǎndào yùnchuán ěxīn

seaside ['si:saɪd] (Brit) N ▸ **the seaside** 海边(邊) hǎibiān

season ['si:zn] N [c] 季节(節) jìjié [个 gè]

seat [si:t] N [c] **1** (chair) 椅子 yǐzi [把 bǎ]; (in car, theatre, cinema) 座 zuò [个 gè] **2** (place) (in train, bus, train) 座位 zuòwèi [个 gè] ▸ **to take a/one's seat** 就座 jiùzuò ▸ **to be seated** (be sitting) 坐 下 zuòxià

seat belt N [c] 安全带(帶) ānquándài [条 tiáo]

second ['sɛkənd] I ADJ 第二的 dì'èr de II ADV [come, finish +] 第二名地 dì'èr míng de III N [c] (unit of time) 秒 miǎo ▸ **second floor** (Brit) 三层(層) sān céng; (US) 二层(層) èr céng

secondary school N [c/U] 中学(學) zhōngxué [所 suǒ]

second-hand ['sɛkənd'hænd] ADJ 二手 的 èrshǒu de

secondly ['sɛkəndlɪ] ADV 其次 qící

secret ['si:krɪt] I ADJ 秘(祕)密的 mìmì de II N [c] 秘(祕)密 mìmì [个 gè]

secretary ['sɛkrətərɪ] N [c] 秘(祕)书(書) mìshū [位 wèi]

section ['sɛkʃən] N [c] 部分 bùfen [个 gè]

security [sɪ'kjuərɪtɪ] N [U] 保安措施 bǎo'ān cuòshī

see [si:] (pt saw, pp seen) VT **1** 看见(見) kànjiàn **2** (meet) 见(見) jiàn **3** [+ film, play] 看 kàn **4** (notice) 意识(識)到 yìshídào ▸ **to see sb doing/do sth** 看 见(見)某人做某事 kànjiàn mǒurén zuò mǒushì ▸ **to go and see sb** 去见(見)某 人 qù jiàn mǒurén ▸ **see you later!** 一 会(會)儿(兒)见(見)! yīhuìr jiàn! ▸ **I see** 我明白 wǒ míngbai

seed [si:d] N [c/U] 籽 zǐ [粒 lì]

seem [si:m] VI 似乎 sìhū ▸ **it seems that...** 看来(來)… kànlái…

seen [si:n] PP of **see**

seldom ['sɛldəm] ADV 不常 bùcháng

select [sɪ'lɛkt] VT 挑选(選) tiāoxuǎn

selection [sɪ'lɛkʃən] N [c] 供选(選)择(擇)的范(範)围(圍) gōng xuǎnzé de fànwéi [个 gè]

self-confidence [sɛlf'kɒnfɪdns] N [U] 自信心 zìxìnxīn

selfie ['sɛlfɪ] N [c] 自拍照 zìpāi zhào [张(張) zhāng] ▸ **to take a selfie** 自拍 zì pāi

selfie stick N [c] 自拍杆 zìpāi gǎn [根 gēn]

selfish ['sɛlfɪʃ] ADJ 自私的 zìsī de

self-service [sɛlf'sə:vɪs] ADJ 自助的 zìzhù de

sell [sɛl] (pt, pp **sold**) VT 卖(賣) mài ▸ **to sell sb sth, sell sth to sb** 将(將)某物卖(賣)给(給)某人 jiāng mǒuwù màigěi mǒurén

semi-final [sɛmɪ'faɪnl] N [c] 半决(決)赛(賽) bànjuésài [场 chǎng]

send [sɛnd] (pt, pp **sent**) VT 1 ▸ **to send sth (to sb)** 将(將)某物发(發)送(给(給)某人) jiāng mǒuwù fāsòng (gěi mǒurén) 2 [+ person] 派遣 pàiqiǎn

senior ['si:nɪə'] ADJ 高级(級)的 gāojí de

senior citizen N [c] 已届(屆)退休年龄(齡)的公民 yǐ jiè tuìxiū niánlíng de gōngmín [位 wèi]

senior high, (US) senior high school N [c] 高中 gāozhōng [所 suǒ]

sense [sɛns] N 1 [c] [of smell, taste] 感觉(覺)官能 gǎnjué guānnéng [种 zhǒng] 2 [U] (good sense) 明智 míngzhì 3 [c] (meaning) 释(釋)义(義) shìyì [个 gè]

sensible ['sɛnsɪbl] ADJ 通情达(達)理的 tōng qíng dá lǐ de; [+ decision, suggestion] 明智的 míngzhì de

sensitive ['sɛnsɪtɪv] ADJ 1 善解人意的 shàn jiě rényì de 2 [+ skin] 敏感的 mǐngǎn de

sent [sɛnt] PT, PP of **send**

sentence ['sɛntns] N [c] (Ling) 句子 jùzi [个 gè]

separate [adj 'sɛprɪt, vb 'sɛpəreɪt] I ADJ [+ section, piece, pile] 分开(開)的 fēnkāi de; [+ rooms] 单(單)独(獨)的 dāndú de II VT (split up) 分开(開) fēnkāi III VI [parents, couple +] 分居 fēnjū ▸ **to be separated** [couple +] 分居 fēnjū

September [sɛp'tɛmbə'] N [c/U] 九月 jiǔyuè; see also/另见 **July**

serial ['sɪərɪəl] N [c] 连(連)续(續)剧(劇) liánxùjù [部 bù]; (in magazine) 连(連)载(載) liánzài [个 gè]

series ['sɪəriːz] (pl **series**) N [c] 1 一系列 yīxìliè [个 gè] 2 (on TV, radio) 系列节(節)目 xìliè jiémù [个 gè]

serious ['sɪərɪəs] ADJ 1 严(嚴)重的 yánzhòng de 2 (sincere) 当(當)真的 dàngzhēn de; (solemn) 严(嚴)肃(肅)的 yánsù de

serve [sə:v] VT 1 (in shop, bar) 招待 zhāodài 2 [+ food, drink, meal] 端上 duānshàng

service ['sə:vɪs] N 1 [c] 服务(務) fúwù [项 xiàng] 2 [c] (train/bus service) 火车(車)/公共汽车(車)营(營)运(運) huǒchē/gōnggòng qìchē yíngyùn [种 zhǒng] 3 [c] (Rel) 仪(儀)式 yíshì [个 gè] ▸ **service included/not included** 含/不含小费(費) hán/bù hán xiǎofèi

service charge N [c] 服务(務)费(費) fúwùfèi [笔 bǐ]

service station N [c] 加油站 jiāyóuzhàn [座 zuò]

set [sɛt] (pt, pp **set**) N 1 [c] [of cutlery, saucepans, books, keys] 套 tào 2 [c] (TV, Rad) 电(電)视(視)机(機) diànshìjī [台 tái] II ADJ [+ routine, time, price] 规(規)定的 guīdìng de III VT 1 (put) 放 fàng 2 [+ table] 摆(擺)放 bǎifàng 3 [+ time, price, rules] 确(確)定 quèdìng 4 [+ alarm] 设(設)定 shèdìng; [+ heating, volume] 调(調)整 tiáozhěng IV VI [sun +] 落山 luòshān ▸ **a chess set** 一副国(國)际(際)象棋 yī fù guójì xiàngqí ▸ **set off** I VI ▸ **to set off (for)** 启(啟)程(前往) qǐchéng (qiánwǎng) II VT [+ alarm] 触(觸)发(發) chùfā ▸ **set out** VI 出发(發) chūfā

settee [sɛ'ti:] N [c] 长(長)沙发(發)椅 chángshāfāyǐ [个 gè]

settle ['sɛtl] VT [+ bill, account, debt] 支付 zhīfù

seven ['sɛvn] NUM 七 qī; see also/另见 **five**

seventeen [sɛvn'ti:n] NUM 十七 shíqī; see also/另见 **fifteen**

seventh ['sɛvnθ] NUM 第七 dìqī; see also/另见 **fifth**

seventy ['sɛvntɪ] NUM 七十 qīshí; see also/另见 **fifty**

several ['sɛvərəl] ADJ, PRON 几(幾)个(個)
jǐ gè

severe [sɪ'vɪər] ADJ 1 [+ pain, damage,
shortage] 严(嚴)重的 yánzhòng de
2 [+ punishment, criticism] 严(嚴)厉(厲)
的 yánlì de

sew [səu] (pt sewed, pp sewn) VI, VT
缝(縫) féng

sewing ['səuɪŋ] N [U] 缝(縫)纫(紉)
féngrèn

sewn [səun] PP of sew

sex [sɛks] N 1 [c] (gender) 性别(別)
xìngbié [种 zhǒng] 2 [U] (lovemaking)
性交 xìngjiāo ▸ to have sex (with sb)
(和某人)性交 (hé mǒurén) xìngjiāo

sexism ['sɛksɪzəm] N [U] 性别(別)歧
视(視) xìngbié qíshì

sexist ['sɛksɪst] ADJ 性别(別)歧视(視)的
xìngbié qíshì de

sexual ['sɛksjuəl] ADJ 性的 xìng de

sexy ['sɛksɪ] ADJ 性感的 xìnggǎn de

shade [ʃeɪd] N 1 [c] 阴(陰)凉(涼)处(處)
yīnliángchù 2 [c] of colour 色度 sèdù
[种 zhǒng] 3 [c] (US) 遮阳(陽)窗帘(簾)
zhēyáng chuānglián [幅 fú]

shadow ['ʃædəu] N [c] 影子 yǐngzi [个 gè]

shake [ʃeɪk] (pt shook, pp shaken) ['ʃeɪkn]
I VT [+ bottle, cocktail, medicine] 摇(搖)晃
yáohuàng; [+ buildings, ground] 使震
动(動) shǐ zhèndòng II VI [person, part of
the body +] 发(發)抖 fādǒu; [building,
table +] 震动(動) zhèndòng; [ground +]
震颤(顫) zhènchàn ▸ to shake one's
head 摇(搖)头(頭)拒绝(絕) yáotóu
jùjué ▸ to shake hands (with sb) (和某
人)握手 (hé mǒurén) wòshǒu

shall [ʃæl] AUX VB 1 (indicating future in 1st
person) ▸ I shall go 我要走了 wǒ yào
zǒu le 2 (in 1st person questions) ▸ shall I/
we open the door? 我/我们(們)把
门(門)打开(開)好吗(嗎)? wǒ/wǒmen
bǎ mén dǎkāi hǎo ma?

shallow ['ʃæləu] ADJ 浅(淺)的 qiǎn de

shame [ʃeɪm] N [U] 耻(恥)辱 chǐrǔ ▸ it is
a shame that... …真遗(遺)憾 …zhēn
yíhàn ▸ what a shame! 太遗(遺)憾了！
tài yíhàn le!

shampoo [ʃæm'puː] N [c/u] 洗发(髮)液
xǐfàyè [瓶 píng]

shape [ʃeɪp] N [c] 形状(狀) xíngzhuàng
[种 zhǒng]

share [ʃɛər] I N [c] 1 (part) 一份 yī fèn
2 (Comm, Fin) 股票 gǔpiào [支 zhī] II VT
1 [+ room, bed, taxi] 合用 héyòng 2 [+ job,
cooking, task] 分担(擔) fēndān
▸ share out VT 平均分配 píngjūn
fēnpèi

shark [ʃɑːk] N [c/u] 鲨(鯊)鱼(魚) shāyú
[条 tiáo]

sharp [ʃɑːp] I ADJ 1 [+ knife, teeth] 锋(鋒)
利的 fēnglì de; [+ point, edge] 尖锐(銳)的
jiānruì de 2 [+ curve, bend] 急转(轉)的
jízhuǎn de II ADV (precisely) ▸ at 2 o'clock
sharp 两(兩)点(點)整 liǎng diǎn zhěng

shave [ʃeɪv] I VT [+ head, legs] 剃毛发(髮)
tì máofà II VI 刮脸(臉) guā liǎn

shaving cream N [U] 剃须(鬚)膏
tìxūgāo

she [ʃiː] PRON 她 tā

she'd [ʃiːd] = she had, she would

sheep [ʃiːp] (pl sheep) N [c] 绵(綿)羊
miányáng [只 zhī]

sheet [ʃiːt] N [c] 1 床单(單) chuángdān
[床 chuáng] 2 [of paper] 一张(張) yī
zhāng

shelf [ʃɛlf] (pl shelves) N [c] (bookshelf) 架
子 jiàzi [个 gè]; (in cupboard) 搁(擱)板
gēbǎn [块 kuài]

shell [ʃɛl] N 1 贝(貝)壳(殼) bèiké [只
zhī] 2 [of tortoise, snail, crab, egg, nut]
壳(殼) ké [个 gè]

she'll [ʃiːl] = she will

shellfish ['ʃɛlfɪʃ] (pl shellfish) I N [c/u]
贝(貝)类(類)海产(產) bèilèi hǎichǎn [种
zhǒng] II NPL (as food) 贝(貝)类(類)海
鲜(鮮) bèilèi hǎixiān

shelter ['ʃɛltər] I N [c] (building) 遮蔽
处(處) zhēbìchù [个 gè] II VI 躲避 duǒbì

shelves ['ʃɛlvz] NPL of shelf

she's [ʃiːz] = she is, she has

shift [ʃɪft] VT 移动(動) yídòng

shin [ʃɪn] N [c] 胫(脛)部 jìngbù

shine [ʃaɪn] (pt, pp shone) VI 照耀
zhàoyào

ship [ʃɪp] N [c] 船 chuán [艘 sōu]

shirt [ʃəːt] N [c] 衬(襯)衫 chènshān [件
jiàn]

shiver ['ʃɪvər] VI 发(發)抖 fādǒu

shock [ʃɔk] I N 1 震惊(驚) zhènhài [种
zhǒng] 2 [U] (Med) 休克 xiūkè 3 [c] (also:
electric shock) 触(觸)电(電) chùdiàn
[次 cì] II VT 使厌(厭)恶(惡) shǐ yànwù

shocked [ʃɔkt] ADJ 感到不快的 gǎndào bùkuài de

shoe [ʃu:] N [c] 鞋 xié [双 shuāng] ▸ a pair of shoes 一双(雙)鞋 yī shuāng xié

shone [ʃɒn] PT, PP of **shine**

shook [ʃuk] PT of **shake**

shoot [ʃu:t] (pt, pp shot) I VT (kill) 向… 开(開)枪(槍) xiàng…kāiqiāng II VI **1** (with gun, bow) ▸ to shoot (at sb/sth) (朝某人/某物) 射击(擊) (cháo mǒurén/mǒuwù) shèjī **2** (Football etc) 射门(門) shèmén

shop [ʃɒp] I N [c] (esp Brit) 商店 shāngdiàn [家 jiā] II VI 购(購)物 gòuwù ▸ to go shopping 去买(買)东(東)西 qù mǎi dōngxi

shop assistant (Brit) N [c] 店员(員) diànyuán [位 wèi]

shopping ['ʃɒpɪŋ] N [U] **1** (activity) 购(購)物 gòuwù **2** (goods) 所购(購)之物 suǒ gòu zhī wù; see also/另见 **shop**

shopping centre, (US) **shopping center** N [c] 购(購)物中心 gòuwù zhōngxīn [个 gè]

shop window N [c] 商店橱(櫥)窗 shāngdiàn chúchuāng [个 gè]

shore [ʃɔ:ʳ] N [c] 岸 àn [个 gè]

short [ʃɔ:t] I ADJ **1** (in time) 短暂(暫)的 duǎnzàn de **2** (in length) 短的 duǎn de **3** (not tall) 矮的 ǎi de II SHORTS NPL **1** (short trousers) 短裤(褲) duǎnkù **2** (esp US: underpants) 男用短衬(襯)裤(褲) nányòng duǎnchènkù ▸ a pair of shorts 一条(條)短裤(褲) yī tiáo duǎnkù

shortage ['ʃɔ:tɪdʒ] N [c/U] 短缺 duǎnquē

shortly ['ʃɔ:tlɪ] ADV 马(馬)上 mǎshàng ▸ shortly after/before sth 某事后(後)/前不久 mǒushì hòu/qián bùjiǔ

short-sighted [ʃɔ:t'saɪtɪd] ADJ (Brit) 近视(視)的 jìnshì de

shot [ʃɒt] I PT, PP of **shoot** II N **1** [c] 射击(擊) shèjī [阵 zhèn] **2** [c] (Football) 射门(門) shèmén [次 cì] **3** (injection) 皮下注射 píxià zhùshè [针 zhēn]

should [ʃud] AUX VB **1** (indicating advisability) ▸ I should go now 我现(現)在应(應)该(該)走了 wǒ xiànzài yīnggāi zǒu le **2** (indicating obligation) 应(應)当(當) yīngdāng **3** (indicating likelihood) ▸ he should be there by now/he should

get there soon 他现(現)在该(該)到那儿(兒)了/他应(應)该(該)很快就到那儿(兒)了 tā xiànzài gāi dào nàr le/tā yīnggāi hěn kuài jiù dào nàr le ▸ you should have been more careful 你本该(該)更加小心 nǐ běn gāi gèngjiā xiǎoxīn ▸ he should have arrived by now 他现(現)在应(應)该(該)到了 tā xiànzài yīnggāi dào le

shoulder ['ʃəuldəʳ] N [c] 肩膀 jiānbǎng [个 gè]

shout [ʃaut] VI (also: shout out) 喊叫 hǎnjiào

show [ʃəu] (pt showed, pp shown) I N [c] **1** (exhibition) 展览(覽) zhǎnlǎn [个 gè] **2** (TV, Rad) 节(節)目 jiémù [个 gè] II VT **1** 表明 biǎomíng ▸ to show sb sth or to show sth to sb 给(給)某人看某物(或)把某物给(給)某人看 gěi mǒurén kàn mǒuwù huò bǎ mǒuwù gěi mǒurén kàn **2** (illustrate, depict) 描述 miáoshù ▸ on show 在展览(覽)中 zài zhǎnlǎn zhōng ▸ to show that… 表明… biǎomíng… ▸ to show sb how to do sth 示范(範)某人如何做某事 shìfàn mǒurén rúhé zuò mǒushì

shower ['ʃauəʳ] N [c] **1** 阵(陣)雨 zhènyǔ [场 cháng] **2** (for washing) 淋浴器 línyùqì [个 gè] II VI 洗淋浴 xǐ línyù ▸ to have or take a shower 洗淋浴 xǐ línyù

shown [ʃəun] PP of **show**

shrank [ʃræŋk] PT of **shrink**

shrimp [ʃrɪmp] N [c] **1** (small) 小虾(蝦) xiǎoxiā [只 zhī]; (US: bigger) 虾(蝦) xiā [只 zhī]

shrink [ʃrɪŋk] (pt shrank, pp shrunk) VI 缩(縮)水 suōshuǐ

shrunk [ʃrʌŋk] PP of **shrink**

shut [ʃʌt] (pt, pp shut) I VT 关(關)上 guānshàng; [+ shop] 关(關)门(門) guānmén; [+ mouth, eyes] 闭(閉)上 bìshàng II VI [shop +] 打烊 dǎyàng III ADJ [+ door, drawer] 关(關)闭(閉)的 guānbì de; [+ shop] 打烊的 dǎyàng de; [+ mouth, eyes] 闭(閉)着(著)的 bìzhe de ▸ shut up VI (inf) 住口 zhùkǒu ▸ shut up! (inf) 闭(閉)嘴! bìzuǐ!

shuttle ['ʃʌtl] N [c] (plane, bus) 穿梭班机(機)/班车(車) chuānsuō bānjī/

bānchē [架/辆 jià/liàng]

shy [ʃaɪ] ADJ 害羞的 hàixiū de

sick [sɪk] ADJ **1** (physically) 患病的 huànbìng de; (mentally) 令人讨(討)厌(厭)的 lìng rén tǎoyàn de **2** ▸ to be sick (vomit) 呕(嘔)吐 ǒutù ▸ to feel sick 感觉(覺)恶(惡)心 gǎnjué ěxīn

sickness [sɪknɪs] N [U] 患病 huànbìng

side [saɪd] I N [c] **1** 边(邊) biān [个 gè] **2** [of building, vehicle] 侧(側)面 cèmiàn [个 gè]; [of body] 体(體)侧(側) tǐcè [边 biān] **3** [of paper, face, brain] 一面 yī miàn [个 gè]; [of tape, record] 面 miàn [个 gè] **4** [of road, bed] 边(邊)缘(緣) biānyuán [个 gè] **5** [of hill, valley] 坡 pō [个 gè] **6** (Brit: team) 队(隊) duì [支 zhī] **7** (in conflict, contest) 一方 yīfāng II ADJ [+ door, entrance] 旁边(邊)的 pángbiān de ▸ on the other side of sth 在某物的另一边(邊) zài mǒuwù de lìng yī biān

side-effect [saɪdɪfekt] N [c] 副作用 fùzuòyòng [个 gè]

sidewalk [saɪdwɔːk] (US) N [c] 人行道 rénxíngdào [条 tiáo]

sigh [saɪ] N [c] 叹(嘆)气(氣) tànqì

sight [saɪt] I N [u] 视(視)力 shìlì **2** [c] (spectacle) 景象 jǐngxiàng [种 zhǒng] II **sights** NPL ▸ the sights 景点(點) jǐngdiǎn

sightseeing [saɪtsiːɪŋ] N [u] 观(觀)光 guāngguāng ▸ to go sightseeing 观(觀)光游(遊)览(覽) guāngguāng yóulǎn

sign [saɪn] I N **1** [c] 指示牌 zhǐshìpái [块 kuài] **2** [c] (also: road sign) 路标(標) lùbiāo [个 gè] **3** [c/u] (indication, evidence) 迹(跡)象 jìxiàng [种 zhǒng] II VT 签(簽)署 qiānshǔ ▸ it's a good/bad sign 这(這)是个(個)好/坏(壞)兆头(頭) zhè shì gè hǎo/huài zhàotou

signal [sɪgnl] I N [c] **1** (to do sth) 信号(號) xìnhào [个 gè] **2** (Rail) 信号(號)机(機) xìnhàojī [部 bù] **3** (Elec) 信号(號) xìnhào [个 gè] II VI (with gesture, sound) ▸ to signal (to sb) (向某人) 示意 (xiàng mǒurén) shìyì

signature [sɪgnətʃəʳ] N [c] 签(簽)名 qiānmíng [个 gè]

sign language N [c/u] 手语(語) shǒuyǔ [种 zhǒng]

signpost [saɪnpəust] N [c] 路标(標) lùbiāo [个 gè]

silence [saɪləns] N [c/u] 寂静(靜) jìjìng [片 piàn] ▸ in silence 鸦(鴉)雀无(無)声(聲) yā què wú shēng

silent [saɪlənt] ADJ [+ person] 沉默的 chénmò de

silk [sɪlk] N [c/u] 丝(絲)绸(綢) sīchóu [块 kuài]

silly [sɪlɪ] ADJ 愚蠢的 yúchǔn de; [+ idea, object] 可笑的 kěxiào de

silver [sɪlvəʳ] I N [u] 银(銀) yín II ADJ [+ spoon, necklace] 银(銀)的 yín de

SIM card [sɪm-] N [c] 手机(機)智能卡 shǒujī zhìnéngkǎ [张 zhāng]

similar [sɪmɪləʳ] ADJ 相似的 xiāngsì de ▸ to be similar to sth 和某事物类(類)似 hé mǒushìwù lèisì

simple [sɪmpl] ADJ **1** (easy) 简(簡)单(單)的 jiǎndān de **2** [+ meal, life, cottage] 简(簡)朴(樸)的 jiǎnpǔ de

simply [sɪmplɪ] ADV **1** (merely) 仅(僅)仅(僅) jǐnjǐn **2** (absolutely) 完全 wánquán

since [sɪns] I ADV (from then onwards) 此后(後) cǐhòu II PREP **1** (from) 自…以来(來) zì…yǐlái **2** (after) 从(從)…以后(後) cóng…yǐhòu III CONJ **1** (from when) 自从(從) zìcóng **2** (after) 从(從)…以后(後) cóng…yǐhòu **3** (as) 因为(為) yīnwèi ▸ since then or ever since 从(從)那时(時)起 cóng nàshí qǐ ▸ I've been here since the end of June 我自6月底以来(來)一直在这(這)儿(兒) wǒ zì liùyuè dǐ yǐlái yīzhí zài zhèr ▸ since it was Saturday, he stayed in bed an extra hour 因为(為)是星期六，他在床上多呆了一小时(時) yīnwèi shì xīngqīliù, tā zài chuáng shàng duō dāile yī xiǎoshí

sincere [sɪnsɪəʳ] ADJ 真诚(誠)的 zhēnchéng de

sincerely [sɪnsɪəlɪ] ADV 由衷地 yóuzhōng de ▸ Yours sincerely or (US) Sincerely yours 谨(謹)上 jǐnshàng

sing [sɪŋ] (pt sang, pp sung) I VI (person +) 唱歌 chànggē; (bird +) 鸣(鳴) míng II VT [+ song] 唱 chàng

Singapore [sɪŋgəpɔːʳ] N 新加坡 Xīnjiāpō

singer [sɪŋəʳ] N [c] 歌手 gēshǒu [位 wèi]

singing [sɪŋɪŋ] N [u] 唱歌 chànggē

single [sɪŋgl] I ADJ **1** (solitary) 单(單)个(個)的 dāngè de **2** (unmarried) 单(單)

身的 dānshēn de **II** N [c] (*Brit*) (*also*: **single ticket**) 单(單)程票 dānchéngpiào [张 zhāng]

singular ['sɪŋɡjulər] ADJ 单(單)数(數)的 dānshù de

sink [sɪŋk] (*pt* **sank**, *pp* **sunk**) **I** N [c] 洗涤(滌)槽 xǐdícáo [个 gè] **II** VI (*ship+*) 沉没(沒) chénmò

sir [sɜːr] N 先生 xiānsheng ▸ **Dear Sir** 亲(親)爱(愛)的先生 Qīn'ài de xiānsheng ▸ **Dear Sir or Madam** 亲(親)爱(愛)的先生或女士 Qīn'ài de xiānsheng huò nǔshì

siren ['saɪərn] N [c] 警报(報)器 jǐngbàoqì [个 gè]

sister ['sɪstər] N [c] 姐妹 jiěmèi [对 duì]; (*elder*) 姐姐 jiějie [个 gè]; (*younger*) 妹妹 mèimei [个 gè] ▸ **my brothers and sisters** 我的兄弟姐妹们(們) wǒde xiōngdì jiěmèimen

sister-in-law ['sɪstərɪnlɔː] (*pl* **sisters-in-law**) N [c] (*husband's sister*) 姑子 gūzi [个 gè]; (*wife's sister*) 姨子 yízi [个 gè]; (*older brother's wife*) 嫂子 sǎozi [位 wèi]; (*younger brother's wife*) 弟媳 dìxí [个 gè]

sit [sɪt] (*pt, pp* **sat**) VI **1** (*also*: **sit down**) 坐下 zuòxià **2** (*be sitting*) 坐 zuò ▸ **sit down** VI 坐下 zuòxià ▸ **to be sitting down** 就座 jiùzuò

site [saɪt] N [c] (*also*: **website**) 网(網)址 wǎngzhǐ [个 gè]

sitting room (*Brit*) N [c] 起居室 qǐjūshì [间 jiān]

situated ['sɪtjueɪtɪd] ADJ ▸ **to be situated in/on/near sth** 位于(於)某物中/上/旁 wèiyú mǒuwù zhōng/shàng/páng

situation [sɪtjuˈeɪʃən] N [c] 情况(況) qíngkuàng [种 zhǒng]

six [sɪks] NUM 六 liù; *see also*/另见 **five**

sixteen [sɪksˈtiːn] NUM 十六 shíliù; *see also*/另见 **fifteen**

sixth [sɪksθ] NUM **1** (*in series*) 第六 dìliù **2** (*fraction*) 六分之一 liù fēn zhī yī; *see also*/另见 **fifth**

sixty ['sɪkstɪ] NUM 六十 liùshí; *see also*/另见 **fifty**

size [saɪz] N **1** [c/u] (*of object*) 大小 dàxiǎo [种 zhǒng]; (*of clothing, shoes*) 尺码(碼) chǐmǎ [个 gè] **2** [u] (*of area, building, task, loss*) 大 dà ▸ **what size shoes do you take?** 你穿几(幾)号(號)的鞋? nǐ chuān jǐ hào de xié?

skate [skeɪt] VI **1** (*ice skate*) 溜冰 liūbīng **2** (*roller skate*) 溜旱冰 liū hànbīng

skateboard ['skeɪtbɔːd] N [c] 滑板 huábǎn [个 gè]

skating ['skeɪtɪŋ] N [u] (*ice-skating*) 冰上运(運)动(動) bīngshàng yùndòng; *see also*/另见 **skate**

skeleton ['skɛlɪtn] N [c] 骨骼 gǔgé [副 fù]

sketch [skɛtʃ] N [c] (*drawing*) 素描 sùmiáo [张 zhāng]

ski [skiː] VI 滑雪 huáxuě ▸ **to go skiing** 去滑雪 qù huáxuě

skiing ['skiːɪŋ] N [u] 滑雪 huáxuě; *see also*/另见 **ski**

skilful, (*US*) **skillful** ['skɪlful] ADJ 老练(練)的 lǎoliàn de; [+ *use, choice, management*] 技巧娴(嫻)熟的 jìqiǎo xiánshú de

skill [skɪl] N **1** [u] (*ability*) 技巧 jìqiǎo **2** [c] (*acquired*) 技能 jìnéng [项 xiàng]

skillful ['skɪlful] (*US*) ADJ = **skilful**

skin [skɪn] N [c/u] (*of person*) 皮肤(膚) pífū; [*of animal*] 皮 pí [张 zhāng]; (*complexion*) 肤(膚)色 fūsè [种 zhǒng]

skip [skɪp] **I** VT [+ *lunch, lecture*] 故意不做 gùyì bù zuò **II** N [c] (*Brit: container*) 无盖用以装运工地废料的废料桶

skirt [skɜːt] N [c] 裙子 qúnzi [条 tiáo]

skull [skʌl] N [c] 颅(顱)骨 lúgǔ [个 gè]

sky [skaɪ] N [c/u] 天空 tiānkōng [片 piàn]

skyscraper ['skaɪskreɪpər] N [c] 摩天大厦(廈) mótiān dàshà [座 zuò]

slap [slæp] **I** N [c] 掌击(擊) zhǎngjī [次 cì] **II** VT 掴(摑) guāi

sled [slɛd] (*US*) N [c] 雪橇 xuěqiāo [副 fù]

sledge [slɛdʒ] (*Brit*) N [c] 雪橇 xuěqiāo [副 fù]

sleep [sliːp] (*pt, pp* **slept**) **I** N **1** [u] 睡眠 shuìmián **2** [c] (*nap*) 睡觉(覺) shuìjiào **II** VI (*be asleep*) 睡 shuì; (*spend the night*) 过(過)夜 guòyè ▸ **to go to sleep** 去睡觉(覺) qù shuìjiào ▸ **sleep with** VT FUS 和…有性关(關)系(係) hé…yǒu xìngguānxì

sleeping bag ['sliːpɪŋ-] N [c] 睡袋 shuìdài [个 gè]

sleeping pill N [c] 安眠药(藥) ānmiányào [片 piàn]

sleet [sli:t] N [U] 雨夹(夾)雪 yǔjiāxuě

sleeve [sli:v] N [c] 袖子 xiùzi [只 zhī]

slept [slɛpt] PT, PP *of* **sleep**

slice [slaɪs] N [c] 片 piàn

slide [slaɪd] (*pt, pp* **slid** [slɪd]) I N [c] **1** (*in playground*) 滑梯 huátī [个 gè] **2** (*Brit*) (*also*: **hair slide**) 发(髮)夹(夾) fàjiā [个 gè] II VI ▶ **to slide down/off/into sth** 滑下/离(離)/进(進)某物 huáxià/lí/jìn mǒuwù

slight [slaɪt] ADJ 微小的 wēixiǎo de

slightly [ˈslaɪtlɪ] ADV 略微地 lüèwēi de

slim [slɪm] I ADJ 苗条(條)的 miáotiao de II VI 节(節)食减(減)肥 jiéshí jiǎnféi

slip [slɪp] I VI [*person +*] 滑跤 huájiāo; [*object +*] 滑落 huáluò II N [c] (*mistake*) 差错(錯) chācuò [个 gè]

slipper [ˈslɪpəˈ] N [c] 拖鞋 tuōxié [只 zhī]

slippery [ˈslɪpərɪ] ADJ 滑的 huá de

slot machine N [c] **1** (*for gambling*) 投币(幣)机(機) tóubìjī [个 gè]; **2** 吃角子老虎机(機) chījiǎozi lǎohǔjī [部 bù]

slow [sləu] I ADJ 慢的 màn de II ADV (*inf*) 缓(緩)慢地 huǎnmàn de ▶ **my watch is 20 minutes slow** 我的表(錶)慢了20分钟(鐘) wǒ de biǎo mànle èrshí fēnzhōng
▶ **slow down** VI 放松(鬆) fàngsōng

slowly [ˈsləulɪ] ADV 慢慢地 mànmàn de

smack [smæk] VT (*as punishment*) 打 dǎ

small [smɔ:l] ADJ **1** 小的 xiǎo de **2** (*young*) 年幼的 niányòu de **3** [*+ mistake, problem, change*] 微不足道的 wēi bù zú dào de

smart [smɑ:t] ADJ **1** (*esp Brit: neat, tidy*) 漂亮的 piàoliang de **2** (*fashionable*) 时(時)髦的 shímáo de **3** (*clever*) 聪(聰)明的 cōngming de

smart phone N [c] 智能手机(機) zhìnéng shǒujī [部 bù]

smash [smæʃ] VT 打碎 dǎsuì

smell [smɛl] (*pt, pp* **smelled** *or* **smelt**) I N [c] 气(氣)味 qìwèi [种 zhǒng] II VT 闻(聞)到 wéndào III VI **1** (*have unpleasant odour*) 发(發)臭 fā chòu **2** ▶ **to smell nice/delicious/spicy** *etc* 闻(聞)起来(來)香/好吃/辣〔等〕wén qǐlái xiāng/hǎochī/là děng ▶ **to smell of** 有…气(氣)味 yǒu…qìwèi

smelt [smɛlt] PT, PP *of* **smell**

smile [smaɪl] I N [c] 微笑 wēixiào [个 gè] II VI ▶ **to smile (at sb)** (对(對)某人) 微笑 (duì mǒurén) wēixiào

smoke [sməuk] I N [U] 烟(煙) yān II VI [*person +*] 吸烟(煙) xīyān III VT [*+ cigarette, cigar, pipe*] 抽 chōu

smoker [ˈsməukəˈ] N [c] 吸烟(煙)者 xīyānzhě [个 gè]

smoking [ˈsməukɪŋ] N [U] 吸烟(煙) xīyān ▶ **"no smoking"** "禁止吸烟(煙)" jìnzhǐ xīyān"

smooth [smu:ð] ADJ (*not rough*) 光滑的 guānghuá de

smoothie [ˈsmu:ðɪ] N [c] 冰沙 bīng shā

smother [ˈsmʌðəˈ] VT 使窒息 shǐ zhìxī

SMS N ABBR (= *short message service*) 短信息服务(務) duǎnxìnxī fúwù

smuggle [ˈsmʌgl] VT 走私 zǒusī ▶ **to smuggle sth in/out** 走私进(進)口/出口某物 zǒusī jìnkǒu/chūkǒu mǒuwù

snack [snæk] N [c] 小吃 xiǎochī [份 fèn]

snail [sneɪl] N [c] 蜗(蝸)牛 wōniú [只 zhī]

snake [sneɪk] N [c] 蛇 shé [条 tiáo]

snapshot [ˈsnæpʃɒt] N [c] 快照 kuàizhào [张 zhāng]

sneakers [ˈsni:kəz] (*US*) NPL 胶(膠)底运(運)动(動)鞋 jiāodǐ yùndòngxié [双 shuāng]

sneeze [sni:z] VI 打喷(噴)嚏 dǎ pēntì

snob [snɒb] (*pej*) N [c] 势(勢)利小人 shìlì xiǎorén [个 gè]

snooker [ˈsnu:kəˈ] N [U] (*Sport*) 英式台(臺)球 yīngshì táiqiú

snore [snɔ:ˈ] VI 打鼾 dǎhān

snow [snəu] I N [U] 雪 xuě II VI 下雪 xiàxuě ▶ **it's snowing** 下雪了 xiàxuě le

snowball [ˈsnəubɔ:l] N [c] 雪球 xuěqiú [个 gè]

snowflake [ˈsnəufleɪk] N [c] 雪花 xuěhuā [朵 duǒ]

snowman [ˈsnəumæn] N [c] 雪人 xuěrén [个 gè] ▶ **to build a snowman** 堆雪人 duī xuěrén

◯ **KEYWORD**

so [səu] I ADV **1** (*thus, likewise*) 这(這)样(樣) zhèyàng ▶ **they do so because...** 他们(們)这(這)样(樣)做是因为(為)… tāmen zhèyàng zuò shì yīnwèi… ▶ **if you don't want to go, say so** 如果你不想去，就说(說)你不想去 rúguǒ nǐ bùxiǎng qù, jiù shuō nǐ bùxiǎng qù ► if so 如果这(這)样(樣) rúguǒ zhèyàng ► I hope/think so 我希望/认(認)为(為)如此 wǒ xīwàng/rènwéi rúcǐ ► so far 迄今为(為)止 qìjīn wéizhǐ ► and so on 等等 děngděng

2 (also) ► so do I/so am I 我也一样(樣) wǒ yě yīyàng

3 如此 rúcǐ ► so quickly/big (that) 如此快/大（以至于(於)） rúcǐ kuài/dà(yǐzhì yú)

4 (very) 非常 fēicháng ► so much 那么(麼)多 nàme duō ► so many 那么(麼)多 nàme duō

5 (linking events) 于(於)是 yúshì ► so I was right after all 那终(終)究我是对(對)的 nà zhōngjiū wǒ shì duì de

II CONJ **1** (expressing purpose) ► so (that) 为(為)的是 wèi de shì ► I brought it so (that) you could see it 我带(帶)过(過)来(來)给(給)你看 wǒ dài guòlái gěi nǐ kàn

2 (expressing result) 因此 yīncǐ ► he didn't come so I left 他没(沒)来(來)，因此我走了 tā méilái, yīncǐ wǒ zǒu le

soaking ['səʊkɪŋ] ADJ (also: soaking wet) [+ person] 湿(濕)透的 shītòu de; [+ clothes] 湿(濕)淋淋的 shīlínlín de

soap [səʊp] N [C/U] **1** 肥皂 féizào [块 kuài] **2** = soap opera

soap opera N [C] 肥皂剧(劇) féizàojù [部 bù]

sober ['səʊbəʳ] ADJ 未醉的 wèi zuì de

soccer ['sɒkəʳ] N [U] 足球 zúqiú

social ['səʊʃl] ADJ **1** 社会(會)的 shèhuì de **2** [+ event, function] 社交的 shèjiāo de

socialism ['səʊʃəlɪzəm] N [U] 社会(會)主义(義) shèhuì zhǔyì

socialist ['səʊʃəlɪst] **I** ADJ 社会(會)主义(義)的 shèhuì zhǔyì de **II** N [C] 社会(會)主义(義)者 shèhuì zhǔyìzhě [位 wèi]

social media N 社交媒体(體) shèjiāo méitǐ

social worker N [C] 社会(會)福利工作者 shèhuì fúlì gōngzuòzhě [位 wèi]

society [sə'saɪətɪ] N [U] 社会(會) shèhuì

sock [sɒk] N [C] 袜(襪)子 wàzi [双 shuāng]

socket ['sɒkɪt] N [C] (Brit) 插座 chāzuò [个 gè]

sofa ['səʊfə] N [C] 沙发(發) shāfā [个 gè]

soft [sɒft] ADJ **1** [+ towel] 松(鬆)软(軟)的 sōngruǎn de; [+ skin] 柔软(軟)的 róuruǎn de **2** [+ bed, paste] 柔软(軟)的 róuruǎn de

soft drink N [C] 软(軟)性饮(飲)料 ruǎnxìng yǐnliào [瓶 píng]

software ['sɒftwɛəʳ] N [U] 软(軟)件 ruǎnjiàn

soil [sɔɪl] N [C/U] 土壤 tǔrǎng [种 zhǒng]

solar power N [U] 太阳(陽)能 tàiyángnéng

sold [səʊld] PT, PP of sell

soldier ['səʊldʒəʳ] N [C] 士兵 shìbīng [位 wèi]

sole [səʊl] N [C] 底 dǐ [个 gè]

solicitor [sə'lɪsɪtəʳ] (Brit) N [C] 律师(師) lùshī [位 wèi]

solid ['sɒlɪd] ADJ **1** (not soft) 坚(堅)实(實)的 jiānshí de **2** (not liquid) 固体(體)的 gùtǐ de **3** [+ gold, oak] 纯(純)质(質)的 chúnzhì de

solution [sə'luːʃən] N [C] 解决(決)方案 jiějué fāng'àn [个 gè]

solve [sɒlv] VT **1** [+ mystery, case] 破解 pòjiě **2** [+ problem] 解决(決) jiějué

⬤ **KEYWORD**

some **I** ADJ **1** (a little, a few) 一些 yīxiē ► some milk/books 一些牛奶/书(書) yīxiē niúnǎi/shū

2 (certain, in contrasts) 某些 mǒuxiē ► some people say that... 有些人说(說)… yǒuxiē rén shuō...

II PRON (a certain amount, certain number) 一些 yīxiē ► I've got some 我有一些 wǒ yǒu yīxiē ► there was/were some left 还(還)剩下一些 hái shèngxià yīxiē ► some of it/them 它的一部分/他们(們)中的一些 tā de yī bùfen/tāmen zhōng de yīxiē

somebody ['sʌmbədɪ] PRON = someone

somehow ['sʌmhaʊ] ADV 不知怎样(樣)地 bùzhī zěnyàng de

someone ['sʌmwʌn] PRON 某人 mǒurén ► I saw someone in the garden 我看见(見)花园(園)里(裡)有人 wǒ kànjiàn huāyuán li yǒu rén ► someone else 别(別)人 biérén

someplace ['sʌmpleɪs] (US) ADV
= **somewhere**

something ['sʌmθɪŋ] PRON 某事物 mǒu
shìwù ▸ **something else** 其他事情 qítā
shìqíng ▸ **would you like a sandwich or
something?** 你要来(來)点(點)三明治
或其他什么(麼)东(東)西吗(嗎)? nǐ yào
lái diǎn sānmíngzhì huò qítā shénme
dōngxi ma?

sometime ['sʌmtaɪm] ADV 某个(個)
时(時)候 mǒugè shíhou

> 请勿将 **sometimes** 和 **sometime**
> 混淆。**sometimes** 表示某事物只发生
> 在某些时候，而不是总是发生。Do you
> visit your sister? — Sometimes...
> Sometimes I wish I still lived in Australia.
> **sometimes** 还可以表示某事物发生在
> 特定情况下，而不是在任何情况下都会
> 发生。Sometimes they stay for a week,
> sometimes just for the weekend.
> **sometime** 表示未来或过去某个不确
> 定或未指明的时间。Can I come and see
> you sometime? ...He started his new job
> sometime last month.

sometimes ['sʌmtaɪmz] ADV 有时(時)
yǒushí

somewhere ['sʌmwɛər] ADV 在某处(處)
zài mǒuchù ▸ **I need somewhere to live**
我需要找个(個)地方住 wǒ xūyào zhǎo
gè dìfang zhù ▸ **I must have lost it
somewhere** 我一定把它丢(丟)在哪儿
(兒)了 wǒ yídìng bǎ bā diū zài nǎr le
▸ **let's go somewhere quiet** 我们(們)去
个(個)安静(靜)的地方吧 wǒmen qù gè
ānjìng de dìfang ba ▸ **somewhere else**
别(別)的地方 bié de dìfang

son [sʌn] N [c] 儿(兒)子 érzi [个 gè]

song [sɒŋ] N [c] 歌曲 gēqǔ [首 shǒu]

son-in-law ['sʌnɪnlɔ:] (pl sons-in-law) N
[c] 女婿 nǚxu [个 gè]

soon [su:n] ADV **1** (in a short time) 不久
bùjiǔ **2** (a short time later) 很快 hěn kuài
3 (early) 早 zǎo ▸ **soon afterwards** 不久
后(後) bùjiǔ hòu ▸ **as soon as** 一…就…
yī...jiù... ▸ **quite soon** 很快 hěn kuài
▸ **see you soon!** 再见(見)! zàijiàn!

sooner ['su:nər] ADV ▸ **sooner or later**
迟(遲)早 chízǎo ▸ **the sooner the better**
越快越好 yuè kuài yuè hǎo

sophomore ['sɒfəmɔ:r] (US) N [c] 二年
级(級)学(學)生 èr niánjí xuésheng [个 gè]

sore [sɔ:r] ADJ 痛的 tòng de

sorry ['sɒrɪ] ADJ 懊悔的 àohuǐ de ▸ (**I'm)
sorry!** (apology) 对(對)不起! duìbuqǐ!
▸ **sorry?** (pardon?) 请(請)再说(講)一遍
qǐng zài jiǎng yí biàn ▸ **to feel sorry for
sb** 对(對)某人表示同情 duì mǒurén
biǎoshì tóngqíng ▸ **to be sorry about
sth** 对(對)某事表示歉意 duì mǒushì
biǎoshì qiànyì ▸ **I'm sorry to hear
that...** 听(聽)到…我很伤(傷)心
tīngdào...wǒ hěn shāngxīn

sort [sɔ:t] **I** N **1** [c] ▸ **sort (of)** 种(種)
类(類) zhǒnglèi [个 gè] **2** [c] (make, brand)
品牌 pǐnpái [个 gè] **II** VT **1** [+ papers, mail,
belongings] 把…分类(類) bǎ...fēnlèi
2 (Comput) 整理 zhěnglǐ ▸ **sort of** (inf)
有点(點)儿(兒) yǒu diǎnr ▸ **all sorts of**
各种(種)不同的 gè zhǒng bùtóng de
▸ **sort out** VT (separate) [+ problem] 解
决(決) jiějué

sound [saund] **I** N [c] 声(聲)音 shēngyīn
[种 zhǒng] **II** VI **1** [alarm, bell +] 响(響)
xiǎng **2** (seem) 听(聽)起来(來) tīng qǐlái
▸ **to make a sound** 出声(聲) chūshēng
▸ **that sounds like an explosion** 听(聽)
起来(來)像是爆炸声(聲)的 tīng qǐlái
xiàng shì bàozhàshēng de ▸ **that
sounds like a great idea** 这(這)主意
听(聽)起来(來)妙极了 zhè zhǔyi tīng
qǐlái miào jí le ▸ **it sounds as if...**
听(聽)起来(來)似乎… tīng qǐlái sìhū...

soup [su:p] N [c/u] 汤(湯) tāng [份 fèn]

sour ['sauər] ADJ **1** (bitter-tasting) 酸的
suān de **2** [+ milk] 酸的 suān de

south [sauθ] **I** N [s/u] 南方 nánfāng
II ADJ 南部的 nánbù de **III** ADV 向南方
xiàng nánfāng ▸ **to the south** 以南 yǐ
nán ▸ **south of...** 在…以南 zài...yǐ nán

South Africa N 南非 Nánfēi

South America N 南美洲 Nán Měizhōu

south-east [sauθ'i:st] **I** N 东(東)南
dōngnán **II** ADJ 东(東)南的 dōngnán de
III ADV 向东(東)南 xiàng dōngnán

southern ['sʌðən] ADJ 南方的 nánfāng
de ▸ **the southern hemisphere** 南半球
nán bànqiú

South Korea N 韩(韓)国(國) Hánguó

South Pole N ▸ **the South Pole** 南
极(極) Nánjí

South Wales N 南威尔(爾)士 Nán
Wēi'ěrshì

south-west [sauθ'wɛst] I N [s/U] 西南 xīnán II ADJ 西南的 xīnán de III ADV 向 西南 xiàng xīnán

souvenir [suːvəˈnɪəʳ] N [c] 纪(紀)念品 jìniànpǐn [件 jiàn]

soy sauce [sɔɪ-] N [U] 酱(醬)油 jiàngyóu

space [speɪs] N 1 [c/U] (gap, place) 空隙 kòngxì [个 gè] 2 [U] (beyond Earth) 太空 tàikōng ▸ to clear a space for sth 为(為)某物腾(騰)地方 wèi mǒuwù téng dìfang

spade [speɪd] N [c] 锹(鍬) qiāo [把 bǎ]

spaghetti [spəˈgɛti] N [U] 意大利面(麵) Yìdàlìmiàn

Spain [speɪn] N 西班牙 Xībānyá

spam [spæm] (Comput) N [U] 垃圾邮(郵) 件 lājī yóujiàn

Spanish [ˈspænɪʃ] I ADJ 西班牙的 Xībānyá de II N [U] (language) 西班牙 语(語) Xībānyáyǔ

spanner [ˈspænəʳ] (Brit) N [c] 扳手 bānshou [个 gè]

spare [spɛəʳ] I ADJ 1 (free) 多余(餘)的 duōyú de 2 (extra) 备(備)用的 bèiyòng de II N [c] = spare part

spare part N [c] 备(備)件 bèijiàn [个 gè]

spare time N [U] 业(業)余(餘)时(時) 间(間) yèyú shíjiān

spat [spæt] PT, PP of spit

speak [spiːk] (pt spoke, pp spoken) I VT [+ language] 讲(講) jiǎng II VI (talk) 讲(講) 话(話) jiǎnghuà ▸ to speak to sb about sth 和某人谈(談)某事 hé mǒurén tán mǒushì

special [ˈspɛʃl] ADJ 1 (important) 特别(別) 的 tèbié de 2 (particular) 专(專)门(門)的 zhuānmén de ▸ we only use these plates on special occasions 我们(們)只 在特别(別)场(場)合才用这(這)些碟子 wǒmen zhǐ zài tèbié chǎnghé cái yòng zhèxiē diézi ▸ it's nothing special 没(沒)什么(麼)特别(別)的 méi shénme tèbié de

speciality [spɛʃɪˈælɪti], (US) **specialty** [ˈspɛʃəlti] N [c] (food) 特制(製)品 tèzhìpǐn [种 zhǒng]; (product) 特产(產) tèchǎn [种 zhǒng]

specially [ˈspɛʃli] ADV 专(專)门(門)地 zhuānmén de

specialty [ˈspɛʃəlti] (US) N = speciality

species [ˈspiːʃiːz] N [c] 种(種) zhǒng [个 gè]

specific [spəˈsɪfɪk] ADJ 1 (fixed) 特定的 tèdìng de 2 (exact) 具体(體)的 jùtǐ de

spectacles [ˈspɛktəklz] NPL 眼镜(鏡) yǎnjìng

spectacular [spɛkˈtækjuləʳ] ADJ [+ view, scenery] 壮(壯)丽(麗)的 zhuànglì de; [+ rise, growth] 惊(驚)人的 jīngrén de; [+ success, result] 引人注目的 yǐn rén zhùmù de

spectator [spɛkˈteɪtəʳ] N [c] 观(觀) 众(眾) guānzhòng [个 gè]

speech [spiːtʃ] N [c] 演说(說) yǎnshuō [场 chǎng]

speed [spiːd] (pt, pp sped [spɛd]) N 1 [c/U] (rate, promptness) 速度 sùdù [种 zhǒng] 2 [U] (fast movement) 快速 kuàisù 3 [c] (rapidity) 迅速 xùnsù ▸ at a speed of 70km/h 以时(時)速70公里 yǐ shísù qīshí gōnglǐ

speed limit (Law) N [c] 速度极(極)限 sùdù jíxiàn [个 gè]

spell [spɛl] (pt, pp spelled or spelt) VT 用 字母拼 yòng zìmǔ pīn ▸ he can't spell 他不会(會)拼写(寫) tā bùhuì pīnxiě

spelling [ˈspɛlɪŋ] N [c] (of word) 拼法 pīnfǎ [种 zhǒng] ▸ spelling mistake 拼 写(寫)错(錯)误(誤) pīnxiě cuòwù

spelt [spɛlt] PT, PP of spell

spend [spɛnd] (pt, pp spent) VT 1 [+ money] 花费(費) huāfèi 2 [+ time, life] 度过(過) dùguò ▸ to spend time/energy on sth 在某事上花时(時)间(間)/精力 zài mǒushì shang huā shíjiān/jīnglì ▸ to spend time/energy doing sth 花时(時) 间(間)/精力做某事 huā shíjiān/jīnglì zuò mǒushì ▸ to spend the night in a hotel 在旅馆(館)度过(過)一晚 zài lǚguǎn dùguò yī wǎn

spent [spɛnt] PT, PP of spend

spicy [ˈspaɪsi] ADJ 辛辣的 xīnlà de

spider [ˈspaɪdəʳ] N [c] 蜘蛛 zhīzhū [只 zhī] ▸ spider's web 蜘蛛网(網) zhīzhūwǎng

spill [spɪl] (pt, pp spilt or spilled) I VT 使溢 出 shǐ yìchū II VI 溢出 yìchū ▸ to spill sth on/over sth 将(將)某物洒(灑)在某 物上 jiāng mǒuwù sǎ zài mǒuwù shang

spinach [ˈspɪnɪtʃ] N [U] 菠菜 bōcài

spine [spaɪn] N [c] 脊柱 jǐzhù [根 gēn]

spit [spɪt] (pt, pp spat) I N [U] (saliva) 唾液 tuòyè II VI 吐唾液 tǔ tuòyè

spite [spaɪt] N [U] 恶(惡)意 èyì ▶ **in spite of** 尽(儘)管 jǐnguǎn

splendid ['splɛndɪd] ADJ (excellent) 极好的 jíhǎo de

split [splɪt] (pt, pp **split**) VT 1 (divide) 把…划(劃)分 bǎ…huàfēn 2 [+ work, profits] 平分 píngfēn
▶ **split up** VI 分手 fēnshǒu

spoil [spɔɪl] (pt, pp **spoiled** or **spoilt**) VT 1 (damage) 损(損)害 sǔnhài 2 [+ child] 溺爱(愛) nìʼài

spoilt [spɔɪlt] I PT, PP of **spoil** II ADJ 宠(寵)坏(壞)的 chǒnghuài de

spoke [spəʊk] PT of **speak**

spoken ['spəʊkn] PP of **speak**

spokesman ['spəʊksmən] (pl **spokesmen**) N [c] 男发(發)言人 nánfāyánrén [位 wèi]

spokeswoman ['spəʊkswʊmən] (pl **spokeswomen**) N [c] 女发(發)言人 nǚfāyánrén [位 wèi]

sponge [spʌndʒ] N [U] 海绵(綿) hǎimián

spoon [spuːn] N [c] 匙 chí [把 bǎ]

sport [spɔːt] N 1 [c] (particular game) 运(運)动(動) yùndòng [项 xiàng] 2 [U] (generally) 体(體)育 tǐyù

sportswear ['spɔːtswɛəʳ] N [U] 运(運)动(動)服 yùndòngfú

spot [spɒt] N [c] 1 (mark) 斑点(點) bāndiǎn [个 gè] 2 (dot) 点(點) diǎn [个 gè] 3 (pimple) 疱点(點) cìdiǎn [个 gè] ▶ **on the spot** (in that place) 在现(現)场(場) zài xiànchǎng; (immediately) 当(當)场(場) dāngchǎng

sprain [spreɪn] VT ▶ **to sprain one's ankle/wrist** 扭伤(傷)脚(腳)踝/手腕 niǔshāng jiǎohuái/shǒuwàn

spray [spreɪ] VT 1 [+ liquid] 喷(噴) pēn 2 [+ crops] 向…喷(噴)杀(殺)虫(蟲)剂(劑) xiàng…pēn shāchóngjì

spread [sprɛd] (pt, pp **spread**) VT 1 ▶ **to spread sth on/over** 把某物摊(攤)在…上 bǎ mǒuwù tān zài…shang 2 [+ disease] 传(傳)播 chuánbō

spreadsheet ['sprɛdʃiːt] N [c] 电(電)子表格 diànzǐ biǎogé [份 fèn]

spring [sprɪŋ] N 1 [c/U] (season) 春季 chūnjì [个 gè] 2 [c] (wire coil) 弹(彈)簧 tánhuáng ▶ **in (the) spring** 在春季 zài chūnjì

spy [spaɪ] N [c] 间(間)谍(諜) jiàndié [个 gè]

spying ['spaɪɪŋ] N [U] 当(當)间(間)谍(諜) dāng jiàndié

square [skwɛəʳ] N [c] 1 正方形 zhèngfāngxíng [个 gè] 2 (in town) 广(廣)场(場) guǎngchǎng [个 gè] 3 (Math) 平方 píngfāng [个 gè] II ADJ 正方形的 zhèngfāngxíng de ▶ **2 square metres** 2平方米 èr píngfāngmǐ

squash [skwɒʃ] I N [U] (Sport) 壁球 bìqiú II VT 把…压(壓)碎 bǎ…yāsuì

squeeze [skwiːz] VT 用力捏 yònglì niē

stab [stæb] VT 刺 cì

stable ['steɪbl] I ADJ (steady) 稳(穩)定的 wěndìng de II N [c] 马(馬)厩(廄) mǎjiù [个 gè]

stadium ['steɪdɪəm] (pl **stadia** ['steɪdɪə] or **stadiums**) N [c] 体(體)育场(場) tǐyùchǎng [个 gè]

staff [stɑːf] N [c] 职(職)员(員) zhíyuán [名 míng]

stage [steɪdʒ] N [c] 1 (in theatre) 舞台(臺) wǔtái [个 gè] 2 (platform) 平台(臺) píngtái [个 gè] ▶ **in the early/final stages** 在早/晚期 zài zǎo/wǎnqī

stain [steɪn] I N [c] 污迹(跡) wūjì [处 chù] II VT 沾污 zhānwū

stainless steel ['steɪnlɪs-] N [U] 不锈(鏽)钢(鋼) bùxiùgāng

stair [stɛəʳ] I N [c] (step) 梯级(級) tījí [层 céng] II **stairs** NPL (flight of steps) 楼(樓)梯 lóutī

stall [stɔːl] N [c] 货(貨)摊(攤) huòtān [个 gè]

stamp [stæmp] I N [c] 1 邮(郵)票 yóupiào [枚 méi] 2 (in passport) 章 zhāng [个 gè] II VT [+ passport, visa] 盖(蓋)章于(於) gàizhāng yú

stand [stænd] (pt, pp **stood**) I VI 1 (be upright) 站立 zhànlì 2 (rise) 站起来(來) zhàn qǐlái 3 ▶ **to stand aside/back** 让(讓)开(開)/退后(後) ràngkāi/tuìhòu II VT ▶ **I can't stand him/it** 我无(無)法容忍他/它 wǒ wúfǎ róngrěn tā/tā ▶ **stand for** VT FUS [abbreviation +] 代表 dàibiǎo ▶ **stand out** VI 醒目 xǐngmù ▶ **stand up** VI (rise) 起立 qǐlì

standard ['stændəd] I N [c] 1 (level) 水平 shuǐpíng [种 zhǒng] 2 (norm, criterion) 标(標)准(準) biāozhǔn [个 gè] II ADJ 1 [+ size] 普通的 pǔtōng de 2 [+ procedure, practice] 标(標)准(準)的

biāozhǔn de **3** [+ model, feature] 规(規)范(範)的 guīfàn de

stank [stæŋk] PT of stink

star [stɑːʳ] N [c] **1** 星 xīng [颗 kē] **2** (celebrity) 明星 míngxīng [个 gè] ▸ a 4-star hotel 4星级(級)旅馆(館) sì xīngjí lǚguǎn

stare [steəʳ] VI ▸ to stare (at sb/sth) 盯着(著) (某人/某物) dīngzhe (mǒurén/mǒuwù)

start [stɑːt] I N [c] 开(開)始 kāishǐ [个 gè] II VT **1** (begin) 开(開)始 kāishǐ **2** [+ business] 创(創)建 chuàngjiàn **3** [+ engine, car] 启(啟)动(動) qǐdòng III VI (begin) 开(開)始 kāishǐ ▸ to start doing or to do sth 开(開)始做某事 kāishǐ zuò mǒushì

▸ **start on** VT FUS 开(開)始 kāishǐ

▸ **start over** (US) VI, VT 重新开(開)始 chóngxīn kāishǐ

▸ **start up** VT 创(創)办(辦) chuàngbàn

starter ['stɑːtəʳ] N [c] (Brit) 开(開)胃菜 kāiwèicài [道 dào]

starve [stɑːv] VI **1** (be very hungry) 挨饿(餓) áiè **2** (die from hunger) 饿(餓)死 èsǐ ▸ I'm starving 我饿(餓)极(極)了 wǒ è jí le

state [steɪt] I N **1** [c] (condition) 状(狀)态(態) zhuàngtài [种 zhǒng] **2** [c] (country) 国(國)家 guójiā [个 gè] **3** [c] (part of country) 州 zhōu [个 gè] II the States NPL (inf) 美国(國) Měiguó

▸ **state of affairs** 事态(態) shìtài

statement ['steɪtmənt] N [c] 声(聲)明 shēngmíng [个 gè]

station ['steɪʃən] N [c] **1** (railway station) 车(車)站 chēzhàn [个 gè] **2** (on radio) 电(電)台(臺) diàntái [个 gè]

statue ['stætjuː] N [c] 塑像 sùxiàng [尊 zūn]

stay [steɪ] I N [c] 逗留 dòuliú [次 cì] II VI **1** (in place, position) 呆(獃)dāi **2** (in town, hotel, someone's house) 逗留 dòuliú **3** (in state, situation) 保持 bǎochí III VT ▸ to stay the night 过(過)夜 guòyè ▸ to stay with sb 在某人家暂(暫)住 zài mǒurén jiā zànzhù

▸ **stay in** VI 呆在家里(裡) dāi zài jiā li

▸ **stay up** VI 不去睡 bù qù shuì

steady ['stɛdɪ] ADJ **1** [+ progress, increase, fall] 稳(穩)定的 wěndìng de **2** [+ job, income] 固定的 gùdìng de

steak [steɪk] N [c/u] 牛排 niúpái [份 fèn]

steal [stiːl] (pt stole, pp stolen) I VT 偷窃(竊) tōuqiè II VI 行窃(竊) xíngqiè

▸ he stole it from me 他从(從)我这(這)里(裡)把它偷走了 tā cóng wǒ zhèlǐ bǎ tā tōuzǒu le

steam [stiːm] I N [u] 蒸汽 zhēngqì II VT 蒸 zhēng

steel [stiːl] I N [u] 钢(鋼)铁(鐵) gāngtiě II CPD (鋼)制(製) gāngzhì

steep [stiːp] ADJ 陡的 dǒu de

steering wheel N [c] 方向盘(盤) fāngxiàngpán [个 gè]

step [stɛp] I N **1** (stage) 阶(階)段 jiēduàn [个 gè] **2** (of stairs) 梯级(級) tījí [层 céng] II VI ▸ to step forward/backward etc 向前/后(後){等}迈(邁)步 xiàng qián/hòu děng màibù

▸ **step aside** = step down

▸ **step down, step aside** VI 辞(辭)职(職) cízhí

stepbrother ['stɛpbrʌðəʳ] N [c] (with shared father) 异(異)母兄弟 yìmǔ xiōngdì [个 gè]; (with shared mother) 异(異)父兄弟 yìfù xiōngdì [个 gè]

stepdaughter ['stɛpdɔːtəʳ] N [c] 继(繼)女 jìnǚ [个 gè]

stepfather ['stɛpfɑːðəʳ] N [c] 继(繼)父 jìfù [位 wèi]

stepmother ['stɛpmʌðəʳ] N [c] 继(繼)母 jìmǔ [位 wèi]

stepsister ['stɛpsɪstəʳ] N [c] (with shared father) 异(異)母姐妹 yìmǔ jiěmèi [个 gè]; (with shared mother) 异(異)父姐妹 yìfù jiěmèi [个 gè]

stepson ['stɛpsʌn] N [c] 继(繼)子 jìzǐ [个 gè]

stereo ['stɛrɪəu] N [c] 立体(體)声(聲)装(裝)置 lìtǐshēng zhuāngzhì [套 tào]

sterling ['stəːlɪŋ] N [u] 英国(國)货(貨)币(幣) Yīngguó huòbì ▸ one pound sterling 一英镑(鎊) yī yīngbàng

stew [stjuː] N [c/u] 炖(燉)的食物 dùn de shíwù [种 zhǒng]

stewardess ['stjuədɛs] N [c] 女乘务(務)员(員) nǚchéngwùyuán [位 wèi]

stick [stɪk] (pt, pp stuck) I N **1** [of wood] 枯枝 kūzhī [根 gēn] **2** (walking stick) 拐(柺)杖 guǎizhàng [根 gēn] II VT ▸ to stick sth on or to sth (with glue etc) 将(將)某物粘贴(貼)在某物上 jiāng

mǒuwù zhāntiē zài mǒuwù shang
▶ **stick out** vi 伸出 shēnchū

sticker ['stɪkəʳ] N [c] 不干(乾)胶(膠)
标(標)签(籤) bùgānjiāo biāoqiān
[个 gè]

sticky ['stɪkɪ] ADJ 1 [+ substance] 黏的
nián de 2 [+ tape, paper] 黏性的
niánxìng de

stiff [stɪf] I ADJ 1 [+ person] 酸(痠)痛的
suāntòng de; [+ neck, arm etc] 僵硬的
jiāngyìng de 2 [+ competition] 激烈的
jīliè de II ADV ▶ **to be bored/scared stiff**
讨(討)厌(厭)/害怕极(極)了 tǎoyàn/
hàipà jí le

still [stɪl] I ADJ 1 [+ person, hands] 不动(動)
的 bùdòng de 2 (Brit: not fizzy) 无(無)
气(氣)泡的 wú qìpào de II ADV 1 (up to
the present) 仍然 réngrán 2 (even) 更
gèng 3 (yet) 还(還) hái 4 (nonetheless)
尽(儘)管如此 jǐnguǎn rúcǐ ▶ **to stand/
keep still** 站着(著)别(別)动(動)/别(別)
动(動) zhànzhe bié dòng/bié dòng ▶ **he
still hasn't arrived** 他还(還)没(沒)到 tā
hái méi dào

sting [stɪŋ] (pt, pp stung) I N [c] 刺 cì [根
gēn] II vT 刺 cì

stink [stɪŋk] (pt stank, pp stunk) I N [c]
恶(惡)臭 èchòu [种 zhǒng] II vI 发(發)
臭 fā chòu

stir [stɜːʳ] vT 搅(攪)动(動) jiǎodòng

stitch [stɪtʃ] N [c] (Med) 缝(縫)针(針)
féngzhēn [枚 méi]

stock [stɔk] N [c] 供应(應)物
gōngyìngwù [种 zhǒng]
▶ **stock up** vi ▶ **to stock up (on or with
sth)** 储(儲)备(備)(某物) chǔbèi
(mǒuwù)

stock exchange N [c] 股票交易所
gǔpiào jiāoyìsuǒ [块 kuài]

stocking ['stɔkɪŋ] N [c] 长(長)统(統)
袜(襪) chángtǒngwà [双 shuāng]

stole [stəul] PT of steal

stolen ['stəuln] PP of steal

stomach ['stʌmək] N [c] 1 (organ) 胃 wèi
[个 gè] 2 (abdomen) 腹部 fùbù [个 gè]

stomach ache N [c/u] 胃痛 wèitòng
[阵 zhèn]

stone [stəun] N 1 [u] 石头(頭) shítou
2 [c] (pebble) 石子 shízǐ [块 kuài]

stood [stud] PT, PP of stand

stop [stɔp] I vT 1 停止 tíngzhǐ 2 (prevent)

阻止 zǔzhǐ II vI 1 [person, vehicle +] 停下
来(來) tíng xiàlái 2 [rain, noise, activity +]
停 tíng III N [c] (for bus, train) 车(車)站
chēzhàn [个 gè] ▶ **to stop doing sth** 停
止做某事 tíngzhǐ zuò mǒushì ▶ **to stop
sb (from) doing sth** 阻止某人做某事
zǔzhǐ mǒurén zuò mǒushì ▶ **stop it!** 住
手！zhùshǒu!

stoplight ['stɔplaɪt] (US) N [c] (in road) 交
通信号(號)灯(燈) jiāotōng xìnhàodēng
[个 gè]

store [stɔːʳ] I N [c] 1 (Brit: large shop) 大商
店 dà shāngdiàn [家 jiā] 2 (US: shop) 店
铺(鋪) diànpù [家 jiā] II vT 1 [+ provisions,
information] 存放 cúnfàng 2 [computer,
brain +] [+ information] 存储(儲) cúnchǔ

storey, (US) **story** ['stɔːrɪ] N [c] 层(層)
céng

storm [stɔːm] N [c] 暴风(風)雨
bàofēngyǔ [场 chǎng]

stormy ['stɔːmɪ] ADJ 有暴风(風)雨的
yǒu bàofēngyǔ de

story ['stɔːrɪ] N [c] 1 (account) 描述
miáoshù [种 zhǒng] 2 (tale) 故事 gùshì
[个 gè] 3 (in newspaper, on news broadcast)
报(報)道 bàodào [条 tiáo] 4 (US) [of
building] = storey

stove [stəuv] N [c] 炉(爐)子 lúzi [个 gè]

straight [streɪt] I ADJ 1 笔(筆)直的 bǐzhí
de 2 [+ hair] 直的 zhí de II ADV 1 [walk,
stand, look +] 直 zhí 2 (immediately) 直接
地 zhíjiē de

straightforward [streɪtˈfɔːwəd] ADJ
简(簡)单(單)的 jiǎndān de

strain [streɪn] I N 1 [c/u] (pressure)
负(負)担(擔) fùdān [个 gè] 2 [c/u]
▶ **back/muscle strain** 背部/肌肉扭
伤(傷) bèibù/jīròu niǔshāng [处 chù]
II vT [+ back, muscle] 扭伤(傷) niǔshāng

strange [streɪndʒ] ADJ 1 (odd) 奇怪的
qíguài de 2 (unfamiliar) [+ person, place]
陌生的 mòshēng de

stranger ['streɪndʒəʳ] N [c] 陌生人
mòshēngrén [个 gè]

strap [stræp] N [c] [of watch, bag] 带(帶)
dài [根 gēn]

straw [strɔː] N 1 [u] 稻草 dàocǎo 2 [c]
(drinking straw) 吸管 xīguǎn [根 gēn]

strawberry ['strɔːbərɪ] N [c] 草莓
cǎoméi [个 gè]

stream [striːm] I N [c] 溪流 xīliú [条

tiáo) II VT (on the internet) 直播 zhíbō

street [stri:t] N [c] 街道 jiēdào [条 tiáo]

streetcar ['stri:tkɑ:ʳ] (US) N [c] 有轨(軌)电(電)车(車) yǒuguǐ diànchē [部 bù]

strength [streŋθ] N 1 [u] 力气(氣) lìqi 2 [u] (of object, material) 强(強)度 qiángdù

stress [stres] I N [c/u] 压(壓)力 yālì [个 gè] II VT [+ point, importance] 强(強)调(調) qiángdiào

stressful ['stresful] ADJ 紧(緊)张(張)的 jǐnzhāng de

stretch [stretʃ] I VI 伸懒(懶)腰 shēn lǎnyāo II VT [+ arm, leg] 伸直 shēnzhí ▶ **stretch out** VT [+ arm, leg] 伸出 shēnchū

strict [strikt] ADJ 1 [+ rule, instruction] 严(嚴)格的 yángé de 2 [+ person] 严(嚴)厉(厲)的 yánlì de

strike [straik] (pt, pp struck) I N [c] 罢(罷)工 bàgōng [场 chǎng] I VT 1 罢(罷)工 bàgōng [场 chǎng] 2 (clock +) 报(報)时(時) bàoshí ▶ **to be on strike** 在罢(罷)工 zài bàgōng

striker ['straikəʳ] N [c] 1 (person on strike) 罢(罷)工者 bàgōngzhě [名 míng] 2 (Football) 前锋(鋒) qiánfēng [个 gè]

string [striŋ] (pt, pp strung) N [c/u] 1 细(細)绳(繩) xìshéng [根 gēn] 2 [c] (on guitar, violin) 弦 xián [根 gēn]

strip [strip] N [c] [of paper, cloth] 狭(狹)条(條) xiátiáo [条 tiáo] I VI (undress) 脱(脫)光衣服 tuōguāng yīfu; (as entertainer) 表演脱(脫)衣舞 biǎoyǎn tuōyīwǔ

stripe [straip] N [c] 条(條)纹(紋) tiáowén [个 gè]

striped ['straipt] ADJ 有条(條)纹(紋)的 yǒu tiáowén de

stroke [strəuk] I N [c] (Med) 中风(風) zhòngfēng [次 cì] II VT [+ person, animal] 抚(撫)摸 fǔmō

stroller ['strəuləʳ] (US) N [c] 婴(嬰)儿(兒)小推车(車) yīng'ér xiǎotuīchē [辆 liàng]

strong [strɔŋ] ADJ 1 [+ person, arms, grip] 有力的 yǒulì de 2 [+ object, material] 牢固的 láogù de 3 [+ wind, current] 强(強)劲(勁)的 qiángjìng de

struck [strʌk] PT, PP of **strike**

struggle ['strʌgl] VI 1 (try hard) 尽(盡)力 jìnlì 2 (fight) 搏斗(鬥) bódòu

stubborn ['stʌbən] ADJ 倔强(強)的 juéjiàng de

stuck [stʌk] I PT, PP of **stick** II ADJ ▶ **to be stuck** [object +] 卡住 qiǎzhù; [person +] 陷于(於) xiànyú

student ['stju:dənt] N [c] 1 (at university) 大学(學)生 dàxuéshēng [名 míng] 2 (at school) 中学(學)生 zhōngxuéshēng [名 míng] ▶ **a law/medical student** 一名法律/医(醫)学(學)学(學)生 yī míng fǎlǜ/yīxué xuésheng

studio ['stju:diəu] N [c] 1 (TV, Rad, Mus) 演播室 yǎnbōshì [个 gè] 2 (of artist) 画(畫)室 huàshì [间 jiān]

study ['stʌdi] I N [c] (room) 书(書)房 shūfáng [间 jiān] II VT [+ subject] 攻读(讀) gōngdú III VI 学(學)习(習) xuéxí

stuff [stʌf] I N [u] 1 (things) 物品 wùpǐn 2 (substance) 东(東)西 dōngxi II VT [+ peppers, mushrooms] 给(給)…装(裝)馅(餡) gěi...zhuāngxiàn; [+ chicken, turkey] 把填料塞入 bǎ tiánliào sāirù

stuffy ['stʌfi] ADJ 闷(悶)热(熱)的 mēnrè de

stung [stʌŋ] PT, PP of **sting**

stunk [stʌŋk] PP of **stink**

stunning ['stʌniŋ] ADJ 1 (impressive) 惊(驚)人的 jīngrén de 2 (beautiful) 极漂亮的 jí piàoliang de

stupid ['stju:pid] ADJ 1 笨的 bèn de 2 [+ question, idea, mistake] 愚蠢的 yúchǔn de

style [stail] N 1 [c] (type) 方式 fāngshì [种 zhǒng] 2 [u] (elegance) 风(風)度 fēngdù 3 [c/u] (design) 样(樣)式 yàngshì [种 zhǒng]

subject ['sʌbdʒikt] N [c] 1 (matter) 主题(題) zhǔtí [个 gè] 2 (Scol) 科目 kēmù [个 gè] 3 (Gram) 主语(語) zhǔyǔ [个 gè]

submarine [sʌbmə'ri:n] N [c] 潜(潛)水艇 qiánshuǐtǐng [艘 sōu]

substance ['sʌbstəns] N [c] 物质(質) wùzhì [种 zhǒng]

substitute ['sʌbstitju:t] I N [c] 1 (person) 代替者 dàitìzhě [位 wèi] 2 (thing) 代用品 dàiyòngpǐn [件 jiàn] II VT ▶ **to substitute sth (for sth)** 用某物代替(某物) yòng mǒuwù dàitì (mǒuwù)

subtitles ['sʌbtaitlz] NPL 字幕 zìmù

subtract [səb'trækt] VT ▶ **to subtract sth**

(from sth) （从(從)某数(數)中） 减(減)去某数(數) (cóng mǒushù zhōng) jiǎnqù mǒushù

suburb ['sʌbə:b] N [c] 郊区(區) jiāoqū [个 gè]

subway ['sʌbweɪ] N [c] (*US: underground railway*) 地铁(鐵) dìtiě [条 tiáo]

succeed [sək'si:d] VI 成功 chénggōng ▸ **to succeed in doing sth** 成功地做某 事 chénggōng de zuò mǒushì

success [sək'ses] N [U/c] 成功 chénggōng ▸ **without success** 一 无(無)所成 yì wú suǒ chéng

successful [sək'sesful] ADJ 成功的 chénggōng de

successfully [sək'sesfəlɪ] ADV 成功地 chénggōng de

such [sʌtʃ] ADJ 1 (*of this kind*) 此类(類)的 cǐ lèi de 2 (*so much*) 这(這)么(麼) zhème ▸ **such a lot of** 那么(麼)多 nàme duō ▸ **such as** (*like*) 像 xiàng

suck [sʌk] VT 含在嘴里(裡)舔吃 hán zài zuǐ lǐ tiǎnchī

sudden ['sʌdn] ADJ 意外的 yìwài de

suddenly ['sʌdnlɪ] ADV 突然 tūrán

suede [sweɪd] N [U] 仿鹿皮 fǎngjǐpí

suffer ['sʌfə'] VI 1 (*due to pain, illness, poverty*) 受损(損)失 shòu sǔnshī 2 (*be badly affected*) 受苦难(難) shòu kǔnàn

sugar ['ʃugə'] N [U/c] 糖 táng [勺 sháo]

suggest [sə'dʒest] VT 建议(議) jiànyì ▸ **to suggest that...** (*propose*) 建 议(議)… jiànyì…

suggestion [sə'dʒestʃən] N [c] 建议(議) jiànyì [条 tiáo] ▸ **to make a suggestion** 提建议(議) tí jiànyì

suicide ['suɪsaɪd] N [U/c] 自杀(殺) zìshā ▸ **a suicide bomber** 人肉炸弹(彈) rénròu zhàdàn ▸ **to commit suicide** 自 杀(殺) zìshā

suit [su:t] I N [c] 西装(裝) xīzhuāng [套 tào] II VT 1 (*be convenient, appropriate*) 对(對)…合适(適) duì…héshì 2 (*colour, clothes +*) 适(適)合 shìhé

suitable ['su:təbl] ADJ 1 [+ *time, place*] 合 适(適)的 héshì de 2 [+ *person, clothes*] 适(適)合的 shìhé de

suitcase ['su:tkeɪs] N [c] 手提箱 shǒutíxiāng [个 gè]

sum [sʌm] N [c] 1 (*amount*) 数(數)额(額) shù'é [笔 bǐ] 2 (*calculation*) 算术(術)

题(題) suànshùtí [道 dào] ▸ **to do a sum** 算术(術) suàn suànshù ▸ **sum up** VI 总(總)结(結) zǒngjié

summarize ['sʌməraɪz] VT 概括 gàikuò

summary ['sʌmərɪ] N [c] 摘要 zhāiyào [个 gè]

summer ['sʌmə'] N [c/U] 夏季 xiàjì [个 gè] ▸ **in (the) summer** 在夏季 zài xiàjì

summit ['sʌmɪt] N [c] 峰顶(頂) fēngdǐng [个 gè]

sun [sʌn] N 1 [s/c] (*in the sky*) 太阳(陽) tàiyáng [轮 lún] 2 [U] (*heat*) 太阳(陽)的 光和热(熱) tàiyáng de guāng hé rè; (*light*) 阳(陽)光 yángguāng

sunbathe ['sʌnbeɪð] VI 晒日光浴 shài rìguāngyù

sunburn ['sʌnbə:n] N [U] 晒斑 shàibān

sunburned ['sʌnbə:nd], **sunburnt** ['sʌnbə:nt] ADJ 晒伤(傷)的 shàishāng de

Sunday ['sʌndɪ] N [c/U] 星期天 xīngqītiān [个 gè]; *see also*/另见 **Tuesday**

sung [sʌŋ] PP *of* **sing**

sunglasses ['sʌngla:sɪz] NPL 墨镜(鏡) mòjìng

sunk [sʌŋk] PP *of* **sink**

sunny ['sʌnɪ] ADJ 晴朗的 qínglǎng de ▸ **it is sunny** 天气(氣)晴朗 tiānqì qínglǎng

sunrise ['sʌnraɪz] N [U] 拂晓(曉) fúxiǎo

sunscreen ['sʌnskri:n] N [c/U] 遮光屏 zhēguāngpíng [个 gè]

sunset ['sʌnset] N 1 [U] (*time*) 傍晚 bàngwǎn 2 [c] (*sky*) 日落 rìluò [次 cì]

sunshine ['sʌnʃaɪn] N [U] 阳(陽)光 yángguāng

suntan ['sʌntæn] I N [c] 晒黑 shàihēi [处 chù] II CPD [+ *lotion, cream*] 防晒 fángshài

super ['su:pə'] (*Brit: inf*) ADJ 极(極)好的 jí hǎo de

supermarket ['su:pəma:kɪt] N [U] 超 级(級)市场(場) chāojí shìchǎng

supervise ['su:pəvaɪz] VT 监(監)督 jiāndū

supper ['sʌpə'] N [c/U] 1 (*early evening*) 晚 餐 wǎncān [顿 dùn] 2 (*late evening*) 夜宵 yèxiāo [顿 dùn]

supply [sə'plaɪ] I VT 提供 tígōng II N [c/U] 供应(應)量 gōngyìngliàng ▸ **to supply sb/sth with sth** 为(為)某人/某

物提供某物 wèi mǒurén/mǒuwù tígōng mǒuwù

support [sə'pɔ:t] VT **1**(morally) 支持 zhīchí **2**(financially) 供养(養) gōngyǎng **3**[+ football team] 支持 zhīchí

supporter [sə'pɔ:tər] N [c] 支持者 zhīchízhě [名 míng]

suppose [sə'pəuz] VT 认(認)为(為) rènwéi ▸ I suppose 我想 wǒ xiǎng ▸ I suppose so/not 我看是/不是(這)样(樣) wǒ kàn shì/bùshì zhèyàng ▸ he's supposed to be an expert 人们(們)以为(為)他是个(個)专(專)家 rénmen yǐwéi tā shì gè zhuānjiā

supposing [sə'pəuzɪŋ] CONJ 假使 jiǎshǐ

sure [fuər] ADJ **1** 有把握的 yǒu bǎwò de **2** ▸ to be sure to do sth (certain) 肯定做某事 kěndìng zuò mǒushì ▸ to make sure that... (take action) 保证(證)… bǎozhèng…; (check) 查明… chámíng… ▸ sure! (inf: of course) 当(當)然了! dāngrán le! ▸ I'm sure of it 我确(確)信 wǒ quèxin ▸ I'm not sure how/why/when 我不能肯定如何/为(為)什么(麼)/什么(麼)时(時)候 wǒ bùnéng kěndìng rúhé/wèi shénme/shénme shíhou

surf [sə:f] I N [U] 拍岸的浪花 pāi'àn de lànghuā II VT ▸ to surf the internet 网(網)上冲(衝)浪 wǎngshang chōnglàng ▸ to go surfing 去冲(衝)浪 qù chōnglàng

surface ['sə:fɪs] N **1** [c] (of object) 表面 biǎomiàn [个 gè] **2** [c] (top layer) 表层(層) biǎocéng [个 gè] ▸ on the surface 在表面上 zài biǎomiàn shang

surfboard ['sə:fbɔ:d] N [c] 冲(衝)浪板 chōnglàngbǎn [块 kuài]

surgeon ['sə:dʒən] N [c] 外科医(醫)师(師) wàikē yīshī [位 wèi]

surgery ['sə:dʒərɪ] N **1** [U] (treatment) 外科手术(術) wàikē shǒushù **2** [c] (Brit: room) 诊(診)所 zhěnsuǒ [家 jiā]

surname ['sə:neɪm] N [c] 姓 xìng [个 gè]

surprise [sə'praɪz] I N **1** [c] (unexpected event) 意想不到的事物 yìxiǎng bùdào de shìwù [个 gè] **2** [U] (astonishment) 诧(詫)异(異) chàyì II VT 使感到意外 shǐ gǎndào yìwài ▸ to my (great) surprise 使我（很）惊(驚)奇的是 shǐ wǒ (hěn) jīngqí de shì

surprised [sə'praɪzd] ADJ 惊(驚)讶(訝)的 jīngyà de

surprising [sə'praɪzɪŋ] ADJ 出人意外的 chū rén yìwài de

surrender [sə'rɛndər] VI 投降 tóuxiáng

surround [sə'raund] VT 包围(圍) bāowéi

surroundings [sə'raundɪŋz] NPL 环(環)境 huánjìng

survey ['sə:veɪ] N [c] 民意测(測)验(驗) mínyì cèyàn [项 xiàng]

survive [sə'vaɪv] VI 幸(倖)存 xìngcún

survivor [sə'vaɪvər] N [c] 幸(倖)存者 xìngcúnzhě [个 gè]

suspect [n 'sʌspɛkt, vb səs'pɛkt] I N [c] 嫌疑犯 xiányífàn [个 gè] II VT **1** [+ person] 怀(懷)疑 huáiyí **2** [+ sb's motives] 质(質)疑 zhìyí **3** (think) 猜想 cāixiǎng ▸ to suspect that... 怀(懷)疑… huáiyí…

suspense [səs'pɛns] N [U] 焦虑(慮) jiāolù

suspicious [səs'pɪfəs] ADJ [+ circumstances, death, package] 可疑的 kěyí de ▸ to be suspicious of or about sb/sth 对(對)某人/某事起疑心 duì mǒurén/mǒushì qǐ yíxīn

swallow ['swɔləu] VT 吞下 tūnxià

swam [swæm] PT of **swim**

swan [swɔn] N [c] 天鹅(鵝) tiān'é [只 zhī]

swap [swɔp] VT ▸ to swap sth (for) (exchange for) （以某物）作交换(換) (yǐ mǒuwù) zuò jiāohuàn; (replace with) 以…替代某物 yǐ…tìdài mǒuwù ▸ to swap places (with sb) （与(與)某人）换(換)位子 (yǔ mǒurén) huàn wèizi

swear word [swɛər-] N [c] 骂(罵)人的话(話) màrén de huà [句 jù]

sweat [swɛt] VI 出汗 chū hàn

sweater ['swɛtər] N [c] 毛衣 máoyī [件 jiàn]

sweatshirt ['swɛtfə:t] N [c] 棉毛衫 miánmáoshān [件 jiàn]

Sweden ['swi:dn] N 瑞典 Ruìdiǎn

sweep [swi:p] (pt, pp swept) VT 扫(掃)sǎo

sweet [swi:t] I N (Brit) **1** [c] (chocolate, mint) 糖果 tángguǒ [颗 kē] **2** [c/U] (pudding) 甜点(點) tiándiǎn [份 fèn] II ADJ **1** (sugary) 甜的 tián de **2** 可爱(愛)的 kě'ài de ▸ sweet and sour 糖醋 tángcù

swept [swept] PT, PP of **sweep**

swerve [swə:v] VI 突然转(轉)向 tūrán zhuǎnxiàng

swim [swɪm] (pt swam, pp swum) I VI [person, animal +] 游水 yóushuǐ **2** (as sport) 游泳 yóuyǒng II VT [+ distance] 游 yóu III N [c] ▶ **to go for a swim** 去游泳 qù yóuyǒng [次 cì] ▶ **to go swimming** 去游泳 qù yóuyǒng

swimming ['swɪmɪŋ] N [U] 游泳 yóuyǒng

swimming pool N [c] 游泳池 yóuyǒngchí [个 gè]

swimsuit ['swɪmsuːt] N [c] 游泳衣 yóuyǒngyī [套 tào]

swing [swɪŋ] (pt, pp swung) I N [c] 秋(鞦)千(韆) qiūqiān [副 fù] II VT [+ arms, legs] 摆(擺)动(動) bǎidòng III VI **1** [pendulum +] 晃动(動) huàngdòng **2** [door +] 转(轉)动(動) zhuǎndòng

switch [swɪtʃ] I N [c] 开(開)关(關) kāiguān [个 gè] II VT (change) 改变(變) gǎibiàn
▶ **switch off** VT 关(關)掉 guāndiào
▶ **switch on** VT [+ light, engine, radio] 开(開)启(啟) kāiqǐ

Switzerland ['swɪtsələnd] N 瑞士 Ruìshì

swollen ['swəulən] ADJ 肿(腫)胀(脹)的 zhǒngzhàng de

swop [swɔp] N, VT = **swap**

sword [sɔːd] N [c] 剑(劍) jiàn [把 bǎ]

swum [swʌm] PP of **swim**

swung [swʌŋ] PT, PP of **swing**

syllabus ['sɪləbəs] (esp Brit) N [c] 教学(學)大纲(綱) jiàoxué dàgāng [个 gè]

symbol ['sɪmbl] N [c] **1** (sign) 象征(徵) xiàngzhēng [种 zhǒng] **2** (Math, Chem) 符号(號) fúhào [个 gè]

sympathetic [sɪmpə'θεtɪk] ADJ 有同情心的 yǒu tóngqíngxīn de

sympathy ['sɪmpəθɪ] N [U] 同情心 tóngqíngxīn

syringe [sɪ'rɪndʒ] N [c] 注射器 zhùshèqì [支 zhī]

system ['sɪstəm] N [c] **1** (organization, set) 系统(統) xìtǒng [个 gè] **2** (method) 方法 fāngfǎ [种 zhǒng]

table ['teɪbl] N [c] 桌子 zhuōzi [张 zhāng]
▶ **to lay** or **set the table** 摆(擺)餐桌 bǎi cānzhuō

tablecloth ['teɪblklɔθ] N [c] 桌布 zhuōbù [块 kuài]

tablespoon ['teɪblspuːn] N [c] 餐匙 cānchí [把 bǎ]

tablet ['tæblɪt] N **1** [c] 药(藥)片 yàopiàn [片 piàn] **2** [c] (computer) 平板电(電)脑(腦) píngbǎn diànnǎo [个 gè]

table tennis N [U] 乒乓球 pīngpāngqiú

tact [tækt] N [U] 机(機)智 jīzhì

tactful ['tæktful] ADJ 老练(練)的 lǎoliàn de

tactics ['tæktɪks] NPL 策略 cèluè

tadpole ['tædpəul] N [c] 蝌蚪 kēdǒu [只 zhī]

taffy ['tæfɪ] (US) N [U] 太妃糖 tàifēitáng

tag [tæg] N [c] **1** (label) 标(標)签(籤) biāoqiān [个 gè] **2** (electronic) 标(標)签(籤) biāoqiān [个 gè]

tail [teɪl] N [c] 尾巴 wěiba [条 tiáo]
▶ **"heads or tails?" — "tails"** "正面还(還)是背面?" "背面" "zhèngmiàn háishì bèimiàn?" "bèimiàn"

tailor ['teɪləʳ] N [c] 裁缝(縫) cáifeng [个 gè]

take [teɪk] (pt took, pp taken) VT **1** [+ holiday, vacation] 度 dù; [+ shower, bath] 洗 xǐ **2** (take hold of) 拿 ná **3** (steal) 偷走 tōuzǒu **4** (accompany) 送 sòng **5** (carry, bring) 携(攜)带(帶) xiédài **6** [+ road] 走 zǒu **7** [+ bus, train] 乘坐

chéngzuò 8 [+ size] 穿 chuān 9 [+ time]
花费(費) huāfèi 10 [+ exam, test] 参(參)
加 cānjiā 11 [+ drug, pill] 服用 fúyòng
▶ don't forget to take your umbrella
别(別)忘了带(帶)雨伞(傘) bié wàngle
dài yǔsǎn

▶ take apart VT (dismantle) [+ bicycle,
radio, machine] 拆开(開) chāikāi
▶ take away VT 1 (remove) 拿走 názǒu
2 (carry off) 带(帶)走 dàizǒu
▶ take back VT [+ goods] 退回 tuìhuí
▶ take down VT (write down) 记(記)
录(錄) jìlù
▶ take off I VI 起飞(飛) qǐfēi II VT
[+ clothes, glasses, make-up] 脱(脫)下
tuōxià
▶ take out VT [+ person] 邀请(請)
yāoqǐng
▶ take up VT 1 [+ hobby, sport] 开(開)始
kāishǐ 2 [+ time, space] 占(佔)用
zhànyòng

takeaway ['teɪkəweɪ] (Brit) N [c] 1 (shop,
restaurant) 外卖(賣)店 wàimàidiàn [家
jiā] 2 (food) 外卖(賣) wàimài [个 gè]

taken ['teɪkən] PP of take

takeoff ['teɪkɔf] N [c] 起飞(飛) qǐfēi
[次 cì]

takeout ['teɪkaut] (US) N [c] 1 (shop,
restaurant) 外卖(賣)店 wàimàidiàn
[家 jiā] 2 (food) 外卖(賣) wàimài
[个 gè]

tale [teɪl] N [c] 故事 gùshì [个 gè]

talent ['tælnt] N [c/u] 才能 cáinéng [种
zhǒng]

talented ['tæləntɪd] ADJ 有才能的 yǒu
cáinéng de

talk [tɔːk] I N 1 [c] (prepared speech) 讲(講)
话(話) jiǎnghuà [次 cì] 2 [u] (gossip)
谣(謠)言 yáoyán 3 [c] (discussion) 交
谈(談) jiāotán [次 cì] II VI 1 (speak)
说(說)话(話) shuōhuà 2 (chat) 聊 liáo
▶ to talk to or with sb 跟某人谈(談)
话(話) gēn mǒurén tánhuà ▶ to talk
about sth 谈(談)论(論)某事 tánlùn
mǒushì
▶ talk over, talk through VT 仔细(細)
商讨(討) zǐxì shāngtǎo

talkative ['tɔːkətɪv] ADJ 健谈(談)的
jiàntán de

talk show N [c] (US) 脱(脫)口秀
tuōkǒuxiù [个 gè]

tall [tɔːl] ADJ 高的 gāo de ▶ he's 6 feet
tall 他6英尺高 tā liù yīngchǐ gāo

tame [teɪm] ADJ 驯(馴)服的 xùnfú de

tampon ['tæmpɔn] N [c] 月经(經)棉栓
yuèjīng miánshuān [个 gè]

tan [tæn] N [c] 晒黑的肤(膚)色 shàihēi
de fūsè [种 zhǒng]

tangerine [tændʒə'riːn] N [c] 红(紅)橘
hóngjú [个 gè]

tank [tæŋk] N [c] 1 (Mil) 坦克 tǎnkè
[辆 liàng] 2 (for petrol, water) 箱 xiāng
[个 gè]

tanker ['tæŋkə'] N [c] 1 (ship) 油轮(輪)
yóulún [艘 sōu] 2 (truck) 油罐车(車)
yóuguànchē [辆 liàng]

tanned [tænd] ADJ 晒黑的 shàihēi de

tap [tæp] N [c] (esp Brit) 龙(龍)头(頭)
lóngtóu [个 gè]

tap-dancing ['tæpdɑːnsɪŋ] N [u] 踢踏
舞 tītàwǔ

tape [teɪp] I N 1 [c] (cassette) 磁带(帶)
cídài [盘 pán] 2 [u] (adhesive) 胶(膠)
带(帶) jiāodài II VT 1 (record) 录(錄)
制(製) lùzhì 2 (attach) 贴(貼) tiē

tape measure N [c] 卷(捲)尺 juǎnchǐ
[把 bǎ]

tape recorder N [c] 录(錄)音机(機)
lùyīnjī [台 tái]

tar [tɑː'] N [u] 沥(瀝)青 lìqīng

target ['tɑːgɪt] N [c] 1 (of missile) 目
标(標) mùbiāo [个 gè] 2 (aim) 目标(標)
mùbiāo [个 gè]

tart [tɑːt] N [c] 果馅(餡)饼(餅)
guǒxiànbǐng [个 gè]

tartan ['tɑːtn] N [c/u] 苏(蘇)格兰(蘭)
方格呢 Sūgélán fānggéní [块 kuài] II ADJ
[+ rug, scarf etc] 苏(蘇)格兰(蘭)方格的
Sūgélán fānggé de

▶ TARTAN

是一种有图案的厚羊毛布料，其图案是
由不同宽度和颜色的直线条垂直交叉组
成。tartan 用来做 kilt ——一种苏格
兰成年男子和男孩子在正式场合穿的特
别的短裙。这种布料起源于在
Highlands (苏格兰高地)——即苏格兰
群山连绵的西北部。在那里，tartan
被作为反抗英国王室的标志，并因此在
1747年至1782年期间被禁用。不同的颜
色和图案代表着苏格兰的不同地区。

task [tɑ:sk] N [c] 任务(務) rènwù [项 xiàng]

taste [teɪst] I N 1 [c] (flavour) 味道 wèidào [种 zhǒng] 2 [c] (sample) 尝(嘗) 试(試) chángshì [次 cì] 3 [u] (choice, liking) 品位 pǐnwèi II VI ▶ to taste of/ like sth 有/像某物的味道 yǒu/xiàng mǒuwù de wèidào

tasty ['teɪstɪ] ADJ 味美的 wèiměi de

tattoo [tə'tu:] N [c] 文身 wénshēn [个 gè]

taught [tɔ:t] PT, PP of teach

Taurus ['tɔ:rəs] N [u] 金牛座 Jīnniú Zuò

tax [tæks] N [c/u] 税(稅) shuì [种 zhǒng]

taxi ['tæksɪ] N [c] 出租车(車) chūzūchē [辆 liàng]

taxi rank (Brit) N [c] 出租车(車)候客站 chūzūchē hòukèzhàn [个 gè]

taxi stand (US) N [c] 出租车(車)候客站 chūzūchē hòukèzhàn [个 gè]

TB N ABBR (= tuberculosis) 肺结(結)核 fèijiéhé

tea [ti:] N [c/u] 1 (drink) 茶 chá [杯 bēi] 2 (dried leaves) 茶叶(葉) cháyè [片 piàn] 3 (Brit: evening meal) 晚饭(飯) wǎnfàn [顿 dùn]

   TEA

英国人和美国人喝的茶大多是红茶。通常茶里要加牛奶，可能还加糖，当然也可以在茶里只放一小片柠檬。花草茶（herbal tea），如薄荷或甘菊茶，正风行起来。tea 还可以指下午小餐，通常有三明治、蛋糕，还有茶。在英国的一些地方，tea 还可以指晚上的正餐。

teach [ti:tʃ] (pt, pp taught) I VT 1 ▶ to teach sb sth, teach sth to sb 教某人某事，将(將)某事教给(給)某人 jiāo mǒurén mǒushì, jiāng mǒushì jiāogěi mǒurén 2 [+ pupils, subject] 教 jiāo II VI (be a teacher) 教书(書) jiāoshū ▶ to teach sb to do sth/how to do sth 教某人做某事/怎样(樣)做某事 jiāo mǒurén zuò mǒushì/zěnyàng zuò mǒushì

teacher ['ti:tʃəʳ] N [c] 教师(師) jiàoshī [位 wèi]

team [ti:m] N [c] 1 [of people, experts, horses] 组(組) zǔ [个 gè] 2 (Sport) 队(隊) duì [个 gè]

teapot ['ti:pɒt] N [c] 茶壶(壺) cháhú [个 gè]

tear¹ [tɛəʳ] (pt tore, pp torn) I N [c] (rip, hole) 裂口 lièkǒu [个 gè] II VT 撕裂 sīliè ▶ **tear up** VT 撕毁(毀) sīhuǐ

tear² [tɪəʳ] N [c] (when crying) 眼泪(淚) yǎnlèi [滴 dī] ▶ **to burst into tears** 哭起来(來) kū qǐlái

tease [ti:z] VT 逗弄 dòunong

teaspoon ['ti:spu:n] N [c] 茶匙 cháchí [把 bǎ]

teatime ['ti:taɪm] (Brit) N [u] 茶点(點)时(時)间(間) chádiǎn shíjiān

tea towel (Brit) N [c] 擦拭布 cāshìbù [块 kuài]

technical ['tɛknɪkl] ADJ 1 [+ problems, advances] 技术(術)的 jìshù de 2 [+ terms, language] 专(專)业(業)的 zhuānyè de

technician [tɛk'nɪʃən] N [c] 技师(師) jìshī [位 wèi]

technological [tɛknə'lɒdʒɪkl] ADJ 工艺(藝)的 gōngyì de

technology [tɛk'nɒlədʒɪ] N [c/u] 工艺(藝)学(學) gōngyìxué [门 mén]

teddy (bear) ['tɛdɪ(-)] N [c] 玩具熊 wánjùxióng [只 zhī]

teenage ['ti:neɪdʒ] ADJ 十几(幾)岁(歲)的 shíjǐ suì de

teenager ['ti:neɪdʒəʳ] N [c] 青少年 qīngshàonián [名 míng]

tee-shirt ['ti:ʃə:t] N = T-shirt

teeth [ti:θ] N PL of tooth

telephone ['tɛlɪfəun] N [c] 电(電)话(話) diànhuà [部 bù]

telephone book, telephone directory N [c] 电(電)话(話)簿 diànhuàbù [个 gè]

telescope ['tɛlɪskəup] N [c] 望远(遠)镜(鏡) wàngyuǎnjìng [架 jià]

television ['tɛlɪvɪʒən] N 1 [c] (also: television set) 电(電)视(視)机(機) diànshìjī [台 tái] 2 [u] (system) 电(電)视(視) diànshì

tell [tɛl] (pt, pp told) VT 1 (inform) ▶ to tell sb sth 告诉(訴)某人某事 gàosù mǒurén mǒushì 2 [+ story, joke] 讲(講)讲 jiǎng ▶ to tell sb to do sth 指示某人做某事 zhǐshì mǒurén zuò mǒushì ▶ to tell sb that... 告诉(訴)某人说(說)… gàosù mǒurén shuō...
▶ **tell off** VT ▶ to tell sb off 斥责(責)某人 chìzé mǒurén

teller ['tɛlər] (US) N [c] (in bank) 出纳(納)员(員) chūnàyuán [名 míng]

telly ['tɛlɪ] (Brit: inf) N [c/u] 电(電)视(視)diànshì [台 tái]

temper ['tɛmpər] N [c/u] 脾气(氣) píqi [种 zhǒng] ▸ **to lose one's temper** 发(發)怒 fānù

temperature ['tɛmprətʃər] N **1** [c/u] (of place) 气(氣)温(溫) qìwēn **2** [u] (of person) 体(體)温(溫) tǐwēn ▸ **to have or be running a temperature** 发(發)烧(燒) fāshāo

temple ['tɛmpl] N [c] 庙(廟)宇 miàoyǔ [座 zuò]

temporary ['tɛmpərərɪ] ADJ 临(臨)时(時)的 línshí de

temptation [tɛmp'teɪʃən] N [c/u] 诱(誘)惑 yòuhuò [种 zhǒng]

tempting ['tɛmptɪŋ] ADJ 诱(誘)人的 yòurén de

ten [tɛn] NUM 十 shí

tend [tɛnd] VI ▸ **to tend to do sth** 倾(傾)向于(於)做某事 qīngxiàng yú zuò mǒushi

tennis ['tɛnɪs] N [u] 网(網)球运(運)动(動) wǎngqiú yùndòng

tennis court N [c] 网(網)球场(場) wǎngqiúchǎng [个 gè]

tennis player N [c] 网(網)球手 wǎngqiúshǒu [位 wèi]

tense [tɛns] I ADJ 紧(緊)张(張)的 jǐnzhāng de II N [c] (Ling) 时(時)态(態) shítài [种 zhǒng]

tension ['tɛnʃən] N **1** [c/u] (of situation) 紧(緊)张(張)的局势(勢) jǐnzhāng de júshì [个 gè] **2** [u] (of person) 焦虑(慮) jiāolǜ

tent [tɛnt] N [c] 帐(帳)篷 zhàngpeng [顶 dǐng]

tenth [tɛnθ] NUM **1** (in series) 第十 dìshí **2** (fraction) 十分之一 shí fēn zhī yī; see also/另见 **fifth**

term [tə:m] N **1** (学(學)期 xuéqī [个 gè] ▸ **in the short/long term** 短/长(長)期 duǎn/chángqī ▸ **to be on good terms with sb** 与(與)某人关(關)系(係)好 yǔ mǒurén guānxì hǎo

terminal ['tə:mɪnl] I ADJ 晚期的 wǎnqī de II N [c] **1** (Comput) 终(終)端 zhōngduān [个 gè] **2** (at airport) 航空站 hángkōngzhàn [个 gè]

terminally ['tə:mɪnlɪ] ADV ▸ **terminally ill** 病入膏肓的 bìng rù gāo huāng de

terrace ['tɛrəs] N [c] **1** (Brit: row of houses) 成排的房屋 chéngpái de fángwū [排 pái] **2** (patio) 平台(臺) píngtái [个 gè]

terraced ['tɛrəst] ADJ [+ house] 成排的 chéngpái de

terrible ['tɛrɪbl] ADJ **1** [+ accident, winter] 可怕的 kěpà de **2** (very poor) 糟糕的 zāogāo de **3** 糟透的 zāotòu de

terribly ['tɛrɪblɪ] ADV **1** (very) 非常 fēicháng **2** (very badly) 差劲(勁)地 chàjìn de

terrific [tə'rɪfɪk] ADJ **1** [+ amount, thunderstorm, speed] 惊(驚)人的 jīngrén de **2** [+ time, party, idea] 极好的 jíhǎo de

terrified ['tɛrɪfaɪd] ADJ 吓(嚇)坏(壞)的 xiàhuài de

terror ['tɛrər] N [u] 恐惧(懼) kǒngjù

terrorism ['tɛrərɪzəm] N [u] 恐怖主义(義) kǒngbù zhǔyì

terrorist ['tɛrərɪst] I N [c] 恐怖分子 kǒngbù fènzǐ [名 míng] II ADJ 恐怖分子的 kǒngbù fènzǐ de

test [tɛst] I N [c] **1** (trial, check) 试(試)验(驗) shìyàn [次 cì] **2** (Med) 检验(驗) jiǎnyàn [次 cì] **3** (Scol) 测(測)验(驗) cèyàn [个 gè] **4** (also: **driving test**) 驾(駕)驶(駛)考试(試) jiàshǐ kǎoshì [次 cì] II VT **1** (try out) 试(試)验(驗) shìyàn **2** (Scol) 测(測)试(試) cèshì

test tube N [c] 试(試)管 shìguǎn [根 gēn]

text [tɛkst] I N **1** [u] (written material) 正文 zhèngwén **2** [c] (book) 课(課)本 kèběn [本 běn] **3** [c] (also: **text message**) 手机(機)短信 shǒujī duǎnxìn [条 tiáo] II VT (on mobile phone) 给…发(發)短消息 gěi...fā duǎnxiāoxi

textbook ['tɛkstbuk] N [c] 课(課)本 kèběn [本 běn]

text message N [c] 短信 duǎnxìn [条 tiáo]

than [ðæn, ðən] PREP (in comparisons) 比 bǐ ▸ **it's smaller than a matchbox** 它比一个(個)火柴盒还(還)小 tā bǐ yī gè huǒcháihé hái xiǎo ▸ **more/less than Paul** 比保罗(羅)多/少 bǐ Bǎoluó duō/shǎo ▸ **more than 20** 20多于(於) 20 duō yú èrshí ▸ **she's older than you think** 她比你想的年纪(紀)要大 tā bǐ nǐ xiǎng de niánjì yào dà

thank [θæŋk] VT [+ *person*] 感谢(謝) gǎnxiè ▸ **thank you (very much)** (非常)感谢(謝)你 (fēicháng) gǎnxiè nǐ ▸ **no, thank you** 不, 谢(謝)谢(謝) bù, xièxie ▸ **to thank sb for (doing) sth** 感谢(謝)某人 (做) 某事 gǎnxiè mǒurén (zuò) mǒushì

thanks [θæŋks] I NPL 感谢(謝) gǎnxiè II INT 谢(謝)谢(謝) xièxie ▸ **many thanks, thanks a lot** 多谢(謝) duōxiè ▸ **no, thanks** 不了, 谢(謝)谢(謝) bù le, xièxie ▸ **thanks to sb/sth** 多亏(虧)某人/某事 duōkuī mǒurén/mǒushì

Thanksgiving (Day) [ˈθæŋksgɪvɪŋ(-)] (*US*) N [C/U] 感恩节(節) Gǎn'ēn Jié [个 gè]

KEYWORD

that [ðæt] (*demonstrative adj, pron: pl* those) I ADJ 那 nà ▸ **that man/ woman/book** 那个(個)男人/女人/那本书(書) nàge nánrén/nǚrén/nà běn shū ▸ **that one** 那一个(個) nà yī gè

II PRON 1 (*demonstrative*) 那 nà ▸ **who's/ what's that?** 那是谁(誰)/那是什么(麼)? nà shì shuí/nà shì shénme? ▸ **is that you?** 是你吗(嗎)? shì nǐ ma? ▸ **that's my house** 那是我的房子 nà shì wǒde fángzi

2 (*relative*) …的 …de ▸ **the man that I saw** 我见(見)过(過)的那个(個)男的 wǒ jiànguo de nàge nán de ▸ **the woman that you spoke to** 和你说(說)过(過)话(話)的那个(個)女的 hé nǐ shuōguo huà de nàge nǚ de

III CONJ 引导宾语从句的关系代词 ▸ **he thought that I was ill** 他以为(為)我病了 tā yǐwéi wǒ bìng le

IV ADV (*so*) 如此 rúcǐ ▸ **that much/bad/ high** 如此多/糟糕/高 rúcǐ duō/zāogāo/gāo

KEYWORD

the [ði:, ðə] DEF ART 1 定冠词, 用于指代已知的人或物 ▸ **the man/girl/house/ book** 男人/女孩/房子/书(書) nánrén/nǚhái/fángzi/shū ▸ **the men/women/ houses/books** 男人/女人/房子/书(書)

nánrén/nǚrén/fángzi/shū ▸ **the best solution** 最好的解决(決)方案 zuìhǎo de jiějué fāng'àn

2 (*in dates, decades*) 表示具体时间 ▸ **the fifth of March** 3月5日 sānyuè wǔ rì ▸ **the nineties** 90年代 jiǔshí niándài 3 (*in titles*) 用于称谓中 ▸ **Elizabeth the First** 伊丽(麗)莎白一世 Yīlìshābái Yīshì

theatre, (*US*) **theater** [ˈθɪətəʳ] N 1 [C] (*building*) 剧(劇)院 jùyuàn [座 zuò] 2 [C] (*Med*) (*also:* **operating theatre**) 手术(術)室 shǒushùshì [间 jiān] 3 [C] (*US*) (*also:* **movie theater**) 电(電)影院 diànyǐngyuàn [家 jiā]

theft [θɛft] N [C/U] 盗(盜)窃(竊) dàoqiè [起 qǐ]

their [ðɛəʳ] ADJ 1 (*of men, boys, mixed group*) 他们(們)的 tāmen de; (*of women, girls*) 她们(們)的 tāmen de; (*of things, animals*) 它们(們)的 tāmen de 2 (*his or her*) 他/她的 tā/tā de

theirs [ðɛəz] PRON (*of men, boys, mixed group*) 他们(們)的 tāmen de; (*of women, girls*) 她们(們)的 tāmen de; (*of animals*) 它们(們)的 tāmen de ▸ **a friend of theirs** 他们(們)/她们(們)的一个(個)朋友 tāmen/tāmen de yī gè péngyou

them [ðɛm, ðəm] PRON (*plural referring to men, boys, mixed group*) 他们(們) tāmen; (*referring to women, girls*) 她们(們) tāmen; (*referring to things and animals*) 它们(們) tāmen

theme park N [C] 主题(題)公园(園) zhǔtí gōngyuán [座 zuò]

themselves [ðəmˈsɛlvz] PL PRON 1 (*referring to men, boys, mixed group*) 他们(們)自己 tāmen zìjǐ; (*referring to girls, women*) 她们(們)自己 tāmen zìjǐ; (*referring to animals*) 它们(們)自己 tāmen zìjǐ 2 (*emphatic: referring to men, boys, mixed group*) 他们(們)本人 tāmen běnrén; (*referring to women, girls*) 她们(們)本人 tāmen běnrén ▸ **they all enjoyed themselves** 他们(們)/她们(們)都玩得很开(開)心 tāmen/tāmen dōu wán de hěn kāixīn ▸ **by themselves** (*unaided*) 他们(們)/她们(們)独(獨)立地 tāmen/tāmen dúlì de; (*alone*) 他们(們)/她们(們)独(獨)自地 tāmen/tāmen dúzì de

then [ðɛn] ADV **1** (at that time) (past) 当(當)时(時) dāngshí; (future) 那时(時) nàshí **2** (after that) 之后(後) zhīhòu ▸ **by then** 到那时(時) dào nàshí ▸ **before then** 在那之前 zài nà zhīqián ▸ **until then** 直到那时(時) zhídào nàshí ▸ **since then** 自从(從)那时(時) zìcóng nàshí ▸ **well/OK then** 好吧 hǎo ba

there [ðɛəʳ] ADV 那儿(兒) nàr ▸ **they've lived there for 30 years** 他们(們)在那儿(兒)住了30年 tāmen zài nàr zhùle sānshí nián ▸ **is Shirley there please?** (on telephone) 请(請)问(問)雪莉在吗(嗎)? qǐng wèn Xuělì zài ma? ▸ **it's over there** 在那边(邊) zài nàbian ▸ **there he is!** 他在那儿(兒)呐! tā zài nàr na! ▸ **there you are** (offering something) 给(給)你 gěi nǐ ▸ **there is/there are** 有 yǒu ▸ **there has been an accident** 发(發)生了一个(個)事故 fāshēng le yī gè shìgù

therefore [ˈðɛəfɔːʳ] ADV 因此 yīncǐ

there's [ðɛəz] = **there is, there has**

thermometer [θəˈmɒmɪtəʳ] N [c] 温(溫)度计(計) wēndùjì [个 gè]

these [ðiːz] I PL ADJ (demonstrative) 这(這)些 zhèxiē II PL PRON 这(這)些 zhèxiē ▸ **these days** 目前 mùqián

they [ðeɪ] PL PRON **1** (referring to men, boys, mixed group) 他们(們) tāmen; (referring to women, girls) 她们(們) tāmen; (referring to animals, things) 它们(們) tāmen **2** (in generalizations) 人们(們) rénmen

they'd [ðeɪd] = **they had, they would**

they'll [ðeɪl] = **they shall, they will**

they're [ðɛəʳ] = **they are**

they've [ðeɪv] = **they have**

thick [θɪk] ADJ **1** [+ slice, line, book, clothes] 厚的 hòu de **2** [+ sauce, mud, fog] 浓(濃)的 nóng de ▸ **it's 20 cm thick** 有20厘(釐)米粗 yǒu èrshí límǐ cū

thief [θiːf] (pl **thieves** [θiːvz]) N [c] 贼(賊) zéi [个 gè]

thigh [θaɪ] N [c] 大腿 dàtuǐ [条 tiáo]

thin [θɪn] ADJ **1** [+ slice, line, book, material] 薄的 báo de **2** [+ person, animal] 瘦的 shòu de

thing [θɪŋ] I N [c] **1** 事 shì [件 jiàn] **2** (physical object) 物品 wùpǐn [件 jiàn] II **things** NPL **1** (belongings) 东(東)西 dōngxi **2** (in general) 情形 qíngxíng ▸ **a strange thing happened** 发(發)生了一件奇怪的事 fāshēngle yī jiàn hěn qíguài de shì ▸ **how are things going?** 情形如何? qíngxíng rúhé?

think [θɪŋk] (pt, pp **thought**) I VI **1** (reflect) 思考 sīkǎo **2** (reason) 想 xiǎng II VT **1** (be of the opinion, believe) 认(認)为(為) rènwéi **2** (believe) 以为(為) yǐwéi ▸ **what do you think of...?** 你认(認)为(為)⋯怎么(麼)样(樣)? nǐ rènwéi...zěnmeyàng? ▸ **to think about sth/sb** 想着(著)某事物/某人 xiǎngzhe mǒu shìwù/mǒurén ▸ **to think of doing sth** 考虑(慮)做某事 kǎolǜ zuò mǒushì ▸ **I think so/not** 我想是/不是的 wǒ xiǎng shì/bùshì de
▸ **think over** VT [+ offer, suggestion] 仔细(細)考虑(慮) zǐxì kǎolǜ

third [θəːd] NUM **1** (in series) 第三 dìsān **2** (fraction) 三份 sānfèn ▸ **a third of** 三分之一 sān fēn zhī yī; see also/另见 **fifth**

thirdly [ˈθəːdlɪ] ADV 第三 dìsān

Third World I N ▸ **the Third World** 第三世界 Dì Sān Shìjiè II ADJ [+ country, debt] 第三世界的 Dì Sān Shìjiè de

thirst [θəːst] N [c/u] 口渴 kǒukě [阵 zhèn]

thirsty [ˈθəːstɪ] ADJ 渴的 kě de

thirteen [θəːˈtiːn] NUM 十三 shísān; see also/另见 **fifteen**

thirteenth [θəːˈtiːnθ] NUM 第十三 dìshísān; see also/另见 **fifth**

thirty [ˈθəːtɪ] NUM 三十 sānshí; see also/另见 **fifty**

 KEYWORD

this [ðɪs] (pl **these**) I ADJ **1** (demonstrative) 这(這) zhè ▸ **this man** 这(這)个(個)男人 zhège nánrén ▸ **this house** 这(這)座房子 zhè zuò fángzi ▸ **this one is better than that one** 这(這)个(個)比那个(個)好 zhège bǐ nàge hǎo **2** (with days, months, years) 这(這)个(個) zhège ▸ **this Sunday/month/year** 这(這)个(個)星期天/本月/今年 zhège xīngqītiān/běnyuè/jīnnián II PRON 这(這)个(個) zhège ▸ **who's/what's this?** 这(這)是谁(誰)/什么(麼)? zhè shì shuí/shénme? ▸ **this is Janet** (in introduction) 这(這)是珍妮特 zhè shì

Zhēnnítè; (on telephone) 我是珍妮特 wǒ shì Zhēnnítè ▸ **like this** 像这(這)个(個)一样(樣)的 xiàng zhège yīyàng de III ADV (demonstrative) ▸ **this much/ high/long** 这(這)么(麼)多/高/长(長) zhème duō/gāo/cháng

thorn [θɔ:n] N [c] 刺 cì [根 gēn]

thorough ['θʌrə] ADJ **1** (+ search, investigation) 彻(徹)底的 chèdǐ de **2** (methodical) (+ person) 细(細)致(緻)的 xìzhì de

those [ðəuz] I PL ADJ 那些 nàxiē II PL PRON 那些 nàxiē ▸ **those people/ books** 那些人/书(書) nàxiē rén/shū ▸ are those yours? 那些是你的吗(嗎)? nàxiē shì nǐ de ma?

though [ðəu] I CONJ (although) 虽(雖)然 suīrán II ADV 但是 dànshì ▸ **even though** 尽(儘)管 jǐnguǎn

thought [θɔ:t] I PT, PP of **think** II N [c] 想法 xiǎngfǎ [个 gè]

thoughtful ['θɔ:tful] ADJ **1** (deep in thought) 深思的 shēnsī de **2** (considerate) 体(體)贴(貼)的 tǐtiē de

thoughtless ['θɔ:tlɪs] ADJ (+ behaviour, words, person) 不体(體)贴(貼)的 bù tǐtiē de

thousand ['θauzənd] NUM ▸ **a or one thousand** 一千 yī qiān ▸ **thousands of** 许(許)许(許)多多 xǔxǔ duō duō

thread [θrɛd] N **1** [c/u] 线(線) xiàn [根 gēn] **2** [c] (in email) 主题(題) zhǔtí [个 gè]

threat [θrɛt] N [c/u] 威胁(脅) wēixié [个 gè]

threaten ['θrɛtn] VT **1** (make a threat against) (+ person) 威胁(脅) wēixié **2** (endanger) (+ life, livelihood) 使受到威胁(脅) shǐ shòudào wēixié

three [θri:] NUM 三 sān; see also/另见 **five**

three-quarters [θri:'kwɔ:təz] I N PL 四分之三 sì fēn zhī sān II ADV ▸ **three-quarters full/empty** 四分之三满(滿)/空 sì fēn zhī sān mǎn/kōng III PRON 四分之三 sì fēn zhī sān ▸ **three-quarters of an hour** 45分钟(鐘) sìshíwǔ fēnzhōng

threw [θru:] PT of **throw**

thriller ['θrɪlə'] N [c] 惊(驚)险(險)片 jīngxiǎn [场 chǎng]

thrilling ['θrɪlɪŋ] ADJ 令人兴(興)奋(奮)的 lìng rén xīngfèn de

throat [θrəut] N [c] **1** (gullet) 咽喉 yānhóu [个 gè] **2** (neck) 脖子 bózi [个 gè] ▸ **to have a sore throat** 嗓子疼 sǎngzi téng

through [θru:] I PREP **1** (+ place) 穿过(過) chuānguò **2** (throughout) (+ time) 整个(個) zhěnggè **3** (coming from the other side of) 穿过(過) chuānguò II ADJ (+ ticket, train) 直达(達)的 zhídá de ▸ **(from) Monday through Friday** (US) (从(從))周(週)一到周(週)五 (cóng) zhōuyī dào zhōuwǔ

throughout [θru:'aut] PREP **1** (+ place) 遍及 biànjí **2** (+ time) 贯(貫)穿 guànchuān

throw [θrəu] (pt threw, pp thrown [θrəun]) VT **1** (toss) (+ stone, ball) 丢(丟) diū **2** (+ person) 抛(拋) pāo ▸ **throw away** VT **1** (+ rubbish) 扔掉 rēngdiào **2** (+ opportunity) 错(錯)过(過) cuòguò ▸ **throw out** VT **1** (+ rubbish) 扔掉 rēngdiào **2** (from team, organization) 赶(趕)走 gǎnzǒu ▸ **throw up** (inf) VI (vomit) 呕(嘔)吐 ǒutù

thru [θru:] (US) = **through**

thumb [θʌm] N [c] 大拇指 dàmǔzhǐ [个 gè]

thumbtack ['θʌmtæk] (US) N [c] 图(圖)钉(釘) túdīng [颗 kē]

thunder ['θʌndə'] N [u] 雷 léi

thunderstorm ['θʌndəstɔ:m] N [c] 雷雨 léiyǔ [阵 zhèn]

Thursday ['θə:zdɪ] N [c/u] 星期四 xīngqīsì [个 gè]; see also/另见 **Tuesday**

tick [tɪk] N **1** [c] (esp Brit: mark) 钩号(號) gōuhào [个 gè] II VI (clock, watch) **1** 嘀嗒作响(響) dīdā zuò xiǎng III VT (esp Brit) (+ item on list) 打钩 dǎ gōu ▸ **tick off** VT (esp Brit) (+ item on list) 给…打钩 gěi...dǎ gōu

ticket ['tɪkɪt] N **1** [c] (for public transport, theatre, raffle) 票 piào [张 zhāng] **2** [c] (Aut) (also: **parking ticket**) 违(違)章停车(車)罚(罰)单(單) wéizhāng tíngchē fádān [张 zhāng]

ticket inspector N [c] 查票员(員) chápiàoyuán [位 wèi]

ticket office N [c] 售票处(處) shòupiàochù [个 gè]

tickle ['tɪkl] VT 挠(撓) náo

tide [taɪd] N [c] 潮汐 cháoxī ▸ **high/low tide** 涨(漲)/落潮 zhǎng/luò cháo

tidy ['taɪdɪ] I ADJ 整洁(潔)的 zhěngjié de II VT (also: **tidy up**) 整理 zhěnglǐ ▸ **tidy up** VT, VI 整理 zhěnglǐ

tie [taɪ] I N [c] **1** (clothing) 领(領)带(帶) lǐngdài [条 tiáo] **2** 淘汰赛(賽) táotàisài [局 jú] **3** (draw) (in competition) 平局 píngjú [个 gè] II VT (also: **tie up**) 扎(紮) zā ▸ **tie up** VT **1** [+ parcel] 捆(綑)绑(綁) kǔnbǎng **2** [+ dog] 拴 shuān **3** [+ person] 捆(綑)绑(綁) kǔnbǎng

tiger ['taɪgə^r] N [c] 老虎 lǎohǔ [只 zhī]

tight [taɪt] I ADJ **1** [+ shoes, clothes] 紧(緊)身的 jǐnshēn de **2** (strict) [+ budget, schedule] 紧(緊)张(張)的 jǐnzhāng de; [+ security, controls] 严(嚴)格的 yángé de II ADV [hold, squeeze, shut +] 紧(緊)紧(緊)地 jǐnjǐn de

tightly ['taɪtlɪ] ADV 紧(緊)紧(緊)地 jǐnjǐn de

tights [taɪts] (Brit) NPL 连(連)裤(褲)袜(襪) liánkùwà

tile [taɪl] N [c] **1** (on roof) 瓦 wǎ [片 piàn] **2** (on floor, wall) 砖(磚) zhuān [块 kuài]

till [tɪl] I N [c] (Brit) 收银(銀)台(臺) shōuyíntái [个 gè] II PREP, CONJ = **until**

timber ['tɪmbə^r] (Brit) N [U] 木材 mùliào

time [taɪm] I N **1** [U] 时(時)间(間) shíjiān **2** [U] (period) 时(時)候 shíhou **3** (by clock) 时(時)间(間) shíjiān **4** [c] (occasion) 次 cì ▸ **to have a good/bad time** 度过(過)一段愉快/不愉快的时(時)光 dùguò yī duàn yúkuài/bù yúkuài de shíguāng ▸ **to spend one's time doing sth** 花时(時)间(間)做某事 huā shíjiān zuò mǒushì ▸ **three times a day** 一日三次 yī rì sān cì ▸ **all the time** 总(總)是 zǒngshì ▸ **at the same time** (simultaneously) 同时(時) tóngshí ▸ **at times** (sometimes) 有时(時) yǒushí ▸ **in time** (for) 正好赶(趕)上(…) zhènghǎo gǎnshàng (…) ▸ **in a week's/month's time** 一周(週)/月以后(後) yī zhōu/yuè yǐhòu ▸ **on time** 准(準)时(時) zhǔnshí ▸ **5 times 5 is 25** 5乘5等于(於)25 wǔ chéng wǔ děngyú èrshíwǔ ▸ **what time is it?, what's the time?** 几(幾)点(點)了? jǐ diǎn le? ▸ **time off** 休假 xiūjià

timetable ['taɪmteɪbl] N [c] **1** (Brit: Rail etc) 时(時)刻表 shíkèbiǎo [个 gè] **2** (Brit: Scol) 课(課)程表 kèchéngbiǎo [个 gè] **3** (programme of events) 计(計)划(劃)表 jìhuàbiǎo [个 gè]

tin [tɪn] N **1** [U] (metal) 锡(錫) xī **2** [c] (Brit: can) 罐 guàn [个 gè] **3** [c] (container: for biscuits, tobacco) 听(聽) tīng

tin opener [-əupnə^r] (Brit) N [c] 开(開)罐器 kāiguànqì [个 gè]

tiny ['taɪnɪ] ADJ 极(極)小的 jí xiǎo de

tip [tɪp] I N [c] **1** (of branch, paintbrush) 顶(頂)端 dǐngduān [个 gè] **2** (to waiter) 小费(費) xiǎofèi [笔 bǐ] **3** (Brit: for rubbish) 弃(棄)置场(場) qìzhìchǎng [个 gè] **4** (advice) 提示 tíshì [个 gè] II VT **1** [+ waiter] 给(給)…小费(費) gěi…xiǎofèi **2** (pour) 倒出 dàochū

tiptoe ['tɪptəu] VI 踮着(著)脚(腳)走 diǎnzhe jiǎo zǒu ▸ **on tiptoe** 踮着(著)脚(腳)走 diǎnzhe jiǎo zǒu

tire ['taɪə^r] N (US) = **tyre**

tired ['taɪəd] ADJ 累的 lèi de ▸ **to be tired of (doing) sth** 厌(厭)倦于(於)(做)某事 yànjuàn yú (zuò) mǒushì

tiring ['taɪərɪŋ] ADJ 令人疲劳(勞)的 lìng rén píláo de

tissue ['tɪʃuː] N [c] (paper handkerchief) 纸(紙)巾 zhǐjīn [张 zhāng]

title ['taɪtl] N **1** [c] (of book, play) 标(標)题(題) biāotí [个 gè] **2** [c] (Sport) 冠军(軍) guànjūn [个 gè]

◯ **KEYWORD**

to [tuː, tə] I PREP **1** (direction) 到 dào ▸ **to France/London/school/the station** 去法国(國)/伦(倫)敦/学(學)校/车(車)站 qù Fǎguó/Lúndūn/xuéxiào/chēzhàn **2** (as far as) ▸ **from here to London** 从(從)这(這)儿(兒)到伦(倫)敦 cóng zhèr dào Lúndūn **3** (position) 向 xiàng ▸ **to the left/right** 向左/右 xiàng zuǒ/yòu **4** (in time expressions) ▸ **it's five/ten/a quarter to five** 差5分/10分/一刻5点(點) chà wǔ fēn/shí fēn/yí kè wǔ diǎn **5** (for, of) 的 de ▸ **a letter to his wife** 给(給)他妻子的一封信 gěi tā qīzi de yī fēng xin **6** (indirect object) ▸ **to give sth to sb**

给(給)某人某物 gěi mǒurén mǒuwù ▶ **to talk to sb** 对(對)某人说(說) duì mǒurén shuō ▶ **a danger to sb** 对(對)某人的危险(險) duì mǒurén de wēixiǎn **7** (towards) ▶ **to be friendly/kind/loyal to sb** 对(對)某人友好/仁慈/忠实(實) duì mǒurén yǒuhǎo/réncí/zhōngshí **8** (in relation to) ▶ **30 miles to the gallon** 每加仑(侖)可行30英里 měi jiālún kě xíng sānshí yīnglǐ ▶ **three goals to two** 3比2 sān bǐ èr **9** (purpose, result) ▶ **to come to sb's aid** 来(來)帮(幫)某人的忙 lái bāng mǒurén de máng **10** (indicating range, extent) ▶ **from... to...** 从(從)…到… cóng...dào... ▶ **from May to September** 从(從)5月到9月 cóng wǔyuè dào jiǔyuè

II WITH VERB **1** (simple infinitive) 与原形动词一起构成动词不定式 ▶ **to go/eat** 走/吃 zǒu/chī **2** (with vb omitted) 用来代替动词不定式或不定式短语，避免重复 ▶ **I don't want to** 我不想 wǒ bù xiǎng **3** (in order to) 为(為)了 wèile ▶ **I did it to help you** 我这(這)么(麼)做是为(為)了帮你 wǒ zhème zuò shì wèile bāng nǐ **4** (equivalent to relative clause) 用作定语 ▶ **I have things to do** 我有事要做 wǒ yǒu shì yào zuò **5** (after adjective etc) 用于某些动词、名词、形容词后构成不定式 ▶ **to be ready to go** 准(準)备(備)走 zhǔnbèi zǒu ▶ **too old/young to do sth** 年纪(紀)太大/太小以至于(於)不能做某事 niánjì tài dà/tài xiǎo yǐzhì yú bùnéng zuò mǒushì ▶ **to and fro** 来(來)来(來)回回地 láilái huíhuí de

toast [təust] N **1** [U] (Culin) 烤面(麵)包 kǎomiànbāo **2** [c] (drink) 祝酒 zhùjiǔ [次 cì] ▶ **a piece** or **slice of toast** 一片烤面(麵)包 yī piàn kǎomiànbāo ▶ **to drink a toast to sb** 为(為)某人干(乾)杯 wèi mǒurén gānbēi

toaster ['təustər] N [c] 烤面(麵)包机(機) kǎomiànbāojī [台 tái]

tobacco [tə'bækəu] N [U] 烟(煙)草 yāncǎo

tobacconist's (shop) [tə'bækənists-] N [c] 烟(煙)草店 yāncǎodiàn [家 jiā]

today [tə'deɪ] I ADV 今天 jīntiān II N [U] 今天 jīntiān ▶ **what day is it today?** 今天星期几(幾)? jīntiān xīngqī jǐ? ▶ **today is the 4th of March** 今天是3月4日 jīntiān shì sān yuè sì rì

toddler ['tɔdlər] N [c] 学(學)步的小孩 xuébù de xiǎohái [个 gè]

toe [təu] N [c] **1** [of foot] 脚(腳)趾 jiǎozhǐ [个 gè] **2** [of shoe, sock] 脚(腳)趾处(處) jiǎozhǐchù [个 gè] ▶ **big/little toe** 大/小脚(腳)趾 dà/xiǎo jiǎozhǐ

toffee ['tɔfɪ] N **1** [U] (Brit: substance) 太妃糖 tàifēitáng **2** [c] (sweet) 奶糖 nǎitáng [颗 kē]

together [tə'gɛðər] ADV **1** (with each other) 一起 yīqǐ **2** (at the same time) 同时(時) tóngshí **3** (combined) 加起来(來) jiā qǐlái ▶ **together with** 连(連)同 liántóng

toilet ['tɔɪlət] N [c] **1** (apparatus) 抽水马(馬)桶 chōushuǐ mǎtǒng [个 gè] **2** (Brit: room) 卫(衛)生间(間) wèishēngjiān [个 gè] ▶ **to go to the toilet** (esp Brit) 上厕(廁)所 shàng cèsuǒ

toilet paper N [U] 卫(衛)生纸(紙) wèishēngzhǐ

toiletries ['tɔɪlətrɪz] NPL 卫(衛)生用品 wèishēng yòngpǐn

toilet roll N [c/U] 卫(衛)生卷(捲)纸(紙) wèishēng juǎnzhǐ [卷 juǎn]

told [təuld] PT, PP of **tell**

toll [təul] N [c] (on road, bridge) 通行费(費) tōngxíngfèi [笔 bǐ]

tomato [tə'mɑ:təu] (pl tomatoes) N [c/U] 西红(紅)柿 xīhóngshì 番茄 fānqié [个 gè]

tomorrow [tə'mɔrəu] I ADV 明天 míngtiān II N [U] 明天 míngtiān ▶ **the day after tomorrow** 后(後)天 hòutiān ▶ **tomorrow morning** 明天早晨 míngtiān zǎochen

ton [tʌn] N [c] **1** (Brit) 英吨(噸) yīngdūn **2** (US) (also: **short ton**) 美吨(噸) měidūn **3** (metric ton) 公吨(噸) gōngdūn

tongue [tʌŋ] N [c] (Anat) 舌头(頭) shétou [条 tiáo]

tonic ['tɔnɪk] N [U] (also: **tonic water**) 奎宁(寧)水 kuíníngshuǐ

tonight [tə'naɪt] ADV N [U] 今晚 jīnwǎn

tonsil ['tɔnsl] N [c] 扁桃体(體) biǎntáotǐ [个 gè]

tonsillitis [tɔnsɪ'laɪtɪs] N [U] 扁桃腺炎 biǎntáoxiànyán

too [tuː] ADV **1** (*excessively*) 太 tài **2** (*also*) 也 yě ▸ **you're from Brooklyn? Me too!** 你从(從)布鲁(魯)克林来(來)? 我也是！ nǐ cóng Bùlǔkèlín lái? Wǒ yě shì!

took [tʊk] PT of **take**

tool [tuːl] N [c] 用具 yòngjù [种 zhǒng]

toolbar ['tuːlbɑːʳ] N [c] (*Comput*) 工具栏(欄) gōngjùlán [个 gè]

tooth [tuːθ] (*pl* **teeth**) N [c] 牙齿(齒) yáchǐ [颗 kē]

toothache ['tuːθeɪk] N [c/u] 牙痛 yátòng [阵 zhèn] ▸ **to have toothache** 牙痛 yátòng

toothbrush ['tuːθbrʌʃ] N [c] 牙刷 yáshuā [把 bǎ]

toothpaste ['tuːθpeɪst] N [c/u] 牙膏 yágāo [管 guǎn]

top [tɒp] I N **1** [c] (*of mountain, building, tree, stairs*) 顶(頂)部 dǐngbù [个 gè] **2** [c] (*of page*) 顶(頂)端 dǐngduān [个 gè] **3** [c] (*of surface, table*) 表面 biǎomiàn [个 gè] **4** [c] (*lid*) (*of box, jar, bottle*) 盖(蓋)子 gàizi [个 gè] **5** [c] (*blouse*) 上衣 shàngyī [件 jiàn] II ADJ **1** [+ *shelf, step, storey, marks*] 最高的 zuì gāo de **2** [+ *executive, golfer*] 顶(頂)级(級)的 dǐngjí de ▸ **at the top of the stairs/page/street** 在楼(樓)梯底端/页(頁)首/街道的尽(盡)头(頭) zài lóutī dǐngduān/yèshǒu/jiēdào de jìntóu ▸ **to be** or **come top** 独(獨)占(佔)鳌(鰲)头(頭) dúzhàn áotóu

topic ['tɒpɪk] N [c] 话(話)题(題) huàtí [个 gè]

torch [tɔːtʃ] N [c] (*Brit*) 手电(電)筒 shǒudiàntǒng [个 gè]

tore [tɔːʳ] PT of **tear¹**

torn [tɔːn] PP of **tear¹**

tortoise ['tɔːtəs] N [c] 乌(烏)龟(龜) wūguī [只 zhǐ]

torture ['tɔːtʃəʳ] I N [u] 酷刑 kùxíng II VT 对(對)…施以酷刑 duì…shī yǐ kùxíng

total ['təʊtl] I ADJ 总(總)的 zǒng de II N [c] 总(總)数(數) zǒngshù [个 gè] ▸ **in total** 总(總)共 zǒnggòng

totally ['təʊtəlɪ] ADV **1** [agree, destroy +] 完全地 wánquán de **2** [+ *different, new*] 绝(絕)对(對)地 juéduì de

touch [tʌtʃ] I N [c] (*contact*) 触(觸)摸 chùmō [次 cì] II VT **1** (*with hand, foot*) 触(觸)摸 chùmō **2** (*move: emotionally*) 感动(動) gǎndòng III VI (*be in contact*) 接触(觸) jiēchù ▸ **to get in touch with sb** 与(與)某人联(聯)系(繫) yǔ mǒurén liánxì ▸ **to lose touch (with sb)** (与(與)某人)失去联(聯)系(繫) (yǔ mǒurén) shīqù liánxì

tough [tʌf] ADJ **1** (*strong, hard-wearing*) [+ *material*] 坚(堅)韧(韌)的 jiānrèn de **2** [+ *meat*] 老的 lǎo de **3** (*physically*) 强(強)壮(壯)的 qiángzhuàng de **4** (*rough*) 无(無)法无(無)天的 wú fǎ wú tiān de

tour [tuəʳ] I N [c] **1** (*journey*) 旅行 lǚxíng [次 cì] **2** [of town, factory, museum] 观(觀)光 guānguāng [次 cì] **3** (*by pop group, sports team*) 巡(巡)回(回)表演 xúnhuí biǎoyǎn [个 gè] II VT [+ *country, city*] 观(觀)光 guānguāng ▸ **to go on a tour of** [+ *region*] 去…旅行 qù…lǚxíng

tourism ['tuərɪzm] N [u] 旅游(遊)业(業) lǚyóuyè

tourist ['tuərɪst] I N [c] 游(遊)客 yóukè [位 wèi] II CPD [+ *season, attraction*] 旅游(遊) lǚyóu

tow [təʊ] VT [+ *vehicle, trailer*] 拖 tuō ▸ **tow away** VT [+ *vehicle*] 拖走 tuōzǒu

toward(s) [tə'wɔːd(z)] PREP **1** (*in direction of*) 朝着(著) cháozhe **2** (*with regard to*) 对(對)于(於) duìyú **3** (*near*) 接近 jiējìn

towel ['tauəl] N [c] 毛巾 máojīn [条 tiáo]

tower ['tauəʳ] N [c] 塔 tǎ [座 zuò]

tower block (*Brit*) N [c] 高楼(樓)大厦(廈) gāolóu dàshà [座 zuò]

town [taun] N [c] 城镇(鎮) chéngzhèn [个 gè]

town hall (*Brit*) N [c] 市政厅(廳) shìzhèngtīng [个 gè]

tow truck (*US*) N [c] 拖车(車) tuōchē [部 bù]

toy [tɔɪ] I N [c] 玩具 wánjù [个 gè] II CPD [+ *train, car*] 玩具 wánjù

trace [treɪs] N [c] [of substance] 痕迹(跡) hénjì [个 gè]; [of person] 踪(蹤)迹(跡) zōngjì [个 gè]

track [træk] N [c] **1** (*path*) 小径(徑) xiǎojìng [条 tiáo] **2** (*Rail*) 轨(軌)道 guǐdào [条 tiáo] **3** (*on tape, record*) 曲目 qǔmù [个 gè]

tracksuit ['træksuːt] (*Brit*) N [c] 运(運)动(動)服 yùndòngfú [套 tào]

tractor ['træktəʳ] N [c] 拖拉机(機) tuōlājī [部 bù]

trade [treɪd] I N 1 [U] (buying and selling) 贸(貿)易 màoyì 2 [c] (skill, job) 谋(謀)生之道 móushēng zhī dào [种 zhǒng] II VT (exchange) ▸ to trade sth (for sth) (esp US) 用某物交换(換)(某物) yòng mǒuwù jiāohuàn (mǒuwù)

trademark ['treɪdmɑːk] N [c] 商标(標) shāngbiāo [个 gè]

trade union (esp Brit) N [c] 工会(會) gōnghuì [个 gè]

tradition [trə'dɪʃən] N [c/U] 传(傳)统(統) chuántǒng [个 gè]

traditional [trə'dɪʃənl] ADJ 传(傳)统(統)的 chuántǒng de

traffic ['træfɪk] N [U] 交通 jiāotōng

traffic circle (US) N [c] 转(轉)盘(盤) zhuànpán [个 gè]

traffic jam N [c] 交通阻塞 jiāotōng zǔsè [阵 zhèn]

traffic lights NPL 红(紅)绿(綠)灯(燈) hónglǜdēng

traffic warden (esp Brit) N [c] 交通管理员(員) jiāotōng guǎnlǐyuán [位 wèi]

tragedy ['trædʒədɪ] N [c/U] 1 (disaster) 极(極)大的不幸 jídà de bùxìng [个 gè] 2 (Theat) 悲剧(劇) bēijù [个 gè]

tragic ['trædʒɪk] ADJ 悲惨(慘)的 bēicǎn de

trailer ['treɪləʳ] N [c] 1 (Aut) 拖车(車) tuōchē [部 bù] 2 (US: caravan) 房式拖车(車) fángshì tuōchē [辆 liàng]

train [treɪn] I N [c] (Rail) 火车(車) huǒchē [辆 liàng] II VT 1 (teach skills to) 培训(訓) péixùn 2 [+ athlete] 培养(養) péiyǎng III VI 1 (learn a skill) 受训(訓)练(練) shòu xùnliàn 2 (Sport) 锻(鍛)炼(鍊) duànliàn

trained [treɪnd] ADJ 经(經)专(專)门(門)训(訓)练(練)的 jīng zhuānmén xùnliàn de

trainee [treɪ'niː] N [c] 1 (apprentice) 受训(訓)者 shòuxùnzhě [位 wèi] 2 (in office, management job) 实(實)习(習)生 shíxíshēng [个 gè]

trainer ['treɪnəʳ] N [c] 1 (Sport) 教练(練) jiàoliàn [位 wèi] 2 (Brit: shoe) 运(運)动(動)鞋 yùndòngxié [双 shuāng]

training ['treɪnɪŋ] N [U] 1 (for occupation) 培训(訓) péixùn 2 (Sport) 训(訓)练(練) xùnliàn

training course N [c] 培训(訓)班 péixùnbān [个 gè]

tram [træm] (Brit) N [c] (also: tramcar) 有轨(軌)电(電)车(車) yǒu guǐ diànchē [辆 liàng]

tramp [træmp] N [c] 流浪者 liúlàngzhě [个 gè]

trampoline ['træmpəliːn] N [c] 蹦床 bèngchuáng [个 gè]

transfer ['trænsfəʳ] N 1 [c/U] [of money, documents] 转(轉)移 zhuǎnyí [次 cì] 2 [c] (Sport) 转(轉)会(會) zhuǎnhuì [次 cì]

transit ['trænzɪt] N 1 ▸ in transit (people) 在途中 zài túzhōng 2 [U] (US) 运(運)输(輸) yùnshū

translate [trænz'leɪt] VT 翻译(譯) fānyì

translation [trænz'leɪʃən] N 1 [c] (text) 译(譯)文 yìwén [篇 piān] 2 [U] (act of translating) 翻译(譯) fānyì

translator [trænz'leɪtəʳ] N [c] 译(譯)者 yìzhě [个 gè]

transparent [træns'pærnt] ADJ 透明的 tòumíng de

transplant [vb træns'plɑːnt, n 'trænsplɑːnt] I VT 1 (Med) 移植 yízhí II N 1 [c/U] (Med: operation) 移植 yízhí [次 cì]

transport [n 'trænspɔːt, vb træns'pɔːt] I N [U] 交通工具 jiāotōng gōngjù II VT 运(運)送 yùnsòng ▸ public transport (esp Brit) 公共交通 gōnggòng jiāotōng

transportation ['trænspɔː'teɪʃən] N [U] (US: transport) 运(運)输(輸) yùnshū

trap [træp] I N [c] 1 陷阱 xiànjǐng [个 gè] II VT 1 [+ animal] 诱(誘)捕 yòubǔ 2 (in building) 困住 kùnzhù

trash [træʃ] N [U] (US) 废(廢)物 fèiwù

trash can (US) N [c] 垃圾桶 lājītǒng [个 gè]

travel ['trævl] I N [U] (travelling) 旅行 lǚxíng II VI 前往 qiánwǎng III VT [+ distance] 走过(過) zǒuguò

travel agency N [c] 旅行社 lǚxíngshè [个 gè]

travel agent N [c] 1 (shop, office) 旅行中介 lǚxíng zhōngjiè [个 gè] 2 (person) 旅行代理人 lǚxíng dàilǐrén [个 gè]

traveller, (US) **traveler** ['trævləʳ] N [c] 旅行者 lǚxíngzhě [位 wèi]

traveller's cheque, (US) **traveler's check** N [c] 旅行支票 lǚxíng zhīpiào [张 zhāng]

travelling, (US) **traveling** ['trævlɪŋ] N [U] 行程 xíngchéng

travel sickness N [U] 晕(暈)车(車)/船/机(機)症 yùnchē/chuán/jī zhèng

tray [treɪ] N [c] 托盘(盤) tuōpán [个 gè]

treasure ['trɛʒə'] N [c] 宝(寶)藏 bǎozàng

treat [triːt] VT **1** (behave towards) [+ person, object] 对(對)待 duìdài **2** (Med) [+ patient, illness] 医(醫)治 yīzhì

treatment ['triːtmənt] N [c/u] (Med) 治疗(療) zhìliáo [次 cì]

treble ['trɛbl] VI 增至三倍 zēng zhì sān bèi

tree [triː] N [c] 树(樹) shù [棵 kē]

tremble ['trɛmbl] VI (with fear, cold) 战(戰)栗(慄) zhànlì

tremendous [trɪ'mɛndəs] ADJ **1** (enormous) 极(極)大的 jí dà de **2** (excellent) 极(極)棒的 jí bàng de

trend [trɛnd] I N [c] **1** (tendency) 趋(趨)势(勢) qūshì **2** (fashion) 潮流 cháoliú II VI 流行 liúxíng

trendy ['trɛndɪ] (inf) ADJ 时(時)髦的 shímáo de

trial ['traɪəl] N [c/u] (Law) 审(審)理 shěnlǐ [次 cì] ▸ **on trial** (Law) 受审(審) shòushěn; (on approval) 试(試)验(驗) shìyàn

triangle ['traɪæŋgl] N [c] (Math) 三角 sānjiǎo [个 gè]

tribe [traɪb] N [c] 部落 bùluò [个 gè]

trick [trɪk] I N [c] **1** (by conjuror) 戏(戲)法 xìfǎ [个 gè] **2** (deception) 伎俩(倆) jìliǎng [个 gè] II VT (deceive) 耍花招 shuǎ huāzhāo

tricky ['trɪkɪ] ADJ 棘手的 jíshǒu de

tricycle ['traɪsɪkl] N [c] 三轮(輪)车(車) sānlúnchē [辆 liàng]

trip [trɪp] I N [c] **1** (journey) 出行 chūxíng [次 cì] **2** (outing) 外出 wàichū [次 cì] II VI (also: **trip up**) 绊(絆)倒 bàndǎo ▸ **to go on a trip** 外出旅行 wàichū lǚxíng

triple ['trɪpl] I ADJ 三部分的 sān bùfen de II VI 三倍于(於) sānbèi yú

triplets ['trɪplɪts] NPL 三胞胎 sānbāotāi

triumph ['traɪʌmf] N [c] 巨大的成功 jùdà de chénggōng [个 gè]

trivial ['trɪvɪəl] ADJ 琐(瑣)碎的 suǒsuì de

troll [trɒl] N (Comput only) 水军(軍) shuǐjūn

trolley ['trɒlɪ] N [c] **1** (Brit) 手推车(車) shǒutuīchē [辆 liàng] **2** (US: vehicle) 电(電)车(車) diànchē [辆 liàng]

trombone [trɒm'bəun] N [c] 长(長)号(號) chánghào [只 zhī]

troop [truːp] I N [c] [of people, animals] 群 qún II **troops** N [c] PL (Mil) 部队(隊) bùduì [支 zhī]

trophy ['trəufɪ] N [c] 奖(獎)品 jiǎngpǐn [个 gè]

tropical ['trɒpɪkl] ADJ 热(熱)带(帶)的 rèdài de

trouble ['trʌbl] N **1** [c/u] (difficulties, bother, effort) 麻烦(煩) máfan [个 gè] **2** [s] (problem) 问(問)题(題) wèntí [个 gè] **3** [U] (unrest) 骚(騷)乱(亂) sāoluàn ▸ **to be in trouble** (with police, authorities) 惹麻烦(煩) rě máfan ▸ **the trouble is...** 问(問)题(題)是… wèntí shì... ▸ **stomach/back trouble** 胃部/背部毛病 wèibù/bèibù máobìng

trousers ['trauzəz] (Brit) NPL 裤(褲)子 kùzi ▸ **a pair of trousers** 一条(條)裤(褲)子 yī tiáo kùzi

trout [traut] N [c/u] 鳟(鱒)鱼(魚) zūnyú [条 tiáo]

truck [trʌk] N [c] 卡车(車) kǎchē [辆 liàng]

truck driver N [c] 卡车(車)司机(機) kǎchē sījī [位 wèi]

true [truː] ADJ 真实(實)的 zhēnshí de

truly ['truːlɪ] ADV (genuinely) 确(確)实(實)地 quèshí de ▸ **yours truly** (in letter) 您忠诚(誠)的 nín zhōngchéng de

trumpet ['trʌmpɪt] N [c] 小号(號) xiǎohào [把 bǎ]

trunk [trʌŋk] I N [c] **1** [of tree] 树(樹)干(幹) shùgàn [个 gè] **2** [of elephant] 象鼻 xiàngbí [个 gè] **3** (US: of car) 后(後)备(備)箱 hòubèixiāng [个 gè] II **trunks** NPL (also: **swimming trunks**) 游泳裤(褲) yóuyǒngkù

trust [trʌst] VT 信任 xìnrèn

truth [truːθ] N [u] 事实(實) shìshí

try [traɪ] I N [c] 尝(嘗)试(試) chángshì [个 gè] II VT (attempt) 试(試) shì III VI (make effort) 努力 nǔlì ▸ **to try to do sth, try doing sth** 尽(盡)力做某事 jìnlì zuò mǒushì ▸ **try on** VT 试(試)穿 shìchuān ▸ **try out** VT 试(試)验(驗) shìyàn

T-shirt ['tiːʃəːt] N [c] 短袖衫 duǎnxiùshān [件 jiàn]

tub [tʌb] N [c] 1 (container) 缸 gāng [个 gè] 2 (US) 浴缸 yùgāng [个 gè]

tube [tjuːb] N 1 [c] (pipe) 管子 guǎnzi [根 gēn] 2 [c] (container) 筒 tǒng [个 gè] 3 (Brit) ▸ the tube (underground) 地铁(鐵) dìtiě

tuberculosis [tjubəːkjuːˈləʊsɪs] N [U] 肺结(結)核 fèijiéhé

Tuesday ['tjuːzdɪ] N [c/U] 星期二 xīngqíʼèr [个 gè] ▸ it is Tuesday 23rd March 今天是3月23号(號)，星期二 jīntiān shì sānyuè èrshísān hào, xīngqíʼèr ▸ on Tuesday 在星期二 zài xīngqíʼèr ▸ on Tuesdays 每个(個)星期二 měigè xīngqíʼèr ▸ every Tuesday 每逢星期二 měi féng xīngqíʼèr ▸ last/next Tuesday 上个(個)/下个(個)星期二 shàng gè/xià gè xīngqíʼèr ▸ Tuesday morning/afternoon/evening 星期二早晨/下午/晚上 xīngqíʼèr zǎochen/xiàwǔ/wǎnshang

tuition [tjuːˈɪʃən] N [U] 1 教学(學) jiàoxué 2 (fees) 学(學)费(費) xuéfèi

tumble dryer (Brit) N [c] 滚(滾)筒干(乾)衣机(機) gǔntǒng gānyījī [台 tái]

tummy ['tʌmɪ] (inf) N [c] 肚子 dùzi [个 gè]

tuna ['tjuːnə] N [c/U] (also: tuna fish) 金枪(槍)鱼(魚) jīnqiāngyú [条 tiáo]

tune [tjuːn] N [c] 曲调(調) qǔdiào [个 gè]

Tunisia [tjuːˈnɪzɪə] N 突尼斯 Tūnísī

tunnel ['tʌnl] N [c] 隧道 suìdào [条 tiáo]

Turk [təːk] N [c] 土耳其人 Tǔěrqírén [个 gè]

Turkey ['təːkɪ] N 土耳其 Tǔěrqí

turkey ['təːkɪ] N [c] 1 (bird) 火鸡(雞) huǒjī [只 zhī] 2 [U] (meat) 火鸡(雞)肉 huǒjī ròu

Turkish ['təːkɪʃ] I ADJ 土耳其的 Tǔěrqí de II N [U] (language) 土耳其语(語) Tǔěrqíyǔ

turn [təːn] I N [c] (in game, queue, series) 机(機)会(會) jīhuì [个 gè] II VT 1 [+ part of body] 转(轉)动(動) zhuàndòng 2 [+ object] 调(調)转(轉) diàozhuǎn 3 [+ handle, key] 转(轉)动(動) zhuàndòng 4 [+ page] 翻 fān III VI 1 (rotate) [object, wheel +] 旋转(轉) xuánzhuǎn 2 (change direction) [person +] 转(轉)身 zhuǎnshēn 3 [vehicle +] 转(轉)向 zhuǎnxiàng ▸ it's my turn to... 轮(輪)到我做… lúndào wǒ zuò... ▸ to take turns or to take it in turns (to do sth) 轮(輪)流做(某事) lúnliú zuò (mǒushì)

▸ **turn around** VI = **turn round**

▸ **turn back** VI 往回走 wǎnghuí zǒu

▸ **turn down** VT [+ heat, sound] 调(調)低 tiáodī

▸ **turn into** VT FUS 变(變)成 biànchéng

▸ **turn off** VT 1 [+ light, radio, tap] 关(關) guān 2 [+ engine] 关(關)掉 guāndiào

▸ **turn on** VT [+ light, radio, tap] 打开(開) dǎkāi

▸ **turn out** VT [+ light, gas] 关(關)掉 guāndiào ▸ **to turn out to be** (prove to be) 原来(來)是 yuánlái shì

▸ **turn round, turn around** VI [person, vehicle +] 调(調)转(轉) diàozhuǎn

▸ **turn up** I VI [person +] 1 露面 lòumiàn 2 [lost object +] 出现(現) chūxiàn II VT [+ radio, heater] 开(開)大 kāi dà

turning ['təːnɪŋ] N [c] (in road) 拐(枴)弯(彎) guǎiwān [个 gè]

turn signal (US) N [U] 指示器 zhǐshìqì [个 gè]

turquoise ['təːkwɔɪz] ADJ [+ colour] 青绿(綠)色的 qīnglǜsè de

turtle ['təːtl] (Brit) N [c] 龟(龜) guī [只 zhī]

tutor ['tjuːtəʳ] N [c] 1 (Brit: Scol) 助教 zhùjiào [位 wèi] 2 (private tutor) 家庭教师(師) jiātíng jiàoshī [位 wèi]

tuxedo [tʌkˈsiːdəʊ] (US) N [c] 男式晚礼(禮)服 nánshì wǎnlǐfú [件 jiàn]

TV N ABBR (= **television**) 电(電)视(視) diànshì

Twitter® ['twɪtəʳ] N 推特 Tuītè

tweet [twiːt] I N 推文 tuīwén II VB 发(發)推文 fā tuīwén

tweezers ['twiːzəz] NPL 镊(鑷)子 nièzi ▸ **a pair of tweezers** 一把镊(鑷)子 yī bǎ nièzi

twelfth [twɛlfθ] NUM (in series) 第十二 dì shíʼèr; see also/另见 **fifth**

twelve [twɛlv] NUM 十二 shíʼèr ▸ **at twelve (o'clock)** (midday) 中午12点(點) zhōngwǔ shíʼèr diǎn; (midnight) 凌晨零点(點) língchén língdiǎn; see also/另见 **five**

twentieth ['twɛntɪɪθ] NUM 第二十 dì'èrshí

twenty ['twɛntɪ] NUM 二十 èrshí
▶ **twenty-one** 二十一 èrshíyī; see also/ 另见 **fifty**

twice [twaɪs] ADV 两(兩)次 liǎng cì
▶ **twice as much/long as** 多/长(長)至 两(兩)倍 duō/chángzhì liǎng bèi

twin [twɪn] I ADJ [+ sister, brother] 孪生的 luánshēng de II N [c] **1**(person) 双(雙)胞胎 shuāngbāotāi [对 duì] **2**(also: **twin room**) 双(雙)人房 shuāngrénfáng [间 jiān]

twist [twɪst] VT **1**(turn) 扭 niǔ **2**[+ ankle] 扭伤(傷) niǔshāng

two [tu:] NUM 二 èr; see also/另见 **five**

two-percent milk [tu:pə'sɛnt-] (US) N [U] 半脱(脫)脂奶 bàntuōzhīnǎi

type [taɪp] I N **1**[c] (sort, kind) 类(類)型 lèixíng [种 zhǒng] **2**[U] (Typ) 字体(體) zìtǐ II VI 打字 dǎzì III VT 在…上打字 zài…shang dǎzì
▶ **type into** VT 录(錄)入 lùrù

typewriter ['taɪpraɪtə'] N [c] 打字机(機) dǎzìjī [台 tái]

typical ['tɪpɪkl] ADJ 典型的 diǎnxíng de

tyre, (US) **tire** ['taɪə'] N [c] 轮(輪)胎 lúntāi [个 gè]

UFO N ABBR (= **unidentified flying object**) 不明飞(飛)行物 bùmíng fēixíngwù

ugly ['ʌglɪ] ADJ 丑(醜)陋的 chǒulòu de

UK N ABBR (= **United Kingdom**) ▶ **the UK** 大不列颠及北爱(愛)尔(爾)兰(蘭)联(聯)合王国(國) Dàbùlièdiān Jí Běi'ài'ěrlán Liánhéwángguó

ulcer ['ʌlsə'] N [c] 溃(潰)疡(瘍) kuìyáng [处 chù]

umbrella [ʌm'brɛlə] N [c] 伞(傘) sǎn [把 bǎ]

umpire ['ʌmpaɪə'] N [c] (Tennis, Cricket) 裁判员(員) cáipànyuán [位 wèi]

UN N ABBR (= **United Nations**) ▶ **the UN** 联(聯)合国(國) Liánhéguó

unable [ʌn'eɪbl] ADJ ▶ **to be unable to do sth** 不能做某事 bùnéng zuò mǒushì

unanimous [ju:'nænɪməs] ADJ 一致同意的 yīzhì tóngyì de

unavoidable [ʌnə'vɔɪdəbl] ADJ 不可避免的 bùkě bìmiǎn de

unbearable [ʌn'bɛərəbl] ADJ 难(難)以忍受的 nányǐ rěnshòu de

uncertain [ʌn'sə:tn] ADJ 不确(確)定的 bù quèdìng de ▶ **to be uncertain about sth** 对(對)某事心无(無)定数(數) duì mǒushì xīn wú dìngshù

uncle ['ʌŋkl] N [c] (father's older brother) 伯父 bófù [位 wèi]; (father's younger brother) 叔父 shūfù [位 wèi]; (father's sister's husband) 姑父 gūfu [位 wèi]; (mother's brother) 舅父 jiùfù [位 wèi]; (mother's sister's husband) 姨父 yífu [位 wèi]

uncomfortable [ʌnˈkʌmfətəbl] ADJ [+ person] 不舒服的 bù shūfu de; [+ chair, room, journey] 不舒适(適)的 bù shūshì de

unconscious [ʌnˈkɒnʃəs] ADJ 失去知觉(覺)的 shīqù zhījué de

under [ˈʌndəʳ] I PREP 1 (beneath) 在…下面 zài…xiàmiàn 2 (less than) [+ age, price] 不到 bù dào II ADV 1 [go, fly +] 从(從)下面 cóng xiàmiàn 2 (in age, price etc) 以下 yǐxià

underground [ˈʌndəɡraund] I N ▶ the underground (Brit: railway) 地铁(鐵) dìtiě II ADJ 地下的 dìxià de

underline [ʌndəˈlaɪn] (Brit) VT 在…下面划(劃)线(線) zài…xiàmiàn huàxiàn

underneath [ʌndəˈniːθ] I ADV 在下面 zài xiàmiàn II PREP 1 在…下面 zài…xiàmiàn 2 (fig) 在…背后(後) zài…bèihòu

underpants [ˈʌndəpænts] NPL 内(內)裤(褲) nèikù

underpass [ˈʌndəpɑːs] N [c] 地下通道 dìxià tōngdào [条 tiáo]

understand [ʌndəˈstænd] VT 明白 míngbai; [+ foreign language] 懂 dǒng

understanding [ʌndəˈstændɪŋ] ADJ 通情达(達)理的 tōng qíng dá lǐ de

understood [ʌndəˈstud] PT, PP of **understand**

underwater [ˈʌndəˈwɔːtəʳ] ADV 在水下 zài shuǐ xià

underwear [ˈʌndəwɛəʳ] N [U] 内(內)衣 nèiyī

undo [ʌnˈduː] (pt undid, pp undone) VT 解开(開) jiěkāi

undress [ʌnˈdrɛs] VI 脱(脫)衣服 tuō yīfu

uneasy [ʌnˈiːzɪ] ADJ 不安的 bù'ān de ▶ to be uneasy about sth 为(為)某事忧(憂)虑(慮) wèi mǒushì yōulù

unemployed [ʌnɪmˈplɔɪd] I ADJ 失业(業)的 shīyè de II NPL ▶ the unemployed 失业(業)者 shīyèzhě

unemployment [ʌnɪmˈplɔɪmənt] N [U] 失业(業) shīyè

unexpected [ʌnɪksˈpɛktɪd] ADJ 意外的 yìwài de

unexpectedly [ʌnɪksˈpɛktɪdlɪ] ADV 意外地 yìwài de

unfair [ʌnˈfɛəʳ] ADJ 不公平的 bù gōngpíng de

unfamiliar [ʌnfəˈmɪlɪəʳ] ADJ 陌生的 mòshēng de

unfashionable [ʌnˈfæʃnəbl] ADJ 过(過)时(時)的 guòshí de

unfit [ʌnˈfɪt] ADJ 不太健康的 bù tài jiànkāng de

unfold [ʌnˈfəuld] VT 展开(開) zhǎnkāi

unfollow [ʌnˈfɒləu] VT (on social media) 取消关(關)注 qǔxiāo guānzhù

unforgettable [ʌnfəˈɡɛtəbl] ADJ 难(難)忘的 nánwàng de

unfortunately [ʌnˈfɔːtʃənətlɪ] ADV 可惜 kěxī

unfriend [ʌnˈfrɛnd] VT (on social media) 删(刪)除好友 shānchú hǎoyǒu

unfriendly [ʌnˈfrɛndlɪ] ADJ 不友善的 bù yǒushàn de

unhappy [ʌnˈhæpɪ] ADJ 愁苦的 chóukǔ de

unhealthy [ʌnˈhɛlθɪ] ADJ 1 [+ person] 身体(體)不佳的 shēntǐ bù jiā de 2 [+ place, diet, lifestyle] 不利于(於)健康的 bù lìyú jiànkāng de

uniform [ˈjuːnɪfɔːm] N [c/U] 制服 zhìfú [套 tào]

uninhabited [ʌnɪnˈhæbɪtɪd] ADJ 无(無)人居住的 wúrén jūzhù de

union [ˈjuːnjən] N [c] (also: trade union) 工会(會) gōnghuì [个 gè]

Union Jack N [c] 英国(國)国(國)旗 Yīngguó guóqí [面 miàn]

unique [juːˈniːk] ADJ 罕有的 hǎnyǒu de

unit [ˈjuːnɪt] N [c] 1 (single whole) 单(單)位 dānwèi [个 gè] 2 (group, centre) 小组(組) xiǎozǔ [个 gè] 3 (in course book) 单(單)元 dānyuán [个 gè]

United Kingdom N ▶ the United Kingdom 大不列颠及北爱(愛)尔(爾)兰(蘭)联(聯)合王国(國) Dàbùlièdiān Jí Běi'ài'ěr'lán Liánhéwángguó

United Nations N ▶ the United Nations 联(聯)合国(國) Liánhéguó

United States (of America) N ▶ the United States (of America) 美利坚(堅)合众(眾)国(國) Měilìjiān Hézhòngguó

universe [ˈjuːnɪvəːs] N [c] 宇宙 yǔzhòu [个 gè]

university [juːnɪˈvəːsɪtɪ] I N [c/U] 大学(學) dàxué [所 suǒ] ▶ to go to

university 上大学(學) shàng dàxué II CPD [+ *student, professor, education, year*] 大学(學) dàxué

unkind [ʌn'kaɪnd] ADJ 刻薄的 kèbó de

unknown [ʌn'nəun] ADJ 1 [+ *fact, number*] 未知的 wèizhī de 2 [+ *writer, artist*] 名不见(見)经(經)传(傳)的 míng bù jiàn jīngzhuàn de

unleaded [ʌn'lɛdɪd] I ADJ 无(無)铅(鉛)的 wúqiān de II N [U] 无(無)铅(鉛)燃料 wúqiān ránliào

unless [ʌn'lɛs] CONJ 除非 chúfēi

unlikely [ʌn'laɪklɪ] ADJ 未必会(會)发(發)生的 wèibì huì fāshēng de ▸ **he is unlikely to win** 他获(獲)胜(勝)的希望不大 tā huòshèng de xīwàng bù dà

unload [ʌn'ləud] VT 1 [+ *objects*] 卸 xiè 2 [+ *car, lorry*] 从(從)…上卸货(貨) cóng…shang xièhuò

unlock [ʌn'lɒk] VT 开(開) kāi

unlucky [ʌn'lʌkɪ] ADJ 1 [+ *person*] 不幸的 bùxìng de 2 [+ *object, number*] 不吉利的 bù jílì de

unmarried [ʌn'mærɪd] ADJ 未婚的 wèihūn de

unnatural [ʌn'nætʃrəl] ADJ 反常的 fǎncháng de

unnecessary [ʌn'nɛsəsərɪ] ADJ 不必要的 bù bìyào de

unpack [ʌn'pæk] I VI 开(開)包 kāibāo II VT [+ *suitcase, bag*] 打开(開)…取出东(東)西 dǎkāi…qǔchū dōngxi

unpleasant [ʌn'plɛznt] ADJ 使人不愉快的 shǐ rén bù yúkuài de; [+ *person, manner*] 令人讨(討)厌(厭)的 lìng rén tǎoyàn de

unplug [ʌn'plʌg] VT 拔去…的插头(頭) báqù…de chātóu

unpopular [ʌn'pɒpjulər] ADJ 不受欢(歡)迎的 bù shòu huānyíng de

unrealistic ['ʌnrɪə'lɪstɪk] ADJ 不切实(實)际(際)的 bù qiè shíjì de ▸ **it is unrealistic to expect that...** 指望…是不切实(實)际(際)的 zhǐwàng…shì bù qiè shíjì de

unreasonable [ʌn'riːznəbl] ADJ 无(無)理的 wúlǐ de

unreliable [ʌnrɪ'laɪəbl] ADJ 1 [+ *person, firm*] 不可信赖(賴)的 bùkě xìnlài de 2 [+ *machine, method*] 不可靠的 bù kěkào de

unroll [ʌn'rəul] VT 展开(開) zhǎnkāi

unscrew [ʌn'skruː] VT 旋开(開) xuánkāi

unsuccessful [ʌnsək'sɛsful] ADJ 1 [+ *attempt, application*] 失败(敗)的 shībài de 2 [+ *person, applicant*] 不成功的 bù chénggōng de

unsuitable [ʌn'suːtəbl] ADJ 1 [+ *place, time, clothes*] 不适(適)宜的 bù shìyí de 2 [+ *candidate, applicant*] 不合适(適)的 bù héshì de ▸ **to be unsuitable for sth/ for doing sth** 不适(適)于(於)某事/做某事 bù shìyú mǒushì/zuò mǒushì

untidy [ʌn'taɪdɪ] ADJ 1 [+ *room*] 不整洁(潔)的 bù zhěngjié de 2 [+ *person, appearance*] 邋遢的 lātā de

until [ən'tɪl] I PREP 直到…时(時) zhídào…shí II CONJ 到…为(為)止 dào…wéizhǐ ▸ **until now** 直到现(現)在 zhídào xiànzài ▸ **until then** 届(屆)时(時) jièshí

unusual [ʌn'juːʒuəl] ADJ 不寻(尋)常的 bù xúncháng de

unwilling [ʌn'wɪlɪŋ] ADJ ▸ **to be unwilling to do sth** 不愿(願)做某事 bù yuàn zuò mǒushì

unwrap [ʌn'ræp] VT 打开(開)…的包装(裝) dǎkāi…de bāozhuāng

KEYWORD

up [ʌp] I PREP 1 (*to higher point on*) 沿…向上 yán…xiàngshàng ▸ **he went up the stairs/the hill/the ladder** 他上了楼(樓)/山/梯子 tā shàngle lóu/shān/tīzi 2 (*along*) 沿着(著) yánzhe 3 (*at higher point on*) 在…高处(處) zài…gāochù; [+ *road*] 在…高远(遠)处(處) zài…gāoyuǎnchù ▸ **they live further up the street** 他们(們)住在这(這)条(條)街那边(邊)儿(兒) tāmen zhù zài zhè tiáo jiē nàbiānr II ADV 1 (*towards higher point*) 往上 wǎngshàng ▸ **the lift only goes up to the 12th floor** 电(電)梯只到12层(層)楼(樓)以上 diàntī zhǐ dào shí'èr céng lóu yǐshàng 2 (*at higher point*) 高高地 gāogāo de ▸ **up here/there** 这(這)/那上面 zhè/nà shàngmian 3 ▸ **to be up** (*be out of bed*) 起床 qǐchuáng

4 (to/in the north) 在/向北方 zài/xiàng běifāng ▶ he often comes up to Scotland 他常北上去苏(蘇)格兰(蘭) tā cháng běishàng qù Sūgélán

5 (approaching) ▶ to go/come/run up (to sb) (朝某人) 走去/走过(過)来(來)/跑去 (cháo mǒurén) zǒuqù/zǒu guòlái/pǎoqù

6 ▶ up to (as far as) 直到 zhídào; (in approximations) 多达(達) duōdá ▶ I can spend up to £100 我可以花到100英镑(鎊) wǒ kěyǐ huādào yìbǎi yīngbàng

7 ▶ up to or until 直到 zhídào ▶ I'll be here up to or until 5.30 pm 我会(會)一直呆到下午5点(點)30分 wǒ huì yīzhí dāidào xiàwǔ wǔ diǎn sānshí fēn ▶ up to now 直到现(現)在 zhídào xiànzài

8 ▶ it is up to you (to decide) 随(隨)便你（决(決)定) suíbiàn nǐ (juédìng)

9 ▶ to feel up to sth/to doing sth 感到能胜(勝)任某事/感到有力气(氣)做某事 gǎndào néng shèngrèn mǒushì/gǎndào yǒu lìqi zuò mǒushì

upcycle [ˈʌpsaɪkl] vT 升级(級)改造 shēng jí gǎi zào

update [vb ʌpˈdeɪt, n ˈʌpdeɪt] I vT 更新 gēngxīn II N [c] 最新信息 zuìxīn xìnxī [条 tiáo]

uphill [ˈʌpˈhɪl] ADV [walk, push +] 往坡上 wǎng pōshang

upload [ʌpˈləʊd] vT (Comput) 上传(傳) shàngchuán

upright [ˈʌpraɪt] ADV [sit, stand +] 挺直地 tǐngzhí de

upset [ʌpˈsɛt] (pt, pp upset) I vT [+ person] 使苦恼(惱) shǐ kǔnǎo II ADJ **1** (unhappy) 心烦(煩)意乱(亂)的 xīn fán yì luàn de **2** [+ stomach] 不舒服的 bù shūfu de ▶ to be upset about sth 为(為)某事感到烦(煩)恼(惱) wèi mǒushì gǎndào fánnǎo

upside down [ʌpsaɪd-] ADV 上下颠(顛)倒地 shàngxià diāndǎo de

upstairs [ʌpˈstɛəz] ADV **1** [be +] 在楼(樓)上 zài lóushang **2** [go +] 往楼(樓)上 wǎng lóushang

up-to-date [ˈʌptəˈdeɪt] ADJ 最新的 zuì xīn de

upwards [ˈʌpwədz] ADV 向上 xiàngshàng

urgent [ˈəːdʒənt] ADJ 紧(緊)急的 jǐnjí de

US N ABBR (= United States) ▶ the US 美国(國) Měiguó

us [ʌs] PRON 我们(們) wǒmen

USA N ABBR (= United States of America) ▶ the USA 美国(國) Měiguó

USB (stick) [juː ɛs biː-] N [c] U盘(盤) U pán [个 gè]

use [n juːs, vb juːz] I N [c/U] (purpose) 用途 yòngtú [种 zhǒng] II vT **1** [+ object, tool] 使用 shǐyòng **2** [+ word, phrase] 应(應)用 yìngyòng ▶ to make use of sth 利用某物 lìyòng mǒuwù ▶ it's no use 没(沒)用的 méiyòng de ▶ it's no use arguing/crying etc 吵/哭〔等〕是没(沒)用的 chǎo/kū děng shì méiyòng de ▶ to be of use (to sb) (对(對)某人) 毫无(無)用处(處) (duì mǒurén) háowú yòngchu ▶ she used to do it 她过(過)去是这(這)么(麼)做的 tā guòqù shì zhème zuò de ▶ I didn't use to or I used not to worry so much 我过(過)去不这(這)么(麼)焦虑(慮) wǒ guòqù bù zhème jiāolǜ ▶ to be used to sth/to doing sth 习(習)惯(慣)于(於)某事/做某事 xíguàn yú mǒushì/zuò mǒushì ▶ to get used to sth/to doing sth 开(開)始习(習)惯(慣)于(於)某事/做某事 kāishǐ xíguàn yú mǒushì/zuò mǒushì

▶ use up vT 用完 yòngwán

useful [ˈjuːsful] ADJ 有用的 yǒuyòng de ▶ to be useful for sth/doing sth 对(對)某事/做某事有帮(幫)助的 duì mǒushì/zuò mǒushì yǒu bāngzhù de

useless [ˈjuːslɪs] ADJ (pointless) 徒劳(勞)的 túláo de

user [ˈjuːzər] N [c] 使用者 shǐyòngzhě [位 wèi]

user-friendly [ˈjuːzəˈfrɛndlɪ] ADJ 易于(於)使用的 yì yú shǐyòng de

username [ˈjuːzəneɪm] N [c] (Comput) 用户名 yònghùmíng [个 gè]

usual [ˈjuːʒuəl] ADJ 惯(慣)常的 guàncháng de ▶ as usual 像往常一样(樣) xiàng wǎngcháng yīyàng ▶ warmer/colder than usual 比平常暖和/冷 bǐ píngcháng nuǎnhuo/lěng

usually [ˈjuːʒuəlɪ] ADV 通常地 tōngcháng de

V

vacancy ['veɪkənsɪ] N [c] *(job)* 空缺 kòngquē [个 gè]; *(hotel room)* 空房 kōngfáng [间 jiān] ▸ "no vacancies" "客满(滿)" "kèmǎn"

vacant ['veɪkənt] ADJ 空着(著)的 kòngzhe de

vacation [və'keɪʃən] N [c] *(esp US)* 休假 xiūjià [次 cì] ▸ to take a vacation 休假 xiūjià ▸ to be/go on vacation 在/去度假 zài/qù dùjià

vaccinate ['væksɪneɪt] VT ▸ to vaccinate sb (against sth) 给 mǒurén jiēzhòng yìmiáo (yùfáng mǒu jíbìng)

vacuum cleaner N [c] *(also: vacuum)* 真空吸尘(塵)器 zhēnkōng xīchénqì [台 tái]

vague [veɪg] ADJ 不清楚的 bù qīngchu de

vain [veɪn] ADJ [+ person] 自负(負)的 zìfù de ▸ in vain 徒然 túrán

Valentine's Day ['væləntaɪnz-] N [c/u] 情人节(節) Qíngrén Jié [个 gè]

valid ['vælɪd] ADJ 有效的 yǒuxiào de

valley ['vælɪ] N [c] 山谷 shāngǔ [个 gè]

valuable ['væljuəbl] ADJ 贵(貴)重的 guìzhòng de

value ['vælju:] N **1** [c/u] *(financial worth)* 价(價)值 jiàzhí [种 zhǒng] **2** [u] *(worth in relation to price)* 价(價)格 jiàgé

van [væn] N [c] *(Aut)* 厢(廂)式运(運)货(貨)车(車) xiāngshì yùnhuòchē [辆 liàng]

vandalism ['vændəlɪzəm] N [u] 蓄意破坏(壞)公物的行为(為) xùyì pòhuài gōngwù de xíngwéi

vandalize ['vændəlaɪz] VT 肆意毁(毀)坏(壞) sìyì huǐhuài

vanish ['vænɪʃ] VI 消失 xiāoshī

vape [veɪp] VI 吸电(電)子烟(煙) xī diànzǐ yān

variety [və'raɪətɪ] N **1** [u] *(diversity)* 多样(樣)性 duōyàngxìng **2** [s] *(range)* [of objects] 若干 ruògān

various ['vɛərɪəs] ADJ 不同的 bùtóng de

vary ['vɛərɪ] **I** VT *(make changes to)* 更改 gēnggǎi **II** VI *(be different)* 有差异(異) yǒu chāyì

vase [vɑːz, US veɪs] N [c] 花瓶 huāpíng [个 gè]

VCR N ABBR (= video cassette recorder) 录(錄)像机(機) lùxiàngjī

VDT *(US)* N ABBR (= visual display terminal) 视(視)频(頻)显(顯)示装(裝)置 shìpín xiǎnshì zhuāngzhì

VDU *(Brit)* N ABBR (= visual display unit) 视(視)频(頻)显(顯)示装(裝)置 shìpín xiǎnshì zhuāngzhì

veal [viːl] N [u] 小牛肉 xiǎoniúròu

vegan ['viːgən] **I** N [c] 纯(純)素食主义(義)者 chún sùshí zhǔyìzhě [个 gè] **II** ADJ [+ diet, restaurant etc] 纯(純)素食的 chún sùshí de

vegetable ['vɛdʒtəbl] N [c] 蔬菜 shūcài [种 zhǒng]

vegetarian [vɛdʒɪ'tɛərɪən] **I** N [c] 素食者 sùshízhě [个 gè] **II** ADJ [+ diet, restaurant etc] 素的 sù de

vehicle ['viːɪkl] N [c] 机(機)动(動)车(車) jīdòngchē [辆 liàng]

vein [veɪn] N [c] 静(靜)脉(脈) jìngmài [条 tiáo]

velvet ['vɛlvɪt] N [c/u] 天鹅(鵝)绒(絨) tiān'éróng [块 kuài]

vending machine ['vɛndɪŋ-] N [c] 自动(動)售货(貨)机(機) zìdòng shòuhuòjī [部 bù]

verb [vəːb] N [c] 动(動)词(詞) dòngcí [个 gè]

versus ['vəːsəs] PREP 对(對) duì

vertical ['vəːtɪkl] ADJ 垂直的 chuízhí de

very ['vɛrɪ] ADV **1** 很 hěn **2** ▸ the very end/beginning 最终(終)/一开(開)始 zuìzhōng/yī kāishǐ ▸ very much so

确(確)实(實)如此 quèshí rúcǐ ▶ **very little** 极少的 jí shǎo de ▶ **there isn't very much (of...)** (⋯)不太多了 (...)bù tài duō le

vest [vɛst] N [c] **1** (Brit: underwear) 汗衫 hànshān [件 jiàn] **2** (US: waistcoat) 马(馬)甲 mǎjiǎ [件 jiàn]

vet [vɛt] N [c] (esp Brit: veterinary surgeon) 兽(獸)医(醫) shòuyī [个 gè]

veterinarian [vɛtrɪ'nɛərɪən] (US) N [c] 兽(獸)医(醫) shòuyī [个 gè]

via ['vaɪə] PREP 经(經)由 jīngyóu

vicar ['vɪkəʳ] N [c] 教区(區)牧师(師) jiàoqū mùshī [位 wèi]

vicious ['vɪʃəs] ADJ **1** [+ attack, blow] 剧(劇)烈的 jùliè de **2** [+ person, dog] 凶残(殘)的 xiōngcán de

victim ['vɪktɪm] N [c] 受害者 shòuhàizhě [个 gè] ▶ **to be the victim of** 成为(為)⋯的受害者 chéngwéi...de shòuhàizhě

victory ['vɪktərɪ] N [c/u] 胜(勝)利 shènglì [次 cì]

video ['vɪdɪəu] I N **1** [c] (film) 录(錄)像 lùxiàng [段 duàn] **2** [u] (system) 录(錄)像 lùxiàng **3** [c] (cassette) 录(錄)像带(帶) lùxiàngdài [盘 pán] **4** [c] (esp Brit: machine) 录(錄)像机(機) lùxiàngjī [台 tái] II VT (esp Brit) 录(錄)下 lùxià

video game N [c] 电(電)子游(遊)戏(戲) diànzǐ yóuxì [种 zhǒng]

video recorder N [c] 录(錄)像机(機) lùxiàngjī [台 tái]

Vietnam ['vjɛt'næm] N 越南 Yuènán

Vietnamese [vjɛtnə'mi:z] (pl **Vietnamese**) I ADJ 越南的 Yuènán de II N **1** [c] (person) 越南人 Yuènánrén [个 gè] **2** [u] (language) 越南语(語) Yuènányǔ

view [vju:] N [c] **1** 景色 jǐngsè [道 dào] **2** (opinion) 看法 kànfǎ [种 zhǒng]

village ['vɪlɪdʒ] N [c] 村庄(莊) cūnzhuāng [个 gè]

vine [vaɪn] N [c] 葡萄藤 pútáoténg [条 tiáo]

vinegar ['vɪnɪgəʳ] N [c/u] 醋 cù [瓶 píng]

vineyard ['vɪnjɑ:d] N [c] 葡萄园(園) pútáoyuán [座 zuò]

violence ['vaɪələns] N [u] 暴力 bàolì

violent ['vaɪələnt] ADJ 暴力的 bàolì de

violin [vaɪə'lɪn] N [c] 小提琴 xiǎotíqín [把 bǎ]

violinist [vaɪə'lɪnɪst] N [c] 小提琴手 xiǎotíqínshǒu [个 gè]

viral [vaɪrəl] ADJ [+ video, tweet] 热(熱)门(門)的 rèmén de ▶ **to go viral** 成为(為)热(熱)门(門)话(話)题(題) chéngwéi rèmén huàtí

virgin ['və:dʒɪn] N [c] 处(處)女 chǔnǚ [个 gè]

Virgo ['və:gəu] N [u] (sign) 处(處)女座 Chǔnǚ Zuò

virus ['vaɪərəs] (Med, Comput) N [c] 病毒 bìngdú [种 zhǒng]

visa ['vi:zə] N [c] 签(簽)证(證) qiānzhèng [个 gè]

visit ['vɪzɪt] I N [c] **1** (to person) 拜访(訪) bàifǎng [次 cì] **2** (to place) 访(訪)问(問) fǎngwèn [次 cì] II VT **1** [+ person] 拜访(訪) bàifǎng **2** [+ place] 游(遊)览(覽) yóulǎn

▶ **visit with** (US) VT FUS 拜访(訪) bàifǎng

visitor ['vɪzɪtəʳ] N [c] **1** (to city, country) 游(遊)客 yóukè [位 wèi] **2** (to person, house) 来(來)客 láikè [位 wèi]

visual ['vɪzjuəl] ADJ 视(視)觉(覺)的 shìjué de

vital ['vaɪtl] ADJ 至关(關)重要的 zhì guān zhòngyào de

vitamin ['vɪtəmɪn, US 'vaɪtəmɪn] N [c] 维(維)生素 wéishēngsù [种 zhǒng]

vivid ['vɪvɪd] ADJ **1** 生动(動)的 shēngdòng de **2** [+ colour, light] 鲜(鮮)艳(豔)的 xiānyàn de

vlog [vlɒg] I N [c] 视(視)频(頻)博客 shìpín bókè II VI 录(錄)制视(視)频(頻)博客 lùzhì shìpín bókè

vlogger ['vlɒgə] N [c] 视(視)频(頻)博主 shìpín bózhǔ [名 míng]

vocabulary [vəu'kæbjulərɪ] N **1** [c/u] [of person] 词(詞)汇(匯)量 cíhuìliàng **2** [c] [of language] 词(詞)汇(匯) cíhuì [个 gè]

vodka ['vɒdkə] N [c/u] 伏特加酒 fútèjiā jiǔ [瓶 píng]

voice [vɔɪs] N [c] 嗓音 sǎngyīn [种 zhǒng]

voice mail N [u] 语(語)音留言 yǔyīn liúyán

volcano [vɒl'keɪnəu] (pl volcanoes) N [c] 火山 huǒshān [座 zuò]

volleyball ['vɒlɪbɔ:l] N [u] 排球 páiqiú

volume ['vɒlju:m] N [u] [of TV, radio,

stereo] 音量 yīnliàng ▶ **volume one/ two** [*of book*] 第一／二册(冊) dìyī/èr cè

voluntary ['vɒləntərɪ] ADJ **1** (*not compulsory*) 自愿(願)的 zìyuàn de **2** [+ *work, worker*] 志愿(願)的 zhìyuàn de

volunteer [vɒlən'tɪəʳ] N [c] (*unpaid worker*) 志愿(願)者 zhìyuànzhě [名 míng] ▶ **to volunteer to do sth** 自愿(願)做某事 zìyuàn zuò mǒushì

vomit ['vɒmɪt] I N [U] 呕(嘔)吐物 ǒutùwù II VT 吐 tù III VI 呕(嘔)吐 ǒutù

vote [vəut] I N [c] 选(選)票 xuǎnpiào [张 zhāng] II VI 投票 tóupiào ▶ **to take a vote on sth** 就某事进(進)行表决(決) jiù mǒushì jìnxíng biǎojué ▶ **to vote for sb** 投某人票 tóu mǒurén piào ▶ **to vote for/against sth** 投票支持/反对(對)某 事 tóupiào zhīchí/fǎnduì mǒushì

voucher ['vautʃəʳ] N [c] 代金券 dàijīnquàn [张 zhāng]

vowel ['vauəl] N [c] 元音 yuányīn [个 gè]

W

wage [weɪdʒ] N [c] (*also*: **wages**) 工 资(資) gōngzī [份 fèn]

waist [weɪst] N [c] **1** 腰 yāo **2** [*of clothing*] 腰身 yāoshēn

waistcoat ['weɪskəut] (*Brit*) N [c] 马(馬) 甲 mǎjiǎ [件 jiàn]

wait [weɪt] I VI 等待 děngdài II N [c] (*interval*) 等待时(時)间(間) děngdài shíjiān [段 duàn] ▶ **to wait for sb/sth** 等候某人/某物 děnghòu mǒurén/ mǒuwù ▶ **wait a minute!** 等一 下！ děng yīxià! ▶ **to keep sb waiting** 让(讓)某人等着(著) ràng mǒurén děngzhe

waiter ['weɪtəʳ] N [c] 男服务(務)员(員) nán fúwùyuán [位 wèi]

waiting list ['weɪtɪŋ-] N [c] 等候者名 单(單) děnghòuzhě míngdān [份 fèn]

waiting room ['weɪtɪŋ-] N [c] 等候室 děnghòushì [间 jiān]

waitress ['weɪtrɪs] N [c] 女服务(務) 员(員) nǚ fúwùyuán [位 wèi]

wake [weɪk] (*pt* **woke** *or* **waked**, *pp* **woken** *or* **waked**)
▶ **wake up** I VT 唤(喚)醒 huànxǐng II VI 醒来(來) xǐnglái

Wales [weɪlz] N 威尔(爾)士 Wēi'ěrshì ▶ **the Prince of Wales** 威尔(爾)士王子 Wēi'ěrshì Wángzǐ

walk [wɔːk] I N [c] 散步 sànbù [次 cì] II VI 走 zǒu III VT [+ *distance*] 走 zǒu ▶ **it's 10 minutes' walk from here** 从(從)这(這)儿(兒)走10分钟(鐘)的路

程 cóng zhèr zǒu yǒu shí fēnzhōng de lùchéng ▸ **to go for a walk** 去散步 qù sànbù

walking ['wɔːkɪŋ] N [U] 步行 bùxíng

wall [wɔːl] N [c] **1** (of building, room) 墙(牆) qiáng [堵 dǔ] **2** (around garden, field) 围(圍)墙(牆) wéiqiáng [圈 quān]

wallet ['wɒlɪt] N [c] 钱(錢)包 qiánbāo [个 gè]

wallpaper ['wɔːlpeɪpəʳ] N [c/u] 墙(牆)纸(紙) qiángzhǐ [张 zhāng]

walnut ['wɔːlnʌt] N [c] (nut) 核桃 hétao [个 gè]

wander ['wɒndəʳ] vɪ 漫游(遊) mànyóu

want [wɒnt] vт **1** (wish for) 想要 xiǎng yào **2** (inf: need) 需要 xūyào ▸ **to want to do sth** 想要做某事 xiǎng yào zuò mǒushì ▸ **to want sb to do sth** 希望某人做某事 xīwàng mǒurén zuò mǒushì

war [wɔːʳ] N [c/u] 战(戰)争(爭) zhànzhēng [场 chǎng]

wardrobe ['wɔːdrəub] N [c] 衣橱(櫥) yīchú [个 gè]

warehouse ['wɛəhaus] N [c] 仓(倉)库(庫) cāngkù [间 jiān]

warm [wɔːm] ADJ **1** [+ meal, soup, water] 温(溫)热(熱)的 wēnrè de; [+ day, weather] 暖和的 nuǎnhuo de **2** [+ clothes, blankets] 保暖的 bǎonuǎn de **3** [+ applause, welcome] 热(熱)情的 rèqíng de ▸ **it's warm** 天很暖和 tiān hěn nuǎnhuo ▸ **are you warm enough?** 你觉(覺)得够(夠)暖和吗(嗎)? nǐ juéde gòu nuǎnhuo ma?
▸ **warm up 1** vɪ [athlete, pianist +] 热(熱)身 rèshēn **II** vт [+ food] 加热(熱) jiārè

warn [wɔːn] vт ▸ **to warn sb that** 警告某人… jǐnggào mǒurén… ▸ **to warn sb not to do sth** 告诫(誡)某人不要做某事 gàojiè mǒurén bùyào zuò mǒushì

warning ['wɔːnɪŋ] N **1** [c] (action, words, sign) 警告 jǐnggào [个 gè] **2** [c/u] (notice) 预(預)兆 yùzhào [个 gè]

was [wɒz] pт of **be**

wash [wɒʃ] **I** vт 洗 xǐ **II** vɪ [person +] 洗净(淨) xǐjìng ▸ **to wash one's face/hands/hair** 洗脸(臉)/手/头(頭)发(髮) xǐ liǎn/shǒu/tóufa ▸ **to have a wash** 洗一下 xǐ yīxià
▸ **wash up** vɪ **1** (Brit: wash dishes) 洗餐具 xǐ cānjù **2** (US: have a wash) 洗一洗 xǐ yī xǐ

washbasin ['wɒʃbeɪsn] N [c] 脸(臉)盆 liǎnpén [个 gè]

washcloth ['wɒʃklɔθ] (US) N [c] 毛巾 máojīn [条 tiáo]

washing ['wɒʃɪŋ] N [U] **1** (dirty) 待洗衣物 dài xǐ yīwù **2** (clean) 洗好的衣物 xǐhǎo de yīwù ▸ **to do the washing** 洗衣服 xǐ yīfu

washing machine N [c] 洗衣机(機) xǐyījī [台 tái]

washing powder (Brit) N [c/u] 洗衣粉 xǐyīfěn [袋 dài]

wasn't ['wɒznt] = **was not**

wasp [wɒsp] N [c] 黄蜂 huángfēng [只 zhī]

waste [weɪst] **I** N **1** [s/u] [of resources, food, money] 浪费(費) làngfèi **2** [U] (rubbish) 废(廢)料 fèiliào **II** vт [+ money, energy, time] 浪费(費) làngfèi; [+ opportunity] 失去 shīqù ▸ **it's a waste of time** 这(這)是浪费(費)时(時)间(間) zhè shì làngfèi shíjiān

wastepaper basket ['weɪstpeɪpə-] (Brit) N [c] 废(廢)纸(紙)篓(簍) fèizhǐlǒu [个 gè]

watch [wɒtʃ] **I** N [c] 手表(錶) shǒubiǎo [块 kuài] **II** vт **1** (look at) 注视(視) zhùshì; [+ match, programme, TV] 看 kàn **2** (pay attention to) 关(關)注 guānzhù **III** vɪ 注视(視) zhùshì ▸ **to watch sb do/doing sth** 看着(著)某人做某事 kànzhe mǒurén zuò mǒushì
▸ **watch out** vɪ 提防 dīfang ▸ **watch out!** (inf) 小心! xiǎoxīn!

water ['wɔːtəʳ] **I** N [U] 水 shuǐ **II** vт [+ plant] 给(給)…浇(澆)水 gěi…jiāoshuǐ ▸ **a drink of water** 一杯水 yī bēi shuǐ

waterfall ['wɔːtəfɔːl] N [c] 瀑布 pùbù [条 tiáo]

watermelon ['wɔːtəmɛlən] N [c] 西瓜 xīguā [个 gè]

waterproof ['wɔːtəpruːf] ADJ 防水的 fángshuǐ de

water-skiing ['wɔːtəskiːɪŋ] N [U] ▸ **to go water-skiing** 去滑水 qù huáshuǐ

wave [weɪv] **I** N [c] **1** [of hand] 挥(揮)动(動) huīdòng [下 xià] **2** (on water) 波浪 bōlàng [个 gè] **II** vɪ 挥(揮)手示意 huīshǒu shìyì **III** vт [+ hand] 挥(揮) huī
▸ **to wave goodbye to sb, wave sb**

goodbye 向某人挥(揮)手告别(別) xiàng mǒurén huīshǒu gàobié

wax [wæks] N [U] 蜡(蠟)là

way [weɪ] I N **1** [c] (route) 路 lù [条 tiáo] **2** [s] (distance) 距离(離) jùlí **3** [c] (direction) 方向 fāngxiàng **4** [c] (manner) 方式 fāngshì [种 zhǒng] **5** [c] (method) 方法 fāngfǎ [个 gè] II **ways** N PL (habits) 习(習)俗 xísú ▶ "which way?" — "this way" "往哪边(邊)?" "这(這)边(邊)" "wǎng nǎbiān?" "zhèbiān" ▶ **on the way** 在路上 zài lùshang ▶ **it's a long way away** 离(離)这(這)儿(兒)很远(遠) lí zhèr hěn yuǎn ▶ **to lose one's way** 迷路 mílù ▶ **the way back** 回去的路 huíqù de lù ▶ **to give way** (break, collapse) 倒塌 dǎotā ▶ **the wrong way round** (Brit) 刚(剛)好相反 gānghǎo xiāngfǎn ▶ **in a way** 在某种(種)程度上 zài mǒu zhǒng chéngdù shang ▶ **by the way...** 顺(順)便说(說)一下... shùnbiàn tí yīxià... ▶ "way in" (Brit) "入口" "rùkǒu" ▶ "way out" (Brit) "出口" "chūkǒu" ▶ **way of life** 生活方式 shēnghuó fāngshì ▶ **do it this way** 这(這)么(麼)做 zhème zuò

we [wi:] PL PRON 我们(們) wǒmen

weak [wi:k] ADJ **1** (虛)弱的 xūruò de **2** [+ tea, coffee, substance] 淡的 dàn de

wealthy ['welθɪ] ADJ 富有的 fùyǒu de

weapon ['wepən] N [c] 武器 wǔqì [种 zhǒng]

wear [weəʳ] (pt **wore**, pp **worn**) VT 穿着(著) chuānzhe; [+ spectacles, jewellery] 戴着(著) dàizhe ▶ **I can't decide what to wear** 我拿不定主意该(該)穿什么(麼) wǒ ná bù dìng zhǔyì gāi chuān shénme
▶ **wear out** VI 耗尽(盡) hàojìn

weather ['weðəʳ] N [U] 天气(氣) tiānqì ▶ **what's the weather like?** 天气(氣)怎么(麼)样(樣)? tiānqì zěnmeyàng?

weather forecast N [c] 天气(氣)预(預)报(報) tiānqì yùbào [个 gè]

web [web] N [c] ▶ **the Web** 互联(聯)网(網) hùliánwǎng [个 gè] ▶ **on the Web** 在互联(聯)网(網)上 zài hùliánwǎng shang

web address N [c] 网(網)络(絡)地址 wǎngluò dìzhǐ [个 gè]

web browser N [c] 网(網)络(絡)浏(瀏)

览(覽)器 wǎngluò liúlǎnqì [个 gè]

webcam ['webkæm] N [c] 网(網)络(絡)摄(攝)像机(機) wǎngluò shèxiàngjī [个 gè]

web page N [c] 网(網)页(頁) wǎngyè [个 gè]

website ['websaɪt] N [c] 网(網)址 wǎngzhǐ [个 gè]

we'd [wi:d] = **we had, we would**

wedding ['wedɪŋ] N [c] 婚礼(禮) hūnlǐ [场 chǎng]

Wednesday ['wednzdɪ] N [c/u] 星期三 xīngqīsān [个 gè]; see also/另见 **Tuesday**

week [wi:k] N [c] 星期 xīngqī [个 gè] ▶ **this/next/last week** 本/下/上周(週) běn/xià/shàngzhōu ▶ **once/twice a week** 一周(週)一次/两(兩)次 yī zhōu yī cì/liǎng cì

weekday ['wi:kdeɪ] N [c] 工作日 gōngzuòrì [个 gè] ▶ **on weekdays** 在工作日 zài gōngzuòrì

weekend [wi:k'end] N [c] 周(週)末 zhōumò [个 gè] ▶ **at the weekend** 在周(週)末 zài zhōumò ▶ **this/next/last weekend** 这(這)个(個)周(週)末/下周(週)末/上周(週)末 zhège zhōumò/xià zhōumò/shàng zhōumò

weigh [weɪ] I VT 称(稱)…的重量 chēng…de zhòngliàng II VI ▶ **she weighs 50kg** 她的体(體)重为(為)50公斤 tāde tǐzhòng wéi wǔshí gōngjīn

weight [weɪt] I N [u] 重量 zhòngliàng II **weights** N PL (in gym) 举(舉)重器械 jǔzhòng qìxiè ▶ **to lose weight** 体(體)重减(減)轻(輕) tǐzhòng jiǎnqīng

welcome ['welkəm] I N [c] 欢(歡)迎 huānyíng II VT 欢(歡)迎 huānyíng ▶ **welcome to Beijing!** 欢(歡)迎到北京来(來)! huānyíng dào Běijīng lái! ▶ **"thank you" — "you're welcome!"** "谢(謝)谢(謝)你。" "别(別)客气(氣)!" "xièxie nǐ" "bié kèqì!" ▶ **to give sb a warm welcome** 热(熱)烈欢(歡)迎某人 rèliè huānyíng mǒurén

well [wel] I N [c] 井 jǐng [口 kǒu] II ADV **1** (to a high standard) 好 hǎo **2** (completely) 充分地 chōngfèn de III ADJ (healthy) 身体(體)好的 shēntǐ hǎo de IV INT 嗯 ng ▶ **to do well** [person +] 做得好 zuò de hǎo; [business +] 进(進)展顺(順)利 jìnzhǎn shùnlì ▶ **well done!** 棒极了! bàng jí le! ▶ **as well** (in addition) 也 yě

▶ **I don't feel well** 我觉(覺)得不舒服 wǒ juéde bù shūfu ▶ **get well soon!** 早日康复(復)! zǎorì kāngfù! ▶ **well, as I was saying...** 那(麼)，像我刚(剛)才所说(說)的… nàme, xiàng wǒ gāngcái suǒ shuō de...

we'll [wiːl] = **we will, we shall**

well-known ['wɛl'nəʊn] ADJ [+ person] 有名的 yǒumíng de; [+ fact, brand] 众(眾)所周知的 zhòng suǒ zhōu zhī de

well-off ['wɛl'ɒf] ADJ 富裕的 fùyù de

Welsh [wɛlʃ] I ADJ 威尔(爾)士的 Wēiěrshì de II N [U] (language) 威尔(爾)士语(語) Wēiěrshìyǔ III NPL ▶ **the Welsh** 威尔(爾)士人 Wēiěrshìrén

went [wɛnt] PT of **go**

were [wəːʳ] PT of **be**

we're [wɪəʳ] = **we are**

weren't [wəːnt] = **were not**

west [wɛst] I N **1** [U/s] (direction) 西方 xīfāng **2** ▶ **the West** (Pol) 西方国(國)家 xīfāng guójiā II ADJ 西部的 xībù de III ADV 向西 xiàng xī ▶ **west of** …以西 …yǐ xī

western ['wɛstən] I ADJ (Geo) 西部的 xībù de II N [c] 西部影片 xībù yǐngpiàn [部 bù]

West Indian I ADJ 西印度群岛(島)的 Xīyìndù Qúndǎo de II N [c] 西印度群岛(島)人 Xīyìndù Qúndǎorén [个 gè]

West Indies [-'ɪndɪz] NPL ▶ **the West Indies** 西印度群岛(島) Xīyìndù Qúndǎo

wet [wɛt] ADJ **1** [+ person, clothes] 湿(濕)的 shī de; [+ paint, cement, glue] 未干(乾)的 wèigān de **2** (rainy) [+ weather, day] 多雨的 duōyǔ de ▶ **to get wet** 弄湿(濕) nòngshī

we've [wiːv] = **we have**

whale [weɪl] N [c] 鲸(鯨) jīng [头 tóu]

KEYWORD

what [wɒt] I PRON **1** 什么(麼) shénme ▶ **what is happening?** 发(發)生了什么(麼)事? fāshēngle shénme shì? ▶ **what is it?** 那是什么(麼)? nà shì shénme? ▶ **what are you doing?** 你在干(幹)什么(麼)? nǐ zài gàn shénme? ▶ **what did you say?** 你说(說)什么(麼)了? nǐ shuō shénme?

2 (in indirect questions/speech: subject, object) 什么(麼) shénme ▶ **do you know what's happening?** 你知道发(發)生了什么(麼)事吗(嗎)? nǐ zhīdào fāshēngle shénme shì ma?

3 (relative) 所…的 suǒ...de ▶ **I saw what was on the table** 我看见(見)了桌上的东(東)西 wǒ kànjiànle zhuō shang de dōngxi

II ADJ **1** 什么(麼) shénme ▶ **what time is it?** 几(幾)点(點)了? jǐdiǎn le? ▶ **what size is this shirt?** 这(這)件衬(襯)衫是几(幾)码(碼)的? zhè jiàn chènshān shì jǐmǎ de?

2 (in exclamations) 多么(麼) duōme ▶ **what a mess!** 真是一团(團)糟! zhēnshì yītuánzāo! ▶ **what a lovely day!** 多么(麼)好的天气(氣)啊! duōme hǎo de tiānqì a!

III INT 什么(麼) shénme ▶ **what, no coffee!** 什么(麼)，没(沒)咖啡了! shénme, méi kāfēi le!

whatever [wɒt'ɛvəʳ] I ADV (whatsoever) 任何 rènhé II PRON ▶ **do whatever is necessary/you want** 做任何必要的/你想做的事情 zuò rènhé bìyào de/nǐ xiǎng zuò de shìqíng

wheat [wiːt] N [U] 小麦(麥) xiǎomài

wheel [wiːl] N [c] **1** 轮(輪) lún [个 gè] **2** (also: **steering wheel**) 方向盘(盤) fāngxiàngpán [个 gè]

wheelchair ['wiːltʃeəʳ] N [c] 轮(輪)椅 lúnyǐ [部 bù]

KEYWORD

when [wɛn] I ADV (interrogative) 什么(麼)时(時)候 shénme shíhou ▶ **when did it happen?** 什么(麼)时(時)候发(發)生的? shénme shíhou fāshēng de? II PRON (relative) ▶ **the day when** 当(當)…的那一天 dāng...de nà yì tiān III CONJ (in time clauses) 当(當)…时(時) dāng...shí ▶ **be careful when you cross the road** 过(過)马(馬)路时(時)要当(當)心 guò mǎlù shí yào dāngxīn ▶ **she was reading when I came in** 当(當)我进(進)来(來)时(時)她正在阅(閱)读(讀) dāng wǒ jìnlái shí tā zhèngzài yuèdú ▶ **I know when it happened** 我知道什么(麼)时(時)候

发(發)生的 wǒ zhīdào shénme shíhou fāshēng de

where [wɛəʳ] I ADV (in or to what place) 在哪里(裡) zài nǎlǐ II CONJ (the place in which) 哪里(裡) nǎlǐ ▸ where are you from? 你是哪里(裡)人? nǐ shì nǎlǐ rén?

whether [ˈwɛðəʳ] CONJ 是否 shìfǒu ▸ I don't know whether to accept or not 我不知道是接受还(還)是不接受 wǒ bù zhīdào shì jiēshòu háishì bù jiēshòu

KEYWORD

which [wɪtʃ] I ADJ **1** (interrogative singular) 哪个(個) nǎge; (plural) 哪些 nǎxiē ▸ which picture do you want? 你要哪幅画(畫)? nǐ yào nǎ fú huà? ▸ which one/ones? 哪个(個)/些? nǎge/xiē? **2** (in indirect questions/speech: singular) 哪个(個) nǎge; (plural) 哪些 nǎxiē ▸ he asked which book I wanted 他问(問)我要哪本书(書) tā wèn wǒ yào nǎ běn shū II PRON **1** (interrogative subject, object) 哪个(個) nǎge ▸ which of these is yours? 这(這)些中的哪个(個)是你的? zhèxiē zhōng de nǎge shì nǐ de? **2** (in indirect questions/speech: subject, object) 哪个(個) nǎge ▸ ask him which of the models is the best 问(問)他哪种(種)型号(號)是最好的 wèn tā nǎ zhǒng xínghào shì zuì hǎo de **3** (relative subject, object) …的那个(個)……de nàge... ▸ the shot which you heard/which killed him 你听(聽)到的那一枪(槍)/杀(殺)死他的那一枪(槍) nǐ tīngdào de nà yī qiāng/shāsǐ tā de nà yī qiāng

while [waɪl] I N [s] 一会(會)儿(兒) yīhuìr II CONJ **1** (during the time that) 在…时(時) zài…shí **2** (although) 虽(雖)然 suīrán ▸ While I'm very fond of him, I don't actually want to marry him. 虽然我很喜欢他,但我真的不想嫁给他。Suīrán wǒ hěn xǐhuan tā, dàn wǒ zhēnde bùxiǎng jiàgěi tā. ▸ for a while 有一会(會)儿(兒) yǒu yīhuìr

whisky, (US) **whiskey** [ˈwɪskɪ] N [c/u] 威士忌酒 wēishìjì jiǔ [瓶 píng]

whisper [ˈwɪspəʳ] VI 低语(語) dīyǔ

whistle [ˈwɪsl] I VI 吹口哨 chuī kǒushào II N [c] **1** (device) 哨子 shàozi [个 gè] **2** (sound) 口哨声(聲) kǒushàoshēng [声 shēng]

white [waɪt] I ADJ **1** 雪白的 xuěbái de; [+ wine] 白的 bái de **2** [+ coffee] 加奶的 jiā nǎi de **3** [+ person] 白种(種)人的 báizhǒngrén de II N **1** [U] (colour) 白色 báisè

KEYWORD

who [huː] PRON **1** 谁(誰) shuí ▸ who is it? 是谁(誰)? shì shuí? ▸ who did you discuss it with? 你和谁(誰)讨(討)论(論)了? nǐ hé shuí tǎolùn le? **2** (in indirect questions/speech: subject, object, after preposition) 谁(誰) shuí ▸ I told her who I was 我告诉(訴)了她我是谁(誰) wǒ gàosùle tā wǒ shì shuí ▸ I don't know who he gave it to 我不知道他把它给(給)了谁(誰) wǒ bù zhīdào tā bǎ tā gěile shuí **3** (relative subject, object) …的那个(個)……de nàge... ▸ the girl who came in 进(進)来(來)的那个(個)女孩 jìnlai de nàge nǚhái ▸ the man who we met in Sydney 我们(們)在悉尼遇到的那个(個)男子 wǒmen zài Xīní yùdào de nàge nánzǐ

whole [həʊl] I ADJ **1** 整个(個)的 zhěnggè de II N [c] **1** (entirety) 整体(體) zhěngtǐ [个 gè] **2** ▸ the whole of sth 某物的全部 mǒuwù de quánbù [个 gè] ▸ the whole (of the) time 所有的时(時)间(間) suǒyǒu de shíjiān ▸ on the whole 大体(體)上 dàtǐ shang

whom [huːm] (frm) PRON **1** (interrogative) 谁(誰) shuí **2** (relative) 所…的那个(個)… suǒ…de nàge… ▸ the man whom I saw/to whom I spoke 我见(見)到的/我跟他说(說)过(過)话(話)的那个(個)男的 wǒ jiàndào de/wǒ gēn tā shuōguo huà de nàge nán de

whose [huːz] I ADJ **1** (interrogative) 谁(誰)的 shuí de **2** (relative) …的 …de II PRON 谁(誰)的 shuí de ▸ whose is this? 这(這)是谁(誰)的? zhè shì shuí de? ▸ whose book is this/coats are these? 这(這)本书(書)是谁(誰)的/这(這)些外

套是谁(誰)的? zhè běn shū shì shuí de/zhèxiē wàitào shì shuí de? ▶ **the woman whose car was stolen** 汽车(車)给(給)偷走的那个(個)女的 qìchē gěi tōuzǒu de nàge nǚ de

KEYWORD

why [waɪ] I ADV 为(為)什么(麼) wèi shénme ▶ **why is he always late?** 为(為)什么(麼)他总(總)是迟(遲)到? wèi shénme tā zǒngshì chídào? ▶ **why not?** 为(為)什么(麼)不呢? wèi shénme bù ne? ▶ **I don't know why** 我不知道为(為)什么(麼) wǒ bù zhīdào wèi shénme
II CONJ 为(為)什么(麼) wèi shénme ▶ **I wonder why he said that** 我想知道他为(為)什么(麼)那么(麼)说(說) wǒ xiǎng zhīdào tā wèi shénme nàme shuō ▶ **the reason why he did it** 他那么(麼)做的原因 tā nàme zuò de yuányīn

wicked ['wɪkɪd] ADJ (evil) [+ person] 邪恶(惡)的 xié'è de; [+ act, crime] 罪恶(惡)的 zuì'è de

wide [waɪd] I ADJ 1 宽(寬)的 kuān de 2 [+ range, variety, publicity, choice] 广(廣)泛的 guǎngfàn de II ADV ▶ **to open sth wide** 张(張)大某物 zhāngdà mǒuwù

widow ['wɪdəu] N [c] 寡妇(婦) guǎfu [个 gè]

widower ['wɪdəuə'] N [c] 鳏(鰥)夫 guānfū [个 gè]

width [wɪdθ] N [c/u] 宽(寬)度 kuāndù

wife [waɪf] (pl **wives**) N [c] 妻子 qīzi [个 gè]

Wi-Fi ['waɪfaɪ] N [u] 无线网络 wúxiàn wǎngluò

wild [waɪld] ADJ 1 野生的 yěshēng de 2 [+ person, behaviour] 狂野的 kuángyě de

wildlife ['waɪldlaɪf] N [u] 野生动(動)物 yěshēng dòngwù

KEYWORD

will [wɪl] I AUX VB 1 ▶ **I will call you tonight** 我今晚会(會)给(給)你打电(電)话(話)的 wǒ jīnwǎn huì gěi nǐ dǎ diànhuà de ▶ **what will you do next?**

下面你要做什么(麼)? xiàmiàn nǐ yào zuò shénme?
2 (in conjectures, predictions) 该(該)是 gāishì ▶ **he'll be there by now** 他现(現)在该(該)到了 tā xiànzài gāi dào le
3 (in commands, requests, offers) ▶ **will you be quiet!** 你安静(靜)点(點)! nǐ ānjìng diǎn!
II N 1 (volition) 意志 yìzhì ▶ **against his will** 违(違)背他的意愿(願) wéibèi tā de yìyuàn
2 (testament) 遗(遺)嘱(囑) yízhǔ [份 fèn] ▶ **to make a will** 立遗(遺)嘱(囑) lì yízhǔ

willing ['wɪlɪŋ] ADJ ▶ **to be willing to do sth** 愿(願)意做某事 yuànyì zuò mǒushi

win [wɪn] (pt, pp **won**) I N [c] 胜(勝)利 shènglì [个 gè] II VT 1 在…中获(獲)胜(勝) zài...zhōng huòshèng 2 [+ prize, medal] 赢(贏)得 yíngdé III VI 获(獲)胜(勝) huòshèng

wind [wɪnd] N [c/u] 风(風) fēng [阵 zhèn]

window ['wɪndəu] N [c] 1 窗户(戶) chuānghu [扇 shàn]; (in shop) 橱(櫥)窗 chúchuāng [个 gè]; (in car, train) 窗 chuāng [个 gè] 2 (Comput) 视(視)窗 shìchuāng [个 gè]

windscreen ['wɪndskri:n] (Brit) N [c] 挡(擋)风(風)玻璃 dǎngfēng bōli [块 kuài]

windshield ['wɪndʃi:ld] (US) N [c] 挡(擋)风(風)玻璃 dǎngfēng bōli [块 kuài]

windsurfing ['wɪndsə:fɪŋ] N [u] 帆板运(運)动(動) fānbǎn yùndòng

windy ['wɪndɪ] ADJ [+ weather, day] 有风(風)的 yǒufēng de ▶ **it's windy** 今天风(風)很大 jīntiān fēng hěndà

wine [waɪn] N [c/u] 葡萄酒 pútáojiǔ [瓶 píng]

wing [wɪŋ] N [c] 1 翅膀 chìbǎng [个 gè]; [of aeroplane] 机(機)翼 jīyì [个 gè] 2 [of building] 侧(側)楼(樓) cèlóu [座 zuò]

wink [wɪŋk] VI [person +] 眨眼 zhǎyǎn ▶ **to give sb a wink, wink at sb** 向某人眨了眨眼 xiàng mǒurén zhǎ le zhǎ yǎn

winner ['wɪnə'] N [c] 获(獲)胜(勝)者 huòshèngzhě [位 wèi]

winter ['wɪntə'] I N [c/u] 冬季 dōngjì [个 gè] II VI 过(過)冬 guòdōng ▶ **in (the) winter** 在冬季 zài dōngjì

wipe [waɪp] VT (dry, clean) 擦 cā ▸ to wipe one's nose 擦鼻子 cā bízi ▸ **wipe up** VT 把…擦干(乾)净(淨) bǎ…cā gānjìng

wire ['waɪər] N [c] (Elec: uninsulated) 电(電)线(線) diànxiàn [根 gēn]; (insulated) 电(電)缆(纜) diànlǎn [条 tiáo]

wise [waɪz] ADJ 睿智的 ruìzhì de

wish [wɪʃ] I N [c] 愿(願)望 yuànwàng [个 gè] II VT 但愿(願) dànyuàn ▸ **best wishes** 良好的祝愿(願) liánghǎo de zhùyuàn ▸ **with best wishes** 祝好 zhùhǎo ▸ **give her my best wishes** 代我向她致意 dài wǒ xiàng tā zhìyì ▸ **to wish to do sth** 想要做某事 xiǎngyào zuò mǒushì

○ **KEYWORD**

with [wɪð, wɪθ] PREP **1** 和…在一起 hé…zài yīqǐ ▸ I was with him 我和他在一起 wǒ hé tā zài yīqǐ ▸ I'll be with you in a minute 请(請)稍等 qǐng shāo děng ▸ we stayed with friends 我们(們)和朋友们(們)在一起 wǒmen hé péngyoumen dāi zài yīqǐ **2** (indicating feature, possession) 有 yǒu ▸ the man with the grey hat/blue eyes 戴着(著)灰帽子/有蓝(藍)眼睛的男人 dàizhe huī màozi/yǒu lán yǎnjing de nánrén **3** (indicating means, substance) 用 yòng ▸ to walk with a stick 拄着(著)拐(枴)杖走 zhǔzhe guǎizhàng zǒu ▸ to fill sth with water 在某物里(裡)装(裝)满(滿)水 zài mǒuwù lǐ zhuāngmǎn shuǐ **4** (indicating cause) ▸ red with anger 气(氣)得涨(漲)红(紅)了脸(臉) qì de zhànghóngle liǎn

without [wɪð'aut] PREP 没(沒)有 méiyǒu ▸ **without a coat** 未穿外套 wèi chuān wàitào ▸ **without speaking** 不曾说(說)话(話) bùcéng shuōhuà

witness ['wɪtnɪs] N [c] (gen, also in court) 目击(擊)者 mùjīzhě [位 wèi]

witty ['wɪtɪ] ADJ 诙(詼)谐(諧)的 huīxié de

wives [waɪvz] NPL of **wife**

woke [wəuk] PT of **wake**

woken ['wəukn] PP of **wake**

wolf [wulf] (pl **wolves** [wulvz]) N [c] 狼 láng [条 tiáo]

woman ['wumən] (pl **women** ['wɪmən]) N [c] 妇(婦)女 fùnǚ [位 wèi]

won [wʌn] PT, PP of **win**

wonder ['wʌndər] I VT ▸ **to wonder whether/why** etc 想知道是否/为(為)什么(麼)(等) xiǎng zhīdào shìfǒu/wèi shénme děng II VI 感到奇怪 gǎndào qíguài

wonderful ['wʌndəful] ADJ 绝(絕)妙的 juémiào de

won't [wəunt] = **will not**

wood [wud] N **1** [U] 木材 mùcái **2** [c] (forest) 树(樹)林 shùlín [棵 kē]

wool [wul] N [U] 羊毛 yángmáo

word [wə:d] N **1** [c] 词(詞)cí [个 gè] **2** [s] (promise) 诺(諾)言 nuòyán ▸ **what's the word for "pen" in French?** "钢(鋼)笔(筆)"这(這)个(個)词(詞)在法语(語)里(裡)怎么(麼)说(說)? "gāngbǐ" zhège cí zài Fǎyǔ li zěnme shuō? ▸ **in other words** 换(換)句话(話)说(說) huàn jù huà shuō

word processing [-'prəusɛsɪŋ] N [U] 文字处(處)理 wénzì chǔlǐ

word processor [-prəusɛsər] N [c] (machine) 文字处(處)理器 wénzì chǔlǐqì [个 gè]

wore [wɔ:r] PT of **wear**

work [wə:k] I N **1** [U] (tasks, duties) 事情 shìqing **2** [U] (job) 工作 gōngzuò II VI **1** (have job, do tasks) 工作 gōngzuò **2** (function) 运(運)行 yùnxíng **3** (be successful) [idea, method +] 起作用 qǐ zuòyòng ▸ **to go to work** 上班 qù shàngbān ▸ **to be out of work** 失业 shīyè ▸ **to work hard** 努力工作 nǔlì gōngzuò ▸ **work out** I VI (Sport) 锻(鍛)炼(鍊) duànliàn II VT (+ answer, solution) 努力找出 nǔlì zhǎochū; (+ plan, details) 制(製)订(訂)出 zhìdìng chū

worker ['wə:kər] N [c] 工人 gōngrén [位 wèi] ▸ **a hard/good worker** 工作努力/良好的人 gōngzuò nǔlì/liánghǎo de rén

work experience N [U] 工作经(經)历(歷) gōngzuò jīnglì

workstation ['wə:ksteɪʃən] N [c] **1** (desk) 工作台(臺) gōngzuòtái [个 gè]

2 (computer) 工作站 gōngzuòzhàn [个 gè]

world [wəːld] I N ▸ **the world** 世界 shìjiè II CPD [+ champion, record, power, authority] 世界 shìjiè; [+ tour] 环(環)球 huánqiú ▸ **all over the world** 全世界 quán shìjiè

World-Wide Web [wəːld'waɪd-] N ▸ **the World-Wide Web** 万(萬)维(維)网(網) Wànwéiwǎng

worn [wɔːn] PP of **wear**

worried ['wʌrɪd] ADJ 闷(悶)闷(悶)不乐(樂)的 mènmèn bù lè de ▸ **to be worried about sth/sb** 担(擔)心某事/某人 dānxīn mǒushì/mǒurén

worry ['wʌrɪ] I N **1** [U] (feeling of anxiety) 忧(憂)虑(慮) yōulǜ **2** [C] (cause of anxiety) 担(擔)心 dānxīn [种 zhǒng] II VT 使担(擔)心 shǐ dānxīn III VI 担(擔)心 dānxīn

worse [wəːs] I ADJ 更坏(壞)的 gèng huài de II ADV (comparative of badly) 更糟地 gèng zāo de III N [s/u] 更坏(壞)的事 gèng huài de shì ▸ **to get worse** 逐渐(漸)恶(惡)化 zhújiàn èhuà

worst [wəːst] I ADJ 最坏(壞)的 zuì huài de II ADV (superlative of badly) 最糟地 zuì zāo de III N 最坏(壞)的事 zuì huài de shì ▸ **at worst** 在最坏(壞)的情况(況)下 zài zuì huài de qíngkuàng xià

worth [wəːθ] I N [U] 价(價)值 jiàzhí II ADJ ▸ **to be worth £50** 值50英镑(鎊) zhí wǔshí yīngbàng ▸ **it's worth it** 这(這)是值得的 zhèshì zhídé de ▸ **400 dollars' worth of damage** 价(價)值400美元的损(損)失 jiàzhí sìbǎi měiyuán de sǔnshī ▸ **it would be (well) worth doing...** (很) 值得做… (hěn) zhídé zuò...

◯ **KEYWORD**

would [wʊd] AUX VB **1** ▸ I **would love to go to Italy** 我很愿(願)意去意大利 wǒ hěn yuànyì qù Yìdàlì ▸ I'**m sure he wouldn't do that** 我确(確)定他不会(會)那么(麼)做的 wǒ quèdìng tā bùhuì nàme zuò de

2 (in offers, invitations, requests) ▸ **would you like a biscuit?** 你要来(來)块(塊)饼(餅)干(乾)吗(嗎)? nǐ yào lái kuàn bǐnggān ma? ▸ **would you ask him to come in?** 你要叫他进(進)来(來)吗(嗎)?

nǐ yào jiàotā jìnlái ma?

3 (be willing to) ▸ **she wouldn't help me** 她不愿(願)意帮(幫)助我 tā bù yuànyì bāngzhù wǒ

4 (in indirect speech) ▸ **he said he would be at home later** 他说(說)他晚点(點)儿(兒)会(會)在家的 tā shuō tā wǎndiǎnr huì zài jiā de

wouldn't ['wʊdnt] = **would not**

wrap [ræp] VT (cover) 包 bāo ▸ **wrap up** VT (pack) 包起来(來) bāo qǐlái

wrapping paper ['ræpɪŋ-] N [U] (gift wrap) 包装(裝)纸(紙) bāozhuāngzhǐ

wreck [rɛk] I N [C] **1** (wreckage, ship) 残(殘)骸 cánhái [个 gè] **2** (US: accident) 事故 shìgù [次 cì] II VT [+ car, building] 摧毁(毀) cuīhuǐ

wrestling ['rɛslɪŋ] N [U] 摔跤 shuāijiāo

wrinkled ['rɪŋkld] ADJ 布(佈)满(滿)皱(皺)纹(紋)的 bùmǎn zhòuwén de

wrist [rɪst] N [C] 手腕 shǒuwàn [个 gè]

write [raɪt] (pt **wrote**, pp **written**) I VT **1** [+ address, number] 写(寫)下 xiěxià **2** [+ letter, note] 写(寫) xiě **3** [+ novel, music] 创(創)作 chuàngzuò **4** [+ cheque, receipt, prescription] 开(開) kāi II VI 写(寫)字 xiězì ▸ **to write to sb** 写(寫)信给(給)某人 xiěxìn gěi mǒurén ▸ **write down** VT 记(記)下 jìxià

writer ['raɪtə] N [C] 作家 zuòjiā [位 wèi]

writing ['raɪtɪŋ] N [U] **1** (sth written) 文字 wénzì **2** (handwriting) 笔(筆)迹(跡) bǐjì ▸ **in writing** 以书(書)面形式 yǐ shūmiàn xíngshì

written ['rɪtn] PP of **write**

wrong [rɒŋ] I ADJ **1** [+ person, equipment, kind, job] 不合适(適)的 bù héshì de **2** [+ answer, information, report] 错(錯)误(誤)的 cuòwù de **3** (morally bad) 不道德的 bù dàodé de II ADV (incorrectly) 错(錯)误(誤)地 cuòwù de ▸ **to be wrong** [answer +] 是错(錯)的 shì cuò de; [person +] 弄错(錯)了 nòng cuò le ▸ **what's wrong?** 出了什么(麼)事? chūle shénme shì? ▸ **what's wrong with you?** 你怎么(麼)了? nǐ zěnme le? ▸ **to go wrong** [plan +] 失败(敗) shībài; [machine +] 发(發)生故障 fāshēng gùzhàng

Z

zebra crossing [ˈziːbrə-] (*Brit*) N [c] 斑马(馬)线(線) bānmǎxiàn [条 tiáo]

zero [ˈzɪərəʊ] (*pl* **zero** *or* **zeroes**) N **1** [u/c] (*number*) 零 líng [个 gè] **2** [u] (*nothing*) 没(沒)有 méiyǒu ▸ **5 degrees below zero** 零下5度 língxià wǔdù

zip [zɪp] N [c] (*Brit: fastener*) 拉链(鏈) lāliàn [条 tiáo]

zip code (*US*) N [c] 邮(郵)政编(編)码(碼) yóuzhèng biānmǎ [个 gè]

zipper [ˈzɪpəʳ] (*US*) N [c] 拉链(鏈) lāliàn [条 tiáo]

zone [zəʊn] N [c] (*area*) 地带(帶) dìdài [个 gè]

zoo [zuː] (*pl* **zoos**) N [c] 动(動)物园(園) dòngwùyuán [个 gè]

zucchini [zuːˈkiːnɪ] (*pl* **zucchini** *or* **zucchinis**) (*US*) N [c/u] 绿(綠)皮西葫芦(蘆) lùpí xīhúlu [个 gè]

Y

yacht [jɒt] N [c] 1 (sailing boat) 帆船 fānchuán [艘 sōu] 2 (luxury craft) 游艇 yóutǐng [艘 sōu]

yard [jɑːd] N [c] (US: garden) 院子 yuànzi

yawn [jɔːn] I vi 打哈欠 dǎ hāqian II N [c] 哈欠 hāqian [个 gè]

year [jɪə] N [c] 1 年 nián 2 (Scol, Univ) 学年 xuénián [个 gè] ▸ **every year** 每年 měi nián ▸ **this year** 今年 jīnnián ▸ **last year** 去年 qùnián ▸ **a or per year** 每年 měi nián ▸ **we lived there for years** 我们（们）在那儿（儿）住了许多年了 wǒmen zài nàr zhùle hǎo duō nián le

yellow [ˈjɛləʊ] I ADJ 黄色的 huángsè de II N [c/u] 黄色 huángsè [种 zhǒng]

yes [jɛs] I ADV 是的 shì de II N [c] (answer) 是 shì

yesterday [ˈjɛstədeɪ] I ADV 昨天 zuótiān II N [U] 昨天 zuótiān ▸ **the day before yesterday** 前天 qiántiān

yet [jɛt] I ADV (up to now: with negative) 还（还）hái; (in questions) 已经（经）yǐjīng II CONJ 然而 rán'ér ▸ **they haven't finished yet** 他们（们）还（还）没（没）完工 tāmen hái méi wángōng ▸ **yet again** 又一次 yòu yī cì

yog(h)urt [ˈjɒɡət] N [c/u] 酸奶 suānnǎi [瓶 píng]

you [juː] PRON 1 (singular) 你 nǐ; (plural) 你们（们）nǐmen 2 任何人 rènhérén ▸ **you never know** 谁（谁）知道 shéi(shuí) zhīdào

young [jʌŋ] ADJ 幼小的 yòuxiǎo de ▸ **my younger brother/sister** 我的弟弟/妹妹 wǒde dìdì/mèimei

your [jɔː] ADJ (of one person) 你的 nǐ de; (of more than one person) 你们的 nǐmen de

yours [jɔːz] PRON (of one person) 你的 nǐ de; (of more than one person) 你们的 nǐmen de ▸ **is this yours?** 这是你/你们的（吗）? zhè shì nǐ/nǐmen de ma? ▸ **yours sincerely/faithfully** 你真挚的/忠实的 nǐ zhēnzhì de/zhōngshí de

yourself [jɔːˈsɛlf] PRON 1 你自己 nǐ zìjǐ 2 (you) 你 nǐ ▸ **by yourself** (unaided) 独（独）立地 dú(dú) lìde; (alone) 独（独）自地 dú(dú) zìde

yourselves [jɔːˈsɛlvz] PL PRON 1 你们自己 nǐmen zìjǐ 2 (you) 你们（们）nǐmen ▸ **by yourselves** (unaided) 独（独）立地 dú(dú) lìde; (alone) 独（独）自地 dú(dú) zìde

youth club N [c] 青年俱乐部 qīngnián jùlèbù [个 gè]

youth hostel N [c] 青年招待所 qīngnián zhāodàisuǒ [个 gè]

Yugoslavia [ˌjuːɡəʊˈslɑːvɪə] N (formerly) 南斯拉夫 Nánsīlāfū

wrote [rəut] PT *of* **write**
WWW (*Comput*) N ABBR (= World-Wide
 Web) 万(萬)维(維)网(網) Wànwéiwǎng

Xmas [ˈɛksməs] N ABBR (= Christmas)
 圣(聖)诞(誕)节(節) Shèngdàn Jié
X-ray [ˈɛksreɪ] **I** N [c] (*photo*) X光照片 X
 guāng zhàopiàn [张 zhāng] **II** VT 用X光
 检(檢)查 yòng X guāng jiǎnchá ▶**to
 have an X-ray** 做一次X光检(檢)查 zuò
 yī cì X guāng jiǎnchá